Lecture Notes in Computer Sci

Commenced Publication in 1973
Founding and Former Series Editors:
Gerhard Goos, Juris Hartmanis, and Jan van Leeuwen

Editorial Board

Advanced Research in Computing and Software Science

Subline of Lectures Notes in Computer Science

Subline Series Editors

Subline Advisory Board

Zhong Shao (Ed.)

Programming Languages and Systems

23rd European Symposium on Programming, ESOP 2014
Held as Part of the European Joint Conferences
on Theory and Practice of Software, ETAPS 2014
Grenoble, France, April 5-13, 2014
Proceedings

 Springer

Volume Editor

Zhong Shao
Yale University
New Haven, CT, USA
E-mail: zhong.shao@yale.edu

ISSN 0302-9743   e-ISSN 1611-3349
ISBN 978-3-642-54832-1   e-ISBN 978-3-642-54833-8
DOI 10.1007/978-3-642-54833-8
Springer Heidelberg New York Dordrecht London

Library of Congress Control Number: 2014934144

LNCS Sublibrary: SL 1 – Theoretical Computer Science and General Issues

Typesetting: Camera-ready by author, data conversion by Scientific Publishing Services, Chennai, India

Printed on acid-free paper

Springer is part of Springer Science+Business Media (www.springer.com)

Foreword

ETAPS 2014 was the 17th instance of the European Joint Conferences on Theory and Practice of Software. ETAPS is an annual federated conference that was established in 1998, and this year consisted of six constituting conferences (CC, ESOP, FASE, FoSSaCS, TACAS, and POST) including eight invited speakers and two tutorial speakers. Before and after the main conference, numerous satellite workshops took place and attracted many researchers from all over the globe.

ETAPS is a confederation of several conferences, each with its own Program Committee (PC) and its own Steering Committee (if any). The conferences cover various aspects of software systems, ranging from theoretical foundations to programming language developments, compiler advancements, analysis tools, formal approaches to software engineering, and security. Organizing these conferences in a coherent, highly synchronized conference program, enables the participation in an exciting event, having the possibility to meet many researchers working in different directions in the field, and to easily attend the talks of different conferences.

The six main conferences together received 606 submissions this year, 155 of which were accepted (including 12 tool demonstration papers), yielding an overall acceptance rate of 25.6%. I thank all authors for their interest in ETAPS, all reviewers for the peer reviewing process, the PC members for their involvement, and in particular the PC co-chairs for running this entire intensive process. Last but not least, my congratulations to all authors of the accepted papers!

ETAPS 2014 was greatly enriched by the invited talks of Geoffrey Smith (Florida International University, USA) and John Launchbury (Galois, USA), both unifying speakers, and the conference-specific invited speakers (CC) Benoît Dupont de Dinechin (Kalray, France), (ESOP) Maurice Herlihy (Brown University, USA), (FASE) Christel Baier (Technical University of Dresden, Germany), (FoSSaCS) Petr Jančar (Technical University of Ostrava, Czech Republic), (POST) David Mazières (Stanford University, USA), and finally (TACAS) Orna Kupferman (Hebrew University Jerusalem, Israel). Invited tutorials were provided by Bernd Finkbeiner (Saarland University, Germany) and Andy Gordon (Microsoft Research, Cambridge, UK). My sincere thanks to all these speakers for their great contributions.

For the first time in its history, ETAPS returned to a city where it had been organized before: Grenoble, France. ETAPS 2014 was organized by the Université Joseph Fourier in cooperation with the following associations and societies: ETAPS e.V., EATCS (European Association for Theoretical Computer Science), EAPLS (European Association for Programming Languages and Systems), and EASST (European Association of Software Science and Technology). It had support from the following sponsors: CNRS, Inria, Grenoble INP, PERSYVAL-Lab and Université Joseph Fourier, and Springer-Verlag.

The organization team comprised:

General Chair: Saddek Bensalem
Conferences Chair: Alain Girault and Yassine Lakhnech
Workshops Chair: Axel Legay
Publicity Chair: Yliès Falcone
Treasurer: Nicolas Halbwachs
Webmaster: Marius Bozga

The overall planning for ETAPS is the responsibility of the Steering Committee (SC). The ETAPS SC consists of an executive board (EB) and representatives of the individual ETAPS conferences, as well as representatives of EATCS, EAPLS, and EASST. The Executive Board comprises Gilles Barthe (satellite events, Madrid), Holger Hermanns (Saarbrücken), Joost-Pieter Katoen (chair, Aachen and Twente), Gerald Lüttgen (treasurer, Bamberg), and Tarmo Uustalu (publicity, Tallinn). Other current SC members are: Martín Abadi (Santa Cruz and Mountain View), Erika Ábrahám (Aachen), Roberto Amadio (Paris), Christel Baier (Dresden), Saddek Bensalem (Grenoble), Giuseppe Castagna (Paris), Albert Cohen (Paris), Alexander Egyed (Linz), Riccardo Focardi (Venice), Björn Franke (Edinburgh), Stefania Gnesi (Pisa), Klaus Havelund (Pasadena), Reiko Heckel (Leicester), Paul Klint (Amsterdam), Jens Knoop (Vienna), Steve Kremer (Nancy), Pasquale Malacaria (London), Tiziana Margaria (Potsdam), Fabio Martinelli (Pisa), Andrew Myers (Boston), Anca Muscholl (Bordeaux), Catuscia Palamidessi (Palaiseau), Andrew Pitts (Cambridge), Arend Rensink (Twente), Don Sanella (Edinburgh), Vladimiro Sassone (Southampton), Ina Schäfer (Braunschweig), Zhong Shao (New Haven), Gabriele Taentzer (Marburg), Cesare Tinelli (Iowa), Jan Vitek (West Lafayette), and Lenore Zuck (Chicago).

I sincerely thank all ETAPS SC members for all their hard work in making the 17th ETAPS a success. Moreover, thanks to all speakers, attendants, organizers of the satellite workshops, and Springer for their support. Finally, many thanks to Saddek Bensalem and his local organization team for all their efforts enabling ETAPS to return to the French Alps in Grenoble!

January 2014   Joost-Pieter Katoen

Preface

This volume contains the proceedings of the 23rd European Symposium on Programming (ESOP 2014). The conference took place in Grenoble, France, during April 8–10, 2014, as part of the European Joint Conferences on Theory and Practice of Software (ETAPS).

ESOP is an annual conference devoted to the art and science of programming. The conference solicits contributions on fundamental issues concerning the specification, analysis, and implementation of systems and programming languages.

The 2014 conference attracted 138 abstracts and 109 full submissions. For each submission, we solicited at least three reviews from the Program Committee members and external reviewers. After an intensive electronic meeting over two weeks, the Program Committee accepted 27 papers for presentation.

In addition, this volume also contains two invited papers, "Composable Transactional Objects: A Position Paper" by Maurice Herlihy and Eric Koskinen, and "Application-Scale Secure Multiparty Computation" by John Launchbury, Dave Archer, Thomas Dubuisson, and Eric Mertens. Maurice Herlihy presented his paper as the ESOP invited talk and John Launchbury presented his paper as one of the two ETAPS-wide invited talks in Grenoble.

I would like thank my fellow Program Committee members for their hard work on selecting a high quality and stimulating program of contributed papers. I also wish to thank the numerous external reviewers, without whom running such a large conference would be impossible. Finally, together with my colleagues on the Program Committee, I want to thank the authors of all submissions for entrusting us with their work and the authors of the accepted papers for their diligent work in preparing their final versions and their conference presentations.

I acknowledge the use of the EasyChair conference system and the support of the ETAPS 2014 General Chair, Saddek Bensalem, and the ETAPS Steering Committee and its Chair, Joost-Pieter Katoen, with regard to all the administrative work.

January 2014   Zhong Shao

Conference Organization

Program Chair

Zhong Shao   Yale University, USA

Program Committee

Zena Ariola	University of Oregon, USA
Gavin Bierman	Microsoft Research, UK
Viviana Bono	University of Turin, Italy
Luis Caires	Universidade Nova de Lisboa, Portugal
Avik Chaudhuri	Facebook, USA
Koen Claessen	Chalmers University of Technology, Sweden
Isil Dillig	University of Texas, Austin, USA
Roberto Giacobazzi	University of Verona, Italy
Alexey Gotsman	IMDEA Software Institute, Spain
Martin Hofmann	LMU Munich, Germany
Zhenjiang Hu	National Institute of Informatics, Japan
Joxan Jaffar	National University of Singapore, Singapore
Neel Krishnaswami	University of Birmingham, UK
Paul-André Melliès	CNRS and Université Paris Diderot, France
Todd Millstein	University of California, Los Angeles, USA
Tobias Nipkow	TU Munich, Germany
David Pichardie	ENS Cachan, France
Francois Pottier	INRIA Rocquencourt, France
Tom Schrijvers	Ghent University, Belgium
David Van Horn	University of Maryland, USA
Martin Vechev	ETH Zurich, Switzerland
Philip Wadler	University of Edinburgh, UK
Nobuko Yoshida	Imperial College London, UK
Steve Zdancewic	University of Pennsylvania, USA

Additional Reviewers

Andreas Abel	Giovanni Bernardi	Edwin Brady
Aws Albarghouthi	Jean-Philippe Bernardy	Marco Carbone
Jade Alglave	Yves Bertot	Giuseppe Castagna
Davide Ancona	Frédéric Besson	Bor-Yuh Evan Chang
Thibaut Balabonski	Laura Bocchi	Arthur Charguéraud

Wei Chen
James Cheney
Chiachun Lin
Wei-Ngan Chin
Adam Chlipala
Horation Cirstea
Pierre Clairambault
David Cock
Pierre-Louis Curien
Ugo Dal Lago
Olivier Danvy
Gwenaël Delaval
Delphine Demange
M. Dezani-Ciancaglini
Pietro Di Gianantonio
Alessandra Di Pierro
Thomas Dillig
Thomas Dinsdale-Young
Paul Downen
Gregory Duck
Anton Ekblad
Kento Emoto
Sebastian Erdweg
Nikita Frolov
Carsten Fuhs
Marco Gaboardi
Marc Geilen
Samir Genaim
Giorgio Ghelli
Dan Ghica
Elena Giachino
Georges Gonthier
Denis Gopan
Andrew Gordon
Philipp Haller
Makoto Hamana
Ichiro Hasuo
Willem Heijltjes
Fritz Henglein
Atsushi Igarashi
Kazuhiro Inaba
Jun Inoue
Bart Jacobs

Barry Jay
Alan Jeffrey
Jacob Johannsen
Steffen Jost
Ohad Kammar
Andrew Kennedy
Steven Keuchel
M. Kirkedal Thomsen
Naoki Kobayashi
Nicolas Koh
Igor Konnov
Laura Kovacs
Arun Lakhotia
Ivan Lanese
Xavier Leroy
Sam Lindley
Francesco Logozzo
Carlos Lombardi
Gregory Malecha
Louis Mandel
Isabella Mastroeni
Kazutaka Matsuda
Damiano Mazza
Massimo Merro
Jan Midtgaard
Fabrizio Montesi
Garrett Morris
Markus Müller-Olm
Keisuke Nakano
Carlos Olarte
Bruno Oliveira
Hugo Pacheco
Luca Padovani
Michele Pagani
Long Pang
Matthew Parkinson
Mathias Peron
Gustavo Petri
Andreas Podelski
Andrei Popescu
Louis-Noel Pouchet
Marc Pouzet
Matthias Puech

Jorge Pérez
Willard Rafnsson
Robert Rand
Francesco Ranzato
Julian Rathke
António Ravara
Didier Remy
Dan Rosen
Claudio Russo
Andrey Rybalchenko
Andrew Santosa
Gabriel Scherer
Dave Schmidt
Alan Schmitt
Klaus Schneider
Aleksy Schubert
Ulrich Schöpp
Peter Sestoft
Vilhelm Sjöberg
Christian Skalka
Nick Smallbone
Marcelo Sousa
Matthieu Sozeau
Manu Sridharan
Stephen Strickland
Josef Svenningsson
Bernardo Toninho
Hugo Torres Vieira
Aaron Turon
Nikos Tzevelekos
Christian Urban
Benoît Valiron
Daniele Varacca
Panagiotis Vekris
Björn Victor
Dimitrios Vytiniotis
Guido Wachsmuth
Meng Wang
Stephanie Weirich
Eran Yahav
Roland Yap
Jooyong Yi
Florian Zuleger

Table of Contents

Semantics

Concurrency

Linear Types

Program Verification II

Network and Process Calculi

Program Analysis

Composable Transactional Objects:
A Position Paper

Maurice Herlihy[1] and Eric Koskinen[2]

[1] Brown University, Providence, RI, USA
[2] New York University, New York, NY, USA

Abstract. Memory transactions provide programmers with a convenient abstraction for concurrent programs: a keyword (such as atomic) designating a region of code that appears, from the perspective of concurrent threads, to execute atomically. Unfortunately, existing implementations in the form of software transactional memory (STM) are often ineffective due to their monolithic nature: every single read or write access is automatically tracked and recorded.

In this statement, we advocate a transactional model of programming without a heavyweight software transactional memory, and describe some related, open research challenges. We suggest that a model based on *persistent data structures* could permit a variety of transactional algorithms to coexist in a library of *composable transactional objects*. Applications are constructed by snapping these objects together to form atomic transactions, in much the same way that today's Java programmers compose their applications from libraries such as java.util.concurrent.

We report preliminary results developing this library in ScalaSTM, and discuss the challenges ahead.

Keywords: Composable transactional objects, transactional memory, persistent, multicore.

1   Introduction

Existing transactional memory systems (hardware [3,11,12], software [9,18,6], or hybrid [5,16]) detect conflicts at a *read-write* level: each transaction keeps track of a *read set*, the locations it read, and a *write set*, the locations it wrote. Two transactions are deemed to conflict if one's write set intersects the other's read or write set. The TM run-time typically intercepts all memory accesses, tracks each transaction's read and write sets, and delays or restarts transactions that encounter conflicts.

There is an increasing realization that tracking read-write conflicts is *inefficient*, because each and every memory access must be monitored for conflict and recorded for potential roll-back, and *ineffective*, because *false conflicts* frequently arise when read and write sets inadvertently intersect in a harmless way. For example, consider an object that generates unique identifiers. Logically, there is no reason that concurrent identifier requests should conflict. If the generator is

Z. Shao (Ed.): ESOP 2014, LNCS 8410, pp. 1–7, 2014.

implemented in a natural way as a counter, however, then today's STM systems will unnecessarily detect a conflict. Perhaps as a result, performance remains a barrier to widespread use of today's STMs.

In this position paper, we propose an alternative research direction, based on libraries of *composable transactional objects*, which we are currently building using ScalaSTM [1]. Our goal here is to outline a research vision, calling attention to open problems and new directions.

In this alternate direction, the unity of our library is not ensured by a monolithic STM but instead defined at a higher level: *persistent objects* [7]. Informally, this property ensures that one can reconstruct (some or all) earlier versions of the object even after it has been modified. The notion of persistent objects allows us to combine diverse transactional algorithms into composable objects that "snap together" to form atomic transactions. Our prior work on *transactional boosting* [10], is an example of how one might implement a composable transactional object, replacing bit-level read-write conflicts with a high-level notion of conflicts between non-commutative methods of abstract data types.

2   Overview

We advocate a move away from the pervasive notion that transactional synchronization must be done on the basis of *read-write conflicts*. Synchronization based entirely on read-write conflicts has three drawbacks: (*i*) it can limit concurrency through false conflicts, (*ii*) it can burden performance by instrumenting too many memory accesses, and (*iii*) it can hamper recovery by requiring bit-wise copying of large amounts of data.

Nonetheless, a library of transactional objects is only useful if the objects can be combined together. In this section we describe a new route toward a library of composable transactional objects via the notion of *persistent* objects. Let's begin with an example object.

Example Transactional Object. Consider the object in Fig. 1 that implements transactions via *boosting* [10]. This figure (see the original paper [10] for a more systematic explanation) shows part of the (Scala) code for a highly-concurrent transactional key-value map that provides put() and get() methods. The base object is the ConcurrentSkipListMap class from the java.util.concurrent library. For transactional synchronization, the key insight is that method calls for distinct keys commute, so concurrent transactions that operate on distinct keys can proceed in parallel, even if their underlying read and write sets conflict. In this code, transactional isolation is provided by our AbstractLock class, which associates each key value (via an internal hash table) with an abstract lock. Abstract locks are strict two-phase locks: each method call acquires the lock associated with its key (Line 6), to be released when the transaction commits or aborts (Line 7). If the transaction eventually aborts, the run time system is requested to restore the previous binding if there was one (Line 10), or to remove the new binding if there wasn't (Line 12). Finally, the new binding is placed in the map (Line 14).

```
1   import java. util . concurrent. ConcurrentSkipListMap
2   class BoostedSkipList[Key,Value] {
3     private val abstractLock = new AbstractLock()
4     private val map = new ConcurrentSkipListMap[Key, Value]()
5     def put(key: Key, value: Value, t = Transaction.current ): Unit = {
6       abstractLock lock key
7       Transaction .onExit ( () => abstractLock unlock key )
8       if (map containsKey key) {
9         var oldValue = map.get(key)
10        Transaction .onAbort(() => map.put(key, oldValue))
11      } else {
12        Transaction .onAbort(() => map remove key)
13      }
14      map.put(key, value)
15    }
16    ...
17  }
```

Fig. 1. A boosted Concurrent Skip List

We have "boosted" a highly complex and highly optimized skip-list map implementation, written by someone else, from being thread-safe to transaction-safe, without rewriting a line of its code. Because the base ConcurrentSkipListMap class provides its own thread-level synchronization, it is safe for concurrent threads to make put() calls concurrently at Line 14. Moreover, there is no need for an underlying STM to intercept and track each low-level read and write access, nor to block or roll back transactions whose read and write sets overlap. Here, transaction recovery is implemented by logging and replaying inverse operations, potentially a much more compact and efficient means of recovery than the usual STM technique of manipulating large, bit-level *before* and *after* images. Deadlocks are detected and resolved using the *Dreadlocks* deadlock detection algorithm [14] developed for this purpose. Finally, this boosted implementation satisfies *opacity* [8], a correctness condition that ensures that all transactions, even those doomed to abort, observe a consistent memory state.

3   Persistent Data Structures

Boosting marks an escape from the monolithic approach present in today's STMs. While there is a substantial performance improvement, we have lost the uniformity of a monolithic STM. It is natural to wonder: how can such transactional objects interoperate with other objects that, themselves, may utilize (possibly different) transactional algorithms?

We argue that we can elevate the common conceptual framework that unifies diverse transactional algorithms. A boosted object can coexist with a transactional object built, for example, in a speculative manner (as discussed next).

And so on. This is what Java programmers, who today combine myriad lock/lock-free java.util.concurrent objects, would expect of a library of transactional objects. We argue that this can be done with objects that are persistent:

Definition 1 (Persistent Object [7]). *A mutable data object is* persistent *if one can reconstruct earlier versions even after the object has been modified. It is said to be* partially persistent *if only some versions can be reconstructed, and it is* confluently persistent *if new versions created by concurrent activities can be merged in a meaningful way.*

Informally, persistent objects allow us to scroll backwards and forwards through time, giving us a great deal of flexibility at run-time to serialize concurrent object operations. Of course a completely persistent object is impractical. So this leads us to research questions such as: *Which* earlier versions must persist? *For how long* must they persist?

Let's look at an example. Here is how one can make a boosted object be persistent. If the object retains the undo logs of committed transactions, then any earlier version can be reconstructed by cloning the base object, and replaying the undo log back to the desired version.

Our use of persistent objects as a basis for both transactional synchronization and semantics is an attempt to combine the well-known benefits of functional programming with the unavoidable need for high-level mutable state, much in the spirit of our earlier work on transactional Haskell [9].

4   Optimism

In boosting, transactions apply method calls directly to the base object, relying on an operation-based undo log to roll back failed transactions. In this way, synchronization in boosting is *pessimistic*, because transactions check for conflicts before calling a method. An alternative is *optimistic* (or *speculative*) synchronization, where transactions check for conflicts only at the end. (Checking for conflicts is often called *validation*.) Many STM systems (for example, TL2 [6]) operate this way: updates to shared memory are deferred until commit. Optimistic synchronization can reduce costs if conflicts are sufficiently rare.

Here is another scenario where deferred updates might be attractive. In a non-uniform memory access (NUMA) architecture, threads can access local memory quickly, and remote memory more slowly. In such a situation, each thread might operate on its own local copy of the base object. When it commits after validation, it propagates its changes (in the form of an operation-based redo log) to the other threads. The Barrelfish [2] operating system is organized around a similar philosophy.

Optimistic synchronization involves objects that are *confluently persistent* [7]: new object versions can be created by concurrent activities as long as those versions can be merged in a meaningful way. Usually, operations can be merged as long as they commute, but weaker properties, involving left- and right-movers, can also be used [15].

This move toward composable transactional objects enables us to incorporate other transactional features such as checkpoints and nested transactions. We can even model *dependent* transactions [17], where one transaction releases its results to another before committing, and the second transaction's commit depends on the first's.

5 Preliminary Results and the Road Ahead

We have embodied our ideas in library of composable transactional objects, implemented in ScalaSTM. Our implementation replaces the existing heavyweight run-time that mediates all transactional memory interactions with a much less obtrusive structure. Our system provides only the following services:

- onCommit() registers a closure to be called when a top-level transaction commits. Closures are called in first-in-first-out order, useful for redo logs.
- onAbort() registers a closure to be called when a transaction (nested or top-level) aborts. Closures are called in last-in-first-out order, useful for undo logs.
- onExit() registers a closure to be called when a top-level transaction commits or aborts, useful for releasing abstract locks, certain kinds of I/O, and memory management.
- onValidate() registers a Boolean-valued closure to be called before a top-level transaction commits or aborts. A transaction commits only if all such return values are *true*. This service is useful for speculative synchronization.

Versioning. At the implementation level, object versions are indexed by transaction identifiers. At all times, there is a unique system-wide identifier for the latest committed transaction, which indexes the latest committed state for each object. Operations of composable transactional objects take a transaction identifier as a default argument, with the currently executing transaction as the default. Objects are confluently persistent in the sense that they can permit concurrent method calls to the committed version, provided the object implementation is capable of merging them, based on commutativity or other type-specific properties. When a thread commits a transaction, it installs that transaction as the latest committed transaction, when it aborts, it discards that transaction and the versions it indexes do not become accessible to the other threads. A long read-only transaction is one that executes under a committed transaction, running against a set of object versions "frozen" at that time. (Not all objects will provide access to older versions.)

Challenges. Our next step is to finish a comprehensive implementation of composable transactional objects with a wide range of transactional algorithms. There are then some open research challenges, including:

1. Investigating trade-offs between granularity and performance in data structure design, and port benchmarks such as STAMP [4] to ScalaSTM.

2. Investigating how special support can be added to aid long-running (in particular, read-only) transactions.
3. Exploring other novel control structures, such as the retry construct for conditional transactional synchronization, and the orElse construct for composing conditional synchronization (as introduced in Transactional Haskell [9]). Elsewhere [13], we described how boosting can be extended to support these and other useful control structures, but a more general approach to composable transactional objects will require rethinking and extending these mechanisms.
4. Exploiting hardware transactions, of the kind recently provided by Intel Haswell [12] and soon to be provided by the IBM Power architecture [3].
5. Developing accessible verification techniques to ensuring the correctness of these objects which we believe will be used widely.

References

1. ScalaSTM, http://nbronson.github.io/scala-stm/
2. Baumann, A., Barham, P., Dagand, P.-E., Harris, T., Isaacs, R., Peter, S., Roscoe, T., Schüpbach, A., Singhania, A.: The multikernel: a new os architecture for scalable multicore systems. In: Proceedings of the ACM SIGOPS 22nd Symposium on Operating Systems Principles, SOSP 2009, pp. 29–44. ACM, New York (2009)
3. Cain, H.W., Michael, M.M., Frey, B., May, C., Williams, D., Le, H.: Robust architectural support for transactional memory in the power architecture. In: Proceedings of the 40th Annual International Symposium on Computer Architecture, ISCA 2013, pp. 225–236. ACM, New York (2013)
4. Cao Minh, C., Trautmann, M., Chung, J., McDonald, A., Bronson, N., Casper, J., Kozyrakis, C., Olukotun, K.: An effective hybrid transactional memory system with strong isolation guarantees. In: Proceedings of the 34th Annual International Symposium on Computer Architecture, ISCA 2007 (June 2007)
5. Damron, P., Fedorova, A., Lev, Y., Luchangco, V., Moir, M., Nussbaum, D.: Hybrid transactional memory. In: Proceedings of the 12th International Conference on Architectural Support for Programming Languages and Operating Systems (ASPLOS-XII), pp. 336–346. ACM Press, New York (2006)
6. Dice, D., Shalev, O., Shavit, N.N.: Transactional locking II. In: Dolev, S. (ed.) DISC 2006. LNCS, vol. 4167, pp. 194–208. Springer, Heidelberg (2006)
7. Driscoll, J.R., Sarnak, N., Sleator, D.D., Tarjan, R.E.: Making data structures persistent. J. Comput. Syst. Sci. 38(1), 86–124 (1989)
8. Guerraoui, R., Kapalka, M.: On the correctness of transactional memory. In: Proceedings of the 13th ACM SIGPLAN Symposium on Principles and practice of parallel programming, PPoPP 2008, pp. 175–184. ACM, New York (2008)
9. Harris, T., Marlow, S., Peyton-Jones, S.L., Herlihy, M.: Composable memory transactions. Commun. ACM 51(8), 91–100 (2008)
10. Herlihy, M., Koskinen, E.: Transactional boosting: a methodology for highly-concurrent transactional objects. In: Proceedings of the 13th ACM SIGPLAN Symposium on Principles and Practice of Parallel Programming, PPoPP 2008, pp. 207–216. ACM, New York (2008)
11. Herlihy, M., Moss, J.E.B.: Transactional memory: architectural support for lock-free data structures. In: Proceedings of the 20th Annual International Symposium on Computer Architecture, ISCA 1993, pp. 289–300. ACM Press (1993)

12. Intel Corporation. Transactional Synchronization in Haswell (September 8, 2012), http://software.intel.com/en-us/blogs/2012/02/07/ transactional-synchronization-in-haswell/ (retrieved from)
13. Koskinen, E., Herlihy, M.: Checkpoints and continuations instead of nested transactions. In: Proceedings of the Twentieth Annual Symposium on Parallelism in Algorithms and Architectures, SPAA 2008, pp. 160–168. ACM, New York (2008)
14. Koskinen, E., Herlihy, M.: Dreadlocks: efficient deadlock detection. In: Proceedings of the Twentieth Annual Symposium on Parallelism in Algorithms and Architectures, SPAA 2008, pp. 297–303. ACM, New York (2008)
15. Koskinen, E., Parkinson, M., Herlihy, M.: Coarse-grained transactions. In: Proceedings of the 37th Annual ACM SIGPLAN-SIGACT Symposium on Principles of Programming Languages, POPL 2010, pp. 19–30. ACM, New York (2010)
16. Moravan, M.J., Bobba, J., Moore, K.E., Yen, L., Hill, M.D., Liblit, B., Swift, M.M., Wood, D.A.: Supporting nested transactional memory in logtm. In: Proceedings of the 12th International Conference on Architectural Support for Programming Languages and Operating Systems (ASPLOS-XII), pp. 359–370. ACM Press, New York (2006)
17. Ramadan, H.E., Roy, I., Herlihy, M., Witchel, E.: Committing conflicting transactions in an stm. In: PPOPP, pp. 163–172 (2009)
18. Saha, B., Adl-Tabatabai, A.-R., Hudson, R.L., Minh, C.C., Hertzberg, B.: McRT-STM: a high performance software transactional memory system for a multi-core runtime. In: Proceedings of the Eleventh ACM SIGPLAN Symposium on Principles and Practice of Parallel Programming, PPoPP 2006, pp. 187–197. ACM, New York (2006)

Application-Scale Secure Multiparty Computation

John Launchbury, Dave Archer, Thomas DuBuisson, and Eric Mertens

Galois, Inc*

Abstract. Secure multiparty computation (MPC) permits a collection
of parties to compute a collaborative result without any of the parties
or compute servers gaining any knowledge about the inputs provided by
other parties, except what can be determined from the output of the
computation. In the form of MPC known as linear (or additive) sharing,
computation proceeds on data that appears entirely random. Operations
such as addition or logical-XOR can be performed purely locally, but operations such as multiplication or logical-AND require a network communication between the parties. Consequently, the computational overhead
of MPC is large, and the cost is still measured in orders of magnitude
slowdown with respect to computing in the clear. However, efficiency improvements over the last few years have shifted the potential applicability
of MPC from just micro benchmarks to user-level applications.

To assess how close MPC is to real world use we implement and assess two very different MPC-based applications—secure email filtering
and secure teleconference VoIP. Because the computation cost model is
very different from traditional machines, the implementations required a
significantly different set of algorithmic and compiler techniques. We describe a collection of the techniques we found to be important, including
SAT-based circuit optimization and an optimized table lookup primitive.

1 Introduction

It is scarcely possible to read the news without seeing yet another reason to
be able to perform computation on encrypted data. The cryptography community has long known that some kinds of computations on encrypted data are
possible—at least in principle. This was notably demonstrated by Yao's seminal
work on secure multiparty computation [Y86], and most radically by Gentry's
work on fully homomorphic encryption (FHE) [G09]. While FHE is very new
and still far from practical, there has been significant effort in the last few years
to make MPC usable in practice.

MPC computations permit a collection of parties to compute a collaborative
result, without any of the parties gaining any knowledge about the inputs provided by other parties (other than what is derivable from the final result of the

---

* This material is based upon work supported by the Defense Advanced Research
Projects Agency through the U.S. Office of Naval Research under Contract N00014-
11-C-0333. The views expressed are those of the author and do not reflect the official
policy or position of the Department of Defense or the U.S. Government.

computation). In recent years, the variant of MPC called *linear shared computation* has been producing significant performance wins [BLW08, LAD12, DKL+13].

When we say "performance wins", we should put it in context: on test cases such as securely decrypting AES-encrypted text, we have been seeing linear sharing achieving execution times of around 3–30ms per 128-bit block, which corresponds to a slowdown of around four to five orders of magnitude compared with computation in the clear. Significant though this slowdown is, it compares well with Yao and especially with FHE, whose current slowdowns appear to be respectively around six and nine orders of magnitude in our experience.

There are two fundamental reasons why secure computation proceeds more slowly than computation in the clear. First, all secure computations have to be performed generically across all possible input and internal values (otherwise information is revealed), though there are neat algorithms which can sometimes amortize this somewhat across multiple accesses. Second, the multi-party schemes (both Yao and linear sharing) require significant network communication, typically growing linearly with the size of the function being evaluated.

MPC protocols can be targeted to different security models, but the performance cost in establishing and maintaining the security for particular models can vary significantly. The simplest security model used for secure computation is *honest but curious* [G04], where the separate parties are assumed to follow the protocol honestly, but may at the same time attempt to learn secrets by looking at internal values of the computation, including any communications. This security model is appropriate for settings such as preventing information leakage by individuals with administrator access, or after a cyber snooping break-in. There are also fairly generic techniques for augmenting honest-but-curious protocols to provide more stringent security guarantees (such as against malicious adversaries who intend to subvert the computation), so the honest-but-curious protocol may be seen as a significant first step towards constructing more secure versions.

1.1   Contributions of This Paper

In this paper, we address the challenge of scaling secure computation to a level required by applications. We implement two: a mail filter, which matches encrypted email texts against regular expressions, and VoIP teleconference calling, which merges and clips multiple audio streams in real-time.

To implement these, we used the *ShareMonad*, a Haskell-embedded domain-specific language for programming secure multiparty computations, with a linear-sharing backend [LAD12]. The ShareMonad view considers the secure multiparty computational substrate as an *MPC-machine*—an abstract machine with highly non-standard interface and performance properties. The implementation comes with a variety of ad-hoc techniques for minimizing expensive operations, either by reducing the overhead of individual operations (through exploiting opportunities for SIMD-like parallelization), or by hiding residual latencies involved in network-based operations. To scale to the size and performance required by our target applications, we further developed the backend optimizations. In particular:

– We developed and implemented many compile-time optimizations, including SAT-based reasoning to replace (expensive) AND-operations with (cheap) XOR-operations, and balancing and packing of global operations to minimize the number and size of network communications.

– We also created a new version of the table lookup primitive, introduced in [LAD12]. This performs secret lookup of an n-bit index in a public table using $log(n)$ global operations (as before), but where each global operation now communicates no more than $2^{1+n/2}$ individual bits. We also optimize the local computations involved in the table-lookup with some pre-computation on the table. Together, these make a huge difference in both computation and network performance. In effect, the compiler uses the table lookup protocol as a mechanism for building custom wide-word instructions that are generated based on the program.

2   Background

The secure computation scheme we use is simple linear (arithmetic) sharing across three peer machines acting as the compute servers. For the protocols we discuss, the three machines run the same code as each other, and communicate (and hence synchronize) between themselves in a cyclic pattern, as shown in Figure 1. Some more complex protocols require less uniform computation and communication patterns, but we won't need them here.

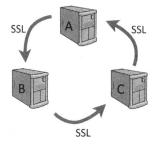

Fig. 1. Machine Configuration

The diagram shows the links protected with SSL. The critical point is that the links are protected by some mechanism, otherwise a network snooper could access the three random shares of a value and so reconstruct the original. For performance and thread-safe reasons, we use a homegrown commsec package instead of OpenSSL, that is 3× faster on small messages.

In an *arithmetic* sharing scheme, private (secret) values never exist concretely but instead are represented by three separate *shared* values, each of which lives on one of the peer servers. A value is shared between the machines in a form that is dependent on its type. Fixed-width integer types (e.g Int16, Int32, etc) are shared arithmetically. Thus, a true value x in Int16 will be shared as three randomly drawn values x_A, x_B, x_C such that $x = x_A + x_B + x_C$ (*mod* 2^{16}). The shares are produced originally by generating x_A and x_B randomly from a uniform distribution, and then defining $x_C = x - x_A - x_B$. Despite x_C being computed, each one of the three numbers exhibit the properties of being fully random, and knowledge of any two of the numbers provides absolutely zero knowledge about the original private value[1]. Subsequently, the computational protocols maintain the share property through the calculations that are performed.

Sharing is lifted to structured types as follows: tuples of private values are shared component-wise, and fixed-length sequences of values (i.e. lists or arrays) are shared element-wise. Thus, a private value of a sequence $[x, y, z]$ will be shared as three (equal length) sequences of randomly drawn values $[x_A, y_A, z_A]$, $[x_B, y_B, z_B], [x_C, y_C, z_C]$ such that $x = x_A + x_B + x_C$, and so on. Sequences of bits are a special case of more general sequences. They need to be handled in an efficient way (else the overhead can kill many algorithmic improvements), so we treat fixed-width bit-vectors (represented as unsigned integers in the Share-Monad library) as if they were sequences of individual bits (i.e. elements of Int1, where multiplication is just boolean AND, and addition is XOR). Thus, a private value x in Word8 (a bit-vector of length 8) will be shared as three randomly drawn values x_A, x_B, x_C such that $x = x_A \oplus x_B \oplus x_C$ (where $\oplus$ is bitwise xor).

To add together two private numbers which are represented by shares, we can simply add together the component shares and we are done. To multiply two private numbers, we have to compute nine partial products of their shares (Fig. 2).

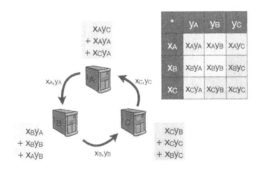

Fig. 2. Computing the Partial Products

Each machine already has the values it needs to enable it to compute one of the entries on the diagonal. If each machine also communicates its shares of x and y to its neighbor (according to the pattern in Fig. 1), then every partial product in the matrix can be computed by somebody. All three machines are

---

[1] Even if given two of the values, x_A and x_C say, every possible value for x has equal probability, depending entirely on the value of x_B.

operating loosely in lockstep, so all are executing the same instruction at around the same time. On receiving the neighbor's value, each machine computes three partial products, XORs them together, and now has a share of the full product.

We need an additional refinement. If we performed multiple multiplications in a sequence, we could easily end up rotating particular share values to all three servers. This would then reveal enough information to reconstruct a private value, and so violate security. To avoid this, we take an extra step and re-randomize the shares before communication. Because of this, each use of multiply communicates re-randomized shares, and so no information accumulates. Cryptographically, this makes the multiply operation *universally composable*, that is, we can use it repeatedly without fear of violating security. As the addition operation requires no communication, it automatically has this property.

3   Applications

We selected two target applications: a secure mail filter, and secure VoIP teleconference calling. They exhibit a significant divergence in application characteristics. The mail server is a batch process that evaluates regular expressions, and the VoIP system is a soft real-time system using simple audio algorithms. We describe each of the applications, including their set-up, and then turn to consider how to scale the secure computation components in each.

3.1   Secure Mail Filter

In the secure mail filter architecture in Fig. 3, the sender S writes an email in Thunderbird. We created a plug-in that encrypts the email, and sends an encrypted email package to a stock mail server.

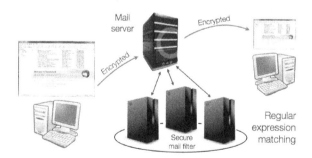

Fig. 3. Architecture of the Secure Mail Filter

We also created a "milter" plug-in for the mail server using the standard mail filter interface. The mail server automatically passes the encrypted email package to the plug-in, which is just a coordinator component that forwards the package to each of three cooperating share servers and awaits their responses.

As we shall see in a moment, the share servers each open the encrypted package (to the extent that they are able), extract random shares of the encrypted email, and together engage in a cooperative secure computation to analyze encrypted e-mail. When they have done their work, they return a random share of their boolean response to the plug-in, who XORs them together to obtain the mail filter response. If the answer is in the affirmative, the mail server forwards the message packet on to the recipient R. Otherwise, the mail server informs S of the rejection.

Communicating with the Share Servers. The sender S constructs an encrypted packet of data such that each of the recipients can extract exactly what they need, and no more than they should. In particular, neither the mail server nor the plug-in filter coordinating component should be allowed to know the content of the email. The three share servers A, B and C should each be able to obtain a random share of the original email, and the ultimate receiver of the email, R, should be able to read the whole thing—assuming the message is permitted through the email filter.

To accomplish all this, S uses a stream cipher encryption algorithm, Enc, such as AES in counter mode, together with a public-key system, Pub, such as RSA. S randomly generates three share-keys k_A, k_B and k_C, for the three share servers, and then computes a pseudo-random stream $\overline{k_A} = Enc_{k_A}(\overline{0})$ (the stream of zeroes encrypted using the stream cipher), and similarly computes pseudo-random streams $\overline{k_B}$ and $\overline{k_C}$. Using these streams as one-time pads, S creates a cipher text of the email message $CT = m \oplus \overline{k_A} \oplus \overline{k_B} \oplus \overline{k_C}$.

S now constructs and sends a package containing CT, together with targeted encryptions of the keys, namely $Pub_R(k_A, k_B, k_C)$, $Pub_A(k_A)$, $Pub_B(k_B)$, and $Pub_C(k_C)$, where $Pub_A(\_)$ is encryption using A's public key, and likewise for B, C, and R.

On receipt of the package, each of the servers A, B and C obtains the respective keys k_A, k_B and k_C (using their private keys), and now each can locally compute a copy of their designated pseudo-random stream: A computes $\overline{k_A}$ and B and C likewise. Using these streams, each of A, B, and C can construct a share of the original email message m: share $m_A = \overline{k_A} \oplus CT$, share $m_B = \overline{k_B} \oplus CT$, and share $m_C = \overline{k_C} \oplus CT$. The XOR ($\oplus$) of these three is the original message m as all the pseudo-random streams will cancel out.

Note than none of the servers are able to reconstruct m itself. In contrast, should the message pass the filter and be sent on, the recipient R will be able to reconstruct m, because it has been sent the keys that generate the three one-time pads.

The Secure Computation. The decision as to whether to send the email to the recipient or not is to be based on the result of evaluating a regular expression. For example, a filter for rejecting emails containing paragraphs with particular security markings might start to look something like this:

```
.*(((TOP|)SECRET)|TS|S)--SI--NO(CON|CONTRACTOR|FORN|FOREIGN).*
```

Each of the three share servers will know the regular expressions being used, but such details may be kept private from everyone else if desired.

There are many ways to evaluate regular expressions in plain text. For the secure setting we chose an algorithm based on non-deterministic finite automata (NFA), as opposed to selecting on the DFA algorithms. As every step of the algorithm has to operate over the whole of the state anyway (so as not to reveal which states are active), it makes sense to have many of those states active during computation[2].

For concreteness we used an efficient NFA algorithm that has been beautifully described in Haskell [FHW10]. The clarity of the description made it particularly easy to re-express the algorithm in our Haskell-based share language. We do not need to describe the algorithm in detail here. Suffice it to say that the algorithm uses a tree representation of the regular expression to represent the state, with each node of the tree flagged (or not) if the corresponding position in the regular expression is a match for the portion of the string consumed so far.

Fig. 4 shows an example for the regular expression (xy)*x after consuming just the input "x".

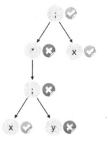

Fig. 4. Match-Annotated Regular Expression

For each new input character, the algorithm computes how to update the set of matched flags. That is, the matching function updates the flag-states on receipt of each new input character to produce a new flag-state for the computation on any remaining input characters. The flag corresponding to the top of the tree indicates whether the input so far has matched the entire regular expression.

3.2 Application 2: Secure VoIP Teleconference

For the second application we selected a client-server VoIP teleconference application that performs audio mixing of encrypted audio streams in real time.

---

[2] It would be interesting future work to explore the alternative choice: select a DFA algorithm, expand the NFA state set into a corresponding DFA state set (which can be significantly larger), and then use locality of the active state to gain amortized complexity improvements in the resulting secure computation.

As Fig. 5 shows, the architecture we used for the VoIP application is very similar to the mail filter application. This allowed us to re-use parts of the infrastructure even though the characteristics of the underlying computation were very different.

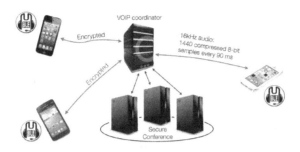

Fig. 5. Architecture of the Secure VoIP Teleconference

The client is a slightly modified open-source iOS-based implementation of the popular Mumble application[Mum], running on iPhone 5s, iPad Mini, and iPad Touch devices. The server is a modified open-source Linux-based implementation of the uMurmur VoIP server application, together with three share servers to perform the encrypted merges.

As with the mail filter setup, we communicate to the share servers by negotiating temporary keys, but with two differences. First, we negotiate temporary keys just once at the start of the audio stream and use the same keys throughout. Second, each client will generate a pair of keys for each server, one for the audio stream sent to the server, the other for the stream being received.

Each client samples audio into a 16kHz PCM data stream of 16-bit fixed point values. These are encoded by logarithmic compression to 8-bit uLAW samples. To tolerate processing and transmission latencies, the clients collect samples into 1440-sample packets, each packet containing 90ms of audio.

To transmit the audio, each client encrypts each audio packet by XORing the data with the XOR of the three pseudo-random streams, as with the mail filter. Similarly, the share servers each receive the data and extract their individual share of the audio packet by XORing it with their individual pseudo-random stream.

In each 90ms epoch, the share servers will compute multiple result streams— one for each client—by merging all the streams except for the client's own input audio stream. This saves us having to do echo-cancellation, but means the computation has to be repeated n times (for n clients). For each-8 bit packet of compressed audio, the computation is as shown in Fig. 6.

For each encrypted compressed sample in the packet, the share servers have to (1) decompress the sample to reform a 16 bit PCM sample, (2) add the decompressed value to the corresponding values in the packets from the other clients,

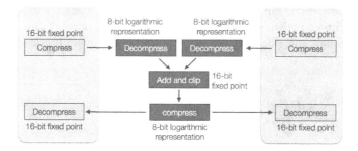

Fig. 6. Data Processing of Audio Packets

making sure that overflow or underflow are handled by graceful clipping, and (3) recompress the resulting 16-bit output audio sample into 8-bits for sending to the client. All of this has to be done cooperatively as the samples are encrypted throughout.

This process is repeated for each client packet received during the epoch. Thus for four clients, each share server has to perform 23,040 secure add-and-clip computations[3] every 90ms!

At the end of each 90ms epoch, the three share servers all XOR the result with the output key for each client, and send each result to the respective client. On receipt, each uMurmur client performs a matching decryption, and the samples in the resulting decrypted audio packet are uLAW decoded into 16 bit PCM format and inserted into a queue for audio playback.

4   Scaling the Secure Computation

Now that we have the structure of the applications, we turn our attention to ensuring the secure computation can scale to provide sufficient performance. Our notion of "sufficient" is not rigorous here; it is intended to reflect whether the results are even in the vicinity of being practical or not.

4.1   Secure Mail Filter

As with many EDSLs, the ShareMonad can produce many different kinds of interpretations of its "programs". One of the interpretations is an abstract representation of the arithmetic and/or logical "circuit" described in the ShareMonad program. In effect, it represents a partial evaluation of the program, leaving behind only the portion that needs to be executed securely.

As we noted earlier, in a step-by-step algorithm like regular expression matching—where each step consumes another input character—the circuit takes two kinds of input: the state of the computation from previous steps, and the new character being consumed. In turn it delivers a value representing the state

---
[3] 23,040 = 1440 samples × 4 input packets × 4 distinct audio result streams.

after this character has been considered. The updated state is used as the input state for the next character (Fig. 7). We also have shown extracting a boolean representing whether the whole regular expression has been matched.

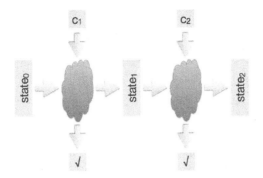

Fig. 7. Two Steps of the Recognizer

This is a raw circuit representing a single step of the recognizer. There is much we can do with the circuit to optimize it for execution. We group these in two phases: Simplification and Scheduling.

Simplification. The most expensive operation is AND (i.e. boolean "multiply"), so we apply many transformations to remove as many of these as possible. A representative set of simplifying transformations is shown in Table 1.

Table 1. Simplification Transformations

	Precondition	Before	After
Idempotence		$a \wedge a$	a
Factorization		$(a \wedge b) \oplus (a \wedge c)$	$a \wedge (b \oplus c)$
Constants	$c \neq d$	$(x = c) \wedge (x = d)$	F
Assoc. and commut.		$a \wedge (b \wedge a))$	$a \wedge b$
Redundancy	$a \Rightarrow b$	$a \wedge b$	a
Eliminate AND	$a \vee b$	$a \wedge b$	$\neg(a \oplus b)$

Most of the transformations are straightforward to implement. The last two deserve special mention, specifically because of the preconditions. These have to be proven to hold before the transformation is valid. We use the DepQBF solver [LB10] to verify whether the precondition holds, and only perform the transformation accordingly. Fig. 8 shows a small example of the kinds of improvements we get using these transformations.

In this case, the three ANDS we had before optimizations were reduced to one, the four state variables were also reduced down to one, and significantly, whereas

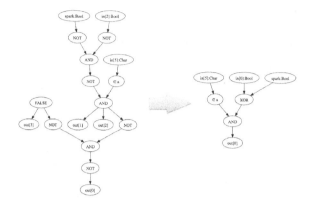

Fig. 8. Example of the Effects of Simplification

the original circuit would have required three rounds of communication, the optimized circuit only requires one. Obviously this is a very simplistic example, but the same kinds of result show up on much larger examples.

Unfortunately, the use of the logic solver is fairly time consuming (during compile time). To keep it manageable, we iterate it in the context of state-functions like the regular expression recognizer. That is, we optimize the circuit for one character; we then combine that circuit with itself to get a circuit for two characters (like in Fig. 7), which we then simplify and optimize. We then repeat the composition to get a circuit for four characters, then eight, and so on.

When do we stop going around this Simplify-Compose cycle? When we reach a point of diminishing returns. Fig 9 shows the effect of running this cycle over the recognizer circuit we get for a regular expression of the form:

```
.*(((TOP|)SECRET)|TS|S)--(ROCKYBEACH|STINGRAY).*
.*(((TOP|)SECRET)|TS|S)--SI--NO(CON|CONTRACTOR|FORN|FOREIGN).*
.*(((TOP|)SECRET)|TS|S|R|RESTRICTED)--(AE1|DS1|MT1|ST1)--LIMDIS.*
.*ac*cb.*
```

As the table shows, by the time we have composed two copies of the recognizer circuit the state is as small as it ever will be, but other measures are still improving. Through to the point where we have eight copies composed together, all the measures are still increasing by less than a factor of two, even though the input size is doubling. This starts to change in the transition from 8 to 16. At 16 copies of the recognizer, we have more than doubled the number of gates (because our heuristics are timing out on some of the larger circuits), and even the most crucial measure—the number of communication rounds—almost doubles too. Thus we can see that there is not much to choose between 8 or 16 copies of the recognizer, though we choose to use the 16 circuit because of the importance of minimizing the number of communication rounds. Multiple communication rounds causes the computation to stutter, introducing significant overheads.

input	unoptimized				optimized			
	ands	xors	state	comms	ands	xors	state	comms
1	203	0	358	10	149	15	119	4
2	388	0	358	12	277	27	117	5
4	756	0	358	14	493	53	117	6
8	1492	0	358	19	949	104	117	9
16	2964	0	358	33	1,950	212	117	17

Fig. 9. Optimization across Multiple Input Characters

Notably, our simplify-compose cycle has been very effective: have reduced the number of communications from 10 per character (unoptimized) to scarcely more than 1 per character.

Scheduling. It seems natural to perform each AND computation as early as its inputs become available. However, as Fig. 10 shows by graphing number of bits against communication round, this can lead to unbalanced communication patterns.

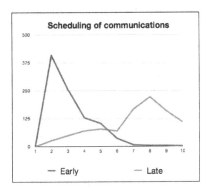

Fig. 10. Effect of Early vs. Late Scheduling

The graph shows an early spike in the number of bits being communicated (as many gates can be evaluated), with a long later tail in which very few bits are communicated. If we were just doing one computation this wouldn't matter as the number of bits is small, but we plan to do thousands of these together. In order to maximize flexibility in packing many copies of an execution together, we would like these communications to be as evenly balanced as possible. It turns out that the equally simple (but counter-intuitive) approach of scheduling each AND computation as late as possible produces less extreme peaks in the balance of communications, so we adopt this by default. It may be worth putting in additional effort to balance the communications more evenly still, but we have not done this.

Once we have scheduled the communications, we gather all the bits and pack them into 32 or 64 bit words in order to perform all the XOR and communication operations at the word level.

4.2   Secure VoIP Teleconference

When we turn our attention to the VoIP teleconference application, it turns out that the circuit characteristics are so different from the regular-expression circuits that we had to take a completely different tack.

Our first implementation was a direct implementation of the algorithm, where we decompressed the compressed audio samples to 16-bit values, added and clipped, and then recompressed. Unfortunately the result was running at about 12 seconds of computations for each 90ms audio sample!

The problem was in the combination of addition and clipping. Addition of 16-bit values can be done very efficiently so long as the values are stored as integers modulo 2^{16} (or larger). However, clipping required comparison operations. These are expensive unless the value is stored as a sequence of separate bits (i.e. not an arithmetic encoding). Whichever encoding is chosen, at least one of the operations is expensive.

We needed a different approach. We were able to take advantage of one significant characteristic of the computation: there are not many bits of input. The whole decompress-add-clip-recompress function on two streams takes 16 bits of input and delivers 8 bits of output. This is a classic opportunity for the oblivious lookup table we introduced previously [LAD12] (though we would have to work to make it scale well to 16 bits of input). The lookup table works as follows: we compute all possible values of the function in the clear, store them in the table, and perform shared access to the table at run time. The shared access works from randomized shares of the index value and delivers randomized shares of the table entry. In this case the whole secure computation reduces to oblivious table lookup.

Lookup Tables. Table lookup (i.e. simple array indexing) becomes tricky when no individual server actually knows what index to look up. Instead, each share server has a random share of the index value (i.e. a random value which if XORed with the random values from the other share servers would represent the real value). The servers have to do a cooperative computation to be able to obtain random shares of the the content of the table at the appropriate location.

Note that the lookup algorithm has to act on all the entries of the table otherwise a server must have had *some* information as to what the index value was. Consequently, we should look to express the lookup protocol as some computation across the whole table. In fact, the form is very simple if we have a cooperative demux protocol that maps a binary representation of a value into a linear, unary representation.

In plaintext, a demux function would map a binary representation of a value into a unary representation. For example, a 4-bit demux would take a 4-bit value and produce a 16-bit value (i.e. 2^4-bits) in which exactly one bit was set to 1, the other bits all being 0. So, for example, with the convention that the demux bits are numbered from left to right:

```
demux 0000 = 1000000000000000
demux 1000 = 0000000010000000
demux 1111 = 0000000000000001
```

and so on.

Still in the plaintext version, the table lookup is now just a kind of "inner product" between the result of the demux function and the table itself (see Figure 11), where the multiply operation is bit-masking. The result of the demux is used to mask the corresponding table entry (i.e. return the entry or 0), and the results across the whole table are XORed together. Only one bit resulting from demux will be set, and this bit will select exactly the single row of the table corresponding to the original index.

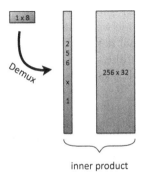

Fig. 11. Inner Product with Demux

We now simulate the plaintext algorithm with a randomized share version. The shared demux computation would map a *share* of a 4-bit value, to a *share* of a 16-bit value. That is, if $x = x_A \oplus x_B \oplus x_C$, if $d = demux(x)$, and if d_A, d_B, and d_C are the result of running the demux protocol on the x_i's, then $d = d_A \oplus d_B \oplus d_C$. For example, if we compute the demux of 0x8, again going from 4-bits to 16-bits, then (subject to randomness) the d_i might be as follows:

```
d_A = 1011001011101011
d_B = 0011010011001101
d_C = 1000011010100110
          ^
```

Notice that only the indicated 9th position (representing the value 8) has odd parity across all three shares; every other position has even parity.

Correctness of indexing is easy to establish. Each d_i is a randomized share of the true demux d. That is, for each bit position j in the demux shares, $d_A(j) \oplus$

$d_B(j) \oplus d_C(j) = d(j)$. Thus all these XORs will be 0 except for the single bit position corresponding to the original index, which will have value 1. The mask operation of the "inner product" function (written here as M) distributes across $\oplus$, so that $M(d_A(j) \oplus d_B(j) \oplus d_C(j), e) = M(d_A(j), e) \oplus M(d_B(j), e) \oplus M(d_C(j), e)$. This means that we can compute the inner product operations locally on each share machine. Demux is the only part that needs to be computed cooperatively.

Demux. In plaintext, demux can be expressed as a divide and conquer algorithm, satisfying the equation $demux(bs{+}{+}cs) = demux(bs)\#demux(cs)$, where $++$ is sequence concatenation, and $\#$ is cartesian product on sequences of bits.

For example, if demux "10" is given by "0010" and demux "01" is given by "0100", then demux "1001" is given by "0000 0000 1000 0000", which is the linearization of the product table between the two.

In our previous work, we had expressed the cartesian product as a parallel multiply by expanding each of the smaller demuxes into structures the same size as the result [LAD12]. The advantage was that we could just use the generic multiply protocol. The downside was that the amount of communication is proportional to the size of the final demux. This was fine for small tables (we were previously only doing lookup tables with 256 elements), but now our tables are starting to become large (with 65536 elements), and the communication bandwidth dominates.

We note that bit-level cartesian product ($\#$) distributes over XOR ($\oplus$) just like AND ($\&$) does, so the multiplication table is identical to the table for AND. We replicate the implementation of shared multiply—but using cartesian product on bits sequences—to produce a direct implementation of shared cartesian product. This means that our communications grow much slower than before. In fact, for a table with 2^n entries, we require $log(n)$ communications, communicating $O(2^{n/2})$ bits. In this case, where n is 16, we have 4 rounds of communication, and around 700 bits per server being communicated.

The cartesian product $\#$ operation is specified recursively using the divide and conquer pattern above. We find it valuable to leave the final expression unexpanded. That is, if p_i and q_i are the randomized shares of the demuxes of the upper and lower 8 bits of the original 16-bit index, then the shares of the outermost call of $\#$ returns the value $(p_A\#q_B) \oplus (p_B\#q_B) \oplus (p_B\#q_A)$, and correspondingly for the other shares. Instead of computing the final $\#$ we create an abstract representation of the computation, or rather of $(p_A\#q_B)\oplus(p_B\#(q_B\oplus q_A))$. We can use this unexpanded definition of $\#$ to act as a pair of 2-dimensional indices into the table, as indicated in Fig. 12. This unexpanded definition of $\#$ reduces the size of the demux value used in the "inner product": we now demux two 256-bit values directly, instead of constructing one large 65535-bit value.

In exchange for the not having to construct the 64k value explicitly, we must perform twice as many local XORs as we have to compute the "inner product" of the table twice. As before, we use the indices to mask out table entries and XOR the remainder. This calculation over the table requires $2 \times 64k$ operations, which can still be expensive even though they are purely local. We have a further

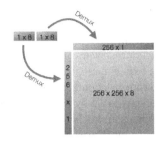

Fig. 12. Two Dimensional Demux

optimization whereby we chunk the table in four rows at a time, and precompute the selective XORs of these rows. This expands the table by a factor of 4, but cuts the table computation time in half.

5   Assessment

Our goal was to test whether we were able to scale secure computation to the levels required by applications. This is a fuzzy standard, but we can still do qualitative assessments against it. We assess architecture, algorithmics, and performance.

The architecture and infrastructure aspects of secure computation were able to be integrated well. In both applications, despite having many different timing and structure characteristics, we were able to adapt the application server to interact with a secure computation engine in order to perform the core operations securely. The bandwidth and latency requirements between the client(s) and the server were scarcely altered.

Regarding algorithmics, the mail filter application was surprisingly easy. We had to apply careful thought to find a version of the algorithm that would suit the oblivious computation world, but once selected, the conversion to use secure flags rather than plaintext flags was straightforward. This would not have been the case if the algorithm used the flags to determine where to branch, but for us it did not.

The VoIP application was tougher. Our first transcription of the algorithm into the secure computation world was so slow that we initially despaired of ever getting it to be relevant. However, the fact that it operates on small data items turned out to be crucial. Once we thought to express the core of the algorithm as a table lookup, the expression of the algorithm became trivial, though we still had to work hard to get performance.

As for performance, we have to conclude that we are only just reaching the point of usability. In the mail filter case, we are able to send a 1 page email, analyze it with the regular expression described earlier, and obtain a response in 30-60 seconds. We believe that there are a number of improvements we could still apply (including increasing the use of parallel processing) that could reduce this by up to another order of magnitude perhaps, at which point it is indeed starting to become practically relevant.

For the VoIP teleconference application, we conducted experiments both in Oregon and Virginia, hosting our servers in the Amazon EC2 cloud instance geographically closest to each experiment. In the first experiment, we conducted audio teleconferences with up to four clients, using spoken voice as the audio content. Audio was reliably understandable by all participating speakers, though we noted the presence of audible clicks and other artifacts. In the second experiment, we streamed recorded music into an iPad Mini client via the device microphone, and an audience of approximately 60 listened to the output audio stream on a second client, an iPhone 5s. Except for occasional distortion corresponding to spikes in network latency, audience members noted that audio quality was good, approximating what might be expected of broadcast radio.

6 Related Work

The classic "real world" example of secure computation is a Danish beet auction in 2008 [BCD+08]. There, 1200 Danish farmers submitted randomized bids to three servers that were run by distinct agencies. Each of the agencies was considered well motivated to follow the multi-party protocols honestly, and the confidentially built into the MPC protocols provided sufficient reassurance to the famers, 78% of whom agreed that, "it is important that my bids are kept confidential."

Our table lookup has many aspects in common with private information retrieval (PIR) algorithms [CGKS95], except that we are working with peer machines rather than a client querying a distributed database. The $O(\sqrt{n})$ growth in communication bandwidth we see (where n here is the size of the table, not of the index), is directly comparable to that of PIRs. It will be interesting to see whether the peer case can be conveniently generalized to more servers as with PIRs.

The Sharemind system [BLW08] is built on the same principles as the system described here. It too has three servers, and performs arithmetic sharing. In some dimensions, the Sharemind system is more fully engineered than our ShareMonad EDSL, in that it comprises a stand alone input language SecreC (i.e. much of C, along with annotations for secrecy), a compiler, a low-level virtual machine interpreter, and theorem proving support for privacy proofs. On the other hand, the fact that we built an EDSL on Haskell means that we are able to bypass most of those components and inherit them from the host language directly.

The SPDZ system [DKL+13] uses a similar computation model, except that it works with precomputed multiplication triples. This provides two advantages: it allows the online computation phase to work with any number of parties, and it provides for covert security (a cheating party is extremely likely to be caught).

The relative performances of Sharemind, SPDZ and our ShareMonad are hard to determine with accuracy, but there is some evidence they are all within factor of two of each other, which in this world means roughly comparable (given that we are all still discovering order of magnitude improvements!).

7   Conclusion

In all existing manifestations of computation on private values, multiplication (both arithmetic and boolean) is exceedingly expensive compared with every other operation. In arithmetic sharing (the setting of this paper) the expense comes from the network communications and coordination required. In Yao garbling, the expense arises because conjunctions are represented by encrypted gate tables that have to be created, communicated and evaluated. In fully homomorphic encryption, the expense comes from multiplications dramatically increasing the noise within the crypto value. These force the programmer to trade off between using larger security parameters or requiring more frequent noise reset operations, which entail evaluating a homomorphic encrypted instance of the decrypt operation.

When optimizing computations in MPC or FHE computational models, we need to approach multiplications with the same mindset we use for disk accesses—how do we minimize them, block them together, and hide the latencies they incur? Some of these performance-improving techniques can be implemented within the secure computation technique itself—for example, all the MPC and FHE approaches are moving to produce SIMD versions of the basic multiply operation (e.g. [SF11])—but that only goes so far. The rest of the optimizations have to come from programming and/or compilation techniques that are designed to optimize for this strange execution model.

This paper continues to explore the kind of algorithmic rethinking and compiler transformation that are required, but much more is needed before secure computation is fully practical.

References

[BLW08]   Bogdanov, D., Laur, S., Willemson, J.: Sharemind: a framework for fast privacy-preserving computations. In: Jajodia, S., Lopez, J. (eds.) ESORICS 2008. LNCS, vol. 5283, pp. 192–206. Springer, Heidelberg (2008)

[BCD+08] Bogetoft, P., Christensen, D.L., Damgård, I., Geisler, M., Jakobsen, T., Krøigaard, M., Nielsen, J.D., Nielsen, J.B., Nielsen, K., Pagter, J., Schwartzbach, M., Toft, T.: Secure Multiparty Computation Goes Live. In: Dingledine, R., Golle, P. (eds.) FC 2009. LNCS, vol. 5628, pp. 325–343. Springer, Heidelberg (2009)

[CGKS95] Chor, B., Goldreich, O., Kushilevitz, E., Sudan, M.: Private Information Retrieval. In: Proc. of IEEE Conference on the Foundations of Computer Science (FOCS) (1995)

[DKL+13] Damgaard, I., Keller, M., Larraia, E., Pastro, V., Scholl, P., Smart, N.: Practical Covertly Secure MPC for Dishonest Majority or: Breaking the SPDZ Limits. In: Crampton, J., Jajodia, S., Mayes, K. (eds.) ESORICS 2013. LNCS, vol. 8134, pp. 1–18. Springer, Heidelberg (2013)

[G09]   Gentry, C.: Fully homomorphic encryption using ideal lattices. In: ACM Symposium on Theory of Computing (STOC 2009) (2009)

[G04]   Goldreich, O.: Foundations of Cryptography. Basic Applications, vol. 2. Cambridge University Press (2004)

[LAD12]   Launchbury, J., Adams-Moran, A., Diatchki, I.: Efficient Lookup-Table Protocol in Secure Multiparty Computation. In: Proc. International Conference on Functional Programming (ICFP) (2012)

[LB10]   Lonsing, F., Biere, A.: DepQBF: A Dependency-Aware QBF Solver. JSAT 7, 2–3 (2010)

[Mum]   http://mumble.sourceforge.net

[SF11]   Smart, N.P., Vercauteren, F.: Fully homomorphic SIMD operations (2011) Manuscript at, http://eprint.iacr.org/2011/133

[Y86]   Yao, A.C.: How to generate and exchange secrets. In: Proceedings of the 27th IEEE Symposium on Foundations of Computer Science (1986)

[FHW10]   Fischer, S., Huch, F., Wilke, T.: A Play on Regular Expressions: Functional Pearl. In: Proceedings of the International Conference on Functional Programming, ICFP 2010 (2010)

An Array-Oriented Language with Static Rank Polymorphism

Justin Slepak, Olin Shivers, and Panagiotis Manolios

Northeastern University
{jrslepak,shivers,pete}@ccs.neu.edu

Abstract. The array-computational model pioneered by Iverson's languages APL and J offers a simple and expressive solution to the "von Neumann bottleneck." It includes a form of rank, or dimensional, polymorphism, which renders much of a program's control structure implicit by lifting base operators to higher-dimensional array structures. We present the first formal semantics for this model, along with the first static type system that captures the full power of the core language.

The formal dynamic semantics of our core language, Remora, illuminates several of the murkier corners of the model. This allows us to resolve some of the model's *ad hoc* elements in more general, regular ways. Among these, we can generalise the model from SIMD to MIMD computations, by extending the semantics to permit functions to be lifted to higher-dimensional arrays in the same way as their arguments.

Our static semantics, a dependent type system of carefully restricted power, is capable of describing array computations whose dimensions cannot be determined statically. The type-checking problem is decidable and the type system is accompanied by the usual soundness theorems. Our type system's principal contribution is that it serves to extract the implicit control structure that provides so much of the language's expressive power, making this structure explicitly apparent at compile time.

1 The Promise of Rank Polymorphism

Behind every interesting programming language is an interesting model of computation. For example, the lambda calculus, the relational calculus, and finite-state automata are the computational models that, respectively, make Scheme, SQL and regular expressions interesting programming languages. Iverson's language APL [7], and its successor J [10], are interesting for this very reason. That is, they provide a notational interface to an interesting model of computation: loop-free, recursion-free array processing, a model that is becoming increasingly relevant as we move into an era of parallel computation.

APL and J's array-computation model is important for several reasons. First, the model provides a solution to Backus's "von Neumann bottleneck" [1]. Instead of using iteration or recursion, all operations are automatically aggregate operations. This lifting is the fundamental control flow mechanism. The iteration space associated with array processing is reified as the shape of the arrays being

Z. Shao (Ed.): ESOP 2014, LNCS 8410, pp. 27–46, 2014.

processed. Though the paradigm is not without implementation challenges of its own, it at least holds out the promise of eliminating the heroic measures required by modern compilers (*e.g.*, the construction of program-dependency graphs and their difficult associated decision procedures [20]) to extract parallelism through the serialised program's obfuscatory encoding.

Second, operator lifting provides a form of polymorphism based on operands' *rank*, or dimensionality. An operation defined for arguments of one rank is automatically defined for arguments of any higher rank. They are thus parameterized over the ranks of their inputs. The operator for scalar addition is also used for adding a vector to a matrix, a scalar to a three-dimensional array, and so forth.

Third, despite its great expressive power, the core computation model is sub-Turing. Lifting operations to work on aggregate structures means the control structure is embedded in the data structure. With a finite data structure representing the program's control structure, all iteration is bounded. Thus APL's computational model has the potential to occupy a "sweet spot" in language design: increased analytic power without surrendering significant expressiveness.

1.1   Addressing the Model's Shortcomings

Iverson received a Turing award for the design of APL, and the language is often cited as an example of beautiful design [4]. Yet the language—and its accompanying model of computation—has received little study from the formal-semantics research community. Iverson worked almost entirely isolated from the rest of the programming-language research community, even adopting his own private nomenclature for his *sui generis* language mechanisms. Iverson never developed a formal semantics, or a static type system for his language designs. The beautiful, crystalline structure of the core language accreted non-general *ad hoc* additions. For example, APL's reduction operator is able to correctly handle empty vectors when the function being folded across the vector is a built-in primitive such as addition or min: base cases are provided for these functions. Programmers who wish to reduce empty vectors with programmer-defined functions, however, are out of luck.

We address many of the shortcomings of the model and its associated language. First, we define a core language that expresses the essence of the rank-polymorphic array-processing model, along with a formal semantics for the language. Besides eliminating ambiguity and pinning down the corner cases, developing the formal semantics enabled us to replace some of APL and J's *ad hoc* machinery with regular, general mechanisms. Our treatment of higher-order functions, for example, is much more general; this, in turn, allows us to extend the basic array-lifting model to permit arrays of functions (that is, in the function position of a function application) as well as arrays of arguments. This effectively generalises the language's computational model from SIMD to MIMD.

With the essence of the array-computational model captured by our untyped core language and its dynamic semantics, we then develop Remora, a language whose static type system makes the rank polymorphism of a program term explicit. Our type system is a significant result for four reasons:

Soundness. We provide a safety theorem connecting the well-typed term judgement to the dynamic semantics of the language. Our type system guarantees that a well-typed term will never become stuck due to the shape or rank of an array argument failing to meet the requirements of its operator.

Expressiveness. It permits typing a term that produces an array whose shape is itself a computed value. Our type system is based on Xi's Dependent ML[18] and tuned to the specific needs of Remora's rank polymorphism.

Decidability. Despite its expressive power, the dependent elements of Remora's type system are constrained to make the type-checking problem decidable.

Control structure. It exposes the iteration space. Recall that the point of Iverson's rank polymorphism is to permit programmers to write programs using element operators that are automatically lifted to operate across the iteration space of the aggregate computation. This means that Remora's static types make the implicit, unwritten iteration structure of a Remora term explicit. In short, our static semantics provides the key "hook" by which compilers can reason about the structure of the computation.

We have implemented the semantics we present using PLT Redex [6]. Our hope (for future work) is that we can exploit this type information to compile programs written in the rank-polymorphic array computation model efficiently: either by translating the reified iteration-space axes of an array back to a serialised, nested-loop computation, or by parallelising the program.

Note that Remora is not intended as a language comfortable for human programmers to write array computations. It is, rather, an explicitly typed, "essential" core language on which such a language could be based.

2   Background: Array-Oriented Programming

2.1   Iverson's Model

The essence of Iverson's array-oriented programming model, which appeared in APL [7] and was later expanded in its successor J [10], is treating all data as regular, *i.e.*, hyperrectangular, arrays. The individual scalar elements of an array, such as numbers or booleans, are referred to as *atoms*. Every r-dimensional array has a *shape*, which is a vector of length r giving the dimensions of the hyperrectangle in which its atoms are laid out. The value r is called the array's *rank*: for example, a matrix has rank 2, a vector has rank 1, and a scalar is taken to have rank 0. An array can be represented using only its shape and its atoms.

The notation we will use for arrays looks like $[2, 3, 5]_3$, meaning a 3-vector whose atoms are 2, 3, and 5. A rank 0 array will be written $[12]_\bullet$, with $\bullet$ denoting an empty shape vector. We write $[9, 8, 7, 6, 5, 4]_{2,3}$ for a 2×3 matrix, $[2, 4, 6, 8, 1, 3, 5, 7]_{2,2,2}$ for a $2 \times 2 \times 2$ array, and so on. For readability, it is sometimes convenient to write arrays in a matrix-like layout:

$$\begin{bmatrix} 9 & 8 & 7 \\ 6 & 5 & 4 \end{bmatrix}_{2,3}$$

An array may also be written with unevaluated expressions:

$$\left[(-\ 10\ 1)\ (-\ 10\ 2)\ (-\ 10\ 3)\right]_3$$

Rank Polymorphism and Frame/Cell Decomposition. An array can be viewed at several different ranks. A 4×3 numeric matrix can be viewed as a 4×3 *frame* of scalar *cells*, a 4-element frame of 3-vector cells, or a scalar frame whose single cell is a 4×3 matrix. More generally, a rank-r array can be viewed $r + 1$ different ways: from a rank r *frame* containing rank 0 *cells* to a rank 0 frame containing a single rank r cell.

Every function has an expected rank for each of its arguments. The expected rank can be a natural number n, indicating that the argument should be viewed as containing rank n cells contained in a frame of unspecified rank. Simple arithmetic functions such as + and log expect arguments with rank 0, *i.e.*, scalars. Applying a function expecting a rank n input to an array of higher rank n' applies the function to the array's n-cells, collecting the multiple outputs into the remaining $n' - n$ dimensional frame. A function can also have expected rank of ∞; such functions consume an entire array of arbitrarily high rank, so they are never lifted. For example, length extracts the first element of an array's shape vector—how long the array is. The programmer may write a function with negative argument rank $-n$. Lifting then breaks arguments into a rank n frame around cells of unspecified rank (the "$-n$-cells"), and then the function's body processes each cell. A function with -1 argument rank which finds its argument's length effectively extracts the second dimension instead of the first.

$$* \ [1,2,3]_3 \ [10]_\bullet \qquad \mapsto \quad * \ [1,2,3]_3 \ [10,\underline{10},\underline{10}]_{\underline{3}} \ \mapsto [(*\ 1\ 10), (*\ 2\ 10), (*\ 3\ 10)]_3$$

$$+ \ [10,20,30]_3 \ \begin{bmatrix} 1\ 2 \\ 3\ 4 \\ 5\ 6 \end{bmatrix}_{3,2} \ \mapsto \ + \ \begin{bmatrix} 10\ \underline{10} \\ 20\ \underline{20} \\ 30\ \underline{30} \end{bmatrix}_{3,\underline{2}} \ \begin{bmatrix} 1\ 2 \\ 3\ 4 \\ 5\ 6 \end{bmatrix}_{3,2} \ \mapsto \ \begin{bmatrix} (+\ 10\ 1)\ (+\ 10\ 2) \\ (+\ 20\ 3)\ (+\ 20\ 4) \\ (+\ 30\ 5)\ (+\ 30\ 6) \end{bmatrix}_{3,2}$$

Fig. 1. Automatic expansion of array arguments

To lift a function of multiple arguments, the frames must be brought into agreement by duplicating the cells of the smaller-framed argument (the new elements are underlined in Figure 1). After this duplication, all arguments' frames are the same; this permits the cell-wise function application. The way argument arrays are expanded to the same frame means that function application is only valid if one argument's frame is a prefix of the other argument's frame. This is the *prefix agreement* rule introduced by J.

Manipulating the Iteration Space. Under this implicit lifting, the iteration space is the argument frame rather than a sequence of loop indices. The programmer is not required to consider the shape of the array as would be necessary when operating on a nested vector with nested calls to map. A function written to alter an RGB pixel can be used as-is to make the same transformation on every pixel in an image or video. If the transformation is the same for all three color channels, it can simply be written as a scalar function. Generalizing the lifting to multiple arguments, an interpolation function can be used on a matrix of "low" and "high" points with a vector of estimated points. J also includes several second-order operators for manipulating the iteration space. For example, `reduce` collapses the -1-cells of an array to a single -1-cell using a specified binary operator, such as using $*$ to transform $[2, 4, 5]_3$ into $2 * 4 * 5$. The `prefix` and `suffix` operators apply a function to the successive prefixes or suffixes of an array, viewing the array as a list of cells with unspecified rank. The results are then put together as cells in a list. A `sum` function could be applied by `prefix` to $[2, 4, 5]_3$ to compute the running sum, $[2, 6, 11]_3$. Some operations such as convolution make use of a sliding window iteration pattern, using a `window` operator which applies a given function over a sliding window of a given shape and assembles the results in a frame corresponding to possible window positions.

The programmer can use the `rerank` operator to change the argument rank of a function. The vector-matrix sum example in Figure 1 effectively treats the vector as a column by duplicating its 0-cells. If $+$ is reranked to expect a vector argument, the 1-cell (*i.e.*, the entire vector) is duplicated, so it is used as a row vector. This reorientation technique generalizes to higher-ranked arrays.

By reranking `append`, the programmer can stitch together arrays by sequencing them on a chosen axis. For example, applying `append` to two matrices will place the vectors (*i.e.*, rows) of one matrix after those of the other. This requires that they have the same number of columns. It produces a matrix with as many rows as the two arguments combined. If `append` is reranked to 1, then it acts on corresponding pairs of vectors, so the two matrices are required to have the same number of rows. Each scalar in a row corresponds to one column in the matrix. Thus the number of columns in the resulting matrix is the sum of the numbers of columns in the argument matrices. Reranking also allows the programmer to `reduce` along any chosen axis. The argument is split into cells of the chosen rank, each cell is `reduce`d along its major axis, and the results are reassembled in the wrapper function's frame.

Boxes. Wrapping an array in a *box* makes it appear scalar, even if it contains a non-scalar array. This makes it possible to safely produce and consume non-regular arrays. Boxes are handled explicitly—a common pattern in J code for operating on boxed data is to compose `box`, the desired operator, and `unbox`.

2.2   Related Work

Originally, APL implicitly lifted scalar functions to aggregate functions via pointwise application, either on a scalar and an aggregate or on two aggregates of the same shape. APL was later enriched with attribution of rank to functions, meaning the rank a function expects its arguments to have. This led to the "frame of cells" view of an array and gave a sensible way to lift functions defined only for aggregates to operate on aggregates of even higher rank. J uses the more general lifting rule, prefix agreement, which allows the aggregate lifting to handle arrays of non-identical shape. J retains APL's distinction between data, first-order functions, and second-order functions. Implicit aggregate lifting is still limited to first-order functions.

The design of J still handles many situations through specially-chosen default behavior. For example, 0 and the space character are designated as "fill" elements and used to pad shape-mismatched cells resulting from an application so that they can all be assembled into the same frame. An unfortunate consequence is that applying the composition of two functions may have a different result from applying one function and then the other.

Thatte [16] described automatic lifting based on using coercion to insert `map`, `transpose`, etc. where needed, but this system is limited to lifting scalar operations. It cannot, for example, automatically construct vector-matrix addition.

Ragan-Kelley *et al.* present Halide [14], a language for graphics processing. In Halide, the computation to do at each pixel is written separately from the strategy for ordering and parallelizing the pixels' instances of that computation. This is a similar idea to Single Assignment C's `WITH`-loops [15]. Halide is, however, designed specifically for image processing pipelines rather than general numeric programming, which limits its lifting to the pixel-to-image case.

Xi's Dependent ML [18] addressed the intractability of static type checking in dependently-typed languages by limiting type indices to a separate, simpler language. This technique makes it possible to check type equivalence without having to check equivalence of program terms, which themselves may include indexed types which must be checked for equivalence, and so on. An index erasure pass converts a well-typed Dependent ML program into an ML program with the same behavior. By adding singleton types for numbers, bounds checking for array accesses can be done by the type system instead of at run time [19].

Like Remora, Trojahner and Grelck's Qube [17] uses a type system based on Dependent ML to statically verify structural constraints in array computation. However, Remora and Qube differ significantly in both their dynamic and static semantics. Qube, strictly speaking, does not address the "von Neumann" bottleneck: programmers still specify their programs down at the scalar-computation level, using expressions that explicitly index elements from arrays. The structure of the loop is also specific to the function being lifted and the array arguments to which it is being applied, whereas Remora's implicit lifting frees the programmer from having to specify this detail.

Qube's type system, then, is a device for guaranteeing dynamic safety, but does not support the implicit lifting that gives APL its noted elegance and concision. Qube's heavy use of explicit array indexing necessitates the use of singleton and range types, which in turn restrict the programmer's ability to write code that depends on user input.

Blelloch *et al.* created NESL [2,3], which focuses on explicit mapping over nested one-dimensional arrays. Arrays need not be rectangular—they can be *jagged*. It is possible, for example, to have a 2-array whose elements are a 4-array and a 5-array. Instead of naïvely breaking a parallel map into a task for each sub-array, the NESL compiler uses a vectorization transformation to treat nested arrays as flat vectors. This makes it possible to split the aggregate operation at places other than sub-array boundaries, removing the load imbalance that had previously been associated with mapping over jagged arrays. Data Parallel Haskell [5] has adopted this vectorization technique. Haskell's existing list comprehensions are extended into parallel array comprehensions [13]. NESL and DPH are still based on explicit looping which does not uniformly handle arrays of varying rank as APL/J and Remora do.

More recent work by Keller *et al.* [11] shows how to use Haskell's type system to handle operations involving regular arrays in a shape-polymorphic way. Instances of the typeclass of Shapes provide functions for extracting the rank and size of an array of that shape as well as for indexing into the array. Functions on arrays can be parameterized over the shape type and can effectively place lower bounds on the ranks of arrays they accept. This system prevents errors caused by underranked arguments but not those caused by mismatch in individual dimensions and does not support the full prefix agreement rule.

Jay and Cockett [9] separated the shape of a data structure from its type. For operations whose result shape is dependent only on argument shape, it is possible to evaluate the shape portion of a program separately from the data portion. Jay puts this to work in FISh [8], where arrays have both shape and element type. Evaluating only the shapes of a program ensures that shape-related errors cannot happen at run time, but requiring operators to determine their output shapes only from their argument shapes is unworkably restrictive. For example, it disallows critical functions such as iota, reshape, and readvec.

3   An Untyped Array Language

In J, functions are not first-class, and automatic lifting is restricted to first-order functions. Lifting a function-producing function would allow the application to produce an array of result functions. For example, in Figure 2, we apply a higher-order function, curry-add, to two vectors. The result of the first application is a vector of functions, which we then apply to a vector of numbers. In order to do this, we must extend the lifting rule.

Function application itself can be thought of as an operation with expected ranks—that is, in a function-application expression, both function and argument can be arrays, as shown in the second half of Figure 2. Application requires a rank 0 array of functions and requires the arguments to have ranks expected by those functions. All functions in the array must agree as to their argument ranks. $[(\text{curry-add } 1), (\text{curry-add } 2)]_2$ is a 2-vector of functions which both expect rank 0 arguments. This gives 2 as the frame for both the function and argument arrays. Now that the function and argument arrays have the same frame, each function in the array is applied to corresponding cells in the argument arrays. We then have $[((\text{curry-add } 1) \ 20), ((\text{curry-add } 2) \ 30)]_2$.

The generalized lifting rule provides a way to express a kind of MIMD computation not expressible in APL: the program can dynamically construct

$$\left(\begin{bmatrix}\texttt{curry-add}\end{bmatrix}_\bullet \begin{bmatrix}1\\2\end{bmatrix}_2\right) \begin{bmatrix}20\\30\end{bmatrix}_2 \mapsto \begin{bmatrix}(\texttt{curry-add } 1)\\(\texttt{curry-add } 2)\end{bmatrix}_2 \begin{bmatrix}20\\30\end{bmatrix}_2 \mapsto \begin{bmatrix}((\texttt{curry-add } 1)\ 20)\\((\texttt{curry-add } 2)\ 30)\end{bmatrix}_2$$

$$\begin{bmatrix}\texttt{sum}\\\texttt{length}\end{bmatrix}_2 \begin{bmatrix}8\\9\\6\end{bmatrix}_3 \mapsto \begin{bmatrix}\texttt{sum}\\\texttt{length}\end{bmatrix}_2 \begin{bmatrix}8\ 9\ 6\\8\ 9\ 6\end{bmatrix}_{2,3} \mapsto \begin{bmatrix}(\texttt{sum } [8\ 9\ 6]_3)\\(\texttt{length } [8\ 9\ 6]_3)\end{bmatrix}_2$$

Fig. 2. Lifting the implicit `apply`

and apply an array of distinct functions. In computing a vector mean, we require both the `sum` and the `length`. We can apply $[\texttt{sum}, \texttt{length}]_2$ to a vector, $[8, 9, 6]_3$. The functions consume vectors, so there is only one argument cell. Duplicating this cell transforms the argument vector into a matrix, $[8, 9, 6, 8, 9, 6]_{2,3}$. Pointwise application then produces a vector of applications, $[(\texttt{sum } [8, 9, 6]_3), (\texttt{length } [8, 9, 6]_3)]_2$.

3.1   Syntax

Figure 3 presents the syntax and semantic domains for our untyped array language. We use $t \ldots$ to denote a possibly empty sequence, t_1 through t_k. Thus $t\, t' \ldots$ represents a guaranteed-nonempty sequence. We may also use $f(t) \ldots$ to represent $f(t_1)$ through $f(t_k)$. Expressions include arrays, variables, application forms, and a `let`-like form for extracting the contents of a box. An array is either a sequence of elements tagged with a sequence of naturals representing its shape or a box containing any expression. Array elements are a broader syntactic class than expressions, including base values (noted as b) and functions. Arrays are allowed to syntactically contain sub-arrays; nested arrays are reduced to non-nested arrays during evaluation. λ-abstractions can only be applied to arrays, so variables can only represent arrays. A function is either a primitive operator (noted as π) or a λ-abstraction.

$$
\begin{aligned}
e &::= \alpha \mid x \mid (e\, e \ldots) \mid (\textbf{unbox}\ (x = e)\ e) & \textit{(exressions)}\\
\alpha &::= [l \ldots]_{n \ldots} \mid (\textbf{box}\ e) & \textit{(arrays)}\\
l &::= b \mid f \mid e & \textit{(array elements)}\\
b &\quad \text{base values} &\\
f &::= \pi \mid (\lambda\ [(x\ \rho) \ldots]\ e) & \textit{(functions)}\\
\pi &\quad \text{primitive operators} &\\
\rho &::= z \mid \infty & \textit{(argument ranks)}\\
z &\in \mathbb{Z} \qquad n, m \in \mathbb{N} & \textit{(numbers)}\\
v &::= b \mid f \mid [b \ldots]_{n \ldots} \mid [f \ldots]_{n \ldots} \mid (\textbf{box}\ v) \mid [(\textbf{box}\ v) \ldots]_{m,n \ldots} & \textit{(value forms)}\\
E &::= \square \mid (v \ldots E\ e \ldots) \mid [v \ldots E\ l \ldots]_{n \ldots} \mid (\textbf{box}\ E) & \textit{(evaluation contexts)}\\
&\quad \mid (\textbf{unbox}\ (x = E)\ e) &
\end{aligned}
$$

Fig. 3. Syntax, value domain and evaluation contexts of the untyped array language

The value forms are arrays with all elements fully evaluated. This allows them to contain base values or functions but not application forms or variables. A box is a value as long as it has a value for its contents. An array of box values is also a value as long as the array is not itself a scalar (*i.e.*, its shape vector must be nonempty). A scalar array containing a box reduces to the box itself.

The built-in operators include conventional scalar operations, such as +, sqrt, AND, *etc.* These all expect their arguments to have rank 0. The common list operations—head, tail, init, last, and append—have argument rank ∞ so that they can be used to build and destructure arrays of any rank (by reranking at finite argument rank). The operations for manipulating the iteration space described earlier (prefix, reduce, *etc.*) have argument rank ∞ for both the function and data arrays they consume, and they can be reranked to any natural or negative rank.

3.2   Semantics

Figure 4 gives the operational semantics, and figure 5 defines metafunctions used by the semantics.

The β rule (analogous to β-reduction in the call-by-value λ-calculus) requires that the function's argument ranks match the ranks of the arrays being passed to it. Similarly, the δ rule applies a scalar containing a built-in operator to arguments which have the operator's expected argument ranks.

The *nat*, *lift*, and *map* rules form the steps involved in lifting function application for function and argument arrays of higher rank. The *nat* rule is used in cases where some functions in an application form have infinite or negative argument rank. Primitives are tagged with the appropriate natural argument ranks so that subsequent uses of *Argrank* $[\![\cdot]\!]$ on this occurrence of the primitive will recognize it as having the natural rank it takes on for this particular application.

The *lift* rule expands the function and argument arrays into the application frame by repeating their cells. In cases where function and argument arrays' frames are not all prefixes of a single frame, we have a shape mismatch—function application cannot proceed, so evaluation is stuck (this would raise a "length error" in J).

After an application has been naturalized and lifted, the *map* rule converts function application in which the function and argument arrays are all over-ranked by the same amount to an array of function applications. In the resulting array, each application will have a scalar in function position, and all arguments will have that function's expected rank. We apply *Cells* to each argument array to produce a list of lists of cells. Transposing the nested list produces a nested list where the first entry contains all of the arguments' first cells, the second entry contains all of the arguments' second cells, and so on. Each of these lists is used as the arguments for the corresponding cell (*i.e.*, single function) of the function array. The reduction step produces an array of application forms whose shape is the frame of the original application form.

After the application forms generated by *map* reduction have been evaluated, we have an array of arrays. The *collapse* rules transform a nested array into a non-nested array. If the inner arrays' shapes differ, we have a shape mismatch, and evaluation is stuck (this would induce J's "filling" behavior mentioned in 2.2, potentially causing unexpected results). For $collapse_1$, the resulting array contains the concatenated atoms of the inner arrays. Its shape results from prepending the shape of the outer array onto the shape of the inner arrays. In the case of a scalar array containing a box, $collapse_2$ reduces to just the box.

Once a box's contents are evaluated, the *unbox* rule substitutes that value into another expression. A function with an unbox form in its body can be used to post-process another operation's result cells to make sure their shapes match.

The Empty-Frame Dilemma. We require separate rules, $lift_0$ and map_0, for cases where an application form's principal frame shape contains one or more zeroes. Such a frame contains *no cells*, so the lifted function is not applied at all. With no cells to generate, the result is an empty array, but there is no clear way to choose the shape of the result array. That is, both a $2 \times 0 \times 7 \times 24$ array and a $2 \times 0 \times 365$ array are empty arrays—they both have no elements. But they are not at all the same array. If we are lifting a function across a 2×0 frame of argument cells, how can we determine the shape of the result cells? The resulting array's shape must at least start with the principal frame. The rest of the shape is left to a nondeterministic choice, but a language may choose to make a stronger guarantee about how $m \ldots$ will be chosen.

For example, in J, when a function is lifted to apply over an empty frame, it is probed (at run time) by applying it to a cell whose atoms are all 0 or the space character ' ' to determine the result cell shape (the cell itself is then discarded). Unfortunately, this is not safe with an effectful function or one whose result shapes are input-dependent, and it relies on having a bounded number of data types. It is one of J's more awkward corner cases, one that we will be able to resolve cleanly by means of the type system developed in the next section.

Another option is to always consider the resulting cell shape to be scalar unless some concrete cells are available to show otherwise. Lifted functions are often functions on scalars, and this allows scalar operations to behave as expected on empty arrays. The reduction rules could also be changed to make applying in an empty frame a dynamic error.

3.3   Sample Code

We present here several examples of code in our untyped language. As noted earlier, it is intended as a core, not surface, language.

A well-known case of manipulating the iteration space is sum:

$$(\lambda\ [(\texttt{xs}\ 1)]\ ([\texttt{reduce}]_\bullet\ [+]_\bullet\ ([\texttt{append}]_\bullet\ [0]_1\ \texttt{xs})))$$

We can take advantage of automatic lifting for a simple dotprod operator:

$$(\lambda\ [(\texttt{xs}\ 1)\ (\texttt{ys}\ 1)]\ ([\texttt{sum}]_\bullet\ ([*]_\bullet\ \texttt{xs}\ \texttt{ys})))$$

Applying term abstraction:
$$([(\lambda\ [(x\ n)\ \ldots]\ e)]_\bullet\ v\ \ldots)$$
$$\mapsto_\beta\ e\,[(x \leftarrow v)\ \ldots]$$
where $n_j = Rank\,[\![v_j]\!]$, for each j

Applying primitive operator:
$$([\pi]_\bullet\ v\ \ldots)$$
$$\mapsto_\delta\ \delta(\pi, v\ \ldots)$$
where $\langle n\ \ldots \rangle = Argrank\,[\![\pi]\!]$
$\quad\quad n_j = Rank\,[\![v_j]\!]$, for each j

Rewriting with natural argument ranks:
$$([f\ \ldots]_{n\,\ldots}\ v\ \ldots)$$
$$\mapsto_{nat}\ ([f'\ \ldots]_{n\,\ldots}\ v\ \ldots)$$
where $Argrank\,[\![f_j]\!] \notin \mathbb{N}^k$ for some j
$\quad\quad f' = Naturalize\,[\![f, v\ \ldots]\!]$

Pointwise application:
$$([f\ \ldots]_{n\,\ldots}\ v\ \ldots)$$
$$\mapsto_{map}\ [([f]_\bullet\ \alpha\ \ldots)\ \ldots]_{n\,\ldots}$$
where $f\ \ldots$ is a nonempty sequence
$\quad\langle n\ \ldots \rangle = Argrank\,[\![f_j]\!]$, for each j
$\quad 0 < k = Rank\,[\![v_j]\!] - n_j$, for each j
$\quad ((\alpha\ \ldots)\ \ldots) = (Cells_n\,[\![v]\!]\ \ldots)^\top$

Duplicating cells:
$$([f\ \ldots]_{n\,\ldots}\ v\ \ldots)$$
$$\mapsto_{lift}\ \left(Dup_{0,n'\,\ldots}\ [\![f\ \ldots]_{n\,\ldots}]\!\ Dup_{\rho,n'\,\ldots\,m'\,\ldots}\ [\![v]\!]\ \ldots\right)$$
where $\langle \rho\ \ldots \rangle = Argrank\,[\![f_j]\!]$, for each j
$\quad \rho_j \in \mathbb{N}$ for each j
$\quad 0 \notin n'\ \ldots = Max\,[\![n\ \ldots, Frame_\rho\,[\![v]\!]\ \ldots]\!]$
$\quad$ the ρ_j-cells of v_j have shape $m'\ \ldots$
$\quad Rank\,[\![v_j]\!] - \rho_j$ is not the same for all j

Empty frame:
$$([f\ \ldots]_{n\,\ldots}\ v\ \ldots)$$
$$\mapsto_{lift_0}\ [\,]_{n'\,\ldots\,m\,\ldots}$$
where $\langle \rho\ \ldots \rangle = Argrank\,[\![f_j]\!]$, for each j
$\quad \rho_j \in \mathbb{N}$ for each j
$\quad 0 \in n'\ \ldots = Max\,[\![n\ \ldots,$
$\quad\quad\quad\quad\quad\quad\quad Frame_\rho\,[\![v]\!]\,, \ldots]\!]$
$\quad Rank\,[\![v_j]\!] - \rho_j$ not same for all j
$\quad m\ \ldots$ chosen nondeterministically

Empty function:
$$([\,]_{n\,\ldots}\ v\ \ldots)$$
$$\mapsto_{map_0}\ [\,]_{n\,\ldots\,m\,\ldots}$$
where $m\ \ldots$ chosen nondeterministically

Converting nested to non-nested:
$$[\alpha\ \ldots]_{n\,\ldots}$$
$$\mapsto_{collapse_1}\ [Atoms\,[\![\alpha]\!]\ \ldots]_{n\,\ldots\,Shape[\![\alpha]\!]}$$
where no α contains a var or app form
$\quad$ no α is a box
$\quad$ all α have the same shape

Converting scalar of boxes to box:
$$[box\ v]_\bullet\ \mapsto_{collapse_2}\ box\ v$$

Extracting the contents of a box:
$$(unbox\ x = (box\ v)\ e)\ \mapsto_{unbox}\ e[x \leftarrow v]$$

Fig. 4. Small-step operational semantics for an untyped array language

We can convolve a signal with a filter by using `dotprod` with the reverse of one argument in a sliding `window` over the other:

```
(λ[(filter 1) (signal 1)]
  ([window]• ([length]• filter)
          [(λ [(seg 1)] ([dotprod]• seg ([reverse]• filter)))]• signal))
```

$Rank : Val \rightharpoonup \mathbb{N}$
$Rank \; [\![[l \ldots]_{n \ldots}]\!] = length(n \ldots)$

$Argrank : Fun \rightarrow Rank^*$
$Argrank \; [\![(\lambda \; [(x \; \rho) \ldots] \, e)]\!] = \rho \ldots$

$Naturalize : Fun \times Val^* \rightharpoonup Fun$
$Naturalize \; [\![(\lambda \; [(x \; \rho) \ldots] \, e), v \ldots]\!]$
$= (\lambda \; [(x \; n) \ldots] \, e)$
where $n_i = \rho_i$ if $\rho_i \in \mathbb{N}$
    $n_i = Rank \; [\![v_i]\!] + \rho_i$ if $-\rho_i \in \mathbb{N}$
    $n_i = Rank \; [\![v_i]\!]$ if $\rho_i = \infty$

$Frame : Rank \times Val \rightharpoonup \mathbb{N}^*$
$Frame_\rho \; [\![[l \ldots]_{m \ldots \; n \ldots}]\!] = (m \ldots)$
where $length(n \ldots) = \rho$

$Max : \mathbb{N}^{**} \rightharpoonup \mathbb{N}^*$
$Max \; [\![(n \ldots)]\!] = n \ldots$
$Max \; [\![(n_0 \ldots), (n_1 \ldots) \ldots, (n_m \ldots)]\!]$
$= (n_0 \ldots)$
if $Max \; [\![(n_1 \ldots) \ldots, (n_m \ldots)]\!] \sqsubseteq (n_0 \ldots)$
$= Max \; [\![(n_1 \ldots) \ldots, (n_m \ldots)]\!]$
if $(n_0 \ldots) \sqsubseteq (n_1 \ldots)$

$Dup : Rank \times \mathbb{N}^* \times Val \rightarrow Val$
$Dup_{\rho, \; n \ldots \; m \ldots} \; [\![[l \ldots]_{d \ldots}]\!]$
$= [\![((l' \ldots)^k \ldots]_{n \ldots \; m \ldots}$
where $length(m \ldots) = \rho$
    $k = \prod_{j=1}^{\rho} n_j$
    $((l' \ldots) \ldots) = Cells_\rho \; [\![[l \ldots]_{d \ldots}]\!]$

$Cells : \mathbb{N} \times Val \rightharpoonup Val^*$
$Cells_n \; [\![[l_1 \ldots l_m \; l_{m+1} \ldots l_{2m} \ldots l_{p-m+1} \ldots l_p]_{c \ldots \; d \ldots}]\!]$
$= [l_1 \ldots l_m]_{d \ldots} \; [l_{m+1} \ldots l_{2m}]_{d \ldots} \ldots [l_{p-m+1} \ldots l_p]_{d \ldots},$
where $length(d \ldots) = n$
    $\prod_{i=1}^{n}(d_i) = m$

Fig. 5. Metafunctions used in array semantics

Iverson included many composition forms and operators. However, λ allows the programmer or library implementor to define them. A simple compose operator for two unary functions can be defined as:

$$(\lambda \; [(\texttt{f} \; 0)(\texttt{g} \; 0)] \; [(\lambda \; [(\texttt{x} \; \infty)] \; (\texttt{f} \; (\texttt{g} \; \texttt{x})))]_\bullet)$$

J's fork form applies two functions (referred to as "tines") to the same input and then applies a third function to their results:

$$(\lambda \; [(\texttt{f} \; 0)(\texttt{g} \; 0)(\texttt{h} \; 0)] \; ([(\lambda \; [(\texttt{x} \; \infty)] \; (\texttt{f} \; (\texttt{g} \; \texttt{x}) \; (\texttt{h} \; \texttt{x})))]_\bullet)$$

A simple use of fork is computing the arithmetic mean:

$$(\lambda \; [(\texttt{xs} \; 1)] \; (([\texttt{fork}]_\bullet \; [/]_\bullet \; [\texttt{sum}]_\bullet \; [\texttt{length}]_\bullet) \; \texttt{xs})$$

The fork divides the sum of its input by its length. The outer λ modifies the argument rank of the resulting function, so the function produced by fork is only applied to lists.

J also uses a hook form (based on the **S** combinator) for applying a binary function to an argument and a transformed version of that same argument.

$$(\lambda \; [(\texttt{f} \; 0)(\texttt{g} \; 0)] \; ([(\lambda[(\texttt{x} \; \infty)] \; (\texttt{f} \; \texttt{x} \; (\texttt{g} \; \texttt{x})))]_\bullet)$$

Without a general recursion operator, iota can be used as a limited form of the classical **unfold**, allowing primitive recursion. Using iota to write factorial:

$$(\lambda\,[(\mathbf{n}\ 0)]$$
$$(\text{unbox}\ (\text{xs} = ([\text{iota}]_\bullet\ [\mathbf{n}]_1))$$
$$([\text{reduce}]_\bullet\ [*]_\bullet\ ([+]_\bullet\ [1]_\bullet\ (\text{append}\ [0]_1\ \text{xs})))))$$

First, the input scalar is wrapped in a singleton vector and passed to iota to produce a boxed vector containing $[0, \ldots, \mathbf{n} - 1]$. If $n = 0$, this vector is empty, and later operations would have an empty frame, so we append 0. We then add 1 to get a vector containing $[1, 1, \ldots, \mathbf{n}]$. Reducing by $*$ gives $\mathbf{n}!$.

We can use iota to evaluate a polynomial at a particular point, which uses arguments of differing rank:

$$(\lambda\,[(\text{coeffs}\ 1)\ (\mathbf{x}\ 0)]$$
$$(\text{unbox}\ (\mathbf{i} = ([\text{iota}]_\bullet\ ([\text{length}]_\bullet\ \text{coeffs})))$$
$$([\text{reduce}]_\bullet\ [+]_\bullet\ ([*]_\bullet\ \text{coeffs}([\char94]_\bullet\ \mathbf{x}\ \mathbf{i})))))$$

We can also construct an iteration space with **reshape**, which is convenient if we only need a single atom duplicated many times. The following **repeat** operator uses **compose** iterated over a vector containing a single duplicated atom to produce a function which applies that atom a given number of times.

$$(\lambda\,[(\mathbf{f}\ \infty)\ (\mathbf{n}\ 0)]$$
$$(\text{unbox}\ (\text{fs} = ([\text{reshape}]_\bullet\ [\mathbf{n}]_1\ \mathbf{f}))$$
$$([\text{reduce}]_\bullet\ [\text{compose}]_\bullet\ ([\text{append}]_\bullet\ [\text{id}]_\bullet\ \text{fs}))))$$

Bounded looping with **repeat** can be used for finding the transitive closure of an adjacency matrix. This example uses two additional functions which can be defined in terms of λ. The **dup** function transforms a binary function into a unary one which duplicates its argument and passes two copies to the underlying binary function. We also use **compose'**, a variation on the compose function defined above which produces a binary function, passing two arguments of ranks 1 and ∞ to its second input function and the result to its first input function.

$$(\lambda\,[(\text{adj}\ 2)]$$
$$((\text{repeat}\ (\text{hook or}\ (\text{dup}\ ([\text{compose'}]_\bullet$$
$$[(\lambda\,[(\text{xs}\ \infty)]\ (\text{reduce or true xs}))]_\bullet$$
$$[(\lambda\,[(\mathbf{x}\ 1)\ (\mathbf{y}\ \infty)]\ (\text{and}\ \mathbf{x}\ \mathbf{y}))]_\bullet)))$$
$$(\text{lg}\ (\text{length adj})))\ \text{adj}))$$

The function constructed by **compose'** applies **and** to each row of its first argument (this treats it as a column) and its entire second argument. The result is a rank 3 array whose matrices are combined using **or** to produce a matrix analogous to the matrix product of the original two arguments. Wrapping this function with **dup** creates a unary function which transforms a matrix into its "boolean product" with itself. The **hook** of **or** and this adjacency matrix transformation is a function which updates an adjacency matrix to allow paths twice as long. Finally, this process is **repeat**ed $(\text{lg}\ (\text{length adj})) = log_2(|V|)$ times.

4   Types for Array-Oriented Programming

In order to eliminate shape-mismatch errors, our type system must be capable of tracking arrays' shapes. Dependent typing has been used in the past to implement lists whose types specify their lengths via a natural number index. This generalizes to an array type which is indexed by a list of natural numbers to specify its shape. If types can contain arbitrary term expressions, checking whether two types are equivalent can require checking whether two terms are equivalent. In order to keep type checking tractable, we use the technique of defining a separate language of type indices, demonstrated by Xi *et al.* in Dependent ML [18]. Separating the term and index languages eliminates the mutual dependence between type checking and evaluation. An index language should be powerful enough to express the desired type properties, but also simple enough that checking index equivalence is tractable. In Dependent ML's case, index equivalence is checked via integer linear programming. The constraint domain associated with our index language also includes lists of natural numbers; this combination of theories is still decidable [12].

4.1   Syntax

Figure 6 gives the syntax for Remora. It includes several new expression and element forms. They are introduction and elimination forms for universal types ($T\lambda$ and T-APP), dependent products ($I\lambda$ and I-APP), and dependent sums (PACK and UNPACK). Dependent sums effectively replace boxes from the untyped language. A type or index abstraction or application form can be used as an element, and it is a valid expressions as long as its underlying element is also a valid expression. Multiple type or index abstraction forms in an array can each be given separate type or index arguments to produce functions of the same type. Remora's arrays can have a type annotation rather than just a shape annotation. This ensures that a concrete type can be determined for an empty array. For non-empty arrays (those of the form $[l\ l'\ \dots]$), a shape annotation is sufficient, and the type can be reconstructed by inspecting the array elements. It is assumed that similar type annotations for all expression forms will be generated in type checking, but these are not included in the regular program syntax.

Types include base types such as Num or Bool (noted as B) and arrays of a given shape and element type (noted as $A_\iota\tau$). An index can be a Nat (*n.b.*, different from Num), a Shape (noted as $(S\ \iota\ \dots)$), or the sum of two indices.

4.2   Static Semantics

The typing, kinding, and sorting rules are given in Figures 7 and 8. Types are ascribed to elements (which can themselves be arrays). Rules for base types are straightforward, but an example rule for numbers is given in Figure 7.

The kind judgment is simply a well-formedness check—all well-formed types are of a single kind. K-ARRAY accepts an array type as well-formed if its underlying type is well formed and its index is a Shape. K-UNIV binds type variables,

$$
\begin{aligned}
e \quad ::= \quad & \alpha \mid x \mid (e\ e'\ \ldots) \mid (\mathrm{T}\lambda\,[x\,\ldots]\,e) \mid (\text{T-APP}\ e\ \tau\ \ldots) && \textit{(exressions)} \\
\mid \quad & (\mathrm{I}\lambda\,[(x\ \gamma)\,\ldots]\,e) \mid (\text{I-APP}\ e\ \iota\ \ldots) \mid (\text{PACK}\ \iota\ \ldots\ e)^\tau \mid (\text{UNPACK}\ (\langle x\ \ldots\mid y\rangle = e)\ e') \\
\alpha \quad ::= \quad & [l\,\ldots]^\tau \mid [l\ l'\,\ldots]^\iota && \textit{(arrays)} \\
l \quad ::= \quad & b \mid f \mid e \mid (\mathrm{T}\lambda\,[x\,\ldots]\,l) \mid (\text{T-APP}\ l\ \tau\ \ldots) \mid (\mathrm{I}\lambda\,[(x\ \gamma)\,\ldots]\,l) && \textit{(array elements)} \\
\mid \quad & (\text{I-APP}\ l\ \iota\ \ldots) \\
f \quad ::= \quad & \pi \mid (\lambda\,[(x\ \tau)\,\ldots]\ e) && \textit{(functions)} \\
\tau, \sigma \quad ::= \quad & B \mid x \mid \mathrm{A}_\iota\tau \mid (\tau\ \ldots \rightarrow \sigma) \mid (\forall[x\,\ldots]\,\tau) \mid (\Pi\,[(x\ \gamma)\,\ldots]\,\tau) && \textit{(types)} \\
\mid \quad & (\Sigma\,[(x\ \gamma)\,\ldots]\,\tau) \\
\iota, \kappa \quad ::= \quad & n \mid x \mid (\mathrm{S}\,\iota\ \ldots) \mid (+\,\iota\ \kappa) && \textit{(indices)} \\
\gamma \quad ::= \quad & \text{Nat} \mid \text{Shape} && \textit{(index sorts)} \\
z \quad \in \quad & \mathbb{Z} && \textit{(numbers)} \\
n, m \quad \in \quad & \mathbb{N} \\
v \quad ::= \quad & [b\,\ldots]^\tau \mid [f\,\ldots]^\tau \mid b \mid f \mid (\mathrm{T}\lambda\,[x\,\ldots]\,l) \mid (\mathrm{I}\lambda\,[(x\ \gamma)\,\ldots]\,l) && \textit{(value forms)} \\
\mid \quad & (\text{PACK}\ \iota\ \ldots\ v) \mid [(\text{PACK}\ \iota\ \ldots\ v)\,\ldots]^{\mathrm{A}(\mathrm{s}\ m\ n\,\ldots)^\tau} \\
E \quad ::= \quad & \Box \mid (v\ \ldots\ E\ e\ \ldots) \mid [v\ \ldots\ E\ l\ \ldots]^\tau \mid (\text{T-APP}\ E\ \tau\ \ldots) && \textit{(evaluation contexts)} \\
\mid \quad & (\text{I-APP}\ E\ \iota\ \ldots) \mid (\text{PACK}\ \iota\ \ldots\ E)^\tau \mid (\text{UNPACK}\ (\langle x\ \ldots\mid y\rangle = E)\ e) \\
\Gamma \quad ::= \quad & \cdot \mid \Gamma, (x : \tau) && \textit{(type environments)} \\
\Delta \quad ::= \quad & \cdot \mid \Delta, x && \textit{(kind environments)} \\
\Theta \quad ::= \quad & \cdot \mid \Theta, (x :: \gamma) && \textit{(sort environments)}
\end{aligned}
$$

Fig. 6. Syntax for Remora

and K-DPROD and K-DSUM bind index variables at specific sorts. A variable introduced in a universal type is only allowed to stand for a non-array type. This is necessary in order to express polymorphic input types like "any scalar," $\mathrm{A}_{(\mathrm{S})}\mathrm{t}$ (with t bound by some $\forall$). Otherwise, $\mathrm{A}_{(\mathrm{S})}\mathrm{t}$ could describe any array type.

S-SHAPE requires that a shape be built from Nats. Constructing an index with $+$ requires that the summands be Nats, and the result will also be a Nat.

T-APP must identify the frame associated with an application form, which requires identifying the frames associated with the individual terms in the application form. Recall that for a *map* reduction, the frames of every term in the application must be the same, and for a *lift* reduction, there must be one frame which is prefixed by every other frame. Once every term's frame has been determined, the next step is to find the largest frame, with the order given by $x \sqsubseteq y$ iff x is a prefix of y. This will be the frame into which the results of the lifted function will be assembled. If the set of frames has no maximum, then the function application term is ill-typed.

The type equivalence relation $\cong$ is a congruence based on relating nested array types and non-nested array types. An array of type $\mathrm{A}_{(\mathrm{S}\ m\,\ldots)}(\mathrm{A}_{(\mathrm{S}\ n\,\ldots)}\tau)$ is equivalent to an array of type $\mathrm{A}_{(\mathrm{S}\ m\,\ldots\ n\,\ldots)}\tau$. This is the transformation which will be made by a *collapse* step at run time and suggests that the fully-collapsed version of a type is its canonical form. The reverse is analogous to breaking an array

$$\boxed{\Gamma; \Delta; \Theta \vdash l : \tau}$$

$$\frac{}{\Gamma; \Delta; \Theta \vdash num : \text{Num}} \quad (\text{T-Num}) \qquad \frac{(x : \tau) \in \Gamma}{\Gamma; \Delta; \Theta \vdash x : \tau} \quad (\text{T-Var})$$

$$\frac{\tau \cong \sigma \quad \Gamma; \Delta; \Theta \vdash l : \tau}{\Gamma; \Delta; \Theta \vdash l : \sigma} \quad (\text{T-Equiv}) \qquad \frac{\begin{array}{c} \Gamma; \Delta; \Theta \vdash l_j : \tau \quad \text{for each } l_j \in l \dots \\ Product \, [\![n \dots]\!] = Length \, [\![elt \dots]\!] \end{array}}{\Gamma; \Delta; \Theta \vdash [l \dots]^{\text{A}_{(\text{S } n \dots)}\tau} : \text{A}_{(\text{S } n \dots)}\tau} \quad (\text{T-Array})$$

$$\frac{\Gamma, (x : \tau) \dots ; \Delta; \Theta \vdash e : \sigma}{\begin{array}{c} \Gamma; \Delta; \Theta \vdash (\lambda \, [(x \, \tau) \dots] \, e) : \\ (\tau \dots \to \sigma) \end{array}} \quad (\text{T-Abst}) \qquad \frac{\begin{array}{c} \Gamma; \Delta; \Theta \vdash e : \text{A}_\iota \, (\sigma \dots \to \tau) \\ \Gamma; \Delta; \Theta \vdash e'_j : \text{A}_{\kappa_j} \sigma_j \quad \text{for each } j \\ \iota' = Max \, [\![\iota, \kappa \dots]\!] \end{array}}{\Gamma; \Delta; \Theta \vdash (e \, e' \dots) : \text{A}_{\iota'}\tau} \quad (\text{T-App})$$

$$\frac{\Gamma; \Delta, x \dots ; \Theta \vdash e : \tau}{\begin{array}{c} \Gamma; \Delta; \Theta \vdash (\text{T}\lambda \, [x \dots] \, e) : \\ (\forall \, [x \dots] \, \tau) \end{array}} \quad (\text{T-TAbst}) \qquad \frac{\begin{array}{c} \Gamma; \Delta; \Theta \vdash l : (\forall \, [x \dots] \, \sigma) \\ \Delta; \Theta \vdash \tau_j \quad \text{for each } j \\ \text{no } \tau_j \text{ is an array type} \end{array}}{\begin{array}{c} \Gamma; \Delta; \Theta \vdash (\text{T-APP } l \, \tau \dots) : \\ \sigma[(x \leftarrow_t \tau) \dots] \end{array}} \quad (\text{T-TApp})$$

$$\frac{\Gamma; \Delta; \Theta, (x :: \gamma) \dots \vdash e : \tau}{\begin{array}{c} \Gamma; \Delta; \Theta \vdash (\text{I}\lambda \, [(x) \dots] \, e) : \\ (\Pi \, [(x \, \gamma) \dots] \, \tau) \end{array}} \quad (\text{T-IAbst}) \qquad \frac{\begin{array}{c} \Gamma; \Delta; \Theta \vdash e : (\Pi \, [(x \, \gamma) \dots] \, \tau) \\ \Gamma; \Delta; \Theta \vdash \iota_j :: \gamma_j \quad \text{for each } j \end{array}}{\begin{array}{c} \Gamma; \Delta; \Theta \vdash (\text{I-APP } e \, \iota \dots) : \\ \tau[(x \leftarrow_i \iota) \dots] \end{array}} \quad (\text{T-IApp})$$

$$\frac{\begin{array}{c} \Gamma; \Delta; \Theta \vdash e : \tau \, [(x \leftarrow \iota) \dots] \\ \Gamma; \Delta; \Theta \vdash \iota_j :: \gamma_j \quad \text{for each } j \end{array}}{\Gamma; \Delta; \Theta \vdash (\text{PACK } \iota \dots e) : (\Sigma \, [(x \, \gamma) \dots] \, \tau)} \quad (\text{T-Pack})$$

$$\frac{\begin{array}{c} \Gamma; \Delta; \Theta \vdash e : (\Sigma \, [(x \, \gamma) \dots] \, \sigma) \\ \Gamma, y : \sigma; \Delta; \Theta, (x :: \gamma) \dots \vdash e' : \tau \\ \Delta; \Theta \vdash \tau \end{array}}{\Gamma; \Delta; \Theta \vdash (\text{UNPACK } (\langle x \dots | y \rangle = e) \, e') : \tau} \quad (\text{T-Unpack})$$

Fig. 7. Type judgment for Remora

into its cells. This type equivalence allows us to express restrictions on a part of a function argument's shape. For example, append has type:

$$\forall [t] \, \Pi \, [(\text{m Nat})(\text{n Nat})(\text{d Shape})] \\ \left(\text{A}_{(\text{S m})} \, (\text{A}_\text{d} \, t) \right) \, \left(\text{A}_{(\text{S n})} \, (\text{A}_\text{d} \, t) \right) \to \left(\text{A}_{(\text{S } (+ \text{ m n}))} \, (\text{A}_\text{d} \, t) \right)$$

In the untyped language, append has argument rank ∞, but it still requires its arguments to have the same shape except for their first dimensions. Any two

$$\boxed{\Delta; \Theta \vdash \tau}$$

$$\frac{}{\Delta; \Theta \vdash B} \; \text{(K-Base)} \qquad \frac{x \in \Delta}{\Delta; \Theta \vdash x} \; \text{(K-Var)} \qquad \frac{\Delta; \Theta \vdash \tau \quad \Theta \vdash \iota :: \text{Shape}}{\Delta; \Theta \vdash \mathsf{A}_\iota \tau} \; \text{(K-Array)}$$

$$\frac{\Delta; \Theta \vdash \tau_j \text{ for each } j \quad \Delta; \Theta \vdash \sigma}{\Delta; \Theta \vdash (\tau \dots \to \sigma)} \; \text{(K-Fun)} \qquad \frac{\Delta; \Theta, (x :: \gamma) \dots \vdash \tau}{\Delta; \Theta \vdash (\Pi \; [(x \; \gamma) \dots] \; \tau)} \; \text{(K-DProd)}$$

$$\frac{\Delta; \Theta, (x :: \gamma) \dots \vdash \tau}{\Delta; \Theta \vdash (\Sigma \; [(x \; \gamma) \dots] \; \tau)} \; \text{(K-DSum)} \qquad \frac{\Delta, x \dots; \Theta \vdash \tau}{\Delta; \Theta \vdash (\forall \; [x \dots] \; \tau)} \; \text{(K-Univ)}$$

$$\boxed{\Theta \vdash \iota :: \gamma}$$

$$\frac{n \in \mathbb{N}}{\Theta \vdash n :: \text{Nat}} \; \text{(S-Nat)} \qquad \frac{(x :: \gamma) \in \Theta}{\Theta \vdash x :: \gamma} \; \text{(S-Var)} \qquad \frac{\Theta \vdash \iota_j :: \text{Nat for each } j}{\Theta \vdash (\mathsf{S} \; \iota \dots) :: \text{Shape}} \; \text{(S-Shape)}$$

$$\frac{\Theta \vdash \iota :: \text{Nat} \quad \Theta \vdash \kappa :: \text{Nat}}{\Theta \vdash (+ \; \iota \; \kappa) :: \text{Nat}} \; \text{(S-Plus)}$$

Fig. 8. Kind and index sort judgments for Remora

array types which have the same atom type and whose shapes differ only in the first dimension can be described using **append**'s argument types.

4.3 Dynamic Semantics

The reduction relation is given in Figure 9. It assumes every expression has been annotated with its type (most of these type annotations can be generated mechanically). This run time type information is needed to determine the correct output cell shape for a function application with an empty frame, so type annotations are kept up to date during reduction (they subsume the untyped language's shape tags). We use $x[(y \leftarrow_e z) \dots]$, $x[(y \leftarrow_t z) \dots]$, and $x[(y \leftarrow_i z) \dots]$ for substitution of term, type, and index variables respectively. The untyped language's box and nonscalar array of boxes value forms are replaced with analogous sum and nonscalar array of sums. We replace the evaluation contexts for **box** and **unbox** with analogous contexts for **PACK** and **UNPACK**.

Remora's β, δ, and *collapse* rules are essentially unchanged from the untyped language, so they are not repeated. The implicit lifting is now type-directed, instead of rank-directed. Types include enough information to determine the correct cell shape for any application form, solving the empty-frame dilemma from 3.2 and eliminating the nondeterminism.

$T\beta$ and $I\beta$ substitute types and indices for the appropriate type and index variables. This substitution must be applied to both the body of the type or index abstraction as well as to its type annotation. Explicit type and index application

Pointwise application:

$$\left([f\ \dots]^{A\left(s\ n_f\ \dots\right)\left(A\left(s\ n_a\ \dots\right)\tau\ \dots\to\tau'\right)}\ {}_v^{A\left(s\ n_f\ \dots\ n_a\ \dots\right)\tau}\ \dots\right)^{A\left(s\ n_f\ \dots\ n_c\ \dots\right)\tau'}$$

$$\mapsto_{map}\ \left[\left([f]^{A(s)\left(A\left(s\ n_a\ \dots\right)\tau\ \dots\to\tau'\right)}\ {}_\alpha^{A\left(s\ n_a\ \dots\right)\tau}\ \dots\right)^{\tau'}\ \dots\right]^{A\left(s\ n_f\ \dots\right)\tau'}$$

where $\rho = length\left(n_f\ \dots\right) > 0$
$$((\alpha\ \dots)\ \dots) = ((Cells_\rho\ [\![v]\!])\ \dots)^\top$$

Duplicating cells:

$$\left([f\ \dots]^{A(s\ m\ \dots)\left(A(s\ n\ \dots)\tau\ \dots\to\tau'\right)}\ {}_v^{A(s\ m'\ \dots)\tau}\ \dots\right)^\sigma$$

$$\mapsto_{lift}\ \left(Dup_{\left(A(s\ n\ \dots)\tau\ \dots\to\tau'\right),\iota}\ [\![[f\ \dots]]\!]\ Dup_{A(s\ m'\ \dots)\tau,\iota}\ [\![v]\!]\ \dots\right)^\sigma$$

where $(m\ \dots), (m'\ \dots)\ \dots$ not all equal
$$\iota = Max\ [\![(m\ \dots), (m'\ \dots)\ \dots]\!]$$

Applying a type abstraction:

$$\left(\text{T-APP}\ (T\lambda\ [x\ \dots]\ e^\tau)^{\left(\forall[x\ \dots]\tau\right)}\ \sigma\ \dots\right)^{\tau[(x\ \leftarrow_t\ \sigma)\ \dots]}\ \mapsto_{T\beta}\ e^\tau\ [(x\ \leftarrow_t\ \sigma)\ \dots]$$

Applying an index abstraction:

$$\left(\text{I-APP}\ (I\lambda\ [(x\ \gamma)\ \dots]\ e^\tau)^{\left(\Pi[(x\ \gamma)\ \dots]\tau\right)}\ \iota\ \dots\right)^{\tau[(x\ \leftarrow_i\ \iota)\ \dots]}\ \mapsto_{I\beta}\ e^\tau\ [(x\ \leftarrow_i\ \iota)\ \dots]$$

Projecting from a dependent sum:

$$\left(\text{UNPACK}\ \left(\langle x\ \dots\ |y\rangle = (\text{PACK}\ \iota\ \dots\ v^\tau)^{\tau'}\right)\ e^\sigma\right)^\sigma\ \mapsto_{proj}\ e^\sigma\ [(x\ \leftarrow_i\ \iota)\ \dots\ (y\ \leftarrow_e\ v)]$$

Fig. 9. Small-step operational semantics for Remora

effectively replace *naturalize* steps from the untyped language. Finally, *project* substitutes a dependent sum's witnesses and contents in the body expression.

The sample programs given in section 3.3 are straightforward to express in Remora. The translation involves adding type and index abstractions and applications and replacing rank annotations with type annotations.

4.4   Type Soundness

We expect a type system which ascribes shapes to arrays to only ascribe shapes that the arrays will actually have once computed.

Theorem 1 (Type soundness). *If* $\vdash l : \tau$, *then one of:*

- *There is some* v *such that* $l \mapsto^* v$
- l *diverges*
- *There exist some* $E, \pi, v\ \dots$ *such that* $l \mapsto^* E[((\pi\ v\ \dots))]$, *where* $\vdash \pi : (\sigma\ \dots \to \sigma')$, *and* $\vdash v_i : \sigma_i$ *for each* i

That is, a well-typed program completes, diverges, or produces an error due to partial primitive operations, such as division by zero.

5   Future Work

The transition from a core semantics modeled in PLT Redex to a complete programming system requires a more flexible surface language and a compiler. In moving from the untyped core language to Remora, the added code is mostly type and index applications. Type inference would be necessary in order to make a surface language based on Remora practical. An interesting challenge in this setting is that the different type and index arguments can produce different behavior (*e.g.*, reducing an entire matrix versus reducing its 1-cells).

An implementation of Remora could use type information to inform decisions about how to parallelize aggregate operations. With a cost model for analyzing when different cells in an application frame are likely to take significantly different amounts of time, a compiler could choose between statically breaking up a task and leaving the allocation to a work-stealing run-time system.

Stream-like computation is often convenient for tasks such as signal processing, and it could be expressed by generalizing array types to allow an unbounded dimension. Implicit lifting still has a sensible meaning, as do `foldl`, `scan`, and `window`. This would allow us to extend Iverson's rank-polymorphic control mechanism to Turing-equivalent programs requiring `while`-loop computation (for example, iterating a numeric solver to a given tolerance).

6   Conclusion

We have given a formal reduction semantics for Iverson's rank polymorphism which addresses several shortcomings of the model. Remora generalizes automatic operator lifting to include first-class functions and MIMD computation. Embedding the core ideas of APL and J in a setting based on λ-calculus combines the expressive power of both models. Our type system rules out errors due to mismatching argument shapes and still gives the programmer enough freedom to write code whose result shape cannot be determined until run time.

References

1. Backus, J.: Can programming be liberated from the von Neumann style?: a functional style and its algebra of programs. Commun. ACM 21(8), 613–641 (1978)
2. Blelloch, G.: NESL: A nested data-parallel language (version 3.1). Tech. rep. (1995)
3. Blelloch, G., Chatterjee, S., Hardwick, J.C., Sipelstein, J., Zagha, M.: Implementation of a portable nested data-parallel language. Journal of Parallel and Distributed Computing 21, 102–111 (1994)
4. Brooks, F.P.: The Design of Design: Essays from a Computer Scientist. Addison-Wesley (2010)
5. Chakravarty, M.M.T., Leshchinskiy, R., Peyton Jones, S., Keller, G., Marlow, S.: Data parallel haskell: a status report. In: DAMP 2007: Workshop on Declarative Aspects of Multicore Programming, ACM Press (2007)
6. Felleisen, M., Findler, R.B., Flatt, M.: Semantics Engineering with PLT Redex, 1st edn. MIT Press (2009)

7. Iverson, K.E.: A programming language. John Wiley & Sons, Inc., New York (1962)
8. Jay, C.B.: The fish language definition. Tech. rep. (1998)
9. Jay, C.B., Cockett, J.: Shapely types and shape polymorphism. In: Sannella, D. (ed.) ESOP 1994. LNCS, vol. 788, pp. 302–316. Springer, Heidelberg (1994)
10. Jsoftware, Inc.: Jsoftware: High-performance development platform, http://www.jsoftware.com/
11. Keller, G., Chakravarty, M.M., Leshchinskiy, R., Peyton Jones, S., Lippmeier, B.: Regular, shape-polymorphic, parallel arrays in haskell. In: Proceedings of the 15th ACM SIGPLAN International Conference on Functional Programming, ICFP 2010, pp. 261–272. ACM, New York (2010)
12. Nelson, G., Oppen, D.C.: Simplification by cooperating decision procedures. ACM Trans. Program. Lang. Syst. 1(2), 245–257 (1979)
13. Peyton Jones, S., Leshchinskiy, R., Keller, G., Chakravarty, M.M.: Harnessing the multicores: Nested data parallelism in haskell. In: FSTTCS, vol. 2, pp. 383–414 (2008)
14. Ragan-Kelley, J., Adams, A., Paris, S., Levoy, M., Amarasinghe, S., Durand, F.: Decoupling algorithms from schedules for easy optimization of image processing pipelines. ACM Trans. Graph. 31(4), 32:1–32:12 (2012)
15. Scholz, S.B.: Single assignment c: efficient support for high-level array operations in a functional setting. J. Funct. Program. 13(6), 1005–1059 (2003)
16. Thatte, S.: A type system for implicit scaling. Sci. Comput. Program. 17(1-3), 217–245 (1991), http://dx.doi.org/10.1016/0167-6423(91)90040-5
17. Trojahner, K., Grelck, C.: Dependently typed array programs don't go wrong. Journal of Logic and Algebraic Programming 78(7), 643–664 (2009)
18. Xi, H.: Dependent types in practical programming. Ph.D. thesis, Pittsburgh, PA, USA (1998) aAI9918624
19. Xi, H., Pfenning, F.: Eliminating array bound checking through dependent types. In: Proceedings of the ACM SIGPLAN 1998 Conference on Programming Language Design and Implementation, PLDI 1998, pp. 249–257. ACM, New York (1998)
20. Zima, H., Chapman, B.: Supercomputers for Parallel and Vector Computers. ACM Press (1990)

Gradual Typing for Annotated Type Systems

Peter Thiemann and Luminous Fennell

University of Freiburg, Germany
{fennell,thiemann}@informatik.uni-freiburg.de

Abstract. Annotated type systems include additional information in types to make them more expressive and to gather intensional information about programs. Gradual types enable a seamless transition between statically and dynamically checked properties of values. Gradual annotation typing applies the ideas of gradual typing to the annotation part of a type system.

We present a generic approach to transform a type system with annotated base types into a system which gradualizes the information contained in the annotations. We prove generic type safety for the gradualized extensions and similar generic versions of the blame theorem for a calculus with run-time annotations. We relate this calculus to a more efficient calculus which elides run-time annotations in the statically annotated parts. We further introduce and prove correct a syntactic transformation that eliminates run-time annotation tests by enlarging the statically annotated parts.

1 Introduction

Refinement type systems have been proposed by a number of researchers to sharpen the guarantees of existing type systems. Examples are Freeman and Pfennings's system to distinguish empty and non-empty lists by type [8], Pessaux and Leroy's exception analysis [21], Jackson's dependency analysis [14], Chin and coworkers' type qualification framework [3], and many others.

In each case, the type language is extended with annotations that either abstract semantic properties of values beyond the capabilities of the underlying type language or they express properties that are not locally checkable. An example of the latter kind are type systems for dimension analysis [15,23] that formalize a notion of parametricity that cannot be checked on single values [16]. Haskell DSLs that employ phantom types provide further examples [18].

Annotated type and effect systems [20,29] play an important role in program analysis where the annotations serve to express intensional information about data. Example uses are race detection and locking [7,1] and, prominently, information flow analysis [10] (using just one example of many). Languages like Java include annotation frameworks that are often used dynamically. An instance of such a framework could be promoted to gradual checking using a suitable extension of our approach. Similar ideas have been pursued in the past [30,4].

Gradual typing [27,25] is concerned with controlling the boundary between static and dynamic typing. A gradual type system provides cast operations that

Z. Shao (Ed.): ESOP 2014, LNCS 8410, pp. 47–66, 2014.

reveal sufficient static type information to improve the efficiency of otherwise dynamically typed programs.

Recent work has considered a number of variations on gradual typing that are not directly related to dynamic typing. For example, Disney and Flanagan [5] as well as Fennell and Thiemann [6] consider gradual information flow, Wolff and coworkers consider gradual typestate [33], and Sergey and Clarke proposed gradual ownership types [24], which are further discussed in the related work.

This proliferation of gradual systems begs the question if there is a common structure underlying all these gradual systems. In this work, we give a partial answer by outlining **a generic approach to "gradualize" existing annotated type systems that support annotations on base types.** Our proposed method is geared towards functional programming, therefore it cannot be expected to handle the gradualized object-oriented systems [33,24] (for example, gradual typestate requires dealing with linearity, which we did not consider).

Scope and limitations: Our approach applies to all properties that can be expressed by additional tokens on base-type values at run time: dimensions, phantom types, security labels, sanitization, representation restrictions (e.g., serializable), and so on. Extensional properties (e.g., refinements) that may be expressed with a predicate as in a subset type $\{x \in B \mid \Phi(x)\}$ are also expressible in our framework by taking a set of predicates as annotations. However, run-time tokens are not needed for establishing a gradual system with subset types because the predicates may just be checked during run time. In exceptional cases, checking a predicate at run time may be too expensive, in which case our approach could be used to handle a run-time token that asserts Φ.

Contributions. We claim that the essence of gradualization for an annotated type system consists of (a) specifying a calculus with run-time annotations and checking, (b) introducing cast operations to stage annotation checking, and (c) eliminating the statically checked annotations. We substantiate this claim in the context of a statically-typed call-by-value lambda calculus, where only base types carry annotations. For this calculus, we prove type soundness and a blame theorem (roughly: only casts at the dynamic→static boundary can fail).

We discuss two approaches to simplify run-time annotations. One of them yields an efficient run-time model where statically checked annotations are erased.

We propose a compile-time transformation to eliminate run-time checks and prove its correctness.

Overview. After some motivating examples (Section 2), we specify a generic base-type annotated type systems and prove generic type safety and blame theorems (Section 3). Subsections 3.5 and 3.6 discuss alternative treatments of annotations including erasure. Section 4 introduces and proves correct the transformation rules to decrease the amount of dynamic checking. We wrap up with a discussion of related work (Section 5) and a conclusion.

2 Gradual Refinement Typing at Work

We demonstrate how gradual typing can remedy problems with overly conservative type-checking in two scenarios: a type system with dimension analysis and a type system that distinguishes encrypted and plaintext data.

2.1 Dimensions

Type systems with dimensions guard the programmer from mixing up measurements of different dimensions that are represented with a common numeric type [15]. For illustration we consider an ML-like language with simple types where numbers carry a dimension annotation. The following function, calculating an estimated time to arrival, is well-typed in this language.

```
fun eta (dist : float[m]) (vel:float[m/s]) : float[s] =
    dist / vel
```

The annotated type float[u] represents an integer of dimension u where u ranges over the free abelian group generated by the SI base dimensions: m, s, kg, and so on. The neutral element is written as 1. The next example does not type check, because the typing of _ - _ requires the same dimension for both arguments.

```
fun eta_broken (dist : float[m]) (vel : float[m/s]) =
    dist - vel
```

Each gain in safety costs flexibility. Thus, all published dimension type systems support dimension polymorphism. However, there are examples where polymorphism is not sufficient as in the definition of the power function on meters.[1]

```
fun pow_m (x : float[m]) (y : int[1]) =
    if y == 0 then 1[S(1)] else x * pow_m x (y - 1)
```

This definition does not type-check in a system based on simple types. Polymorphism does not help, either, because the dimension of the result depends on the parameter y as in float[m^y]. Nevertheless, pow_m is useful to define generic operations on geometric objects, like the n-dimensional volume and the $n - 1$-dimensional surface of an n-dimensional hypercube given its base length c:

```
fun   nVolume (n : int[1]) (c : float[m]) =
    pow_m c n
fun   nSurface (n : int[1]) (c : float[m]) =
    (2 * n) * nVolume (n-1) c
```

A gradual annotation for such functions avoids the complexity of dependent types and preserves some guarantees about the annotation. In our system, the function pow_m could be modified to have type

```
pow_mg : float[m] → int[1] → float[?]
```

---

[1] The annotation S(1) indicates a statically checked dimensionless number.

The ? annotation marks the annotation of the result type as *dynamic* and indicates that the run-time system needs to check the consistent use of the dynamic dimension of the value. The programmer has to insert casts of the form $e : t \rightsquigarrow t'$, where t is the type of e and t' is the destination type. Casts only switch type annotations from static to dynamic or vice versa. Here is the implementation of pow_m in the gradual system:

```
1 fun pow_mg (x : float[m]) (y : int[1]) =
2     if y == 0 then 1[D(1)]
3     else (x : float[m] ⤳ float[?]) * pow_mg x (y - 1)
```

The cast x : float[m] ⤳ float[?] in line 3 converts x of type float[m] to destination type float[?] with a dynamic dimension initialized by the dimensionless 1[D(1)]. At run time, values of dynamic dimension are marked with a D, as illustrated in line 2. The dynamically annotated result can be reintegrated into statically verified code by casting the dynamic annotation to a static one:

```
fun volume3d : float[m³] =
  (nVolume 3 2[m]) : float[?] ⤳ float[m³]
```

While it is possible to write type incorrect programs that cannot be sensibly executed, the run-time system rejects illegal casts. For example, the expression (nVolume 3 2[m]) : float[?] ⤳ float[m²] evaluates to 8[D(m³)] : float[?] ⤳ float[m²]. As the computed dimension D(m³) is incompatible to the expected dimension m², the cast fails and stops a computation with a potentially flawed result.

2.2 Tracking Encrypted Data

Custom type annotations are also useful to track certain operations on data throughout the program. As an example, consider the following program fragment that operates on encrypted as well as plaintext data.

```
1 val prog (encrypt : int → int)
2          (decrypt : int → int)
3          (inc : int → int)
4          (sendPublic : int → unit)
5          (displayLocal : int → unit)
6          (v : int) : unit =
7     displayLocal (decrypt v)
8     let v' = inc (decrypt v) in
9     sendPublic (encrypt v')
10    let v'' = ... in
11    sendPublic v''
```

It is parameterized by the operations for encryption, decryption, and increment and also receives a value. It is crucial that the operations are not applied arbitrarily: only encrypted data should be sent over the public channel (lines 9 and 11), incrementation only yields a sensible result on plaintext data (line 8), and only encrypted values should be decrypted to avoid gibberish (line 7).

If such a program grows sufficiently complex, these restrictions should be checked in a principled way. A lightweight way of doing so is to add suitable annotations to the type language and have them statically checked as much as possible. The types in the signature of prog could be enhanced with annotations indicating whether a number is encrypted ($\bullet$) or in plaintext ($\circ$).

```
val prog (encrypt : int° → int•)
         (decrypt : int• → int°)
         (inc : int° → int°)
         (sendPublic : int• → unit)
         (displayLocal : int° → unit)
         (v : int•) : unit = ...
```

A programmer can easily program against such an annotated signature. However, there might be legacy code that might not fit the more restrictive annotated typing discipline, even if it performs correctly dynamically. For example, the following procedure uses a boolean flag in order to distinguish encrypted data from plaintext:

```
fun prog' (is_encrypted : bool)
          encrypt decrypt inc sendPublic displayLocal v =
  let v' = if is_encrypted
           then encrypt (inc (decrypt v))
           else inc v
  if is_encrypted then sendPublic v' else displayLocal v'
```

Most type systems ignore conditional control flow and therefore would reject prog'. But, as in Section 2.1, it is possible to use the gradual typing approach for programs that are written in such a "dynamic style" by inserting suitable casts:

```
val prog_safe : (int° → int•) → (int• → int°) →
                (int° → int°) →
                (int• → unit) → (int° → unit) →
                int• → unit =
  (prog' true) : ((int? → int?) → (int? → int?) → ...)
              ⤳ ((int° → int•) → (int• → int°) → ...)
```

The last line casts the legacy program prog' to the type of prog_safe. All interface functions passed to prog' are assumed to accept and return dynamic numbers of type int?. To work correctly, the program prog' has to be recompiled with the gradual type on the left. The gradual annotated type system accepts prog_safe and the run-time system checks the correct use of the encryption operations dynamically. The underlying unannotated type system still rules out type errors on arithmetic operations, like calling prog' with a string as last argument.

3   The Generic Calculus with Base Type Annotations

The generic calculus λ^{BA} relies on a *base type annotation algebra* $\mathcal{A}$ with the same signature $\Sigma = (\oplus, \ldots)$ as the primitive operations on base types.

$$t ::= B[a] \mid t \to t \qquad\qquad v ::= b[a] \mid \lambda x.e$$
$$e ::= b[a] \mid e \oplus e \mid x \mid \lambda x.e \mid e\, e \qquad E ::= [\,] \mid E \oplus e \mid v \oplus E \mid E\, e \mid v\, E$$

Fig. 1. Syntax: types, expressions, values, evaluation contexts

Thus, $\mathcal{A} = (A, \oplus_A, \dots)$ where A is the carrier set and each $(\oplus_A) : A \times A \hookrightarrow A$ is a partial function on A. Partiality is needed, e.g., for dimension analysis where addition is only sensible for arguments with the same dimension.

3.1 Static Annotated Typing

Figure 1 defines the syntax of λ^{BA}. A type t, is either a base type B annotated with an annotation $a \in A$, a function type, or any other standard type. In the term language e, base type values b carry a corresponding annotation. The remaining term constructors are as usual. Values v and evaluation contexts E are defined in the standard way.

Lambda expressions are interpreted as call-by-value functions, hence they reduce with the β_v reduction rule where $e[x \mapsto v]$ denotes the capture-avoiding substitution of v for x in e.

BA-S-BetaV
$$(\lambda x.e)\, v \longrightarrow e[x \mapsto v]$$

The evaluation of primitive operations is governed by another Σ algebra $(B, \oplus_B, \dots)$ where, again, $(\oplus_B) : B \times B \hookrightarrow B$ is a partial function. The dynamics for $\oplus$ check if the annotations of the arguments are combinable with $\oplus_A$ and execute the operation using its interpretation $\oplus_B$ on base-type values. We write $b_1 \oplus_B b_2 =: b$ as a shorthand for $(b_1, b_2) \in dom(\oplus_B)$ and $b_1 \oplus_B b_2 = b$.

BA-S-Op
$$\frac{b_1 \oplus_B b_2 =: b \qquad a_1 \oplus_A a_2 =: a}{b_1[a_1] \oplus b_2[a_2] \longrightarrow b[a]}$$

This rule may fail for two reasons, either the annotations are incompatible $(a_1, a_2) \notin dom(\oplus_A)$ or the operation is not defined on the particular argument values, i.e., $(b_1, b_2) \notin dom(\oplus_B)$. The example of dimension analysis demonstrates that the two conditions are independent. In the computation $3[m]/0[m]$, the division of the dimensions is defined, but $3/0$ is undefined.

The corresponding typing rule checks the annotations and the rule for constants just matches the annotations.

BA-T-Const
$$\Gamma \vdash b[a] : B[a]$$

BA-T-Op
$$\frac{\Gamma \vdash e_1 : B[a_1] \qquad \Gamma \vdash e_2 : B[a_2] \qquad a_1 \oplus_A a_2 =: a}{\Gamma \vdash e_1 \oplus e_2 : B[a]}$$

Type soundness of the annotated type system implies that well-typed operations make the run-time check on annotations in rule BA-S-Op obsolete. Consequently the run-time annotations on well-typed programs could be erased. The erasure of statically verified annotations is further discussed in Section 3.6.

3.2   Gradual Annotated Typing

Our execution model from Subsection 3.1 equips all base-type values with run-time value annotations. For gradualization, we transition to a calculus λ_G^{BA} where value annotations are categorized as either static or dynamic and the operations on them are lifted from the original annotation algebra. Subsections 3.5 and 3.6 discuss the drawbacks of alternative approaches and demonstrate how the efficiency of annotation handling at run time can be improved.

Before we continue, it is important to realize that gradual annotation typing is different to gradual typing or dynamic typing. In dynamic typing, primitive operations, like addition, have a fixed low-level type, say, `int->int->int`. To execute these operations requires dynamic arguments to be unwrapped and results to be wrapped in a dynamic container. For that reason, gradual typing [27] starts with a type system that exposes these low-level types and introduces casts to revert to type dynamic if the low-level types do not match.

In annotated gradual typing, we take the low-level typing of operations for granted: an addition on integers may certainly be executed, **but** it may be forbidden because of non-matching dimension annotations, say. In particular, it is not desirable to even define a translation that introduces casts because the same addition operation may be used polymorphically with arguments of different (but matching) dimensionality.

Gradualization requires two different extensions of the annotation algebra, one for type annotations and one for value annotations. Type annotations in the gradual system, ta, are drawn from $\mathcal{A}^? = (A^?, \oplus, \dots)$ where $A^? = A \cup \{?\}$ and an operation is lifted from $\mathcal{A}$ by insisting that any ? argument makes the result ?, or that all arguments are in A, in which case the operation works as before.

$$? \oplus_{A^?} \_ = ?$$
$$\_ \oplus_{A^?} ? = ?$$
$$a_1 \oplus_{A^?} a_2 = a \quad a_1, a_2 \in A, (a_1 \oplus_A a_2) =: a$$

Apart from drawing type annotations from this extended algebra, the type language is unchanged.

The refined algebra $\mathcal{A}^+ = (A^+, \oplus, \dots)$ stages the value annotations using $A^+ = \mathbf{D}(A) + \mathbf{S}(A)$, the disjoint union of two copies of A tagged with $\mathbf{D}$ and $\mathbf{S}$, where $\mathbf{D}$ annotations are only checked dynamically and $\mathbf{S}$ annotations are (also) checked statically. The operations are lifted to $\mathcal{A}^+$ by insisting that results are static unless any dynamic argument is present. In any case, they apply the underlying operation from $\mathcal{A}$.

$$\mathbf{D}(a_1) \oplus_{A^+} V(a_2) = \mathbf{D}(a) \quad (a_1 \oplus_A a_2) =: a$$
$$V(a_1) \oplus_{A^+} \mathbf{D}(a_2) = \mathbf{D}(a) \quad (a_1 \oplus_A a_2) =: a$$
$$\mathbf{S}(a_1) \oplus_{A^+} \mathbf{S}(a_2) = \mathbf{S}(a) \quad (a_1 \oplus_A a_2) =: a$$

Here and in the following, the meta variables $V, V_1, V_2, \dots$ range over $\mathbf{D}$ and $\mathbf{S}$ and meta variables $va, va_1, \dots$ range over annotations of the shape $V(a)$.

The term language is extended by type (annotation) casts.

$$e ::= \cdots \mid e : t \leadsto^p t$$

BA-SG-Op

$$\frac{b_1 \oplus b_2 =: b \qquad va_1 \oplus_{A+} va_2 =: va}{b_1[va_1] \oplus b_2[va_2] \longrightarrow b[va]}$$

BA-SG-Cast-Base

$$\frac{V_1(a) \prec ta_1 \qquad V_2(a) \prec ta_2}{(b[V_1(a)] : B[ta_1] \rightsquigarrow^p B[ta_2]) \longrightarrow b[V_2(a)]}$$

BA-SG-Cast-Fun

$$v : (t_1 \to t_2) \rightsquigarrow^p (t_1' \to t_2') \longrightarrow \lambda x.(v(x : t_1' \rightsquigarrow^{\overline{p}} t_1)) : t_2 \rightsquigarrow^p t_2'$$

Fig. 2. Dynamics of the gradual annotation calculus

They modify the annotations but leave the shape of types intact. The *blame label* p on the cast indicates the source of the potential error. Blame labels come with an involutory operation $\overline{}$ that flips the polarity of the blame between positive $p = \overline{\overline{p}}$ and negative $\overline{p}$. When a cast error arises during execution, the blame's polarity indicates whether it is the cast expression that violates the typing assertions of the cast (positive blame) or the context (negative blame).

Figure 2 contains the dynamics of the calculus. Base type operations are unsurprising (BA-SG-Op). They just switch to the new algebras. For functions, β_v reduction is kept unchanged (BA-S-BetaV). It remains to consider casts.

The base type cast BA-SG-Cast-Base checks the annotation and converts between their **S** and **D** shapes while keeping the underlying annotation a. The relation $\prec$ expresses compatibility of a value annotation with a type annotation. Any dynamic value annotation is compatible with the type annotation ? and a static value annotation of the form $\mathbf{S}(a)$ is compatible with a.

$$\mathbf{D}(a) \prec ? \qquad \mathbf{S}(a) \prec a$$

Type casts at non-base types are treated by decomposing the cast into its constituent casts and distributing them according to the type constructor, exemplified with casting of values of function type BA-SG-Cast-Fun. Due to the contravariance of the function type, the polarity of the blame on the function argument flips but the polarity on the function result remains the same.

With respect to λ^{BA}, the typing rule for operations changes and the rule for casts gets added. Even the rule for operations just switches the handling of the annotations to the algebra $\mathcal{A}^?$. The rule for constants needs to be slightly adjusted to require the compatibility of annotations.

BA-TG-Op

$$\frac{\Gamma \vdash_G e_1 : B[a_1] \qquad \Gamma \vdash_G e_2 : B[a_2] \qquad (a_1 \oplus_{A^?} a_2) =: a}{\Gamma \vdash_G e_1 \oplus e_2 : B[a]}$$

BA-TG-Const

$$\frac{V(a) \prec ta}{\Gamma \vdash b[V(a)] : ta}$$

The typing rule for casts enforces that casts are only executed for compatible annotated types as indicated by a compatibility relation.

BA-TG-Cast

$$\frac{\Gamma \vdash_G e : t_1 \qquad t_1 \sim t_2}{\Gamma \vdash_G (e : t_1 \rightsquigarrow^p t_2) : t_2}$$

$$B[?] \sim B[ta] \qquad B[ta] \sim B[?] \qquad B[ta] \sim B[ta] \qquad \frac{t_1 \sim t'_1 \quad t_2 \sim t'_2}{t_1 \to t_2 \sim t'_1 \to t'_2}$$

Fig. 3. Compatibility

The compatibility relation $\sim$ (Figure 3) ensures that two types have the same underlying structure and that direct casts between statically annotated types are ruled out. This relation is reflexive and symmetric, but not transitive. For a transitive compatibility, $B[a] \sim B[?]$ and $B[?] \sim B[a']$ would imply $B[a] \sim B[a']$ if $a \neq a'$. Using the annotation algebra for dimensions, such a cast could try to convert metres to seconds (and would always fail). Intransitive compatibility makes it harder to write obviously faulty code by only allowing casts between static and dynamic annotations. Furthermore, if $B[a] \sim B[a']$ for $a \neq a'$, then the BA-SG-CAST-BASE rule would fail on a static cast that should be disallowed by the type system. Also, the formulation of the technical results in Section 3.3 would get more complicated (particularly Definition 1).

3.3 Results

We have established type soundness for the gradual calculus. The most interesting part of the result is the progress lemma because it comes with a characterization of the possibly failing terms, the dynamically stuck terms.

Definition 1. *A term e is* dynamically stuck *if*

1. $e = E[b[\boldsymbol{D}(a)] : B[?] \rightsquigarrow^p B[a']]$ *where* $a \neq a'$,
2. $e = E[b_1[V_1(a_1)] \oplus b_2[V_2(a_2)]]$ *where* $(a_1, a_2) \notin dom(\oplus_A)$ *and* $V_i = \boldsymbol{D}$ *for some* $i \in \{1, 2\}$,
3. $e = E[b_1[V_1(a_1)] \oplus b_2[V_2(a_2)]]$ *where* $(a_1, a_2) \in dom(\oplus_A)$ *but* $(b_1, b_2) \notin dom(\oplus_B)$.

The core reason for being dynamically stuck is either a failing cast of a dynamically annotated value to a statically annotated one, where the provided annotation is not the expected one, or a failing attempt at a dynamically checked operation. For the failing cast, we also say that it *raises blame p* according to the blame label attached to the cast. A third case arises when $\oplus_B$ is partial, but its occurrence depends on the abstraction implemented by the annotation algebra. It is thus independent of gradual typing.

Lemma 1 (Progress). *If* $\cdot \vdash_G e : t$ *then either e is a value or* $(\exists e')\ e \longrightarrow e'$ *or e is a dynamically stuck term.*

Lemma 2 (Preservation).
If $\cdot \vdash_G e : t$ *and* $e \longrightarrow e'$, *then* $\cdot \vdash_G e' : t$.

$$B[ta] <:^\circ B[ta] \qquad\qquad B[ta] <:^+ B[ta]$$

$$B[a] <:^\circ B[?] \qquad\qquad B[a] <:^+ B[?] \qquad\qquad B[ta_1] <:^- B[ta_2]$$

$$\frac{t_2' <:^\circ t_1' \quad t_1 <:^\circ t_2}{t_1' \to t_1 <:^\circ t_2' \to t_2} \qquad \frac{t_2' <:^+ t_1' \quad t_1 <:^- t_2}{t_1' \to t_1 <:^- t_2' \to t_2} \qquad \frac{t_2' <:^- t_1' \quad t_1 <:^+ t_2}{t_1' \to t_1 <:^+ t_2' \to t_2}$$

Fig. 4. Cast-related subtyping relations

Following Wadler and Findler's Blame Calculus [32], the subsequent development works towards a blame theorem for λ_G^{BA}. The blame theorem is a sharpening of progress which further examines the nature of the casts [31,32]. It gives sufficient conditions on casts to ensure that all blame falls on the dynamically checked parts of the program.

Casts are classified according to a number of subtyping relations which are not meant to be used for subsumption: plain subtyping, positive subtyping, and negative subtyping. Figure 4 defines them for gradual annotated typing.

Plain subtyping classifies casts that perform safe conversions and thus never cause a run-time error: A cast from t to t' is safe if $t <:^\circ t'$. Intuitively, casts are safe if they are trivial, or inject statically checked expressions into dynamic code. In the latter case, the dynamic code has the complete freedom and responsibility to use the statically typed results adequately. Examples of such safe injections are $e : B[a] \rightsquigarrow^p B[?]$, or $e : B[a] \to B[a] \rightsquigarrow^p B[a] \to B[?]$. Trying to inject a dynamic value into static code (e.g. $e : B[?] \rightsquigarrow^p B[a]$) could result in a run-time error, which is unsafe. Plain subtyping on base-types allows the identity conversion and a conversion from a static annotation to a dynamic one. Blame subtyping for function types is contravariant in the parameter type. A cast like $e : B[?] \to B[a] \rightsquigarrow^p B[a] \to B[a]$ is considered safe because it relies on the function's original type which already claims full responsibility for the parameter.

As in Wadler and Findler's work, plain subtyping may be factored into positive subtyping $<:^+$ and negative subtyping $<:^-$. If positive (negative) subtyping $t_1 <:^{+(-)} t_2$ holds then a cast from t_1 to t_2 with label p does not result in a run-time error that raises blame p ($\bar{p}$). Positive subtyping is analogous to plain subtyping on base types but relaxes the restriction on function parameters to *negative* subtyping. Negative subtyping only restricts type annotations for function parameters (via positive subtyping), as only function casts may invert blame labels.

Lemma 3. *The relations* $<:^+$, $<:^-$, *and* $<:^\circ$ *are reflexive and transitive.*

Further, plain subtyping is the intersection of positive and negative subtyping.

Lemma 4. $<:^\circ = <:^+ \cap <:^-$.

$$x \text{ sf } p \qquad \frac{e_1 \text{ sf } p \quad e_2 \text{ sf } p}{e_1 \, e_2 \text{ sf } p} \qquad \frac{e \text{ sf } p}{\lambda x.e \text{ sf } p} \qquad b[va] \text{ sf } p \qquad \frac{e_1 \text{ sf } p \quad e_2 \text{ sf } p}{e_1 \oplus e_2 \text{ sf } p}$$

$$\frac{e \text{ sf } p \quad q \notin \{p, \overline{p}\}}{e : t_1 \leadsto^q t_2 \text{ sf } p} \qquad \frac{e \text{ sf } p \quad t_1 <:^+ t_2}{e : t_1 \leadsto^p t_2 \text{ sf } p} \qquad \frac{e \text{ sf } p \quad t_1 <:^- t_2}{e : t_1 \leadsto^{\overline{p}} t_2 \text{ sf } p}$$

Fig. 5. Safety with respect to p

The next step towards showing a blame theorem consists of defining a set of expressions that is safe for a certain blame label p. The judgment $e \text{ sf } p$ in Figure 5 characterizes this set. It guarantees that all cast operations in e that involve the label p (or $\overline{p}$) use types that are related by positive (negative) subtyping. Fortunately, safety is an invariant under reduction.

Lemma 5. *If e sf p and $e \longrightarrow e'$, then e' sf p.*

The blame theorem states that an irreducible term, which is safe for p, cannot be stuck on a cast labeled p. An irreducible term, which is safe for p and $\overline{p}$, cannot be stuck on a cast labeled p or $\overline{p}$.

Lemma 6. *If e sf p and $\neg(\exists e') \, e \longrightarrow e'$, then e cannot have the form $E[b[D(a)] : B[?] \leadsto^p B[a']]$, where $a \neq a'$.*

Theorem 1 (Blame). *If e sf p and e sf $\overline{p}$ and $\neg(\exists e') \, e \longrightarrow e'$, then e cannot have the form $E[b[D(a)] : B[?] \leadsto^p B[a']]$ or $E[b[D(a)] : B[?] \leadsto^{\overline{p}} B[a']]$, where $a \neq a'$.*

3.4 Subtyping

A reflexive and transitive conversion relation $\precsim$ on the annotation algebra for base types induces a subtyping relation on the corresponding annotated type system. The required subsumption rule is standard.

$$\frac{a_1 \precsim a_2}{B[a_1] <: B[a_2]} \qquad \frac{t_1' <: t_1 \quad t_2 <: t_2'}{t_1 \to t_2 <: t_1' \to t_2'} \qquad \frac{\Gamma \vdash e : t \quad t <: t'}{\Gamma \vdash e : t'}$$

In the presence of conversion, the static annotation on a value need no longer be equal to the static annotation on its type. Hence, the type-level operation $\oplus_{A?}$ and the value-level operation $\oplus_A$ may yield different results because they are applied to different arguments, albeit related by $\precsim$. This observation leads to the requirement that $\oplus_A$ must be monotonic with respect to $\precsim$. In particular, if $a_1 \precsim a_1'$, $a_2 \precsim a_2'$, and $a_1' \oplus_A a_2' =: a'$, then $a_1 \oplus_A a_2 =: a$ and $a \precsim a'$. Otherwise, reduction may get stuck on a well-typed term and type preservation may fail.

To see that, consider $b_i[a_i] : B[a_i']$ where $a_i \precsim a_i'$ ($i = 1, 2$). If $a_1' \oplus_A a_2' =: a'$, then the term $b_1[a_1] \oplus b_2[a_2] : B[a']$ is well-typed. However, the reduction of $\oplus$ gets stuck unless $a_1 \oplus_A a_2 =: a$ holds and type preservation fails unless $a \precsim a'$.

For the gradual system, the subtyping relation needs to be extended to ? annotations. They are not convertible with any other annotation so that annotations cannot become dynamic (and vice versa) without an explicit cast.

$$B[?] <:_G B[?]$$

In particular, having $B[a] \not<:_G B[?]$ prevents the unintentional introduction of dynamic values. The remaining cases are as in the static system.

Nothing else needs to change, except that the compatibility relation between value annotations and type annotations that is used in the static checking of casts (Figure 2) has to reflect the possible conversion.

$$\frac{a \precsim a'}{\mathbf{S}(a) \prec a'}$$

In the presence of subtyping, one might contemplate to slacken the compatibility relation $\sim$ and admit the cast between annotations that are related by subtyping. That is, the axiom $B[ta] \sim B[ta]$ would be refined to $B[ta] \sim B[ta']$ if $ta \precsim ta'$ or $ta' \precsim ta$. However, this refined axiom introduces the danger that casts that do not involve ? may raise blame at run time: Each downcast involves a runtime check. The blame theorem can be refined to distinguish safe upcasts and unsafe downcasts by including the conversion relation in the blame subtyping of static base-types: $B[a] <:^\circ B[a']$ and $B[a] <:^+ B[a']$ whenever $a \precsim a'$.

3.5 Alternative Modeling

A notion of gradual typing could also be introduced without an extended algebra, just with the plain annotation algebra $\mathcal{A}$ for value annotations. The compatibility relation between value annotations and type annotations would relate any value annotation to ? and otherwise be the equality on plain annotations:

$$a \prec' ? \qquad a \prec' a$$

With this change, the cast operation (as in BA-SG-CAST-BASE) would never modify any annotation. The dynamics of operations would correspond to BA-S-OP. The definition of dynamically stuck terms (Definition 1) would change as follows.

Definition 2. *A term e is stuck if*

1. *$e = E[b[a] : B[?] \rightsquigarrow^p B[a']]$ where $a \neq a'$,*
2. *$e = E[b_1[a_1] \oplus b_2[a_2]]$ where $(a_1, a_2) \notin dom(\oplus_A)$,*
3. *$e = E[b_1[a_1] \oplus b_2[a_2]]$ where $(a_1, a_2) \in dom(\oplus_A)$ but $(b_1, b_2) \notin dom(\oplus_B)$.*

Comparing Definitions 1 and 2 shows that the plain annotation algebra weakens the progress result. While cases 1 and 3 yield the same information as cases 1 and 3 in Definition 1, case 2 has become ambiguous: In case 2 of Definition 1 it is clear that the annotation mismatch is caused by an attempt to apply $\oplus$ in a dynamically typed fragment. With Definition 2 the annotation mismatch can no longer be located; it might be in a statically typed part of the program.

We conclude that the simplified approach is weaker than the $\mathcal{A}^+$-approach presented in Section 3.2 because it yields a less informative progress result that only makes an ambiguous statement about a key part of the type system.

3.6 Annotation Erasure

Using the $\mathcal{A}^+$-approach, we may define an erasure translation that avoids the passing of annotations at run time in the statically checked parts of a program. In the target calculus of this translation, the cast operations amount to adding or removing run-time annotations. The syntax of this calculus extends the syntax for base type refinements with unannotated base-type values:

$$e ::= b \mid \dots \qquad v ::= b \mid \dots$$

The erasure translation $|\cdot|$ only acts on annotated base-type values and extends homomorphically to the remaining syntactic constructs:

$$|b[\mathbf{S}(a)]| = b \qquad |b[\mathbf{D}(a)]| = b[a]$$

Besides rule BA-S-Op, there is an additional computation rule for unannotated base-type values:

BA-S-Op
$$\frac{b_1 \oplus_B b_2 =: b \qquad a_1 \oplus_A a_2 =: a}{b_1[a_1] \oplus b_2[a_2] \longrightarrow' b[a]}$$

BA-SG-Op'
$$\frac{b_1 \oplus_B b_2 =: b}{b_1 \oplus b_2 \longrightarrow' b}$$

Reduction of base type casts is best presented as three separate rules.

BA-SG-Cast-Trivial
$$(v : B[ta] \rightsquigarrow^p B[ta]) \longrightarrow' v$$

BA-SG-Cast-ToDyn
$$(b : B[a] \rightsquigarrow^p B[?]) \longrightarrow' b[a]$$

BA-SG-Cast-FromDyn
$$(b[a] : B[?] \rightsquigarrow^p B[a]) \longrightarrow' b$$

Trivial casts are discarded. A cast from a static type into a dynamic one adds the annotation of the static type as a run-time annotation. A cast from dynamic to static strips off the run-time annotation, provided it matches that of the static destination type.

Progress for this calculus needs yet another notion of stuck terms.

Definition 3. *A term e is* stuck *if*

1. $e = E[b[a] : B[?] \rightsquigarrow^p B[a']]$ *where* $a \neq a'$,
2. $e = E[b_1[a_1] \oplus b_2[a_2]]$ *where* $(a_1, a_2) \notin dom(\oplus_A)$,
3. $e = E[b_1 \oplus b_2]$ *where* $(b_1, b_2) \notin dom(\oplus_B)$.

This definition is again unsatisfactory. The first and second cases correspond to Definition 1. However, in the third case, computations with unannotated base-type values never check their annotation. Hence, the condition imposed by the static typing rule for primitive operations does not correspond to a run-time restriction, which trivializes preservation and progress.

We conclude that this calculus is also unsuitable to prove a strong progress result and we see that as a further indication in favor of the $\mathcal{A}^+$-approach.

However, it is possible to relate the $\mathcal{A}^+$-approach with the erasure approach, which amounts to an efficient implementation. For typed expressions, the evaluation relations $\longrightarrow$ and $\longrightarrow'$ simulate each other in lockstep.

Lemma 7. *Let e be a closed expression.*

1. *If $e \longrightarrow e'$, then $|e| \longrightarrow' |e'|$.*
2. *If $\cdot \vdash_G e : t$ and $|e| \longrightarrow' e''$, then $e \longrightarrow e'$ and $e'' = |e'|$.*

As an example that typing is essential for item 2 in the lemma, consider the expression $1[S(m)] + 1[S(kg)]$ in the calculus for dimensions. It is not typeable and it is stuck at rule BA-SG-OP. However, its erasure $|1[S(m)]+1[S(kg)]| = 1+1$ reduces to 2 using $\longrightarrow'$.

4   Eliminating Run-Time Checks

A gradually typed program with manually inserted casts can be improved by a type-preserving transformation, $e \Longrightarrow e'$, that increases the amount of statically handled annotations and decreases the number of dynamic checks without eliminating potential annotation mismatches. Thus, the transformed program should be equivalent to the original one, but with less dynamic annotation handling.

To express the results of the transformation concisely, we introduce a new kind of term $e ::= (\!|p|\!) \mid \ldots$ where $(\!|p|\!)$ is an *exception package* that carries blame label p. An exception package is generated by failing cast expressions, it is propagated upwards through evaluation contexts, and it has any type.

$$\frac{a \neq a'}{b[\mathbf{D}(a)] : B[?] \rightsquigarrow^p B[a'] \longrightarrow (\!|p|\!)} \qquad \frac{e \longrightarrow (\!|p|\!)}{E[e] \longrightarrow (\!|p|\!)} \qquad \Gamma \vdash_G (\!|p|\!) : t$$

4.1   Transformation Rules

In a typed term, any cast may be executed on a base type constant b. The result e' is either the same value b with a different annotation or an exception $(\!|p|\!)$. Exceptions may be promoted across evaluation contexts.

BA-TR-CONST
$$\frac{b[va] : B[ta] \rightsquigarrow^p B[ta'] \longrightarrow e'}{b[va] : B[ta] \rightsquigarrow^p B[ta'] \Longrightarrow e'}$$

BA-TR-BLAME
$$E[(\!|p|\!)] \Longrightarrow (\!|p|\!)$$

If a cast is applied to a dynamic operation $\oplus$, then the annotations of the arguments can be determined from the annotation of the result if $\oplus_A$ is locally injective. Only in this case, the cast can be propagated to the arguments.

BA-TR-OP
$$\frac{\oplus_A^{-1}(a) = \{(a_1, a_2)\}}{e_1 \oplus e_2 : B[?] \rightsquigarrow^p B[a] \Longrightarrow (e_1 : B[?] \rightsquigarrow^p B[a_1]) \oplus (e_2 : B[?] \rightsquigarrow^p B[a_2])}$$

The blame annotation gets propagated to the arguments to preserve the error messages. A typical example where this rule is applicable is an addition expression in the system for dimensions, where the annotations of both arguments are equal to the annotation of the result.

If a cast is applied to a lambda expression, then the expression can be transformed analogously to the dynamics for the cast (rule BA-SG-CAST-FUN). However, the cast on the result is pushed inside to the body of the lambda to be able to continue the transformation.

BA-TR-FUN
$$(\lambda x.e) : (t_1 \rightarrow t_2) \rightsquigarrow^p (t_1' \rightarrow t_2') \Longrightarrow \lambda x.(\lambda x.(e : t_2 \rightsquigarrow^p t_2'))(x : t_1' \rightsquigarrow^{\overline{p}} t_1)$$

Any cast applied to a function application may be pushed towards the function, which might enable rule BA-TR-FUN.

BA-TR-APP
$$\frac{e_2 : t_2}{(e_1\, e_2) : t \rightsquigarrow^p t' \Longrightarrow (e_1 : t_2 \rightarrow t \rightsquigarrow^p t_2 \rightarrow t')\, e_2}$$

The interplay between BA-TR-APP and BA-TR-FUN may generate identity casts, which may safely be omitted.

BA-TR-ID
$$e : t \rightsquigarrow^p t \Longrightarrow e$$

It also makes sense to consider transforming casts nested in elimination positions. If both operands of an operation are (positive) casts to dynamic, then these casts can be merged and propagated to the result. The blame labels need not be preserved because a positive cast on a base type never fails. The transformation arbitrarily chooses the left operand's blame label.

BA-TR-OP-ELIM
$$\frac{a_1 \oplus_A a_2 =: a}{(e_1 : B[a_1] \rightsquigarrow^{p_1} B[?]) \oplus (e_2 : B[a_2] \rightsquigarrow^{p_2} B[?]) \Longrightarrow e_1 \oplus e_2 : B[a] \rightsquigarrow^{p_1} B[?]}$$

We may also state rules for lifting casts out of function bodies and out of function applications. However, the overall approach of our transformation is to start at the root of a term and to push casts as far inside as possible. This approach does not require such lifting rules. Applying our rules exhaustively in a top-down manner results in a term where each casts is either applied to a variable, to an application of a primitive operation, or to another cast. However, we stress that each transformation step is correct in any context.

To further optimize the resulting term additionally requires an approach for merging two casts into one. A few special cases of this merge can be stated easily. However, a satisfactory treatment of cast composition requires a different representation of casts and a careful consideration of blame propagation. There are at least two alternatives for this representation, either threesomes [28] or coercions [11], but their introduction is not in scope of this paper.

4.2   Contextual Equivalence and Bisimulation

To prove the correctness of the transformation rules, we establish that they are contextual equivalences in λ_G^{BA}. Two expressions e_1 and e_2 are contextually equivalent if they behave the same in every context [19].

Now, for all contexts C, if

1. there exists v such that $C[e_1] \longrightarrow^* v$ and $C[e_2] \longrightarrow^* v$, or
2. there exists p such that $C[e_1] \longrightarrow^* (\!|p|\!)$ and $C[e_2] \longrightarrow^* (\!|p|\!)$, or
3. $C[e_1] \Uparrow$ iff $C[e_2] \Uparrow^2$

then e_1 and e_2 are contextually equivalent, written $e_1 \simeq e_2$.

As contextual equivalence is hard to prove directly, we prove it via bisimulation. To this end, we define a notion of observations $\alpha ::= @v \mid b[a] \mid (\!|p|\!)$ for λ_G^{BA} programs. An observation on a function type is the application of a value $@v$. On a base type, we may observe the annotated base-type value $b[a]$. On a failing computation, we observe the blame label raised $(\!|p|\!)$. This observation is possible at any type.

Based on this notion of observations, we define a labeled transition system. Basic values are emitted as observations and their transition yields a non-terminating expression $\mathbf{0}$ with an empty derivation tree. Blame exceptions are treated in the same way. At function type, a transition is only possible on a function which is applied to a value of suitable type. This treatment is an adaptation of the call-by-value variation of Gordon's applicative bisimulation theory [9].

$$
\text{LT-Base} \qquad \text{LT-Blame} \qquad \frac{\text{LT-App} \atop \cdot \vdash_G v : t' \to t \quad \cdot \vdash_G v' : t'}{v \overset{@v'}{\Longmapsto} v\, v'} \qquad \frac{\text{LT-Comp} \atop e \longrightarrow e' \quad e' \overset{\alpha}{\Longmapsto} e''}{e \overset{\alpha}{\Longmapsto} e''}
$$

$$
b[a] \overset{b[a]}{\Longmapsto} \mathbf{0} \qquad (\!|p|\!) \overset{(\!|p|\!)}{\Longmapsto} \mathbf{0}
$$

This definition of the labeled transition relation is adequate because an expression can make a transition if and only if it either terminates in a value or in a blame exception.

Lemma 8. $e \overset{\alpha}{\Longmapsto} e'$ *iff either there exists v such that $e \longrightarrow^* v$ or there exists p such that $e \longrightarrow^* (\!|p|\!)$.*

From the labeled transition system, we define bisimilarity as usual. For a relation $\mathcal{S} \subseteq Exp \times Exp$, define two functions:

$$
[\mathcal{S}] := \{(e_1, e_2) \mid (\exists \alpha, e_1')\ e_1 \overset{\alpha}{\Longmapsto} e_1' \Rightarrow (\exists e_2')\ e_2 \overset{\alpha}{\Longmapsto} e_2', e_1' \mathcal{S} e_2'\}
$$
$$
\langle \mathcal{S} \rangle := [\mathcal{S}] \cap [\mathcal{S}^{op}]^{op}
$$

Here, $\mathcal{S}^{op} = \{(e_2, e_1) \mid (e_1, e_2) \in \mathcal{S}\}$ is the opposite relation to $\mathcal{S}$. Both functions are easily checked to be monotone, so we can take their greatest fixpoint $\sim\ =\ \nu\mathcal{S}.\langle\mathcal{S}\rangle$, which is the bisimilarity relation for the calculus λ_G^{BA}.

Lemma 9.

1. $\sim$ *is an equivalence relation.*
2. *Evaluation steps are bisimilar:* $\longrightarrow\ \subseteq\ \sim$.

---

2 $e \Uparrow$ if for each e' such that $e \longrightarrow^* e'$ there exists e'' such that $e' \longrightarrow e''$.

Using Gordon's adaptation [9] of Howe's method [12], it can be shown that bisimilarity is a congruence and that it coincides with contextual equivalence.

The soundness of the transformation rules is proven by strong coinduction. As a corollary, we obtain that each transformation rule is a contextual equivalence in λ_G^{BA}.

5 Related Work

Disney and Flanagan [5] have applied gradual typing to a type system for information flow. They have proved type safety, noninterference, and a blame theorem. Their approach is tailored to the particular system. They do not systematically transform the annotation strategy of an existing system, but define notions like positive and negative subtyping directly on the existing annotations.

Gradual typing has made an impact on object-oriented language design, so the following related work comes from that area. As our method is mainly geared towards functional programming, it is not directly applicable. In addition, each of the related work items addresses a very specific point for gradualization that is deeply intertwined with the rest of the language design considered.

Typestate is a refinement of an (imperative object) type that changes as a program progresses. There are distinguished operations that change the typestate and the typestate governs which operations are available. Gradual typestate by Wolff and coworkers [33] addresses the problem that a program with typestate requires extensive type annotations to indicate the typestate transitions (e.g., on function arguments) and to manage sharing: if a function obtains two aliases to a typestate object, then applying different operations to them may lead to unsoundness. The gradual version of the system allows to replace typestate-related annotations by Dyn and performs the corresponding state and permission checks at run time. The authors prove type soundness and define a semantics by translating to a lower level calculus. The construction of the gradual extension is closely tied to the particulars of the system, in particular with the handling of aliasing. The aliasing aspect is not considered in our work.

The goal of gradual ownership types by Sergey and Clarke [24], also from the realm of object-oriented programming, is to enable a smooth migration from systems without control of ownership to static control of ownership. They apply the ideas of gradual typing to express heap properties instead of properties of values or (single) objects. One motivation is in avoiding the excessive annotation overhead that comes with other ownership type systems. In the construction of the system, the particular dynamic enforcement mechanism is an ad-hoc design. In this system, assignments have to be checked in order to prevent unwanted paths in the object graph.

Ina and Igarashi have considered gradual typing for generics [13]. Their system extends gradual typing to an object-oriented language with bounded subtyping. As such it discusses an extension to parameterized types, not to annotated. Thus, the required dynamic checks are tests on the run-time type of an object, not for additional properties.

Tobin-Hochstadt and Felleisen [31] were the first to investigate the boundaries of static and dynamic checking with a blame theorem. Wadler and Findler's subsequent analysis of blame [32] has been a major source of inspiration. We managed to transfer their results to a wide range of annotated type systems. Hybrid type checking [17] is a system based on dependent types and base-type refinements, which are described by arbitrary predicates. Dynamic checks (casts) serve to manifest refinements in types where they can be exploited in static checking. Here, the dynamically annotated type is essentially one where the predicate is true. Subtyping needs to be checked with a theorem prover. In contrast, our approach is geared toward refining types with additional properties that are not just predicates on the values of a base type.

The transformation of programs with coercions has been considered by Henglein [11]. Different to the discussion in our paper, his calculus employs coercion expressions that are built from primitive coercions on base types using functorial operations. Furthermore, he develops an equational theory of coercions and of expressions with coercions. His theory is not directly linked with contextual equivalence.

A coercion calculus with blame has been investigated by Siek, Garcia, and Taha [26]. They consider design alternatives for higher-order casts, where they also analyze the problem of merging two casts at run time. One of their options is to fail early, when casts are composed. In a program transformation as we consider it in Section 4, such a behavior would yield false positives when processing dead code.

Siek and Wadler [28] discuss a variation of the blame calculus where arbitrarily long compositions of casts are compressed into a single, equivalent threesome cast. They also show the equivalence of threesomes and a normalizing coercion calculus. A mechanism like that should be integrated in our simplifying transformation. We leave it to future work because it would require a reworking of the annotated cast mechanism, either in terms of coercions or in terms of threesomes.

Rastogi and coworkers [22] develop an algorithm for type inference in Action-Script that also aims to eliminate run-time checks, similar to our transformation. Their approach is not based on program transformation. Instead, their algorithm replaces the dynamic type with type variables and globally computes and solves set constraints that overapproximate the flows of types to contexts. The algorithm preserves run-time errors with respect to the original untyped program but sacrifices blame guarantees for improved precision. In contrast, our transformation preserves errors and blame as each transformation preserves contextual equivalence.

6   Conclusion

We show that annotated type systems, where the annotation is restricted to base types, can be gradualized by applying a simple procedure. The core of our approach is the definition of a generic gradual annotated type system based on an annotation algebra. We demonstrate its applicability by instantiating it to several examples. The technical results (type soundness and blame theorems) for the generic gradual systems have generic reusable proofs that can be instantiated to each annotation algebra.

Specific semantic properties still require extra work: the generic results hold, even if the dynamic manipulation of the annotations is total nonsense. For example, a sound gradual security type system requires that the handling of dynamic annotations guarantees noninterference, but the specifics are not prescribed by our framework.

Our type system can be extended in several directions. Annotations may be added to each type constructor: this extension is necessary for an information flow analysis that can guarantee noninterference. The calculus may be extended with annotation polymorphism, which diminishes the need for the dynamic handling of annotations. Also the whole system may be based on a calculus with ML-style polymorphism.

References

1. Abadi, M., Flanagan, C., Freund, S.N.: Types for safe locking: Static race detection for Java. ACM TOPLAS 28(2), 207–255 (2006)
2. Castagna, G. (ed.): ESOP 2009. LNCS, vol. 5502. Springer, Heidelberg (2009)
3. Chin, B., Markstrum, S., Adsul, B.: Inference of user-defined type qualifiers and qualifier rules. In: Sestoft, P. (ed.) ESOP 2006. LNCS, vol. 3924, pp. 264–278. Springer, Heidelberg (2006)
4. Darwin, I.F.: Annabot: A static verifier for java annotation usage. Adv. Software Engineering (2010)
5. Disney, T., Flanagan, C.: Gradual information flow typing. In: STOP 2011 (2011)
6. Fennell, L., Thiemann, P.: Gradual security typing with references. In: Cortier, V., Datta, A. (eds.) CSF, pp. 224–239. IEEE (2013)
7. Flanagan, C., Freund, S.N.: Type-based race detection for Java. In: Proceedings of the 2000 ACM SIGPLAN Conference on Programming Language Design and Implementation (PLDI), pp. 219–232. ACM Press (June 2000); 35(5) of SIGPLAN Notices
8. Freeman, T., Pfenning, F.: Refinement types for ML. In: Proc. PLDI 1991, pp. 268–277. ACM (June 1991)
9. Gordon, A.D.: Bisimilarity as a theory of functional programming. Theoretical Computer Science 228(1-2), 5–47 (1999)
10. Heintze, N., Riecke, J.G.: The SLam calculus: Programming with security and integrity. In: Cardelli, L. (ed.) Proc. 25th ACM Symp. POPL, pp. 365–377. ACM Press (January 1998)
11. Henglein, F.: Dynamic typing: Syntax and proof theory. Science of Computer Programming 22, 197–230 (1994)
12. Howe, D.: Proving congruence of bisimulation in functional programming languages. Information and Computation 124(2), 103–112 (1996)
13. Ina, L., Igarashi, A.: Gradual typing for generics. In: Lopes, C.V., Fisher, K. (eds.) OOPSLA, pp. 609–624. ACM (2011)
14. Jackson, D.: Aspect: Detecting bugs with abstract dependences. ACM Trans. Softw. Eng. Methodol. 4(2), 109–145 (1995)

15. Kennedy, A.: Dimension types. In: Sannella, D. (ed.) ESOP 1994. LNCS, vol. 788, pp. 348–362. Springer, Heidelberg (1994)
16. Kennedy, A.J.: Relational parametricity and units of measure. In: Jones, N. (ed.) Proc. 1997 ACM Symp. POPL, pp. 442–455. ACM (January 1997)
17. Knowles, K.L., Flanagan, C.: Hybrid type checking. ACM Trans. Program. Lang. Syst. 32(2) (2010)
18. Leijen, D., Meijer, E.: Domain-specific embedded compilers. In: 2nd Conference on Domain-Specific Languages. USENIX (October 1999), http://usenix.org/events/dsl99/index.html
19. Morris Jr., J.H.: Lambda Calculus Models of Programming Languages. PhD thesis. MIT Press (December 1968)
20. Nielson, F.: Annotated type and effect systems. Computing Surveys 28(2), 344–345 (1996)
21. Pessaux, F., Leroy, X.: Type-based analysis of uncaught exceptions. In: Aiken, A. (ed.) Proc. 26th ACM Symp. POPL, pp. 276–290. ACM Press (January 1999)
22. Rastogi, A., Chaudhuri, A., Hosmer, B.: The ins and outs of gradual type inference. In: Proc. 39th ACM Symp. POPL, pp. 481–494. ACM Press (January 2012)
23. Rittri, M.: Dimension inference under polymorphic recursion. In: Peyton Jones, S. (ed.) Proc. FPCA 1995, pp. 147–159. ACM (June 1995)
24. Sergey, I., Clarke, D.: Gradual ownership types. In: Seidl, H. (ed.) ESOP 2012. LNCS, vol. 7211, pp. 579–599. Springer, Heidelberg (2012)
25. Siek, J.G., Taha, W.: Gradual typing for objects. In: Ernst, E. (ed.) ECOOP 2007. LNCS, vol. 4609, pp. 2–27. Springer, Heidelberg (2007)
26. Siek, J.G., Garcia, R., Taha, W.: Exploring the design space of higher-order casts. In: Castagna [2], pp. 17–31
27. Siek, J.G., Taha, W.: Gradual typing for functional languages. In: Scheme and Functional Programming Workshop (September 2006)
28. Siek, J.G., Wadler, P.: Threesomes, with and without blame. In: Palsberg, J. (ed.) Proc. 37th ACM Symp. POPL, pp. 365–376. ACM Press (January 2010)
29. Solberg, K.L.: Annotated Type Systems for Program Analysis. PhD thesis, Odense University, Denmark. Also technical report DAIMI PB-498, Comp. Sci. Dept. Aarhus University (July 1995)
30. Tang, D., Plsek, A., Vitek, J.: Static checking of safety critical Java annotations. In: Kalibera, T., Vitek, J. (eds.) JTRES. ACM International Conference Proceeding Series, pp. 148–154. ACM (August 2010)
31. Tobin-Hochstadt, S., Felleisen, M.: Interlanguage migration: From scripts to programs. In: Dynamic Languages Symposium, DLS 2006, pp. 964–974. ACM (2006)
32. Wadler, P., Findler, R.B.: Well-typed programs can't be blamed. In: Castagna [2], pp. 1–16
33. Wolff, R., Garcia, R., Tanter, É., Aldrich, J.: Gradual typestate. In: Mezini, M. (ed.) ECOOP 2011. LNCS, vol. 6813, pp. 459–483. Springer, Heidelberg (2011)

Staged Composition Synthesis

Boris Düdder, Moritz Martens, and Jakob Rehof

Technical University of Dortmund, Faculty of Computer Science

Abstract. A framework for composition synthesis is provided in which metalanguage combinators are supported and the execution of synthesized programs can be staged into composition-time code generation (stage 1) and run-time execution (stage 2). By extending composition synthesis to encompass both object language (L1) and metalanguage (L2) combinators, composition synthesis becomes a powerful and flexible framework for the generation of L1-program compositions. A system of modal intersection types is introduced into a combinatory composition language to control the distinction between L1- and L2-combinators at the type level, thereby exposing the language distinction to composition synthesis. We provide a theory of correctness of the framework which ensures that generated compositions of component implementations are well typed and that their execution can be staged such that all metalanguage combinators can be computed away completely at stage 1, leaving only well typed L1-code for execution at stage 2. Our framework has been implemented, and we report on experiments.

1 Introduction

Composition synthesis [1–5] is based on the idea of using inhabitation in combinatory logic [6] with intersection types [7] as a foundation for computing compositions from a repository of components. We can regard a combinatory type judgement $\Gamma \vdash e : \tau$ as modeling the fact that combinatory expression e can be obtained by composition from a repository Γ of components which are exposed as combinator symbols and whose interfaces are exposed as combinator types enriched with intersection types that specify semantic properties of components. The decision problem of inhabitation, often indicated as $\Gamma \vdash ? : \tau$, is the question whether a combinatory expression e exists such that $\Gamma \vdash e : \tau$ (such an expression e is called an inhabitant of τ). An algorithm (or semi-algorithm) for solving the inhabitation problem searches for inhabitants and can be used to synthesize them. Under the propositions-as-types correspondence, inhabitation is the question of provability in a Hilbert-style presentation of a propositional logic, where Γ represents a propositional theory, τ represents a proposition to be proved, and e is a proof.

Following [8, 9], a level of *semantic types* is introduced to specify component interfaces and synthesis goals so as to direct synthesis by means of semantic concepts. Semantic types are not necessarily checked against component implementations (this is regarded as an orthogonal issue). In the combinatory approach

Z. Shao (Ed.): ESOP 2014, LNCS 8410, pp. 67–86, 2014.

of [1–5] semantic types are represented by intersection types [7]. In addition to being inherently component-oriented, it is a possible advantage of the type-based approach of composition synthesis that types can be naturally associated with code at the API-level. We think of intersection types as hosting a two-level type system, consisting of *native types* and *semantic types*. Native types are types of the implementation language, whereas semantic types are abstract, application-dependent conceptual structures, drawn, e.g., from a taxonomy of semantic concepts. For example, in the specification

$$X : ((\mathtt{real} \times \mathtt{real}) \cap \mathit{Cart} \to (\mathtt{real} \times \mathtt{real}) \cap \mathit{Pol}) \cap \mathit{Isom}$$

native types ($\mathtt{real}$, $\mathtt{real} \times \mathtt{real}$, . . .) are enriched with semantic types (in the example, $\mathit{Cart}, \mathit{Pol}, \mathit{Isom}$) by means of intersections. Semantic types express intended properties of the component (combinator) X — e.g., that it is an isometry transforming Cartesian to polar coordinates. We can think of semantic types as organized in any system of finite-dimensional feature spaces (e.g., $\mathit{Cart}, \mathit{Pol}$ are features of coordinates, Isom is a feature of functions) whose elements can be mapped onto the native API using intersections, at any level of the type structure.

In this paper we develop a framework for *staged composition synthesis* (SCS) in which *compositional metalanguage* components, implemented in a distinct language suitable for metaprogramming, can be introduced into composition synthesis. The introduction of metalanguage combinators adds power and flexibility to composition synthesis in several respects, including the ability to define special purpose composition operators, higher-order functional abstraction, native language code template substitution and code-generating operators.

In more detail, we assume here that we have a (possibly low-level) component implementation language L1 in which we can execute programs at runtime, referred to as the *native language*. Following the ideas summarized in [4], components written in L1 can be exposed for composition synthesis through a combinatory environment $\mathscr{C}$ in which named components are exposed as semantically typed combinator symbols $(X : \phi)$, where X is the name of the component and ϕ° is the native type of the component in the language L1 (the map $()^\circ$ erases semantic type information). So we assume for each $(X : \phi) \in \mathscr{C}$ that we have a native implementation program T_X with $\vdash_{\mathsf{L1}} T_X : \phi^\circ$, where $\vdash_{\mathsf{L1}}$ formalizes the type system of L1, and where the implementation T_X is associated with the typed combinator symbol $(X : \phi)$. Composition of L1-components from the environment $\mathscr{C}$ can be formalized in a corresponding combinatory logic, C1. We take a simple monomorphic imperative first-order language as our exemplary native language L1.

In our SCS framework we want to enhance our ability to compute compositions of L1-programs by introducing *templates* of L1-program fragments and expressions into which we can substitute other L1-program expressions to build complex L1-programs from simpler ones. To realize this idea in full, we need a possibly different language, L2, referred to as the *compositional metalanguage*, which is suited for the metaprogramming tasks involved in computing over L1-templates. Since a central task here is to perform substitutions into L1-templates we take the λ-calculus as our exemplary L2-language. In order to formalize this situation, we introduce type variables (type templates) and special program expression template variables u into L1 to serve as substitutable placeholders for L1-expressions inside other L1-expressions. Moreover, we introduce a type system $\vdash_{L2}$ for the metalanguage L2. Now, if we could compose *both* L1-programs *and* L2-programs that compose L1-programs, we could achieve more flexible and powerful forms of composition, since we can implement special code-generating L1-composition operators in L2, depending on situation and purpose. This situation is formalized by introducing a combinatory logic, C2, in which compositions of L2-programs are computed. In this combinatory logic C2, implemented L2-components are exposed in combinatory environments $\mathscr{D}$ analogously to the way L1-components are exposed in environments $\mathscr{C}$ in C1. We now have two implementation languages, L1 and L2, exposed for combinatory composition through associated combinatory logics, C1 and C2. In this system, we need a phase distinction between *composition time* computations in L2 and *runtime* computations in L1: we first (stage 1) perform composition time computations in the metalanguage L2 which produce L1-programs to be executed at runtime (stage 2). Since our focus is entirely on the generation of L1-compositions, we shall focus on L2-computations here.

Main Technical Contributions. Since composition synthesis is entirely type-directed, we need to expose the language- and phase distinction between L1 and L2 to synthesis at the type level. We solve this problem by exploiting the ideas of *staged computation* introduced by Davies and Pfenning [10], using modal types of the form $\Box\tau$ to describe "code of type τ". In our setting, such a type can appear in an L2-program manipulating L1-code to describe L1-code with L1-type τ. The type system ensures that L2-computations over L1-code is sound, i.e., that L2-implementations of type $\Box\tau$ can be computed away completely at composition time in L2 leaving a well typed L1-program (of type τ) as a result.

Our main technical innovation is the design and theory of semantic types at the combinatory logic level (C1 and C2), which are based on a novel system of *modal intersection types*. Such types can be superimposed onto implementation language types (L1 and L2) to express semantic properties of components to control composition. The basic challenge here is to achieve a design which allows such highly expressive semantic types to coexist with a guarantee of *implementation type correctness* (cf. Thm. 1), i.e., that synthesized compositions remain well typed in the implementation languages under semantic type erasure, even though compositions are constructed in a much more expressive type system of intersection types.

Our framework has been implemented in an extension of the (CL)S (Combinatory Logic Synthesizer) tool, and we report on the results of experiments using the tool for SCS.

Organization of the Paper. The remainder of this paper is organized as follows. In Sec. 2 we introduce the native language L1 and the metalanguage L2 (some definitions are placed in App.(s) A and B at the end of the paper).

Semantic types are defined in Sec. 3, and the combinatory logics C1 and C2 are defined in Sec. 4. In Sec. 5 we consider a simple example to illustrate SCS. In Sec. 6 we develop the theory of implementation type correctness, and Sec. 7 is devoted to the inhabitation algorithm underlying our extension of (CL)S, and experiments with the tool are discussed in Sec. 8. Related work is discussed in Sec. 9, and Sec. 10 concludes the paper.

2   Implementation Languages

We introduce an exemplary native language L1 and a compositional metalanguage L2, referred to collectively as implementation languages. In distinction to the framework of Davies and Pfenning [10] we have two distinct languages, which are highly independent of each other (regarding both operational semantics and type systems). Moreover, we only wish to distinguish exactly two stages of computation, *runtime* computation in the native language and *composition time* computation in the metalanguage (in [10] arbitrary levels of stages exist within a single language, and our framework can also be thus generalized). Our goal is a framework in which the native language is largely substitutable – native programs are regarded as "black boxes" that are exposed as expressions box T to the language L2 with L2-types of the form $\Box\tau$ (where τ is an L1-type), but other than that the theory of L2 is agnostic of the nature of programs T and types τ of L1.

For concreteness, we fix a simply typed first-order core language as an exemplary native implementation language L1 shown in Fig. 5, App. A, but (as mentioned) L1 can be exchanged easily. The only requirements on the design of L1 are that L1 should be typed, it should contain functions and function application, the language should satisfy preservation of types under appropriate term substitution (see substitution Lem. 1, App. A, for L1), and that well typed L1-programs can be executed at a later runtime stage (with which we are not further concerned, here). The native language consists of template expressions T containing template variables ranged over by u. Other native expressions or templates can be substituted for template variables. The type structure consists of a set $\mathbb{T}_0$ of *value types* ranged over by t_0, reference types t_1 and the set of *native template types* $\mathbb{T}_1$, ranged over by τ in which value types can be substituted for type variables ranged over by $\alpha, \beta, \gamma, \ldots \in \mathbb{V}$ (cf. App. A). We do not specify an operational semantics for L1, since it is altogether standard, and we are mainly concerned with computations in the metalanguage which we will consider next.

The compositional metalanguage L2 is a standard λ-calculus with simple types extended with *modal types* as introduced by Davies and Pfenning [10] to distinguish computational stages at the type level. In our setting, we can intuitively understand an L2-type $\Box\tau$ ($\tau \in \mathbb{T}_1$) as meaning "L1-code with L1-type τ". The set $\mathbb{T}_2$ denotes *metalanguage types*, ranged over by σ. The modal type constructor $\Box$ is a special covariant constructor.

$$\mathbb{T}_2 \ni \sigma ::= \Box\tau \mid \sigma \to \sigma'$$

Compositional metalanguage terms are terms M of the $\lambda_e^{\square\to}$-calculus [10]:

$$M ::= \text{box } T \mid \text{letbox } u : \tau = M_1 \text{ in } M_2 \mid x \mid \lambda x : \sigma.M \mid (M_1 M_2)$$

Compositional metalanguage expressions are typed by the system L2 shown in Fig. 1. Judgements are of the form $\Delta; \Gamma \vdash_{L2} M : \sigma$, where Δ contains L1-bindings $(u : \tau)$ of native template variables to L1-types, and Γ is the standard λ-calculus type environment of bindings $(x : \sigma)$ of λ-variables to L2-types.

The rule ($\square$I) together with the environment Δ provide the interface between L1 and L2. According to this rule, native templates T that are well typed with native template types in L1 can be injected into L2 by being placed in the scope of the box-operator. Importantly, the rule requires that we only inject native *expressions* T with no free native program variables (but possibly with free template variables) into L2. As shown in [10], this discipline ensures that we can soundly substitute native expressions into native templates in L2-computations. The dual rule ($\square$E) discharges assumptions in Δ using the letbox construct. As detailed in App. B, this construct performs substitution of native templates into native template variables under L2-computation.

$$\frac{}{\Delta; (\Gamma, x : \sigma) \vdash_{L2} x : \sigma} (\text{var})$$

$$\frac{\Delta; (\Gamma, x : \sigma) \vdash_{L2} M : \sigma'}{\Delta; \Gamma \vdash_{L2} \lambda x : \sigma.M : \sigma \to \sigma'} (\to\text{I}) \qquad \frac{\Delta; \Gamma \vdash_{L2} M_1 : \sigma \to \sigma' \quad \Delta; \Gamma \vdash_{L2} M_2 : \sigma}{\Delta; \Gamma \vdash_{L2} (M_1 M_2) : \sigma'} (\to\text{E})$$

$$\frac{\Delta; \emptyset \vdash_{L1} T : \tau}{\Delta; \Gamma \vdash_{L2} \text{box } T : \square\tau} (\square\text{I}) \qquad \frac{\Delta; \Gamma \vdash_{L2} M_1 : \square\tau \quad (\Delta, u : \tau); \Gamma \vdash_{L2} M_2 : \sigma}{\Delta; \Gamma \vdash_{L2} \text{letbox } u : \tau = M_1 \text{ in } M_2 : \sigma} (\square\text{E})$$

Fig. 1. Metalanguage L2

The operational semantics of L2 are summarized in App. B. As a consequence of theorems in [10] (subject reduction, Thm. 4, and eliminability, Thm. 5, see App. B), typability in system L2 implies that reducing, in L2, an expression of type $\square\tau$ to normal form results in a well typed native L1-program in the scope of a box-constructor. In sum, it is guaranteed for a well typed closed L2-term of type $\square\tau$ that *composition-time* reduction to normal form in L2 computes all L2-term occurrences away and leaves only a well typed boxed L1-program as a result. That L1-term can then be executed at the next stage (*run-time*).

3 Semantic Types

We introduce a level of semantic types, which are special structures of modal intersection types, to be used in the combinatory logics C1 and C2 (Sec. 4).

The sets $\mathfrak{S}_i$ of *semantic types* of level i ($i = 1, 2$) are ranged over by $\mathfrak{t}$ and $\mathfrak{s}$, respectively. Type variables of level 1 are ranged over by $\mathfrak{a} \in \mathbb{V}_{\mathfrak{S}_1}$, and type variables of level 2 are ranged over by $\mathfrak{b} \in \mathbb{V}_{\mathfrak{S}_2}$. We assume that $\mathbb{V}$, $\mathbb{V}_{\mathfrak{S}_1}$ and $\mathbb{V}_{\mathfrak{S}_2}$ are disjoint sets. We assume sets of semantic type constants $\mathbb{D}_1$ and $\mathbb{D}_2$, with $\mathbb{D}_1$ and $\mathbb{D}_2$ disjoint from each other and from the constants of L1.

The set $\mathfrak{S}_1$ contains a copy[1] of $\mathbb{T}_1$ built from distinct sets of variables $\mathbb{V}_{\mathfrak{S}_1}$ and constants $\mathbb{D}_1$ and closed under intersection. The set $\mathfrak{S}_2$ is built analogously, as a copy of $\mathbb{T}_2$ over distinct variables in $\mathbb{V}_{\mathfrak{S}_2}$ and constants in $\mathbb{D}_2$:

$$\mathfrak{S}_1 \ni \mathfrak{t} ::= \mathfrak{a} \mid d_1 \mid \mathfrak{t} \to \mathfrak{t}' \mid \mathfrak{t} \cap \mathfrak{t}' \qquad \mathfrak{S}_2 \ni \mathfrak{s} ::= \mathfrak{b} \mid d_2 \mid \mathfrak{s} \to \mathfrak{s}' \mid \mathfrak{s} \cap \mathfrak{s}' \mid \Box \mathfrak{t}$$

The set of *semantic L1-types* $\mathbb{S}_1$ is ranged over by ϕ, and the set of *semantic L2-types* $\mathbb{S}_2$ is ranged over by ψ:

$$\mathbb{S}_1 \ni \phi ::= \tau \mid \phi \cap \mathfrak{t} \mid \mathfrak{t} \cap \phi \mid \phi \to \phi' \mid \phi \cap \phi' \qquad \mathbb{S}_2 \ni \psi ::= \sigma \mid \psi \cap \mathfrak{s} \mid \mathfrak{s} \cap \psi \mid \Box \phi \mid \psi \to \psi' \mid \psi \cap \psi'$$

We follow the convention that $\to$ is right-associative and that $\cap$ binds stronger than $\to$. Type expressions are implicitly considered as equivalence classes modulo commutativity, associativity and idempotency of $\cap$. We let $\vartheta, \varrho, \upsilon$ range over $\mathbb{S}_1 \cup \mathbb{S}_2 \cup \mathfrak{S}_1 \cup \mathfrak{S}_2$. Notice that $\mathbb{T}_1$ and $\mathbb{T}_2$ are disjoint, $\mathbb{S}_1$ and $\mathbb{S}_2$ are disjoint, and $\mathbb{T}_i \subseteq \mathbb{S}_i$. An *atom* is a type variable or a type constant, and we let A range over atoms.

The semantic type structure allows for maximal freedom in combining semantic types with "underlying" (see Def. 3, Sec. 6) implementation types and allows us to treat the semantic types as a distinct kind from implementation types. The type structures $\mathbb{T}_0$ and $\mathfrak{S}_i$ are treated as different kinds in the following definition of type substitution, which ensures that the sets $\mathbb{T}_i$, $\mathbb{S}_i$, and $\mathfrak{S}_i$ ($i = 1, 2$) are closed under substitutions.

Definition 1. *A type substitution is a map* $S : \mathbb{V} \cup \mathbb{V}_{\mathfrak{S}_1} \cup \mathbb{V}_{\mathfrak{S}_2} \to \mathbb{T}_0 \cup \mathfrak{S}_1 \cup \mathfrak{S}_2$ *satisfying the following conditions:* $\forall \alpha \in \mathbb{V}. \, S(\alpha) \in \mathbb{T}_0$, $\forall \mathfrak{a} \in \mathbb{V}_{\mathfrak{S}_1}. \, S(\mathfrak{a}) \in \mathfrak{S}_1$, *and* $\forall \mathfrak{b} \in \mathbb{V}_{\mathfrak{S}_2}. \, S(\mathfrak{b}) \in \mathfrak{S}_2$.

The following definition is standard for intersection types [7]. We tacitly assume that the sets $\mathbb{D}_1$ and $\mathbb{D}_2$ can be equipped with partial orders $\leq_{\mathbb{D}_i}$ in which case axioms $d_i \leq_{\mathbb{D}_i} d_i' \Rightarrow d_i \leq d_i'$ are added to the axiomatization of subtyping.

Definition 2. *Subtyping* $\leq$ *is the least preorder (reflexive and transitive relation) on* $\mathbb{S}_1 \cup \mathbb{S}_2 \cup \mathfrak{S}_1 \cup \mathfrak{S}_2$, *satisfying the following conditions:*

$$\vartheta \cap \varrho \leq \vartheta, \quad \vartheta \cap \upsilon \leq \upsilon, \quad (\vartheta \to \varrho) \cap (\vartheta \to \upsilon) \leq \vartheta \to \varrho \cap \upsilon,$$
$$\vartheta \leq \vartheta' \wedge \varrho \leq \varrho' \Rightarrow \vartheta' \to \varrho \leq \vartheta \to \varrho', \quad \vartheta \leq \vartheta' \wedge \varrho \leq \varrho' \Rightarrow \vartheta \cap \varrho \leq \vartheta' \cap \varrho',$$
$$(\Box \vartheta) \cap (\Box \varrho) \leq \Box(\vartheta \cap \varrho), \quad \vartheta \leq \varrho \Rightarrow \Box \vartheta \leq \Box \varrho.$$

We say that ϑ *and* ϱ *are* equal, *written* $\vartheta = \varrho$, *if* $\vartheta \leq \varrho$ *and* $\varrho \leq \vartheta$. *We write* $\vartheta \equiv \varrho$, *if* ϑ *and* ϱ *are syntactically identical.*

---

[1] Function types of $\mathfrak{S}_1$ and $\mathbb{S}_1$ below are not restricted to be first order, since our system is developed for the general case. If L1 happens to be restricted to a first-order system, as in our example case, our semantic type framework is more general.

The following distributivity properties follow from the axioms of subtyping:

$$(\vartheta \to \varrho) \cap (\vartheta \to \upsilon) = \vartheta \to \varrho \cap \upsilon, \quad (\vartheta \to \varrho) \cap (\vartheta' \to \varrho') \leq (\vartheta \cap \vartheta') \to (\varrho \cap \varrho'),$$
$$(\Box\vartheta) \cap (\Box\varrho) = \Box(\vartheta \cap \varrho).$$

4   Combinatory Logic and Composition Synthesis

We introduce combinatory logics C1 and C2 in which components implemented in L1 and L2 can be exposed as combinator symbols. The combinatory rules of C1 are standard for combinatory logic with intersection types [11], and the rules of C2 are extended (in rule ($\Box$I)) according to the modal extension of L2. Combinatory C1-terms are defined by $e ::= X \mid (e_1 e_2)$. Environments $\mathscr{C}$ are finite sets of bindings of the form $(X : \phi)$ with $\phi \in \mathbb{S}_1$. The combinatory logic C1 is defined by the rules of Fig. 2. Combinatory C2-terms are defined by $E ::= F \mid (E_1 E_2) \mid$ box e. Environments $\mathscr{D}$ are finite sets of bindings of the form $(F : \psi)$ with $\psi \in \mathbb{S}_2$. The combinatory logic C2 is defined by the rules of Fig. 3. Note carefully, that the rules ($\leq$) for C1 (resp. C2) are restricted to types in $\mathbb{S}_1$ (resp. $\mathbb{S}_2$) as shown by use of the metavariable ϕ (resp. ψ). This restriction is necessary for Thm. 1 to go through.

$$\frac{}{\mathscr{C}, X : \phi \vdash_{\text{C1}} X : S(\phi)}(\text{var}) \qquad \frac{\mathscr{C} \vdash_{\text{C1}} e_1 : \phi \to \phi' \quad \mathscr{C} \vdash_{\text{C1}} e_2 : \phi}{\mathscr{C} \vdash_{\text{C1}} (e_1 e_2) : \phi'}(\to\text{E})$$

$$\frac{\mathscr{C} \vdash_{\text{C1}} e : \phi \quad \mathscr{C} \vdash_{\text{C1}} e : \phi'}{\mathscr{C} \vdash_{\text{C1}} e : \phi \cap \phi'}(\cap\text{I}) \qquad \frac{\mathscr{C} \vdash_{\text{C1}} e : \phi \quad \phi \leq \phi'}{\mathscr{C} \vdash_{\text{C1}} e : \phi'}(\leq)$$

Fig. 2. Combinatory logic C1

$$\frac{}{\mathscr{C}; (\mathscr{D}, F : \psi) \vdash_{\text{C2}} F : S(\psi)}(\text{var})$$

$$\frac{\mathscr{C}; \mathscr{D} \vdash_{\text{C2}} E_1 : \psi \to \psi' \quad \mathscr{C}; \mathscr{D} \vdash_{\text{C2}} E_2 : \psi}{\mathscr{C}; \mathscr{D} \vdash_{\text{C2}} (E_1 E_2) : \psi'}(\to\text{E}) \qquad \frac{\mathscr{C}; \mathscr{D} \vdash_{\text{C2}} E : \psi \quad \mathscr{C}; \mathscr{D} \vdash_{\text{C2}} E : \psi'}{\mathscr{C}; \mathscr{D} \vdash_{\text{C2}} E : \psi \cap \psi'}(\cap\text{I})$$

$$\frac{\mathscr{C}; \mathscr{D} \vdash_{\text{C2}} E : \psi \quad \psi \leq \psi'}{\mathscr{C}; \mathscr{D} \vdash_{\text{C2}} E : \psi'}(\leq) \qquad \frac{\mathscr{C} \vdash_{\text{C1}} e : \phi}{\mathscr{C}; \mathscr{D} \vdash_{\text{C2}} \text{box } e : \Box\phi}(\Box\text{I})$$

Fig. 3. Combinatory logic C2

In composition synthesis (see [4] for a general introduction), we are concerned with the *relativized inhabitation problem*: Given $\mathscr{C}$, $\mathscr{D}$ and ψ, does there exist a combinatory term E such that $\mathscr{C}; \mathscr{D} \vdash_{\text{C2}} E : \psi$? We use the notation $\mathscr{C}; \mathscr{D} \vdash_{\text{C2}} ? : \psi$

to specify the problem. The inhabitation relation in combinatory logic can be used as a foundation for component-oriented synthesis, since an inhabitation algorithm can be employed to compute program terms E (inhabitants) by combinatory composition. Here we think of $\mathscr{C}$ and $\mathscr{D}$ as component repositories and ψ as a synthesis goal specification.

It should be noted that the expressive power of the inhabitation relation is enormous: it is undecidable even in simple types. The reason is that the relation is not confined to a fixed base but is *relativized* to arbitrary environments $\mathscr{C}$, $\mathscr{D}$ ([4] contains a survey of the relevant results). We can indeed consider the inhabitation relation as an operational semantics for a Turing-complete abstract logic programming language [12] at the level of interface types, as suggested in [4]. Or, we can restrict the relation to ensure that search for inhabitants always terminates. We consider algorithmic aspects of the relation in Sec. 7.

We emphasize again that our design of semantic types must be understood in conjunction with the theory of implementation type correctness given by Thm. 1 (Sec. 6), which guarantees preservation of typability of compositions in the implementation languages under semantic type erasure (Def. 3). The semantic type structure in Sec. 3 is a restricted yet very general structure still allowing Thm. 1 to go through. The fundamental challenge here is to ensure that implementation language typability is guaranteed even though compositions are constructed in a much more expressive intersection type theory. Freely combining semantic types with implementation types under intersection and subtyping will not work — as a simple example, one would derive $\{X : \texttt{bool} \cap (d \to d'), Y : \texttt{int} \cap d\} \vdash (XY) : d'$ (where d, d' are semantic type constants in $\mathfrak{S}_1$ and $\texttt{bool}, \texttt{int}$ are L1-types) which does not type check when semantic types are erased. Our system prevents such problems by ensuring that semantic types have sufficient support (see Def. 4) in the implementation language (in the example above, using rule $\leq$ to derive $X : d \to d'$ is not allowed even though $\texttt{bool} \cap (d \to d') \leq d \to d'$, since $d \to d'$ is not a member of $\mathbb{S}_1$).

5   Example

We introduce a simple example adapted from [4] and extended with our modal types to illustrate a few basic features of the formal system. For ease of reading, we write $\mathfrak{S}_1$-types in *blue* font (as in *Cel*) and $\mathfrak{S}_2$-types in *red* font (as in *Conv*). Programs and combinators in L1 are written in green typewriter font. Whenever convenient we use the shorthand notation $\tilde{\tau}$ to denote an $\mathbb{S}_1$-type consisting of the L1-type τ intersected with an associated semantic type variable $\mathfrak{a}_\tau$ from $\mathfrak{S}_1$, so, for example, $\tilde{\alpha}$ denotes the type $\alpha \cap \mathfrak{a}_\alpha$. L1-types are written in black typewriter font, for example, $\texttt{R}$ which denotes the type of reals.

Let $\mathscr{C}$ contain the combinators (we freely extend the L1-type language by type constructors — below, $(\cdot, \cdot)$ is a pair-constructor whereas $D((\cdot, \cdot), \cdot, \cdot)$ is a constructor for a data-structure):

$$\begin{aligned}
&\text{O} \quad : \text{TrObj} \\
&\text{Tr} \quad : \text{TrObj} \to D((R, R) \cap Cart, R \cap Gpst, R \cap Cel) \\
&\text{tmp} : D((R, R), R, R \cap a) \to R \cap a \cap ms
\end{aligned}$$

The environment $\mathscr{C}$ could be part of a semantic repository of components to track (Tr) an object (O) by giving the Cartesian coordinates ($Cart$) of the tracked object (TrObj) at a given point in time ($Gpst$) and its temperature (Cel). There is also a function tmp which projects the temperature. Its result type has the semantic component ms which is intended to indicate that the datum (in this case, a real number) represents a measurement. Let $\mathscr{D}$ contain the combinators

$$\begin{aligned}
&\bullet \qquad : \Box(\tilde{\beta} \to \tilde{\gamma}) \to \Box(\tilde{\alpha} \to \tilde{\beta}) \to \Box(\tilde{\alpha} \to \tilde{\gamma}) \\
&\text{cl2fh} : (\Box(R \cap Cel) \to \Box(R \cap Fh)) \cap Conv \\
&\Diamond \qquad : \Box(\tilde{\alpha} \cap ms) \to (\Box\tilde{\alpha} \to \Box\tilde{\beta}) \cap Conv \to \Box(\tilde{\beta} \cap ms)
\end{aligned}$$

with the following bindings to implementations in L2:

$$\begin{aligned}
\bullet \quad &\triangleq \lambda G : \Box(\beta \to \gamma).\lambda F : \Box(\alpha \to \beta). \\
&\quad \text{letbox } f : \alpha \to \beta = F \text{ in} \\
&\qquad \text{letbox } g : \beta \to \gamma = G \text{ in box } (\text{fn } y : \alpha => (g \ (f \ y))) \\
\text{cl2fh} \quad &\triangleq \lambda z : \Box R. \\
&\quad \text{letbox } u : R = z \text{ in} \\
&\qquad \text{box let } x : R = u \text{ in } x * (9 \text{ div } 5) + 32 \\
\Diamond \quad &\triangleq \lambda z : \Box\alpha.\lambda F : \Box\alpha \to \Box\beta.(F \ z)
\end{aligned}$$

The semantic $\mathfrak{S}_2$-type $Conv$ of the combinator cl2fh expresses the idea that the corresponding function acts as a unit conversion. The type of the combinator $\Diamond$ uses this type and the $\mathfrak{S}_1$-type ms to express the idea that a conversion can be applied to a measurement to produce something which is still a measurement.

Suppose we ask for a function composable from the component repositories $\mathscr{C}$ and $\mathscr{D}$ which measures the temperature of an object in Celsius. We can formalize this query as the inhabitation problem $\mathscr{C}; \mathscr{D} \vdash_{\text{C2}} ? : \Box(\text{TrObj} \to (R \cap Cel \cap ms))$ which has the solution $(\text{box tmp}) \bullet (\text{box Tr}) : \Box(\text{TrObj} \to (R \cap Cel \cap ms))$ where we write $\bullet$ in infix notation. Performing the L2-reduction $(\text{box tmp}) \bullet (\text{box Tr}) \longmapsto^*$ box $(\text{fn } y : \text{TrObj} => (\text{tmp } (\text{Tr } y)))$ we see that L1-code implementing such a function is produced.

If we ask for $\mathscr{C}; \mathscr{D} \vdash_{\text{C2}} ? : \Box(R \cap Fh \cap ms)$, the solution is, again writing $\Diamond$ in infix notation, $(\text{box } (\text{tmp } (\text{Tr O}))) \ \Diamond \ \text{cl2fh}$ with the L2-reduction

$$(\text{box } (\text{tmp } (\text{Tr O}))) \Diamond \text{cl2fh} \longmapsto^* \text{box let } x : R = \text{tmp } (\text{Tr O}) \text{ in } x * (9 \text{ div } 5) + 32$$

If we add c2f : $(R \cap Cel \cap ms) \to (R \cap Fh \cap ms)$ to $\mathscr{C}$, we get the additional solution, box $(\text{c2f } (\text{tmp } (\text{Tr O})))$, for the same inhabitation goal. If we further add the modal apply combinator mapply : $\Box(\tilde{\alpha} \to \tilde{\beta}) \to \Box\tilde{\alpha} \to \Box\tilde{\beta}$ with definition

$$\begin{aligned}
\text{mapply} \triangleq \ &\lambda F : \Box(\alpha \to \beta).\lambda z : \Box\alpha. \\
&\text{letbox } f : \alpha \to \beta = F \text{ in} \\
&\quad \text{letbox } u : \alpha = z \text{ in box } (f \ u)
\end{aligned}$$

to $\mathscr{D}$ we also get `mapply` (box `c2f`) (`mapply` ((box `tmp`) • (box `Tr`))(box `0`)) reducing in L2 to the L1-program box (`c2f` ((`fn y : TrObj` => (`tmp` (`Tr y`))) `0`)). These examples illustrate that the inhabitation relation determines the possible placements of the box-constructor, in each case determining a specific "division of labor" between L1 and L2. Furthermore, higher-order abstraction in L2 adds considerable power to composition and generation of first-order L1-code.

All examples have been automated by an inhabitation algorithm in our combinatory logic synthesis framework (CL)S as discussed in Sec.(s) 7 and 8.

6   Implementation Type Correctness

Correctness of our framework is based on a conservative extension theorem (Thm. 1) showing that combinatory compositions performed over restricted (supported or grounded, Def. 4) environments can be transformed into well typed L1-expressions. The proof of Thm. 1 depends on a series of technical lemmas which can be found in [13]. Here, we only present the necessary definitions and the theorem. We explain how it constitutes a theory of implementation type correctness for SCS. The following notion relates semantic types to implementation types.

Definition 3 (Erasure). *For type expressions $\vartheta \in \mathbb{S}_i$ we define the erasure of ϑ, written ϑ°, $(i = 1, 2)$, as follows.*

$$
\begin{aligned}
\vartheta^\circ &\equiv \vartheta, \text{ when } \vartheta \in \mathbb{T}_1 \cup \mathbb{T}_2 \\
(\vartheta \cap \mathfrak{u})^\circ &\equiv \vartheta^\circ \text{ when } \mathfrak{u} \in \mathfrak{S}_1 \cup \mathfrak{S}_2 \\
(\mathfrak{u} \cap \vartheta)^\circ &\equiv \vartheta^\circ \text{ when } \mathfrak{u} \in \mathfrak{S}_1 \cup \mathfrak{S}_2 \\
(\vartheta \to \varrho)^\circ &\equiv \vartheta^\circ \to \varrho^\circ \\
(\vartheta \cap \varrho)^\circ &\equiv \vartheta^\circ \cap \varrho^\circ \\
(\Box \vartheta)^\circ &\equiv \Box \vartheta^\circ
\end{aligned}
$$

For combinatory environments $\mathscr{C}, \mathscr{D}$ we lift $()^\circ$ by pointwise application to the types in the environment, $\mathscr{C}^\circ = \{(X : \phi^\circ) \mid (X : \phi) \in \mathscr{C}\}$ and similarly for $\mathscr{D}^\circ$.

It can be shown that $\vartheta_1 = \vartheta_2$ implies $\vartheta_1{}^\circ = \vartheta_2{}^\circ$, hence the operation $()^\circ$ is a well defined function on equivalence classes with respect to $=$. The function $()^\circ$ erases semantic types in $\mathfrak{S}_1 \cup \mathfrak{S}_2$ from semantic L1- and L2-types in $\mathbb{S}_1 \cup \mathbb{S}_2$.

We introduce combinatory expressions over combinator symbols of C1 and C2, subscripted with types from $\mathbb{T}_1$ and $\mathbb{T}_2$, respectively, as follows.

$$
f ::= X_\tau \mid (f_1 f_2) \qquad\qquad g ::= F_\sigma \mid (g_1 g_2) \mid \mathsf{box}\ f
$$

For a C1-environment $\mathscr{C}$ in which all bindings are of the form $(X : \bigcap_{j \in J} \tau_j)$ (intersections of types in $\mathbb{T}_1$) and a C2-environment $\mathscr{D}$ in which all bindings are of the form $(F : \bigcap_{j \in J} \sigma_j)$ (intersections of types in $\mathbb{T}_2$) we define the $\mathbb{T}_1$-environment $\mathscr{C}^+$ and the $\mathbb{T}_2$-environment $\mathscr{D}^+$ by

$$
\begin{aligned}
\mathscr{C}^+ &= \{(X_{\tau_j} : \tau_j) \mid j \in J, (X : \textstyle\bigcap_{j \in J} \tau_j) \in \mathscr{C}\} \\
\mathscr{D}^+ &= \{(F_{\sigma_j} : \sigma_j) \mid j \in J, (F : \textstyle\bigcap_{j \in J} \sigma_j) \in \mathscr{D}\}
\end{aligned}
$$

We can consider such environments $\mathscr{C}^+$ and $\mathscr{D}^+$ as L1-environments, resp. L2-environments, by considering (possibly through a mapping, which we shall leave implicit) the symbols X_τ (resp. F_σ) as L1-variables (resp. L2-variables).

We define an erasure function $()^-$ mapping these expressions back to combinator expressions of C1, respectively C2:

$$X_\tau^- \equiv X \qquad\qquad F_\sigma^- \equiv F$$
$$(f_1 f_2)^- \equiv (f_1^- f_2^-) \qquad (g_1 g_2)^- \equiv (g_1^- g_2^-)$$
$$(\mathsf{box}\ f)^- \equiv \mathsf{box}\ f^-$$

The following definition is central for Thm. 1. The concepts of supported and grounded types capture relations between semantic types and their "underlying" (under erasure) implementation language types.

Definition 4 (Supported, grounded). *For $\vartheta \in \mathbb{S}_i$ ($i = 1, 2$) we say that ϑ is supported if $\vartheta = \bigcap_{j \in J} \vartheta_j$ with $\vartheta_j \in \mathbb{T}_i$ for $j \in J$. We say that ϑ is grounded if $\vartheta^\circ \in \mathbb{T}_i$. An environment $\mathscr{C}$ or $\mathscr{D}$ is said to be supported (grounded) if all types appearing in the environment are supported (grounded).*

We say that a derivation in C1 or C2 is *monomorphic*, if all applications of rule (var) use the identity substitution (combinatory logics restricted to such derivations are finite combinatory logics, in the sense of [1]). For a derivation tree D in C1 or C2, let $\mathcal{S}_D(X)$ (resp. $\mathcal{S}_D(F)$) be the set of substitutions S such that S is applied in an application in D of rule (var) of the form $\mathscr{C}', X : \phi \vdash_{\mathsf{c1}} X : S(\phi)$ (resp. $\mathscr{C}; (\mathscr{D}', F : \psi) \vdash_{\mathsf{c2}} F : S(\psi)$). We let $\mathscr{C}^D$, resp. $\mathscr{D}^D$, denote the *exponentiated* environments defined as follows:

$$\mathscr{C}^D = \{(X : \bigcap_{S \in \mathcal{S}_D(X)} S(\phi) \mid (X : \phi) \in \mathscr{C}\}$$
$$\mathscr{D}^D = \{(F : \bigcap_{S \in \mathcal{S}_D(F)} S(\psi) \mid (F : \psi) \in \mathscr{D}\}$$

We write $\mathscr{C} \vdash_{\mathsf{c1}}^D e : \phi$ whenever $\mathscr{C} \vdash_{\mathsf{c1}} e : \phi$ is derivable by derivation D, and similarly for $\mathscr{C}; \mathscr{D} \vdash_{\mathsf{c2}}^D E : \psi$. It can be shown that exponentiation preserves supportedness of environments. We write $()^{\circ D} = (()^\circ)^D$ and $()^{\circ D+} = ((()^\circ)^D)^+$. We can now state the conservative extension theorem.

Theorem 1 (Conservative extension).

1. *Suppose that $\mathscr{C}^\circ$ and $\mathscr{D}^\circ$ are supported and that ϕ and ψ are grounded. Then*
   (a) If $\mathscr{C} \vdash_{\mathsf{c1}}^D e : \phi$ then $\emptyset; \mathscr{C}^{\circ D+} \vdash_{\mathsf{L1}} f : \phi^\circ$ for some f with $f^- \equiv e$.
   (b) If $\mathscr{C}; \mathscr{D} \vdash_{\mathsf{c2}}^D E : \psi$ then $\emptyset; \mathscr{C}^{\circ D+}, \mathscr{D}^{\circ D+} \vdash_{\mathsf{L2}} g : \psi^\circ$ for some g with $g^- \equiv E$.
2. *Suppose that $\mathscr{C}, \mathscr{D}, \phi$, and ψ are grounded. Then*
   (a) If $\mathscr{C} \vdash_{\mathsf{c1}}^D e : \phi$ with D monomorphic then $\emptyset; \mathscr{C}^\circ \vdash_{\mathsf{L1}} e : \phi^\circ$.
   (b) If $\mathscr{C}; \mathscr{D} \vdash_{\mathsf{c2}}^D E : \psi$ with D monomorphic then $\emptyset; \mathscr{C}^\circ, \mathscr{D}^\circ \vdash_{\mathsf{L2}} E : \psi^\circ$.

We use the theorem to show that inhabitants obtained by composition in C1 and C2 from environments whose erasure represent well typed programs in L1 and L2 can be translated back to well typed expressions of L1 and L2 by type instantiations.

Assume that we have sets of combinator symbols $\mathcal{X}$ and $\mathcal{F}$, and assume that $X \in \mathcal{X}$ and $F \in \mathcal{F}$ are associated with implementations T_X and M_F in L1 and L2, respectively, such that

$$\emptyset; \emptyset \vdash_{\mathsf{L1}} T_X : \tau_X \text{ for } X \in \mathcal{X} \qquad \emptyset; \emptyset \vdash_{\mathsf{L2}} M_F : \sigma_F \text{ for } F \in \mathcal{F}$$

and exposed in combinatory environments as

$$\mathscr{C} = \{(X : \phi_X) \mid X \in \mathcal{X}\} \qquad \mathscr{D} = \{(F : \psi_F) \mid F \in \mathcal{F}\}$$

with $(\phi_X)^\circ = \tau_X$ and $(\psi_F)^\circ = \sigma_F$. Then $\mathscr{C}$ and $\mathscr{D}$ are grounded, hence $\mathscr{C}^\circ$ and $\mathscr{D}^\circ$ are supported and $\mathscr{C}^{\circ D+}$ and $\mathscr{D}^{\circ D+}$ are grounded.

Suppose now that $\mathscr{C} \vdash_{\mathsf{C1}}^D e : \phi$ with ϕ grounded. It follows from Thm. 1 that we have $\emptyset; \mathscr{C}^{\circ D+} \vdash_{\mathsf{L1}} f : \phi^\circ$ for some f with $f^- \equiv e$. Since all combinators in $\mathscr{C}^{\circ D+}$ have the form $(X_{S(\tau_X)} : S(\tau_X))$ with $(X : \phi_X) \in \mathscr{C}$ and $(\phi_X)^\circ \equiv \tau_X$, it follows by Lem. 1, App. A that we have $\emptyset; \emptyset \vdash_{\mathsf{L1}} f' : \phi^\circ$ where

$$f' \equiv f[X_{S(\tau_X)} := S(T_X)]$$

Similarly, if $\mathscr{C}; \mathscr{D} \vdash_{\mathsf{C2}} E : \psi$ with ψ grounded, we have $\emptyset; \mathscr{C}^{\circ D+}, \mathscr{D}^{\circ D+} \vdash_{\mathsf{L2}} g : \phi^\circ$ with bindings in $\mathscr{D}^{\circ D+}$ all of the form $(F_{S(\sigma_F)} : S(\sigma_F))$ with $(F : \psi_F) \in \mathscr{D}$ and $(\psi_F)^\circ \equiv \sigma_F$. Hence, by Lem. 2, App. B we have $\emptyset; \emptyset \vdash_{\mathsf{L2}} g' : \psi^\circ$ where

$$g' \equiv g[X_{S(\tau_X)} := S(T_X)][F_{S(\sigma_F)} := S(M_F)]$$

7   Inhabitation

We provide a theoretical semi-decision procedure for solving the relativized inhabitation problems for C1 and C2, which is a decision procedure for bounded variants of the inhabitation problem. The procedure underlies the optimized implementation in the (CL)S system discussed in Sec. 8. To explain the procedure we need a few definitions.

Definition 5. *A path π is a type of the form $\pi ::= A \mid \Box\pi \mid \vartheta \to \pi$. A type ϑ is called* organized, *if it is an intersection of paths, i.e., $\vartheta \equiv \bigcap_{i \in I} \pi_i$. The length of a path $\vartheta_1 \to \cdots \to \vartheta_n \to \varrho$ (where ϱ is not a function type) is defined to be n. We let $\|\vartheta\|$ denote the maximal length of a path in ϑ (assuming ϑ is organized). For a type $\vartheta \equiv \vartheta_1 \to \cdots \to \vartheta_n \to \varrho$ we let $arg_i(\vartheta) \equiv \vartheta_i$ for $1 \le i \le n$, and we let $tgt_n(\vartheta) \equiv \varrho$. Finally, $\mathbb{P}_m(\vartheta)$ denotes the set of paths of length at least m in ϑ (assuming ϑ is organized).*

It is easy to see that any type ϑ is equal to a polynomially sized organized type [2], and, whenever convenient, we shall tacitly assume that types are organized. Figure 4 is a semi-decision procedure for the inhabitation problem $\mathscr{C}; \mathscr{D} \vdash_{\mathsf{C2}}? : \psi$. It adapts the results of [2] to modal intersection types, and its correctness follows from the path lemmas presented in [13]. We use the notation of [2] where CHOOSE and OR denote nondeterministic choice and FORALL denotes universal branching of an alternating Turing-machine (ATM) [14]. By restriction to

```
        Input :  𝒞, 𝒟, ϑ
1  loop :
2  IF (ϑ ∈ 𝕊₁)THEN
3      CHOOSE (X : φ) ∈ 𝒞
4      CHOOSE 𝒮 ⊆_fin 𝕍 → 𝕋₀ ∪ 𝔖₁ ∪ 𝔖₂
5      φ' := ⋂{S(φ) | S ∈ 𝒮}
6      CHOOSE m ∈ {0, ..., ‖φ'‖};
7      CHOOSE P ⊆ ℙ_m(φ');
8      IF (⋂_{π∈P} tgt_m(π) ≤ ϑ) THEN
9          IF (m = 0) THEN ACCEPT;
10         ELSE
11             FORALL(i = 1 ... m)
12                 ϑ := ⋂_{π∈P} arg_i(π);
13             GOTO loop;
14 ELSE
15     IF (ϑ = □φ) THEN
16         GOTO case1 OR GOTO case2
17     ELSE GOTO case2
18     case1 :
19         ϑ := φ; GOTO loop
20     case2 :
21         CHOOSE (F : ψ) ∈ 𝒟;
22         CHOOSE 𝒮 ⊆_fin 𝕍 → 𝕋₀ ∪ 𝔖₁ ∪ 𝔖₂
23         ψ' := ⋂{S(ψ) | S ∈ 𝒮}
24         CHOOSE m ∈ {0, ..., ‖ψ'‖};
25         CHOOSE P ⊆ ℙ_m(ψ');
26         IF (⋂_{π∈P} tgt_m(π) ≤ ϑ) THEN
27             IF (m = 0) THEN ACCEPT;
28         ELSE
29             FORALL(i = 1 ... m)
30                 ϑ := ⋂_{π∈P} arg_i(π);
31             GOTO loop;
```

Fig. 4. ATM semi-decision procedure for $\mathscr{C}; \mathscr{D} \vdash_{c2}? : \vartheta$

monomorphic derivations [1] or by bounding the size of substitutions to depth k in derivations [2] the semi-decision procedure shown in Fig. 4 becomes a decision procedure (cf. Thm. 2).

The restriction to grounded types in Thm. 1 does not limit the theoretical expressive power of the inhabitation relation:

Theorem 2 (Complexity). *Inhabitation in* C1 *and* C2 *is* $(k + 2)$-EXPTIME-*complete with bound* k *(as in [2]) and* EXPTIME-*complete in the monomorphic case (as in [1]).*

The proof of the theorem can be found in [13] which also contains comments explaining why the restriction has no theoretical impact on expressiveness (which may seem surprising).

8   Experiments with (CL)S

We implemented the presented framework in the context of the (CL)S tool[2] [3, 4], using F# and C#. The inhabitation algorithm is configured for the bound $k = 0$ [2], limiting type instantiations to atomic types or intersections of such. We implemented an optimized version of the ATM in Fig. 4 and an L2-interpreter. We used them to solve suitable inhabitation problems and to generate L1-programs from resulting inhabitants. We provide a first experimental evaluation of our implementation by discussing three examples. The experiments were conducted on a computer with 8 GB main memory, Intel Core i5 (2.66 GHz), and Windows 8, using the .NET-Framework 4.0. For reasons of space we cannot provide all details, here.[3] In particular, it is not possible to present the L2-implementations of all $\mathcal{D}$-combinators or the generated L1-code, confining discussion to a few interesting combinators. Note that we extend the type language of L1 with type constructors of arbitrary arity that do not distribute over $\cap$.

We first extend the L1-repository $\mathscr{C}$ introduced in Sec. 5 to the tracking-scenario discussed in [4, Fig. 8], allowing to project a tracked object to its coordinates, for example. Furthermore, we add the following L2-combinators with associated implementations to $\mathscr{D}$:[4]

$$\texttt{avgFun} : \Box(\texttt{TrObj} \to R \cap \mathfrak{a} \cap ms) \to \Box[\texttt{TrObj}] \to \Box(R \cap \mathfrak{a} \cap Avg \cap ms)$$
$$\texttt{dist} : \Box((R, R) \cap Cart) \to \Box((R, R) \cap Cart) \to \Box(R \cap dist)$$

Here, $\texttt{avgFun}$ uses code of a function that extracts a measured real value (with semantic property $\mathfrak{a}$) from a tracked object and code of an array of such objects to produce code of a real that is an average. Similarly, $\texttt{dist}$ calculates distances between two coordinates. Using (CL)S, we solved various inhabitation questions for this scenario. For example, $\texttt{dist}(\texttt{box } \texttt{cdn}(\texttt{pos}(\texttt{TrV}(0))), \texttt{box } \texttt{cdn}(\texttt{pos}(\texttt{TrV}(0))))$ solves $\mathscr{C}; \mathscr{D} \vdash_{C2}? : \Box(R \cap dist)$ and has L1-code of type real describing a distance between objects. All synthesis-requests of this form were answered in ≤ 250ms.

Second, we consider $\mathscr{C}_2$ and $\mathscr{D}_2$ for synthesizing sorting routines for arrays of objects with a given order relation. Assume $\mathscr{C}_2$ only contains an L1-combinator $\texttt{lessThan} : ((R, R) \to \texttt{bool}) \cap incTO$ deciding the standard total order $\leq_{\mathbb{R}}$ on $\mathbb{R}$, where $incTO$ is a semantic type stating that $\leq_{\mathbb{R}}$ is an increasing total order. The repository $\mathscr{D}_2$ contains the combinators with associated implementations:

$$\texttt{S} \quad : \big(\Box((\tilde{\alpha}, \tilde{\alpha}) \to \texttt{bool}) \to \Box([\tilde{\alpha}] \to [\tilde{\alpha}])\big) \cap \big(\Box\mathfrak{a} \to \Box(\top \to \mathfrak{a} \cap Sorted)\big)$$
$$\texttt{swap} : \big(\Box((\tilde{\alpha}, \tilde{\beta}) \to \gamma) \to \Box((\tilde{\beta}, \tilde{\alpha}) \to \gamma)\big) \cap \big(\Box\mathfrak{a} \to \Box Rev(\mathfrak{a})\big)$$
$$\varPhi \quad : \big(\Box((\tilde{\alpha}, \tilde{\alpha}) \to \texttt{bool}) \to \Box((\tilde{\alpha}, \tilde{\alpha}) \to \texttt{bool})\big) \cap$$
$$\big(\Box Rev(incTO) \to \Box decTO\big) \cap \big(\Box Rev(decTO) \to \Box incTO\big)$$

The combinator S contains an L1-template for bubble sort. Its first type component states that, given L1-code of a binary relation, S produces L1-code of

---

[2] http://www-seal.cs.tu-dortmund.de/seal/cls_en.shtml
[3] We refer to [13] for a comprehensive discussion of the examples and generated code.
[4] $[\vartheta]$ is a unary type constructor representing an array of objects of type ϑ.

a function mapping an array into an array. The semantic (second) component expresses that S returns code of a function that sorts an array without any distinguishing properties (we introduce $\top$ as a top element for semantic types for this purpose) according to the semantic property of the relation. Thus, if the relation happens to be a decreasing total order (i.e., $\mathfrak{a}$ gets instantiated with $decTO$), then S returns code of a function that sorts a typed array in decreasing order. The combinator swap is the modal version of the λ-calculus combinator that swaps the arguments of a function with a semantic property expressing that it reverses the order of arguments (Rev). The type of the combinator Φ (a purely logical combinator whose implementation is the identity function) expresses the idea that the reversal of an increasing total order is decreasing, and vice versa. The inhabitation question $\mathscr{C}_2; \mathscr{D}_2 \vdash_{\mathsf{C2}}? : \square([\mathsf{R}] \to [\mathsf{R}] \cap decTO \cap Sorted)$ produces the following inhabitant: $\mathsf{S}(\Phi(\mathsf{swap}(\mathsf{box\ lessThan})))$. Its $\longmapsto^*$-reduction results in a corresponding L1-sorting routine. The subterm $\Phi(\mathsf{swap}(\mathsf{box\ lessThan}))$ creates an L1-function of the form $\mathsf{fn}\ (x, y)\ :\ (\mathsf{R}, \mathsf{R})\ =>\ \mathsf{lessThan}(y, x)$. Semantically, this function reverses an increasing order into a decreasing order. It is passed to the implementation of S as an argument. Asking the inhabitation question above in (CL)S and carrying out the $\longmapsto^*$-reduction produced a bubble sort-based implementation of a corresponding sorting routine (24 lines of L1-code) within 150ms. Changing the inhabitation question by replacing $decTO$ by $incTO$, the algorithm produces a sorting routine in increasing order. In [13] we extended the repositories in various ways, e.g., we synthesized a sorting routine for topologically sorting nodes of a directed acyclic graph.

Our last example combines the previous two scenarios and highlights the power of our framework for exploiting compositional design and higher order abstraction in synthesizing a non-trivial L1-program. Our goal is to synthesize code of a function which, when given an array of tracked objects, first calculates the average temperature of the tracked objects. This requires the synthesis of the function $(\mathsf{box\ tmp}) \bullet (\mathsf{box\ Tr})$ of Sec. 5. This function is then passed to a higher order L2-combinator that uses it to produce code which, when given an array of tracked objects, calculates their average temperature. The average temperature is then used to produce a function that filters out all objects from the array whose temperature is below average. The remaining array is sorted in decreasing order (with regard to temperature).[5] We assume that $\mathscr{D}_3$ contains the combinator filterAndSort which will be the top-level combinator for the inhabitant realizing the desired function.[6] Amongst others filterAndSort requires an argument whose type is given by the following combinator:

$$\mathsf{largerThanAvg} : \square([\tilde{\alpha}] \to \tilde{\beta} \cap Cel \cap Avg) \to \square(((\tilde{\beta}, \tilde{\beta}) \to \mathsf{bool}) \cap decTO) \to$$
$$\square[\tilde{\alpha}] \to \square(\tilde{\alpha} \to \tilde{\beta} \cap Cel) \to \square(\tilde{\alpha} \to \mathsf{bool})$$

This combinator requires code which calculates an average temperature of an array of objects of type α, code of a decreasing total order, code of an array

---

[5] For example, if the tracked objects are reefer containers it is necessary to take action on those containers first that are the furthest above average.

[6] A complete discussion of this example can be found in [13].

of objects of type α, and code of a function that returns the temperature of an object of type α. It calculates the average temperature of the objects in the array by using the function provided as a first argument. Then it uses the total order and the temperature-function to compare the temperature of an object to the average temperature, returning true if it is larger than the average. The question $\mathscr{C}_3; \mathscr{D}_3 \vdash_{C_2}? : \Box([\text{TrObj}] \to [\text{TrObj}] \cap decTO \cap Sorted)$ resulted in:

$$\texttt{filterAndSort}((\texttt{box tmp}) \bullet (\texttt{box TrV}),$$
$$\Phi(\texttt{swap}(\texttt{box lessThan})), \texttt{avgFun}, \texttt{largerThanAvg}, \texttt{F})$$

As can be seen, `largerThanAvg` is an argument for `filterAndSort`. There is an interesting interaction between these two combinators. The L2-implementation of `filterAndSort` uses its *other* arguments to compute code with types of the arguments required by `largerThanAvg`. The L2-implementation of `filterAndSort` binds this code to names then passed to `largerThanAvg`. Thus, `largerThanAvg` indirectly uses functionality created by higher-order applications occurring in `filterAndSort` even though `largerThanAvg` exists *outside* `filterAndSort`. This is possible because `filterAndSort` takes `largerThanAvg` as argument and can thus provide it with bindings. The time required for synthesis and $\longmapsto^*$-reduction was approximately 9s and resulted in 61 lines of L1-code.

We conclude the discussion of $(\mathsf{CL})\mathsf{S}$ by mentioning an important principle for optimization of the inhabitation algorithm. Line 5 of the ATM (Fig. 4) indicates that the complexity arises from the construction of *all* possible type substitutions. Thus, one possible heuristic for optimization is to reduce the number of substitutions that actually have to be constructed. Using the fact that inhabitants must be well typed in L1 (cf. Thm. 1) the number of relevant type substitutions can be drastically decreased. This principle was used to optimize the inhabitation algorithm of $(\mathsf{CL})\mathsf{S}$ and showed major impact on runtime. The above initial experiments with SCS are encouraging, but further experiments, optimization heuristics, and engineering are needed.

9 Related Work

The idea of a staged approach to component-oriented synthesis does not appear to have been considered before. Our development of SCS would not, however, have been possible without the benefit of the modal analysis by Davies and Pfenning [10] of staged computation and their calculus $\lambda_e^{\Box\to}$. Not only can we transfer results from $\lambda_e^{\Box\to}$ to ensure semantic correctness (eliminability), but, interestingly, it turns out that modal types constitute a perfect instrument for exposing both the language- and phase distinction of staged computation to synthesis in combinatory logic.

Composition synthesis based on combinatory logic [6] with intersection types [7] was introduced and developed in [1–5]. The $(\mathsf{CL})\mathsf{S}$-tool has been under development since 2011 and has been applied in several application scenarios, including generation of GUI and of control programs for LegoNXT robots [3].

Several optimizations have been implemented in the tool, including optimizations based on DFS-look-ahead strategies with subtype matching [5].

Composition synthesis is in deep accord with recent movements, in technically quite different branches of synthesis, towards component-orientation, where synthesis is considered relative to a given library of components (rather than construction from scratch) [15]. Our approach can be broadly compared in spirit (rather than in technology) to synthesis of loop free programs [16]. The combinatory approach is fundamentally different, at a technical level, from such approaches that are based on either temporal logic, automata theory, or traditional program logics.

Our approach is related to adaptation synthesis via proof counting [8, 9], where semantic types are combined with proof search in a specialized proof system. In particular, we follow [8, 9] in using semantic specifications at the interface level. The idea of adaptation synthesis [8] is related to our notion of composition synthesis, however our logic is different, our design of semantic types with intersection types is novel, and the algorithmic methods are different (in [8] the specification language used is a typed predicate logic). Semantic intersection types can be compared to refinement types [17], but semantic types do not need to stand in a refinement relation to implementation types (as can be seen from our examples, this is important). Still, refinement types are a great source of inspiration for how semantic types can be used in specifications in many interesting situations.

10 Conclusion

We have introduced a framework for SCS based on modal intersection type systems and inhabitation in combinatory logic, and we have provided a theory of its correctness. The framework has been implemented in a prototype extension of the (CL)S system and has been used in experiments with SCS. Further work includes optimizations of the algorithm, in particular by exploiting the conservative extension property, more experimentation, and applications.

Acknowledgement. We thank our reviewers for very helpful reviews.

A Native Language L1

The native template language L1 is simultaneously defined and typed by the system shown in Fig. 5 below. It is a simply typed first order imperative core language with local references, extended with template variables u. The type structure consists of a set $\mathbb{T}_0$ of *value types* ranged over by t_0, reference types t_1 and the set of *native template types* $\mathbb{T}_1$, ranged over by τ. Value types are type variables ranged over by $\alpha, \beta, \gamma, \ldots$ drawn from the set $\mathbb{V}$, or type constants b including $*$ (unit type), **bool**, **int** and **real**.

$$\mathbb{T}_0 \ni t_0 ::= \alpha \mid b \qquad \mathbb{T}_0 \ni t_1 ::= \mathbf{ref}\ t_0 \qquad \mathbb{T}_1 \ni \tau ::= t_0 \mid t_0 \to t_0$$

Native *program variables*, disjoint from template variables u, are ranged over by x, and t ranges over all types (of the kind t_0, t_1, or τ). Judgements have the form $\Delta; \Sigma \vdash_{\text{L1}} T : t$, where the environment Δ contains bindings $(u : \tau)$ of template variables, and the environment Σ contains bindings $(x : t)$ of program variables. *Native expressions* are template expressions T such that $\emptyset; \Sigma \vdash_{\text{L1}} T : t$ for some Σ and t. That is, native expressions do not contain any free template variables. *Native programs* are template expressions T such that $\emptyset; \emptyset \vdash_{\text{L1}} T : \tau$ for some τ. That is, native programs are closed expressions with no free variables and with types in $\mathbb{T}_1$. We assume in rule (cnst) further program constants c_t including the constant ref for creating references.[7]

$$\frac{}{\Delta; (\Sigma, \mathrm{x} : t) \vdash_{\text{L1}} \mathrm{x} : t}(\text{var}) \qquad \frac{}{\Delta; \Sigma \vdash_{\text{L1}} \mathrm{c}_t : t}(\text{cnst})$$

$$\frac{}{(\Delta, u : \tau); \Sigma \vdash_{\text{L1}} u : \tau}(\text{mvar}) \qquad \frac{}{\Delta; \Sigma \vdash_{\text{L1}} \mathrm{skip} : *}(\text{skip})$$

$$\frac{\Delta; \Sigma \vdash_{\text{L1}} \mathrm{x} : \mathrm{ref}\ t_0}{\Delta; \Sigma \vdash_{\text{L1}}\, !\mathrm{x} : t_0}(\text{rd}) \qquad \frac{\begin{array}{c}\Delta; \Sigma \vdash_{\text{L1}} T : t_0 \\ \Delta; \Sigma \vdash_{\text{L1}} \mathrm{x} : \mathrm{ref}\ t_0\end{array}}{\Delta; \Sigma \vdash_{\text{L1}} \mathrm{x} := T : *}(\text{wr})$$

$$\frac{\begin{array}{c}\Delta; \Sigma \vdash_{\text{L1}} T : \mathrm{bool} \\ \Delta; \Sigma \vdash_{\text{L1}} T_1 : t_0 \quad \Delta; \Sigma \vdash_{\text{L1}} T_2 : t_0\end{array}}{\Delta; \Sigma \vdash_{\text{L1}} \mathrm{if}\ T\ \mathrm{then}\ T_1\ \mathrm{else}\ T_2 : t_0}(\text{if}) \qquad \frac{\begin{array}{c}\Delta; \Sigma \vdash_{\text{L1}} T : \mathrm{bool} \\ \Delta; \Sigma \vdash_{\text{L1}} T_1 : *\end{array}}{\Delta; \Sigma \vdash_{\text{L1}} \mathrm{while}\ T\ \mathrm{do}\ T_1 : *}(\text{wh})$$

$$\frac{\begin{array}{c}\Delta; \Sigma \vdash_{\text{L1}} T_1 : * \\ \Delta; \Sigma \vdash_{\text{L1}} T_2 : t_0\end{array}}{\Delta; \Sigma \vdash_{\text{L1}} T_1; T_2 : t_0}(\text{seq}) \qquad \frac{\Delta; \Sigma \vdash_{\text{L1}} T_1 : t \quad \Delta; (\Sigma, \mathrm{x} : t) \vdash_{\text{L1}} T_2 : t_0}{\Delta; \Sigma \vdash_{\text{L1}} \mathrm{let}\ \mathrm{x} : t = T_1\ \mathrm{in}\ T_2 : t_0}(\text{let})$$

$$\frac{\Delta; (\Sigma, \mathrm{x} : t_0) \vdash_{\text{L1}} T : t_0'}{\Delta; \Sigma \vdash_{\text{L1}} \mathrm{fn}\ \mathrm{x} : t_0 => T\ : t_0 \to t_0'}(\text{fn}) \qquad \frac{\Delta; \Sigma \vdash_{\text{L1}} T_1 : t_0 \to t_0' \quad \Delta; \Sigma \vdash_{\text{L1}} T_2 : t_0}{\Delta; \Sigma \vdash_{\text{L1}} (T_1\ T_2) : t_0'}(\to\text{E})$$

Fig. 5. Native template language L1

The following lemma can be proven as in [10] by induction on a derivation of the typing judgement. Notice the restriction to an empty environment Σ in the first assumption of the second property (see [10]).

Lemma 1 (Substitution).

1. *If* $\Delta; \Sigma \vdash_{\text{L1}} T : t$ *and* $\Delta; (\Sigma, \mathrm{x} : t) \vdash_{\text{L1}} T' : t'$ *then* $\Delta; \Sigma \vdash_{\text{L1}} T'[\mathrm{x} := T] : t'$.
2. *If* $\Delta; \emptyset \vdash_{\text{L1}} T : \tau$ *and* $(\Delta, u : \tau); \Sigma \vdash_{\text{L1}} T' : t$ *then* $\Delta; \Sigma \vdash_{\text{L1}} T'[u := T] : t$.
3. *Let* $S : \mathbb{V} \to \mathbb{T}_0$. *If* $\Delta; \Sigma \vdash_{\text{L1}} T : \tau$ *then* $S(\Delta); S(\Sigma) \vdash_{\text{L1}} S(T) : S(\tau)$.

---

[7] Reference types ref t_0 cannot escape local scopes by the type rules of L1, which simplifies our theory of intersection types (Sec. 3) which are unsound in the presence of unrestricted references [18]. The restriction can be lifted in several ways [18–20], but for brevity we shall not do so here.

B   Operational Semantics of L2

The language and type system of L2 is identical to the calculus $\lambda_e^{\square\to}$ introduced by Davies and Pfenning in [10], only our level L1 is decoupled from L2 in that it is distinguished as a different language with a type system and semantics of its own, and we use only a fully boxed fragment of the type language in which L2-types σ are generated from boxed types of L1 (of the form $\square\tau$).[8]

The operational semantics of L2 is exactly the reduction relation $\longmapsto$ (and its reflexive transitive closure $\longmapsto^*$) defined for $\lambda_e^{\square\to}$ in [10]. Computation is generated by β-reduction and the letbox-reduction rule (called $\square\beta$ in [10]):

$$\text{letbox } u = \text{box } T \text{ in } M \longmapsto M[u := T]$$

together with congruences with respect to all contexts except for the context box T. The reduction of letbox-expressions substitute template expressions box T into template variables u in L2-expressions M. This rule allows L2-programs to perform code substitution into L1-code. However, a boxed expression can itself be the result of L2-computations, as captured in the congruence rule

$$\frac{M_1 \longmapsto M_1'}{\text{letbox } u = M_1 \text{ in } M_2 \longmapsto \text{letbox } u = M_1' \text{ in } M_2}$$

as can the L2-expression into which substitution is performed:

$$\frac{M_2 \longmapsto M_2'}{\text{letbox } u = M_1 \text{ in } M_2 \longmapsto \text{letbox } u = M_1 \text{ in } M_2'}$$

Because the relation $\longmapsto$ is *not* a congruence with respect to box-expressions (reduction does not "go under" box) it is possible to semantically decouple L1-expressions under the box-operator from the language level L2 (the contents of such boxed expressions are treated as black boxes). We refer the reader to [10] for full details of the semantics.

The type system imposes a strict phase distinction, in that metalanguage terms and only such can be reduced under $\longmapsto$ in L2, and, by subject reduction, expressions cannot "go wrong" under reduction (for example, by applying a boxed term, or by unboxing an unboxed term). Subterm occurrences in the scope of a box-constructor are, in the parlance of [10], *persistent*, in that they cannot be executed under metalanguage (L2) reduction. Term occurrences other than persistent term occurrences are called *eliminable* [10]. It is shown in [10] (subject reduction, Thm. 4, and eliminability, Thm. 5) that one has:

1. If $\Delta; \Gamma \vdash_{L2} M : \sigma$ and $M \longmapsto^* M'$ then $\Delta; \Gamma \vdash_{L2} M' : \sigma$
2. If $\emptyset; \emptyset \vdash_{L2} M : \square\tau$ and $M \longmapsto^* M'$ and M' is irreducible, then M' contains no eliminable term occurrences.

Lemma 2 (Substitution [10]).

1. *If $\Delta; \emptyset \vdash_{L2} M : \sigma$ and $\Delta; (\Gamma, x : \sigma) \vdash_{L1} M' : \sigma'$ then $\Delta; \Gamma \vdash_{L2} M'[x := M] : \sigma'$*
2. *Let $S : \mathbb{V} \to \mathbb{T}_0$. If $\Delta; \Gamma \vdash_{L2} M : \sigma$ then $S(\Delta); S(\Gamma) \vdash_{L2} S(M) : S(\sigma)$.*

---

[8] This restriction is not essential, but it simplifies our presentation.

References

1. Rehof, J., Urzyczyn, P.: Finite Combinatory Logic with Intersection Types. In: Ong, L. (ed.) TLCA 2011. LNCS, vol. 6690, pp. 169–183. Springer, Heidelberg (2011)
2. Düdder, B., Martens, M., Rehof, J., Urzyczyn, P.: Bounded Combinatory Logic. In: Proceedings of CSL 2012, Schloss Dagstuhl. LIPIcs, vol. 16, pp. 243–258 (2012)
3. Düdder, B., Garbe, O., Martens, M., Rehof, J., Urzyczyn, P.: Using Inhabitation in Bounded Combinatory Logic with Intersection Types for GUI Synthesis. In: Proceedings of ITRS 2012 (2012)
4. Rehof, J.: Towards Combinatory Logic Synthesis. In: 1st International Workshop on Behavioural Types, BEAT 2013. ACM (January 22, 2013)
5. Düdder, B., Martens, M., Rehof, J.: Intersection Type Matching with Subtyping. In: Hasegawa, M. (ed.) TLCA 2013. LNCS, vol. 7941, pp. 125–139. Springer, Heidelberg (2013)
6. Hindley, J.R., Seldin, J.P.: Lambda-calculus and Combinators, an Introduction. Cambridge University Press (2008)
7. Barendregt, H., Coppo, M., Dezani-Ciancaglini, M.: A Filter Lambda Model and the Completeness of Type Assignment. Journal of Symbolic Logic 48(4), 931–940 (1983)
8. Haack, C., Howard, B., Stoughton, A., Wells, J.B.: Fully Automatic Adaptation of Software Components Based on Semantic Specifications. In: Kirchner, H., Ringeissen, C. (eds.) AMAST 2002. LNCS, vol. 2422, pp. 83–98. Springer, Heidelberg (2002)
9. Wells, J.B., Yakobowski, B.: Graph-Based Proof Counting and Enumeration with Applications for Program Fragment Synthesis. In: Etalle, S. (ed.) LOPSTR 2004. LNCS, vol. 3573, pp. 262–277. Springer, Heidelberg (2005)
10. Davies, R., Pfenning, F.: A Modal Analysis of Staged Computation. Journal of the ACM 48(3), 555–604 (2001)
11. Dezani-Ciancaglini, M., Hindley, R.: Intersection Types for Combinatory Logic. Theoretical Computer Science 100(2), 303–324 (1992)
12. Miller, D., Nadathur, G., Pfenning, F., Scedrov, A.: Uniform Proofs as a Foundation for Logic Programming. Ann. Pure Appl. Logic 51(1-2), 125–157 (1991)
13. Düdder, B., Martens, M., Rehof, J.: A Theory of Staged Composition Synthesis (Extended Version). Technical Report 843, Faculty of Computer Science, TU Dortmund (2013), http://www-seal.cs.tu-dortmund.de/seal/downloads/research/cls/TR843-SCS.pdf
14. Chandra, A.K., Kozen, D.C., Stockmeyer, L.J.: Alternation. Journal of the ACM 28(1), 114–133 (1981)
15. Lustig, Y., Vardi, M.Y.: Synthesis from Component Libraries. In: de Alfaro, L. (ed.) FOSSACS 2009. LNCS, vol. 5504, pp. 395–409. Springer, Heidelberg (2009)
16. Gulwani, S., Jha, S., Tiwari, A., Venkatesan, R.: Synthesis of Loop-free Programs. In: Proceedings of PLDI 2011, pp. 62–73. ACM (2011)
17. Freeman, T., Pfenning, F.: Refinement Types for ML. In: Proceedings of PLDI 1991, pp. 268–277. ACM (1991)
18. Davies, R., Pfenning, F.: Intersection Types and Computational Effects. In: ICFP, pp. 198–208 (2000)
19. Dezani-Ciancaglini, M., Giannini, P., Della Rocca, S.R.: Intersection, Universally Quantified, and Reference Types. In: Grädel, E., Kahle, R. (eds.) CSL 2009. LNCS, vol. 5771, pp. 209–224. Springer, Heidelberg (2009)
20. Dezani-Ciangaglini, M., Ronchi Della Rocca, S.: Intersection and Reference Types. Essays dedicated to Henk Barendregt on the occasion of his 60'th birthday, pp. 77–86 (2007)

Overlapping and Order-Independent Patterns
Definitional Equality for All

Jesper Cockx, Frank Piessens, and Dominique Devriese

DistriNet, KU Leuven, Belgium
`firstname.lastname@cs.kuleuven.be`

Abstract. Dependent pattern matching is a safe and efficient way to write programs and proofs in dependently typed languages. Current languages with dependent pattern matching treat overlapping patterns on a first-match basis, hence the order of the patterns can matter. Perhaps surprisingly, this order-dependence can even occur when the patterns do not overlap. To fix this confusing behavior, we developed a new semantics of pattern matching which treats all clauses as definitional equalities, even when the patterns overlap. A confluence check guarantees correctness in the presence of overlapping patterns. Our new semantics has two advantages. Firstly, it removes the order-dependence and thus makes the meaning of definitions clearer. Secondly, it allows the extension of existing definitions with new (consistent) evaluation rules. Unfortunately it also makes pattern matching harder to understand theoretically, but we give a theorem that helps to bridge this gap. An experimental implementation in Agda shows that our approach is feasible in practice too.

Keywords: Type theory, dependent pattern matching, overlapping patterns, confluence, Agda.

1 Introduction

Pattern matching is a mechanism to write programs by case distinction and recursion. Definitions by pattern matching are given by a set of equalities called *clauses*, for example:

$$
\begin{aligned}
&\texttt{plus} : \texttt{Nat} \to \ \texttt{Nat} \to \texttt{Nat} \\
&\texttt{plus zero} \quad\ n \ \ = n \\
&\texttt{plus (suc } m) \, n \ \ = \texttt{suc (plus } m \ n)
\end{aligned}
\tag{1}
$$

If the patterns of the clauses of a definition overlap, it is customary to choose the first clause that gives a match. This is the *first-match semantics* of pattern matching. For example, in the following definition the last clause cannot hold as a definitional equality but holds only when the first two clauses don't match:

$$
\begin{aligned}
&\texttt{equal} : \texttt{Nat} \to \ \texttt{Nat} \quad\ \to \texttt{Bool} \\
&\texttt{equal zero} \quad\ \texttt{zero} \quad = \texttt{true} \\
&\texttt{equal (suc } m) \, (\texttt{suc } n) = \texttt{equal } m \ n \\
&\texttt{equal } m \qquad\ n \qquad\ = \texttt{false}
\end{aligned}
\tag{2}
$$

Z. Shao (Ed.): ESOP 2014, LNCS 8410, pp. 87–106, 2014.

In a language with dependent types, pattern matching allows us to write not just programs, but also proofs. For example, the following is a proof that plus m zero $\equiv m$ for all m : Nat:[1]

$$
\begin{aligned}
&\text{lemma} : (m : \text{Nat}) \to \text{plus } m \text{ zero} \equiv m \\
&\text{lemma zero} \quad\;\; = \text{refl} \\
&\text{lemma (suc } m) \; = \text{cong suc (lemma } m)
\end{aligned}
\tag{3}
$$

If we are not careful, it is very well possible to give incorrect proofs by pattern matching. For example, a case analysis might be incomplete, or a recursive proof might become infinitely large when we expand it. This leads to an inconsistent logic. Hence certain restrictions are put on definitions by pattern matching to ensure totality [Coq92]. These restrictions allow us to translate definitions by pattern matching to type theory with only the theoretically simpler *eliminators* plus the K axiom [GMM06]. This ensures that definitions by pattern matching are correct with respect to the core theory, but also limits the expressiveness of the language.

In order to guarantee completeness, it is required that patterns must form a *covering*, i.e. arise as the patterns at the leaves of a *case tree*. An example of a case tree for a function half : Nat $\to$ Nat is given in Fig. 1. This case tree shows that the patterns zero, suc zero, and suc (suc k) together form a covering, ensuring completeness of functions that use these patterns.

$$
\begin{array}{ll}
\text{half} : \text{Nat} & \to \text{Nat} \\
\text{half}\;\; \text{zero} & = \text{zero} \\
\text{half}\;\; (\text{suc zero}) & = \text{zero} \\
\text{half}\;\; (\text{suc (suc } n)) & = \text{suc (half } n)
\end{array}
\qquad
n \left\{
\begin{array}{l}
\text{zero} \mapsto \text{zero} \\
(\text{suc } \underline{m}) \left\{
\begin{array}{l}
\text{suc zero} \mapsto \text{zero} \\
\text{suc (suc } k) \mapsto \text{suc (half } k)
\end{array}
\right.
\end{array}
\right.
$$

Fig. 1. Case trees such as the one on the right are used to check completeness. In each internal node, one variable is chosen and replaced by all possible constructors of its type applied to fresh variables.

Some languages with dependent pattern matching (such as Agda [Nor07]) allow more general pattern sets, but translate them to a covering internally. In this translation, overlapping patterns are treated on a first-match basis, hence the result of the translation depends on the order of the clauses.

Perhaps surprisingly, this order-dependence occurs even when the patterns do not overlap. For example, if we define disjunction on booleans as in [Ab12]:

$$
\begin{array}{lll}
\text{or} : \text{Bool} \to \text{Bool} & \to \text{Bool} \\
\text{or}\;\; \text{false}\;\; \text{false} & = \text{false} \\
\text{or}\;\; \text{true}\;\; \text{false} & = \text{true} \\
\text{or}\;\; x \qquad\quad \text{true} & = \text{true}
\end{array}
\tag{4}
$$

---

[1] The *identity type* $a \equiv b$ expresses equality of two terms $a, b : A$. Here refl is a proof that $m \equiv m$ and cong f p is a proof that $f\,x \equiv f\,y$ if p is a proof that $x \equiv y$.

then it does not satisfy the definitional equality[2] or x true $=$ true, while this is the case if the last clause is given first instead, leading to unexpected results for an inexperienced user. This is a sign of bad abstraction.

The goal of this paper is to make dependent pattern matching more amenable to equational reasoning. We do this by interpreting each clause directly as a definitional equality, even when the patterns overlap. In particular, our interpretation does not depend on the order of the patterns. This also allows us to give definitions with overlapping patterns, which can be used to extend a function with extra evaluation rules. For example, we allow the following definition:

$$
\begin{aligned}
&\text{plus}: \text{Nat} \to \text{Nat} && \to \text{Nat} \\
&\text{plus} \ \ \text{zero} \ \ y && = y \\
&\text{plus} \ \ (\text{suc } x) \, y && = \text{suc } (\text{plus } x \, y) \qquad\qquad (5)\\
&\text{plus} \ \ x \qquad\quad \text{zero} && = x \\
&\text{plus} \ \ x \qquad\quad (\text{suc } y) && = \text{suc } (\text{plus } x \, y)
\end{aligned}
$$

While all the examples in this introduction only use simple types, our approach is general enough to cope with *inaccessible patterns*, which are specific to dependent pattern matching. Section 6 includes two examples of dependent functions with overlapping patterns.

By making all clauses hold as definitional equalities, definitions by pattern matching feel more like mathematical definitions, rather than sequential program instructions. However, we lose the ability to translate pattern matching to the use of eliminators, making it more complex to understand theoretically.

Contributions

- We present an extended form of dependent pattern matching that allows patterns that do not necessarily form a covering (e.g. they might overlap), while treating all clauses as definitional equalities.
- We give a generalized criterion for completeness of overlapping patterns.
- We describe a simple criterion that can be used to check the confluence of definitions with overlapping patterns.
- We verify the feasibility of our approach by extending the Agda language, and give some simple examples that show how overlapping patterns can be used to add extra computation rules to existing functions.
- We formulate and prove a theoretical result that gives for every definition of a function f with overlapping patterns another definition of a function f' of which the patterns form a covering such that f' is extensionally equal to f.

Outlook. In Sect. 2, we give our notations and conventions for this paper. In Sect. 3, we describe the three problems with dependent pattern matching in current languages that we try to solve. In Sect. 4, we give a general description of our extended form of dependent pattern matching. In Sect. 5, we describe how the correctness of these extended definitions by pattern matching can be

---

[2] Two terms are called *definitionally equal* if they have the same normal form.

checked. In Sect. 6, we give some examples of how our extended form of pattern matching can be used. In Sect. 7, we give a theoretical result that says that each definition that uses our extension is extensionally equal to a classical one.

2   Conventions and Terminology

Type Theory. As our version of type theory, we use Luo's Unified Theory of Dependent Types (UTT) with dependent products, inductive families, and universes [Luo94]. We omit the meta-level logical framework and the impredicative universe of propositions because they are not needed for our current work. The formal rules of the version of UTT we use are summarized in Fig. 2.

$$\frac{}{\epsilon \ \textbf{valid}} \ \text{(Ctx-empty)} \qquad \frac{\Gamma \vdash A : Set_i \qquad x \notin FV(\Gamma)}{\Gamma(x : A) \ \textbf{valid}} \ \text{(Ctx-ext)}$$

$$\frac{\Gamma \ \textbf{valid} \qquad x : A \in \Gamma}{\Gamma \vdash x : A} \ \text{(Var)} \qquad \frac{\Gamma \vdash t : A_1 \qquad \Gamma \vdash A_1 = A_2 : Set_i}{\Gamma \vdash t : A_2} \ \text{(=Ty)}$$

$$\frac{\Gamma \ \textbf{valid}}{\Gamma \vdash \epsilon : \epsilon} \ \text{(List-empty)} \qquad \frac{\Gamma \vdash \bar{t} : \Delta \qquad \Gamma \vdash t : A[\Delta \mapsto \bar{t}]}{\Gamma \vdash \bar{t} \, t : \Delta(x : A)} \ \text{(List-ext)} \ + \text{ equality rule}$$

$$\frac{\Gamma \ \textbf{valid}}{\Gamma \vdash Set_i : Set_{i+1}} \ \text{(Set)} \qquad \frac{\Gamma \vdash A : Set_i \qquad \Gamma(x : A) \vdash B : Set_j}{\Gamma \vdash (x : A) \to B : Set_{\max(i,j)}} \ \text{(Π)} \ + \text{ equality rule}$$

$$\frac{\Gamma(x : A) \vdash t : B}{\Gamma \vdash \lambda(x : A). \, t : (x : A) \to B} \ \text{(λ)} \qquad\qquad + \text{ equality rule}$$

$$\frac{\Gamma(x : A) \vdash B : Set_i \qquad \Gamma \vdash f : (x : A) \to B \qquad \Gamma \vdash t : A}{\Gamma \vdash f \, t : B[x \mapsto t]} \ \text{(App)} \ + \text{ equality rule}$$

$$\frac{\Gamma(x : A) \vdash t : B \qquad \Gamma \vdash s : A}{(\lambda(x : A). \, t) \, s = t[x \mapsto s] : B[x \mapsto s]} \ \text{(β)} \qquad \frac{\Gamma \vdash f : (x : A) \to B \qquad x \notin FV(f)}{\lambda(x : A). \, f \, x = f : (x : A) \to B} \ \text{(η)}$$

$$+ \text{ reflexivity, symmetry, and transitivity rules for } =$$

Fig. 2. The core formal rules of UTT, including dependent function types $(x : A) \to B$, an infinite hierarchy of universes $Set_0, Set_1, Set_2, \ldots$, and $\beta\eta$-equality

Contexts and Substitutions. We use Greek capitals $\Gamma, \Delta, \ldots$ for contexts, capitals $T, U, \ldots$ for types, and small letters $t, u, \ldots$ for terms. A list of terms is indicated by a bar above the letter: $\bar{t}$. Contexts double as the type of such a list of terms, so we can write for example $\bar{t} : \Gamma$ where $\Gamma = (m : \text{Nat})(p : m \equiv \text{zero})$ and $\bar{t} = \text{zero refl}$. The simultaneous substitution of the terms $\bar{t}$ for the variables in the context Γ is written as $[\Gamma \mapsto \bar{t}]$. We denote substitutions by small greek letters $\sigma, \tau, \ldots$ The identity substitution is written as $[]$, and the forward composition of two substitutions σ and τ is written as $\sigma; \tau$.

Inductive Families. Inductive families are (dependent) types inductively defined by a number of *constructors*, for example Nat is defined by the constructors zero : Nat and suc : Nat → Nat. Inductive families can also have *parameters* and *indices*, for example Vec A n is an inductive family with one parameter $A : Set$, one index $n : $ Nat, and two constructors nil : Vec A zero and cons : $(n : $ Nat$) \to A \to$ Vec A $n \to$ Vec A (suc n). A formal treatment of inductive families can be found in [Dyb94]. For our purposes, it suffices to know that inductive families are introduced by the rules given in Fig. 3.

$$\frac{\Gamma \text{ valid}}{\Gamma \vdash D : \Psi\Delta \to Set_l} \text{ (Data)} \qquad\qquad \frac{\Gamma \text{ valid}}{\Gamma \vdash c_k : \Psi\Phi_k \to D\ \bar{\imath}_k} \text{ (Cons)}$$

Fig. 3. Introduction rules for an inductive family D with parameters Ψ, indices Δ, and constructors $c_k : \Phi_k \to D\ \bar{\imath}_k$ for $k = 1, \ldots, n$

Definitional and Propositional Equality. In (intensional) type theory, there are two distinct notions of equality. On the one hand, two terms s and t are *definitionally equal* (or *convertible*) if $\Gamma \vdash s = t : T$. On the other hand, two terms s and t are *propositionally equal* if we can prove their equality, i.e. if we can give a term of type $s \equiv_T t$. Propositional equality was introduced by Martin-Löf [ML84]. In UTT, it can be defined as an inductive family with two parameters $A : Set_i$ and $a : A$, one index $b : A$, and one constructor refl : $a \equiv_A a$.

When working with type theory in dependently typed languages such as Agda or Coq, it is more convenient to work with definitional equalities rather than propositional ones. This is because (in intensional type theory) definitional equality can be checked automatically, while propositional equality has to be proven and applied manually. When working with terms with free variables however, not all propositionally equal terms are definitionally equal, so the propositional equality is often necessary.

Definitions by Pattern Matching. A definition by pattern matching of a function f consists of a number of equalities called *clauses*, which are of the form $f\ \bar{p} = t$ where $\bar{p}$ is a list of patterns and t is a term called the *right-hand side*. A *pattern* is a term or a list of terms that is built from only (fully applied) constructors and variables, which we call the pattern variables. In dependent pattern matching, patterns can also contain *inaccessible patterns*, which can occur when there is only one type-correct term possible in a given position. As in [Nor07], we mark inaccessible patterns as $\lfloor t \rfloor$. For example, let Square n be an inductive family with one index $n : $ Nat and one constructor sq : $(m : $ Nat$) \to$ Square m^2. Then $\lfloor m^2 \rfloor$ (sq m) is a pattern of type $(n : $ Nat$)(p : $ Square $n)$. Any other pattern $\lfloor t \rfloor$ (sq m) would be ill-typed, so the use of an inaccessible pattern is justified.

We see patterns as a distinct syntactic class rather than a special kind of terms. We can convert a pattern p to a term by taking the *underlying term* $\lceil p \rceil$ defined as follows:

$$\lceil x \rceil = x \qquad \lceil c\, p_1\, \ldots\, p_n \rceil = c\, \lceil p_1 \rceil\, \ldots\, \lceil p_n \rceil \qquad \lceil \lfloor t \rfloor \rceil = t \qquad (6)$$

A term t *matches* a pattern p if there exists a substitution σ such that $\lceil p \rceil \sigma = t$.

A pattern $\bar{p} : \Delta$ is called *linear* if each pattern variable occurs exactly once in an accessible position in $\bar{p}$. It is called *respectful* [GMM06] if for each list of terms $\bar{a} : \Delta$ that matches all the accessible parts of $\bar{p}$, we have that $\bar{a}$ matches all the inaccessible parts of $\bar{p}$ as well. Patterns are required to be linear and respectful in order to have decidable pattern matching in the presence of inaccessible patterns.

Formally, we write $\Gamma | \Phi \vdash \bar{p} : \Delta$ **pattern** to express that, in the context Γ, $\bar{p}$ is a pattern of type Δ with pattern variables from the context Φ. A definition by pattern matching of a function $f : \Delta \to T$ in a context Γ then consists of a set of clauses of the form $f\, \bar{p} = t$ where $\Gamma | \Phi \vdash \bar{p} : \Delta$ **pattern** is linear and respectful and $\Gamma \Phi (f : \Delta \to T) \vdash t : T[\Delta \mapsto \lceil \bar{p} \rceil]$. In order to ensure correctness, definitions by pattern matching are required to have three additional properties:

Completeness. For each closed list of terms $\bar{s} : \Delta$, there must be a pattern $\bar{p}$ such that $\bar{s}$ matches $\bar{p}$. This is required in order to have canonicity, i.e. that any closed normal form of an inductive family is constructor-headed.

Termination. There can be no $\bar{s} : \Delta$ such that there is an infinite sequence of evaluation steps $f\, \bar{s} \longrightarrow t_1 \longrightarrow t_2 \longrightarrow \ldots$ where f occurs in each of the t_i. This is required in order to have strong normalization.

Confluence. If $f\, \bar{s} \longrightarrow^* t_1$ and $f\, \bar{s} \longrightarrow^* t_2$, there should exist a term t such that $t_1 \longrightarrow^* t$ and $t_2 \longrightarrow^* t$. This is required in order to have the Church-Rosser property.

If these three requirements are satisfied, we can add f to the theory by the rules given in Fig. 4.

$$\frac{\Gamma\ \textbf{valid}}{\Gamma \vdash f : \Phi \to T}\ \text{(Func)} \qquad\qquad \frac{\Gamma \vdash \bar{s} = \lceil \bar{p}_k \rceil \sigma : \Phi}{\Gamma \vdash f\, \bar{s} = t_k \sigma : T[\Phi \mapsto \bar{s}]}\ \text{(Clause)}$$

Fig. 4. Rules for a function $f : \Phi \to T$ defined by the clauses $f\, \bar{p}_k = t_k$ for $k = 1, \ldots, n$

Respectfulness can be checked step by step by context splitting (see Sect. 2.1 of [Nor07]), completeness is checked by constructing a case tree, and termination can be achieved by requiring that definitions are structurally recursive. Confluence is a non-issue as long as first-match semantics are used, because then only one clause is ever applicable at the same time. When we drop the first-match semantics, the checks for respectfulness and termination stay valid, but those for completeness and confluence need to be updated. We will do this in Sect. 5.

Case Trees. Definitions by pattern matching can be represented by a *case tree*. A case tree tells us how the patterns of a definition are built by introducing constructors step by step. Each leaf node of a splitting tree corresponds to a clause of the definition. For example, consider the function `parity` (7) given by Achim Jung on the Agda mailing list[3]. It can be represented by the case tree given in Fig. 5.

$$
m\ n
\begin{cases}
\text{zero } \underline{n}
\begin{cases}
\text{zero zero} \mapsto \text{true} \\
\text{zero (suc } \underline{n})
\begin{cases}
\text{zero (suc zero)} \mapsto \text{false} \\
\text{zero (suc (suc } n)) \mapsto \text{parity zero } n
\end{cases}
\end{cases} \\[2em]
(\text{suc } m)\ \underline{n}
\begin{cases}
(\text{suc } \underline{m})\ \text{zero}
\begin{cases}
(\text{suc zero) zero} \mapsto \text{false} \\
(\text{suc (suc } m))\ \text{zero} \mapsto \text{parity } m \text{ zero}
\end{cases} \\
(\text{suc } m)\ (\text{suc } n) \mapsto \text{parity } m\ n
\end{cases}
\end{cases}
$$

Fig. 5. This case tree corresponds precisely to the definition of `parity` (7)

$$
\begin{aligned}
&\text{parity} : \text{Nat} \rightarrow & \text{Nat} & \rightarrow \text{Bool} \\
&\text{parity zero} & \text{zero} & = \text{true} \\
&\text{parity zero} & (\text{suc zero}) & = \text{false} \\
&\text{parity zero} & (\text{suc (suc } n)) & = \text{parity zero } n \\
&\text{parity (suc zero)} & \text{zero} & = \text{false} \\
&\text{parity (suc (suc } m)) & \text{zero} & = \text{parity } m \text{ zero} \\
&\text{parity (suc } m) & (\text{suc } n) & = \text{parity } m\ n
\end{aligned}
\tag{7}
$$

Using case trees has a number of advantages. Firstly, the patterns at the leaves of a case tree always form a covering, hence they are complete. Secondly, they give an efficient method to evaluate functions defined by pattern matching. Thirdly, each internal node in a case tree corresponds exactly to the application of an eliminator for an inductive family, so they are a useful intermediate step in the translation of dependent pattern matching to pure type theory (without pattern matching) as done in [GMM06].

In section 2.2 of [Nor07], it is described how a case tree can be constructed from a given (complete) set of clauses. When dealing with overlapping patterns, the algorithm chooses whatever pattern comes first. In other words, the resulting case tree follows the first-match semantics of pattern matching.

Termination Checking. In order to guarantee termination, functions are required to be *structurally recursive*. This means that the arguments of recursive calls should be *structurally smaller* than the pattern on the left-hand side. The structural order $\prec$ is defined in Fig. 6. For functions with multiple arguments, the function should be structurally recursive on one of its arguments, i.e. there should be some k such that $s_k \prec \lceil p_k \rceil$ for each clause $f\ \bar{p} = t$ and each recursive call $f\ \bar{s}$ in t.

---

[3] https://lists.chalmers.se/pipermail/agda/2012/004397.html, last visited on 15 January 2014.

$$\frac{}{t_i \prec c\, t_1 \;\ldots\; t_n} \qquad \frac{f \prec t}{f\, s \prec t} \qquad \frac{r \prec s \qquad s \prec t}{r \prec t}$$

Fig. 6. The structural order $\prec$ can be used to check termination [GMM06]. The most important property of the structural order is that it is well-founded, because this guarantees that structurally recursive functions are indeed terminating.

We lack the space to do justice to the large amount of research on termination checking. For some more sophisticated approaches, see for example size-change termination [LJB01], type-based termination [Bla04], and almost-full relations [VCW12].

3   Problem Statement

When deciding which definitions by pattern matching are allowed, there is a conflict between theory and practice. From a theoretical perspective, we want to be able to write definitions by pattern matching in function of eliminators as in [GMM06], because this guarantees correctness of the definitions. From a practical perspective, we want to be able to write overlapping definitions that follow the first-match semantics, because this reduces the number of clauses required in some cases. In an attempt to reconcile these two goals, [Nor07] allows patterns to overlap but translates definitions to a case tree internally using the first-match semantics. However, the representation of function definitions as case trees and the translation to a case tree specifically introduce a number of new problems which we describe in this section.

Clauses Are Split Too Much. When constructing a case tree from a set of clauses, the constructed case tree is not always the one the user intended. An example of this behavior was given by the definition of `or` (4) in the introduction. As another example, when we translate the definition (7) to a case tree using the algorithm from [Nor07], we won't get the case tree in Fig. 5 but rather the one given in Fig. 7. Note that in this case tree, the constructors are introduced in a different order. The result is that the single clause `parity` (suc m) (suc n) = `parity` $m\, n$ has been split in the following two clauses:

$$\text{parity (suc zero)} \quad (\text{suc } n) = \text{parity zero } n$$
$$\text{parity (suc (suc } m)) (\text{suc } n) = \text{parity (suc } m) \, n$$

This means that a term of the form `parity` (suc m) (suc n), where m and n are free variables, won't evaluate to `parity` $m\, n$, even though it should according to the input clauses. This impedes equational reasoning and can be very confusing to the unsuspecting user. If the last clause was placed first instead, then the correct covering would have been reconstructed. So although the patterns of this definition form a covering, their order nevertheless influences the result!

$$
\underline{m}\ n
\begin{cases}
\text{zero } \underline{n}
\begin{cases}
\text{zero zero} \mapsto \text{true} \\
\text{zero (suc } \underline{n})
\begin{cases}
\text{zero (suc zero)} \mapsto \text{false} \\
\text{zero (suc (suc } n)) \mapsto \text{parity zero } n
\end{cases}
\end{cases} \\
(\text{suc } \underline{m})\ n
\begin{cases}
(\text{suc zero) } \underline{n}
\begin{cases}
(\text{suc zero) zero} \mapsto \text{false} \\
(\text{suc zero) (suc } n) \mapsto \text{parity zero } n
\end{cases} \\
(\text{suc (suc } m)) \underline{n}
\begin{cases}
(\text{suc (suc } m)) \text{ zero} \mapsto \text{parity } m \text{ zero} \\
(\text{suc (suc } m)) (\text{suc } n) \mapsto \text{parity (suc } m)\ n
\end{cases}
\end{cases}
\end{cases}
$$

Fig. 7. In contrast to the case tree in Fig. 5, this case tree of the `parity` function does not include the definitional equality `parity (suc` m`) (suc` n`) = parity` m n

Not All Complete Pattern Sets Form a Covering. The second problem is that not all complete pattern sets form a covering, hence they cannot be represented precisely by a case tree. Consider for example the following definition of `majority` due to Gérard Berry:

$$
\begin{array}{llll}
\texttt{majority} : \texttt{Bool} \rightarrow \texttt{Bool} \rightarrow \texttt{Bool} & \rightarrow \texttt{Bool} \\
\texttt{majority true} & \texttt{true} & \texttt{true} & = \texttt{true} \\
\texttt{majority } x & \texttt{false} & \texttt{true} & = x \\
\texttt{majority true} & y & \texttt{false} & = y \\
\texttt{majority false} & \texttt{true} & z & = z \\
\texttt{majority false} & \texttt{false} & \texttt{false} & = \texttt{false}
\end{array}
\tag{8}
$$

It is clear that the patterns of this definition are complete and do not overlap, yet there is no case tree representing exactly this definition. Instead, it is translated to the case tree given in Fig. 8. We can see that in the case tree, the clause

$$
\underline{x}\ y\ z
\begin{cases}
\text{true } \underline{y}\ z
\begin{cases}
\text{true true } \underline{z}
\begin{cases}
\text{true true true} \mapsto \text{true} \\
\text{true true false} \mapsto \text{true}
\end{cases} \\
\text{true false } \underline{z}
\begin{cases}
\text{true false true} \mapsto \text{true} \\
\text{true false false} \mapsto \text{false}
\end{cases}
\end{cases} \\
\text{false } \underline{y}\ z
\begin{cases}
\text{false true } z \mapsto z \\
\text{false false } \underline{z}
\begin{cases}
\text{false false true} \mapsto \text{false} \\
\text{false false false} \mapsto \text{false}
\end{cases}
\end{cases}
\end{cases}
$$

Fig. 8. Case tree constructed from the definition of `majority` (8). It does not include the definitional equality `majority` x `false true =` x.

`majority` x `false true =` x has been split into the following two clauses:

$$
\begin{array}{l}
\texttt{majority true\ false true} = \texttt{true} \\
\texttt{majority false false true} = \texttt{false}
\end{array}
\tag{9}
$$

So we have lost the definitional equality `majority` x `false true =` x. Note that no case tree corresponds precisely to the definition (8), so this problem is inherent to the representation of definitions by case trees.

Overlapping Patterns Can Be Useful. It would sometimes be useful to define a function with overlapping clauses that are all interpreted as definitional equalities, for example definition (5) of `plus`. Currently, such definitions are not allowed because the last two clauses are 'unreachable'. Yet in order to evaluate `plus` m `zero` or `plus` m (`suc` n) where m is not in constructor form, we need the last two clauses. For example, with definition (5) of `plus`, it is easy to define the function `plus-comm` that proves the commutativity of `plus`:

$$
\begin{aligned}
&\texttt{plus-comm} : (m : \texttt{Nat}) \to (n : \texttt{Nat}) \to \texttt{plus}\ m\ n \equiv \texttt{plus}\ n\ m\\
&\texttt{plus-comm}\ \ \texttt{zero}\qquad\ n\qquad\ \ = \texttt{refl}\\
&\texttt{plus-comm}\ \ (\texttt{suc}\ m)\quad\ n\qquad\ \ = \texttt{cong suc}\ (\texttt{plus-comm}\ m\ n)
\end{aligned}
\tag{10}
$$

In contrast, to give this proof for the standard definition of `plus`, the Agda standard library first needs a lemma to prove that `plus` m (`suc` n) $\equiv$ `suc` (`plus` m n), and then the proof itself still takes approximately eight lines. So the overlapping patterns of `plus` allow us to give shorter and more straightforward proofs than before. Note that no case tree can contain overlapping patterns, so again this restriction is inherent to the representation by case trees.

4   Allowing More General Pattern Sets

To fix these problems, we extend pattern matching in order to allow more general pattern sets than just coverings. In particular, we allow the patterns in a definition to overlap. Instead of following the first-match semantics, these definitions follow 'any-match semantics', i.e. any clause can be used to evaluate the function at any time. In practice, this means that evaluation of a function application doesn't block when pattern matching gets stuck on a free variable. Instead, evaluation continues with the next clause. This gives us 'what-you-see-is-what-you-get' pattern matching where all clauses hold as definitional equalities.

By extending pattern matching in this way, we solve all three above problems. All clauses are treated as definitional equalities, so their order doesn't matter. We don't need patterns to form a covering, so there is no need to split clauses. Overlapping patterns are allowed, so there is no need to discard them. However, our approach also has some drawbacks:

- First of all, we lose the first-match semantics. This doesn't restrict the functions we can define, but it requires us to write longer definitions in some cases. This problem is unavoidable if we want clauses to be order-independent.
- We also lose the ability to translate definitions to pure type theory with eliminators. To guarantee correctness (completeness, termination, and confluence), we thus need to reason about the definitions directly.
- Finally, we lose the ability to represent functions by case trees, hence the ability to evaluate them efficiently. It is however possible to extend case trees with *catchall subtrees* that allow us to represent these more general definitions by case trees. See the first author's master thesis [Coc13] for a full description.

5   Checking Definitions with Overlapping Patterns

The standard technique for checking termination doesn't depend on the fact that the patterns form a covering, but those for completeness and confluence do. In this section, we describe how to check completeness and confluence in the presence of overlapping patterns.

Completeness. To check whether a set of (overlapping) patterns is complete, we just try to build a case tree for it using the coverage algorithm from section 2.2 of [Nor07]. Because this algorithm can only split patterns or discard them, we know that it preserves completeness. Hence if the construction of a case tree succeeds, we know that the patterns we started from are complete. More formally, we have the following (equivalent) criterion for completeness:

Proposition 1. *Let Δ be a valid context and P be a set of lists of patterns of the same type Δ. If there exists a covering O such that for each $\bar{q} \in O$, there exists a $\bar{p} \in P$ such that $\bar{p} \supseteq \bar{q}^4$, then P is complete.*

Proof. Since the covering O is complete, each closed list of terms $\bar{t} : \Delta$ matches a $\bar{q} \in O$, i.e. there exists a substitution τ such that $\bar{t} = \lceil \bar{q} \rceil \tau$. By assumption, there exists a $\bar{p}$ such that $\bar{p} \supseteq \bar{q}$, i.e. there exists a substitution σ such that $\lceil \bar{p} \rceil \sigma = \lceil \bar{q} \rceil$. Then we have $\bar{t} = \lceil \bar{p} \rceil \sigma \tau$. This holds for any $\bar{t} : \Delta$, hence the set of patterns P is complete. $\square$

The fact that we can reuse the existing coverage algorithm means we don't have to change our intuition about when a function definition is complete. It also means we can re-use existing code for coverage checking.

Confluence. To ensure the confluence of a definition with overlapping patterns, we want that whenever a term matches the patterns of two clauses, then they also give the same result for that term. In order to check whether two patterns overlap, we will use unification. A *unifier* of two terms a and b is a substitution σ such that $a\sigma = b\sigma$. A *most general unifier* of a and b is a unifier σ such that for each other unifier σ', there exists a substitution τ such that $\sigma' = \sigma; \tau$. The question whether unifiers exist is called the *unification problem*. In general, this is an undecidable problem. There exist unification algorithms (see for example [McB00]) but they can give up in case the problem is too hard. We say that the algorithm *succeeds positively* if it finds a most general unifier, that it *succeeds negatively* if it concludes there exist no unifiers, and that it *fails* otherwise.

We make the following observation: let $\bar{p}_1$ and $\bar{p}_2$ be two patterns that have a most general unifier σ and let $\bar{p} = \bar{p}_1 \sigma = \bar{p}_2 \sigma$. Then a term $\bar{t}$ matches $\bar{p}$ if and only if it matches both $\bar{p}_1$ and $\bar{p}_2$. Also, if there is no unifier of $\bar{p}_1$ and $\bar{p}_2$, then there is no term $\bar{t}$ that matches both $\bar{p}_1$ and $\bar{p}_2$. So if we require that the unification of each pair of patterns (with all pattern variables as the flexible

---

^{4} We write $\bar{p} \supseteq \bar{q}$ ($\bar{q}$ is a *specialization* of $\bar{p}$) if there exists a substitution σ on the pattern variables of $\bar{p}$ such that $\lceil \bar{q} \rceil = \lceil \bar{p} \rceil \sigma$.

variables) succeeds (either positively or negatively) then we are able to check whether two patterns overlap. This is the idea behind the following proposition.

Proposition 2. *Let $f : \Delta \to T$ be defined by a set of clauses which are structurally recursive on the k'th argument. Assume that for each pair of clauses $f\ \bar{p}_1 = t_1$ and $f\ \bar{p}_2 = t_2$ we have that unification of $\bar{p}_1$ and $\bar{p}_2$ succeeds (either positively or negatively). Moreover, assume that if it succeeds positively with result σ, then $t_1\sigma$ and $t_2\sigma$ have the same normal form. Then the definition of f is confluent.*

Proof. Let $\bar{u} : \Delta$ be a normal form, we prove that $f\ \bar{u}$ has a unique normal form by structural induction on the k'th component u_k. So suppose that this is true for all normal forms $\bar{v} : \Delta$ with $v_k \prec u_k$, and suppose $f\ \bar{u} \longrightarrow s_1$ and $f\ \bar{u} \longrightarrow s_2$. Then there exist clauses $f\ \bar{p}_1 = t_1$, $f\ \bar{p}_2 = t_2$ and substitutions τ_1, τ_2 such that $\lceil \bar{p}_1 \rceil \tau_1 = \bar{u} = \lceil \bar{p}_2 \rceil \tau_2$, $t_1\tau_1 = s_1$ and $t_2\tau_2 = s_2$. In particular we have that $\tau = \tau_1; \tau_2$ is a unifier of $\bar{p}_1$ and $\bar{p}_2$, so unification of $\bar{p}_1$ and $\bar{p}_2$ cannot succeed negatively. Unification of $\bar{p}_1$ and $\bar{p}_2$ cannot fail by assumption, hence it must succeed positively with result the most general unifier σ and moreover there must exist a normal form t such that $t_1\sigma \longrightarrow^* t$ and $t_2\sigma \longrightarrow^* t$. Because σ is a most general unifier of $\bar{p}_1$ and $\bar{p}_2$, there exists a substitution τ' such that $\tau = \sigma; \tau'$. This implies $s_1 = t_1\tau = (t_1\sigma)\tau' \longrightarrow^* t\tau'$ and $s_2 = t_2\tau = (t_2\sigma)\tau' \longrightarrow^* t\tau'$. By the induction hypothesis, all recursive calls to f in $t_1\tau$ and $t_2\tau$ have a unique normal form, hence the (shared) normal form $t\tau'$ of $t_1\tau$ and $t_2\tau$ is unique. We can conclude that the definition of f is confluent.   □

Note that in order to check confluence of a recursive function, we need to know that the definition has already passed the termination checker. This is because we need to evaluate the function in question in order to check confluence.

It can happen that the unification of two patterns fails while checking confluence. However, unification of patterns consisting of only constructors and variables always succeeds (either positively or negatively). So this problem can only occur if an inaccessible pattern overlaps with a constructor pattern or another inaccessible pattern.

6   Implementation and Examples

Our extended form of pattern matching, as well as the confluence checker, have been implemented as an experimental modification to the Agda compiler. The implementation allows choosing between the standard semantics and ours for each definition separately by the use of a new keyword `overlapping`. We do not give the details of the implementation here, but instead give some examples of definitions with overlapping patterns. In particular, we add extra evaluation rules to some standard definitions. This can make it easier to prove propositions that mention these functions, as in the proof of `plus-comm` (10). We also give an example where our confluence check fails unexpectedly.

Concatenation of Vectors. Here is a definition of the concatenation `concat` on vectors that uses overlapping patterns:

$$\begin{aligned}
&\texttt{concat} : (m : \textsf{Nat})\ (n : \textsf{Nat})\ (v : \textsf{Vec}\ A\ m)\ (w : \textsf{Vec}\ A\ n) \rightarrow \textsf{Vec}\ A\ (\texttt{plus}\ m\ n) \\
&\texttt{concat}\ \lfloor\texttt{zero}\rfloor\quad n \qquad\ \texttt{nil} \qquad\qquad w\ \ = w \\
&\texttt{concat}\ m \qquad\ \lfloor\texttt{zero}\rfloor\ v \qquad\qquad\ \texttt{nil} = v \\
&\texttt{concat}\ \lfloor\texttt{suc}\ m\rfloor\ n \qquad (\texttt{cons}\ m\ a\ v)\ w\ \ = \texttt{cons}\ m\ a\ (\texttt{concat}\ m\ n\ v\ w)
\end{aligned}$$
$$(11)$$

Note that for the first clause to be of correct type, we need that $\texttt{plus}\ \texttt{zero}\ n = n$; while for the second clause we need that $\texttt{plus}\ m\ \texttt{zero} = m$. So this definition of `concat` relies upon the fact that the definition of `plus` has overlapping clauses.

Transitivity of the Propositional Equality. The definition of the propositional equality $\equiv_A$ as an inductive family only provides reflexivity of the relation. In order to prove that $\equiv_A$ is symmetric and transitive, we have to give a proof ourselves. For example, here is a proof of transitivity:

$$\begin{aligned}
&\texttt{trans} : (x : A)\ (y : A)\ (z : A)\ (p : x \equiv y)\ (q : y \equiv z) \rightarrow x \equiv z \\
&\texttt{trans}\ \ \lfloor y\rfloor\quad \lfloor y\rfloor\quad z \qquad \texttt{refl} \qquad q \qquad\ = q \\
&\texttt{trans}\ \ x \qquad \lfloor y\rfloor\quad \lfloor y\rfloor\quad p \qquad\quad \texttt{refl}\quad = p
\end{aligned}$$
$$(12)$$

We again use overlapping patterns in order to increase the number of evaluation rules. This ensures that both proofs of the form $\texttt{trans}\ \texttt{refl}\ p$ and $\texttt{trans}\ p\ \texttt{refl}$ are automatically simplified to p, saving us from proving them ourselves. This also shows that the confluence checker works in the presence of inaccessible patterns.

A Counterexample: Multiplication. Here is another function on natural numbers, multiplication:

$$\begin{aligned}
&\texttt{mult} : \textsf{Nat} \rightarrow\ \textsf{Nat} \quad\ \rightarrow \textsf{Nat} \\
&\texttt{mult}\ \ \texttt{zero}\quad y \qquad = \texttt{zero} \\
&\texttt{mult}\ \ (\texttt{suc}\ x)\ y \qquad = \texttt{plus}\ (\texttt{mult}\ x\ y)\ y \\
&\texttt{mult}\ \ x \qquad\quad \texttt{zero}\ = \texttt{zero} \\
&\texttt{mult}\ \ x \qquad\quad (\texttt{suc}\ y) = \texttt{plus}\ x\ (\texttt{mult}\ x\ y)
\end{aligned}$$
$$(13)$$

Let us focus on the confluence of the second and the fourth clause. After unification of the patterns, the right-hand sides become respectively:

$$\texttt{plus}\ (\texttt{mult}\ x\ (\texttt{suc}\ y))\ (\texttt{suc}\ y) \longrightarrow^* \texttt{suc}\ (\texttt{plus}\ (\texttt{plus}\ x\ (\texttt{mult}\ x\ y))\ y)$$

$$\texttt{plus}\ (\texttt{suc}\ x)\ (\texttt{mult}\ (\texttt{suc}\ x)\ y) \longrightarrow^* \texttt{suc}\ (\texttt{plus}\ x\ (\texttt{plus}\ (\texttt{mult}\ x\ y)\ y))$$

We see that the right-hand sides do not have the same normal form, but are only equal *up to associativity* of `plus`. Hence this definition does not satisfy our criterion for confluence (Proposition 2). It is however possible to prove that the right-hand sides are *propositionally* equal. But to obtain confluence, we need them to have the same normal form, i.e. they must be *definitionally* equal. To solve this problem, we would have to introduce a new evaluation rule of the form

$$\text{plus } (\text{plus } x \, y) \, z \longrightarrow \text{plus } x \, (\text{plus } y \, z)$$

Such rules are currently not allowed in type theory, and it is not clear how to add them in a sound way. Hence we refrain from allowing definitions such as (13) in the current work.

7   Link with Non-overlapping Definitions

We have shown that overlapping function definitions can be useful, but we also have to worry about soundness. For definitions by pattern matching whose patterns form a covering, this is done by translating the definition to repeated application of eliminators [GMM06]. If the patterns of a definition do not form a covering however, there is no hope to proceed in this way.

In this section, we prove that each new function definition we introduce is equivalent to an old one. In order to formulate the proposition, we first have to define what we mean by 'equivalent'. It is not realistic to ask that they are definitionally or propositionally equal, because both are *intensional* equalities: they care about how functions are defined, not just about their values. To solve this problem, we assume the functional extensionality axiom, which expresses that two functions are equal when they have equal values for equal inputs. This is achieved by adding for each pair of functions $f_1, f_2 : (x : A) \to B \, x$ the following constant:

$$\text{Ext} : ((x : A) \to f_1 \, x \equiv f_2 \, x) \to f_1 \equiv f_2 \tag{14}$$

This constant was introduced by [Hof95]. Now we can state our main theorem:

Theorem 3. *Assume the functional extensionality axiom (14). If a function $\Gamma \vdash f : \Delta \to T$ is defined by a set of clauses that satisfy the criteria for completeness (see Proposition 1), termination (i.e. the definition is structurally recursive), and confluence (see Proposition 2); then we can define a function $\Gamma \vdash f' : \Delta \to T$ whose patterns form a covering such that $\Gamma \vdash eq_f : f \equiv f'$ where eq_f only contains functions whose patterns form a covering as well.*

The equality proof eq_f given by this theorem is internal to the language, rather than meta-theoretical. In principle, this could cause problems because we don't prove consistency of the extended language. However, note the following:

– Functions with overlapping patterns cannot occur inside the equality proof. So possible inconsistencies arising from non-confluent definitions do not invalidate the theorem.
– The function f is not required to be terminating, but only structurally recursive, which is easily checked and requires no further proof. It would be better to be independent of the specific termination criterion, but this would introduce a circularity in the proof.

- While we need reductions in order to typecheck a function and hence to check its completeness, a function can never occur in its own type. Hence we do not need to know the definition is confluent in order to check completeness.

In order to prove this theorem, we use the heterogeneous equality $a \cong_{A,B} b$ introduced by McBride [McB00]. It allows the expression of equality between terms of different types, but still only allows a proof if the types are equal. Heterogeneous equality can be defined as an inductive family with two parameters $A : Set_i$ and $a : A$, *two* indices $B : Set_i$ and $b : B$, and one constructor $\mathtt{refl} : a \cong_{A,A} a$. In contrast to [McB00], this definition uses the standard elimination principle (which McBride calls $\mathtt{eqIndElim}$). We will work with the heterogeneous equality by means of pattern matching, this is equivalent with using $\mathtt{eqIndElim}$ together with the K axiom [GMM06]. We will use the following fact about the heterogeneous equality:

- For any type A and terms $x, y : A$, we have:

$$\mathtt{hom\text{-}to\text{-}het} : x \equiv y \to x \cong y \tag{15}$$

$$\mathtt{het\text{-}to\text{-}hom} : x \cong y \to x \equiv y \tag{16}$$

Assuming extensionality, we additionally have the following facts:

- For all $f_1 : (x : A_1) \to B_1 \, x$ and $f_2 : (x : A_2) \to B_2 \, x$, we have:

$$\begin{aligned}\lambda\text{-}\mathtt{cong} : (A_1 \cong A_2) \to \\ ((x_1 : A_1)(x_2 : A_2) \to x_1 \cong x_2 \to f_1 \, x_1 \cong f_2 \, x_2) \to \\ f_1 \cong f_2\end{aligned} \tag{17}$$

- For all $t_1 : A_1$, $t_2 : A_2$, $f_1 : (x : A_1) \to B_1$ and $f_2 : (x : A_2) \to B_2$, we have:

$$\begin{aligned}\mathtt{ap\text{-}cong} : ((x_1 : A_1)(x_2 : A_2) \to x_1 \cong x_2 \to B_1 \, x_1 \cong B_2 \, x_2) \to \\ f_1 \cong f_2 \to t_1 \cong t_2 \to f_1 \, t_1 \cong f_2 \, t_2\end{aligned} \tag{18}$$

- For all $B_1 : A_1 \to Set_i$ and $B_2 : A_1 \to Set_i$ we have:

$$\begin{aligned}\Pi\text{-}\mathtt{cong} : (A_1 \cong A_2) \to \\ ((x_1 : A_1)(x_2 : A_2) \to x_1 \cong x_2 \to B_1 \, x_1 \cong B_2 \, x_2) \to \\ ((x_1 : A_1) \to B_1 \, x_1) \cong ((x_2 : A_2) \to B_2 \, x_2)\end{aligned} \tag{19}$$

The last three facts are used mainly as a tool to 'push' our (heterogeneous) propositional equalities through all syntactic constructs. For a machine-checked proof of these facts in Agda, please refer to the extended version of this paper on the first author's website.

Proof (of Theorem 3). We start by giving the definition of the function f'. Let P be the set of patterns in the definition of f. Because the clauses of f satisfy the criterion for completeness (Proposition 1), there exists a covering O such that for each $\bar{q} \in O$, there exists a $\bar{p} \in P$ such that $\bar{p} \supseteq \bar{q}$. In other words, for all $\bar{q} \in O$ there exists a clause $f \, \bar{p} = t$ of f and a substitution σ such that $\bar{p}\sigma = \bar{q}$.

This means we have $\Gamma\Psi(f : \Delta \to T) \vdash t : T[\Delta \mapsto \lceil \bar{p}\rceil]$ where Ψ is the context of pattern variables of $\bar{p}$. Let t' be the term t where all occurrences of f have been replaced by f'. The function f' is defined by the clauses $f' \bar{q} = t'\sigma$ for all $\bar{q} \in O$. We check that this is a valid definition:

- Let Φ be the context of pattern variables of $\bar{q}$. We have $\Gamma\Phi(f' : \Delta \to T) \vdash t'\sigma : T[\Delta \mapsto \lceil \bar{q}\rceil]$ by α-renaming and the fact that $\bar{p}\sigma = \bar{q}$, so the clauses of f' are valid.
- The set of patterns O is a covering, hence the patterns are complete.
- The arguments of all recursive calls $f \bar{s}$ in the right-hand side of a clause $f \bar{p} = t$ satisfy $\bar{s} \prec \lceil \bar{p}\rceil$. Note that if $s \prec t$, then also $s\sigma \prec t\sigma$ for any substitution σ (by induction on the definition of $\prec$). This gives us that $\bar{s}\sigma \prec \lceil \bar{p}\rceil\sigma = \lceil \bar{q}\rceil$. This implies that the definition of f' is structurally recursive, hence it is terminating.
- The patterns in O do not overlap, hence the definition of f' is confluent.

Now we define $\tilde{eq}_f$ such that $\Gamma \vdash \tilde{eq}_f : f \cong f'$. By extensionality (14) it is sufficient to give a term $\Gamma \vdash \tilde{eq}_{f(\Delta)} : \Delta \to f \Delta \cong f' \Delta$. In order to do this, we use pattern matching with the same pattern set O used in the definition of f'. Let $\Gamma|\Phi \vdash \bar{q} : \Delta$ **pattern** be one of these patterns, the return type of $\tilde{eq}_{f(\Delta)}$ for that pattern becomes $f \lceil \bar{q}\rceil \cong f' \lceil \bar{q}\rceil$.

On the one hand, by definition of O there exists a clause $f \bar{p} = t$ of f and a substitution σ such that $\bar{p}\sigma = \bar{q}$. This implies that $\Gamma \vdash f \lceil \bar{q}\rceil = t\sigma : T[\Delta \mapsto \lceil \bar{q}\rceil]$. On the other hand, there is a clause $f' \bar{q} = t'\sigma$ of f', hence $\Gamma \vdash f' \lceil \bar{q}\rceil = t'\sigma : T[\Delta \mapsto \lceil \bar{q}\rceil]$. So we are left to give a term of type $t\sigma \cong t'\sigma$ in the context $\tilde{\Gamma} = \Gamma\Phi(\tilde{eq}_{f(\Delta)} : \Delta \to f \Delta \cong f' \Delta)$.

Note that the bound variables in t and t' with the same name do not necessarily have the same type, because occurrences of f in the types have been replaced by f'. In order to avoid confusion between these variables, we α-rename all bound variables x in t' to their primed variants x'.

In order to proceed, we first fix some notations. Let Ξ be a context such that $\tilde{\Gamma}\Xi$ **valid**. We denote with Ξ' the context Ξ where each variable x has been replaced by its primed version x' and each occurrence of f has been replaced by f'. If $\tilde{\Gamma}\Xi \vdash a : A$, then a' denotes the term a where each variable from the context Ξ has been replaced by x' and each occurrence of f has been replaced by f'. Note that $\tilde{\Gamma}\Xi' \vdash a' : A'$, and that this can be proven by using the same tree of inference rules. One further notation we use is $\Xi \cong \Xi'$ for the context expressing pairwise equality between the variables in Ξ and Ξ'. For example, if $\Xi = (n : \text{Nat})(v : \text{Vec } n)$ and $\Xi' = (n' : \text{Nat})(v' : \text{Vec } n')$, then $\Xi \cong \Xi' = (eq_n : n \cong n')(eq_v : v \cong v')$.

In order to prove $t\sigma \cong t'\sigma$ in the context $\tilde{\Gamma}$, we give for all contexts Ξ and all terms $\tilde{\Gamma}\Xi \vdash a : A$ a proof $\tilde{\Gamma}\Xi\Xi'(\Xi \cong \Xi') \vdash eq_a : a \cong a'$. As long as a is not a recursive call of the form $f \bar{u}$, we proceed by induction on the derivation of $\tilde{\Gamma}\Xi \vdash a : A$ (and hence also that of $\tilde{\Gamma}\Xi' \vdash a' : A'$). See Fig. 2, Fig. 3, and Fig. 4 for the relevant rules.

Var rule. In this case we have $a = x$ for some variable x from the context $\tilde{\Gamma}\Xi$. If it comes from $\tilde{\Gamma}$, we have $a' = x$ and hence $\tilde{\Gamma}\Xi\Xi'(\Xi \cong \Xi') \vdash \mathtt{refl} : x \cong x$. If on the other hand it comes from Ξ, we have $a' = x'$ and $eq_x : x \cong x' \in (\Xi \cong \Xi')$, hence $\tilde{\Gamma}\Xi\Xi'(\Xi \cong \Xi') \vdash eq_x : x \cong x'$ (where $eq_x : x \cong x' \in \Xi \cong \Xi'$).

=Ty rule. In this case we just proceed with the induction on the derivation of the first assumption of the rule.

Set rule. In this case we have $a = Set_i$ for some i, hence also $a' = Set_i$. So we have $\tilde{\Gamma}\Xi\Xi'(\Xi \cong \Xi') \vdash \mathtt{refl} : Set_i \cong Set_i$.

Π rule. In this case we have $a = (x : U) \to V$ and $a' = (x' : U') \to V' = (x' : U') \to V'[x \mapsto x']$. By the induction hypothesis, we have $\tilde{\Gamma}\Xi\Xi'(\Xi \cong \Xi') \vdash eq_U : U \cong U'$ and $\tilde{\Gamma}\Xi(x : U)\Xi'(x' : U')(\Xi \cong \Xi')(eq_x : x \cong x') \vdash eq_V : V \cong V'[x \mapsto x']$. This gives us $\tilde{\Gamma}\Xi\Xi'(\Xi \cong \Xi') \vdash \Pi\text{-cong } eq_U\ (\lambda x\ x'\ eq_x.\ eq_V) : (x : U) \to V \cong (x' : U') \to V'[x \mapsto x']$.

λ rule. In this case we have $a = \lambda(x : U).\ v$ and $a' = \lambda(x' : U').\ v'[x \mapsto x']$. By the induction hypothesis, we have $\tilde{\Gamma}\Xi\Xi'(\Xi \cong \Xi') \vdash eq_U : U \cong U'$ and $\tilde{\Gamma}\Xi(x : U)\Xi'(x' : U')(\Xi \cong \Xi')(eq_x : x \cong x') \vdash eq_v : v \cong v'[x \mapsto x']$. This gives us $\tilde{\Gamma}\Xi\Xi'(\Xi \cong \Xi') \vdash \lambda\text{-cong } eq_U\ (\lambda x\ x'\ eq_x.\ eq_v) : \lambda(x : U).\ v \cong \lambda(x' : U').\ v'[x \mapsto x']$.

App rule. In this case we have $a = g\ u$ and $a' = g'\ u'$. By the induction hypothesis, we have $\tilde{\Gamma}\Xi(x : U)\Xi'(x' : U')(\Xi \cong \Xi')(eq_x : x \cong x') \vdash eq_V : V \cong V'[x \mapsto x']$, $\tilde{\Gamma}\Xi\Xi'(\Xi \cong \Xi') \vdash eq_g : g \cong g'$, and $\tilde{\Gamma}\Xi\Xi'(\Xi \cong \Xi') \vdash eq_u : u \cong u'$. This gives us $\tilde{\Gamma}\Xi\Xi'(\Xi \cong \Xi') \vdash \mathtt{ap\text{-}cong}\ (\lambda x\ x'\ eq_x.\ eq_V)\ eq_g\ eq_u : g\ u \cong g'\ u'$.

Cons rule. In this case we have $a = c$ and $a' = c$ for a constructor c. This gives us $\tilde{\Gamma}\Xi\Xi'(\Xi \cong \Xi') \vdash \mathtt{refl} : c \cong c$.

Data rule. In this case we have $a = D$ and $a' = D$ for an inductive family D. Hence we have $\tilde{\Gamma}\Xi\Xi'(\Xi \cong \Xi') \vdash \mathtt{refl} : D \cong D$.

Func rule. In this case we have $a = g$ and $a' = g$ for a defined function g distinct from f and f'. Then we have $\tilde{\Gamma}\Xi\Xi'(\Xi \cong \Xi') \vdash \mathtt{refl} : g \cong g$.

In the end, we reach a recursive call: $a = f\ \bar{u}$ and $a' = f'\ \bar{u}'$. In this case, we recursively call the proof $\tilde{eq}_{f(\Delta)}$ which we are in the process of defining: $\tilde{\Gamma}\Xi\Xi'(\Xi \cong \Xi') \vdash \tilde{eq}_{f(\Delta)}\ \bar{u} : f\ \bar{u} \cong f'\ \bar{u}$. This call is structurally recursive because the recursive call to f in a is. By continuing the induction as above we also get $\tilde{\Gamma}\Xi\Xi'(\Xi \cong \Xi') \vdash eq_{\bar{u}} : \bar{u} \cong \bar{u}'$. By applying $\mathtt{ap\text{-}cong}$ repeatedly, we get $\tilde{\Gamma}\Xi\Xi'(\Xi \cong \Xi') \vdash eq_{f'(\bar{u})} : f'\ \bar{u} \cong f'\ \bar{u}'$, and by transivity of $\cong$, we get $\tilde{\Gamma}\Xi\Xi'(\Xi \cong \Xi') \vdash eq_{f(\bar{u})} : f\ \bar{u} \cong f'\ \bar{u}'$, completing the definition of $\tilde{eq}_{f(\Delta)}$ and hence also that of $\tilde{eq}_f$. Finally, by $\mathtt{het\text{-}to\text{-}hom}$ (16), we get eq_f such that $\Gamma \vdash eq_f : f \equiv f'$, finishing the proof. $\qquad\square$

8   Related Work

Dependent pattern matching was introduced by Coquand in [Coq92]. A big step toward its practical usefulness was the introduction of the 'with' construct by [MM04]. On a more fundamental level, [GMM06] shows that definitions by dependent pattern matching can be translated to pure type theory with the K axiom. Real languages with dependent pattern matching include Agda [Nor07], Coq [Soz10], and Idris [Bra13].

- In [Ken90], *tightest-match semantics* for overlapping patterns are used. To ensure confluence, they require for each pair of overlapping patterns that their unification is also part of the definition. In contrast to our current work, they do not look at the right-hand sides to check confluence.
- In the Calculus of Algebraic Constructions [BJO99] general well-typed rewriting rules are allowed. However, in order to prove confluence they have to assume that the left-hand sides of the rewrite rules do not overlap.
- In deduction modulo [DHK03], overlapping rewriting rules are allowed, but confluence is usually assumed or proven manually.
- In systems based on the LF logical framework and the $\lambda\Pi$-calculus (for example Twelf [PS99]), there can be overlapping clauses, but definitions are not required to be confluent. Instead backtracking is utilized to generate all possible solutions.
- In Isabelle/HOL, it is possible to define functions by pattern matching such that the result doesn't depend on the order of the patterns [Kra06]. In contrast to our work, they don't deal with dependent pattern matching, and they don't give a concrete algorithm for confluence checking.
- Even though we provide more definitional equalities than the standard formulation of pattern matching, some will always be missing. Another possibility would be to add a better support for coercion by propositional equality proofs, as supported for example by OTT [AMS07].
- The recent work on adding equations for neutral terms [ABM13] starts from a motivation similar to ours, but doesn't focus on pattern matching in specific.

9   Conclusion and Future Work

The main goal of this paper is to make dependent pattern matching more intuitively usable for specialists and non-specialists alike. We do this by extending the semantics of pattern matching in order to allow overlapping patterns. Because all clauses are interpreted as definitional equalities, these definitions behave as one would expect them to. This also makes pattern matching more amenable to equational reasoning. Type theory supports equational reasoning in the language itself by means of the identity type, so this is not just a theoretical advantage, but also a practical one.

In practice, a typical user would probably start by giving a non-overlapping definition and add overlapping clauses when he has a need for them. For example, when giving the clause `concat` $v\ \epsilon = v$ for the concatenation operator on vectors, the type checker complains that the length `plus` n `zero` of the left-hand side does not equal the length n of the right-hand side. The user can then add the clause `plus` n `zero` $= n$ to the definition of `plus`, after which the clause for `concat` passes the type checker. This blends well with the typical interactive development of dependently typed programs in dependently typed programming languages.

The current implementation is still very experimental. It would be interesting to give a full implementation that is compatible with extensions of pattern matching such as wildcard patterns, 'with'-expressions [MM04], and coinductive data types. It should also be possible to implement the pattern matching described in this paper in other languages with dependent pattern matching such as Coq.

One limit to our approach is that the confluence checker doesn't always see that a definition is confluent. This occurs when inaccessible patterns overlap with constructor patterns or other inaccessible patterns. This could be solved by improving the unification algorithm for patterns. Another case where the confluence check fails, is the definition of multiplication (13). This problem is not easily solved by improving the confluence checker, however. Rather, it depends crucially on the question whether we want to see $l + (m + n)$ and $(l + m) + n$ as 'the same' even if l, m and n are free variables.

When designing a dependently-typed programming language, a balance needs to be found w.r.t. the definitional equality. It typically includes at least β-equivalence for functions, but e.g. Agda additionally has definitional η-equivalence for functions and record types [Nor07]. Strengthening definitional equality generally increases programmer convenience but makes equality and type-checking harder for the compiler to decide and may exclude certain models of the theory. When adding functions defined by pattern matching to the theory, definitional equality needs to be extended with their computational behaviour as in the Clause rule of Fig. 4. In this setting, our work can be seen as allowing functions with overlapping reduction rules that cannot be reduced to the non-overlapping rules of data type eliminators. Our new compromise is that we allow overlapping reduction rules as long as confluence can be checked definitionally. We think our approach strikes an interesting new balance between having too little and too many definitional equalities: have any less evaluation rules, and overlapping clauses cannot all hold as definitional equalities; have any more, and extra equalities have to be introduced to regain confluence.

As with any modification to type theory, there is the question of soundness. We think that Theorem 3 gives a step in the right direction, but it is an interesting question whether any extra requirements are needed in order to give a definitive answer. A practical use of this theorem is *program extraction*: since we have $f \cong f'$, these functions both give the same results for *closed* arguments. In a compiled program, only closed terms are evaluated so we can freely replace f by f'. Because f' can be compiled to a case tree, this increases the efficiency of the extracted program.

Acknowledgments. This research is partially funded by the Research Fund KU Leuven, and by the Research Foundation - Flanders under grant number G004321N. Jesper Cockx and Dominique Devriese both hold a Ph.D. fellowship of the Research Foundation - Flanders (FWO).

References

Ab12.   Abel, A.: Agda: equality,
         http://www2.tcs.ifi.lmu.de/~abel/Equality.pdf
ABM13.   Allais, G., Boutillier, P., McBride, C.: New equations for neutral terms.
         Dependently-Typed Programming (2013)

AMS07.   Altenkirch, T., McBride, C., Swierstra, W.: Observational equality, now! Programming languages meets program verification (2007)

BJO99.   Blanqui, F., Jouannaud, J., Okada, M.: The calculus of algebraic constructions. Rewriting Techniques and Applications (1999)

Bla04.   Blanqui, F.: A type-based termination criterion for dependently-typed higher-order rewrite systems. Rewriting Techniques and Applications (2004)

BP85.   Bachmair, L., Plaisted, D.A.: Termination orderings for associative-commutative rewriting systems. Journal of Symbolic Computation 1, 4 (1985)

Bra13.   Brady, E.: Idris, a General Purpose Dependently Typed Programming Language: Design and Implementation. JFP 23(5) (2013)

Coc13.   Cockx, J.: Overlapping and order-independent patterns in type theory. Master thesis, KU Leuven (2013)

Coq92.   Coquand, T.: Pattern matching with dependent types. Types for proofs and programs (1992)

DHK03.   Dowek, G., Hardin, T., Kirchner, C.: Theorem proving modulo. Journal of Automated Reasoning (2003)

Dyb94.   Dybjer, P.: Inductive families. Formal Aspects of Computing 6(4) (1994)

GMM06.   Goguen, H., McBride, C., McKinna, J.: Eliminating dependent pattern matching. Algebra, Meaning, and Computation (2006)

Hof95.   Hofmann, M.: Extensional concepts in intensional type theory. PhD thesis, University of Edinburgh (1995)

Hud89.   Hudak, P.: Conception, evolution, and application of functional programming languages. ACM Computing Surveys 21(3) (1989)

Ken90.   Kennaway, R.: The specificity rule for lazy pattern-matching in ambiguous term rewrite systems. In: Jones, N.D. (ed.) ESOP 1990. LNCS, vol. 432, pp. 256–270. Springer, Heidelberg (1990)

Kra06.   Krauss, A.: Partial recursive functions in higher-order logic. Automated Reasoning (2006)

LJB01.   Lee, C.S., Jones, N.D., Ben-Amram, A.M.: The size-change principle for program termination. ACM SIGPLAN Notices 36(3) (2001)

Luo94.   Luo, Z.: Computation and reasoning: a type theory for computer science. International Series of Monographs on Computer Science 11 (1994)

McB00.   McBride, C.: Dependently typed functional programs and their proofs. PhD thesis, University of Edinburgh (2000)

ML84.   Martin-Löf, P.: Intuitionistic type theory. Studies in Proof Theory 1 (1984)

MM04.   McBride, C., McKinna, J.: The view from the left. JFP 14(1) (2004)

Nor07.   Norell, U.: Towards a practical programming language based on dependent type theory. PhD Thesis, Chalmers University of Technology (2007)

PS99.   Pfenning, F., Schürmann, C.: System description: Twelf - a meta-logical framework for deductive systems. In: Ganzinger, H. (ed.) CADE 1999. LNCS (LNAI), vol. 1632, pp. 202–206. Springer, Heidelberg (1999)

Soz10.   Sozeau, M.: Equations: A dependent pattern-matching compiler. In: Kaufmann, M., Paulson, L.C. (eds.) ITP 2010. LNCS, vol. 6172, pp. 419–434. Springer, Heidelberg (2010)

VCW12.   Vytiniotis, D., Coquand, T., Wahlstedt, D.: Stop when you are almost-full. In: Beringer, L., Felty, A. (eds.) ITP 2012. LNCS, vol. 7406, pp. 250–265. Springer, Heidelberg (2012)

Verified Compilation for Shared-Memory C

Lennart Beringer[1], Gordon Stewart[1], Robert Dockins[2],
and Andrew W. Appel[1]

[1] Princeton University
[2] Portland State University

Abstract. We present a new architecture for specifying and proving optimizing compilers in the presence of shared-memory interactions such as buffer-based system calls, shared-memory concurrency, and separate compilation. The architecture, which is implemented in the context of CompCert, includes a novel interaction-oriented model for C-like languages, and a new proof technique, called *logical simulation relations*, for compositionally proving compiler correctness with respect to this interaction model. We apply our techniques to CompCert's primary memory-reorganizing compilation phase, Cminorgen. Our results are formalized in Coq, building on the recently released CompCert 2.0.

1 Introduction

Shared-memory cooperation—the coordinated use of memory by several static or dynamic execution units—occurs ubiquitously in systems software. *Sequential* applications exchange pointers across module boundaries; *concurrent* threads interact via memory synchronization and by communicating pointers to shared data; nearly all programs communicate via memory with libraries and make pointer-valued system calls. Correct compilers—that preserve program safety and functional specifications—must respect a program's effects on memory.

Yet optimizing compilers for system languages such as C routinely perform code transformations that *alter* memory behavior. They relocate or eliminate load and store operations, they coalesce allocation events (especially as local variables are formulated into a stack frame), and they delete and insert loads, stores, stack allocations, and stack frees. For example, consider the CompCert verified optimizing C compiler [Ler11]. To limit pointer aliasing and perform efficient register allocation, CompCert identifies in an early compiler phase all local variables whose addresses are not taken. These unaddressed variables are shifted from in-memory blocks in function stack frames to register-allocated compiler temporaries. The variables are thus "removed from memory" (though some may later be spilled back into memory after register allocation).

Optimizing transformations are important for generating efficient code, yet also complicate the compiler's specification as it relates to memory. Correctness of any phase that adjusts the memory layout must preserve the program's memory behavior. However, it is not clear what "preservation of memory behavior" means when the compiler may introduce or remove memory effects. The difficulties are even more acute when translation units may be *separately compiled*, since

Z. Shao (Ed.): ESOP 2014, LNCS 8410, pp. 107–127, 2014.

a pointer passed as an argument between modules may need to be translated depending on the (intermediate) languages in which the modules are expressed.

To address these issues, we present a novel framework for specifying C-like languages—imperative languages with low-level memory models—and their translations. The framework consists of two major components.

First, we develop a new interaction model, *core semantics*, that describes communication between execution threads with pointer exchange. A thread, or *core*, might represent true concurrency, or a sequential call to an external function. Crucially, our model is *language-independent*, separating thread-local data such as the control stack and local environment from global data such as shared memory. The caller of an external function thus need not know in which language the invoked function is implemented—a necessary precondition even for the *specification* of separate compilation and linking.

Second, we introduce *logical simulation relations (LSRs)*, a notion of compiler correctness that supports the core semantics model. Critically important—and a major contribution of our work—is a proof that LSRs compose transitively. Transitivity is essential for compositional verification of multiphase compilers.

We develop our framework in the concrete setting of CompCert. CompCert is an ideal testbed for three reasons: (i) it is the only publicly available optimizing C compiler that is equipped with a formal specification and correctness proof; (ii) CompCert provides a uniform memory model across all intermediate languages, a prerequisite for meaningful pointer communication; and (iii) CompCert punts on shared-memory cooperation, by disallowing communication of pointers to dynamically allocated data. CompCert's transitivity proof is dependent on this restriction, but in consequence, even basic interactions with system calls such as Linux `read` and `write` cannot be validated. Our framework reformulates CompCert's correctness theorem to lift these restrictions.

Contributions and Outline

i. We provide a detailed analysis of the tensions that result when proving compiler correctness in the shared-memory setting (§2). Our analysis is conducted in the concrete setting of CompCert and its memory model.

ii. We present *core semantics*, a new execution model for C-like languages (§3). Core semantics capture the interactions between a running thread, or core, and its environment via calls to external functions. Unlike in current CompCert, our execution model enables pointer sharing at interaction points.

iii. We develop (§4) a language-independent notion of shared-memory compiler correctness, called *logical simulation relations (LSRs)*, that is compatible with all three classes of memory transformations employed by CompCert. Our model of compiler correctness is *transitively composable*, a result that is necessary for the verification of multiphase compilers.

iv. Our approach requires minimal changes to CompCert's existing machine-checked correctness proofs. We demonstrate a proof adaptation for the hardest case, Cminorgen (§6).

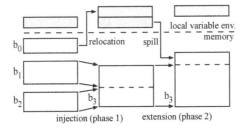

Fig. 1. CompCert block-level memory transformations

v. Our operational-semantic model supports the soundness proof of expressive program logics. For example, we have formalized the soundness proof of a step-indexed program logic for C light [A+14], but could support XCAP-like syntactic models [NS06] just as well. Section 5 briefly describes the connection of the C light logic to the techniques of this paper.

2   Technical Challenges and Approach

The technical challenges inherent in adapting CompCert to support shared memory lie in three major areas: the CompCert memory model, the Comp-Cert correctness proofs, and the compiler's specification of external functions. This section motivates, with examples, the main technical challenges in each of these three areas, and outlines our solutions.

2.1   The CompCert C Memory Model

The semantics of pointer arithmetic, pointer comparison, and other "messy" features of C led Leroy, Blazy *et al.* to strike a balance in the design of CompCert's memory model [LB08,L+12] between concreteness and abstraction. Concreteness is necessary to model C's low-level memory behavior, such as aliasing and partial overlap of word-sized loads due to pointer arithmetic. Abstraction is needed for high-level reasoning. These competing requirements have led to a memory model—for use in operational semantics—that is elegant, yet inherently complex.

CompCert models memory as a set of *blocks*, the sizes of which are fixed at allocation time. Addresses are pairs of a block-number and an *offset*, which is an integer pointing to a particular location within the block. Pointer arithmetic is allowed within blocks but not across blocks. CompCert allocates a fresh block for each local variable, thus permitting pointer arithmetic *within* a local (array or struct) variable, but not across them. A stack-allocated char array of size n would be allocated an n-byte block, whereas a local integer variable occupies a block of size 4 (on 32-bit architectures).

This memory model is used in all operational semantics from C, through several intermediate languages, to assembly language. Because CompCert may alter a program's memory layout during compilation, the model must also support *memory transformations.* The transformations include (1) removal from function activation records of scalar local variables that are never addressed with the & operator, and (2) spilling of local variables that could not be register-allocated. Figure 1 depicts these transformations schematically. In CompCert's variable relocation phase (labeled *injection* in the diagram), local variables that are never addressed (here, block 0) are moved from memory into a local variable environment. Additionally in this phase, CompCert coalesces the distinct memory blocks of the local variables for each function activation (here, blocks 1 and 2) into a single block representing the entire activation record (block 3). It is sound to merge blocks—thus permitting more pointer arithmetic in the target program than in the source program—because we assume that the source program did not go wrong: *i.e.*, did not do forbidden cross-variable pointer arithmetic.

To model phase (1), CompCert introduces a generic form of memory embedding called *memory injection*: a block-wise partial function of the form $\mathcal{B} \rightharpoonup \mathcal{B} \times \mathcal{Z}$. Here $\mathcal{B}$ is a countable set of blocks. The second component $\mathcal{Z}$ of the result pair is an integer offset that is applied, in the resulting memory, uniformly to every address in the mapped block. For example, assuming four byte blocks in the source language, the memory injection in phase (1) would be specified as, $b_0 \mapsto \mathsf{None}$ $b_1 \mapsto \mathsf{Some}\ (b_3, 4)$ $b_2 \mapsto \mathsf{Some}\ (b_3, 0)$.

Block b_0 is unmapped because it is not addressed, block b_1 is mapped to block b_3 at offset 4 and block b_2 is mapped to block b_3 at offset 0. Thus a load from block b_1 at offset 0 becomes a load from block b_3 at offset 4 after the transformation.

Variables in the local variable environment do not have addresses, but may be spilled back into memory in phase (2) (labeled *extension* in Figure 1) after register allocation. Spilling requires that certain (stack-frame) blocks be *extended* (here, block 3) to make room for the spilled variables. Extension of a block is modeled by a change in *memory permissions*, which record the level of access allowed (read, write, etc.) at a particular memory location.

CompCert 1.x's[1] memory injections and memory extensions did not compose. This was not a problem for CompCert 1.x because memory was not exposed at external calls. We discuss the solution for CompCert 2.x in Section 4.1.

Permission Changes. A different limitation of CompCert 1.x is its operational model of memory-access permissions: at each abstract block number, a range $lo \dots hi$ of addresses could be read or written. Calling a function would allocate a new (stack) block, returning would deallocate (without reusing block numbers).

Consider a source-level program logic for shared-memory concurrency, such as Concurrent Separation Logic [O'H07], in which we prove that a synchronization

---

[1] We describe as **CompCert 1.x** early versions of CompCert dating from 2006 in which Leroy *et al.* focused on whole-program single-threaded execution. Certain releases between 1.0 and 2.0 have incorporated several technical suggestions that resulted from the work reported in this paper and from discussions with Leroy. We describe as **CompCert 2.x** the 2.0 release, incorporating these changes, and near-future CompCert versions in which other adjustments to the specification may be made to improve compositionality of shared-memory interaction. Of course, between CompCert 1.0 and 2.0, Leroy *et al.* made many other unrelated enhancements.

operation (lock acquire/release) adds or removes write or read permission to some set of addresses. To communicate the *result* of the program-logic reasoning to CompCert, without embedding the entire program logic into CompCert, we now use a finer-grain permission structure in the operational semantics: byte by byte, read or write [L+12]. External functions (such as lock-acquire, lock-release) may change the permissions in arbitrary and nondeterministic ways.[2] Reasoning in the program logic ensures that the source program (with its operational permission changes) is safe. These permissions in the operational semantics will not exist physically when executing the compiled program.

CompCert 1.x could not permit this; it could not even permit general system calls such as `brk` to change memory permissions; `malloc` and `free` could not be modeled as system calls, so had to be special built-ins. The new permission model allows for expressive proofs about correct compilation of synchronized shared-memory programs.

2.2   The CompCert Correctness Proofs

The correctness proofs of the CompCert phases generally take the form of *forward simulations* to deterministic languages. By proving receptiveness of the source language, CompCert recovers event trace equivalence from the forward simulation proofs, for a limited class of events not containing pointers to stack or heap data. For shared-memory interaction, the events in CompCert 1.x's event traces are simply too inexpressive; but we *will* use forward simulations.[3]

A forward simulation proof consists of a *measured simulation relation* between the states of the source and target languages and a proof that the simulation relation can be re-established over execution steps. For example, in the proof of CompCert's variable relocation phase, the simulation relation asserts that the values of variables that have been removed from memory match the contents of the blocks from which the variables were relocated. That is, a four byte load from block b_0 in Figure 1 should produce the same value as evaluation of the associated local variable in the environment that results after the injection. "Measured" means the simulations allow multiple source language steps to correspond to zero target language steps, as long as there is a well-founded order on source language states that decreases at each step.

---

[2] CompCert need not know which external functions do what; any external call may change memory permissions. Standard optimizing compilers such as `gcc` behave consistently with similar conservative assumptions. In principle, one could tell CompCert that lock-acquire only increases permissions, and lock-release only decreases them; then CompCert could hoist loads/stores past these calls (down, and up, respectively).

[3] Forward simulations are adequate because: We determinize multithreading with an external oracle (schedule), we transform racy loads/stores into "external calls" (which the compiler cannot remove or reschedule). Nonracy loads/stores are thread-modular by Dijkstra/Hoare (Pthreads) locking, modeled by (implicit virtual) permission transfers at acquire/release events; load/store without permission is "stuck" in the source program. In summary, no unmatched target behaviors are possible.

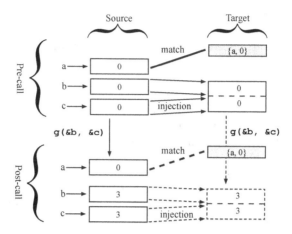

Fig. 2. Schematic CompCert simulation diagram for f's call to external function g. Compilation goes left-to-right; execution goes top-to-bottom.

CompCert 1.x permits calls to *external functions* that take numeric parameters and do not access shared memory. For whole-program embedded applications without an operating system, such an external function could drive an actuator or read a scalar value from a sensor. But more generally in the C language, external functions are just those that are declared within the current module (as **extern**) but defined, or implemented, in another.

```
//Module A
extern void g(int *d, int *e);

int f(void) {
    int a=0, b=0, c=0;
    g(&b, &c);
    return a + b + c;
}
```

```
//Module B

void g(int *d, int *e) {
    *d = 3;
    *e = 3;
}
```

For example, module A above declares an external function g taking two integer pointers as parameters and returning void. It also defines an *internal* function f calling g with the addresses of f's local variables b and c as arguments. Module B defines g to perform side effects on the pointers that are passed.

Now imagine CompCert compiles module A through its variable relocation phase, with external module B remaining uncompiled. The memory state before and after the memory injection, just before external function g is called, is shown in the top half of Figure 2. The simulation invariant, pre-call, says that the value in memory at address &a in the source (*i.e.*, before variable relocation) equals the value of the variable a in the local variable environment in the target, after variable relocation. In the diagram, we depict this constraint as a bold line labeled "match" connecting the two boxes along the compilation axis.

To preserve semantics, CompCert needs to show that at the point of the external call, g will succeed in the injected memory state assuming it succeeded before memory injection, and that the "match" relation can be re-established after the call, assuming it held initially. This proof corresponds to the completion of the lower half of the diagram in Figure 2. We must find a state that (1) results from running g with injected arguments; (2) is the injection of the lower left state; and (3) satisfies the match invariant with respect to the lower left. But an issue arises when we attempt to establish (3). To retain expressiveness, we must give external functions the freedom to mutate memory. On the other hand, simulation proofs for modules such as A should be able to safely assume that certain portions of memory remain unchanged by external calls. For example, the value in memory at address &a above, which is private to module A because the location has not been leaked as a parameter to g, should match the value assigned to a in the local variable environment both before and after the call to function g. How to reconcile these opposing concerns?

2.3   External Functions

CompCert 1.x maintains a distinction between "public" and "private" memory, but does so in a way that restricts the kinds of external functions that may be defined. To see why, consider CompCert 1.13's specification of external calls, modeled as a relation on the function arguments, the initial memory, the return value, and the final memory. We call this relation ec_sem, for external-call semantics. The axiom for external calls is: Suppose

- ec_sem ge $\overrightarrow{v_1}$ m_1 rv_1 m_1'; inject j m_1 m_2 (we use notation $m_1 \rightarrowtail_j m_2$ for this);
- block validity, and permissions (see below) are suitably preserved; we use notation forward m_1 m_1' for this; and
- val_list_inject j $\overrightarrow{v_1}$ $\overrightarrow{v_2}$ (notation: $\overrightarrow{v_1} \rightarrowtail_j \overrightarrow{v_2}$);

that is, in the *source language*, in global environment ge, calling a particular function with parameters $\overrightarrow{v_1}$ and memory m_1 yields return-value rv_1 and memory m_1'; and there is a source-to-target memory injection j injecting $\overrightarrow{v_1}$ into $\overrightarrow{v_2}$, and m_1 into m_2. Then there must exist a post-call injection j' extending j (notation $j \leq j'$), and rv_2 and m_2' such that:

- ec_sem ge $\overrightarrow{v_2}$ m_2 rv_2 m_2'; forward m_2 m_2'; $rv_1 \rightarrowtail_{j'} rv_2$; $m_1' \rightarrowtail_{j'} m_2'$;
- unchOn (loc_unmapped j) m_1 m_1'; and unchOn (loc_out_of_reach j m_1) m_2 m_2'.

That is, at every external function call (ec_sem ge $\overrightarrow{v_1}$ m_1 rv_1 m_1') one can complete the simulation diagram (ec_sem ge $\overrightarrow{v_2}$ m_2 rv_2 m_2') for compiler phases that adjust the memory representation via a memory injection. (CompCert imposes a similar restriction in the memory extension case.) Also, on locations such as &a that are unmapped by the memory injection, the memory remains unmodified (unchOn, "unchanged on") in the pre-transformation execution. Memory locations in the post-transformation states that have empty permission initially, before the injection is applied (loc_out_of_reach j m_1), must remain unmodified by the external function call.

There are two problems with these restrictions. The first is that they impose a big-step semantics on external calls. Clause ec_sem ge $\vec{v_2}$ m_2 rv_2 m'_2 requires that the external function terminate, in one step, when executed in m_2. This requirement is incompatible with external functions implemented by potentially nonterminating code, or that might block in a concurrent setting.

The second problem lies with the restrictions on how external function calls may mutate memory (clauses beginning unchOn. . .). The unchOn P m m' clauses have two effects. They ensure that (1) external calls do not modify, in the pre-compilation memories m_1 and m'_1, locations which are unmapped by the memory injection j (loc_unmapped); and (2) they ensure that external calls do not modify locations in m_2 which were unreachable in m_1 under j (loc_out_of_reach). The problem here is that CompCert is using injections both to specify the memory transformations performed by the compiler, and to axiomatize the behavior of external function calls. In other words, restrictions on which locations external calls may mutate are keyed to the compiler transformations themselves. (Locations mapped by a memory injection are made public, whereas unmapped locations, e.g., &a in the example above, remain private.) Unfortunately, this dual-purpose use of memory injections (and extensions) fails to account for situations in which the external function is *itself* code, perhaps a second CompCert translation unit, that is compiled independently from the calling module.

To illustrate the issues that arise when external functions are compiled, consider the case in which the function g of module B *itself* contains an unaddressed local variable, say h, which is relocated out of memory by CompCert's variable relocation phase.

```
void g(int *d, int *e) {      //Module B'
  int h = <expr>; *d = h; *e = <expr>;
}
```

By the above axiom, module B' must not mutate memory blocks that are subsequently removed from memory by compilation (here, the block containing variable h). Yet this is exactly what module B' does when it assigns to h. Indeed, since h is a private local variable, the modification is perfectly acceptable behavior.

3   Core Semantics

The first major part of our solution is to define a uniform, protocol-oriented interface to languages that interact with their environments. Imagine a multithread shared-memory execution. One can spawn a new thread; a thread may yield (or block on a synchronization) and perhaps later resume; eventually a thread may exit. We use this model not only for concurrency but also for sequential calls to separately compiled functions (spawn a new "thread" to run the call, block until it returns) and for a single thread running in an operating-system context with system calls. When a thread yields (or calls a sequential external function), its local state including stack and registers will be preserved until it resumes, but the state of most of memory may have changed arbitrarily upon resumption.

Core semantics (Figure 3) are a general formulation of a thread protocol. At a high level, a core semantics (G, C, M) is a partitioning of a thread's state into a *global environment* (G), a *local* part (C), which we call the *core state*, or *core*, and which typically includes both the control continuation and local variable environment, and a shared part (M), which we typically identify with shared memory. V is the type of values, and $\mathcal{F}$ is the type of external function names.

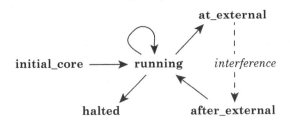

Fig. 3. Core Semantics interface

The types G (global environment), C (core state), and M (memory) are parameters to the interface. $\mathcal{F}$ is the type of external function identifiers. V is the type of values, and $\mathbb{T}$ is Coq's type of propositions, Prop. The names initial_core, at_external, after_external, halted are not constructors, but are (proved) disjoint predicates.

$$\text{initial\_core} : G \to V \to \text{list } V \to \text{option } C$$
$$\text{at\_external} : C \to \text{option } (\mathcal{F} \times \text{list } V)$$
$$\text{after\_external} : \text{option } V \to C \to \text{option } C$$
$$\text{halted} : C \to \text{option } V$$
$$\text{corestep} : G \to C \to M \to C \to M \to \mathbb{T}$$

With this partitioning comes a step relation (corestep) on core states and memories that defines the small-step operational model of the core semantics. We will often write the **corestep** relation as $ge \vdash \langle c, m \rangle \longmapsto \langle c', m' \rangle$. The global environment ge maps functions to their definitions and does not vary.

In a (concurrently or sequentially) multithreaded system, different cores could have different core types (C) and different **corestep** relations. This permits interoperation of modules written in different languages. But such a surrounding system, modeling (respectively) a scheduler or a linker, is not needed for specifying compilation. This is an important separation of concerns.

To enforce the protocol described above, we divide core states into the five *lifetime* stages. *Initial* cores result directly from the creation of the thread or initialization of the program using initial_core. Typically, an initial core contains an empty local environment, together with a control continuation consisting of a single function call (the V parameter in the definition), with arguments (list V). For a standalone program, this function is `main`; for a thread, it is the function that was forked; for a call to a separately compiled module, it is the called function. At_external cores are those initiating an external function call. In C terminology, external functions are just functions that are declared within the current translation unit or module but which are defined elsewhere (*e.g.*, in a module that is later linked to the current one). After_external cores result from resumption of the thread or program after an external call. In the transition from after_external to a running state, a core is expected to incorporate the return value (option $\mathcal{V}$) into its local variables (in its own language-dependent way). Halted cores are just that: threads or programs that have terminated normally, yielding an optional return value (option $\mathcal{V}$). Finally, *running* cores are neither blocked on an external function call nor halted.

Preemption. The core semantics protocol is nonpreemptive—it does not *directly* model thread preemption that may result from interrupt handling. We can make this simplification—even though the underlying machine-language system may do preemption—because we write well-synchronized *race-free* code. Our source-level program logic verifies a stronger property than race-freedom: every memory access is performed with permission, and synchronization ensures that no two threads have conflicting permissions to a given address. Race-free programs running in a nonpreemptive semantics soundly approximate race-free programs in an interleaving semantics. Moreover, we are interested ultimately in proving correctness of the logic and compilation toolchain with respect to weak memory models—on such machines, *interleaving* is not even the right model. Race-free programs have sequentially consistent behavior on all well-behaved weakly consistent machines.[4] In our approach, the compiler correctness theorems can be oblivious of preemption and weak cache coherence—they just follow the rules of operational memory permissions.

3.1   Example: C Light

As an example of a core semantics, we show CompCert C light. This high-level subset of C is the target of CompCert's first translation phase (from the full CompCert C language). It serves as a natural interface between CompCert, user-level program logics, and verified static analyses.

Figure 4 gives the syntax of C light. The syntax of expressions a is standard. In the statement syntax, `for` and `while` loops have already been translated (in an earlier compiler phase) to combinations of the more primitive Sloop and Sbreak constructs. The details of local control flow (loop, if, break, continue, switch, goto) are standard CompCert 1.13 Clight, and not relevant to (or changed by) our work on external interaction.

Functions F are either internal (defined in the current translation unit) or external (declared here but defined elsewhere). Internal functions comprise a record containing the function return type, a list of function parameters with their types, a local variable environment for address-taken variables, a temporaries environment for the rest of the function variables, and the function body. External functions comprise an external function identifier f, a list of argument

---

[4] This is not a theorem, it's better than a theorem: it is the *definition* of "well-behaved" for weakly consistent memory models.

Statements:

$$s ::= \text{Sskip} \qquad\qquad \text{no-op}$$

$\mid$	Sassign a_1 a_2	lval ← rval
$\mid$	Sset id a	temp ← rval
$\mid$	Scall $optid$ a $\overrightarrow{a}$	function call
$\mid$	Sbuiltin $optid$ f $\overrightarrow{\tau}$ $\overrightarrow{a}$	intrinsic
$\mid$	Ssequence s_1 s_2	sequence
$\mid$	Sifthenelse a s_1 s_2	conditional
$\mid$	Sloop s_1 s_2	infinite loop
$\mid$	Sbreak $\mid$ Sreturn a_{opt}	break/return
$\mid$	Scontinue s	continue stmt.
$\mid$	Switch s $\mid$ Slabel l s $\mid$ Sgoto l	

Internal Functions:

$$F_i ::= \{ \text{ returnType } \tau; \quad \text{fun. ret. type}$$

params $\overrightarrow{(id, \tau)}$;	params./types
locals ρ_v;	local var. env.
temps ρ_t;	temp. env.
body s $\}$	function body

Internal & External Fun. Definitions:

$$\tau ::= \text{int} \mid \text{float} \mid \text{long} \mid \text{single}$$
$$F ::= \text{Internal } F_i$$
$$\mid \text{External } f \ \overrightarrow{\tau} \ \tau$$

Fig. 4. Syntax of C light

types $\overrightarrow{\tau}$ and a return type τ, where τ is int, float, long, or single (single-precision floats). External functions do not contain a function body. The core semantics for C light will stop at external calls and yield control to the execution environment.

Semantics. Figure 5 shows our reformulation of the internal and external function call rules of the C light operational semantics. The operational semantics is a three-place relation on global environments $ge : G$, initial configurations $\langle c, m \rangle$ and final configurations $\langle c', m' \rangle$. Here c is a core state; m is a CompCert memory. The relation $ge \vdash a \Downarrow_{\rho_v, \rho_t, m} v$ denotes big-step evaluation of expression a to value v in global environment ge, local variable environment ρ_v, temporaries environment ρ_t, and memory m.

We instantiate the type C of the core semantics interface to C light as follows.

$$c \in C ::= \text{RunState } \rho_v \ \rho_t \ \kappa \qquad\qquad \text{"running" states}$$
$$\mid \text{ExtCallState } f \ sig \ \overrightarrow{v} \ optid \ \rho_v \ \rho_t \ \kappa \qquad \text{at\_external states}$$

RunStates are normal execution states. ExtCallStates are calls to an external function f, with arguments $\overrightarrow{v}$. Parameter $optid$ is an optional return value variable (= None when the function has void return type). The control continuation κ is a stack of suspended commands and function activations. In the ExtCallState constructor, sig is the external function type signature.

Next, we define the at_external function of the core semantics interface as a straightforward match on a core state c, returning Some $(f, \overrightarrow{v})$ when c is an ExtCallState, and None otherwise.

After_external takes as arguments an optional return value v_{ret} (again, None is used for void functions) and a core state c. If c is an ExtCallState and the return value is not None, then the temporary environment is updated to reflect the new return value. After_external will return None if c is not a proper external call state or if the return value and return variable are incompatible.

Readers familiar with CompCert 1.x will observe the proximity of our definition to Leroy *et al.*'s presentation: our adaptation removes the memory

$$\frac{ge \vdash a \Downarrow_{\rho_v,\rho_t,m} v_f \quad ge \vdash \overrightarrow{a} \Downarrow_{\rho_v,\rho_t,m} \overrightarrow{v} \quad ge[v_f] = \mathsf{Some}\ (\mathsf{Internal}\ F_i)}{\mathsf{typeOf}\ F_i = \mathsf{Tfunction}\ \overrightarrow{\tau}\ \tau \quad \mathsf{allocVars}\ \rho_{\emptyset}\ m\ (\mathsf{locals}\ F_i) = (\rho'_v, m')}$$

$$\frac{\mathsf{bindParams}\ (\mathsf{params}\ F_i)\ \overrightarrow{v}\ (\mathsf{initTempEnv}\ (\mathsf{temps}\ F_i)) = \mathsf{Some}\ \rho'_t}{ge \vdash \langle\mathsf{RunState}(\rho_v, \rho_t, \mathsf{Scall}\ optid\ a\ \overrightarrow{a} \cdot \kappa), m\rangle \longmapsto}$$
$$\langle\mathsf{RunState}(\rho'_v, \rho'_t, \mathsf{body}\ F_i \cdot \mathsf{Sreturn}\ \mathsf{None} \cdot \mathsf{Kcall}\ optid\ F_i\ \rho_v\ \rho_t\ \kappa), m'\rangle$$

$$\text{(SCALLINTERNAL)}$$

$$\frac{ge \vdash a \Downarrow_{\rho_v,\rho_t,m} v_f \quad ge \vdash \overrightarrow{a} \Downarrow_{\rho_v,\rho_t,m} \overrightarrow{v} \quad ge[v_f] = \mathsf{Some}\ (\mathsf{External}\ f\ \overrightarrow{\tau}\ \tau)}{ge \vdash \langle\mathsf{RunState}(\rho_v, \rho_t, \mathsf{Scall}\ optid\ a\ \overrightarrow{a} \cdot \kappa), m\rangle \longmapsto}$$
$$\langle\mathsf{ExtCallState}(f, \overrightarrow{\tau}, \tau, \overrightarrow{v}, optid, \rho_v, \rho_t, \kappa), m\rangle$$

$$\text{(SCALLEXTERNAL)}$$

Fig. 5. Internal and external call rules from the operational semantics of C light

components from the two state constructors RunState and ExtCallState and adds the definitions of after_external and so on. The operational semantics (not shown) arises by refactoring the existing definition in accordance with these state representation changes and removing the rule for external function calls: such calls are now handled by the generic core-semantics interface.

4 Logical Simulation Relations

To adapt compiler correctness to the core semantics of Section 3 in a composable way, we take inspiration from the well established notion of type-indexed logical relations. Given a pair of core semantics, our notion of compiler correctness takes the form of a forward simulation, a correspondence relation between cores that is structure-preserving in source-to-target direction. Given the absence of sufficiently expressive type structure, *preservation of structure* in our case amounts to compatibility with the cores' lifetime stages.

CompCert distinguishes among three kinds of translations: *memory equality passes* leave memory unaffected but may modify the representation or operational behavior of cores; *memory extension passes* may enlarge existing memory blocks (by increasing the block size during allocation) and increase the definedness of memory-held values, but do not add or remove blocks; *memory injection passes* may discard or merge blocks by eliminating or coalescing allocation instructions. Our simulation relation accordingly defines distinct clauses for the three cases. Definition 1 below details the clause for injection passes, where $j, j', \ldots : \mathcal{B} \rightharpoonup \mathcal{B} \times \mathcal{Z}$ indicate block relocations (*e.g.*, $j\ b = (b', z)$ relocates block b to a contiguous region in block b', starting at offset z), $j \le j'$ indicates inclusion of relocations, $j \bowtie_{m_1;m_2} j'$ denotes that for any entry $j'\ b_1 = (b_2, z)$ not present in j, blocks $b_{\{1,2\}}$ must be unallocated in $m_{\{1,2\}}$, and $m_1 \rightarrowtail_j m_2$ indicates that m_2 is m_1's image under j (and similarly for $\overrightarrow{v_1} \rightarrowtail_j \overrightarrow{v_2}$).

Definition 1 (Measured Forward Simulation (Injection Case)). *Let M be the type of CompCert memories; $L_1 = (G_1, C_1, M)$ be the source core semantics; $L_2 = (G_2, C_2, M)$ be the target core semantics; $ge_1 : G_1$ be some source global environment; $ge_2 : G_2$ be some target global environment.*

Then we say there is a measured forward simulation for injections *from L_1 to L_2 (notation $L_1 \preceq_{\mathsf{Inj}} L_2$) if there exist a well-founded-order $<$ and a family of relations $(\sim_j) : C_1 \to M \to C_2 \to M \to \mathbb{T}$ on cores and memory states, indexed by memory injections, such that the following hold.*

1. *If* initial_core $ge_1 \ u_1 \ \overrightarrow{v_1} = $ Some c_1; entryPoints $u_1 \ u_2 \ sig$; $m_1 \rightarrowtail_j m_2$; and $\overrightarrow{v_1} \rightarrowtail_j \overrightarrow{v_2}$ then there exists c_2 such that initial_core $ge_2 \ u_2 \ \overrightarrow{v_2} = $ Some c_2 and $\langle c_1, m_1 \rangle \sim_j \langle c_2, m_2 \rangle$.

2. *If* halted $c_1 = $ Some v_1 and $\langle c_1, m_1 \rangle \sim_j \langle c_2, m_2 \rangle$ then there exists v_2 such that halted $c_2 = $ Some v_2, $v_1 \rightarrowtail_j v_2$, and $m_1 \rightarrowtail_j m_2$.

3. *If* $ge_1 \vdash \langle c_1, m_1 \rangle \longmapsto \langle c_1', m_1' \rangle$ then for all c_2, j, m_2 such that $\langle c_1, m_1 \rangle \sim_j \langle c_2, m_2 \rangle$, there exist c_2', m_2', j' for which $j \leq j'$; $j \bowtie_{m_1;m_2} j'$; and $\langle c_1', m_1' \rangle \sim_{j'} \langle c_2', m_2' \rangle$; and either
   - $ge_2 \vdash \langle c_2, m_2 \rangle \longmapsto^+ \langle c_2', m_2' \rangle$; or
   - $ge_2 \vdash \langle c_2, m_2 \rangle \longmapsto^* \langle c_2', m_2' \rangle$ and $c_1' < c_1$.

4. *If* $\langle c_1, m_1 \rangle \sim_j \langle c_2, m_2 \rangle$ and at_external $c_1 = $ Some $(f, \overrightarrow{v_1})$ then $m_1 \rightarrowtail_j m_2$, and there exists $\overrightarrow{v_2}$ with $\overrightarrow{v_1} \rightarrowtail_j \overrightarrow{v_2}$ and at_external $c_2 = $ Some $(f, \overrightarrow{v_2})$.

5. *If* $\langle c_1, m_1 \rangle \sim_j \langle c_2, m_2 \rangle$ and at_external $c_1 = $ Some $(f, \overrightarrow{v_1})$, then for all m_1', m_2', j', v_1', v_2' with $j \leq j'$; $j \bowtie_{m_1;m_2} j'$; $m_1' \rightarrowtail_{j'} m_2'$; $v_1' \rightarrowtail_{j'} v_2'$ and
   - forward $m_1 \ m_1'$; forward $m_2 \ m_2'$;
   - unchOn (loc_unmapped j) $m_1 \ m_1'$; unchOn (loc_out_of_reach $j \ m_1$) $m_2 \ m_2'$

   there exist c_1', c_2' such that
   - after_external (Some v_1') $c_1 = $ Some c_1';
   - after_external (Some v_2') $c_2 = $ Some c_2'; and $\langle c_1', m_1' \rangle \sim_{j'} \langle c_2', m_2' \rangle$.

The definition contains one clause for each protocol stage of core semantics:

Initial Cores. Clause 1, the base case, requires L_2 to match any L_1-initial core, given matching memories and arguments and related entry points.

Halted Cores. Symmetrically, clause 2 propagates termination from L_1 to L_2 for any $\sim_j$-related states, guaranteeing correspondence with respect to j for final memories and return values.

Core Steps. Clause 3 handles core steps, following the pattern of CompCert 1.x's forward simulations. An L_1 step may be matched by empty or nonempty sequences of L_2 core steps. In order to prevent infinite stuttering, the well-founded measure $<$ over core states c must decrease each time a possibly empty sequence is chosen. Since c_1 and c_2 may allocate new blocks during execution, resulting in larger memories m_1' and m_2', the relocation map j may also be extended to j' (notation $j \leq j'$) to account for the new blocks (under condition $j \bowtie_{m_1;m_2} j'$).

External Steps. The most interesting clauses concern the interaction of a core semantics with its environment. Clause 4 requires that L_2 match any call performed by L_1 with a call to the same function, with corresponding arguments.

Function Returns (Clause 5). In contrast to formulations using logical relations or $\top\top$-closure, we do not explicitly impose a simulation relation on environments. Instead, we require that the cores be ready to accept (and to re-establish the match relation on) nearly any pair of memories and return values the environments happen to return.[5] As a consequence, a compilation is considered correct *independent* of the termination behavior of its environment.

More precisely, given a call in L_1 (and, necessarily, a corresponding call in L_2, by Clause 4), we mandate that the match relation $\sim$ be re-established (and the resumption of normal execution succeed in both languages) whenever the environments yield back with return values v_1' and v_2' and updated memories m_1' and m_2' that are related by a relocation map j'. Here j' is an extension of the relocation map j provided at the time of the calls, meaning it agrees with j wherever j was defined, but may relocate new, freshly allocated blocks.

In accordance with the restrictions on external calls in CompCert, however, we assume that the evolution of memories across calls satisfies some basic conditions: forward m m' requires that an evolution $m \rightsquigarrow m'$ does not invalidate (*i.e.*, return to the allocation pool) any block that was previously allocated, and at most decreases the maximum permissions of the block's individual locations.[6] Blocks may of course be freed, but in CompCert's memory model, freed blocks are never re-allocated (each new allocation takes a fresh block-number from a countable set of positive numbers). The unchOn conditions impose a frame discipline, by confining the effects of the commands to addresses specifiable using j. In particular, unchOn (loc_unmapped j) m_1 m_1' requires that m_1' contain identical values as m_1 in all blocks b outside the preimage of j, while unchOn (loc_out_of_reach j m_1) m_2 m_2' imposes preservation of values at m_2 address whose preimage under j has empty Max permission.

In addition to the clauses in Definition 1, our formal definition imposes some structural conditions on the relation $\langle c_1, m_1 \rangle \sim_j \langle c_2, m_2 \rangle$, such as a constraint that global environments be suitably preserved (notation preservesGlobals ge_1 j), and that all blocks mentioned by j be valid in the respective memories. We omit the details of these clauses from our presentation.

We denote simulations for extension and equality passes by $L_1 \preceq_{\mathsf{Ext}} L_2$ and $L_1 \preceq_{\mathsf{Eq}} L_2$, respectively—the definitions of these notions mirror that of $L_1 \preceq_{\mathsf{Inj}} L_2$, but we omit the details. We write . $\preceq$. for the union of all three relations.

4.1   Transitive Composition of Simulations

In order to verify a multiphase compiler in a modular way, it is critically important to *transitively compose* correctness proofs of individual compiler phases.

---

[5] This is an important point! The authors of a compiler such as gcc or CompCert make few assumptions about the environment, or about separately compiled modules. They do not want their reasoning about compiler correctness entangled with specifications of the programs to be linked with.

[6] The current permission at each memory location may fluctuate arbitrarily so long as it does not exceed the Max permission.

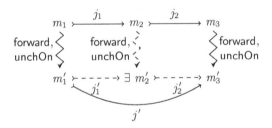

Fig. 6. Interpolation lemma for composing injection phases $L_1 \preceq_{\mathsf{Inj}} L_2$ and $L_2 \preceq_{\mathsf{Inj}} L_3$. Solid lines represent assumptions; dashed lines represent constraints that the constructed m_2' has to satisfy. Similar lemmas have been validated in Coq for all combinations of injection and extension passes.

That is, we would like to prove that $L_1 \preceq L_3$ holds whenever $L_1 \preceq L_2$ and $L_2 \preceq L_3$. In the following, we summarize our Coq proof of this result.

A *cooperative core semantics* is a core semantics such that $ge \vdash \langle c, m \rangle \longmapsto \langle c', m' \rangle$ implies forward $m\ m'$.

Theorem 1. *For cooperative L_1, L_2, L_3, suppose $L_1 \preceq L_2$ and $L_2 \preceq L_3$. Then there exists a simulation $L_1 \preceq L_3$.*

The proof of this result proceeds by case distinction on $L_1 \preceq L_2$ and $L_2 \preceq L_3$, yielding nine cases. The resulting simulation is of type . $\preceq_{\mathsf{Inj}}$. whenever at least one hypothesis is an injection, is of type . $\preceq_{\mathsf{Eq}}$. if both hypotheses are equalities, and is of type . $\preceq_{\mathsf{Ext}}$. otherwise. Each case consists of subgoals according to the clauses in Definition 1 (or the similar clauses in case of . $\preceq_{\mathsf{Ext}}$. and . $\preceq_{\mathsf{Eq}}$.).

The most interesting subgoals are those for the after_external-clauses.[7] In order to establish the desired relation $\langle c_1', m_1' \rangle \sim_{j'} \langle c_3', m_3' \rangle$ between the return states in languages L_1 and L_3, one would like to appeal to the corresponding relations that are inductively given for $L_1 \preceq L_2$ and $L_2 \preceq L_3$. However, in order for these induction hypotheses to apply, one must provide a suitable intermediate state $\langle c_2', m_2' \rangle$, and in particular the memory m_2'. Figure 6 depicts this situation for the case in which both compiler phases are injection passes. As illustrated in the figure, we require the existence of a post-call memory m_2' in L_2 such that m_1' can be injected to m_2' (via an extension j_1' of j_1) and m_2' can be injected to m_3' via j_2', such that $j' = j_2' \circ j_1'$ ($j_2 \circ j_1$ defines injection composition). This is assuming j_1 injects m_1 to m_2, j_2 injects m_2 to m_3, and j' injects m_1' to m_3'.

Prior to CompCert 2.0, memory injections did not compose, *i.e.* $m_1 \longmapsto_{j_2 \circ j_1} m_3$ did not follow from $m_1 \longmapsto_{j_1} m_2$ and $m_2 \longmapsto_{j_2} m_3$. Because the simulations did not expose memory, transitive compiler correctness did not require this property to hold. In CompCert 2.0, Leroy respecified injections to facilitate such composition, based on a suggestion of Tahina Ramananandro. The interpolation lemma

---

[7] Indeed, a principal result of this paper is that one *can* reason about the interaction between the memory manipulations of the compiler and the memory effects of external function calls.

provides the counterpart to this composition, by guaranteeing that the post-call injection $m_1' \rightarrowtail_{j'} m_3'$ can be split into some m_2', j_1', and j_2' with $m_1' \rightarrowtail_{j_1'} m_2'$ and $m_2' \rightarrowtail_{j_2'} m_3'$. Moreover, these items can be constructed in such a way that the evolution $m_2 \rightsquigarrow m_2'$ inherits the appropriate forward and unchOn properties from the extremal evolutions $m_1 \rightsquigarrow m_1'$ and $m_3 \rightsquigarrow m_3'$. Our proofs of the interpolation lemmas suggested a handful of additional alterations to the memory model, which we communicated to Leroy. These included a subtle refinement to the treatment of permissions across external calls and a tweak to the definition of unchOn. Leroy installed these modifications in CompCert 2.0, and we formally validated the interpolation lemma in Coq. That is, we have proved that intermediate memories m_2', and injections j_1' and j_2' with the required properties can indeed be constructed.[8] Having proved similar lemmas for the cases where one or both of the phases are memory extension translations, we combined the interpolation lemmas to a Coq proof of Theorem 1.

The evolutions $m_i \rightsquigarrow m_i'$ in Figure 6 are stated purely extensionally, in terms of forward and unchOn. The alternative would be a requirement to preserve sequences of memory operations—but the question of *which sequences* we'd want to preserve would take us back exactly to square one: simply requiring *all* sequences to be preserved prevents the compiler from optimizing redundant loads/stores and from reordering loads/stores once we refine external calls into (compilable) code. On the other hand, any other equivalence would itself require extensional justification, so nothing would be gained by considering such sequences.

5   Semantics Preservation

As Section 4 showed, LSRs support phase-by-phase verification of a compiler such as CompCert. But what end-to-end result do LSRs guarantee?

This section answers this question, by stating and proving a strong semantics preservation theorem implied by LSRs. In order to simplify the presentation of this theorem, we deal here only with closed programs, *i.e.*, those whose calls to external functions have been fully resolved after linking. But LSRs imply a strong semantics preservation theorem for open programs as well.

We prove semantics preservation as a corollary of safety preservation, under the following definition of program safety.

---

[8] Differences between injections and extensions mean that the intermediate memories differ slightly between these cases, although several auxiliary lemmas are shared. As a consequence of our work, it became apparent that under certain conditions, namely the absence of pointers to previously unallocated blocks, memory extensions are special cases of memory injections. This opens the potential to unify the two notions across the entire CompCert development, and hence to coalesce all interpolation lemmas. The price is that all languages would have to (be proven to) preserve the absence of such wild pointers throughout execution. At present, it is unclear which way CompCert will eventually go, so we adopt the status quo for the time being.

Definition 2 (Safety). *A program $\langle c, m \rangle$ is* safe *for n steps with postcondition Q and in global environment ge when either*

- *$n = 0$, or*
- *$n \neq 0$ and if* halted *$c =$* Some *v then $Q(v, m)$ else there exist c', m' such that $ge \vdash \langle c, m \rangle \longmapsto \langle c', m' \rangle$ and $\langle c', m' \rangle$ is safe for $n - 1$ steps.*

A program $\langle c, m \rangle$ is safe *iff it is safe for all n.*

In particular, if $\langle c, m \rangle$ is safe with postcondition Q, then $\langle c, m \rangle$ will either infinite loop or halt in a state (return value and memory) satisfying Q.

We state safety preservation in terms of this definition of safety as follows.

Theorem 2 (Safety Preservation). *Let M be the type of CompCert memories; $L_1 = (G_1, C_1, M)$ be the source semantics; $L_2 = (G_2, C_2, M)$ be the target semantics; $\langle c_1, m_1 \rangle$ be a configuration of L_1; and $\langle c_2, m_2 \rangle$ be a configuration of L_2. Assume that L_1 and L_2 are deterministic, and that $L_1 \preceq_{\mathsf{Inj}} L_2$ holds with $\langle c_1, m_1 \rangle \sim_j \langle c_2, m_2 \rangle$ for some injection j. Then for all postconditions Q up to injection, if $\langle c_1, m_1 \rangle$ is safe for Q then $\langle c_2, m_2 \rangle$ is safe for Q.*

By "postconditions Q up to injection," we mean the set of predicates on return values and memories that remain true under injection of their arguments. Formulating Theorem 2 with respect to . $\preceq_{\mathsf{Inj}}$. is appropriate since this is the type of simulation one obtains when composing all translation phases of CompCert. In the Verified Software Toolchain [App11], a proof of $\{P\}c\{Q\}$ in our C light program logic [A$^+$14] and soundness of the logic together give us the required safety theorem for source-language C light configurations.

As a corollary of Theorem 2 and from termination preservation, we get the following semantics preservation result.

Corollary 1 (Semantics Preservation). *For any execution of L_1 starting in an initial state (module entry point) and resulting in a halted state, and for any observation Q up to injection one could make of that halted state, there is a unique execution starting from the initial state of L_2 that terminates in a unique halted state also satisfying the predicate Q.*

These top-level theorems concern fully linked programs, but our results on LSRs allow the extensions of these theorems to the situation in which a thread interacts with its environment using shared-memory interaction, provided external functions are equipped with suitable up-to-injection specifications. To get an even stronger result regarding fully separate compilation, some additional constraints need to be imposed on CompCert's specification: that all assumptions made in the *External Steps* clause are established by the *Core Steps* clause.

6   Backwards Compatibility

Although CompCert 2.0's top-level correctness theorems still say very little about the memory transformations performed by the compiler, many of the compiler's internal invariants—established in proofs of individual compiler phases—make more precise statements about these memory transformations. In order to maximize the reuse of CompCert's proof infrastructure, it is desirable to preserve as many of these internal invariants as possible.

To evaluate our approach, we adapted the proof of one of the trickiest compilation passes, Cminorgen, to the simulation structures of Section 4. The main task of Cminorgen is to remove from activation records any local variables that are not address-taken (these local variables are allocated in registers, or occasionally spilled back into activation records after CompCert's register allocation pass). Because the Cminorgen pass significantly reorganizes memory, CompCert 2.0 proves Cminorgen as an injection pass.

First, we refactored the source and target languages of the transformation, Csharpminor and Cminor, as described for C light in Section 3.1. This involved isolating the memory component from the core data and giving definitions for the core semantics interface from Figure 3. Next, we adapted the proof, by exposing the memory injection in a match relation that described the evolution of the call stack, and reassembling the main inductive argument. While most instruction forms were rather easy to adapt, the rule for internal function calls required a slight strengthening of invariants in order to establish the $j \bowtie_{m_1;m_2} j'$ condition of clause 3 from Definition 1. In contrast, the case for external functions, which in CompCert 1.x and 2.0 was rather involved, disappeared completely since external function calls are now handled by the core semantics interface.

That the adaptation of the Cminorgen proof, one of CompCert's most complicated phases, to our setting was reasonably straightforward indicates that our proof techniques will scale to the remainder of CompCert. Indeed, many of CompCert's phases make no adaptations to the memory layout at all. For these phases, all that is needed is to adapt the source and target languages to the core semantics interface of Section 3, and its strengthening to cooperative semantics.

7   Related Work

Some of the most appealing treatments of compiler correctness to-date have been developed in the setting of ML-like languages or (typed) lambda-calculi [Plo73,Rey74]. Proof techniques such as logical relations or $\top\top$-closure exploit type structure to capture the relationship between code and its execution context, supporting advanced language features such as higher-order functions, existential or recursive types, polymorphism, and references. But the property of transitive compositionality has often been difficult to obtain.

Inspired in part by Pitts and Stark's work on *Kripke logical relations* [PS98], recent years have seen progress on supporting local state in the form of mutable references [ADR09,DNB10,HDNV12,HNDV13]. State transition systems, which are similar in some respects to our protocol-oriented semantics, figure prominently in many of the recent approaches as a means of specifying invariants on local state. However, this work has all been done in the context of strongly typed functional languages, *e.g.*, System F extended with recursive types and mutable references. Our context and goals are different: we apply logical simulation relations to the problem of verified separate compilation of a weakly typed language (C), in the context of a realistic optimizing compiler (CompCert). The application to CompCert is one of the major contributions of our work.

Arguably, the most closely related work to ours is Hur *et al.*'s integration of bisimulations and Kripke logical relations [HDNV12]. Hur *et al.* achieve compositionality for the rich setting of $F^{\mu!}$, but employ a highly nonstandard construction: the cardinalities of the syntactic categories for types and values, and of the semantic interpretation of the type **nat**, are exploited to construct "bad" values that have little motivation from a typed perspective (these values occur in the logical relation at function type position, despite being integers) and are then used to "artificially" block certain executions in the intermediate language L_2. In contrast, although being far from trivial, the proofs of our interpolation lemmas have significantly more constructive content.

A strength of Hur *et al.*'s contribution is to capture the intricate interactions between global (shared) and local knowledge. Hur *et al.*'s analysis is formulated using *relation-transition systems* (RTS's), an evolution of the authors' earlier work on using state transition systems to index Kripke-worlds in step-indexed logical relations [ADR09,DNB10]. Our protocol-oriented interaction model shares many of the features of RTS's but is used to specify the "operational ground truth".

Progress has also been made in extending logical relations to low-level code, and to compilation [BH09,BH10]. One of the challenges is to transform high-level type structure into well-behavedness at the low level even in the presence of more fine-grained observation contexts. Again, the situation for our work is different, as the C language does not provide us with much high-level type structure to start with. It is indeed the memory model, not type structure, that constitutes the *lingua franca* between *C* modules, and the use of a *uniform* memory model across all stages of compilation is a crucial feature of CompCert.

Recently, Liang *et al.* [LFF12] have explored applications of rely-guarantee reasoning [Jon83] to proving the correctness of concurrent program transformations. In that work, rely-guarantee conditions were used to model the interactions of a program thread with its concurrent context. There are natural extensions of these ideas to separate compilation in the CompCert setting. Indeed, we are actively exploring a rely-guarantee simulation proof method that would allow separate compilation of linked modules even in the presence of mutually recursive inter-module dependencies. In the CompCert setting, rely conditions correspond to the assumptions CompCert currently makes about the behaviors of external function calls, and which we expose in Clause 5 of measured forward simulations (Definition 1, Section 4). Adapting CompCert to support symmetric guarantees about compiled code is much trickier. Solving these issues is active research.

Our work on verified compilation of concurrent programs has goals similar to those of CompCertTSO [ŠVZN+11] but with a quite different method. Instead of modeling a specific relaxed memory model, *e.g.*, x86-TSO, as CompCert-TSO does, we prove—by instrumenting the CompCert languages with memory permissions—that data race freedom is preserved by compilation. For programs proved data race free in our concurrent separation logic we will therefore get correctness guarantees with respect to even *weaker* memory models than x86-TSO, *e.g.*, the POWER and ARM models. Our approach even permits CompCert to optimize nonsynchronizing loads and stores, *e.g.*, hoist loads/stores, eliminate redundant load/stores, when they do not cross synchronization operations.

8 Conclusion

Compositional compilation is not an easy problem. In this paper, we attack the problem "at scale," in the intensely practical CompCert compiler. In this setting, we show that core semantics and LSRs, together with the program logic [A$^+$14], enable end-to-end verification of C programs that interact via shared memory. But our approach to "how to specify a compiler" is significant beyond just Comp-Cert, and will be relevant to optimizing compilation of any C-like language.

Acknowledgments. We thank the members of the Princeton programming languages group and the ESOP anonymous reviewers for their comments on earlier drafts of this paper. We are indebted to Xavier Leroy and Tahina Ramananandro for many enlightening technical conversations.

This material is based on research sponsored by the DARPA under agreement number FA8750-12-2-0293. The U.S. Government is authorized to reproduce and distribute reprints for Governmental purposes notwithstanding any copyright notation thereon. The views and conclusions contained herein are those of the authors and should not be interpreted as necessarily representing the official policies or endorsements, either expressed or implied, of DARPA or the U.S. Government.

References

A$^+$14. Appel, A.W., et al.: Program logics for certified compilers, Cambridge (2014)

ADR09. Ahmed, A., Dreyer, D., Rossberg, A.: State-dependent representation independence. In: POPL (2009)

Appl11. Appel, A.W.: Verified software toolchain. In: Barthe, G. (ed.) ESOP 2011. LNCS, vol. 6602, pp. 1–17. Springer, Heidelberg (2011)

BH09. Benton, N., Hur, C.-K.: Biorthogonality, step-indexing and compiler correctness. In: ICFP, New York, pp. 97–108 (2009)

BH10. Benton, N., Hur, C.-K.: Realizability and compositional compiler correctness for a polymorphic language. Tech. Report MSR-TR-2010-62, Microsoft Research (2010)

DNB10. Dreyer, D., Neis, G., Birkedal, L.: The impact of higher-order state and control effects on local relational reasoning. ACM SIGPLAN Notices 45, 143–156 (2010)

HDNV12. Hur, C.-K., Dreyer, D., Neis, G., Vafeiadis, V.: The marriage of bisimulations and Kripke logical relations. In: POPL (2012)

HNDV13. Hur, C.-K., Neis, G., Dreyer, D., Vafeiadis, V.: Parametric bisimulations: A logical step forward, draft (2013)

Jon83. Jones, C.B.: Tentative steps toward a development method for interfering programs. TOPLAS 5(4), 596–619 (1983)

L+12.   Leroy., X., et al.: The CompCert memory model, version 2. Tech. Report
         RR-7987, INRIA (2012)
LB08.   Leroy, X., Blazy, S.: Formal verification of a C-like memory model and its
         uses for verifying program transformations. JAR 41(1) (2008)
Ler11.   Leroy, X.: The CompCert verified compiler, software & ann. proof (2011)
LFF12.   Liang, H., Feng, X., Fu, M.: A rely-guarantee-based simulation for verifying
         concurrent program transformations. In: POPL (2012)
NS06.   Ni, Z., Shao, Z.: Certified assembly programming with embedded code
         pointers. In: POPL (2006)
O'H07.   O'Hearn, P.W.: Resources, concurrency and local reasoning. Theoretical
         Computer Science 375(1), 271–307 (2007)
Plo73.   Plotkin, G.: Lambda-definability and logical relations, School of Artificial
         Intelligence, University of Edinburgh (1973)
PS98.   Pitts, A., Stark, I.: Operational reasoning for functions with local state.
         Higher Order Operational Techniques in Semantics, 227–273 (1998)
Rey74.   Reynolds, J.: On the relation between direct and continuation semantics.
         Automata, Languages and Programming, 141–156 (1974)
ŜVZN+11. Ševčik, J., Vafeiadis, V. Zappa Nardelli, F. Jagannathan, S., and Sewell,
         P.: Relaxed-memory concurrency and verified compilation. ACM SIGPLAN
         Notices 46(1), 43–54 (2011)

Verifying an Open Compiler
Using Multi-language Semantics

James T. Perconti and Amal Ahmed

Northeastern University

Abstract. Existing verified compilers are proved correct under a closed-world assumption, i.e., that the compiler will only be used to compile *whole* programs. We present a new methodology for verifying correct compilation of program *components*, while formally allowing linking with target code of arbitrary provenance. To demonstrate our methodology, we present a two-pass type-preserving open compiler and prove that compilation preserves semantics. The central novelty of our approach is that we define a combined language that embeds the source, intermediate, and target languages and formalizes a semantics of interoperability between them, using boundaries in the style of Matthews and Findler. Compiler correctness is stated as contextual equivalence in the combined language.

Note to reader: We use blue, red, and purple to typeset terms in various languages. This paper will be difficult to follow unless read/printed in color.

1 Introduction

There has been remarkable progress on formally verified compilers over the last few years, with researchers proving the correctness of increasingly sophisticated compilers for increasingly realistic languages. The most well known instance of this is the Comp-Cert compiler [1,2] which uses the Coq proof assistant to both implement and verify a multi-pass optimizing compiler from C to PowerPC, ARM, and x86 assembly, proving that the compiler preserves semantics of source programs. Several other compiler-verification efforts have successfully followed CompCert's lead and basic methodology, for instance, focusing on multithreaded Java [3], just-in-time compilation [4], and C with relaxed memory concurrency [5].

Unfortunately, these projects prove compiler correctness under a *closed-world* assumption, that is, assuming that the verified compiler will always compile *whole* programs. Despite the immense effort put into verification, the compiler correctness theorem provides no guarantees about correct compilation of *components*. This whole-program assumption is completely unrealistic since most software systems today are comprised of many components written in different languages compiled to a common target, as well as runtime-library routines that may be handwritten in the target language. We need compiler correctness theorems applicable to the way we actually use these compilers.

Formally verifying that components are compiled correctly—often referred to as *compositional compiler correctness*—is a challenging problem. A key difficulty is that, in the setting of compiling components, it is not clear how to even state the compiler correctness theorem. CompCert's compiler correctness theorem is easy to state thanks to

Z. Shao (Ed.): ESOP 2014, LNCS 8410, pp. 128–148, 2014.

the whole program assumption: informally, it says that if a source program P_S compiles to a target program P_T, then running P_S and P_T results in the same trace of observable events. The same sort of theorem does not make sense when we compile a component e_S to a component e_T: we cannot "run" a component since it is not a complete program.

Intuitively, we want the compiler correctness theorem to say that if a component e_S compiles to e_T, then some desired relationship $e_S \simeq e_T$ holds between e_S and e_T. The central question is: how do we *formally specify* $e_S \simeq e_T$? To answer this question, we must consider how the compiled component is actually used: it needs to be linked with some e_T', creating a whole program that can be run. Informally, the compiler correctness theorem should guarantee that if we link e_T with e_T', then the resulting target-level program should correspond to the source component e_S linked with e_T'. But, formally speaking, how can one link a source component with a target component and what are the rules for running the resulting source-target hybrid? These questions demand a *semantics of interoperability* between the source and target languages. We give our semantics of interoperability as a multi-language operational model. We then define $e_S \simeq e_T$ as a contextual equivalence in that model.

There are two other important issues to consider when evaluating a compositional compiler correctness theorem and its supporting formalism. The first is the degree of *horizontal compositionality* that the model allows, that is, which target components e_T' may formally be linked with a compiled component. At the lower end of the horizontal compositionality spectrum are *fully abstract* compilers. Full abstraction states that the compiler both preserves and reflects contextual equivalence. Hence, a fully abstract compiler preserves all of the source language's abstractions, and compiled components are only allowed to link with components that can be expressed in the source language.

But real systems often link together components from multiple languages with different guarantees and different expressive power. We are particularly interested in supporting interoperability between parametric typed languages like ML and low-level languages like C. Thus, full abstraction is often too restrictive. To support the whole programs that we actually run, the compiler correctness theorem should formally support linking with as large a class of programs as possible, and in particular, should not require an e_T' to have been compiled from the same source language as e_T.

Abandoning full abstraction in favor of greater horizontal compositionality does not require giving up all the guarantees of the source language. The compiler and its verification framework can be designed to preserve the source-level equivalences that are critically needed without forbidding all foreign behavior. To show that different levels of abstraction preservation are possible, we will deliberately pick a target language that is more expressive than the source and design our compiler so that it is *not* fully abstract. Our focus in this paper is on how to preserve the representation independence and information hiding guarantees provided by type abstraction in our source language.

The second important issue for a compiler correctness framework is that we want to be able to verify multi-pass compilers. For example, if we have a two-pass compiler that compiles a source component e_S to an intermediate-language component e_I to a target component e_T, we should be able to verify each pass separately, showing $e_S \simeq e_I$ and $e_I \simeq e_T$, and then compose these results to get a correctness theorem for the whole compiler saying $e_S \simeq e_T$. This is typically referred to as *vertical compositionality*.

We will show that our approach of using a multi-language operational model succeeds at both horizontal and vertical compositionality. In particular, we validate our methodology by applying it to a two-pass type-preserving compiler. The compiler deals with three languages: our source language F (System F with existential and recursive types), an intermediate language C (the target of a typed closure conversion pass), and our target language A (the target of a heap allocation pass).[1] The target language A allows tuples and closures to live only on the heap and supports both mutable and immutable references. Our closure conversion pass translates F components of type τ to C components of type $\tau^{\mathcal{C}}$, where $\tau^{\mathcal{C}}$ denotes the type translation of τ. The subsequent allocation pass translates C components of type τ to A components of type $\tau^{\mathcal{A}}$, where $\tau^{\mathcal{A}}$ is the type translation of τ.

To define the semantics of interoperability between these languages, we embed them all into one language, FCA, and add syntactic boundary forms between each pair of adjacent languages, in the style of Matthews and Findler [7] and of Ahmed and Blume [8]. For instance, the term $\mathcal{CF}^{\tau}(\mathsf{e_F})$ allows an F component $\mathsf{e_F}$ of type τ to be used as a C component of type $\tau^{\mathcal{C}}$, while $^{\tau}\mathcal{FC}(\mathsf{e_C})$ allows a C component $\mathsf{e_C}$ of translation type $\tau^{\mathcal{C}}$ to be used as an F component of type τ. Similarly, we have boundary forms $\mathcal{AC}$ and $\mathcal{CA}$ for the next language pair. Non-adjacent languages can interact by stacking up boundaries: for example, $\mathcal{FC}(\mathcal{CA}\,\mathsf{e_A})$ (abbreviated $\mathcal{FCA}(\mathsf{e_A})$) allows an A component $\mathsf{e_A}$ to be embedded in an F term.

FCA *Design Principles.* Our goal is for the FCA interoperability semantics to give us a useful specification of when a component in one of the underlying languages should be considered equivalent to a component in another language. We realize that goal by following three principles.

First, we define the operational semantics of FCA so that the original languages are *embedded* into FCA unchanged: running an FCA program that's written solely in one of the embedded languages is identical to running it in that language alone. For instance, execution of the A program $\mathsf{e_A}$ proceeds in exactly the same way whether we use the operational semantics of A or the augmented semantics for FCA.

Next, we ensure that the typing rules are similarly embedded: a component that contains syntax from only one underlying language should typecheck under that language's individual type system if and only if it typechecks under FCA's type system.

The final property we need is *boundary cancellation*, which says that wrapping two opposite language boundaries around a component yields the same behavior as the underlying component with no boundaries. For example, any $\mathsf{e_F} : \tau$ must be contextually equivalent to $^{\tau}\mathcal{FC}(\mathcal{CF}^{\tau}\mathsf{e_F})$, and any $\mathsf{e_C} : \tau^{\mathcal{C}}$ must be equivalent to $\mathcal{CF}^{\tau}(^{\tau}\mathcal{FC}\mathsf{e_C})$.

Compiler Correctness. We state the correctness criterion for our compiler as a contextual equivalence. For each pass of the compiler from a source S to a target T, where S and T interoperate via boundaries $\mathcal{ST}$ and $\mathcal{TS}$, define our source-target relationship by

$$e_S \simeq e_T \overset{\text{def}}{=} e_S \approx^{ctx}_{\mathsf{FCA}} {}^{\tau}\mathcal{ST}(e_T) : \tau.$$

We prove that if $e_S : \tau$ compiles to e_T, then $e_S \simeq e_T$. Since contextual equivalence is transitive, our framework achieves vertical compositionality immediately: it is easy

---

[1] We have extended our F to A compiler with a code-generation pass to an assembly language, much like Morrisett *et al.*'s stack-based TAL [6]. We will report on that work in a future paper.

to combine the two correctness proofs for the individual compiler passes, giving the overall correctness result that if e_F compiles to e_A, then $e_F \simeq e_A$, or

$$e_F \approx^{ctx}_{FCA} {}^\tau \mathcal{FCA}(e_A) : \tau.$$

Reasoning About Linking. Our approach enjoys a strong horizontal compositionality property: we can link with any target component e'_A that has an appropriate type, with no requirement that e'_A was produced by any particular means or from any particular source language. Specifically, if e_F expects to be linked with a component of type τ' and compiles to e_A, then e_A will expect to be linked with a component of type $((\tau')^C)^A$. If e'_A has this type, then using our compiler correctness theorem, we can conclude that

$$(e_F \ {}^{\tau'}\mathcal{FCA}(e'_A)) \approx^{ctx} \mathcal{FCA}(e_A \ e'_A),$$

or equivalently,

$$\mathcal{ACF}(e_F \ {}^{\tau'}\mathcal{FCA}(e'_A)) \approx^{ctx} e_A \ e'_A.$$

The right-hand side of this equality is exactly the A program we ultimately want to run, and the left-hand side is an FCA program that models that program.

Contributions. Our main contributions are our methodology and that we have proven correctness for an open multi-pass compiler. We have designed a multi-language semantics that lets us state a strong compiler-correctness theorem, and to prove the theorems, we have developed a logical relation for proving contextual equivalences between FCA components. The most significant technical challenges were related to interoperability between languages with type abstraction, specifically, in designing the multi-language semantics so it preserves type abstraction between languages (§5), and in designing the parts of the logical relation that model the handling of type abstraction in a multi-language setting (§9).

Due to space constraints, we elide various technical details and omit proofs. All definitions, lemmas, and proofs are spelled out in full detail in the accompanying technical report [9], available at: http://ccs.neu.edu/home/amal/voc/

2   Related Work: Benton-Hur Approach

Before beginning our technical development, we compare our methodology to the only prominent existing approach to compositional compiler correctness.

To eliminate the closed-world assumption, Benton and Hur [10] advocate setting up a logical relation between the source and target languages, specifying when a source term semantically approximates target code and vice versa. We will refer to a logical relation that relates terms from two *different* languages as a *cross-language* logical relation. The relation is defined by induction on source-language types. Benton and Hur verified a compiler from the simply-typed λ-calculus with recursion [10]—and later, from System F with recursion [11]—to an SECD machine, proving that if source component e_S compiles to target code e_T, then e_S and e_T are logically related. Later, Hur and Dreyer [12] used essentially the same approach to prove correctness of a compiler from an idealized ML to assembly.

However, the Benton-Hur (henceforth, BH) approach suffers from serious drawbacks in both vertical and horizontal compositionality. First, the cross-language framework does not scale to a multi-pass compiler. Both Benton-Hur and Hur-Dreyer handle only a single pass. To achieve vertical compositionality in the BH style, one would have to define separate cross-language logical relations relating the source and target of each compiler pass, and then prove that the logical relations compose transitively in order to establish that the correctness of each pass implies correctness for the entire compiler. But this kind of transitive composition of cross-language logical relations has been an open problem for some time. (We'll discuss recent work towards addressing this problem in §11.)

The second drawback to the BH approach is its limited horizontal compositionality. Consider the situation where a verified compiler from language S to language T is used to compile a source component e_S to some target code e_T. The BH compiler correctness theorem tells us that e_S and e_T are logically related. We wish to link the compiled code e_T with some other target code e'_T and verify the resulting program. To do this using the BH framework, we must now *come up with a source-level component e'_S* and show that it is logically related to e'_T. This is an onerous requirement: while it may be reasonable to come up with e'_S when the given e'_T is very simple, it seems almost impossible when e'_T consists of hundreds of lines of assembly! Further, if e'_T is compiled from some other source language R, it may not even be possible to write down an e'_S in language S that is related to e'_T.

Technically speaking, the BH approach does support linking with any target code that can be proved logically related to a source component. But it cannot support linking with any components that are not expressible in the source language. And we contend that even for the theoretically-allowed cases, in practice the approach is limited to allowing linking between only very simple components or components that were all compiled from the same source language.

Overcoming BH Limitations. By reasoning about components in the FCA setting, we can overcome both limitations of the BH framework. We have already pointed out that our framework admits vertical compositionality thanks to the transitivity of contextual equivalence.

For the second limitation of the BH approach, consider a target component e'_A. While the BH approach would need to find a related source component to fit e'_A into their framework, we only need to find an FCA component that looks like a source component. Specifically, we can use e'_A itself in a source context by wrapping it in appropriate boundaries: $\mathcal{FCA}(e'_A)$.

3   The Languages

We begin our technical development with a few notes on typesetting and notational conventions. We typeset the terms, types, and contexts of our various languages as follows:

- F (System <u>F</u>) in a blue sans-serif font;
- C (<u>C</u>losure conversion) in a red bold font with serifs;
- A (<u>A</u>llocation) in a purple sans-serif bold font.

For each of our languages, we will use the metavariable e for *components* and t for *terms*. In the first two languages, F and C, terms and components coincide, but the distinction will be meaningful in language A. Similarly, all languages use τ for types, v for values, E for evaluation contexts, and C for general contexts. We write $\mathrm{fv}(e)$

$\tau ::= \alpha \mid \text{unit} \mid \text{int} \mid \forall[\overline{\alpha}].(\overline{\tau}) \to \tau \mid \langle \overline{\tau} \rangle \mid \exists \alpha.\tau \mid \mu\alpha.\tau$

$e ::= t$

$t ::= x \mid () \mid n \mid t\,p\,t \mid \text{if0}\,t\,t\,t \mid \lambda[\overline{\alpha}](\overline{x{:}\tau}).t \mid t[\overline{\tau}]\,\overline{t} \mid \langle \overline{t} \rangle \mid \pi_i(t) \mid \text{pack}\langle\tau,t\rangle\,\text{as}\,\exists\alpha.\tau$
$\qquad \mid \text{unpack}\,\langle\alpha,x\rangle = t\,\text{in}\,t \mid \text{fold}_{\mu\alpha.\tau}\,t \mid \text{unfold}\,t$

$p ::= + \mid - \mid *$

$v ::= () \mid n \mid \lambda[\overline{\alpha}](\overline{x{:}\tau}).t \mid \langle \overline{v} \rangle \mid \text{pack}\langle\tau,v\rangle\,\text{as}\,\exists\alpha.\tau \mid \text{fold}_{\mu\alpha.\tau}\,v$

$E ::= [\cdot] \mid E\,p\,t \mid v\,p\,E \mid \text{if0}\,E\,t\,t \mid E[\overline{\tau}]\,\overline{t} \mid v[\overline{\tau}]\,\overline{v}\,E\,\overline{t} \mid \ldots$

$\boxed{e \longmapsto e'}\quad E[\lambda[\overline{\alpha}](\overline{x{:}\tau}).t\,[\overline{\tau'}]\,\overline{v}] \longmapsto E[t[\overline{\tau'/\alpha}]\,[\overline{v/x}]] \qquad \ldots$

$\boxed{\Delta;\Gamma \vdash e : \tau}\ \text{where}\ \Delta ::= \cdot \mid \Delta,\alpha\ \text{and}\ \Gamma ::= \cdot \mid \Gamma,x{:}\tau$

$\tau ::= \alpha \mid \text{unit} \mid \text{int} \mid \forall[\overline{\alpha}].(\overline{\tau}) \to \tau \mid \langle \overline{\tau} \rangle \mid \exists \alpha.\tau \mid \mu\alpha.\tau$

$e ::= t$

$t ::= x \mid () \mid n \mid t\,p\,t \mid \text{if0}\,t\,t\,t \mid \lambda[\overline{\alpha}](\overline{x{:}\tau}).t \mid t\,[]\,\overline{t} \mid t[\overline{\tau}] \mid \langle \overline{t} \rangle \mid \pi_i(t)$
$\qquad \mid \text{pack}\langle\tau,t\rangle\,\text{as}\,\exists\alpha.\tau \mid \text{unpack}\,\langle\alpha,x\rangle = t\,\text{in}\,t \mid \text{fold}_{\mu\alpha.\tau}\,t \mid \text{unfold}\,t$

$p ::= + \mid - \mid *$

$v ::= () \mid n \mid \lambda[\overline{\alpha}](\overline{x{:}\tau}).t \mid \langle \overline{v} \rangle \mid \text{pack}\langle\tau,v\rangle\,\text{as}\,\exists\alpha.\tau \mid \text{fold}_{\mu\alpha.\tau}\,v \mid v[\overline{\tau}]$

$E ::= [\cdot] \mid \ldots \mid E\,[]\,\overline{t} \mid v[\overline{\tau}]\,\overline{v}\,E\,\overline{t} \mid E[\overline{\tau}] \mid \ldots$

$\boxed{e \longmapsto e'}\quad E[\lambda[\overline{\alpha}](\overline{x{:}\tau}).t\,[\overline{\tau'}]\,\overline{v}] \longmapsto E[t[\overline{\tau'/\alpha}]\,[\overline{v/x}]] \qquad \ldots$

$\boxed{\Delta;\Gamma \vdash e : \tau}\ \text{where}\ \Delta ::= \cdot \mid \Delta,\alpha\ \text{and}\ \Gamma ::= \cdot \mid \Gamma,x{:}\tau$

$$\frac{\overline{\alpha};\overline{x{:}\tau} \vdash t : \tau'}{\Delta;\Gamma \vdash \lambda[\overline{\alpha}](\overline{x{:}\tau}).t : \forall[\overline{\alpha}].(\overline{\tau}) \to \tau'} \qquad \frac{\Delta;\Gamma \vdash t : \forall[].(\overline{\tau}) \to \tau' \quad \Delta;\Gamma \vdash \overline{t} : \overline{\tau}}{\Delta;\Gamma \vdash t\,[]\,\overline{t} : \tau'}$$

$$\frac{\Delta;\Gamma \vdash t : \forall[\beta,\overline{\alpha}].(\overline{\tau}) \to \tau' \quad \Delta \vdash \tau_0}{\Delta;\Gamma \vdash t[\tau_0] : \forall[\overline{\alpha}].(\overline{\tau[\tau_0/\beta]}) \to \tau'[\tau_0/\beta]} \qquad \ldots$$

$\tau ::= \alpha \mid \text{unit} \mid \text{int} \mid \exists \alpha.\tau \mid \mu\alpha.\tau \mid \text{ref}\,\psi \mid \text{box}\,\psi$

$\psi ::= \forall[\overline{\alpha}].(\overline{\tau}) \to \tau \mid \langle \tau,\ldots,\tau \rangle$

$e ::= (t, H)$

$t ::= x \mid () \mid n \mid t\,p\,t \mid \text{if0}\,t\,t\,t \mid \ell \mid t\,[]\,\overline{t} \mid t[\tau] \mid \text{pack}\langle\tau,t\rangle\,\text{as}\,\exists\alpha.\tau \mid \text{unpack}\,\langle\alpha,x\rangle = t\,\text{in}\,t$
$\qquad \mid \text{fold}_{\mu\alpha.\tau}\,t \mid \text{unfold}\,t \mid \text{ralloc}\,\langle\overline{t}\rangle \mid \text{balloc}\,\langle\overline{t}\rangle \mid \text{read}[i]\,t \mid \text{write}\,t\,[i] \leftarrow t$

$p ::= + \mid - \mid *$

$v ::= () \mid n \mid \text{pack}\langle\tau,v\rangle\,\text{as}\,\exists\alpha.\tau \mid \text{fold}_{\mu\alpha.\tau}\,v \mid \ell \mid v[\tau]$

$E ::= (E_t, \cdot) \qquad E_t ::= [\cdot] \mid \ldots \mid \text{balloc}\,\langle\overline{v}, E_t, \overline{t}\rangle \mid \ldots$

$h ::= \lambda[\overline{\alpha}](\overline{x{:}\tau}).t \mid \langle v,\ldots,v \rangle \qquad H ::= \cdot \mid H, \ell \mapsto h$

$\boxed{\langle H \mid e \rangle \longmapsto \langle H' \mid e' \rangle}\ \text{Reduction Relation (selected cases)}$

$$\langle H \mid (t, (H', \ell \mapsto h)) \rangle \longmapsto \langle H, \ell' \mapsto h \mid (t[\ell'/\ell], H'[\ell'/\ell]) \rangle \qquad \text{if } \ell' \notin \text{dom}(H)$$

$$\langle H \mid E[\ell\,[\overline{\tau'}]\,\overline{v}] \rangle \longmapsto \langle H \mid E[t[\overline{\tau'/\alpha}]\,[\overline{v/x}]] \rangle \qquad\qquad \text{if } H(\ell) = \lambda[\overline{\alpha}](\overline{x{:}\tau}).t$$

$\boxed{\Psi \vdash h : \psi}\ \text{where}\ \Psi ::= \cdot \mid \Psi, \ell :\,^{\text{ref}}\psi \mid \Psi, \ell :\,^{\text{box}}\psi$

$\boxed{\Psi \vdash H : \Psi'}\ \text{which implies}\ \text{dom}(\Psi) \cap \text{dom}(\Psi') = \emptyset$

$\boxed{\Psi;\Delta;\Gamma \vdash e : \tau}\ \text{where}\ \Delta ::= \cdot \mid \Delta,\alpha\ \text{and}\ \Gamma ::= \cdot \mid \Gamma,x{:}\tau$

$$\frac{\Psi \vdash H : \Psi' \quad (\Psi,\Psi');\Delta;\Gamma \vdash t : \tau}{\Psi;\Delta;\Gamma \vdash (t, H) : \tau} \qquad \ldots$$

$$\frac{\Psi;\Delta;\Gamma \vdash \overline{t} : \overline{\tau}}{\Psi;\Delta;\Gamma \vdash \text{balloc}\,\langle\overline{t}\rangle : \text{box}\,\langle\overline{\tau}\rangle} \qquad \frac{\Psi;\Delta;\Gamma \vdash t : \text{box}\,\langle\tau_0,\ldots\tau_i\ldots,\tau_n\rangle}{\Psi;\Delta;\Gamma \vdash \text{read}[i]\,t : \tau_i}$$

Fig. 1. Definition of F (top), C (middle), and A (bottom)

to denote the free term variables of e and ftv(e) (or ftv(τ)) to denote the free type variables of e (or of type τ). We use a line above a syntactic element to indicate a list of repeated instances of this element, e.g., $\overline{\alpha} = \alpha_1, \ldots, \alpha_n$ for $n \geq 0$. When the arities of different lists are required to match up in a definition or inference rule, these constraints will usually be obvious from context. Whenever two environments (e.g. Δ or Γ or Ψ) are joined by a comma, this should be interpreted as a *disjoint* union.

Source Language. Our source language F is System F with recursive types, existential types, and tuples. The syntax of types and terms in F is shown in Figure 1 (top). We combine type- and term-level abstractions of arbitrary arity into a single binding form $\forall[\overline{\alpha}].(\overline{\tau}) \to \tau'$, abbreviating $\forall[].(\overline{\tau}) \to \tau'$ as $\overline{\tau} \to \tau'$. We define a small-step operational semantics for F (written $e \longmapsto e'$) using evaluation contexts E to lift the primitive reductions to a standard left-to-right call-by-value semantics for the language. The reduction rules are standard; we show only the application rule.

F's typing judgment has the form $\Delta; \Gamma \vdash e : \tau$. The type environment Δ tracks the type variables in scope. The value environment Γ tracks the term variables in scope along with their types τ, which must be well formed under Δ (written $\Delta \vdash \tau$ and defined as ftv$(\tau) \subseteq \Delta$). The typing rules are standard and hence omitted.

Intermediate Language. Our intermediate language C, shown in Figure 1 (middle), is nearly identical to F, with two exceptions. First, since this language is the target of closure conversion, functions are not allowed to contain free type or term variables. Second, we allow the partial application of a function to a type. Hence, C terms include $t[\tau]$ and we consider $v[\tau]$ to be a value.

The reduction relation $e \longmapsto e'$ is identical to that of F, and the typing judgment $\Delta; \Gamma \vdash e : \tau$ differs only in the rules for abstraction and application which are shown in the figure. Note that the body of a C function must typecheck in an environment that contains only the function's formal arguments.

Target Language. Our target A must serve as a target for heap allocation. Its design is similar to the language λ^A from [13]. Since we are compiling a source language without mutable references, it would suffice for A to provide only immutable references to functions and tuples that must now live on the heap. However, to provide a concrete illustration of the ability to link with target code that cannot be expressed in the source language, we augment A with mutable references to tuples.

The language A is shown in Figure 1 (bottom). Functions in A are stored only in immutable cells on the heap, while tuples are stored in heap cells that can be either mutable or immutable. We use ψ for the types of these *heap values* h. Mutable and immutable references have types ref ψ and box ψ, respectively. The terms ralloc $\langle \overline{t} \rangle$ and balloc $\langle \overline{t} \rangle$—which allocate mutable and immutable cells, respectively—each allocate a new location ℓ and initialize it to the given tuple. The instructions read$[i]\ \ell$ and write $\ell\ [i] \leftarrow v$ respectively read from and write the value v to the i-th slot in the tuple (of length n) stored at ℓ, assuming $0 \leq i < n$. The type system ensures that writes are only performed on mutable tuples.

Unlike F and C, the syntax of A distinguishes components e from terms t. A component e pairs a term t with a *heap fragment* H. H can contain functions and tuples that t may use by referring to locations in H. Intuitively, we need this notion of components because a bare term t is not as expressive as C component. In particular, A does not provide any way to dynamically allocate a location and initialize it to a function. We discuss how the compiler produces components with heap fragments in §4.

Heap fragments are assigned heap types Ψ. A heap fragment may reference locations that are to be linked in by another component, so the judgment $\Psi \vdash H : \Psi'$ includes an external heap type Ψ as an environment used in assigning H the type Ψ'. Here, Ψ' must provide types for exactly the locations in H. Each h in H must typecheck under the disjoint union of the two heap types (Ψ, Ψ'). Similarly, a component (t, H) can reference both external locations and those bound by H, that is, locations in the domain of either the external heap type Ψ or of H.

Our operational semantics for A is a relation between configurations $\langle H \mid e \rangle$. Any code or data in the internal heap fragment of component e must be loaded into memory before it can be run. We formally capture this with a reduction rule that "loads" a component by merging its internal heap fragment with the external heap. When loading a component (t, H), we must rename the locations bound in H so that they do not conflict with the external heap. After the loading step, the term component t can be evaluated using standard reduction rules.

The structure of A components also entails a small change to the structure of evaluation contexts, which are defined in two layers: contexts E expect components e, and term contexts E_t expect terms t. Terms are plugged into term contexts in the obvious way. Plugging a component-level evaluation context $E = (E_t, \cdot)$ with a component e is defined by $(E_t, \cdot)[(t, H)] = (E_t[t], H)$

4   The Compiler

Compiling F to C. Closure conversion collects a function's free term variables in a tuple called the *closure environment* that is passed as an additional argument to the function, thus turning the function into a closed term. The closed function is paired with its environment to create a *closure*. The basic idea of typed closure conversion goes back to Minamide *et al.* [14], whom we follow in using an existential type to abstract the type of the environment. This ensures that two functions with the same type but different free variables still have the same type after closure conversion: the abstract type hides the fact that the closures' environments have different types.

We must also rewrite functions to take their free type variables as additional arguments. However, instead of collecting these types in a type environment as Minamide *et al.* do, we follow Morrisett *et al.* [13] and directly substitute the types into the function. Like the latter, we adopt a *type-erasure* interpretation, which means that since all types are erased at run time the substitution of types into functions has no run-time effect.

Our closure-conversion pass compiles F terms of type τ to C terms of type τ^C. Figure 2 (top) presents the type translation τ^C and some of the compilation rules. Since this is closure conversion, the only interesting parts are those that involve functions. The omitted rules are defined by structural recursion on terms.

Compiling C to A. Our second compiler pass combines hoisting of functions with explicit allocation of tuples. It takes a C component (that is, just a C term t) of type τ, and produces an A term t as well as a heap fragment H with all the hoisted functions.

$\boxed{\tau^{\mathcal{C}}}$ Type Translation

$$\alpha^{\mathcal{C}} = \alpha \quad \mathrm{unit}^{\mathcal{C}} = \mathrm{unit} \quad \mathrm{int}^{\mathcal{C}} = \mathrm{int} \quad \forall[\overline{\alpha}].(\overline{\tau}) \to \tau'^{\mathcal{C}} = \exists\beta.\langle(\forall[\overline{\alpha}].(\beta,\overline{\tau^{\mathcal{C}}}) \to \tau'^{\mathcal{C}}),\beta\rangle$$

$$\exists\alpha.\tau^{\mathcal{C}} = \exists\alpha.\tau^{\mathcal{C}} \qquad \mu\alpha.\tau^{\mathcal{C}} = \mu\alpha.\tau^{\mathcal{C}} \qquad \langle\tau_1,\ldots,\tau_n\rangle^{\mathcal{C}} = \langle\tau_1{}^{\mathcal{C}},\ldots,\tau_n{}^{\mathcal{C}}\rangle$$

$\boxed{\Delta;\Gamma \vdash e:\tau \leadsto e}$ Compiler (implies $\Delta^{\mathcal{C}};\Gamma^{\mathcal{C}} \vdash e:\tau^{\mathcal{C}}$)

$$\frac{x:\tau \in \Gamma}{\Delta;\Gamma \vdash x:\tau \leadsto x} \qquad \frac{}{\Delta;\Gamma \vdash ():\mathrm{unit} \leadsto ()} \qquad \frac{}{\Delta;\Gamma \vdash n:\mathrm{int} \leadsto n}$$

$$\frac{\begin{array}{c} y_1,\ldots,y_m = \mathrm{fv}(\lambda[\overline{\alpha}](\overline{x:\tau}).t) \qquad \beta_1,\ldots,\beta_k = \mathrm{ftv}(\lambda[\overline{\alpha}](\overline{x:\tau}).t) \\ \Delta,\overline{\alpha};\Gamma,\overline{x:\tau} \vdash t:\tau' \leadsto t \qquad \tau_{\mathrm{env}} = \langle(\Gamma(y_1))^{\mathcal{C}},\ldots,(\Gamma(y_m))^{\mathcal{C}}\rangle \\ v = \lambda[\overline{\beta},\overline{\alpha}](z:\tau_{\mathrm{env}},\overline{x:\tau^{\mathcal{C}}}).(t[\pi_1(z)/y_1]\cdots[\pi_m(z)/y_m]) \end{array}}{\begin{array}{c} \Delta;\Gamma \vdash \lambda[\overline{\alpha}](\overline{x:\tau}).t:\forall[\overline{\alpha}].(\overline{\tau}) \to \tau' \leadsto \\ \mathrm{pack}\langle\tau_{\mathrm{env}},\langle v[\overline{\beta}],\langle\overline{y}\rangle\rangle\rangle \text{ as } \exists\alpha'.\langle(\forall[\overline{\alpha}].(\alpha',\overline{\tau^{\mathcal{C}}}) \to \tau'^{\mathcal{C}}),\alpha'\rangle \end{array}}$$

$$\frac{\Delta;\Gamma \vdash t_0:\forall[\overline{\alpha}].(\overline{\tau_1}) \to \tau_2 \leadsto t_0 \quad \Delta \vdash \overline{\tau} \quad \Delta;\Gamma \vdash \overline{t}:\overline{\tau_1[\tau/\alpha]} \leadsto \overline{t}}{\Delta;\Gamma \vdash t_0[\overline{\tau}]\,\overline{t}:\tau_2[\overline{\tau/\alpha}] \leadsto \mathrm{unpack}\,\langle\beta,z\rangle = t_0 \text{ in } \pi_1(z)\,[\overline{\tau^{\mathcal{C}}}]\,\pi_2(z),\overline{t}}$$

$\boxed{\tau^{\mathcal{A}}}$ Type Translation

$$\alpha^{\mathcal{A}} = \alpha \quad \mathrm{unit}^{\mathcal{A}} = \mathrm{unit} \quad \mathrm{int}^{\mathcal{A}} = \mathrm{int} \quad \forall[\overline{\alpha}].(\overline{\tau}) \to \tau'^{\mathcal{A}} = \mathrm{box}\,\forall[\overline{\alpha}].(\overline{\tau^{\mathcal{A}}}) \to \tau'^{\mathcal{A}}$$

$$\exists\alpha.\tau^{\mathcal{A}} = \exists\alpha.\tau^{\mathcal{A}} \qquad \mu\alpha.\tau^{\mathcal{A}} = \mu\alpha.\tau^{\mathcal{A}} \qquad \langle\tau_1,\ldots,\tau_n\rangle^{\mathcal{A}} = \mathrm{box}\,\langle(\tau_1{}^{\mathcal{A}}),\ldots(\tau_n{}^{\mathcal{A}})\rangle$$

$\boxed{\Delta;\Gamma \vdash e:\tau \leadsto (t,H:\Psi)}$ Compiler (implies $\cdot \vdash H:\Psi$, and $\cdot;\Delta^{\mathcal{A}};\Gamma^{\mathcal{A}} \vdash (t,H):\tau^{\mathcal{A}}$)

$$\frac{x:\tau \in \Gamma}{\Delta;\Gamma \vdash x:\tau \leadsto (x,\cdot:\cdot)} \qquad \frac{}{\Delta;\Gamma \vdash ():\mathrm{unit} \leadsto ((),\cdot:\cdot)} \qquad \cdots$$

$$\frac{\overline{\alpha};\overline{x:\tau} \vdash t:\tau' \leadsto (t,H:\Psi)}{\begin{array}{c} \Delta;\Gamma \vdash \lambda[\overline{\alpha}](\overline{x:\tau}).t:\forall[\overline{\alpha}].(\overline{\tau}) \to \tau' \leadsto \\ (\ell,(H,\ell \mapsto \lambda[\overline{\alpha}](\overline{x:\tau^{\mathcal{A}}}).t):(\Psi,\ell:{}^{\mathrm{box}}\forall[\overline{\alpha}].(\overline{\tau^{\mathcal{A}}}) \to \tau'^{\mathcal{A}})) \end{array}}$$

$$\frac{\Delta;\Gamma \vdash t_1:\tau_1 \leadsto (t_1,H_1:\Psi_1) \quad \cdots \quad \Delta;\Gamma \vdash t_n:\tau_n \leadsto (t_n,H_n:\Psi_n)}{\begin{array}{c} \Delta;\Gamma \vdash \langle t_1,\ldots,t_n\rangle:\langle\tau_1,\ldots,\tau_n\rangle \leadsto \\ (\mathrm{balloc}\,\langle t_1,\ldots,t_n\rangle,(H_1,\ldots,H_n):(\Psi_1,\ldots,\Psi_n)) \end{array}}$$

Fig. 2. Compiler from F to C (top) and from C to A (bottom)

The component (t,H) is the overall output, and has type $\tau^{\mathcal{A}}$ under an empty external heap. The heap fragment generated by the compiler does not contain tuples: the compiler translates C tuples by generating **balloc** expressions, not by putting them in a static heap fragment. The type translation and interesting parts of the term translation are shown in Figure 2 (bottom).

5   F and C Interoperability

5.1   The Basics

We now present a formal semantics for interoperability between F and C. For now, we define a combined language FC; in §6, we will extend this to FCA. Our FC multi-language system embeds the languages F and C so that both languages have natural access to foreign values (i.e., values from the other language). In particular, we want F components of type τ to be usable as C components of type τ^C, and vice versa. To allow cross-language communication, FC extends the original F and C with syntactic boundaries, written $^\tau\mathcal{F}C\,e$ (C inside, F outside) and $\mathcal{C}\mathcal{F}^\tau e$ (F inside, C outside).

The interesting cases in the semantics of boundaries are those that handle universal and existential types. These must be defined carefully to ensure that type abstraction is not broken as values pass between languages. First, though, we explain the general principles of our boundary semantics by looking at the cases for simple types and their translations.

CF *Boundary Semantics.* A term $\mathcal{C}\mathcal{F}^\tau e$ has type τ^C if e has type τ. To evaluate this boundary term, FC's operational semantics require first that e be reduced to a value v (using F reduction rules). Then a type-directed meta-function is applied to v, yielding a value in C of type τ^C (written $\mathbf{CF}^\tau(v) = v$). An important restriction on this meta-function, which we call the *value translation*, is that it is only defined for *closed* values. This is sufficient for our needs because it is used only by the FC operational semantics, and substitution-based reduction relations are defined only for closed programs. We can still write FC programs with free variables appearing under boundaries, but by the time we evaluate the boundary term, we will have supplied values for all of these free variables.

At base types, value translation is easy: for example, translating a value n of type int yields the same integer in C, n. Most of the other types are translated simply by structural recursion.

The interesting case is the case for function types. Consider the translation of a value v of type $\tau \to \tau'$. As per the type translation, this should produce a value of type $\exists\beta.\langle((\beta,\tau^C) \to \tau'^C),\beta\rangle$. Since v is closed, we can simply use unit for the type β of the closure environment:
$$\mathbf{CF}^{\tau \to \tau'}(v) = \text{pack}\langle\text{unit},\langle v,()\rangle\rangle \text{ as } \exists\beta.\langle((\beta,\tau^C) \to \tau'^C),\beta\rangle$$
We must still construct the underlying function v for this closure, which we can do using boundary terms and the original function v:
$$v = \lambda(z:\text{unit}, x:\tau^C).\mathcal{C}\mathcal{F}^{\tau'}(v\,^\tau\mathcal{F}C\,x).$$
The function we build simply translates its argument from C to F, applies v to the translated argument, and finally translates the result back into C.

The full translation rule for functions must also handle type arguments and requires some additional machinery, which we will discuss momentarily.

FC *Boundary Semantics.* The term $^\tau\mathcal{F}C\,e$ has type τ when e has type τ^C. As before, to evaluate a boundary term, we first evaluate the component under the boundary, this time to a value v. Then we apply a value translation $^\tau\mathbf{FC}(v) = v$ that yields an F value v of type τ. Again, this translation is only defined for closed values of translation type.

Let us consider the type $\tau \to \tau'$ again. A closure v of type $(\tau \to \tau')^{\mathcal{C}}$ must be translated to an F function that first translates its argument from F to C, then unpacks the closure v and applies the code to its environment and the translated argument, and finally translates the result back from C to F:

$$^{\tau \to \tau'}\mathbf{FC}(v) = \lambda(x\!:\!\tau).{}^{\tau'}\mathcal{FC}(\text{unpack } \langle \beta, y \rangle = v \text{ in } \pi_1(y) \, \pi_2(y) \, \mathcal{CF}^{\tau}x)$$

In both function cases, notice that the direction of the conversion (and the boundary used) reverses for function arguments.

5.2 Handling Abstract Types

Now that we have established the general structure of boundary rules, we come to the interesting cases, those for abstract types.

FC *Type Abstraction.* Consider the type $\forall[\alpha].(\alpha) \to \alpha$. Since $\alpha^{\mathcal{C}} = \alpha$, the translation of this type is

$$(\forall[\alpha].(\alpha) \to \alpha)^{\mathcal{C}} = \exists\beta.\langle(\forall[\alpha].(\beta, \alpha) \to \alpha), \beta\rangle.$$

If we naively try to extend the function case of the value translation given above, we get the following:

$$^{\forall[\alpha].(\alpha) \to \alpha}\mathbf{FC}(v) = \lambda[\alpha](x\!:\!\alpha).{}^{\alpha}\mathcal{FC}(\text{unpack } \langle \beta, y \rangle = v \text{ in } \pi_1(y) \, [\alpha^{\mathcal{C}}] \, \pi_2(y) \, \mathcal{CF}^{\alpha}x)$$

Note that we have not expanded $\alpha^{\mathcal{C}}$ in the application produced by this translation. It would expand to a C type variable α, but we cannot allow this, because that α would be unbound! What we really want is that when α is instantiated with a concrete type τ, the positions inside language C where that type is needed receive $\tau^{\mathcal{C}}$.

We resolve this by making two changes to our system: first, we add a type $\lceil\alpha\rceil$ (which may be read as "α suspended in C") that allows an F type variable to appear in a C type. The F type variable α needs to be translated, but the translation is *delayed* until α is instantiated with a concrete type. We enforce this semantics in the definition of type substitution: $\lceil\alpha\rceil[\tau/\alpha] = \tau^{\mathcal{C}}$.

Second, we adjust the type translation to turn F type variables into suspended type variables instead of C type variables. We call this modified version of the type translation the *boundary type translation*, and notate it by $\tau^{\langle\mathcal{C}\rangle}$. Formally, the rule for type variables in the compiler's type translation is replaced by the rule $\alpha^{\langle\mathcal{C}\rangle} = \lceil\alpha\rceil$ in the boundary type translation. We only want to suspend free type variables, so when we translate a type that contains bound variables, we need to restore the behavior of the compiler's type translation when we translate the binding position. We can do this using a substitution, e.g., $(\exists\alpha.\tau)^{\langle\mathcal{C}\rangle} = \exists\alpha.(\tau^{\langle\mathcal{C}\rangle}[\alpha/\lceil\alpha\rceil])$. Thus the boundary type translation preserves the binding structure of the type to which it is applied.

With these two changes, we can correct the example above by replacing the appearance of $\alpha^{\mathcal{C}}$ with $\alpha^{\langle\mathcal{C}\rangle}$, and we get a sensible translation from C to F for values of type $(\forall[\alpha].(\alpha) \to \alpha)^{\mathcal{C}}$.

CF *Type Abstraction.* Next, consider translating values of type $\forall[\alpha].(\alpha) \to \alpha$ from F into C. Once again, the existing machinery is not quite sufficient. Here is a naive attempt:

$$\mathbf{CF}^{\forall[\alpha].(\alpha) \to \alpha}(v) = \text{pack}\langle\text{unit}, \langle v, () \rangle\rangle \text{ as } (\forall[\alpha].(\alpha) \to \alpha)^{\langle\mathcal{C}\rangle}$$
$$\text{where } v = \lambda[\alpha](z\!:\!\text{unit}, x\!:\!\alpha).\mathcal{CF}^{\alpha}(v\,[\alpha]\,{}^{\alpha}\mathcal{FC}x).$$

$$\begin{array}{llll}
\tau ::= \cdots \mid \mathsf{L}\langle\tau\rangle & \tau ::= \cdots \mid \lceil\alpha\rceil & \tau ::= \tau \mid \tau & \\
t ::= \cdots \mid {}^{\tau}\mathcal{FC}\,e & t ::= \cdots \mid \mathcal{CF}^{\tau}e & e ::= e \mid e & \\
v ::= \cdots \mid {}^{\mathsf{L}\langle\tau\rangle}\mathcal{FC}v & v ::= \cdots & v ::= v \mid v & \Delta ::= \cdot \mid \Delta,\alpha \mid \Delta,\alpha \\
E ::= \cdots \mid {}^{\tau}\mathcal{FC}\,E & E ::= \cdots \mid \mathcal{CF}^{\tau}E & E ::= E \mid E & \Gamma ::= \cdot \mid \Gamma,x{:}\tau \mid \Gamma,x{:}\tau
\end{array}$$

$\boxed{\tau^{\langle\mathcal{C}\rangle}}$ Boundary Type Translation

$$\forall[\overline{\alpha}].(\overline{\tau}) \to \tau'^{\langle\mathcal{C}\rangle} = \exists\beta.\left\langle\left(\forall[\overline{\alpha}].(\beta, \overline{\tau^{\langle\mathcal{C}\rangle}\lceil\alpha/\lceil\alpha\rceil\rceil}) \right) \to \tau'^{\langle\mathcal{C}\rangle}\overline{\lceil\alpha/\lceil\alpha\rceil\rceil}\right), \beta\right\rangle$$

$$\alpha^{\langle\mathcal{C}\rangle} = \lceil\alpha\rceil \qquad \mathsf{unit}^{\langle\mathcal{C}\rangle} = \mathsf{unit} \qquad \mathsf{int}^{\langle\mathcal{C}\rangle} = \mathsf{int} \qquad \exists\alpha.\tau^{\langle\mathcal{C}\rangle} = \exists\alpha.(\tau^{\langle\mathcal{C}\rangle}[\alpha/\lceil\alpha\rceil])$$

$$\mu\alpha.\tau^{\langle\mathcal{C}\rangle} = \mu\alpha.(\tau^{\langle\mathcal{C}\rangle}[\alpha/\lceil\alpha\rceil]) \qquad \langle\overline{\tau}\rangle^{\langle\mathcal{C}\rangle} = \langle\overline{\tau^{\langle\mathcal{C}\rangle}}\rangle \qquad \mathsf{L}\langle\tau\rangle^{\langle\mathcal{C}\rangle} = \tau$$

Type Substitution: $\lceil\alpha\rceil[\tau/\alpha] = \tau^{\langle\mathcal{C}\rangle}$

$\boxed{\Delta;\Gamma \vdash e:\tau}$ Include F and C rules, with environments replaced by $\Delta;\Gamma$

$$\dfrac{\Delta;\Gamma \vdash e:\tau^{\langle\mathcal{C}\rangle}}{\Delta;\Gamma \vdash {}^{\tau}\mathcal{FC}\,e:\tau} \qquad\qquad \dfrac{\Delta;\Gamma \vdash e:\tau}{\Delta;\Gamma \vdash \mathcal{CF}^{\tau}e:\tau^{\langle\mathcal{C}\rangle}}$$

$\boxed{\mathbf{CF}^{\tau}(\mathsf{v}) = v}$ Value Translation $\mathbf{CF}^{\mathsf{unit}}(()) = ()$ $\mathbf{CF}^{\mathsf{int}}(\mathsf{n}) = n$ $\mathbf{CF}^{\mathsf{L}\langle\tau\rangle}({}^{\mathsf{L}\langle\tau\rangle}\mathcal{FC}\mathsf{v}) = v$

$$\mathbf{CF}^{\forall[\overline{\alpha}].(\overline{\tau}) \to \tau'}(\mathsf{v}) = \mathsf{pack}\langle\mathsf{unit},\langle v, ()\rangle\rangle \text{ as } (\forall[\overline{\alpha}].(\overline{\tau}) \to \tau')^{\langle\mathcal{C}\rangle}$$
$$\text{where } v = \lambda[\overline{\alpha}](z{:}\mathsf{unit}, x{:}\overline{\tau^{\langle\mathcal{C}\rangle}\lceil\alpha/\lceil\alpha\rceil\rceil}).\mathcal{CF}^{\tau'\overline{[\mathsf{L}\langle\alpha\rangle/\alpha]}}(\mathsf{v}\,\overline{[\mathsf{L}\langle\alpha\rangle]}\,\overline{{}^{\tau[\mathsf{L}\langle\alpha\rangle/\alpha]}\mathcal{FC}x})$$

$$\mathbf{CF}^{\exists\alpha.\tau}(\mathsf{pack}\langle\tau',\mathsf{v}\rangle \text{ as } \exists\alpha.\tau) = \mathsf{pack}\langle\tau'^{\langle\mathcal{C}\rangle},v\rangle \text{ as } \exists\alpha.\tau^{\langle\mathcal{C}\rangle} \qquad \text{where } \mathbf{CF}^{\tau[\tau'/\alpha]}(\mathsf{v}) = v$$

$$\mathbf{CF}^{\mu\alpha.\tau}(\mathsf{fold}_{\mu\alpha.\tau}\mathsf{v}) = \mathsf{fold}_{\mu\alpha.\tau^{\langle\mathcal{C}\rangle}} v \qquad\qquad \text{where } \mathbf{CF}^{\tau[\mu\alpha.\tau/\alpha]}(\mathsf{v}) = v$$

$$\mathbf{CF}^{\langle\tau_1,\ldots,\tau_n\rangle}(\langle\mathsf{v}_1,\ldots,\mathsf{v}_n\rangle) = \langle v_1,\ldots,v_n\rangle \qquad\qquad \text{where } \mathbf{CF}^{\tau_i}(\mathsf{v}_i) = v_i$$

$\boxed{{}^{\tau}\mathbf{FC}(\mathsf{v}) = v}$ Value Translation ${}^{\mathsf{unit}}\mathbf{FC}(()) = ()$ ${}^{\mathsf{int}}\mathbf{FC}(\mathsf{n}) = n$ ${}^{\mathsf{L}\langle\tau\rangle}\mathbf{FC}(\mathsf{v}) = {}^{\mathsf{L}\langle\tau\rangle}\mathcal{FC}\mathsf{v}$

$$^{\forall[\overline{\alpha}].(\overline{\tau}) \to \tau}\mathbf{FC}(\mathsf{v}) = \lambda[\overline{\alpha}](\overline{x{:}\tau}).{}^{\tau}\mathbf{FC}(\mathsf{unpack}\,\langle\beta,y\rangle = \mathsf{v}\text{ in }\pi_1(y)\,[\overline{\lceil\alpha\rceil}]\,\pi_2(y), \overline{\mathcal{CF}^{\tau}x})$$

$$^{\exists\alpha.\tau}\mathbf{FC}(\mathsf{pack}\langle\tau',\mathsf{v}\rangle \text{ as } \exists\alpha.\tau^{\langle\mathcal{C}\rangle}) = \mathsf{pack}\langle\mathsf{L}\langle\tau'\rangle,v\rangle \text{ as } \exists\alpha.\tau \qquad \text{where } {}^{\tau[\mathsf{L}\langle\tau'\rangle/\alpha]}\mathbf{FC}(\mathsf{v}) = v$$

$$^{\mu\alpha.\tau}\mathbf{FC}(\mathsf{fold}_{\mu\alpha.\tau^{\langle\mathcal{C}\rangle}} \mathsf{v}) = \mathsf{fold}_{\mu\alpha.\tau} v \qquad\qquad \text{where } {}^{\tau[\mu\alpha.\tau/\alpha]}\mathbf{FC}(\mathsf{v}) = v$$

$$^{\langle\tau_1,\ldots,\tau_n\rangle}\mathbf{FC}(\langle\mathsf{v}_1,\ldots,\mathsf{v}_n\rangle) = \langle v_1,\ldots,v_n\rangle \qquad\qquad \text{where } {}^{\tau_i}\mathbf{FC}(\mathsf{v}_i) = v_i$$

$\boxed{e \longmapsto e'}$ Include F and C rules, replacing eval. contexts E, E with E.

$$\dfrac{\mathbf{CF}^{\tau}(\mathsf{v}) = v}{E[\mathcal{CF}^{\tau}\mathsf{v}] \longmapsto E[v]} \qquad\qquad \dfrac{{}^{\tau}\mathbf{FC}(\mathsf{v}) = v \quad \tau \neq \mathsf{L}\langle\tau\rangle}{E[{}^{\tau}\mathcal{FC}\mathsf{v}] \longmapsto E[v]}$$

Fig. 3. FC multi-language system (extends F and C from Figure 1)

This time, we have translated the binder for α into a C binder for α, but we are left with free occurrences of α in the result! This is not a suitable translation, as we must produce a closed value. Note that the boundary terms in the body of v expect to be annotated with a type that translates to α.

To fix this problem, we introduce a *lump type* $\mathsf{L}\langle\tau\rangle$ that allows us to pass C values to F terms as opaque lumps. The introduction form for the lump type is the boundary term ${}^{\mathsf{L}\langle\tau\rangle}\mathcal{FC}e$, and the elimination form is $\mathcal{CF}^{\mathsf{L}\langle\tau\rangle}e$. A pair of opposite boundaries at lump type cancel, to yield the underlying C value. We extend the boundary type translation by defining $\mathsf{L}\langle\tau\rangle^{\langle\mathcal{C}\rangle} = \tau$.

Now the three free occurrences of α in v can be replaced with $\mathsf{L}\langle\alpha\rangle$, yielding a well-typed translation.

Summary. With the additional tools of lumps, suspensions, and the boundary type translation, we have now developed everything needed for the FC multi-language system. Figure 3 presents more of the details, including the complete value translations.

The syntax of FC simply combines the syntax of F with that of C, and adds boundaries, lumps, and suspensions. The type judgment combines the type rules for F and C, but with the environments replaced by environments that can contain variables from both languages. We also add rules to typecheck boundary terms.

The cases of the value translations we have not yet covered mostly proceed by structural recursion, but note that the cases for existential types need to make use of lumps and suspensions (the suspensions are introduced by the boundary type translation) in ways that are dual to the function cases.

The reduction relation combines the reduction rules from F and C and adds rules for boundaries. The boundary reduction rules use the value translations to produce a value in the other language.

$$\tau ::= \cdots \mid L\langle\tau\rangle \qquad \tau ::= \cdots \mid \lceil\alpha\rceil \mid \lfloor\alpha\rfloor \qquad \tau ::= \cdots \mid \tau$$
$$t ::= \cdots \mid {}^{\tau}\mathcal{C}\mathcal{A}\,e \qquad t ::= \cdots \mid \mathcal{A}\mathcal{C}^{\tau}e \qquad e ::= \cdots \mid e \qquad \qquad \Delta ::= \cdots \mid \Delta, \alpha$$
$$v ::= \cdots \mid {}^{L\langle\tau\rangle}\mathcal{C}\mathcal{A}\,v \qquad v ::= \cdots \qquad\qquad v ::= \cdots \mid v \qquad \Gamma ::= \cdots \mid \Gamma, x : \tau$$
$$E ::= \cdots \mid {}^{\tau}\mathcal{C}\mathcal{A}\,E \qquad E_t ::= \cdots \mid \mathcal{A}\mathcal{C}^{\tau}E \qquad E ::= \cdots \mid E$$

$\boxed{\tau^{\langle\mathcal{A}\rangle}}$ Boundary Type Translation

$$\forall[\overline{\alpha}].(\overline{\tau}) \to \tau'^{\langle\mathcal{A}\rangle} = \text{box}\,\forall[\overline{\alpha}].(\overline{\tau^{\langle\mathcal{A}\rangle}[\alpha/\lceil\alpha\rceil]}) \to \tau'^{\langle\mathcal{A}\rangle}[\alpha/\lceil\alpha\rceil]$$

$$\alpha^{\langle\mathcal{A}\rangle} = \lceil\alpha\rceil \qquad \cdots \qquad L\langle\tau\rangle^{\langle\mathcal{A}\rangle} = \tau \qquad \lceil\alpha\rceil^{\langle\mathcal{A}\rangle} = \lceil\alpha\rceil$$

Type Substitution: $\lceil\alpha\rceil[\tau/\alpha] = (\tau^{\langle\mathcal{C}\rangle})^{\langle\mathcal{A}\rangle} \qquad \lceil\alpha\rceil[\tau/\alpha] = \tau^{\langle\mathcal{A}\rangle}$

$\boxed{\Psi;\Delta;\Gamma \vdash e : \tau}$ Include A rules and add Ψ to existing rules

$$\frac{\Psi;\Delta;\Gamma \vdash e : \tau^{\langle\mathcal{A}\rangle}}{\Psi;\Delta;\Gamma \vdash {}^{\tau}\mathcal{C}\mathcal{A}\,e : \tau} \qquad\qquad \frac{\Psi;\Delta;\Gamma \vdash e : \tau}{\Psi;\Delta;\Gamma \vdash \mathcal{A}\mathcal{C}^{\tau}e : \tau^{\langle\mathcal{A}\rangle}}$$

$\boxed{\mathbf{AC}^{\tau}(v, H) = (v, H')}$ Value Translation (selected cases) $\mathbf{AC}^{\text{unit}}((), H) = ((), H)$

$\mathbf{AC}^{\forall[\overline{\alpha}].(\overline{\tau}) \to \tau'}(v, H) = (\ell, (H, \ell \mapsto h))$

where $h = \lambda[\overline{\alpha}](x : \tau^{\langle\mathcal{A}\rangle}[\alpha/\lceil\alpha\rceil]).\mathcal{A}\mathcal{C}^{\tau'[L\langle\alpha\rangle/\alpha]}v\,[\overline{L\langle\alpha\rangle}]\,\overline{\tau^{[L\langle\alpha\rangle/\alpha]}\mathcal{C}\mathcal{A}\,x}$

$\mathbf{AC}^{\langle\overline{\tau}\rangle}(\langle\overline{v}\rangle, H_1) = (\ell, (H_{n+1}, \ell \mapsto \langle\overline{v}\rangle))$ where $\mathbf{AC}^{\tau_i}(v_i, H_i) = (v_i, H_{i+1})$

$\boxed{{}^{\tau}\mathbf{CA}(v, H) = (v, H')}$ Value Translation (selected cases) ${}^{\text{unit}}\mathbf{CA}((), H) = ((), H)$

${}^{\forall[\overline{\alpha}].(\overline{\tau}) \to \tau'}\mathbf{CA}(v, H) = (\lambda[\overline{\alpha}](\overline{x : \tau}).{}^{\tau'}\mathbf{CA}(v\,[\overline{\lceil\alpha\rceil}]\,\overline{\mathcal{A}\mathcal{C}^{\tau}x}), H)$

${}^{\langle\overline{\tau}\rangle}\mathbf{CA}(\ell, H_1) = (\langle\overline{v}\rangle, H_{n+1})$ where $H_1(\ell) = \langle\overline{v}\rangle$ and ${}^{\tau_i}\mathbf{CA}(v_i, H_i) = (v_i, H_{i+1})$

$\boxed{\langle H \mid e\rangle \longmapsto \langle H' \mid e'\rangle}$ Lift FC rules to new config.; replace E with E

$$\frac{\mathbf{AC}^{\tau}(v, H) = (v, H')}{\langle H \mid E[\mathcal{A}\mathcal{C}^{\tau}v]\rangle \longmapsto \langle H' \mid E[v]\rangle} \qquad \frac{{}^{\tau}\mathbf{CA}(v, H) = (v, H') \quad \tau \neq L\langle\tau\rangle}{\langle H \mid E[{}^{\tau}\mathcal{C}\mathcal{A}\,v]\rangle \longmapsto \langle H' \mid E[v]\rangle}$$

Fig. 4. FCA multi-language system (extends Figures 1 and 3)

6   C and A Interoperability

The extensions to FC for interoperability with A are given in Figure 4. The principles discussed in the development of FC still apply, but here we need to handle the presence of the heap. Specifically, since functions and tuples in A are contained in the heap, the value translations need access to the program's memory. Going from C to A, the value translation may allocate new memory for functions and tuples; going from A to C requires looking up the contents of locations and translating those contents to functions or tuples in C. Thus, we pass the current memory as an argument to the translations, and return a memory that may have had additional locations allocated. Memory cells allocated by boundaries are always immutable.

Aside from this change, the extension for the new language mostly follows what we did for FC: we augment the syntax with boundaries between C and A, a lump type $L\langle \tau \rangle$ for opaquely embedding A values into C, and suspensions of type variables into A. Note that we need the boundary type translation from C to A to handle both C type variables α and suspended F type variables $\lceil \alpha \rceil$. Thus A has both $\lceil \alpha \rceil$ and $\lceil \alpha \rceil$ as suspension types. The boundary type translation $\tau^{\langle A \rangle}$ works similarly to $\tau^{\langle C \rangle}$. The figure shows the function case and the cases involving lumps and suspensions. The type judgment merges the A type rules with the FC type rules, but where the latter are modified to add the extra environment Ψ, and adds type rules for boundaries. Finally, the reduction relation for FCA lifts the FC reductions to use the configuration from A, with a program heap. We also add the reduction rules from A and a pair of boundary reduction rules that utilize the value translations.

7   Compiler Correctness

As mentioned in §1, we state compiler correctness in terms of FCA contextual equivalence. Below, we formally define contextual equivalence for FCA components and then present our compiler correctness theorems. We discuss how to prove these theorems in §9 and give a longer discussion and the full proofs in the technical report [9].

7.1   FCA Contextual Equivalence

A general context C is an FCA component with a hole. A component e can be plugged into the context only if it is from the same language as the hole. Since contexts can contain boundaries, e need not be from the same language as the outermost layer of C. The syntax of general contexts is given in Figure 5 (top). Contexts for F and C forms are standard. In A, we need contexts to be able to have their hole in either the term part of a component, or in the body of a function contained in the heap fragment. So in addition to contexts C that produce components, we have context forms C_t and C_H that produce terms and heap fragments, respectively.

When plugging an A component (t, H) into a context C, the heap fragment H is placed at the innermost component-level layer of C—that is, at the language boundary closest to the hole—and merged with the heap fragment already in that position. To formalize this, the A portion of the definition of plugging a component into a context is given in Figure 5 (middle). The definition of plugging for F and C contexts is standard.

$$C ::= [\cdot] \mid C \, p \, t \mid \cdots \mid \lambda[\overline{\alpha}](\overline{x:\tau}).C \mid \cdots \mid {}^\tau\mathcal{F}C \, C$$
$$C ::= [\cdot] \mid \cdots \mid \lambda[\overline{\alpha}](\overline{x:\tau}).C \mid \cdots \mid \mathcal{C}\mathcal{F}^\tau C \mid {}^\tau\mathcal{C}\mathcal{A} \, C$$
$$C ::= (C_t, H) \mid (t, C_H)$$
$$C_t ::= [\cdot] \mid \cdots \mid \mathcal{A}\mathcal{C}^\tau C \qquad C_H ::= C_H, \ell \mapsto h \mid H, \ell \mapsto \lambda[\overline{\alpha}](\overline{x:\tau}).C_t$$
$$C ::= C \mid C \mid C$$

$C[e]$	Context Plugging (A cases shown)

$$(C_t, H)[e] = \begin{cases} (C_t[t], (H, H')) & e = (t, H') \wedge C_t \text{ contains no language boundaries} \\ (C_t[e], H) & \text{otherwise} \end{cases}$$

$$(t, C_H)[e] = \begin{cases} (t, (C_H[t'], H')) & e = (t', H') \wedge C_H \text{ contains no language boundaries} \\ (t, C_H[e]) & \text{otherwise} \end{cases}$$

$$[\cdot][t] = t \qquad\qquad (C_t \, p \, t)[e] = (C_t[e]) \, p \, t \qquad \cdots$$

$$(C_H, \ell \mapsto h)[e] = (C_H[e]), \ell \mapsto h$$

$$(H, \ell \mapsto \lambda[\overline{\alpha}](\overline{x:\tau}).C_t)[e] = H, \ell \mapsto \lambda[\overline{\alpha}](\overline{x:\tau}).(C_t[e])$$

$\vdash C : (\Psi; \Delta; \Gamma \vdash \tau) \rightsquigarrow (\Psi'; \Delta'; \Gamma' \vdash \tau')$	Context Typing (omitted)

Contextual Equivalence

$$\Psi; \Delta; \Gamma \vdash e_1 \approx^{ctx} e_2 : \tau \overset{\text{def}}{=} \Psi; \Delta; \Gamma \vdash e_1 : \tau \wedge \Psi; \Delta; \Gamma \vdash e_2 : \tau \wedge$$
$$\forall C, H, \Psi', \tau'. \vdash C : (\Psi; \Delta; \Gamma \vdash \tau) \rightsquigarrow (\Psi'; \cdot; \cdot \vdash \tau') \wedge \vdash H : \Psi'$$
$$\implies (\langle H \mid C[e_1]\rangle \downarrow \iff \langle H \mid C[e_2]\rangle \downarrow)$$

Fig. 5. General Contexts & Contextual Equivalence for FCA

Given this notion of general contexts, contextual equivalence for FCA is standard (see Figure 5, bottom). It says that two components e_1 and e_2 are contextually equivalent under environments Ψ, Δ, Γ and at type τ if the following hold: First, both components must typecheck under Ψ, Δ, Γ at type τ. Second, if C is a context that expects to be given a component that typechecks under Ψ, Δ, Γ at type τ, and produces a resulting program that is closed but expects to be run with a heap of type Ψ', then $C[e_1]$ and $C[e_2]$ have the same termination behavior when we run them with any initial heap H that has type Ψ'.

7.2 Compiler Correctness

We can now state our main result: compiler-correctness theorems for both passes of our compiler.

Theorem 1 (Closure Conversion is Semantics-Preserving). *If* $\overline{\alpha}; \overline{x:\tau'} \vdash e : \tau \rightsquigarrow e$, *then* $\cdot; \overline{\alpha}; \overline{x:\tau'} \vdash e \approx^{ctx} {}^\tau\mathcal{F}C(e[\lceil\overline{\alpha}\rceil/\alpha][\mathcal{C}\mathcal{F}^\tau x/x]) : \tau$.

Theorem 2 (Allocation is Semantics-Preserving). *If* $\overline{\alpha}; \overline{x:\tau'} \vdash e : \tau \rightsquigarrow (t, H : \Psi)$, *then* $\cdot; \overline{\alpha}; \overline{x:\tau'} \vdash e \approx^{ctx} {}^\tau\mathcal{C}\mathcal{A}(t[\lceil\overline{\alpha}\rceil/\alpha][\mathcal{A}\mathcal{C}^{\tau'} x/x], H) : \tau$.

The formal theorems are essentially as we described our compiler correctness results in §1, with only one additional subtlety: we need to perform a substitution so that the free variables of the original component match those of the compiled component. Recall that the compiler turns free type and term variables α and x into type and term variables α and x from the next language, whereas FCA needs the binding structure of components to be preserved, including free variables being in the language prescribed by the type environments Δ and Γ. To get the free variables of the two components back into sync, we substitute suspended type variables for translated type variables, and we substitute boundary terms for translated term variables. Note that we do not need to perform a substitution in the heap fragment produced by the allocation pass, since heap values must be closed anyway.

We could equivalently have stated these theorems with the substitution on the other side, and the environments correspondingly translated; e.g.

$$\cdot; \overline{\alpha}^{\mathcal{C}}; \overline{x : \tau'}^{\mathcal{C}} \vdash \overline{e[L\langle\alpha\rangle/\alpha]}\,[\hat{\tau}' \mathcal{F C} x / x] \approx^{ctx} {}^{\hat{\tau}} \mathcal{F C}\, e : \hat{\tau},$$

where $\hat{\tau} = \tau\overline{[L\langle\alpha\rangle/\alpha]}$ and $\hat{\tau}' = \tau'\overline{[L\langle\alpha\rangle/\alpha]}$.

It also does not matter which side the boundary term is placed on: boundary cancellation lemmas allow us to prove as a corollary that, for example,

$$\cdot; \overline{\alpha}; \overline{x : \tau} \vdash \mathcal{C F}^{\tau} e \approx^{ctx} \overline{e[\lceil\alpha\rceil/\alpha]}\,[\mathcal{C F}^{\tau'} x / x] : \tau^{\langle\mathcal{C}\rangle}.$$

Since we want to ensure that type variables in the environment remain tied to their free occurrences in the result type, this version of the theorem uses the boundary type translation $\tau^{\langle\mathcal{C}\rangle}$ for the result type (instead of the compiler's type translation $\tau^{\mathcal{C}}$).

Contextual equivalence is transitive, so we can easily chain these theorems together to prove correctness for the full compiler:

Corollary 1 (Compiler Correctness). *If* $\overline{\alpha}; \overline{x : \tau'} \vdash e : \tau \rightsquigarrow e \rightsquigarrow e$, *then*

$$\cdot; \overline{\alpha}; \overline{x : \tau'} \vdash e \approx^{ctx} {}^{\tau} \mathcal{F C A}(e\overline{[\lceil\alpha\rceil/\alpha]}[\mathcal{A C F}^{\tau'} x / x]) : \tau.$$

8 An Example

We can use our compiler correctness theorem to make statements about linking with arbitrary A components, as long as they have translation type. In this section, we present an example showing how our framework allows linking both with A components that cannot be expressed in F, and with those that can. To keep our example concise, we use variable substitution as a simple notion of linking.

Consider the component

$$e = (\lambda g : \text{unit} \rightarrow \text{int}. \ (g\ ()) * (g\ ()))\ x,$$

where $\cdot; \cdot; (x : \text{unit} \rightarrow \text{int}) \vdash e : \text{int}$. In F alone, only divergent or constant functions can have type unit $\rightarrow$ int, but if we are compiling to A before linking, we could be given a component that makes use of A's mutable references.

Putting e through the first compiler pass, we get a C component that contains several administrative reductions. The complete result of compilation is shown in the technical report, but for readability, we pretend that e compiles to

$$e = (\lambda g : \exists\alpha.\langle(\alpha, \text{unit})\rightarrow\text{int}, \alpha\rangle.(\text{unpack } \langle\beta, z\rangle = g \text{ in } (\pi_1(z)\ \pi_2(z)\ ())))$$
$$* (\text{unpack } \langle\beta, z\rangle = g \text{ in } (\pi_1(z)\ \pi_2(z)\ ()))))\ x,$$

which is equivalent to the actual result of compilation, and has exactly the same function body as the closure produced by the compiler.

The second pass brings us to an A component $e = (t, H)$, where $t = \ell\, x$ and $H = \ell \mapsto \lambda g : \exists \alpha.\text{box } \langle \text{box } (\alpha, \text{unit}) \rightarrow \text{int}, \alpha \rangle$.

$$((\text{unpack } \langle \beta, z \rangle = g \text{ in } ((\text{read}[1]\, z)\ (\text{read}[2]\, z)\ ())) *$$
$$(\text{unpack } \langle \beta, z \rangle = g \text{ in } ((\text{read}[1]\, z)\ (\text{read}[2]\, z)\ ())))).$$

By compiler correctness, we know that
$$\cdot; \cdot; (x : \text{unit} \rightarrow \text{int}) \vdash e \approx^{ctx}\ {}^{\text{int}}\mathcal{FCA}(e[\mathcal{ACF}^{\text{unit} \rightarrow \text{int}}x/x]) : \text{int}.$$

Equivalently,
$$\cdot; \cdot; (x : \tau) \vdash \mathcal{ACF}^{\text{int}}(e[^{\text{unit} \rightarrow \text{int}}\mathcal{FCA}\, x/x]) \approx^{ctx} e : \text{int},$$

where $\tau = \text{unit} \rightarrow \text{int}^{\langle \mathcal{C} \rangle \langle \mathcal{A} \rangle} = \exists \alpha.\text{box } \langle \text{box } (\alpha, \text{unit}) \rightarrow \text{int}, \alpha \rangle$.

Suppose we want to instantiate x with the following A component, which creates a function that uses a mutable reference to return the number of times it has been called:

$e' = (\text{pack} \langle \text{ref int}, \text{balloc } \langle \ell, \text{ralloc } \langle 0 \rangle \rangle \rangle \text{ as } \tau,$

$\quad \ell \mapsto \lambda(x : \text{ref int}, z : \text{unit}).\ \text{let } y = \text{read}[1]\, x \text{ in let } z = \text{write } x\, [1] \leftarrow y + 1 \text{ in } y + 1).$

We would then have
$$\cdot; \cdot; \cdot \vdash \mathcal{ACF}^{\text{int}}(e[^{\text{unit} \rightarrow \text{int}}\mathcal{FCA}\, e'/x]) \approx^{ctx} e[e'/x] : \text{int},$$

The right-hand side of this equivalence is exactly the pure-A program that we would ultimately run, and the left-hand side is an FCA program that models it. Note that on either side of the equation, the function exported by e' will be applied to the unit value twice, returning 1 the first time and 2 the second time. An F function could not exhibit this behavior. This demonstrates how our framework allows for linking with components that are not expressible in F.

If we want instead to link with a different A component $\hat{e}$ that was compiled from an F component $\hat{e}$, we can still make the statement
$$\cdot; \cdot; \cdot \vdash \mathcal{ACF}^{\text{int}}(e[^{\text{unit} \rightarrow \text{int}}\mathcal{FCA}\, \hat{e}/x]) \approx^{ctx} e[\hat{e}/x] : \text{int},$$

but we can also simplify this statement using our additional knowledge of $\hat{e}$. Our compiler correctness theorem tells us that
$$\cdot; \cdot; \cdot \vdash \mathcal{ACF}^{\text{unit} \rightarrow \text{int}}\, \hat{e} \approx^{ctx} \hat{e} : \tau.$$

From this, we can infer that
$$\cdot; \cdot; \cdot \vdash \mathcal{ACF}^{\text{int}}(e[^{\text{unit} \rightarrow \text{int}}\mathcal{FCA}(\mathcal{ACF}^{\text{unit} \rightarrow \text{int}}\, \hat{e})/x]) \approx^{ctx} e[\hat{e}/x] : \text{int}.$$

Applying boundary cancellation yields
$$\cdot; \cdot; \cdot \vdash \mathcal{ACF}^{\text{int}}(e[\hat{e}/x]) \approx^{ctx} e[\hat{e}/x] : \text{int}.$$

Now we are essentially equating the pure-A program with a pure-F program, since the only multi-language element in this statement is the integer boundary at the outermost level, which merely converts an n to n. This demonstrates that when we do have source-language equivalents for all our target-level components, our framework allows us to model target-level linking with source-level linking.

9   Proving Compiler Correctness

To prove the compiler correctness theorem, we design a step-indexed Kripke logical relation as a sound and complete model of contextual equivalence in FCA. Our logical relation extends that of Dreyer *et al.* [15] with the ability to handle multi-language type abstraction. We give an overview of the logical relation and a more detailed discussion of its novel features in the technical report [9]. In this section, we briefly discuss the high-level ideas behind our model's novel elements.

A logical-relations model provides a *relational value interpretation* of each type τ. This relation, which we denote $\mathcal{V}[\![\tau]\!]$, specifies when two values of type τ should be considered related or equivalent. When τ has free type variables, an environment ρ holds *arbitrary relational interpretations* for those abstract types. The relations in ρ capture the invariants of different instantiations of polymorphic values, which allows us to prove parametricity properties.

The interpretation $\mathcal{V}[\![\alpha]\!]\rho$ is defined by just looking up $\rho(\alpha)$. To prove important properties of $\mathcal{V}[\![\tau]\!]\rho$ for all types, we must ensure those properties hold in the α case by constraining the relations we can put into ρ to require these properties to hold upfront. Interpretations that satisfy these properties are called *candidates* or *admissible relations*.

In our multi-language setting, the two key properties we need to require for admissibility are boundary cancellation and the *bridge lemma*. The bridge lemma states that, given a pair of values v_1 and v_2 related according to the interpretation $\mathcal{V}[\![\tau]\!]\rho$, the $\mathbf{CF}^{\tau}$ translations of those values must be related according to $\mathcal{V}[\![\tau^{\langle C \rangle}]\!]\rho$. Similarly, given values v_1 and v_2 related according to $\mathcal{V}[\![\tau^{\langle C \rangle}]\!]\rho$, their $^{\tau}\mathbf{FC}$ translations must be related according to $\mathcal{V}[\![\tau]\!]\rho$. (We also require the analogous properties for the second pass.)

The type translation of α is $\lceil \alpha \rceil$, so in order for the bridge lemma to hold at type α, we need a suitable definition of $\mathcal{V}[\![\lceil\alpha\rceil]\!]\rho$, which necessarily will depend on $\rho(\alpha)$. One naïve definition we tried is the set of translations of values from $\rho(\alpha)$, roughly:

$$\mathcal{V}[\![\lceil\alpha\rceil]\!]\rho = \{(v_1, v_2) \mid (v_1, v_2) \in \rho(\alpha) \wedge \mathbf{CF}(v_i) = v_i\}.$$

While this definition does let us prove the bridge lemma at type α, it does not satisfy boundary cancellation: if v_1 and $\dot{v}_2$ are related according to this definition of $\mathcal{V}[\![\lceil\alpha\rceil]\!]\rho$, it is not necessarily the case that $\mathbf{CA}(\mathbf{AC}(v_1))$ and v_2 are related.

All the ways we tried to define $\mathcal{V}[\![\lceil\alpha\rceil]\!]\rho$ by a simple formula in terms of $\rho(\alpha)$ failed for similar reasons. Instead of giving a uniform definition, we took the viewpoint that if the properties of $\rho(\alpha)$ must be given *a priori*, then the particular relations with those properties that instantiate $\mathcal{V}[\![\alpha]\!]\rho$ and $\mathcal{V}[\![\lceil\alpha\rceil]\!]\rho$ should be given *a priori* as well. Specifically, in our model, an interpretation $\rho(\alpha)$ is not just given by a relation on F values, but by a triple containing the relation on F values, a relation on C values to serve as its "translation" and instantiate $\mathcal{V}[\![\lceil\alpha\rceil]\!]\rho$, and a relation on A values to instantiate $\mathcal{V}[\![\lceil\alpha\rceil]\!]\rho$. Similarly, an interpretation $\rho(\alpha)$ is given by a pair containing a C-level relation and an A-level relation. For $\rho(\alpha)$, since A is the target language, only one relation is needed.

This strategy moves the burden for defining the "translations" of candidate relations to the places in our proof development where individual candidates are needed. But in all these places, there is some specific information available about the relation, so it was not difficult to construct them.

10   Discussion and Future Work

Software is composed from components written in different languages because different languages are suited to different tasks. We have provided a novel methodology for verifying *open, multi-pass* compilers, one that yields a stronger theorem than any existing work, allowing target-level linking with components of arbitrary provenance regardless of whether the component can be expressed in the source language compiled by the verified compiler.

Adding Compiler Passes. Adding more intermediate languages to our compiler pipeline requires extending the multi-language model with new boundary forms and translation rules, and extending the logical relation with new clauses. Our aim is that the proof structure should be as modular as possible, so that the major lemmas and the correctness proof for one compiler pass can be completed independently of the rest of the pipeline. Presently, since our admissible relations design requires relations from multiple languages, we have a small number of places where a proof about one pass is affected by the other languages and passes. We hope to improve our proof engineering so that proofs for existing passes are unaffected when the compiler pipeline is changed.

Compiling to Assembly. We have extended our compiler with a code-generation pass that translates A components to a stack-based typed assembly language, T. The latter is similar to Morrisett *et al.*'s stack-based TAL [6] but with a type system that tracks more information. Informally, the T type system allows us to track calls and returns of semantic "functions" that may span multiple basic blocks, and to determine the "return type" of such functions. With this information, we are able to give a formal definition of contextual equivalence for T that makes distinctions about assembly at an appropriate level of granularity. That is, we relate assembly language components comprised of any number of basic blocks, rather than relating individual basic blocks. An equivalence relation based on individual blocks would be too fine grained; for instance, it would be unable to relate two components with an unequal number of basic blocks that may have been produced by compiling two equivalent source terms. We are working on the proofs for this pass and will report on it in a future paper.

Mutable References. Consider adding mutable references to F and C. For the first compiler pass, we would extend the type translation with $(\text{ref } \tau)^{\mathcal{C}} = \text{ref } \tau^{\mathcal{C}}$. When defining interoperability at type ref τ, it doesn't make sense to convert an F location ℓ into a fresh C location ℓ (and vice versa) since it would lead to duplication of mutable cells in the interoperating languages and these would be impossible to keep in sync. One solution is to treat a wrapped location (e.g., $^{\text{ref } \tau}\mathcal{FC}\ell$) as a value form. Operations on these wrapped locations can be performed by reduction rules such as these:

$$!(^{\text{ref } \tau}\mathcal{FC}\ell) \longmapsto {}^{\tau}\mathcal{FC}(!\ell) \quad (^{\text{ref } \tau}\mathcal{FC}\ell) := \mathsf{v} \longmapsto {}^{\text{unit}}\mathcal{FC}(\ell := \mathcal{CF}^{\tau}\mathsf{v}),$$

where $!\mathsf{v}$ is a dereference and $\mathsf{v} := \mathsf{v}'$ is an assignment. Passing references between C and A can be done analogously. While these interoperability semantics are straightforward, we expect to find nontrivial challenges in designing a logical relation to properly handle the wrapped-location value forms they introduce.

Supporting Realistic Interoperability. We are particularly interested in supporting target-level interoperability between a language with parametric polymorphism such as ML and languages without type abstraction such as Scheme or C. For instance, given a generic tree library compiled from ML, we want to allow code compiled from Scheme or C to be able to use the library but ensure that such use cannot invalidate ML's parametricity guarantees by inspecting values that have abstract type on the ML side. In this paper, we have shown how to preserve ML's parametricity guarantees part-way through the compiler. Going forward we wish to develop a gradually typed assembly language that, following Matthews and Ahmed [16], uses dynamic sealing on the untyped side to enforce parametricity guarantees provided by type abstraction on the typed side.

11 Related Work

The literature on compiler verification spans over four decades but is mostly limited to whole-program compilation; we refer the reader to the bibliography by Dave [17] for compilers for first-order languages, and to Chlipala [18] for compilers for higher-order functional languages. We have already discussed the existing work [10,12] on compositional compiler correctness in §2. Here we focus on other closely related work.

Dreyer et al. have recently been working on Relational Transition Systems (RTS's) [19] that may provide an alternative cross-language specification technique that is designed to make it possible to prove transitivity. Regardless, it is still not easy to do: see their technical report [20] where they prove transitivity for their *single-language* RTS system for an idealized ML. It is a non-trivial task to do this for multiple cross-language RTS's. Additionally, even if the RTS approach proves effective for verifying a multi-pass compiler, it still does not address the problem of linking with a component e'_T for which there is no related source-level e'_S.

The design of our multi-language system builds on that of Ahmed and Blume [8], who developed a boundary-based multi-language system embedding the source (STLC) and target (System F) of CPS translation. Ahmed and Blume did not have type abstraction in the source language, which meant that they did not have to make use of lumps or suspensions, nor design a logical relation to handle these. Our semantics preservation proof is analogous to theirs. However, since they were interested in fully abstract CPS translation, they designed their type translation to disallow linking compiled code with target components whose behavior cannot be expressed at the source level. The additional work that they do to prove full abstraction provides a roadmap for how to extend our methodology to prove full abstraction in a setting where the type translation enforces it.

Acknowledgements. We would like to thank Nick Benton, whose views on compositional compiler correctness have been an inspiration to us. In particular, our thinking has been influenced by Benton and Hur's introduction [11], which eloquently lays out desirable features of a compiler correctness specification. We would also like to thank Aaron Turon for helpful feedback on an earlier version of this paper. This research was supported by the National Science Foundation (grant CCF-1203008).

References

1. Leroy, X.: Formal certification of a compiler back-end or: programming a compiler with a proof assistant. In: POPL (2006)
2. Leroy, X.: A formally verified compiler back-end. J. Automated Reasoning 43(4), 363–446 (2009)
3. Lochbihler, A.: Verifying a compiler for Java threads. In: Gordon, A.D. (ed.) ESOP 2010. LNCS, vol. 6012, pp. 427–447. Springer, Heidelberg (2010)

4. Myreen, M.O.: Verified just-in-time compiler on x86. In: POPL 2010 (2010)
5. Sevcik, J., Vafeiadis, V., Nardelli, F.Z., Jagannathan, S., Sewell, P.: Relaxed-memory concurrency and verified compilation. In: POPL 2011 (2011)
6. Morrisett, G., Crary, K., Glew, N., Walker, D.: Stack-based typed assembly language. J. Functional Programming 12(1), 43–88 (2002)
7. Matthews, J., Findler, R.B.: Operational semantics for multi-language programs. In: POPL 2007 (2007)
8. Ahmed, A., Blume, M.: An equivalence-preserving CPS translation via multi-language semantics. In: ICFP 2011 (2011)
9. Perconti, J.T., Ahmed, A.: Verifying an open compiler using multi-language semantics (technical report) (January 2014), http://ccs.neu.edu/home/amal/voc/
10. Benton, N., Hur, C.K.: Biorthogonality, step-indexing and compiler correctness. In: ICFP 2009 (2009)
11. Benton, N., Hur, C.K.: Realizability and compositional compiler correctness for a polymorphic language. Technical Report MSR-TR-2010-62, Microsoft Research (April 2010)
12. Hur, C.K., Dreyer, D.: A Kripke logical relation between ML and assembly. In: POPL 2011 (2011)
13. Morrisett, G., Walker, D., Crary, K., Glew, N.: From System F to typed assembly language. ACM TOPLAS 21(3), 527–568 (1999)
14. Minamide, Y., Morrisett, G., Harper, R.: Typed closure conversion. In: POPL 1996 (1996)
15. Dreyer, D., Neis, G., Birkedal, L.: The impact of higher-order state and control effects on local relational reasoning. J. Functional Programming 22(4&5), 477–528 (2012)
16. Matthews, J., Ahmed, A.: Parametric polymorphism through run-time sealing, or, theorems for low, low prices! In: Drossopoulou, S. (ed.) ESOP 2008. LNCS, vol. 4960, pp. 16–31. Springer, Heidelberg (2008)
17. Dave, M.A.: Compiler verification: A bibliography. ACM SIGSOFT Software Engineering Notes 28(6) (2003)
18. Chlipala, A.: A verified compiler for an impure functional language. In: POPL 2010 (2010)
19. Hur, C.K., Dreyer, D., Neis, G., Vafeiadis, V.: The marriage of bisimulations and Kripke logical relations. In: POPL 2012 (2012)
20. Hur, C.K., Dreyer, D., Neis, G., Vafeiadis, V.: The marriage of bisimulations and Kripke logical relations. Technical report, Max Planck Institute for Software Systems (January 2012)

Impredicative Concurrent Abstract Predicates

Kasper Svendsen and Lars Birkedal

Aarhus University
{ksvendsen,birkedal}@cs.au.dk

Abstract. We present impredicative concurrent abstract predicates –
iCAP – a program logic for modular reasoning about concurrent, higher-
order, reentrant, imperative code. Building on earlier work, iCAP uses
protocols to reason about shared mutable state. A key novel feature of
iCAP is the ability to define impredicative protocols; protocols that are
parameterized on arbitrary predicates, including predicates that themselves refer to protocols. We demonstrate the utility of impredicative
protocols through a series of examples, including the specification and
verification, *in the logic*, of a spin-lock, a reentrant event loop, and
a concurrent bag implemented using cooperation, against *modular*
specifications.

1 Introduction

It is well-known that modular specification and verification of concurrent higher-
order imperative programs is very challenging. Recently good progress has been
made on reasoning about subsets of these language features. For instance, concurrent abstract predicates [8] has proved useful for reasoning about shared
mutable data structures in a concurrent setting and state transition systems [10]
have proved useful for reasoning about higher-order functions and shared mutable data structures and, very recently, also concurrency [23].

Internal and External Sharing. The logics referred to above extend rely-
guarantee versions of separation logic [24,11] with protocols governing access to
shared mutable state. These logics are sufficiently expressive to verify implementations of abstract data structures that use sharing *internally* against abstract
specifications that hide this *internal sharing*. However, in practice programmers
often also use shared mutable data structures to facilitate *external* sharing –
the sharing of a mutable data structure through another shared mutable data
structure. A lock is the canonical example of a data structure used to facilitate
external sharing. In higher-order separation logic we can easily express *specifications* that support reasoning about external sharing, by parameterizing our
specifications with assertions that describe the external resources shared through
the data structure. However, without imposing severe predicativity restrictions
(as in our earlier [21]), verifying implementations against such higher-order specifications *in the logic* is currently impossible!

To illustrate, consider a simple lock. We can specify a lock in higher-order separation logic by parameterizing our lock specification with a resource invariant

Z. Shao (Ed.): ESOP 2014, LNCS 8410, pp. 149–168, 2014.
© Springer-Verlag Berlin Heidelberg 2014

R that describes the resources protected by the lock (the *externally* shared resources):

$$\{R\} \text{ new Lock() } \{\text{isLock}(R, \text{ret})\}$$
$$\{\text{isLock}(R, x)\} \text{ x.Acquire() } \{\text{locked}(R, x) * R\}$$
$$\{\text{locked}(R, x) * R\} \text{ x.Release() } \{\text{isLock}(R, x)\}$$

$$\text{isLock}(R, x) \Leftrightarrow \text{isLock}(R, x) * \text{isLock}(R, x)$$

Here isLock and locked are abstract predicates; $\text{isLock}(R, x)$ expresses that x is a lock protecting the resource invariant R and $\text{locked}(R, x)$ expresses that the lock x is indeed locked. Acquiring the lock grants ownership of R, while releasing the lock requires the client to relinquish ownership of R. Since the resource invariant R is universally quantified, this is a very strong specification; in particular, the client is free to instantiate R with any assertion, *including assertions about other shared resources or even the lock itself*. In Section 2.2 we will see that resource invariants that refer to the lock itself are useful for reasoning about reentrancy.

There has been some previous work on logics for languages with *built-in* locks [12,14]. In [14] the built-in locks were shown to satisfy a similar higher-order specification, as part of the logic's soundness proof. However, to reason about libraries in general (not just built-in locks), we, of course, need to able to verify that implementations satisfy such specifications in the logic.

Our first contribution is a new program logic, *impredicative Concurrent Abstract Predicates* or *iCAP*, that is sufficiently expressive to support modular reasoning about both internal *and* external sharing. It is the first logic that can verify implementations of synchronization primitives, such as locks, against such higher-order specifications *in the logic*.

Layered and Recursive Abstractions. One of the main objectives of iCAP is to support modular reasoning about *libraries* consisting of concurrent, higher-order, reentrant, imperative code. In iCAP we have focused on two types of modularity that are both important in programming practice. The first type is simply the ability to build layers of abstractions; for instance, we want to be able to reason about a hashtable library implemented using a linked list library through an abstract linked list specification and hide this internal use of the linked list abstraction in the abstract hashtable specification. The second type of modularity is more challenging, namely the ability to build recursive abstractions; for instance, we want to be able to verify *reentrant libraries* against an abstract specification that allows clients to register callbacks that can themselves use the abstract library specification to reason about calls into the library.

To illustrate the problem of modular reasoning about reentrant libraries, consider an *event loop library* satisfying the interface given below.[1]

---

[1] The first line declares a delegate type (a type-safe function pointer type) by the name handler for delegates that do not take any arguments and do not return anything.

```
public delegate void handler();

interface IEventLoop {
  void loop();
  void signal();
  void when(handler f);
}
```

This library allows clients to emit an event using the `signal` method, to register an event handler using the `when` method and start the event loop using the `loop` method. Crucially, this library explicitly allows event handlers to emit events and thereby schedule themselves for execution once again! We have simplified this example to focus on the main difficulty introduced by reentrancy – namely that clients can *tie Landin's knot through the library* – however, this pattern is *ubiquitous* in the real world. For instance, event-driven code is ubiquitous in GUI applications and high-performance network applications as a way of implementing asynchronous I/O [1,18].

To support *modular* reasoning about such examples and in particular the event loop, we need a logic that is sufficiently expressive to (1) define an abstract event loop specification that allows clients to register callbacks that emit events *and reason about these callbacks using the same abstract specification* and (2) allow implementors to verify an implementation of the event loop against the abstract event loop specification.

In Section 2.2 we explain how to verify an implementation against such an abstract specification, by defining the memory footprint of the event loop implementation recursively. In iCAP we achieve this using *guarded recursion*. One of the implementations we consider uses the lock module and thus, as we shall see, the recursively defined predicate involves the abstract isLock predicate. To the best of our knowledge, iCAP is the first program logic that supports such modular reasoning about layered and recursive abstractions, and a key technical contribution of our work is the model used to show the soundness of this expressive logic, in particular, the ability to define predicates recursively *across abstraction boundaries*.

Fine-Grained Concurrency. Fine-grained concurrent ADTs allow multiple threads to interleave memory operations on the underlying data representation, with the goal of reducing critical sections as much as possible, often down to basic compare-and-swap operations. Sophisticated fine-grained concurrent ADTs also employ *cooperation* [23] among threads and in particular the technique of *helping*, where one thread may help another complete its operation [13].

Conceptually, separation logic achieves modular reasoning about shared mutable state through the notion of resources that describe *information* about some part of the state and assert certain *rights* to modify this part of the state. To support *modular* reasoning about ADTs we need abstract specifications that allow *clients* to define high-level ADT resources with a notion of rights expressed in terms of the operations provided by the ADT rather than rights to modify the underlying data representation. Previous CAP-based techniques for reasoning about fine-grained concurrent data structures have either not scaled to handle implementations that employed helping [21], or have verified implementations with helping against *non-modular* specifications [8] that imposed a fixed notion of rights – choosen by the module *implementor* – on clients.

In iCAP, using impredicative protocols, we can verify fine-grained concurrent ADTs implemented with helping against *modular* specifications that allow *clients* to define high-level ADT resources. In Section 2.3 we present an example to show how this is done.

Details and proofs can be found in the accompanying appendix and technical report available at:

https://bitbucket.org/logsem/public/wiki/icap

1.1   Summary of Contributions

In summary, our contributions include the design of a new sound program logic, iCAP, for *modular* reasoning about concurrent, higher-order, reentrant, imperative programs. In particular, iCAP supports modular reasoning about internal and external sharing, layered and recursive abstractions, and fine-grained cooperative implementations of concurrent data structures.

iCAP's expressiveness derives from the fact that it is a *higher-order* logic supporting guarded recursion and impredicative protocols. The presence of these features means that soundness of iCAP is non-trivial. Thus a key technical contribution of our work is our soundness proof of iCAP, which uses a novel model construction that we explain in Section 3.

2   Examples

2.1   Internal and External Sharing – A Lock

Following concurrent separation logic and its descendants [16,12,14], assertions in iCAP describe resources that may potentially be shared between several threads according to some protocol. A key feature of iCAP is that it supports full higher-order quantification over assertions in specifications. This means that we can give the following general abstract specification for a lock, which we explained informally in the introduction.

$$\exists \mathsf{isLock}, \mathsf{locked} : \mathsf{Prop} \times \mathsf{Val} \to \mathsf{Prop}.\ \forall R : \mathsf{Prop}.\ \mathsf{stable}(R) \ \Rightarrow$$
$$\{R\}\,\mathbf{new}\ \mathsf{Lock}(-)\,\{\mathsf{ret}.\ \mathsf{isLock}(R, \mathsf{ret})\}$$
$$\wedge\ \{\mathsf{isLock}(R, x)\}x.\mathsf{Acquire}(-)\,\{\mathsf{locked}(R, x) * R\}$$
$$\wedge\ \{\mathsf{locked}(R, x) * R\}x.\mathsf{Release}(-)\,\{\mathsf{ret}.\ \mathsf{emp}\}$$
$$\wedge\ \mathsf{valid}(\forall x : \mathsf{Val}.\ \mathsf{isLock}(R, x) \Leftrightarrow \mathsf{isLock}(R, x) * \mathsf{isLock}(R, x))$$
$$\wedge\ \forall x : \mathsf{Val}.\ \mathsf{stable}(\mathsf{isLock}(R, x)) \wedge \mathsf{stable}(\mathsf{locked}(R, x))$$

In this formal specification Prop is the type of iCAP assertions, which includes assertions about shared resources. The specification thus explicitly requires the resource invariant R to be stable (invariant under any changes to the state the environment is permitted to make). The existentially quantified predicates isLock and locked are used to support modular reasoning about internal sharing, whereas the universally quantified predicate R is used to support modular reasoning about external sharing.

This specification asserts the existence of a lock representation predicate that is *parametric* in the resource invariant R. This allows us to use the lock representation predicate itself when defining resource invariants and thus to define recursive resource invariants. Had we simply asserted that for each resource invariant R, there exists a *non-parametric* lock representation predicate isLock$_R$, this would *not* be possible! As we will see in Section 2.2, the above *third-order* lock specification and the ability to define recursive resource invariants is critical for reasoning about the reentrancy of a multi-threaded event loop.

To verify an implementation against this specification we have to provide concrete instantiations for the parametric isLock and locked predicates and prove that the implementation satisfies the specification with these concrete instantiations. Since this specification explicitly allows clients to define recursive resource invariants, most of the difficulty in verifying an implementation boils down to defining the parametric isLock and locked predicates. In iCAP this is trivial using impredicative protocols.

A Spin-Lock. The implementation we have in mind is a simple spin-lock; it maintains a single boolean field, locked, which is true if and only if the lock is currently held. When the lock is unlocked, the lock owns the resource invariant R. Once the lock has been locked, only the *exclusive* owner of the locked resource is allowed to unlock the lock! We can express this protocol formally using iCAP.

iCAP extends separation logic with shared regions. Resources in shared regions are — as the name implies — shared between all clients. Upon allocation of a new shared region, we can pick a protocol of our choice, describing what resources the shared region must own. A protocol consists of a labelled transition system, labelled with *action identifiers*, and an assertion for each abstract state in the transition system that describes the resources the shared region must own in the given state. The transitions then specify how the abstract states of the region are allowed to evolve and the labels how different clients are allowed to evolve the states. In particular, for a client to change the state from s_1 to s_2, the client must own permissions to labels along a path from s_1 to s_2.

In the case of the spin-lock, for each instance of the spin-lock, we introduce a new shared region that governs that spin-lock and the resources protected by that lock. The labelled transition system that governs a spin-lock is very simple: it contains two abstract states — locked (L) and unlocked (U) — and the two obvious transitions:

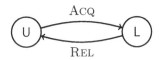

The next step is to define an assertion for each abstract state describing the resources owned by the spin-lock region (conceptually, the lock) in the given state. This is mostly straightforward. When the lock is locked, the lock owns the locked field, which contains true. However, when the lock is unlocked, the lock owns both the locked field, which contains false, and the resource invariant R:

$$I(n, R, x)(L) \stackrel{\text{def}}{=} x.\text{locked} \mapsto \text{true} \qquad I(n, R, x)(U) \stackrel{\text{def}}{=} x.\text{locked} \mapsto \text{false} * R * [\text{REL}]_1^n$$

To capture that only the owner of the locked resource is allowed to unlock the lock, we also let the lock take full ownership of the REL transition for the given region, when the lock is unlocked. Formally this is expressed using an action assertion, $[\alpha]_\pi^n$. Here π is a fraction between 0 and 1, and $[\alpha]_\pi^n$ asserts π-ownership of the α action on region n. When the client locks the lock, the client can thus take ownership of both the resource invariant R and the exclusive (1) permission to transition the shared region back into the unlocked state. Note that this spin-lock protocol is parameterized over an arbitrary resource invariant R provided by the client and is thus an *impredicative protocol*.

With these ingredients we are now ready to instantiate isLock. The isLock predicate asserts that there exists a shared region governed by the above spin-lock protocol, that is either in the unlocked or locked state; and furthermore, it asserts *non-exclusive* permission to the ACQ action. Formally, this is expressed as follows (where T_{lock} refers to the labelled transition system above):

$$\text{isLock}(R, x) \stackrel{\text{def}}{=} \exists n : \text{RId.} \ [\text{ACQ}]_-^n * \text{rintr}(I(n, R, x), n) * \text{region}(\{L, U\}, T_{lock}, n)$$

The region assertion, $\text{region}(X, T, n)$, asserts that there exists a region with region identifier n, whose labelled transition system is T and that the current abstract state of region n is a member of the set X. The labelled transition system T is represented as a function from action identifiers to relations on abstract states; see the appendix for details. To specify the spin-lock protocol we also need to specify what resources the spin-lock must own in the different abstract states. This is expressed using the region interpretation assertion, $\text{rintr}(I, n)$, which takes as argument a predicate I, indexed by the abstract states of the given region. We use $[\alpha]_-^n$ as shorthand for $\exists \pi. \ [\alpha]_\pi^n$ to express non-exclusive ownership of an action α.

This illustrates the use of iCAP's impredicative protocols for defining the concrete instantion of isLock for a spin-lock. Now that isLock has been defined, the actual verification of the spin-lock implementation with this concrete instantiation follows the structure of the original CAP proof of a spin-lock [8]. One crucial difference is that iCAP features enough proof rules to carry out the proof *in the logic*, including stability proofs. In the appendix, we show in detail how to verify the spin-lock implementation with this concrete instantiation using the formal iCAP proof system.

Compared to earlier work on concurrent abstract predicates [8,9,21], in iCAP we simplify the description of protocols, by describing them using state transition systems. This presentation is inspired by earlier work by Dreyer et. al. on protocols for reasoning about local state in higher-order programs [10]. We believe this description of protocols is a useful conceptual simplification compared to the original CAP presentation [8], in particular since protocols can now easily be drawn. However, we stress that this presentation also simplifies stability proofs in the program logic, since they only have to refer to abstract states in the transition system. The iCAP stability obligations for the verification of the spin-lock are thus significantly easier to prove that the corresponding stability obligations from the original spin-lock CAP proof.

2.2   Layered and Recursive Abstractions – An Event Loop

The previous example illustrated how iCAP's impredicative protocols allow modular reasoning about internal and external sharing. In this section we illustrate how higher-order logic and guarded recursion allow modular reasoning about layered and recursive abstractions.

A Single-Threaded Event Loop. Recall the *reentrant* event loop library from the introduction. We can express an abstract event loop specification for single-threaded event loops that explicitly allows clients to reason about event handlers using the same event loop specification as follows:

$$\exists \mathsf{eloop} : \mathsf{Val} \to \mathsf{Prop}.$$

$$\{\mathsf{emp}\}\,\mathbf{new}\ \mathsf{EventLoop}(-)\,\{\mathsf{ret}.\ \mathsf{eloop}(\mathsf{ret})\}$$

$$\wedge\ \{\mathsf{eloop}(\mathsf{x})\}\mathsf{x}.\mathsf{loop}(-)\,\{\mathsf{eloop}(\mathsf{x})\}$$

$$\wedge\ \{\mathsf{eloop}(\mathsf{x})\}\mathsf{x}.\mathsf{signal}(-)\,\{\mathsf{eloop}(\mathsf{x})\}$$

$$\wedge\ \{\mathsf{eloop}(\mathsf{x}) * \mathsf{f} \mapsto \{\mathsf{eloop}(\mathsf{x})\}\{\mathsf{eloop}(\mathsf{x})\}\}\mathsf{x}.\mathsf{when}(\mathsf{f})\,\{\mathsf{eloop}(\mathsf{x})\}$$

This specification asserts the existence of an abstract event loop resource, eloop, which is created by creating a new event loop instance and preserved by all event loop methods. The when method for registering event handlers requires that the given event handler satisfies the nested Hoare triple

$$\mathsf{f} \mapsto \{\mathsf{eloop}(\mathsf{x})\}\{\mathsf{eloop}(\mathsf{x})\},$$

thereby explicitly allowing event handlers to use the abstract eloop resource to emit events. In a sense this is a very *weak* specification, in that it only allows us to reason about memory safety of our clients. However, in the presence of reentrancy, verifying an implementation against this simplified specification is highly non-trivial and beyond almost all current program logics.[2]

To define a concrete eloop resource, imagine a concrete implementation that maintains a set of pending events and a set of registered handlers, as sketched below.

```
class EventLoop : IEventLoop {
    private Set<event> signals;
    private Set<handler> handlers;

    ...
}
```

---

[2] The exception being our own HOCAP [21], which, however, had other severe restrictions compared to iCAP.

To allow the event loop to call registered event handlers, the eloop resource must assert that the registered event handlers satisfy some specification. To allow event handlers to emit events, this specification must itself refer to the eloop resource. In iCAP we can express this recursion by guarding the recursive occurence of the eloop resource and defining eloop by *guarded recursion* (note the use of the "later" ($\triangleright$) connective, which serves as a guard):

$$\text{eloop} = \text{fix}(\ \lambda \text{eloop} : \text{Val} \rightarrow \text{Prop}.\ \lambda x : \text{Val}.\ \exists y, z : \text{Val}.\ \exists A, B : \mathcal{P}_{fin}(\text{Val}).$$

$$x.\text{signals} \mapsto y * x.\text{handlers} \mapsto z * \text{set}(y, A) * \text{set}(z, B) *$$

$$\forall b \in B.\ \triangleright b \mapsto \{\text{eloop}(x)\}\{\text{eloop}(x)\})$$

This event loop resource asserts exclusive ownership of the signals field, the handlers field, the set of pending events, the set of registered handlers, and that all registered handlers satisfy the specification $f \mapsto \{\text{eloop}(x)\}\{\text{eloop}(x)\}$, one step later.

In our operational semantics each atomic statement takes one step to execute and executing a method or delegate call executes one atomic statement before the body of the method or delegate is executed. Hence, to verify a call to a method or delegate, it suffices to know the specification of the method or delegate body, one step later. We can thus verify calls from the event loop to the registered event handlers using the guarded eloop resource defined above.

Note that eloop is *not* definable by induction, as the recursive argument is not applied to a structurally smaller argument, nor by Tarski's fixed-point theorem, as nested Hoare triples are contravariant in the pre-condition and covariant in the postcondition.

As with the lock example, the interesting part of the verification of a reentrant event loop is the definition of the event loop resource. Once the event loop resource has been defined, the verification is routine. The real challenge is defining a logic and accompanying model that supports such recursive resource definitions!

A Multi-threaded Event Loop. The single-threaded event loop example illustrated the use of guarded recursion for reasoning about recursive abstractions. To make the example even more challenging and truly illustrate the power of impredicative protocols, let us now consider a *multi-threaded* reentrant event loop library. The abstract event loop specification remains the same, expect with the added axiom that the abstract event loop resource is freely duplicable (thus allowing any number of clients to use the event loop concurrently):

$$\text{valid}(\forall x : \text{Val}.\ \text{eloop}(x) \Leftrightarrow \text{eloop}(x) * \text{eloop}(x))$$

As for the implementation, imagine a lock-based implementation that extends the previous implementation with a lock that protects the set of pending events and the set of registered event handlers. Conceptually, we thus have a library that allows clients to tie Landin's knot *through a reference protected by a lock*. To verify the single-threaded implementation, we needed to refer to eloop to specify the registered handlers when defining eloop. Likewise, now eloop must assert the existence of a lock that protects the registered event handlers that are again specified in terms of eloop (note the use of isLock):

$$\begin{aligned}
\mathsf{eloop} = \mathsf{fix}(\ &\lambda \mathsf{eloop} : \mathsf{Val} \to \mathsf{Prop}.\ \lambda \mathsf{x} : \mathsf{Val}.\ \exists \mathsf{l} : \mathsf{Val}.\ \mathsf{x.lock} \mapsto \mathsf{l} * \\
&\mathsf{isLock}(\mathsf{l}, \exists \mathsf{y}, \mathsf{z} : \mathsf{Val}.\ \exists A, B : \mathcal{P}_{fin}(\mathsf{Val}). \\
&\mathsf{x.signals} \mapsto \mathsf{y} * \mathsf{x.handlers} \mapsto \mathsf{z} * \mathsf{set}(\mathsf{y}, A) * \mathsf{set}(\mathsf{z}, B) * \\
&\forall b \in B.\ \rhd\, b \mapsto \{\mathsf{eloop}(\mathsf{x})\}\{\mathsf{eloop}(\mathsf{x})\}))
\end{aligned}$$

This definition is extremely interesting! First of all, it illustrates the true power of the third-order lock specification to define *recursive* resource invariants *that refer back to the lock itself*. This is only possible because the abstract lock specification asserts the existence of a *parameterized* lock representation predicate; thus allowing us to *define the resource invariant in terms of the lock itself* (the resource invariant we use for the lock is the argument given to isLock, which refers to eloop, which again refers to isLock).

This example also illustrates the ability of iCAP to combine layered and recursive abstractions; in this example we are reasoning about the recursive event loop abstraction in terms of the lock abstraction defined in Section 2.1. In particular, the eloop representation predicate is defined in terms of an *abstract* isLock representation predicate. To ensure that eloop is well-defined we thus have to prove guardedness across an abstraction boundary (i.e., that the recursive occurence of eloop inside the abstract isLock assertion is guarded). This is automatically enforced in iCAP (!), and thus iCAP supports modular reasoning about guardedness. Semantically, this is enforced in the interpretation of the iCAP function space, which intuitively does not consist of all set-theoretic functions, but only those functions that are suitably non-expansive. Note that these intracies in the model are abstracted away by the iCAP logic and the proof in iCAP of the well-definedness of the eloop predicate above is completely trivial and just follows from the fact that the recursive occurrence of eloop is under a $\rhd$ guard.

These two event loop examples illustrate how we can reason about recursive abstractions in iCAP and also exemplify the power of impredicative protocols. For presentation purposes we considered the core part of a simple example — we emphasize that this style of reasoning also scales to full functional verification of complicated examples such as the joins library [19], which combines layered and recursive abstractions with internal and external sharing in a higher-order, concurrent, reentrant, imperative library. We have previously verified a lock-based joins implementation in HOCAP against an abstract joins specification with an explicit predicative stratification [20]. In iCAP, using impredicative protocols, we can verify the joins implementation against a much *simpler* and more *expressive* joins specification. Furthermore, in HOCAP we could not verify a fine-grained implementation of the joins library; in iCAP this is now possible using the techniques explained in the following.

2.3   Fine-Grained Concurrency – A Concurrent Bag

In this section we illustrate how iCAP supports *modular* reasoning about advanced concurrent ADTs by verifying a fine-grained implementation of a concurrent bag, implemented using helping, against a *modular* ADT specification.

We start by recalling our specification pattern from HOCAP [21] for expressing modular ADT specifications that allow clients to define a high-level ADT resources with a notion of rights that matches the client's intended use. Next, we sketch how to verify a fine-grained implementation with helping of a concurrent bag against an abstract bag specification expressed using this specification pattern. See the associated technical report for the full proof.

A Modular ADT Specification. Recall that in a sequential setting, one typically specifies data structure operations by relating an abstraction of the initial and terminal state of the operation through an abstract representation predicate. For instance, we might specify a Push method for an unordered bag as follows:

$$\{\mathsf{bag}(\mathsf{x}, A)\}\ \mathsf{x.Push(y)}\ \{\mathsf{bag}(\mathsf{x}, A \cup \{\mathsf{y}\})\}$$

This says that if, initially, the bag contains the elements in the multiset A, then, upon termination, the bag contains the elements in A and y. Crucially, this specification relates the abstract initial and terminal effects of the *entire* Push method.

In a concurrent setting we can reason modularly about implementations that satisfy that for each intermediate state in its execution, there exists some abstract state describing the concrete state and the method contains zero or more atomic instructions that modify the abstract state. Following our earlier work [21], the idea now is to allow clients to reason about the abstract initial and terminal state for each of these *atomic instructions*, rather than the abstract initial and terminal state of the *entire method*. By allowing clients to reason about the atomic instructions that modify the abstract state, clients can define their own high-level ADT resources with a notion of rights expressed in terms of the abstract state.

Technically, we achieve this using a *phantom field*, shared between the concurrent ADT and any clients, that stores the current abstract state of an instance. Phantom fields play a similar role as ghost/auxiliary variables [17], in that they are fields used only for specification purposes. We use $\mathsf{x}_f \overset{\pi}{\mapsto} v$ to assert fractional ownership of phantom field f on object x with fraction π. By splitting ownership of the phantom field we ensure that the concurrent ADT and any clients agree on the current abstract state. To allow clients to reason about the atomic instructions that modify the abstract state (and thus the phantom field), we further parameterize the specification of each method with a *view shift*. View shifts describe updates to the instrumented state that do not affect the concrete state. View shifts can thus be used to update phantom fields, allocate new regions and change the abstract state of a region, potentially transferring ownership of some resource in the process. We use $P \sqsubseteq Q$ to express that P can be view shifted to Q. See the appendix for proof rules relating to phantom fields and view shifts.

A Modular Bag Specification. We present part of the bag specification in Figure 1; we now explain it. We only include an operation to create the bag and a push operation, the specification for a pop method is similar and omitted.

$$\exists \mathsf{bag} : \mathsf{RId} \times \mathsf{Val} \to \mathsf{Prop}.$$

$$\{\mathsf{emp}\} \; \mathbf{new} \; \mathsf{Bag}(-) \; \{\mathsf{ret}. \; \exists \mathsf{n} : \mathsf{RId}. \; \mathsf{bag}(\mathsf{n}, \mathsf{ret}) * \mathsf{ret}_{\mathsf{cont}} \overset{1/2}{\mapsto} \emptyset\}$$

$$\forall \mathsf{P}, \mathsf{Q} : \mathsf{Val} \times \mathsf{Val} \to \mathsf{Prop}. \; \forall \mathsf{n} : \mathsf{RId}.$$

$$(\forall \mathsf{X} : \mathcal{P}_m(\mathsf{Val}). \; \forall \mathsf{x}, \mathsf{y} : \mathsf{Val}.$$

$$\mathsf{x}_{\mathsf{cont}} \overset{1/2}{\mapsto} \mathsf{X} * \mathsf{P}(\mathsf{x}, \mathsf{y}) \sqsubseteq^{RId \setminus \{\mathsf{n}\}} \mathsf{x}_{\mathsf{cont}} \overset{1/2}{\mapsto} (\mathsf{X} \cup \{\mathsf{y}\}) * \mathsf{Q}(\mathsf{x}, \mathsf{y})) \; \Rightarrow$$

$$\{\mathsf{bag}(\mathsf{n}, \mathsf{x}) * \mathsf{P}(\mathsf{x}, \mathsf{y})\} \; \mathsf{x}.\mathsf{Push}(\mathsf{y}) \; \{\mathsf{bag}(\mathsf{n}, \mathsf{x}) * \mathsf{Q}(\mathsf{x}, \mathsf{y})\}$$

Fig. 1. Part of a modular bag specification

In the case of the Push method, assuming it only contains a single atomic instruction that "commits" the push, we can express this formally by relating the effects of the Push method with an arbitrary "push" view shift provided by the client, see Lines 3–6 in Figure 1. The view shift expresses what should happen at the client side when the abstract state of the push operation takes place. The assertion $\mathsf{x}_{\mathsf{cont}} \overset{1/2}{\mapsto} \mathsf{X}$ asserts half-ownership of the phantom field cont, which contains the current abstract state of the bag. By letting the data structure own half and clients share the other half (clients get the other half by calling the **new** method), clients can impose a protocol on the abstract state that matches their intended notion of rights through their half of the phantom field. Since updating the phantom field requires both halves, this forces clients to prove that the abstract effects of any call to the Push method satisfies any protocols clients may have imposed.

We call the view shift in the premise of the above rule a "push" view shift because it requires the client to update the initial abstract state from X to $\mathsf{X} \cup \{\mathsf{y}\}$, for any abstract state X. Conceptually, this view shift is thus an atomic "push" method at the instrumented level and the push specification expresses that the Push method simulates any such "push" view shift provided by the client. The universally quantified predicates P and Q allow the client to relate its local state with the abstract initial and terminal state of the atomic instruction that "commits" the push. We refer to P and Q as *synchronization pre- and postconditions.*

In [21] we had to impose severe restrictions on P and Q due to the lack of impredicative protocols, but with iCAP, there are no restrictions on P and Q, resulting in *much simpler* and *more expressive* refinable specifications.

Finally we comment on the superscript on the view shifts and the region identifier n argument to the bag predicate, $\mathsf{bag}(\mathsf{n}, \mathsf{x})$. In iCAP, when reasoning about an atomic instruction, we can "open" a shared region and move the shared resources into our local state for the duration of the atomic instruction, provided we obey the protocol imposed by the region. Clearly, it is only sound to "open" each region once for each atomic instruction (opening a region twice results in two local copies of the shared region's resources).[3] Since the "push" view shifts provided by the client are used during the atomic instruction that "commits" the push, we have to ensure that the client does not "open" the module's region with its view shifts. We thus parameterize the bag predicate with a region identifier n to reveal that the bag module may use region n. As discussed in the appendix, this allows us to express, qua the superscript on the view shift, that the view shift provided by the client should not open the region n.

Now we have explained how to give a modular, refinable, specification to a concurrent data structure. We now sketch how iCAP can be used to verify that a sophisticated fine-grained concurrent implementation using cooperation actually meets the modular bag specification. iCAP is the first program logic that supports verification of such sophisticated implementations against such modular specifications (in particular, in our earlier work [21] we could not deal with implementations using cooperation).

To reduce contention on the main data structure used to implement the bag, a thread seeking to push an element (the "pusher") may offer the push operation to other threads, using a side-channel. If a thread seeking to pop (the "popper") then comes along, it may notice and accept the push-offer, without touching the main data structure at all. By accepting the push-offer the popper also completes the operation of the pusher, and in that sense it has *helped* the pusher. The heart of the verification is the protocol used for handling offers. In our case, that protocol can be described using the following labelled transition system, denoted T_{offer}:

Intuitively, pending means that an offer has been made and it is waiting for somebody to accept it, accepted means that the offer has been accepted, ack'ed means that we have acknowledged that somebody has accepted the offer, and revoked is used for the case where we revoke the offer (since no one accepted it and now we will re-attempt to push).

The interpretation of the states of T_{offer} are as follows:

$$I_{offer}(n, P, Q, b, x, y)(\text{pending}) \stackrel{\text{def}}{=} x.\text{state} \mapsto 0 * P(b, y) *$$
$$spec(\forall X : \mathcal{P}_m(\text{Val}). \ \forall x, y : \text{Val}.$$
$$x_{cont} \stackrel{1/2}{\mapsto} X * P(x, y) \sqsubseteq^{RId\backslash\{n\}} x_{cont} \stackrel{1/2}{\mapsto} (X \cup \{y\}) * Q(x, y))$$

---

[3] See the appendix for a concrete counterexample.

$$\mathsf{I}_{\mathit{offer}}(\mathsf{n},\mathsf{P},\mathsf{Q},\mathsf{b},\mathsf{x},\mathsf{y})(\mathsf{accepted}) \stackrel{\mathrm{def}}{=} \mathsf{x}.\mathsf{state} \mapsto 1 * \mathsf{Q}(\mathsf{b},\mathsf{y})$$

$$\mathsf{I}_{\mathit{offer}}(\mathsf{n},\mathsf{P},\mathsf{Q},\mathsf{b},\mathsf{x},\mathsf{y})(\mathsf{revoked}) \stackrel{\mathrm{def}}{=} \mathsf{x}.\mathsf{state} \mapsto 2$$

$$\mathsf{I}_{\mathit{offer}}(\mathsf{n},\mathsf{P},\mathsf{Q},\mathsf{b},\mathsf{x},\mathsf{y})(\mathsf{ack'ed}) \stackrel{\mathrm{def}}{=} \mathsf{x}.\mathsf{state} \mapsto 1$$

Here b refers to the bag, x refers to the offer, y is the value on offer, and P and Q are the pusher's synchronization pre- and postconditions.

The interpretations of the states contain information about the value of program variable state, which is used by the implementation to keep track of which state the offer is in. The point to notice, however, is that the pending state contains both the pusher's synchronization precondition, $P(b,y)$, and the pusher's "push" view shift, and the accepted state contains the pusher's synchronization postcondition, $Q(b,y)$. To accept an offer (transition the abstract state from pending to accepted) the popper thus has to perform the pusher's "push" view shift. Conceptually, the offer protocol "transfers" the pusher's view shift to the popper.

Note how the combination of view shifts and impredicative protocols together allows us to prove that the fine-grained implementation with helping meets the modular bag specification.

See the accompanying technical report for the full proof.

3   Model

In this section we present a model of iCAP. Soundness of iCAP is non-trivial. Indeed, in our earlier work on HOCAP [21], we discovered that a recent proposal for a higher-order variant of concurrent abstract predicates [9] was unsound. This led us to consider only predicative protocols in [21], which simplified the construction of a sound model, but also resulted in much *weaker* and more *complicated* specifications and proofs. Here instead, we follow ideas from models of impredicative type systems with higher-order store, e.g. [2,4], and define our model of iCAP using a *guarded-recursively defined space of protocols*. We define our model in the type theory and logic of the topos of trees [4]. This has the advantage that most of the model construction is done as if we were working with ordinary sets, except for those places where we need to guard some recursive definitions for well-definedness. More importantly, it makes it straightforward to define a higher-order logic, since the recursively defined space of protocols is now simply a type in the type theory of the topos of trees, which already includes function and powerset types! The resulting program logic includes the later operator from the ambient type theory. As we have already seen, we use this later operator to define guarded-recursive assertions and protocols. It can also be used to define guarded-recursive specifications. We emphasize that readers need not be familiar with [4] in order to understand the present paper.

Topos of Trees. The internal language of the topos of trees is an intuitionistic higher-order logic over a simply-typed term language extended with subset types and guarded-recursive types. This internal language features a new type former

▶, pronounced later, for defining guarded-recursive types, and a new logical connective ▷, also pronounced later, for defining guarded-recursive predicates. (For readers who are familiar with the use of theorem provers, such as Coq, for formalizing models of logics or programming languages, it may be helpful to think of the type theory of the topos of trees as playing the rôle of the Coq type theory.) The point of using the guarded type theory and logic is that it makes it easy to define the space of protocols, which needs to be recursively defined. Crucially, this results in a type in the guarded type theory, and thus, since that type theory includes higher function types, we can then easily define the interpretation of the function spaces in iCAP.[4] The guarded type theory also includes types of the form ΔX, for any ordinary set X. Such types ΔX are referred to as constant sets. We define the non-recursive part of the model in the category of sets and use these as constant sets to construct the recursive part of the model in the topos of trees.

The presentation of the iCAP model is inspired by the Views framework [7] and models of impredicative type systems, e.g., [5], with higher-order store.

The Views framework provides a general way of relating a *concrete semantics* with an *instrumented semantics* and constructing a separation logic over the instrumented semantics. In our case the concrete semantics is a subset of C# with an interleaving semantics. The instrumented semantics extends the concrete C# states with phantom fields, shared regions, and protocols and enforces that clients respect the protocols governing shared resources.

The model of iCAP is defined in Figure 2, and is defined over countably infinite and disjoint set of action identifiers, AId, state identifiers, SId, object identifiers, OId, closure identifiers CId, region identifiers RId, class names CN, field names FN, and method names MN.

Instrumented states ($m \in \mathcal{M}$) are tuples consisting of three components: a local state, a shared state and an action model. We use $m.l, m.s$ and $m.a$ to refer to the first, second and third component of m. The local state ($l \in LS$) consists of a partial C# heap, a partial phantom heap and a capability map. The partial C# heap and phantom heaps specify the current value and permissions to heap cells and phantom fields, respectively. The capability map specifies action permissions on shared regions. In particular, it records the fractional permission the client owns on each region and action identifier. The shared state ($s \in SS$) specifies the current abstract state of each allocated region and the labelled transition system governing the given region. We use $s(r).s$ and $s(r).p$ to refer to the state and labelled transition system of region r of a shared state s. The set of abstract states, AS, consists of pairs of local and shared state. Finally, the action model ($\varsigma \in AMod$) specifies the interpretation of the abstract states of each allocated region. Since the interpretation of each abstract state is given by a general assertion, which is itself a subset of instrumented states, a naive

---

[4] If we had worked in the category of sets and used step-indexing directly, we would have had to define an appropriate notion of function space between the resulting indexed space of protocols and itself, and that would essentially amount to unrolling the definition from the topos of trees model.

Semantic domains in the category of Sets

$$Cap \stackrel{\text{def}}{=} \{f : (RId \times AId) \to [0,1] \mid \exists R \subseteq_{fin} RId.\ \forall r \in RId \setminus R.\ \forall \alpha \in AId.\ f(r, \alpha) = 0\}$$

$$Heap \stackrel{\text{def}}{=} (OId \times FN \rightharpoonup_{fin} Val) \times (OId \rightharpoonup_{fin} CN) \times (CId \rightharpoonup_{fin} OId \times MN)$$

$$PHeap \stackrel{\text{def}}{=} \{(pc, ph) \in (OId \times FN \to [0,1]) \times (OId \times FN \rightharpoonup_{fin} Val) \mid$$
$$\forall o \in OId.\ \forall f \in FN.\ pc(o, f) = 0 \Rightarrow (o, f) \notin dom(ph)\}$$

$$l \in LS \stackrel{\text{def}}{=} PHeap \times Heap \times Cap \qquad\qquad LTS \stackrel{\text{def}}{=} AId \to \mathcal{P}(SId \times SId)$$

$$s \in SS \stackrel{\text{def}}{=} RId \rightharpoonup_{fin} (SId \times LTS) \qquad\qquad AS \stackrel{\text{def}}{=} LS \times SS$$

Semantic domains in the topos of trees

$$RIntr \cong \blacktriangleright((\Delta SId \times (\Delta RId \rightharpoonup_{fin} RIntr)) \to_{mon} \mathcal{P}^{\uparrow}(\Delta AS)) \qquad s \in Spec \stackrel{\text{def}}{=} \Omega$$

$$\varsigma \in AMod \stackrel{\text{def}}{=} \Delta RId \rightharpoonup_{fin} RIntr \qquad m \in \mathcal{M} \stackrel{\text{def}}{=} \Delta LS \times \Delta SS \times AMod \qquad p \in Prop \stackrel{\text{def}}{=} \mathcal{P}^{\uparrow}(\mathcal{M})$$

where the ordering on $\mathcal{M}$ is R_{RId} and the ordering on ΔAS is

$$m_1 \leq m_2 \quad \text{iff} \quad m_1.l \leq m_2.l \wedge m_1.s \leq m_2.s \wedge m_1.a \leq m_2.a$$

Interference relation

$$acts(l, r) \stackrel{\text{def}}{=} \{\alpha \mid \pi_3(l)(r, \alpha) < 1\}$$

$$upds(l, r, p) \stackrel{\text{def}}{=} \{(s_1, s_2) \mid \exists \alpha \in acts(l, r).\ (s_1, s_2) \in p(\alpha)\}$$

$$R_A \stackrel{\text{def}}{=} \{((l_1, s_1), (l_2, s_2)) \mid l_1 \leq l_2 \wedge \forall r \in dom(s_1).$$
$$((r \in A \wedge (s_1(r).s, s_2(r).s) \in \overline{upds(l_1, r, s_1(r).p)})$$
$$\vee\ s_1(r).s = s_2(r).s \wedge s_1(r).p = s_2(r).p\}$$

where $\overline{(-)}$ denotes the transitive, reflexive closure.

Orderings

$$l_1 \leq l_2 \quad \text{iff} \quad \exists l_3.\ l_2 = l_1 \bullet_{LS} l_3$$
$$s_1 \leq s_2 \quad \text{iff} \quad \forall r \in dom(s_1).\ r \in dom(s_2) \wedge s_1(r) = s_2(r)$$
$$\varsigma_1 \leq \varsigma_2 \quad \text{iff} \quad \forall r \in dom(\varsigma_1).\ r \in dom(\varsigma_2) \wedge \varsigma_1(r) = \varsigma_2(r)$$

Composition

$$x \bullet_= y \stackrel{\text{def}}{=} x \quad \text{if } x = y \qquad\qquad f \bullet_+ g \stackrel{\text{def}}{=} \lambda x.\ f(x) + g(x) \quad \text{if } \forall x.\ f(x) + g(x) \leq 1$$

$$f \bullet_{\cup} g \stackrel{\text{def}}{=} f \cup g \qquad\qquad\qquad\qquad \text{if } dom(f) \cap dom(g) = \emptyset$$

$$f \bullet_? g \stackrel{\text{def}}{=} f \cup g \qquad\qquad\qquad\qquad \text{if } \forall x \in dom(f) \cap dom(g).\ f(x) = g(x)$$

$$\bullet_{Heap} \stackrel{\text{def}}{=} \bullet_{\cup} \times \bullet_= \times \bullet_= \qquad\qquad\qquad \bullet_{PHeap} \stackrel{\text{def}}{=} \bullet_+ \times \bullet_?$$

$$\bullet_{LS} \stackrel{\text{def}}{=} \bullet_{PHeap} \times \bullet_{Heap} \times \bullet_+ \qquad\qquad \bullet_{\mathcal{M}} \stackrel{\text{def}}{=} \bullet_{LS} \times \bullet_= \times \bullet_=$$

Erasure

$$\lfloor (s, \varsigma) \rfloor_r \stackrel{\text{def}}{=} \{l \in LS \mid (l, s) \in app(\varsigma(r))(s(r).s, \varsigma)\}$$

$$\lfloor (l, s, \varsigma) \rfloor_A \stackrel{\text{def}}{=} \{h \in Heap \mid \exists l', sr : dom(s) \cap A \to LS.$$
$$h = l'.h \wedge l' = l \bullet \Pi_{r \in dom(s) \cap A} sr(r) \wedge$$
$$\forall r \in dom(s) \cap A.\ sr(r) \in \lfloor (s, \varsigma) \rfloor_r\}$$

Fig. 2. Model of iCAP

definition of *AMod* in set theory is not well-defined. Instead, we let *RIntr* (the type of interpretations of abstract states for a single region) denote a solution to the following guarded-recursive equation

$$RIntr \cong \blacktriangleright((\Delta SId \times (\Delta RId \rightharpoonup_{fin} RIntr)) \rightarrow_{mon} \mathcal{P}^{\uparrow}(\Delta AS))$$

Here ΔSId is the constant set of state identiers, ΔRId is the constant set of region identifiers, ΔAS is the constant set of abstract states, and $\mathcal{P}^{\uparrow}(\Delta AS)$ consistst of the upwards-closed subsets of ΔAS with respect to the ordering shown in Figure 2. Note the use of the $\blacktriangleright$ operator, which acts as a guard, and ensures that *RIntr* is well-defined (unique up to isomorphism). Using *RIntr* we can then define the type of action models as the type of finite functions from region identifiers to region interpretations: $AMod \stackrel{def}{=} \Delta RId \rightharpoonup_{fin} RIntr$. From the above isomorphism we can define the following abstraction and application functions to fold and unfold elements of *RIntr*:

$$lam : (\Delta SId \times AMod \rightarrow_{mon} \mathcal{P}^{\uparrow}(\Delta AS)) \rightarrow RIntr$$

$$app : RIntr \rightarrow (\Delta SId \times AMod \rightarrow_{mon} \mathcal{P}^{\uparrow}(\Delta AS))$$

Crucially, because of the guard, if we unfold a folded element x, we get back the element x, one step later: $app \circ lam = \triangleright$, where $\triangleright$ refers to the pointwise lifting of $\triangleright$ to function spaces.

Assertions in iCAP are modeled as upwards-closed subsets of instrumented states (see the definition of *Prop* in Figure 2), where the upwards-closure expresses that assertions should be closed under allocation of new regions and extensions of the local state. Assertions in the specification logic are simply modeled as assertions in the topos of trees. The function types of iCAP are simply modeled using the function space in the guarded type theory! (We emphasize again that this is one of the advantages of using the topos of trees as the ambient theory in which to define the model of iCAP; if we had worked in ordinary sets, then iCAP types could not simply be interpreted as sets,[5] they would have to be indexed families of sets, and then the iCAP function space would also have to be appropriate families of functions satisfying certain naturality conditions.

Interference Relation and Stability. The interference relation, R_A, specifies how the environment is allowed to modify the *abstract state* of shared regions. The interference relation is indexed by a set of region identifiers, A, of regions that are allowed to change. R_{RId} thus allows the environment to change the abstract state using any path in the labelled transition system governing the region, along actions not exclusively owned by the client. R_A is defined in Figure 2 in terms of two functions, *acts* and *upds*. The *acts* function specifies the actions not exclusively owned by the client and the *upds* function specifies the set of transitions labelled with actions not exclusively owned by the client.

Unlike previous models of CAP, this interference relation is expressed entirely in terms of *abstract states* and is completely independent of the interpretation

---

[5] Why? Because then we could not guarantee the existence of guarded recursive predicates involving higher-order functions (such as the eloop predicate from Section 2.2).

of these abstract states. This is why stability in iCAP is also expressed at the abstract level and why it is much simpler than previous versions of CAP. An assertion is A-stable if it is closed under R_A:

$$stable_A(p) \overset{\text{def}}{=} (R_A \times id_{AMod})(p) \subseteq p$$

where $R(p) = \{m' \in \mathcal{M} \mid \exists m \in p. (m, m') \in R\}$. Intuitively, an assertion is A-stable if it is closed under interference from the environment on regions in A. An assertion is thus stable if it is RId-stable.

Erasure. The relation between the instrumented semantics and the concrete semantics is expressed through an erasure function, $\lfloor - \rfloor_A$, that maps instrumented states to sets of concrete states. Like the interference relation, the erasure is indexed by a set of region identifiers, A, of regions to erase. The erasure works by picking a concrete state l_r for each allocated region $r \in A$ that satisfies the interpretation of the current abstract state of the given region, and composing all these states with the current local state. The erasure is defined in terms of a single-region erasure, $\lfloor - \rfloor_r$, that defines the set of concrete states satisfying the interpretation of the current abstract state of region r. Note that this is expressed in terms of the application function, app, introduced earlier for unfolding a region interpretation.

View shifts describe changes at the instrumented level that preserves the state at the concrete level. An A-view shift $p \sqsubseteq^A q$ describes a view shift that is only allowed to modify regions in A. We can express this formally (and build-in framing) by requiring the view shift to preserve all A-stable frames r:

$$p \sqsubseteq^A q \overset{\text{def}}{=} \forall r \in Prop. \; stable_A(r) \Rightarrow \lfloor p * r \rfloor_A \subseteq \lfloor q * r \rfloor_A$$

The operational semantics of the underlying programming language is defined in terms of a labelled thread pool evaluation relation, $\overset{a}{\rightarrow}$, and an action semantics, $[\![-]\!]$. The labelled thread pool evaluation relation, $\overset{a}{\rightarrow}$, defines the local effects (i.e., stack effects) of executing a single thread for one step of execution, while the action semantics defines the global effects (i.e., heap effects) of executing an atomic action. Atomic satisfaction expresses what it means for an atomic action a to satisfy a given Hoare specification:

$$a \; sat^A \; \{p\} \{q\} \overset{\text{def}}{=} \forall r \in Prop. \; \forall m \in \mathcal{M}. \; \forall h, h' \in Heap.$$
$$m \in p * \triangleright r \wedge h \in \lfloor m \rfloor_A \wedge h' \in [\![a]\!](h) \wedge stable_A(r)$$
$$\Rightarrow \exists m' \in \mathcal{M}. \; \triangleright (m' \in q * r \wedge h' \in \lfloor m' \rfloor_A)$$

This is the case, if, executing a from any initial concrete state h in the erasure of p there exists an abstract state in q that erases to the terminal concrete state $h' \in [\![a]\!](h)$, and preserves $\triangleright r$, for all stable frames r. Intuitively, the $\triangleright$ operator expresses that executing an atomic action corresponds to one step of execution in the operational semantics.

Safety, $safe(s, p, q)$, extends satisfaction from atomic actions to statements s. Intuitively, it expresses that every step of s at the concrete level has a corresponding step at the abstract level. Formally, $safe$ is defined using guarded recursion to establish the connection between steps in the underlying operational semantics and steps in the topos of trees. See the accompanying technical report for the formal definition.

Interpretation. Most of the interpretation of iCAP is fairly straightforward and reduces directly to the topos of trees. For instance, conjunction in iCAP is interpreted using conjunction in the topos of trees: $p \wedge q \stackrel{\text{def}}{=} \{m \in \mathcal{M} \mid m \in p \wedge m \in q\}$. The most interesting case is the interpretation of the region interpretation assertion, $\text{rintr}(-)$:

$$\text{rintr}(I, r) \stackrel{\text{def}}{=} \{(l, s, \varsigma) \in \mathcal{M} \mid r \in dom(\varsigma) \wedge \forall x \in \Delta(SId).$$
$$\forall \varsigma' \geq \varsigma. \; app(\varsigma(r))(x, \varsigma') = \rhd(\lambda(l, s). \; I(x)(l, s, \varsigma'))\}$$

Readers familiar with models of ML references may understand this region interpretation assertion by analogy to the ref type constructor of ML, which can be modelled by a similar equation [2,4].[6] The reference type in ML describes a simple invariant for a single location, which expresses that the values stored at that location are always of the given type. With iCAP we can describe invariants given by a protocol and covering a region of memory (varying according to the protocol).

4   Logic

In the accompanying appendix we introduce a formal proof system for iCAP and in the accompanying technical report we present the entire proof system. We stress that the logic contains sufficient proof rules for proving all the examples sketched in this paper, *including all stability proofs and all proofs about atomic instructions!*

In the accompanying technical report we prove that iCAP is sound with respect to the model described in the previous section. As a corollary of this soundness theorem it follows that if $\Gamma \mid - \vdash (\Delta).\{P\}s\{Q\}$, then

$$\forall \vartheta \in [\![\Gamma]\!]. \; safe(s, [\![\Gamma; \Delta \vdash P : \text{Prop}]\!](\vartheta), [\![\Gamma; \Delta \vdash Q : \text{Prop}]\!](\vartheta)).$$

5   Discussion

We have presented iCAP, the first program logic for modular reasoning about higher-order concurrent imperative programs that supports full impredicative quantification over general predicates, including predicates describing protocols over shared regions of memory. We have presented examples illustrating how iCAP supports modular reasoning about internal and external sharing, layered

---

[6] Think of ς as the world in models of references; then the equation says that, for all future worlds, the interpretation of the region recorded in the world agrees with the interpretation given by I.

and recursive abstractions, and fine-grained concurrent ADTs implemented using helping, entirely in the logic.

We have discussed related work on program logics along the way. As an alternative to program logics, there has also been several recent advances on using relational models for reasoning about concurrent programs. In particular, Liang et. al. [15] presented a simulation relation based on rely-guarantee to verify program transformations for a first-order concurrent imperative language; Birkedal et. al. [5] presented a logical relations model for verifying effect-based program transformations for a higher-order concurrent imperative language, and Turon et. al. [23,22] extended [5] with an extension of the protocols of Dreyer et. al. [10] to allow for relational refinement proofs of sophisticated fine-grained concurrent algorithms, including cooperation. To reason about cooperation, the model and logic of Turon et. al. [23,22] uses specification code (i.e., an expression of the programming language) as a transferrable resource. This is similar to how view shifts are transferred here to reason about cooperation; the difference is that here we do not use code (since we are not proving refinement), but allow for transfer of more abstract specifications given by view shifts. The model in [23] is defined using step-indexing and involves an indexed definition of what essentially amounts to a recursively defined space of protocols, similar in spirit to the one we are using in this paper. However, the model in [23] does not support impredicative protocols, technically since island predicates (corresponding to region predicates) in *loc. cit.* have a restriction on how they can be parameterized. It is probably possible to lift this restriction, but one would still need a richer notion of model in order to model impredicative higher-order logic, essentially since constant sets would no longer suffice. As explained earlier, we use the type theory of the topos of trees as our metatheory for that purpose.

In this paper we have focused on the foundational issue of establishing soundness of a new very expressive logic for reasoning about higher-order concurrent imperative programs. Future work includes implementing a tool for interactive verification of programs using iCAP. We plan to do so in Coq, following the approaches of the Bedrock [6] and Charge! [3] tools, which have been successful in using Coq tactics to automate large parts of formal reasoning.

Acknowledgements. This research was supported in part by the ModuRes Sapere Aude Advanced Grant from The Danish Council for Independent Research for the Natural Sciences (FNU).

References

1. Node.js, http://www.nodejs.org
2. Appel, A.W., Melliès, P.-A., Richards, C.D., Vouillon, J.: A Very Modal Model of a Modern, Major, General Type System. In: Proceedings of POPL (2007)
3. Bengtson, J., Jensen, J.B., Birkedal, L.: Charge! In: Beringer, L., Felty, A. (eds.) ITP 2012. LNCS, vol. 7406, pp. 315–331. Springer, Heidelberg (2012)

4. Birkedal, L., Møgelberg, R., Schwinghammer, J., Støvring, K.: First Steps in Synthetic Guarded Domain Theory: Step-Indexing in the Topos of Trees. In: Proceedings of LICS (2011)
5. Birkedal, L., Sieczkowski, F., Thamsborg, J.: A Concurrent Logical Relation. In: Proceedings of CSL (2012)
6. Chlipala, A.: Mostly-Automated Verification of Low-Level Programs in Computational Separation Logic. In: Proceedings of PLDI (2011)
7. Dinsdale-Young, T., Birkedal, L., Gardner, P., Parkinson, M., Yang, H.: Views: Compositional Reasoning for Concurrent Programs. In: Proceedings of POPL (2013)
8. Dinsdale-Young, T., Dodds, M., Gardner, P., Parkinson, M.J., Vafeiadis, V.: Concurrent Abstract Predicates. In: D'Hondt, T. (ed.) ECOOP 2010. LNCS, vol. 6183, pp. 504–528. Springer, Heidelberg (2010)
9. Dodds, M., Jagannathan, S., Parkinson, M.J.: Modular reasoning for deterministic parallelism. In: Proceedings of POPL, pp. 259–270 (2011)
10. Dreyer, D., Neis, G., Birkedal, L.: The Impact of Higher-Order State and Control Effects on Local Relational Reasoning. In: Proceedings of ICFP (2010)
11. Feng, X., Ferreira, R., Shao, Z.: On the Relationship between Concurrent Separation Logic and Assume-Guarantee Reasoning. In: De Nicola, R. (ed.) ESOP 2007. LNCS, vol. 4421, pp. 173–188. Springer, Heidelberg (2007)
12. Gotsman, A., Berdine, J., Cook, B., Rinetzky, N., Sagiv, M.: Local Reasoning for Storable Locks and Threads. In: Shao, Z. (ed.) APLAS 2007. LNCS, vol. 4807, pp. 19–37. Springer, Heidelberg (2007)
13. Herlihy, M., Shavit, N.: The Art of Multiprocessor Programming. Morgan Kaufmann (2008)
14. Hobor, A., Appel, A.W., Nardelli, F.Z.: Oracle semantics for concurrent separation logic. In: Drossopoulou, S. (ed.) ESOP 2008. LNCS, vol. 4960, pp. 353–367. Springer, Heidelberg (2008)
15. Liang, H., Feng, X., Fu, M.: A rely-guarantee-based simulation for verifying concurrent program transformations. In: POPL (2012)
16. O'Hearn, P.W.: Resources, Concurrency and Local Reasoning. Theor. Comput. Sci. 375(1-3), 271–307 (2007)
17. Owicki, S.S.: Axiomatic Proof Techniques for Parallel Programs. PhD thesis, Cornell (1975)
18. Provos, N., Mathewson, N.: libevent – an event notification library, http://www.monkey.org/~provos/libevent
19. Russo, C.V.: The Joins Concurrency Library. In: Hanus, M. (ed.) PADL 2007. LNCS, vol. 4354, pp. 260–274. Springer, Heidelberg (2007)
20. Svendsen, K., Birkedal, L., Parkinson, M.: Joins: a Case Study in Modular Specification of a Concurrent Reentrant Higher-order Library. In: Castagna, G. (ed.) ECOOP 2013. LNCS, vol. 7920, pp. 327–351. Springer, Heidelberg (2013)
21. Svendsen, K., Birkedal, L., Parkinson, M.: Modular Reasoning about Separation of Concurrent Data Structures. In: Felleisen, M., Gardner, P. (eds.) ESOP 2013. LNCS, vol. 7792, pp. 169–188. Springer, Heidelberg (2013)
22. Turon, A., Dreyer, D., Birkedal, L.: Unifying Refinement and Hoare-Style Reasoning in a Logic for Higher-Order Concurrency. In: Proceedings of ICFP (2013)
23. Turon, A., Thamsborg, J., Ahmed, A., Birkedal, L., Dreyer, D.: Logical Relations for Fine-Grained Concurrency. In: Proceedings of POPL (2013)
24. Vafeiadis, V., Parkinson, M.: A Marriage of Rely/Guarantee and Separation Logic. In: Caires, L., Vasconcelos, V.T. (eds.) CONCUR 2007. LNCS, vol. 4703, pp. 256–271. Springer, Heidelberg (2007)

Local Reasoning for the POSIX File System

Philippa Gardner, Gian Ntzik, and Adam Wright

Imperial College London
{p.gardner,gian.ntzik08,adam.wright07}@imperial.ac.uk

Abstract. We provide a program logic for specifying a core subset of the sequential POSIX file system, and for reasoning abstractly about client programs working with the file system.

Keywords: file systems, POSIX, local reasoning, separation logic.

1 Introduction

Local reasoning, in the style of separation logic, was introduced to reason about programs that manipulate the RAM memory model. Local reasoning has strong modular properties, which means that it scales. Many forms of *abstract* local reasoning have been introduced to specify structured data libraries: e.g. abstract predicates for linked lists [20], concurrent abstract predicates for abstract concurrent sets [7, 24, 23], and context logic for complex structured data such as the DOM [13]. Despite these advances, there are many other properties of real-world libraries that naturally resonate with this local-reasoning approach but have yet to be studied.

We study abstract local reasoning for the POSIX file system [2]. POSIX has an English specification which naturally describes commands which globally follow directory paths to locally update files or directories[1]. There has been much work on traditional reasoning techniques for specifying POSIX, such as the well-known Z specification [18]. However, the global path constraints associated with this work are substantial. Our aim is to use local reasoning to minimise the global path constraints. POSIX is an interesting test case for abstract local reasoning. It has enough emphasis on local update to suggest that the advantages of local reasoning might apply. However, the complexity of the data combined with concurrency, global paths and local update means that the application of local reasoning to this example is not straightforward.

Current work on abstract local reasoning cannot specify POSIX. For example, context logic works well for reasoning about sequential update of complex data, such as the W3C DOM library for XML update [13, 5, 22]. However, it has no mechanism for reasoning about global paths, it does not extend simply to concurrency, and it does not integrate well with ideas from separation logic. Concurrent abstract predicates [7, 24, 23] work well for reasoning abstractly about

---

[1] Both files and directories are called 'files' in POSIX. We use the term 'entries' to denote either directories or files.

Z. Shao (Ed.): ESOP 2014, LNCS 8410, pp. 169–188, 2014.
© Springer-Verlag Berlin Heidelberg 2014

simple concurrent data structures. However, they do not extend to complex data structures since the implementation details leak into the abstraction [12].

We introduce structural separation logic (SSL) for reasoning abstractly about complex structured data. SSL provides more fine-grained reasoning than context logic, leading to straightforward reasoning about disjoint concurrency and a natural integration with separation logic. Here, we demonstrate SSL by reasoning about POSIX. In [25, 12], we provide the general theory which relies substantially on ideas from the views framework [6][2]. SSL combines fine-grained local reasoning about e.g. directory fragments with global path constraints about the overall structured data. The global path constraints limit the use of the frame rule in our sequential setting, and specify stability requirements of the environment in the concurrent setting. We illustrate our ideas using absolute linear paths, called paths in this paper. In future, it will be very interesting to study general paths (with the backwards .. and symbolic links) as part of our abstract local reasoning agenda, since they walk right across the directory structure.

In this paper, we use SSL to reason about the sequential POSIX file system, demonstrating that our axioms correspond to the English description given in the POSIX standard. We identify a core subset of POSIX, which is both faithful to the standard and a natural subset with which to introduce our reasoning. We model various structures of the file-system state as standard heaps: file heaps mapping file identifiers (inodes) to bytes; and file-descriptor heaps mapping file descriptors to input/output related data. Separation logic can reason about these heap structures. We require SSL to reason about the directory structure, which we regard as a tree-shaped hierarchy[3]. SSL naturally integrates with separation logic, enabling us to reason about directories and the standard heap within the same logic. We demonstrate this integrated reasoning by verifying natural safety properties of a client software installer. Although we concentrate on sequential POSIX in this paper, our results immediately extend to POSIX with disjoint concurrency. In future, we will explore POSIX with shared-memory concurrency.

Related Work. There has been substantial work on formal specifications of file systems [15, 18, 9, 4], leading to a verification challenge by Joshi and Holzmann [17, 10]. It is not feasible to give a comprehensive account of this work in the space available; such an account will be in Ntzik's thesis [19]. Here, we concentrate on demonstrating the advantages of local directory tree reasoning compared with first-order global tree reasoning and reasoning about heap structures with paths as addresses.

A natural question is whether we might use first-order reasoning as in [8], rather than local reasoning in the style of separation logic. For our program-logic application, first-order reasoning leads to scalability problems. Consider one case of a first-order specification of the `rename(p/a, p'/b)` command:

---

[2] Previous work on segment logic [14] was too complicated, because we needed views.

[3] In general, files and directories can be hard linked more than once. Most implementations only allow files to be linked more than once. This is a sensible choice as, for example, cycles generated by directory hard links are not detected by recursive traversal programs. We therefore regard POSIX as a tree-shaped hierarchy.

$$\{\,resolve(p, d[t + a[t']] \wedge resolve(p', d'[t'' \wedge \neg exists(b)]) \wedge \neg \exists p''.\ p' = p/a/p''\,\}$$

$$\texttt{rename(p/a, p'/b)}$$

$$\{\,resolve(p, d[t]) \wedge resolve(p', d'[t'' + b[t']]) \wedge \neg \exists p''.\ p' = p/a/p''\,\}$$

In the precondition, the assertion $resolve(p, d[t + a[t']])$ states that path p resolves to the directory d containing the subdirectory a and list t of unknown entries. The assertion $resolve(p', d'[t'' \wedge \neg exists(b)])$ states that path p' resolves to directory d' with no b entry. Finally, the assertion $\neg \exists p''.\ p' = p/a/p''$ is a path constraint, stating that path p' cannot be a descendant of p/a which would be an error case in POSIX. In the postcondition, the assertions state that the directory a has gone from d, and a new directory b has been created under directory d' with the contents of the old a.

Now consider program $\texttt{rename(p/a, p'/b)}$; $\texttt{rename(p''/c, p'''/d)}$. In this case, we need path constraints in the precondition stating the following properties: path p' is not a descendant of path p/a; p''' is not a descendant of p''/c; and, in addition, p''/c is not a descendant of p/a since directory a has been removed. These syntactic path checks mushroom as more rename commands are added. Hence, this style of reasoning does not scale. Those familiar with separation logic might recognise that this example is analogous to Reynolds' original list example for justifying separation logic [21].

A completely different approach, used in much of the work on the formal specification of file systems in Z [18] and other methods [15], is to treat paths as heap addresses. Define the set of heaps as $\text{PATHS} \overset{\text{fin}}{\rightharpoonup} \text{BYTES} \cup \mathcal{P}(\text{FNAMES})$, mapping paths to byte sequences in the file case or sets of names in the directory case. This approach requires significant global constraints: for example, in the specification of $\texttt{rename(p/a, p/a')}$ not only we would replace p/a with p/a' in the heap, but also every descendant $p/a/p'$ with $p/a'/p'$ in order to preserve path consistency.

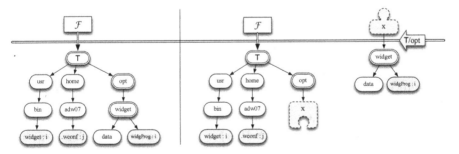

Fig. 1. The left-hand diagram represents a complete directory; the right, the same directory instrumented with abstract addresses

2 Example Specifications

We focus on the sequential POSIX file system in this paper, in particular studying a core fragment of 16 commands. Although this fragment is small, it includes most of the primitive commands that manipulate the structure and perform input-output (IO) and a large proportion of the file system commands can be implemented using them.

First consider the English description of the rmdir command[4]:

[r := rmdir(path)] Remove the directory identified by path and set r to 0. The directory must be empty.

Intuitively, this command traverses the *global* structure, using the global path path to identify the location of the update. It then performs *local* update, removing the empty directory whilst leaving the rest of the file system unchanged.

We capture this combination of global traversal and local update using structural separation logic. Consider figure 1. The left-hand side illustrates part of a standard structured heap, consisting of a heap cell with address $\mathcal{F}$ whose structured value is a complete directory tree. The right-hand side illustrates part of an abstract heap, consisting of the heap cell $\mathcal{F}$ whose value is now an incomplete directory tree with *body address* x, and an abstract heap cell with *abstract address* x whose value is a pair consisting of a *path promise* 'T/opt' and, in this case, a complete subdirectory. The path promise provides the stability condition that body address x must be at the end of 'T/opt'. This promise to x allows us to reason locally about the abstract heap cell x whilst retaining the knowledge of its location in the global structure. Notice that the two heaps illustrated in figure 1 describe the same state, in that they differ only in the instrumentation added by abstract addresses. We move from the left-hand to the right-hand view of the state using *abstract allocation* which creates a new abstract heap cell containing the subdirectory; the converse is *abstract deallocation*.

With structured separation logic (SSL), we can reason about such abstract heap cells. For example, the assertion $subdir(\alpha@P, A[\varnothing])$ describes the ownership of the abstract heap cell with address given by logical variable α and value given by the path promise P and empty subdirectory $A[\varnothing]$. Using this assertion, we are able to provide an axiomatic specification of the rmdir command:

$$\{ expr(\textbf{path}, P/A) \land var(\textbf{r}, -) \star \mathcal{E} \star subdir(\alpha@P, A[\varnothing]) \}$$
$$\textbf{r} := \texttt{rmdir(path)}$$
$$\{ var(\textbf{r}, 0) \star \mathcal{E} \star subdir(\alpha@P, \varnothing) \}$$

In the precondition, the assertion for the abstract heap cell at α describes the subdirectory resource necessary for the command to succeed, plus the stable information that the subdirectory is to be found under global path P. In addition, the precondition contains assertions about path expressions and variables. The *expression assertion* $expr(\textbf{path}, P/A)$ is a pure assertion which states that expression path has logical expression P/A as its value. This logical expression describes an arbitrary path P followed by the directory or file name A. The *variable assertion* $var(\textbf{r}, -)$ states that the program variable r has some

---

[4] This description only presents the case when the operation succeeds. When the command fails, for example if path does not identify an existing file or directory, the result is to assign -1 to r and set the global variable errno to ENOENT. We give the full error specifications in our technical report [11]. In this paper we discuss such cases only when required by an example.

arbitrary value, and $\mathcal{E}$ describes the extra variable resource necessary for **path** to be evaluated. This follows the standard variables-as-resource approach [3]

The postcondition states that variable **r** now has value 0, whilst the abstract heap cell α is empty with the path promise P. Notice that we do *not* remove the abstract heap cell α. If the axiom destroyed this cell, the associated α body address (which must exist in some data in the frame) would have no matching cell address. This would break the stability of the system, where a cell address always matches with a body address at the appropriate path promise. The additional variable resource predicate $\mathcal{E}$ is unchanged between the pre and postconditions.

The specification of **rmdir** is *small* in that the precondition intuitively describes local ownership of the minimum resource needed to safely run the command: the variables **r** and those needed to evaluate **path** given by $\mathcal{E}$; and the abstract cell address α with the subdirectory being updated. It also describes the global information that only (incomplete) directories satisfying path promise P associated with α can be framed on. To illustrate this, consider the complete directory $dir(\mathcal{F}, \top[C+D[A[\varnothing]]])$, the path P = $\top/D/A$ and the proof derivation:

$\{ \, expr(\mathbf{path}, \top/D/A) \wedge var(\mathbf{r}, -) * \mathcal{E} * dir(\mathcal{F}, \top[C + D[A[\varnothing]]]) \, \}$
// abstract allocation
$\{ \, expr(\mathbf{path}, \top/D/A) \wedge var(\mathbf{r}, -) * \mathcal{E} * \exists \alpha. \, (dir(\mathcal{F}, \top[C+D[\alpha]]) * subdir(\alpha@\top/D, A[\varnothing])) \, \}$
// existential elimination and frame rule and apply the axiom
$\{ \, expr(\mathbf{path}, \top/D/A) \wedge var(\mathbf{r}, -) * \mathcal{E} * subdir(\alpha@\top/D, A[\varnothing]) \, \}$
`r := rmdir(path)`
$\{ \, var(\mathbf{r}, 0) * \mathcal{E} * subdir(\alpha@\top/D, \varnothing) \, \}$
// existential, frame rule reapplication
$\{ \, var(\mathbf{r}, 0) * \mathcal{E} * \exists \alpha. \, (dir(\mathcal{F}, \top[C + D[\alpha]]) * subdir(\alpha@\top/D, \varnothing)) \, \}$
// abstract deallocation
$\{ \, var(\mathbf{r}, 0) * \mathcal{E} * dir(\mathcal{F}, \top[C + D[\varnothing]]) \, \}$

The initial precondition contains the assertion $dir(\mathcal{F}, \top[C+D[A[\varnothing]]])$ describing a complete directory tree at the file-system root $\top$, with arbitrary contents captured by the logical variable C and a directory named D that contains the empty directory A. This precondition does not match the precondition of **rmdir**, and so we take the following steps. First, we abstractly allocate a new abstract heap cell containing the A directory, existentially quantifying the abstract address α to ensure that the address is fresh. Then, we apply the standard Hoare logic existential elimination to set aside the existential binding of α, and use the frame rule to set aside the resource that **rmdir** does not need. We are now in a position to match **rmdir**'s precondition, where $\top/D$ is P. After applying the axiom we can reintroduce the resource and binding set aside with frame and existential elimination, and abstractly deallocate the cell with address α.

Now consider the **unlink** command and its English specification:

[**r** := **unlink(path)**] Remove the link to the file identified by **path**.
Using SSL, we can formalise the English specification in a similar fashion, with the following small axiom:

$$\{ \, expr(\mathbf{path}, P/A) \wedge var(\mathbf{r}, -) * \mathcal{E} * subdir(\alpha@P, A : I) \}$$
$$\mathbf{r} := \mathbf{unlink(path)}$$
$$\{ \, var(\mathbf{r}, 0) * \mathcal{E} * subdir(\alpha@P, \varnothing) \}$$

In the precondition, $subdir(\alpha@P, A : I)$ states that a file named A is found at abstract cell address α at the end of path P. The file data is not included in the precondition, but can be found at file inode I. When the last link to a file is removed, the file will no longer be accessible by any path, and we assume garbage collection will remove any associated file data.

Finally, consider the **stat** command, which returns meta-data about the file or directory identified by the path argument. In this paper, we take that meta-data to be just the file type, D for directory and F for file. There is one axiom for each file type; the directory case is:

$$\{\, expr(\textbf{path}, P/A) \wedge var(\textbf{t}, -) \star \mathcal{E} \star subdir(\alpha@P, A[\beta]) \,\}$$
$$\textbf{t:=stat(path)}$$
$$\{\, var(\textbf{t}, D) \star \mathcal{E} \star subdir(\alpha@P, A[\beta]) \,\}$$

Notice that the specification uses *body address* β in $A[\beta]$ to specify that the content of A is not changed by the command. It does not need more detailed knowledge of the contents of A since the command does not require this knowledge to determine that the entry is a directory.

The commands discussed so far are enough to implement the POSIX command **r := remove(path)**. According to its POSIX description, this command removes the file or empty directory identified by the **path** argument. In figure 2 we implement **remove** and derive its specification. Notice that the derived specification exactly matches the English description obtained from POSIX. Following the same process, we can use the core fragment of this paper to "discover" formal specifications of many more complex commands of POSIX.

$\{\, expr(\textbf{path}, P/A) \wedge var(\textbf{r}, -) \star \mathcal{E} \star subdir(\alpha@P, (A : I \vee A[\varnothing])) \,\}$
r := remove(path) $\triangleq$ **local t {**
  t := stat(path);
  $\{\, \exists T.\ expr(\textbf{path}, P/A) \wedge var(\textbf{r}, -) \star var(\textbf{t}, T) \star \mathcal{E} \star subdir(\alpha@P, (A : I \wedge T = F) \vee (A[\varnothing] \wedge T = D)) \,\}$
  if t = F
    $\{\, expr(\textbf{path}, P/A) \wedge var(\textbf{r}, -) \star \mathcal{E} \star subdir(\alpha@P, A : I) \,\}$
    r := unlink(path);
    $\{\, var(\textbf{r}, 0) \star \mathcal{E} \star subdir(\alpha@P, \varnothing) \,\}$
  else if t = D
    $\{\, expr(\textbf{path}, P/A) \wedge var(\textbf{r}, -) \star \mathcal{E} \star subdir(\alpha@P, A[\varnothing]) \,\}$
    r := rmdir(path);
    $\{\, var(\textbf{r}, 0) \star \mathcal{E} \star subdir(\alpha@P, \varnothing) \,\}$
  else r := -1;
  $\{\, var(\textbf{r}, 0) \star var(\textbf{t}, -) \star \mathcal{E} \star subdir(\alpha@P, \varnothing) \,\}$
}
$\{\, var(\textbf{r}, 0) \star subdir(\alpha@P, \varnothing) \,\}$

Fig. 2. An implementation of **remove** and the derived specification

3   File System Specification

We provide an axiomatic specification of our sequential POSIX commands using SSL.

3.1 Abstract Program State

An abstract program state comprises: an abstract *file-system heap*, which represents the directory tree and associated files, as might intuitively reside on a hard disk; a *process heap*, which represents the computer memory during execution; and a *variable store*, which represents the values of program variables.

File-System Heaps. Abstract file-system heaps are abstract heaps whose cells contain partial directories. Directories are defined using a set of *inodes* INODES, ranged over by $\iota, \kappa, \cdots$, and a set of file names FNAMES, ranged over by A, B, $\cdots$, for naming directories and files. Both sets are defined as in POSIX. Our partial directories are instrumented by body addresses (context holes), drawn from the countably infinite set of abstract addresses ABSADDRS, ranged over by $x, y, z, \cdots$, with $(\text{FNAMES} \cup \{\mathcal{F}\} \cup \text{INODES}) \cap \text{ABSADDRS} = \varnothing$ where $\mathcal{F}$ is the distinguished address of the root directory.

Definition 1 (Directories). *The set of* unrooted directories, UDIRS, *is:*

$$ud ::= \varnothing \mid a : \iota \mid a[ud] \mid ud + ud \mid x$$

where $\varnothing$ is the empty list of entries, $a : \iota$ is a file link associating file name $a \in$ FNAMES with inode $\iota \in$ INODES, $a[ud]$ is a directory named a containing unrooted abstract directory ud, $+$ is directory composition and $x \in$ ABSADDRS is a body address. The directories have sibling-unique names, body addresses are unique, and $+$ is commutative and associative with identity $\varnothing$.

There is a distinguished $\top \notin$ FNAMES representing the root directory of the file-system tree. The set of rooted directories, RDIRS, is defined as RDIRS $\triangleq \{\top[ud] \mid ud \in \text{UDIRS}\}$. The set of directories, $d \in$ DIRS, is defined by DIRS $\triangleq$ UDIRS $\cup$ RDIRS. Each directory entry has a type DETYPES $\triangleq \{F, D\}$, where F denotes a hard link to a file and D a directory.

Each body address can be replaced by entries via *context application*.

Definition 2 (Context application). *The* addresses function, $addrs : \text{DIRS} \to \mathcal{P}(\text{ABSADDRS})$ *describes the set of body addresses in a directory. Context application is the function $\circ : \text{ABSADDRS} \to (\text{DIRS} \to \text{UDIRS}) \to \text{DIRS}$ defined by:*

$$d_1 \circ_x ud_2 = \begin{cases} d_1[ud_2/x] & x \in \text{addrs}(d_1) \wedge \text{addrs}(d_1) \cap \text{addrs}(ud_2) \subseteq \{x\} \\ undefined & otherwise \end{cases}$$

where $d_1[ud_2/x]$ is the substitution of ud_2 for x in d_1. The function is defined only if the result is in DIRS.

Many POSIX commands refer to entries in the file system tree by *absolute linear paths* through the directory tree. General paths (with .. and symbolic links) are complex but we should be able to handle general paths using a combination of promises and *obligations* discussed in the conclusions: the abstract address x will have the promise that the part of the path in the context is stable, and the obligation to keep the part of the path in the context stable.

Definition 3 (Paths and Resolution). *The set of relative paths, RELPATHS, is defined by:*

$$rp ::= \epsilon \mid a \mid rp/rp$$

where $a \in$ FNAMES *and the path composition* / *is associative with identity* ϵ. *The set of absolute paths is* ABPATHS $\triangleq \{\top\} \cup \{\top/rp \mid rp \in$ RELPATHS$\}$. *The set of abstract paths is* ABSPATHS $= \{p/x \mid p \in$ ABPATHS$, x \in$ ABSADDRS$\}$. *The set of paths,* $p \in$ PATHS, *is* PATHS $\triangleq$ RELPATHS $\cup$ ABPATHS $\cup$ ABSPATHS.

The path resolution *function* resolve : PATHS $\times$ DIRS $\rightharpoonup$ DIRS *is defined by:*

$$
\begin{aligned}
\text{resolve}(a, d + a : \iota) &= a : \iota & \text{resolve}(a/rp, d_1 + a[d_2]) &= \text{resolve}(rp, d_2) && \textit{if } rp \not\equiv \epsilon \\
\text{resolve}(a, d_1 + a[d_2]) &= a[d_2] & \text{resolve}(\top, \top[d]) &= \top[d] \\
\text{resolve}(x, x + d) &= x & \text{resolve}(\top/rp, \top[d]) &= \text{resolve}(rp, d) && \textit{if } rp \not\equiv \epsilon
\end{aligned}
$$

In all other cases, the result is undefined.

A file-system heap is the union of three finite partial functions: from distinguished address $\mathcal{F}$ to the root directory which might be partial; from abstract addresses to absolute paths (expressing where the corresponding body address lies) and directories; and from inodes to byte sequences representing file contents. We construct file-system heaps in two phases: first, we define *pre-file-system heaps*; then, we define well-formedness conditions to give the full definition.

Definition 4 (Pre-file-system Heap). *Let* BYTES *be the set of finite byte sequences. A pre-file-system heap,* $pfs \in$ PREFS, *is a function in the set*

$$(\{\mathcal{F}\} \rightharpoonup \{\epsilon\} \times \text{RDIRS}) \sqcup (\text{ABSADDRS} \overset{fin}{\rightharpoonup} \text{ABPATHS} \times \text{DIRS}) \sqcup (\text{INODES} \overset{fin}{\rightharpoonup} \text{BYTES})$$

Let inodes(d) *denote the set of all inodes occurring in directory* d. *A pre-file-system-heap,* pfs, *is* complete *if:* $dom(pfs) \cap$ ABSADDRS $= \varnothing$; $pfs(\mathcal{F}) = (\epsilon, rd)$; $addrs(rd) = \varnothing$; *and* inodes(rd) $\subseteq \mathbf{dom}(pfs)$[5].

Pre-file-system heaps may use abstract addresses incorrectly. For example, two separate partial directories at different addresses may contain the same body address, or the path promises may not correctly identify the location of the directory. We define a *collapse relation*, with which we give a well-formedness condition that ensures addresses are used correctly. The collapse relation intuitively states that we can connect a cell address to the matching body address with context application, if the paths match, as illustrated in figure 3.

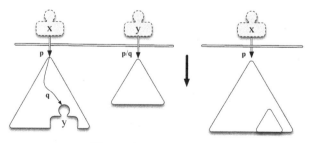

Fig. 3. Collapse relation

---

[5] Complete pre-file-system-heaps are thus simple DAGs, with sharing occurring only at the leaves in the sense that two separate file names can point to the same inode.

Definition 5 (Collapse Relation). *The one-step collapse relation,* $\downarrow \subseteq$ PREFS$\times$ PREFS, *relates* $pfs_1 \downarrow pfs_2$ *if and only if there is some address addr* $\in$ ABSADDRS $\cup$ $\{\mathcal{F}\}$ *and unique* $y \in$ ABSADDRS *such that:*

1. $pfs_1(addr) = (p, d)$ *and* $pfs_1(y) = (p_y, d_y)$;
2. $y \in addrs(d)$;
3. *there is some* $q \in$ PATHS *such that* $p_y = p/q$;
4. resolve$(q, d) = y$;
5. $pfs_2 = pfs_1[addr \mapsto (p, d \circ_y d_y)]/y^6$.

Let $\downarrow^*$ *be the reflexive, transitive closure of* $\downarrow$.

Using collapse, we can detect all pre-file-system heaps that use invalid addressing. Given *pfs*, the correct use of abstract addressing falls into three cases:

1. *pfs* is complete, and is thus trivially uses abstract addresses correctly.
2. *pfs* uses abstract addresses, but is related via collapse to a complete abstract file system. In this case, the complete system it is related to must be unique (see [25] for details).
3. *pfs* uses abstract addresses, but is not immediately related to a complete file system. However, at least one other pre-abstract file system *pfs'* can be found such that the union of the two *does* collapse to a complete file system (as in case 2). In this case, *pfs* is a *partial* file-system heap, missing some data, but still using abstract addressing in a consistent way.

With the collapse relation, we can now define file-system heaps.

Definition 6 (File-system Heaps). *The set of* file-system heaps, FS *ranged by fs, is defined as:*

$$\text{FS} = \left\{ pfs \in \text{PREFS} \mid \exists pfs', pfs'' \in \text{PREFS}. \ pfs \sqcup pfs' \downarrow^* pfs'' \wedge pfs'' \text{ is complete} \right\}$$

Process Heaps. The *process heap* represents the contents of the heap during program execution. It contains structures used for controlling access to files and directories: *open file descriptions* and *directory streams*. An open file description is a record holding information that controls file accesses: the inode and current offset of an open file. It is used to support the commands **read**, **write**, **lseek** and **close**. The heap addresses of open file descriptions, in POSIX terminology called *file descriptors*, are given by the set OFADDRS and ranged by $f, g, \ldots$.

A directory stream is an abstract data structure that captures the set of the entries in a given directory and supports the **opendir**, **readdir** and **closedir** commands. For example, when **opendir(p)** is used, a fresh *directory stream address* from the set DSADDRS is allocated and mapped to a directory stream, which provides a snapshot of the entry names in the directory given by path **p**. Here, we deviate from POSIX. The **readdir** command returns the names of entries contained within a directory. POSIX allows a high degree of non-determinism when using **readdir** on a directory whilst modifying its contents: one may see some changes; all changes; or none. Specifying the full behaviour is possible, but complex. To aid comprehension, we chose a *snapshot semantics*.

---

6 That is, pfs_2 is equal to the function obtained from pfs_1 by removing y from the domain, mapping $addr$ to $(p, d \circ_y d_y)$, and leaving the other mappings the same.

Definition 7 (Process Heaps). *A process heap, denoted* $\text{ph} \in \text{PH}$, *is a partial function in the set* $(\text{DSADDRS} \overset{fin}{\rightharpoonup} \mathcal{P}(\text{FNAMES})) \sqcup (\text{OFADDRS} \overset{fin}{\rightharpoonup} (\text{INODES} \times \mathbb{N}))$

Variable Stores. Variables are assigned values through a *variable store*, σ : VARS $\rightarrow$ VALUES, with the set of variable stores denoted Σ. Variables are dynamically typed, with values drawn from the set:

$$\text{VALUES} \triangleq \begin{array}{c} \mathbb{Z} \uplus \{\textbf{true}, \textbf{false}\} \uplus \text{RELPATHS} \uplus \text{ABPATHS} \uplus \text{BYTES} \uplus \text{INODES} \\ \uplus \text{OFADDRS} \uplus \text{DSADDRS} \uplus \text{DETYPES} \end{array}$$

Definition 8 (Abstract Program States). *Given the sets of file-system heaps* FS, *process heaps* PH *and variable stores* Σ, *the set of* abstract program states, *as* $\in$ ASTATES, *is defined as:* ASTATES $\triangleq$ FS $\times$ PH $\times$ Σ.

3.2   Programming Language

We define a standard imperative sequential WHILE language with calls to POSIX commands. *Program expressions* are used as the rvalue of assignments and as parameters to control-flow commands. They consist of the standard literals, variable lookup, arithmetic and boolean operations, and path concatenation Expr/Expr. Expression evaluation $[\![\cdot]\!]_\sigma$: EXPR $\rightarrow$ Σ $\rightharpoonup$ VALUES is mostly standard[7]. Our core POSIX commands can be classified into *structural* commands that manipulate the file system structure, *primitive IO* commands that read and write the contents of files, and *state* commands for querying the type of files.

Definition 9 (Core Fragment & Programming Language). *The core POSIX fragment consists of structural commands* $\mathbb{C}_{Str} \in \text{COMM}_{Str}$, *IO commands* $\mathbb{C}_{IO} \in \text{COMM}_{IO}$, *and state commands* $\mathbb{C}_{Stat} \in \text{COMM}_{Stat}$:

$$\mathbb{C}_{Str} ::= \begin{array}{l} \texttt{r := mkdir(path)| r := rmdir(path)| r := link(existing, new)} \\ \texttt{| r := unlink(path)| r := rename(old, new)} \end{array}$$

$$\mathbb{C}_{IO} ::= \begin{array}{l} \texttt{dir := opendir(path)| fn := readdir(dir) | closedir(dir)} \\ \texttt{| fd := open(path, flags)| buffer := read(fd, size)} \\ \texttt{| size := write(fd, buffer)} \\ \texttt{| offset' := lseek(fd, offset, whence) | close(fd)} \end{array}$$

$$\mathbb{C}_{Stat} ::= \texttt{t := stat(path)}$$

The commands, $\mathbb{C} \in \text{COMM}$, *of the programming language are:*

$$\mathbb{C} ::= \begin{array}{l} \texttt{var := Expr | local var in } \mathbb{C} \texttt{ | if Expr then } \mathbb{C} \texttt{ else } \mathbb{C} \\ \texttt{| while Expr do } \mathbb{C} \texttt{ | skip | } \mathbb{C} \texttt{ ; } \mathbb{C} \texttt{ | } \mathbb{C}_{Str} \texttt{ | } \mathbb{C}_{IO} \texttt{ | } \mathbb{C}_{Stat} \end{array}$$

In POSIX, the commands are specified as C function interfaces. Here, we adapt them to a simple imperative programming style for simplicity. Details relating to the semantics of C are thus abstracted. We have formally specified all the commands of this fragment using SSL in [11]. Here, we present specifications for those commands that are used in our examples.

---

[7] Concatenation: $[\![\text{Expr}/\text{Expr}']\!]_\sigma \triangleq [\![\text{Expr}]\!]_\sigma/[\![\text{Expr}']\!]_\sigma$ iff $[\![\text{Expr}']\!]_\sigma \notin \text{ABPATHS}$.

3.3   Assertions

We describe assertions for reasoning about POSIX programs.[8] Analogous to programs using variables and expressions, assertions use logical variables and expressions. Logical variables are mapped to values by a logical environment, $e \in \text{LENV}$, extending program values with directories, paths, abstract addresses, and sets of these values. Logical expressions, denoted by E, E', are defined and evaluated similarly to program expressions, disallowing program variables. We denote logical variables with block capitals $A, B, X, Y, \ldots$, except for abstract address variables denoted $\alpha, \beta, \ldots$.

Cell Assertions		Directory Assertions	ϕ
Directory Tree	$dir(\mathcal{F}, \phi)$	Empty Entry	$\varnothing$
Subdirectory	$subdir(\alpha @ E, \phi)$	File Type Entry	$E : I$
File	$file(I, E)$	Directory Type Entry	$E[\phi]$
File Descriptor	$fd(X, I, E)$	File System Root	$\top[\phi]$
Directory Stream	$ds(X, E)$	Logical Expression	E
Heap	$ptr(E, E)$	Entry List	$\phi + \phi$
Variable	$var(\mathtt{var}, E)$	Context Application	$\phi \circ_\alpha \phi$
Expression	$expr(\mathtt{Expr}, E)$	Path Resolution	$@E$

Fig. 4. Assertion language

Assertions, $P, Q \in \text{ASRTS}$, are constructed from: the standard first-order logic connectives and quantifiers; the *separating conjunction* of separation logic, $P * Q$, and its unit, emp; and the cell assertions of figure 4 which describe file-system heaps, process heaps and variable stores. Key is the subdirectory assertion, $subdir(\alpha @ E, \phi)$, which combines *local* information ϕ about the partial directory at α, and *global* information about the environment using path promise E. It states that, at abstract cell address given by α, there is a partial subdirectory satisfying directory assertion ϕ (to be explained) which can be rejoined with the main directory using body address α which must be at the end of path expression E. The splitting and joining of partial directories gives rise to novel allocation and deallocation axioms, discussed in Section 3.4.

The file assertion, $file(I, E)$, describes the file with inode address given by the logical variable I and contents given by the byte sequence described by logical expression E. The next three cell assertions describe elements of the process heap and are directly lifted from definition 7. The final two describe the contents of the variable store. The assertion $var(\mathtt{var}, E)$, describes program variable $\mathtt{var}$ with its value given by the logical expression E. Our core program commands accept parameters given by program expressions. The pure assertion $expr(\mathtt{Expr}, E)$ states that the program expression $\mathtt{Expr}$ evaluates to the value of the logical expression E. The evaluation requires that we own all the variables used in the expression. Since in an arbitrary expression the variables are unknown, we will

---

[8] We have been asked whether ramified separation logic for reasoning about dags might be worth exploring [16]. It uses the sepish connective to say that there is possibly some shared dag structure, but where it is not determined. Here, the dag structure is fully determined at the leaves, so ramified separation logic is not appropriate.

typically use this assertion in conjunction with an *exact* assertion $\mathcal{E}$, leading to assertions of the form $expr(\text{Expr}, E) \wedge \mathcal{E}$, where $\mathcal{E}$ captures all the variable resource required to evaluate Expr.

Directory assertions, $\phi, \psi \in \text{DIRASRTS}$, are constructed from the standard first-order connectives and quantifiers, and the directory assertions of figure 4 describing the structure of directories, context application and path resolution. Most have been directly lifted from the structure of directories (definition 1). *Context application*, $\phi \circ_\alpha \psi$, taken from context logic, describes a directory tree that can be separated into an partial directory satisfying ϕ, with abstract body address α bound in the assertion, and a partial directory satisfying ψ. The assertion $@E$ describes directories in which the path given by E resolves.

Definition 10 (Derived Assertions). *The standard first-order logic assertions are derived from* $\Rightarrow$ *and* **false**. *Additionally, we define the following:*

$$\Diamond\phi \triangleq \mathbf{true} \circ_\alpha \phi \qquad\qquad \Diamond\phi \triangleq \mathbf{true} + \phi$$
$$complete \triangleq \neg\exists\alpha. \Diamond\alpha \qquad\qquad top\_complete \triangleq \neg\exists\alpha. \Diamond\alpha$$
$$entry(A) \triangleq A[\mathbf{true}] \vee \exists I. (A : I) \qquad\qquad top(\phi) \triangleq \phi \wedge top\_complete$$

$$can\_create(A) \triangleq (\neg \Diamond entry(A)) \wedge top\_complete$$
$$names(S) \triangleq \forall A. (A \in S \iff \Diamond entry(A)) \wedge top\_complete$$

The assertion $\Diamond\phi$ is read "somewhere ϕ", and describes directories containing some directory satisfying ϕ. The assertion $\Diamond\phi$ is similar, restricted to siblings. The assertion *complete* describes directories that do not contain any abstract body addresses and thus no subdirectory is missing; *top_complete* is similar, but restricted to siblings. The assertion $top(\phi)$ states that the directory entries satisfy ϕ, and that no sibling entries have been split away. The assertion *can_create*(A) states that an entry named A can be safely created at the current sibling level (used for commands that create new entries such as `mkdir`). Finally, *names*(S) states that every name in the set S is present as an entry.

3.4   Program Logic

We describe our program logic for reasoning about our core fragment of sequential POSIX, comprising standard rules from separation logic, axioms for specifying the POSIX commands (Figure 5), and *abstract allocation and deallocation* axioms 11. The abstract allocation and deallocation axioms are similar to normal heap allocation and deallocation axioms, but instead of introducing and deleting fresh heap cells, they introduce and delete abstract heap cells in order to split and recombine partial directories. They are essential for our local reasoning about directories, and are only possible due to the recent technological advances of the views framework [6]. For uniformity, we give these as axioms over the *id* command, which has no operational effect. It is a technical device to enable the small axioms in Figure 5 to be used whenever required.

Definition 11 (Abstract allocation and deallocation axioms). *The axioms for* abstract allocation *and* abstract deallocation *are, respectively:*

$$\{ subdir(\alpha@\text{P}, (\phi_1 \wedge @\text{Q}/\beta) \circ_\beta \phi_2) \}$$
$$id$$
$$\{ \exists\gamma. (subdir(\alpha@\text{P}, (\phi_1 \wedge @\text{Q}/\beta) \circ_\beta \gamma) \star subdir(\gamma@\text{P}/\text{Q}, \phi_2)) \}$$

$$\big\{\exists \gamma.\,\big(subdir(\alpha @ \text{P}, (\phi_1 \wedge @ \text{Q}/\beta) \circ_\beta \gamma) \star subdir(\gamma @ \text{P}/\text{Q}, \phi_2)\big)\big\}$$
$$id$$
$$\big\{subdir\big(\alpha @ \text{P}, (\phi_1 \wedge @ \text{Q}/\beta) \circ_\beta \phi_2\big)\big\}$$

The first axiom is *abstract allocation*. The precondition states that there is a partial directory at cell α with path promise P. This partial directory can be viewed as an application of two separate parts: the context directory described by ϕ_1 which contains a relative path Q ending in body address β, applied via β to the subdirectory described by ϕ_2. The postcondition states that directory really can be separated into its two subparts: the subdirectory satisfying ϕ_2 is "allocated" into its own abstract heap cell γ whose corresponding body address is at absolute path P/Q; and the context directory at α satisfying ϕ_1 with γ replacing β. *Abstract deallocation* is the converse: if we know that γ is at the end of path Q in a directory that is itself at the end of path P, it is safe to combine the two using context application.

We justify the abstract allocation and deallocation axioms by referring to the collapse relation in Definition 5. Abstract allocation is the assertion equivalent of "expanding" by one step, in that the result introduces one additional abstract address, but still collapses to the same complete heap. Deallocation is the equivalent of a single collapse step, and will still result in the same complete file system. Therefore, whilst abstract (de)allocation changes the abstract addressing in use by a file system, it does not change the underlying file system.

Figure 5 provides the axioms for specifying the commands used in our software installer example, plus the axioms for **rename** as it is the most challenging command. The complete set of axioms is given in [11]. Each axiom must be *stable* with respect to both abstract addresses and path promises. Axioms cannot introduce or remove abstract addresses, and must not invalidate any path promises that have been issued. Commands that alter paths (for example, **rename**) ensure this later point by requiring that the subdirectories described by the preconditions contain no abstract body addresses. Commands such as **rename** and **stat** have multiple axioms, each covering a different behaviour specified in POSIX depending on the precondition state[9].

Consider the **mkdir(path)** command. According to its POSIX description, it creates a new empty directory identified by **path**. An existing entry with the same name must not already exist. In our precondition, **path** evaluates to a path of the form P/B/A. The subdirectory assertion $subdir(\alpha @ \text{P}, \text{B}[\text{C} \wedge can\_create(\text{A})])$ states that the subdirectory B must be at abstract address α found at the end of path P with contents C where the predicate $can\_create(\text{A})$ (definition 10) states that it is safe to create a new entry A. In the postcondition, the assertion $subdir(\alpha @ \text{P}, \text{B}[\text{C} + \text{A}[\varnothing]])$ states that the empty directory A has indeed been created. Note that in the case we create a new directory directly under the root, in the path expression P will be an empty path and B will be ⊤.

Now consider **link(existing, new)**, which creates a new hard link with path **new** to the file identified by the path **existing**. Its first axiom is similar to that of **mkdir**. In the precondition, it has two subdirectory assertions, one

---

[9] The preconditions in such cases are mutually exclusive.

$$\left\{\begin{array}{l} expr(\texttt{path}, \text{P/B/A}) \wedge var(\texttt{r}, -) \star \mathcal{E} \\ \star\; subdir(\alpha@\text{P}, \text{B}[\text{C} \wedge can\_create(\text{A})]) \end{array}\right\}$$
$$\texttt{r := mkdir(path)}$$
$$\left\{ var(\texttt{r}, 0) \star \mathcal{E} \star subdir(\alpha@\text{P}, \text{B}[\text{C} + \text{A}[\varnothing]]) \right\}$$

$$\left\{\begin{array}{l} expr(\texttt{path}, \text{P/A}) \wedge var(\texttt{r}, -) \\ \star\; \mathcal{E} \star subdir(\alpha@\text{P}, \text{A}[\varnothing]) \end{array}\right\}$$
$$\texttt{r := rmdir(path)}$$
$$\left\{ var(\texttt{r}, 0) \star \mathcal{E} \star subdir(\alpha@\text{P}, \varnothing) \right\}$$

$$\left\{\begin{array}{l} expr(\texttt{existing}, \text{P/A}) \wedge expr(\texttt{new}, \text{P}'/\text{D/B}) \\ \wedge\; var(\texttt{r}, -) \star \mathcal{E} \star subdir(\alpha@\text{P}, \text{A} : \text{I}) \\ \star\; subdir(\beta@\text{P}', \text{D}[\text{C} \wedge can\_create(B)]) \end{array}\right\}$$
$$\texttt{r := link(existing, new)}$$
$$\left\{\begin{array}{l} var(\texttt{r}, 0) \star \mathcal{E} \star subdir(\alpha@\text{P}, \text{A} : \text{I}) \\ \star\; subdir(\beta@\text{P}', \text{D}[\text{C} + \text{B} : \text{I}]) \end{array}\right\}$$

$$\left\{\begin{array}{l} expr(\texttt{existing}, \text{P/D/A}) \\ \wedge\; expr(\texttt{new}, \text{P/D/B}) \wedge var(\texttt{r}, -) \star \mathcal{E} \\ \star\; subdir(\alpha@\text{P}, \text{D}[(\text{C} + \text{A} : \text{I}) \wedge can\_create(\text{B})]) \end{array}\right\}$$
$$\texttt{r := link(existing, new)}$$
$$\left\{ var(\texttt{r}, 0) \star \mathcal{E} \star subdir(\alpha@\text{P}, \text{D}[\text{C} + \text{A} : \text{I} + \text{B} : \text{I}]) \right\}$$

$$\left\{\begin{array}{l} expr(\texttt{path}, \text{P/A}) \wedge var(\texttt{r}, -) \\ \star\; \mathcal{E} \star subdir(\alpha@\text{P}, \text{A} : \text{I}) \end{array}\right\}$$
$$\texttt{r := unlink(path)}$$
$$\left\{ var(\texttt{r}, 0) \star \mathcal{E} \star subdir(\alpha@\text{P}, \varnothing) \right\}$$

$$\left\{\begin{array}{l} expr(\texttt{old}, \text{P/A}) \wedge expr(\texttt{new}, \text{P}'/\text{D/B}) \\ \wedge var(\texttt{r}, -) \star \mathcal{E} \star subdir(\alpha@\text{P}, \text{A}[\text{C} \wedge complete]) \\ \star\; subdir(\beta@\text{P}', \text{D}[\text{C}' \wedge can\_create(\text{B})]) \end{array}\right\}$$
$$\texttt{r := rename(old, new)}$$
$$\left\{\begin{array}{l} var(\texttt{r}, 0) \star \mathcal{E} \star subdir(\alpha@\text{P}, \varnothing) \\ \star\; subdir(\beta@\text{P}', \text{D}[\text{C}' + \text{B}[\text{C}]]) \end{array}\right\}$$

$$\left\{\begin{array}{l} expr(\texttt{old}, \text{P/D/A}) \wedge expr(\texttt{new}, \text{P/D/B}) \\ \wedge\; var(\texttt{r}, -) \star \mathcal{E} \\ \star\; subdir\left(\alpha@\text{P}, \text{D}\left[\begin{array}{l}(\text{C} + \text{A}[\text{C}' \wedge complete]) \\ \wedge\; can\_create(\text{B}) \end{array}\right]\right) \end{array}\right\}$$
$$\texttt{r := rename(old, new)}$$
$$\left\{ var(\texttt{r}, 0) \star \mathcal{E} \star subdir(\alpha@\text{P}, \text{D}[\text{C} + \text{B}[\text{C}']]) \right\}$$

$$\left\{\begin{array}{l} expr(\texttt{old}, \text{P/A}) \wedge expr(\texttt{new}, \text{P}'/\text{B}) \\ \wedge\; var(\texttt{r}, -) \star \mathcal{E} \\ \star\; subdir(\alpha@\text{P}, \text{A}[\text{C} \wedge complete]) \\ \star\; subdir(\beta@\text{P}', \text{B}[\varnothing]) \end{array}\right\}$$
$$\texttt{r := rename(old, new)}$$
$$\left\{\begin{array}{l} var(\texttt{r}, 0) \star \mathcal{E} \star subdir(\alpha@\text{P}, \varnothing) \\ \star\; subdir(\beta@\text{P}', \text{B}[\text{C}]) \end{array}\right\}$$

$$\left\{\begin{array}{l} expr(\texttt{old}, \text{P/A}) \wedge expr(\texttt{new}, \text{P}'/\text{B}) \\ \wedge\; var(\texttt{r}, -) \star \mathcal{E} \star subdir(\alpha@\text{P}, \text{A} : \text{I}) \\ \star\; subdir(\beta@\text{P}', \text{B} : \text{I}') \end{array}\right\}$$
$$\texttt{r := rename(old, new)}$$
$$\left\{\begin{array}{l} var(\texttt{r}, 0) \star \mathcal{E} \star subdir(\alpha@\text{P}, \varnothing) \\ \star\; subdir(\beta@\text{P}', \text{B} : \text{I}) \end{array}\right\}$$

$$\left\{\begin{array}{l} expr(\texttt{old}, \text{P/D/A}) \wedge expr(\texttt{new}, \text{P/D/B}) \\ \wedge\; var(\texttt{r}, -) \star \mathcal{E} \\ \star\; subdir\left(\alpha@\text{P}, \text{D}\left[\begin{array}{l}(\text{C} + \text{A} : \text{I}) \\ \wedge\; can\_create(\text{B}) \end{array}\right]\right) \end{array}\right\}$$
$$\texttt{r := rename(old, new)}$$
$$\left\{\begin{array}{l} var(\texttt{r}, 0) \star \mathcal{E} \\ \star\; subdir(\alpha@\text{P}, \text{D}[\text{C} + \text{B} : \text{I}]) \end{array}\right\}$$

$$\left\{\begin{array}{l} expr(\texttt{old}, \text{P/A}) \wedge expr(\texttt{new}, \text{P}'/\text{D/B}) \\ \wedge\; var(\texttt{r}, -) \star \mathcal{E} \star subdir(\alpha@\text{P}, \text{A} : \text{I}) \\ \star\; subdir(\beta@\text{P}', \text{D}[\text{C} \wedge can\_create(B)]) \end{array}\right\}$$
$$\texttt{r := rename(old, new)}$$
$$\left\{\begin{array}{l} var(\texttt{r}, 0) \star \mathcal{E} \star subdir(\alpha@\text{P}, \varnothing) \\ \star\; subdir(\beta@\text{P}', \text{D}[\text{C} + \text{B} : \text{I}]) \end{array}\right\}$$

$$\left\{\begin{array}{l} expr(\texttt{old}, \text{P/A}) \wedge expr(\texttt{new}, \text{P/A}) \\ \wedge\; var(\texttt{r}, -) \star \mathcal{E} \\ \star\; subdir(\alpha@\text{P}, \text{C} \wedge entry(\text{A})) \end{array}\right\}$$
$$\texttt{r := rename(old, new)}$$
$$\left\{ var(\texttt{r}, 0) \star \mathcal{E} \star subdir(\alpha@\text{P}, \text{C}) \right\}$$

$$\left\{\begin{array}{l} expr(\texttt{path}, \text{P/A}) \wedge var(\texttt{t}, -) \star \mathcal{E} \\ \star\; subdir(\alpha@\text{P}, \text{A}[\beta]) \end{array}\right\}$$
$$\texttt{t := stat(path)}$$
$$\left\{ var(\texttt{t}, \text{D}) \star \mathcal{E} \star subdir(\alpha@\text{P}, \text{A}[\beta]) \right\}$$

$$\left\{\begin{array}{l} expr(\texttt{path}, \text{P/A}) \wedge var(\texttt{t}, -) \\ \star\; \mathcal{E} \star subdir(\alpha@\text{P}, \text{A} : \text{I}) \end{array}\right\}$$
$$\texttt{t := stat(path)}$$
$$\left\{ var(\texttt{t}, \text{F}) \star \mathcal{E} \star subdir(\alpha@\text{P}, \text{A} : \text{I}) \right\}$$

$$\left\{\begin{array}{l} expr(\texttt{path}, \text{P/D}) \wedge var(\texttt{dir}, -) \star \mathcal{E} \\ \star\; subdir(\alpha@\text{P}, \text{D}[top(\text{C})]) \end{array}\right\}$$
$$\texttt{dir := opendir(path)}$$
$$\left\{\begin{array}{l} \exists \text{H}.\; var(\texttt{dir}, \text{H}) \star \mathcal{E} \\ \star\; subdir(\alpha@\text{P}, \text{D}[\text{C} \wedge names(\text{A})]) \\ \star\; ds(\text{H}, \text{A}) \end{array}\right\}$$

$$\left\{\begin{array}{l} var(\texttt{dir}, \text{H}) \star var(\texttt{fn}, -) \\ \star\; ds(\text{H}, \text{A}) \wedge \text{A} \neq \{\} \end{array}\right\}$$
$$\texttt{fn := readaddr(dir)}$$
$$\left\{\begin{array}{l} var(\texttt{fn}, \text{B}) \star var(\texttt{dir}, \text{H}) \\ \star\; ds(\text{H}, (\text{A} \smallsetminus \{\text{B}\})) \wedge \text{B} \in \text{A} \end{array}\right\}$$

$$\left\{\begin{array}{l} var(\texttt{dir}, \text{H}) \star var(\texttt{fn}, -) \\ \star\; ds(\text{H}, \{\}) \end{array}\right\}$$
$$\texttt{fn := readaddr(dir)}$$
$$\left\{\begin{array}{l} var(\texttt{dir}, \text{H}) \star var(\texttt{fn}, \epsilon) \\ \star\; ds(\text{H}, \{\}) \end{array}\right\}$$

$$\left\{ var(\texttt{dir}, \text{H}) \star ds(\text{H}, \text{A}) \right\}$$
$$\texttt{closedir(dir)}$$
$$\left\{ var(\texttt{dir}, \text{H}) \right\}$$

Fig. 5. Axioms for some POSIX commands

for each path. The assertion $subdir(\alpha@P, A:I)$ states that the existing path P/A identifies a file link named A to the file with inode address I. The assertion $subdir(\beta@P', D[C \wedge can\_create(B)])$ states, as in mkdir, that an entry with the name we want to create does not already exist. In the postcondition, the assertion $subdir(\beta@P', D[C + B:I])$ states that this new entry has been created with another file link to the same file. Note that, in this first axiom, the update takes place between two different directories; in the second, they take place within the same directory.

The rename(old,new) command moves and/or renames the entry identified by the path old to that identified by new. Consider the first axiom where old is a directory and new does not exist. In the precondition, the assertion $subdir(\alpha@P, A[C \wedge complete])$ states that the subdirectory A must be complete and the assertion $subdir(\beta@P', D[C' \wedge can\_create(B)])$ states that it is possible to create the new directory B under D. The only path constraints are that the global paths P and P' must exist in the underlying global directory, thus restricting the application of the frame rule. In contrast to the first-order rename axiom discussed in related work, we do not require any additional path constraints to ensure that P' is not a descendant of P/A. It comes automatically from the separating conjunction.

Finally, the dir:=opendir(path) command allocates a new directory stream for the directory identified by path and assigns its address to dir. In the precondition, the assertion $top(C)$ (definition 10) states that the entries of the identified subdirectory D are complete at the top level. In the postcondition, the assertion $subdir(\alpha@P, D[C \wedge names(A)])$ declares the set A of all the entries of the directory D, and uses it in the assertion $ds(H, A)$ to describe the allocated directory stream at H. Elements of the directory stream are obtained via the readdir command, for which we have two cases: one when the directory stream is not empty; and one where it is. Note that readdir non-deterministically selects which entry name to return and remove from the A set. This mirrors the fact the order of directory entries is implementation defined in POSIX. The closedir(dir) command simply deallocates the directory stream given by dir.

Sequential Soundness. We believe it is enough to justify our axiomatic specification by comparing it with the POSIX English standard, since the descriptions are naturally close. However, this is perhaps a controversial point. In [11], we give a standard soundness result for sequential programs (no external processes modifying the file system), providing an operational semantics and proving soundness in the style of the views framework [6].

4   Software Installer

We now demonstrate our reasoning by considering a *software installer*. New software is typically provided as a bundle, either downloaded onto the users file system or provided on some media containing a file system. The goal is to place the bundle's contents correctly in the users' file system which may involve other tasks such as removing any previous installations and dealing with incompatible user files. Installers are a common class of client programs that perform complex manipulation of file system structure.

Here, we develop an installer for the fictional software "Widget v2". It supersedes "Widget v1", but is incompatible with any v1 user configuration files. Widget v2 consists of a program executable, '*widgProg*' and a data file, '*widgData*'. Following common conventions [1], we place the files in 'т/*opt*/*widget*/' and create a link from 'т/*usr*/*bin*/*widget*' to 'т/*opt*/*widget*/*widgProg*'. An example situation the installer may encounter is that in figure 1, where v1 exists and the user '*adw07*' has a configuration file.

Even though our installer is fictional, it follows a common workflow found in real practice. In our example, this workflow translates to the following steps:

① Test if entries already exist at the locations we wish to place Widget v2 files. If they exist, we expect 'т/*usr*/*bin*/*widget*' to be a file and 'т/*opt*/*widget*' to be a directory. If this is the case, we remove them. If it is not, the installer aborts without modifying the system to avoid damaging other components.

② Check for v1 configuration files in home directories, and remove them where they exist as they are assumed to be incompatible.

③ Copy Widget v2 files to the target location on the file system.

④ Make a link to the Widget v2 executable, so the user can run it.

Before implementing the installer we need to consider errors. So far, our specifications describe only when commands succeed. However, commands can also fail with an error result. Our installer relies on the **stat** command returning an error when a path does not exist. We consider error specifications for the entire subset in [11]. Here, we discuss only the ENOENT error for **stat**, triggered when a path does not resolve to a file or directory. To describe a file system in which a path cannot resolve, we define the following:

$$\text{ENOENT}(P) \triangleq P \equiv \epsilon \vee (\exists P', A, B, P''. \; P \equiv P'/A/B/P''. \; subdir(\alpha @ P', A[can\_create(B)]))$$

This predicate states that the path P has a prefix which can be resolved, but a suffix which *cannot*. All paths which do not resolve will satisfy this specification and with it, we can give the following error axiom for **stat**:

$$\big\{ \, expr(\textbf{path}, P) \wedge var(\textbf{t}, -) \star var(\textbf{errno}, -) \star \mathcal{E} \star S \wedge \text{ENOENT}(P) \, \big\}$$
$$\textbf{t} \; \texttt{:=} \; \texttt{stat(path)}$$
$$\big\{ \, var(\textbf{t}, -1) \star var(\textbf{errno}, \text{ENOENT}) \star \mathcal{E} \star S \, \big\}$$

In the precondition we use the predicate on the value of **path** to assert that we are in the error case. Note that we capture the state satisfying the predicate in the logical variable S. In the postcondition, this state is preserved and the global variable **errno** is assigned the error value, for which we use the same name as the predicate for convenience.

To remove an existing Widget installation (point ②) we need to be able to remove non-empty directories, but **rmdir** only removes empty directories. We can implement a program **rmdirRec** that recursively removes all the directories entries before removing the directory itself. The specification is:

$$\big\{ \, expr(\textbf{path}, P/A) \wedge var(\textbf{r}, -) \star \mathcal{E} \star subdir(\alpha @ P, A[complete]) \, \big\}$$
$$\textbf{r} \; \texttt{:=} \; \texttt{rmdirRec(path)}$$
$$\big\{ \, var(\textbf{r}, 0) \star \mathcal{E} \star subdir(\alpha @ P, \varnothing) \, \big\}$$

Finally, to copy files (point ④), we can implement the program `fileCopy` with the following specification:

$$\left\{ \begin{array}{c} expr(\text{source}, \text{P}/\text{A}) \wedge expr(\text{target}, \text{P}'/\text{D}) \wedge var(\text{r}, -) \star \mathcal{E} \\ \star\ subdir(\alpha@\text{P}, \text{A}:\text{I}) \star subdir(\beta@\text{P}', \text{D}[\text{C} \wedge can\_create(\text{A})]) \star file(\text{I}, \text{SD}) \end{array} \right\}$$

$$\text{r} := \text{fileCopy(source, target)}$$

$$\left\{ \begin{array}{c} \exists \text{I}'.\ var(\text{r}, 0) \star \mathcal{E} \star subdir(\alpha@\text{P}, \text{A}:\text{I}) \star subdir(\beta@\text{P}', \text{D}[\text{C} + \text{A}:\text{I}']) \\ \star\ file(\text{I}, \text{SD}) \star file(\text{I}', \text{SD}) \end{array} \right\}$$

We have implemented both `rmdirRec` and `fileCopy` and derived their specifications in [11].

The installation of a simple, two file program is a surprisingly complex task. We therefore specify our intuitions about good behaviour and prove that our installer matches them. First, we develop abstractions to assist us in the specifications. We use the following predicates to assert that entries may or may not exist within a given directory resource:

$$out(\text{C}, \text{A}) \triangleq top(\text{C}) \wedge \neg \diamondsuit entry(\text{A}) \qquad in(\text{C}, \text{A}) \triangleq \text{C} + entry(\text{A})$$
$$infile(\text{C}, \text{A}) \triangleq \text{C} + \exists \text{I}.\ \text{A}:\text{I}$$

The first predicate describes directory entries C in which an entry named A does not exist, whereas the second describes entries C in which it does. $infile(\text{C}, \text{A})$ is more specific and describes directory entries C with an A file entry.

We build a precondition for our installer out of several sub-assertions with the help of the above predicates. In these, the assertion $+_{X \in E}\ \phi$ is the iterated version of $+$, interpreted as $\phi_1 + \cdots + \phi_{|E|}$ where each ϕ_i has X bound to a distinct member of E.

$$src_{\text{Pre}} \triangleq subdir(\delta@\text{IL}, \text{widgProg}:\text{J} + \text{widgData}:\text{K}) \star file(\text{J}, \text{PROG}) \star file(\text{K}, \text{DAT})$$

$$home_{\text{Pre}} \triangleq subdir\big(\alpha@\text{T}, \text{home}\left[+_{(\text{N}, \text{C}) \in \text{H}}\ \text{N}\left[infile(\text{C}, .wconf) \vee out(\text{C}, .wconf)\right]\right]\big)$$

$$bin_{\text{Pre}} \triangleq subdir\big(\gamma@\text{T}/usr, \text{bin}\left[in(\text{B}, \text{widget}) \vee out(\text{B}, \text{widget})\right]\big)$$

$$opt_{\text{Pre}} \triangleq subdir\big(\beta@\text{T}, \text{opt}\left[top(\text{T}) + (\varnothing \vee \text{widget}[\text{T}_w \wedge complete])\right]\big)$$

Each of these describes the states that parts of the file system may be in for the installer to run safely. The directory entries and file data that make up the Widget v2 installation sources are described by src_{Pre}. We require them to be in a location given by the variable `il`. $home_{\text{Pre}}$ captures all the home directories of the system, along with the fact that some of them will contain a v1 '.wconf' configuration file. The bin_{Pre} resource captures the UNIX executables directory, that may contain a 'widget' entry. Finally, opt_{Pre} describes the target installation directory, which may already contain a previous installation, which we require to be complete, as it will be deleted.

We combine these descriptions into a precondition, where we also snapshot the initial state in the logical variable W, to show that nothing changes in the event of an error.

$$P_i \triangleq var(\text{il}, \text{IL}) \star var(\text{r}, -) \star var(\text{errno}, -) \wedge \text{W} \wedge src_{\text{Pre}} \star home_{\text{Pre}} \star bin_{\text{Pre}} \star opt_{\text{Pre}}$$

If the installer errors, we expect the file system to be unchanged. If it succeeds, we expect Widget v1 to be installed successfully. There should be no other outcome. We describe a successful installation with the following sub-assertions:

$\{\,P_i\,\}$

```
r := installWidgetV2 ≙
local t1, t2, hDir, user {
```

  $\{\, var(\text{t1}, -) \star var(\text{t2}, -) \star var(\textbf{errno}, -) \star bin_{\text{Pre}} \star opt_{\text{Pre}} \,\}$

```
    // Check for preexisting files (point ①). The installer expects T/usr/bin/widget
    // to be a file and T/opt/widget to be a directory, if they exist.
    t1 := stat('T/usr/bin/widget'); t2 := stat('T/opt/widget');
```

  $\left\{ \begin{array}{l} var(\text{t1}, \text{T1}) \wedge (\text{T1} = \text{F} \vee \text{D} \vee -1) \star var(\text{t2}, \text{T2}) \wedge (\text{T2} = \text{F} \vee \text{D} \vee -1) \\ \star\, var(\textbf{errno}, \text{E}) \wedge ((\text{T1} = -1 \vee \text{T2} = -1) \Rightarrow \text{E} = \text{ENOENT}) \star bin_{\text{Pre}} \star opt_{\text{Pre}} \end{array} \right\}$

```
    if t1 = D ∨ t2 = F
        // There are preexisting entries, but not of a previous installation.
        // The installer ends here without any modifications.
        r = -1;
    else
        // Either previous entries do not exist, or they are of a previous installation.
```

    $\{\, var(\text{r}, -) \star var(\text{t1}, \text{F}) \vee var(\text{t1}, -1) \star var(\text{t2}, \text{D}) \vee var(\text{t2}, -1) \star bin_{\text{Pre}} \star opt_{\text{Pre}} \,\}$

```
        if t1 = F
            // Remove previous installation executable.
            r := unlink('T/usr/bin/widget');
        if t2 = D
            // Remove previous installation directory. We apply the rmdirRec specification.
```

      $\{\, var(\text{t2}, \text{D}) \star var(\text{r}, -) \star subdir(\beta@\text{T}, \text{opt}[\text{T} + \text{widget}[\text{T}_w \wedge complete]]) \,\}$

```
            r := rmdirRec('T/opt/widget');
```

      $\{\, var(\text{t2}, \text{D}) \star var(\text{r}, 0) \star subdir(\beta@\text{T}, \text{opt}[\text{T}]) \,\}$

    $\left\{ \begin{array}{l} var(\text{r}, 0) \star var(\text{t1}, \text{F}) \vee var(\text{t1}, -1) \star var(\text{t2}, \text{D}) \vee var(\text{t2}, -1) \\ \star\, subdir(\gamma@\text{T}/usr, \text{bin}[\text{B}]) \star subdir(\beta@\text{T}, \text{opt}[\text{T}]) \end{array} \right\}$

```
        // Remove any stale Widget configuration files (point ②)
```

    $\{ var(\text{hDir}, -) \star var(\text{user}, -) \star subdir(\alpha@\text{T}, \text{home}[+_{(\text{N},\text{C})\in\text{H}} \text{N}[infile(\text{C}, .\text{wconf}) \vee out(\text{C}, .\text{wconf})]]) \}$

```
        hDir := opendir('T/home');
        user := readdir(hDir);
```

    $\left\{ \begin{array}{l} \exists \text{HD}, \text{U}, \text{Us}. \; var(\text{hDir}, \text{HD}) \star var(\text{user}, \text{U}) \star ds(\text{HD}, \text{Us}) \\ \star\, subdir(\alpha@\text{T}, \text{home}[+_{(\text{N},\text{C})\in\text{H}} \text{N}[out(\text{C}, .\text{wconf}) + \text{N} \in \text{Us} \Rightarrow (\varnothing \vee \exists \text{I}. .\text{wconf}:\text{I}) \wedge \text{N} \notin \text{Us} \Rightarrow \varnothing]]) \end{array} \right\}$

```
    while user ≠ ε
        // We iterate over every user's home directory and delete the file.
        // If the file does not exist, then unlink returns -1 as in stat.
        r := unlink('T/home'/user/'.wconf'); user := readdir(hDir);
    closedir(hDir);
    // In the end, there are no Widget V1 configuration files.
```

  $\{\, subdir(\alpha@\text{T}, \text{home}[+_{(\text{N},\text{C})\in\text{H}} \text{N}[\text{C} \wedge can\_create(.\text{wconf})]]) \,\}$

```
    // Now we create the new installation, copy the new Widget files
    // and link the executable (Points ③ and ④)
```

  $\left\{ \begin{array}{l} var(\text{r}, -) \star var(\text{il}, \text{IL}) \star subdir(\delta@\text{IL}, v2Dir_{\text{Pre}}) \star subdir(\alpha@\text{T}, \text{home}_{\text{Post}}) \\ \star\, subdir(\gamma@\text{T}/usr, \text{bin}[\text{B}]) \star subdir(\beta@\text{T}, \text{opt}[\text{T}]) \star file(\text{J}, \text{PROG}) \star file(\text{K}, \text{DAT}) \end{array} \right\}$

```
    r := mkdir('T/opt/widget');
    r := fileCopy(il/'widgProg', 'T/opt/widget');
    r := fileCopy(il/'widgData', 'T/opt/widget');
    r := link('T/opt/widget/widgProg', 'T/usr/bin/widget'); r := 0
```

  $\left\{ \begin{array}{l} \exists \text{J}', \text{K}'. \; var(\text{r}, 0) \star var(\text{il}, \text{IL}) \star src_{\text{Pre}} \star home_{\text{Post}} \\ \star\, subdir(\beta@\text{T}, \text{opt}[\text{T} + \text{widget}[\text{widgProg}:\text{J}' + \text{widgData}:\text{K}']]) \\ \star\, subdir(\gamma@\text{T}/usr, \text{bin}[\text{B} + \text{widget}:\text{J}']) \star file(\text{J}', \text{PROG}) \star file(\text{K}', \text{DAT}) \end{array} \right\}$

```
}
```

$\left\{ \begin{array}{l} \exists \text{R}, \text{J}', \text{K}'. \; var(\text{il}, \text{IL}) \star var(\text{r}, \text{R}) \star var(\textbf{errno}, -) \wedge (\text{R} = -1 \Rightarrow \text{W}) \\ \wedge\, \text{R} = 0 \Rightarrow (src_{\text{Pre}} \star home_{\text{Post}} \star opt_{\text{Post}}(\text{J}', \text{K}') \star bin_{\text{Post}}(\text{K}') \star v2Files_{\text{Post}}(\text{J}', \text{K}')) \end{array} \right\}$

$\{\,Q_i\,\}$

Fig. 6. Widget v2 software installer

$v2Files_{\text{Post}}(\text{J}, \text{K}) \triangleq file(\text{J}, \text{PROG}) \star file(\text{K}, \text{DAT})$

$\qquad home_{\text{Post}} \triangleq subdir\left(\alpha_{@\text{T}}, \text{home}\left[+_{(\text{N},\text{C})\in \text{H}} \text{N}\left[\text{C} \wedge can\_create(.\text{wconf})\right]\right]\right)$

$\qquad bin_{\text{Post}}(\text{J}) \triangleq subdir\left(\gamma_{@\text{T}/usr}, \text{bin}[\text{B} + \text{widget} : \text{J}]\right)$

$\qquad opt_{\text{Post}}(\text{J}, \text{K}) \triangleq subdir\left(\beta_{@\text{T}}, \text{opt}[\text{T} + \text{widget}[\text{widgProg} : \text{J} + \text{widgDat} : \text{K}]]\right)$

The postcondition is built from these sub-assertions.

$$Q_i \triangleq \begin{array}{l} \exists \text{R}, \text{J}', \text{K}'.\ var(\texttt{il}, \text{IL}) \star var(\mathbf{r}, \text{R}) \star var(\texttt{errno}, -) \wedge (\text{R} = -1 \Rightarrow \text{W}) \\ \wedge\ \text{R} = 0 \Rightarrow \big(src_{\text{Pre}} \star home_{\text{Post}} \star opt_{\text{Post}}(\text{J}', \text{K}') \star bin_{\text{Post}}(\text{J}') \star v2Files_{\text{Post}}(\text{J}', \text{K}')\big) \end{array}$$

Note that if the installer fails, the return variable $\mathbf{r}$ has value -1 and the state of the file system is the same as in the precondition, captured by the logical variable W. Otherwise, $\mathbf{r}$ is 0 and the state changes according to the sub-assertions that we have defined.

Our installer implementation, along with a proof that it meets its specification, $\{P_i\}\texttt{installWidgetV2}\{Q_i\}$, is given in figure 6. Throughout the proof we make implicit use of the frame rule to temporarily discard irrelevant state, and at the points of axiom application we implicitly use abstract allocation/deallocation.

5   Conclusions and Future Work

The POSIX file system provides an interesting challenge for local reasoning: complex abstract data update with global absolute paths for identifying the place to do local update. We give a natural axiomatic specification of the sequential POSIX file system using SSL; the general theory is in [25, 12]. We verify safety properties for a client software installer, demonstrating integrated reasoning for the file system and the heap. Our POSIX reasoning provides an illustrative example of reasoning about global access and local update; other natural applications include identifying the ith element of a list [25] and querying the DOM.

The promises in our POSIX reasoning are naturally stable. Wright has also explored the combination of promises and *obligations*: promises on abstract heap cells give information about what can be relied upon by the environment; obligations gives information about what data fragments must guarantee; sometimes both are needed for stability. In this paper, the only obligations are that the abstract cell and body addresses must be preserved. In general, understanding obligations is hard. A natural test example would be to extend the core POSIX fragment presented here with non-linear paths (.. and symbollic links), where the paths can move back and forth over the structure. We also believe obligations will be useful for file-access permissions and shared-memory concurrency.

Acknowledgements. We acknowledge funding from an EPSRC DTA (Ntzik, Wright) and EPSRC programme grant EP/H008373/1 (Gardner, Ntzik and Wright). We also thank Pedro da Rocha Pinto, Ramana Kumar, Azalea Raad, Tom Ridge and Mark Wheelhouse for many interesting discussions.

References

[1] Filesystem Hierarchy Standard Group. Filesystem hierarchy standard
[2] POSIX.1-2008, IEEE 1003.1-2008, The Open Group Base Specifications Issue 7
[3] Variables as resource in separation logic. Electronic Notes in Theoretical Computer Science 155, 247–276 (2006)
[4] Arkoudas, K., Zee, K., Kuncak, V., Rinard, M.: Verifying a File System Implementation. In: Davies, J., Schulte, W., Barnett, M. (eds.) ICFEM 2004. LNCS, vol. 3308, pp. 373–390. Springer, Heidelberg (2004)
[5] Calcagno, C., Gardner, P., Zarfaty, U.: Context logic and tree update. SIGPLAN Not. (2005)
[6] Dinsdale-Young, T., Birkedal, L., Gardner, P., Parkinson, M., Yang, H.: Views: compositional reasoning for concurrent programs. In: POPL (2013)
[7] Dinsdale-Young, T., Dodds, M., Gardner, P., Parkinson, M.J., Vafeiadis, V.: Concurrent abstract predicates. In: D'Hondt, T. (ed.) ECOOP 2010. LNCS, vol. 6183, pp. 504–528. Springer, Heidelberg (2010)
[8] Fisher, K., Foster, N., Walker, D., Zhu, K.Q.: Forest: a language and toolkit for programming with filestores. In: ICFP (2011)
[9] Freitas, L., Fu, Z., Woodcock, J.: POSIX file store in Z/Eves: an experiment in the verified software repository. In: IEEE International Conference on Engineering of Complex Computer Systems (2007)
[10] Freitas, L., Woodcock, J., Butterfield, A.: POSIX and the verification grand challenge: A roadmap. In: ICECCS (2008)
[11] Gardner, P., Ntzik, G., Wright, A.: Local Reasoning for the POSIX File System. Technical report, Imperial College London (2014), http://www.doc.ic.ac.uk/~gn408/POSIXFS/
[12] Gardner, P., Raad, A., Wheelhouse, M., Wright, A.: Abstract Local Reasoning for Concurrent Libraries. In preparation (2014)
[13] Gardner, P., Smith, G., Wheelhouse, M., Zarfaty, U.: Local Hoare reasoning about DOM. In: PODS (2008)
[14] Gardner, P., Wheelhouse, M.: Small specifications for tree update, http://www.doc.ic.ac.uk/~pg/papers/move.pdf
[15] Hesselink, W.H., Lali, M.: Formalizing a hierarchical file system. In: REFINE (2009)
[16] Hobor, A., Villard, J.: The ramifications of sharing in data structures. In: POPL (2013)
[17] Joshi, R., Holzmann, G.J.: A mini challenge: build a verifiable filesystem. Form. Asp. Comput. (2007)
[18] Morgan, C., Sufrin, B.: Specification of the UNIX Filing System. IEEE Transactions on Software Engineering (1984)
[19] Ntzik, G.: Local Reasoning about File Systems. PhD thesis (expected, 2014)
[20] Parkinson, M., Bierman, G.: Separation logic and abstraction. In: POPL (2005)
[21] Reynolds, J.C.: Separation logic: A logic for shared mutable data structures. In: LICS (2002)
[22] Smith, G.: Local Reasoning about Web Programs. PhD thesis (2011)
[23] Svendsen, K., Birkedal, L.: Impredicative concurrent abstract predicates. In: Shao, Z. (ed.) ESOP 2014. LNCS, vol. 8410, pp. 149–168. Springer, Heidelberg (2014)
[24] Turon, A., Dreyer, D., Birkedal, L.: Unifying refinement and hoare-style reasoning in a logic for higher-order concurrency. In: ICFP (2013)
[25] Wright, A.: Structural Separation Logic. PhD thesis, Imperial College London (2013)

A Coq Formalization of the Relational Data Model[*]

Véronique Benzaken[1], Évelyne Contejean[2], and Stefania Dumbrava[1]

[1] Université Paris Sud, LRI, France
[2] CNRS, LRI, Université Paris Sud, France

Abstract. In this article, we propose a Coq formalization of the relational data model which underlies relational database systems. More precisely, we present and formalize the data definition part of the model including integrity constraints. We model two different query language formalisms: relational algebra and conjunctive queries. We also present logical query optimization and prove the main "database theorems": algebraic equivalences, the homomorphism theorem and conjunctive query minimization.

1 Introduction

Current data management applications and systems involve increasingly massive data volumes. Surprisingly, while the amount of data stored and managed by data engines has drastically increased, little attention has been devoted to ensure that those are reliable. Obtaining strong guarantees requires the use of formal methods and mature tools. A very promising approach consists in using proof assistants such as Coq [10]. Among such systems, relational database management systems (RDBMS) are the most widespread, motivating our choice to focus on the formalization of the relational data model.

The relational model serves different related purposes: it allows to *represent* information through *relations*, to *refine* the represented information by further restricting it through *integrity constraints*. It also provides ways to *extract* information through *query languages* based on either algebra (relational algebra queries) or first-order logic (conjunctive queries). Two different equivalent versions of the relational model exist: the *unnamed* and the *named* ones. In the *unnamed* setting, the specific attributes of a relation are ignored: only the arity (*i.e.*, the number of attributes) of a relation is available to query languages. In the *named* setting, attributes are viewed as an *explicit part* of a database and are used by query languages and integrity constraints. In practice, systems such as Oracle, DB2, PostgreSQL or Microsoft Access, rely on the *named* version of the model. They do it for several reasons. First, because for modeling purposes, names carry much more semantics than column numbers. Second, query optimizers do exploit auxiliary data structures such as indexes natively based on attributes names for physical optimization purposes (exploiting different algorithms and/or indexes). We thus chose to formalize this version.

---

[*] This work is partially supported by ANR project Typex n° 11BS0200702.

Z. Shao (Ed.): ESOP 2014, LNCS 8410, pp. 189–208, 2014.
© Springer-Verlag Berlin Heidelberg 2014

1.1   Related Work

The first attempt in that direction is found in Gonzalia [5,6]. This work investigates different formalizations of the *unnamed* version of the model and only addresses data definition and relational algebra aspects. A more recent formalization is found in Malecha *et al.*, [8] which addresses the problem of designing a fully verified, lightweight *implementation* of a relational database system. The authors prove that their implementation meets the specification, all the proofs being written and verified in the Ynot [3] extension of Coq. However, they implemented only a *single-user* database system. Both works chose a very unrealistic data model, the unnamed version, and gave only a *partial* modeling, insofar as conjunctive queries, serious optimization techniques, as well as integrity constraint aspects, are left for future work. Any modeling aiming at being a realistic full-fledged specification of the relational model has to include all of them.

1.2   Contributions

Our long term purpose is to *prove* that *existing* systems conform to their specifications and to *verify* that programs that make intensive use of database queries are correct and *not to implement* a RDBMS in Coq. So, the first essential step is to formalize the relational model of data. We first formalize the data definition part of the model, relational algebra and conjunctive queries. Since the latter play a central role in optimization, as they admit an *exact* equivalent optimized form, we provide both a formal specification and a certified version of the algorithm that translates relational algebra queries into conjunctive queries. We then present logical query optimization, for both query formalisms, and prove the main "databases theorems": algebraic equivalences, the homomorphism theorem and conjunctive query minimization. We also provide a certified algorithm for such a minimization. As integrity constraints are central to database technology at the design level, to build relation structures (called *schemas* in the database dialect) enjoying good properties, and at the compiler and optimizer levels, to generate optimizations, we thus specify the integrity constraints part of the relational model. We model functional and general dependencies which are considered by the database community as the most important constraints. We then deal with the problem of implication, *i.e.*, inferring all logically implied constraints from a given set. Inferring *all* constraints is important, as these are intensively used for design and optimization purposes, and since, in the absence of some of them, the compiler could miss further optimizations. We provide a formal Coq proof that the inference system for functional dependencies, *a.k.a.*, Armstrong's system, is sound, complete and terminating. We formalize and prove the correctness of the procedure for deducing new general dependencies, *a.k.a.*, the *chase*. The informal presentation of all concepts is directly taken from reference textbooks on the topic [1,11,9]. Our formalization achieves a high degree of abstraction and modularity and is, to our knowledge, the most realistic mechanization of classic database theory to date. A last but not least contribution is that through this formalization process, we also bring insight both to the database and to the Coq communities. To this extent, we emphasize, throughout this article, the subtleties, which were hidden (or even missing) in textbooks. Finally, we would like to stress that this formalization step is not a mere Coq exercise of style but a needed phase in the realistic verification of full fledged database management systems, and there is no way around it.

1.3   Organization

In Section 2, we present and formalize the *named version* of the relational model, in Section 3, we model relational algebra, and conjunctive queries, we formalize and extract an algorithm translating algebra queries into conjunctive ones. In Section 4, we present the logical query optimization and prove the main "database theorems": algebraic equivalences, tableaux query minimization and the homomorphism theorem. We discuss and formalize the constraint part of the model in Section 5. We conclude by drawing lessons and giving perspectives in Section 6.

2   Data Representation

Intuitively, in the relational model, data is represented by tables (relations) consisting of rows (tuples), with uniform structure and intended meaning, each of which gives information about a specific entity. For example, assuming we want to describe movies, we can represent each movie by a tuple, whose fields (attributes) could be the movie title, its director and one of its actors. Note that we will have as many rows as there are actors for a given movie. Then, assuming that movies are screened in specific locations, these could be described by a theater name, an address and a phone number. Last, one should be able to find in the Pariscope journal[1] which theater features which movie on which schedule.

2.1   Attributes, Domains, Values

Quoting [1], a set *attribute* of (names for) attributes is fixed and equipped with a total order $\leq_{\mathtt{att}}$. When different attributes should have distinct domains (or types), a mapping, *dom*, from *attribute* to *domain* is assumed. Further, an infinite set *value* is fixed. Usually, the set of attributes is assumed to be countably infinite but in our formal development this assumption was not needed. We also assume several distinct domain names (*e.g.*, "string", "integer"), which belong to set *domain*. In the database context, *domain* corresponds to the Coq notion of type. In order to have a decidable equality, we rather used our own type : **Type**. In our setting, *dom* is called type_of_attribute. Each value has a formal type (obtained by the function type_of_value) which belongs to type. All these assumptions are gathered in a Coq record Tuple.Rcd, whose contents will be enriched throughout this section.

---

[1] The Pariscope is a Parisian journal for advertising cultural events.

```
Module Tuple.                    type : Type;
Record Rcd : Type :=             value : Type;                         (* Default Values. *)
 mk_R {                          (* Typing attributes and values. *)   default_value : type → value;
  (* Basic ingredients,          type_of_attribute : attribute →      ... }.
    attributes, types and values *)  type;                            End Tuple.
  attribute : Type;              type_of_value : value → type;
```

We illustrate these definitions with our running movie example. Recall that our purpose is *not* to store an actual database schema or instance in Coq, rather the following example is intended to be a *proof of concept*.

```
Inductive attribute :=                 | Value_Z : Z → value.              Definition type_of_value v :=
 | Title | Director | Actor | Theater  Definition type_of_attribute x :=   match v with
 | Address | Phone | Schedule.         match x with                       | Value_string _ ⇒ type_string
Inductive type :=                      | Title | Director | Actor | Theater | Value_nat _ ⇒ type_nat
 | type_string | type_nat | type_Z.    | Address | Phone ⇒ type_string    | Value_Z _ ⇒ type_Z
Inductive value :=                     | Schedule ⇒ type_nat             end.
 | Value_string : string → value       end.
 | Value_nat : nat → value
```

There is also a more generic modeling for attributes, and in that case, for the sake of readability, we could use the Coq notations shown in [2].

2.2 Tuples

In the named perspective, tuples are characterized by their relevant attributes (for example {Title, Director, Actor} for movies). We call this the tuple's *support*. Following textbooks, we naturally model support's by finite sets. To this end, we mainly used Letouzey's MSet library [7]. To be as modular as possible, we still dissociate the specification of finite sets from the implementation. The specification is given by a record Fset.Rcd parametrized by the elements' type and contains a comparison function elt_compare. From now on, we use the notation $\stackrel{set}{=}$ to denote set equivalence, which is actually the usual mathematical extensional equality for sets: $\forall s\ s', s \stackrel{set}{=} s' \iff (\forall e, e \in s \iff e \in s')$. For the sake of readability, the usual sets operators will be denoted with their usual mathematical notations ($\cap$, $\cup$, $\setminus$, $\in$, ...). Extending the record Tuple.Rcd, we further assume:

```
Module Tuple.                              support_mk_tuple_ok :
Record Rcd : Type := mk_R {                 ∀ V f, support (mk_tuple V f) ≝set V;
 (** Basic ingredients,                    dot_mk_tuple_ok :
   attributes, domains and values *)        ∀ a V f, a ∈ V → dot (mk_tuple V f) a = f a;
 ...                                        FTuple : Fset.Rcd tuple;
 A : Fset.Rcd attribute;                   tuple_eq_ok : ∀ t1 t2 : tuple,
 (** tuples *)                              (Fset.elt_compare FTuple t1 t2 = Eq) ⟷
 tuple : Type;                              (support t1 ≝set support t2 ∧
 support : tuple → set A;                   ∀ a, a ∈ (support t1) → dot t1 a = dot t2 a)
 dot : tuple → attribute → value;
 mk_tuple : set A → (attribute → value) → tuple;  }
```

where A models finite sets of attribute's. We still keep the type of tuples abstract and assume the existence of two functions: support, returning the relevant tuple attributes, and dot, the associated field extraction. These functions allow to characterize tuple equivalence (tuple_eq_ok) since a tuple t behaves as the pair (support t, dot t). Further, we assume the existence of the mk_tuple function which builds tuples. This and the previous modeling of attribute induce a notion of tuple well-typedness. A tuple t is well-typed if and only if for any attribute a in its support the type of the value t.a is the type of attribute a:

Definition well_typed_tuple (t : tuple) := ∀ a, a ∈ (support t) → type_of_value (dot t a)= type_of_attribute a.

However and surprisingly, such a notion was useless to prove all the results stated in theoretical textbooks. This is an a posteriori justification of the *relevance* of the assumption that it suffices to use a unique domain for values. The previously presented record Tuple.Rcd captures exactly the abstract behavior of tuples *i.e.*, the needed properties for proving all the theorems presented hereafter. To illustrate the generality and flexibility of our specification, we give, in [2], different possible implementations for tuples. All of them satisfy the required properties and are orthogonal to the implementation of attributes. Among others, one implements tuples as pairs containing a set of attributes and a function, and sticks to the abstract definition. For instance, another one implements tuples as association lists between attributes and values.

2.3 Relations, Schemas and Instances

A distinction is made between the *database schema*, which specifies the structure of the database, and the database *instance*, which specifies its actual content: sets of tuples. In textbooks, each table is called a *relation* and has a *name*. A set relname of relation names, equipped with a suitable comparison function specified by ORN, is thus assumed. The structure of a table is given by a relation name and a *finite* set of attributes: its *sort*. The relation name, together with its sort, is called the *relation schema*. A *database schema* is a non-empty finite set of relation schemas. We choose to model database schemas with a function basesort which associates to each relname its sort. We adopted this representation because it is the most *abstract* and makes no further choices on any *concrete implementation* (*e.g.*, association lists or finite maps or even functions) of function basesort.

Module DatabaseSchema.
Record Rcd attribute (A : Fset.Rcd attribute) : Type :=
mk_R { (** names for relations *) relname : Type; ORN : Oset.Rcd relname; basesort : relname → set A}.
End DatabaseSchema.

More precisely, the basesort function will be used to relate the support of tuples (in the instance they belong to) and the structure of the corresponding relation name.

Definition well_sorted_instance (I : relname → setT) :=
    ∀ (r : relname) (t : tuple), t ∈ (I r) → support t $\overset{set}{=}$ basesort r.

It is important to mention that, in all our further development, the notion of well-sorted instance resulted *central to the correctness* of many theorems.

3   Queries

Queries allow the extraction of information from tables. The result of a query is also a table or a collection of tables. Information extraction is usually performed by a query language, the standard being SQL or QBE. All these languages rely on a more formal basis: *relational algebra* or *first-order logic*. Both formalisms are based on the notion of tuples. Thus, we assume the existence of a record T of type Tuple.Rcd, for representing tuples, as well as of a record DBS of type DatabaseSchema.Rcd, for representing base relations. Moreover, we assume that T and DBS use the same representation, A, for finite sets of attributes. This is achieved by parameterizing DBS by (A T). For the sake of readability, we shall omit all extra (implicit) record arguments and denote by setA and setT finite sets of attributes and tuples respectively.

3.1   Relational Algebra

Relational algebra consists of a set of (algebraic) operators with relations as operands. The algebra we shall consider in this article is the *SPJRU(ID)*, where S stands for selection, P for projection, J for natural join, R for renaming and last U for union. Though intersection (I) and difference (D) are not part of the SPJRU minimal algebra, we decided to include them at this point, as they are usually part of commercial query languages. In the context of the named version, the natural way to combine relations is the natural join, whereas in the unnamed one it is the Cartesian product. The complete definition of queries is given in Figure 1. In our development, we chose, as far as possible, *not to embed proofs* in types. Hence, types are much more concise and readable.

```
Inductive query : Type :=
  | Query_ Basename : relname → query
  | Query_ Sigma : formula → query → query
  | Query_ Pi : setA → query → query
  | Query_ NaturalJoin : query → query → query
  | Query_ Rename : renaming → query → query
  | Query_ Union : query → query → query
  | Query_ Inter : query → query → query
  | Query_ Diff : query → query → query
with variable : Type :=
  | Var : query → varname → variable
with term : Type :=
  | Term_ Constant : value → term
```

```
  | Term_ Dot : variable → attribute → term
with atom : Type :=
  | Atom_ Eq : term → term → atom
  | Atom_ Le : term → term → atom
with formula : Type :=
  | Formula_ Atom : atom → formula
  | Formula_ And : formula → formula → formula
  | Formula_ Or : formula → formula → formula
  | Formula_ Not : formula → formula
  | Formula_ Forall : variable → formula → formula
  | Formula_ Exists : variable → formula → formula.
```

Fig. 1. Queries

Syntax. Base relations are queries. Concerning the selection operator, in textbooks, it has the form $\sigma_{A=a}$ or $\sigma_{A=B}$, where $A, B \in attribute$ and $a \in value$. The notation $A = a$ ($A = B$ resp.,) is improper and corresponds to $x.A = a$ ($x.A = x.B$ resp.,) where x is a free variable. Given a set of tuples $\mathcal{I}$, with the same support S, we shall call S the *sort* of $\mathcal{I}$. The selection applies to any set of tuples $\mathcal{I}$ of sort S, (with $A, B \in S$) and yields an output of sort S. The semantics of the operator is $\sigma_f(\mathcal{I}) = \{t \mid t \in \mathcal{I} \wedge f\{x \to t\}\}$ where $f\{x \to t\}$ stands for "t satisfies formula f", x being the only free variable of f. Formula satisfaction is based on the standard underlying interpretation. Since, in another context (database program verification) we use general first-order formulas, we chose to model selection's (filtering) conditions with them, rather than restricting ourselves to the simpler case found in textbooks. We first introduce names for variables:

Inductive varname : Set := VarN : N → varname.

Then formulas are built in the standard way from equality and inequality atoms which compare either constants or tuples' field extractions. However, one should notice that variables are used to denote tuples in the output of specific queries, therefore containing information about the query itself. For example variable x below is intended to represent any tuple in the Movies relation while formula f corresponds to x ∈ Movies ⇒ x.Director = "Fellini".

Notation x := (Var (Query_Basename Movies) (VarN 0)).
Definition f := (* x ∈ Movies ⇒ x.Director = "Fellini" *)
    (Formula_Atom (Atom_Eq (Term_Dot x Director) (Term_Constant (Coq_string "Fellini")))).

The projection operator has the form $\pi_{\{A1,...,An\}}$, $n \geq 0$ and operates on all inputs, $\mathcal{I}$, whose sort contains the subset of attributes $W = \{A_1, \ldots, A_n\}$ and produces an output of sort W. The semantics of projection is $\pi_W(\mathcal{I}) = \{t|_W \mid t \in \mathcal{I}\}$ where the notation $t|_W$ represents the tuple obtained from t by keeping only the attributes in W. Remember that setA denotes finite sets of attributes and embeds as an implicit argument (A T), the record representing all types and operations on finite sets. Depending on the actual implementation of sets, this definition may contain some proofs in the setA data type. For instance the proof that a set is an AVL tree may be part of the type. The natural join operator, denoted ⋈, takes arbitrary inputs $\mathcal{I}_1$ and $\mathcal{I}_2$ having sorts V and W, respectively, and produces an output with sort equal to $V \cup W$. The semantics is, $\mathcal{I}_1 \bowtie \mathcal{I}_2 = \{t \mid \exists v \in \mathcal{I}_1, \exists w \in \mathcal{I}_2, t|_V = v \land t|_W = w\}$. When $sort(\mathcal{I}_1) = sort(\mathcal{I}_2)$, then $\mathcal{I}_1 \bowtie \mathcal{I}_2 = \mathcal{I}_1 \cap \mathcal{I}_2$, and when $sort(\mathcal{I}_1) \cap sort(\mathcal{I}_2) = \emptyset$, then $\mathcal{I}_1 \bowtie \mathcal{I}_2$ is the cross-product of $\mathcal{I}_1$ and $\mathcal{I}_2$. The join operator is associative and commutative. An attribute renaming for a finite set V of attributes is a one-one mapping from V to *attribute*. In textbooks, an attribute renaming g for V is specified by the set of pairs $(a, g(a))$, where $g(a) \neq a$; this is usually written as $a_1 a_2 \ldots a_n \to b_1 b_2 \ldots b_n$ to indicate that $g(a_i) = b_i$ for each $i \in [1, n], n \geq 0$. A renaming operator for inputs over V is an expression ρ_g, where g is an attribute renaming for V; this maps to outputs over $g[V]$. Precisely, for $\mathcal{I}$ over V, $\rho_g(\mathcal{I}) = \{v \mid \exists u \in \mathcal{I}, \forall a \in V, v(g(a)) = u(a)\}$. We made a different more abstract choice to model this operator. To avoid proofs in types, we made no assumptions on the "renaming" function except for its type attribute → attribute in the inductive definition. However, the one-to-one assumption will explicitly appear as an hypothesis for some theorems. Set operators can be applied over sets of tuples, $\mathcal{I}_1, \mathcal{I}_2$, with the same sort. As standard in mathematics, $\mathcal{I}_1 \cup \mathcal{I}_2$ (resp. $\mathcal{I}_1 \cap \mathcal{I}_2, \mathcal{I}_1 \setminus \mathcal{I}_2$) is the set having this same sort and containing the union (resp., intersection, difference) of the two sets of tuples. Sort compatibility constraints are absent in our modeling so as to avoid proofs and will be enforced in the semantics part.

Semantics. We present our Coq modeling of query evaluation. We, hence, have to explicitly describe constraints about sorts, which were, deliberately, left out of the query syntax. For base queries, the sort corresponds to the basesort of the relation name, for selections, the sort is left unchanged and for joins, the sort is as expected the union of sorts. The cases which are of interest are projections, renaming and set theoretic operators. For projections, rather than imposing that the set W of attributes on which we project, be a subset of the sort of q1, we chose to define the sort of Query_Pi W q1 as their intersection (W ∩ sort q1). For renaming, we check that the corresponding function rho behaves as expected, *i.e.*, that it is a one-to-one mapping over attributes in q1; otherwise the sort of the query is empty. Last, for set theoretic operators, if the input's sorts are not compatible, the sort of the query is empty. This is formally defined by:

```
Fixpoint sort (q : query) : setA := match q with          else ∅
  | Query_Basename r ⇒ basesort r                         | Query_Union q1 q2 | Query_Inter q1 q2
  | Query_Sigma _q1 ⇒ sort q1                             | Query_Diff q1 q2 ⇒
  | Query_Pi W q1 ⇒ W ∩ sort q1                              let sort_q1 := sort q1 in
  | Query_Join q1 q2 ⇒ sort q1 ∪ sort q2                       if sort_q1 =ˢᵉᵗ_? sort q2
  | Query_Rename rho q1 ⇒                                        then sort_q1
     let sort_q1 := sort q1 in                                  else ∅
     if one_to_one_renaming_bool sort_q1 rho             end.
     then fset_map A A rho sort_q1
```

At this point we are ready to interpret queries. We first assume an interpretation for base relations. When we shall prove the usual structural equivalence theorems (Section 4) for query optimization, we shall impose that queries' results are *well-sorted*. This means that all tuples in an instance or query evaluation must have the *same* support which is the sort of the query. This property is inherited from base instances as stated below:

```
Lemma well_sorted_query : ∀ (I : relname → setT), well_sorted_instance I →
     ∀ (q : query) (t : tuple), t ∈ (eval_query I q) → support t =ˢᵉᵗ sort q.
```

Query evaluation is inductively defined from a given interpretation I for base relations. We sketch its structure (the complete definition of eval_query is given in [2]) in order to emphasize the fact that the same tests as for sorts, are performed. For example, for renaming, if the corresponding function is not suitable, the query evaluates to the empty set of tuples.

```
Fixpoint eval_query I (q : query) : setT := match q with     | Query_Union q1 q2 ⇒
  | Query_Basename r ⇒ I r                                       if sort q1 =ˢᵉᵗ_? sort q2
  | Query_Sigma f q1 ⇒ ...                                       then (eval_query I q1) ∪ (eval_query I q2)
  | Query_Pi W q1 ⇒ ...                                          else ∅
  | Query_Join q1 q2 ⇒ ...                                    | Query_Inter q1 q2 ⇒ if sort q1 =ˢᵉᵗ_? sort q2 ...
  | Query_Rename rho q1 ⇒                                     | Query_Diff q1 q2 ⇒ if sort q1 =ˢᵉᵗ_? sort q2 ...
     let sort_q1 := sort q1 in                              end.
     if one_to_one_renaming_bool sort_q1 rho
     then ...
     else ∅
```

Our definition enjoys the standard properties stated in all database textbooks which are expressed in our framework by the following lemmas. We only present some of them ; the full list, as well as the complete code, is given in [2]. In particular, the way terms, atoms and formulas are interpreted is detailed. For the sake of readability we used some syntactic sugar, such as $\overset{I}{=}$, $\in_I$, as well as f {x → t}, for the interpretation of formula f under assignment x → t.

Notation query_eq q1 q2 := (eval_query I q1 $\overset{set}{=}$ eval_query I q2).

Infix " $\overset{I}{=}$ " := query_eq.

Notation "t '$\in_I$' q" := t $\in$ (eval_query I q).

Lemma mem_Basename : $\forall$ I r t, t $\in_I$ (Query_Basename r) $\longleftrightarrow$ t $\in$ (I r).

Lemma mem_Inter : $\forall$ I q1 q2, sort q1 $\overset{set}{=}$ sort q2 $\rightarrow$ $\forall$ t, t $\in_I$ (Query_Inter q1 q2) $\longleftrightarrow$ (t $\in_I$ q1 $\bigwedge$ t $\in_I$ q2).

Lemma mem_Sigma : $\forall$ I, well_sorted_instance I $\rightarrow$ $\forall$ f x q t, set_of_attributes_f f $\subseteq$ sort q $\rightarrow$

   Fset.elements FV (free_variables_f f) = x :: nil $\rightarrow$

   (t $\in_I$ (Query_Sigma f q) $\longleftrightarrow$ (t $\in_I$ q $\bigwedge$ f {x $\rightarrow$ t} = true)).

Lemma mem_Pi : $\forall$ I, well_sorted_instance I $\rightarrow$

   $\forall$ W q t, t $\in_I$ Query_Pi W q $\longleftrightarrow$ $\exists$t', (t' $\in_I$ q $\bigwedge$ t $\overset{t}{=}$ mk_tuple (W $\cap$ sort q) (dot t')).

Lemma mem_Join : $\forall$ I, well_sorted_instance I $\rightarrow$ $\forall$ q1 q2 t,

   t $\in_I$ Query_Join q1 q2 $\longleftrightarrow$

     $\exists$t1, $\exists$t2, (t1 $\in_I$ q1 $\bigwedge$ t2 $\in_I$ q2 $\bigwedge$ ($\forall$ a, a $\in$ sort q1 $\cap$ sort q2 $\rightarrow$ dot t1 a = dot t2 a) $\bigwedge$

     t $\overset{t}{=}$ mk_tuple (sort q1 $\cup$ sort q2) (fun a $\Rightarrow$ if a $\in_?$ (sort q1) then dot t1 a else dot t2 a)).

Lemma mem_Rename : $\forall$ I, well_sorted_instance I $\rightarrow$ $\forall$ rho q, one_to_one_renaming (sort q) rho $\rightarrow$

   $\forall$ t, t $\in_I$ (Query_Rename rho q) $\longleftrightarrow$ ($\exists$ t', t' $\in_I$ q $\bigwedge$ t $\overset{t}{=}$ rename_tuple rho t').

Lemma NaturalJoin_Inter : $\forall$ I, well_sorted_instance I $\rightarrow$ $\forall$ q1 q2, sort q1 $\overset{set}{=}$ sort q2 $\rightarrow$

   Query_NaturalJoin q1 q2 $\overset{I}{=}$ Query_Inter q1 q2.

Those lemmas highlight the heterogeneous nature of relational operators. In order to prove that they enjoy their usual semantics, on the one hand, the purely set theoretic ones, only need sort compatibility conditions, on the other hand, the database ones need well-sortedness. Interestingly, the lemma, NaturalJoin_Inter, bridging both worlds, needs both.

3.2 Conjunctive Queries

In this context, the query language is slightly different. Rather than relying on algebraic operators, queries are expressed by logical formulas of the form $\{(a_1, \ldots, a_n) \mid \exists b_1, \ldots \exists b_m, P_1 \wedge \ldots \wedge P_k\}$, where the a_i, b_i denote variables which will be interpreted by values and where P_i's denote either equalities or membership to a base relation. For example the query: "Which of "Fellini" 's movies are played at the cinema "Action Christine" ?" expressed by the following relational algebra expression:

$$\pi_{\{\text{Title, Director, Actor}\}}(\sigma_{\substack{x.\text{Director}=\text{"Fellini"} \wedge \\ x.\text{Theater} = \text{"Action Christine"}}} (\text{Movies} \bowtie \text{Pariscope}))$$

will be:

$$\left\{ (t, d, a) \mid \begin{array}{l} \exists th, \exists t', \exists s, \text{Movies}(t, d, a) \wedge \text{Pariscope}(th, t', s) \\ \wedge t = t' \wedge d = \text{"Fellini"} \wedge th = \text{"Action Christine"} \end{array} \right\}$$

Quoting [1], "if we blur the difference between a variable and a constant, the body of a conjunctive query can be seen as an instance with additional constraints". This leads to the notion of extended tuples mapping attributes to either *constants* or *variables*. Hence, a *tableau* over a schema is defined exactly as was the notion of an instance over this schema, except that it contains extended tuples. A *conjunctive query* is simply a pair *(T, s)* where T is a tableau and s, an extended tuple called the *summary* of the query. Variables occurring in s are called *distinguished variables* or *distinguished symbols* in textbooks.

The summary s in query *(T, s)* represents the answer to the query which consists of all tuples for which the pattern described by T is found in the database. This formulation of queries is closest to the QBE visual form. Equality conditions are embedded in the tableau itself as shown by the following example:

Title	Director	Actor	Theater	Schedule	
t	''Fellini''	a			Movies
t			''Action Christine''	s	Pariscope
t	d	a			summary

Syntax. The formal way to "blur" the differences between variables and constants (value's in our modeling) is achieved by embedding them in a single Coq type tvar.

Inductive tvar : Type := Tvar : nat → tvar | Tval : value → tvar.
Inductive trow : Type := Trow : relname → (attribute → tvar) → trow.

Notice that a row, modeled by type trow, is tagged by a relation name (its first argument) and gathers variables and constants thanks to its second argument. For instance the first row of the above query is:

Trow Movies (fun a : attribute ⇒ match a with | Title ⇒ Tvar 0 | Director ⇒ Tval "Fellini" | ... end)

A tableau is a set of trow's. This set is built using a comparison function similar to the one for tuples. Next a summary is tagged by a set of relevant attributes and maps attribute's to tvar's. Last a conjunctive query consists of a tableau and a summary.

Notation setR := (Fset.set (Ftrow T DBS)).
Definition tableau := SetR.
Inductive summary : Type := Summary : setA → (attribute → tvar) → summary.
Definition tableau_query := (tableau * summary)

Semantics. Let us grasp, through our former example, the semantics of such queries. This query is expressed by the summary

Summary (mk_set A (Title :: Director :: Actor :: nil))
  (fun a : attribute ⇒ match a with | Title ⇒ Tvar 0 | Director ⇒ Tvar 1 | ... end)

and its result consists in the set of movies

mk_set A ((mk_movie "Casanova" "Fellini" "Donald Sutherland") ::
          (mk_movie "La strada" "Fellini" "Giulietta Masini") :: nil)

This set is computed by composing the summary function with some mappings from variables in the tableau rows to values, hence mapping summaries to tuples. Thus, we first need to define the notion of valuation which, as usual, maps variables to values. More precisely, in our case, as we embedded variables and constants in a single abstract type tvar, and because variables are characterized by their nat identifier, the type of valuation is nat→ value. Hence applying a valuation (thanks to apply_valuation) on constants consists in applying the identity function.

Definition valuation := nat → value.
Definition apply_valuation (ν : valuation) (x : tvar) : value := match x with | Tvar n ⇒ ν n | Tval c ⇒ c end.
Notation "ν '⟦' x '⟧'" := (apply_valuation ν x).

Valuations naturally extend to trow's and summary's, yielding tuples, and to tableaux, yielding sets of tuples.

Definition apply_valuation_t (ν : valuation) (x : trow) : tuple :=
  match x with Trow r f ⇒ mk_tuple (basesort r) (fun a ⇒ ν ⟦f a⟧) end.
Notation " ν '⟦' x '⟧$_t$'" := (apply_valuation_t ν x).
Definition apply_valuation_s (ν : valuation) (x : summary) : tuple :=
  match x with Summary V f ⇒ mk_tuple V (fun a ⇒ ν ⟦f a⟧) end.
Notation " ν '⟦' x '⟧$_s$'" := (apply_valuation_s ν x).

Given a query (T, s), its result on instance $\mathcal{I}$ is given by $\{t \mid \exists \nu, \nu(T) \subseteq \mathcal{I} \wedge t = \nu(s)\}$ where ν is a valuation. In our development, we characterize this set by the predicate is_a_solution I (T, s), where $\overset{t}{=}$ denotes the equivalence of tuples.

Inductive is_a_solution (I : relname → setT) : tableau_query → tuple → Prop :=
  | Extract : ∀ (ST : tableau) (s : summary) (ν : valuation),
      (∀ (r : relname) (f : attribute → tvar), (Trow r f) ∈ ST → ν ⟦Trow r f⟧$_t$ ∈$_I$ (Query_Basename r)) →
      ∀ (t : tuple), t $\overset{t}{=}$ ν ⟦s⟧$_s$ → is_a_solution I (ST, s) t.

3.3   From Algebra Queries to Conjunctive Queries

The two formalisms presented are not exactly equivalent except in the case where relational queries are only built with selections, projections and joins. In this case there is an *apparently straightforward* way to construct the corresponding conjunctive query. We give hereafter the algorithm found in [11] as it is presented. If we try to apply this algorithm on the following relational expression $\sigma_{A=B}(r) \bowtie \sigma_{B=C}(r)$, we obtain for E_1 and E_2 the following tableaux:
$\dfrac{x_1 \; x_1 \; x_2 \; \text{r}}{x_1 \; x_1 \; x_2}$ and $\dfrac{y_1 \; y_2 \; y_2 \; \text{r}}{y_1 \; y_2 \; y_2}$. Given those two tableaux whatever renaming we choose to apply to the second one as stated in [11] there is no way to be in the situation described by the algorithm, *i.e.*, *if both (T_1, s_1) and (T_2, s_2) have distinguished symbols in the summary column for attribute A then those symbols are the same.* We fixed this source of incompleteness by using *unification*

Given an SPJ algebraic expression, a conjunctive query equivalent to this expression is inductively constructed using the following rules. The base case consists in a relation $r(A_1, \ldots, A_n)$ the corresponding tableau consists in a single row and summary which are exactly the same with one variable for each A_i. Assume that we have an expression of the form $\pi_W(E)$ and that we have constructed (T, s) for E, then to reflect the projection, all the distinguished variables that are not in W are deleted from s. For selections $\sigma_f(E)$ where f is either of the form $A = B$ or $A = c$, in the former case, the distinguished symbols for columns A and B in the summary and the tableau are identified, in the latter, the distinguished variable for A is replaced by c. For joins $E_1 \bowtie E_2$, it is assumed without loss of generality that if both (T_1, s_1) and (T_2, s_2) have distinguished symbols in the summary column for attribute A then those symbols are the same, but that otherwise (T_1, s_1) and (T_2, s_2) have no symbols in common. Then the tableau for $E_1 \bowtie E_2$ has a summary in which a column has a distinguished symbol a if a appears as a distinguished symbol in that column of s_1 or s_2 or both. The new tableau has as rows all the rows of T_1 and T_2.

Fig. 2. Ullman's book algorithm presentation

instead of renaming. If we unify the two summaries of our example, we obtain
$x_2 \mapsto x_1; y_1 \mapsto x_1; y_2 \mapsto x_1$ yielding the tableau $\dfrac{x_1 \; x_1 \; x_1 \; r}{x_1 \; x_1 \; x_1}$ which indeed
corresponds to what is expected in terms of semantics. The unify function, given
in [2], is readable but the proofs of its soundness (the result of unify is a unifier) and completeness (whenever there is a unifier, unify finds it) took more
than 4000 lines of code. Thanks to it we are able to express the translation
algorithm, also given in [2], which is sound and complete and handles all SPJ
queries. If the selection condition is a conjunction of equalities, a preprocess-
ing step, expand_query, transforms it into a sequence of selections whose conditions are equalities. The translation yields either an equivalent query, EmptyRel
when the original query has no solution or NoTranslation when the input query
is not SPJ. The translation algorithm relies on several auxiliary functions. The
first one, fresh_row n r, is used for the base case and generates a row, Trow r fr,
tagged by relation name r. Function fr maps attributes to fresh variables starting
from index n. The second one rename t1 t2 is used for selections with condition
t1 = t2 and returns either None if t1 and t2 are distinct constants or Some rho
where rho is a substitution which replaces one of the t1 and t2 by the other
one, avoiding to replace a constant by a variable. In that case rho is applied
to the whole tableau. The only case where unify is needed is for joins. In this
case the translation is applied to both operands and then compatibility on common attributes is ensured by applying the resulting substitution to the whole
query. The following lemma states that the algorithm behaves as expected.

Our formalization helped us in
making precise the exact behavior
of the translation algorithm. In the
informal presentation taken from
textbooks, an *underlying assumption* is made about *freshness of*

```
Lemma algebra_to_tableau_expand_is_complete :
  ∀ (q : query) (n : nat) (I : relname → setT),
    well_sorted_instance I →
    match algebra_to_tableau (S n) (expand_query q) with
    | TQ _ Ts ⇒
        ∀ t, is_a_solution I Ts t ⟷ t ∈ (eval_query I q)
    | EmptyRel ⇒ ∀ t, t ∈ (eval_query I q) → False
    | NoTranslation ⇒ translatable_q q = false
  end.
```

variables for the base case, which is quite tedious to handle at the formal level.
To our knowledge our algorithm is the *first one* for such a translation which is
formally specified and fully proved.

4   Logical Optimization

4.1   Optimizing Relational Algebra Queries

Query optimization exploits algebraic equivalences. Such equivalences are found
in all textbooks and in particular in [9]. We list the most classical ones hereafter.

$$\sigma_{f_1 \wedge f_2}(q) \equiv \sigma_{f_1}(\sigma_{f_2}(q)) \quad (1) \qquad \pi_{W_1}(\pi_{W_2}(q)) \equiv \pi_{W_1}(q) \qquad \text{if } W_1 \subseteq W_2 \;(5)$$

$$\sigma_{f_1}(\sigma_{f_2}(q)) \equiv \sigma_{f_2}(\sigma_{f_1}(q)) \quad (2) \qquad \pi_W(\sigma_f(q)) \equiv \sigma_f(\pi_W(q)) \qquad \text{if } Att(f) \subseteq W \;(6)$$

$$(q_1 \bowtie q_2) \bowtie q_3 \equiv q_1 \bowtie (q_2 \bowtie q_3) \,(3) \qquad \sigma_f(q_1 \bowtie q_2) \equiv \sigma_f(q_1) \bowtie q_2 \quad \text{if } Att(f) \subseteq sort(q_1) \,(7)$$

$$q_1 \bowtie q_2 \equiv q_2 \bowtie q_1 \qquad (4) \qquad \sigma_f(q_1 \nabla q_2) \equiv \sigma_f(q_1) \nabla \sigma_f(q_2) \,_{\text{where } \nabla \text{ is } \cup, \cap \text{ or } \setminus}(8)$$

All these have been formally proved and their formal statements are given in [2]. Although not technically involved, all the proofs relied on the assumption that instances are *well sorted*. To illustrate this, we give the formal statement of (7).

Lemma Sigma_NaturalJoin_comm : ∀ I, well_sorted_instance I → ∀ f q1 q2, set_of_attributes_f f ⊆ sort q1 →

  Query_Sigma f (Query_NaturalJoin q1 q2) $\overset{I}{=}$ Query_NaturalJoin (Query_Sigma f q1) q2.

4.2 Optimizing Conjunctive Queries

For the algebraic queries that are expressible by a conjunctive query, there exists an exact optimization technique. In this case, query optimization is based on the following consideration: the number of lines in the tableau corresponds to the number of joins (plus one) in the relational expression. Therefore, the optimization consists in reducing this number of lines. This is achieved through the notions of tableaux containment and equivalence and finally through a minimality condition. More precisely, let (T_1, s_1) and (T_2, s_2) be two conjunctive queries, (T_1, s_1) is contained in (T_2, s_2) written $(T_1, s_1) \subseteq (T_2, s_2)$ iff (T_1, s_1) and (T_2, s_2) have the same set of attributes, and, for all relations' instances, solutions of (T_1, s_1) are included in the set of solutions of (T_2, s_2). This inclusion relation naturally induces an equivalence. $(T_1, s_1) \equiv (T_2, s_2)$ iff $(T_1, s_1) \subseteq (T_2, s_2)$ and $(T_2, s_2) \subseteq (T_1, s_1)$. This is formalized in Coq by:

Definition is_contained_instance I Ts1 Ts2 := ∀ (t : tuple), is_a_solution I Ts1 t → is_a_solution I Ts2 t.
Definition is_contained Ts1 Ts2 := ∀ I, is_contained_instance I Ts1 Ts2.
Definition are_equivalent Ts1 Ts2 := is_contained Ts1 Ts2 ∧ is_contained Ts2 Ts1.

These semantic notions can be checked syntactically relying on tableaux's substitutions. A (tableau) substitution θ is a mapping from variables to variables or constants. The following database theorem expresses this syntactical characterization of containment.

Theorem 1 (Tableaux Homomorphism). *If (T_1, s_1) and (T_2, s_2) are conjunctive queries, $(T_1, s_1) \subseteq (T_2, s_2)$ iff there exists a substitution tableau θ such that for all line t tagged by relation name r in T_2, $\theta(t)$ occurs tagged by r in T_1, and $\theta(s_2) = s_1$. θ is called a tableau homomorphism from (T_2, s_2) to (T_1, s_1).*

We first give the definition of substitution in our setting and then formally define the application of a substitution to a variable. This notion extends to trow's and summary's. Then we provide the formal definition of tableau homomorphism and state the homomorphism theorem.

Definition substitution := nat → tvar.
Definition apply_subst_tvar (θ : substitution) (x : tvar) := match x with Tvar n ⇒ θ n | Tval _ ⇒ x end.
Notation "θ '[' x ']_v'" := (apply_subst_tvar θ x).
Definition tableau_homomorphism (θ : substitution) Ts2 Ts1 :=
match Ts1, Ts2 with (T1, s1), (T2, s2) ⇒ (fset_map Ftrow Ftrow (fun t ⇒ θ [t]_t) T2) ⊆ T1 ∧ θ [s2]_s $\overset{s}{=}$ s1
end.
Theorem Homomorphism_theorem :
  ∀ Ts1 Ts2, (∃ θ , tableau_homomorphism θ Ts2 Ts1) ⟷ is_contained Ts1 Ts2.

We briefly sketch the proof of the homomorphism theorem. Interestingly in textbooks a lot of material is hidden. Namely, the notion of *fresh constants* is central to the proof in order to be able to define a list of such *distinct* fresh constants for each variable present in the query. We assume therefore

Hypothesis fresh : (Fset.set Ftvar) → value.
Hypothesis fresh_is_fresh : ∀ lval, (Tval (fresh lval)) ∈ lval → False.

This implies that domains are *infinite*. Based on fresh constants we define a variable assignment μ from variables to new fresh abstract constants on (T_1, s_1). We then show that μ is a solution of (T_1, s_1) w.r.t. the interpretation I which contains exactly $\mu(T_1)$. Thanks to the definition of tableaux containment, μ is a solution of (T_2, s_2) w.r.t. I. Hence there is an assignment ν which corresponds to a solution of (T_2, s_2), $\nu(s_2) = \mu(s_1) \wedge (\forall t_2\, r, t_2 : r \in T_2 \Rightarrow \nu(t_2) \in I(r))$, that is $\nu(s_2) = \mu(s_1) \wedge (\forall t_2\, r,\ t_2 : r \in T_2 \Rightarrow \exists t_1,\ t_1 : r \in T_1 \wedge \nu(t_2) = \mu(t_1))$. By construction μ admits an inverse function defined over the variables of (T_1, s_1). What remains to show is that $x \mapsto \mu^{-1}(\nu(x))$ is an homomorphism from (T_2, s_2) to (T_1, s_1). The main difficulties encountered in Coq were to properly define the notion of query solution, to build the variable assignment μ as a function from the fresh function and to prove that μ is injective.

At this point, based on the homomorphism theorem, given a conjunctive query, we shall explicitly construct an equivalent minimal one. Indeed another, well known, database theorem states that for each conjunctive query there exists a minimal equivalent query among its sub-queries. A sub-query of (T, s) is simply (T', s) such that $T' \subseteq T$. Hence, the optimization process consists in inspecting all equivalent sub-tableaux and among those keeping a minimal one.

Definition min_tableau Ts Ms :=
    are_equivalent Ts Ms ⋀ (∀ Ts', are_equivalent Ts Ts' → cardinal (fst Ms) ≤ cardinal (fst Ts')).
Lemma tableaux_optimisation : ∀ T s, {T' | min_tableau (T, s) (T', s)}.

More precisely, the corner stone of the algorithm is to find an homomorphism from the initial tableau to a given sub-tableau. To do so we used a function abstract_matching. All further details are given in [2]. Not only do we *prove* this result but we also provide a *certified algorithm* to build this minimal tableau both in Coq and by *extraction* from tableaux_optimization in OCaml.

5   Integrity Constraints

Constraints are captured by the theory of dependencies which deal with the semantics of data. For example, returning to our running example, we may know that there is only one director associated with each movie title. Such properties are called *functional dependencies* because the values of some attributes of a tuple uniquely determine the values of other attributes of that tuple. Let us further assume that we have another relation: *Showings(Theater, Screen, Title, Snack)* which contains tuples *(th, sc, ti, sn)* if the theater *th* is showing the movie *ti* on the screen *sc* and if the theater *th* offers snack *sn*. Intuitively, one would expect a certain independence between the *Screen-Title* attributes, on the one hand, and the *Snack* attribute, on the other, for a given value of *Theater*. For example, if *(Action Christine, 1, Casanova, Coffee)* and *(Action Christine, 2, M, Tea)* are in *Showings*, we also expect *(Action Christine, 1, Casanova, Tea)* and *(Action Christine, 2, M, Coffee)* to be present. Such dependencies are called tuple generating dependencies. Functional and tuple generating dependencies fall under the wider class of *general dependencies* which we model and that also capture inclusion dependencies which correspond to foreign key constraints in real systems. First we introduce functional dependencies, then we present the class of general dependencies. An important problem concerning dependencies is that of the so called *logical implication*: given a set of constraints, what other constraints could be inferred ? Armstrong's system that allows to deduce, in the functional case, all dependencies implied by a given set, is sound, complete and terminating. We then detail the chase, a procedure that allows to infer general dependencies, and prove its soundness.

5.1   Functional Dependencies

A *functional dependency (fd)* expresses a constraint between schema attribute sets. Specifically, given a database schema R, an instance r of R and attribute sets V and W (in the sort of R), a functional dependency $V \hookrightarrow W$ over r, denoted $r \models V \hookrightarrow W$, *holds* if $\forall t_1\ t_2, t_1 \in r \Rightarrow t_2 \in r \Rightarrow t_1|_V = t_2|_V \Rightarrow t_1|_W = t_2|_W$.

Let F be a set of functional dependencies over a given schema R. A functional dependency $d = X \hookrightarrow Y$ is *semantically implied* by F, denoted $F \models d$, if $\forall r : R, (r \models F \Rightarrow r \models d)$. This is formally defined in Coq by:

```
Inductive fd : Type := FD : setA → setA → fd.
Notation "V '↪' W" := (FD V W).
Definition fd_sem (ST : setT) (d : fd) := match d with | V ↪W ⇒
∀ t1 t2, t1 ∈ ST → t2 ∈ ST → (∀ x, x ∈ V → dot T t1 x = dot T t2 x)
                → ∀ y, y ∈ W → dot T t1 y = dot T t2 y
end.
```

Armstrong's inference system $\mathcal{A}$ is modeled via the dtree inductive definition, representing a derivation tree, whose branches are the axioms above and the D_ax rule, for deriving dependencies already in the context and where setF denotes the type of sets of dependencies.

```
Inductive dtree (F : setF) : fd → Type :=
 | D_Ax : ∀X Y, (X ↪Y) ∈ F → dtree F (X ↪Y)
 | D_Refl : ∀X Y, Y ⊆ X → dtree F (X ↪Y)
 | D_Aug : ∀X Y Z XZ YZ, XZ ≝(X ∪ Z) → YZ ≝(Y ∪ Z) → dtree F (X ↪Y) → dtree F (XZ ↪YZ)
 | D_Trans : ∀X Y Y' Z, Y ≝Y' → dtree F (X ↪Y) → dtree F (Y' ↪Z) → dtree F (X ↪Z).
Theorem Armstrong_soundness : ∀F d (t : dtree F d) ST, (∀ f, f ∈ F → fd_sem ST f) → fd_sem ST d.
```

This theorem is formally proven by an easy induction on the derivation tree. The completeness proof borrows from [11] the central idea of building a *model* M. Given a set of dependencies F and a set of attributes X, M consists of two tuples t0 and t1, which only agree on the closure attribute set $[X]_F^+$. The constructive proof of completeness is simply based on the fact that if $F \models X \hookrightarrow Y$, since M is a model of F, then M is a model of $X \hookrightarrow Y$.

```
Lemma Armstrong_completeness : ∀U F X Y, X ⊆U → Y ⊆U → (∀ ST,(∀ t, t ∈ ST → support T t ≝U)
   → (∀ f, f ∈ F → fd_sem ST f) → fd_sem ST (X ↪Y)) → (dtree F (X ↪Y)).
```

Interestingly, while for soundness the hypotheses did not make any assumption on the finiteness of the attribute universe, for the completeness, this assumption was needed. All intermediate lemmas are given in [2] and the main theorem explicitly mentions the fact that all sets of attributes are included in the finite universe U and that the values zero and one are distinct.

5.2 General Dependencies

Constraints described in textbooks (functional, join or inclusion dependencies) are first-order logic sentences of the form

$$\forall x_1 \ldots \forall x_n(\phi(x_1, \ldots, x_n) \Rightarrow \exists z_1 \ldots \exists z_k \psi(x_1, \ldots, x_n, z_1, \ldots, z_k)),$$

where ϕ is a (possibly empty) conjunction of atoms and ψ an atom. In both ϕ and ψ, one finds relation atoms of the form $r(w_1, \ldots, w_l)$ and equality atoms of the form $w = w'$, where each of the $w, w', w_1, \ldots, w_l$ is a variable or a constant. Inclusion dependencies can be expressed by $\forall x_1 \ldots \forall x_n(r_1(x_1, \ldots, x_n) \Rightarrow r_2(x_1, \ldots, x_n))$. According to textbooks, the semantics of such formulas is the natural one. There is a strong relationship between general dependencies and tableaux which provides a convenient notation for expressing and working with dependencies. For example the functional dependency $A \hookrightarrow B$ on relation $r(A, B)$, is represented by the following formula $\forall v, v_1, v_2 \; r(v, v_1) \wedge r(v, v_2) \Rightarrow v_1 = v_2$ and

conjunctive query

$$\begin{array}{ll} A & B \\ v & v_1 \; r \\ v & v_2 \; r \\ \hline v_1 & = v_2 \end{array}$$

. When the right part of the implication is a relation predicate, the last line is a summary and such dependencies are referred as "tuple generating" while the other ones are referred as "equality generating". We model this by the following inductive definition of gd, according to whether ϕ is a relation predicate or an equality, we use two constructors TupleGen or EqGen.

Notation "s1 '$\overset{r}{=}$' s2" := *(** equivalence of rows **)* (Fset.elt_compare Ftrow s1 s2 = Eq).
Inductive gd := TupleGen : setR → trow → gd | EqGen : setR → tvar → tvar → gd.

The natural semantics is provided by:

Inductive gd_sem : gd → setT → Prop :=
| TupleGenSem : ∀ (SR : setR) (s : trow) (ST : setT), (∀ (ν : valuation), (∀ x, x ∈ SR → (ν [[x]]_t) ∈ ST) →
        ∃ν_e , (∀ x, x ∈ variables_tableau SR → ν_e [[x]] = ν [[x]]) ⋀ ν_e [[s]]_t ∈ ST) →
gd_sem (TupleGen SR s) ST
| EqGenSem : ∀ (SR : setR) x1 x2 (ST : setT),
        (∀ (ν : valuation), (∀ x, x ∈ SR → ν [[x]]_t ∈ ST) → ν [[x1]] = ν [[x2]]) → gd_sem (EqGen SR x1 x2) ST.

The only subtle point in this definition is that it is stated for tableaux, but corresponds exactly to the semantics of logical formulas. Due to the particular form of the latter, given a valuation ν assigning values to the x's we extend it by ν_e over the existentially quantified z's.

5.3 The Chase

We present the so-called *chase* a procedure for reasoning about dependencies and used to determine logical implication between sets of dependencies. More precisely, given a set D of dependencies and a dependency d over a given schema, the chase allows to decide whether $D \models d$. The intuition is that the chase starts assuming that the tableau part of d is satisfied and consists in applying all dependencies in D. If the conclusion of d is inferred then we have a proof that

$$
\begin{array}{llll}
A & B & C & D \\
a_1 & b_1 & c_1 & d_1 \\
a_1 & b_2 & c_2 & d_2 \\
\hline
a_1 & b_1 & c_2 & d_3 \\
\end{array}
\qquad
\begin{array}{llll}
A & B & C & D \\
a_2 & b_3 & c_3 & d_4 \\
a_3 & b_3 & c_4 & d_5 \\
\hline
\multicolumn{4}{l}{d_4 = d_5} \\
\end{array}
\qquad
\begin{array}{llll}
A & B & C & D \\
a_4 & b_4 & c_5 & d_6 \\
a_4 & b_5 & c_6 & d_7 \\
\hline
a_4 & b_6 & c_5 & d_7 \\
\end{array}
\qquad
\begin{array}{llll}
A & B & C & D \\
a_4 & b_4 & c_5 & d_6 \\
a_4 & b_5 & c_6 & d_7 \\
\end{array}
\qquad
\begin{array}{llll}
A & B & C & D \\
a_4 & b_4 & c_5 & d_6 \\
a_4 & b_5 & c_6 & d_7 \\
a_4 & b_5 & c_5 & d_8 \\
\end{array}
\qquad
\begin{array}{llll}
A & B & C & D \\
a_4 & b_4 & c_5 & d_6 \\
a_4 & b_5 & c_6 & d_7 \\
a_4 & b_5 & c_5 & d_7 \\
\end{array}
$$

$$
tg_1 \qquad\qquad eg_2 \qquad\qquad tg \qquad\qquad (i) \qquad\qquad (ii) \qquad\qquad (iii)
$$

Fig. 3. Applying Dependencies

$D \models d$. The main result stated in the literature is that, any instance of the schema, satisfying d' and $chase(d, d')$ (the dependency obtained by applying d' to d), also satisfies d. All the magic resides in the definition of "applying a dependency". Assume that we want to prove that dependencies tg_1 and eg_2 in Figure 3 imply dependency tg, where we omit to tag the rows as a single relation name r is assumed. To do so, we apply them to instance (i) (indeed the tableau part of tg). More precisely, applying tg_1 to (i) consists in finding a mapping ν such that $\{\nu(a_1, b_1, c_1, d_1), \nu(a_1, b_2, c_2, d_2)\} \subseteq (i)$. For instance in this case we can choose, among other mappings, $\nu(a_1) = a_4, \nu(b_1) = b_5, \nu(c_1) = c_6, \nu(d_1) = d_7, \nu(b_2) = b_4, \nu(c_2) = c_5, \nu(d_2) = d_6$. Tuple $\nu(a_1, b_1, c_2, d_3)$ is then added to (i) yielding (ii). There is a subtlety: as d_3 appears only in the summary, d_3 is existentially quantified therefore $\nu(d_3)$ is a fresh variable (d_8). Then applying eg_2 to (ii) makes d_7 and d_8 equal in (iii). Again, as b_6 is existentially quantified in tg, it can be instantiated by b_5 and allows to conclude that since the tuple to be generated in tg occurs in (iii), tg is implied.

We *tried to formalize* what is very informally provided by textbooks with the following inference rules. Let d and d' be respectively $\forall \vec{x}, \phi(\vec{x}) \Rightarrow \exists \vec{z}, \psi(\vec{x} \cup \vec{z})$ and $\forall \vec{x'}, \phi'(\vec{x'}) \Rightarrow \exists \vec{z'}, \psi'(\vec{x'} \cup \vec{z'})$. For applying d' to d we first need to find a mapping ν such that $\nu(\phi'(\vec{x'}))$ seen as a set of atoms is a subset of $\phi(\vec{x})$. Depending on the form of ψ', we get

1. if $\psi' \equiv y_1' = y_2'$ then let ρ be the renaming: $\{\nu(y_2') \mapsto \nu(y_1')\}$ and $chase(d, d')$ is $\forall \vec{x}, \rho(\phi(\vec{x}) \Rightarrow \exists \vec{z}, \psi(\vec{x} \cup \vec{z}))$.
2. if $\psi' \equiv r'(\vec{y'})$ then $chase(d, d')$ is $\forall \vec{x}, \phi(\vec{x}) \wedge \nu(r'(\vec{y'})) \Rightarrow \exists \vec{z}, \psi(\vec{x} \cup \vec{z})$.

However the above version is faulty due to variable's capture for $\nu(r'(\vec{y'}))$ by $\forall \vec{x}$ which naturally arose in the second case as shown by the following counter-example. Let d be $\forall y\, z, r(y, y, z) \Rightarrow r(y, y, y)$ and d' be $\forall x\, y, r(x, x, y) \Rightarrow \exists z, r(x, z, x)$. With mapping $\nu = \{x \mapsto y, y \mapsto z\}$, the above definition yields:

$$chase(d, d') \equiv \forall y\, z, r(y, y, z) \wedge r(y, z, y) \Rightarrow r(y, y, y).$$

Consider the instance $\mathcal{I} = \{(a, a, b), (a, c, a)\}$. We have $\mathcal{I} \models d'$, and $\mathcal{I} \models chase(d, d')$ since there is no μ such that $\mu(y, y, z) \in \mathcal{I} \wedge \mu(y, z, y) \in \mathcal{I}$. But $\mathcal{I} \not\models d$ as shown by $\mu_1 = \{y \mapsto a, z \mapsto b\}$ since $\mu_1(y, y, z) = (a, a, b) \in \mathcal{I}$ and $\mu_1(y, y, y) = (a, a, a) \notin \mathcal{I}$. This counter-example does not affect the essence of the theorem but emphasizes the fact that humans naturally perform α-conversion in order to avoid capture; therefore when defining the chase in Coq we had to seriously take this into account.

Since variables (in the gd's) are indexed by integers, in order to avoid captures, we generate fresh variables for renaming, starting from the maximum index of all variables in the constraints which is computed thanks to the function max_var_chase. Then, avoid_capture_trow max_n phi' psi' computes a renaming for the variables which are in psi' and not in phi'. The chase may yield three different results: the first one is when there is at least one ν producing a new constraint, the second captures the fact that no such mappings exist, then the third one corresponds to the fact that the current dependency tries to identify two distinct constants. There is one further subtle point to detail. Given a pair of dependencies, there may exist several mapping ν's, thus, in order to avoid the design of a lazy matching function, we chose to apply them at once. The first case applies an equality generating dependency EqGen SR x1 x2. It consists in iterating the replacement of νx1 by νx2 for all such ν's. The second case applies a tuple generating dependency TupleGen SR s. In that case we simply add all νs to current tableau. The only point is to avoid capture for existential variables and also to avoid interference between the different mappings. This has the unfortunate consequence that the chase step given in [2] as well as soundness proofs are intricate. As the chase terminates only for a specific class of dependencies (the one with no existential quantifiers), we defined a kind of "for loop" in order to iterate the application of a set of dependencies over d a fixed number of times. At this point the algorithm stops with a (potentially) new dependency. If this dependency is trivial (i.e., either of the form $\forall \vec{x}, \phi(\vec{x}) \Rightarrow y = y$ or $\forall \vec{x}, \phi(\vec{x}) \Rightarrow \exists \vec{z}, \psi(\vec{x} \cup \vec{z})$ where there exists a substitution σ for z's such that $\psi(\vec{x} \cup \sigma(\vec{z}))$ is an atom of $\phi(\vec{x})$) then the initial set of dependencies implies d. Last the result that the chase procedure is sound is established by

```
Inductive res : Type := Res : gd → res | NoProgress | Fail.
...
Definition var_in_query x SR := match x with Tvar _ ⇒ x ∈ variables_gd SR | Tval _ ⇒ True end.
Lemma chase_is_sound :
    ∀ST n D d d', chase n d D = Res d' →
        match d with TupleGen __⇒ True | EqGen SR1 x1 x2 ⇒ var_in_query x1 SR1 ⋀ var_in_query x2 SR1 end
        → (∀ gd, List.In gd D → gd_sem gd ST) → gd_sem d' ST → gd_sem d ST.
```

Doing the proof, the main subtle point was to avoid variables' capture through iteration. Again, it was during this proof step that we discovered that the textbooks were imprecise not to say faulty. The needed functions and technical lemmas are given in [2].

6   Conclusion, Lessons and Perspectives

This article provides a specification of the relational model, a first, *unavoidable*, step towards verifying relational database management systems with the Coq proof assistant. Our specification is the first that covers the named version of the relational model, both algebra and conjunctive queries, logical optimization for both languages, and, finally, dependencies (both functional and general). The whole development consists of 21,000 loc. It makes a clear distinction between specification and implementation, achieved thanks to a parametrization of the data definition part of the model – attributes, tuples, relations and constraints – by modules whose interface is independent from the concrete implementation (e.g., Letouzey's finite sets). This allowed us to reach a very modular and reusable library. From the data definition point of view, our modeling is very close to the one found in textbooks as well as in real systems and is expressive and versatile enough to allow us to express the main algorithms and to prove the database theorems. In particular, we gave a completely certified version of the algorithm that translates an SPJ query into a conjunctive one, a proof of the main relational structural equivalences, a proof of the homomorphism theorem and based on this proof a certified version of the tableaux minimization algorithm, its extraction in OCaml and finally we modeled and certified Armstrong's system for functional dependencies and the chase procedure for which we also extracted an OCaml algorithm.

We learned several lessons both from the database and Coq sides. There are two different aspects in our work: one concerns modeling, the second is about proving properties and algorithms' correctness. On the side of proofs, the article does not bring very new insights except expliciting technical points such as freshness, unification in the translation, avoiding variables' capture. This is not new for Coq users or even the functional programming community. However it is worth precising that for the database theoreticians and practitioners as well. Such aspects are never mentioned in text books nor appear explicitly in implementations (usually written in C). The real challenge was to model. Our contribution, unlike, [8,6], is almost complete. We were able to model all these various aspects because our very first choices for attributes, tuples were adequate. Such choices were not trivial nor immediate and neither [8] nor [5] made them hence they never reached the generality we achieved. Obviously once the right choices are done, the whole seems simple.

In a first version of our development, we heavily used dependent types and proofs in types. In particular, they expressed that tuples and queries were well-typed by construction. But, we experienced a lot of problems with type conversion in proofs. In all algorithms given in the article, it is *crucial* to check equality (or congruence). In Coq one can only check equality between two terms which belong to the *same* Type. With dependent types, there are two possibilities: either to use type conversion or John Major equality (fortunately we fall in the decidable case). Both are very cumbersome. Moreover, in order to debug we needed to run the algorithms with well-typed terms (*i.e.*, with hand-written proofs embedded in types). The benefits of our approach are three (i) with it, it is easier and lighter to write algorithms and perform case analysis in proofs (ii) it is closer to main stream programming languages in which real systems are encoded (iii) it precisely allows to locate where well-typedness is needed. Surprisingly, we discovered that types, in the usual sense, were not useful, rather, the notion of *well-sortedness* was indeed crucial. This is an a posteriori justification of the fact that in all theoretical books values range in a unique domain. Specifying the main algorithms and proving the "database theorems" for tableaux and the chase led us to thoroughly make explicit some notions or definitions which were either unclear or at least very sloppy. For example, freshness or variables' capture are almost completely left aside in textbooks. However, such notions are *central to the correctness* of the results, as shown by our counter-example.

The long term goal of our work is to verify data intensive systems with the Coq proof assistant and the Why3 [4] program verification suite. We shall extend our work in several directions. First for the specification part we shall capture other data models such as JSon, XML etc to mechanize the semantics of languages such as JAQL or Pig. Then, we shall model all the relational normalization theory for logical schema design. Based on our library, another line of research will consist in verifying an SQL compiler and optimizer against our specification. SQL compilers not only transform queries into relational algebra (as far as possible) yielding an AST whose nodes are labeled by relational operators and leaves are base relations, but, they also choose the "best" access method to evaluate the query. To do so they rely on the fact that different algorithms for joins or selections do exist (sort-merge joins, hash-based, nested loops) and on different access paths to actual data (for example indexes). They generate so called query evaluation plans and choose, according to a cost model, the most efficient one. We plan to verify those algorithms using our formalization and Why3. We shall also handle transactions and concurrency control, updates and database triggers as well as security and privacy aspects.

Acknowledgements. We are very grateful to Arthur Charguéraud for his helpful comments.

References

1. Abiteboul, S., Hull, R., Vianu, V.: Foundations of Databases. Addison-Wesley (1995)
2. Benzaken, V., Contejean, E., Dumbrava, S.: A Relational Library (2013), http://datacert.lri.fr/esop/html/Datacert.AdditionalMaterial.html
3. Chlipala, A., Malecha, J.G., Morrisett, G., Shinnar, A., Wisnesky, R.: Effective interactive proofs for higher-order imperative programs. In: Hutton, G., Tolmach, A.P. (eds.) ICFP, pp. 79–90. ACM (2009)
4. Filliâtre, J.-C., Paskevich, A.: Why3 - where programs meet provers. In: Felleisen, M., Gardner, P. (eds.) ESOP 2013. LNCS, vol. 7792, pp. 125–128. Springer, Heidelberg (2013)
5. Gonzalia, C.: Relations in Dependent Type Theory. Ph.D. thesis, Chalmers Göteborg University (2006)
6. Gonzalia, C.: Towards a formalisation of relational database theory in constructive type theory. In: Berghammer, R., Möller, B., Struth, G. (eds.) RelMiCS 2003. LNCS, vol. 3051, pp. 137–148. Springer, Heidelberg (2004)
7. Letouzey, P.: A library for finite sets
8. Malecha, G., Morrisett, G., Shinnar, A., Wisnesky, R.: Toward a verified relational database management system. In: ACM Int. Conf. POPL (2010)
9. Ramakrishnan, R., Gehrke, J.: Database management systems, 3rd edn. McGraw-Hill (2003)
10. The Coq Development Team: The Coq Proof Assistant Reference Manual (2010), http://coq.inria.fr, http://coq.inria.fr
11. Ullman, J.D.: Principles of Database Systems, 2nd edn. Computer Science Press (1982)

On Probabilistic Applicative Bisimulation and Call-by-Value λ-Calculi[*]

Raphaëlle Crubillé[1] and Ugo Dal Lago[2]

[1] ENS-Lyon
raphaelle.crubille@ens-lyon.fr
[2] Università di Bologna & INRIA
dallago@cs.unibo.it

Abstract. Probabilistic applicative bisimulation is a recently introduced coinductive methodology for program equivalence in a probabilistic, higher-order, setting. In this paper, the technique is applied to a typed, call-by-value, lambda-calculus. Surprisingly, the obtained relation coincides with context equivalence, contrary to what happens when call-by-name evaluation is considered. Even more surprisingly, full-abstraction only holds in a symmetric setting.

Keywords: lambda calculus, probabilistic computation, bisimulation, coinduction.

1 Introduction

Traditionally, an algorithm is nothing but a finite description of a sequence of deterministic primitive instructions, which solve a computational problem when executed. Along the years, however, this concept has been generalized so as to reflect a broader class of effective procedures and machines. One of the many ways this has been done consists in allowing probabilistic choice as a primitive instruction in algorithms, this way shifting from usual, deterministic computation to a new paradigm, called probabilistic computation. Examples of application areas in which probabilistic computation has proved to be useful include natural language processing [19], robotics [28], computer vision [3], and machine learning [22]. Sometimes, being able to "flip a fair coin" while computing is a *necessity* rather than an alternative, like in computational cryptography (where, e.g., secure public key encryption schemes are bound to be probabilistic [10]).

Any (probabilistic) algorithm can be executed by concrete machines only once it takes the form of a *program*. And indeed, various probabilistic programming languages have been introduced in the last years, from abstract ones [15,26,21] to more concrete ones [23,11]. A quite common scheme consists in endowing any deterministic language with one or more primitives for probabilistic choice, like binary probabilistic choice or primitives for distributions.

Viewing algorithms as functions allows a smooth integration of distributions into the playground, itself nicely reflected at the level of types through monads [12,26]. As a matter of fact, some existing probabilistic programming languages [23,11] are designed

---

[*] The authors are partially supported by the ANR project 12IS02001 PACE.

Z. Shao (Ed.): ESOP 2014, LNCS 8410, pp. 209–228, 2014.

around the λ-calculus or one of its incarnations, like Scheme. This, in turn has stimulated foundational research about probabilistic λ-calculi, and in particular about the nature of program equivalence in a probabilistic setting. This has already started to produce some interesting results in the realm of denotational semantics, where adequacy and full-abstraction results have recently appeared [7,9].

Not much is known about operational techniques for probabilistic program equivalence, and in particular about coinductive methodologies. This is in contrast with what happens for deterministic or nondeterministic programs, when various notions of bisimulation have been introduced and proved to be adequate and, in some cases, fully abstract [1,20,18]. A recent paper by Alberti, Sangiorgi and the second author [5] generalizes Abramsky's applicative bisimulation [1] to $\Lambda_\oplus$, a call-by-name, untyped λ-calculus endowed with binary, fair, probabilistic choice [6]. Probabilistic applicative bisimulation is shown to be a congruence, thus included in context equivalence. Completeness, however, fails, the counterexample being exactly the one separating bisimulation and context equivalence in a nondeterministic setting. Full abstraction is then recovered when pure, deterministic λ-terms are considered, as well as when another, more involved, notion of bisimulation, called coupled logical bisimulation, takes the place of applicative bisimulation.

In this paper, we proceed with the study of probabilistic applicative bisimulation, analysing its behaviour when instantiated on call-by-value λ-calculi. This investigation brings up some nice, unexpected results. Indeed, not only the non-trivial proof of congruence for applicative bisimulation can be adapted to the call-by-value setting, which is somehow expected, but applicative bisimilarity turns out to precisely characterize context equivalence. This is quite surprising, given that in nondeterministic λ-calculi, both when call-by-name and call-by-value evaluation are considered, applicative bisimilarity is a congruence, but *finer* than context equivalence [18]. There is another, even less expected result: the aforementioned correspondence does not hold anymore if we consider applicative *simulation* and the contextual *preorder*.

Technically, the presented results owe much to a recent series of studies about probabilistic bisimulation for labelled Markov processes [8,29], i.e., labelled probabilistic transition systems in which the state space is continuous (rather than discrete, as in Larsen and Skou's labelled Markov chains [17]), but time stays discrete. More specifically, the way we prove that context equivalent terms are bisimilar goes by constructively showing how each *test* of a kind characterizing probabilistic bisimulation can be turned into an equivalent *context*. If, as a consequence, two terms are not bisimilar, then any test the two terms satisfy with different probabilities (of which there must be at least one) becomes a context in which the two terms converge with different probabilities. This helps understanding the discrepancies between the probabilistic and nondeterministic settings, since in the latter the class of tests characterizing applicative bisimulation is well-known to be quite large [20]. The mismatch between the symmetric and asymmetric cases is also clarified — again, the language of tests characterizing similarity is strictly more general than the one characterizing bisimilarity [29].

The whole development is done in a probabilistic variation on PCF with lazy lists, called PCFL$_\oplus$. Working with an applied calculus allows to stay closer to concrete programming languages, this way facilitating exemplification, as in Section 2 below.

Infinitary data structures are there to show that probabilistic applicative bisimulation works well in a setting where coinduction plays a key rôle.

2   Some Motivating Examples

In this section, we want to show how λ-calculus can naturally express probabilistic programs. More importantly, we will argue that checking the equivalence of some of the presented programs is not only interesting from a purely theoretical perspective, but corresponds to a proof of *perfect security* in the sense of Shannon [27].

Let's start from the following very simple programs:

$$NOT = \lambda x.\text{if } x \text{ then } \underline{\text{false}} \text{ else } \underline{\text{true}} : \textbf{bool} \rightarrow \textbf{bool};$$
$$ENC = \lambda x.\lambda y.\text{if } x \text{ then } (NOT\ y) \text{ else } y : \textbf{bool} \rightarrow \textbf{bool} \rightarrow \textbf{bool};$$
$$GEN = \underline{\text{true}} \oplus \underline{\text{false}} : \textbf{bool}.$$

The function ENC computes exclusive disjunction as a boolean function, but can also be seen as the encryption function of a one-bit version of the so-called One-Time Pad cryptoscheme (OTP in the following). On the other hand, GEN is a term reducing probabilistically to one of the two possible boolean values, each with probability $\frac{1}{2}$, and is meant to be a way to generate a random key for the same scheme.

One of the many ways to define perfect security of an encryption scheme consists is setting up an *experiment* [16]: the adversary generates two messages, of which one is randomly chosen, encrypted, and given back to the adversary who, however, should not be able to guess whether the first or the second message have been chosen (with success probability strictly greater than $\frac{1}{2}$). This can be seen as the problem of proving the following two programs to be context equivalent:

$$EXP = \lambda x.\lambda y.ENC\ (x \oplus y)\ GEN : \textbf{bool} \rightarrow \textbf{bool} \rightarrow \textbf{bool};$$
$$RND = \lambda x.\lambda y.\underline{\text{true}} \oplus \underline{\text{false}} : \textbf{bool} \rightarrow \textbf{bool} \rightarrow \textbf{bool};$$

where $\oplus$ is a primitive for fair, probabilistic choice. Analogously, one could verify that any adversary is not able to distinguish an experiment in which the *first* message is chosen from an experiment in which the *second* message is chosen. This, again, can be seen as the task of checking whether the following two terms are context equivalent:

$$EXP_{FST} = \lambda x.\lambda y.ENC\ x\ GEN : \textbf{bool} \rightarrow \textbf{bool} \rightarrow \textbf{bool};$$
$$EXP_{SND} = \lambda x.\lambda y.ENC\ y\ GEN : \textbf{bool} \rightarrow \textbf{bool} \rightarrow \textbf{bool}.$$

But how could we actually *prove* two programs to be context equivalent? The universal quantification in its definition, as is well known, turns out to be burdensome in proofs. The task can be made easier by way of various techniques, including context lemmas and logical relations. Later in this paper, we show how the four terms above can be proved equivalent by way of applicative bisimulation, which is proved sound (and complete) with respect to context equivalence in Section 4 below.

Before proceeding, we would like to give examples of terms having the same type, but which are *not* context equivalent. We will do so by again referring to perfect security. The kind of security offered by the OTP is unsatisfactory not only because keys cannot be shorter than messages, but also because it does not hold in presence of multiple encryptions, or when the adversary is *active*, for example by having an access to an encryption oracle. In the aforementioned scenario, security holds if and only if the following two programs (both of type $\textbf{bool} \rightarrow \textbf{bool} \rightarrow \textbf{bool} \times (\textbf{bool} \rightarrow \textbf{bool}))$ are context equivalent:

$$EXP_{FST}^{CPA} = \lambda x.\lambda y.(\lambda z.\langle ENC\ x\ z, \lambda w.ENC\ w\ z \rangle)\, GEN;$$
$$EXP_{SND}^{CPA} = \lambda x.\lambda y.(\lambda z.\langle ENC\ y\ z, \lambda w.ENC\ w\ z \rangle)\, GEN.$$

It is very easy, however, to realize that if $C = (\lambda x.(\textsf{snd}\,(x))(\textsf{fst}\,(x)))([\cdot]\ \underline{\textsf{true}}\ \underline{\textsf{false}})$, then $C[EXP_{FST}^{CPA}]$ reduces to $\underline{\textsf{true}}$, while $C[EXP_{SND}^{CPA}]$ reduces to $\underline{\textsf{false}}$, both with probability 1. In other words, the OTP is not secure in presence of active adversaries, and for very good reasons: having access to an oracle for encryption is essentially equivalent to having access to an oracle for *decryption*.

3   Programs and Their Operational Semantics

In this section, we will present the syntax and operational semantics of $\textsf{PCFL}_\oplus$, the language on which we will define applicative bisimulation. Due to lack of space, we cannot give all the details, which are anyway available in [4]. Moreover, $\textsf{PCFL}_\oplus$ is identical to Pitts' PCFL [24], except for the presence of a primitive for binary probabilistic choice.

3.1   Terms and Types

The terms of $\textsf{PCFL}_\oplus$ are built up from constants (for boolean and integer values, and for the empty list) and variables, using the usual constructs from PCF, and binary choice. In the following, $\mathcal{X} = \{x, y, \ldots\}$ is a countable set of variables and $\mathcal{O}$ is a finite set of binary arithmetic operators including at least the symbols $+, \leq$, and $=$.

Definition 1. Terms *are expressions generated by the following grammar:*

$$M, N ::= x \mid \underline{n} \mid \underline{b} \mid \textsf{nil} \mid \langle M, M \rangle \mid M :: M \mid \lambda x.M \mid \textsf{fix}\,x.\,M$$
$$\mid M \oplus M \mid \textsf{if}\,M\,\textsf{then}\,M\,\textsf{else}\,M \mid M\,\textsf{op}\,M \mid \textsf{fst}\,(M) \mid \textsf{snd}\,(M)$$
$$\mid \textsf{case}\,M\,\textsf{of}\,\{\textsf{nil} \rightarrow M \mid h :: t \rightarrow M\} \mid M\,M,$$

where $x, h, t \in \mathcal{X}, n \in \mathbb{N}, b \in \mathbb{B} = \{\,\textsf{true}, \textsf{false}\,\}$, *and* $\textsf{op} \in \mathcal{O}$.

In what follows, we consider terms of $\textsf{PCFL}_\oplus$ as α-equivalence classes of syntax trees. The set of free variables of a term M is indicated as $FV(M)$. A term M is closed if $FV(M) = \emptyset$. The (capture-avoiding) substitution of N for the free occurrences of x in M is denoted $M[N/x]$.

The constructions from PCF have their usual meanings. The operator $(\cdot :: \cdot)$ is the constructor for lists, $\textsf{nil}$ is the empty list, and $\textsf{case}\,L\,\textsf{of}\,\{\textsf{nil} \rightarrow M \mid h :: t \rightarrow N\}$ is a list destructor. The construct $M \oplus N$ is a binary choice operator, to be interpreted probabilistically, as in $\Lambda_\oplus$ [6].

Example 1. Relevant examples of terms are $\Omega = (\text{fix}\,x.\,x)\,\underline{0}$, and $I = \lambda x.x$: the first one always diverges, while the second always converges (to itself). In between, one can find terms that converge with probability between 0 and 1, excluded, e.g., $I \oplus \Omega$, and $I \oplus (I \oplus \Omega)$.

We are only interested in well-formed terms, i.e., terms to which one can assign a type.

Definition 2. Types *are given by the following grammar:*

$$\sigma, \tau ::= \gamma \mid \sigma \to \sigma \mid \sigma \times \sigma \mid [\sigma]; \qquad \gamma, \delta ::= \mathbf{bool} \mid \mathbf{int}.$$

The set of all types is $\mathcal{Y}$. Please observe that the language of types we consider here coincides with the one of Pitts' PCFL [24]. An alternative typing discipline for probabilistic languages (see, e.g. [26]), views probability as a *monad*, this way reflecting the behaviour of programs in types: if σ is a type, $\square\sigma$ is the type of probabilistic distributions over σ, and the binary choice operator always produces elements of type $\square\sigma$.

We assume that all operators from $\mathcal{O}$ take natural numbers as input, and we associate to each operator op $\in \mathcal{O}$ its *result type* $\gamma_{\text{op}} \in \{\mathbf{bool}, \mathbf{int}\}$ and its semantics $\overline{\text{op}}$: $\mathbb{N} \times \mathbb{N} \to X$ where X is either $\mathbb{B}$ or $\mathbb{N}$, depending on γ_{op}. A *typing context* Γ is a finite partial function from variables to types. $dom(\Gamma)$ is the domain of the function Γ. If $x \notin dom(\Gamma), (x : \sigma, \Gamma)$ represents the function which extends Γ to $dom(\Gamma) \cup \{x\}$, by associating σ to x.

Definition 3. *A typing judgement is an assertion of the form* $\Gamma \vdash M : \sigma$, *where* Γ *is a context,* M *is a term, and* σ *is a type. Typing rules are standard, and the most interesting ones are in Figure 1.*

$$\frac{\Gamma \vdash M : \mathbf{int} \qquad \Gamma \vdash M : \mathbf{int}}{\Gamma \vdash M \text{ op } M : \gamma_{\text{op}}} \qquad \frac{\Gamma \vdash M : \sigma \qquad \Gamma \vdash N : \sigma}{\Gamma \vdash M \oplus N : \sigma}$$

$$\frac{\Gamma, x : \sigma \to \tau \vdash M : \sigma \to \tau \qquad x \notin dom(\Gamma)}{\Gamma \vdash \text{fix}\,x.\,M : \sigma \to \tau} \qquad \frac{\Gamma \vdash T : [\sigma] \qquad \Gamma \vdash H : \sigma}{\Gamma \vdash H :: T : [\sigma]}$$

$$\frac{\Gamma \vdash L : [\sigma] \qquad \Gamma \vdash M : \tau \qquad \Gamma, h : \sigma, t : [\sigma] \vdash N : \tau}{\Gamma \vdash \text{case } L \text{ of } \{\text{nil} \to M \mid h :: t \to N\} : \tau}$$

Fig. 1. Type Assignment in $\text{PCFL}_\oplus$ — Rule Selection

Please notice that any term of which we want to form the fixpoint needs to be a function. If σ is a type and Γ is a typing context, then $\mathcal{T}^\sigma = \{t \mid \emptyset \vdash t : \sigma\}$, $\mathcal{T} = \{t \mid \exists \sigma, t \in \mathcal{T}^\sigma\}$, $\mathcal{T}^\sigma_\Gamma = \{t \mid \Gamma \vdash t : \sigma\}$. Terms in $\mathcal{T}^\sigma$ are said to be the *closed terms* (also called *programs*) of type σ.

3.2   Operational Semantics

Because of the probabilistic nature of choice in $PCFL_\oplus$, a program does not evaluate to a value, but to a probability distribution of values. Therefore, we need the following notions to define an evaluation relation.

Definition 4. Values *are terms of the following form:*

$$V ::= \underline{n} \mid \underline{b} \mid \text{nil} \mid \lambda x.M \mid \text{fix}\,x.\,M \mid M :: M \mid \langle M, M \rangle.$$

We will call $\mathcal{V}$ *the set of values, and we note* $\mathcal{V}^\sigma = \mathcal{V} \cap \mathcal{T}^\sigma$. *A* value distribution *is a function* $\mathcal{D} : \mathcal{V} \to [0,1]$, *such that* $\sum_{V \in \mathcal{V}} \mathcal{D}(V) \leq 1$. *Given a value distribution* $\mathcal{D}$, *we will note* $S(\mathcal{D})$ *the set of those values* V *such that* $\mathcal{D}(V) > 0$. *A value distribution* $\mathcal{D}$ *is said* finite *whenever* $S(\mathcal{D})$ *has finite cardinality. If* V *is a value, we note* $\{V^1\}$ *the value distribution* $\mathcal{D}$ *such that* $\mathcal{D}(W) = 1$ *if* $W = V$ *and* $\mathcal{D}(V) = 0$ *otherwise. Value distributions can be ordered pointwise.*

We first give an *approximation* semantics, which attributes *finite* probability distributions to terms, and only later define the actual semantics, which will be the least upper bound of all distributions obtained through the approximation semantics. Big-step semantics is given by way of a binary relation $\Downarrow$ between closed terms and value distributions, which is defined by some rules, of which we only give the most interesting ones in Figure 2. This evaluation relation, by the way, is the natural extension to $PCFL_\oplus$

$$\frac{}{M \Downarrow \emptyset} \qquad \frac{}{V \Downarrow \{V^1\}} \qquad \frac{M \Downarrow \mathcal{D} \qquad N \Downarrow \mathcal{E}}{M \text{ op } N \Downarrow \sum_{\underline{n} \in S(\mathcal{D}), \underline{m} \in S(\mathcal{E})} \mathcal{D}(\underline{n})\mathcal{E}(\underline{m})\{\overline{\text{op}}(m,n)^1\}}$$

$$\frac{M \Downarrow \mathcal{K} \qquad N \Downarrow \mathcal{F} \qquad \{P[V/x] \Downarrow \mathcal{E}_{P,V}\}_{\lambda x.P \in S(\mathcal{K}), V \in S(\mathcal{F})}}{\{Q[\text{fix}\,x.\,Q/x]V \Downarrow \mathcal{G}_{Q,V}\}_{\text{fix}\,x.\,Q \in S(\mathcal{K}), V \in S(\mathcal{F})}}$$

$$MN \Downarrow \sum_{V \in S(\mathcal{F})} \mathcal{F}(V) \left(\sum_{\lambda x.P \in S(\mathcal{K})} \mathcal{K}(\lambda x.P)\mathcal{E}_{P,V} + \sum_{\text{fix}\,x.\,Q \in S(\mathcal{K})} \mathcal{K}(\text{fix}\,x.\,Q)\mathcal{G}_{Q,V} \right)$$

$$\frac{M \Downarrow \mathcal{D} \qquad N \Downarrow \mathcal{E} \qquad L \Downarrow \mathcal{F}}{\text{if } M \text{ then } N \text{ else } L \Downarrow \mathcal{D}(\underline{\text{true}})\mathcal{E} + \mathcal{D}(\underline{\text{false}})\mathcal{F}} \qquad \frac{M \Downarrow \mathcal{D} \qquad N \Downarrow \mathcal{E}}{M \oplus N \Downarrow \frac{1}{2}\mathcal{D} + \frac{1}{2}\mathcal{E}}$$

Fig. 2. Evaluation — Rule Selection

of the evaluation relation given in [6] for the untyped probabilistic λ-calculus. Please observe how function arguments are evaluated before being passed to functions. Moreover, $M :: N$ is a value even if M or N are not, which means that lists are *lazy* and potentially infinite.

Proposition 1. *Call-by-value evaluation preserves typing, that is: if* $M \Downarrow \mathcal{D}$, *and* $M \in \mathcal{T}^\sigma$, *then for every* $V \in S(\mathcal{D})$, $V \in \mathcal{V}^\sigma$.

Lemma 1. *For every term M, if $M \Downarrow \mathscr{D}$, and $M \Downarrow \mathscr{E}$, then there exists a distribution $\mathscr{F}$ such that $M \Downarrow \mathscr{F}$ with $\mathscr{D} \leq \mathscr{F}$, and $\mathscr{E} \leq \mathscr{F}$.*

Proof. The proof is by induction on the structure of derivations for $M \Downarrow \mathscr{D}$.

Definition 5. *For any closed term M, we define the* big-steps semantics *$[\![M]\!]$ of M as* $\sup_{M \Downarrow \mathscr{D}} \mathscr{D}$.

Since distributions form an ω-complete partial order, and for every M the set of those distributions $\mathscr{D}$ such that $M \Downarrow \mathscr{D}$ is a countable directed set, this definition is well-posed, and associates a unique value distribution to every term.

The distribution $[\![M]\!]$ can be obtained equivalently by taking the least upper bound of all finite distributions $\mathscr{D}$ for which $M \Rightarrow \mathscr{D}$, where $\Rightarrow$ is a binary relation capturing *small-step* evaluation of terms. More about it can be found in [4].

Example 2. Approximation semantics does not allow to derive any assertion about Ω, and indeed $[\![\Omega]\!] = \emptyset$. Similarly, $[\![I]\!] = \{I^1\}$. Recursion allows to define much more interesting programs, e.g. $M = (\text{fix}\, x. (\lambda y.y) \oplus \lambda y.x(y + \underline{1}))\,\underline{0}$. Indeed, $[\![M]\!](\underline{n}) = \frac{1}{2^{n+1}}$ for every $n \in \mathbb{N}$, even if $M \not\Downarrow [\![M]\!]$.

3.3 Relations

A *typed relation* is a family $\mathcal{R} = (\mathcal{R}_\sigma^\Gamma)_{\sigma,\Gamma}$, where each $\mathcal{R}_\sigma^\Gamma$ is a binary relation on $\mathcal{T}_\sigma^\Gamma$. Sometime, $M \,\mathcal{R}_\sigma^\Gamma\, N$ will be noted as $\Gamma \vdash M \,\mathcal{R}_\sigma\, N$ (or as $\Gamma \vdash M \,\mathcal{R}\, N : \sigma$). The notions of symmetry, reflexivity, transitivity and compatibility can all be extended to typed relations in the natural way. Since being compatible can be seen as being reflexive on ground types and stable by the constructors of the language, the following is easy to prove:

Proposition 2. *Let $\mathcal{R}$ be a typed relation. If $\mathcal{R}$ is compatible, then $\mathcal{R}$ is reflexive.*

Any typed relation capturing a notion of equivalence should be a congruence, this way being applicable at any point in the program, possibly many times:

Definition 6. *Let $\mathcal{R}$ be a typed relation. Then $\mathcal{R}$ is said to be a* precongruence *relation if $\mathcal{R}$ is transitive and compatible, and $\mathcal{R}$ is said to be a* congruence *relation if $\mathcal{R}$ is symmetric, transitive and compatible.*

We write $\mathscr{R}$ for the set of type-indexed families $\mathcal{R} = (\mathcal{R}_\sigma)_\sigma$ of binary relations $\mathcal{R}_\sigma$ between the terms in $\mathcal{T}^\sigma$.

3.4 Context Equivalence

The general idea of context equivalence is the following: two terms M and N are equivalent if any occurrence of M in any program L can be replaced with N without changing the observable behaviour of L. The notion of a context allows us to formalize this idea.

Definition 7. *A context is a term containing a unique hole $[\cdot]$. Given a context C and a term M, $C[M]$ is the term obtained by substituting the unique hole in C with M.*

When defining context equivalence, we work with *closing* contexts, namely those contexts C such that $C[M]$, and $C[N]$ are closed terms (where M and N are the possibly open terms being compared). In the following, we will use judgements in the form $\Gamma \vdash C(\Delta; \sigma) : \tau$, which informally means that if M is a term of type σ under the typing context Δ, then the hole of C can be filled by M, obtaining a term of type τ under the typing context Γ. Correct assertions of this form can be derived by a formal system, which we cannot present for lack of space, but which can be anyway found in [4].

Example 3. Example of derivable judgments of the just described form are $\emptyset \vdash \lambda x.[\cdot]$ $(x : \sigma; \tau) : (\sigma \to \tau)$ and $\emptyset \vdash ((\lambda x.\underline{\text{true}})[\cdot])(\emptyset; \sigma) : \textbf{bool}$.

Here, following [7,5], we consider that the observable behaviour of a program M is its *probability of convergence* $\sum [\![M]\!] = \sum_V [\![M]\!](V)$. We now have all the ingredients necessary to define what context equivalence is:

Definition 8. *The* contextual preorder *is the typed relation $\leq$ given by: for every* $M, N \in \mathcal{T}_\tau^\Gamma$, $\Gamma \vdash M \leq N : \tau$ *if for every context C such that $\emptyset \vdash C(\Gamma; \tau) : \sigma$, it holds that $\sum [\![C[M]]\!] \leq \sum [\![C[N]]\!]$. Context equivalence is the typed relation $\equiv$ given by stipulating that $\Gamma \vdash M \equiv N : \sigma$ iff $\Gamma \vdash M \leq N : \sigma$ and $\Gamma \vdash N \leq M : \sigma$.*

Another way to define context equivalence would be to restrain ourselves to contexts of **bool** and **int** type in the definition of context equivalence: this is the so-called *ground* context equivalence. In a call-by-value setting, however, this gives exactly the same relation, since any non-ground context can be turned into a ground context inducing the same probability of convergence. A similar argument holds for a notion of equivalence in which one observes the obtained (ground) *distribution* rather than merely its sum. The following can be proved in a standard way:

Proposition 3. $\leq$ *is a typed relation, which is reflexive, transitive and compatible.*

Because of the quantification over all contexts, it is usually difficult to show that M and N are two context equivalent terms. In the next sections, we will introduce another notion of equivalence, and we show that it is included in context equivalence.

4 Applicative Bisimulation

In this section, we introduce the notions of similarity and bisimilarity for $\mathsf{PCFL}_\oplus$. We proceed by instantiating probabilistic bisimulation as developed by Larsen and Skou for a generic labelled Markov chain in [17]. A similar use was done for a call-by-name untyped probabilistic λ-calculus $\Lambda_\oplus$ in [5].

4.1 Larsen and Skou's Probabilistic Bisimulation

Preliminary to the notion of (bi)simulation, is the notion of a *labelled Markov chain* (LMC in the following), which is a triple $\mathcal{M} = (\mathcal{S}, \mathcal{L}, \mathcal{P})$, where $\mathcal{S}$ is a countable set of *states*, $\mathcal{L}$ is a set of *labels*, and $\mathcal{P}$ is a *transition probability matrix*, i.e., a function $\mathcal{P} : \mathcal{S} \times \mathcal{L} \times \mathcal{S} \to \mathbb{R}$ such that for every state $s \in \mathcal{S}$ and for every label $l \in \mathcal{L}$, $\sum_{t \in \mathcal{S}} \mathcal{P}(s, l, t) \leq 1$. Following [8], we allow the sum above to be smaller than 1, modelling divergence this way. The following is due to Larsen and Skou [17]:

Definition 9. *Given* $(\mathcal{S}, \mathcal{L}, \mathcal{P})$ *a labelled Markov chain, a* probabilistic simulation *is a preorder relation R on $\mathcal{S}$ such that $(s, t) \in R$ implies that for every $X \subseteq \mathcal{S}$ and for every $l \in \mathcal{L}$, $\mathcal{P}(s, l, X) \leq \mathcal{P}(t, l, R(X))$, with $R(X) = \{y \mid \exists x \in X \text{ such that } x\,R\,y\}$. Similarly, a* probabilistic bisimulation *is an equivalence relation R on $\mathcal{S}$ such that $(s, t) \in R$ implies that for every equivalence class E modulo R, and for every $l \in \mathcal{L}$, $\mathcal{P}(s, l, E) = \mathcal{P}(t, l, E)$.*

Insisting on bisimulations to be equivalence relations has the potential effect of not allowing them to be formed by just taking unions of other bisimulations. The same can be said about simulations, which are assumed to be partial orders. Nevertheless:

Proposition 4. *If $(R_i)_{i \in I}$ is a collection of probabilistic (bi)simulations, then the reflexive and transitive closure of their union, $(\cup_{i \in I} R_i)^*$, is a (bi)simulation.*

A nice consequence of the result above is that we can define *probabilistic similarity* (noted $\precsim$) simply as the relation $\precsim = \bigcup\{R \mid R \text{ is a probabilistic simulation}\}$. Analogously for the largest probabilistic bisimulation, that we call *probabilistic bisimilarity* (noted $\smile$), defined as $\smile = \bigcup\{R \mid R \text{ is a probabilistic bisimulation}\}$. A property of probabilistic bisimulation which does not hold in the usual, nondeterministic, setting, is the following:

Proposition 5. $\smile = \precsim \cap \precsim^{op}$.

4.2   A Concrete Labelled Markov Chain

Applicative bisimulation will be defined by instantiating Definition 9 on a specific LMC, namely the one modelling evaluation of PCFL$_\oplus$ programs.

Definition 10. *The labelled Markov chain $\mathcal{M}_\oplus = (\mathcal{S}_\oplus, \mathcal{L}_\oplus, \mathcal{P}_\oplus)$ is given by:*
- *A set of states $\mathcal{S}_\oplus$ defined as follows:*

$$\mathcal{S}_\oplus = \{(M, \sigma) \mid M \in \mathcal{T}^\sigma\} \uplus \{(\hat{V}, \sigma) \mid V \in \mathcal{V}^\sigma\},$$

  where terms and values are taken modulo α-equivalence. A value V in the second component of $\mathcal{S}_\oplus$ is distinguished from one in the first by using the notation $\hat{V}$.
- *A set of labels $\mathcal{L}_\oplus$ defined as follows:*

$$\mathcal{V} \uplus \mathcal{Y} \uplus \mathbb{N} \uplus \mathbb{B} \uplus \{nil, hd, tl\} \uplus \{fst, snd\} \uplus \{eval\},$$

  where, again, terms are taken modulo α-equivalence, and $\mathcal{Y}$ is the set of types.
- *A transition probability matrix $\mathcal{P}_\oplus$ such that:*
  - *For every $M \in \mathcal{T}^\sigma$, $\mathcal{P}_\oplus((M, \sigma), \sigma, (M, \sigma)) = 1$, and similarly for values.*
  - *For every $M \in \mathcal{T}^\sigma$, and any value $V \in \mathsf{S}(\llbracket M \rrbracket)$, $\mathcal{P}_\oplus\left((M, \sigma), eval, (\hat{V}, \sigma)\right) = \llbracket M \rrbracket(V)$.*
  - *If $V \in \mathcal{V}^\sigma$ then certain actions from $\mathcal{L}_\oplus$ are enabled and produce the natural outcomes depending on the shape of σ. As a an example, if $\sigma = \tau \to \theta$, and $V = \lambda x.M$, then for each $W \in \mathcal{V}^\tau$, $\mathcal{P}_\oplus\left((\hat{V}, \tau \to \theta), W, (M[W/x], \theta)\right) = 1$. As another example, if $\sigma = \mathbf{int}$, then there is $k \in \mathbb{N}$ such that $V = \underline{k}$ and $\mathcal{P}_\oplus\left((\hat{V}, \mathbf{int}), k, (\hat{V}, \mathbf{int})\right) = 1$. The other cases are similar, and more details are in [4].*

For all s, l, t such that $\mathcal{P}_\oplus(s, l, t)$ is not defined above, we have $\mathcal{P}_\oplus(s, l, t) = 0$.

Please observe that if $V \in \mathcal{V}^\sigma$, both (V, σ) and $(\hat{V}, \sigma)$ are states of the Markov chain $\mathcal{M}_\oplus$. A similar Markov chain was used in [5] to define bisimilarity for the untyped probabilistic λ-calculus $\Lambda_\oplus$. We use here in the same way actions which apply a term to a value, and an action which models term evaluation, namely *eval*.

4.3   The Definition

We would like to see any simulation (or bisimulation) on the LMC $\mathcal{M}_\oplus$ as a family in $\mathcal{R}$. As can be easily realized, indeed, any (bi)simulation on $\mathcal{M}_\oplus$ cannot put in correspondence states (M, σ) and (N, τ) where $\sigma \neq \tau$, since each such pair exposes its second component as an action. Moreover, $(\hat{V}, \sigma)$ is (bi)similar to $(\hat{W}, \sigma)$ iff (V, σ) is (bi)similar to (W, σ). This then justifies the following:

Definition 11. *A probabilistic applicative simulation (a PAS in the following), is a family* $(\mathcal{R}_\sigma) \in \mathcal{R}$ *such that there exists a probabilistic simulation R on the LMC $\mathcal{M}_\oplus$ such that for every type σ, and for every $M, N \in \mathcal{T}^\sigma$ it holds that $M \; \mathcal{R}_\sigma \; N \Leftrightarrow (M, \sigma) \; R \; (N, \sigma)$. A probabilistic applicative bisimulation (PAB in the following) is defined similarly, requiring R to be a bisimulation rather than a simulation.*

The greatest simulation and the greatest bisimulation on $\mathcal{M}_\oplus$ are indicated with $\precsim$, and $\frown$, respectively. In other words, $\precsim_\sigma$ is the relation $\{(M, N) \mid (M, \sigma) \precsim (N, \sigma)\}$, while $\frown_\sigma$ is the relation $\{(M, N) \mid (M, \sigma) \frown (N, \sigma)\}$. Terms having the same semantics need to be bisimilar:

Lemma 2. *Let $(\mathcal{R}_\sigma) \in \mathcal{R}$ be defined as follows: $M \; \mathcal{R}_\sigma \; N \Leftrightarrow M, N \in \mathcal{T}^\sigma \wedge [\![M]\!] = [\![N]\!]$. Then $(\mathcal{R}_\sigma)$ is a PAB.*

As a consequence, if $M, N \in \mathcal{T}^\sigma$ are such that $[\![M]\!] = [\![N]\!]$, then $M \frown_\sigma N$.

Example 4. For all σ, M, N such that $\emptyset \vdash M, N : \sigma$ and $[\![N]\!] = \emptyset$, we have that $M \precsim_\sigma N$ implies $[\![M]\!] = \emptyset$. For every terms M, N such that $x : \tau \vdash M : \sigma$, and $\emptyset \vdash N : \tau$, we have, as a consequence of Lemma 2, that $(\lambda x.M)N \frown_\sigma M[N/x]$.

We have just defined applicative (bi)simulation as a family $(\mathcal{R}_\sigma)_\sigma$, each $\mathcal{R}_\sigma$ being a relation on closed terms of type σ. We can extend it to a *typed* relation, by the usual open extension:

Definition 12. *1. If $\Gamma = x_1 : \tau_1, \ldots, x_n : \tau_n$ is a context, a Γ-closure makes each variable x_i to correspond to a value $V_i \in \mathcal{V}^{\tau_i}$ (where $1 \leq i \leq n$). The set of Γ-closures is CC_Γ. For every term $\Gamma \vdash M : \sigma$ and for every Γ-closure ξ, $M\xi$ is the term in $\mathcal{T}^\sigma$ obtained by substituting the variables in Γ with the corresponding values from ξ.*
2. Let be $\mathcal{R} = (\mathcal{R}_\sigma) \in \mathcal{R}$. We define the open extension of $(\mathcal{R}_\sigma)$ as the typed relation $\mathcal{R}_\circ = (\mathcal{P}_\sigma^\Gamma)$ where $\mathcal{P}_\sigma^\Gamma \subseteq \mathcal{T}_\sigma^\Gamma \times \mathcal{T}_\sigma^\Gamma$ is defined by stipulating that $M \; \mathcal{P}_\sigma^\Gamma \; N$ iff for every $\xi \in CC_\Gamma$, $(M\xi) \; \mathcal{R}_\sigma \; (N\xi)$.

Definition 13 (Simulation Preorder and Bisimulation Equivalence). *The typed relation $\precsim_\circ$ is said to be the* simulation preorder. *The typed relation $\frown_\circ$ is said to be* bisimulation equivalence.

4.4 Bisimulation Equivalence Is a Congruence

In this section, we want to show that $\leftrightsquigarrow_{o}$ is actually a congruence, and that $\precsim_{o}$ is a precongruence. In view of Proposition 5, it is enough to show that the typed relation $\precsim_{o}$ is a precongruence, since $\leftrightsquigarrow_{o}$ is the intersection of $\precsim_{o}$ and the opposite relation of $\precsim_{o}$. The key step consists in showing that $\precsim_{o}$ is compatible. This will be carried out by the Howe's Method, which is a general method for establishing such congruence properties [14].

The main idea of Howe's method consists in defining an auxiliary relation $\precsim_{o}^{H}$, such that it is easy to see that it is compatible, and then prove that $\precsim_{o} = (\precsim_{o}^{H})^{+}$.

Definition 14. *Let $\mathcal{R}$ be a typed relation. The relation $\mathcal{R}^{H}$ is defined by a set of rules, of which we report a selection in Figure 3. The others can be found in [4], and are anyway identical to the analogous ones from [24].*

$$\frac{\Gamma, x : \sigma \vdash x \,\mathcal{R}\, M : \sigma}{\Gamma, x : \sigma \vdash x \,\mathcal{R}^{H}\, M : \sigma} \qquad \frac{\Gamma \vdash \underline{n} \,\mathcal{R}\, M : \mathbf{int}}{\Gamma \vdash \underline{n} \,\mathcal{R}^{H}\, M : \mathbf{int}}$$

$$\frac{\Gamma \vdash M \,\mathcal{R}^{H}\, N : \mathbf{int} \qquad \Gamma \vdash L \,\mathcal{R}^{H}\, P : \mathbf{int} \qquad \Gamma \vdash (N \,\mathsf{op}\, P) \,\mathcal{R}\, R : \gamma_{\mathsf{op}}}{\Gamma \vdash (M \,\mathsf{op}\, L) \,\mathcal{R}^{H}\, R : \gamma_{\mathsf{op}}}$$

$$\frac{\Gamma, x : \sigma \vdash M \,\mathcal{R}^{H}\, N : \tau \qquad \Gamma \vdash (\lambda x.N) \,\mathcal{R}\, L : \sigma \to \tau}{\Gamma \vdash (\lambda x.M) \,\mathcal{R}^{H}\, L : \sigma \to \tau}$$

$$\frac{\Gamma, x : \sigma \vdash M \,\mathcal{R}^{H}\, N : \sigma \qquad \Gamma \vdash (\mathsf{fix}\, x.\, N) \,\mathcal{R}\, L : \sigma}{\Gamma \vdash (\mathsf{fix}\, x.\, M) \,\mathcal{R}^{H}\, L : \sigma}$$

$$\frac{\Gamma \vdash M \,\mathcal{R}^{H}\, N : \sigma \to \tau \qquad \Gamma \vdash L \,\mathcal{R}^{H}\, P : \sigma \qquad \Gamma \vdash (NP) \,\mathcal{R}\, R : \tau}{\Gamma \vdash (ML) \,\mathcal{R}^{H}\, R : \tau}$$

Fig. 3. Howe's Construction — Rule Selection

We are now going to show, that if the relation $\mathcal{R}$ we start from satisfies minimal requirements, namely that it is reflexive and transitive, then the transitive closure $(\mathcal{R}^{H})^{+}$ of the Howe's lifting is guaranteed to be a precongruence which contains $\mathcal{R}$. This is a direct consequence of the following results, whose proofs are standard inductions (see.[4] for some more details):

- Let $\mathcal{R}$ be a reflexive typed relation. Then $\mathcal{R}^{H}$ is compatible.
- Let $\mathcal{R}$ be transitive. Then:

$$(\Gamma \vdash M \,\mathcal{R}^{H}\, N : \sigma) \wedge (\Gamma \vdash N \,\mathcal{R}\, L : \sigma) \Rightarrow (\Gamma \vdash M \,\mathcal{R}^{H}\, L : \sigma)$$

- If $\mathcal{R}$ is reflexive and $\Gamma \vdash M \,\mathcal{R}\, N : \sigma$, then $\Gamma \vdash M \,\mathcal{R}^{H}\, N : \sigma$.
- If $\mathcal{R}$ is compatible, then so is $\mathcal{R}^{+}$.

We can now apply the Howe's construction to $\precsim_\circ$, since it is clearly reflexive and transitive. The points above then tell us that $\precsim_\circ^H$, and $(\precsim_\circ^H)^+$ are both compatible. What we are left with, then, is proving that $(\precsim_\circ^H)^+$ is also a simulation. The following is a crucial step towards proving it:

Lemma 3 (Key Lemma). *For every terms M, N, the following hold:*

- *If $\emptyset \vdash M \precsim_\circ^H N : \sigma \to \tau$, then for every $X_1 \subseteq \mathcal{T}_{x:\sigma}^\tau$ and $X_2 \subseteq \mathcal{T}_{x:\sigma \to \tau}^\tau$, it holds that $[\![M]\!](\lambda x.X_1 \bigcup \mathrm{fix}\, x.\, X_2) \leq [\![N]\!](\precsim_\circ (\lambda x.Y_1 \bigcup \mathrm{fix}\, x.\, Y_2))$, where $Y_1 = \{L \in \mathcal{T}_{x:\sigma}^\tau \mid \exists P \in X_1.x : \sigma \vdash P \precsim_\circ^H L : \tau\}$ and $Y_2 = \{L \in \mathcal{T}_{x:\sigma \to \tau}^{\sigma \to \tau} \mid \exists P \in X_2.x : \sigma \to \tau \vdash P \precsim_\circ^H L : \sigma \to \tau\}$.*
- *If $\emptyset \vdash M \precsim_\circ^H N : \sigma \times \tau$, then for every $X \subseteq \mathcal{V}^{\sigma \times \tau}$ we have: $[\![M]\!](X) \leq [\![N]\!](\precsim_\circ(Y))$, where $Y = \{\langle L, P\rangle \mid \exists \langle R, T\rangle \in X \wedge \emptyset \vdash R \precsim_\circ^H L : \sigma \wedge \emptyset \vdash T \precsim_\circ^H P : \tau\}$.*
- *If $(\emptyset \vdash M \precsim_\circ^H N : [\sigma])$ then it holds that $[\![M]\!](\mathrm{nil}) \leq [\![N]\!](\mathrm{nil})$ and for every $X \subseteq \mathcal{V}^{[\sigma]}$, $[\![M]\!](X) \leq [\![N]\!](\precsim_\circ(Y))$ where Y is the set of those $K :: L$ such that there are H, T with $H :: T \in X$, $\emptyset \vdash H \precsim_\circ^H K : \sigma$, and $\emptyset \vdash T \precsim_\circ^H L : [\sigma]$.*
- *$\emptyset \vdash M \precsim_\circ^H N : \mathbf{int} \Rightarrow \forall k \in \mathbb{N}, [\![M]\!](\underline{k}) \leq [\![N]\!](\underline{k})$.*
- *$\emptyset \vdash M \precsim_\circ^H N : \mathbf{bool} \Rightarrow \forall b \in \mathbb{B}, [\![M]\!](\underline{b}) \leq [\![N]\!](\underline{b})$.*

The Key Lemma can be proved with tools very similar to the ones employed in [5] for an analogous result in an untyped call-by-name setting. Details can be found in [4]. A careful look at its statement reveals that, indeed, what it says is that $\precsim_\circ^H$ satisfies the axioms of a simulation when instantiated on the concrete LMC $\mathcal{M}_\oplus$.

A consequence of the Key Lemma, then, is that $(\precsim_\circ^H)^+$ is an applicative bisimulation, thus included in the largest one, namely $\precsim_\circ$. Since the latter is itself included in $\precsim_\circ^H$, we obtain that $\precsim_\circ = (\precsim_\circ^H)^+$. But $(\precsim_\circ^H)^+$ is a precongruence, and we get the main result of this section: $\precsim_\circ$ is a precongruence.

Theorem 1 (Soundness). *The typed relation $\precsim_\circ$ is a precongruence relation included in $\leq$. Analogously, $\backsim_\circ$ is a congruence relation included in $\equiv$.*

4.5 Back to Our Examples

We now have all the necessary tools to prove that the example programs from Section 2 are indeed context equivalent. As an example, let us consider again the following terms:

$$EXP_{FST} = \lambda x.\lambda y.ENC\ x\ GEN : \mathbf{bool} \to \mathbf{bool} \to \mathbf{bool};$$
$$EXP_{SND} = \lambda x.\lambda y.ENC\ y\ GEN : \mathbf{bool} \to \mathbf{bool} \to \mathbf{bool}.$$

One can define the relations $\mathcal{R}_{\mathbf{bool}}, \mathcal{R}_{\mathbf{bool} \to \mathbf{bool}}, \mathcal{R}_{\mathbf{bool} \to \mathbf{bool} \to \mathbf{bool}}$ by stipulating that $\mathcal{R}_\sigma = X_\sigma \times X_\sigma \cup ID_\sigma$ where

$$X_{\mathbf{bool}} = \{(ENC\ \underline{\mathrm{true}}\ GEN), (ENC\ \underline{\mathrm{false}}\ GEN)\};$$
$$X_{\mathbf{bool} \to \mathbf{bool}} = \{(\lambda y.ENC\ y\ GEN), (\lambda y.ENC\ \underline{\mathrm{true}}\ GEN), (\lambda y.ENC\ \underline{\mathrm{false}}\ GEN)\};$$
$$X_{\mathbf{bool} \to \mathbf{bool} \to \mathbf{bool}} = \{EXP_{FST}, EXP_{SND}\};$$

and for every type σ, ID_σ is the identity on $\mathcal{T}^\sigma$. When σ is not one of the types above, $\mathcal{R}_\sigma$ can be set to be just ID_σ. This way, the family $(\mathcal{R}_\sigma)$ can be seen as a relation R on the state space of $\mathcal{M}_\oplus$ (since any state in the form $(\hat{V}, \sigma)$ can be treated as (V, σ)). But R is easily seen to be a bisimulation. Indeed:

- All pairs of terms in $\mathcal{R}_{\mathbf{bool}}$ have the same semantics, since $[\![ENC \text{ } \underline{\text{true}} \text{ } GEN]\!]$ and $[\![ENC \text{ } \underline{\text{false}} \text{ } GEN]\!]$ are both the uniform distribution on the set of boolean values.
- The elements of $X_{\mathbf{bool}\to\mathbf{bool}}$ are values, and if we apply any two of them to a fixed boolean value, we end up with two terms $\mathcal{R}_{\mathbf{bool}}$ puts in relation.
- Similarly for $X_{\mathbf{bool}\to\mathbf{bool}\to\mathbf{bool}}$: applying any two elements of it to a boolean value yields two elements which are put in relations by $X_{\mathbf{bool}\to\mathbf{bool}}$.

Being an applicative bisimulation, $(\mathcal{R}_\sigma)_\sigma$ is included in $\sim$. And, by Theorem 1, we can conclude that $EXP_{FST} \equiv EXP_{SND}$. Analogously, one can verify that $EXP \equiv RND$.

5   Full Abstraction

Theorem 1 tells us that applicative bisimilarity is a sound way to prove that certain terms are context equivalent. Moreover, applicative bisimilarity is a congruence, and can then be applied in any context yielding bisimilar terms. In this section, we ask ourselves *how close* bisimilarity and context equivalence really are. Is it that the two coincide?

5.1   LMPs, Bisimulation, and Testing

The concept of probabilistic bisimulation has been generalized to the continuous case by Edalat, Desharnais and Panangaden, more than ten years ago [8]. Similarity and bisimilarity as defined in the aforementioned paper were later shown to exactly correspond to appropriate, and relatively simple, notions of *testing* [29]. We will make essential use of this characterization when proving that context equivalence is included in bisimulation. And this section is devoted to giving a brief but necessary introduction to the relevant theory. For more details, please refer to [29] and to [4].

In the rest of this section, $\mathscr{A}$ is a fixed set of labels. The first step consists in giving a generalization of LMCs in which the set of states is not restricted to be countable:

Definition 15. *A labelled Markov process (LMP in the following) is a triple $\mathcal{C} = (\mathcal{X}, \Sigma, \mu)$, consisting of a set $\mathcal{X}$ of states, a σ-field Σ on $\mathcal{X}$, and a transition probability function $\mu : \mathcal{X} \times \mathscr{A} \times \Sigma \to [0, 1]$, such that:*
- *for all $x \in \mathcal{X}$, and $a \in Act$, the naturally defined function $\mu_{x,a}(\cdot) : \Sigma \to [0, 1]$ is a subprobability measure;*
- *for all $a \in Act$, and $A \in \Sigma$, the naturally defined function $\mu_{(\cdot),a}(A) : \mathcal{X} \to [0, 1]$ is measurable.*

The notion of (bi)simulation can be smoothly generalized to the continuous case:

Definition 16. *Let $(\mathcal{X}, \Sigma, \mu)$ be a LMP, and let R be a reflexive relation on $\mathcal{X}$. We say that R is a simulation if it satisfies Condition 1 below, and we say that R is a bisimulation if it satisfies both conditions 1 and 2:*
1. *If $x \mathrel{R} y$, then for every $a \in \mathscr{A}$ and for every $A \in \Sigma$ such that $A = R(A)$, it holds that $\mu_{x,a}(A) \leq \mu_{y,a}(A)$.*
2. *If $x \mathrel{R} y$, then for every $a \in \mathscr{A}$ and for every $A \in \Sigma$, $\mu_{x,a}(\mathcal{X}) = \mu_{y,a}(\mathcal{X})$.*

We say that two states are bisimilar if they are related by some bisimulation.

We will soon see that there is a natural way to turn any LMC into a LMP, in such a way that (bi)similarity stays the same. Before doing so, however, let us introduce the notion of a *test*:

Definition 17. *The* test language $\mathscr{T}$ *is given by the grammar* $t ::= \omega \mid a \cdot t \mid \langle t, t \rangle$, *where* $a \in \mathscr{A}$.

Please observe that tests are *finite* objects, and that there isn't any disjunctive nor any negative test in $\mathscr{T}$. Intuitively, ω is the test which always succeeds, while $\langle t, s \rangle$ corresponds to making two copies of the underlying state, testing them independently according to t and s and succeeding iff *both* tests succeed. The test $a \cdot t$ consists in performing the action a, and in case of success performing the test t. This can be formalized as follows:

Definition 18. *Given a labelled Markov Process* $\mathcal{C} = (\mathcal{X}, \Sigma, \mu)$, *we define an indexed family* $\{P_{\mathcal{C}}(\cdot, t)\}_{t \in \mathscr{T}}$ *(such that* $P_{\mathcal{C}}(\cdot, t) : \mathcal{X} \to \mathbb{R}$) *by induction on the structure of* t:

$$P_{\mathcal{C}}(x, \omega) = 1; \qquad P_{\mathcal{C}}(x, a \cdot t) = \int P_{\mathcal{C}}(\cdot, t) d\mu_{x,a}; \qquad P_{\mathcal{C}}(x, \langle t, s \rangle) = P_{\mathcal{C}}(x, t) \cdot P_{\mathcal{C}}(x, s).$$

From our point of view, the key result is the following one:

Theorem 2 ([29]). *Let* $\mathcal{C} = (\mathcal{X}, \Sigma, \mu)$ *be a LMP. Then* $x, y \in \mathcal{X}$ *are bisimilar iff* $P_{\mathcal{C}}(x, t) = P_{\mathcal{C}}(y, t)$ *for every test* $t \in \mathscr{T}$.

5.2   From LMPs to LMCs

We are now going to adapt Theorem 2 to LMCs, thus getting an analogous characterization of probabilistic bisimilarity for them.

Let $\mathcal{M} = (\mathcal{X}, \mathscr{A}, \mathcal{P})$ be a LMC. The function $\mu_{\mathcal{M}} : \mathcal{X} \times \mathscr{A} \times \mathscr{P}(\mathcal{X}) \to [0, 1]$ is defined by $\mu_{\mathcal{M}}(s, a, X) = \sum_{x \in X} \mathcal{P}(s, a, x)$. This construction allows us to see any LMC as a LMP:

Lemma 4. *Let* $\mathcal{M} = (\mathcal{X}, \mathscr{A}, \mathcal{P})$ *be a LMC. Then* $(\mathcal{X}, \mathscr{P}(\mathcal{X}), \mu_{\mathcal{M}})$ *is a LMP, that we denote as* $\mathcal{C}_{\mathcal{M}}$.

But how about bisimulation? Do we get the same notion of equivalence this way? The answer is positive:

Lemma 5. *Let* $\mathcal{M} = (\mathcal{X}, \mathscr{A}, \mathcal{P})$ *be a LMC, and let* R *be an equivalence relation over* $\mathcal{X}$. *Then* R *is a bisimulation with respect to* $\mathcal{M}$ *if and only if* R *is a bisimulation with respect to* $\mathcal{C}_{\mathcal{M}}$. *Moreover, two states are bisimilar with respect to* $\mathcal{M}$ *iff they are bisimilar with respect to* $\mathcal{C}_{\mathcal{M}}$.

Let $\mathcal{M} = (\mathcal{X}, \mathscr{A}, \mathcal{P})$ be a LMC. We define an indexed family $\{P_{\mathcal{M}}(\cdot, t)\}_{t \in \mathscr{T}}$ by $P_{\mathcal{M}}(x, t) = P_{\mathcal{C}_{\mathcal{M}}}(x, t)$, the latter being the function from Definition 18 applied to the Markov process $\mathcal{C}_{\mathcal{M}}$. As a consequence of the previous results in this section, we get that:

Theorem 3. *Let* $\mathcal{M} = (\mathcal{X}, \mathscr{A}, \mathcal{P})$ *be a LMC. Then two states* $x, y \in \mathcal{X}$ *are bisimilar if and only if for all tests* $t \in \mathscr{T}$, $P_{\mathcal{M}}(x, t) = P_{\mathcal{M}}(y, t)$.

The last result derives appropriate expressions for the $P_{\mathcal{M}}(\cdot,\cdot)$, which will be extremely useful in the next section:

Proposition 6. *Let $\mathcal{M} = (\mathcal{X},\mathscr{A},\mathcal{P})$ be a LMC. For all $x \in \mathcal{X}$, and $t \in \mathscr{T}$, we have:*

$$P_{\mathcal{M}}(x,\omega) = 1; \qquad P_{\mathcal{M}}(x, a \cdot t) = \sum_{s \in \mathcal{X}} \mathcal{P}(x,a,s) \cdot P_{\mathcal{M}}(s,t); \qquad P_{\mathcal{M}}(x,\langle t,s\rangle) = P_{\mathcal{M}}(x,t) \cdot P_{\mathcal{M}}(x,s).$$

5.3 Every Test Has an Equivalent Context

We are going to consider the labelled Markov chain $\mathcal{M}_{\oplus}$ defined previously. We know that two programs M and N in $\mathcal{T}^{\sigma}$ are bisimilar if and only if the states (M,σ) and (N,σ) have exactly the same probability to succeed for the tests in $\mathscr{T}$, measured according to $P_{\mathcal{M}}(\cdot,\cdot)$. Proving that context equivalence is included in bisimulation boils down to show that if M and N have exactly the same convergence probability for all contexts, then they have exactly the same success probability for all tests. Or, more precisely, that for a given test t, and a given type σ, there exists a context C, such that for every term M of type σ, the success probability of t on (M,σ) is *exactly* the convergence probability of $C[M]$. However, we should take into account states in the form $(\hat{V},\sigma) \in \mathcal{S}_{\oplus}$, where V is a value. The formalisation of the just described idea is the following Lemma:

Lemma 6. *Let σ be a type, and t a test. Then there are contexts C_t^{σ}, and D_t^{σ} such that $\emptyset \vdash C_t^{\sigma}(\emptyset;\sigma)$: **bool**, $\emptyset \vdash D_t^{\sigma}(\emptyset;\sigma)$: **bool**, and for every $M \in \mathcal{T}^{\sigma}$ and every $V \in \mathcal{V}^{\sigma}$, it holds that*

$$P_{\mathcal{M}_{\oplus}}((M,\sigma),t) = \sum [\![C_t^{\sigma}[M]]\!]; \qquad P_{\mathcal{M}_{\oplus}}((\hat{V},\sigma),t) = \sum [\![D_t^{\sigma}[V]]\!].$$

The proof of Lemma 6 is by induction on the structure of the test t. If $t = \omega$, we can take $(\lambda x.\underline{\text{true}})(\lambda x.[\cdot])$ for C_t^{σ}, and D_t^{σ}, since it always converges. If $t = \langle t,s\rangle$, we want to have a context which makes two copies of a term M, and applies t to the first copy and s to the second copy; this strategy can of course be implemented. The most delicate case is the one in which $t = a \cdot s$. We consider here only the case where $a = eval$. We take $D_t^{\sigma} = (\lambda x.[\cdot])\Omega$, since $eval$ is aimed to be applied only to states of the form (M,σ). If D_s^{σ} is the context associated to s for values of type σ, we take $C_t^{\sigma} = (\lambda x.D_s^{\sigma}[x])[\cdot]$. Since the evaluation is call-by-value, the reduction of $C_t^{\sigma}[M]$ is done in the following way: first M is evaluated , and then the context D_s^{σ} is applied to the result of the evaluation of M. So the probability of convergence of $C_t^{\sigma}[M]$ is equal to $\sum_{V \in \mathcal{V}^{\sigma}} ([\![M]\!](V) \cdot (\sum[\![D_s^{\sigma}[V]]\!]))$, which is precisely what we wanted. Please observe that it couldn't be done similarly in a call-by-name setting, since $((\lambda x.B[x])[\cdot])[M]$ has there the same probability of convergence that $B[M]$.

It follows from Lemma 6 that if two well-typed closed terms are context equivalent, they are bisimilar:

Theorem 4. *Let M, N be terms such that $\emptyset \vdash M \equiv N : \sigma$. Then $\emptyset \vdash M \backsim_{\circ} N : \sigma$.*

Proof. Let t be a test. We have that, since $M \equiv N$,

$$P_{\mathcal{M}_{\oplus}}((M,\sigma),t) = \sum [\![C_t^{\sigma}[M]]\!] = \sum [\![C_t^{\sigma}[N]]\!] = P_{\mathcal{M}_{\oplus}}((N,\sigma),t),$$

where C_t^σ is the context from Lemma 6. By Theorem 3, (M, σ) and (N, σ) are bisimilar. So $\emptyset \vdash M \leadsto_\circ N : \sigma$ which is the thesis.

We can now easily extend this result to terms in $\mathcal{T}_\sigma^\Gamma$, which gives us Full Abstraction: bisimilarity and context equivalence indeed coincide.

Theorem 5 (Full Abstraction). *Let M and N be terms in $\mathcal{T}_\sigma^\Gamma$. Then $\Gamma \vdash M \equiv N : \sigma$ iff $\Gamma \vdash M \leadsto_\circ N : \sigma$.*

5.4 The Asymmetric Case

Theorem 5 establishes a precise correspondence between bisimulation and context equivalence. This is definitely not the end of the story — surprisingly enough, indeed, *simulation* and the contextual *preorder* do not coincide, and this section gives a counterexample, namely a pair of terms which can be compared in the context preorder but which are not similar.

Let us fix the following terms: $M = \lambda x.\lambda y.(\Omega \oplus I)$ and $N = \lambda x.(\lambda y.\Omega) \oplus (\lambda y.I)$. Both these terms can be given the type $\sigma = \mathbf{bool} \to \mathbf{bool} \to \mathbf{bool} \to \mathbf{bool}$ in the empty context. The first thing to note is that M and N cannot even be compared in the simulation preorder:

Lemma 7. *It is not the case that $\emptyset \vdash M \precsim_\circ N : \sigma$ nor that $\emptyset \vdash N \precsim_\circ M : \sigma$.*

We now proceed by proving that M and N can be compared in the *contextual* preorder. We will do so by studying their dynamics seen as terms of $\Lambda_\oplus$ [6] (in which the only constructs are variables, abstractions, applications and probabilistic choices, and in which types are absent) rather than terms of $\mathsf{PCFL}_\oplus$. We will later argue why this translates back into a result for $\mathsf{PCFL}_\oplus$. This detour allows to simplify the overall treatment without sacrificing generality. From now on, then M and N are seen as pure terms, where Ω takes the usual form $(\lambda x.xx)(\lambda x.xx)$.

Let us introduce some notation now. First of all, three terms need to be given names as follows: $L = \lambda y.(\Omega \oplus I)$, $L_0 = \lambda y.\Omega$, and $L_1 = \lambda y.I$. If $b = b_1, \ldots, b_n \in \{0, 1\}^n$, then L_b denotes the sequence of terms $L_{b_1} \cdots L_{b_n}$. If P is a term, $P \Rightarrow^p$ means that there is distribution $\mathscr{D}$ such that $P \Rightarrow \mathscr{D}$ and $\sum \mathscr{D} = p$ (where $\Rightarrow$ is small-step approximation semantics [6]; see [4] for more details).

The idea, now, is to prove that in any term P, if we replace an occurrence of M by an occurrence of N, we obtain a term R which converges with probability smaller than the one with which P converges. We first need an auxiliary lemma, which proves a similar result for L_0 and L_1.

Lemma 8. *For every term P, if $(P[L_0/x]) \Rightarrow^p$, then there is another real number $q \geq p$ such that $(P[L_1/x]) \Rightarrow^q$.*

Proof. First, we can remark that, for every term P and any variable z which doesn't appear in P, $P[L_0/x] = (P[\lambda y.z/x])[\Omega/z]$, and $P[L_1/x] = (P[\lambda y.z/x])[I/z]$. It is thus enough to show that for every term R, if $(R[\Omega/x]) \Rightarrow^p$, then there is $q \geq p$ such that $(R[I/x]) \Rightarrow^q$. This is an induction on the proof of $(R[\Omega/x]) \Rightarrow^p$, i.e., an induction on the structure of a derivation of $(R[\Omega/x]) \Rightarrow \mathscr{D}$ where $\sum \mathscr{D} = p$. Some interesting cases:

- If $(R[\Omega/x]) = V$ is a value, then the term $(R[I/x])$ is a value too. So we have $(R[I/x]) \Rightarrow \{(R[I/x])^1\}$, and so $(R[I/x]) \Rightarrow^1$, and the thesis holds.
- Suppose that the derivation looks as follows:

$$\frac{(R[\Omega/x]) \to \overline{T} \qquad T_i \Rightarrow \mathscr{E}_i}{(R[\Omega/x]) \Rightarrow \sum_{1 \le i \le k} \frac{1}{k} \cdot \mathscr{E}_i}$$

Then there are two possible cases :
- If $R[\Omega/x] \to T_1, \ldots, T_k$, but the involved redex is *not* Ω, then we can easily prove that each T_i can be written in the form $U_i[\Omega/x]$, where

$$R[\Omega/x] \to U_1[\Omega/x], \ldots, U_k[\Omega/x].$$

Similarly $R[I/x] \to U_1[I/x], \ldots, U_k[I/x]$. We can then apply the induction hypothesis to each of the derivations for $U_i[\Omega/x]$.
- The interesting case is when the active redex in $R[\Omega/x]$ is Ω. Since we have $\Omega \to \Omega$, we have $R[\Omega/x] \to R[\Omega/x]$, and so $\overline{T} = T_1 = R[\Omega/x]$, and $\mathscr{D} = \mathscr{E}_1$. We can apply the induction hypothesis to $T_1 \Rightarrow \mathscr{E}_1$, and the thesis follows.

This concludes the proof.   □

We are now ready to prove the central lemma of this section, which takes a rather complicated form just for the sake of its inductive proof:

Lemma 9. *Suppose that P is a term and suppose that $(P[M, L/x, \overline{y}]) \Rightarrow^p$, where $\overline{y} = y_1, \ldots, y_n$. Then for every $b \in \{0,1\}^n$ there is p_b such that $(P[N, L_b/x, \overline{y}]) \Rightarrow^{p_b}$ and $\sum_b \frac{p_b}{2^n} \ge p$.*

Proof. This is an induction on the proof of $(P[M, L/x, \overline{y}]) \Rightarrow^p$, i.e., an induction on the structure of a derivation of $(P[M, L/x, \overline{y}]) \Rightarrow \mathscr{D}$ where $\sum \mathscr{D} = p$:
- If $P[M, L/x, \overline{y}]$ is a value, then:
  - either $p = 1$, but we can also choose p_b to be 1 for every b, since the term $P[N, L_b/x, \overline{y}]$ is a value, too;
  - or $p = 0$, and in this case we can fix p_b to be 0 for every b.
- If $P[M, L/x, \overline{y}] \to R_1, \ldots, R_k$, but the involved redex has *not* M nor L as functions, then we are done, because one can easily prove in this case that each R_i can be written in the form $T_i[M, L/x, \overline{y}]$, where

$$P[N, L_b/x, \overline{y}] \to T_1[N, L_b/x, \overline{y}], \ldots, T_k[N, L_b/x, \overline{y}].$$

It suffices, then, to apply the induction hypothesis to each of the derivations for $T_i[M, L/x, \overline{y}]$, easily reaching the thesis;
- The interesting case is when the active redex in $P[M, L/x, \overline{y}]$ has either M or L (or, better, occurrences of them coming from the substitution) in functional position.
  - If M is involved, then there are a term R and a variable z such that

$$P[M, L/x, \overline{y}] \to R[M, L, L/x, \overline{y}, z];$$
$$P[N, L_b/x, \overline{y}] \to R[N, L_b, L_0/x, \overline{y}, z], \to R[N, L_b, L_1/x, \overline{y}, z].$$

This, in particular, means that we can easily apply the induction hypothesis to $R[M, L, L/x, \overline{y}, z]$.

- If, on the other hand L is involved in the redex, then there are a term R and a variable z such that

$$P[M, L/x, \overline{y}] \to R[M, L, \Omega/x, \overline{y}, z], R[M, L, I/x, \overline{y}, z].$$

Moreover, the space of all sequences b can be partitioned into two classes of the same cardinality 2^{n-1}, call them B_B and B_G; for every $b \in B_B$, we have that $P[N, L_b/x, \overline{y}]$ is diverging, while for every $b \in B_G$, we have that

$$P[N, L_b/x, \overline{y}] \to R[N, L_b, I/x, \overline{y}, z].$$

Observe how for any $b \in B_B$ there is $\hat{b} \in B_G$ such that b and $\hat{b}$ agree on every bit except one, which is 0 in b and 1 in $\hat{b}$. Now, observe that $p = \frac{q}{2}$ where $R[M, L, I/x, \overline{y}, z] \Rightarrow^q$. We can then apply the induction hypothesis and obtain that $q \leq \sum_b \frac{q_b}{2^n}$ where $R[N, L_b, I/x, \overline{y}, z] \Rightarrow^{q_b}$. Due to Lemma 8, we can assume without losing generality that $q_b \leq q_{\hat{b}}$ for every $b \in B_B$. Now, fix $p_b = 0$ if $b \in B_B$ and $p_b = q_b$ if $b \in B_G$. Of course $(P[N, L_b/x, \overline{y}]) \Rightarrow^{p_b}$. But moreover,

$$p = \frac{q}{2} \leq \frac{1}{2} \sum_b \frac{q_b}{2^n} \leq \frac{1}{2} \sum_{b \in B_G} \frac{2 \cdot q_b}{2^n} = \sum_{b \in B_G} \frac{q_b}{2^n} = \sum_b \frac{p_b}{2^n}.$$

This concludes the proof.   □

From what we have seen so far, it is already clear that for any context C, it cannot be that $\sum [\![C[M]]\!] > \sum [\![C[N]]\!]$, as this would mean that for a certain term P, $P[M/x]$ would converge to a distribution $\mathscr{D}$ whose sum p is higher than the sum of any distribution to which $P[N/x]$ converges, and this is in contradiction with Lemma 9: simply consider the case where $n = 0$.

But how about $\mathsf{PCFL}_\oplus$? Actually, there is an embedding $\langle\!\langle \cdot \rangle\!\rangle$ of $\mathsf{PCFL}_\oplus$ into $\Lambda_\oplus$ such that for every $P \in \mathcal{T}^\sigma$, it holds that $\sum [\![P]\!] = \sum [\![\langle\!\langle P \rangle\!\rangle]\!]$ (again, see [4] for more details). As a consequence there cannot be any $\mathsf{PCFL}_\oplus$ context contradicting what we have said in the last paragraph. Summing up,

Theorem 6. *The simulation preorder $\precsim_o$ is not fully abstract.*

The careful reader may now wonder whether a result akin to Theorem 3 exists for *simulation* and testing. Actually, there *is* such a result [29], but for a different notion of test, which not only, like $\mathcal{T}$, includes conjunctive tests, but also *disjunctive* ones. Now, anybody familiar with the historical developments of the quest for a fully abstract model of PCF [25,2] would immediately recognize disjunctive tests as something which cannot be easily implemented by terms.

6   A Comparison with Call-by-Name

Actually, $\mathsf{PCFL}_\oplus$ could easily be endowed with call-by-name rather than call-by-value operational semantics. The obtained calculus, then, is amenable to a treatment similar to the one described in Section 4. Full abstraction, however, holds neither for simulation nor for bisimulation. These results are given in more detail in [4], and are anyway among the major contributions of [5]. The precise correspondence between testing and bisimulation described in Section 5.2 shed some further light on the gap between call-by-value and call-by-name evaluation. In both cases, indeed, bisimulation can be characterized by testing as given in Definition 17. What call-by-name evaluation misses, however, is the capability to copy a term *after* having evaluated it, a feature which is instead available if parameters are passed to function evaluated, as in call-by-value. In a sense, then, the tests corresponding to bisimilarity are the same in call-by-name, but the calculus turns out to be too poor to implement all of them. We conjecture that the subclass of tests which are implementable in a call-by-name setting are those in the form $\langle t_1, \ldots, t_n \rangle$ (where each t_i is in the form $a_i^1 \cdot \ldots \cdot a_i^{m_i} \cdot \omega$), and that full abstraction can be recovered if the language is endowed with an operator for *sequencing*.

7 Conclusions

In this paper, we study probabilistic applicative bisimulation in a call-by-value scenario, in the meantime generalizing it to a typed language akin to Plotkin's PCF. Actually, some of the obtained results turn out to be surprising, highlighting a gap between the symmetric and asymmetric cases, and between call-by-value and call-by-name evaluation. This is a phenomenon which simply does not show up when applicative bisimulation is defined over deterministic [1] nor over nondeterministic [18] λ-calculi. The path towards these results goes through a characterization of bisimilarity by testing which is known from the literature [29]. Noticeably, the latter helps in finding the right place for probabilistic λ-calculi in the coinductive spectrum: the corresponding notion of test is more powerful than plain trace equivalence, but definitely less complex than the infinitary notion of test which characterizes applicative bisimulation in presence of nondeterminism [20].

Further work includes a broader study on (not necessarily coinductive) notions of equivalence for probabilistic λ-calculi. As an example, it would be nice to understand the relations between applicative bisimulation and logical relations (e.g. the ones defined in [13]). Another interesting direction would be the study of notions of *approximate* equivalence for λ-calculi with restricted expressive power. This would be a step forward getting a coinductive characterization of computational indistinguishability, with possibly nice applications for cryptographic protocol verification.

References

1. Abramsky, S.: The Lazy λ-Calculus. In: Turner, D. (ed.) Research Topics in Functional Programming, pp. 65–117. Addison Wesley (1990)
2. Berry, G., Curien, P.-L.: Sequential algorithms on concrete data structures. Theor. Comput. Sci. 20, 265–321 (1982)
3. Comaniciu, D., Ramesh, V., Meer, P.: Kernel-based object tracking. IEEE Trans. on Pattern Analysis and Machine Intelligence 25(5), 564–577 (2003)
4. Crubille, R., Dal Lago, U.: On Probabilistic applicative bisimulation for call-by-value lambda calculi (long version) (2014), http://arxiv.org/abs/1401.3766

5. Dal Lago, U., Sangiorgi, D., Alberti, M.: On coinductive equivalences for higher-order probabilistic functional programs. In: POPL, pp. 297–308 (2014)
6. Dal Lago, U., Zorzi, M.: Probabilistic operational semantics for the lambda calculus. RAIRO - Theor. Inf. and Applic. 46(3), 413–450 (2012)
7. Danos, V., Harmer, R.: Probabilistic game semantics. ACM Trans. Comput. Log. 3(3), 359–382 (2002)
8. Desharnais, J., Edalat, A., Panangaden, P.: Bisimulation for labelled markov processes. Inf. Comput. 179(2), 163–193 (2002)
9. Ehrhard, T., Tasson, C., Pagani, M.: Probabilistic coherence spaces are fully abstract for probabilistic PCF. In: POPL, pp. 309–320 (2014)
10. Goldwasser, S., Micali, S.: Probabilistic encryption. J. Comput. Syst. Sci. 28(2), 270–299 (1984)
11. Goodman, N.D.: The principles and practice of probabilistic programming. In: POPL, pp. 399–402 (2013)
12. Gordon, A.D., Aizatulin, M., Borgström, J., Claret, G., Graepel, T., Nori, A.V., Rajamani, S.K., Russo, C.V.: A model-learner pattern for bayesian reasoning. In: POPL, pp. 403–416 (2013)
13. Goubault-Larrecq, J., Lasota, S., Nowak, D.: Logical relations for monadic types. Mathematical Structures in Computer Science 18(6), 1169–1217 (2008)
14. Howe, D.J.: Proving congruence of bisimulation in functional programming languages. Inf. Comput. 124(2), 103–112 (1996)
15. Jones, C., Plotkin, G.D.: A probabilistic powerdomain of evaluations. In: LICS, pp. 186–195 (1989)
16. Katz, J., Lindell, Y.: Introduction to Modern Cryptography. Chapman & Hall Cryptography and Network Security Series. Chapman & Hall (2007)
17. Larsen, K.G., Skou, A.: Bisimulation through probabilistic testing. Inf. Comput. 94(1), 1–28 (1991)
18. Lassen, S.B.: Relational Reasoning about Functions and Nondeterminism. PhD thesis, University of Aarhus (1998)
19. Manning, C.D., Schütze, H.: Foundations of statistical natural language processing, vol. 999. MIT Press (1999)
20. Ong, C.-H.L.: Non-determinism in a functional setting. In: LICS, pp. 275–286 (1993)
21. Park, S., Pfenning, F., Thrun, S.: A probabilistic language based on sampling functions. ACM Trans. Program. Lang. Syst. 31(1) (2008)
22. Pearl, J.: Probabilistic reasoning in intelligent systems: networks of plausible inference. Morgan Kaufmann (1988)
23. Pfeffer, A.: IBAL: A probabilistic rational programming language. In: IJCAI, pp. 733–740. Morgan Kaufmann (2001)
24. Pitts, A.: Operationally-based theories of program equivalence. In: Semantics and Logics of Computation, pp. 241–298. Cambridge University Press (1997)
25. Plotkin, G.D.: LCF considered as a programming language. Theor. Comput. Sci. 5(3), 223–255 (1977)
26. Ramsey, N., Pfeffer, A.: Stochastic lambda calculus and monads of probability distributions. In: POPL, pp. 154–165 (2002)
27. Shannon, C.: Communication theory of secrecy systems. Bell System Technical Journal 28, 656–715 (1949)
28. Thrun, S.: Robotic mapping: A survey. Exploring artificial intelligence in the new millennium, 1–35 (2002)
29. van Breugel, F., Mislove, M.W., Ouaknine, J., Worrell, J.: Domain theory, testing and simulation for labelled markov processes. Theor. Comput. Sci. 333(1-2), 171–197 (2005)

Grounding Synchronous Deterministic Concurrency in Sequential Programming*

Joaquín Aguado[1], Michael Mendler[1], Reinhard von Hanxleden[2], and Insa Fuhrmann[2]

[1] Otto-Friedrich-Universität Bamberg, Germany
[2] Christian-Albrechts-Universität zu Kiel, Germany

Abstract. Using a new domain-theoretic characterisation we show that Berry's constructive semantics is a conservative approximation of the recently proposed *sequentially constructive* (SC) model of computation. We prove that every Berry-constructive program is deterministic and deadlock-free under sequentially admissible scheduling. This gives, for the first time, a natural interpretation of Berry-constructiveness for shared-memory, multi-threaded programming in terms of synchronous cycle-based scheduling, where previous results were cast in terms of synchronous circuits. This opens the door to a direct mapping of Esterel's signal mechanism into boolean variables that can be set and reset under the programmer's control within a tick. We illustrate the practical usefulness of this mapping by discussing how *signal reincarnation* is handled efficiently by this transformation, which is of linear complexity in program size, in contrast to earlier techniques that had quadratic overhead.

Keywords: Concurrency, Constructiveness, Determinism, Mealy Reactive Systems, Synchronous Programming, Esterel.

1 Introduction

If traditional main-stream programming was largely single-threaded and sequential, the new multi-core processing age raises the incentives for concurrent programming. However, multi-threaded, shared memory programming is notoriously difficult because of data races (write-write, read-write conflicts) which jeopardise the functional correctness and predictability of program behaviour. The main-stream answer to avoid the non-determinism are elementary synchronisation primitives, such as monitors, semaphores and locks. Stemming from the early days of concurrent programming, these general-purpose operators are safe in the hands of an expert, at least for systems of limited complexity, but not necessarily in the hands of the novice or for complex systems [1,2].

An approach which does not rely on synchronisation through low-level primitives is the *synchronous model* of computation (SMoC). SMoC is a disciplined

---

* This work is part of the PRETSY project and supported by the German Science Foundation (DFG HA 4407/6-1 and ME 1427/6-1).

Z. Shao (Ed.): ESOP 2014, LNCS 8410, pp. 229–248, 2014.

scheduling regime based on *logical clocks* and *signals* as the key synchronisation mechanisms. To ensure determinism and bounded response, it enforces a strict cycle-based communication pattern between concurrent threads, which abstracts the principle of deterministic input-output Mealy machines.

A synchronous computation, consisting of a system and an environment, is generally described by an ordered sequence of *reaction instants*, each one occurring at a global clock *tick* acting as a synchronisation barrier. In a synchronous program, these ticks are derived from explicit clocks, as in Lustre [3] or Signal [4], or from statements such as Esterel's [5] pause, which establish precisely identifiable global configurations of the system in question. What happens, then, between two ticks, *i. e.*, within a *macro-step*, is a change from one system configuration to the next. This change results from the combined execution of the system's individual statements or *micro-steps*. The environment perceives macro-steps as atomic (instantaneous) computations. The environment's observations and interactions can only occur at globally consistent configurations delimited by the clock tick. This modelling is known as the *Synchrony Hypothesis*.

This abstraction has led to the family of *synchronous languages* [6], which have been used successfully in particular in safety-critical embedded systems, such as avionics applications. The synchrony abstraction naturally leads to a fixed-point semantics, where all variables that are computed as part of a reaction have a unique value throughout the reaction. In data-flow oriented synchronous languages, such as Lustre, this means that for each variable there must be a unique defining equation, leading to a declarative programming style. In imperative, control-flow oriented languages, such as Esterel, SyncCharts [7] or Quartz [8], the synchrony abstraction means that a signal must not be modified after it has been read ("write-before-read"). This protocol leads to the notion of *constructiveness*, also referred to as *causality*; a program is considered constructive if and only if this "write-before-read" protocol is neither too stringent, to avoid deadlocks, nor too lax, to avoid non-determinism. Programs that are not constructive must be rejected at compile time. This compile-time reasoning, which eliminates deadlock and non-determinism is one of the strengths of synchronous programming.

The synchrony abstraction has proven to be useful in practice, and its sound mathematical basis allows formal reasoning and verification. The SMoC construction principles—used so far mainly in synchronous languages—can be naturally generalised and be mapped to familiar, sequential programming concepts as used in C or Java. This not only allows a fresh look at existing synchronous languages, including more efficient compilation strategies, but also leads to natural extensions that allow a familiar, sequential programming style. In this vein, we recently introduced the notion of *sequential constructiveness* (SC) to integrate SMoC with mainstream sequential languages such as Java or C [9,10]. The idea is to reconstruct signals and their synchronisation properties in terms of variables and scheduling constraints on variable accesses. SC leaves more control to the programmer than traditional SMoC. It exploits the fact that the program-prescribed sequencing of statements can typically be implemented reliably by the compiler on the run-time system. This assumption is not usually made in traditional SMoC. The SMoC advantage is that it offers more robustness with respect to the admissible run-time models regarding reordering of statements, while SC is more permissive and more flexible to use in the context of sequential programming.

Contributions. In this paper, we investigate the formal relationship between SC and SMoC which has been discussed only informally before. Our results offer an interpretation of SC as a clocked scheduling protocol which, within a single clock tick, supports arbitrary sequences of concurrent init-update-read accesses on shared variables. This reduces the number of required clock cycles compared to SMoC which does not permit such repetitions.

- We introduce the class of Δ_0 or *strongly Berry-constructive programs* for multi-threaded shared memory programs in which one concurrent init-update-read cycle is permitted and initialisations are under the programmer's control. This generalises *Berry-constructiveness* for Esterel which we identify as a relaxation Δ_1 in which all initialisations are implicit.
- We present Δ_0 and Δ_1 in the form of fixed point analyses in abstract domains of signal statuses. Concretely, Δ_1 is equivalent to ternary analysis, which is known to be related to delay-insensitive Boolean circuits, while Δ_0 refines this naturally in a 10-valued lattice domain of approximation intervals $I(\mathbb{D})$. This brings a novel characterisation of Berry's must-cannot analysis that suggests extensions to other data types.
- We show that both Δ_0 and Δ_1 are properly included in SC, referred to as Δ_*, which permits arbitrarily many repetitions of concurrent init-update-read cycles. This proves formally that SC is indeed a conservative extension of Esterel thus solving an open problem [9].
- Finally, to illustrate the usefulness of SC (beyond Δ_1) we show by example how two initialisations during one tick implement efficiently some forms of signal reincarnation, known in SMoC as the "schizophrenia" problem. Earlier work suggests that code transformations for separating signal incarnations require at least quadratic-size code duplication [11,12,13]. This is a consequence of working at the $\Delta_{0,1}$ level. We show that in Δ_*, a code transformation that separates signal incarnations can be implemented in linear size.

Overview. Sec. 2 provides the technical setup for our results. We start with a brief discussion on how synchronous signals can be represented using variables in shared memory multi-threading. We illustrate the SC model of synchronous computation and its role for the proper sequencing of signal initialisation (Sec. 2.1). This is followed by the definition of a kernel language for pure boolean programs of single synchronous instants (Sec. 2.2), the formal definition of its operational semantics and the notion of sequential constructiveness, called Δ_*-constructiveness (Sec. 2.3). Sec. 3 contains our main results, where we introduce the Δ_0 and Δ_1 levels of abstraction for SC for approximating Δ_*-constructiveness. We study their relationship and connect Δ_1 with Berry's notion of constructiveness introduced for Esterel. Finally, Sec. 4 discusses related work, Sec. 5 sums up the paper and provides an outlook. Further material on the theory outlined in this paper, such as detailed proofs and expository examples can be found in [14].

2   Model and Δ_* Constructiveness of Boolean SC

Synchronous computations relate to classical automata in the sense that macro-steps correspond to automata transitions and clock ticks separate automata states at which system and environment can synchronize and communicate with each other. At this level of modelling, where a macro-step appears as an atomic interaction, the SMoC can be analysed by means of well-known FSM techniques. However, synchronous programming languages generate Mealy automata whose outputs depend instantaneously on the inputs. Thus, multiple accesses to the same object cannot necessarily be sequentially separated by the ticks of the macro-level clock. Here, the coordination of variable accesses raises problems of causality, initialisation, reincarnation and schizophrenia within macro steps.

2.1   Grounding Synchronous Signals in Sequential Variables

Before a formal treatment of the subject matter in later sections, we will set the stage by comparing signals, a key SMoC concept to achieve deterministic concurrency, with variables, familiar from sequential languages as C and Java. We here use a C-like language, called SCL [9], which extends C by synchronous primitives, such as pause to delineate ticks as in Esterel.

A *signal* is per default *absent* in each tick, unless it is *emitted*, in which case it becomes *present* in the current tick. Fig. 1a shows schizo-strl, an example of how signals are used in Esterel, taken from [13]. In the initial tick, the present S statement emits O if S is present; however, as S has not been emitted yet, O is not emitted. The pause statement then terminates the current tick. In the next tick, the emit S makes S present, however, the local scope of S is left immediately afterwards. When, after looping around, the scope of S is re-entered, a fresh instance of S is in place that has not been emitted yet, so the test for the presence of S fails again.

Signals that may become absent and present in the same tick, such as S in schizo-strl, are called *schizophrenic*. Schizophrenic signals bring a risk for non-determinism, for example, when synthesizing hardware, as signal wires must have a stable voltage. Thus a number of strategies have been proposed to eliminate schizophrenia by code transformations [11,12,13]. These transformations essentially duplicate loop bodies when they contain local signal scopes that might be left and re-entered in the same tick, as illustrated in schizo-cured-strl in Fig. 1b. This approach "cures" the schizophrenia problem, but could lead to an exponential code increase (each loop nesting level can double the code size, and the nesting level can be linear in the size of the program). This can be improved by distinguishing surface and depth [11] of a (compound) statement S, where S in this case is the body of the loop. The *surface* is the part that can be executed in the same tick when entering S, and the *depth* is the part of S that can be executed in subsequent ticks. The schizo-cured2-strl version in Fig. 1c illustrates this approach which, however, can still lead to a quadratic code size increase in the worst case (the recursive code expansion due to loops can only happen in the depth copy of the loop body, not anymore in the surface copy).

```
1   module schizo−strl
2   output O;
3
4   loop
5     signal S in
6       present S
7         then
8           emit O
9       end;
10      pause;
11      emit S;
12    end;
13  end loop
14  end module
```

(a) The original Esterel version [13]. The *output signal* O is communicated to the environment at each tick. The *local signal* S is not observable from the outside.

```
1   module schizo−cured−strl
2   output O;
3
4   loop
5     signal S in
6       present S then
7         emit O
8       end;
9       pause;
10      emit S;
11    end;
12    signal S' in
13      present S' then
14        emit O
15      end;
16      pause;
17      emit S';
18    end;
19  end loop
```

(b) Esterel version with schizophrenia cured by duplicating the loop body (exponential complexity). Just for clarity, we renamed the second copy of S to S'.

```
1   module schizo−cured2−strl
2   output O;
3
4   loop
5     % Surface
6     signal S in
7       present S then
8         emit O
9       end;
10    end;
11
12    % Depth
13    signal S' in
14      pause;
15      emit S';
16    end;
17  end loop
```

(c) Esterel version with schizophrenia cured by splitting the loop body into surface and depth (quadratic complexity).

```
1   schizo−seq−scl
2     (output bool O)
3   {
4     while (true) {
5       bool S;
6
7       // Surf init
8       S = false;
9       O = S;
10      pause;
11      // Depth init
12      S = false;
13      // Emit
14      S = true;
15    }
16  }
```

(d) An SCL version, still sequential, with boolean flags O and S. S is explicitly initialised to false ("absent") when entering its scope ("surface initialisation") and at the subsequent tick ("depth initialisation").

```
1   schizo−conc−scl
2     (output bool O)
3   {
4     while (true) {
5       bool S, _Term;
6
7       _Term = false;
8       fork
9         O = S;
10        pause;
11        S = true; // Emit
12        _Term = true;
13      par
14        while (true) {
15          S = false; // Init
16          if (_Term)
17            break;
18          pause;
19        }
20      join ;
21    }
22  }
```

(e) SCL version with initialisations of S in a separate thread concurrent to the scope of S.

```
1   schizo−conc−cured−scl
2     (output bool O)
3   {
4     while (true) {
5       bool S, _Term;
6
7       S = false;  // Surf init
8       _Term = false;
9       fork
10        O = S;
11        pause;
12        S = true; // Emit
13        _Term = true;
14      par
15        do {
16          pause;
17          S = false; // Depth init
18        } while (!_Term);
19      join ;
20    }
21  }
```

(f) SCL version with separate surface and depth initialisations of S to cure schizophrenia (linear complexity).

Fig. 1. The schizo example illustrating the correspondence between Esterel signals and boolean, sequentially controlled variables

The schizophrenia issue that arises at the signal-based view (as in Esterel) can be elegantly handled by the variable-based approach (as in SCL). The signals used in schizo-strl can be replaced by boolean variables that are explicitly set to false (absent) before they are possibly updated to true (present). The schizo-seq-scl code in Fig. 1d shows a functionally equivalent version of schizo-strl that replaces signals O and S by boolean variables of the same name. *False* is interpreted as signal absence and *true* as signal presence.

To fully emulate signals, we need to allow concurrent writes, but must make sure that *initialising* writes (S = false) precede non-initialising, or *updating* writes (S = true). With such an *init-update-read* protocol [10,9], for concurrent (not sequential!) variable accesses in place, we can emulate signals even in a concurrent setting, as is illustrated in the schizo-conc-scl code in Fig. 1e. This is still equivalent to the non-concurrent schizo-seq-scl, but uses concurrency for separating the initialisation of S from the original code. The point of this example is two-fold: 1) it illustrates how to handle signals in a concurrent setting, and 2) it presents a way to initialise signals in a way that scales up well to signal scopes that contain an arbitrary number of tick boundaries (pause statements) that would otherwise each require an explicit initialisation of every signal at every pause statement. In schizo-conc-scl, the back-and-forth scheduling between the concurrent threads that puts everything in the right order is induced by the aforementioned init-update-read protocol. With the advantage of having direct access to the signal initialisation we can cure schizophrenia of signals efficiently by just duplicating the reincarnated initialisation statement, again into surface and depth initialisation. This results in the schizo-conc-cured-scl code in Fig. 1f which only incurs a linear cost in code expansion over the original Esterel.

2.2   Language and Terminology

For our further elaborations, we need a language that focuses on the micro-steps. Programs in this language, called *combinational programs* or *cprogs* for short, contain the necessary control structures for capturing multiple variable accesses as they occur inside macro-steps, and abstract syntactic and control particularities of existing synchronous languages not directly related to our analysis. This not only provides generality but also avoids over-complicating our formal treatment. A cprog is *pure* in the sense that it manipulates Boolean *variables* from a finite set V carrying values in $\mathbb{B} = \{0, 1\}$. The values 0 and 1 emulate the synchronous signal statuses, respectively, of absent (initialised) and present (updated) through appropriate scheduling constraints. The syntax of cprogs is given by the BNF

$$P := \epsilon \mid {\mathchoice{}{}{}{}}_{\mathsf{i}}s \mid !s \mid s \ ? \ P : P \mid P \| P \mid P \ ; \ P.$$

Intuitively, the *empty* statement ϵ is a cprog that terminates instantaneously. The *reset* ¡s ("unemit s", initialise) and *set* !s ("emit s", update) constructs modify the value of $s \in V$ to 0 or 1, respectively. The *conditional* control $s \ ? \ P : Q$ has the usual interpretation: depending on the value 1 or 0 of the guard variable s

either P or Q is executed. *Parallel* composition $P \| Q$ forks P and Q, so both are executed concurrently. This composition terminates (joins) when both threads terminate. When just one of the two threads in $P \| Q$ terminates, the computation continues from the statements of the other thread until it terminates, too. In the *sequential* composition $P \,;\, Q$ the statements of P are first executed until P terminates. Then the control is transferred to Q which determines the behaviour of the composition thereafter. A more elaborate language handling loops and sequential pausing is treated in [14].

2.3 SC Operational Semantics and Δ_*-Constructiveness

An executing cprog, called a *process*, is a triple $T = \langle T.id, T.prog, T.next \rangle$. The *identifier* $T.id$ locates the process in the sequential-concurrent control flow with respect to other processes. As described in [14] a preorder $T_1.id \prec T_2.id$ expresses that T_2 has been instantiated sequentially after T_1. If $T_1.id \npreceq T_2.id$ and $T_2.id \npreceq T_1.id$, where $\preceq$ is the reflexive closure of $\prec$, then both processes are *concurrent*. The *current-program* $T.prog$ is the expression that defines the next action of T. The *next-control* $T.next$ is a list of future program fragments that are converted into actions sequentially after $T.prog$ has terminated.

A *configuration* (Σ, ρ) consists of the *global memory* ρ storing the current value $\rho(x) \in \mathbb{B}$ for each variable $x \in V$, and the *process pool* Σ, which is a finite set of processes with distinct identifiers. We call $T \in \Sigma$ *active* if $T.id$ is $\preceq$-maximal in Σ, otherwise T is *waiting*. In a given configuration (Σ, ρ) every active process $T \in \Sigma$ can be selected to execute its action, thereby producing a *micro-step* $T : (\Sigma, \rho) \to_{\mu s} (\Sigma', \rho')$. Since the resulting configuration (Σ', ρ') is uniquely determined by the process T, we may write $(\Sigma', \rho') = T(\Sigma, \rho)$.

In a *micro-sequence* the scheduler runs through a succession $(\Sigma_{i+1}, \rho_{i+1}) = T_{i+1}(\Sigma_i, \rho_i)$, $0 \le i < k$, of micro-steps obtained from the interleaving of process executions. We let $\twoheadrightarrow_{\mu s}$ be the reflexive and transitive closure of $\to_{\mu s}$. That is, we write $R : (\Sigma_0, \rho_0) \twoheadrightarrow_{\mu s} (\Sigma_k, \rho_k)$ to express that there exists a micro-sequence $R = T_1, T_2, \ldots, T_k$, not necessarily maximal, from configuration (Σ_0, ρ_0) to (Σ_k, ρ_k). A *(synchronous) instant*, abbreviated $R : (\Sigma_0, \rho_0) \Longrightarrow_{\mu s} (\Sigma_k, \rho_k)$, is a *maximal* micro-sequence R that reaches a final *quiescent* configuration in which all the processes have terminated, i. e., in which $\Sigma_k = \emptyset$.

Let us explain the operational semantics of SC by way of an example, for formal definitions see [14]. Consider the second tick of program schizo-conc-cured-scl (Fig. 1f), which starts immediately after the pauses in lines $L11$ and $L17$, concurrently. As a cprog this is expressed by $P_0 := (L11 \| L17) \,;\, L7$ where $L7$ stands for the code executed from line $L7$ after completion of the join wrapping around the while loop. The sub-expressions are $L11 = !s \,;\, !term$, $L17 = ¡s \,;\, term \,?\, \epsilon : L16$. We start in the configuration (Σ_0, ρ_0) where ρ_0 gives value 0 to every variable and the process pool consists of a single process $\Sigma = \{T_0\}$ with $T_0 = \langle 0, P_0, [\,] \rangle$. Since T_0 is active it can induce the micro-step $(\Sigma_0, \rho_0) \to_{\mu s} (\Sigma_1, \rho_0)$ where $\Sigma_1 = \{T_1\}$ with $T_1 = \langle 0, L11 \| L17, [L7] \rangle$. Notice how this action has split up the sequential cprog P_0 into the current-program $L11 \| L17$ and the next-control $[L7]$. Executing T_1, we obtain $(\Sigma_1, \rho_0) \to_{\mu s} (\Sigma_2, \rho_0)$, where $\Sigma_2 = \{T_{20}, T_{21}, T_{22}\}$ has forked the parent $T_{20} = \langle 0, \epsilon, [L7] \rangle$ and the two children $T_{21} = \langle 0.l.0, L11, [\,] \rangle$ and $T_{22} = \langle 0.r.0, L17, [\,] \rangle$. Since $0 \preceq 0.l.0$ and $0 \preceq 0.r.0$ but $0.l.0 \npreceq 0.r.0$ and $0.r.0 \npreceq 0.l.0$ the two children are are concurrent with each other and active in Σ_2, whereas the parent T_{20} is waiting. The parent plays the role of a join in the sense that it cannot execute until T_{21} and T_{22} terminate. The top-level operators of both $T_{21}.prog = L11$ and $T_{22}.prog = L17$ are sequential compositions. Executing these does not change the memory, so both processes are *confluent* with each other. Any scheduling order results in the same configuration $(\Sigma_2, \rho_0) \twoheadrightarrow_{\mu s} (\Sigma_4, \rho_0)$ with $\Sigma_4 = \{T_{20}, T_{31}, T_{32}\}$, where $T_{31} = \langle 0.l.0, !s, [!term] \rangle$ and $T_{32} = \langle 0.r.0, ¡s, [term \; ? \; \epsilon : L16] \rangle$ are active. In (Σ_4, ρ_0) we have conflicting concurrent writes as $T_{31}.prog$ sets the variable s and $T_{32}.prog$ resets it. Now the scheduling order matters. The "init-update-read" protocol resolves the nondeterminism, as the initialisation of T_{32} is always performed first and only then the update by T_{31}. So, $(\Sigma_4, \rho_0) \twoheadrightarrow_{\mu s} (\Sigma_6, \rho_{11})$ results from scheduling T_{32} followed by T_{31}, where the memory is $\rho_{11}(s) = 1$ and the process pool $\Sigma_6 = \{T_{20}, T_{41}, T_{42}\}$, with $T_{41} = \langle 0.l.1, !term, [\,] \rangle$ and $T_{42} = \langle 0.r.1, term \; ? \; \epsilon : L16, [\,] \rangle$. In configuration (Σ_6, ρ_{11}) there is a race between the reading of $term$ by T_{42} and the writing to $term$ by T_{41}. Again, the "init-update-read" protocol fixes the choice. It forces the run-time system to schedule first the set operation $!term$ of T_{41}, whereupon this child terminates and disappears from the process pool. Then, the conditional test T_{42} is scheduled which selects its 'then'-branch ϵ and then terminates, too. Therefore, we reach the configuration (Σ_9, ρ_{21}) with $\Sigma_9 = \{T_{20}\}$ with memory $\rho_{21}(s) = \rho_{21}(term) = 1$. This brings back the parent $T_{20} = \langle 0, \epsilon, [L7] \rangle$ as the only active process so that the next configuration is (Σ_{10}, ρ_{21}) with $\Sigma_{10} = \{\langle 1, L7, [\,] \rangle\}$. At this point we have come around the while loop and continue to execute program schizo-conc-cured-scl (Fig. 1f) from line $L7$ expressed by the cprog $L7 := ¡s \; ; \; (¡term \; ; \; o = s \; ; \; L11 \, \| \, L16)$, where $o = s$ is an abbreviation for $s \; ? \; !o : ¡o$. This generates a determinate final configuration (Σ_{21}, ρ_0) with $\Sigma_{21} = \emptyset$ considering that for the current macro-step the pauses $L11$ and $L16$ behave like ϵ, i.e., they terminate instantaneously.

Roughly, a cprog P is Δ_*-constructive if the "init-update-read" scheduling does not deadlock and all such admissible executions of P produce the same final memory. The following Defs. 1 and 2 make this formal.

Definition 1 (Confluence and Init-Update-Read Precedence)
Let $R : (\Sigma_0, \rho_0) \twoheadrightarrow_{\mu s} (\Sigma_k, \rho_k)$ be a micro-sequence and $R = T_1, T_2, \ldots, T_k$. Pick any two processes T_{i_1} and T_{i_2} and let $j = min(i_1, i_2) - 1$:

- *T_{i_1} and T_{i_2} are confluent in R if there is no micro-sequence $(\Sigma_j, \rho_j) \twoheadrightarrow_{\mu s} (\Sigma', \rho')$ such that (i) $T_{i_1}, T_{i_2} \in \Sigma'$ are both active and (ii) $T_{i_1}(T_{i_2}(\Sigma', \rho')) \neq T_{i_2}(T_{i_1}(\Sigma', \rho'))$.*
- *T_{i_1} precedes T_{i_2} if T_{i_1} and T_{i_2} are concurrent and either: (i) T_{i_1} performs a reset $¡s$ or set $!s$ on a variable s that is read (tested) by T_{i_2}, or (ii) T_{i_1} performs a reset $¡s$ on a variable s on which T_{i_2} performs a set $!s$.*

Definition 2 (Δ_*-Admissibility and Δ_*-Constructiveness)

- A micro-sequence $R = T_1, T_2, \ldots, T_n$ is Δ_*-admissible or SC-admissible, if whenever T_{i_1} precedes T_{i_2}, then $i_1 < i_2$ or both T_{i_1}, T_{i_2} are confluent in R.
- A cprog P is Δ_*-constructive, or SC-constructive, if for all configurations (Σ_0, ρ_0) with $\Sigma_0 = \{\langle 0, P, [] \rangle\}$ we have: (i) there exists a Δ_*-admissible synchronous instant $(\Sigma_0, \rho_0) \Longrightarrow_{\mu s} (\emptyset, \rho_k)$ and (ii) every Δ_*-admissible synchronous instant leads to the same final configuration $(\emptyset, \rho_k)$.

A cprog that is not Δ_*-constructive is $P_1 := (x\ ?\ !y : !y) \parallel (y\ ?\ !x : !x)$. From initial $\rho_0(x) = \rho_0(y) = 0$ all schedules force a concurrent, non-confluent, write $!y$ or $!x$ sequentially after a read x? or y?. Hence, the protocol deadlocks. Another not Δ_*-constructive program is $P_2 := (x\ ?\ \epsilon : !y) \parallel (y\ ?\ \epsilon : !x)$, which does not deadlock but has two Δ_*-admissible schedules with different results.

3 $\Delta_{0/1}$-Constructiveness: An Abstraction for Δ_*-Analysis

In earlier work [10] we have presented a simple static cycle criterion for the analysis of SC-constructiveness, called *ASC-schedulability*. Since the ASC test is purely static it cannot deal with data dependencies. This unnecessarily rejects programs as non-constructive even when the causality cycles are not executable in the run-time control flow. We now introduce an approximation to Δ_*-constructiveness which does account for data dependencies. It can deal with the difference of a variable retaining its original initial value from the initial memory (pristine), being initialised to 0 and then either remaining 0 (signal absence) or being set to 1 (signal presence). This includes monotonic value changes from 0 to 1 but is restricted to a single "init-update-read" cycle within a logical tick rather than arbitrarily many as would be permitted by Δ_*-constructiveness.

3.1   Abstract Value Domain $I(\mathbb{D})$ and Environments

Our constructiveness analysis takes place in an abstract domain of information values which describe the sequential and concurrent interaction of signals. Instead of distinguishing just two signal statuses "absent" and "present" as in the traditional SMoC, we consider the sequential behaviour of a variable (during each instant) as taking place in a linearly ordered 4-valued domain $\mathbb{D} = \{\bot \leq 0 \leq 1 \leq \top\}$. The linear ordering $\leq$ captures a trajectory through a *single* instance of the init-update protocol. Every declared variable starts off initially in status $\bot$ (pristine). It can later be *reset* (initialised) to 0 and then, possibly, *set* (updated) to 1. On the other hand, changes from status 1 back to 0 are not permitted. Any attempt to reset a variable sequentially after it has been set results in the value $\top$, denoting a model crash. The status $\top$ for a variable x indicates that more than one init-update cycle is necessary to analyse the final response of x. If this is intended, then an analysis for $\Delta_{\geq 2}$ may resolve the case. Clearly, $\leq$ induces a lattice structure over $\mathbb{D}$ with minimum $\bot$, maximum $\top$ and the join (max) and meet (min) operations obtained in the obvious fashion.

In the analysis we operate on predictions of variable values. Possible statuses of variables are approximated by closed *intervals* $I(\mathbb{D}) = \{[a,b] \mid a,b \in \mathbb{D}, a \leq b\}$ over $\mathbb{D}$. An interval $[a,b] \in I(\mathbb{D})$ in this 10-valued domain corresponds to the set $set([a,b]) = \{x \mid a \leq x \leq b\} \subseteq \mathbb{D}$ which, if $a < b$, denotes *uncertain* information, *i. e.*, a potential non-deterministic response. Such a general interval represents an approximation to the final (stable) state of a variable from its two ends, the lower bound a and the upper bound b. An interval $[a,b]$ associated with a variable $x \in V$ can thus be read as follows: *"the execution ensures that x has at least status a, yet it cannot be excluded that some statements might be executed which could increase the status of x up to b"*. In this vein, the intervals $[a,a]$ correspond to *decided*, or *crisp*, statuses which are naturally identified with the values a, *i. e.*, $\mathbb{D} \subset I(\mathbb{D})$. A variable $s \in V$ with status $\gamma \in I(\mathbb{D})$ is denoted by s^γ.

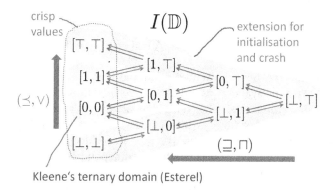

Fig. 2. Interval domain $I(\mathbb{D})$ of signal variable statuses

On the constructive value domain $I(\mathbb{D})$ we can define two natural orderings: The *point-wise* ordering $[a_1,b_1] \preceq [a_2,b_2]$ iff $a_1 \leq a_2$ and $b_1 \leq b_2$ and the *(inverse) inclusion* ordering $[a_1,b_1] \sqsubseteq [a_2,b_2]$ iff $set([a_2,b_2]) \subseteq set([a_1,b_1])$ endow $I(\mathbb{D})$ with a full lattice structure for $\preceq$ and a lower semi-lattice structure for $\sqsubseteq$. The *point-wise* lattice $\langle I(\mathbb{D}), \preceq \rangle$ has minimum element $[\bot,\bot]$, the minimum for the *inclusion* semi-lattice $\langle I(\mathbb{D}), \sqsubseteq \rangle$ is $[\bot,\top]$.

The element $[\top,\top]$ is a maximal element for both orderings but it is the maximum only for $\preceq$. For $\sqsubseteq$ all singleton intervals $[a,a]$ are maximal. Join $\vee$ and meet $\wedge$ for the $\preceq$-lattice are obtained in the point-wise manner: $[a_1,b_1] \vee [a_2,b_2] := [max(a_1,a_2), max(b_1,b_2)]$ and $[a_1,b_1] \wedge [a_2,b_2] := [min(a_1,a_2), min(b_1,b_2)]$. In the inclusion $\sqsubseteq$-lattice the meet $\sqcap$ is $[a_1,b_1] \sqcap [a_2,b_2] := [min(a_1,a_2), max(b_1,b_2)]$. The semi-lattice $\langle I(\mathbb{D}), \sqsubseteq \rangle$ does not possess joins, but it is *consistent complete*, *i. e.*, whenever in a nonempty subset $\emptyset \neq X \subseteq I(\mathbb{D})$ any two elements $x_1, x_2 \in X$ have an upper bound $y \in I(\mathbb{D})$, $x_1 \sqsubseteq y$ and $x_2 \sqsubseteq y$, then there exists the least upper bound $\sqcup X = \sqcap \{y \mid \forall x \in X. \; x \sqsubseteq y\}$. This will give us least fixed points.

Fig. 2 illustrates the two-dimensional lattice structure of $I(\mathbb{D})$. The vertical direction (upwards) corresponds to $\preceq$ and captures the sequential dimension of the statuses. The horizontal direction (right-to-left) is the inclusion ordering $\sqsubseteq$

and expresses the degree of precision of the approximation. The most precise status description is given by the crisp values on the left side, which are $\sqsubseteq$-maximal and make up the embedded domain $\mathbb{D}$. The least precise information value is the interval $[\bot, \top]$ on the right.

Observe that the well-known ternary domain for the fixed-point analysis of Pure Esterel [15] or constructive Boolean circuits [16] is captured, as indicated in Fig. 2, by the inner part with values $[0,0]$ ("absent"), $[1,1]$ ("present") and $[0,1]$ ("undefined"). In ternary analysis all signal variables are implicitly assumed initialised, hence no need for $\bot$. Moreover, since there is no reset operator and thus programs cannot fail the monotonic single-change requirement, there is no need for $\top$. This ternary fragment of $I(\mathbb{D})$ corresponds to three-valued Kleene logic with $\vee$ disjunction and $\wedge$ logical conjunction. Fig. 2 visualises clearly how the 10-valued domain $I(\mathbb{D})$ offers an extended playground to represent the logic of explicit initialisation.

The statuses of variables are kept in *environments* $E : V \to I(\mathbb{D})$ mapping each variable $x \in V$ to an interval $E(x) \in I(\mathbb{D})$. The orderings and (semi-)lattice operations are lifted to environments by stipulating $E_1 \trianglelefteq E_2$ iff $E_1(x) \trianglelefteq E_2(x)$ for $\trianglelefteq \in \{\preceq, \sqsubseteq\}$ and $(E_1 \odot E_2)(x) = E_1(x) \odot E_2(x)$ for $\odot \in \{\vee, \wedge, \sqcap\}$ and all $x \in V$. If $E(x) = [a,b]$ then we will also write $x^{[a,b]} \in E$ and further $x^\gamma \in E$ when $E(x) = [\gamma, \gamma]$.

It is natural to identify the values $[a,b] \in I(\mathbb{D})$ with *constant* environments such that $[a,b](x) = [a,b]$ for all $x \in V$. An environment E is called *decided*, or *crisp*, if $E(x) \in \mathbb{D}$; *ternary* if $E(x) \in \{0, 1, [0,1]\}$; and *crash-free* if $E(x) \preceq 1$ for all variables $x \in V$. Every environment can be separated into its lower projection $low(E) := \{x^{[a,\top]} \mid x^{[a,b]} \in E\}$ and upper projection $upp(E) := \{x^{[\bot,b]} \mid x^{[a,b]} \in E\}$ so that $E = \sqcap\{X \mid low(E) \sqsubseteq X \text{ and } upp(E) \sqsubseteq X\}$. We use the set-like notation $\{x_1^{\gamma_1}, x_2^{\gamma_2}, \ldots, x_n^{\gamma_n}\}$ for *finite* environments that explicitly set the status γ_i for the listed variables x_i and implicitly define the status $\bot$ for all other variables $z \in V \setminus \{x_1, x_2, \ldots, x_n\}$. Then, $\{\} = \bot$ is the neutral element for $\vee$.

3.2 Δ_0 and Δ_1-Constructiveness

The classes of Δ_0 and Δ_1 constructiveness over-approximate Δ_* for pure SC programs by performing an abstract program simulation in $I(\mathbb{D})$. The denotational semantics of a cprog P is given by a function $\langle\!\langle P \rangle\!\rangle_C^S$, called *Extended Berry Response Function* that determines constructive (non-speculative) information on the instantaneous response of P to an external stimulus consisting of a *sequential* environment S and a *concurrent* environment C. The sequential context S can be thought of as an initialisation under which P is activated. It represents knowledge about the value of variables sequentially before P is started. In contrast, the parallel environment C contains the external stimulus which is concurrent with P. The lower bound $low \langle\!\langle P \rangle\!\rangle_C^S$ of the response tells us what P *must* write to the variables and the upper bound $upp \langle\!\langle P \rangle\!\rangle_C^S$ is the level that the variables *may* reach upon execution of P. The function $\langle\!\langle P \rangle\!\rangle_C^S$ is defined by recursion on the structure of the cprog P as seen in Fig. 3.

$$\langle\!\langle \epsilon \rangle\!\rangle_C^S \quad := S$$

$$\langle\!\langle s \; ? \; P : Q \rangle\!\rangle_C^S := \begin{cases} \langle\!\langle P \rangle\!\rangle_C^S & \text{if } s^1 \in C \\ \langle\!\langle Q \rangle\!\rangle_C^S & \text{if } s^0 \in C \\ S \vee upp\langle\!\langle P \rangle\!\rangle_C^S \vee upp\langle\!\langle Q \rangle\!\rangle_C^S \\ & \text{otherwise} \end{cases}$$

$$\langle\!\langle \mathsf{i}s \rangle\!\rangle_C^S \quad := \begin{cases} S \vee \{s^\top\} & \text{if } 1 \preceq S(s) \\ S \vee \{s^0\} & \text{if } S(s) \preceq 0 \\ S \vee \{s^{[0,\top]}\} & \text{otherwise} \end{cases}$$

$$\langle\!\langle !s \rangle\!\rangle_C^S \quad := S \vee \{s^1\}$$

$$\langle\!\langle P \; ; \; Q \rangle\!\rangle_C^S \quad := \begin{cases} \langle\!\langle Q \rangle\!\rangle_C^{\langle\!\langle P \rangle\!\rangle_C^S} \\ \text{if } cmpl\langle P, C \rangle = \{0\} \\ \langle\!\langle P \rangle\!\rangle_C^S \vee upp\left(\langle\!\langle Q \rangle\!\rangle_C^{\langle\!\langle P \rangle\!\rangle_C^S}\right) \\ \text{otherwise} \end{cases}$$

$$\langle\!\langle P \| Q \rangle\!\rangle_C^S := \langle\!\langle P \rangle\!\rangle_C^S \vee \langle\!\langle Q \rangle\!\rangle_C^S$$

Fig. 3. Abstract analysis for cprogs

The definition of $\langle\!\langle P \; ; \; Q \rangle\!\rangle_C^S$ involves computing a set of completion codes $cmpl\langle P, C \rangle$. For cprogs we only need one code 0 for "instantaneous" termination. Informally, $cmpl\langle P, C \rangle = \{0\}$ iff P is guaranteed to execute to completion without getting blocked by a conditional test $s \; ? \; P' : Q'$ where guard s does not evaluate to a crisp value 0 or 1 in C. The precise definition can be found in [14].

- The empty cprog $\langle\!\langle \epsilon \rangle\!\rangle_C^S$ just passes out its sequential stimulus S.
- The result of resetting a variable $\langle\!\langle \mathsf{i}s \rangle\!\rangle_C^S$ depends on whether the sequential stimulus S already contains a status 1 for s or not. If $1 \preceq S(s)$, then the sequential status of s is one of the intervals $S(s) \in \{1, [1, \top], \top\}$. This indicates that s *must* have been set sequentially before the execution of the reset $\mathsf{i}s$. Hence, we must crash s since a change from 1 to 0 falls outside of the $\langle\!\langle \_ \rangle\!\rangle$ model. All other variables $x \neq s$ retain their status from S. This is what $(S \vee \{s^\top\})(s) = \top$ achieves. If $S(s) \preceq 0$ then the sequential status of s is one of $S(s) \in \{\bot, [0, \bot], 0\}$. This says that s *cannot* have been set before and so we can execute the reset by returning $(S \vee \{s^0\})(s) = 0$. Finally, the remaining cases are $S(s) = [a, b]$, where $a < 1$ and $b \geq 1$. These statuses say that s *may* have been set before. So, the execution of $\mathsf{i}s$ *may* crash the model, whence the result $S \vee \{s^{[0,\top]}\}$ forces the status of s to be $[0, \top]$.
- Setting a variable $\langle\!\langle !s \rangle\!\rangle_C^S$ updates the sequential environment S with the status s^1 for variable s if $S(\mathbf{s}) \preceq 1$ and preserves the crash if $S(s) = \top$.
- The response of a parallel $\langle\!\langle P \| Q \rangle\!\rangle_C^S$ is obtained by letting each of the child threads P, Q react to the S and C environments, independently, and then combine their responses using $\vee$.
- The result of a branching test $s \; ? \; P : Q$ can only be predicted if and when the value of s has been firmly established as a crisp 0 or 1 under all possible SC-admissible schedules. The decision value for s is taken from the concurrent environment C. Accordingly, if $s^1 \in C$ then $\langle\!\langle s \; ? \; P : Q \rangle\!\rangle_C^S$ behaves like $\langle\!\langle P \rangle\!\rangle_C^S$ and if $s^0 \in C$ the result of the evaluation is $\langle\!\langle Q \rangle\!\rangle_C^S$. As long as the value of s is still undecided, *i. e.*, if $s^0 \notin C$ and $s^1 \notin C$, we cannot know if branch P or Q will be executed. However, at least the write accesses

already recorded in the sequential environment S *must* become effective. This gives the condition $low \langle\!\langle s\ ?\ P : Q \rangle\!\rangle^S_C = low(S)$ for the lower bound. A write access *may* be produced by $s\ ?\ P : Q$ if it *may* be generated by S or by one of the branches P or Q. This implies $upp \langle\!\langle s\ ?\ P : Q \rangle\!\rangle^S_C = upp(S) \vee upp \langle\!\langle P \rangle\!\rangle^S_C \vee upp \langle\!\langle Q \rangle\!\rangle^S_C$ for the upper bound. Both can be expressed by the single equation $\langle\!\langle s\ ?\ P : Q \rangle\!\rangle^S_C = S \vee upp \langle\!\langle P \rangle\!\rangle^S_C \vee upp \langle\!\langle Q \rangle\!\rangle^S_C$.

- If $0 \in cmpl \langle P, C \rangle$ then the overall response $\langle\!\langle P\ ;\ Q \rangle\!\rangle^S_C$ is that of Q reacting to the concurrent stimulus C using the response $\langle\!\langle P \rangle\!\rangle^S_C$ as the sequential stimulus. If $0 \notin cmpl \langle P, C \rangle$ this means that some conditional test on the execution path in P cannot be decided in C. Thus, it is not known yet if P will terminate and Q will be executed. Therefore, we can only say a variable *must* be written by $P\ ;\ Q$, if it *must* be written by P. This leads to $low \langle\!\langle P\ ;\ Q \rangle\!\rangle^S_C = low \langle\!\langle P \rangle\!\rangle^S_C$. As regards upper bounds, a variable *may* be written if it *may* be written by Q with the response of P as its sequential stimulus: $upp \langle\!\langle P\ ;\ Q \rangle\!\rangle^S_C = upp \langle\!\langle Q \rangle\!\rangle^{\langle\!\langle P \rangle\!\rangle^S_C}_C$. One can show that both lower and upper bound equations can be combined into $\langle\!\langle P\ ;\ Q \rangle\!\rangle^S_C = \langle\!\langle P \rangle\!\rangle^S_C \vee upp \langle\!\langle Q \rangle\!\rangle^{\langle\!\langle P \rangle\!\rangle^S_C}_C$.

While $\langle\!\langle P \rangle\!\rangle^S_C$ describes the instantaneous behaviour of P in a compositional fashion, the constructive response of P running by itself is obtained by the least fixed point

$$\mu C. \langle\!\langle P \rangle\!\rangle^S_C = \bigsqcup_{i \geq 0} C_i, \qquad (1)$$

where $C_0 := [\bot, \top]$ and $C_{i+1} := \langle\!\langle P \rangle\!\rangle^S_{C_i}$. The fixed point (1) lets P communicate with itself by treating P as its own *concurrent* context. The fixed point exists, because the completion set $cmpl \langle P, S \rangle$ and the functional $\langle\!\langle P \rangle\!\rangle^S_C$ are well-behaved. In particular, $\langle\!\langle P \rangle\!\rangle^S_C$ is monotonic in both S, C with respect to $\sqsubseteq$ and it is monotonic and inflationary in S for $\preceq$. For a detailed exposition of the technical background the reader is referred to [14].

Definition 3. *A cprog P is Δ_0-constructive, or strongly Berry-constructive, iff* $\forall x \in V. (\mu C. \langle\!\langle P \rangle\!\rangle^{\bot}_C)(x) \in \{\bot, 0, 1\}$. *A cprog P is Δ_1-constructive, or Berry-constructive, iff* $\forall x \in V. (\mu C. \langle\!\langle P \rangle\!\rangle^0_C)(x) \in \{0, 1\}$.

As stated in Def. 3, a cprog is Δ_0-constructive if its $\langle\!\langle \_ \rangle\!\rangle$ fixed point is crisp and associates with every variable a unique reaction status $\bot$ (pristine, unchanged), 0 (initialised by reset and not updated) or 1 (updated by set and never re-initialised later). The crisp status $\top$ is excluded because it indicates that the variable is re-initialised by P after having been updated. This is not tracked by Δ_0 and requires Δ_* analysis capabilities. The difference between the two forms of Berry-constructiveness Δ_0 and Δ_1 is whether we run the simulation with the sequential stimulus $\bot$ or 0, respectively. Because of its default initialisation, Δ_1 is less restrictive and therefore contains more programs than Δ_0. However, if the initialisation is added then both notions coincide.

Theorem 1 (Relationship between Δ_0, Δ_1 and Δ_*)

1. *Every Δ_0-constructive cprog is both Δ_1-constructive and Δ_*-constructive with the same final response.*
2. *Let $P^{init} = Init$; P or $P^{init} = Init \parallel P$, where $Init$ is the cprog which resets every variable. If P is Δ_1-constructive, then P^{init} is Δ_0-constructive and the Δ_1-response of P is identical to the Δ_0-response of P^{init}.*

By Thm. 1 every Δ_0-constructive cprog is also Δ_*-constructive. On the other hand, there are Δ_*-constructive cprogs which are not Δ_0-constructive. The reason is essentially that (i) Δ_0 requires constructive initialisation of every signal variable, where Δ_* permits implicit initialisation through memory and (ii) that Δ_0 requires a monotonic status change, where Δ_* permits re-initialisation. A simple example for (i) is $P_3 = x$? $!x : !x$. For every initial memory ρ_0, P_3 admits exactly one (Δ_*-admissible) schedule, ending up with memory $\rho_k(x) = 1$, whence P_3 is Δ_*-constructive. However, P_3 is not Δ_0-constructive since $\mu C.\langle\!\langle P_3 \rangle\!\rangle_C^\perp = \{x^{[\perp,1]}\}$. An example for (ii) is $P_4 = !x$; $_{\text{¡}}x$ which is Δ_*-constructive for the same reason, but not Δ_0-constructive since it forces a reset of x sequentially after a set. In the fixed point we get a crash $\mu C.\langle\!\langle P_4 \rangle\!\rangle_C^\perp = \{x^\top\}$. Note, neither P_3 nor P_4 is Δ_1-constructive, viz. $\mu C.\langle\!\langle P_3 \rangle\!\rangle_C^0 = \{x^{[0,1]}\}$ and $\mu C.\langle\!\langle P_4 \rangle\!\rangle_C^0 = \{x^\top\}$.

The benefit of (i) and (ii) is that Δ_0 provides stronger constructiveness guarantees making it more robust under scheduling non-determinism. It does not depend on initial memory and proper isolation of successive "init-update-read" phases. In fact, the restriction (ii) of Δ_0 to monotonic status changes (from $0 \rightarrow 1$ but not $1 \rightarrow 0$) is the definitive feature of signals in traditional SMoC as exemplified by the constructive semantics [15] of the Esterel language [5] or of Quartz [8]. On the other hand, in these languages constraint (i) does not exist because initialisation is not done by the program but the run-time system. Specifically, Esterel's semantics assumes that all signals are reset to 0 by default, at the beginning of every instant.

Our Δ_0 semantics is more general, in the sense that it verifies proper initialisation as part of the constructiveness analysis. It holds the programmer responsible for proper initialisation, not the compiler or the run-time system. However, one can emulate initialisation directly by running the fixed point over $\langle\!\langle \_ \rangle\!\rangle$ in the sequential environment $S = 0$ instead of $S = \perp$ which is what Δ_1 does. For instance, $P_5 = x$? $!y : !y$ is Δ_1-constructive with $\mu C.\langle\!\langle P_5 \rangle\!\rangle_C^0 = \{x^0, y^1\}$ but not Δ_0-constructive since $\mu C.\langle\!\langle P_5 \rangle\!\rangle_C^\perp = \{y^{[\perp,1]}\}$.

The following Prop. 1 shows that Δ_1 precisely coincides with Berry's notion of constructiveness for Pure Esterel [15] whose semantics is given in terms of a set $must(P, C) \subseteq V$ of signals that $must$ be emitted by P under C and a set $cannot(P, C) \subseteq V$ which cannot be emitted by P in environment C.

Proposition 1 (Semantics of Pure Esterel). *For reset-free cprog P and ternary environment C, $s \in must(P, C)$ iff $s^1 \in \langle\!\langle P \rangle\!\rangle_C^0$ and $s \in cannot(P, C)$ iff $s^0 \in \langle\!\langle P \rangle\!\rangle_C^0$. It follows that a reset-free cprog P is constructive in Berry's sense iff it is Δ_1-constructive and the response coincides in both semantics.*

Let P be a Δ_1-constructive cprog and $Init$; P the instrumented version of P where $Init$ resets every variable. In refinement of Thm. 1(2) one can show that $\mu C.\, \langle\!\langle P \rangle\!\rangle_C^0 = \mu C.\, \langle\!\langle Init \; ; \; P \rangle\!\rangle_C^\perp = \mu C.\, \langle\!\langle Init \; ; \; P^* \rangle\!\rangle_C^\perp$, where P^* is P with all occurrences of a reset $\dot{\mathfrak{f}}x$ substituted by ϵ. This implies that $Init \; ; \; P^*$ is Δ_0-constructive, whence by Thm. 1(1) $Init \; ; \; P^*$ is Δ_*-constructive with the same response. Together with Prop. 1 this proves the conjecture [9] that sequentially constructive cprogs conservatively extend Esterel. Also, we can extract from every Δ_0-constructive cprog P an equivalent constructive Esterel program P^*.

4   Related Work

In terms of programming languages, the work presented here is at the interface between synchronous concurrent languages and C-like sequential languages, and is strongly influenced by both worlds. Edwards [17] and Potop-Butucaru et al. [18] provide good overviews of compilation challenges and approaches for concurrent languages, including synchronous languages. They discuss efficient mappings from Esterel to C, thus their work is related to ours in the sense that we present a means to express Esterel-style signal behaviour and deterministic concurrency directly with variables in a C-like language. However, a key difference is that we do not "compile away" the concurrency as part of our signal-to-variable mapping, but fully preserve the original, concurrent semantics with shared variables.

Coming from the other, C-like side, there have been several proposals that extend C or Java with synchronous concurrency constructs. Reactive C [19] is an extension of C that employs the concepts of ticks and preemptions, but does not provide true concurrency. FairThreads [20] are an extension introducing concurrency via native threads. Precision Timed C (PRET-C) [21] and Synchronous C [22] provide macros for defining synchronous concurrent threads. Synchronous C also permits dynamic thread scheduling, and thus would be a suitable implementation target for the analyses discussed here. SHIM [23], another C-like language, provides concurrent Kahn process networks with CCS-like rendezvous communication [24] and exception handling. SHIM has also been inspired by synchronous languages, but it does not use the synchronous programming model, instead relying on communication channels for synchronisation. None of these language proposals claims and proves to embed and conservatively extend the concept of Esterel-style constructiveness into shared variables as we do here. As far as these language proposals include signals, they come as "closed packages" that do not, for example, allow to separate initialisations from updates.

As traditional sequential, single-core execution platforms are being replaced by multi-core/processing architectures, determinism is no longer a trade secret of synchronous programming but has become an important issue in shared memory concurrent programming. Powerful techniques have recently been developed to verify program determinism statically. For Java with structured parallelism, the tool DICE by Vechev et al. [25] performs static analysis to check that concurrent tasks do not interfere on shared array accesses. Leung et al. [26] present a *test amplification* technique based on a combination of instrumented test execution and static data-flow analysis to verify that the memory accesses of cyclic, barrier-synchronised, CUDA C++ threads do not overlap during a clock cycle (barrier interval). For polyhedral X10 programs with finish/async parallelism and affine loops over array-based data structures, Yuki *et al.* [27] describe an exact algorithm for static race detection that ensures deterministic execution.

These recently published analyses [25,26,27] are targeted at data-intensive, array/pointer/based code building on powerful arithmetical models and decision procedures for memory separation. Yet, they address determinism in more limited models of communication. SMoC constructiveness concerns the determinism and reactivity of "control-parallel" rather than "data-parallel" synchronous programs and permits instantaneous communication between threads during a single tick. The challenge is to deal with feedbacks and reaction to absence, as in circuit design, which is difficult. The causality of SMoC memory accesses cannot necessarily be captured in terms of regular affine arithmetics as done in the polyhedral model of [25,27] or reduced to a "small core of configuration inputs" as in [26]. Further, analyses such as [25,26,27] verify race-freedom for maximally strong data conflicts: Within the barrier no write must ever compete with a concurrent read or another conflicting write. Soundness of the analysis is straightforward under such full isolation. Full thread isolation is fine for Moore-style communication but does not hold in SMoCs whose hallmark is the Mealy model. Threads do in fact share variables during a clock phase and multi-emissions are permitted. Analysing SMoC determinism, therefore, is tricky and argueing soundness of the constructivity analysis in SMoCs (e.g., our Thm. 1) is non-trivial. This is particularly true if reaction to absence is permitted, as in our work, which introduces non-monotonic system behaviour on which the standard (naive) fixed-point techniques fail.

For functional programming languages, traditionally abstracting from the impurity of low-level scheduling, determinism on concurrent platforms also has become an issue. For instance, Kuper *et al.* [28] extend the IVar/LVar approach in Haskell to provide deterministic shared data-structures permitting multiple concurrent reads and writes. This extension, dubbed *LVish*, adds asynchronous event handlers and explicit value freezing to implement negative data queries. Since the negative information is transient, run-time exceptions are possible due to the race between freezing and writing. However, all error-free executions produce the same result which is called *quasi-determinism*. Because of the instantaneous communication and the negative information carried by the value status of shared data, the quasi-deterministic model of [28] is similar in spirit to our approach. However, there are at least two differences: First, our programming model deals with first-order imperative programs on boolean data, while [28] considers higher-order λ-functions on more general "*atomistic*" data structures. Second, our $\Delta_{0,1,*}$ constructivity includes *reactivity*, which is a liveness property, whereas [28] only address the safety property of non-interference. Our *two-dimensional* lattice $I(\mathbb{D})$ seems richer than the lifted domain $Freeze(\mathbb{D})$ of [28] which only distinguishes between the "unfrozen" statuses $[\bot, \top]$, $[0, \top]$, $[1, \top]$, $[\top, \top]$ (lower information) and the "frozen" statuses $[\bot, \bot]$, $[0, 0]$, $[1, 1]$ (crisp information). There do not seem to be genuine upper bound approximations expressible in *Freeze*($\mathbb{D}$). It will be interesting to study the exact relationship between the two models.

Coming back to SMoCs, there is already a large body of related work investigating different notions of constructiveness, in the literature also referred to as causality. Causal Esterel programs on pure signals satisfy a strong scheduling invariant: they can be translated into constructive circuits which are *delay-insensitive* [29] under the non-inertial delay model, which can be fully decided using ternary Kleene algebra [16]. This makes Malik's work on causality analysis of cyclic circuits [30] applicable to the constructiveness analysis of combinational Esterel programs. This has been extended by Shiple *et al.* [31] to state-based systems, as induced by Esterel's pause operator, thus handling sequential programs as well. The algebraic transformations proposed by Schneider *et al.* [32] increase the class of programs considered constructive by permitting different levels of partial evaluation. However, none of these approaches separates initialisations and updates or permits sequential writes within a tick as we do here. Recently, Mandel *et al.*'s *clock domains* [33] and Gemünde's *clock refinement* [34] provide sequences of micro-level computations within an outer clock tick. This also increases sequential expressiveness albeit in an upside-down fashion compared to our approach. Our work on SC aims to reconstruct the scope of a synchronous instant on top of the primitive notion of sequential composition. In the clock refinement approach clocks are the only sequencing mechanism, so micro-level sequencing is implemented in terms of lower-level clocks.

An acknowledged strength of synchronous languages is their formal foundation [6], which facilitates formal verification, timing analyses, and inclusion results of the type presented here. Our algebraic approach based on $I(\mathbb{D})$ generalises the "must-cannot" analysis for constructiveness [15] and the ternary analysis for synchronous control flow [35] and circuits [30,31]. The extension lies in the ability to deal with non-initialisation ($\bot$) and re-initialisation ($\top$) in sequential control flow, which the analyses [15,35,30,31] cannot handle. Due to the two-sided nature of intervals our semantics permits the modelling of instantaneous reaction to absence, a definitive feature of Esterel-style synchrony for control-flow languages. In contrast, the *balance equations* (see, e.g., [36]) or the *clock calculus* (see, e.g., [3]) of synchronous reactive data flow do not handle reaction to absence. These analyses are concerned with inter-tick causality (i.e., in which ticks a signal is present) rather than intra-tick causality (i.e., presence or absence in a given tick) which we focus on here. Reflected into $I(\mathbb{D})$, Lustre clocks collapse the signal status (within a tick) to either $\bot$ (value not initialised or computed) or $[0, \top]$ (value computed). However, since each program abstracts to a continuous function on $I(\mathbb{D})$-valued environments our model fits naturally into the Kahn-style fixed-points semantics and scheduling analysis for synchronous block diagrams [37,38].

5   Conclusion and Outlook

On the theoretical side, we have identified an abstract value domain $I(\mathbb{D})$ with special topological features. First, it has an interval structure in which lower and upper bounds are indispensable when dealing with the non-monotonic nature

causality analysis (cf. [39]). The generality of this domain makes it possible to handle co-/contra-variant fixed point computations by means of approximations in the intervals much in the style of Berry's must and cannot constructiveness analysis. Second, this domain has two complementary dimensions $\preceq$ and $\sqsubseteq$ which makes it sensitive not only to the concurrent but also the sequential interaction of a synchronous object. This is in contrast to Esterel, Quartz or ternary simulation where all micro-steps are considered concurrent. With this at hand, we have given a new functional interpretation $\langle\!\langle \_ \rangle\!\rangle$ to Berry's behavioural semantics of Esterel and have proven that SC (Δ_*) is indeed a conservative extension of Esterel. In view of Prop. 1 we propose to consider the Extended Berry Response Function $\langle\!\langle \_ \rangle\!\rangle$ as the analogue of Berry's ternary constructive semantics in the SC setting. It matches Berry's semantics on initialised programs (Δ_1) and additionally verifies constructive initialisation on general programs (Δ_0).

It should not be difficult to generalise the linear data structure $\mathbb{D}$ to capture signal protocols that span more than only one "init-update-read" cycle in order to define similar analyses for Δ_2, Δ_3 and so on. Here we introduce the essential ideas for Δ_0/Δ_1 only, anticipating generalisations to richer sequential data types in follow-up work.

On the practical side, we have shown how to emulate signals with variables, even in a concurrent setting. Furthermore, we can do so with constant code size increase per signal, $i.\,e.$, with overall code size increase that is at worst linear in the size of the program. Like in the sequential case, the transformation still properly handles schizophrenia. Thus, for schizophrenic signals, this is a clear improvement over existing techniques for eliminating schizophrenia at the Esterel level. Note that here we focus on handling schizophrenia for signals. This does not address reincarnation in general, $i.\,e.$, the repeated execution of statements within a tick; this still must be addressed separately by one of the existing techniques [11,12,13].

More fundamentally, emulating signals by plain, standard variables closes a conceptual gap between programming and implementation. The statements of the variable-based program can be mapped directly to the run-time behaviour of a software implementation, or alternatively to the gate-and-wire structure of a hardware implementation. There are no implicit mechanisms, such as default absence, that a programmer has no control over and that must be delegated to a synthesis tool. Every synchronous language ultimately depends on sequential variable accesses somewhere downstream in the compilation path. For uniformity, therefore, it is expedient to build on notions of constructiveness which are sensitive to micro-step sequential behaviour such as Δ_0, Δ_1, ..., Δ_*, at the outset.

References

1. Hansen, P.B.: Java's insecure parallelism. SIGPLAN Not. 34, 38–45 (1999)
2. Lee, E.A.: The problem with threads. IEEE Computer 39, 33–42 (2006)
3. Caspi, P., Pilaud, D., Halbwachs, N., Plaice, J.A.: Lustre: a declarative language for programming synchronous systems. In: Proceedings of the 14th ACM SIGACT-SIGPLAN Symposium on Principles of Programming Languages (POPL 1987), Munich, Germany, pp. 178–188. ACM (1987)

4. Guernic, P.L., Goutier, T., Borgne, M.L., Maire, C.L.: Programming real time applications with SIGNAL. Proceedings of the IEEE 79, 1321–1336 (1991)
5. Berry, G., Gonthier, G.: The Esterel synchronous programming language: Design, semantics, implementation. Science of Computer Programming 19, 87–152 (1992)
6. Benveniste, A., Caspi, P., Edwards, S.A., Halbwachs, N., Guernic, P.L., de Simone, R.: The Synchronous Languages Twelve Years Later. In: Proc. IEEE, Special Issue on Embedded Systems, Piscataway, NJ, USA, vol. 91, pp. 64–83. IEEE (2003)
7. André, C.: SyncCharts: A visual representation of reactive behaviors. Technical Report RR 95–52, rev. RR 96–56, I3S, Sophia-Antipolis, France (1996)
8. Schneider, K.: The synchronous programming language Quartz. Internal report, Department of Computer Science, University of Kaiserslautern, Kaiserslautern, Germany (2010), http://es.cs.uni-kl.de/publications/datarsg/Schn09.pdf
9. von Hanxleden, R., Mendler, M., Aguado, J., Duderstadt, B., Fuhrmann, I., Motika, C., Mercer, S., O'Brien, O., Roop, P.: Sequentially Constructive Concurrency—A conservative extension of the synchronous model of computation. Technical Report 1308, Christian-Albrechts-Universität zu Kiel, Department of Computer Science (2013)) ISSN 2192-6247
10. von Hanxleden, R., Mendler, M., Aguado, J., Duderstadt, B., Fuhrmann, I., Motika, C., Mercer, S., O'Brien, O.: Sequentially Constructive Concurrency—A conservative extension of the synchronous model of computation. In: Proc. Design, Automation and Test in Europe Conference (DATE 2013), Grenoble, France, pp. 581–586. IEEE (2013)
11. Berry, G.: The foundations of Esterel. In: Plotkin, G., Stirling, C., Tofte, M. (eds.) Proof, Language, and Interaction: Essays in Honour of Robin Milner, pp. 425–454. MIT Press, Cambridge (2000)
12. Schneider, K., Wenz, M.: A new method for compiling schizophrenic synchronous programs. In: International Conference on Compilers, Architecture, and Synthesis for Embedded Systems (CASES), Atlanta, Georgia, USA, pp. 49–58. ACM (2001)
13. Tardieu, O., de Simone, R.: Curing schizophrenia by program rewriting in Esterel. In: Proceedings of the Second ACM-IEEE International Conference on Formal Methods and Models for Codesign (MEMOCODE 2004), San Diego, CA, USA (2004)
14. Aguado, J., Mendler, M., von Hanxleden, R., Fuhrmann, I.: Grounding synchronous deterministic concurrency in sequential programming. Technical report, Christian-Albrechts-Universität zu Kiel, Department of Computer Science (2014) ISSN 2192-6247
15. Berry, G.: The Constructive Semantics of Pure Esterel. Draft Book, Version 3.0, Centre de Mathématiques Appliqées, Ecole des Mines de Paris and INRIA, 2004 route des Lucioles, 06902 Sophia-Antipolis CDX, France (2002), http://www-sop.inria.fr/members/Gerard.Berry/Papers/EsterelConstructiveBook.zip
16. Mendler, M., Shiple, T.R., Berry, G.: Constructive boolean circuits and the exactness of timed ternary simulation. Formal Methods in System Design 40, 283–329 (2012)
17. Edwards, S.A.: Tutorial: Compiling concurrent languages for sequential processors. ACM Transactions on Design Automation of Electronic Systems 8, 141–187 (2003)
18. Potop-Butucaru, D., Edwards, S.A., Berry, G.: Compiling Esterel, vol. 86. Springer, P.O. Box 17, 3300 AA Dordrecht, The Netherlands (2007)
19. Boussinot, F.: Reactive C: An extension of C to program reactive systems. Software Practice and Experience 21, 401–428 (1991)
20. Boussinot, F.: Fairthreads: mixing cooperative and preemptive threads in C. Concurrency and Computation: Practice and Experience 18, 445–469 (2006)

21. Andalam, S., Roop, P.S., Girault, A.: Deterministic, predictable and light-weight multithreading using pret-c. In: Proceedings of the Conference on Design, Automation and Test in Europe (DATE 2010), Dresden, Germany, pp. 1653–1656 (2010)
22. von Hanxleden, R.: SyncCharts in C—A Proposal for Light-Weight, Deterministic Concurrency. In: Proceedings of the International Conference on Embedded Software (EMSOFT 2009), Grenoble, France, pp. 225–234. ACM (2009)
23. Tardieu, O., Edwards, S.A.: Scheduling-independent threads and exceptions in SHIM. In: Proceedings of the International Conference on Embedded Software (EMSOFT 2006), Seoul, South Korea, pp. 142–151. ACM (2006)
24. Hoare, C.A.R.: Communicating Sequential Processes. Prentice Hall, Upper Saddle River (1985)
25. Vechev, M., Yahav, E., Raman, R., Sarkar, V.: Automatic verification of determinism for structured parallel programs. In: Cousot, R., Martel, M. (eds.) SAS 2010. LNCS, vol. 6337, pp. 455–471. Springer, Heidelberg (2010)
26. Leung, A., Gupta, M., Agarwal, Y., Gupta, R., Jhala, R., Lerner, S.: Verifying GPU kernels by test amplification. In: Programming Language Design and Implementation, PLDI 2012, pp. 383–394. ACM, New York (2012)
27. Yuki, T., Feautrier, P., Rajopadye, S., Saraswat, V.: Array dataflow analysis for polyhedral X10 programs. In: Principles and Practice of Parallel Programming, PPoPP 2013, pp. 23–34. ACM, New York (2013)
28. Kuper, L., Turon, A., Krishnaswami, N.R., Newton, R.R.: Freeze after writing: Quasi-deterministic parallel programming with LVars. In: Principles of Programming Languages, POPL 2014. ACM, New York (2014)
29. Brzozowski, J.A., Seger, C.J.H.: Asynchronous Circuits. Springer, New York (1995)
30. Malik, S.: Analysis of cyclic combinational circuits. IEEE Transactions on Computer-Aided Design of Integrated Circuits and Systems 13, 950–956 (1994)
31. Shiple, T.R., Berry, G., Touati, H.: Constructive Analysis of Cyclic Circuits. In: Proc. European Design and Test Conference (ED&TC 1996), Paris, France, Los Alamitos, California, USA, pp. 328–333. IEEE Computer Society Press (1996)
32. Schneider, K., Brandt, J., Schüle, T., Türk, T.: Improving constructiveness in code generators. In: Maraninchi, F., Pouzet, M., Roy, V. (eds.) Int'l Workshop on Synchronous Languages, Applications, and Programming, SLAP 2005, Edinburgh, Scotland, UK. ENTCS, pp. 1–19 (2005)
33. Mandel, L., Pasteur, C., Pouzet, M.: Time refinement in a functional synchronous language. In: ACM SIGPLAN Int. Symp. on Principles and Practice of Declarative Programming, PPDP 2013, pp. 169–180. ACM, New York (2013)
34. Gemünde, M.: Clock Refinement in Imperative Synchronous Languages. PhD thesis, University of Kaiserslautern (2013)
35. Schneider, K., Brandt, J., Schuele, T.: Causality analysis of synchronous programs with delayed actions. In: Conference on Compilers, Architecture, and Synthesis for Embedded Systems (CASES), Washington, D.C., USA, pp. 179–189. ACM (2004)
36. Lee, E.A., Messerschmitt, D.G.: Synchronous data flow. In: Proceedings of the IEEE, vol. 75, pp. 1235–1245. IEEE Computer Society Press (1987)
37. Edwards, S.A., Lee, E.A.: The Semantics and Execution of a Synchronous Block-Diagram Language. In: Science of Computer Programming, vol. 48, Elsevier (2003), http://www1.cs.columbia.edu/~sedwards/papers/edwards2003semantics.pdf
38. Pouzet, M., Raymond, P.: Modular static scheduling of synchronous data-flow networks: an efficient symbolic representation. In: EMSOFT, pp. 215–224 (2009)
39. Aguado, J., Mendler, M.: Constructive semantics for instantaneous reactions. Theoretical Computer Science 241, 931–961 (2011)

The Duality of Construction

Paul Downen and Zena M. Ariola

University of Oregon
{pdownen,ariola}@cs.uoregon.edu

Abstract. We explore the duality of construction and deconstruction in the presence of different evaluation strategies. We characterize an evaluation strategy by the notion of substitutability, given by defining what is a value and a co-value, and we present an equational theory that takes the strategy as a parameter. The theory may be extended with new logical connectives, in the form of user-defined data and co-data types, which are duals of one another. Finally, we explore a calculus with composite evaluation strategies that allow for more flexibility over evaluation order by mingling multiple primitive strategies within a single program.

1 Introduction

Over two decades ago, Filinski [5] discovered the dual relationship between the call-by-value and call-by-name evaluation strategies by relating programs that produce information with continuations that consume information. Since then, this duality has been studied from the perspective of category theory [5,10] and proof theory [3,11,12]. In particular, the sequent calculus has provided a fruitful foundation for this study, due to the inherent duality in the form of sequent judgments: assumptions act as inputs and conclusions act as outputs. This notion has been formalized [3,11] as foundational calculi which execute at the level of an abstract machine. For example, the inference rule for implication on the left of a sequent is viewed as the typing rule for a call-stack in a Krivine machine.

More recently [13,8,4], polarization in logic has been used as a type-based account of evaluation order, which divides types into two classifications, positive and negative, based on properties of their inference rules. On the one hand, positive types are defined by their rules of introduction, *i.e.*, construction, and are given a call-by-value interpretation. The use of a positively typed value is given by cases over the possible constructions, in the style of data types in functional languages like ML. On the other hand, negative types are defined by their rules of elimination, *i.e.*, observation, and are given a call-by-name interpretation. In order to produce a negatively typed value, we must consider all possible observations, giving us a message-passing programming style. If there is ever an apparent ambiguity on the evaluation order of a program, the type is consulted and the order is determined by considering the type's polarity.

The primary focus on either introduction or elimination divides programs into two parts: concrete programs that are constructed and abstract programs defined by cases. This division describes the behavior of programs as an interaction

Z. Shao (Ed.): ESOP 2014, LNCS 8410, pp. 249–269, 2014.

between construction and deconstruction, with two dual ways of orienting the roles between a consumer and a producer: data with concrete producers and abstract consumers, and co-data with abstract producers and concrete consumers. In high-level languages, both data and co-data are useful tools for organizing information in programs, and may be interpreted by different evaluation strategies: we may want strictly evaluated terms defined by dynamic dispatch on their observations (as in an object-oriented language), and likewise we may want lazily evaluated terms that are defined by construction (as in Haskell). Polarized logic can account for this behavior by translating a program into one with polarities to provide the desired evaluation order, much like how a continuation-passing style transformation can define the evaluation order for a language.

The goal of this paper is to provide a general account of the data and co-data definitional paradigms along with an equational theory that directly supports evaluation according to different strategies, expressing both the duality between strategies and the two paradigms. A better understanding of the data and (co-)data paradigms may eventually lead to a more suitable foundation for studying the design of languages that contain both functional and object-oriented features. Since the sequent calculus exposes details that appear in abstract machines while still maintaining high-level reasoning principles, it may serve as a bridge between programming languages and their low-level representations, for example as an intermediate language in a compiler.

We develop a sequent calculus that is parameterized by a chosen evaluation strategy, similar to the parametric λ-calculus [9], which guides the notion of substitution in the calculus. The goal of choosing a strategy is to eliminate the fundamental inconsistency of the calculus by eliminating the single point of conflict between producers and consumers. The equational theory is untyped since any conflicts that arise are resolved by the strategy, meaning that we do not need to consult the type of a program during evaluation. We begin by examining the core calculus (Section 3) which expresses the impact of an evaluation strategy on the behavior of a program as a restriction of what may be substituted for a variable. We take notions of call-by-name and call-by-value as our primary examples for characterizing strategies, but also show a characterization of call-by-need and its dual, demonstrating that there are more than two possible strategies.

Atop the core calculus of substitution, we consider functions (Section 4) and describe their behavior in terms of β and η rules. Unlike in the λ-calculus and previous formulations of the sequent calculus [3,11], these same rules apply in every evaluation strategy, and we show that they provide a complete definition of functions. Next, we extend the language with basic data and co-data types (Section 5), illustrating two forms of pairs ($\otimes$, &) and two forms of sums ($\oplus$, $\mathbin{⅋}$) that correspond to similar concepts in Girard's linear logic [6] and polarized logic [13,4]. As with functions, we give a similar $\beta\eta$ characterization of the basic (co-)data types that does not reference the chosen evaluation strategy, and show that this characterization derives the various "lifting" (ς) rules of Wadler's sequent calculus [11,12]. Finally, we use the common $\beta\eta$ theme in order to present a general notion of user-defined data and co-data types (Section 6) which encompasses all of the previous types. On the one hand, since we are working in an untyped setting, (co-)data type declarations are used for introducing new ways to form structures and abstractions in a program, independently of a static type system. On the other hand, (co-)data type declarations are inspired by logic and may be seen as describing a static type system for the parametric sequent calculus.

We also consider how to compose several strategies into a single composite strategy (Section 7). This allows a single program to be written with call-by-name and call-by-value parts, or any other combination of two (or more) strategies. To maintain consistency of the calculus, we separate the (co-)data types into different *kinds* that denote different strategies, so that well-kinded programs are consistent. When considering only one strategy, this degenerates into the previous untyped equational theory, and for two strategies the approach is similar to Zeilberger's [14] "bi-typed" system, except generalized to also work with any number of additional strategies like call-by-need (or its dual).

Our contributions are: (1) We develop a parametric equational theory for the sequent calculus that may be instantiated by various strategies. We express the essence of a strategy by what may be substituted for a (co-)variable. In other words, a strategy is identified by a choice of values and co-values. (2) We enrich the sequent calculus with user-defined data and co-data types, whose behavior are defined exclusively in terms of β and η principles that do not refer to the chosen strategy. These two principles provide the basis for all user-defined (co-)data types, and may be used to derive other properties like Wadler's ς rules [11]. (3) We give call-by-value and call-by-name strategies for the equational theory that are sound and complete with respect to known CPS transformations [3] and their extension with user-defined (co-)data types. (4) We generalize the known duality of call-by-value and call-by-name evaluation in the sequent calculus [3,11] to be parametric over evaluation strategies and types, giving a mechanical procedure for generating the dual language for any choice of connectives and evaluation strategy, as expressed in the parametric calculus. (5) We exhibit that the parametric theory supports more intricate notions of evaluation strategy by instantiating it with a call-by-need strategy and generating its dual. (6) We illustrate how to compose two or more primitive strategies, such as call-by-value, call-by-name, and call-by-need, into a single composite strategy, so that a program may selectively choose and switch between several evaluation strategies at run-time.

2 Introduction to the Sequent Calculus

When implementing an evaluator for the λ-calculus, it becomes necessary to find the next reduction, or step, to perform in a term. Searching for the next reduction is not always trivial, since it may be buried deep inside the syntax of the term. For instance, consider the syntax tree for the term $(((\lambda x.M)\ N_1)\ N_2)\ N_3$ as shown in Figure 1(a), where the name α is a placeholder for the rest of the surrounding context. The next step is to call the function $(\lambda x.M)$ with the argument N_1, but

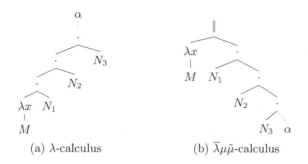

(a) λ-calculus   (b) $\overline{\lambda}\mu\tilde{\mu}$-calculus

Fig. 1. Re-association of the abstract-syntax tree for function calls

the term for this function call is at the bottom of the tree, and to reach it we need to search past the function calls with N_3 and N_2 as arguments. As an alternate representation of the same program, we can re-associate the syntax tree so that the next step to perform is located at the top of the tree, as shown in Figure 1(b). Imagine that we take hold of the edge connecting the function to its call and drag it upward so that the rest of the tree hangs off both sides of the edge, turning the context inside out. Syntactically, this amounts to converting the evaluation context into a term in its own right, *i.e.*, a *co-term*. Written out sequentially using Curien and Herbelin's $\overline{\lambda}\mu\tilde{\mu}$-calculus [3], the re-associated program is the *command* $\langle \lambda x.M \| N_1 \cdot N_2 \cdot N_3 \cdot \alpha \rangle$, where $\cdot$ builds a call-stack and associates to the right. From the perspective of the Curry-Howard correspondence, this change in orientation in the syntax of programming languages corresponds with a similar change in the structure of proofs. Just as the λ-calculus corresponds with natural deduction, the $\overline{\lambda}\mu\tilde{\mu}$-calculus corresponds with the sequent calculus.

Fundamentally, the $\overline{\lambda}\mu\tilde{\mu}$-calculus describes computation as the interaction between a term and a co-term. For example, if we evaluate the program in Figure 1(b) according to a call-by-name strategy, where a function call is performed without evaluating the argument, we get the reduction

$$\langle \lambda x.M \| N_1 \cdot N_2 \cdot N_3 \cdot \alpha \rangle \twoheadrightarrow \langle M\{N_1/x\} \| N_2 \cdot N_3 \cdot \alpha \rangle$$

where we take the first argument, N_1, in the co-term and substitute it for x in the body of the function. Afterward, we evaluate the interaction between $M\{N_1/x\}$ and the remaining co-term. Alternatively, we may want to consider a call-by-value strategy, where we evaluate N_1 before calling the function. As a way to keep reduction at the top of the syntax tree, a $\tilde{\mu}$-abstraction can give a name to N_1. The co-term $\tilde{\mu}x.\langle M \| N_2 \cdot N_3 \cdot \alpha \rangle$ should be read as **let** $x = \square$ **in** $(M\ N_2\ N_3)$ in the context α. Therefore, we can make the call-by-value reduction

$$\langle \lambda x.M \| N_1 \cdot N_2 \cdot N_3 \cdot \alpha \rangle \twoheadrightarrow \langle N_1 \| \tilde{\mu}x.\langle M \| N_2 \cdot N_3 \cdot \alpha \rangle \rangle$$

with the understanding that we must first fully evaluate N_1 to a value before substituting it for x in $\langle M \| N_2 \cdot N_3 \cdot \alpha \rangle$. In addition to $\tilde{\mu}$-abstraction, we have the dual notion of μ-abstraction that allows a term to name its co-term.

Therefore, we can close off the command by introducing α, giving us the term $\mu\alpha.\langle(\lambda x.M)\|N_1 \cdot N_2 \cdot N_3 \cdot \alpha\rangle$.

The $\overline{\lambda}\mu\tilde{\mu}$-calculus takes implication (functions) as its only logical connective (type constructor). However, we want to explore a variety of other connectives in the sequent calculus. Furthermore, once we have a method for declaring new type constructors, functions just become another instance of a user-defined type. For this reason, we temporarily forgo functions and more closely examine the core language of substitution.

3   The Parametric $\mu\tilde{\mu}$ Core

We now consider the μ and $\tilde{\mu}$-abstractions which lie at the heart of the $\overline{\lambda}\mu\tilde{\mu}$-calculus. More specifically, programs in the $\mu\tilde{\mu}$-calculus are defined as follows:

$$c \in Command ::= \langle v\|e\rangle \quad v \in Term ::= x \mid \mu\alpha.c \quad e \in CoTerm ::= \alpha \mid \tilde{\mu}x.c$$

The μ and $\tilde{\mu}$-abstractions, $\mu\alpha.c$ and $\tilde{\mu}x.c$ respectively, embody the primitive variable binding structure of the language, giving a name to a (co-)term in an underlying command. It follows that during evaluation, these abstractions implement a notion of substitution. The μ axiom gives control to the term (producer) by substituting the co-term for a co-variable, whereas the $\tilde{\mu}$ gives control to the co-term (consumer) by performing the opposite substitution:

$$(\mu) \qquad \langle\mu\alpha.c\|e\rangle = c\{e/\alpha\} \qquad (\tilde{\mu}) \qquad \langle v\|\tilde{\mu}x.c\rangle = c\{v/x\}$$

As is, this theory is not consistent, as shown by the fact that the μ and $\tilde{\mu}$ axioms fight for control in the command $\langle\mu\alpha.c\|\tilde{\mu}x.c'\rangle$[1]. To restore consistency, we can give priority to one axiom over the other [3]:

> Call-by-value consists in giving priority to the (μ) axiom, while call-by-name gives priority to the $(\tilde{\mu})$ axiom.

In lieu of considering two (or more) different theories that place restrictions where necessary, we instead give a single parametric equational theory that does not assume a particular evaluation strategy *a priori*. The theory is parameterized by a choice of *strategy*, $\mathcal{S}$, which is defined as a set of *values* and *co-values* that are subsets of terms and co-terms, respectively. The axioms for the parametric core $\mu\tilde{\mu}_{\mathcal{S}}$-calculus are given in Figure 2, where the meta-variables V and E range over the set of values and co-values given by $\mathcal{S}$, respectively. In addition to the substitution axioms, $\tilde{\mu}_V$ and μ_E, we also have extensionality axioms, η_μ and $\eta_{\tilde{\mu}}$, that eliminate trivial μ- and $\tilde{\mu}$-abstractions. Note that all equations follow the usual restrictions to avoid capture of static variables. For instance, α is not a free variable of v in the η_μ axiom of Figure 2.

Since the μ_E and $\tilde{\mu}_V$ axioms are restricted by the strategy, carefully chosen combinations of values and co-values may avoid the fundamental inconsistency of the calculus. The simplest consistent choice of (co-)values that we can make is to always exclude either μ or $\tilde{\mu}$-abstractions, as shown in Figure 3. We can

---

[1] If $\alpha \notin FV(c)$ and $x \notin FV(c')$ then $\langle\mu\alpha.c\|\tilde{\mu}x.c'\rangle = c, c'$, equating arbitrary c and c'.

$$(\mu_E) \quad \langle \mu\alpha.c \| E \rangle = c\,\{E/\alpha\} \qquad\qquad (\eta_\mu) \quad \mu\alpha.\langle v \| \alpha \rangle = v$$
$$(\tilde{\mu}_V) \quad \langle V \| \tilde{\mu}x.c \rangle = c\,\{V/x\} \qquad\qquad (\eta_{\tilde{\mu}}) \quad \tilde{\mu}x.\langle x \| e \rangle = e$$

Fig. 2. The parametric equational theory $\mu\tilde{\mu}_S$

$$V \in Value_\mathcal{N} ::= v \quad E \in CoValue_\mathcal{N} ::= \alpha \quad V \in Value_\mathcal{V} ::= x \quad E \in CoValue_\mathcal{V} ::= e$$

Fig. 3. Call-by-name ($\mathcal{N}$) and call-by-value ($\mathcal{V}$) strategies of $\mu\tilde{\mu}_S$

then form a core call-by-name evaluation strategy, $\mathcal{N}$, by letting every term be a value, and restricting co-values to just co-variables. Dually, we have a core call-by-value evaluation strategy, $\mathcal{V}$, by letting every co-term be a co-value, and restricting values to just variables. To disambiguate the different instances of the parametric equational theory $\mu\tilde{\mu}_S$, we write $\mu\tilde{\mu}_\mathcal{N} \vdash c = c'$ and $\mu\tilde{\mu}_\mathcal{V} \vdash c = c'$ to mean that c and c' are equated by the $\mathcal{N}$ and $\mathcal{V}$ instances of the parametric theory, respectively. Notice that in both the $\mathcal{N}$ and $\mathcal{V}$ strategies, (co-)variables are considered co-values, which is a condition we always assume to hold when speaking of strategies in general. Moreover, the $\mu\tilde{\mu}_S$ equational theory is closed under substitution of (co-)values for (co-)variables.

Finally, we can also give a *continuation-passing style* (CPS) transformation that maps sequent calculus programs to the λ-calculus. The CPS transformation can be used as a reference point for reasoning about the correctness of the equational theory through the usual β and η axioms in the resulting λ-calculus term. In Figure 4, we recount the call-by-name and call-by-value CPS transformations given in [3] for the core calculus, denoted $[\![\_]\!]^\mathcal{N}$ and $[\![\_]\!]^\mathcal{V}$. The $\mu\tilde{\mu}_\mathcal{N}$ and $\mu\tilde{\mu}_\mathcal{V}$ equational theories are sound and complete with respect to $\beta\eta$ equality of the λ-calculus terms resulting from the $[\![\_]\!]^\mathcal{N}$ and $[\![\_]\!]^\mathcal{V}$ transformations, respectively.

4   Functions

Having first laid out the core $\mu\tilde{\mu}_S$-calculus, we consider the behavior of functions in more detail. Using the same notation as the $\overline{\lambda}\mu\tilde{\mu}$-calculus [3], we extend the core $\mu\tilde{\mu}_S$-calculus with the following syntax, giving us the $\mu\tilde{\mu}_S^{\rightarrow}$-calculus:

$$v \in Term ::= \ldots \mid \lambda x.v \qquad\qquad e \in CoTerm ::= \ldots \mid v \cdot e$$

Functions are expressed as λ-abstraction terms ($\lambda x.v$), the same as in the λ-calculus. A function call, on the other hand, is represented by the co-term $v \cdot e$, where v stands for the function's argument and e for the calling context, which we first saw in Section 2. Additionally, we may extend our core call-by-name and call-by-value strategies from Figure 3 to account for functions, as shown in Figure 5. In the call-by-value strategy $\mathcal{V}$, we admit λ-abstractions as values and continue to let every co-term be a co-value. In the call-by-name strategy $\mathcal{N}$, we continue to let every term be a value, and admit the co-term $v \cdot E$ as a co-value, representing a λ-calculus context of the form $E[\square\ v]$.

$$[\![\langle v \| e \rangle]\!]^{\mathcal{N}} \triangleq [\![e]\!]^{\mathcal{N}} \, [\![v]\!]^{\mathcal{N}} \qquad\qquad [\![\langle v \| e \rangle]\!]^{\mathcal{V}} \triangleq [\![v]\!]^{\mathcal{V}} \, [\![e]\!]^{\mathcal{V}}$$

$$[\![\alpha]\!]^{\mathcal{N}} \triangleq \lambda x.x \, \alpha \qquad [\![x]\!]^{\mathcal{N}} \triangleq x \qquad\qquad [\![x]\!]^{\mathcal{V}} \triangleq \lambda \alpha.\alpha \, x \qquad [\![\alpha]\!]^{\mathcal{V}} \triangleq \alpha$$

$$[\![\tilde{\mu}x.c]\!]^{\mathcal{N}} \triangleq \lambda x.[\![c]\!]^{\mathcal{N}} \quad [\![\mu\alpha.c]\!]^{\mathcal{N}} \triangleq \lambda \alpha.[\![c]\!]^{\mathcal{N}} \qquad [\![\mu\alpha.c]\!]^{\mathcal{V}} \triangleq \lambda \alpha.[\![c]\!]^{\mathcal{V}} \quad [\![\tilde{\mu}x.c]\!]^{\mathcal{V}} \triangleq \lambda x.[\![c]\!]^{\mathcal{V}}$$

Fig. 4. Call-by-name ($\mathcal{N}$) and call-by-value ($\mathcal{V}$) CPS transformations of $\mu\tilde{\mu}_S$

$$V \in Value_{\mathcal{N}} ::= v \qquad\qquad V \in Value_{\mathcal{V}} ::= x \mid \lambda x.v$$

$$E \in CoValue_{\mathcal{N}} ::= \alpha \mid v \cdot E \qquad\qquad E \in CoValue_{\mathcal{V}} ::= e$$

Fig. 5. Call-by-name ($\mathcal{N}$) and call-by-value ($\mathcal{V}$) strategies of $\mu\tilde{\mu}_S^{\rightarrow}$

Now, we need to determine which axioms to add to our equational theory in order to give a complete account for the run-time behavior of functions. It is obvious we need an axiom for β reduction, as given in [3] for $\overline{\lambda}\mu\tilde{\mu}$, since that is the primary computational rule for functions. In addition, we also consider an axiom for η equality, giving functions a notion of extensionality similar to the λ-calculus. We therefore extend the core $\mu\tilde{\mu}_S$ equational theory from Figure 2 with the two rules for functions in Figure 6 to obtain the $\mu\tilde{\mu}_S^{\rightarrow}$-calculus.

Notice that unlike in [3,11], these rules define the behavior of functions independently of the strategy since the $\beta^{\rightarrow}$ and $\eta^{\rightarrow}$ axioms do not reference V or E — the evaluation strategy is implemented by the core $\mu\tilde{\mu}_S$-calculus alone.

We should ask ourselves if these rules make sense computationally, so that a consistent strategy for the core calculus is still consistent when extended with functions. The $\beta^{\rightarrow}$ axiom is applicable to any command between a λ-abstraction and a call, and dissolves the function call into a $\tilde{\mu}$ binding, thereby relying on the consistency of the strategy in the core $\mu\tilde{\mu}_S$-calculus. For example, with the call-by-value strategy $\mathcal{V}$, the $\tilde{\mu}$-abstraction bears the responsibility of ensuring that the argument v' to a function call is a value before substituting it into the body of the function — if v' is the non-value $\mu\alpha.c$ then it gets to go first by means of the μ_E rule. On the other hand, the $\eta^{\rightarrow}$ axiom is restricted to apply only to variables. Intuitively, the $\eta^{\rightarrow}$ axiom states that an unknown function is indistinguishable from a λ-abstraction. Recall that the core $\mu\tilde{\mu}_S$ theory is closed under substitution of values for variables, so the usual $\eta^{\rightarrow}$ axiom that applies to values is derivable within the equational theory. This restriction is crucial for preserving consistency of certain strategies, like the $\mathcal{V}$ strategy, and comes out for free from the meaning of $\tilde{\mu}$-abstractions in the core calculus.

We should also ask ourselves if these rules are complete enough to describe the other behavioral properties of functions. For instance, previous reduction systems for the sequent calculus [11,8] include a family of ς rules that lift sub-computations to the top of a command. For implication, this takes the form of axioms that lift out the sub-expressions of a function call:

$$(\varsigma_x^{\rightarrow}) \quad v \cdot e = \tilde{\mu}f.\langle v \| \tilde{\mu}x.\langle f \| x \cdot e \rangle \rangle \qquad (\varsigma_\alpha^{\rightarrow}) \quad V \cdot e = \tilde{\mu}f.\langle \mu\alpha.\langle f \| V \cdot \alpha \rangle \| e \rangle$$

$$(\beta^{\rightarrow}) \qquad \langle \lambda x.v \| v' \cdot e \rangle = \langle v' \| \tilde{\mu} x.\langle v \| e \rangle \rangle \qquad (\eta^{\rightarrow}) \qquad \lambda x.\mu \alpha.\langle z \| x \cdot \alpha \rangle = z$$

Fig. 6. The β and η axioms of the $\mu \tilde{\mu} \vec{s}$ equational theory

$$[\![\lambda x.v]\!]^{\mathcal{N}} \triangleq \lambda(x,\beta).[\![v]\!]^{\mathcal{N}} \beta \qquad\qquad [\![\lambda x.v]\!]^{\mathcal{V}} \triangleq \lambda \alpha.\alpha \; \lambda(x,\beta).[\![v]\!]^{\mathcal{V}} \beta$$

$$[\![v \cdot e]\!]^{\mathcal{N}} \triangleq \lambda x.[\![e]\!]^{\mathcal{N}} \lambda \beta.x \; ([\![v]\!]^{\mathcal{N}}, \beta) \qquad [\![v \cdot e]\!]^{\mathcal{V}} \triangleq \lambda x.[\![v]\!]^{\mathcal{V}} \lambda y.x \; (y, [\![e]\!]^{\mathcal{V}})$$

Fig. 7. Call-by-name ($\mathcal{N}$) and call-by-value ($\mathcal{V}$) CPS transformations of functions

The ς rules are necessary for making progress with some programs. For example, call-by-value evaluation of the command $\langle z \| \mu \alpha.c \cdot e \rangle$ cannot proceed by β reduction, and since the non-value argument $\mu \alpha.c$ is buried inside of a function call, it needs to be lifted out for it to take control so that evaluation can continue. A course-grained version of the lifting axiom, which lifts out both parts of a function call

$$(\varsigma^{\rightarrow}) \qquad\qquad v \cdot e = \tilde{\mu} f.\langle v \| \tilde{\mu} x.\langle \tilde{\mu} \alpha.\langle f \| x \cdot \alpha \rangle \| e \rangle \rangle$$

is easily derived from the $\eta_{\tilde{\mu}}$, $\eta^{\rightarrow}$, and $\beta^{\rightarrow}$ axioms as follows:

$$v \cdot e =_{\eta_{\tilde{\mu}}} \tilde{\mu} f.\langle f \| v \cdot e \rangle =_{\eta^{\rightarrow}} \tilde{\mu} f.\langle \lambda x.\mu \alpha.\langle f \| x \cdot \alpha \rangle \| v \cdot e \rangle =_{\beta^{\rightarrow}} \tilde{\mu} f.\langle v \| \tilde{\mu} x.\langle \mu \alpha.\langle f \| x \cdot \alpha \rangle \| e \rangle \rangle$$

Furthermore, the $\varsigma^{\rightarrow}$ axiom can be broken down into the more atomic rules within the existing equational theory. The derivation of $\varsigma_{\alpha}^{\rightarrow}$ from $\varsigma^{\rightarrow}$ is a consequence of the $\tilde{\mu}_V$ axiom, and we can derive the $\varsigma_x^{\rightarrow}$ axiom as follows:

$$v \cdot e =_{\varsigma^{\rightarrow}} \tilde{\mu} f.\langle v \| \tilde{\mu} x.\langle \mu \alpha.\langle f \| x \cdot \alpha \rangle \| e \rangle \rangle$$
$$=_{\tilde{\mu}_V} \tilde{\mu} f.\langle v \| \tilde{\mu} x.\langle f \| \tilde{\mu} f'.\langle x \| \tilde{\mu} x'.\langle \mu \alpha.\langle f' \| x' \cdot \alpha \rangle \| e \rangle \rangle \rangle \rangle =_{\varsigma^{\rightarrow}} \tilde{\mu} f.\langle v \| \tilde{\mu} x.\langle f \| x \cdot e \rangle \rangle$$

Therefore, the combination of $\beta^{\rightarrow}$ and $\eta^{\rightarrow}$ axioms is powerful enough in the parametric equational theory $\mu \tilde{\mu} \vec{s}$ to express other known behavioral properties of functions that are needed for certain strategies.

We can achieve a more concrete sense of completeness for the specific cases of call-by-name and call-by-value functions by extending our core CPS transformations for the $\mathcal{N}$ and $\mathcal{V}$ strategies, as in $\overline{\lambda} \mu \tilde{\mu}$ [3] and shown in Figure 7, with clauses that handle function abstractions and calls. The $\mu \tilde{\mu} \vec{\mathcal{N}}$ and $\mu \tilde{\mu} \vec{\mathcal{V}}$ equational theories are sound and complete with respect to the $[\![\_]\!]^{\mathcal{N}}$ and $[\![\_]\!]^{\mathcal{V}}$ CPS transformations, respectively. This was previously known to hold for two separate and disjoint subsets of $\overline{\lambda} \mu \tilde{\mu}$ [3], but we now show that the correspondence holds for the full $\mu \tilde{\mu} \vec{\mathcal{N}}$- and $\mu \tilde{\mu} \vec{\mathcal{V}}$-calculi using the equational theories given by the strategies presented here.

Theorem 1. $\mu \tilde{\mu} \vec{s} \vdash c = c'$ *if and only if* $\beta \eta \vdash [\![c]\!]^{\mathcal{S}} = [\![c']\!]^{\mathcal{S}}$, *for* $\mathcal{S} = \mathcal{V}$ *or* $\mathcal{N}$.

Therefore, it turns out that the combination of the $\beta^{\rightarrow}$ and $\eta^{\rightarrow}$ axioms alone really do give a complete account of functions in the sequent calculus. Furthermore, both of these axioms do not reference the strategy: all of the details regarding order of evaluation has been taken care of by the core $\mu \tilde{\mu}_s$-calculus.

Remark 1. Now that we have a logical connective to work with, we can compare our use of strategies for determining evaluation order with the use of types in polarized logic. Take the usual ambiguous command, $\langle \mu\alpha.c \| \tilde{\mu}x.c' \rangle$, in which both sides appear to be fighting for control, and let's assume that the term and co-term belong to the type $A \to B$. One way to resolve the conflict is to assume that the $\eta^{\to}$ rule, corresponding to the reversibility of implication introduction in a proof or the universal property of exponentials in a category, is as strong as possible. Under this assumption, we can use the $\eta^{\to}$ rule to expand any term of type $A \to B$ into a λ-abstraction. Therefore, the ambiguous command is actually equivalent to the unambiguous command $\langle \lambda y.v \| \tilde{\mu}x.c' \rangle$, where $v = \mu\beta.\langle \mu\alpha.c \| y \cdot \beta \rangle$, and the conflict has been resolved in favor of the consumer. This goes to show that under the polarized view of types, in which the η rules are taken to be as strong as possible, the type of the active (co-)terms in a command can be used to determine evaluation order. Since the η rules for negative types like $A \to B$ apply to terms, then every term must be equivalent to a value, leading to a call-by-name interpretation. Dually, the η rules for positive types apply to co-terms, so every co-term must be a co-value, giving us a call-by-value interpretation. In contrast, the strategy based interpretation allows the user of the equational theory to choose what is considered a (co-)value, and the logical η rules are weakened so that they are consistent with the choice of strategy.

5 Basic Data and Co-data Structures

So far, our approach has been to characterize the behavior of functions in terms of β and η axioms alone, giving us a complete axiomatization for functions in the sequent calculus. All other details relevant to computation, such as when to lift out sub-computations in a function call, are derived from the primitive β and η principles. Furthermore, the β and η rules did not directly reference the strategy, but instead the meaning of the strategy is entirely defined by the core $\mu\tilde{\mu}_S$ calculus. To demonstrate the general applicability of this approach, and to build toward a more complete language, we should also account for pairs and disjoint unions, giving us a notion of products and sums in the sequent calculus. As a test to see if our formulation of the β and η axioms are sufficient, we will derive similar lifting rules, ς, as those described in Section 4 for functions.

We begin by considering sums ($\oplus$) in the $\mu\tilde{\mu}_S$-calculus. As per the usual approach in functional programming languages (based on natural deduction style), terms are injected into the sum as $\iota_1(v)$ or $\iota_2(v)$, and later analyzed by cases in the form **case** v **of** $\iota_1(x) \Rightarrow v_1 | \iota_2(y) \Rightarrow v_2$. In the sequent setting, we can keep the same terms, and reify the context for case analysis into the co-term $\tilde{\mu}[\iota_1(x).c_1 | \iota_2(y).c_2]$. Our goal now is to characterize the dynamic behavior of sums in terms of β and η axioms. Performing β reduction is implemented by a straightforward case analysis, matching the tag of the term with the appropriate branch of the co-term. For the η rule, we want to recognize a trivial case analysis that rebuilds the sum exactly as it was. Therefore, to extend the core $\mu\tilde{\mu}_S$-calculus with sums, we include the following two axioms:

$$(\beta^{\oplus}) \qquad\qquad \langle \iota_i(v) \| \tilde{\mu}[\iota_1(x).c_1 | \iota_2(x).c_2] \rangle = \langle v \| \tilde{\mu}x.c_i \rangle$$

$$(\eta^{\oplus}) \qquad\qquad \tilde{\mu}[\iota_1(x).\langle \iota_1(x) \| \alpha \rangle | \iota_2(y).\langle \iota_2(y) \| \alpha \rangle] = \alpha$$

Notice in particular that under call-by-value evaluation, the β axiom is applicable even when $\iota_i(v)$ is not a value, which is not directly allowed in Wadler's [11] call-by-value sequent calculus but is sound with respect to the CPS transformation. As with the β rule for functions, we are relying on the fact that a $\tilde{\mu}$-abstraction establishes the correct evaluation order, so that the underlying term will only be substituted if it is a value. Additionally, substitution of a co-value for α means that the η axiom for sums is also applicable to co-values. Because of the ability to substitute a co-value for a co-variable, we end up with a stronger η axiom for sums than we may have otherwise considered in natural deduction, corresponding to (**case** v **of** $\iota_1(x) \Rightarrow E[\iota_1(x)] | \iota_2(x) \Rightarrow E[\iota_2(x)]) = E[v]$ where E is an evaluation context of the chosen strategy. Restricting the η axiom to co-variables captures the fact that languages which impose restrictions on co-values have a correspondingly restricted notion of sums, as observed by Filinski for call-by-name languages [5]. To test that this combination of β and η axioms completely defines the behavior of sums, we derive Wadler's [12] lifting rule: $(\varsigma^{\oplus}) \quad \iota_i(v) = \mu\alpha.\langle v \| \tilde{\mu}x.\langle \iota_i(x) \| \alpha \rangle \rangle$

$$\iota_i(v) =_{\eta_\mu, \eta^{\oplus}} \mu\alpha.\langle \iota_i(v) \| \tilde{\mu}[\iota_1(x).\langle \iota_1(x) \| \alpha \rangle | \iota_2(x).\langle \iota_2(x) \| \alpha \rangle] \rangle =_{\beta^{\oplus}} \mu\alpha.\langle v \| \tilde{\mu}x.\langle \iota_i(x) \| \alpha \rangle \rangle$$

The fact that we have unrestricted β reduction for sums is crucial for deriving the $\varsigma^{\oplus}$ axiom. If we were only allowed to work with values, then the second step of the derivation would not be possible.

Next, we would like to formulate products ($\otimes$) that correspond to eager pairs in the call-by-value setting. Constructing a pair can be given straightforwardly as (v_1, v_2), following natural deduction style. Suppose now that we choose to define the co-terms as the projections $\pi_1[e]$ and $\pi_2[e]$, to correspond with the natural deduction terms $\pi_1(v)$ and $\pi_2(v)$. In order to implement eager pairs using this formulation, we would be forced to restrict β reduction to commands of the form $\langle (V_1, V_2) \| \pi_i[e] \rangle$, since we can only project out of an eager product when both components are values. This restriction on the β axiom makes it impossible to derive the appropriate lifting axioms for eager products, which means that the β and η axioms would be necessarily incomplete. The fundamental problem is that this formulation of pairs does not give us a $\tilde{\mu}$-abstraction to rely on for evaluating the sub-terms, forcing us to infect the β rule with details about evaluation order. Instead, we define the co-term as a case abstraction, $\tilde{\mu}(x, y).c$, which corresponds to case analysis on the structure of a pair in natural deduction, **case** v **of** $(x, y) \Rightarrow v'$. As before, β reduction decomposes the structure, and the η axiom recognizes a trivial case abstraction that immediately rebuilds the pair:

$$(\beta^{\otimes}) \quad \langle (v_1, v_2) \| \tilde{\mu}(x, y).c \rangle = \langle v_1 \| \tilde{\mu}x.\langle v_2 \| \tilde{\mu}y.c \rangle \rangle \quad (\eta^{\otimes}) \quad \tilde{\mu}(x, y).\langle (x, y) \| \alpha \rangle = \alpha$$

Notice that the β axiom is strong enough to break apart any pair (v_1, v_2) without throwing anything away, allowing us to still evaluate the two sub-terms eagerly afterward with the $\tilde{\mu}$-abstractions generated by the β rule. For instance, in the call-by-value strategy $\mathcal{V}$, the command $\langle (V, \mu\_.c') \| \tilde{\mu}(x, \_).c \rangle$ rightly reduces to c'. Additionally, because the β axiom breaks apart a pair containing (potentially) non-values, it must give an order to the bindings of the elements, thereby determining an order of evaluation between them. In the β rule presented here, we (arbitrarily) give priority to the first component of the pair. We can now pass our test by deriving a lifting rule for products that pulls out the two components so that they may be evaluated: $(\varsigma^{\otimes})$ $(v_1, v_2) = \mu\alpha.\langle v_1 \| \tilde{\mu}x.\langle v_2 \| \tilde{\mu}y.\langle (x, y) \| \alpha \rangle \rangle \rangle$

$$(v_1, v_2) =_{\eta_\mu, \eta^\otimes} \mu\alpha.\langle (v_1, v_2) \| \tilde{\mu}(x, y).\langle (x, y) \| \alpha \rangle \rangle =_{\beta\otimes} \mu\alpha.\langle v_1 \| \tilde{\mu}x.\langle v_2 \| \tilde{\mu}y.\langle (x, y) \| \alpha \rangle \rangle \rangle$$

As with functions, we derive Wadler's [12] more atomic rules that lift out one term at a time:

$$(\varsigma_x^{\otimes})\ \ (v_1, v_2) = \mu\alpha.\langle v_1 \| \tilde{\mu}x.\langle (x, v_2) \| \alpha \rangle \rangle \quad (\varsigma_x^{\otimes})\ \ (V_1, v_2) = \mu\alpha.\langle v_2 \| \tilde{\mu}y.\langle (V_1, y) \| \alpha \rangle \rangle$$

The symmetry of the sequent calculus points out a dual formulation of pairs and sums. This corresponds to the two forms of conjunction and disjunction in Girard's linear logic [6] and polarized logic [13,4]. Taking the mirror image of sums ($\oplus$) gives a formulation of products ($\&$) using projection as primitive that computes either the first or the second component on demand. The mirror image of products ($\otimes$) gives us a "classical" disjunction ($\mathbin{⅋}$), resulting in a lazier sum which only evaluates the term as it is needed, once both branches of its co-term have been reduced to co-values. The syntax and axioms for these connectives are exactly dual to those given above. The $\&$ connective has terms of the form $\mu(\pi_1[\alpha].c_1 | \pi_2[\beta].c_2)$ and the co-terms $\pi_1[e]$ and $\pi_2[e]$, and the $\mathbin{⅋}$ connective has the term $\mu[\alpha, \beta].c$ and the co-term $[e_1, e_2]$. For example, $\mu(\pi_1[\alpha].\langle 1 \| \alpha \rangle | \pi_2[\beta].\langle 2 \| \beta \rangle)$ is a $\&$ product that immediately returns 1 or 2 when asked, and given a $\&$ product x, we may swap its responses by intercepting and reversing the messages it receives: $\mu(\pi_1[\alpha].\langle x \| \pi_2[\alpha] \rangle | \pi_2[\beta].\langle x \| \pi_1[\beta] \rangle)$. Additionally, a $\mathbin{⅋}$ term may return a result to one of the two branches by responding to one of the provided co-variables, for example responding with 1 to the left branch is written $\mu[\alpha, \beta].\langle 1 \| \alpha \rangle$. Intuitively, $\oplus$ and $\&$ express the concept of choice (the choice to produce either the first or second or the choice to ask for the first or second), whereas $\otimes$ and $\mathbin{⅋}$ are about an amalgamation of two sub-parts.

To finish off the development, we also extend our call-by-value and call-by-name strategies to account for the new (co-)terms. We extend the sets of $\mathcal{V}$ values and $\mathcal{N}$ co-values as

$$V \in Value_{\mathcal{V}} ::= \ldots | (V, V') | \iota_i(V) | \mu(\pi_1[\alpha].c | \pi_2[\beta].c') | \mu[\alpha, \beta].c$$
$$E \in CoValue_{\mathcal{N}} ::= \ldots | \tilde{\mu}(x, y).c | \tilde{\mu}[\iota_1(x).c | \iota_2(y).c'] | \pi_i[E] | [E, E']$$

and continue to accept every co-term as a $\mathcal{V}$ co-value and every term as a $\mathcal{N}$ value. Notice in particular that the $\mathcal{V}$ strategy has a notion of eager and non-eager pairs: the concrete $\otimes$ term, (v, v'), will eagerly evaluate its sub-terms before becoming a value, whereas the abstract & term, $\mu(\pi_1[\alpha].c|\pi_2[\beta].c')$, is a value that is waiting for a message before running one of its sub-commands. The meanings of functions and & are similar in call-by-value, where we eagerly evaluate a term down to an abstraction and then stop. On the other hand, the $\mathcal{N}$ strategy implements the idea of a strict and non-strict sum: the $\oplus$ case abstraction is a co-value that forces evaluation of its term, whereas the $\mathcal{R}$ co-structure only forces evaluation of its term when both branches are co-values, so that they are strict in their input. This fundamental difference of the two views on disjunction has been previously observed by Selinger [10], who pointed out that in call-by-name, the two forms of disjunction cannot be isomorphic to one another. We also have the dual property, that there are two fundamentally different forms of products in call-by-value: a concrete pair and an abstract pair.

6   User-Defined Data and Co-data Types

By this point, we have arrived at a common pattern for adding basic (co-)data types to the core $\mu\tilde{\mu}_S$-calculus, which we will now generalize to user-defined types, similar to Herbelin's notion of generalized connectives [7]. We will take the data or co-data nature of a type constructor as a fundamental ingredient to its definition, therefore allowing the user to declare new data types (with concrete terms) and co-data types (with abstract terms). These are two dual ways of approaching data structures in programming languages: data corresponds to ordinary data types in functional languages like ML, whereas co-data is more akin to an interface for abstract objects that defines a fixed set of allowable observations or messages. The utility of definition by observations has been previously shown for infinite structures [1]. We present (co-)data declarations in the style of a statically typed language, like Haskell. However, since we are focused on an equational theory in an untyped setting, we use the declarations as a way to extend the language with new syntactic forms for structures and abstractions and to extend the theory with rules defining their operational meaning.

6.1   Defining Basic Data and Co-data Types

We first approach user-defined (co-)data types by example, and observe how the basic type constructors we have considered so far fit within the same general framework. To express the declarations in their full generality, we use a richer notation than that provided for ordinary algebraic data types in ML. Therefore, consider how the syntax of GADT declarations in Haskell can be applied to ordinary algebraic data types. For instance, the basic Either and Both (a tuple of two components) type constructors in Haskell are declared using GADT notation as follows:

$$\textbf{data}\,\textsf{Either}\,A\,B\,\textbf{where}$$
$$\textsf{Left} : A \to \textsf{Either}\,A\,B$$
$$\textsf{Right} : B \to \textsf{Either}\,A\,B$$

$$\textbf{data}\,\textsf{Both}\,A\,B\,\textbf{where}$$
$$\textsf{Pair} : A \to B \to \textsf{Both}\,A\,B$$

data $A \oplus B$ **where**

    $\iota_1 : A \vdash A \oplus B|$

    $\iota_2 : B \vdash A \oplus B|$

data $A \otimes B$ **where**

    pair $: A, B \vdash A \otimes B|$

data 1 **where**

    unit $: \ \vdash 1|$

data 0 **where**

data $A - B$ **where**

    uncall $: A \vdash A - B|B$

codata $A \ \& \ B$ **where**

    $\pi_1 : |A \ \& \ B \vdash A$

    $\pi_2 : |A \ \& \ B \vdash B$

codata $A \ \mathbin{⅋} \ B$ **where**

    split $: |A \ \mathbin{⅋} \ B \vdash A, B$

codata $\bot$ **where**

    tp $: | \bot \ \vdash$

codata $\top$ **where**

codata $A \to B$ **where**

    call $: A|A \to B \vdash B$

Fig. 8. Declarations for basic (co-)data types

The declaration of Either A B corresponds with the sequent declaration of $A \oplus B$ in Figure 8, both of which introduce a data type with two constructors: one accepting an input of type A and the other an input of type B. However, the sequent declaration separates input from output with entailment, $\vdash$, rather than a function arrow, and explicitly distinguishes the result produced by the constructor as $A \oplus B|$. Similarly, the constructor Pair from the declaration of Both A B can be seen as a curried form of the constructor pair from $A \otimes B$. In addition, the data declarations of 1 and 0 in Figure 8 correspond to the usual unit and empty types in functional programming languages.

However, the rest of the declarations in Figure 8 step outside the usual notion of data type in functional programming languages, and illustrate the various possibilities for defining new type constructors in the sequent calculus. The co-data declaration for $A \ \& \ B$ introduces a pair that is uniquely defined by their first and second projections, which consume the distinguished input written as $|A \ \& \ B$, rather than by a structure containing two elements. The declaration for $A \ \mathbin{⅋} \ B$ demonstrates that a (co-)constructor in the sequent calculus may have multiple outputs. The co-data declarations for $\top$ and $\bot$ give a dual notion of the unit and empty types, respectively, where the unit is an abstract object with no possible observations, and the empty type has one observation that produces no output. We can also express implication, $A \to B$, and its dual, $A - B$, as user-defined types that make use of both input and output at the same time.

6.2 Defining New Data and Co-data Types

Next, we consider how to introduce a new data type to the $\mu\tilde{\mu}_{\mathcal{S}}$-calculus, in its full generality. A data type is defined by cases over a set of *constructors*, $\mathsf{K}_1, \ldots, \mathsf{K}_n$. The general form of declaration for the new data type $\mathsf{F}(\overrightarrow{X})$, where $\overrightarrow{X}$ are zero

$$\textbf{data } \mathsf{F}(\overrightarrow{X_j}^{\,j}) \textbf{ where} \qquad\qquad \textbf{codata } \mathsf{G}(\overrightarrow{X_j}^{\,j}) \textbf{ where}$$

$$\mathsf{K}_1 : \overrightarrow{A_{1j}}^{\,j} \vdash \mathsf{F}(\overrightarrow{X_j}^{\,j}) | \overrightarrow{B_{1j}}^{\,j} \qquad\qquad \mathsf{H}_1 : \overrightarrow{A_{1j}}^{\,j} | \mathsf{G}(\overrightarrow{X_j}^{\,j}) \vdash \overrightarrow{B_{1j}}^{\,j}$$

$$\dots \qquad\qquad\qquad \dots$$

$$\mathsf{K}_n : \overrightarrow{A_{nj}}^{\,j} \vdash \mathsf{F}(\overrightarrow{X_j}^{\,j}) | \overrightarrow{B_{nj}}^{\,j} \qquad\qquad \mathsf{H}_n : \overrightarrow{A_{nj}}^{\,j} | \mathsf{G}(\overrightarrow{X_j}^{\,j}) \vdash \overrightarrow{B_{nj}}^{\,j}$$

Fig. 9. The general forms of (co-)data declarations in $\mu\tilde{\mu}_{\mathcal{S}}^{\mathcal{F}}$

$$(\beta^{\mathsf{F}}) \quad \langle \mathsf{K}_i(\overrightarrow{e_j}^{\,j}, \overrightarrow{v_j}^{\,j}) \| \tilde{\mu}[\overline{\mathsf{K}_i(\overrightarrow{\alpha_{ij}}^{\,j}, \overrightarrow{x_{ij}}^{\,j}).c_i}^{\,i}] \rangle = \langle \mu\overrightarrow{\alpha_{ij}}^{\,j}.\langle \overrightarrow{v_j}^{\,j} \| \tilde{\mu}\overrightarrow{x_{ij}}^{\,j}.c_i \rangle \| \overrightarrow{e_j}^{\,j} \rangle$$

$$(\eta^{\mathsf{F}}) \quad \tilde{\mu}[\overline{\mathsf{K}_i(\overrightarrow{\alpha_{ij}}^{\,j}, \overrightarrow{x_{ij}}^{\,j}).\langle \mathsf{K}_i(\overrightarrow{\alpha_{ij}}^{\,j}, \overrightarrow{x_{ij}}^{\,j}) \| \gamma \rangle}^{\,i}] = \gamma$$

$$(\beta^{\mathsf{G}}) \quad \langle \mu(\overline{\mathsf{H}_i[\overrightarrow{x_{ij}}^{\,j}, \overrightarrow{\alpha_{ij}}^{\,j}].c_i}^{\,i}) \| \mathsf{H}_i[\overrightarrow{v_j}^{\,j}, \overrightarrow{e_j}^{\,j}] \rangle = \langle \overrightarrow{v_j}^{\,j} \| \tilde{\mu}\overrightarrow{x_{ij}}^{\,j}.\langle \mu\overrightarrow{\alpha_{ij}}^{\,j}.c_i \| \overrightarrow{e_j}^{\,j} \rangle \rangle$$

$$(\eta^{\mathsf{G}}) \quad \mu(\overline{\mathsf{H}_i[\overrightarrow{x_{ij}}^{\,j}, \overrightarrow{\alpha_{ij}}^{\,j}].\langle z \| \mathsf{H}_i[\overrightarrow{x_{ij}}^{\,j}, \overrightarrow{\alpha_{ij}}^{\,j}] \rangle}^{\,i}) = z$$

Fig. 10. The β and η axioms for (co-)data of the $\mu\tilde{\mu}_{\mathcal{S}}^{\mathcal{F}}$ equational theory

or more type variables[2], is given in Figure 9. The type variables may appear in any of the types $\vec{A}$ and $\vec{B}$, and each constructor has $\mathsf{F}(\vec{X})$ as the distinguished output type on the right of the sequent. Syntactically, each constructor builds a new term not only from other terms, as per usual in a functional programming language, but also possibly from co-terms that represent reified contexts. The data declaration for $\mathsf{F}(\vec{X})$ introduces the family of data structures, $\mathsf{K}_i(\vec{e}, \vec{v})$, as new terms and the single case abstraction, $\tilde{\mu}[\overline{\mathsf{K}(\vec{\alpha}, \vec{x}).c}]$, as the new co-term of that type. In addition to the syntax for the data type $\mathsf{F}(\vec{X})$, we also have two primitive axioms, β^{F} and η^{F} shown in Figure 10. Following the same pattern as pairs and sums, the axioms are strategy independent and rely on μ and $\tilde{\mu}$ in $\mu\tilde{\mu}_{\mathcal{S}}$ to manage evaluation order. Binding the sequence of terms $\vec{v} = v_1, v_2, \dots, v_n$ to the sequence of variables $\vec{x} = x_1, x_2, \dots, x_n$ is defined as

$$\langle \vec{v} \| \tilde{\mu} \vec{x}.c \rangle \triangleq \langle v_1 \| \tilde{\mu} x_1.\langle v_2 \| \tilde{\mu} x_2. \dots. \langle v_n \| \tilde{\mu} x_n.c \rangle \dots \rangle \rangle$$

and analogously for binding a sequence of co-terms to co-variables. The β^{F} axiom performs case analysis by looking up the appropriate command to run based on the constructor and binding the sub (co-)terms of the structure by matching it with the appropriate pattern. The η^{F} axiom states that an unknown co-value γ is treated the same as a trivial case abstraction that re-constructs all matched structures and forwards them along to γ. As before, we have a family of axioms that lift out sub-(co-)terms in a data structure, which can be derived by following the same pattern shown in Section 5 for products and sums.

---

[2] We write $\overrightarrow{X_i}^{\,i}$ to mean a sequence $X_1, \dots, X_n$ of zero or more elements indexed by i. The index is left implicit when it is clear from context.

$$\left(\mathbf{data}\, \mathsf{F}(\overrightarrow{X})\, \mathbf{where}\, \overrightarrow{\mathsf{K} : \overrightarrow{A} \vdash \mathsf{F}(\overrightarrow{X}) | \overrightarrow{B}} \right)^{\circ} \triangleq \mathbf{codata}\, \mathsf{F}(\overrightarrow{X})\, \mathbf{where}\, \overrightarrow{\mathsf{K} : \overrightarrow{B} | \mathsf{F}(\overrightarrow{X}) \vdash \overrightarrow{A}}$$

$$\left(\mathbf{codata}\, \mathsf{G}(\overrightarrow{X})\, \mathbf{where}\, \overrightarrow{\mathsf{H} : \overrightarrow{A} | \mathsf{G}(\overrightarrow{X}) \vdash \overrightarrow{B}} \right)^{\circ} \triangleq \mathbf{data}\, \mathsf{G}(\overrightarrow{X})\, \mathbf{where}\, \overrightarrow{\mathsf{H} : \overrightarrow{B} \vdash \mathsf{G}(\overrightarrow{X}) | \overrightarrow{A}}$$

$$\langle v \| e \rangle^{\circ} \triangleq \langle e^{\circ} \| v^{\circ} \rangle$$

$$(\mu\alpha.c)^{\circ} \triangleq \tilde{\mu}\alpha^{\circ}.c^{\circ} \quad (\mathsf{K}(\overrightarrow{e}, \overrightarrow{v}))^{\circ} \triangleq \mathsf{K}[\overrightarrow{e^{\circ}}, \overrightarrow{v^{\circ}}] \quad (\mu(\overrightarrow{\mathsf{H}[\overrightarrow{x}, \overrightarrow{\alpha}].c}))^{\circ} \triangleq \tilde{\mu}[\overrightarrow{\mathsf{H}(\overrightarrow{x^{\circ}}, \overrightarrow{\alpha^{\circ}}).c^{\circ}}]$$

$$(\tilde{\mu}x.c)^{\circ} \triangleq \mu x^{\circ}.c^{\circ} \quad (\mathsf{H}[\overrightarrow{v}, \overrightarrow{e}])^{\circ} \triangleq \mathsf{H}(\overrightarrow{v^{\circ}}, \overrightarrow{e^{\circ}}) \quad (\tilde{\mu}[\overrightarrow{\mathsf{K}(\overrightarrow{\alpha}, \overrightarrow{x}).c}])^{\circ} \triangleq \mu(\overrightarrow{\mathsf{K}(\overrightarrow{\alpha^{\circ}}, \overrightarrow{x^{\circ}}).c^{\circ}})$$

Fig. 11. The duality operation for the $\mu\tilde{\mu}_{\mathcal{S}}^{\mathcal{F}}$-calculus

Introducing a new co-data type to the $\mu\tilde{\mu}_{\mathcal{S}}$-calculus follows the same general pattern, but with a twist. Instead of defining a co-data type $\mathsf{G}(\overrightarrow{X})$, by its constructors, which produce a data structure as output, it is defined by cases over its possible *co-constructors* which build concrete co-structures on the side of co-terms. The co-structures can be thought of as observations or messages that are sent to and analyzed by abstract terms of type $\mathsf{G}(\overrightarrow{X})$. It follows that the co-data declaration mirrors the general form of a data declaration, as shown in Figure 9. Likewise, the syntax introduced for the co-data type $\mathsf{G}(\overrightarrow{X})$ is dual to the data form. We now have a family of co-data structures, $\mathsf{H}_i[\overrightarrow{v}, \overrightarrow{e}]$, as new co-terms, and a single new term, $\mu(\overrightarrow{\mathsf{H}[\overrightarrow{x}, \overrightarrow{\alpha}].c})$. This term is a co-case abstraction which responds to a co-data structure, *i.e.*, a message, by giving a command to perform for every possible case.

Following the exchanged roles between term and co-term, the primitive β^{G} and η^{G} axioms are mirror images of their counterparts for data types, as seen in Figure 10. The β^{G} axiom performs case analysis on a co-constructor, matching the co-structure to the given pattern and running the appropriate command given by the abstract term. The η^{G} axiom wraps an unknown value z in a co-case abstraction that just forwards every co-structure to that original value. We also have a family of axioms that lift out sub-(co-)terms in a co-data structure, which exactly mirror the derived lifting axioms for data types.

6.3 Duality and Strategies for User-Defined Co-data Types

We also extend the duality relationship of Curien and Herbelin [3] and Wadler [11] to be parametric over evaluation strategies and user-defined (co-)data types. The duality operation, given in Figure 11, transforms a program in the $\mu\tilde{\mu}_{\mathcal{S}}^{\mathcal{F}}$-calculus into its dual in the $\mu\tilde{\mu}_{\mathcal{S}^{\circ}}^{\mathcal{F}^{\circ}}$-calculus. The duality operation flips the roles of a program, mapping terms into co-terms, co-terms into terms, and exchanges the two sides of a command. The dual of a set of declared (co-)data types, $\mathcal{F}$, is given by the dual of each (co-)data type declaration of $\mathcal{F}$. In addition, we can automatically generate the dual of a strategy, $\mathcal{S}^{\circ}$, by taking the point-wise dual of the values and co-values of $\mathcal{S}$. Notice that the double dual of a (co-)data declaration is identical to the original declaration. This gives us soundness and involution of duality that is parametric in evaluation strategy and (co-)data types.

$$V \in Value_\mathcal{V} ::= x \mid \mathsf{K}_i(\overrightarrow{e}, \overrightarrow{V}) \mid \mu(\overrightarrow{\mathsf{H}(\overrightarrow{x}, \overrightarrow{\alpha}).c}) \qquad E \in CoValue_\mathcal{V} ::= e$$

$$V \in Value_\mathcal{N} ::= v \qquad E \in CoValue_\mathcal{N} ::= \alpha \mid \tilde{\mu}[\overrightarrow{\mathsf{K}(\overrightarrow{\alpha}, \overrightarrow{x}).c}] \mid \mathsf{H}_i[\overrightarrow{v}, \overrightarrow{E}]$$

Fig. 12. Call-by-value ($\mathcal{V}$) and call-by-name ($\mathcal{N}$) strategies of $\mu\tilde{\mu}_\mathcal{S}^\mathcal{F}$

$$[\![\mathsf{K}_i(\overrightarrow{e}, \overrightarrow{v})]\!]^\mathcal{V} = \lambda\alpha.[\![v_1]\!]^\mathcal{V}\lambda x_1.\ldots [\![v_n]\!]^\mathcal{V}\lambda x_n.\alpha \ \mathsf{K}_i(\overrightarrow{[\![e]\!]^\mathcal{V}}, \overrightarrow{x})$$

$$[\![\mu(\overrightarrow{\mathsf{H}[\overrightarrow{x}, \overrightarrow{\alpha}].c})]\!]^\mathcal{V} = \lambda\beta.\beta \ \lambda\gamma.\mathbf{case}\,\gamma\,\mathbf{of}\,\overrightarrow{\mathsf{H}(\overrightarrow{x}, \overrightarrow{\alpha})} \Rightarrow \overrightarrow{[\![c]\!]^\mathcal{V}}$$

$$[\![\tilde{\mu}[\overrightarrow{\mathsf{K}(\overrightarrow{\alpha}, \overrightarrow{x}).c}]]\!]^\mathcal{V} = \lambda z.\mathbf{case}\,z\,\mathbf{of}\,\overrightarrow{\mathsf{K}(\overrightarrow{\alpha}, \overrightarrow{x})} \Rightarrow \overrightarrow{[\![c]\!]^\mathcal{V}}$$

$$[\![\mathsf{H}_i[\overrightarrow{v}, \overrightarrow{e}]]\!]^\mathcal{V} = \lambda x.[\![v_1]\!]^\mathcal{V}\lambda y_1.\ldots [\![v_n]\!]^\mathcal{V}\lambda y_n.x \ \mathsf{H}_i(\overrightarrow{y}, \overrightarrow{[\![e]\!]^\mathcal{V}})$$

Fig. 13. Call-by-value ($\mathcal{V}$) CPS transformation of $\mu\tilde{\mu}_\mathcal{S}^\mathcal{F}$

Theorem 2.   – If $\mu\tilde{\mu}_\mathcal{S}^\mathcal{F} \vdash c = c'$ then $\mu\tilde{\mu}_{\mathcal{S}^\circ}^{\mathcal{F}^\circ} \vdash c^\circ = c'^\circ$.
 – $c^{\circ\circ} \triangleq c$, $\mathcal{S}^{\circ\circ} \triangleq \mathcal{S}$, and $\mathcal{F}^{\circ\circ} \triangleq \mathcal{F}$.

It is worthwhile to pause over the statement of this theorem: for *every* strategy and collection of (co-)data types under which two commands are equated, the strategy and (co-)data types obtained from their duals equate the dual commands. In addition to recognizing a duality between two hand-crafted strategies and sets of connectives, like for $\mathcal{N}$ and $\mathcal{V}$, this theorem demonstrates a mechanical procedure for generating the semantic dual of *any* strategy and *any* set of (co-)data types, as well as the dual to any theory given as an instance of $\mu\tilde{\mu}_\mathcal{S}^\mathcal{F}$.

Finally, we need to choose an evaluation strategy for each newly declared (co-)data type. We can do this generically across user-defined (co-)data by deciding on a schema for extending the sets of values and co-values based on (co-)data declarations. For our call-by-value strategy $\mathcal{V}$, we can say that data structures are values if every sub-term is a value, abstract terms are values, and every co-term is a co-value, as shown in Figure 12. This schema agrees with the definition of our call-by-value strategy for all the previously considered (co-)data types, and gives us exactly the same equational theory as we had before. We can provide a schema for our call-by-name evaluation strategy $\mathcal{N}$ in the dual way. In this case, we say that co-structures are co-values if every sub-co-term is a co-value, abstract co-terms are co-values, and every term is a value. Likewise, this schema agrees with the previous definition of our call-by-name strategy.

In addition, we extend the basic call-by-value CPS transformation $[\![\_]\!]^\mathcal{V}$ with clauses for the newly declared (co-)data types by encoding (co-)structures and (co-)case abstractions into a CPS λ-calculus extended with user-defined data types, à la ML, as given in Figure 13.

The call-by-name CPS transformation is defined as the dual of the call-by-value transformation, $[\![\_]\!]^\mathcal{N} = [\![\_^\circ]\!]^\mathcal{V}$. It follows that the call-by-value and call-by-name equational theories are sound and complete with respect to the call-by-value and call-by-name CPS transformations, respectively.

$$V \in Value_{\mathcal{LV}} ::= x \mid \mathsf{K}_i(\overrightarrow{E}, \overrightarrow{V}) \mid \mu(\overrightarrow{\mathsf{H}[\overrightarrow{x}, \overrightarrow{\alpha}].c}) \qquad C_{\mathcal{LV}} \in Context_{\mathcal{LV}} ::= \square \mid \langle v \| \tilde{\mu}x.C_{\mathcal{LV}} \rangle$$

$$E \in CoValue_{\mathcal{LV}} ::= \alpha \mid \tilde{\mu}[\overrightarrow{\mathsf{K}(\overrightarrow{x}, \overrightarrow{\alpha}).c}] \mid \mathsf{H}_i[\overrightarrow{v}, \overrightarrow{E}] \mid \tilde{\mu}x.C_{\mathcal{LV}}[\langle x \| E \rangle]$$

Fig. 14. The $\mathcal{LV}$ strategy for $\mu\tilde{\mu}_{\mathcal{S}}^{\mathcal{F}}$

$$V \in Value_{\mathcal{LN}} ::= x \mid \mathsf{K}_i(\overrightarrow{e}, \overrightarrow{V}) \mid \mu(\overrightarrow{\mathsf{H}[\overrightarrow{x}, \overrightarrow{\alpha}].c}) \mid \mu\alpha.C_{\mathcal{LN}}[\langle V \| \alpha \rangle]$$

$$E \in CoValue_{\mathcal{LN}} ::= \alpha \mid \tilde{\mu}[\overrightarrow{\mathsf{K}(\overrightarrow{x}, \overrightarrow{\alpha}).c}] \mid \mathsf{H}_i[\overrightarrow{V}, \overrightarrow{E}] \quad C_{\mathcal{LN}} \in Context_{\mathcal{LN}} ::= \square \mid \langle \mu\alpha.C_{\mathcal{LN}} \| e \rangle$$

Fig. 15. The $\mathcal{LN}$ strategy for $\mu\tilde{\mu}_{\mathcal{S}}^{\mathcal{F}}$

Theorem 3. $\mu\tilde{\mu}_{\mathcal{S}}^{\mathcal{F}} \vdash c = c'$ *if and only if* $\beta\eta \vdash [\![c]\!]^{\mathcal{S}} = [\![c']\!]^{\mathcal{S}}$, *for* $\mathcal{S} = \mathcal{V}$ *or* $\mathcal{N}$.

The parametric $\mu\tilde{\mu}_{\mathcal{S}}$-calculus extended with user-defined (co-)data types encompasses Wadler's dual sequent calculus [12], where conjunction and disjunction are mapped to the $A \oplus B$ and $A \otimes B$ data types for the call-by-value calculus, and to the $A \& B$ and $A \,\mathscr{Y}\, B$ co-data types for the call-by-name calculus. Additionally, negation is mapped to the co-data type form of negation for call-by-value, and to the data type form of negation for call-by-name.

Remark 2. So far, we have focused our attention only on two evaluation strategies: the $\mathcal{N}$ strategy for call-by-name and the $\mathcal{V}$ strategy for call-by-value. However, there are other strategies that can be studied by this parametric approach. For instance, we can adapt the "lazy value" strategy [2], $\mathcal{LV}$, to the parametric $\mu\tilde{\mu}_{\mathcal{S}}$-calculus with user-defined (co-)data types as shown in Figure 14. The $\mathcal{LV}$ strategy uses the same notion of value as in $\mathcal{V}$, but restricts co-values to only those co-terms that "need" a value in order to continue. In this way, the $\mathcal{LV}$ behaves in a call-by-name manner by first prioritizing the co-term, and only evaluates terms when demanded. The intuition is that in a context like $\langle v_1 \| \tilde{\mu}y_1.\langle v_2 \| \tilde{\mu}y_2.\square \rangle \rangle$, v_1 and v_2 are delayed computations whose results are bound to y_1 and y_2 so that they are shared. The co-term $\tilde{\mu}x.\langle v_1 \| \tilde{\mu}y_1.\langle v_2 \| \tilde{\mu}y_2.\langle x \| E \rangle \rangle \rangle$ is strict since $\langle x \| E \rangle$ is the actively running command and it needs the value of x in order to continue, making the whole $\tilde{\mu}$-abstraction a co-value. In the command $\langle \mu\alpha.c_1 \| \tilde{\mu}x.c_2 \rangle$, we begin to evaluate c_2 as if we performed a call-by-name substitution until the value of x is demanded (in a command like $C_{\mathcal{LV}}[\langle x \| E \rangle]$), and then switch to evaluating c_1 by the μ_E rule. The call-by-need $\mathcal{LV}$ strategy demonstrates that there are more than two possible strategies of interest, and that more subtle concerns about evaluation order, such as sharing the results of computations in a non-strict setting, is captured by the parametric $\mu\tilde{\mu}_{\mathcal{S}}$-calculus.

Furthermore, the procedure illustrated by Theorem 2 can be used to mechanically generate a strategy dual to call-by-need, $\mathcal{LN}$, as shown in Figure 15. In this setting, priority is initially given to the producer, but we still share the work needed to reduce a consumer. This strategy may be thought of as call-by-value with a delayed form of control effects, so that a continuation is reduced first before being copied. Delayed control effects introduce new values of the form $\mu\alpha.\langle\mu\beta.\langle V\|\alpha\rangle\|e\rangle$, where we are returning the value V from inside a delayed capture of e. $\mathcal{LN}$ implements the dual form of sharing as call-by-need: it behaves like call-by-value but only captures strict contexts in the sense of call-by-name.

7   Composing Multiple Strategies

We have now seen how to reason about data and co-data in the sequent calculus according to multiple different evaluation strategies by capturing the essence of the strategy as the parameter to the equational theory. The parameter for the strategy fixes evaluation order once and for all as a global property of the language. However, can we also allow for a program to make use of more than one strategy at a time? Or put another way, can we take several independently consistent strategies and compose them together into a composite strategy for the parametric equational theory, while still maintaining consistency?

The problem calls for a more subtle approach than just taking the union of two or more strategies. For example, if we take the simple union of the call-by-name $\mathcal{N}$ and call-by-value $\mathcal{V}$ strategies, so a (co-)term is a (co-)value if it fits either the $\mathcal{N}$ or $\mathcal{V}$ notions of (co-)value, then the combined strategy considers *every* term and co-term to be a (co-)value. In the command $\langle\mu\alpha.c\|\tilde\mu x.c'\rangle$, we could consider the term to be a value by $\mathcal{N}$ criteria and the co-term to be a co-value by $\mathcal{V}$ criteria, leading back to the fundamental inconsistency we were trying to avoid. The issue is that allowing a $\mathcal{N}$ (co-)term interact with a $\mathcal{V}$ (co-)term opens the door for further inconsistencies, even though the two strategies are perfectly consistent in isolation. The solution comes by disallowing (co-)terms from different strategies from interacting directly with one another. If the strategy $\mathcal{S}$ is consistent, then we know that every command is interpreted consistently if we evaluate *both* the term and co-term by $\mathcal{S}$. Our goal is to ensure that every command consistently interprets both term and co-term by the same strategy, and that this consistency is maintained by the rules of the equational theory.

One approach for ensuring that terms only communicate with co-terms following the same strategy is to think about types. We can take all the types which classify programs and put them into different universes, or *kinds*, so that each kind represents one primitive strategy. However, a full static typing discipline is more than necessary for ensuring that programs are consistent. After all, we were able to consistently reason about untyped programs by using a single global strategy, and ideally we would like to keep this property when possible. Therefore, we relax the typing relationship by collapsing all of the types for a particular kind into a single universal type. The notion of having more than one universal type for untyped evaluation is similar to Zeilberger's [14] "bi-typed" system, except that we admit more than two universes, thereby allowing a program to make use of more than two primitive evaluation strategies at a time and in other combinations like call-by-value and call-by-need. To make the strategy for interpreting a (co-)term apparent from its syntax, we explicitly annotate (co-)variables with their kind. An inference system for checking kinds of the core

$$\frac{c :: (\Gamma \vdash \alpha :: \mathcal{S}, \Delta)}{\Gamma \vdash \mu\alpha^{\mathcal{S}}.c :: \mathcal{S}|\Delta} \; \frac{\Gamma, x :: \mathcal{S} \vdash x^{\mathcal{S}} :: \mathcal{S}|\Delta}{} \qquad \frac{c :: (\Gamma, x :: \mathcal{S} \vdash \Delta)}{\Gamma|\tilde{\mu}x^{\mathcal{S}}.c :: \mathcal{S} \vdash \Delta} \; \frac{\Gamma|\alpha^{\mathcal{S}} :: \mathcal{S} \vdash \alpha :: \mathcal{S}, \Delta}{} \qquad \frac{\Gamma \vdash v :: \mathcal{S}|\Delta \quad \Gamma|e :: \mathcal{S} \vdash \Delta}{\langle v\|e\rangle :: (\Gamma \vdash \Delta)}$$

Fig. 16. Type-agnostic kind system for the core calculus

calculus, shown in Figure 16, resembles the type system for $\overline{\lambda}\mu\tilde{\mu}$ [3] except at one level up. The most interesting rule is the cut rule for forming commands that only allows v and e to interact if they both belong to a type of the same kind, ensuring that we interpret v and e according to the same strategy.

In order to allow for user-defined (co-)data types in the presence of multiple primitive strategies, we need to consider kinds when declaring a new (co-)data type. We will illustrate (co-)data declaration with explicit, multiple kinds by example in lieu of presenting the general form. We can declare a strict pair $A \otimes B$, where both components are evaluated eagerly, by annotating the declaration in Figure 8 so that A, B, and $A \otimes B$ belong to the kind $\mathcal{V}$:

$$\mathbf{data}\,(A : \mathcal{V}) \otimes (B : \mathcal{V}) : \mathcal{V}\,\mathbf{where}\,\mathsf{pair} : A : \mathcal{V}, B : \mathcal{V} \vdash A \otimes B : \mathcal{V}|$$

The annotated declaration for $A \otimes B \;:\; \mathcal{V}$ introduces the term $\mathsf{pair}(v, v')$ and co-term $\tilde{\mu}[\mathsf{pair}(x^{\mathcal{V}}, y^{\mathcal{V}}).c]$. In addition, the declaration extends the set of $\mathcal{V}$ values with $\mathsf{pair}(V, V')$, where V and V' are $\mathcal{V}$ values, as intended. We are also at liberty to declare a pair using more interesting combinations of strategies, as expressed by kinds. For example, we can introduce a lazy pair $\mathsf{MixedProduct}(A, B)$ of the kind $\mathcal{N}$ where the first component is evaluated strictly:

$$\mathbf{data}\,\mathsf{MixedProduct}(A : \mathcal{V}, B : \mathcal{N}) : \mathcal{N}\,\mathbf{where}$$
$$\mathsf{MixedPair} : A : \mathcal{V}, B : \mathcal{N} \vdash \mathsf{MixedProduct}(A, B) : \mathcal{N}|$$

The declaration of $\mathsf{MixedProduct}(A, B) : \mathcal{N}$ introduces the term $\mathsf{MixedPair}(v, v')$ and co-term $\tilde{\mu}[\mathsf{MixedPair}(x^{\mathcal{V}}, y^{\mathcal{N}}).c]$, both of which are taken to be $\mathcal{N}$ (co-)values. The interesting interplay between the $\mathcal{V}$ and $\mathcal{N}$ strategies in a $\mathsf{MixedProduct}$ is revealed during β reduction:

$$\langle \mathsf{MixedPair}(v, v')\|\tilde{\mu}[\mathsf{MixedPair}(x^{\mathcal{V}}, y^{\mathcal{N}}).c]\rangle =_{\beta, \tilde{\mu}_V} \langle v\|\tilde{\mu}x^{\mathcal{V}}.c\,\{v'/y^{\mathcal{N}}\}\rangle$$

The intended behavior is that after breaking apart the mixed pair, v is evaluated eagerly until it is reduced to a value according to the $\mathcal{V}$ strategy, after which the value is substituted for $x^{\mathcal{V}}$. On the other hand, v' is interpreted according to the $\mathcal{N}$ strategy, so that it is already a value and may be substituted immediately.

Observe that the parametric equational theory instantiated with multiple strategies $\vec{\mathcal{S}}$ and type constructors $\mathcal{F}$, written $\mu\tilde{\mu}_{\vec{\mathcal{S}}}^{\mathcal{F}}$, preserves the well-kindedness of commands and (co-)terms. The axioms in need of the most care are the η axioms, which only apply to variables of the appropriate kind. For instance, the η axiom for $A \otimes B$ of the kind $\mathcal{V}$ only applies to a co-variable $\alpha^{\mathcal{V}}$, whereas the η axiom for $\mathsf{MixedProduct}(A, B)$ of the kind $\mathcal{N}$ only applies to $\alpha^{\mathcal{N}}$.

Theorem 4. *If $\vec{S}$ are consistent strategies, then $\mu\tilde{\mu}_{\vec{S}}^{F}$ is consistent for well-kinded commands and (co-)terms.*

8   Conclusion

The parametric theory provides a direct framework for reasoning about the behavior of programs with both data and co-data in the sequent calculus. We may understand the meaning of a sequent calculus program using both data structures and message-passing in terms of the intended evaluation strategy. As future work, we would like to develop the theory of the sequent calculus so that it may provide a foundation for objects as a form of co-data, giving us a framework where a notion of object-oriented programming is expressed as the dual paradigm to functional programming. This will involve extending the theory with more advanced features such as inductive and co-inductive forms of self-reference, subtyping, and parametric polymorphism. In addition, we would like to study the suitability of the sequent calculus as an intermediate language in a compiler. Since the sequent calculus provides a framework in which low-level implementation details can be better expressed than in the λ-calculus, we want to study its impact on reasoning about optimizations and program analysis.

Acknowledgments. We would like to thank Pierre-Louis Curien, Hugo Herbelin, and Alexis Saurin for their helpful input and discussion in early versions of this paper, and to acknowledge the support of INRIA and Paris Diderot University while both authors were visiting Paris, where this work was carried out. The authors have also been supported by NSF grant CCF-0917329 and INRIA Équipe Associée SEMACODE.

References

1. Abel, A., Pientka, B., Thibodeau, D., Setzer, A.: Copatterns: programming infinite structures by observations. In: POPL 2013 (2013)
2. Ariola, Z.M., Herbelin, H., Saurin, A.: Classical call-by-need and duality. In: Ong, L. (ed.) TLCA 2011. LNCS, vol. 6690, pp. 27–44. Springer, Heidelberg (2011)
3. Curien, P.-L., Herbelin, H.: The duality of computation. In: International Conference on Functional Programming, pp. 233–243 (2000)
4. Curien, P.-L., Munch-Maccagnoni, G.: The duality of computation under focus. In: Calude, C.S., Sassone, V. (eds.) TCS 2010. IFIP AICT, vol. 323, pp. 165–181. Springer, Heidelberg (2010)
5. Filinski, A.: Declarative Continuations and Categorical Duality. Master thesis, DIKU, Danmark (August 1989)
6. Girard, J.-Y.: Linear logic. Theoretical Computer Science 50, 1–102 (1987)
7. Herbelin, H.: Duality of computation and sequent calculus: a few more remarks (2012), http://pauillac.inria.fr/~herbelin/publis/full-dual-lk.pdf
8. Munch-Maccagnoni, G.: Focalisation and classical realisability. In: Grädel, E., Kahle, R. (eds.) CSL 2009. LNCS, vol. 5771, pp. 409–423. Springer, Heidelberg (2009)

9. Ronchi Della Rocca, S., Paolini, L.: The Parametric λ-Calculus: a Metamodel for Computation. Springer (2004)
10. Selinger, P.: Control categories and duality: on the categorical semantics of the lambda-mu calculus. MSCS 11(2), 207–260 (2001)
11. Wadler, P.: Call-by-value is dual to call-by-name. In: Proceedings of ICFP, pp. 189–201. ACM (2003)
12. Wadler, P.: Call-by-value is dual to call-by-name – reloaded. In: Giesl, J. (ed.) RTA 2005. LNCS, vol. 3467, pp. 185–203. Springer, Heidelberg (2005)
13. Zeilberger, N.: On the unity of duality. Annals of Pure Applied Logic 153(1-3), 66–96 (2008)
14. Zeilberger, N.: The Logical Basis of Evaluation Order and Pattern-Matching. PhD thesis, Carnegie Mellon University (2009)

Deriving Pretty-Big-Step Semantics
from Small-Step Semantics

Casper Bach Poulsen and Peter D. Mosses

Department of Computer Science, Swansea University, Swansea, UK
{cscbp,p.d.mosses}@swansea.ac.uk

Abstract. Big-step semantics for languages with abrupt termination and/or divergence suffer from a serious duplication problem, addressed by the novel 'pretty-big-step' style presented by Charguéraud at
ESOP'13. Such rules are less concise than corresponding small-step rules,
but they have the same advantages as big-step rules for program correctness proofs. Here, we show how to automatically derive pretty-big-step
rules directly from small-step rules by 'refocusing'. This gives the best
of both worlds: we only need to write the relatively concise small-step
specifications, but our reasoning can be big-step as well as small-step.
The use of strictness annotations to derive small-step congruence rules
gives further conciseness.

Keywords: structural operational semantics, SOS, Modular SOS,
pretty-big-step semantics, small-step semantics, big-step semantics, natural semantics, refocusing.

1 Introduction

Structural operational semantics (SOS) are typically given in either small-step
(Plotkin 2004) or big-step (Kahn 1987) style. Big-step rules evaluate terms by
relating them to their computed values, whereas small-step evaluation involves
partly evaluated terms. Both styles are powerful frameworks for formalizing operational semantics, and each has its own merits and limitations. For example,
small-step semantics is usually preferred for process algebras (Milner 1980), interleaving, and type soundness proofs (Pierce 2002; Wright and Felleisen 1994),
whereas the big-step style is more suitable for proving correctness of program
transformations (Charguéraud 2013; Leroy and Grall 2009). An equally important concern is the effort involved in specifying the semantics: rules should be
concise, but comprehensible. But which style requires less effort?

The answer to this question depends not only on conciseness, but also on the
application, i.e., on features of the specified language and properties that the
semantics will be used to reason about. When the language involves abrupt termination, Charguéraud (2013) recently noted that big-step semantics (also called
natural semantics) duplicate premises and rules to propagate abrupt termination and/or divergence. In contrast, the small-step style allows for more concise

Z. Shao (Ed.): ESOP 2014, LNCS 8410, pp. 270–289, 2014.

specifications involving abrupt termination, and there is no need to specify propagation of divergence. However, this would seem of little consolation if the use of the semantics requires big-step reasoning. Charguéraud provides an alternative by showing how to decompose big-step rules into simpler *pretty-big-step* rules. Such rules allow for more concise specifications without sacrificing the ability to do big-step reasoning. The style also incorporates coinductive reasoning similar to *coinductive big-step semantics* (Leroy and Grall 2009).

Table 1 illustrates the difference between big-step, pretty-big-step, and small-step SOS rules for subtracting natural numbers. In the small-step SOS rules we use a state variable a to propagate exceptions. By matching on the exception

Table 1. Comparison of big-step, pretty-big-step, and small-step SOS rules for partially defined subtraction of natural numbers ($\mathbb{N}$)

Big-step SOS $\boxed{t \Rightarrow b}$

$$t ::= \mathsf{minus}(t, t) \mid n \qquad n \in \mathbb{N} \qquad b ::= n \mid \mathsf{exc}(n)$$

$$\frac{t_1 \Rightarrow n_1 \qquad t_2 \Rightarrow n_2 \qquad n_1 \geq n_2 \qquad n = n_1 - n_2}{\mathsf{minus}(t_1, t_2) \Rightarrow n} \ [\textsc{Big1}]$$

$$\frac{t_1 \Rightarrow n_1 \qquad t_2 \Rightarrow \mathsf{exc}(n')}{\mathsf{minus}(t_1, t_2) \Rightarrow \mathsf{exc}(n')} \ [\textsc{Big2}]$$

$$\frac{t_1 \Rightarrow n_1 \qquad t_2 \Rightarrow n_2 \qquad n_1 < n_2}{\mathsf{minus}(t_1, t_2) \Rightarrow \mathsf{exc}(0)} \ [\textsc{Big3}] \qquad \frac{t_1 \Rightarrow \mathsf{exc}(n')}{\mathsf{minus}(t_1, t_2) \Rightarrow \mathsf{exc}(n')} \ [\textsc{Big4}]$$

Pretty-big-step SOS $\boxed{e \Downarrow o}$

$$t ::= \mathsf{minus}(t, t) \mid n \qquad n \in \mathbb{N} \qquad e ::= t \mid \mathsf{minus1}(o, t) \mid \mathsf{minus2}(n, o) \qquad o ::= n \mid \mathsf{exc}(n)$$

$$\frac{t_1 \Downarrow o_1 \qquad \mathsf{minus1}(o_1, t_2) \Downarrow o}{\mathsf{minus}(t_1, t_2) \Downarrow o} \ [\textsc{Pretty1}] \qquad \frac{t_2 \Downarrow o_2 \qquad \mathsf{minus2}(n_1, o_2) \Downarrow o}{\mathsf{minus1}(n_1, t_2) \Downarrow o} \ [\textsc{Pretty2}]$$

$$\frac{n_1 \geq n_2 \qquad n = n_1 - n_2}{\mathsf{minus2}(n_1, n_2) \Downarrow n} \ [\textsc{Pretty3}] \qquad \frac{n_1 < n_2}{\mathsf{minus2}(n_1, n_2) \Downarrow \mathsf{exc}(0)} \ [\textsc{Pretty4}]$$

$$\frac{\mathsf{abort}(o_1)}{\mathsf{minus1}(o_1, t_2) \Downarrow o_1} \ [\textsc{Pretty5}] \qquad \frac{\mathsf{abort}(o_2)}{\mathsf{minus2}(n_1, o_2) \Downarrow o_2} \ [\textsc{Pretty6}]$$

$$\frac{}{\mathsf{abort}(\mathsf{exc}(n))} \ [\textsc{Abort}]$$

Small-step SOS $\boxed{\langle t, a \rangle \to \langle t', a' \rangle}$

$$t ::= \mathsf{minus}(t, t) \mid n \qquad n \in \mathbb{N} \qquad a ::= \tau \mid \mathsf{exc}(n)$$

$$\frac{\langle t_1, \tau \rangle \to \langle t_1', a' \rangle}{\langle \mathsf{minus}(t_1, t_2), \tau \rangle \to \langle \mathsf{minus}(t_1', t_2), a' \rangle} \ [\textsc{Small1}]$$

$$\frac{\langle t_2, \tau \rangle \to \langle t_2', a' \rangle}{\langle \mathsf{minus}(n_1, t_2), \tau \rangle \to \langle \mathsf{minus}(n_1, t_2'), a' \rangle} \ [\textsc{Small2}]$$

$$\frac{n_1 \geq n_2 \qquad n = n_1 - n_2}{\langle \mathsf{minus}(n_1, n_2), \tau \rangle \to \langle n, \tau \rangle} \ [\textsc{Small3}] \qquad \frac{n_1 < n_2}{\langle \mathsf{minus}(n_1, n_2), \tau \rangle \to \langle 0, \mathsf{exc}(0) \rangle} \ [\textsc{Small4}]$$

state, rather than explicit exception terms, we can abruptly terminate as soon as an exception state is entered.

As the table illustrates, pretty-big-step rules eliminate the duplicate premise evaluating t_1 to n_1 in the big-step rules. However, both the big-step and pretty-big-step rules are less concise than their small-step counterparts – even more so if we generate small-step *congruence rules*, i.e., rules which perform a single contraction in the context of a term, such as [SMALL1] and [SMALL2], from *strictness annotations*, as used in the K-framework (Roşu and Şerbănuţă 2010).

We could ask ourselves: does (pretty-)big-step reasoning always come at the cost of less concise specifications? In this paper we answer this question in the negative. We show how we can have our cake and eat it by writing concise specifications in small-step style and automatically deriving their pretty-big-step counterparts. This allows us to do both small-step and big-step reasoning based on the same semantics. Our derivation differs in two ways from Charguéraud's manual transformation:

1. rather than transforming big-step rules into pretty-big-step rules, we transform small-step rules into pretty-big-step rules; and
2. our transformation is fully mechanical and has been automated.

Our pretty-big-step rules are derived by *refocusing* (Danvy and Nielsen 2004), which allows us to go from reduction-based (small-step) to reduction-free (big-step) evaluation (Danvy 2008b). We have previously adapted the techniques of Danvy and Nielsen to Modular SOS (MSOS) to generate efficient prototype interpreters (Bach Poulsen and Mosses 2014). Here, we extend and combine that with research in pretty-big-step semantics and modular semantics specification to make the following contributions to semantics engineering and its applications:

- We compare the effort required to extend a language with exceptions for big-step, pretty-big-step, and (modular) small-step semantics (Sect. 2). Our conclusion is that small-step MSOS specifications are more concise than corresponding pretty-big-step (SOS) and big-step (SOS and MSOS) specifications.
- We demonstrate that pretty-big-step semantics is within the range of refocusing by extending the diagram from (Danvy 2008a, p. 131) by the highlighted box and arrows[1]:

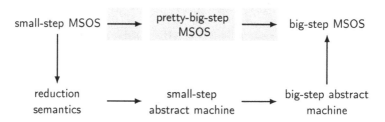

---
[1] Danvy (2008a) gave arrows for SOS rather than MSOS. The extension to MSOS follows from the correspondence between SOS and MSOS (Mosses 2004, Proposition 3 and 4).

By unfolding a refocused small-step semantics as described in Sect. 3 we derive pretty-big-step rules with fewer intermediate terms than Charguéraud's original formulation and which do not require auxiliary predicates.

- We adapt strictness annotations to MSOS (Sect. 4). By comparing the number of rules and premises required to specify an example language involving a considerable number of language features, we conclude that small-step MSOS with strictness annotations can be significantly more concise than the pretty-big-step style.

We claim that refocusing small-step MSOS specifications with strictness annotations gives the best of both the small-step and the big-step worlds: a concise specification format from which somewhat less concise pretty-big-step rules, amenable to the big-step proof techniques pioneered by Charguéraud (2013) and Leroy and Grall (2009), can be mechanically derived.

2   The Language and Its Semantics

We recall and contrast big-step semantics, pretty-big-step semantics, and small-step SOS and MSOS, and illustrate that small-step semantics is more concise than big-step semantics. Following Charguéraud (2013) and Leroy and Grall (2009), the language here considered is the call-by-value λ-calculus extended with constants. We consider the problem of extending this language with exceptions.

2.1   Big-Step Semantics

We give an environment-based semantics for the big-step semantics of the call-by-value λ-calculus based on closures[2]. Judgments take the form $\rho \vdash t \Rightarrow v$, asserting that, under environment ρ, t evaluates to v. Environments $\rho : Var \to Val$ map variables to values, and $\mathbb{N}$ are the natural numbers.

$$Val \ni v ::= n \mid \mathsf{clo}(x, t, \rho) \qquad n \in \mathbb{N} \qquad x \in Var$$

$$\frac{}{\rho \vdash v \Rightarrow v} \text{ [B1]} \qquad \frac{\rho(x) = v}{\rho \vdash \mathsf{var}(x) \Rightarrow v} \text{ [B2]} \qquad \frac{}{\rho \vdash \mathsf{abs}(x, t) \Rightarrow \mathsf{clo}(x, t, \rho)} \text{ [B3]}$$

$$\frac{\rho \vdash t_1 \Rightarrow \mathsf{clo}(x, t, \rho') \qquad \rho \vdash t_2 \Rightarrow v \qquad \rho'[x \mapsto v] \vdash t \Rightarrow v'}{\rho \vdash \mathsf{app}(t_1, t_2) \Rightarrow v'} \text{ [B4]}$$

Following Charguéraud (2013), we introduce an exception term for abruptly terminating evaluation. Under this extension, our judgment becomes $\rho \vdash t \Rightarrow b$ and now asserts that, under environment ρ, t results in the *behaviour* b. The grammar and rules immediately above are extended by:

$$Behaviour \ni b ::= v \mid \mathsf{exc}(v)$$

---

[2] By using closures we avoid the need to specify substitution.

$$\frac{\rho \vdash t_1 \Rightarrow \mathsf{exc}(v')}{\rho \vdash \mathsf{app}(t_1, t_2) \Rightarrow \mathsf{exc}(v')}\ [\text{B5}] \qquad \frac{\rho \vdash t_1 \Rightarrow \mathsf{clo}(x, t, \rho') \qquad \rho \vdash t_2 \Rightarrow \mathsf{exc}(v')}{\rho \vdash \mathsf{app}(t_1, t_2) \Rightarrow \mathsf{exc}(v')}\ [\text{B6}]$$

$$\frac{\rho \vdash t_1 \Rightarrow \mathsf{clo}(x, t, \rho') \qquad \rho \vdash t_2 \Rightarrow v \qquad \rho'[x \mapsto v] \vdash t \Rightarrow \mathsf{exc}(v')}{\rho \vdash \mathsf{app}(t_1, t_2) \Rightarrow \mathsf{exc}(v')}\ [\text{B7}]$$

In order to propagate the exception, the premise evaluating t_1 to a closure $\mathsf{clo}(x, t, \rho')$ becomes duplicated between the rules [B4], [B6], and [B7], the premise evaluating t_2 to a value v is duplicated between [B4] and [B7], and the number of rules defining the application construct grows from one ([B3]) to four ([B3]–[B7]). This is the *duplication problem* with abrupt termination in big-step semantics.

As illustrated by Charguéraud (2013) and Leroy and Grall (2009), a similar duplication problem arises if we express divergence following Cousot and Cousot (1992), e.g., by introducing a 'divergence relation' coinductively defined by rules similar to [B4]–[B7] above. Coinductive big-step semantics (Leroy and Grall 2009) avoids the duplication problem with divergence in big-step semantics by giving a dual (inductive and coinductive) interpretation of the same set of rules. Coinductive big-step semantics does not, however, offer any obvious solutions to the duplication problem with abrupt termination. Pretty-big-step semantics does.

2.2 Pretty-Big-Step Semantics

Charguéraud defines pretty-big-step rules as "rules that consider the evaluation of at most one subterm at a time" and are syntax-directed (Charguéraud 2013, Sect. 2.1), i.e., the initial term (conclusion source) for each rule is syntactically distinct. Using pretty-big-step rules, duplicate premises are eliminated:

$$Outcome \ni o ::= b \mid \mathsf{div} \qquad Intermediate \ni e ::= t \mid \mathsf{app1}(o, t) \mid \mathsf{app2}(v, o)$$

$$\frac{}{\rho \vdash v \Downarrow v}\ [\text{P1}] \qquad \frac{\rho(x) = v}{\rho \vdash \mathsf{var}(x) \Downarrow v}\ [\text{P2}] \qquad \frac{}{\rho \vdash \mathsf{abs}(x, t) \Downarrow \mathsf{clo}(x, t, \rho)}\ [\text{P3}]$$

$$\frac{\rho \vdash t_1 \Downarrow o_1 \qquad \rho \vdash \mathsf{app1}(o_1, t_2) \Downarrow o}{\rho \vdash \mathsf{app}(t_1, t_2) \Downarrow o}\ [\text{P4}] \qquad \frac{\rho \vdash t_2 \Downarrow o_2 \qquad \rho \vdash \mathsf{app2}(v_1, o_2) \Downarrow o}{\rho \vdash \mathsf{app1}(v_1, t_2) \Downarrow o}\ [\text{P5}]$$

$$\frac{\rho'[x \mapsto v] \vdash t \Downarrow o}{\rho \vdash \mathsf{app2}(\mathsf{clo}(x, t, \rho'), v) \Downarrow o}\ [\text{P6}] \qquad \frac{\mathsf{abort}(o)}{\rho \vdash \mathsf{app1}(o, t_2) \Downarrow o}\ [\text{P7}]$$

$$\frac{\mathsf{abort}(o)}{\rho \vdash \mathsf{app2}(v, o) \Downarrow o}\ [\text{P8}] \qquad \frac{}{\mathsf{abort}(\mathsf{exc}(v))}\ [\text{Abort-Exc}]$$

$$\frac{}{\mathsf{abort}(\mathsf{div})}\ [\text{Abort-Div}]$$

Here, e denotes *intermediate terms*. Like coinductive big-step semantics, each pretty-big-step rule has a dual interpretation: inductive and coinductive. Thus, the judgment $\rho \vdash e \Downarrow o$ asserts that, under environment ρ, t either terminates with, or *coevaluates* to, an *outcome* o. An outcome is either a behaviour b (e.g., an exception or a value), or div, the term representing divergence which is only derivable under a coinductive interpretation. The abort(o) auxiliary predicate allows abrupt termination or divergence to be propagated in a generic way.

While pretty-big-step rules eliminate duplicate premises, they also introduce additional terms in the grammar of the language (app1(o,t) and app2(v,o)), an auxiliary predicate (abort(o)), and the number of rules compared to big-step semantics has increased from seven to eight.

2.3   Small-Step SOS

We now compare big-step and pretty-big-step semantics to small-step SOS. Consider the following small-step SOS rules for the call-by-value λ-calculus without exceptions:

$$\frac{\rho(x) = v}{\rho \vdash \mathsf{var}(x) \to v} \;\text{[S1]} \qquad\qquad \frac{}{\rho \vdash \mathsf{abs}(x,t) \to \mathsf{clo}(x,t,\rho)} \;\text{[S2]}$$

$$\frac{\rho \vdash t_1 \to t_1'}{\rho \vdash \mathsf{app}(t_1,t_2) \to \mathsf{app}(t_1',t_2)} \;\text{[S3]} \qquad \frac{\rho \vdash t_2 \to t_2'}{\rho \vdash \mathsf{app}(v_1,t_2) \to \mathsf{app}(v_1,t_2')} \;\text{[S4]}$$

$$\frac{\rho'[x \mapsto v] \vdash t \to t'}{\rho \vdash \mathsf{app}(\mathsf{clo}(x,t,\rho'),v) \to \mathsf{app}(\mathsf{clo}(x,t',\rho'),v)} \;\text{[S5]} \qquad \frac{}{\rho \vdash \mathsf{app}(\mathsf{clo}(x,v',\rho'),v) \to v'} \;\text{[S6]}$$

The small-step judgment $\rho \vdash t \to t'$ asserts that, under environment ρ, t makes a transition to t', which need not be a value. This formulation uses two more rules than the big-step style specification before adding exceptions (Sect. 2.1). This is in part due to the two congruence rules [S3] and [S4] which propagate the result of doing a contraction inside a subterm. Section 4.3 shows how these can be replaced by a strictness annotation.

Following Plotkin (2004), evaluation in a small-step SOS is given by (possibly infinite) sequences of transition steps in an underlying *labelled terminal transition system* (LTTS). The LTTS for the SOS with the rules [S1]–[S6] above is given by $\langle \textit{Term}, \mathbf{1}, \to, \textit{Val} \rangle$, where $\to \,\subseteq\, \textit{Term} \times \mathbf{1} \times \textit{Term}$ is the transition relation that our rules inductively define, and $\mathbf{1}$ denotes the singleton set containing a unit label that is implicitly present on all transitions. Divergence in small-step SOS corresponds to an infinite sequence of transition steps in the underlying LTTS.

To extend our small-step semantics with exceptions, we could follow Charguéraud (2013) in introducing an exception term. This would require us to introduce rules propagating exceptions similarly to the pretty-big-step rules. An alternative, following Mosses (2004), is to model exceptions as signals in the label of the transition relation. In this approach, a top-level term abruptly terminates evaluation if an exception signal is propagated to the top-level. Here, we take a different approach and model exceptions as *states* in the configurations of the underlying LTTS. Updating our relation, the judgment $\rho \vdash \langle t, a \rangle \to \langle t', a' \rangle$ asserts that, under environment ρ, the *configuration* $\langle t, a \rangle$ makes a transition to

$\langle t', a' \rangle$, where $a ::= \tau \mid \mathsf{exc}(v)$. Our small-step rules are updated to propagate the exception state:

$$\frac{\rho(x) = v}{\rho \vdash \langle \mathsf{var}(x), \tau \rangle \to \langle v, \tau \rangle} \; [\mathrm{S1'}] \qquad \frac{}{\rho \vdash \langle \mathsf{abs}(x, t), \tau \rangle \to \langle \mathsf{clo}(x, t, \rho), \tau \rangle} \; [\mathrm{S2'}]$$

$$\frac{\rho \vdash \langle t_1, \tau \rangle \to \langle t_1', a' \rangle}{\rho \vdash \langle \mathsf{app}(t_1, t_2), \tau \rangle \to \langle \mathsf{app}(t_1', t_2), a' \rangle} \; [\mathrm{S3'}] \qquad \frac{\rho \vdash \langle t_2, \tau \rangle \to \langle t_2', a' \rangle}{\rho \vdash \langle \mathsf{app}(v_1, t_2), \tau \rangle \to \langle \mathsf{app}(v_1, t_2'), a' \rangle} \; [\mathrm{S4'}]$$

$$\frac{\rho'[x \mapsto v] \vdash \langle t, \tau \rangle \to \langle t', a' \rangle}{\rho \vdash \langle \mathsf{app}(\mathsf{clo}(x, t, \rho'), v), \tau \rangle \to \langle \mathsf{app}(\mathsf{clo}(x, t', \rho'), v), a' \rangle} \; [\mathrm{S5'}]$$

$$\frac{}{\rho \vdash \langle \mathsf{app}(\mathsf{clo}(x, v', \rho'), v), \tau \rangle \to \langle v', \tau \rangle} \; [\mathrm{S6'}]$$

Here, τ indicates that no exception is being thrown. By matching on the exception state for each transition at the top-level of our LTTS, we can decide whether evaluation should continue (in case of a τ state), or whether to terminate (in case of an exception).

2.4   Small-Step Modular SOS

Unlike pretty-big-step semantics, introducing abrupt termination in the small-step SOS in previous subsection did not increase the number of rules. Unlike big-step semantics, nor did introducing abrupt termination result in duplication of premises. To introduce the exception state, we did, however, reformulate all of our rules. If we use MSOS instead of ordinary SOS, we do not need to update our rules at all. The MSOS rules corresponding to the small-step SOS rules [S1]–[S6] in the previous subsection are:

$$\frac{\rho(x) = v}{\mathsf{var}(x) \xrightarrow{\{\mathbf{env} = \rho, -\}} v} \; [\mathrm{M1}] \qquad \frac{}{\mathsf{abs}(x, t) \xrightarrow{\{\mathbf{env} = \rho, -\}} \mathsf{clo}(x, t, \rho)} \; [\mathrm{M2}]$$

$$\frac{t_1 \xrightarrow{\ell} t_1'}{\mathsf{app}(t_1, t_2) \xrightarrow{\ell} \mathsf{app}(t_1', t_2)} \; [\mathrm{M3}] \qquad \frac{t_2 \xrightarrow{\ell} t_2'}{\mathsf{app}(v_1, t_2) \xrightarrow{\ell} \mathsf{app}(v_1, t_2')} \; [\mathrm{M4}]$$

$$\frac{t \xrightarrow{\{\mathbf{env} = \rho'[x \mapsto v], \dots\}} t'}{\mathsf{app}(\mathsf{clo}(x, t, \rho'), v) \xrightarrow{\{\mathbf{env} = \rho, \dots\}} \mathsf{app}(\mathsf{clo}(x, t', \rho'), v)} \; [\mathrm{M5}] \qquad \frac{}{\mathsf{app}(\mathsf{clo}(x, v', \rho'), v) \xrightarrow{\{-\}} v'} \; [\mathrm{M6}]$$

The judgment $t \xrightarrow{\ell} t'$ asserts that, under label ℓ, t reduces to t'. Labels in MSOS are comprised of label components, such as $\mathbf{env} = \rho$ in the rules above, and are denoted using Standard ML syntax for record patterns (Milner et al. 1997). Whereas SOS requires auxiliary entities to be explicitly propagated, even for rules that don't explicitly use them, MSOS uses label variables to refer to label components that are not explicitly needed. In the rules above, '...' is an example of such a variable. The '—' in the rules above is a variable with a special meaning in MSOS: it says that no *side-effects* occur in the step. For example, if '—' refers to, say, a pair of read-write store label components $\langle \mathbf{sto} = \sigma, \mathbf{sto'} = \sigma' \rangle$, where $\mathbf{sto} = \sigma$ is the store before the transition, and $\mathbf{sto'} = \sigma'$ is the store resulting from making the transition, the '—' variable requires that the state is not updated, i.e., that $\sigma = \sigma'$.

While side-effects (or lack hereof) on auxiliary entities in SOS are explicitly propagated, side-effects in MSOS are propagated by *label composition*. Formally, a label is a morphism in a product category, the members of the product being the label components. Propagating side-effects between transitions corresponds to composition in the product category. 'No side-effects' (or *unobservability*) is represented by identity morphisms. Recalling that composition in a product category corresponds to taking the product of compositions for each of the corresponding individual members of the product (Pierce 1991), composing two labels corresponds to propagating the side-effects for each of the underlying label components. We briefly recall the basic label component categories for MSOS and their composition principles:

Read-only: modelled by a *discrete category* where objects only have identity morphisms. This corresponds to environments which may be inspected but not changed. Composition principle for read-only entities ro: $ro \circ ro = ro$.

Read-write: modelled by a *preorder category* where morphisms between objects constitute a preorder. Corresponds to stores which may be inspected and changed by a transition. Each morphism is a pair; e.g., $\langle rw, rw' \rangle$. Composition principle for read-write entities $\langle rw, rw' \rangle$: $\langle rw', rw'' \rangle \circ \langle rw, rw' \rangle = \langle rw, rw'' \rangle$.

Write-only: modelled by a *free monoid* considered as a category with a single object. The morphisms are (possibly empty) sequences of observable actions and signals. One of the identity arrows corresponds to the unobservable action τ (the empty sequence); all others represent observable sequences of actions. Composition principle for write-only entities wo': $wo'_2 \circ wo'_1 = wo'_1 \bullet wo'_2$ where $\bullet$ is the composition operator in the monoid

By convention, readable label components are labelled by unprimed indices, such as $\mathbf{env}$, and writable label components are labelled by primed indices, such as $\mathbf{sto'}$. For example, for the two labels $\ell_1 = \{\mathbf{env} = \rho, \mathbf{sto} = \sigma, \mathbf{sto'} = \sigma\}$ and $\ell_2 = \{\mathbf{env} = \rho, \mathbf{sto} = \sigma, \mathbf{sto'} = \sigma'\}$, their composition $\ell_2 \circ \ell_1$ is given by the label $\{\mathbf{env} = \rho, \mathbf{sto} = \sigma, \mathbf{sto'} = \sigma'\}$.

Following Mosses (2004), evaluation in MSOS corresponds to (possibly infinite) sequences of transition steps in an underlying *generalized transition system*. The generalized transition system for the MSOS given by rules [M1]–[M6] above is a tuple $\langle \textit{Term}, \mathbb{L}, \rightarrow, \textit{Val} \rangle$, where $\mathbb{L}$ is a product category consisting of a single discrete category, corresponding to the read-only label component $\mathbf{env} = \rho$.

In a similar style to Leroy and Grall (2009), the iteration of this GTS can be expressed by a relation $\rightarrow^*$ for which judgments take the form $t \xrightarrow{\ell}{}^* v$, asserting that term t evaluates to value v under label ℓ. $\rightarrow^*$ is defined by the rules:

$$\frac{}{v \xrightarrow{\{-\}}{}^* v} \; [\text{MRefl}] \qquad \frac{t \xrightarrow{\ell_1} t' \quad t' \xrightarrow{\ell_2}{}^* v}{t \xrightarrow{\ell_2 \circ \ell_1}{}^* v} \; [\text{MTrans}]$$

To extend our semantics with exceptions, we extend the product category $\mathbb{L}$ by a new read-write label component $\langle \mathbf{exc} = a, \mathbf{exc}' = a' \rangle$, where $a ::= \tau \mid \mathsf{exc}(v)$. There are several ways of inhibiting further evaluation after an exception state is entered in MSOS. One is to follow the approach taken in our SOS rules and explicitly modify our rules such that each transition only matches when $\mathbf{exc} = \tau$. Another way, which does not require the modification of our transition rules, is to update the evaluation rules [MREFL] and [MTRANS] as we illustrate in Sect. 3.1.

Table 2. Required number of rules, premises, and rule modifications in order to express abrupt termination. Rule modifications are counted by comparing with the corresponding semantics without abrupt termination, where we count each reformulated existing rule and each introduction of a new rule for previously defined constructs.

Variant	(exceptions)	Rules	Premises	Modifications
Big-step	terms	7 ([B1]–[B7])	10	3
	states	6	7	3
Pretty-big-step	terms	8 ([P1]–[P8])	8	2
	states	8	8	2
Small-step SOS	terms	8	4	2
	states	6 ([S1']–[S6'])	4	6
Small-step MSOS	terms	8	4	2
	states	6 ([M1]–[M6])	4	0

Table 2 summarizes the effort required to specify and update our semantics. From this, we can see that SOS with exception labels requires fewer rules and premises to handle abrupt termination than big-step and pretty-big-step rules. This is in part due to the fact that we followed Charguéraud (2013) in using explicit exception terms rather than exception states. By refocusing our small-step MSOS rules in Sect. 3.2, we demonstrate how to derive more concise pretty-big-step rules based on small-step MSOS. Deriving pretty-big-step MSOS rules in this fashion also reduces the need for intermediate terms and auxiliary predicates.

3   From Small-Step to Pretty-Big-Step Modular SOS

After introducing some preliminary requirements, we show how to derive pretty-big-step rules from small-step rules by refocusing.

3.1   Preliminaries

To ensure the correctness of our derivation, we require that:

1. the small-step MSOS is syntax-directed; and
2. exception states are explicitly recognizable at the top-level of the semantics.

The first requirement ensures that derived pretty-big-step rules are syntax-directed. The second ensures that abrupt termination is propagated correctly in derived pretty-big-step rules.

Syntax-Directed Evaluation. Following Charguéraud (2013), rules are syntax-directed if the initial configuration (i.e., the conclusion source term) of each rule is distinct from all other rules. In MSOS rules, an initial configuration consist of the initial (conclusion source) term together with the readable label components in the conclusion. The small-step MSOS rules from the previous section are not syntax-directed: e.g., for some value v and term t, $\mathsf{app}(v,t)$ matches the conclusions of both [M3] and [M4]. Rather than introducing intermediate terms, like in Sect. 2.2, we modify the abstract syntax to distinguish terms and values:

$$Val \ni v ::= n \mid \mathsf{clo}(x,e,\rho) \qquad n \in \mathbb{N} \qquad x \in Var$$

$$Term \ni t ::= \mathsf{var}(x) \mid \mathsf{app}(e,e) \mid \mathsf{abs}(x,e)$$

$$Expr \ni e ::= \mathsf{term}(t) \mid \mathsf{val}(v)$$

Using this abstract syntax, values are no longer instances of terms. However, terms and values are both instances of *expressions* in *Expr*. To avoid the tedium of writing out the constructor names term and val each time we need them, we will leave them implicit, like Charguéraud (2013), and simply write t instead of $\mathsf{term}(t)$, and v instead of $\mathsf{val}(v)$. We revise our relations and rules from Sect. 2.4 to reflect the updated abstract syntax:

$$\frac{}{v \xrightarrow{\{-\}}{}^* v} \text{[EREFL]} \qquad \frac{t \xrightarrow{\ell_1} e \qquad e \xrightarrow{\ell_2}{}^* v}{t \xrightarrow{\ell_2 \circ \ell_1}{}^* v} \text{[ETRANS]} \qquad \boxed{e \xrightarrow{\ell}{}^* e} \; \boxed{t \xrightarrow{\ell} e}$$

$$\frac{\rho(x) = v}{\mathsf{var}(x) \xrightarrow{\{\mathbf{env}=\rho,-\}} v} \text{[E1]} \qquad \frac{}{\mathsf{abs}(x,e) \xrightarrow{\{\mathbf{env}=\rho,-\}} \mathsf{clo}(x,e,\rho)} \text{[E2]}$$

$$\frac{t_1 \xrightarrow{\ell} e_1}{\mathsf{app}(t_1,e_2) \xrightarrow{\ell} \mathsf{app}(e_1,e_2)} \text{[E3]} \qquad \frac{t_2 \xrightarrow{\ell} e_2}{\mathsf{app}(v_1,t_2) \xrightarrow{\ell} \mathsf{app}(v_1,e_2)} \text{[E4]}$$

$$\frac{t \xrightarrow{\{\mathbf{env}=\rho'[x \mapsto v],...\}} e}{\mathsf{app}(\mathsf{clo}(x,t,\rho'),v) \xrightarrow{\{\mathbf{env}=\rho,...\}} \mathsf{app}(\mathsf{clo}(x,e,\rho'),v)} \text{[E5]} \qquad \frac{}{\mathsf{app}(\mathsf{clo}(x,v',\rho'),v) \xrightarrow{\{-\}} v'} \text{[E6]}$$

These rules are syntax-directed: $\mathsf{app}(v,t)$ only matches the conclusion of [E4].

Exception State Recognition. Consider the extension of our language by a $\mathsf{throw}(v)$ construct for throwing exceptions:

$$t ::= ... \mid \mathsf{throw}(v) \qquad\qquad v ::= ... \mid \mathsf{unit}$$

$$\frac{}{\mathsf{throw}(v) \xrightarrow{\{\mathbf{exc}=\tau,\mathbf{exc}'=\mathsf{exc}(v),-\}} \mathsf{unit}} \text{[E7]}$$

We expect evaluation of the term $\mathsf{app}(\mathsf{abs}(x,\mathsf{var}(x)),\mathsf{throw}(42))$ to abruptly terminate after reducing $\mathsf{throw}(42)$. However, using [ETRANS] as defined above, this is not what happens. First, $\mathsf{abs}(x, \mathsf{var}(x))$ is evaluated to the closure $\mathsf{clo}(x, \mathsf{var}(x), \emptyset)$, where $\emptyset$ is the empty environment. The next step throws the exception, giving the subject term $\mathsf{app}(\mathsf{clo}(x, \mathsf{var}(x), \emptyset), \mathsf{unit})$ and label $\{\mathbf{exc} = \tau, \mathbf{exc}' = \mathsf{exc}(42), \ldots\}$. Rather than abruptly terminate at this point, the exception is forward propagated by label composition, whereafter evaluation of the subject term $\mathsf{app}(\mathsf{clo}(x, \mathsf{unit}, \emptyset), \mathsf{unit})$ and label $\{\mathbf{exc} = \mathsf{exc}(42), \mathbf{exc}' = a, \ldots\}$ continues. We update our evaluation rules to terminate when $\mathbf{exc} = \mathsf{exc}(v)$:

$$a ::= \tau \mid \mathsf{exc}(v)$$

$$\cfrac{t \xrightarrow{\{\mathbf{exc}=\tau, \mathbf{exc}'=a, X_1\}} e \qquad e \xrightarrow{\ell_2}{}^* e'}{t \xrightarrow{\ell_2 \circ \{\mathbf{exc}=\tau, \mathbf{exc}'=a, X_1\}}{}^* e'} \text{ [TRANS]} \qquad\qquad \cfrac{}{e \xrightarrow{\{\mathbf{exc}=\mathsf{exc}(v), \mathbf{exc}'=\mathsf{exc}(v), -\}}{}^* e} \text{ [EXC]}$$

By the definition of label composition, the conclusion of the first rule only matches transitions with $\mathbf{exc} = \tau$, since the result of composing an arbitrary label with $\{\mathbf{exc} = \tau, \mathbf{exc}' = a, X_1\}$ is a label with $\mathbf{exc} = \tau$. The initial configurations for [TRANS] and [EXC] are distinct and hence syntax-directed.

Evaluating the subject term $\mathsf{app}(\mathsf{clo}(x, \mathsf{var}(x), \emptyset), \mathsf{throw}(42))$ under [TRANS] and [EXC] changes the exception state from τ to $\mathsf{exc}(42)$, after which only [EXC] matches the rule. Evaluation therefore abruptly terminates with label $\{\mathbf{exc} = \tau, \mathbf{exc}' = \mathsf{exc}(42), \ldots\}$ and term $\mathsf{app}(\mathsf{clo}(x, \mathsf{var}(x), \emptyset), \mathsf{unit})$.

It is equally straightforward to extend our language with a catch construct for catching and handling exceptions. We give a syntax-directed definition by introducing an $\mathsf{eq}(e, e)$ construct for checking syntactic equality for values and an $\mathsf{if}(e, e, e)$ construct for checking the outcome of the $\mathbf{exc}'$ label component:

$$t ::= \ldots \mid \mathsf{if}(e, e, e) \mid \mathsf{eq}(e, e) \mid \mathsf{catch}(e, e) \qquad v ::= \ldots \mid \mathsf{true} \mid \mathsf{false} \mid a$$

$$\cfrac{t \xrightarrow{\ell} e}{\mathsf{if}(t, e_1, e_2) \xrightarrow{\ell} \mathsf{if}(e, e_1, e_2)} \text{ [E8]} \qquad\qquad \cfrac{}{\mathsf{if}(\mathsf{true}, e_1, e_2) \xrightarrow{\{-\}} e_1} \text{ [E9]}$$

$$\cfrac{}{\mathsf{if}(\mathsf{false}, e_1, e_2) \xrightarrow{\{-\}} e_2} \text{ [E10]} \qquad\qquad \cfrac{t_1 \xrightarrow{\ell} e_1}{\mathsf{eq}(t_1, e_2) \xrightarrow{\ell} \mathsf{eq}(e_1, e_2)} \text{ [E11]}$$

$$\cfrac{t_2 \xrightarrow{\ell} e_2}{\mathsf{eq}(v_1, t_2) \xrightarrow{\ell} \mathsf{eq}(v_1, e_2)} \text{ [E12]} \qquad\qquad \cfrac{v_1 = v_2}{\mathsf{eq}(v_1, v_2) \xrightarrow{\{-\}} \mathsf{true}} \text{ [E13]}$$

$$\cfrac{v_1 \neq v_2}{\mathsf{eq}(v_1, v_2) \xrightarrow{\{-\}} \mathsf{false}} \text{ [E14]} \qquad\qquad \cfrac{}{\mathsf{catch}(v_1, e_2) \xrightarrow{\{-\}} v_1} \text{ [E15]}$$

$$\cfrac{t_1 \xrightarrow{\{\mathbf{exc}=\tau, \mathbf{exc}'=a, X\}} e_1}{\mathsf{catch}(t_1, e_2) \xrightarrow{\{\mathbf{exc}=\tau, \mathbf{exc}'=\tau, X\}} \mathsf{if}(\mathsf{eq}(a, \tau), \mathsf{catch}(e_1, e_2), \mathsf{app}(e_2, a))} \text{ [E16]}$$

The resulting semantics is syntax-directed and explicitly recognizes abrupt termination at the top-level.

3.2 Deriving Pretty-Big-Step Rules by Refocusing

Following our previous work (Bach Poulsen and Mosses 2014), refocusing a small-step MSOS involves extending the MSOS evaluation rules from previous section by a refocusing rule. Renaming [EREFL] to [REFL], the evaluation rules extended by the [REFOCUS] rule are:

$$\frac{}{v \xrightarrow{\{-\}}{}^* v}\ [\text{REFL}] \qquad \frac{t \xrightarrow{\{\mathbf{exc}=\tau,\mathbf{exc}'=a,X_1\}} e \qquad e \xrightarrow{\ell_2}{}^* e'}{t \xrightarrow{\ell_2 \circ \{\mathbf{exc}=\tau,\mathbf{exc}'=a,X_1\}}{}^* e'}\ [\text{TRANS}]$$

$$\frac{}{e \xrightarrow{\{\mathbf{exc}=\mathrm{exc}(v),\mathbf{exc}'=\mathrm{exc}(v),-\}}{}^* e}\ [\text{EXC}] \qquad \frac{t \xrightarrow{\ell}{}^* e}{t \xrightarrow{\ell} e}\ [\text{REFOCUS}]$$

Introducing the [REFOCUS] rule allows evaluation to occur inside derivation trees, as opposed to always at the top-level. However, it also breaks syntax-direction: the initial configuration of [REFOCUS] matches that of every other transition rule. To get the effect of refocusing while preserving syntax-direction, we unfold the refocusing rule and replace our transition rules by the derived rules corresponding to the partial derivation for each transition rule $[r]$:

$$\frac{\dfrac{\dfrac{P_1 \quad \cdots \quad P_n}{t \xrightarrow{\{\mathbf{exc}=\tau,\mathbf{exc}'=a,X_1\}} e}\ [r] \qquad e \xrightarrow{\ell_2}{}^* e'}{t \xrightarrow{\ell_2 \circ \{\mathbf{exc}=\tau,\mathbf{exc}'=a,X_1\}}{}^* e'}\ [\text{TRANS}]}{t \xrightarrow{\ell_2 \circ \{\mathbf{exc}=\tau,\mathbf{exc}'=a,X_1\}} e'}\ [\text{REFOCUS}]$$

$$\sim \qquad \frac{P_1 \quad \cdots \quad P_n \qquad e \xrightarrow{\ell_2}{}^* e'}{t \xrightarrow{\ell_2 \circ \{\mathbf{exc}=\tau,\mathbf{exc}'=a,X_1\}} e'}$$

Noticing that we have to propagate the label components $\mathbf{exc}=\tau, \mathbf{exc}'=a$ many times, we introduce the notation $\|X\|$ for abbreviating $\{\mathbf{exc}=\tau, \mathbf{exc}'=a, X\}$.

Returning to our running example, *refocusing* the [E3] rule from Sect. 3.1 Gives the following partial derivation and derived (*refocused*) rule [ER3]:

$$\frac{\dfrac{\dfrac{t_1 \xrightarrow{\|X_1\|} e_1}{\mathsf{app}(t_1, e_2) \xrightarrow{\|X_1\|} \mathsf{app}(e_1, e_2)}\ [\text{E3}] \qquad \mathsf{app}(e_1, e_2) \xrightarrow{\ell_2}{}^* e'}{\mathsf{app}(t_1, e_2) \xrightarrow{\ell_2 \circ \|X_1\|}{}^* e'}\ [\text{TRANS}]}{\mathsf{app}(t_1, e_2) \xrightarrow{\ell_2 \circ \|X_1\|} e'}\ [\text{REFOCUS}]$$

$$\sim \qquad \frac{t_1 \xrightarrow{\|X_1\|} e_1 \qquad \mathsf{app}(e_1, e_2) \xrightarrow{\ell_2}{}^* e'}{\mathsf{app}(t_1, e_2) \xrightarrow{\ell_2 \circ \|X_1\|} e'}\ [\text{ER3}]$$

The refocused rules corresponding to [E1]–[E7] are:

$$\frac{\rho(x) = v}{\mathsf{var}(x) \xrightarrow{\|\mathbf{env}=\rho,-\|} v} \text{ [ER1]} \qquad\qquad \frac{}{\mathsf{abs}(x,e) \xrightarrow{\|\mathbf{env}=\rho,-\|} \mathsf{clo}(x,e,\rho)} \text{ [ER2]}$$

$$\frac{t_1 \xrightarrow{\|X_1\|} e_1 \qquad \mathsf{app}(e_1,e_2) \xrightarrow{\ell_2}{}^* e'}{\mathsf{app}(t_1,e_2) \xrightarrow{\ell_2 \circ \|X_1\|} e'} \text{ [ER3]} \qquad \frac{t_2 \xrightarrow{\|X_1\|} e_2 \qquad \mathsf{app}(v_1,e_2) \xrightarrow{\ell_2}{}^* e'}{\mathsf{app}(v_1,t_2) \xrightarrow{\ell_2 \circ \|X_1\|} e'} \text{ [ER4]}$$

$$\frac{t \xrightarrow{\|\mathbf{env}=\rho'[x \mapsto v], X_1\|} e \qquad \mathsf{app}(\mathsf{clo}(x,e,\rho'),v) \xrightarrow{\ell_2}{}^* e'}{\mathsf{app}(\mathsf{clo}(x,t,\rho'),v) \xrightarrow{\ell_2 \circ \|\mathbf{env}=\rho, X_1\|} e'} \text{ [ER5]}$$

$$\frac{}{\mathsf{app}(\mathsf{clo}(x,v',\rho'),v) \xrightarrow{\|-\|} v'} \text{ [ER6]} \qquad \frac{}{\mathsf{throw}(v) \xrightarrow{\{\mathbf{exc}=\tau, \mathbf{exc}'=\mathbf{exc}(v), -\}} \mathsf{unit}} \text{ [ER7]}$$

Our refocused rules are very closely related to pretty-big-step rules. Like pretty-big-step rules, each refocused rule:

- relates a term to a value or an exception state;
- reduces a single subterm at a time; and
- is syntax-directed.

A significant difference is that our refocused rules mutually define both $\rightarrow^*$ and $\rightarrow$. However, we can observe that each ordinary transition step ($\rightarrow$) either maps a term to an exception state, or maps a term to a value. From this, it follows that the top-level application of [TRANS] has the form:

$$\frac{t \xrightarrow{\|X_1\|} e \qquad \dfrac{}{e \xrightarrow{\ell_2}{}^* e'} \text{ [R]}}{t \xrightarrow{\ell_2 \circ \|X_1\|}{}^* e'} \text{ [TRANS]}$$

Either e is going to be a value v, in which case [R]=[REFL]. Otherwise, for the label $\ell_2 = \{\mathbf{exc} = a, \mathbf{exc}' = a', \dots\}$ it is the case that $a \neq \tau$, whereby [R]=[EXC]. Therefore, in a semantics with refocused rules, all applications of [TRANS] match the derived rule:

$$\frac{t \xrightarrow{\|X\|} e}{t \xrightarrow{\|X\|}{}^* e} \text{ [TTRANS]}$$

By applications of [REFOCUS] and [TTRANS], each occurrence of an ordinary step ($\rightarrow$) can be replaced by a transitive step ($\rightarrow^*$). Replacing ordinary steps gives the MSOS pretty-big-step rules in Table 3. These rules describe the same language as the pretty-big-step rules given in (Charguéraud 2013, Fig. 2). In contrast to Charguéraud's pretty-big-step semantics, we have not introduced any intermediate terms or auxiliary predicates.

The correctness of the derivations presented in this section have been tested by using the MSOS Derivation Tool (Bach Poulsen and Mosses 2014) to generate and compare executable interpreters for the small-step semantics, its refocused, and its pretty-big-step counterpart. The generated interpreters and test suite are available online[3]. Sections 5 and 6 suggest future directions for a more formal treatment of correctness.

---

[3] www.plancomps.org/bachpoulsen2014a

Table 3. Derived pretty-big-step rules for [E1]–[E16]

$$\frac{}{v \xrightarrow{\{-\}}^* v} \text{[EPREFL]} \qquad\qquad \frac{}{e \xrightarrow{\{\mathbf{exc}=\mathbf{exc}(v),\mathbf{exc'}=\mathbf{exc}(v),-\}}^* e} \text{[EPEXC]}$$

$$\frac{\rho(x) = v}{\mathsf{var}(x) \xrightarrow{\|\mathbf{env}=\rho,-\|}^* v} \text{[EP1]} \qquad\qquad \frac{}{\mathsf{abs}(x,e) \xrightarrow{\|\mathbf{env}=\rho,-\|}^* \mathsf{clo}(x,e,\rho)} \text{[EP2]}$$

$$\frac{t_1 \xrightarrow{\|X_1\|}^* e_1 \quad \mathsf{app}(e_1,e_2) \xrightarrow{\ell_2}^* e'}{\mathsf{app}(t_1,e_2) \xrightarrow{\ell_2\circ\|X_1\|}^* e'} \text{[EP3]} \qquad \frac{t_2 \xrightarrow{\|X_1\|}^* e_2 \quad \mathsf{app}(v_1,e_2) \xrightarrow{\ell_2}^* e'x}{\mathsf{app}(v_1,t_2) \xrightarrow{\ell_2\circ\|X_1\|}^* e'} \text{[EP4]}$$

$$\frac{t \xrightarrow{\|\mathbf{env}=\rho'[x\mapsto v],X_1\|}^* e \quad \mathsf{app}(\mathsf{clo}(x,e,\rho'),v) \xrightarrow{\ell_2}^* e'}{\mathsf{app}(\mathsf{clo}(x,t,\rho'),v) \xrightarrow{\ell_2\circ\|\mathbf{env}=\rho,X_1\|}^* e'} \text{[EP5]}$$

$$\frac{}{\mathsf{app}(\mathsf{clo}(x,v',\rho'),v) \xrightarrow{\|-\|}^* v'} \text{[EP6]} \qquad \frac{}{\mathsf{throw}(v) \xrightarrow{\{\mathbf{exc}=\tau,\mathbf{exc'}=\mathbf{exc}(v),-\}}^* \mathsf{unit}} \text{[EP7]}$$

$$\frac{t \xrightarrow{\|X_1\|}^* e \quad \mathsf{if}(e,e_1,e_2) \xrightarrow{\ell_2}^* e'}{\mathsf{if}(t,e_1,e_2) \xrightarrow{\ell_2\circ\|X_1\|}^* e'} \text{[EP8]} \qquad \frac{e_1 \xrightarrow{\ell}^* e'}{\mathsf{if}(\mathsf{true},e_1,e_2) \xrightarrow{\ell}^* e'} \text{[EP9]}$$

$$\frac{e_2 \xrightarrow{\ell}^* e'}{\mathsf{if}(\mathsf{false},e_1,e_2) \xrightarrow{\ell}^* e'} \text{[EP10]} \qquad \frac{t_1 \xrightarrow{\|X_1\|}^* e_1 \quad \mathsf{eq}(e_1,e_2) \xrightarrow{\ell_2}^* e'}{\mathsf{eq}(t_1,e_2) \xrightarrow{\ell_2\circ\|X_1\|}^* e'} \text{[EP11]}$$

$$\frac{t_2 \xrightarrow{\|X_1\|}^* e_2 \quad \mathsf{eq}(v_1,e_2) \xrightarrow{\ell_2}^* e'}{\mathsf{eq}(v_1,t_2) \xrightarrow{\ell_2\circ\|X_1\|}^* e'} \text{[EP12]} \qquad \frac{v_1 = v_2}{\mathsf{eq}(v_1,v_2) \xrightarrow{\{-\}}^* \mathsf{true}} \text{[EP13]}$$

$$\frac{v_1 \neq v_2}{\mathsf{eq}(v_1,v_2) \xrightarrow{\{-\}}^* \mathsf{false}} \text{[EP14]} \qquad \frac{}{\mathsf{catch}(v_1,e_2) \xrightarrow{\{-\}}^* v_1} \text{[EP15]}$$

$$\frac{t_1 \xrightarrow{\|\mathbf{exc}=\tau,\mathbf{exc'}=a,X_1\|}^* e_1 \quad \mathsf{if}(\mathsf{eq}(a,\tau),\mathsf{catch}(e_1,e_2),\mathsf{app}(e_2,a)) \xrightarrow{\ell_2}^* e'}{\mathsf{catch}(t_1,e_2) \xrightarrow{\ell_2\circ\|\mathbf{exc}=\tau,\mathbf{exc'}=\tau,X_1\|}^* e'} \text{[EP16]}$$

4   Scaling Up to Real Languages

Our running example in this paper has been the λ-calculus with exceptions. This section illustrates how the derivation in Sect. 3.2 scales up to other language features.

4.1   Side-Effects

We have already shown how to derive pretty-big-step rules for semantics with exceptions. Other kinds of abrupt termination can be handled in a similar way. Small-step MSOS rules with output channels (such as printing) and mutable storage impose no additional constraints when deriving pretty-big-step rules by refocusing. To demonstrate, we extend our language with printing and ML-style references. To handle these features, we introduce two new label components: a read-write label component $\langle \mathbf{sto} = \sigma, \mathbf{sto'} = \sigma \rangle$, where $\sigma : Loc \to Val$ are stores mapping *locations* (such as memory addresses) to values; and a write-only label component $\mathbf{out'} = [v]$ containing a (possibly empty) list of printed values. The extended language is:

$$t ::= \ldots \mid \mathsf{print}(e) \mid \mathsf{ref}(e) \mid \mathsf{deref}(e) \mid \mathsf{assign}(e, e) \qquad v ::= \ldots \mid l \qquad l \in Loc$$

$$\frac{t \xrightarrow{\ell} e}{\mathsf{print}(t) \xrightarrow{\ell} \mathsf{print}(e)} \text{ [E17]} \qquad \frac{}{\mathsf{print}(v) \xrightarrow{\{\mathbf{out'}=[v], -\}} \mathsf{unit}} \text{ [E18]}$$

$$\frac{t \xrightarrow{\ell} e}{\mathsf{ref}(t) \xrightarrow{\ell} \mathsf{ref}(e)} \text{ [E19]} \qquad \frac{l \notin \mathrm{dom}(\sigma)}{\mathsf{ref}(v) \xrightarrow{\{\mathbf{sto}=\sigma, \mathbf{sto'}=\sigma[l \mapsto v], -\}} l} \text{ [E20]}$$

$$\frac{t \xrightarrow{\ell} e}{\mathsf{deref}(t) \xrightarrow{\ell} \mathsf{deref}(e)} \text{ [E21]} \qquad \frac{\sigma(l) = v}{\mathsf{deref}(l) \xrightarrow{\{\mathbf{sto}=\sigma, \mathbf{sto'}=\sigma, -\}} v} \text{ [E22]}$$

$$\frac{t_1 \xrightarrow{\ell} e_1}{\mathsf{assign}(t_1, e_2) \xrightarrow{\ell} \mathsf{assign}(e_1, e_2)} \text{ [E23]} \qquad \frac{t_2 \xrightarrow{\ell} e_2}{\mathsf{assign}(l, t_2) \xrightarrow{\ell} \mathsf{assign}(l, e_2)} \text{ [E24]}$$

$$\frac{}{\mathsf{assign}(l, v) \xrightarrow{\{\mathbf{sto}=\sigma, \mathbf{sto'}=\sigma[l \mapsto v], -\}} v} \text{ [E25]}$$

No modification of our evaluation rules is necessary. These syntax-directed rules are straightforwardly refocused and unfolded into pretty-big-step rules as described in Sect. 3.2.

4.2   C-Style for-Loops

Following Charguéraud (2013), we illustrate how to express a C-style for-loop construct. We recall Charguéraud's pretty-big-step rules, and compare with a corresponding small-step formulation and its derived pretty-big-step MSOS counterpart.

A C-style for-loop, $\mathsf{for}(e_1, e_2, e_3)$, continually evaluates body e_3 of a loop, until the condition e_1 no longer holds. Between each iteration of the for-loop, *incrementer* e_2 is evaluated. Charguéraud gives pretty-big-step rules that reflect this as follows:

$$t ::= \mathsf{for}(e, e, e) \mid v \qquad Intermediate \ni e ::= t \mid \mathsf{for}(i, o, t, t, t) \quad i \in \{1, 2, 3\}$$

$$b ::= v \mid \mathsf{exc}(v) \qquad o ::= \langle b, \sigma \rangle \mid \mathsf{div}$$

$$\frac{\langle t_1, \sigma \rangle \Downarrow o_1 \qquad \langle \text{for}(1, o_1, t_1, t_2, t_3), \sigma \rangle \Downarrow o}{\langle \text{for}(t_1, t_2, t_3), \sigma \rangle \Downarrow o} \qquad \frac{}{\langle \text{for}(1, \langle \text{false}, \sigma \rangle, t_1, t_2, t_3), \sigma' \rangle \Downarrow \langle \text{unit}, \sigma \rangle}$$

$$\frac{\langle t_3, \sigma \rangle \Downarrow o_3 \qquad \langle \text{for}(2, o_3, t_1, t_2, t_3), \sigma \rangle \Downarrow o}{\langle \text{for}(1, \langle \text{true}, \sigma \rangle, t_1, t_2, t_3), \sigma' \rangle \Downarrow o} \qquad \frac{\langle t_2, \sigma \rangle \Downarrow o_2 \qquad \langle \text{for}(3, o_2, t_1, t_2, t_3), \sigma \rangle \Downarrow o}{\langle \text{for}(2, \langle \text{unit}, \sigma \rangle, t_1, t_2, t_3), \sigma' \rangle \Downarrow o}$$

$$\frac{\langle \text{for}(t_1, t_2, t_3), \sigma \rangle \Downarrow o}{\langle \text{for}(3, \langle \text{unit}, \sigma \rangle, t_1, t_2, t_3), \sigma' \rangle \Downarrow o} \qquad \frac{\text{abort}(o)}{\langle \text{for}(i, o, t_1, t_2, t_3), \sigma \rangle \Downarrow o}$$

$$\frac{}{\text{abort}(\text{exc}(v))}$$

In small-step MSOS, a corresponding specification of for-loops is in terms of the conditional $\text{if}(e, e, e)$ defined in Sect. 3.1 rules [E8]–[E10], and sequential composition $\text{seq}(e, e)$:

$$t ::= \ldots \mid \text{seq}(e, e) \mid \text{for}(e, e, e)$$

$$\frac{t_1 \xrightarrow{\ell} e_1}{\text{seq}(t_1, e_2) \xrightarrow{\ell} \text{seq}(e_1, e_2)} \text{ [E26]} \qquad \frac{}{\text{seq}(v_1, e_2) \xrightarrow{\{-\}} e_2} \text{ [E27]}$$

$$\frac{}{\text{for}(e_1, e_2, e_3) \xrightarrow{\{-\}} \text{if}(e_1, \text{seq}(e_3, \text{seq}(e_2, \text{for}(e_1, e_2, e_3))), \text{unit})} \text{ [E28]}$$

Deriving the pretty-big-step MSOS rules gives:

$$\frac{t_1 \xrightarrow{\|X_1\|}^* e_1 \qquad \text{seq}(e_1, e_2) \xrightarrow{\ell_2}^* e'}{\text{seq}(t_1, e_2) \xrightarrow{\ell}^* e'} \text{ [EP26]} \qquad \frac{e_2 \xrightarrow{\|X_1\|}^* e'}{\text{seq}(v_1, e_2) \xrightarrow{\|X_1\|}^* e'} \text{ [EP27]}$$

$$\frac{\text{if}(e_1, \text{seq}(e_3, \text{seq}(e_2, \text{for}(e_1, e_2, e_3))), \text{unit}) \xrightarrow{\|X\|}^* e}{\text{for}(e_1, e_2, e_3) \xrightarrow{\|X\|}^* e} \text{ [EP28]}$$

These pretty-big-step rules correspond to Charguéraud's rules. In fact, we can derive Charguéraud's pretty-big-step rules directly from these rules. Replacing a rule by the derived rule(s) corresponding to all possible partial derivations is trivially correct. We can compress transitions, similar to (Danvy 2008b), by unfolding the rightmost 'continuation' premise in pretty-big-step rules. This corresponds to *striding* as described in (Bach Poulsen and Mosses 2014). Transition compressing [EP28] once gives:

$$\frac{e_1 \xrightarrow{\|X_1\|}^* e_1' \qquad \text{if}(e_1', \text{seq}(e_3, \text{seq}(e_2, \text{for}(e_1, e_2, e_3))), \text{unit}) \xrightarrow{\ell_2}^* e}{\text{for}(e_1, e_2, e_3) \xrightarrow{\ell_2 \circ \|X_1\|}^* e} \text{ [EP28']}$$

$$\frac{}{\text{for}(\text{false}, e_2, e_3) \xrightarrow{\{-\}}^* \text{unit}} \text{ [EP29]} \qquad \frac{\text{seq}(e_3, \text{seq}(e_2, \text{for}(e_1, e_2, e_3))) \xrightarrow{\ell}^* e}{\text{for}(\text{true}, e_2, e_3) \xrightarrow{\ell}^* e} \text{ [EP30]}$$

If we continue doing this, we get a set of classic big-step rules. Decomposing the derived big-step rules into pretty-big-step rules, as described by Charguéraud (2013), we obtain a set of rules that coincides with the pretty-big-step semantics for C-style for loops given in the beginning of this subsection.

4.3 Strictness Annotations

Inspired by the K-framework (Roşu and Şerbănuţă 2010), we can use strictness annotations to automatically generate congruence rules. For example, for application in the λ-calculus:

$$t ::= \ldots$$
$$| \quad \mathsf{app}(e, e) \qquad [\mathsf{seq\text{-}strict}]$$
$$| \quad \ldots$$

The **seq-strict** annotation automatically generates congruence rules for evaluating each sub-term fully in left-to-right order. Recall the original rules defining $\mathsf{app}(e, e)$:

$$\frac{t_1 \xrightarrow{\ell} e_1}{\mathsf{app}(t_1, e_2) \xrightarrow{\ell} \mathsf{app}(e_1, e_2)} \; [\mathrm{E3}] \qquad \frac{t_2 \xrightarrow{\ell} e_2}{\mathsf{app}(v_1, t_2) \xrightarrow{\ell} \mathsf{app}(v_1, e_2)} \; [\mathrm{E4}]$$

$$\frac{t \xrightarrow{\{\mathbf{env} = \rho'[x \mapsto v], \ldots\}} e}{\mathsf{app}(\mathsf{clo}(x, t, \rho'), v) \xrightarrow{\{\mathbf{env} = \rho, \ldots\}} \mathsf{app}(\mathsf{clo}(x, e, \rho'), v)} \; [\mathrm{E5}] \qquad \frac{}{\mathsf{app}(\mathsf{clo}(x, v', \rho'), v) \xrightarrow{\{-\}} v'} \; [\mathrm{E6}]$$

We can omit [E3] and [E4], since these congruence rules correspond exactly to the rules generated by **seq-strict**.

To generate congruence rules for subterm positions $n_1, n_2, \ldots$ numbered in the order they should be evaluated, we use the annotation $\mathbf{strict}(n_1 \; n_2 \; \ldots)$. E.g., $\mathsf{if}(e, e, e)$ can be specified as:

$$t ::= \ldots$$
$$| \quad \mathsf{if}(e, e, e) \qquad [\mathbf{strict(1)}]$$
$$| \quad \ldots$$

$$\frac{}{\mathsf{if}(\mathsf{true}, e_1, e_2) \xrightarrow{\{-\}} e_1} \; [\mathrm{E9}]$$

$$\frac{}{\mathsf{if}(\mathsf{false}, e_1, e_2) \xrightarrow{\{-\}} e_2} \; [\mathrm{E10}]$$

This annotation automatically generates rule [E8] from Sect. 3.1.

Table 4. Comparison of number of rules and premises for strictness annotated small-step, ordinary small-step, and derived pretty-big-step MSOS

Variant	Explicit rules	Premises	Generated rules	Generated premises
Strictness-annotated small-step MSOS	20	9	31	20
Small-step MSOS	31	20	31	20
Pretty-big-step MSOS	30	35	30	35

Table 4 summarizes how the use of strictness annotations reduces the number of explicitly specified rules by a third. As expected, small-step specifications are more concise than their pretty-big-step counterparts. By deriving the pretty-big-step rules automatically as described in this paper, we get the best of both worlds: a concise small-step specification format, and derived pretty-big-step rules that can be used for (pretty-)big-step reasoning.

5 Related Work

As illustrated throughout this paper, specifications in small-step MSOS require less effort to specify than corresponding big-step and pretty-big-step specifications. By automatic derivation, it is possible to apply both small-step and (pretty-)big-step reasoning to the same semantics. Many other authors have considered the relationship between small-step and big-step semantics.

Danvy et al. (2004; 2008a; 2008b) have explored this relationship by inter-deriving functional programs implementing many different semantic styles by provably correct transformations. Refocusing (Danvy and Nielsen 2004) was originally formulated for reduction semantics (Felleisen and Hieb 1992), but is also applicable to the K-framework, whose *heating* and *cooling* rules closely resemble reduction contexts (Roşu and Şerbănuţă 2010).

Recently, Ciobâcă (2013) described a means of deriving big-step semantics automatically from small-step semantics. His transformation essentially corresponds to the derivation we describe here. Unlike this work, his transformation does not describe the intermediate steps involved in the derivation, and is defined for substitution-based small-step semantics, which are transformed into substitution-based classic big-step rules. The correctness of Ciobâcă's transformation is based on notions of *star-soundness* and *star-completeness*. Comparing with Leroy and Grall's proof method for relating small-step and big-step semantics, these notions coincide with their proof method (Leroy and Grall 2009, Theorem 9)[4]. Star-soundness corresponds to the helper lemmas required for the "easy induction" used by Leroy and Grall, which holds for semicompositional semantics in the sense of Jones (2004). Similarly, star-completeness says that a big-step can be decomposed into a small-step followed by a big-step on the resulting term, corresponding to the second step of the "only if" part of Leroy and Grall's proof. The decomposition of a big-step into a small-step followed by a big-step is correct when the semantics is either confluent or deterministic, which corresponds to the unique decomposition requirement of refocusing in reduction semantics, and to Ciobâcă's requirement that the semantics is confluent.

We have taken a syntactic approach to deriving pretty-big-step semantics by describing each of the intermediate steps involved in the derivation. To ensure correct derivations, we required (Sect. 3.1) that:

1. the small-step semantics is syntax-directed; and
2. exception states are explicitly recognizable at the top-level of the semantics.

By insisting that our semantics is syntax-directed we avoid the issue of having to prove unique decomposition, as is required for refocusing in reduction semantics (Xiao et al. 2001). Syntax-direction implies determinism, which in turn

---

[4] See also their Coq proofs: `http://gallium.inria.fr/~xleroy/coindsem/`

implies unique decomposition. Whereas Ciobâcă and Danvy and Nielsen prove their transformations correct, we have so far relied on testing by generating executable interpreters using the MSOS Derivation Tool (Bach Poulsen and Mosses 2014) and comparing their outputs for example programs.

6   Conclusion and Future Directions

Small-step MSOS requires less effort than big-step and pretty-big-step rules to specify. We have shown that pretty-big-step semantics is within the range of refocusing, and that it is therefore possible to automatically derive pretty-big-step rules. In our examples, the derived pretty-big-step rules do not require auxiliary predicates, and are more concise than the pretty-big-step rules one would specify manually.

Future work includes exploring whether all pretty-big-step semantics are derivable by refocusing, and whether refocusing always yields a pretty-big-step semantics. A first step towards answering these questions is to mechanically verify, using, e.g., Coq, the correctness criteria for the derivation presented in Sect. 3.2[5]. Existing work by Leroy and Grall (2009), Ciobâcă (2013), and Sieczkowski et al. (2011) are notable sources of reference for aiding such mechanization.

Acknowledgements. We would like to thank Martin Churchill, Paolo Torrini, and the anonymous referees for their useful comments. This work was supported by an EPSRC grant (EP/I032495/1) to Swansea University in connection with the *PLanCompS* project (www.plancomps.org).

References

Bach Poulsen, C., Mosses, P.D.: Generating specialized interpreters for modular structural operational semantics. In: LOPSTR 2013. LNCS, Springer, Heidelberg (to appear, 2014)

Charguéraud, A.: Pretty-big-step semantics. In: Felleisen, M., Gardner, P. (eds.) ESOP 2013. LNCS, vol. 7792, pp. 41–60. Springer, Heidelberg (2013)

Ciobâcă, Ş.: From small-step semantics to big-step semantics, automatically. In: Johnsen, E.B., Petre, L. (eds.) IFM 2013. LNCS, vol. 7940, pp. 347–361. Springer, Heidelberg (2013)

Cousot, P., Cousot, R.: Inductive definitions, semantics and abstract interpretations. In: POPL 1992, pp. 83–94. ACM (1992)

Danvy, O.: Defunctionalized interpreters for programming languages. In: Hook, J., Thiemann, P. (eds.) ICFP 2008, pp. 131–142. ACM (2008a)

Danvy, O.: From reduction-based to reduction-free normalization. In: Koopman, P., Plasmeijer, R., Swierstra, D. (eds.) AFP 2008. LNCS, vol. 5832, pp. 66–164. Springer, Heidelberg (2009)

---

[5] Preliminary work on a Coq mechanization of the correctness proofs for the derivations in Sect. 3 and 4 is available online: www.plancomps.org/bachpoulsen2014a

Danvy, O., Nielsen, L.R.: Refocusing in reduction semantics. BRICS Research Series RS-04-26, Dept. of Comp. Sci., Aarhus University (2004)

Felleisen, M., Hieb, R.: The revised report on the syntactic theories of sequential control and state. Theor. Comput. Sci. 103(2), 235–271 (1992)

Jones, N.D.: Transformation by interpreter specialisation. Sci. Comput. Program. 52(1-3), 307–339 (2004)

Kahn, G.: Natural semantics. In: Brandenburg, F.J., Wirsing, M., Vidal-Naquet, G. (eds.) STACS 1987. LNCS, vol. 247, pp. 22–39. Springer, Heidelberg (1987)

Leroy, X., Grall, H.: Coinductive big-step operational semantics. Inf. Comput. 207(2), 284–304 (2009)

Milner, R.: A Calculus of Communication Systems. LNCS, vol. 92. Springer, Heidelberg (1980)

Milner, R., Tofte, M., Macqueen, D.: The Definition of Standard ML. MIT Press, Cambridge (1997)

Mosses, P.D.: Modular structural operational semantics. J. Log. Algebr. Program. 60-61, 195–228 (2004)

Pierce, B.C.: Basic Category Theory for Computer Scientists. MIT Press (1991)

Pierce, B.C.: Types and programming languages. MIT Press (2002)

Plotkin, G.D.: A structural approach to operational semantics. J. Log. Algebr. Program. 60-61, 17–139 (2004)

Roşu, G., Şerbănuţă, T.F.: An overview of the K semantic framework. J. Log. Algebr. Program. 79(6), 397–434 (2010)

Sieczkowski, F., Biernacka, M., Biernacki, D.: Automating derivations of abstract machines from reduction semantics. In: Hage, J., Morazán, M.T. (eds.) IFL 2011. LNCS, vol. 6647, pp. 72–88. Springer, Heidelberg (2011)

Wright, A., Felleisen, M.: A syntactic approach to type soundness. Inf. Comput. 115(1), 38–94 (1994)

Xiao, Y., Sabry, A., Ariola, Z.M.: From syntactic theories to interpreters: Automating the proof of unique decomposition. Higher-Order and Symbolic Computation 14(4), 387–409 (2001)

Communicating State Transition Systems
for Fine-Grained Concurrent Resources

Aleksandar Nanevski[1], Ruy Ley-Wild[2], Ilya Sergey[1], and Germán Andrés Delbianco[1]

[1] IMDEA Software Institute, Spain
{aleks.nanevski,ilya.sergey,german.delbianco}@imdea.org
[2] LogicBlox, USA
ruy.leywild@logicblox.com

Abstract. We present a novel model of concurrent computations with shared memory and provide a simple, yet powerful, logical framework for uniform Hoare-style reasoning about partial correctness of coarse- and fine-grained concurrent programs. The key idea is to specify arbitrary resource protocols as communicating *state transition systems* (STS) that describe valid states of a resource and the transitions the resource is allowed to make, including transfer of heap ownership.

We demonstrate how reasoning in terms of communicating STS makes it easy to crystallize behavioral invariants of a resource. We also provide *entanglement* operators to build large systems from an arbitrary number of STS components, by interconnecting their lines of communication. Furthermore, we show how the classical rules from the Concurrent Separation Logic (CSL), such as scoped resource allocation, can be generalized to fine-grained resource management. This allows us to give specifications as powerful as Rely-Guarantee, in a concise, scoped way, and yet regain the compositionality of CSL-style resource management. We proved the soundness of our logic with respect to the denotational semantics of action trees (variation on Brookes' action traces). We formalized the logic as a shallow embedding in Coq and implemented a number of examples, including a construction of coarse-grained CSL resources as a modular composition of various logical and semantic components.

1 Introduction

There are two main styles of program logics for shared-memory concurrency, customarily divided according to the supported kind of granularity of program interference. Logics for coarse-grained concurrency such as Concurrent Separation Logic (CSL) [12,14] restrict the interference to critical sections only, but generally lead to more modular specifications and simpler proofs of program correctness. Logics for fine-grained concurrency, such as Rely-Guarantee (RG) [8] admit arbitrary interference, but their specifications have traditionally been more monolithic, as we shall illustrate. In this paper, we identify the essential ingredients required for compositional specification of concurrent programs, and combine them in a novel way to reconcile the two approaches. We present a semantic model and a logic that enables specification and reasoning about fine-grained programs, but in the style of CSL. To describe our contribution more precisely, we first compare the relevant properties of CSL and RG.

Z. Shao (Ed.): ESOP 2014, LNCS 8410, pp. 290–310, 2014.

CSL employs *shared resources* and associated *resource invariants* [13], to abstract the interference between threads. A resource r is a chunk of shared state, and a resource invariant I is a predicate over states, which holds of r whenever all threads are outside the critical section. By mutual exclusion, when a thread enters a critical section for r, it acquires ownership and hence exclusive access to r's state. The thread may mutate the shared state and violate the invariant I, but it must restore I before releasing r and leaving the critical section, as given by the following CSL rule [2].

$$\frac{\Gamma \vdash \{p * I\}\, c\, \{q * I\}}{\Gamma, r : I \vdash \{p\} \text{ with } r \text{ do } c\, \{q\}} \text{ CRITSECCSL}$$

Γ is a context of currently existing resources. The rule for parallel composition assumes that forked threads don't share any state beyond that of the resources in Γ, and may divide the private state of the parent thread disjointly among the children.

$$\frac{\Gamma \vdash \{p_1\}\, c_1\, \{q_1\} \qquad \Gamma \vdash \{p_2\}\, c_2\, \{q_2\}}{\Gamma \vdash \{p_1 * p_2\}\, c_1 \parallel c_2\, \{q_1 * q_2\}} \text{ PARCSL}$$

A private heap of a thread may be promoted into a freshly allocated shared resource in a scoped manner by the following rule.

$$\frac{\Gamma, r : I \vdash \{p\}\, c\, \{q\}}{\Gamma \vdash \{p * I\} \text{ resource } r \text{ in } c\, \{q * I\}} \text{ RESOURCECSL}$$

One may see from these rules that resources are abstractions that promote modularity. In particular, one may verify a thread wrt. the smallest resource context required. By context weakening, the introduction of new resources will not invalidate the existing verification. Thread-local resources can be hidden from the environment by the RESOURCECSL rule.

In RG, the interaction between threads is directly specified by the rule for parallel composition.[1]

$$\frac{R \vee G_2, G_1 \vdash \{p\}\, c_1\, \{q_1\} \qquad R \vee G_1, G_2 \vdash \{p\}\, c_2\, \{q_2\}}{R, G_1 \vee G_2 \vdash \{p\}\, c_1 \parallel c_2\, \{q_1 \wedge q_2\}} \text{ PARRG}$$

The rely transition R and guarantee transitions G_1 and G_2 are relations on states. A rely specifies the thread's expectations of state transitions made by its environment. A guarantee specifies the state transitions made by the thread itself. The disjunctive combinations of R and G's in the rule captures the idea we call *forking shuffle*, whereby upon forking, the thread c_1 becomes part of the environment for c_2 and vice-versa.

RG is more expressive than CSL because transitions can encode arbitrary protocols on shared state, whereas CSL is specialized to a fixed mutual exclusion protocol on critical sections. But, CSL is more compositional in manipulating resources. Where a CSL resource invariant specifies the behavior of an individual chunk of shared state, the transitions in RG treat the whole state as monolithically shared. Feng's work on Local Rely Guarantee (LRG) [5] has made first steps in improving RG in this respect.

---

[1] In the presence of heaps, the rule is more complicated [6, 18], but we elide the issue here.

1.1 Contributions

We propose that a logic for fine-grained concurrency can be based on a notion of a *fine-grained resource*. Fine-grained resources serve as buildings blocks for program specification, and generalize CSL-style coarse-grained resource management. A fine-grained resource is specified by a resource invariant, as in CSL, but it also adds transitions in the form of relations between resource states. Thus, it is best viewed as a *state transition system* (STS), where the resource invariant specifies the state space. We identify a number of properties that an STS has to satisfy to specify a fine-grained resource, and refer to such STSs as *concurroids*. We refer to our generalization of CSL as Fine-grained CSL (FCSL).

There are two main ideas that we build on in FCSL, and which separate FCSL from LRG and other recent related work [4, 15, 17] (see Section 6 for details): (a) *subjectivity* and (b) *communication*. Subjectivity [10] means that each state of a concurroid STS describes not only the shared resource, but also *two* abstractions of it that represent the views of the state by the thread, and by its environment, respectively. Subjectivity will enable us to capture the idea of forking shuffle by a rule for parallel composition akin to PARCSL (but with a somewhat generalized notion of separating conjunction ($*$) [10]), rather than in the monolithic style of PARRG.

To compositionally build large systems out of a number of smaller ones, we make concurroids communicate. In addition to standard for STS *internal* transitions between states, concurroids contain *external* transitions. These may be thought of as "wires" whose one end is connected to a state in the STS, but whose other end is dangling, representing either an "input" into or an "output" out of the STS. Concurroids can be *entangled*, *i.e.*, composed by interconnecting their dangling wires of opposite polarity, where the interconnections serve to transfer heap ownership between concurroids. Communication and entanglement endow FCSL with the compositionality of CSL. For example, entanglement generalizes the notion of adding a resource to the context Γ in RESOURCECSL. We also rely on entanglement to formulate a rule generalizing the scoped resource allocation of RESOURCECSL. More precisely, our contributions are:

– We identify STSs with subjectively-shaped states (concurroids) and a number of algebraic properties, as a natural model for scalable concurrency verification. We show how communication enables composing larger STSs out of smaller ones.
– We present FCSL—a simple and expressive logic for fine-grained resources that combines expressivity of RG with the compositional resource management of CSL.
– We illustrate FCSL by showing how to implement a coarse-grained resource of CSL by a fine-grained resource of FCSL in which an explicit spin lock protects the resource's state. We also implemented examples such as ticketed locks, that go beyond coarse-grained CSL resources, and present them in the extended version [11].
– We implemented FCSL [11] as a shallow embedding within the type theory of the Calculus of Inductive Constructions (*i.e.*, Coq [1, 16]). Thus, FCSL naturally reconciles with features such as higher-order functions, abstract predicates, modules and functors. We formally instantiated the whole stack of abstractions: the semantic model is formalized in Coq, FCSL is built on top of the semantic model, CSL is built on top of FCSL, and then verified programs are built on top of CSL.

2   An Overview of Fine-Grained Resources

There are three different aspects along which fine-grained resources can be composed: space (*i.e.*, states), ownership, and time (*i.e.*, transitions). In this section, we describe how to represent these aspects in the assertion logic of FCSL.

Space. The heap belonging to a fine-grained resource,[2] is explicitly identified by a *resource label*. We use assertions in the "points-to" style of separation logic, to name resources and identify their respective heaps. For example, the assertion

$$\ell_1 \overset{j}{\mapsto} h_1 * \ell_2 \overset{j}{\mapsto} h_2$$

describes a state in which the heaps h_1 and h_2 are associated with the resources labeled ℓ_1 and ℓ_2, respectively. The connective $*$ ensures that ℓ_1 and ℓ_2 are distinct labels, and that h_1 and h_2 are disjoint heaps. The superscript j indicates that the heaps are *joint* (shared), *i.e.*, can be accessed by any thread, even though they are owned by the resources ℓ_1 and ℓ_2, respectively.

The heaps h_1 and h_2 are not described by means of points-to assertions, but are built using operators for singleton heaps $x \to v$ and disjoint union $\uplus$. For example, the heap of the resource lock, which explicitly encodes a coarse-grained resource with the resource invariant I [12] may be described by the assertion

$$\text{lock} \overset{j}{\mapsto} ((lk \to b) \uplus h) \wedge \text{if } b \text{ then } h = \text{empty else } I \ h. \tag{1}$$

The assertion exposes the fact that the heap owned by lock contains a boolean pointer lk encoding a lock that protects the heap h. The conditional conjunct is a *pure* (*i.e.*, label-free) assertion, which describes an aspect of the ownership transfer protocol of CSL. When the lock is not taken (i.e. $b = \text{false}$), the heap h satisfies the resource invariant. When the lock is taken, the heap is transfered to the private ownership of the locking thread, so h equals the empty heap, but lk remains in the ownership of lock.

Ownership. Data in FCSL may be owned by a resource, as illustrated above, or by individual threads. The thread-owned data, however, is also associated with a resource, which it refines with *thread-relative* information. For example, the resource lock owns a pointer lk which operationally implements a lock. However, just knowing that the lock is taken or not is not enough for reasoning purposes; we need to know which thread has taken it, if any. Thus, we associate with each thread an extra bit of lock-related information, Own or Ȯwn, which will identify the lock-owning thread as follows.

Following the idea of *subjectivity* [10], FCSL assertions are interpreted in a thread-relative way. We use *self* to name the interpreting thread, and *other* to name the combination of all other threads running concurrently with *self* (*i.e.*, the environment of *self*). We use two different assertions to describe thread-relative views: $\ell \overset{s}{\mapsto} v$ and $\ell \overset{o}{\mapsto} v$. The first is true in the *self* thread, if *self*'s view of the resource ℓ is v. The second is true in

---

[2] Or just resource for short. Later on, we explicitly identify CSL resources as *coarse-grained*.

the *self* thread, if *other*'s view of the resource ℓ is v. In this sense, the $\ell \overset{j}{\mapsto} v$ describes the resource's view of the data. In the case of lock, the thread that acquired the lock will validate the assertion:

$$\text{lock} \overset{s}{\mapsto} \text{Own} \wedge \text{lock} \overset{j}{\mapsto} (lk \to \text{true}),$$

while the symmetric assertion holds in all other threads at the same moment of time:

$$\text{lock} \overset{j}{\mapsto} (lk \to \text{true}) \wedge \text{lock} \overset{o}{\mapsto} \text{Own}.$$

In general, the values of the *self* and *other* views for *any resource* are elements of some resource-specific *partial commutative monoid* (PCM) [10]. A PCM is a set with a commutative and associative operation • with a unit element. • combines the *self* and *other* views into a view of the parallel composition of *self* and *other* threads. The • operation is commutative and associative because parallel composition of threads is commutative and associative, and the unit element models the view of the idle thread. Partiality models impossible thread combinations. For example, the elements of $O = \{\overline{\text{Own}}, \text{Own}\}$ represent thread-relative views of the lock lk. O forms a PCM under the operation defined as $x \bullet \overline{\text{Own}} = \overline{\text{Own}} \bullet x = x$, with Own • Own undefined. The unit element is $\overline{\text{Own}}$, and the undefinedness of the last combination captures that two threads can't simultaneously own the lock. Notice that heaps form a PCM under disjoint union, with the empty heap as unit. Thus, they too obey the discipline required of the general *self* and *other* components.

Anticipating lock-related examples in Section 3, we combine thread-relative views of the lock with thread-relative views of the lock-protected heap h. We parametrize the resource lock by a PCM U, which the user may choose depending on the application. Then we use assertions over *pairs*, such as lock $\overset{s}{\mapsto} (m_S, a_S)$ and lock $\overset{o}{\mapsto} (m_O, a_O)$, to express that $m_S, m_O \in O$ are views of the lock lk, and $a_S, a_O \in U$ are views of the heap h. The following assertion illustrates how the different FCSL primitives combine. It generalizes (1) and defines the valid states of the resource lock.

$$\begin{aligned} &\text{lock} \overset{s}{\mapsto} (m_S, a_S) \wedge \text{lock} \overset{o}{\mapsto} (m_O, a_O) \wedge \text{lock} \overset{j}{\mapsto} ((lk \to b) \uplus h) \wedge \\ &\text{if } b \text{ then } h = \text{empty} \wedge m_S \bullet m_O = \text{Own else } I (a_S \bullet a_O) h \wedge m_S \bullet m_O = \overline{\text{Own}} \end{aligned} \quad (2)$$

The assertion states that if the lock is taken ($b = \text{true}$) then the heap h is given away, otherwise it satisfies the resource invariant I. In either case, the thread-relative views m_S, m_O, a_S and a_O are consistent with the resource's views of lk and h. Indeed, notice how m_S, m_O and a_S, a_O are first •-joined (by the •-operations of O and U, respectively) and then related to b and h; the former implicitly by the conditional, the latter explicitly, by the resource invariant I, which is now parametrized by $a_S \bullet a_O$.

Private heaps. In addition to a private view of a resource, a thread may own a private heap as well. We describe such thread-private heaps by means of the same thread-relative assertions, but with a different resource label. We consider a dedicated resource for *private heaps*, with a dedicated label priv. Then we can write, say, priv $\overset{s}{\mapsto} x \to 4$ to describe a heap consisting of a pointer x private to the *self* thread. By definition, priv $\overset{j}{\mapsto}$ empty, *i.e.*, the *joint* heap of the priv resource is always empty.

Time. Fine-grained reasoning requires characterization of the possible changes the threads can make to the state. We encode such a characterization as relations between states of possibly *multiple resources* (*i.e.*, using multiple labels). For example, coarse-grained resources require that upon successful acquisition, the resource's heap is trans-fered into the private ownership of the acquiring thread. In our fine-grained encoding, the transition can be represented as follows:

$$\text{priv} \overset{s}{\mapsto} h_{\mathsf{S}} \quad * (\text{lock} \overset{s}{\mapsto} (\cancel{\text{Own}}, \mathsf{a}_{\mathsf{S}}) \wedge \text{lock} \overset{j}{\mapsto} ((lk \to \text{false}) \uplus h)) \rightsquigarrow$$
$$\text{priv} \overset{s}{\mapsto} (h_{\mathsf{S}} \uplus h) * (\text{lock} \overset{s}{\mapsto} (\text{Own}, \mathsf{a}_{\mathsf{S}}) \wedge \text{lock} \overset{j}{\mapsto} (lk \to \text{true})) \tag{3}$$

This transition preserves heap *footprints*, in the sense that the domain of the combined heaps in the source of the transition equals the domain in the target of the transition. We refer to such transitions as *internal*. Footprint preservation is an essential property, as it facilitates composing and framing transitions. In particular, adding additional labels and heaps with non-overlapping footprint to a source of an internal transition is guaranteed to produce non-overlapping footprints in the target of the transition as well.

We also consider *external* transitions that *can* acquire and release heaps. We use external transitions to build internal ones. For example, the above internal transition over priv and lock resources can be obtained as an interconnection (to be defined in Section 4) of two external transitions, each operating on an individual label.

$$\text{priv} \overset{s}{\mapsto} h_{\mathsf{S}} \overset{+h}{\rightsquigarrow} \text{priv} \overset{s}{\mapsto} (h_{\mathsf{S}} \uplus h)$$
$$\text{lock} \overset{s}{\mapsto} (\cancel{\text{Own}}, \mathsf{a}_{\mathsf{S}}) \wedge \text{lock} \overset{j}{\mapsto} ((lk \to \text{false}) \uplus h) \overset{-h}{\rightsquigarrow} \text{lock} \overset{s}{\mapsto} (\text{Own}, \mathsf{a}_{\mathsf{S}}) \wedge \text{lock} \overset{j}{\mapsto} lk \to \text{true} \tag{4}$$

The transition over priv takes a heap h as an input and attaches it to the *self* heap. The transition over lock gives the heap h as an output. When interconnected, the two transitions exchange the ownership of h between the lock and priv, producing (3).

A *concurroid* is an STS that formally represents a collection of resources. Each state of the STS contains a number of components, identified by the labels naming the in-dividual resources. Each concurroid contains one internal transition, and an arbitrary number of external ones. The internal transition describes how threads specified by the concurroid may change their state in a single step. The external transitions are the "dan-gling wires", which provide means for composing different concurroids by *entangling* them, *i.e.*, interconnecting (some or all of) their dually polarized external transitions, to obtain a larger concurroid.

For example, if P is the concurroid for private heaps (containing a single label priv), and $L_{\{\text{lock},lk,I\}}$ is the concurroid for a lock (with a single label lock, lock pointer lk and protected heap described by the coarse-grained resource invariant I), we could con-struct the entangled concurroid $CSL_{\{\text{lock},lk,I\}} = P \rtimes L_{\{\text{lock},lk,I\}}$ that captures the heap ownership-exchange protocol (3) of CSL for programs with *one coarse-grained re-source*.[3] The entanglement can be iterated, to obtain an STS for *two coarse-grained resources* $CSL_{\{\text{lock},lk,I\},\{\text{lock}',lk',I'\}} = CSL_{\{\text{lock},lk,I\}} \rtimes L_{\{\text{lock}',lk',I'\}}$, and so on. In this way, con-curroids generalize the notion of resource context from the RESOURCECSL rule, with entanglement modeling the addition of new resources to the context.

---

[3] The formal definition of the $\rtimes$ is postponed until Section 4.

Fig. 1. Semantics of selected FCSL assertions

$$w \models \top \quad \text{iff always}$$
$$w \models \ell \overset{s}{\mapsto} v \quad \text{iff valid } w, \text{ and } w.\, s = \ell \to v$$
$$w \models \ell \overset{j}{\mapsto} h \quad \text{iff valid } w, \text{ and } w.\, j = \ell \to h$$
$$w \models \ell \overset{o}{\mapsto} v \quad \text{iff valid } w, \text{ and } w.\, o = \ell \to v$$
$$w \models p \wedge q \quad \text{iff } w \models p \text{ and } w \models q$$
$$w \models p * q \quad \text{iff valid } w, \text{ and } w = w_1 \uplus w_2, \text{ and } w_1 \models p \text{ and } w_2 \models q$$
$$w \models p \mathbin{-\!\!*} q \quad \text{iff for every } w_1, \text{ valid } w \uplus w_1 \text{ and } w_1 \models p \text{ implies } w \uplus w_1 \models q$$
$$w \models p \circledast q \quad \text{iff valid } w, \text{ and } w.\, s = s_1 \uplus s_2, \text{ and}$$
$$[s_1 \mid w.\, j \mid s_2 \circ w.\, o] \models p \text{ and } [s_2 \mid w.\, j \mid s_1 \circ w.\, o] \models q$$
$$w \models \text{this } w' \quad \text{if } w = w'$$
$$\models p \downarrow h \quad \text{iff for every valid } w, w \models p \text{ implies } \lfloor w \rfloor = h$$

3 Reasoning with Concurroids

Auxiliary Definitions. A PCM-map is a finite map from labels (isomorphic to nat) to $\Sigma_{\mathrm{U:pcm}}\mathbb{U}$. It associates each label with a pair of a PCM $\mathbb{U}$ and a value $v \in \mathbb{U}$. A heap-map is a finite map from labels to heaps. If m_1, m_2 are PCM-maps, then $m_1 \circ m_2$ is defined as empty $\circ$ empty = empty, and $((\ell \to_{\mathbb{U}} v_1) \uplus m_1') \circ ((\ell \to_{\mathbb{U}} v_2) \uplus m_2') = (\ell \to_{\mathbb{U}} v_1 \bullet v_2) \uplus (m_1' \circ m_2')$, and undefined otherwise. By overloading the notation, we define state w as a triple $[s \mid j \mid o]$, where s, o are PCM-maps, and j is a heap-map. We abbreviate $[\ell \to v_s \mid \ell \to v_j \mid \ell \to v_o]$ with $\ell \to [v_s \mid v_j \mid v_o]$. w is valid if $w.\, s$, $w.\, j$, $w.\, o$ have the same domain as PCM-maps, $w.\, s \circ w.\, o$ is defined, and the heaps in $w.\, s$, $w.\, j$ and $w.\, o$ are disjoint (if $w.\, s$ and $w.\, o$ contain heaps in their codomain). State flattening $\lfloor w \rfloor$ is the disjoint union of all such heaps. $w_1 \uplus w_2$ is the pairwise disjoint union of component maps of w_1 and w_2. The semantics of the main FCSL assertions is provided in Figure 1. The subjective assertions ($e.g.$, $w \models \ell \overset{s}{\mapsto} v$) constrain the value of one state component, assuming others to be existentially quantified over.

FCSL specifications take the form of Hoare 4-tuple $\{p\}\, c\, \{q\}\, @\, U$ expressing that the thread c has a precondition p, postcondition q, in a state space and under transitions defined by the concurroid U, which in FCSL takes the role of a resource context from CSL. We next present the characteristic inference rules of FCSL.

Parallel Composition. The rule for parallel composition in FCSL is similar to PARCSL, with Γ replaced by a concurroid U, which we will define formally in Section 4.

$$\frac{\{p_1\}\, c_1\, \{q_1\}\, @\, U \qquad \{p_2\}\, c_2\, \{q_2\}\, @\, U}{\{p_1 \circledast p_2\}\, c_1 \parallel c_2\, \{q_1 \circledast q_2\}\, @\, U} \ \text{PAR}$$

The PAR rule uses *subjective separating conjunction* $\circledast$ (see [10] and Figure 1) to split the state of $c_1 \parallel c_2$ into two. The split states contain the same labels, and equal *joint* portions, but the *self* and *other* portions are recombined to match the thread-relative views of c_1 and c_2. When the parent thread forks the children c_1 and c_2, the PCM values in the parent's *self* components are split between the children (similarly $*$ splits heaps in CSL), while the children's *other* component are implicitly induced to preserve overall

$\bullet$-total (*i.e.*, c_1's *other* view includes c_2's *self* view, and vice versa). For example, in the case of one label ℓ, we have

$$\ell \overset{s}{\mapsto} a \bullet b \wedge \ell \overset{o}{\mapsto} c \implies (\ell \overset{s}{\mapsto} a \wedge \ell \overset{o}{\mapsto} c \bullet b) \circledast (\ell \overset{s}{\mapsto} b \wedge \ell \overset{o}{\mapsto} c \bullet a).$$

The implication encodes the idea of a forking shuffle from RG, but via states, rather than transitions as in RG. It allows us to use the *same* concurroid U to specify the transitions of both c_1 and c_2 in PAR, much like PARCSL uses the same context Γ. Essentially, we rely on the recombination of views to select the transitions of U available to each of c_1 and c_2, instead of providing distinct transitions for c_1 and c_2 as in PARRG.

We commonly encounter cases where the *other* views are existentially abstracted, hence the conjuncts $\ell \overset{o}{\mapsto} -$ are omitted. In those cases, we have the simplified bi-implication:

$$\ell \overset{s}{\mapsto} a \bullet b \iff \ell \overset{s}{\mapsto} a \circledast \ell \overset{s}{\mapsto} b \qquad (5)$$

The implications generalize to $\circledast$-separated assertions with more than one distinct label.

We illustrate PAR and $\circledast$ with the example of concurrent incrementation [10, 13] in a setting of a concurroid $CSL_{lock,lk,I}$ (*i.e.*, private state and one lock). The lock lk protects a shared integer pointer x, that is, the resource invariant is $I (a : nat) (h : heap) \widehat{=} h = x \to a$. For the nat argument, we chose the PCM structure under addition; thus, an assertion lock $\overset{s}{\mapsto} (-, a_S)$ expresses that the *self* thread has added a_S to x, and dually for lock $\overset{o}{\mapsto} (-, a_O)$. Therefore, whenever the lock is not taken, x stores the sum $a_S + a_O$. This follows from interpreting $\bullet$ with $+$ in the lock state invariant (2).

Procedure incr(n) acquires the lock to ensure exclusive access to x, increments x by n, and releases the lock. In FCSL, it has the following specification:

$$\left\{ \text{priv} \overset{s}{\mapsto} \text{empty} * \text{lock} \overset{s}{\mapsto} (\text{Own}, 0) \right\} \text{incr}(n) \left\{ \text{priv} \overset{s}{\mapsto} \text{empty} * \text{lock} \overset{s}{\mapsto} (\text{Own}, n) \right\} @ CSL_{lock,lk,I}$$

The specification states that incr runs in an empty private heap (hence by framing, in any larger heap), the lock is not owned by the calling thread initially, and will not be owned in the end. The addition of calling thread to x increases from 0 to n (hence by framing, from m to $m + n$). We now prove that incr(i) $\|$ incr(j) increments x by $i + j$.

$$\left\{ \text{priv} \overset{s}{\mapsto} \text{empty} * \text{lock} \overset{s}{\mapsto} (\text{Own}, 0) \right\}$$
$$\left\{ \text{priv} \overset{s}{\mapsto} \text{empty} \cup \text{empty} * \text{lock} \overset{s}{\mapsto} (\text{Own} \bullet \text{Own}, 0 + 0) \right\}$$
$$\left\{ (\text{priv} \overset{s}{\mapsto} \text{empty} * \text{lock} \overset{s}{\mapsto} (\text{Own}, 0)) \circledast (\text{priv} \overset{s}{\mapsto} \text{empty} * \text{lock} \overset{s}{\mapsto} (\text{Own}, 0)) \right\}$$
$$\left\{ \text{priv} \overset{s}{\mapsto} \text{empty} * \text{lock} \overset{s}{\mapsto} (\text{Own}, 0) \right\} \Big\| \left\{ \text{priv} \overset{s}{\mapsto} \text{empty} * \text{lock} \overset{s}{\mapsto} (\text{Own}, 0) \right\}$$
$$\text{incr}(i) \qquad\qquad\qquad \text{incr}(j)$$
$$\left\{ \text{priv} \overset{s}{\mapsto} \text{empty} * \text{lock} \overset{s}{\mapsto} (\text{Own}, i) \right\} \Big\| \left\{ \text{priv} \overset{s}{\mapsto} \text{empty} * \text{lock} \overset{s}{\mapsto} (\text{Own}, j) \right\}$$
$$\left\{ (\text{priv} \overset{s}{\mapsto} \text{empty} * \text{lock} \overset{s}{\mapsto} (\text{Own}, i)) \circledast (\text{priv} \overset{s}{\mapsto} \text{empty} * \text{lock} \overset{s}{\mapsto} (\text{Own}, j)) \right\}$$
$$\left\{ \text{priv} \overset{s}{\mapsto} \text{empty} * \text{lock} \overset{s}{\mapsto} (\text{Own}, i + j) \right\}$$

The proof uses the bi-implication (5) to move between $\circledast$-separated assertions and $\bullet$-joined views. The proof is compositional in the sense that the same verification of incr is used as a black box in both parallel threads, with the subproofs merely instantiating the parameter n with i and j respectively.

Injection. The PAR rule requires c_1 and c_2 to share the same concurroid U, which describes the totality of their resources. If the threads use different concurroids, they first must be brought into a common entanglement, via the rule INJECT.

$$\frac{\{p\}\, c\, \{q\}@U \qquad r \text{ stable under } V}{\{p * r\}\, \text{inject}\, c\, \{q * r\}@U \bowtie V}\ \text{INJECT}$$

If c is verified wrt. concurroid U, it can be *injected* (i.e. coerced) into a larger concurroid $U \bowtie V$. In programs, we use the explicit coercion inject to describe the change of "type" from U to $U \bowtie V$. Reading the rule bottom-up, it says we can ignore V, as V's transitions and c operate on disjointly-labeled state. V may change U's state by communication, but the change is bounded by U's external transitions. Thus, we are justified in verifying c against U alone. In this sense, INJECT may be seen as generalizing the rule for resource context weakening of CSL.

The connective $*$ splits the state according to labels of U and V; p and q describe the part labeled by U, and r describes the part labeled by V. Since r describes both the prestate and poststate, it has to be *stable* [11] under V; that is, determine a subset of V's states that remains fixed under transitions the *other* thread takes over the labels from V.

We illustrate INJECT and stability by verifying incr. To set the stage, we need atomic commands for reading from and writing to a pointer x. These have the following obvious specification relative to the concurroid P for private state:

$$\left\{\text{priv} \overset{s}{\mapsto} x \to v\right\}\ \text{read } x\ \left\{\text{priv} \overset{s}{\mapsto} x \to v \wedge res = v\right\}@P$$
$$\left\{\text{priv} \overset{s}{\mapsto} x \to -\right\}\ \text{write } x\, v\ \left\{\text{priv} \overset{s}{\mapsto} x \to v\right\}@P$$

The commands for acquiring and releasing lock exchange ownership of the protected pointer x. Thus, they have specifications relative to the concurroid $CSL_{\text{lock},lk,I} = P \bowtie L_{\text{lock},lk,I}$, which we have already used before.

$$\left\{\text{priv} \overset{s}{\mapsto} \text{empty} * \text{lock} \overset{s}{\mapsto} (\overline{\text{Own}}, 0)\right\}$$
$$\text{acquire}$$
$$\left\{\exists a_O. \text{priv} \overset{s}{\mapsto} x \to a_O * (\text{lock} \overset{s}{\mapsto} (\text{Own}, 0) \wedge \text{lock} \overset{o}{\mapsto} (-, a_O))\right\}@CSL_{\text{lock},lk,I}$$

$$\left\{\text{priv} \overset{s}{\mapsto} x \to a_S + a_O * (\text{lock} \overset{s}{\mapsto} (\text{Own}, 0) \wedge \text{lock} \overset{o}{\mapsto} (-, a_O))\right\}$$
$$\text{release}$$
$$\left\{\text{priv} \overset{s}{\mapsto} \text{empty} * \text{lock} \overset{s}{\mapsto} (\overline{\text{Own}}, a_S)\right\}@CSL_{\text{lock},lk,I}$$

acquire assumes that lock is not taken, and that the *self* thread so far has added 0 to x. Thus, the overall contents of x is $0 + a_O = a_O$, where a_O is the addition of the *other* threads. Note that acquire does not have to be atomic:[4] as implemented, it just spins on lk, and after acquisition, x is transferred into the private heap of *self*. a_O must be existentially quantified, because *other*'s may add to x while acquire is spinning.

---

[4] The implementation of acquire and release relies on atomic actions (Section 5), specific for a particular concurroid, *e.g.* $CSL_{\text{lock},lk,I}$.

release assumes that lock is taken by *self*, and that prior to taking lock, *self* and *other* have added 0 and a_O to x, respectively. After acquiring x, *self* has mutated it, so that its contents is $a_S + a_O$. After releasing, x is moved from the private heap to the *joint* portion of lock. The postcondition does not mention x, as once in *joint*, x's contents becomes unstable. Indeed, *other* may acquire the lock and change x after release terminates. However, *other* can't change the *self* view of x, which is now set to a_S.

The following proof outline presents the implementation and verification of incr(n).

$$\left\{ \text{priv} \overset{s}{\mapsto} \text{empty} * \text{lock} \overset{s}{\mapsto} (\text{Own}, 0) \right\}$$

acquire;

$$\left\{ \exists a_O.\text{priv} \overset{s}{\mapsto} x \to a_O * (\text{lock} \overset{s}{\mapsto} (\text{Own}, 0) \wedge \text{lock} \overset{o}{\mapsto} (-, a_O)) \right\}$$

$res \leftarrow$ inject (read x);

$$\left\{ \exists a_O.\text{priv} \overset{s}{\mapsto} x \to a_O \wedge res = a_O * (\text{lock} \overset{s}{\mapsto} (\text{Own}, 0) \wedge \text{lock} \overset{o}{\mapsto} (-, a_O)) \right\}$$

inject (write x ($res + n$));

$$\left\{ \exists a_O.\text{priv} \overset{s}{\mapsto} x \to n + a_O * (\text{lock} \overset{s}{\mapsto} (\text{Own}, 0) \wedge \text{lock} \overset{o}{\mapsto} (-, a_O)) \right\}$$

release

$$\left\{ \text{priv} \overset{s}{\mapsto} \text{empty} * \text{lock} \overset{s}{\mapsto} (\text{Own}, n) \right\}$$

INJECT is used twice, to coerce read and write from the concurroid P to $CSL_{\text{lock},lk,I}$. These commands manipulate the contents of priv, but retain the framing predicate lock $\overset{s}{\mapsto}$ (Own, 0) $\wedge$ lock $\overset{o}{\mapsto}$ $(-, a_O)$. This predicate is stable wrt. $L_{\text{lock},lk,I}$. Intuitively, because *self* owns lock, *other* can't acquire x and add to it. Thus, no matter what *other* does, a_O and the framing predicate remain invariant.

To simplify the proof, we have not emphasized the invariance of a_O between calls to acquire and release, even though it is the case (we could do it using the rule EXIST from Figure 2). However, this invariance is what allowed us to calculate the contribution of *self* to x as n (*i.e.*, final contents of x minus a_O). Without tracking a_O, we would not know how much of the final contents of x is attributable to *self*, and how much to *other*.

Hiding. refers to the ability to construct a concurroid V from the thread-private heap, in a scope of a thread c. The children forked by c can interfere on V's state, respecting V's transitions, but V is hidden from the environment of c. To the environment, V's state changes look like changes of the private heap of c. In this sense, hiding generalizes the RESOURCECSL rule to fine-grained resources.

$$\frac{\left\{ \text{priv} \overset{s}{\mapsto} h * p \right\} c \left\{ \text{priv} \overset{s}{\mapsto} h' * q \right\} @(P \bowtie U) \bowtie V \qquad \text{(omitted side condition on } U \text{ and } V\text{)}}{\{ \Psi\, g\, h * (\Phi(g) \twoheadrightarrow p) \} \text{hide}_{\Phi,g}\, c\, \{ \exists g'. \Psi\, g'\, h' * (\Phi(g') \twoheadrightarrow q) \} @ P \bowtie U} \text{ HIDE}$$

$$\text{where } \Psi\, g\, h = \exists k\text{:heap. priv} \overset{s}{\mapsto} h \cup k \wedge \Phi(g) \downarrow k$$

Since installing V consumes a chunk of private heap, the rule requires the overall concurroid to support private heaps, *i.e.*, to be an entanglement $P \bowtie U$, where P is the concurroid for private heaps, and U is arbitrary (it is also possible to generalize the rule so as to be not tied to the specific concurroid P, see [11]). The omitted side condition on U and V is essential for the existence of entanglement and will be explained in Section 5. When U is of no interest, we set it to the empty concurroid E (Section 4), for which $P \bowtie E = P$.

In programs, we use the explicit coercion $\text{hide}_{\Phi,g}$ to indicate the change of type from $(P \bowtie U) \bowtie V$ to $P \bowtie U$. The annotation $\Phi(g)$ corresponds to a set of *concrete states* of a concurroid V to be created. Its parameter g is a meaningful abstraction of such a set (*e.g.*, (m_S, a_S) for the $L_{(\text{lock},lk,I)}$ concurroid) and can be thought of as an "abstract state". In the rule HIDE, g is the initial abstract state, *i.e.*, upon creation, the state of V satisfies $\Phi(g)$. In the premise of the HIDE rule, the predicates $\text{priv} \overset{s}{\mapsto} -$ describe the behavior of c on the private heaps, while p and q describe the state of the labels belonging to U and V. In the conclusion, $\Psi\, g\, h$ and $\Psi\, g'\, h'$ map the abstract states g and g' into private heaps h and h'. This follows from the definition of Ψ, in which $\Phi(g) \downarrow k$ indicates that states satisfying $\Phi(g)$ *erase* to the private heap k (see Figure 1). Thus, changes that c imposes on abstract states, appear as changes to private heaps for $\text{hide}_{\Phi,g}\, c$.

In the conclusion, the assertion $\Phi(g) \twoheadrightarrow p$ states that attaching any state satisfying $\Phi(g)$ to the chunk of the initial state identified by the labels from U produces a state in which p holds, "compensating" for the component k in Ψ. That is, p corresponds to an abstract state g and c can be safely executed in such a state. The rule guarantees that if c terminates with a postcondition q, then q corresponds to some abstract state g'.

We illustrate the rule with a proof outline for program $\text{hide}_{\Phi,g}\,(\text{incr}(n))$. We show how to choose Φ and g so that the program implements the following functionality. It starts with only the concurroid P, and the private heap containing pointers lk and x. It locally installs $L_{\text{lock},lk,I}$, which makes x a shared pointer, protected by the lock lk. It runs $\text{incr}(n)$, after which the local concurroid is disposed, and lk and x return to the private heap. We prove that if initially $x \to 0$, then in the end $x \to n$. The abstract states are pairs (m_S, a_S), encodings of the *self* views of the concrete state of lock. Φ maps a *self* view into a predicate on the full state of lock, specifying *joint* and *other* views as well.

$$\Phi(m_S, a_S) = \text{lock} \overset{s}{\mapsto} (m_S, a_S) \wedge \text{lock} \overset{o}{\mapsto} (\text{Own}, 0)\,\wedge$$
$$\text{if } m_S = \text{Own then lock} \overset{j}{\mapsto} ((lk \to \text{false}) \cup (x \to a_S)) \text{ else lock} \overset{j}{\mapsto} (lk \to \text{true})$$

We choose the initial state $g = (m_S, a_S) = (\text{Own}, 0)$: indicating that the lock is installed with lk unlocked, and x set to 0.

The proof outline uses the facts that $\Phi(\text{Own}, a_S) \downarrow lk \to \text{false} \cup x \to a_S$, and thus $\Psi(\text{Own}, a_S)$ empty $= \text{priv} \overset{s}{\mapsto} lk \to \text{false} \cup x \to 0$. Also, $\Phi(m_S, a_S) \twoheadrightarrow \text{lock} \overset{s}{\mapsto} (m'_S, a'_S)$ is equivalent to $(m_S, a_S) = (m'_S, a'_S)$ in the label-free state.

$$\left\{ \text{priv} \overset{s}{\mapsto} lk \to \text{false} \cup x \to 0 \right\} @ P$$
$$\{ \Psi(\text{Own}, 0) \text{ empty} \} @ P$$
$$\left\{ \Psi(\text{Own}, 0) \text{ empty} * (\Phi(\text{Own}, 0) \twoheadrightarrow \text{lock} \overset{s}{\mapsto} (\text{Own}, 0)) \right\} @ P\ (= P \bowtie E)$$
$$\text{hide}_{\Phi,(\text{Own},0)} \left\{ \text{priv} \overset{s}{\mapsto} \text{empty} * \text{lock} \overset{s}{\mapsto} (\text{Own}, 0) \right\} @ CSL_{\text{lock},lk,I}\ (= P \bowtie E \bowtie L_{\text{lock},lk,I})$$
$$\qquad \text{incr}(n)$$
$$\left\{ \text{priv} \overset{s}{\mapsto} \text{empty} * \text{lock} \overset{s}{\mapsto} (\text{Own}, n) \right\} @ CSL_{\text{lock},lk,I}$$
$$\left\{ \exists g_2.\, \Psi\, g_2 \text{ empty} * (\Phi\, g_2 \twoheadrightarrow \text{lock} \overset{s}{\mapsto} (\text{Own}, n)) \right\} @ P$$
$$\{ \Psi(\text{Own}, n) \text{ empty} \} @ P$$
$$\left\{ \text{priv} \overset{s}{\mapsto} lk \to \text{false} \cup x \to n \right\} @ P$$

The soundness of HIDE depends on a number of semantic properties of Φ [11]. The most important one is that states in the range of Φ have fixed *other* views for every label ℓ of V; equivalently, that environment threads for the program $\mathsf{hide}_{\Phi, g_1}\ c$ do not interfere with c on the states of V: all interference on V is *hidden* within the hide-section.

$$\text{if } w_1 \models \Phi\ g_1 \wedge (\ell \overset{o}{\mapsto} v_1 * \top) \text{ and } w_2 \models \Phi\ g_2 \wedge (\ell \overset{o}{\mapsto} v_2 * \top) \text{ then } v_1 = v_2$$

Concretely for our example, $\Phi\ g \wedge (\mathsf{lock} \overset{o}{\mapsto} v)$ implies $v = (\mathsf{Own}, 0)$, thus the above property clearly holds.

4   Concurroids Abstractly

A concurroid is a 4-tuple $V = (\mathcal{L}, \mathcal{W}, \tau, \mathcal{E})$ where: (1) $\mathcal{L}$ is a set of labels, where a label is a nat; (2) $\mathcal{W}$ is the *set of states*, each state $w \in \mathcal{W}$ having the structure described in Section 3; (3) τ is the *internal transition*, which is a relation on $\mathcal{W}$; (4) $\mathcal{E}$ is a set of pairs (α, ρ), where α and ρ are *external transitions* of V. An external transition is a function, mapping a heap h into a relation on $\mathcal{W}$. The components must satisfy a further set of requirements, discussed next.

State Properties. Every state $w \in \mathcal{W}$ is valid as defined in Figure 1, and its label footprint is $\mathcal{L}$, i.e. $\mathsf{dom}\ (w.\,s) = \mathsf{dom}\ (w.\,j) = \mathsf{dom}\ (w.\,o) = \mathcal{L}$. Additionally, $\mathcal{W}$ satisfies the property:

$$\textit{Fork-join closure: } \forall t{:}\text{PCM-map.}\ w \triangleleft t \in \mathcal{W} \iff w \triangleright t \in \mathcal{W},$$
$$\text{where } w \triangleleft t = [t \circ w.\,s \mid w.\,j \mid w.\,o], \text{and } w \triangleright t = [w.\,s \mid w.\,j \mid t \circ w.\,o]$$

The property requires that $\mathcal{W}$ is closed under the realignment of *self* and *other* components, when they exchange a PCM-map t between them. Such realignment is part of the definition of $\circledast$, and thus appears in proofs whenever the rule PAR is used, i.e. whenever threads fork or join. Fork-join closure ensures that if a parent thread forks in a state from $\mathcal{W}$, then the child threads are supplied with states which also are in $\mathcal{W}$, and dually for joining.

Transition Properties. A concurroid transition γ is a relation on $\mathcal{W}$ satisfying:

$$\textit{Guarantee: } (w, w') \in \gamma \implies w.\,o = w'.\,o$$
$$\textit{Locality: } \quad \forall t{:}\text{PCM-map.}\ w.\,o = w'.\,o \implies (w \triangleright t, w' \triangleright t) \in \gamma \implies (w \triangleleft t, w' \triangleleft t) \in \gamma$$

Guarantee restricts γ to only modify the *self* and *joint* components. Therefore, γ describes the behavior of a viewing thread in the subjective setting, but not of the thread's environment. In the terminology of Rely-Guarantee logics [5, 6, 8, 18], γ is a *guarantee* relation. To describe the behavior of the thread's environment, i.e. obtain a *rely* relation, we merely *transpose* the *self* and other components of γ:

$$\gamma^{\top} = \{(w_1^{\top}, w_2^{\top}) \mid (w_1, w_2) \in \gamma\}, \text{ where } w^{\top} = [w.\,o \mid w.\,j \mid w.\,s].$$

In this sense, FCSL transitions always encode *both* guarantee and rely relations.

Locality ensures that if γ relates states with a certain *self* components, then γ also relates states in which the *self* components have been simultaneously *framed* by a PCM-map t, *i.e.*, enlarged according to t. It thus generalizes the notion of locality from separation logic [14], with a notable difference. In separation logic, the frame t materializes out of nowhere, whereas in FCSL, t has to be appropriated from *other*; that is, taken out from the ownership of the environment.

An *internal* transition τ is a transition which is *reflexive* and preserves heap footprints. An *acquire* transition α, and a *release* transition ρ are functions mapping heaps to transitions which extend and reduce heap footprints, respectively, as formalized below. An external transition is either an acquire or a release transition. If $(\alpha, \rho) \in \mathcal{E}$, then α is an acquire transition, and ρ is a release transition.

$$\textit{Footprint preservation:}\quad (w, w') \in \tau \implies \text{dom} \lfloor w \rfloor = \text{dom} \lfloor w' \rfloor$$
$$\textit{Footprint extension:}\quad \forall h\text{:heap.}\, (w, w') \in (\alpha\, h) \implies \text{dom} (\lfloor w \rfloor \uplus h) = \text{dom} \lfloor w' \rfloor$$
$$\textit{Footprint reduction:}\quad \forall h\text{:heap.}\, (w, w') \in (\rho\, h) \implies \text{dom} (\lfloor w' \rfloor \uplus h) = \text{dom} \lfloor w \rfloor$$

Internal transitions are reflexive so that programs specified by such transitions may be *idle* (*i.e.*, transition from a state to itself). Footprint preservation requires internal transitions to preserve the domains of heaps obtained by state flattening. Internal transitions may exchange the ownership of subheaps between the *self* and *joint* components, or change the contents of individual heap pointers, or change the values of non-heap (*i.e.*, auxiliary) state, which flattening erases. However, they cannot add new pointers to a state or remove old ones, which is the task of external transitions, as formalized by Footprint extension and reduction.

Example 1 (The concurroid for private state). $P = (\{\text{priv}\}, \mathcal{W}_P, \tau_P, \{(\alpha_P, \rho_P)\})$, with

$$\mathcal{W}_P = \{\, \text{priv} \to [h_S \mid \text{empty} \mid h_O] \mid h_S \text{ and } h_O \text{ disjoint heaps} \,\}, \text{ and}$$
$$(w, w') \in \tau_P \iff w.\,s = \text{priv} \to h_S, w'.\,s = \text{priv} \to h'_S, \text{dom } h_S = \text{dom } h'_S, w.\,o = w'.\,o$$
$$(w, w') \in \alpha_P\, h \iff w.\,s = \text{priv} \to h_S, w'.\,s = \text{priv} \to h_S \uplus h, w.\,o = w'.\,o$$
$$(w, w') \in \rho_P\, h \iff w.\,s = \text{priv} \to h_S \uplus h, w'.\,s = \text{priv} \to h_S, w.\,o = w'.\,o$$

The internal transition admits arbitrary footprint-preserving change to the private heap h_S, while the acquire and release transitions simply add and remove the heap h from h_S.

Example 2 (The concurroid for a lock). $L_{\text{lock},lk,I} = (\{\text{lock}\}, \mathcal{W}_L, \tau_L, \{(\alpha_L, \rho_L)\})$, with $\mathcal{W}_L = \{\, w \mid w \models \text{assertion (2)} \,\}$, and (assuming $w.\,o = w'.\,o$ everywhere):

$$(w, w') \in \tau_L \iff w = w'$$
$$(w, w') \in \alpha_L\, h \iff w.\,s = \text{lock} \to (\text{Own}, a_S), w.\,j = \text{lock} \to (lk \to \text{true}),$$
$$w'.\,s = \text{lock} \to (\overline{\text{Own}}, a'_S), w'.\,j = \text{lock} \to ((lk \to \text{false}) \uplus h)$$
$$(w, w') \in \rho_L\, h \iff w.\,s = \text{lock} \to (\overline{\text{Own}}, a_S), w.\,j = \text{lock} \to ((lk \to \text{false}) \uplus h),$$
$$w'.\,s = \text{lock} \to (\text{Own}, a_S), w'.\,j = \text{lock} \to (lk \to \text{true})$$

The internal transition admits no changes to the state w. The α_L transition corresponds to unlocking, and hence to the acquisition of the heap h. It flips the ownership bit from Own to $\overline{\text{Own}}$, the contents of the lk pointer from true to false, and adds the heap h to the resource state. The ρ_L transition corresponds to locking, and is dual to α_L. When locking, the ρ_L transition keeps the auxiliary view a_S unchanged. Thus, the resource "remembers" the auxiliary view at the point of the last lock. Upon unlocking, the α_L transition changes this view into a'_S, where a'_S is some value that is coherent with the acquired heap h, i.e., which makes the resource invariant I ($a_S \bullet a_O$) h hold, and thus, the whole state belongs to $\mathcal{W}_L$.

Entanglement. Let $U = (\mathcal{L}_U, \mathcal{W}_U, \tau_U, \mathcal{E}_U)$ and $V = (\mathcal{L}_V, \mathcal{W}_V, \tau_V, \mathcal{E}_V)$, be concurroids. The entanglement $U \bowtie V$ is a concurroid with the label component $\mathcal{L}_{U \bowtie V} = \mathcal{L}_U \cup \mathcal{L}_V$. The state set component combines the individual states of U and V by unioning their labels, while ensuring that the labels contain only non-overlapping heaps.

$$\mathcal{W}_{U \bowtie V} = \{w \cup w' \mid w \in \mathcal{W}_U, w' \in \mathcal{W}_V, \text{and } \lfloor w \rfloor \text{ disjoint from } \lfloor w' \rfloor\}$$

To define the transition components of $U \bowtie V$, we first need the auxiliary concept of transition interconnection. Given transitions γ_U and γ_V over $\mathcal{W}_U$ and $\mathcal{W}_V$, respectively, the interconnection $\gamma_1 \bowtie \gamma_2$ is a transition on $\mathcal{W}_{U \bowtie V}$ which behaves as γ_U (resp. γ_V) on the part of the states labeled by U (resp. V).

$$\gamma_1 \bowtie \gamma_2 = \{(w_1 \cup w_2, w'_1 \cup w'_2) \mid (w_i, w'_i) \in \gamma_i, w_1 \cup w_2, w'_1 \cup w'_2 \in \mathcal{W}_{U \bowtie V}\}.$$

The internal transition of $U \bowtie V$ is defined as follows, where id_U is the diagonal of $\mathcal{W}_U$.

$$\tau_{U \bowtie V} = (\tau_U \bowtie \mathrm{id}_V) \cup (\mathrm{id}_U \bowtie \tau_V) \cup \bigcup_{h, (\alpha_U, \rho_U) \in \mathcal{E}_U, (\alpha_V, \rho_V) \in \mathcal{E}_V} (\alpha_U \, h \bowtie \rho_V \, h) \cup (\alpha_V \, h \bowtie \rho_U \, h).$$

Thus, $U \bowtie V$ steps internally whenever U steps and V stays idle, or when V steps and U stays idle, or when there exists a heap h which U and V exchange ownership over by synchronizing their external transitions.

Example 3. The transitions α_p of P and ρ_L of $L_{\mathrm{lock},lk,I}$ have already been described in display (4) of Section 2, but using assertions, rather than semantically. The display (3) of Section 2 presents the interconnection $\alpha_P \, h \bowtie \rho_L \, h$, which moves h from $L_{\mathrm{lock},lk,I}$ to P, and is part of the definition of $\tau_{P \bowtie L_{\mathrm{lock},lk,I}}$. The latter further allows moving h in the opposite direction ($\alpha_L \, h \bowtie \rho_P \, h$), independent stepping of P ($\tau_P \bowtie \mathrm{id}_L$) and of $L_{\mathrm{lock},lk,I}$ ($\mathrm{id}_P \bowtie \tau_L$).

The external transitions of $U \bowtie V$ are those of U, framed wrt. the labels of V.

$$\mathcal{E}_{U \bowtie V} = \{(\lambda h. (\alpha_U \, h) \bowtie \mathrm{id}_V, \lambda h. (\rho_U \, h) \bowtie \mathrm{id}_V) \mid (\alpha_U, \rho_U) \in \mathcal{E}_U\}$$

We note that $\mathcal{E}_{U \bowtie V}$ somewhat arbitrarily chooses to frame on the transitions of U rather than those of V. In this sense, the definition interconnects the external transitions of U and V, but it keeps those of U "open" in the entanglement, while it "shuts down" those of V. The notation $U \bowtie V$ is meant to symbolize this asymmetry. The asymmetry is important for our example of encoding CSL resources, as it enables us to iterate the (non-associative) addition of new resources as $((P \bowtie L_{\mathrm{lock}_1, lk_1, I_1}) \bowtie L_{\mathrm{lock}_2, lk_2, I_2}) \bowtie \cdots$ while keeping the external transitions of P open to exchange heaps with new resources.

Clearly, many ways exist to interconnect transitions of two concurroids and select which transitions to keep open. In our implementation, we have identified several operators implementing common interconnection choices, and proved a number of equations and properties about them (*e.g.*, all of them validate an instance of the INJECT rule). We also show a version of the INJECT rule with a different operator ($\ltimes$) [11]. However, as none of these operators is needed for the examples in this paper, we omit them.

Lemma 1. *$U \bowtie V$ is a concurroid.*

We can also reorder the iterated addition of lock concurroids.

Lemma 2 (Exchange law). *$(U \bowtie V) \bowtie W = (U \bowtie W) \bowtie V$.*

We close the section with the definition of the concurroid E which is the right unit of the entanglement operator $\bowtie$. E is defined as $E = (\emptyset, \mathcal{W}_E, id, \emptyset)$, where $\mathcal{W}_E$ contains only the empty state (i.e. the state with no labels).

5   Language and Logic

In the tradition of axiomatic program logics, the language of FCSL splits into purely functional expressions e (v when the expression is a value), and commands c with the effects of divergence, state and concurrency. We also include procedures F, for commands with arguments.

FCSL Commands. A command c satisfies the Hoare tuple $\{p\} c : A \{q\} @ U$ if c's effect on states respects the internal transition of the concurroid U, c is *memory-safe* when executed from a state satisfying p, and concurrently with any environment that respects the transitions (internal and external) of U. Furthermore, if c terminates, it returns a value of type A in a state satisfying q. Formally, q may use a dedicated variable *res* of type A to name the return result.[5] FCSL uses a *procedure tuple*, $\forall x{:}B.\,\{p\}\,f\,(x) : A\,\{q\}@U$, to specify a potentially recursive higher-order procedure f taking an argument x of type B to a result of type A. The assertions p and q may depend on x. FCSL does not treat first-order looping commands, as these are special cases of recursive procedures. In the case of recursive procedures, p and q in the procedure tuple together correspond to a loop invariant, and typically are provided by the programmer.

The syntax of commands and procedures is as follows.

$$c ::= x \leftarrow c_1; c_2 \mid c_1 \parallel c_2 \mid \text{if } e \text{ then } c_1 \text{ else } c_2 \mid F(e) \mid \text{return } v \mid \text{act } a \mid \text{inject } c \mid \text{hide}_{\Phi, g} \, c$$
$$F ::= f \mid \text{fix } f.\,x.\,c$$

Commands and procedures include *atomic actions* act a, a monadic unit return v that returns v and terminates, a monadic bind (*i.e.* sequential composition) $x \leftarrow c_1; c_2$ that runs c_1 then substitutes its result v_1 for x to run c_2 (we write $c_1; c_2$ when $x \notin \text{FV}(c_2)$), parallel composition $c_1 \parallel c_2$, a conditional, a procedure application $F(e)$, a procedure variable f, a fixed-point construct for recursion, and injection and hiding commands.

Judgments and Inference Rules. The FCSL judgments are *hypothetical* under a context Γ that maps *program variables* x to their type and *procedure variables* f to their specification. We allow each specification to depend on the variables declared to the left.

$$\Gamma ::= \cdot \mid \Gamma, x{:}A \mid \Gamma, \forall x{:}B.\{p\}f(x) : A\,\{q\}@U$$

---

[5] When $A = \text{unit}$, we suppress the type and the variable *res*, as we did in previous sections.

Fig. 2. FCSL inference rules

$$\frac{\Gamma \vdash \{p\} c_1 : B \{q\}@U \qquad \Gamma, x : B \vdash \{[x/res]q\} c_2 : A \{r\}@U \qquad x \notin \mathsf{FV}(r)}{\Gamma \vdash \{p\} x \leftarrow c_1; c_2 : A \{r\}@U} \ \text{SEQ}$$

$$\frac{\Gamma \vdash \{p_1\} c_1 : A_1 \{q_1\}@U \qquad \Gamma \vdash \{p_2\} c_2 : A_2 \{q_2\}@U}{\Gamma \vdash \{p_1 \circledast p_2\} c_1 \parallel c_2 : A_1 \times A_2 \{[\pi_1\, res/res]q_1 \circledast [\pi_2\, res/res]q_2\}@U} \ \text{PAR} \qquad \frac{\forall x{:}B. \{p\} f(x) : A \{q\}@U \in \Gamma}{\Gamma \vdash \forall x{:}B. \{p\} f(x) : A \{q\}@U} \ \text{HYP}$$

$$\frac{\Gamma \vdash \{p_1\} c : A \{q_1\}@U \qquad \Gamma \vdash (p_1, q_1) \sqsubseteq (p_2, q_2)}{\Gamma \vdash \{p_2\} c : A \{q_2\}@U} \ \text{CONSEQ} \qquad \frac{\Gamma \vdash \{p\} c : A \{q\}@U \qquad r \text{ stable under } U}{\Gamma \vdash \{p \circledast r\} c : A \{q \circledast r\}@U} \ \text{FRAME}$$

$$\frac{\Gamma \vdash \{e = \mathsf{true} \wedge p\} c_1 : A \{q\}@U \qquad \Gamma \vdash \{e = \mathsf{false} \wedge p\} c_2 : A \{q\}@U}{\Gamma \vdash \{p\} \text{ if } e \text{ then } c_1 \text{ else } c_2 : A \{q\}@U} \ \text{IF}$$

$$\frac{\Gamma \vdash \{p_1\} c : A \{q_1\}@U \qquad \Gamma \vdash \{p_2\} c : A \{q_2\}@U}{\Gamma \vdash \{p_1 \wedge p_2\} c : A \{q_1 \wedge q_2\}@U} \ \text{CONJ} \qquad \frac{\Gamma \vdash \{p\} c : A \{q\}@U \qquad \alpha \notin \mathrm{dom}\,\Gamma}{\Gamma \vdash \{\exists \alpha{:}B. p\} c : A \{\exists \alpha{:}B. q\}@U} \ \text{EXIST}$$

$$\frac{\Gamma \vdash e : A \qquad p \text{ stable under } U}{\Gamma \vdash \{p\} \text{ return } e : A \{p \wedge res = e\}@U} \ \text{RET} \qquad \frac{\Gamma, \forall x{:}B. \{p\} f(x) : A \{q\}@U, x{:}B \vdash \{p\} c : A \{q\}@U}{\Gamma \vdash \forall x{:}B. \{p\} (\mathrm{fix}\, f.\, x.\, c)(x) : A \{q\}@U} \ \text{FIX}$$

$$\frac{\Gamma \vdash \forall x{:}B. \{p\} F(x) : A \{q\}@U \qquad \Gamma \vdash e : B}{\Gamma \vdash \{[e/x]p\} F(e) : A \{[e/x]q\}@U} \ \text{APP} \qquad \frac{\Gamma \vdash \{p\} c : A \{q\}@U \qquad r \text{ stable under } V}{\Gamma \vdash \{p * r\} \text{ inject } c : A \{q * r\}@U \bowtie V} \ \text{INJECT}$$

$$\frac{\Gamma \vdash \left\{ \mathrm{priv} \overset{s}{\mapsto} h * p \right\} c \left\{ \mathrm{priv} \overset{s}{\mapsto} h' * q \right\}@(P \bowtie U) \bowtie V \qquad P, U \text{ and } V \text{ have disjoint sets of labels}}{\Gamma \vdash \{\Psi\, g\, h * (\Phi(g) \mathbin{-\!*} p)\} \, \mathrm{hide}_{\Phi,g}\, c \, \{\exists g'. \Psi\, g'\, h' * (\Phi(g') \mathbin{-\!*} q)\}@P \bowtie U} \ \text{HIDE}$$

$$\text{where } \Psi\, g\, h = \exists k{:}\mathrm{heap.}\ \mathrm{priv} \overset{s}{\mapsto} h \cup k \wedge \Phi(g) \downarrow k$$

$$\frac{a = (U, A, \sigma, \mu) \text{ is an action} \qquad \Gamma \vdash (\sigma \wedge \mathrm{this}\, w, \lambda w'. (w, w', res) \in \mu) \sqsubseteq (p, q) \qquad p, q \text{ stable under } U}{\Gamma \vdash \{p\} \text{ act } a : A \{q\}@U} \ \text{ACTION}$$

Γ does not bind logical variables. In first-order Hoare logics, logical variables are implicitly universally quantified with global scope. In FCSL, we limit their scope to the Hoare tuples in which they appear. This is required for specifying recursive procedures, where a logical variable may be instantiated differently in each recursive call [9]. We also assume a formation requirement on Hoare tuples $\mathsf{FLV}(p) \supseteq \mathsf{FLV}(q)$, *i.e.*, that all free logical variables of the postcondition also appear in the precondition.

The inference rules of the Hoare tuple judgments for commands and procedures are presented in Figure 2. We note that the assertions and the annotations in the rules (*e.g.*, Φ in the HIDE rule) may freely use the variables in Γ. To reduce clutter, we silently assume the checks that all such specification level-entities are well-typed in their respective contexts Γ.

We have already discussed PAR, INJECT and HIDE rules in their versions where the return type $A = \mathsf{unit}$. The generalization to arbitrary A is straightforward. A side condition of HIDE ensures that the sets of labels of P, U and V don't clash, so the entanglement $(P \bowtie U) \bowtie V$ is defined. The rule FRAME is a special case of PAR when c_2 is taken to be the idle thread (*i.e.*, $c_2 = \mathsf{return}()$). Just like in the rule RET, we need to prove the framing assertion r stable, to account for the interference of the *other* threads. The rule FIX requires proving a Hoare tuple for the procedure body, under a hypothesis that the recursive calls satisfy the same tuple. The procedure APPlication rule uses the typing judgment for expressions $\Gamma \vdash e : A$, which is the customary one from a typed λ-calculus, so we omit its rules; in our formalization in Coq, this judgment will correspond to the CiC's typing judgment. The CONSEQ rule uses the judgment $\Gamma \vdash (p_1, q_1) \sqsubseteq (p_2, q_2)$, which generalizes the customary side conditions $p_2 \implies p_1$ for strengthening the precondition and $q_1 \implies q_2$ for weakening the postcondition, to deal with the local scope of logical variables [11]. The other rules are standard from Hoare logic, except the ACTION rule for *atomic actions*. We devote the rest of the section to it.

Atomic Actions. Actions perform atomic steps from state to state, such as, *e.g.*, realigning the boundaries between, or changing the contents of *self*, *joint* and *other* state components. The actions thus serve to *synchronize* the changes to operational state (*i.e.*, heaps), with changes to the logical information required for verification (*i.e. auxiliary*, or *abstract*, parts of the state: a_S, a_O, *etc.*). If the logical information is erased, that is, if the states are flattened to heaps, then an action implements a single atomic memory operation such as looking up or mutating a heap pointer, CAS-ing over a heap pointer, or performing some other atomic *Read-Modify-Write* operation [7, § 5.6]. How an action manipulates the logical state is up to the user, depending on the application: we provide a formal definition of actions, and require that user's choices adhere to the definition.

An action is a 4-tuple $a = (U, A, \sigma, \mu)$ where: (1) the concurroid U whose internal transition a respects, (2) the type A of the action's return value, (3) the predicate σ on states describing the states in which the action could be executed, and (4) the relation μ relating the initial state, the ending state, and the ending result of the action. σ and μ are given in a large-footprint style, giving fully the heaps and the auxiliaries they accept.

For example, consider the action **release** used in Section 3 to release a lock and transfer the pointer x from a private heap of a thread to the ownership of the lock resource. This action is over the entangled concurroid $CSL_{\text{lock},lk,I} = P \bowtie L_{\text{lock},lk,I}$ as it transfers the ownership of $(x \to -)$. Its return value type is $A = \text{unit}$. It can be executed in states in which the lock is taken by the *self* thread, and the pointer x is in the private heap. The contents of x is $a_S + a'_S + a_O$, for some a_S and a'_S, so that once x is transfered to the ownership of the lock resource, it satisfies the resource invariant. Thus:

$$w \in \sigma \iff w = \text{priv} \to [x \to (a_S + a'_S + a_O) \uplus h_S \mid \text{empty} \mid h_O] \uplus$$
$$\text{lock} \to [(\text{Own}, a'_S) \mid lk \to \text{true} \mid (\text{Own}, a_O)]$$

$$(w, w', res) \in \mu \iff w = \text{priv} \to [x \to (a_S + a'_S + a_O) \uplus h_S \mid \text{empty} \mid h_O] \uplus$$
$$\text{lock} \to [(\text{Own}, a'_S) \mid lk \to \text{true} \mid (\text{Own}, a_O)] \land$$
$$w' = \text{priv} \to [h_S \mid \text{empty} \mid h_O] \uplus$$
$$\text{lock} \to [(\text{Own}, a_S + a'_S) \mid lk \to \text{false} \uplus x \to (a_S + a'_S + a_O) \mid (\text{Own}, a_O)]$$

Once the states are flattened into heaps, the σ and μ components of **release** reduce to describing the behavior of a memory mutation on the pointer lk. For example, the relation $\lfloor \mu \rfloor = \{(\lfloor w \rfloor, \lfloor w' \rfloor, r) \mid (w, w', r) \in \mu\}$ relates (h, h', r) iff

$$h = (x \to (a_S + a'_S + a_O)) \uplus h_S \uplus (lk \to \text{true}) \uplus h_O$$
$$h' = (x \to (a_S + a'_S + a_O)) \uplus h_S \uplus (lk \to \text{false}) \uplus h_O$$

Thus, operationally, **release** can be implemented as a single mutation to the lk pointer.

The inference rule ACTION takes an action $a = (U, A, \sigma, \mu)$ and checks that a satisfies that σ can be strengthened into p and μ can be weakened into q. As μ is not a postcondition itself, but a relation taking input states, we first introduce a fresh logical variable w to name the input state using a predicate this. Then the predicate expressing post states for the action is computed out of μ and w, and it is this predicate that's weakened into q. p and q must be stable wrt. U, in order to account for the possibility that an interference of the environment appears just before, or just after, the action is executed.

Soundness and Implementation. We have established the soundness of FCSL by exhibiting a denotational model based on *action trees* [10, 11], which are a variation on Brookes' action trace semantics, so we can formulate the following theorem.

Theorem 1. *FCSL is sound with respect to the denotational model of action trees.*

We developed the model in the logics of Calculus of Inductive Constructions, thus, the model is a shallow embedding in Coq, and its implementation is available on-line [11]. The implementation also defines denotational semantics for constructs and ascribes them types corresponding to rules in Figure 2. These type ascriptions require proofs, and together establish soundness of the logic, although rules/types in the implementation differ somewhat from those in Figure 2, facilitating encoding in Coq: (1) they use binary postconditions, (2) pre-/postconditions are in higher-order logic over heaps and PCMs, instead of notation from Figure 1, (3) they infer weakest-pre-/strongest-postconditions and (4) assertions are stabilized. The correspondence between the implementation and Figure 2 is straightforward, but established by hand.

6   Related Work

FCSL builds on the previous work on subjective auxiliary state and SCSL logic [10]. The SCSL logic contained the distinction between *self* and *other* views, which was essential for compositional implementation of *auxiliary state*. However, it contained exactly one coarse-grained resource, with no ability to create and dispose new resources. In contrast, FCSL can introduce any number of fine-grained resources in a scoped way.

The work on Concurrent Abstract Predicates (CAP) [4] introduces a notion of *shared region* that serves a similar purpose as concurroids, in that regions circumscribe a chunk of shared heap with a protocol governing its evolution. A *protocol* is defined by a set of atomic actions, which are RG-style transitions on private state and a region. In addition to heaps, regions may contain abstract capabilities that identify enabled actions. Thus there is a subtle mutual recursion in a protocol definition between an action and the capability to perform the action. A recurring pattern for this approach is quantification over *all* possible capabilities and placing them in a shared region, to be used up if needed in the execution of the protocol. The CAP framework could atomically change only one region; a restriction lifted in the recent work on Views [3] and HOCAP [15] that introduced *view shifts* to synchronize changes in several regions. Once allocated, CAP's regions have dynamically-scoped lifetime, and they can be disposed by a particular thread if it collects all corresponding region's capabilities. To the best of our knowledge, HOCAP does not allow the removal or scoped hiding of a shared region.

In contrast with CAP and their successors, FCSL does not require capabilities to perform actions, as these are naturally represented in the *self* and *other* views associated with a resource (and can also be seen as auxiliary state). Such auxiliary state is simpler than capabilities; it is not subject to ownership transfer, and there is no need to quantify over all capabilities. In our experience, this simplicity extends to the specification of invariants and transitions, and to the proofs of stability. In FCSL, synchronizing changes over a number of concurroids is achieved directly at the level of transitions by means of entanglement, and at the level of programs by allowing actions to be defined over any concurroid, including entangled ones. Thus, no view shifts are required. The burden of stability proofs is further reduced in FCSL by formulating private heaps as a separate concurroid that one may, but need not, entangle with. Thus, when an action manipulates only the internal state of a resource, the attendant stability proofs can ignore private heaps, *e.g.*, the take action of a ticketed lock [4, 11]. Moreover, the communication in FCSL makes it possible for concurroids to pass heaps between each other directly, rather than going through private state. While the current paper does not present examples that exploit this ability, we have found it useful when verifying in FCSL a more advanced example of readers-writers, which we will present in future work.

CaReSL [17] uses the same notion of shared region as CAP, though it specifies the transitions in a manner closer to FCSL, namely by means of STS's. CaReSL does not directly provide subjective *self* and *other* views of a resource, but it provides a notion of *tokens*, whose ownership is exchanged between a thread and its environment. CaReSL assertions explicitly allow statements only about self-owned tokens, not *other*-owned ones. Thus, reasoning about the lack of logical changes to environment-owned data has to be encoded with a level of indirection, potentially quantifying over all tokens, similar to CAP's quantification over capabilities. A frequent side condition in CaReSL rules is that various assertions are *token-pure*, which does not have a direct correspondent in FCSL. Similar to CAP, CaReSL currently allows actions that work over only a single region, and will require an extension akin to view shifts to enable synchronized updates. CaReSL does not consider removal or scoped hiding of shared regions, although it can be emulated by introducing an empty "final" protocol state. Instead of stability checks in FCSL, in CaReSL one may stabilize assertions by composing them with environment stepping. In our experience, this does not change the proofs: the same obligations reappear in proofs out of stabilized hypotheses. On the other hand, CaReSL can reason about fine-grained data structure by means of refinement (a generalization of linearizability). FCSL supports higher-order functions by means of shallow embedding into CiC [1, 16], but we have not considered linearizability so far, which is future work.

Feng's Local Rely-Guarantee (LRG) [5] is, to the best of our knowledge, the first work that reconciled fine-grained reasoning in the style of RG with framing and hiding at the level of transitions (similar to our INJECT and HIDE). We differ from LRG in that we introduce communication and subjectivity into the mix; thus our injection and hiding rules take *self* and *other* views into account. The latter are a compositional form of auxiliary state, whereas LRG in practice has to use the classical, non-compositional form of auxiliary state [10, 13].

7   Conclusion and Future Work

We presented *concurroids*—a novel model for scalable shared-memory concurrency verification, based on communicating STS, and FCSL—a logic for concurroids.

In the future work, we are going to build a number of concurroids to encode common programming patterns. For example, dynamic allocation and deallocation of memory can be encoded via an allocator concurroid (without extensions of FCSL), and similarly for dynamic allocation and deallocation of locks. We hope to investigate if concurroids can be endowed with analogues of channel relabeling and restriction operators from process algebras, to provide finer control over interconnection and closure of external transitions. Finally, we plan to consider refinement which allows weakening the ascribed concurroid U of a program, to a coarser-grained concurroid V, if U can be shown to simulate V. One could then verify fine-grained concurrent ADTs against V, and afterwards hide the granularity by switching to U.

Acknowledgments. We thank Anindya Banerjee, Thomas Dinsdale-Young and the ESOP 2014 anonymous reviewers for their comments. This research was partially supported by Spanish MINECO projects TIN2012-39391-C04-01 Strongsoft, TIN2010-20639 Paran10, AMAROUT grant PCOFUND-GA-2008-229599, and Ramon y Cajal grant RYC-2010-0743.

References

1. Bertot, Y., Castéran, P.: Interactive Theorem Proving and Program Development. Coq'Art: The Calculus of Inductive Constructions. Springer (2004)
2. Brookes, S.: A semantics for concurrent separation logic. Th. Comp. Sci. 375(1-3) (2007)
3. Dinsdale-Young, T., Birkedal, L., Gardner, P., Parkinson, M.J., Yang, H.: Views: compositional reasoning for concurrent programs. In: POPL 2013 (2013)
4. Dinsdale-Young, T., Dodds, M., Gardner, P., Parkinson, M.J., Vafeiadis, V.: Concurrent abstract predicates. In: D'Hondt, T. (ed.) ECOOP 2010. LNCS, vol. 6183, pp. 504–528. Springer, Heidelberg (2010)
5. Feng, X.: Local rely-guarantee reasoning. In: POPL 2009 (2009)
6. Feng, X., Ferreira, R., Shao, Z.: On the relationship between concurrent separation logic and assume-guarantee reasoning. In: De Nicola, R. (ed.) ESOP 2007. LNCS, vol. 4421, pp. 173–188. Springer, Heidelberg (2007)
7. Herlihy, M., Shavit, N.: The art of multiprocessor programming. M. Kaufmann (2008)
8. Jones, C.B.: Tentative steps toward a development method for interfering programs. ACM Trans. Prog. Lang. Syst. 5(4) (1983)
9. Kleymann, T.: Hoare logic and auxiliary variables. Formal Asp. Comput. 11(5) (1999)
10. Ley-Wild, R., Nanevski, A.: Subjective auxiliary state for coarse-grained concurrency. In: POPL 2013 (2013)
11. Nanevski, A., Ley-Wild, R., Sergey, I., Delbianco, G.A.: Supporting Material, http://software.imdea.org/~aleks/fcsl/
12. O'Hearn, P.W.: Resources, concurrency, and local reasoning. Th. Comp. Sci. 375(1-3) (2007)
13. Owicki, S.S., Gries, D.: Verifying properties of parallel programs: An axiomatic approach. Commun. ACM 19(5) (1976)

14. Reynolds, J.C.: Separation logic: A logic for shared mutable data structures. In: LICS (2002)
15. Svendsen, K., Birkedal, L., Parkinson, M.: Modular reasoning about separation of concurrent data structures. In: Felleisen, M., Gardner, P. (eds.) ESOP 2013. LNCS, vol. 7792, pp. 169–188. Springer, Heidelberg (2013)
16. The Coq Development Team. The Coq Proof Assistant Reference Manual - Version V8.4 (2012), http://coq.inria.fr/
17. Turon, A., Dreyer, D., Birkedal, L.: Unifying refinement and Hoare-style reasoning in a logic for higher-order concurrency. In: ICFP 2013 (2013)
18. Vafeiadis, V., Parkinson, M.: A marriage of rely/guarantee and separation logic. In: Caires, L., Vasconcelos, V.T. (eds.) CONCUR 2007. LNCS, vol. 4703, pp. 256–271. Springer, Heidelberg (2007)

Checking Linearizability of Encapsulated Extended Operations*

Oren Zomer[1], Guy Golan-Gueta[1], G. Ramalingam[2], and Mooly Sagiv[1]

[1] Tel Aviv University, Tel Aviv, Israel
[2] Microsoft Research, Bangalore, India

Abstract. Linearizable objects (data-structures) provide operations that appear to execute atomically. Modern mainstream languages provide many linearizable data-structures, simplifying concurrent programming. In practice, however, programmers often find a need to execute a sequence of operations (on linearizable objects) that executes atomically and write *extended operations* for this purpose. Such extended operations are a common source of atomicity bugs.

This paper focuses on the problem of verifying that a set of extension operations (to a linearizable library) are themselves linearizable. We present several reduction theorems that simplify this verification problem enabling more efficient verification.

We first introduce the notion of an *encapsulated extension*: this is an extension that (a) does not introduce new shared state (beyond the shared state in the base linearizable library), and (b) accesses or modifies the shared state only through the base operations. We show that encapsulated extensions are widely prevalent in real applications.

We show that linearizability of encapsulated extended operations can be verified by considering only histories with one occurrence of an extended operation, interleaved with atomic occurrences of base and extended operations. As a consequence, this verification needs to consider only histories with two threads, whereas general linearizability verification requires considering histories with an unbounded number of threads.

We show that when the operations satisfy certain properties, each extended operation can be verified independently of the others, enabling further reductions.

We have implemented a simple static analysis algorithm that conservatively verifies linearizabilty of encapsulated extensions of Java concurrent maps. We present empirical results illustrating the benefits of the reduction theorems.

Keywords: concurrency, linearizability, atomicity, verification, composition, extension.

* Zomer, Gueta, and Sagiv were funded by the European Research Council under the European Unions Seventh Framework Program (FP7/2007-2013) / ERC grant agreement no. [321174-VSSC].

Z. Shao (Ed.): ESOP 2014, LNCS 8410, pp. 311–330, 2014.

1 Introduction

Concurrent programs are challenging to write. To ease the programmer's burden, modern programming platforms provide libraries of efficient concurrent data structures. These libraries provide operations that are guaranteed to be *atomic*, while hiding the complexity of the implementation from clients.

Unfortunately, clients often need to atomically perform some computation that may invoke multiple library operations. Programmers end up extending a linearizable data type by defining new custom atomic operations, which we refer to as *extended operations*. Figure 1 and Figure 2 are real world examples of linearizable operations that extend the Java *ConcurrentMap* interface. As shown in [1], such extended operations are a common source of concurrency bugs. In this paper, we consider the problem of verifying the correctness of an extension of a linearizable data-structure. Specifically, we wish to verify that the extension of the data-structure is linearizable [2].

Encapsulated Extension. In this paper, we identify a restricted class of extensions of a data-structure, inspired by the examples in [1]. This class is realistic and includes many commonly found extensions. As we show, this class is also amenable to more efficient verification. An extension is said to be *encapsulated* if it satisfies the following two restrictions:

Encapsulation. The extension methods do not directly access or modify any global (shared) state. Instead, extension methods access shared state only via operations of the underlying data-structure that is being extended.

Open Environment. All of the operations of the underlying data-structure are exposed to the clients: i.e., none of the underlying operations are hidden by the extension.

A Simple Verification Approach. Informally, an execution in which multiple threads invoke a data-structure's operations concurrently is said to be *linearizable* if each invoked operation appears to execute instantaneously, with the result that the data-structure's operations appear to be executed sequentially (without any overlap). The data-structure is said to be *linearizable* if all possible concurrent executions involving the data-structure are linearizable.

Consider a data-structure with core methods $m_1, \ldots, m_n$ that has been extended by adding extension methods $em_1, \ldots, em_k$. We can verify that the extended ADT is linearizable by considering all executions of the following "driver" program, and verifying that each of these executions is linearizable (We write $s_1|s_2$ to indicate that either s_1 or s_2 may be executed non-deterministically). For simplicity we have omitted parameters and return-values in this code template.

```
Val computeIfAbsent(Key k) {
  Val temp1, temp2 ;
  temp1 = this.get(k) ;
  if (temp1 == null) {
    temp2 = hardLocalPureStateComputation(k) ;
    temp1 = this.putIfAbsent(k, temp2) ;
    if (temp1 == null) temp1 = temp2 ;
  }
  return temp1 ;
}
```

Fig. 1. A linearizable operation that extends Java *ConcurrentMap*. The pure computation can be, for example if k is an integer, evaluating the square of k. The get operation in *ConcurrentMap* returns the value mapped from the given key (initialized to null). The putIfAbsent operation in *ConcurrentMap* atomically checks whether the given key is mapped to null: if it is mapped to null, the operation immediately maps the key to the given value and returns null, otherwise the operation returns the non-null value that the key is mapped to without changing the map.

```
void inc(Class<?> key) {
  for (;;) {
    Integer i = this.get(key);
    if (i == null) {
      if (this.putIfAbsent(key, 1) == null) return;
    } else {
      if (this.replace(key, i, i + 1)) return;
    }
  }
}
```

Fig. 2. An extended encapsulated operation over Java *ConcurrentMap* from *OpenJDK 7*, class: *ThrowingTasks*. The replace operation atomically checks whether the given key is mapped to the first value: if it is mapped to that value, the operation immediately remaps the key to the second value and returns true, otherwise the operation returns false without changing the map.

```
while (∗) do {
  create new thread to execute {
    while (∗) do {
      m₁() | · · · | mₙ() | em₁() | · · · | emₖ();
    }
  }
}
```

Incremental Verification. Suppose the core ADT (consisting only of the core methods) is known to be linearizable. We can then exploit this to simplify the driver program as shown below, replacing each call to a core method m_i by "atomic s_i", where s_i is the sequential specification for m_i. (Note that this replacement is done within the code for any extension method em_j as well, even though that is not shown below.)

```
while (∗) do {
  create new thread to execute {
    while (∗) do {
      atomic {s₁()} | ⋯ | atomic{sₙ()} | em₁() | ⋯ | emₖ();
    }
  }
}
```

Note that this reduction is valid only because of the "encapsulation" assumption stated earlier. If the code for extended operations directly accesses or manipulates the shared state (of the underlying data-structure), this reduction is invalid. However, accessing this shared state via the core operations is fine.

Reduction to Two Threads. As we show in the paper, it is not necessary to consider all executions of the preceding driver program. Using induction, we show that it suffices to consider a single occurrence of any one extended operation and replace other occurrences of an extended operation em_i by an atomic execution of its sequential specification es_i. If the implementations and specifications do not depend on thread identifiers (such as Java *ThreadLocal* class), we can rewrite the driver program so that it contains only two threads (since all atomic executions of operations can be treated as executed by the same thread). This gives us the following simplified driver program:

```
// Thread 1 (Environment thread)
while (∗) do {
 atomic { s₁() } | ⋯ | atomic { sₙ() } | atomic { es₁() } | ⋯ | atomic { esₖ() };
}
||
// Thread 2 (Nonatomic extension method)
{ em₁() | ⋯ | emₖ(); }
```

Note that such a reduction is not possible for general linearizability verification. Consider the simple example shown in Figure 3, which is not linearizable. However, all histories of this example with less than K threads are linearizable. Hence, the verifier will find a counterexample only when it considers executions with K threads.

Proving linearizability is intractable even for finite systems, in general [3]. However, bounding the number of threads reduces the complexity of linearizability verification (see [3]).

Further Reductions. We then describe additional conditions (explained later) that, when satisfied, allow us to verify the linearizability of the extension operations em_1 to em_k independent of each other. These conditions, in fact, allow us to verify the linearizability of the executions produced by the following driver program, for each i, independently.

```
// Environment thread
while (∗) do {
    atomic { s₁() } | ··· | atomic { sₙ() };
}
||
// One nonatomic extension method:
{ emᵢ() }
```

Such a reduction is not always valid, even when we have only one extension operation, as demonstrated by the example in Figure 4. This extension method sets a boolean register to true and returns the original value. This method is not linearizable. Assume that the initial value of the register is false and that there are two concurrent invocations of the extension method. It is possible for both invocations to return a value of false, which is not possible in any sequential execution. However, any execution that contains only one occurrence of the extension method (along with any number of occurrences of the core methods **read** and **write**) can be shown to be linearizable.

```
int s = 0;
// Specifications:
//   return value must be true.
// K is a constant value larger
// than 1.
boolean incReadAssertDec() {
    s++;
    boolean b = (s < K);
    s−−;
    return b;
}
```

Fig. 3. A simple example of a method which is linearizable for up to K threads. (we assume that the operations on s are atomic.)

```
boolean readAndWriteTrue() {
    boolean temp = this.read() ;
    if (!temp) {
        this.write(true) ;
    }
    return temp ;
}
```

Fig. 4. An extension of the interface of a boolean register. The base object has a boolean value and two atomic base-operations: **read()** that returns the boolean value and **write(x)** that overwrites it and returns nothing. This encapsulated extended operation is an incorrect implementation of a simple test-and-set operation.

Empirical Evaluation. Java's concurrent maps are widely used, not surprisingly, since they are a higher-level shared memory abstraction. Our empirical study shows that encapsulated extensions over maps are widely used, and that the reductions described above are applicable to many of these extensions, simplifying the verification. We have implemented a static checker for verifying linearizability of encapsulated extensions of the Java concurrent map.

However, we did not find encapsulated extensions over other interesting data structures, such as queues, stacks and deques, in which non-linearizability might cause errors. The implementations of these data-structures, such as Java *ConcurrentLinkedQueue* and *ConcurrentLinkedDeque*, do not provide methods for "conditional modifications" like *ConcurrentMap*'s `putIfAbsent` and `replace`. For this reason, in most real-world scenarios, the programmer must call external synchronization mechanisms (such as locks and transactions) in order to implement linearizable extensions. This type of extensions contradicts our Encapsulation requirement and therefore it is not in the range of this paper. On the other hand, if those data structures had provided base operations for "conditional modifications", we could write interesting encapsulated extensions on top of them, as demonstrated in [4].

2   Concurrent Objects and Linearizability

In this section we review standard terminology relating to concurrent objects (without extended operations) and *linearizability* (as in [2]).

A concurrent execution of an object is modeled by a *history*, which is a finite sequence of method *invocation* and *response events*. We write a *method invocation* as $[_{t.m(arg)}$ where t is a thread name, m is a method name and *arg* denotes the values of actual argument values of the method. We write a *method response* as $]_{t.m}/b$ where t is a thread name, m is a method name and b is the return value. We sometimes write $t.m(arg)/b$ instead of writing the sequence of the two events $[_{t.m(arg)}$, $]_{t.m}/b$ (this is used as a short way to represent an invocation which is immediately followed by its corresponding response). For convenience, we assume that a unique identifier is attached to every event in a history.

A response *matches* an invocation if they have the same thread name and the same method name. A *method call* in a history h is a pair consisting of an invocation and the next matching response in h. An invocation is *pending* in h if no matching response follows the invocation. *complete(h)* is the subsequence of h consisting of all non-pending invocations and all responses. A history h is *complete* if $h = complete(h)$.

A history h is *sequential* if the first event of h is an invocation, and each invocation, except possibly the last, is immediately followed by a matching response.

A *thread subhistory* $h|t$ of history h is the subsequence of all events in h whose thread names are t. Two histories h and h' are *equivalent* if for every thread t, $h|t = h'|t$.

Definition 1 (well formed history). *A history h is* well formed *if each thread subhistory of h is sequential.*

We assume that all histories that represent object executions are well formed — because, given a concurrent object x, well formed histories represent all reasonable behaviors of x (see [2]).

Definition 2 (Linearization of a history). *We say that a sequential history s is a linearization of a history h, if there exists a history h' such that the following conditions are satisfied:*

- h' is constructed by appending zero or more responses to h.
- $complete(h')$ is equivalent to s.
- If a response event e precedes an invocation event e' in h, then the same is true in s.

Definition 3 (Sequential Specification). *A sequential specification of a concurrent object is a set of sequential histories.*

A sequential specification is used to describe the legal behaviors of an object in the absence of concurrency.

Definition 4 (Linearizable Object). *We say that an object x is linearizable with respect to a sequential specification S, if for any feasible history h of x there exists $s \in S$, such that s is a linearization of h.*

Note that, from the above definition, if x is linearizable with respect to S then any feasible sequential history of x is in S. Furthermore, intuitively, any feasible history of x can be seen as a history in which each method call is *atomic*.

3   Linearizability of Encapsulated Extensions

In this section we generalize the model from Section 2 for encapsulated extensions of a linearizable object and present our reduction theorem for proving linearizablity of encapsulated extensions.

3.1   The Problem

Let BASE be a specification describing a (base) linearizable object. An encapsulated extension of BASE consists of a set of extension methods (including their implementation). The only global (shared) state accessed by the extension methods is the state of BASE, which can be accessed only via the methods of BASE.

Extended Histories. Consider an execution of an arbitrary concurrent client program that uses the extended object. For our purposes, it suffices to focus on the invocation and response events of the (base and extended) operations of the object. Hence, we model an execution of the object by an *extended-history*, defined to be a finite sequence of method *invocation* and *response events* in which the events can be divided into two types:
(i) *basic events*: represent invocations and responses of base methods of the given object ;
(ii) *extension events*: represent invocations and responses of the extended methods.
Each event in an extended-history is either a basic event or an extension event (and not both). As in Section 2, we assume that a unique identifier is attached to each event in an extended-history.

Figure 5 shows an example for 3 extended histories. In this figure, the events that refer to the *inc* method are extension events and the other events are basic events.

Internal Events. Let h be an extended-history that contains an extension invocation event e_{inv}. We say that a basic event e is executed by e_{inv} in h, if e and e_{inv} have the same thread name, and one of the following conditions is satisfied: (1) e appears between e_{inv} and the next matching response of e_{inv}; (2) e_{inv} is pending in h, and e appears after e_{inv}. We write $h|e_{inv}$ to denote the subsequence of h of all events that are executed by e_{inv}. We say that a basic event e is internal in h if e is executed by an extension invocation event in h.

For example, in the extended-history h_1 from Figure 5, the events that are marked with an underline are executed by the extension event $[_{t_1.inc(c)}$ and therefore they are internal events in h_1. Together they form the subsequence $h_1|[_{t_1.inc(c)}$.

Two Perspectives. An *object perspective* of an extended-history h, denoted by $obj(h)$, is the maximal subsequence of h such that $obj(h)$ does not contain extension events. A *client perspective* of an extended-history h, denoted by $client(h)$, is the maximal subsequence of h such that $client(h)$ does not contain internal events. Figure 5 shows the two perspectives of an extended history.

Definition 5 (well formed extended-history). *We say that an extended-history h is* well formed *if: (1) both $obj(h)$ and $client(h)$ are well formed histories, (2) for every extension invocation e_{inv} in h that is non-pending, $h|e_{inv}$ is complete.*

In the sequel, we consider only well-formed extended-histories.

Definition 6 (Sequential Specification). *A* sequential specification *of an object with extended operations is a set of extended-histories S such that every $s \in S$ is sequential and does not contain internal events.*

h: $[_{t_1.inc(c)}, \underline{t_1.get(c)/null}, t_2.put(c,7)/null, \underline{t_1.putIfAbsent(c,1)/7, t_1.get(c)/7, t_1.replace(c,7,8)/true},]_{t_1.inc}/\emptyset, t_2.get(c)/8$

$client(h)$: $[_{t_1.inc(c)}, t_2.put(c,7)/null,]_{t_1.inc}/\emptyset, t_2.get(c)/8$

$obj(h)$: $t_1.get(c)/null, t_1.putIfAbsent(c,1)/7, t_1.get(c)/7, t_1.replace(c,7,8)/true, t_2.get(c)/8$

Fig. 5. Example for 3 extended histories of a Map with the extended operation from Figure 2. The histories are executed by threads t_1 and t_2.

Semantics of an Encapsulated Extension. An implementation of a linearizable object x with extended operations defines a set of possible extended histories H_x, defined as follows.

Define an *operation history* (for an extended method m) to be an extended history consisting of an invocation event e of m, followed by a sequence of internal events executed by e, optionally followed by a matching response of e. The semantics of the implementation of m, denoted $[\![m]\!]$ can be formally represented as a set of operation histories (denoting possible executions of a single invocation of m).

Given an extended history h and an extended invocation event e in h, define $h[e]$ to be the sequence $e(h|e)$ if e is pending in h and the sequence $e(h|e)e'$, if e' is the next matching response of e in h. Thus, $h[e]$ represents the operation history corresponding to e.

An extension x of a sequential specification BASE consists of a set of extension operations $m_1, \cdots, m_k$. The set of extended histories H_x is defined to be the set of all well-formed extended histories h such that (a) $obj(h) \in$ BASE, and (b) For any invocation event e, of an extension operation m_i, in h, we have $h[e] \in [\![m_i]\!]$.

The above definition captures the possible behaviors of x when used with any linearizable implementation of BASE. The following definition thus captures the intuition that x should work correctly when used with any correct implementation of BASE.

Definition 7 (Linearizable Encapsulated Extension). *We say that the encapsulated extension x is linearizable with respect to a sequential specification S, if for every $h \in H_x$ there exists $s \in S$ such that s is a linearization of client(h).*

3.2   The Reduction Theorem

Properties of Extended-Objects. It can be checked that the set H_x satisfies the following properties, for any extended history h:

(1) if $h \in H_x$ and h' is a well-formed subsequence of h such that $obj(h) = obj(h')$, every internal event in h' is executed by the same extension invocation in h' as in h, and every extension response in h' matches the same extension invocation in h' as in h, then $h' \in H_x$.
(2) if $obj(h) \in H_x$ and for every extension invocation event e_{inv} there is $h' \in H_x$ in which $h[e_{inv}] = h'[e_{inv}]$, then $h \in H_x$.

Condition (1) means that we can create a history in H_x by omitting some of the extension invocation events with their next matching responses (or without them if they are pending). This ensures that the behaviour of the concurrent object is not affected by the extended events. This condition is satisfied because the concurrent object's state is only accessed by its client API.

Condition (2) means that the behavior of an extended method only depends on its arguments and its interaction with the base object. This condition is satisfied because the only shared state (between threads) is the state of the concurrent object.

Reduction Theorem. Let e_{inv} be an invocation event in an extended-history h. We say that e_{inv} is *interrupted* if there exists an event e in h such that: (i) e_{inv}

and e have a different thread name; (ii) e appears after e_{inv}; (iii) e does not appear after the matching response of e_{inv}. For example, in the extended-history h_1 from Figure 5, the event $e_{inc} = [_{t_1.inc(c)}$ is interrupted because the events of $t_2.put(c, 7)/null$ appear between e_{inc} and its matching response.

We write $\#(h)$ to denote the number of interrupted invocation events in h. We write H_x^k to denote $\{h \in H_x \mid \#(h) \leq k\}$, and H_x^0 to denote the subset of sequential histories. $client\left[H_x^0\right] = \left\{client(h) \mid h \in H_x^0\right\}$ is the client perspective of the sequential histories.

We present our reduction theorem below, treating the implementation of the extension itself as its sequential specification. Specifically, we consider the case where $client\left[H_x^0\right]$ is the sequential specification for the extension. In [4] we present a generalization of this theorem which handles general specifications.

Theorem 1 (Reduction Theorem). *If the set H_x^1 is linearizable with respect to $client\left[H_x^0\right]$, then the set H_x is linearizable with respect to $client\left[H_x^0\right]$.*

Proof (Sketch). We use induction to show that for any $n \geq 1$, H_x^n is linearizable with respect to $client\left[H_x^0\right]$. Let's assume that for some $k \geq 1$, H_x^k is linearizable, and prove that H_x^{k+1} is linearizable. Let $h \in H_x^{k+1}$ be a history with $\#(h) = k+1$ which contains an interrupted extension invocation e_{inv}. Let's assume that e_{inv} is not pending and has a matching response e_{res} (the case in which e_{inv} is pending can be shown in a similar way).

Using condition (1), we can remove e_{inv} and e_{res} from h, and get a new history $h' \in H_x$ with $\#(h') = k$. Notice that all internal method calls $h|e_{inv}$ are not internal in h', and appear in $client(h')$. By the induction hypothesis, $client(h')$ is linearizable — let s' be its linearization. s' also contains the subsequence $h|e_{inv}$.

$s' \in client\left[H_x^0\right]$, so let $h'' \in H_x^0$ be a history such that $client(h'') = s'$. We know that $\#(h'') = 0$, and we also know that $h|e_{inv}$ is a subsequence of $client(h'')$.

Let's add e_{inv} to h'' right before the beginning of the subsequence, and e_{res} right after the end of the subsequence, and denote the new history by $\hat{h}$.

$obj(\hat{h}) = obj(h'') \in H_x$, and for any invocation $e'_{inv} \neq e_{inv}$ in $\hat{h}$ we know that $\hat{h}[e'_{inv}] = h''[e'_{inv}]$. Furthermore, for e_{inv} in $\hat{h}$ we know that $\hat{h}[e_{inv}] = h[e_{inv}]$. Together, we can apply condition (2), so $\hat{h} \in H_x$.

$\#(\hat{h}) \leq \#(h'')+1 = 1$, so by the induction hypothesis $client(\hat{h})$ is linearizable. $client(\hat{h})$ can be created from $client(h)$ by omitting some pending invocations, appending matching responses to other pending invocations, and moving e_{inv} and e_{res} closer to each other. The order of operations in $client(\hat{h})$ preserves the order of operations in $client(h)$, and therefore the linearization of $client(\hat{h})$ is also a linearization of $client(h)$, which means that $client(h)$ is linearizable.

The complete proof is presented in [4].

4   Non-interfering Linearizable Extensions

In this section, we consider conditions under which different linearizable extensions of a concurrent object do not interfere with each other. Specifically, let

$em_1, \cdots, em_k$ be encapsulated extended operations of a concurrent object $Base$. Suppose that, for each i, $\{em_i\} \cup Base$ is linearizable. We present sufficient conditions under which $\{em_1, \cdots, em_k\} \cup Base$ is guaranteed to be linearizable. When these conditions hold, verifying linearizability of an encapsulated extension is further simplified as each extended operation can be independently verified. Many extended operations in the programs in our empirical studies satisfy these conditions.

Recall that a method call is a pair of events of the form $[_{t.m(a)}]_{t.m}/b$ which we also refer as $t.m(a)/b$. In the sequel, we may refer to $m(a)/b$ when the thread name is irrelevant or can be understood from the context.

Given a sequence $\alpha = c_1 \cdots c_m$, where each c_i is a method call of the form $m_i(a_i)/b_i$, we define $t.\alpha$ to be the sequential history $t.c_1 \cdots t.c_m$. We denote $\mathcal{M}$ to the set of base method calls, and $\mathcal{M}_E$ to denote the set of both base method calls and extension method calls.

4.1 Replaceability

We first introduce a notion of *replaceability*.

Let $c \in \mathcal{M}_E$ be some method call and let $M \subseteq \mathcal{M}_E$ be a set of method calls. We say that $c \propto M$ if for every concurrent history $\alpha(t.c)\beta$ in $client[H_x]$ there is some $c' \in M$ such that $\alpha(t.c')\beta$ is in $client[H_x]$. For example:

$$\texttt{readAndWriteTrue()/false} \propto \{\texttt{write(true)/ok}\}$$

$$\texttt{computeIfAbsent}(3)/4 \propto \{\texttt{get}(3)/4\}$$

$$\texttt{computeIfAbsent}(3)/9 \propto \{\texttt{get}(3)/9, \texttt{put}(3,9)/\texttt{null}\} \ [1]$$

We say that a method call c is *replacement equivalent to* M if $c \propto M$ and for every $c' \in M$ we have $c' \propto \{c\}$. We say that c is *replaceable by* M if c is replacement equivalent to some subset of M. We say that a method is *replaceable by* M if each of its method calls is replaceable by M.

Recall that H_x^1 denotes the set of extended histories of x containing at most one occurrence of an interrupted invocation event. For any set of method calls $M \subseteq \mathcal{M}_E$, let H_M^1 denote the subset of histories from H_x^1 in which all the uninterrupted operations are in M.

Lemma 1. *If c is replaceable by a set of method calls M, and all the histories in H_M^1 are linearizable, then all the histories in $H_{M \cup \{c\}}^1$ are linearizable.*

Proof. Assume that all histories in H_M^1 are linearizable. Consider any history $h \in H_{M \cup \{c\}}^1$. Replace all (uninterrupted) appearances of c with other calls from M to get a history h' in H_M^1. Let s' be a linearization of h'. Replace the replacement calls back by c to get a sequential history s, which will be a linearization of h.

Corollary 1. *If every method call in $\mathcal{M}_E \setminus M$ (of an extended operation) is replaceable by M, then H_x is linearizable iff H_M^1 is linearizable.*

---

[1] The pure computation in $\texttt{computeIfAbsent}$ calculates the square of the given key.

Discussion. Consider the examples `computeIfAbsent` (Figure 1) and `inc` (Figure 2). Each of these extension operations are replaceable (by the base map method calls). For example, the method call `computeIfAbsent(3)/9` is replaceable because in any history we can replace such uninterrupted call with a call to `put` or `get`, as appropriate:

$$\texttt{computeIfAbsent}(3)/9 \propto \{\texttt{get}(3)/9, \texttt{put}(3,9)/\texttt{null}\}$$

and in any other history with these calls, we can replace them back:

$$\texttt{get}(3)/9 \propto \{\texttt{computeIfAbsent}(3)/9\}$$

$$\texttt{put}(3,9)/\texttt{null} \propto \{\texttt{computeIfAbsent}(3)/9\}$$

It follows from the above corollary that these two extension operations are non-interfering. To verify that an extension consisting of this pair of operations is linearizable it suffices to verify that the two extensions consisting of each of these operations separately is linearizable.

Not only does the corollary help decouple the verification of multiple extension operations, it also helps simplify the verification of an extension consisting of a single operation. This is because the set of histories $H^1_{\mathcal{M}}$ we need to check is smaller than the set H_x even when the extension consists of a single operation.

Just as we expect, the above corollary does not apply to the example in Fig. 4. As explained in Section 1, $H^1_{\mathcal{M}}$ (i.e., the set of histories with at most one invocation of `readAndWriteTrue`) is linearizable for this example, but the extension is not linearizable. Corollary 1 does not apply because `readAndWriteTrue()/false` is not replaceable — we can take any history in *client* $[H_x]$ and replace a method call `readAndWriteTrue()/false` with the method call `write(true)/ok` to get a new history in *client* $[H_x]$, however, in some histories in *client* $[H_x]$ we cannot replace a method call `write(true)/ok` back with `readAndWriteTrue()/false` and get a history in *client* $[H_x]$ (consider histories where the state of the register before the call is `true`).

4.2   Composition Closure

A sequence of method calls β is said to be *atomically equivalent* to a method call c if for all α, γ, we have $\alpha(t.\beta)\gamma \in obj\,[H_x]$ iff $\alpha(t.c)\gamma \in obj\,[H_x]$. We say that a set of method calls M is *composition-closed* if every sequence of calls from M is atomically equivalent to a single call in M.

Example. A *Generic Register* is a register with three linearizable base operations: `read()` that returns the register's value, `write(x)` that changes the register's value to `x` and returns the register's old value (an unconditional "*swap*"), and a unique operation `compareAndSwap(expect,new)` that changes the register's value to `new` if it equals `expect`, and returns the register's old value (whether it changed or not).

In this example, the sequence $\texttt{write}(7)/0 \; \texttt{write}(8)/7$ is atomically equivalent to the call $\texttt{write}(8)/0$. Furthermore, any sequence of $\texttt{read}$ and $\texttt{write}$ over a generic register (with at least one $\texttt{write}$):

$$m_1(args_1)/b_1 \ldots m_k(args_k)/b_k$$

is atomically equivalent to $\texttt{write}(args_j)/b_1$, where j is the index of the last $\texttt{write}$ — this single operation makes the change of the whole sequence atomically, and returns the value of the register before the sequence. Hence, the set of all method calls to $\{\texttt{read}, \texttt{write}\}$ is composition-closed. This composition-closure property holds even if we include the $\texttt{compareAndSwap}$ operation.

Lemma 2. *The set of all base method calls of a generic register is composition-closed.*

Now let's look at encapsulated operations over any $\mathcal{M}$ that is composition-closed:

Lemma 3. *If $\mathcal{M}$ is composition-closed, then every encapsulated extended operation of the object is replaceable by $\mathcal{M}$.*

Proof. In any extended history, an uninterrupted call of the encapsulated extended operation can be replaced by its internal base operation calls. This sequence of base calls is atomically equivalent to a single base call which can replace it, and vice versa.

By combining Lemma 3 with Corollary 1, we get:

Corollary 2. *Let $\mathcal{M}$, the set of all base method calls of a concurrent object, be composition-closed. For any encapsulated extension x of this object, if $H^1_{\mathcal{M}}$ is linearizable, then H_x (and x) is linearizable.*

The immediate implication of Corollary 2 on the generic register example is that checking the linearizability of $H^1_{\{read()/b,write(a)/b,compareAndSwap(a,b)/c\}}$ guarantees the linearizability of H_x. We can further reduce the set of histories that need to be checked by noticing that every $\texttt{compareAndSwap}(a,b)/c$ is replaceable by the set of $\texttt{read}$ and $\texttt{write}$ operations:

Corollary 3. *For encapsulated extended operations over a generic register, verifying the linearizability of the histories in $H^1_{\{read()/b,write(a)/b\}}$ guarantees the linearizability of every history in H_x.*

In Section 5.2 we show that verifying the linearizability of many real world methods can be reduced to verifying linearizability of encapsulated extended operations over a generic register.

4.3   Further Reductions

Let's look at some history $h \in H^1_{\mathcal{M}}$, assuming $\mathcal{M}$ is composition-closed. Let's assume that there is a sequence $s \in \mathcal{M}^*$ of successive base operations in h, and the interrupted encapsulated operation does not call any internal operations during that sequence, i.e., its thread is idle. The sequence of base operations is atomically equivalent to some single base operation $m(a)/b \in \mathcal{M}$ that can replace s and give a new history $h' \in H^1_{\mathcal{M}}$. Verifying the linearizability of h' guarantees that h is linearizable, because we can take the linearization of h' and replace $m(a)/b$ back with s.

Let $\overline{H^1_{\mathcal{M}}} \subseteq H^1_{\mathcal{M}}$ be the subset of histories where between every two uninterrupted base operations, the interrupted encapsulated operation must have called an internal operation. By induction, we can conclude:

Lemma 4. *If $\mathcal{M}$ is composition-closed, then verifying the linearizability of $\overline{H^1_{\mathcal{M}}}$ guarantees the linearizability of $H^1_{\mathcal{M}}$, and therefore guarantees the linearizability of H_x.*

Corollary 4. *For encapsulated extended operations over a generic register, verifying the linearizability of the histories in $\overline{H^1_{\{read()/b,write(a)/b\}}}$ guarantees the linearizability of every history in H_x.*

Corollary 4 subsumes the results of Corollary 3.

In every history $\overline{h} \in \overline{H^1_{\mathcal{M}}}$, between every two uninterrupted base operations, there must be an internal operation of the interrupted call. This means that if $\overline{h}$ is linearizable, the linearization point of the interrupted call may be seen as if it happened in one of its internal operations (or in its invocation/response) — we look at the uninterrupted calls with the linearization points that precede and succeed the one of the interrupted call, find an internal operation (of the interrupted call) that reside between them, and move the linearization point of the interrupted call inside it, without breaking the total order of the linearization points.

Lemma 5. *If $\mathcal{M}$ is composition-closed and $\overline{H^1_{\mathcal{M}}}$ is linearizable, then we can linearize every history in $\overline{H^1_{\mathcal{M}}}$ using linearization points that reside in the same thread.*

Notice the necessity of $\mathcal{M}$ being composition-closed. Figure 6 is an artificial example for a replaceable encapsulated operation over a base data-structure that is not composition-closed — the sequence `increase()/ok increase()/ok` is not atomically equivalent to any single operation. In this linearizable example, some histories can be linearized only by picking a linearization point that resides in a different thread, such as:

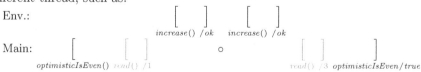

```
boolean optimisticIsEven() {
    int temp1, temp2;
    temp1 = read();
    if (temp1 % 2 == 0) {
        return true;
    }
    temp2 = read();
    if (temp1 == temp2) {
        return false;
    }
    else {
        return true;
    }
}
```

$$\texttt{optimisticIsEven}()/\texttt{true} \propto \{\texttt{read}()/x \mid x \text{ is even}\}$$
$$\forall x \text{ even} : \texttt{read}()/x \propto \{\texttt{optimisticIsEven}()/\texttt{true}\}$$
$$\texttt{optimisticIsEven}()/\texttt{false} \propto \{\texttt{read}()/x \mid x \text{ is odd}\}$$
$$\forall x \text{ odd} : \texttt{read}()/x \propto \{\texttt{optimisticIsEven}()/\texttt{false}\}$$

Fig. 6. An encapsulated extended operation over an integer register with two base operations: `read()` that returns the register's value and `increase()` that increases its value by one. `optimisticIsEven()` is replaceable by the base methods.

5 On the Applicability of the Reduction

5.1 Checking Encapsulation of Extended Operations

Checking that a method is an encapsulated extension can be done conservatively by checking that: (1) The method does not access global mutable variables, and (2) all external methods invoked by an encapsulated method are either base-methods or pure.

Out of 109 methods used [5], 55 methods were identified as encapsulated operations, using the technique described in [6]. The base data-structure in all of the 55 methods was the linearizable Java `ConcurrentMap` interface.

5.2 Checking Composition Closure

In general, checking that an encapsulated operation is replaceable (as defined in Section 4) can be hard. It requires verifying all sequential executions, which is undecidable. In contrast, checking composition closure can be done once and for all for a given base data structure. Unfortunately, the Java `ConcurrentMap`, which is heavily used, does not satisfy this closure property since a sequence of operations on different keys is not necessarily equivalent to any single `ConcurrentMap` operation.

We observed 52 out of the 55 operations employ maps in a limited fashion: any single invocation of the operation is guaranteed to invoke map operations on only one key (Note that different execution paths may, however, operate on different keys — Figure 7 is an interesting example which illustrates this). Such operations are guaranteed to be replaceable by `ConcurrentMap`'s base operations. In fact, the code can be syntactically replaced by an equivalent extended encapsulated operation over a generic register as follows:

$$\text{map.get}(k) \Rightarrow \text{reg.read}()$$
$$\text{map.put}(k, v) \Rightarrow \text{reg.write}(v)$$
$$\text{map.remove}(k) \Rightarrow \text{reg.write}(null)$$
$$\text{map.putIfAbsent}(k, v) \Rightarrow \text{reg.compareAndSwap}(null, v)$$
$$\text{map.replace}(k, v1, v2) \Rightarrow (\text{reg.compareAndSwap}(v1, v2) == v1)$$

Intuitively, checking the linearizability of the new method is equivalent to checking the linearizability of the original method.

The other 3 out of the 55 operations employ either use `size` and `clean` or more than one key and therefore are not considered.

```
final FxLanguage DEFAULT = ...
final ConcurrentMap<FxLanguage, FxValueRenderer> renderers = ...

FxValueRenderer getInstance(FxLanguage language) {
    if (language == null) {
        // default renderer always exists
        return renderers.get(DEFAULT);
    }
    if (!renderers.containsKey(language)) {
        renderers.putIfAbsent(language, new FxValueRendererImpl(language));
    }
    return renderers.get(language);
}
```

Fig. 7. An extended encapsulated operation from *Flexive*, class: *FxValueRendererFactory*. In every execution path, only a single key is used. This example is **not** linearizable — consider the following history: $[_{A.getInstance(L)}, A.containsKey(L)/false, A.putIfAbsent(L, Fx_A)/null, B.put(L, Fx_B)/Fx_A, A.get(L)/Fx_B,]_{A.getInstance/Fx_B}$.

5.3 Checking Linearizaibility via Abstract Interpretation

We implemented a conservative tool to check the linearizability of the 52 examples using the abstract interpreter described in [4]. The tool employs our theoretical results by checking only histories with 2 threads in which the extended operation run once. We verified 24 examples as linearizable (Table 1) and detected 27 linearizabilty violations (Table 2). Our implementation failed to verify one linearizable example due to the abstraction, and issued a false alarm (see Figure 8) — The reason for the failure is an over approximation that did not store the correlations between objects and constants, such as `osFamily` and `"windows"`/`"unix"`.

Table 1. Encapsulated operations verified as linearizable by the static analysis method presented in [4]

Application Name	Class Name	Code Lines	Verification Time	Abstract States
Apache ServiceMix	SimpleLockManager	11	2375 (ms)	49
Clojure	Namespace	8	2329 (ms)	49
Cometdim	ChatService	7	2169 (ms)	49
DWR	AbstractMapContextScope	14	2357 (ms)	49
ehcache-spring-annotation	CacheAttributeSourceImpl	11	2466 (ms)	49
FindBugs	Profiler	8	2451 (ms)	54
Granite	ExternalizerFactory	14	2559 (ms)	49
GWTEventService	DefaultUserManager	11	1702 (ms)	14
Hazelcast	Log4jFactory	12	2450 (ms)	49
ifw2	PropertyNavigator	14	2794 (ms)	91
ifw2	ReflectiveClone	11	2310 (ms)	49
ifw2	ClassInfo	10	2326 (ms)	49
Jboss	AOPLogger	14	2404 (ms)	49
Jetty	AbstractBayeux	12	2450 (ms)	49
Jetty	OortChatService	7	2185 (ms)	47
Jetty	OortChatService	7	2341 (ms)	47
Jexin	ActiveTemplateMap	8	2341 (ms)	47
Jsefa	InitialConfiguration	14	2388 (ms)	49
Keyczar	StreamCache	12	2502 (ms)	49
OpenJDK	ThrowingTasks	12	3776 (ms)	98
Tammi	StaticPersisterFactory	18	3308 (ms)	122
ProjectTrack	MethodCallRecorder	8	2326 (ms)	48
ProjectTrack	MethodCallRecorder	8	2357 (ms)	49
Yasca	Profiler	8	2356 (ms)	49

Table 2. Encapsulated operations with non-linearizability reports issued by the static analysis. The bold row (autoandroid) is the benchmark from Figure 8 that raised a false alarm.

Application Name	Class Name	Code Lines	Verification Time	Abstract States
Adobe BlazeDS	FIFOMessageQueue	10	1498 (ms)	17
Adobe BlazeDS	FIFOMessageQueue	10	1452 (ms)	17
Annsor	Annsor	11	1405 (ms)	12
Apache Cassandra	SuperColumn	15	1529 (ms)	12
Apache Cassandra	ColumnFamily	21	1498 (ms)	12
Apache MyFaces Trinidad	SessionChangeManager	5	1297 (ms)	8
Apache Tomcat	ApplicationContext	9	1343 (ms)	9
Apache Tomcat	ApplicationContext	8	1374 (ms)	12
Apache Tomcat	ReplicatedContext	6	1436 (ms)	9
Apache CXF	ClassResourceInfo	12	1483 (ms)	24
autoandroid	**AndroidTools**	**16**	**1342 (ms)**	**17**
dyuproject	StandardConvertorCache	10	1438 (ms)	17
dyuproject	StandardConvertorCache	11	1437 (ms)	20
Flexive	MessageBean	7	1390 (ms)	8
Flexive	FxValueRendererFactory	10	1655 (ms)	19
GlassFish	BeanManager	13	1531 (ms)	13
Gridkit	ReflectionPofSerializer	14	1455 (ms)	12
GWTEventService	AutoIncrementFactory	4	1266 (ms)	7
Hazelcast	ClientEndpoint	8	1655 (ms)	12
Hudson	Hudson	10	1307 (ms)	12
JRipples	HessianSkeletonProviderImpl	21	1483 (ms)	19
memcache-client	SockIOpool	10	1327 (ms)	8
Tammi	StaticVariableRegistry	14	1389 (ms)	11
RestEasy	XmlJAXBContextFinder	8	1395 (ms)	13
RestEasy	JsonJAXBContextFinder	5	1732 (ms)	12
RestEasy	JsonJAXBContextFinder	5	1436 (ms)	12
Torque-spring	PersistenceManagerFactory	8	1529 (ms)	12
Webmill	ContextNavigator	9	1545 (ms)	12

```
public static AndroidTools forOsFamily(String osFamily) {
  AndroidTools instance = androidTools.get(osFamily);
  if (instance == null) {
    AndroidTools newInstance = null;
    if (osFamily.equals("windows")) {
      newInstance = new WindowsAndroidTools();
    } else if (osFamily.equals("unix")) {
      newInstance = new UnixAndroidTools();
    } else {
      throw new UnsupportedOperationException(
        "Don't_know_how_to_start_android_tools_on_" + osFamily);
    }
    instance = androidTools.putIfAbsent(osFamily,newInstance);
    if (instance == null) instance = newInstance;
  }
  return instance;
}
```

Fig. 8. Application Name: *autoandroid*, Class Name: *AndroidTools*. A linearizable encapsulated operation that the verification failed to verify, due to impreciseness of our abstraction.

6   Related Work

Linearizability checking tools can be very effective in identifying bugs and a substantial body of work exists in this space, as discussed below. A distinguishing aspect of our work is that we focus on a special case, namely verifying linearizability of encapsulated extensions of a linearizable object. This problem was motivated by [1] which shows that extended operations of linearizable collections are widespread and are a source of concurrency bugs. While [1] presents a dynamic tool for checking linearizability of extended operations, we focus on static verification of the same.

Modular Reasoning. The basic techniques we utilize have a long history in the literature on modular reasoning techniques for concurrent systems. The idea of using a general client over-approximating the thread environment is common in modular verification. Previous work represented the environment as invariants [7] or relations [8] on the shared state. This idea has also been used early on for automatic compositional verification [9]. In addition, this approach has led to the notion of thread-modular verification for model checking systems with finitely-many threads [10], and has also been applied to the domain of heap-manipulating programs with coarse-grained concurrency [11]. The main ideas in these works is to approximate the thread environment.

Exploiting Atomicity of Methods. [12] shows that schedules where linearizable operations are executed with interruptions need not be generated. This can reduce the number of interleavings that need to be explored. This insight has also been discussed and made use of in the preemption sealing work of [13]. [14,15] use the atomicity proof to simplify the correctness proofs of multithreaded programs. [16] presents a proof calculus for reasoning about concurrent programs with atomic sections. It would be interesting to see if such a proof calculus can be used to simplify the proofs of our reduction theorems.

Dynamic Tools for Finding Linearizabilty Violations. Vyrd [17] is a dynamic checking tool that checks a property similar to linearizability. Line-Up [18] is a dynamic linearizability checker that enumerates schedules.

Static Linearizability Verification. [19] manually proves correctness of several interesting concurrent data structure implementations using rely-guarantee reasoning. The PVS system has been successfully used to semi-automatically verify linearizability [20,21,22] of several interesting programs.

[23] pioneered the idea of using abstract interpretation [24] to develop an automatic over-approximation for checking linearizability. Thus, the algorithm can prove linearizability in certain programs but may fail due to overly conservative abstraction. [25,26] generalize [23] using a thread-centric approach to programs with unbounded number of threads. [27] combines the idea of bounded difference with rely guarantee reasoning and shape abstractions in order to perform fast linearizability checks.

Composing Linearizable Operations. Recently several interesting techniques for enforcing atomicity of sequences of linearizable operations were developed. [28] employs a variation of the join-calculus to compose operations via DCAS. [29,6] synthesize locks to enforce atomicity and deadlock freedom. In contrast to these approaches, we focus on understanding the complexity of verifying the linearizability of a special useful class of composed operations.

References

1. Shacham, O., Bronson, N.G., Aiken, A., Sagiv, M., Vechev, M.T., Yahav, E.: Testing atomicity of composed concurrent operations. In: OOPSLA, pp. 51–64 (2011)
2. Herlihy, M.P., Wing, J.M.: Linearizability: a correctness condition for concurrent objects. TOPLAS 12(3) (1990)
3. Alur, R., McMillan, K.L., Peled, D.: Model-checking of correctness conditions for concurrent objects. Inf. Comput. 160(1-2), 167–188 (2000)
4. Zomer, O., Golan-Gueta, G., Ramalingam, G., Sagiv, M.: Checking linearizability of encapsulated extended operations. Technical report, Tel Aviv University (2013), http://www.cs.tau.ac.il/~ggolan/papers/ESOP14TechRep.pdf
5. Shacham, O.: Verifying Atomicity of Composed Concurrent Operations. PhD thesis, Tel Aviv University (2012)
6. Golan-Gueta, G., Ramalingam, G., Sagiv, M., Yahav, E.: Concurrent libraries with foresight. In: PLDI, pp. 263–274 (2013)
7. Hoare, C.A.R.: Towards a theory of parallel programming. Operating System Techniques (1972)
8. Jones, C.B.: Specification and design of (parallel) programs. In: IFIP Congress (1983)

9. Clarke Jr., E.: Synthesis of resource invariants for concurrent programs. TOPLAS 2(3), 338–358 (1980)
10. Flanagan, C., Qadeer, S.: Thread-modular model checking. In: Ball, T., Rajamani, S.K. (eds.) SPIN 2003. LNCS, vol. 2648, pp. 213–224. Springer, Heidelberg (2003)
11. Gotsman, A., Berdine, J., Cook, B., Sagiv, M.: Thread-modular shape analysis. In: Proceedings of the 2007 ACM SIGPLAN Conference on Programming Language Design and Implementation, PLDI 2007, pp. 266–277. ACM, New York (2007)
12. Filipovic, I., O'Hearn, P., Rinetzky, N., Yang, H.: Abstraction for concurrent objects. Theoretical Computer Science 411(51-52), 4379–4398 (2010)
13. Ball, T., Burckhardt, S., Coons, K.E., Musuvathi, M., Qadeer, S.: Preemption sealing for efficient concurrency testing. In: Esparza, J., Majumdar, R. (eds.) TACAS 2010. LNCS, vol. 6015, pp. 420–434. Springer, Heidelberg (2010)
14. Flanagan, C., Qadeer, S.: A type and effect system for atomicity. In: PLDI, pp. 338–349 (2003)
15. Musuvathi, M., Qadeer, S.: Iterative context bounding for systematic testing of multithreaded programs. In: PLDI, pp. 446–455 (2007)
16. Elmas, T., Qadeer, S., Tasiran, S.: A calculus of atomic actions. In: POPL, pp. 2–15 (2009)
17. Elmas, T., Tasiran, S., Qadeer, S.: Vyrd: verifying concurrent programs by runtime refinement-violation detection. In: PLDI, pp. 27–37 (2005)
18. Burckhardt, S., Dern, C., Musuvathi, M., Tan, R.: Line-up: a complete and automatic linearizability checker. In: PLDI, pp. 330–340 (2010)
19. Vafeiadis, V., Herlihy, M., Hoare, T., Shapiro, M.: Proving correctness of highly-concurrent linearisable objects. In: PPoPP (2006)
20. Doherty, S., Groves, L., Luchangco, V., Moir, M.: Formal verification of a practical lock-free queue algorithm. In: de Frutos-Escrig, D., Núñez, M. (eds.) FORTE 2004. LNCS, vol. 3235, pp. 97–114. Springer, Heidelberg (2004)
21. Colvin, R., Groves, L., Luchangco, V., Moir, M.: Formal verification of a lazy concurrent list-based set algorithm. In: Ball, T., Jones, R.B. (eds.) CAV 2006. LNCS, vol. 4144, pp. 475–488. Springer, Heidelberg (2006)
22. Gao, H., Hesselink, W.H.: A formal reduction for lock-free parallel algorithms. In: Alur, R., Peled, D.A. (eds.) CAV 2004. LNCS, vol. 3114, pp. 44–56. Springer, Heidelberg (2004)
23. Amit, D., Rinetzky, N., Reps, T.W., Sagiv, M., Yahav, E.: Comparison under abstraction for verifying linearizability. In: Damm, W., Hermanns, H. (eds.) CAV 2007. LNCS, vol. 4590, pp. 477–490. Springer, Heidelberg (2007)
24. Cousot, P., Cousot, R.: Abstract interpretation: A unified lattice model for static analysis of programs by construction of approximation of fixed points. In: POPL, pp. 238–252 (1977)
25. Berdine, J., Lev-Ami, T., Manevich, R., Ramalingam, G., Sagiv, M.: Thread quantification for concurrent shape analysis. In: Gupta, A., Malik, S. (eds.) CAV 2008. LNCS, vol. 5123, pp. 399–413. Springer, Heidelberg (2008)
26. Manevich, R., Lev-Ami, T., Sagiv, M., Ramalingam, G., Berdine, J.: Heap decomposition for concurrent shape analysis. In: Alpuente, M., Vidal, G. (eds.) SAS 2008. LNCS, vol. 5079, pp. 363–377. Springer, Heidelberg (2008)
27. Vafeiadis, V.: Automatically proving linearizability. In: Touili, T., Cook, B., Jackson, P. (eds.) CAV 2010. LNCS, vol. 6174, pp. 450–464. Springer, Heidelberg (2010)
28. Turon, A.: Reagents: expressing and composing fine-grained concurrency. In: PLDI, pp. 157–168 (2012)
29. Hawkins, P., Aiken, A., Fisher, K., Rinard, M.C., Sagiv, M.: Concurrent data representation synthesis. In: PLDI, pp. 417–428 (2012)

Bounded Linear Types in a Resource Semiring

Dan R. Ghica and Alex I. Smith

University of Birmingham, UK

Abstract. Bounded linear types have proved to be useful for automated resource analysis and control in functional programming languages. In this paper we introduce a bounded linear typing discipline on a general notion of resource which can be modeled in a semiring. For this type system we provide both a general type-inference procedure, parameterized by the decision procedure of the semiring equational theory, and a (coherent) categorical semantics. This could be a useful type-theoretic and denotational framework for resource-sensitive compilation, and it represents a generalization of several existing type systems. As a non-trivial instance, motivated by hardware compilation, we present a complex new application to calculating and controlling timing of execution in a (recursion-free) higher-order functional programming language with local store.

1 Resource-Aware Types and Semantics

The two important things about a computer program are what it computes and what resources it needs to carry out the computation successfully. Correctness of the input-output behavior of programs has been, of course, the object of much research from various conceptual angles: logical, semantical, type-theoretical and so on. Resource analysis has been conventionally studied for algorithms, such as time and space complexity, and for programs has long been a part of research in compiler optimization.

An exciting development was the introduction of semantic [1] and especially type theoretic [14] characterizations of resource consumption in functional programming languages. Unlike algorithmic analyses, type based analysis are formal and can be statically checked for implementations of algorithms in concrete programming languages. Unlike static analysis, a typing mechanism is compositional which means that it supports, at least in principle, separate compilation and even a foreign function interface: it is an analysis based on signatures rather than implementations.

Linear logic and typing, because of the fine-grained treatment of resource-sensitive structural rules, constitute an excellent framework for resource analysis, especially in its bounded fragment [13], which can logically characterize polynomial time computation. Bounded Linear Logic (BLL) was subsequently extended to improve its flexibility while retaining poly-time [5] and further extensions to linear *dependent* typing were used to completely characterize complexity of evaluation of functional programs [4].

Z. Shao (Ed.): ESOP 2014, LNCS 8410, pp. 331–350, 2014.

Such analyses use *time* as a motivating example, but can be readily adapted to other *consumable* resources such as energy or network traffic. What they have in common is a *monadic* view of resources, tracking their global usage throughout the execution of the term.

A complementary view on resource sensitivity is the *co-monadic* one, as advocated by Melliès and Tabareau [18]. The intuition is that the type system tracks how much resource a term needs in order to execute successfully. This is quite typical when controlling *reusable* resources which can be allocated and de-allocated at runtime, the typical example of which is *memory*, especially *local* (stack-allocated) memory. In fact this resource-sensitive approach is key in giving a better semantic understanding of higher-order state [17]. This view of resources is instrumental in facilitating the compilation of functional-imperative programming languages directly for resource-constrained runtimes, such as electronic circuits [8].

2   Bounded Linear Types Over a Semiring

Types are generated by the grammar $\theta ::= \sigma \mid (J \cdot \theta) \multimap \theta$, where σ is a fixed collection of base types and $J \in \mathcal{J}$, where $(\mathcal{J}, +, \times, \mathbf{0}, \mathbf{1})$ is a semiring. We will always take $\cdot$ to bind strongest so we will omit the brackets.

Let $\Gamma = x_1{:}J_1{\cdot}\theta_1, \ldots, x_n{:}J_n{\cdot}\theta_n$ be a list of identifiers x_i and types θ_i, annotated with semiring elements J_i. Let $fv(M)$ be the set of free variables of term M, defined in the usual way. The typing rules are:

$$\frac{}{x : \mathbf{1} \cdot \theta \vdash x : \theta} \text{ Identity}$$

$$\frac{\Gamma \vdash M : \theta}{\Gamma, x : J \cdot \theta' \vdash M : \theta} \text{ Weakening}$$

$$\frac{\Gamma, x : J \cdot \theta \vdash M : \theta'}{\Gamma \vdash \lambda x.M : J \cdot \theta \multimap \theta'} \text{ Abstraction}$$

$$\frac{\Gamma \vdash M : J \cdot \theta \multimap \theta' \qquad \Gamma' \vdash N : \theta}{\Gamma, J \cdot \Gamma' \vdash MN : \theta'} \text{ Application}$$

$$\frac{\Gamma, x : J \cdot \theta, y : K \cdot \theta \vdash M : \theta'}{\Gamma, x : (J + K) \cdot \theta \vdash M[x/y] : \theta'} \text{ Contraction}$$

In *Weakening* we have the side condition $x \notin fv(M)$, and in *Application* we require $\mathrm{dom}(\Gamma) \cap \mathrm{dom}(\Gamma') = \emptyset$. In the *Application* rule we use the notation

$$J \cdot (x_1 : K_1 \cdot \theta_1, \ldots, x_n : K_n \cdot \theta_n) \triangleq x_1 : (J \times K_1) \cdot \theta_1, \ldots, x_n : (J \times K_n) \cdot \theta_n \quad (1)$$

Note. For the sake of simplicity we take operations in the semiring to be resolved *syntactically* within the type system. So types such as $2 \cdot A$ and $(1 + 1) \cdot A$ are taken to be syntactically equal. In the context of type-checking this is reasonable because semiring actions are always constants that the type-checker can calculate with. If we were to allow resource variables, i.e. some form of resource-based polymorphism (cf. [5]) then a new structural rule would be required to handle type congruences induced by the semiring theory:

$$\frac{\Gamma, x : J \cdot \theta' \vdash M : \theta \qquad J =_{\mathcal{J}} J'}{\Gamma, x : J' \cdot \theta' \vdash M : \theta} \; \text{Semiring}$$

But in our current system this level of formalization is not worth the complication.

2.1 Examples

Bounded Linear Logic. If we take $\mathcal{J}$ to be *resource polynomials* we obtain BLL. A *monomial* is any finite product of binomial coefficients $\prod_{i=1}^{n} \binom{x_i}{n_i}$; a resource polynomial is a finite sum of monomials. They are closed under sum and product and have a semiring structure. The *Axiom* of BLL is not quite the same as ours, as we require a unit action on the type of the variable, whereas in BLL any bound can be introduced, hence the whimsical name of *Waste of Resources* for the BLL Axiom. In our system a wasteful axiom is admissible only if a resource can be decomposed as a sum involving the unit resource, by using a combination of contraction and weakening.

$$\frac{\dfrac{x : \mathbf{1} \cdot \theta \vdash x : \theta}{y : J \cdot \theta, x : \mathbf{1} \cdot \theta \vdash x : \theta}}{x : (J + 1) \cdot \theta \vdash x : \theta}$$

The intuition of this restriction is that we need *at least* an unit of resource in order to use x.

Syntactic Control of Concurrency (SCC). It is possible to use a comonadic notion of resource to bound the number of threads used by a parallel programming language [10]. This has the advantage of identifying programs with finite-state models, with applications in automated verification [9] and in hardware synthesis [11]. If we instantiate $\mathcal{J}$ to the semiring of natural numbers we obtain SCC. However, SCC includes an additive conjunction rule to model *sequentiality*:

$$\frac{\Gamma \vdash M : \theta \qquad \Gamma \vdash N : \theta'}{\Gamma \vdash \langle M, N \rangle : \theta \times \theta'}$$

This allows to distinguish between sequential and concurrent programming language constants, e.g.: seq $:!_1 \cdot \text{com} \times !_1 \cdot \text{com} \multimap \text{com}$ versus par $:!_1 \cdot \text{com} \multimap !_1 \cdot \text{com} \multimap \text{com}$. This is an idea borrowed from Reynolds's *Syntactic Control of Interference* (SCI) [23].

This distinction between sequential and parallel composition becomes interesting when contraction is involved, e.g.

$$\lambda x.\text{seq}\langle x, x \rangle :!_1 \cdot \text{com} \multimap \text{com} \quad \text{vs.} \quad \lambda x.\text{par } x\, x :!_2 \cdot \text{com} \multimap \text{com}. \qquad (2)$$

Note that SCC uses the notation $!_k-$ instead of $k \cdot -$ to indicate resource actions.

Tagged Control of Concurrency (TCC). SCI is akin to SCC where all bounds are set to 1. This means that in SCI the first term in Eqn. 2 can be typed, but the second cannot. Both SCI and SCC are complicated semantically by the presence of the extra additive conjunction because it lacks an adjoint exponential. The complication is also syntactic as the two composition operators have peculiarly different signatures (uncurried vs. curried).

Completing the syntactic and semantic tableau by providing both conjunctions with exponentials leads to *Bunched Typing* [21]. However, it is possible to have an SCI-like type system without using both additive and multiplicative conjunctions, but harnessing the power of an expressive enough set of resources. The elements of the semiring are a system of *tags* corresponding, intuitively, to run-time locks that need to be acquired. A notion of *safety* is introduced for tags, corresponding to the requirement that locks cannot be grabbed more than once. The restrictions on terms of an SCI-like type system can be recovered by imposing the restriction that all tags are safe. The two command compositions, sequential and parallel, have types:

$$\mathsf{seq}_{\tau_1,\tau_2} : \tau_1 \cdot \mathsf{com} \multimap \tau_2 \cdot \mathsf{com} \multimap \mathsf{com} \quad \text{vs.} \quad \mathsf{par}_\tau : \tau \cdot \mathsf{com} \multimap \tau \cdot \mathsf{com} \multimap \mathsf{com},$$

for any (safe) tags τ, τ_1, τ_2 such that $\tau_1 + \tau_2$ is also safe. Note that the two command compositions (sequential and parallel) now have the same type skeleton (com $\multimap$ com $\multimap$ com) and no extra rules are required. The example terms in Eqn. 2 can be written in a more uniform way as:

$$\lambda x.x; x : (\tau_1 + \tau_2) \cdot \mathsf{com} \multimap \mathsf{com} \quad \text{vs.} \quad \lambda x.x \,\|\, x : (\tau + \tau) \cdot \mathsf{com} \multimap \mathsf{com}. \quad (3)$$

As in SCI, the second one is not a valid term, as the tag $(\tau + \tau)$ cannot be safe.

The uniformity of the type skeleton is quite important for practical usage. Under the original SCI, functions that need their arguments to share information must use an uncurried signature, as opposed to functions that disallow that. A syntactic distinction that poses a sometimes difficult burden on the programmer. By contrast, in TCC the tags are inferred automatically by the compiler.

A full description of the type system, its game semantics and an application to hardware compilation is forthcoming [24].

2.2   Modularity

Given two semirings $\mathcal{J}, \mathcal{J}'$ their Cartesian product $\mathcal{J} \times \mathcal{J}'$ is also a semiring with multiplicative unit $(\mathbf{1}, \mathbf{1}')$, additive unit $(\mathbf{0}, \mathbf{0}')$ and addition and multiplication defined component-wise. Because there are many different resources one might want to track in the type system (time, space, energy, bandwidth, etc.) with significantly different properties, the fact that they can be easily combined in a modular way can be a quite appealing feature.

2.3   Type Inference

We present a bound inference algorithm for the abstract system which works by creating a system of constraints to be solved, separately, by an SMT-solver thatcan handle the equational theory of the resource semiring. In the type grammar, for the exponential type $J \cdot \theta \multimap \theta$ we allow J to stand for a concrete element of $\mathcal{J}$ or for a variable in the input program; the bound-inference algorithm will produce a set of constraints such that every model of those constraints gives rise to a typing derivation of the program without resource variables as variables are instantiated to suitable concrete values. Type judgments have form $\Gamma \vdash M : \theta \blacktriangleright \chi$, where χ is a set of equational constraints in the semiring. We also allow an arbitrary set of constants $\mathsf{k} : \theta$, which will allow the definition of concrete programming languages based on the type system. We allow each constant k to introduce arbitrary resource constraints χ_k

$$\frac{}{x : 1 \cdot \theta \vdash x : \theta \blacktriangleright \mathit{true}} \qquad \frac{}{\emptyset \vdash \mathsf{k} : \theta \blacktriangleright \chi_\mathsf{k}}$$

$$\frac{\Gamma \vdash M : \theta \blacktriangleright \chi}{\Gamma, x : J \cdot \theta' \vdash M : \theta \blacktriangleright \chi} \qquad \frac{\Gamma, x : J \cdot \theta \vdash M : \theta' \blacktriangleright \chi}{\Gamma \vdash \lambda x : \theta.M : J \cdot \theta \multimap \theta' \blacktriangleright \chi}$$

$$\frac{\Gamma, x : J_1 \cdot \theta', y : J_2 \cdot \theta'' \vdash M : \theta \blacktriangleright \chi}{\Gamma, x : J \cdot \theta' \vdash M[x/y] : \theta \blacktriangleright \chi \cup \{J = J_1 + J_2\} \cup \overline{\theta' = \theta''}}$$

$$\frac{\Gamma \vdash M : J \cdot \theta \multimap \theta' \blacktriangleright \chi \qquad x_1{:}J_1 \cdot \theta_1, \dots, x_n{:}J_n \cdot \theta_n \vdash N{:}\theta'' \blacktriangleright \chi'}{\Gamma, x_1{:}J_1' \cdot \theta_1, \dots, x_n{:}J_n' \cdot \theta_n \vdash MN{:}\theta' \blacktriangleright \chi \cup \chi' \cup \{J_k' = J \cdot J_k \mid k = 1, n\} \cup \overline{\theta = \theta''}}$$

The constraints of shape $\overline{\theta_1 = \theta_2}$ are to be interpreted in the obvious way, as the set of pairwise equalities between resource bounds used in the same position in the two types:

$$\overline{\sigma = \sigma} \overset{def}{=} \emptyset$$

$$\overline{J_1 \cdot \theta_1 \multimap \theta_1' = J_2 \cdot \theta_2 \multimap \theta_2'} \overset{def}{=} \{J_1 = J_2\} \cup \overline{\theta_1 = \theta_2} \cup \overline{\theta_1' = \theta_2'}.$$

If $\mathcal{M}$ is a model, i.e. a function mapping variables to concrete values, by $\Gamma[\mathcal{M}]$ we write the textual substitution of each variable by its concrete value in a sequent. The following is then true by construction:

Theorem 1. *If $\Gamma \vdash M : \theta \blacktriangleright \chi$ and $\mathcal{M}$ is a model of the system of constraints χ in the semiring $\mathcal{J}$ then $(\Gamma \vdash M : \theta)[\mathcal{M}]$ is derivable.*

2.4 Categorical Semantics

We give an abstract framework suitable for interpreting the abstract type system of Sec. 2. Up to this point the calling discipline of the type system was not relevant, as there are no side-effects, but for giving an interpretation we need to make this choice. In order to remain relevant to our motivating application, hardware compilation, we shall choose the *call-by-name* mechanism, which is used by the *Geometry of Synthesis* compiler.

We require two categories. We interpret *computations* in a symmetric monoidal closed category $(\mathcal{G}, \otimes, I)$ in which the tensor unit I is a terminal object. Let α be the *associator* and λ, ρ be the right and left *unitors*. We write the unique morphism into the terminal object as $!_A : A \to I$. Currying is the isomorphism

$$\Lambda_{A,B,C} : A \otimes B \to C \simeq A \to B \multimap C,$$

and the evaluation morphism is $\mathit{eval}_{A,B} : A \otimes (A \multimap B) \to B$.

We interpret *resources* in a category $\mathcal{R}$ with two monoidal tensors $(\oplus, 0)$ and $(\odot, 1)$ such that:

$$J \odot (K \oplus L) \simeq J \odot K \oplus J \odot L \qquad \text{(r-distributivity)}$$
$$(J \oplus K) \odot L \simeq J \odot L \oplus K \odot L \qquad \text{(l-distributivity)}$$
$$J \odot 0 \simeq 0 \odot J \simeq 0 \qquad \text{(zero)}.$$

The action of resources on computations is modeled by a functor $\cdot : \mathcal{R} \times \mathcal{G} \to \mathcal{G}$ such that the following natural isomorphisms must exist:

$$\delta_{J,K,A} : J {\cdot} A \otimes K {\cdot} A \simeq (J \oplus K) {\cdot} A \tag{4}$$
$$\pi_{R,R',A} : R {\cdot} (R' {\cdot} A) \simeq (R \odot R') {\cdot} A \tag{5}$$
$$\zeta_A : 0 {\cdot} A \simeq I \tag{6}$$
$$\iota_A : 1 {\cdot} A \simeq A \tag{7}$$

and the following diagrams commute:

$$
\begin{array}{ccc}
J {\cdot} A \otimes K {\cdot} A \otimes L {\cdot} A & \xrightarrow{\delta_{J,K,A} \otimes 1_{L {\cdot} A}} & (J \oplus K) {\cdot} A \otimes L {\cdot} A \\
{\scriptstyle 1_{J {\cdot} A} \otimes \delta_{K,L,A}} \downarrow & & \downarrow {\scriptstyle \delta_{J \oplus K, L, A}} \\
J {\cdot} A \otimes (K \oplus L) {\cdot} A & \xrightarrow{\delta_{J,K \oplus L, A}} & (J \oplus K \oplus L) {\cdot} A
\end{array}
\tag{8}
$$

$$
\begin{array}{ccc}
J {\cdot} A \otimes K {\cdot} A & \xrightarrow{\delta_{J,K,A}} & (J \oplus K) {\cdot} A \\
{\scriptstyle J {\cdot} f \otimes K {\cdot} f} \downarrow & & \downarrow {\scriptstyle (J \oplus K) {\cdot} f} \\
J {\cdot} B \otimes K {\cdot} B & \xrightarrow{\delta_{J,K,B}} & (J \oplus K) {\cdot} B
\end{array}
\tag{9}
$$

Natural isomorphism π (Eqn. 5) reduces successive resource actions on computations to a composite resource action, corresponding to the product of the semiring. Natural isomorphism $\delta_{J,K,A}$ in Eqn. 4 is a "quantitative" version of the diagonal morphism in a Cartesian category, which collects the resources of the contracted objects. The commuting diagram in Eqn. 8 stipulates that the order in which we use the "quantitative" diagonal order to contract several objects is irrelevant, and the commuting diagram in Eqn. 9 gives a "quantitative" counterpart for the naturality of the diagonal morphism. Finally, Eqns. 6 and 7 show the connection between the units of the tensors involved.

A direct consequence of the naturality of ρ and I being terminal, useful for proving coherence, is:

Proposition 1. *The following diagram commutes in the category $\mathcal{G}$ for any* $f : B \to C$:

$$
\begin{array}{ccccc}
B \otimes A & \xrightarrow{1_B \otimes !_A} & B \otimes I & \xrightarrow{\rho_B} & B \\
{\scriptstyle f \otimes 1_A} \downarrow & & & & \downarrow {\scriptstyle f} \\
C \otimes A & \xrightarrow{1_C \otimes !_A} & C \otimes I & \xrightarrow{\rho_C} & C.
\end{array}
$$

Computations are interpreted in a canonical way in the category $\mathcal{G}$. Types are interpreted as objects and terms as morphisms, with

$$[\![J \cdot \theta \multimap \theta']\!]_{\mathcal{G}} = ([\![J]\!]_{\mathcal{R}} \cdot [\![\theta]\!]_{\mathcal{G}}) \multimap [\![\theta']\!]_{\mathcal{G}}.$$

From now on, the interpretation of the resource action is written as J instead of $[\![J]\!]_{\mathcal{R}}$ when there is no ambiguity and the subscript of $[\![-]\!]_{\mathcal{G}}$ is left implicit.

Environments are interpreted as

$$[\![\Gamma]\!] = [\![x_1 : J_1 \cdot \theta_1, \ldots x_n : J_n \cdot \theta_n]\!] = J_1 \cdot [\![\theta_1]\!] \otimes \cdots \otimes J_n \cdot [\![\theta_n]\!].$$

Terms are morphisms in $\mathcal{G}$, $[\![\Gamma \vdash M : \theta]\!]$ defined as follows:

$$[\![x : 1 \cdot \theta \vdash x : \theta]\!] = \iota_{[\![\theta]\!]}$$
$$[\![\Gamma, x : J \cdot \theta \vdash M : \theta']\!] = 1_{[\![\Gamma]\!]} \otimes !_{J \cdot [\![\theta]\!]}; \rho_{[\![\Gamma]\!]}; [\![\Gamma \vdash M : \theta]\!]$$
$$[\![\Gamma \vdash \lambda x.M : J \cdot \theta \multimap \theta']\!] = \Lambda_{J \cdot [\![\theta]\!]}([\![\Gamma, x : J \cdot \theta \vdash M : \theta']\!])$$
$$[\![\Gamma, J \cdot \Gamma' \vdash FM : \theta']\!] = ([\![\Gamma \vdash F : J \cdot \theta \multimap \theta']\!] \otimes J \cdot [\![\Gamma' \vdash M : \theta]\!]); eval_{J \cdot [\![\theta]\!], [\![\theta']\!]}$$
$$[\![\Gamma, x : (J + K) \cdot \theta \vdash M[x/y] : \theta']\!] = 1_{[\![\Gamma]\!]} \otimes \delta_{J,K,\theta}; [\![\Gamma, x : J \cdot \theta, y : K \cdot \theta \vdash M : \theta]\!].$$

2.5 Coherence

The main result of this section is the coherence of typing. The derivation trees are not unique because there is choice in the use of the weakening and contraction rules. Since meaning is calculated on a particular derivation tree we need to show that it is independent of it. The coherence conditions for the monoidal category are standard [15], but what is interesting and new is that resource manipulation does not break coherence. The key role is played by the isomorphism δ which is the resource-sensitive version of contraction, which can combine or de-compose resources without loss of information.

The key idea of the proof is that we can bring any derivation tree to a standard form (which we call *stratified*), with weakening and contraction performed as late as possible. A combination of weakenings and contractions can bring a term to linear form, which has a uniquely determined derivation tree. The key result is Lem. 3 which stipulates that the order in which contractions and weakenings are performed is irrelevant.

The following derivation rules is admissible because it is a chain of contractions and weakenings, followed by an abstraction:

$$\frac{x_1 : J_1 \cdot \theta, \ldots, x_n : J_n \cdot \theta, \Gamma \vdash M : \theta'}{\Gamma \vdash \lambda x.M[x/x_i] : (J_1 + \cdots + J_m) \cdot \theta \multimap \theta'} \text{ ACW}$$

where $x, x_j \notin fv(M)$, for some $1 \leq m \leq n$, and all $1 \leq i \leq m$, $m \leq j \leq n$. Variables $x_1, \ldots, x_m$ are contracted into a fresh variable x and dummy variables $x_{m+1}, \ldots, x_n$ can be added.

We denote sequents $\Gamma \vdash M : \theta$ by Σ and derivation trees by ∇. Let $\Lambda(\Sigma) \in \{id, wk, ab, ap, co, acw\}$ be a label on the sequents, indicating whether a sequent is derived using the rule for identity, weakening, etc. If a sequent $\Sigma = \Gamma \vdash M : \theta$ is the root of a derivation tree ∇ we write it Σ^∇ or $\Gamma \vdash^\nabla M : \theta$.

We say that a sequent is *linear* if each variable in the environment Γ occurs freely in the term M exactly once.

Definition 1. *For a linear sequent, we call a* stratified *derivation tree the unique derivation tree produced by the following deterministic algorithm.*

> MN: *The only possible rule is* Application *and, since the judgement* $\Gamma, J \cdot \Delta \vdash MN : \theta$ *is about a linear term, both* $\Gamma \vdash M : J \cdot \theta' \multimap \theta$ *and* $\Delta \vdash N : \theta'$ *are linear and there is only one way* Γ *can be split, unless* $J = 0$. *In this case any resource actions in* Δ *can be chosen, since they will be zeroed by the action of* J. *To keep the algorithm deterministic we choose zeroes. This ensures that every resource action in the derivation of* N *is also* 0.
>
> $\lambda x.M$: *We use AWC to give each occurrence of* $x : J \cdot A$ *in* M *a new (fresh) name* $x_i : J_i : A$. *Each* J_i *is uniquely determined by the context in which* x_i *occurs. Note that it is necessary that* $\sum J_i \leq J$, *otherwise the term cannot be typed.*
>
> x: *The only possible rule is* Weakening.

Lemma 1. *If a linear sequent has a derivation tree then it has a (unique) stratified derivation tree. Moreover, all the sequents occurring in the tree are linear.*

Proof. The proof is almost immediate (by contradiction). Linear derivations cannot use weakening or contractions except where they can be replaced by AWC, so to construct a stratified tree, we just ned to normalise uses of 0.

We now show that any derivation can be reduced to a stratified derivation through applying a series of meaning-preserving tree transformations, which we call *stratifying rules.*

The Weakening rule commutes trivially with all other rules except Identity, Abstraction and Contraction, if they act on the weakened variable. In thes cases we replace the sequence of Weakening followed by Abstraction and/or Contraction with the combined *AWC* rule. The more interesting tree transformation rules are for Contraction.

Contraction commutes with Application. There are two pairs of such rules, one for pushing down contraction in the function and one for pushing down contraction in the argument:

$$\cfrac{\cfrac{\Gamma, x : J \cdot \theta, y : J' \cdot \theta \vdash F : J_1 \cdot \theta_1 \multimap \theta_2}{\Gamma, x : (J + J') \cdot \theta \vdash F[x/y] : J_1 \cdot \theta_1 \multimap \theta_2} \qquad \Gamma' \vdash M : \theta_1}{\Gamma, x : (J + J') \cdot \theta, J_1 \cdot \Gamma' \vdash F[x/y]M : \theta_2}$$

$$\stackrel{AL}{\Longleftrightarrow}$$

$$\cfrac{\cfrac{\Gamma, x : J \cdot \theta, y : J' \cdot \theta \vdash F : J_1 \cdot \theta_1 \multimap \theta_2 \qquad \Gamma' \vdash M : \theta_1}{\Gamma, x : J \cdot \theta, y : J' \cdot \theta, J_1 \cdot \Gamma' \vdash FM : \theta_2}}{\Gamma, x : (J + J') \cdot \theta, J_1 \cdot \Gamma' \vdash (FM)[x/y] : \theta_2}$$

Similarly for pushing down contraction from the argument side and similarly for rules involving weakening:

$$\frac{\Gamma \vdash F : J_1 \cdot \theta_1 \multimap \theta_2 \qquad \dfrac{\Gamma, x : J \cdot \theta, y : J' \cdot \theta \vdash M : \theta_1}{\Gamma, x : (J + J') \cdot \theta \vdash M[x/y] : \theta_1}}{\Gamma, x : (J_1 \times (J + J')) \cdot \theta, \Gamma' \vdash F(M[x/y]) : \theta_2}$$

$$\overset{AR}{\Longleftrightarrow}$$

$$\frac{\dfrac{\Gamma \vdash F : J_1 \cdot \theta_1 \multimap \theta_2 \qquad \Gamma', x : J \cdot \theta, y : J' \cdot \theta \vdash M : \theta_1}{\Gamma, J_1 \cdot \Gamma', x : (J_1 \times J) \cdot \theta, y : (J_1 \times J') \cdot \theta \vdash FM : \theta_2}}{\Gamma, x : (J_1 \times J + J_1 \times J') \cdot \theta, \Gamma' \vdash (FM)[x/y] : \theta_2}$$

Contraction also commutes with Abstraction, if the contracted and abstracted variables are distinct, $x \neq y$:

$$\frac{\dfrac{\Gamma, x : J \cdot \theta, x' : J' \cdot \theta, y : K \cdot \theta' \vdash M : \theta''}{\Gamma, x : (J + J') \cdot \theta, y : K \cdot \theta' \vdash M[x/x'] : \theta''}}{\Gamma, x : (J + J') \cdot \theta \vdash \lambda y.M[x/x'] : K \cdot \theta' \multimap \theta''}$$

$$\overset{CA}{\Longleftrightarrow}$$

$$\frac{\dfrac{\Gamma, x : J \cdot \theta, x' : J' \cdot \theta, y : K \cdot \theta' \vdash M : \theta''}{\Gamma, x : J, x' : J' \cdot \theta \vdash \lambda y.M : K \cdot \theta' \multimap \theta''}}{\Gamma, x : (J + J') \cdot \theta \vdash (\lambda y.M)[x/x'] : K \cdot \theta' \multimap \theta''}$$

The rule for swapping contraction and weakening is (types are obvious and we elide them for concision):

$$\frac{\dfrac{\Gamma, y, z \vdash M}{\Gamma, y \vdash M[y/z]}}{\Gamma, y, x \vdash M[y/z]} \quad \overset{WC}{\Longleftrightarrow} \quad \frac{\dfrac{\Gamma, y, z \vdash M}{\Gamma, y, z, x \vdash M}}{\Gamma, y, x \vdash M[y/z]}$$

The final rule is to zero-out the resource actions of free identifiers used in derivations of functions with zero-types.

$$\frac{\Gamma \vdash M : 0 \cdot \theta \multimap \theta' \qquad \Gamma' \vdash N : \theta}{\Gamma, 0 \cdot \Gamma' \vdash MN : \theta'} \quad \overset{ZO}{\Longleftrightarrow} \quad \frac{\Gamma \vdash M : 0 \cdot \theta \multimap \theta' \qquad 0 \cdot \Gamma' \vdash N : \theta}{\Gamma, 0 \cdot \Gamma' \vdash MN : \theta'}$$

Proposition 2. *The following judgments are syntactically equal*

$$\Gamma, x : \theta, \Gamma' \vdash F[x/y]M : \theta' = \Gamma, x : \theta, \Gamma' \vdash (FM)[x/y] : \theta',$$
$$\Gamma, x : (J_1 \times (J + J')) \cdot \theta, \Gamma' \vdash F(M[x/y]) : \theta_2$$
$$= \Gamma, x : (J_1 \times J + J_1 \times J') \cdot \theta, \Gamma' \vdash (FM)[x/y] : \theta_2,$$
$$\Gamma, x : (J + J') \cdot \theta \vdash \lambda y.M[x/x'] : K \cdot \theta' \multimap \theta'$$
$$= \Gamma, x : (J + J') \cdot \theta \vdash (\lambda y.M)[x/x'] : K \cdot \theta' \multimap \theta''.$$

Proof. The proof of the first two statements is similar. Because Application is linear it means that an identifier y occurs either in F or in M, but not in both.

Therefore $(FM)[x/y]$ is either $F(M[x/y])$ or $(F[x/y])M$. This makes the terms syntactically equal. In any semiring, $J_1 \times (J+J') = J_1 \times J + J_1 \times J'$, which makes the environments equal. Note that semiring equations are resolved syntactically in the type system, as pointed out at the beginning of this section. For the third statement we know that $x \neq y$.

Proposition 3. *If ∇ is a derivation and ∇' is a tree obtained by applying a stratifying rule then ∇' is a valid derivation with the same root $\Sigma^\nabla = \Sigma^{\nabla'}$ and the same leaves.*

Proof. By inspecting the rules and using Prop. 2.

Most importantly, stratifying transformation preserve the meaning of the sequent.

Lemma 2. *If $\nabla \Rightarrow \nabla'$ is a stratifying rule then $[\![\Sigma^\nabla]\!] = [\![\Sigma^{\nabla'}]\!]$.*

Proof. By inspecting the rules. Prop. 3 states that the root sequents are equal and the trees are well-formed. For WC (and the other rules involving the stratification of Weakening) this is an immediate consequence of Prop. 1. For AL and AR the equality of the two sides is an immediate consequence of symmetry in $\mathcal{G}$ and the functoriality of the tensor $\otimes$. For CA the equality of the two sides is an instance of the general property in a symmetric monoidal closed category that $f; \Lambda(g) = \Lambda((f \otimes 1_{B'}); g)$ for any $A \xrightarrow{f} B$, $B \otimes B' \xrightarrow{g} C$. For ZO the equality is given by the (zero) isomorphism in the resource category and the ζ isomorphism (Eqn. 6).

Lemma 3. *If ∇, ∇' are derivation trees consisting only of Contraction and Weakening with a common root Σ then $[\![\Sigma^\nabla]\!] = [\![\Sigma^{\nabla'}]\!]$.*

Proof. Weakening commutes with any other rule (Prop. 1). Changing the order of multiple contraction of the same variable uses the associativity coherence property in Eqn. 8. Changing the order in which different variables are contracted uses the naturality coherence property in Eqn. 9.

The lemma above ensures that the AWC rule is itself semantically coherent.

Lemma 4. *If ∇ is a derivation there exists a stratified derivation tree ∇' which can be obtained from ∇ by applying a (finite) sequence of stratifying tree transformations. Moreover, $[\![\Sigma^\nabla]\!] = [\![\Sigma^{\nabla'}]\!]$.*

Proof. The stratifying transformations push contraction and weakening through any other rules and the derivation trees have finite height. If a contraction or weakening cannot be pushed through a rule it means that the rule is an abstraction on the variable being contracted or weakened, and we replace the rules with AWC. For the weakening and contractions pushed to the bottom of the tree the order is irrelevant, according to Lem. 3 The result is a stratified tree. Next we apply induction on the chain of stratifying rules using Lem. 2 for every rule application and Lem. 3 for the final chain of weakening and contractions.

Theorem 2 (Coherence). *For any derivation trees* ∇_1, ∇_2 *with common root* Σ, $[\![\Sigma^{\nabla_1}]\!] = [\![\Sigma^{\nabla_2}]\!]$.

Proof. Using Lem. 4, ∇_1, ∇_2 must be effectively stratifiable into trees ∇'_1, ∇'_2 with the same root and $[\![\Sigma^{\nabla_i}]\!] = [\![\Sigma^{\nabla'_i}]\!]$ for $i = 1, 2$. We first reduce Σ^{∇_i} to a linear form (using contractions and weakenings) then use Lem. 1. The only difference between ∇'_1, ∇'_2 are the order of the abstractions and permutations at the bottom of the tree, and the choice of names of variables, both of which are semantically irrelevant (Lem. 3).

3   Case Study: Timing Analysis

In the sequel we will present a more complex resource semiring which we shall use in giving a precise type-level analysis of timing. The interpretation of the type $J \cdot \theta \multimap \theta'$ is that the function needs a *schedule of execution* J for the argument in order to execute. Again, note the comonadic interpretation of resources. This type system is interesting in its own right, as a way of capturing timing at the level of the type system. A full blown analysis for timing bounds, as part of a more general approach to certifying resource bounds, has been given before using dependent types [3]. However, this approach only automates the *certification* of the bounds whereas we fully automate the process, at the expense of less precision.

A *schedule* $J = [x_1, x_2, \ldots, x_n]$ is a multiset of *stages* x_i, which are one-dimensional contractive affine transformations over $\mathbb{R}$. This means that our reading of time is a *relative* one. A *contractive* affine transformation is represented as $x_{s,p} = \begin{pmatrix} s & p \\ 0 & 1 \end{pmatrix}$, where $0 \leq s \leq 1$ and $0 \leq s + p \leq 1$.. The value s is a *scaling factor* relative to the unit interval, and p is a *phase change*, i.e. a delay from the time origin. For example, $x_{.25,.5} = \begin{pmatrix} .25 & .5 \\ 0 & 1 \end{pmatrix}$ represents a stage that starts when $\frac{1}{2}$ of the duration has elapsed and lasts for $\frac{1}{4}$ the duration relative to which we are measuring. Some extreme values are $\begin{pmatrix} 1 & 0 \\ 0 & 1 \end{pmatrix}$ which overlaps perfectly to the reference interval or $\begin{pmatrix} 0 & 1 \\ 0 & 1 \end{pmatrix}$ which starts at the end of the reference interval and has zero duration (is instantaneous).

For an example of how schedules are interpreted as type annotations, the type $[x_{.5,0}, x_{.5,.5}] \cdot \mathsf{com} \multimap \mathsf{com}$ is of a function that executes its argument twice. First argument starts instantly and the second starts half-way through its execution; both take $\frac{1}{2}$ of the execution.

In mathematical terms, schedules are the *semigroup semiring of one-dimensional contractive affine transformations*, usually written as $\mathcal{J} = \mathbb{N}[\mathrm{Aff}_1^c]$. This is a canonical construction which has the mathematical properties we desire.

Contractive affine transformations enable composition of timed functions in a natural way, because such transformations compose, by matrix product.

Composing time represented as absolute intervals is perhaps possible, but it complicates the rules of the type system significantly. By using relative timing the rules of the system are clean, at the expense of having a rather complicated final step of elaborating relative into absolute timings for a closed term (i.e. a program), as it will be seen in Sec. 3.3.

When we refer to the timing of a computation, and it is unambiguous from context, we will sometimes use just x to refer to its action on the unit interval $u = [0, 1]$. For example, if we write $x \subseteq x'$ we mean $x \cdot u \subseteq x' \cdot u$, i.e. $[p, s + p] \subseteq [p', s' + p']$, i.e. $p \geq p'$ and $s + p \leq s' + p'$. If we write $x \leq x'$ we mean the Egli-Milner order on the two intervals, $x \cdot u \leq x' \cdot u$, i.e. $p \leq p'$ and $s + p \leq s' + p'$. If we write $x \cap x' = \emptyset$ we mean the two intervals are disjoint, $x \cdot u \cap x' \cdot u = \emptyset$, etc.

Contractive affine transformations form a semigroup with matrix product as multiplication and unit element $I \triangleq \begin{pmatrix} 1 & 0 \\ 0 & 1 \end{pmatrix}$. The semiring of a semigroup $(\mathcal{G}, \times, I)$ is a natural construction from any semiring and any semigroup. In our case the semiring is natural numbers ($\mathbb{N}$), so the semigroup semiring is the set of finitely supported functions $J : \mathrm{Aff}_1^c \to \mathbb{N}$ with

$$\mathbf{0}(x) = 0 \qquad\qquad \mathbf{1}(x) = \begin{cases} 1 & \text{if } x = I \\ 0 & \text{otherwise} \end{cases}$$

$$(J + K)(x) = J(x) + K(x) \qquad (J \times K)(x) = \sum_{\substack{y,z \in \mathrm{Aff}_1^c \\ y \times z = x}} J(y) \times K(z).$$

This is isomorphic to finite multisets over Aff_1^c. We use interchangeably whichever representation is more convenient.

3.1   A Concrete Programming Language

A concrete programming language is obtained by adding a family of functional constants in the style of Idealized Algol [22]. We take commands and integer expressions as the base types, $\sigma ::= \mathsf{com} \mid \mathsf{exp}$.

Ground-type constants are just $n : \mathsf{exp}$ and $\mathsf{skip} : \mathsf{com}$. Ground-type operators are provided with explicit timing information. For example, for commands we have a family of timed composition operators (i.e. schedulers):

$$\mathsf{comp}_{x,y} : [x] \cdot \mathsf{com} \multimap [y] \cdot \mathsf{com} \multimap \mathsf{com}.$$

Both sequential and parallel composition are subsumed by the timed scheduler. Sequential composition is a scheduler in which the arguments are non-overlapping, with the first argument completing before the second argument starts: $\mathsf{seq}_{x,y} = \mathsf{comp}_{x,y}$ where $x \leq y$ and $x \cap y = \emptyset$ (which we write $x < y$). Parallel composition is simply $\mathsf{par}_x = \mathsf{comp}_{x,x}$, with both arguments initiating and completing execution at the same time. Schedulers that are neither purely sequential nor parallel, but a combination thereof, are also possible.

Arithmetic operators and branching (if) are also given explicit timings.

$$\mathsf{op}_{x,y} : [x]\cdot\mathsf{exp} \multimap [y]\cdot\mathsf{exp} \multimap \mathsf{exp},$$

$$\mathsf{if}_{x,y} : [x]\cdot\mathsf{exp} \multimap [y]\cdot\sigma \multimap [y]\cdot\sigma \multimap \sigma, \quad x < y.$$

Note that branching has an additional sequentiality constraint which stipulates that the guard must execute before the branches are allowed to start executing. This is not a type-related constraint, but a language-level constraint.

Assignable variables are handled by separating read and write access, as is common in IDEALIZED ALGOL (IA). Let the type of *acceptors* be defined (syntactically) as the familly $\mathsf{acc}_w \triangleq [w]\cdot\mathsf{exp} \multimap \mathsf{com}$. There is no stand-alone var type, instead the reader and writers to a variable are bound to the same memory location by a block variable constructor with signature:

$$\mathsf{new}_{\sigma,J,w_1,\dots,w_n} : (J\cdot\mathsf{exp} \multimap \mathsf{acc}_{w_1} \multimap \cdots \multimap \mathsf{acc}_{w_n} \multimap \sigma) \multimap \sigma, \quad \sigma \in \{\mathsf{exp}, \mathsf{com}\}.$$

The asymmetric treatment of readers and acceptors is a consequence of using call-by-name: the read operation is an expression thunk with no arguments, but the acceptor needs to evaluate its argument which can take an arbitrary amount of time. For programmer convenience var-typed identifiers can be sugared into the language but, because the read and write schedules of access need to be maintained separately, the contraction rules become complicated (yet routine) so we omit them here.

Example 1. The timings of the IA program $\mathsf{new}\, v.\, v := {!v} + 1$ can be captured by this typing system. First let us write it in a functional-style syntax where the occurrences of v are linearized: $\mathsf{new}(\lambda v_1 \lambda v_2.v_2(\mathsf{add}\, v_1\, 1))$. The type of this linearized local-variable binder is $\mathsf{new} : (\mathsf{exp} \multimap \mathsf{acc} \multimap \mathsf{com}) \multimap \mathsf{com}$.

The next step is to determine schedules of execution for the constants. The typing derivation is

$$\cfrac{v_2:[w]\cdot\mathsf{exp}\multimap\mathsf{com} \vdash v_2:\mathsf{acc}_w \quad \cfrac{\cfrac{v_1:\mathsf{exp} \vdash v_1:\mathsf{exp} \quad \vdash \mathsf{add}_{x,y}:[x]\cdot\mathsf{exp}\multimap[y]\cdot\mathsf{exp}\multimap\mathsf{exp}}{v_1:[x]\cdot\mathsf{exp} \vdash \mathsf{add}_{x,y}\, v_1:[y]\cdot\mathsf{exp}\multimap\mathsf{exp}} \quad \vdash 1:\mathsf{exp}}{v_1:[x]\cdot\mathsf{exp} \vdash \mathsf{add}_{x,y}\, v_1\, 1:\mathsf{exp}}}{\cfrac{v_2:\mathsf{acc}_w, v_1:[w \times x]\cdot\mathsf{exp} \vdash v_2(\mathsf{add}_{x,y}\, v_1\, 1):\mathsf{com}}{\vdash \lambda v_1\lambda v_2.v_2(\mathsf{add}_{x,y}\, v_1\, 1):[w \times x]\cdot\mathsf{exp}\multimap\mathsf{acc}_w\multimap\mathsf{com}}}$$

for any stages x, y, w. To complete the term we need to apply the binder $\mathsf{new}_{\mathsf{com},[w\times x],w}$. Written in a fully sugared notation, this term would be: $\mathsf{new}_{\mathsf{com},[w\times x],w}\, x := {!x} +_{x,y} 1$. We will see later how to choose sensible concrete values for the stages.

3.2 Type Inference for Pipelining

Computing such detailed timings can perhaps be useful when doing real-time computation using programs with higher-order functions without recursion, as this language is expressive enough for implementing, for example, certain digital signal processing algorithms. However, we will look at a different application motivated by hardware compilation: imposing a pipelining discipline via the type system. Pipelining is important because it allows the concurrent use of a hardware component and thus reduces the overall footprint of a program compiled in hardware. Without it, any concurrently used component is systematically replicated, a process called *serialization* [11].

The constraints imposed by the typing system, as seen in Example 1 can be quite loose, and there can be broad choice in selecting concrete values for the stages. In some sense this is a bug, because there can be no principal type, but we will turn it into a handy feature by introducing extra constraints motivated by the *platform* to which we are compiling the program, in this case one relying on pipelining. Thus the overall system of constraints will contain *type*, *language* and *platform* constraints independently of each other, a pleasant degree of modularity. The rest of the section describes the type inference algorithm.

First an observation: the general recipe from Sec. 2.3 cannot be immediately applied because there is no (off-the-shelf) SMT solver for $\mathbb{N}[\mathrm{Aff}_1^c]$. We need to run the SMT in two stages: first we calculate the sizes of the multiset (as in SCC inference), which allows us to reduce constraints in $\mathbb{N}[\mathrm{Aff}_1^c]$ to constraints in Aff_1^c. Then we map equations over Aff_1^c into real-number equations, which can be handled by the SMT solver. There is a final, bureaucratic, step of reconstructing the multi-sets from the real-number values. To fully automate the process we start with the Hindley-Milner type inference to determine the underlying simple-type structure [19].

Multiset size (SCC) type inference is presented in detail elsewhere [11], but we will quickly review it here. We first interpret schedules as natural numbers, representing their number of stages $J \in \mathbb{N}$. Unknown schedules are variables, schedules with unknown stages but fixed size (such as those for operators) are constants. A type derivation results in a constraint system over $\mathbb{N}$ which can be solved by an SMT tool such as Z3 [20]. More precisely, Z3 can attempt to solve the system, but it can be either unsatisfiable in some cases or unsolvable as nonlinear systems of constraints over $\mathbb{N}$ are generally undecidable.

As a practical observation, solving this constraint using general-purpose tools will give an arbitrary solution, if it exists, whereas a "small" solution is preferable. [11] gives a special-purpose algorithm guaranteed to produce solutions that are in a certain sense minimal. To achieve a small solution when using Z3 we set a global maximum bound which we increment on iterated calls to Z3 until the system is satisfied.

Next we instantiate schedules to their known sizes, and to re-run the inference algorithm, this time in order to compute the stages. This proceeds according to the general type-inference recipe, resulting in a system of constraints over the $\mathbb{N}[\mathrm{Aff}_1^c]$ semiring, with the particular feature that all the sizes of all the multisets is known. We only need to specify the schedules for the constants:

$$\overline{\vdash 1 : \mathsf{exp} \blacktriangleright \mathit{true}} \qquad \overline{\vdash \mathsf{skip} : \mathsf{com} \blacktriangleright \mathit{true}}$$

$$\overline{\vdash \mathsf{op}_{x,y} : [x]\cdot\sigma \multimap [y]\cdot\sigma \multimap \sigma \blacktriangleright \{x \neq I, y \neq I\}}$$

$$\vdash \mathsf{if}_{x,y} : [x]{\cdot}\mathsf{exp} \multimap [y]{\cdot}\sigma \multimap [y]{\cdot}\sigma \multimap \sigma \blacktriangleright \{x < y\}$$

$$\vdash\mathsf{new}_{\sigma,J,w_1,\dots,w_n} : (J{\cdot}\mathsf{exp} \multimap \mathsf{acc}_{w_1} \multimap \cdots \multimap \mathsf{acc}_{w_n} \multimap \sigma) \multimap \sigma \blacktriangleright \bigwedge_{i=1,n}\{0 \neq w_i\}$$

In the typing for op we disallow an instant response and in the typing for new we disallow instantanewous write operations.

As mentioned, in the concrete system it is useful to characterize the resource usage of families of constants also by using constraints, which can be combined with the other constraints (of the type system, etc.). The language of constraints itself can be extended arbitrarily, provided that eventually we can represent it into the language of our external SMT solver, Z3. The constraints introduced by the language constants are motivated as follows:

op: We prevent the execution of any of the two arguments to take the full inter- val, because an arithmetic operation cannot be computed instantaneously.

if: The execution of the guard must precede that of the branches.

new: The write-actions cannot be instantaneous.

This allows us to translate the constraints from the semiring theory into real- number constraints. Solving the system (using Z3) gives precise timing bounds for all types. However, this does not guarantee the fact that computations can be pipelined, it just establishes timings. In order to force a pipeline-compatible timing discipline we need to add extra constraints guaranteeing the fact that each timing annotation J is in fact a proper pipeline.

Two stages $x_1, x_2 \in \mathrm{Aff}_1^c$ are *FIFO* if they are Egli-Milner-ordered, $x_1 \leq x_2$. They are *strictly FIFO*, written $x_1 \lhd x_2$ if they are FIFO and they do not start or end at the same time, i.e. if $x_i{\cdot}[0,1] = [t_i, t_i']$ then $t_0 \neq t_0'$ and $t_1 \neq t_1'$.

Definition 2. *We say that a schedule $J \in \mathbb{N}[\mathrm{Aff}_1^c]$ is a pipeline, written* $\mathsf{Pipe}(J)$, *if and only if $\forall x \in \mathrm{Aff}_1^c, J(x) \leq 1$ (i.e. J is a proper set) and for all $x, x' \in J$, either $x \lhd x'$ or $x' \lhd x$ or $x = x'$.*

Given a system of constraints χ over $\mathbb{N}[\mathrm{Aff}_1^c]$, before solving it we augment it with the condition that every schedule is a proper pipeline: for any J used in χ, $\mathsf{Pipe}(J)$. Using the conventional representation (scaling and phase), the usual matrix operations and the pipelining definitions above we can represent χ as a system of constraints over $\mathbb{R}$, and solve it using Z3.

Implementation note. For the implementation, we enforce arbitrary orders on the stages of the pipeline and, if that particular order is not satisfiable then a different (arbitrary) order is chosen and the process is repeated. However, spelling out the constraint for the existence of a pipelining order $\lhd$ for any schedule J would entail a disjunction over all possible such orders, which is $\mathcal{O}(n!)$ in the size of the schedule, for each schedule, therefore not realistic. However, if the systems of constraints have few constants and mostly unknowns, i.e. we are trying to find a schedule rather than accommodate complex known schedules, our experience shows that this pragmatic approach is reasonable.

Example 2. Let us first consider the simple problem of using three parallel adders to compute the sum $fx + fx + fx + fx$ when we know the timings of f. Suppose f : $([(0.5, 0.1); (0.5, 0.2)] \cdot \text{exp} \multimap \text{exp}$, i.e. it is a two-stage pipeline where the execution of the argument takes half the time of the overall execution and have relative delays of 0.1 and 0.2 respectively. We have the choice of using three adders with distinct schedules $+_i : [x_i] \cdot \text{exp} \multimap [y_i] \cdot \text{exp} \multimap \text{exp}$ ($i \in \{1, 2, 3\}$) so that the expression respects the pipelined schedule of execution of f. The way the operators are associated is relevant: $(fx +_2 fx) +_1 (fx +_3 fx)$. Also note that part of the specification of the problem entails that the adders are trivial (single-stage) pipelines. Following the algorithm above, the typing constraints are resolved to the following:

$$+_1 : [(0.5, 0.265625)] \cdot \text{exp} \multimap [(0.5, 0.25)] \cdot \text{exp} \multimap \text{exp}$$
$$+_2 : [(0.5, 0.21875)] \cdot \text{exp} \multimap [(0.5, 0.25)] \cdot \text{exp} \multimap \text{exp}$$
$$+_3 : [(0.5, 0.375)] \cdot \text{exp} \multimap [(0.5, 0.25)] \cdot \text{exp} \multimap \text{exp}$$

In the implementation, the system of constraints has 142 variables and 357 assertions, and is solved by Z3 in circa 0.1 seconds on a high-end desktop machine.

Example 3. Let us now consider a more complex, higher-order example. Suppose we want to calculate the convolution ($*$) of a pipelined function (f : $[(0.5, 0.1); (0.5, 0.2)] \cdot \text{exp} \multimap \text{exp}$) with itself four times. And also suppose that we want to use just two instances of the convolution operator $*_1, *_2$, so we need to perform contraction on it as well. The type skeleton of the convolution operator is ($*$) : $(\text{exp} \to \text{exp}) \to (\text{exp} \to \text{exp}) \to \text{exp} \to \text{exp}$.

The implementation of f and $*$ are unknown, so we want to compute the timings for the term

$$(*_1) : J_1^{vi} \cdot (J_1^i \cdot (J_1^{ii} \cdot \text{exp} \multimap \text{exp}) \to J_1^{iv} \cdot (J_1^{iii} \cdot \text{exp} \multimap \text{exp}) \multimap J_1^v \cdot \text{exp} \multimap \text{exp}),$$
$$(*_2) : J_2^{vi} \cdot (J_2^i \cdot (J_2^{ii} \cdot \text{exp} \multimap \text{exp}) \to J_2^{iv} \cdot (J_2^{iii} \cdot \text{exp} \multimap \text{exp}) \multimap J_2^v \cdot \text{exp} \multimap \text{exp}),$$
$$f : J_3 \cdot ([(0.5, 0.1); (0.5, 0.2)] \cdot \text{exp} \multimap \text{exp}) \vdash (f *_1 f) *_2 (f *_1 f) : \theta.$$

The constraint system has 114 variables and 548 assertions and is solved by Z3 in 0.2 seconds on a high-end desktop machine. The results are:

$$J_1^i = J_1^{iv} = J_2^i = J_2^{iv} = [(1.0, 0.0)]$$
$$J_1^{ii} = J_1^{iii} = J_1^v = J_2^{ii} = J_2^{iii} = J_2^v = [(0.5, 0.1); (0.5, 0.2)]$$
$$J_1^{vi} = J_3 = [(0.5, 0.125); (0.5, 0.25); (0.5, 0.375); (0.5, 0.4375)]$$
$$J_2^{vi} = [(0.25, 0.25); (0.25, 0.5); (0.25, 0.625)]$$

3.3   Absolute Timing

This section is a variation of the type system in order to deal with absolute rather than relative timing. The presentation is more informal, but the formalism of the previous sections can be applied here if desired.

In our main intended application, hardware compilation, relative timing rather than absolute timing is relevant. However, for other applications such as real-time computing absolute timing might be required. We can recover absolute timings for a program (closed term) in two steps. What is interesting here is the introduction of yet another level of constraints, this times imposed by the physical characteristics of the computational platform we use. They come in addition to the structural, language and architectural constraints seen so far.

In the first step we propagate the timing annotations all the way down to the constants. The constants of the language are families indexed by schedules, and this propagation will generate the set of all concrete constants used by a program, with timings given relative to the overall execution of the program. The function $\ulcorner - \urcorner$ takes as arguments a schedule and a term and produces as set of language constants. It is defined inductively on the type derivation as follows:

$$\ulcorner x : \mathbf{1}\cdot\theta \vdash x : \theta \urcorner(J) = \emptyset$$

$$\ulcorner \Gamma, x : K\cdot\theta \vdash M : \theta' \urcorner(J) = \ulcorner \Gamma \vdash M : \theta' \urcorner(J), \quad x \notin fv(M)$$

$$\ulcorner \Gamma \vdash \lambda x.M : K\cdot\theta \multimap \theta' \urcorner(J) = \ulcorner \Gamma, x : K\cdot\theta \vdash M : \theta' \urcorner(J)$$

$$\ulcorner \Gamma, K\cdot\Gamma' \vdash FM : \theta' \urcorner(J) = \ulcorner \Gamma \vdash F : K\cdot\theta \multimap \theta' \urcorner(J) \cup \ulcorner \Delta \vdash M : \theta \urcorner(J \times K)$$

$$\ulcorner \Gamma, x : (K+L)\cdot\theta \vdash M[x/y] : \theta' \urcorner(J) = \ulcorner \Gamma, x : K\cdot\theta, y : L\cdot\theta \vdash M : \theta' \urcorner(J)$$

$$\ulcorner k : \theta \urcorner(J) = \{k : \ulcorner\theta\urcorner([x]) \mid x \in J\}$$

$$\ulcorner K \cdot \theta \multimap \theta' \urcorner(J) = K \cdot \ulcorner\theta\urcorner(J) \multimap \ulcorner\theta'\urcorner(J)$$

$$\ulcorner \sigma \urcorner(J) = J \cdot \sigma.$$

What is the most interesting is the translation of the constants. In the case of our concrete programming language we have, for example:

$$\ulcorner \mathsf{op} : [x] \cdot \mathsf{exp} \multimap [y] \cdot \mathsf{exp} \multimap \mathsf{exp} \urcorner[u] = \mathsf{op} : [u \times x] \cdot \mathsf{exp} \multimap [u \times y] \cdot \mathsf{exp} \multimap [u] \cdot \mathsf{exp}$$

and so on. This is a constant which executes in interval u, and its arguments in $u \times x$ and $u \times y$, which now represent absolute timings. The reasons that we collect these constants is because depending on the concrete target platform some of them may be impossible to implement from a timing point of view. For the operation above (op), if we work out the numbers we get $t_1 = u_1 x_1 + u_1 x_2 + u_2$ and $t_2 = u_1 y_1 + u_1 y_2 + u_2$ as the respective times when the two arguments terminate, which means that the duration in which op must compute the result is before its own termination at $t = u_1 + u_2$, i.e. $\delta t = u_1 - \max(u_1 x_1 + u_1 x_2, u_1 y_1 + u_1 y_2)$. This δt must be greater than a system-defined constant such as the duration of one clock cycle (e.g. 1 ns).

For any program $\vdash M : \mathsf{com}$, its set of constants is $\ulcorner \vdash M : \sigma \urcorner([d])$ where d is an affine (not necessarily contractive) transform defining its total duration. The value of d is not known and must be chosen large enough so that all constants in $\ulcorner M \urcorner[d]$ are implementable.

Example 4. Consider the term $\vdash 1 +_{x,y} (2 +_{u,v} 3) : \mathsf{exp}$. It is quite easy to calculate that

$$\ulcorner \vdash 1 +_{x,y} (2 +_{u,v} 3) : \mathsf{exp} \urcorner ([d]) = \{ + : [d \times x] \cdot \mathsf{exp} \multimap [d \times y] \cdot \mathsf{exp} \multimap [d] \cdot \mathsf{exp},$$
$$+ : [d \times x \times u] \cdot \mathsf{exp} \multimap [d \times x \times v] \cdot \mathsf{exp} \multimap [d \times x] \cdot \mathsf{exp},$$
$$1 : [d \times x] \cdot \mathsf{exp}, 1 : [d \times x \times u] \cdot \mathsf{exp}, 1 : [d \times x \times v] \cdot \mathsf{exp} \}$$

Suppose that all the additions can performed in 1 ns and the constants can be computed instantaneously. These timing constraints are satisfied by $d = \begin{pmatrix} 2 & 0 \\ 0 & 1 \end{pmatrix}$, $y = \begin{pmatrix} 0.5 & 0 \\ 0 & 1 \end{pmatrix}$, and $x, u, v = \begin{pmatrix} 0 & 0 \\ 0 & 1 \end{pmatrix}$.

4 Related Work

The BLL type system has been already generalized by Dal Lago and collaborators to Linear Dependent Types (LDT) [4,6]. This greatly increases the expressiveness of the type system but at the expense of losing decidability. We also generalize BLL but in a different way, by using an abstract notion of resource. It is natural to think of resources as having a monoidal structure, as resources can be *aggregated*. However, we show that the additional structure of a semiring can be employed in a useful way to *scale* resources. Our generalization consists of replacing the family of modalities $!_x A$ of BLL, which are interpreted as A *may be reused less than x times* with a general resource action $R \cdot A$, which is interpreted as A *may use at most R resources*. This is a generalization because R can be simply instantiated to x, giving back BLL. For this abstract type system we show how the problem of type inference can be naturally reduced to a system of constraints parametrized by the equational theory of the resource semiring. Provided this theory is decidable, a type inference algorithm automatically follows.

We also provide a categorical framework, for which we prove the key result of *coherence*. This is the main technical contribution of the paper. Coherence is an essential technical property because denotational interpretations are given inductively on type derivations, which are generally not unique. This means that in the absence of coherence a denotational interpretation cannot make sense. Coherence for a categorical semantics is also the generalization of the subject reduction property used by operational semantics, as substitution is usually interpreted by composition in the category. Resource-awareness has been usually modeled operationally, but game-semantic [7] and, more recently, relational models [16] have been proposed to model resources denotationally.

The same typing framework presented here was developed independently in [2] (published in this volume), but includes resource actions in covariant positions so it could be used to model call-by-value languages. For this larger type system the soundness of the system is proved relative to an operational semantics with so-called *coeffect actions*.

The second part of the paper presents a non-trivial motivating application to timing analysis and automated pipelining of computations in a recursion-free functional programming language with local store, and is meant to illustrate several points. The first one is showing a complex notion of resource in action. The second one is presenting a non-trivial multi-stage type inference algorithm for this resource. The third one is to show a specialization of the type inference algorithm in the case of a concrete programming language when language constants and arbitrary system-level resources can come into play.

5   Conclusion

We have presented an abstract framework for BLL using a more general notion of resource which can be modeled in a semiring, gave a categorical model and a proof of coherence. We gave several instances of this general typing framework, depending on several notions of resource, one of which is a fairly elaborate method for tracking execution time in a higher-order setting. We have not given concrete semantics here, but denotational (game) models of various programming languages that fit this framework have been developed elsewhere [10,12,24].

One methodological feature which seems quite unique for this typing framework, and is amply illustrated in the previous section, is its degree of flexibility and modularity. In addition to the structural constraints imposed by the type system we can freely add language-level constraints (e.g. "the if statement is sequential"), architectural constraints (e.g. "schedules must be pipelines") and physical constraints (e.g. "addition can be performed no faster than 1 ns"). Various passes of the type-inference algorithm collect constraints which, ultimately, are about what language constants are implementable or not within certain resource constraints on a particular physical platform. The modularity of the system is expressed in a different dimension as well. Since the Cartesian product of semirings is a semiring we can easily combine unrelated notions of constraints, which is essential in managing the trade-offs that need to be made in a realistic system.

Acknowledgment. Sec. 2.4 benefited significantly from discussions with Steve Vickers. Olle Fredriksson and Fredrik Nordvall Forsberg provided useful comments. The authors express gratitude for their contribution.

References

1. Boudol, G.: The lambda-calculus with multiplicities (abstract). In: Best, E. (ed.) CONCUR 1993. LNCS, vol. 715, pp. 1–6. Springer, Heidelberg (1993)
2. Brunel, A., Gaboardi, M., Mazza, D., Zdancewic, S.: A core quantitative coeffect calculus. In: Shao, Z. (ed.) ESOP 2014. LNCS, vol. 8410, pp. 351–370. Springer, Heidelberg (2014)
3. Crary, K., Weirich, S.: Resource bound certification. In: POPL 2000, pp. 184–198. ACM, New York (2000)

4. Lago, U.D., Gaboardi, M.: Linear Dependent Types and Relative Completeness. Logical Methods in Computer Science 8(4) (2011)
5. Dal Lago, U., Hofmann, M.: Bounded linear logic, revisited. In: Curien, P.-L. (ed.) TLCA 2009. LNCS, vol. 5608, pp. 80–94. Springer, Heidelberg (2009)
6. Lago, U.D., Petit, B.: The geometry of types. In: Giacobazzi, R., Cousot, R. (eds.) POPL, pp. 167–178. ACM (2013)
7. Dan, R.: Ghica. Slot games: a quantitative model of computation. In: POPL 2005, Long Beach, California, USA, January 12-14, pp. 85–97. ACM (2005)
8. Dan, R.: Ghica. Geometry of Synthesis: a structured approach to VLSI design. In: Hofmann, M., Felleisen, M. (eds.) POPL, pp. 363–375. ACM (2007)
9. Ghica, D.R., Murawski, A.S.: Compositional model extraction for higher-order concurrent programs. In: Hermanns, H., Palsberg, J. (eds.) TACAS 2006. LNCS, vol. 3920, pp. 303–317. Springer, Heidelberg (2006)
10. Ghica, D.R., Murawski, A.S., Luke Ong, C.-H.: Syntactic control of concurrency. Theor. Comput. Sci. 350(2-3), 234–251 (2006)
11. Ghica, D.R., Smith, A.: Geometry of synthesis iii: resource management through type inference. In: Ball, T., Sagiv, M. (eds.) POPL, pp. 345–356. ACM (2011)
12. Ghica, D.R., Smith, A.: From bounded affine types to automatic timing analysis. CoRR, abs/1307.2473 (2013)
13. Girard, J.Y., Scedrov, A., Scott, P.J.: Bounded linear logic: a modular approach to polynomial-time computability. Theoretical Computer Science 97(1), 1–66 (1992)
14. Hofmann, M.: Linear types and non-size-increasing polynomial time computation. In: LICS, pp. 464–473. IEEE Computer Society (1999)
15. Kelly, G.M.: On MacLane's conditions for coherence of natural associativities, commutativities, etc. Journal of Algebra 1(4), 397–402 (1964)
16. Laird, J., Manzonetto, G., McCusker, G., Pagani, M.: Weighted relational models of typed lambda-calculi. In: LICS, pp. 301–310. IEEE Computer Society (2013)
17. Melliès, P.-A., Tabareau, N.: An algebraic account of references in game semantics. Electr. Notes Theor. Comput. Sci. 249, 377–405 (2009)
18. Melliès, P.-A., Tabareau, N.: Resource modalities in tensor logic. Ann. Pure Appl. Logic 161(5), 632–653 (2010)
19. Milner, R.: A theory of type polymorphism in programming. Journal of Computer and System Sciences 17(3), 348–375 (1978)
20. de Moura, L., Bjørner, N.S.: Z3: An efficient SMT solver. In: Ramakrishnan, C.R., Rehof, J. (eds.) TACAS 2008. LNCS, vol. 4963, pp. 337–340. Springer, Heidelberg (2008)
21. O'Hearn, P.W.: On bunched typing. J. Funct. Program. 13(4), 747–796 (2003)
22. Reynolds, J.C.: The essence of ALGOL. In: ALGOL-like Languages, vol. 1, pp. 67–88. Birkhauser Boston Inc. (1997)
23. John, C.: Reynolds. Syntactic control of interference. In: Aho, A.V., Zilles, S.N., Szymanski, T.G. (eds.) POPL, pp. 39–46. ACM Press (1978)
24. Smith, A.: Type-directed hardware synthesis. PhD thesis, University of Birmingham (forthcoming)

A Core Quantitative Coeffect Calculus

Aloïs Brunel[1], Marco Gaboardi[2], Damiano Mazza[1], and Steve Zdancewic[3]

[1] CNRS, UMR 7030, LIPN, Université Paris 13, Sorbonne Paris Cité
[2] University of Dundee
[3] University of Pennsylvania

Abstract. Linear logic is well known for its resource-awareness, which has inspired the design of several resource management mechanisms in programming language design. Its resource-awareness arises from the distinction between linear, single-use data and non-linear, reusable data. The latter is marked by the so-called exponential modality, which, from the categorical viewpoint, is a (monoidal) comonad.

Monadic notions of computation are well-established mechanisms used to express effects in pure functional languages. Less well-established is the notion of comonadic computation. However, recent works have shown the usefulness of comonads to structure context dependent computations. In this work, we present a language $\ell\mathcal{R}$PCF inspired by a generalized interpretation of the exponential modality. In $\ell\mathcal{R}$PCF the exponential modality carries a label—an element of a semiring $\mathcal{R}$—that provides additional information on how a program uses its context. This additional structure is used to express comonadic type analysis.

1 Introduction

Linear Types. The ideas of linear logic [17] have found several applications in programming languages. The most popular aspect of linear logic is certainly the *distinction* it makes between objects that can be used exactly once and objects that can be used several times—zero or more. This distinction allows type systems to introduce the concept of *usage* that can be exploited to reason about *resources* in various contexts such as explicit memory management, complexity analysis or process specification. The explicit manipulation of resources is obtained formally by introducing the so-called *exponential modality* ! that distinguishes two kinds of types *linear* $A, B, \ldots$—for objects that can be used only once—and *non-linear* $!A, !B, \ldots$—for objects that can be used several times.

Monads and Effects. The use of monads in programming languages, originally introduced in category theory, was pioneered by Moggi [29] as a way to structure the semantics of his computational lambda calculus. The use of monads was further advocated by Wadler [40] and they have since found important applications in the development of Haskell. A monad T represents a notion of *computation from a value* that is obtained by distinguishing *value types* $A, B, \ldots$—the types of the language values—from *computation types* $TA, TB, \ldots$—the types of computations over values. From a different perspective a monadic type TA

Z. Shao (Ed.): ESOP 2014, LNCS 8410, pp. 351–370, 2014.

can be seen as a computation that outputs a value of type A and that produces the *effect* described by T on its environment—e.g. a change in the state, input-output operations, *etc. Effect systems* [36] were developed independently as a way to use static type analysis to understand how programs *influence* their environment. Besides this superficial correspondence, monads and effect systems are indeed intimately related as shown by Wadler [41].

Comonads and Coeffects. A comonad is the categorical dual of a monad. While monads have grown very popular in the recent years, comonads are still not well-known and probably less understood. Recent works [38, 39, 33] have proposed to interpret a comonad D as a notion of *value in a context* that is obtained by distinguishing *value types* $A, B, \ldots$—the types of the language values—from *contextual types* $DA, DB, \ldots$—the types of values in contexts. From a different perspective, a comonadic type DA can be seen as a computation that consumes a value of type A producing the *coeffect* described by D on its environment. The coeffect described by D can be seen as a requirement of the program with respect to the environment—*e.g.* the availability of a resource, a specific prerequisite on the input, *etc.* A general theory of *coeffect systems* has not yet been established, but some steps in this direction have been recently proposed [33].

Our Contributions. It is not difficult to see a common pattern here. Indeed, linear types, monads and comonads are all ways to structure computations by interpreting types in two different ways. The correspondence clearly goes farther: as we already said, monad and comonad are dual notions; moreover, it is a well-known fact that the linear logic exponential modality ! has the structure of a (monoidal) comonad [26]; finally, both the computational λ-calculus and the linear λ-calculus can be embedded in the adjoint calculus, where their relations is revealed through an adjunction [6].

Besides these technical similarities, one may wonder if the comonadic structure of the modality ! can also be used to design general comonadic analyses.

The answer we give in the present work is affirmative. Starting from linear logic, we derive a core PCF-like comonadic language, named $\ell\mathcal{R}$PCF, that is able to express at the same time quantitative reasoning and general comonadic reasoning. Our proposal follows a simple remark (which will not surprise linear logic semantics experts): in many concrete models of linear logic several different interpretations of the ! modality (in terms of abstract resources) are possible. In the present work, we make explicit in the syntax these different interpretations by introducing a modality $!_r$ indexed by an element r of an abstract structure $\mathcal{R}$—a *structural semiring*—that naturally arises from the structural rules of linear logic. Interestingly, this abstract structure also permits general coeffect analyses like the ones previously studied by Petricek *et al.* [33].

A key ingredient of $\ell\mathcal{R}$PCF is the presence of explicit *co-handlers* coeff, which are typed primitives performing an action $r \in \mathcal{R}$ on the context. For instance, a first example of a simple co-handler in the context of clocked dataflow programming [38, 39, 33], is the primitive next that shifts the clock of the input signal s one step forward. This operation can be seen as a co-handler requiring that the context be able to provide signal information one step in the future.

To express this requirement in our framework one can add a co-handler next with the associated action 1 on the context. In fact, $\ell\mathcal{R}$PCF is parametrized over the structure $\mathcal{R}$ and the set of co-handlers. Hence, different comonadic analyses may be performed using different primitives and different structures $\mathcal{R}$.

The focus of our work is on providing a framework for specifying sound type analyses even in the presence of operations—like co-handlers—that change the semantics of the language in terms of contextual operations. For this reason, we instrument the language and the operational semantics—presented in the form of an abstract machine—with informations about the *observable* actions of coeffects. This is achieved by adding to the language an explicit observation $(\!-\!)$ that mark where to monitor the behavior of a specific part of the program during the computation. We prove a parametric soundness theorem for the type system with respect to the information collected by the instrumented operational semantics. That is, we associate to each term (through its type derivation) a value in $\mathcal{R}$ and we show that this value approximates the information that can be observed at runtime with the instrumented operational semantics. This result is proved by defining a general quantitative realizability model, based on biorthogonality and parametrized over $\mathcal{R}$. Finally, we sketch a denotational semantics for $\ell\mathcal{R}$PCF in the form of an interpretation of $\ell\mathcal{R}$PCF programs in a categorical structure describing the properties of $\mathcal{R}$.

Summarizing, our contributions are:

- A quantitative comonadic core language inspired by linear logic semantics. This language is parametrized over an abstract structure $\mathcal{R}$ and over a set of coeffect primitives (co-handlers). By instantiating $\mathcal{R}$ with concrete structures and by choosing particular sets of co-handlers we are able to perform several context-dependent analysis.
- A parametrized quantitative realizability technique used to prove the soundness of the different analyses. The realizability is parametrized over $\mathcal{R}$ and the set of coeffect primitives. The soundness is proved with respect to an abstract machine reduction relation.
- The description of a categorical model, based on Melliès's work on parametric comonads [27, 28], showing the abstract structure needed to interpret our language. Such a categorical semantics provides a base for a comparison with usual semantics of linear logic.

2   The $\ell\mathcal{R}$PCF Language

Syntax: Linear Constructors and Coeffects.   The language of $\ell\mathcal{R}$PCF, defined in Fig. 1.a, is a linearized version of PCF (*i.e.*, with explicit constructors for the modalities of linear logic) extended with coeffects.

The !-constructor and `let` bindings are standard in languages designed using the proofs-as-programs correspondence with linear logic. Here, they are used to explicitly track the use of the coeffects in expressions. We consider three kinds of values: numerals $\underline{n}$, abstractions $\lambda x.e$ and expressions of the form $!e$. The latter are useful to delimit the scope of coeffects.

$$e ::= x \mid \lambda x.e \mid e\, e \mid \text{let } !x = e \text{ in } e \mid !e \mid (\!|e|\!) \mid \text{coeff}(e) \mid \qquad \text{(expressions)}$$
$$\underline{n} \mid \text{s}(e) \mid \text{case } e \text{ of } \underline{0} \to e \text{ else } \underline{x+1} \to e \mid \text{fix } x.e$$
$$v ::= \lambda x.e \mid \underline{n} \mid !e \qquad \qquad \text{(values)}$$

$$A ::= \text{Nat} \mid !_r A \mid A \multimap A \qquad\qquad\qquad\qquad r \in \mathcal{R} \quad \text{(types)}$$
$$\Gamma ::= \emptyset \mid \Gamma, x : A \mid \Gamma, x : [A]_r \qquad\qquad\qquad r \in \mathcal{R} \quad \text{(contexts)}$$

$$c ::= (e, \rho) \qquad\qquad\qquad\qquad\qquad\qquad\qquad\qquad \text{(closures)}$$
$$\rho ::= [] \mid \rho \cdot [x/c] \qquad\qquad\qquad\qquad\qquad\qquad \text{(environments)}$$
$$\pi ::= \diamond \mid \langle c \rangle.\pi \mid \langle x, e, \rho \rangle.\pi \mid \langle \text{coeff} \rangle.\pi \mid \langle \text{s} \rangle.\pi \mid \langle e_1, x, e_2, \rho \rangle.\pi \quad \text{(stacks)}$$
$$C ::= (c, \pi) \qquad\qquad\qquad\qquad\qquad\qquad\qquad \text{(configurations)}$$

Fig. 1. $\ell\mathcal{R}$PCF (a) grammar (b) typing (c) abstract machine configurations

The construction $\text{coeff}(e)$ wraps expression e in a *coeffect handler* coeff. Note that coeff is a metavariable, ranging over a (finite) set of *coeffect handler identifiers* or, more simply, *co-handlers*. We leave the set of co-handlers unspecified, as a parameter of $\ell\mathcal{R}$PCF.

Finally, the construct $(\!| - |\!)$ is an *observation*. It has no computational value but makes our quantitative analysis more flexible. By arbitrarily introducing observations in expressions, we can track the behavior of specific subterms during a computation, giving more power to our quantitative soundness result.

Structural Semirings. The other main parameter of $\ell\mathcal{R}$PCF (or, rather, of its type system) is the following algebraic structure.

Definition 1 (Structural semiring). *A structural semiring, denoted in general by $\mathcal{R}$, is a tuple $(\mathcal{R}, +, \mathbf{0}, \star, \mathbf{1}, \preceq)$ such that:*

- *$(\mathcal{R}, +, \mathbf{0}, \star, \mathbf{1})$ is a unit semiring, that is:*
  - *$(\mathcal{R}, +, \mathbf{0})$ is a commutative monoid;*
  - *$(\mathcal{R}, \star, \mathbf{1})$ is a monoid;*
  - *multiplication distributes over addition, i.e., for all $p, q, r \in \mathcal{R}$:*
    - *$r \star (p + q) = r \star p + r \star q$,*
    - *$(p + q) \star r = p \star r + q \star r$;*
  - *$\mathbf{0}$ is absorbing for multiplication: $p \star \mathbf{0} = \mathbf{0} \star p = \mathbf{0}$ for all $p \in \mathcal{R}$.*
- *$(\mathcal{R}, \preceq)$ is a bounded sup-semilattice, that is:*
  - *$\preceq$ is a partial order on $\mathcal{R}$ such that the least upper bound of every two elements $p, q \in \mathcal{R}$ exists and is denoted by $p \vee q$;*
  - *there is a least and greatest element, the latter being denoted by ∞.*

Moreover, the following compatibility conditions hold, for all $p, q, r \in \mathcal{R}$:

- *$\mathbf{0}$ is the least element;*
- *$p \preceq q$ implies $p + r \preceq q + r$, $r \star p \preceq r \star q$ and $p \star r \preceq q \star r$.*

Note that the compatibility conditions imply that ∞ is absorbing for addition and that it is idempotent w.r.t. both operations.

The notion of structural semiring arises naturally from the structural rules of linear logic, hence the name.[1] It is possible to give a categorical generalization of this structure, which is used for describing the denotational models of $\ell\mathcal{R}$PCF (*cf.* Sect. 4).

The presence of least upper bounds is not strictly necessary; it is useful to provide a more precise typing of the **case** construction. Similarly, the existence of a greatest element is postulated only to ensure that fixpoints may be given at least a trivial type.

The following are some notable examples of structural semirings:
- the extended natural numbers $\overline{\mathbb{N}} := \mathbb{N} \cup \{\infty\}$ (usual operations and order);
- the tropical semiring $\mathcal{T} := (\overline{\mathbb{N}}, \min, \infty, +, 0, \geq)$ (note the reversed ordering);
- the arctic semiring $\mathcal{A} := (\overline{\mathbb{N}} \cup \{-\infty\}, \max, -\infty, +, 0, \leq)$;
- the Boolean lattice $\{0, 1\}$, as well as any bounded distributive lattice;
- the probability semiring $\overline{\mathbb{R}}^+$ of non-negative real numbers plus infinity, with the usual operations and order.

Type System.   As mentioned above, the type system of $\ell\mathcal{R}$PCF is parametrized over a structural semiring $\mathcal{R}$. Elements of $\mathcal{R}$ can appear in types (defined in Figure Fig. 1.b) as decorations of the exponential modality, as well as in *discharged types* (of the form $[A]_r$) in typing contexts (also defined in Fig. 1.b). Discharged types are not themselves types; they can appear only in contexts and they cannot be nested.

Each co-handler coeff comes with three pieces of information: its *source type* A_{coeff}, its *target type* B_{coeff} and its *coeffect* $r_{\text{coeff}} \in \mathcal{R}$. It also comes with a *coeffect map* φ_{coeff}, which assigns to every value of type A_{coeff} a value of type B_{coeff}. The coeffect map will be required to satisfy a semantic soundness property, which we will give in Sect. 3. We use the term "map" instead of "function" because we do not want to restrict the kind of transitions (of the abstract machine, to be introduced below) we can consider. For instance, φ_{coeff} may be probabilistic or non-deterministic. We consider only unary co-handlers; n-ary co-handlers could be obtained by combining unary co-handlers with the usual tensor product of linear logic, which we do not include here for brevity.

A typing context Γ is a set of typed variables that are either of the form $x : A$ (*linear* variables) or $x : [A]_r$ (*discharged* variables). Discharged variables are a technical artifact useful to implicitly manage variables in contexts. More specifically, if we denote by $[\Gamma]$ a discharged context (a context containing only discharged variables) we can extend the operation $+$ of the semiring to contexts:

$$\emptyset + \Delta = \Delta$$
$$(x : [A]_p, \Gamma) + (x : [A]_q, \Delta) = x : [A]_{p+q}, (\Gamma + \Delta)$$
$$(x : [A]_p, \Gamma) + \Delta = x : [A]_p, (\Gamma + \Delta) \quad \text{if } x \notin \Delta$$
$$(x : A, \Gamma) + \Delta = x : A, (\Gamma + \Delta) \quad \text{if } x \notin \Delta$$

---

[1] For the acquainted reader: contraction is addition, with weakening being its neutral element; multiplication comes from crossing the context of a promotion rule, with dereliction being its unit.

$$\frac{}{A <: A}\text{ O-I} \qquad \frac{A <: B \quad q \preceq p}{!_p A <: !_q B}\text{ O-B} \qquad \frac{A' <: A \quad B <: B'}{A \multimap B <: A' \multimap B'}\text{ O-L}$$

$$\frac{A <: B \quad q \preceq p}{[A]_p <: [B]_q}\text{ O-D} \qquad \frac{}{\Gamma <: \Gamma}\text{ O-IC} \qquad \frac{\Gamma <: \Delta \quad A <: B}{\Gamma, x : B <: \Delta, x : A}\text{ O-C}$$

$$\frac{}{x : A \vdash x : A}\text{ id} \qquad \frac{\Gamma, x : A \vdash e : B}{\Gamma \vdash \lambda x.e : A \multimap B}\text{ lam} \qquad \frac{\Gamma \vdash e : A \multimap B \quad \Delta \vdash e' : A}{\Gamma + \Delta \vdash e\, e' : B}\text{ app}$$

$$\frac{\Gamma, x : A \vdash e : B}{\Gamma, x : [A]_1 \vdash e : B}\text{ der} \qquad \frac{[\Gamma] \vdash e : B}{r \star [\Gamma] \vdash\, !e\, :\, !_r B}\text{ pr} \qquad \frac{\Gamma \vdash e : !_r A \quad \Delta, x : [A]_r \vdash e' : B}{\Gamma + \Delta \vdash \text{ let } !x = e \text{ in } e' : B}\text{ let}$$

$$\frac{}{\vdash \underline{n} : \text{Nat}}\text{ nat} \qquad \frac{\Gamma \vdash e : \text{Nat}}{\Gamma \vdash \text{s}(e) : \text{Nat}}\text{ succ} \qquad \frac{[\Gamma], x : [A]_p \vdash e : A \quad 1 + p \star q \preceq q}{q \star [\Gamma] \vdash \text{ fix } x.e : A}\text{ fix}$$

$$\frac{\Gamma \vdash e : \text{Nat} \quad \Delta \vdash e_1 : A \quad \Delta, x : \text{Nat} \vdash e_2 : A}{\Gamma + \Delta \vdash \text{ case } e \text{ of } \underline{0} \to e_1 \text{ else } \underline{x+1} \to e_2 : A}\text{ case}$$

$$\frac{\Delta \vdash e : B \quad \Gamma <: \Delta}{\Gamma, \Xi \vdash e : B}\text{ sub} \qquad \frac{[\Gamma] \vdash e : A_{\text{coeff}}}{r_{\text{coeff}} \star [\Gamma] \vdash \text{coeff}(e) : B_{\text{coeff}}}\text{ coeff}$$

$$\frac{\Gamma \vdash e : A}{\Gamma \vdash (\!|e|\!) : A}\text{ obs}$$

Fig. 2. (a) Subtyping rules   (b) Typing rules

Note that the addition of contexts is partial: $\Gamma + \Delta$ is defined only if Γ and Δ do not share any linear variable declaration. In what follows, the use of this operation implicitly means that this condition is met. Similarly, the action of an element $r \in \mathcal{R}$ on a discharged context $[\Gamma]$, denoted by $r \star [\Gamma]$, is defined by induction on the size of $[\Gamma]$ as: $r \star \emptyset = \emptyset$ and $r \star (x : [A]_p, [\Gamma]) = x : [A]_{r \star p}, r \star [\Gamma]$. We also extend to contexts the partial order of $\mathcal{R}$, by introducing *subtyping* between types. A subtyping judgment $A <: B$ can be obtained using the rules in Fig. 2.a. The subtyping rules are rather standard with the exception of rules O-B and O-D, which lift the semiring partial order to types; notice that these rules are contravariant in the elements of the semiring.

As usual, typing judgments are of the form $\Gamma \vdash e : A$, where in our case Γ may contain both linear and discharged variables. The typing rule are in Fig. 2.b.

The rule der introduces a discharged variable starting from a linear variable. This rule may be seen as a quantitative analog of the *dereliction* principle of linear logic: $!A \multimap A$. A way of reading this rule is: "a variable with coeffect **1**

x	$\rho \cdot [x/(e,\rho')]$	π	$\rightarrow_v$	e	ρ'	π
$\lambda x.e$	ρ	$\langle c \rangle.\pi$	$\rightarrow_\lambda$	e	$\rho \cdot [x/c]$	π
$e_1\,e_2$	ρ	π	$\rightarrow_@$	e_1	ρ	$\langle (e_2,\rho) \rangle.\pi$
let $!x = e_1$ in e_2	ρ	π	$\rightarrow_1$	e_1	ρ	$\langle x, e_2, \rho \rangle.\pi$
$!e_1$	ρ_1	$\langle x, e_2, \rho_2 \rangle.\pi$	$\rightarrow_!$	e_2	$\rho_2 \cdot [x/(e_1,\rho_1)]$	π
$s(e)$	ρ	π	$\rightarrow_s$	e	ρ	$\langle s \rangle.\pi$
$\underline{n}$	ρ	$\langle s \rangle.\pi$	$\rightarrow_+$	$\underline{n+1}$	ρ	π
$\left(\begin{array}{l} \text{case } e \text{ of } \underline{0} \rightarrow e_1 \\ \text{else } x+1 \rightarrow e_2 \end{array} \right)$	ρ	π	$\rightarrow_i$	e	ρ	$\langle e_1, x, e_2, \rho \rangle.\pi$
$\underline{0}$	ρ_1	$\langle e_1, x, e_2, \rho_2 \rangle.\pi$	$\rightarrow_z$	e_1	ρ_2	π
$\underline{n+1}$	ρ_1	$\langle e_1, x, e_2, \rho_2 \rangle.\pi$	$\rightarrow_e$	e_2	$\rho_2 \cdot [x/(\underline{n},\rho_1)]$	π
fix $x.e$	ρ	π	$\rightarrow_f$	e	$\rho \cdot [x/(\text{fix } x.e, \rho)]$	π
coeff(e)	ρ	π	$\rightarrow_c$	e	ρ	$\langle \text{coeff} \rangle.\pi$
v	ρ	$\langle \text{coeff} \rangle.\pi$	$\rightarrow_x$	$\varphi_{\text{coeff}}(v)$	ρ	π
$\langle\!| e |\!\rangle$	ρ	π	$\rightarrow_o$	e	ρ	π

Fig. 3. The $\mathcal{K}^{\mathcal{R}}$ machine

is also linear". Similarly, the pr rule corresponds to a quantitative version of the *promotion* rule of linear logic. Note that this rule is in fact a scheme for rules parametrized by an element $r \in \mathcal{R}$. A way of reading this rule is: "if a co-handler whose coeffect is r is to operate on an expression e, then r has to act on the context of e". The rule sub is at the same time the rule for the subtyping and for *weakening* (of the context Ξ); indeed, the system is actually *affine*, not strictly linear. The rule let is responsible for removing discharged variables. This can be seen as an analog (or dual) of the let of the computational λ-calculus. Note that this rule, as well as all the binary rules, uses the operation $+$ to merge the contexts of the two premises. This is because the resulting coeffect is the sum of the coeffects in the two premises.

The rule coeff is the rule for typing co-handler expressions. It is parametrized on the particular co-handler. We could have chosen to have this rule as derivable from an application of the pr rule—introducing an extra !-operator in the expression—and an application of an axiom rule introducing the co-handler. We prefer this formulation so that co-handlers are always applied in expressions—and we also avoid the use of an extra !-operator.

The additive management of the context Δ in the two branches of the case rule is standard for languages inspired by linear logic. Note that the existence of least upper bounds is useful here for type-inference: it allows to find minimal discharged types to build the context Δ. The last rule deserving some explanation is fix. This is parametrized by an element $q \in \mathcal{R}$ that has to satisfy the side condition $1 + q \star p \preceq q$. Note that for every $p \in \mathcal{R}$ the element ∞ satisfies this condition. However, in general there may be other elements satisfying it.

The Abstract Machine. The operational semantics we consider is provided by an adaptation of the Krivine abstract machine [22]. In particular, we extend (in a standard way) Krivine's machine to deal with natural numbers, conditional and fixpoint. The basic components of the machine (closures, environments, stacks, configurations) are defined in Fig. 1.c. Stacks are also assigned a *weight*:

Definition 2 (Weight of a stack). *Let π be a stack. Its weight $w(\pi)$ is the element of $\mathcal{R}$ defined by induction on π as follows:*

- $w(\diamond) = \mathbf{1}$;
- $w(\langle\mathsf{coeff}\rangle.\pi') = w(\pi') \star r_{\mathsf{coeff}}$;
- $w(\kappa.\pi') = w(\pi')$ *in all other cases.*

A *state* of the machine is a pair (C, r), where C is a configuration and $r \in \mathcal{R}$. This latter, called the *observable quantity*, must be seen as the value of a counter. It adds a quantitative aspect to the operational semantics of $\ell\mathsf{RPCF}$.

The transitions of the $\mathcal{K}^{\mathcal{R}}$ machine are given in Fig. 3. The counter of the machine is left untouched by all transitions except the o transition: if $C = (\!(e)\!, \rho, \pi)$ and $C' = (e, \rho, \pi)$, then the state (C, r) evolves to $(C', r + w(\pi))$. We write $C \rightarrow C'$ when we do not want to specify the kind of transition.

In general, we are interested in computations of the shape $((e, [], \diamond), \mathbf{0}) \rightarrow^* ((v, \rho, \diamond), r)$, *i.e.*, computations that evaluate expressions in the empty environment and the empty stack starting with an observable quantity of $\mathbf{0}$. In this case, we can say that r is the *observable quantity* of the computation. The goal of our type analysis is to provide by static analysis a bound to this quantity. This is obtained by a quantitative realizability technique that we present in the next section.

3   Quantitative Realizability

This section presents the construction of a realizability interpretation suitable for modeling $\ell\mathsf{RPCF}$ as parameterized by an arbitrary structural semiring $\mathcal{R}$. However, to soundly handle the fixpoint typing rule, it is necessary to "step index" the construction. Fortunately, such step indexing can itself be smoothly added using a structural semiring.

In the rest of the section we fix an arbitrary structural semiring $\mathcal{R}$ and we consider the structural semiring $\mathcal{R} \oplus \mathcal{T}$, where $\mathcal{T}$ is the tropical semiring defined in Sect. 2. The elements of $\mathcal{R} \oplus \mathcal{T}$, which we denote by α, β, γ, are pairs of the form (p, m) where $p \in \mathcal{R}$ and $m \in \bar{\mathbb{N}}$. The operations and order relation on these elements are (abusively) denoted like the operations and order relation of $\mathcal{R}$: $(p, m) + (q, n) = (p + q, \min(m, n))$ with neutral element $(\mathbf{0}, \infty)$, $(p, m) \star (q, n) = (p \star q, m + n)$ with neutral element $(\mathbf{1}, 0)$, and $(p, m) \preceq (q, n)$ iff $p \preceq q$ and $n \leq m$ (note the reverse ordering on integers).

The elements of $\mathcal{R}$ may be (monotonically) embedded in $\mathcal{R} \oplus \mathcal{T}$ through the additive endomorphism $p \mapsto (p, \infty)$ and the multiplicative endomorphism $p \mapsto (p, 0)$. In the sequel, we tacitly apply such embeddings to treat elements of $\mathcal{R}$ as elements of $\mathcal{R} \oplus \mathcal{T}$, using the suitable endomorphism according to the operation of interest. For instance, given a stack π, we write $\alpha + w(\pi)$ to actually mean $\alpha + (w(\pi), \infty)$, and we write $w(\pi) \star \alpha$ to actually mean $(w(\pi), 0) \star \alpha$.

Orthogonality. In what follows, we associate with each transition $C \rightarrow C'$ of the $\mathcal{K}^{\mathcal{R}}$ machine a function $\theta[C \rightarrow C'] : \mathcal{R} \oplus \mathcal{T} \rightarrow \mathcal{R} \oplus \mathcal{T}$ which is the identity in all cases except:

- when $C \to_f C'$, in which case we set $\theta[C \to C'](p, m) = (p, m + 1)$;
- when $C = (\langle\!\lvert e \rvert\!\rangle, \rho, \pi)$ and $C \to_o C'$, in which case we set $\theta[C \to C'](p, m) = (p + w(\pi), m)$.

Definition 3 (Pole). *A* pole *is a family* $\perp\!\!\!\perp = (\perp\!\!\!\perp_\alpha)_{\alpha \in \mathcal{R} \oplus \mathcal{T}}$ *of sets of configurations such that:*

- Saturation: *if* $C' \in \perp\!\!\!\perp_\alpha$ *and* $C \to C'$, *then* $C \in \perp\!\!\!\perp_{\theta[C \to C'](\alpha)}$;
- Monotonicity: $\alpha \preceq \beta$ *implies* $\perp\!\!\!\perp_\alpha \subseteq \perp\!\!\!\perp_\beta$;
- Approximation: *for all* $p \in \mathcal{R}$, $\perp\!\!\!\perp_{(p,0)}$ *is the set of all configurations and* $\bigcap_{n \in \mathbb{N}} \perp\!\!\!\perp_{(p,n)} = \perp\!\!\!\perp_{(p,\infty)}$;
- Weakening: *for all* α *and* $(e, \rho, \pi) \in \perp\!\!\!\perp_\alpha$, *if* $y_1, \ldots, y_k$ *do not appear free in* e, *then, for all closures* $c_1, \ldots, c_k$, $(e, \rho \cdot [y_1/c_1] \cdots [y_k/c_k], \pi) \in \perp\!\!\!\perp_\alpha$.

Definition 4 (Weighted closures and stacks, orthogonality). *A* weighted closure *(resp.* weighted stack*) is a pair* (c, α) *(resp.* (π, α)*) where* c *is a closure (resp.* π *is a stack) and* $\alpha \in \mathcal{R} \oplus \mathcal{T}$.

Let $((e, \rho), \alpha)$, (π, β) *be a weighted closure and stack, respectively, and let* $\perp\!\!\!\perp$ *be a pole. We define the* orthogonality *relation w.r.t.* $\perp\!\!\!\perp$ *by*

$$((e, \rho), \alpha) \perp (\pi, \beta) \quad iff \quad (e, \rho, \pi) \in \perp\!\!\!\perp_{w(\pi) \star \alpha + \beta}.$$

Intuitively, the pole expresses a notion of correctness, and ortogonality means that the closure (program) and stack (environment) interact correctly. In Sect. 5 we will give explicit examples of poles and clarify this intuition.

The orthogonality relation lifts to sets of weighted closures X and sets of weighted stacks Y as usual: $X^\perp := \{ (\pi, \beta) \mid \forall (c, \alpha) \in X, (c, \alpha) \perp (\pi, \beta) \}$, and $Y^\perp := \{ (c, \alpha) \mid \forall (\pi, \beta) \in Y, (c, \alpha) \perp (\pi, \beta) \}$. The *biorthogonality operator* $(.)^{\perp\perp}$ on sets of weighted closures is then a closure operator.

Lemma 5. *Suppose that* X *is a set of weighted closures or weighted stacks. Then: (i)* $X \subseteq X^{\perp\perp}$; *(ii)* $Y \subseteq X$ *implies* $X^\perp \subseteq Y^\perp$; *(iii)* $X^{\perp\perp\perp} = X^\perp$.

Moreover, it is easy to see that the properties of the pole are transferred to biorthogonally-closed sets of weighted closures:

Lemma 6. *Let* X *be a set of weighted closures. Then:*

1. *if, for all* $n \in \mathbb{N}$, $(c, (p, n)) \in X$, *then* $(c, (p, \infty)) \in X^{\perp\perp}$;
2. *if* $((e, \rho), \alpha) \in X$, $\alpha \preceq \beta$ *and if* $y_1, \ldots, y_k$ *are variables not appearing free in* e, *then* $((e, \rho \cdot [y_1/c_1] \cdots [y_k/c_k]), \beta) \in X^{\perp\perp}$ *for all closures* $c_1, \ldots, c_k$.

Interpretation. We are now going to assign to each type a set of weighted closures. We first define in Fig. 4 two operations $\multimap$ and $!_r$, along with the set Nat (for convenience, we use the same notation as the type).

Definition 7 (Interpretation, realizability, adaptation). *Let* A *be a type. Its* interpretation $\|A\|$ *is the set of weighted closures defined as follows:*

$$\|\mathsf{Nat}\| := \mathsf{Nat}^{\perp\perp} \qquad \|A \multimap B\| := (\|A\| \multimap \|B\|)^{\perp\perp} \qquad \|!_r A\| := (!_r \|A\|)^{\perp\perp}$$

The realizability *relation* $(c, \alpha) \Vdash A$ *is valid if and only if* $(c, \alpha) \in \|A\|$.

Note that realizability depends on the pole. We say that a pole is adapted *if we have* $(\diamond, (\mathbf{0}, \infty)) \in \|A\|^\perp$ *for every type* A.

$$\mathsf{Nat} := \{ \ ((\underline{n}, []), (\mathbf{0}, \infty)) \mid n \in \mathbb{N} \ \}$$
$$X \multimap Y := \{ \ ((\lambda x.e, \rho), \alpha) \mid \forall (c', \beta) \in X, \ ((e, \rho \cdot [x/c']), \alpha + \beta) \in Y^{\perp\perp} \ \}$$
$$r \star X := \{ \ (c, (r \star p, m)) \mid (c, (p, m)) \in X \ \}$$
$$!_r X := \{ \ ((!e, \rho), \alpha) \mid ((e, \rho), \alpha) \in r \star X \ \}$$

Fig. 4. Realizability operations. X and Y are generic sets of weighted closures.

Soundness. We start by introducing the notions needed to state the soundness theorem. We first need to extend the realizability relation to open terms. Then, we will define what it means for a typing judgment and a typing rule to be sound.

Definition 8 (Sound environment). *Suppose γ is a sequence $\gamma_1, \dots, \gamma_n$ of elements of $\mathcal{R} \oplus \mathcal{T}$. We say that an environment $\rho = [x_1/c_1] \cdots [x_n/c_n]$ is γ-sound with respect to $\Gamma = x_1 : A_1, \dots, x_k : A_k, x_{k+1} : [A_{k+1}]_{r_{k+1}}, \dots, x_n : [A_n]_{r_n}$, and we write $(\rho, \gamma) \Vdash \Gamma$, if $(c_i, \gamma_i) \in \|A_i\|$ for $1 \le i \le k$, and $(c_i, \gamma_i) \in r_i \star (\|A_i\|)$ for $k + 1 \le i \le n$.*

In what follows, if γ is a sequence $\gamma_1, \dots, \gamma_n$ of elements of $\mathcal{R} \oplus \mathcal{T}$, we denote by $\sum \gamma$ the element $\gamma_1 + \dots + \gamma_n$ (which is $(\mathbf{0}, \infty)$ if $n = 0$).

Definition 9 (Sound judgment and rules). *Let $p \in \mathcal{R}$. We say that the judgment $\Gamma \vdash e : A$ is p-sound if $(\rho, \gamma) \Vdash \Gamma$ implies $((e, \rho), p + \sum \gamma) \Vdash A$.*

Consider a typing rule R whose premises are the judgments $J_1, \dots, J_n$ and whose conclusion is the judgment K. Let $\phi : \mathcal{R}^n \to \mathcal{R}$. We say that R is ϕ-sound if for all $p_1, \dots, p_n \in \mathcal{R}$ such that J_i is p_i-sound, then K is $\phi(p_1, \dots, p_n)$-sound.

Any judgment obtained by composition of sound rules is itself a sound judgment. Hence, to prove soundness of our type system with respect to the realizability semantics, it will suffice to prove the soundness of each typing rule.

If R is an n-ary rule of our type system, we associate to it a *soundness function* of type $\mathcal{R}^n \to \mathcal{R}$ denoted by $\phi[R]$. The definition is given in Fig. 5, where we use meta-λ-notation. For instance, $\phi[\mathsf{obs}]$ is the function taking an element $p \in \mathcal{R}$ and returning the element $p + 1$ of $\mathcal{R}$.

If δ is a typing derivation of conclusion $\Gamma \vdash e : A$, then we may assign to it a *soundness element* $p[\delta] \in \mathcal{R}$, defined by composing the $\phi[R]$ for each rule R used in δ, inductively. Then, we have the following:

Theorem 10 (Soundness). *The conclusion of every derivation δ is $p[\delta]$-sound.*

The proof of the above result, which we omit here for space reasons, is conditional to the following hypothesis being verified, for every co-handler coeff, which we call *soundness* of coeff:

$$(\pi, \beta) \in \|B_{\mathsf{coeff}}\|^{\perp} \text{ implies } (\langle \mathsf{coeff} \rangle . \pi \beta) \in \|A_{\mathsf{coeff}}\|^{\perp}.$$

$$\phi[\text{id}] := \mathbf{0} \qquad \phi[\text{lam}] := \lambda p.p \qquad \phi[\text{app}] := \lambda(p,q).p + q$$
$$\phi[\text{der}] := \lambda p.p \qquad \phi[\text{pr}] := \lambda p.r \star p \qquad \phi[\text{let}] := \lambda(p,q).p + q$$
$$\phi[\text{nat}] := \mathbf{0} \qquad \phi[\text{succ}] := \lambda p.p \qquad \phi[\text{fix}] := \lambda p.q \star p$$
$$\phi[\text{sub}] := \lambda p.p \qquad \phi[\text{coeff}] := \lambda p.r_{\text{coeff}} \star p \qquad \phi[\text{obs}] := \lambda p.p + 1$$
$$\phi[\text{case}] := \lambda(p,q,r).p + (q \vee r)$$

Fig. 5. Soundness functions of the typing rules of Fig. 2.b. The arity of each function is the same as that of its associated rule; p, q, r correspond to the first, second and third premises, respectively (from left to right).

This is the semantic condition on coeffect maps which we mentioned when we introduced the type system.

In case the pole is adapted, we obtain the following important result:

Corollary 11. *If $\vdash e : A$ via a typing derivation δ, then $(e, [], \diamond) \in \perp\!\!\!\perp_{(p[\delta],\infty)}$.*

Since $C \in \perp\!\!\!\perp_{(p,\infty)}$ usually means "the configuration C uses at most p resources", we have that, for properties that can be expressed using an adapted pole, typing derivations of $\ell\mathcal{R}$PCF imply quantitative bounds on the execution of the typed expression.

4   Categorical Semantics

Our framework has a rich underlying structure that we describe in categorical terms in this section. The first step is introducing bimonoidal categories (formerly called *ring categories* [25]), which are a "categorification" of the notion of semiring. The most synthetic way of defining a bimonoidal category is saying that it is a one-object category enriched over symmetric monoidal categories [19]. Spelled out, this means that a bimonoidal category is a structure $(\mathcal{S}, +, 0, \star, 1, \mathsf{d}^l, \mathsf{d}^r, \mathsf{a}^l, \mathsf{a}^r)$ such that $(\mathcal{S}, +, 0)$ is a symmetric monoidal category, $(\mathcal{S}, \star, 1)$ is a monoidal category and $\mathsf{d}^l, \mathsf{a}^l, \mathsf{d}^r, \mathsf{a}^r$ are structure maps ensuring distibutivity and absorption laws. A certain numer of coherence diagrams are required to commute, of course; the precise definition may be found in [19].

Next, we introduce a notion of parametric comonad, that we take from [27]. In what follows, we will deal with two categories $\mathcal{S}$ and $\mathcal{A}$ and we shall use x, y (resp. a, b) as placeholders for the arguments of a functor of domain $\mathcal{S}$ (resp. $\mathcal{A}$), *e.g.* an endofunctor F of $\mathcal{A}$ will be denoted by $F(a)$, whereas we use p, q, r (resp. A, B) to range over the objects of $\mathcal{S}$ (resp. $\mathcal{A}$).

Definition 12 (Positive action). *A positive action of a monoidal category $(\mathcal{S}, \star, 1)$ on a category $\mathcal{A}$ is a functor $\bullet : \mathcal{S} \times \mathcal{A} \longrightarrow \mathcal{A}$ with two natural* *transformations* $\delta : (x \star y) \cdot a \Longrightarrow x \cdot (y \cdot a)$ *and* $\varepsilon : 1 \cdot a \Longrightarrow a$ *such that the following diagrams commute:*

$$(p \star (q \star r)) \cdot A \xrightarrow{\alpha^* \cdot A} ((p \star q) \star r) \cdot A \xrightarrow{\delta} (p \star q) \cdot (r \cdot A) \qquad (1 \star p) \cdot A \xrightarrow{\lambda^*} p \cdot A \xleftarrow{\rho^*} (p \star 1) \cdot A$$

$$\downarrow^\delta \qquad\qquad\qquad\qquad \downarrow^\delta \qquad\qquad \downarrow^\delta \qquad\qquad \| \qquad\qquad \downarrow^\delta$$

$$p \cdot ((q \star r) \cdot A) \xrightarrow{\qquad\qquad p \cdot \delta \qquad\qquad} p \cdot (q \cdot (r \cdot A)) \qquad 1 \cdot (p \cdot A) \xrightarrow{\varepsilon} p \cdot A \xleftarrow{p \cdot \varepsilon} p \cdot (1 \cdot A)$$

We now generalize Definition 12 to the case of a bimonoidal category acting on a symmetric monoidal category. This should be seen as a categorification of the "raising to a power" action: the natural transormations required correspond to the usual, elementary laws of exponentiation (such as $A^{p+q} = A^p A^q$, $A^0 = I$, and so on). Although not contained in either [27] or [28], the definition was still suggested to the authors by Melliès.

Definition 13 (Exponential action). *Let* $(\mathcal{A}, \otimes, I)$ *be a symmetric monoidal category, and let* $(\mathcal{S}, +, 0, \star, 1)$ *be a bimonoidal category. An* exponential action *of* $\mathcal{S}$ *on* $\mathcal{A}$ *is a positive action* $(\cdot, \delta, \varepsilon)$ *of* $(\mathcal{S}, \star, 1)$ *on* $\mathcal{A}$ *together with four natural transformations* $\mathsf{c} : (x + y) \cdot a \Longrightarrow x \cdot a \otimes y \cdot a$, $\mathsf{w} : 0 \cdot a \Longrightarrow I$, $\mathsf{m} : x \cdot a \otimes x \cdot b \Longrightarrow x \cdot (a \otimes b)$, *and* $\mathsf{n} : I \Longrightarrow x \cdot I$ *such that*

- *for every object* A *of* $\mathcal{A}$, *the natural transformations* $\mathsf{c}^A, \mathsf{w}^A$ *induced by fixing the parameter* A *in* c, w *make the functor* $x \cdot A : (\mathcal{S}, +, 0) \to \mathcal{A}$ *symmetric comonoidal (i.e. oplax monoidal);*
- *for every object* p *of* $\mathcal{S}$, *the natural transformations* $\mathsf{m}^p, \mathsf{n}^p$ *induced by fixing the parameter* p *in* m, n *make the endofunctor* $p \cdot a$ *of* $\mathcal{A}$ *symmetric monoidal.*

Furthermore, we require 12 *diagrams to commute, which are fairly natural but cannot be included for space reasons.*

Definition 14 (Bounded exponential situation). *A* bounded exponential situation *consists of the following data:*

- *a symmetric monoidal closed category* $(\mathcal{A}, \otimes, I, \multimap)$;
- *a bimonoidal category* $(\mathcal{S}, +, 0, \star, 1)$ *with finite coproducts (not necessarily expressed by* +*) and a terminal object, in which* 0 *is initial;*
- *an exponential action* ! *of* $\mathcal{S}^{\mathrm{op}}$ *on* $\mathcal{A}$, *for which we use the notation* $!_p A$ *(with* p *an object of* $\mathcal{S}$ *and* A *an object of* $\mathcal{A}$*).*

A bounded exponential situation is affine *if* I *is terminal in* $\mathcal{A}$.

An affine bounded exponential situation is enough to interpret the typing rules of ℓRPCF (Fig. 2). The category $\mathcal{S}$ is a "category of bounds": it is the generalization of a structural semiring, in which an arrow $p \to q$ may be seen as a proof that $p \preceq q$. In fact, for the sake of this paper, it does not hurt to assume that $\mathcal{S}$ is just a (preordered) structural semiring, *i.e.*, that the monoidal structures are strict and that there is at most one arrow in every homset.

It is obvious how to interpret each type constructor of ℓRPCF as a functor of $\mathcal{A}$. A typing derivation δ of the judgment $x_1 : B_1, \ldots, x_m : B_m, y_1 : [C_1]_{r_1}, \ldots, y_n : [C_n]_{r_n} \vdash e : A$ is interpreted by an arrow $[\![\delta]\!] : [\![B_1]\!] \otimes \cdots \otimes [\![B_m]\!] \otimes !_{r_1} [\![C_1]\!] \otimes \cdots \otimes !_{r_n} [\![C_n]\!] \to [\![A]\!]$ of $\mathcal{A}$, built by induction on the derivation:

- the interpretation of the rules id, lam and app is standard; the only non-standard feature is the $+$ operation on contexts, which is interpreted by means of the natural transformation c.
- The rule der corresponds to the natural transformation ε. The rule pr is just the application of the endofunctor $!_r(-)$, plus the natural transformations δ and m (if the context has more than one variable) or n (if the context is empty). The let rule is just a composition of morphisms.
- The sub rule is intepreted thanks to the contravariance of the action ! in its first argument: $p \preceq q$ corresponds to the existence of an arrow $f : p \to q$ in $\mathcal{S}$, from which we have an arrow $!_f(\mathrm{id}_A) : !_qA \to !_pA$ in $\mathcal{A}$, implementing subtyping. Free weakening is available because I is the terminal object of $\mathcal{A}$.

The intepretation of the type Nat and the PCF-specific constructions (successor, fixpoint...) require a suitable object and morphisms of $\mathcal{A}$, as usual. The interpretation of co-handlers is also dependent on the specific case, and cannot be defined in general.

Notice that, when $\mathcal{S}$ is the one-object category (which is tivially bimonoidal), then an exponential action is just a comonad $(!, \delta, \varepsilon)$, which is monoidal thanks to the natural transformations m and n. In this degenerated case, the conditions of Definition 13 boil down to asking that the natural transformations $\delta, \varepsilon, \mathsf{c}, \mathsf{w}$ are monoidal; that, for every object A of $\mathcal{A}$, $(!A, \mathsf{c}^A, \mathsf{w}^A)$ is a commutative comonoid in the category of free !-coalgebras of $\mathcal{A}$; and that free coalgebra morphisms (such as δ) are also comonoid morphisms. This amounts to giving a model of linear logic in the sense of [4] (and in fact, when $\mathcal{R}$ is the trivial semiring, $\ell\mathcal{R}\mathsf{PCF}$ is just multiplicative-exponential intuitionistic affine logic).

5   Examples

Before introducing the examples, it is worth noticing the importance of observations and coeffects for the evolution of observable quantities in the abstract machine states. First, note that the state changes only when an observation is performed. So, depending on where we place the observation we can obtain different quantitative information about our programs. Moreover, note that in the evaluation of a co-handler-free program the weight of each stack is always $\mathbf{1}$, so the state of the machine contains only an additive information of the shape $\mathbf{1} + \ldots + \mathbf{1}$, where the number of $\mathbf{1}$'s depends on the number of observations encountered in the evaluation. These two remarks are important for understanding the kind of analysis our framework can perform. Indeed, the observable quantities in the abstract machine states are ultimately the only quantities that the type system is able to analyze thanks to the soundness Theorem 10.

We show here the details of three examples and then we conclude by commenting on other examples. We choose three examples that stress different features of our framework: the first example is a classic of linear type systems—complexity analysis—this is helpful to see that we do not loose anything. The second example is inspired by Uustalu and Vene [38, 39] and Petricek *et al.* [33]—signal processing—this example requires an analysis that is quantitative on $\star$ but not on +, differing so from the previous one. Finally, the third example uses an operational semantics that is probabilistic—probability analysis—this shows that the analysis can be performed even when the underlying semantics changes.

In all cases, we will use one of the structural semirings introduced after Definition 1 and we will always use the same pole (or, rather, instances of a pole parametric in the semiring of choice). We first say that a state of the $\mathcal{K}^{\mathcal{R}}$ machine (C', p') is l-fixpoint-reachable from another state (C, p), and we write $(C, p) \twoheadrightarrow^l (C', p')$, if $(C, p) \rightarrow^* (C', p')$ and l is the number of f-transitions in the computation. Then, we set

$$\bot\!\!\!\bot_{(p,m)} := \{\ C \mid \text{whenever } (C, \mathbf{0}) \twoheadrightarrow^l (C', r),\ l < m \text{ implies } r \preceq p\ \}.$$

This pole expresses the following notion of correctness: a configuration is (p, m)-correct if, when evaluated with the quantity $\mathbf{0}$ and left evolving for a number of steps including strictly less than m recursive calls, produces an observable quantity bounded by p. We leave it as an easy (but instructive) exercise to the reader to show that the above definition gives a pole, for any structural semiring $\mathcal{R}$. The fact that it is adapted may be proved by a straightforward induction on types. Then, we have

Fact 15. *If $\vdash e : A$ with a type derivation δ, then any computation of the form $((e, [], \diamond), \mathbf{0}) \rightarrow^* (C, r)$ satisfies $r \preceq p[\delta]$.*

The above fact, which holds regardless of the chosen semiring, is an immediate consequence of Corollary 11 (we just spelled out the property $(e, [], \diamond) \in \bot\!\!\!\bot_{(p[\delta], \infty)}$ for this particular pole). The exact meaning will depend on the coeffects and on the semiring.

Complexity Analysis. As a warm up we sketch how we can use observations to express a simple complexity analysis for coeffect-free programs inspired by [18, 9]. We want to analyze the complexity (in terms of time) of the execution of a closed term on the $\mathcal{K}^{\mathcal{R}}$ machine. We remark two properties of the machine: first, the evaluation of a program e in an empty environment and an empty stack requires environments containing only subterms of e; second, v-transitions are the only ones[2] that increase the overall size of a configuration[3]. Therefore, if e is a closed, observation- and co-handler-free term and n is the number of v-transitions in the computation from $(e, [], \diamond)$ to its normal form, a good estimate of the time complexity of such a computation is $n \cdot \text{size}(e)$. This requires to compute n, which is precisely the quantity that our type system is able to provide.

First of all, we insert observations around each variable of e, obtaining a term e'. This does not alter the computational behavior of e but ensures that each o-transition is followed by an v-transition, so the number of o-transitions of e', which are the ones we can account for, bounds the number of v-transitions of e. Now, we set $\mathcal{R} := \overline{\mathbb{N}}$, with the usual operations and order. We obviously have that $\vdash e : A$ implies $\vdash e' : A$. Call the latter type derivation δ. Recalling Fact 15,

---

[2] Here we consider co-handler-free programs so there are no x-transitions.

[3] For a suitable notion of configurations size [9].

we have that any computation $((e', [], \diamond), \mathbf{0}) \to^* (C, n)$ satisfies $n \leq p[\delta]$. But, as noted above, n is nothing but the number of o-transitions performed in the computation, which in turn are no less than the v-transitions in the evaluation of e, so $p[\delta] \cdot \mathsf{size}(e)$ is the desired complexity bound.

We observe that our analysis for programs including recursion is very limited: the presence of fixpoints is likely to yield $p[\delta] = \infty$. However, as we will discuss below, we expect our approach to be adaptable to the use of dependent types as in [9].

Signal Processing. The second example we consider is signal processing. We take this example from Petricek *et al.* [33] and show how $\ell\mathcal{R}$PCF provides a bound on the number of *look-ahead* operations each program performs for the given inputs. This enables optimization of memory allocation and buffering needs for each input. To make this example interesting, we add to the language a type Sig representing signals as globally clocked streams of natural numbers. We add to the grammar of $\ell\mathcal{R}$PCF terms non-denumerably many constants $s, s', \ldots$, one for each stream, and the nullary typing rule $\vdash s : \mathsf{Sig}$. We denote by $\underline{n} \cdot s$ the stream whose head is $\underline{n}$ and tail s.

We set $\mathcal{R} := \mathcal{A}$, the arctic semiring. We consider two co-handlers: read, with $A_{\mathsf{read}} = \mathsf{Sig}$, $B_{\mathsf{read}} = \mathsf{Nat}$ and $r_{\mathsf{read}} = 0$, and next, with $A_{\mathsf{next}} = \mathsf{Sig}$, $B_{\mathsf{next}} = \mathsf{Sig}$ and $r_{\mathsf{next}} = 1$. Their semantic maps are defined as follows: $\varphi_{\mathsf{read}}(\underline{n} \cdot s) = \underline{n}$ and $\varphi_{\mathsf{next}}(\underline{n} \cdot s) = s$. In other words, read and next return the head and tail of the stream, respectively. In order to check the semantic condition on φ_{read} and φ_{next} which ensure soundness, we need to define the realizability interpretation of the type Sig. This is done as for Nat: abusing the notations, we set $\mathsf{Sig} := \{ ((s, []), (0, \infty)) \mid \forall \text{ streams } s \}$ and $\|\mathsf{Sig}\| := \mathsf{Sig}^{\perp\perp}$. Now, to prove the soundness of φ_{read}, we need to check that, for all $(\pi, (t, m)) \in \|\mathsf{Nat}\|^{\perp} = \mathsf{Nat}^{\perp}$, we have $(\mathsf{read}.\pi, (t, m)) \in \|\mathsf{Sig}\|^{\perp} = \mathsf{Sig}^{\perp}$. This amounts to checking that, for all $((s, []), (0, \infty)) \in \mathsf{Sig}$, we have $(s, [], \mathsf{read}.\pi) \in \perp\!\!\!\perp_{(w(\mathsf{read}.\pi)+t,m)}$. But $w(\mathsf{read}.\pi) = r_{\mathsf{read}} + w(\pi) = w(\pi)$ (remember that multiplication in $\mathcal{A}$ is addition in $\mathbb{N}$), so this follows by saturation. Similarly, for the soundness of next, let $(\pi, (t, m)) \in \mathsf{Sig}^{\perp}$. We need to check that $(\mathsf{next}.\pi, (t, m)) \in \mathsf{Sig}^{\perp}$, which amounts to verifying that, for every stack constant s, $(s, [], \mathsf{next}.\pi) \in \perp\!\!\!\perp_{(w(\mathsf{next}.\pi)+t,m)}$. Now, we know by saturation that $(s, [], \mathsf{next}.\pi) \in \perp\!\!\!\perp_{(w(\pi)+t,m)}$, but $w(\mathsf{next}.\pi) = 1 + w(\pi)$, so $\perp\!\!\!\perp_{(w(\pi)+t,m)} \subseteq \perp\!\!\!\perp_{(w(\mathsf{next}.\pi)+t,m)}$ by monotonicity, which allows us to conclude.

We are now in position to apply the Soundness Theorem 10. From $\vdash (\!|s|\!) : \mathsf{Sig}$ we have $((s, []), (t, \infty)) \in t \star \|\mathsf{Sig}\|$ for all $t \in \mathbb{N}$. Now, suppose that e is a program (with no observations) with a free variable x, and suppose that $x : [\mathsf{Sig}]_t \vdash e : A$ with a typing derivation δ. Theorem 10 gives us that $(e, [x/(\!|s|\!)], \diamond) \in \perp\!\!\!\perp_{(\max(p[\delta],t),\infty)}$. By observing the soundness function of Fig. 5, we realize that if e contains no observation, then $p[\delta]$ is necessarily $\mathbf{0}$, which is equal to $-\infty$ in $\mathcal{A}$. Therefore, $(e, [x/(\!|s|\!)], \diamond)$ is (t, ∞)-correct. So, any computation starting with $((e, [x/(\!|s|\!)], \diamond), -\infty)$ terminates on a state (C, u) such that $u \leq t$. By looking at the transition rules (Fig. 3), we see that u is the maximum (addition in $\mathcal{A}$ is max) of the number of next co-handlers that were present on the stack (multiplication in $\mathcal{A}$ is addition) at each o-transition. But since e contains no observation, o-transitions are possible only when we access the stack s in the environment, and it is not hard to see that the number of next co-handlers on the stack is the number of look-ahead operations performed on s. Therefore, we have

Fact 16. *If $x : [\mathsf{Sig}]_t \vdash e : A$, then e uses at most the first t values of the stack fed to its argument x.*

We hope that the above result gives an idea of the kind of analysis that may be performed for this application. Other more general results can be obtained by placing observations on different subterms. Also, here we considered only terminating computations but for this application one can use a different pole to allow analysis of non-terminating programs as well.

Probabilistic Usage. We now turn to probabilistic setting. Monadic programming languages have been extensively used for describing probabilistic computations. Here we propose something slightly different. We want to consider the situation in which accessing certain memory locations is subjected to probabilistic failures. For this application, we set $\mathcal{R} = \overline{\mathbb{R}}^+$, the probability semiring, and we consider a single co-handler, coflip, with $A_{\mathsf{coflip}} = \mathbb{N}$, $B_{\mathsf{coflip}} = \mathbb{N}$ and $r_{\mathsf{coflip}} = \lambda \in [0, 1]$. The coeffect map $\varphi_{\mathsf{coflip}}$ is the identity, which is obviously sound. However, we change the operational semantics: the x-transition of the $\mathcal{K}^{\mathcal{R}}$ machine, when coflip is on the stack, is executed with probability λ, whereas with probability $1 - \lambda$ the machine halts because of a failure. When we want to model the fact that a variable x in a program e represents a failure-prone memory location, we replace every occurrence of x in e with $\mathsf{coflip}(x)$.[4]

Consider now a closed program e. We define $\mathsf{var}(e)$ as the number of v-transitions in the computation starting from $(e, [], \diamond)$ before a failure occurs or a normal form is reached. Due to the probabilistic nature of the machine, $\mathsf{var}(e)$ is a random variable with values in $\overline{\mathbb{N}}$. Our type system allows us to estimate the expected value of $\mathsf{var}(e)$. Indeed, given such a closed program e and a configuration C, we may define $\mathsf{obs}(e, C)$ as the number of o-transitions in the computation $(e, [], \diamond) \to^* C$, which is a random variable too. It is not hard to the check that the observable quantity $r \in \mathbb{R}^+$ of the computation $((e, [], \diamond), 0) \to^* (C, r)$ is the expected value of $\mathsf{obs}(e, C)$: every time an o-transition is executed, the quantity λ^n is added to the observable quantity, with n being the number of coflip coeffects on the stack. This is the probability of success, *i.e.*, the probability that the evaluation will "survive" in the current environment.

More generally, we define $\mathsf{obs}(e)$ as the number of o-transitions in the longest computation starting from $(e, [], \diamond)$, and we apply the same decoration used in complexity analysis, *i.e.*, we consider programs obtained by inserting observations around every variable of a program. In this way, we know that, if e' is the decoration of e, $\mathsf{var}(e) \leq \mathsf{obs}(e')$ and therefore, applying Fact 15, we have

Fact 17. *Let e be a program (observation-free) and let $\vdash e : A$ through a typing derivation δ. Then, $p[\delta]$ bounds the expected value of $\mathsf{var}(e)$.*

---

[4] For simplicity we used a single co-handler, with a single probability of failure, but of course any number of co-handlers may be used, each with its own probability λ.

Other Analyses. We presented three examples that are representative of some of the reasoning that may be performed in our framework. Other analyses may be obtained in a similar way. For instance, a liveness analysis like the one of [33] may be obtained by considering the Boolean lattice. Furthermore, the scheduling analysis of [16], which uses a semiring of affine transformations, is another application of our framework, independently developed (we discuss this a bit more in Sect. 6).

More interestingly, also the type system for sensitivity analysis from [35] and the one for non-interference analysis of the SLam calculus [20] can be seen as instances of our calculus. Unfortunately, the realizability semantics is not enough expressive for proving the soundness of these analyses. What we need is a relational version of our realizability technique, which we leave for future investigations.

6   Related Work

Indexed Notions of Monads and Comonads. Several works have extended monads with the aim of reasoning about more general effects: indexed monads [41], parametrised monads [2], layered monads [13], etc. Similarly, we aim at providing a theory to reason about general coeffects. Abadi *et al.* [1] use an indexed monad as a basis for their core calculus of dependencies. Similar to our modalities, their indexed monad is useful to capture dependencies between input and output and so to perform several program analysis. Moreover, they provide a generalized soundness result using domain theory. Tate [37] proposes the notion of *producer* to describe general producer effect systems. Interestingly, his notion can be specialized to capture all the other extensions of monads referred above. Tate also mention the notion of *consumptor*, as dual to producer, and he suggest as an example of consumptor the non-linear use of resources. Our development can be seen as a step in the direction of developing a theory of consumptor. Several effect type systems have been used for program analysis [36, 30]. The common aspect with our work is the use of indices in types to track information about the interaction of the program with the environment.

Uustalu and Vene [38, 39] have proposed a general comonadic approach to programming following the idea of values in context. In particular, they showed how to formulate several context dependent programming models in terms of comonadic computations. Extending this approach, the closest work to our own approach, in the motivations as well as in technical terms is certainly [33, 32]. In these papers, the authors present a coeffect system parametrised over a coeffect algebra that has some remarkable similarities with our notion of structural semiring. The main difference is that while we use two monoids for the different operations in the semiring—plus some additional structure—they use instead a semilattice and a monoid. The semilattice operation is idempotent, so they loose in this way the possibility of being quantitative with respect to this operation. Moreover, they consider "global" comonadic information, *i.e.*, applied to the whole context, whereas our information is "local", *i.e.*, on each variable, as customary in linear logic. The global aspect of their approach forces them to introduce an additional operation $\wedge$ in their algebra, needed to split the information in the case of λ-abstraction, which isolates one variable from the context.

However, this operation has no algebraic requirement and in all of the examples they consider we are able to simulate it by means of subtyping. Finally, the most important difference is that they do not provide any soundness result for the analyses that may be performed using their framework (even though they do provide a categorical model), while we prove a parametric soundness theorem.

Linear Indexed Types. The idea of distinguishing between linear, single-use data and non-linear, reusable data has been one of the reason of the success of linear logic. Less attention has attracted the idea, already presented by Girard in [17], of using indexed approximated modalities $!_n$ for *counting* multiple uses of the same resource. The first real attempt on using this kind of modalities is Bounded Linear Logic [18], where modalities are indexed by polynomial expressions. More recently, indexed modalities similar to the ones studied in the present work have been used in [23, 9] for complexity analysis, in [35, 14] for sensitivity analysis in the context of Differential Privacy, and in [16] for automatic scheduling analysis.

Interestingly, the authors of the latter work, inspired by their previous work [15], introduce an abstract type system that is essentially the call-by-name fragment of our $\ell\mathcal{R}$PCF. They also present a categorical model, less general than ours, and prove a coherence theorem for it. However, they do not prove any form of soundness. Therefore, the present paper and [16] (which will be presented at the same conference) are in a way complementary: that work provides a further, highly interesting example of analysis to which our soundness proof applies.

Other indexed modalities, dubbed "subexponentials", have also been used in [31] with the aim of increasing the expressiveness of linear logic programming. However, this use of indexes seems orthogonal to the one studied in the present paper. Another work that, superficially, seems to be related to ours is [24], where the authors introduced a class of denotational models of linear logic parametrized over continuous semirings. However, the connection does not seem to be very strong, because their technical results are totally different. Indeed, the elements of their semiring are used as coefficients for terms in the language.

Realizability and Logical Relations. Realizability and (unary) logical relations are well-establishe reasoning tools. Step-indexing and biorthogonality (also referred as "TT closure") are technical mechanisms that permit to extend the reasoning to consider languages with potentially infinite computations and to consider different properties of programs in a uniform way. Several works have studied step indexing and biorthogonality, see for instance [5, 34]. The extension of realizability for reasoning about quantitative properties has been pioneered in [21] and further developed in [10, 11]. The realizability we use is in the spirit of the quantitative classical realizability proposed by Brunel [7]. Moreover, we use a combination of quantitative realizability with biorthogonality and step indexing similar to the one of [8] with the difference that here the step-indexing is used as usual to control recursion. A last work that has some similarities with ours is [3]. The authors use indexed types, logical relations and parametricity to achieve invariance under changes of data representation. The invariance allows them to capture program properties in a spirit similar to ours. In particular, also their language is parametrized over a choice of basic data types and primitives.

7   Conclusion and Future Work

In our work we focused on showing how indexed linear types, naturally arising from linear logic semantics, can be used to talk about value in context. This suggests that linear logic semantics can be a unifying framework for several program analyses. Several steps however need to be done. A first simple step is to lift the analysis we have presented here to the standard lambda calculus—this can be done in a rather standard way by using the usual call-by-name and call-by-value translation. Moreover, a type inference algorithm parametrized over constraints in $\mathcal{R}$ can be designed in a natural way following D'Antoni *et al.* [12]. A second and more important step is to broaden the scope of the analysis. Indeed, the analysis for the fixpoint and pattern matching are too limited in practice. For this reason we plan to extend our work with polymorphism and a restricted form of dependent types as in [9, 14]. A point that is worth to stress here is that the realizability semantics we have presented is already able to accommodate some of the future presented there. For instance by interpreting basic constants with non-zero quantities we can accommodate basic indexed types.

Acknowledgments. We are grateful to Emilio Jesús Gallego Arias, Jan Hoffmann, Paul-André Melliès, Dominic Orchard, and Tarmo Uustalu for fruitful discussions. This work benefited from partial support of: ANR, under projects Logoi ANR-2010-BLAN-0213-02 (A. Brunel and D. Mazza) and Coquas ANR-12-JS02-006-01 (D. Mazza); the European Community's Seventh Framework Programme FP7/2007-2013 under grant agreement No. 272487 (M. Gaboardi); DARPA Crash program under Contract No. FA8650-10-C-7090 (A. Brunel). The views expressed are those of the authors and do not reflect the official policy or position of the Department of Defense or the U.S. Government.

References

[1] Abadi, M., Banerjee, A., Heintze, N., Riecke, J.: A core calculus of dependency. In: POPL. ACM (1999)

[2] Atkey, R.: Parameterised notions of computation. JFP 19(3-4) (2009)

[3] Atkey, R., Johann, P., Kennedy, A.: Abstraction and invariance for algebraically indexed types. In: POPL. ACM (2013)

[4] Benton, N., Bierman, G.M., Hyland, J.M.E., de Paiva, V.: Term assignment for intuitionistic linear logic. Technical Report 262, University of Cambridge (1992)

[5] Benton, N., Tabareau, N.: Compiling functional types to relational specifications for low level imperative code. In: TLDI. ACM (2009)

[6] Benton, N., Wadler, P.: Linear logic, monads and the lambda calculus. In: LICS. IEEE (1996)

[7] Brunel, A.: Quantitative classical realizability. Inf. and Comp. (to appear, 2013)

[8] Brunel, A., Madet, A.: Indexed realizability for bounded-time programming with references and type fixpoints. In: Jhala, R., Igarashi, A. (eds.) APLAS 2012. LNCS, vol. 7705, pp. 264–279. Springer, Heidelberg (2012)

[9] Dal Lago, U., Gaboardi, M.: Linear dependent types and relative completeness. In: LICS. IEEE (2011)

[10] Dal Lago, U., Hofmann, M.: Bounded linear logic, revisited. In: Curien, P.-L. (ed.) TLCA 2009. LNCS, vol. 5608, pp. 80–94. Springer, Heidelberg (2009)

[11] Dal Lago, U., Hofmann, M.: Realizability models and implicit complexity. TCS 412(20) (2011)

[12] D'Antoni, L., Gaboardi, M., Gallego Arias, E.J., Haeberlen, A., Pierce, B.: Sensitivity analysis using type-based constraints. In: FPCDSL. ACM (2013)

[13] Filinski, A.: Representing layered monads. In: POPL. ACM (1999)

[14] Gaboardi, M., Haeberlen, A., Hsu, J., Narayan, A., Pierce, B.C.: Linear dependent types for differential privacy. In: POPL. ACM (2013)

[15] Ghica, D.R., Smith, A.: Geometry of synthesis III: Resource management through type inference. In: POPL. ACM (2011)

[16] Ghica, D.R., Smith, A. I.: Bounded linear types in a resource semiring. In: Shao, Z. (ed.) ESOP 2014. LNCS, vol. 8410, pp. 331–350. Springer, Heidelberg (2014)

[17] Girard, J.-Y.: Linear logic. TCS 50(1), 1–102 (1987)

[18] Girard, J.-Y., Scedrov, A., Scott, P.: Bounded linear logic. TCS 97(1) (1992)

[19] Guillou, B.: Strictification of categories weakly enriched in symmetric monoidal categories. Theory and Applications of Categories 24(20), 564–579 (2010)

[20] Heintze, N., Riecke, J.G.: The SLam calculus: Programming with secrecy and integrity. In: POPL. ACM (1998)

[21] Hofmann, M., Scott, P.J.: Realizability models for BLL-like languages. TCS 318(1-2) (2004)

[22] Krivine, J.-L.: A call-by-name lambda-calculus machine. HOSC 20(3) (2007)

[23] Dal Lago, U., Schöpp, U.: Functional programming in sublinear space. In: Gordon, A.D. (ed.) ESOP 2010. LNCS, vol. 6012, pp. 205–225. Springer, Heidelberg (2010)

[24] Laird, J., Manzonetto, G., McCusker, G., Pagani, M.: Weighted relational models of typed lambda-calculi. In: LICS. IEEE (2013)

[25] Laplaza, M.: Coherence for distributivity. Lecture Notes in Math. 281 (1972)

[26] Melliès, P.-A.: Categorical semantics of linear logic. Panoramas et Syntheses (2009)

[27] Melliès, P.-A.: Parametric monads and enriched adjunctions. Technical report (2012), http://www.pps.univ-paris-diderot.fr/~mellies/tensorial-logic/

[28] Melliès, P.-A.: The parametric continuation monad. Mathematical Structures in Computer Science (to appear, 2014)

[29] Moggi, E.: Computational lambda-calculus and monads. In: LICS. IEEE (1989)

[30] Nielson, F., Nielson, H.R., Hankin, C.L.: Principles of Program Analysis. Springer (1999)

[31] Nigam, V., Miller, D.: Algorithmic specifications in linear logic with subexponentials. In: PPDP. ACM (2009)

[32] Orchard, D.: Programming contextual computations, Cambridge University (2013)

[33] Petricek, T., Orchard, D., Mycroft, A.: Coeffects: Unified static analysis of context-dependence. In: Fomin, F.V., Freivalds, R., Kwiatkowska, M., Peleg, D. (eds.) ICALP 2013, Part II. LNCS, vol. 7966, pp. 385–397. Springer, Heidelberg (2013)

[34] Pitts, A.M.: Step-indexed biorthogonality: a tutorial example, Dagstuhl (2010)

[35] Reed, J., Pierce, B.C.: Distance makes the types grow stronger: A calculus for differential privacy. In: ICFP. ACM (2010)

[36] Talpin, J.-P., Jouvelot, P.: The type and effect discipline. In: LICS. IEEE (1992)

[37] Tate, R.: The sequential semantics of producer effect systems. In: POPL (2013)

[38] Uustalu, T., Vene, V.: Signals and comonads. J. UCS 11(7) (2005)

[39] Uustalu, T., Vene, V.: Comonadic notions of computation. ENTCS 203 (2008)

[40] Wadler, P.: The essence of functional programming. In: POPL. ACM (1992)

[41] Wadler, P.: The marriage of effects and monads. In: ICFP. ACM (1998)

Measurements in Proof Nets
as Higher-Order Quantum Circuits

Akira Yoshimizu[1], Ichiro Hasuo[1], Claudia Faggian[2], and Ugo Dal Lago[3]

[1] University of Tokyo, Japan
[2] CNRS and Université Paris Diderot, Paris 7, France
[3] Università di Bologna, Italy

Abstract. We build on the series of work by Dal Lago and coauthors and identify proof nets (of linear logic) as higher-order quantum circuits. By accommodating quantum measurement using additive slices, we obtain a comprehensive framework for programming and interpreting quantum computation. Specifically, we introduce a quantum lambda calculus MLLqm and define its geometry of interaction (GoI) semantics—in the style of token machines—via the translation of terms into proof nets. Its soundness, i.e. invariance under reduction of proof nets, is established. The calculus MLLqm attains a pleasant balance between expressivity (it is higher-order and accommodates all quantum operations) and concreteness of models (given as token machines, i.e. in the form of automata).

1 Introduction

Quantum Programming Languages. Quantum computation and quantum communication have been attracting growing attention. The former achieves real breakthrough in computational power—at least for some classes of problems, such as the integer factorization problem (Shor's algorithm) and search problems. While it is often disputed if quantum computation is physically realizable, quantum communication is close to actual deployment in real-world applications. By exploiting the nonlocal character of quantum phenomena (notably *quantum entanglement*), quantum cryptography protocols accomplish *perfect security* that do not rely on any computational assumptions (like Diffie-Hellman).

Compared to the algorithmic aspects, the theory of *quantum programming* is relatively new. For example, quantum algorithms are most often expressed in *quantum circuits* that lack structuring means like recursion or higher-order functions. Consequently we have seen some proposals for quantum programming languages including QCL [19], quantum lambda calculi [21, 23] and most recently Quipper [10]: QCL is imperative and the others are functional.

Our interests are in a quantum lambda calculus as a prototype of functional quantum programming languages. The functional style comes with several advantages. For one, a type system based on resource-sensitive *linear logic* [6] can force *no-cloning* of quantum states via type safety [23]. Moreover, various techniques for classical functional programming can often be "transferred" to the quantum setting, since they are formulated in an abstract mathematical language and hence are generic. For example,

Z. Shao (Ed.): ESOP 2014, LNCS 8410, pp. 371–391, 2014.

in [11, 16, 21] various semantical techniques in the classical setting—such as linear-nonlinear adjunctions, categorical geometry of interaction, and presheaf completion—are applied to quantum calculi, exploiting the categorical genericity of these techniques.

From Quantum Circuits to Proof Nets. The current work relies on another rich body of techniques that are developed in the linear logic community. Specifically we follow the line of [3, 4] where, roughly speaking,

> proof nets are thought of as *extended quantum circuits.*

Proof nets as devised in [6] are a graphical presentation of linear lambda terms (i.e. linear logic proofs) whose principal concern is reduction of terms (i.e. cut-elimination). Proof nets are "extended quantum circuits" in the following sense: (some) wires in proof nets can be naturally identified with those in quantum circuits; and at the same time higher-order computation is naturally accommodated using a linear type system ($A \multimap B \equiv A^\perp \parr B$). This view is hence a quantum version of the one in [22]. See §3.5 for further discussion.

Once a quantum lambda term is presented as a proof net, the *geometry of interaction (GoI)* interpretation [7]—especially its concrete presentation as *token machines* [14]—gives a concrete and operational interpretation of the term as a state transition system. This is a main advantage of the current "proof net and GoI" approach compared to the categorical one taken in [11, 16]: in the latter models tend to be abstract and huge.

A main disadvantage, however, is that it is harder to interpret extra features in a calculus. Such desired features include recursion and accommodation of duplicable classical data by the ! modality; these are all present e.g. in [11]. In fact, in the preceding work [3, 4] of the current approach, even measurements are excluded from the calculi. Hence important (and basic) examples like quantum teleportation cannot be expressed in their calculi.

Contributions. In the current work we present a comprehensive framework for programming and interpreting higher-order quantum computation based on a linear lambda calculus, proof nets and GoI interpretation. More specifically:

- We introduce MLLqm, a linear lambda calculus with quantum primitives (including measurement, unlike [3, 4]).
- We define a notion of *proof net*, into which terms of MLLqm are translated. For accommodating measurements we follow the idea of *(additive) slices* (see e.g. [8]). We also define the reduction of proof nets and prove that it is strongly normalizing.
- We define *token machine semantics* of MLLqm proof nets and prove that it is *sound*, i.e., is invariant under reduction of proof nets. Here we have multiple tokens in a token machine (this is as in [4]); the slices are suitably handled following the token machine semantics in [13] for additives.

Our framework attains a balance between *expressivity* and *concreteness of models* that we find pleasant. On the one hand, the calculus MLLqm is reasonably expressive: it does include all the quantum operations (preparation, unitary transformation, and most importantly, measurement) and is capable of expressing examples like quantum teleportation, which is not possible in the earlier work [3, 4] of the same proof net approach. Moreover, our framework can naturally express higher-order procedures that are essential e.g. in formalizing *quantum pseudo-telepathy games* in quantum game theory. The latter are attracting attention as a useful presentation of quantum nonlocality (see e.g. [9]). On the other hand, while the languages in [11, 16, 21] are much more expressive—they include duplicable classical data (by the ! modality) and/or recursion—their models given in [11, 16] rely on abstract categorical constructions and it is not trivial to describe them in concrete terms. In contrast, our token machine semantics for MLLqm is given explicitly by a transition system.

The current work shares the same interest as [2], in the sense that both aim at pictorial formalisms for operational structures in quantum computation. We follow the linear logic tradition; an advantage is explicit correspondence with a term calculus. In contrast, [2] employs string diagrams for monoidal categories (more specifically compact closed categories with biproducts). The two approaches are not unrelated: there is a body of literature studying monoidal categories as models of linear logic. See [17] for a survey.

Organization of the Paper. After introducing the calculus MLLqm in §2, in §3 we define MLLqm *proof nets* and translate terms into proof nets. As usual, proof nets are defined to be *proof structures* satisfying a certain correctness criterion. We also define reduction (i.e. cut-elimination) of proof nets. In §4 we give GoI semantics to MLLqm proof nets, in the form of token machines. Our main result is soundness of the GoI semantics, i.e. that it is invariant under reduction of proof nets. Quantum teleportation will exemplify these constructions.

Most of the proofs are deferred to the extended version [24]. Familiarity to linear logic techniques like proof nets and token machine semantics is helpful in reading this paper. Our favorite reference is [20].

2   Syntax of Quantum Lambda Calculus MLLqm

We introduce a typed calculus MLLqm. It is a term calculus based on linear logic—specifically *multiplicative linear logic (MLL)* that has connectives $\otimes$, $\mathbin{\rotatebox[origin=c]{180}{\&}}$ and $(\cdot)^{\perp}$. It is further augmented with quantum primitives that are rich enough to express any *quantum operation*. The latter notion is roughly for "what we can do to quantum states" and can be represented as a combination of *preparation*, *unitary transformation* and *measurement*. See [18, Chap. 8] for more details. The name MLLqm stands for "MLL for quantum computation with measurements."

Definition 2.1 (Types of MLLqm**).** *Types of* MLLqm *are defined by the following BNF:*
$$A, B ::= \mathsf{qbit} \mid \mathsf{qbit}^{\perp} \mid A \otimes B \mid A \mathbin{\rotatebox[origin=c]{180}{\&}} B .$$
The syntactic equality shall be denoted by $\equiv$. As is customary in linear logic, we syntactically identify types according to the following rules: $(A \otimes B)^{\perp} \equiv A^{\perp} \mathbin{\rotatebox[origin=c]{180}{\&}} B^{\perp}$, $(A \mathbin{\rotatebox[origin=c]{180}{\&}} B)^{\perp} \equiv A^{\perp} \otimes B^{\perp}$, and $(A^{\perp})^{\perp} \equiv A$. We write $A \multimap B$ for $A^{\perp} \mathbin{\rotatebox[origin=c]{180}{\&}} B$ and $A^{\otimes n}$ for $(\cdots (A \otimes A) \otimes A) \cdots) \otimes A$ (here $\otimes$ occurs $n - 1$ times).

Definition 2.2 (Terms of MLLqm**).** *Terms of* MLLqm *are defined by:*
$$M, N, L ::= \quad x \mid \lambda x^{A}.M \mid MN \mid \langle M, N \rangle \mid \lambda \langle x^{A}, y^{B} \rangle.M$$
$$\mid \mathsf{new}_{|\varphi\rangle} \mid \mathsf{U} \mid \mathsf{if\ meas}\ M\ \mathsf{then}\ N\ \mathsf{else}\ L\ .$$
Here x is an element of a fixed countable set **Var** *of variables.* $\mathsf{new}_{|\varphi\rangle}$ *is a constant for each normalized vector $|\varphi\rangle$ in $\mathbb{C}^{2}$ and designates preparation of a qubit.* U *is a constant*

for each 2^n-dimension unitary matrix, where $n \in \mathbb{N}$. Measurements meas *occur only in conditionals. Note that in variable binders λx^A and $\lambda\langle x^A, y^B\rangle$, variables x, y come with explicit type labels. This is to ensure Lem. 2.5.*

Remark 2.3. *The constructor* if meas M then N else L *is intended for "classical control": operationally, the qubit represented by M is* actually measured *before going on to evaluate N or L.*

This is not to be confused with "quantum control." In quantum circuits, it is well-known that any measurement can be postponed to the end of a circuit (the principle of deferred measurement, *[18, §4.4]). This is possible by use of* controlled operations *like* CNOT *[18, §4.3]. We shall stick to classical control because, in the current higher-order setting, it is not clear how to simulate classical control by quantum control, or how to systematically construct quantum controlled operations.*

Definition 2.4 (Typing rules of MLLqm). *Typing rules of MLLqm are shown below. A context Γ in a type judgment is a set $\{x_1 : A_1, \ldots, x_n : A_n\}$ of variables and their types. We write its* domain $\{x_1, \ldots, x_n\}$ *as $|\Gamma|$. The juxtaposition Γ, Δ of contexts denotes their union and we assume $|\Gamma| \cap |\Delta| = \emptyset$.*

$$\frac{}{x : A \vdash x : A} \text{ ax} \qquad \frac{\Gamma, x : A \vdash M : B}{\Gamma \vdash \lambda x^A.M : A \multimap B} \multimap I_1 \qquad \frac{\Gamma, x : A, y : B \vdash M : C}{\Gamma \vdash \lambda\langle x^A, y^B\rangle.M : A \otimes B \multimap C} \multimap I_2$$

$$\frac{\Gamma \vdash M : A \multimap B \quad \Delta \vdash N : A}{\Gamma, \Delta \vdash MN : B} \multimap E \qquad \frac{\Gamma \vdash M : A \quad \Delta \vdash N : B}{\Gamma, \Delta \vdash \langle M, N\rangle : A \otimes B} \otimes I$$

$$\frac{}{\vdash \mathsf{new}_{|\varphi\rangle} : \mathsf{qbit}} \text{ new} \qquad \frac{}{\vdash \mathsf{U} : \mathsf{qbit}^{\otimes n} \multimap \mathsf{qbit}^{\otimes n}} \mathsf{U}_n$$

$$\frac{\Gamma \vdash M : \mathsf{qbit} \quad \Delta \vdash N : A \quad \Delta \vdash L : A}{\Gamma, \Delta \vdash \text{ if meas } M \text{ then } N \text{ else } L : A} \text{ meas}$$

The rule $\multimap I_2$ replaces the usual $\otimes E$ rule that is problematic in the current linear setting. The following will enable inductive translation of terms into proof nets.

Lemma 2.5. *A derivable type judgment $\Gamma \vdash M : A$ has a unique derivation.* □

3   MLL Proof Nets with Quantum Nodes

In this section we introduce the notion of proof nets tailored for the calculus MLLqm. It is based on MLL proof nets [6] (see also [20]) and has additional nodes that correspond to quantum primitives (preparation, unitary transformation and measurement). Among them, (conditionals based on) measurements are the most challenging to model; we follow the idea of *additive slices* that are successfully utilized e.g. in [15].

As usual, we start with the notion of *proof structures* as graphs consisting of certain nodes. Then *proof nets* are defined to be those proof structures which comply with a *correctness criterion* (like Danos & Regnier's in [5]). We define translation of MLLqm terms into proof structures, which we prove to be proof nets. Moreover, we define reduction of proof structures, which we think of as one operational semantics of MLLqm terms. It is shown that proof nets are reduced to proof nets, and that reduction of proof nets is strongly normalizing (SN). Note that recursion is not in MLLqm.

3.1 MLLqm Proof Structures

In addition to the usual nodes in MLL proof nets, we introduce three kinds of nodes for quantum computation: new (preparation of a single qubit), U (unitary transformations/gates), and if (conditionals according to measurement of a qubit). An if node is as shown on the right. It is like a *box* in standard proof nets.

an if node

An if node will appear in a proof structure in the form where the two dashed boxes on its top are filled with "internal" proof structures. Such a combination of an if node and two (internal) proof structures shall be called a meas *node*. Overall, in MLLqm proof structures we allow the following seven kinds of nodes (Fig. 1).

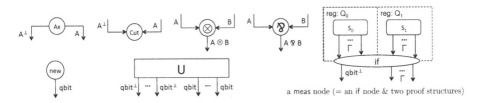

a meas node (= an if node & two proof structures)

Fig. 1. Nodes of MLLqm proof structures

Note that nodes and proof structures are defined by mutual induction: in a proof structure there is a meas node, in whose dashed boxes there are other internal proof structures, and so on. We will make this precise in Def. 3.1. In Fig. 1, a unitary gate node for a 2^n-dimension unitary matrix U has n-many qbit edges and n-many qbit$^\perp$ edges. Γ denotes a finite sequence of types. In a meas node, the qbit$^\perp$-typed edge sticking out to the down-left is called a *query edge*.

As usual, incoming edges of a node are called *premises* and outgoing edges are called *conclusions*. A proof structure is roughly a graph that consists of nodes in Fig. 1, and

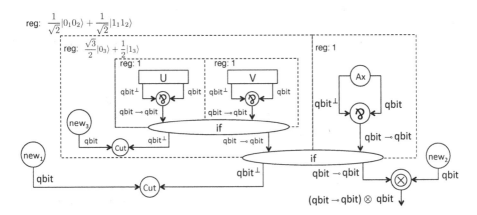

Fig. 2. An example of proof structure

is augmented with a quantum state called a *quantum register*, whose functionality we shall explain by an example.

See Fig. 2. The outermost proof structure (we say it is of *level* 0) has two new nodes, a cut node, a ⊗ node and a meas node. Its quantum register is a state of a 2-qubit system; each qubit corresponds to a certain new node and the correspondence is designated by indices. Therefore our intention is that each proof structure has a quantum register whose size is the number of new nodes, and that the proof structure explicitly carries the content of the quantum register. Such pairing of computational structure (proof structures here) and quantum registers is inspired by the operational semantics of [21], where a term of a calculus and a quantum state together form a quantum closure.

Definition 3.1 (MLLqm **proof structure**). *Let S be a directed finite graph consisting of nodes in Fig. 1; Q be a quantum register of length $n \in \mathbb{N}$ (that is, a normalized vector in $\mathbb{C}^{2^n}$); k be the number of new nodes in S; and l be a bijection $\{$the new nodes in $S\} \xrightarrow{\cong} \{1, 2, \dots, k\}$. A triple (S, Q, l) satisfying*

- *each edge in S is well-typed;*
- *no incoming edge in S is dangling; and*
- *$n = k$*

is called a proof structure. *The types on the dangling outgoing edges in S are called the* conclusions *of S.*

Let (S_0, Q_0, l_0) and (S_1, Q_1, l_1) be proof structures with the same conclusions, say Γ. We call a triple $\big($if node, $(S_0, Q_0, l_0), (S_1, Q_1, l_1)\big)$ a meas node *and regard it as a node with conclusions* qbit$^\perp$, Γ. *Each of the proof structures (S_0, Q_0, l_0) and (S_1, Q_1, l_1) is called a* branch *of the* meas *node.*

The outermost proof structure is said to be of level 0 *and the branches of a* meas *node of level n are said to be of* level $n + 1$.

We emphasize again that the above definitions of proof structures and meas nodes are mutually inductive. We allow meas nodes nested only finitely many times. The bijection l in a proof structure (S, Q, l) gives indices to new nodes and designates correspondences between new nodes and qubits in a quantum register Q.

For example, in Fig. 2 the unitary gate nodes U and V belong to level 2. The quantum state that corresponds to the node new$_3$ is in the level-1 register. Note that it is invisible from level 0.

Finally we define *slices* for MLLqm proof structures, like usual additive slices. We will employ this notion later in §4.

Definition 3.2 (Slicing and slices). *Let $\mathcal{N} = (S, Q, l)$ be an MLLqm proof structure. A slicing is a function $b : \{$all if nodes in S (of any level)$\} \to \{0, 1\}$. Abusing notation, a slice $b(\mathcal{N})$ is a graph obtained by deleting the unselected branch of each* if *node according to the slicing b, i.e. if $b(v) = 0$ delete the branch on the right and if $b(v) = 1$ delete the branch on the left for each* if *node v. Note that a slice is not a proof structure.*

3.2 Reduction of MLLqm Proof Structures

We now introduce reduction rules for MLLqm proof structures. Following the Curry-Howard intuition that normalization of a proof is computation, a reduction step is thought of as a step in quantum computation.

Definition 3.3 (Reduction rules of MLLqm proof structures). Reduction rules *are shown in Fig. 3. The first two are standard in MLL proof nets; the latter three are new. In the unitary gate rule, the unitary matrix* $U^{j_1,\dots,j_m}$ *acts on* $j_1,\dots,j_m$-*th qubits in the same way as* U *does, and leaves other qubits unchanged. The last two rules occur probabilistically, where the resulting quantum registers* $|\varphi'_0\rangle, |\varphi'_1\rangle$ *and probabilities* $\sum_j |\alpha_j|^2, \sum_j |\beta_j|^2$ *defined in the obvious way. Explicitly:*

$$|\varphi_0\rangle = \sum_j \alpha_j \left(|\psi_j^0\rangle \otimes |0\rangle \otimes |\chi_j^0\rangle\right), \quad |\varphi'_0\rangle = \sum_j \frac{\alpha_j}{\sqrt{\sum_k |\alpha_k|^2}} \left(|\psi_j^0\rangle \otimes |\chi_j^0\rangle\right),$$
$$|\varphi_1\rangle = \sum_j \beta_j \left(|\psi_j^1\rangle \otimes |1\rangle \otimes |\chi_j^1\rangle\right), \quad |\varphi'_1\rangle = \sum_j \frac{\beta_j}{\sqrt{\sum_k |\beta_k|^2}} \left(|\psi_j^1\rangle \otimes |\chi_j^1\rangle\right),$$

$$(1)$$

where $|\psi_j^b\rangle$ *of length* $m-1$ *and* m *is the index of the* new *node that is measured. The other rules occur with probability* 1. *In* meas *rules, the indexing function* l *is suitably updated too.*

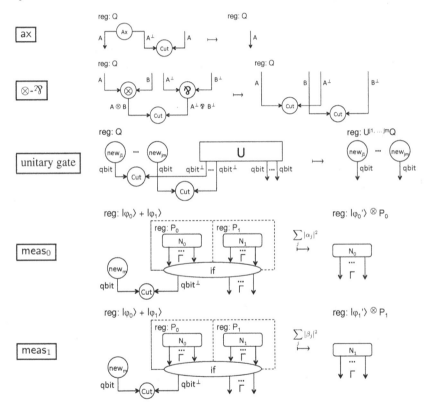

Fig. 3. Reduction rules of MLLqm proof structures

3.3   MLLqm Proof Nets and the Correctness Criterion

Our view of MLLqm proof structures is that they are "extended quantum circuits" that allow formalization of higher-order quantum computation.

As usual with proof structures, however, Def. 3.1 does not exclude proof structures that carries no computational contents—to put it technically, those which have cut nodes that cannot be eliminated. This is mainly due to vicious "feedback loops," as seen in the proof structure on the right. We exclude such feedback loops by imposing a *correctness criterion* that is similar to Danos and Regnier's "connected and acyclic" one [5]. Then *proof nets* are proof structures that comply with the correctness criterion.

In the current quantum setting the challenge is to devise a graph-theoretic correctness condition for unitary gate nodes. We follow the idea in [4].

Definition 3.4 (Correctness graphs with quantum nodes). *Let* $\mathcal{N} = (\mathcal{S}, \mathcal{Q}, l)$ *be a proof structure. A* correctness graph *of* $\mathcal{N}$ *is an undirected graph obtained by applying the following operations to* $\mathcal{S}$.

- *Ignore directions of all edges.*
- *For each* $\mathfrak{N}$ *node, choose one of the two premises and disconnect the other.*
- *For each unitary gate node, choose an arbitrary bijective correspondence between the sets of* qbit$^\perp$ *edges and* qbit *edges. Remove the node and connect each correspondent pair of edges.*
- *For each* meas *node, ignore its branches.*

Here is an example. The correctness graphs for the proof structure on the right are the four undirected graphs below. There are two choices for the $\mathfrak{N}$ node and two for the unitary gate node.

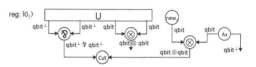

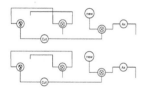
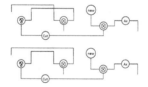

Definition 3.5 (MLLqm **proof nets**). *A correctness graph is said to* satisfy the correctness criterion *if it is acyclic and connected.*

A proof structure $\mathcal{N}$ *is called a* proof net *if each of its correctness graphs satisfies the correctness criterion and every branch in it is a proof net.*

Lemma 3.6. *If a proof net* $\mathcal{N}$ *reduces to another proof structure* $\mathcal{N}'$ *(according to the rules in Def. 3.3), then* $\mathcal{N}'$ *is also a proof net.*   □

3.4   Translation of MLLqm Terms into Proof Nets

We assign a proof structure $[\![\Gamma \vdash M : A]\!]$ to each derivable type judgment $\Gamma \vdash M : A$. This turns out to satisfy the correctness criterion. Lem. 2.5 allows for the definition of $[\![\Gamma \vdash M : A]\!]$ by induction on derivation.

Definition 3.7 (Translation of terms into proof nets). *For each derivable type judgment* $\Gamma \vdash M : A$*, a proof structure* $[\![\Gamma \vdash M : A]\!]$ *is defined inductively as in Fig. 4–5.*

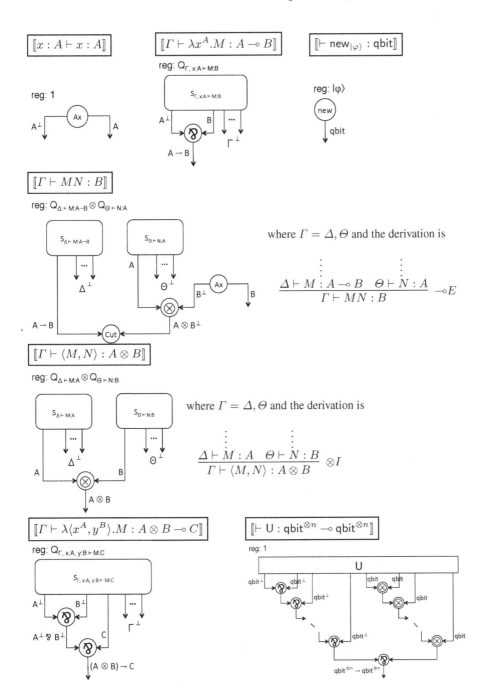

Fig. 4. Proof net translation of MLLqm terms—part I

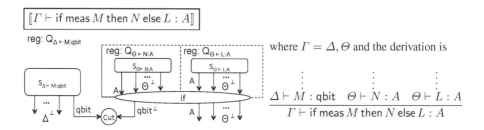

Fig. 5. Proof net translation of MLLqm terms—part II

Here we let $[\![\Gamma \vdash M : A]\!] = (\mathcal{S}_{\Gamma\vdash M:A}, Q_{\Gamma\vdash M:A}, l_{\Gamma\vdash M:A})$; and Γ denotes a sequence $A_1, A_2, \ldots, A_n$ of types. In each case, the types A_j in the context Γ of $\Gamma \vdash M : A$ appear as their dual $A_j{}^\perp$ in the conclusions of $\mathcal{S}_{\Gamma\vdash M:A}$.

The indexing l between new nodes and quantum registers are merged in the obvious way, in the cases of $[\![\Gamma \vdash \langle M, N\rangle : A \otimes B]\!]$ and $[\![\Gamma \vdash MN : B]\!]$.

Lemma 3.8. *For any derivable type judgment* $\Gamma \vdash M : A$*, the proof structure* $[\![\Gamma \vdash M : A]\!]$ *is a proof net.* ☐

Hence, regarding MLLqm proof structures as a rewriting system for quantum computation, it is sufficient to consider solely proof nets. This rewriting system exhibits the following pleasant properties (Thm. 3.9–3.10).

Theorem 3.9 (Termination of reduction). *The reduction of* MLLqm *proof nets is terminating.* ☐

Regarding reduction of proof nets as cut elimination, it is natural to expect all the cut nodes to disappear after reduction terminates. This is unfortunately not the case and we have the following restricted result (Thm. 3.10). The condition in Thm. 3.10 corresponds to the condition that a term of MLLqm is *closed*, i.e. has no free variable. Intuitively, it states that a proof net "executes all computation steps" if the whole input is given.

Theorem 3.10 (Strong normalization). *Let* $\mathcal{N} = (\mathcal{S}, Q, l)$ *be an* MLLqm *proof net. If no type containing* qbit$^\perp$ *occurs in the conclusions of* $\mathcal{S}$*, then every maximal sequence of reductions from* $\mathcal{N}$ *reaches a proof net that contains no cut nodes, no unitary gate nodes, or no* if *nodes.* ☐

Remark 3.11. *For MLL proof nets, one of the purposes to introduce correctness criteria in [5,6] is to characterize those proof structures which arise from some proof in sequent calculus. Therefore the converse of Lem. 3.8—so-called* sequentialization—*is also proved in [6]. It allows (re)construction of sequent calculus proofs from proof nets.*

However, sequentialization fails for MLLqm*. Consider the following reduction; the original proof net is the translation of the term* CNOT$\langle$new$_{|0\rangle}$, new$_{|0\rangle}\rangle$*.*

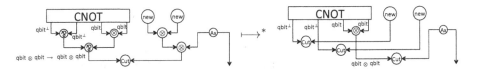

After two $\otimes$-$\mathfrak{N}$ reductions we do not yet get rid of the CNOT node; it is easily seen that there is no MLLqm term that gives rise to the resulting proof net.

This is a phenomenon that reflects the nonlocal character of MLLqm; and ultimately the nonlocality of quantum entanglement is to blame.

Sequentialization fails in general. Those proof nets which are sequentializable include: the net $\llbracket \Gamma \vdash M : A \rrbracket$ (trivially); and the normal form of the net $\llbracket \Gamma \vdash M : A \rrbracket$ for a closed term M. The latter is because Thm. 3.10 says that in that case the normal form is merely an MLL proof net with new nodes.

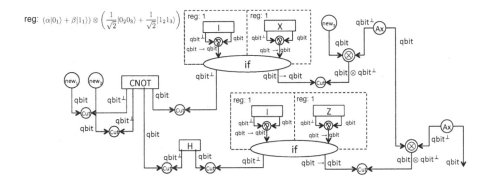

Fig. 6. Quantum teleportation (after some reductions irrelevant to the quantum part)

3.5 Examples and Discussion

As syntax sugar we write $\langle x_1, x_2, x_3 \rangle \equiv \langle x_1, \langle x_2, x_3 \rangle \rangle$ and $\lambda \langle x_1^{A_1}, x_2^{A_2}, x_3^{A_3} \rangle . M \equiv \lambda \langle x_1^{A_1}, y^{A_2 \otimes A_3} \rangle . ((\lambda \langle x_2^{A_2}, x_3^{A_3} \rangle . M) y)$, where y is a fresh variable. Let

$B := \lambda \langle x^{\mathsf{qbit}}, y^{\mathsf{qbit}}, z^{\mathsf{qbit}} \rangle . \Big((\lambda \langle v^{\mathsf{qbit}}, w^{\mathsf{qbit}} \rangle . \langle \mathsf{H} v, w, z \rangle)(\mathsf{CNOT} \langle x, y \rangle) \Big)$,

$C := \lambda \langle s^{\mathsf{qbit}}, t^{\mathsf{qbit}}, u^{\mathsf{qbit}} \rangle . (\text{if meas } s \text{ then } \mathsf{Z} \text{ else } \mathsf{I}) \big((\text{if meas } t \text{ then } \mathsf{X} \text{ else } \mathsf{I}) u \big)$, and

$\beta_{00} := \mathsf{CNOT} \langle \mathsf{H} \, \mathsf{new}_{|0\rangle}, \mathsf{new}_{|0\rangle} \rangle$

where H is the Hadamard gate, CNOT is the controlled not gate, I is the identity matrix, and Z and X are the Pauli matrices. The term β_{00} denotes one of the Bell state; and the terms B and C represent the quantum circuits on the right, respectively. Quantum teleportation of one qubit $\alpha|0\rangle + \beta|1\rangle$ (where $\alpha, \beta \in \mathbb{C}$) is then described as a MLLqm term $T := \big(\lambda x^{\mathsf{qbit}} . C(B \langle x, \beta_{00} \rangle) \big) \, \mathsf{new}_{\alpha|0\rangle + \beta|1\rangle}$.

The term T is closed and has the type qbit. Its proof net translation $\llbracket \vdash T : \mathsf{qbit} \rrbracket$, after some reductions that are irrelevant to the quantum part, is shown in Fig. 6.

It is not hard to notice the similarity between the proof net in Fig. 6 and the presentation by a quantum circuit. In general, when we translate a first-order MLLqm term the resulting proof net looks quite much like a quantum circuit. Notice that the term T is indeed first-order.

It is when higher-order functions are involved that our linear logic based approach shows its real advantage. For example, the proof net in the figure below receives a transformation $\mathcal{E}$ of a qubit into a qubit as an input; and feeds $\mathcal{E}$ with either $H|\varphi\rangle$ or $|\psi\rangle$, according to the outcome of the measurement of $|\chi\rangle$. (It is straightforward to write down an MLLqm term that gives rise to this proof net. Explicitly, the term is:

if meas new$_{|\chi\rangle}$ then $(\lambda f^{\text{qbit}\multimap\text{qbit}}.f\,(\text{H new}_{|\phi\rangle}))$ else $(\lambda f^{\text{qbit}\multimap\text{qbit}}.f\,\text{new}_{|\psi\rangle})$.) This is a "quantum circuit with a hole," so to speak; our current MLLqm framework can express, execute and reason about such procedures in a structural manner.

4 Token Machine Semantics for MLLqm Proof Nets

In this section we go on to introduce token machine semantics for MLLqm proof nets and prove its soundness, that is, the semantics is invariant under reduction of proof nets.

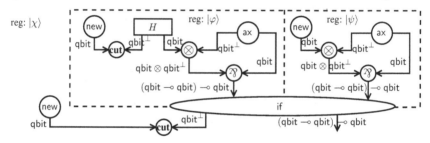

Token machines are one presentation of Girard's *geometry of interaction* [7]. Unlike the original presentation by C^*-algebras, token machines as devised in [14] are (concrete) automata and carry a strong operational flavor. For more details see [20].

The MLLqm token machines are different from the usual MLL ones in that it employs multiple tokens. Intuitively one token corresponds to one qubit; and they are required to synchronize when they go beyond a unitary gate node. This is one way how quantum entanglement (hence nonlocality) can be taken care of in token machine semantics. Use of multiple tokens is already in [4] where the style is called *wave-style token machine*. Multiple tokens inevitably results in *nondeterminism* in small-step behaviors of machines (which token moves first?). We prove confluence of small-step behaviors, and also uniqueness of big-step behaviors as its consequence. This is like in [4].

In the current work we go beyond [4] and interpret measurements too. For that purpose we rely on the ideas developed in linear logic towards accommodating additive connectives: namely *(additive) slicing* of proof nets, and *weights* in token machines. See e.g. [8, 13].

4.1 Tokens

We start with usual definitions. We follow [13] most closely. The presentation in [20] is essentially the same.

Definition 4.1 (Context). *A* context *is defined by the following BNF:*
$$C ::= [\,] \mid C \otimes A \mid A \otimes C \mid C \,\mathregular{⅋}\, A \mid A \,\mathregular{⅋}\, C \ ,$$
where A is a type of MLLqm. *Note that every context has exactly one* hole $[\,]$. *The type obtained by substituting a type A for the hole in a context C is denoted by $C[A]$. A context C is called a* context for A *if the type A is obtained by substituting some type B for the hole $[\,]$, i.e. $A \equiv C[B]$. The negation $C^{\perp}$ of a context C is defined in a natural way, e.g.* $(\mathsf{qbit} \otimes [\,])^{\perp} := \mathsf{qbit}^{\perp} \,\mathregular{⅋}\, [\,]$.

Definition 4.2 (Token). *Given a proof net $\mathcal{N} = (\mathcal{S}, \mathcal{Q}, l)$, a* token *is a 4-tuple (A, C, D, ζ) where*
- *A is an edge of $\mathcal{S}$ (we abuse notations and identify an edge and the type occurrence A assigned to it; no confusion is likely),*
- *C is a context for A,*
- *D is a* direction, *that is an element of $\{\Uparrow, \Downarrow\}$, and*
- *$\zeta \in \mathbb{N}$.*

Intuitively, a token is a particle moving around the given proof net. The type occurrence A of a token indicates on which edge the token is. The context C designates which base type in A the token is concerned about. An example is $A \equiv \mathsf{qbit}^{\perp} \,\mathregular{⅋}\, \mathsf{qbit}$ and $C \equiv [\,] \,\mathregular{⅋}\, \mathsf{qbit}$; token machine semantics is defined in such a way that a token's context determines which edge to take when the token hits a fork, namely a $\mathregular{⅋}$ node. The direction D of a token specifies whether it is going up or down along the edge.

Finally, the natural number ζ is a feature that is not in usual MLL proof nets: it records to which qubit of a quantum register the token corresponds. When a token is deployed the initial value of ζ is 0, meaning that the token does not yet know which qubit it corresponds to. When it hits a new node new_j, its index j is recorded in ζ.

4.2 The Token Machine $\mathcal{T}_{\mathcal{N}}$

Our goal is to construct a transition system (called a *token machine*) $\mathcal{T}_{\mathcal{N}}$ for a given MLLqm proof net $\mathcal{N}$. As an example, one state of the token machine is depicted below.

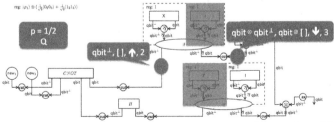

A state of $\mathcal{T}_{\mathcal{N}}$ is roughly the data that specifies the tokens in the proof net $\mathcal{N}$ (how many of them, their locations, their contexts, etc.).

In the current setting of MLLqm a state carries much more data, in fact. For example it has a slicing, which is depicted by hatching the unselected branches in the above figure. It may feel strange that the selection of branches are specified even before the relevant qubits are measured: a *probability*—that is also carried by a state of a token machine ($p = 1/2$ in the above figure)—represents the likelihood of the slicing actually taken. The formal definition is as follows.

Definition 4.3 (State). *Given a proof net* $\mathcal{N} = (\mathcal{S}, Q_{\mathcal{N}}, l)$, *a state of the token machine* $\mathcal{T}_{\mathcal{N}}$ *is a 5-tuple* $(Q, p, b, T_{\mathsf{pr}}, T_{\mathsf{ms}})$ *where*

- *Q is a quantum register,*
- *p is a probability, i.e. a real number satisfying* $0 \leq p \leq 1$,
- *b is a slicing,*
- T_{pr} *is a finite set of tokens (called* principal *tokens),*
- T_{ms} *is another finite set of tokens (called* measurement *tokens).*

A quantum register Q of a state is related to $Q_{\mathcal{N}}$ (that of the proof net) but not necessarily the same—this will be clarified by definitions below of the transition relation and the initial states of $\mathcal{T}_{\mathcal{N}}$.

We go on to define the transition structure $\to_{\mathcal{N}}$ of $\mathcal{T}_{\mathcal{N}}$ (Def. 4.4). We note that transitions $\to_{\mathcal{N}}$ form a binary relation between states—without any labels or probabilities assigned to transitions. Hence $\mathcal{T}_{\mathcal{N}}$ is simply a Kripke frame. We shall refer to the transitions $\to_{\mathcal{N}}$ in $\mathcal{T}_{\mathcal{N}}$ also as the *small-step semantics* of $\mathcal{T}_{\mathcal{N}}$.

The rules in Def. 4.4 are fairly complicated so their intuitions are stated first. The rules mainly describe how token(s) "move around the net." Almost every rule moves only one token. An exception is the U-Apply rule: it makes tokens "synchronized" and moves them at once. The if-Meas rule deletes one measurement token. The U-Apply and if-Meas rules also act on the quantum register and the probability of a state, reflecting the quantum effects of the corresponding operations. A slicing b is left untouched by transitions.

Definition 4.4 (Transition $\to_{\mathcal{N}}$ of the token machine $\mathcal{T}_{\mathcal{N}}$). *The transition relation* $\to_{\mathcal{N}}$ *between states of the token machine* $\mathcal{T}_{\mathcal{N}}$ *is defined by the rules as in Fig. 7–8. Each rule except the U-Apply and if-Meas rules is divided into two rules, one for principal tokens and the other for measurement tokens.*

For each rule, we informally depict the intended movement of token(s) too.

Hatching over a branch means the branch is not selected by the slicing.

Lemma 4.5 (One-step confluence). *Let* $\mathcal{N} = (\mathcal{S}, Q, l)$ *be an* MLLqm *proof net. The transition relation* $\to_{\mathcal{N}}$ *of its token machine* $\mathcal{T}_{\mathcal{N}}$ *is one-step confluent. That is, if both* $s \to_{\mathcal{N}} s_1$ *and* $s \to_{\mathcal{N}} s_2$ *hold, then either* $s_1 = s_2$ *or there exists a state* s' *such that* $s_1 \to_{\mathcal{N}} s'$ *and* $s_2 \to_{\mathcal{N}} s'$. □

4.3 Big-Step Semantics of $\mathcal{T}_{\mathcal{N}}$

We identify the "computational content" of a proof net $\mathcal{N}$ to be the *big-step semantics* of the token machine $\mathcal{T}_{\mathcal{N}}$ that is defined below. The big-step semantics is intuitively the correspondence between an *initial state* $s \in I_{\mathcal{N}}$ and a *final state* $s' \in F_{\mathcal{N}}$, such

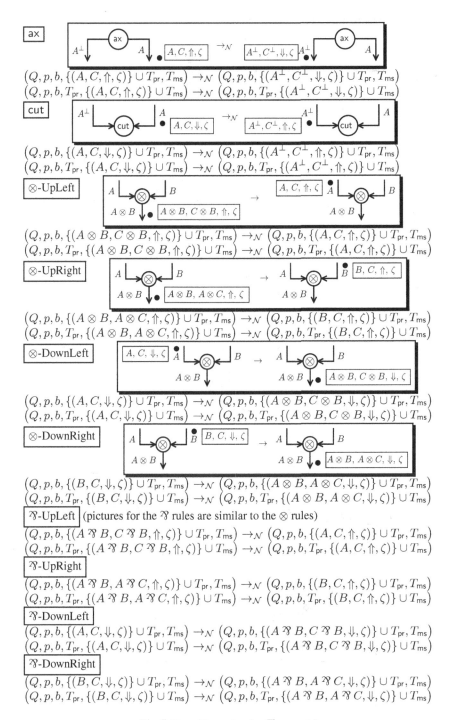

$(Q,p,b,\{(A,C,\Uparrow,\zeta)\}\cup T_{\mathsf{pr}},T_{\mathsf{ms}}) \to_{\mathcal{N}} (Q,p,b,\{(A^\perp,C^\perp,\Downarrow,\zeta)\}\cup T_{\mathsf{pr}},T_{\mathsf{ms}})$

$(Q,p,b,T_{\mathsf{pr}},\{(A,C,\Uparrow,\zeta)\}\cup T_{\mathsf{ms}}) \to_{\mathcal{N}} (Q,p,b,T_{\mathsf{pr}},\{(A^\perp,C^\perp,\Downarrow,\zeta)\}\cup T_{\mathsf{ms}})$

$(Q,p,b,\{(A,C,\Downarrow,\zeta)\}\cup T_{\mathsf{pr}},T_{\mathsf{ms}}) \to_{\mathcal{N}} (Q,p,b,\{(A^\perp,C^\perp,\Uparrow,\zeta)\}\cup T_{\mathsf{pr}},T_{\mathsf{ms}})$

$(Q,p,b,T_{\mathsf{pr}},\{(A,C,\Downarrow,\zeta)\}\cup T_{\mathsf{ms}}) \to_{\mathcal{N}} (Q,p,b,T_{\mathsf{pr}},\{(A^\perp,C^\perp,\Uparrow,\zeta)\}\cup T_{\mathsf{ms}})$

$(Q,p,b,\{(A\otimes B,C\otimes B,\Uparrow,\zeta)\}\cup T_{\mathsf{pr}},T_{\mathsf{ms}}) \to_{\mathcal{N}} (Q,p,b,\{(A,C,\Uparrow,\zeta)\}\cup T_{\mathsf{pr}},T_{\mathsf{ms}})$

$(Q,p,b,T_{\mathsf{pr}},\{(A\otimes B,C\otimes B,\Uparrow,\zeta)\}\cup T_{\mathsf{ms}}) \to_{\mathcal{N}} (Q,p,b,T_{\mathsf{pr}},\{(A,C,\Uparrow,\zeta)\}\cup T_{\mathsf{ms}})$

$(Q,p,b,\{(A\otimes B,A\otimes C,\Uparrow,\zeta)\}\cup T_{\mathsf{pr}},T_{\mathsf{ms}}) \to_{\mathcal{N}} (Q,p,b,\{(B,C,\Uparrow,\zeta)\}\cup T_{\mathsf{pr}},T_{\mathsf{ms}})$

$(Q,p,b,T_{\mathsf{pr}},\{(A\otimes B,A\otimes C,\Uparrow,\zeta)\}\cup T_{\mathsf{ms}}) \to_{\mathcal{N}} (Q,p,b,T_{\mathsf{pr}},\{(B,C,\Uparrow,\zeta)\}\cup T_{\mathsf{ms}})$

$(Q,p,b,\{(A,C,\Downarrow,\zeta)\}\cup T_{\mathsf{pr}},T_{\mathsf{ms}}) \to_{\mathcal{N}} (Q,p,b,\{(A\otimes B,C\otimes B,\Downarrow,\zeta)\}\cup T_{\mathsf{pr}},T_{\mathsf{ms}})$

$(Q,p,b,T_{\mathsf{pr}},\{(A,C,\Downarrow,\zeta)\}\cup T_{\mathsf{ms}}) \to_{\mathcal{N}} (Q,p,b,T_{\mathsf{pr}},\{(A\otimes B,C\otimes B,\Downarrow,\zeta)\}\cup T_{\mathsf{ms}})$

$(Q,p,b,\{(B,C,\Downarrow,\zeta)\}\cup T_{\mathsf{pr}},T_{\mathsf{ms}}) \to_{\mathcal{N}} (Q,p,b,\{(A\otimes B,A\otimes C,\Downarrow,\zeta)\}\cup T_{\mathsf{pr}},T_{\mathsf{ms}})$

$(Q,p,b,T_{\mathsf{pr}},\{(B,C,\Downarrow,\zeta)\}\cup T_{\mathsf{ms}}) \to_{\mathcal{N}} (Q,p,b,T_{\mathsf{pr}},\{(A\otimes B,A\otimes C,\Downarrow,\zeta)\}\cup T_{\mathsf{ms}})$

⅋-UpLeft (pictures for the ⅋ rules are similar to the ⊗ rules)

$(Q,p,b,\{(A\,⅋\,B,C\,⅋\,B,\Uparrow,\zeta)\}\cup T_{\mathsf{pr}},T_{\mathsf{ms}}) \to_{\mathcal{N}} (Q,p,b,\{(A,C,\Uparrow,\zeta)\}\cup T_{\mathsf{pr}},T_{\mathsf{ms}})$

$(Q,p,b,T_{\mathsf{pr}},\{(A\,⅋\,B,C\,⅋\,B,\Uparrow,\zeta)\}\cup T_{\mathsf{ms}}) \to_{\mathcal{N}} (Q,p,b,T_{\mathsf{pr}},\{(A,C,\Uparrow,\zeta)\}\cup T_{\mathsf{ms}})$

⅋-UpRight

$(Q,p,b,\{(A\,⅋\,B,A\,⅋\,C,\Uparrow,\zeta)\}\cup T_{\mathsf{pr}},T_{\mathsf{ms}}) \to_{\mathcal{N}} (Q,p,b,\{(B,C,\Uparrow,\zeta)\}\cup T_{\mathsf{pr}},T_{\mathsf{ms}})$

$(Q,p,b,T_{\mathsf{pr}},\{(A\,⅋\,B,A\,⅋\,C,\Uparrow,\zeta)\}\cup T_{\mathsf{ms}}) \to_{\mathcal{N}} (Q,p,b,T_{\mathsf{pr}},\{(B,C,\Uparrow,\zeta)\}\cup T_{\mathsf{ms}})$

⅋-DownLeft

$(Q,p,b,\{(A,C,\Downarrow,\zeta)\}\cup T_{\mathsf{pr}},T_{\mathsf{ms}}) \to_{\mathcal{N}} (Q,p,b,\{(A\,⅋\,B,C\,⅋\,B,\Downarrow,\zeta)\}\cup T_{\mathsf{pr}},T_{\mathsf{ms}})$

$(Q,p,b,T_{\mathsf{pr}},\{(A,C,\Downarrow,\zeta)\}\cup T_{\mathsf{ms}}) \to_{\mathcal{N}} (Q,p,b,T_{\mathsf{pr}},\{(A\,⅋\,B,C\,⅋\,B,\Downarrow,\zeta)\}\cup T_{\mathsf{ms}})$

⅋-DownRight

$(Q,p,b,\{(B,C,\Downarrow,\zeta)\}\cup T_{\mathsf{pr}},T_{\mathsf{ms}}) \to_{\mathcal{N}} (Q,p,b,\{(A\,⅋\,B,A\,⅋\,C,\Downarrow,\zeta)\}\cup T_{\mathsf{pr}},T_{\mathsf{ms}})$

$(Q,p,b,T_{\mathsf{pr}},\{(B,C,\Downarrow,\zeta)\}\cup T_{\mathsf{ms}}) \to_{\mathcal{N}} (Q,p,b,T_{\mathsf{pr}},\{(A\,⅋\,B,A\,⅋\,C,\Downarrow,\zeta)\}\cup T_{\mathsf{ms}})$

Fig. 7. Transition rules for $\mathcal{T}_{\mathcal{N}}$—part I

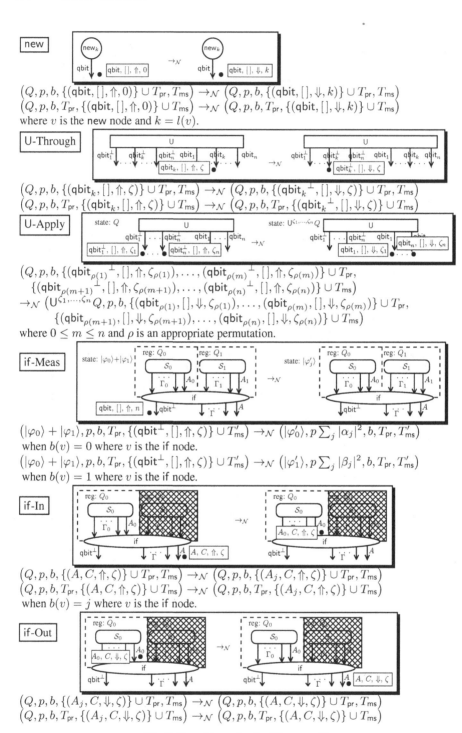

$$\left(Q, p, b, \{(\mathsf{qbit}, [\,], \Uparrow, 0)\} \cup T_{\mathsf{pr}}, T_{\mathsf{ms}}\right) \to_{\mathcal{N}} \left(Q, p, b, \{(\mathsf{qbit}, [\,], \Downarrow, k)\} \cup T_{\mathsf{pr}}, T_{\mathsf{ms}}\right)$$
$$\left(Q, p, b, T_{\mathsf{pr}}, \{(\mathsf{qbit}, [\,], \Uparrow, 0)\} \cup T_{\mathsf{ms}}\right) \to_{\mathcal{N}} \left(Q, p, b, T_{\mathsf{pr}}, \{(\mathsf{qbit}, [\,], \Downarrow, k)\} \cup T_{\mathsf{ms}}\right)$$
where v is the new node and $k = l(v)$.

$$\left(Q, p, b, \{(\mathsf{qbit}_k, [\,], \Uparrow, \zeta)\} \cup T_{\mathsf{pr}}, T_{\mathsf{ms}}\right) \to_{\mathcal{N}} \left(Q, p, b, \{(\mathsf{qbit}_k{}^\perp, [\,], \Downarrow, \zeta)\} \cup T_{\mathsf{pr}}, T_{\mathsf{ms}}\right)$$
$$\left(Q, p, b, T_{\mathsf{pr}}, \{(\mathsf{qbit}_k, [\,], \Uparrow, \zeta)\} \cup T_{\mathsf{ms}}\right) \to_{\mathcal{N}} \left(Q, p, b, T_{\mathsf{pr}}, \{(\mathsf{qbit}_k{}^\perp, [\,], \Downarrow, \zeta)\} \cup T_{\mathsf{ms}}\right)$$

$$\left(Q, p, b, \{(\mathsf{qbit}_{\rho(1)}{}^\perp, [\,], \Uparrow, \zeta_{\rho(1)}), \ldots, (\mathsf{qbit}_{\rho(m)}{}^\perp, [\,], \Uparrow, \zeta_{\rho(m)})\} \cup T_{\mathsf{pr}}, \right.$$
$$\left. \{(\mathsf{qbit}_{\rho(m+1)}{}^\perp, [\,], \Uparrow, \zeta_{\rho(m+1)}), \ldots, (\mathsf{qbit}_{\rho(n)}{}^\perp, [\,], \Uparrow, \zeta_{\rho(n)})\} \cup T_{\mathsf{ms}}\right)$$
$$\to_{\mathcal{N}} \left(\mathsf{U}^{\zeta_1, \ldots, \zeta_n} Q, p, b, \{(\mathsf{qbit}_{\rho(1)}, [\,], \Downarrow, \zeta_{\rho(1)}), \ldots, (\mathsf{qbit}_{\rho(m)}, [\,], \Downarrow, \zeta_{\rho(m)})\} \cup T_{\mathsf{pr}}, \right.$$
$$\left. \{(\mathsf{qbit}_{\rho(m+1)}, [\,], \Downarrow, \zeta_{\rho(m+1)}), \ldots, (\mathsf{qbit}_{\rho(n)}, [\,], \Downarrow, \zeta_{\rho(n)})\} \cup T_{\mathsf{ms}}\right)$$
where $0 \le m \le n$ and ρ is an appropriate permutation.

$$\left(|\varphi_0\rangle + |\varphi_1\rangle, p, b, T_{\mathsf{pr}}, \{(\mathsf{qbit}^\perp, [\,], \Uparrow, \zeta)\} \cup T'_{\mathsf{ms}}\right) \to_{\mathcal{N}} \left(|\varphi'_0\rangle, p \sum_j |\alpha_j|^2, b, T_{\mathsf{pr}}, T'_{\mathsf{ms}}\right)$$
when $b(v) = 0$ where v is the if node.
$$\left(|\varphi_0\rangle + |\varphi_1\rangle, p, b, T_{\mathsf{pr}}, \{(\mathsf{qbit}^\perp, [\,], \Uparrow, \zeta)\} \cup T'_{\mathsf{ms}}\right) \to_{\mathcal{N}} \left(|\varphi'_1\rangle, p \sum_j |\beta_j|^2, b, T_{\mathsf{pr}}, T'_{\mathsf{ms}}\right)$$
when $b(v) = 1$ where v is the if node.

$$\left(Q, p, b, \{(A, C, \Uparrow, \zeta)\} \cup T_{\mathsf{pr}}, T_{\mathsf{ms}}\right) \to_{\mathcal{N}} \left(Q, p, b, \{(A_j, C, \Uparrow, \zeta)\} \cup T_{\mathsf{pr}}, T_{\mathsf{ms}}\right)$$
$$\left(Q, p, b, T_{\mathsf{pr}}, \{(A, C, \Uparrow, \zeta)\} \cup T_{\mathsf{ms}}\right) \to_{\mathcal{N}} \left(Q, p, b, T_{\mathsf{pr}}, \{(A_j, C, \Uparrow, \zeta)\} \cup T_{\mathsf{ms}}\right)$$
when $b(v) = j$ where v is the if node.

$$\left(Q, p, b, \{(A_j, C, \Downarrow, \zeta)\} \cup T_{\mathsf{pr}}, T_{\mathsf{ms}}\right) \to_{\mathcal{N}} \left(Q, p, b, \{(A, C, \Downarrow, \zeta)\} \cup T_{\mathsf{pr}}, T_{\mathsf{ms}}\right)$$
$$\left(Q, p, b, T_{\mathsf{pr}}, \{(A_j, C, \Downarrow, \zeta)\} \cup T_{\mathsf{ms}}\right) \to_{\mathcal{N}} \left(Q, p, b, T_{\mathsf{pr}}, \{(A, C, \Downarrow, \zeta)\} \cup T_{\mathsf{ms}}\right)$$

Fig. 8. Transition rules for $\mathcal{T}_{\mathcal{N}}$—part II

that s reaches s' via a succession of $\to_\mathcal{N}$. By confluence of $\to_\mathcal{N}$ (Lem. 4.5) such s' is shown to be unique if it exists (Prop. 4.12); hence the big-step semantics is given as a partial function $I_\mathcal{N} \rightharpoonup F_\mathcal{N}$. Later in §4.4 we will show *soundness*, that is, the big-step semantics is invariant under the reduction of proof nets (as defined in §3), modulo certain "quantum effects."

We start with singling out some states of $\mathcal{T}_\mathcal{N}$ as *initial* and *final*.

Notation 4.6 (Q_b^v). *Let* $\mathcal{N} = (\mathcal{S}, Q_\mathcal{N}, l)$ *be an* MLLqm *proof net, b be a slicing of $\mathcal{N}$, and v be an* if *node in* $\mathcal{S}$. *By* Q_b^v *we denote the quantum register associated with the branch designated by b.*

Hence Q_b^v is a quantum register inside a dashed box attached to the if node v.

Definition 4.7 (Initial states). *Let* $\mathcal{N} = (\mathcal{S}, Q_\mathcal{N}, l)$ *be an* MLLqm *proof net. A state $s = (Q, p, b, T_{\mathsf{pr}}, T_{\mathsf{ms}})$ of $\mathcal{T}_\mathcal{N}$ is said to be* initial *if:*

- $Q = Q_\mathcal{N} \otimes \left(\bigotimes_{v \in V} Q_b^v \right)$ *where V is the set of all* if *nodes in the slice $b(\mathcal{N})$ (of any level; recall Def. 3.2).*
- *A token (A, C, D, ζ) belongs to T_{pr} if and only if*
  - *A is a conclusion edge of level 0 (recall that we denote an edge by its type occurrence);*
  - *$C[\mathsf{qbit}] \equiv A$; $D = \Uparrow$; and $\zeta = 0$.*
- *A token (A, C, D, ζ) belongs to T_{ms} if and only if*
  - *$A \equiv \mathsf{qbit}^\perp$, a query edge (one sticking left-down from an* if *node) in a branch remaining in the slice $b(\mathcal{N})$;*
  - *$C \equiv [\,]$; $D = \Downarrow$; and $\zeta = 0$.*

The set of initial states is denoted by $I_\mathcal{N}$.

In an initial state, every principal token is at one of the conclusion edges (of level 0), waiting to go up. Measurement tokens are at query edges of any level (but only those which are in the slice $b(\mathcal{N})$). The quantum register Q keeps track not only of the level-0 register $Q_\mathcal{N}$ but also of "internal" registers (again which are in the slice $b(\mathcal{N})$).

Definition 4.8 (Final states). *Let* $\mathcal{N} = (\mathcal{S}, Q_\mathcal{N}, l)$ *be an* MLLqm *proof net. A state $s = (Q, p, b, T_{\mathsf{pr}}, T_{\mathsf{ms}})$ of $\mathcal{T}_\mathcal{N}$ is said to be* final *if:*
- *each principal token $(A, C, D, \zeta) \in T_{\mathsf{pr}}$ satisfies*
  - *A is a conclusion edge;*
  - *$C[\mathsf{qbit}] = A$; and $D = \Downarrow$.*
- *$T_{\mathsf{ms}} = \emptyset$.*

Therefore in a final state, all the principal tokens are back at conclusion edges, and all the measurement tokens are gone. Recall that the if-Meas transition in Def. 4.4 deletes a measurement token.

Definition 4.9 (Token machine). *The* token machine *for an* MLLqm *proof net $\mathcal{N}$ is the 4-tuple $\mathcal{T}_\mathcal{N} = (S_\mathcal{N}, I_\mathcal{N}, F_\mathcal{N}, \to_\mathcal{N})$ where $S_\mathcal{N}$ is the set of states (Def. 4.3), $I_\mathcal{N}$ and $F_\mathcal{N}$ are the sets of initial and final states (Def. 4.7–4.8), and $\to_\mathcal{N} \subseteq S_\mathcal{N} \times S_\mathcal{N}$ is the (small-step) transition relation (Def. 4.4).*

In what follows, the transitive closure of $\to_\mathcal{N}$ is denoted by $\to_\mathcal{N}^+$.

Definition 4.10 (Big-step semantics). *Let* $\mathcal{N}$ *be an* MLLqm *proof net. The* big-step semantics *of the token machine* $\mathcal{T}_{\mathcal{N}}$, *denoted by* $[\![\mathcal{N}]\!]$, *is the partial function* $[\![\mathcal{N}]\!]$: $I_{\mathcal{N}} \rightharpoonup F_{\mathcal{N}}$ *defined by* $[\![\mathcal{N}]\!](s) := \begin{cases} s' \in F_{\mathcal{N}} & \text{if } s \to_{\mathcal{N}}^{+} s'; \\ \bot & \text{otherwise.} \end{cases}$

Prop. 4.12 below exhibits the legitimacy of this definition (as a partial function). It is not *total* but *partial* in general: partiality arises when the conclusion contains a qbit$^{\bot}$. For the proof nets translated from *closed* MLLqm terms, it is always total (Cor. 4.16).

Lemma 4.11 (Termination of transition). *Let* $\mathcal{N} = (\mathcal{S}, Q, l)$ *be an* MLLqm *proof net. There is no infinite sequence of small-step transitions* $\to_{\mathcal{N}}$ *in* $\mathcal{T}_{\mathcal{N}}$. □

Proposition 4.12 (Unique final state). *Let* $\mathcal{N} = (\mathcal{S}, Q, l)$ *be an* MLLqm *proof net. If* $s \to_{\mathcal{N}}^{+} s_0$ *and* $s \to_{\mathcal{N}}^{+} s_1$ *with* $s_0, s_1 \in F_{\mathcal{N}}$, *then* $s_0 = s_1$. □

4.4 Soundness of the Token Machine Semantics

Soundness of the big-step semantics—that it is invariant under the reduction of proof nets—holds only modulo certain quantum effects. The latter are formalized as follows, as suitable transformations of token machine states.

Definition 4.13 ($\overline{\mathsf{U}}$). *Let* $\mathcal{N} = (\mathcal{S}, Q_{\mathcal{N}}, l)$ *be an* MLLqm *proof net. Assume that there is a unitary gate node* U *in* $\mathcal{N}$ *for which the unitary gate reduction rule in Fig. 3 can be applied, resulting in the proof net* $\mathcal{N}'$. *In this case, we define a function* $\overline{\mathsf{U}} : S_{\mathcal{N}} \to S_{\mathcal{N}'}$ *by* $\overline{\mathsf{U}}(Q, p, b, T_{\mathsf{pr}}, T_{\mathsf{ms}}) := (\mathsf{U}^{j_1, \dots, j_m} Q, p, b, T_{\mathsf{pr}}, T_{\mathsf{ms}})$.

Definition 4.14 ($\overline{\mathsf{meas}}$). *Let* $\mathcal{N} = (\mathcal{S}, Q_{\mathcal{N}}, l)$ *be an* MLLqm *proof net. Assume that there is an* if *node* v *in* $\mathcal{N}$ *to which the* meas0 *and* meas1 *rules in Fig. 3 are applicable, resulting in nets* $\mathcal{N}_0$ *and* $\mathcal{N}_1$, *respectively.*

First we define functions $\overline{\mathsf{meas}}_{|0\rangle}^{v} : I_{\mathcal{N}} \to I_{\mathcal{N}_0}$ *and* $\overline{\mathsf{meas}}_{|1\rangle}^{v} : I_{\mathcal{N}} \to I_{\mathcal{N}_1}$, *by*

$\overline{\mathsf{meas}}_{|0\rangle}^{v} (|\varphi_0\rangle + |\varphi_1\rangle), p, b, T_{\mathsf{pr}}, \{(qbit^{\bot}, [], \Downarrow, \zeta)\} \cup T_{\mathsf{ms}}) := (|\varphi_0'\rangle, p \sum_j |\alpha_j|^2, b_0, T_{\mathsf{pr}}, T_{\mathsf{ms}})$,

$\overline{\mathsf{meas}}_{|1\rangle}^{v} (|\varphi_0\rangle + |\varphi_1\rangle), p, b, T_{\mathsf{pr}}, \{(qbit^{\bot}, [], \Downarrow, \zeta)\} \cup T_{\mathsf{ms}}) := (|\varphi_1'\rangle, p \sum_j |\beta_j|^2, b_1, T_{\mathsf{pr}}, T_{\mathsf{ms}})$,

where b_j *is defined by* $b_j(u) := b(u)$ *on every* if *node* u *in the proof net* $\mathcal{N}_j$ ($j \in \{0, 1\}$). *Here the token* $(qbit^{\bot}, [], \Downarrow, \zeta)$ *in the definition is on the query edge of* v, *and* $|\varphi_0\rangle, |\varphi_0'\rangle, |\varphi_1\rangle, |\varphi_1'\rangle$ *are registers as in (1) in §3.2.*

Finally we define a function $\overline{\mathsf{meas}}^{v} : I_{\mathcal{N}} \to I_{\mathcal{N}_0} + I_{\mathcal{N}_1}$ *by* (+ *denotes disjoint union*)

$$\overline{\mathsf{meas}}^{v}(s) := \begin{cases} \overline{\mathsf{meas}}_{|0\rangle}^{v}(s) & \text{if } b(v) = 0, \\ \overline{\mathsf{meas}}_{|1\rangle}^{v}(s) & \text{if } b(v) = 1, \end{cases} \quad \text{where } s = (|\varphi\rangle, p, b, T_{\mathsf{pr}}, T_{\mathsf{ms}}).$$

Intuitively, the function $\overline{\mathsf{meas}}^{v}$ "deletes" the if node v together with relevant entries in the slicing b. A quantum register and a probability are updated too, in an obvious manner.

Using these state transformations our main result is stated as follows.

Theorem 4.15 (Soundness). *Let* $\mathcal{N} \mapsto \mathcal{N}'$ *be a reduction of* MLLqm *proof nets. Then,*

1. $[\![\mathcal{N}]\!] = [\![\mathcal{N}']\!]$ *if the reduction is by the* ax-cut *or the* $\otimes$-$\invamp$ *rule.*
2. $[\![\mathcal{N}]\!] = [\![\mathcal{N}']\!] \circ \overline{\mathsf{U}}$ *if the reduction is by the unitary gate rule, where* U *is the corresponding unitary matrix.*

3. $[\![\mathcal{N}]\!] \simeq ([\![\mathcal{N}_0]\!] + [\![\mathcal{N}_1]\!]) \circ \overline{\mathsf{meas}}^v$ *if the reduction is by one of the* meas *rules. In this case there must be another reduction possible due to the other* meas *rule, and we denote the resulting two proof nets by* $\mathcal{N}_0$ *and* $\mathcal{N}_1$ ($\mathcal{N}'$ *is one of these). The function* $[\![\mathcal{N}_0]\!] + [\![\mathcal{N}_1]\!]$ *means case-distinction (recall the type* $I_\mathcal{N} \to I_{\mathcal{N}_0} + I_{\mathcal{N}_1}$ *of* $\overline{\mathsf{meas}}^v$). *Here the equivalence* $\simeq$ *is a natural identification of final states of* $\mathcal{T}_\mathcal{N}, \mathcal{T}_{\mathcal{N}_0}$ *and* $\mathcal{T}_{\mathcal{N}_1}$. *That is,* $F \simeq G \overset{def.}{\Longleftrightarrow} \forall x. F(x) \sim G(x)$ *and*

$$s \sim s' \overset{def.}{\Longleftrightarrow} s = s' \quad \text{disregarding slicings.}$$

Pictorially, the statements 2. *and* 3. *say the following diagrams commute:*

$$
\begin{array}{ccc}
I_\mathcal{N} & \xrightarrow{\;[\![\mathcal{N}]\!]\;} & F_\mathcal{N} \\
\overline{\mathsf{u}}\downarrow & \parallel & \parallel \\
I_{\mathcal{N}'} & \xrightarrow{\;[\![\mathcal{N}']\!]\;} & F_{\mathcal{N}'}
\end{array}
\qquad
\begin{array}{ccc}
I_\mathcal{N} & \xrightarrow{\qquad [\![\mathcal{N}]\!] \qquad} & F_\mathcal{N} \\
\overline{\mathsf{meas}}^v\downarrow & & \downarrow\sim \\
I_{\mathcal{N}_0} + I_{\mathcal{N}_1} & \xrightarrow{\;[\![\mathcal{N}_0]\!]+[\![\mathcal{N}_1]\!]\;} & F_{\mathcal{N}_0} + F_{\mathcal{N}_1}
\end{array}\ .
\qquad \square
$$

Thm. 4.15 together with Thm. 3.10 yield the following corollary (Cor. 4.16). This corollary implies that the computation of a closed term ends *with a result.*

Corollary 4.16. *Let* $\mathcal{N}$ *be a proof net with no* $\mathsf{qbit}^\perp$ *in its conclusions. Then the big-step semantics* $[\![\mathcal{N}]\!]$ *is total.* $\square$

4.5   Example

As a concrete example we briefly look at the token machine for the proof net for quantum teleportation (Fig. 6); we shall demonstrate that the qubit $\alpha|0_1\rangle + \beta|1_1\rangle$ ("stored" in the node new_1) is transmitted correctly.

The initial states of our interests are the following four:

$$\left(Q, 1, b_{ij}, \{ (\mathsf{qbit}, [\,], \Uparrow, 0) \}, \{ (\mathsf{qbit}_x{}^\perp, [\,], \Downarrow, 0), (\mathsf{qbit}_z{}^\perp, [\,], \Downarrow, 0) \} \right) \ ,$$

where Q is the quantum register $(\alpha|0_1\rangle + \beta|1_1\rangle) \otimes \left(\frac{1}{\sqrt{2}}|0_2 0_3\rangle + \frac{1}{\sqrt{2}}|1_2 1_3\rangle \right)$ and $i, j \in \{0, 1\}$. Each initial state (with a different slicing b_{ij}) corresponds to possible outcomes of the two measurements. Note that each has the probability 1.

It is straightforward to see that each of the four initial states is led to the final state $(\alpha|0\rangle + \beta|1\rangle, 1/4, b_{ij}, \{(\mathsf{qbit}, [\,], \Downarrow, 3)\}, \emptyset)$, with the qubit $\alpha|0\rangle + \beta|1\rangle$ assigned to the node new_3. The probabilities (1/4 each) add up to 1 with the four initial states together, a fact which witnesses that the original qubit is successfully transmitted with the probability 1.

5   Conclusions and Future Work

We introduced the notion of MLLqm proof net. It is the first one that accommodates measurements as proof structures, and has suitable features for expressing higher-order computation thus going beyond quantum circuits.

The GoI semantics with measurements in this paper is also the first one, which was mentioned in [4] as one of future work. The ideas of using a form of "weakening" to capture measurements (qubits are deleted) and that states of a token machine carry probabilities are new and clean, while the overall structure of the machine follows the usual notion of slice used in linear logic.

As future work, one direction is to accommodate duplicable data, namely the bit type. Although linear logic has a standard tool—the ! modality—to handle such data, there are subtle problems coming from the no-cloning property, nonlocality, etc. Another is to accommodate recursion. We expect to be able to adapt the techniques developed in [14] and [12].

Acknowledgments. Thanks are due to Kentaro Honda, Tristan Roussel, and Alexis Saurin for useful discussions. A.Y. and I.H. are supported by Grants-in-Aid for Young Scientists (A) No. 24680001, and by Aihara Innovative Mathematical Modeling Project, FIRST Program, JSPS/CSTP. C.F. is supported by the ANR project ANR-2010-BLAN-021301 LOGOI.

References

1. 19th IEEE Symposium on Logic in Computer Science (LICS 2004), Turku, Finland, July 14-17. Proceedings. IEEE Computer Society (2004)
2. Abramsky, S., Coecke, B.: A categorical semantics of quantum protocols. In: LICS [1], pp. 415–425
3. Dal Lago, U., Faggian, C.: On multiplicative linear logic, modality and quantum circuits. In: Jacobs, B., Selinger, P., Spitters, B. (eds.) QPL. EPTCS, vol. 95, pp. 55–66 (2011)
4. Dal Lago, U., Zorzi, M.: Wave-style token machines and quantum lambda calculi (2013)
5. Danos, V., Regnier, L.: The structure of multiplicatives. Arch. for Math. Logic 28(3), 181–203 (1989)
6. Girard, J.Y.: Linear logic. Theor. Comput. Sci. 50, 1–102 (1987)
7. Girard, J.Y.: Geometry of interaction 1: Interpretation of system F. Logic Colloquium 88 (1989)
8. Girard, J.Y.: Proof-nets: The parallel syntax for proof-theory. In: Logic and Algebra, pp. 97–124. Marcel Dekker (1996)
9. Gisin, N., Methot, A.A., Scarani, V.: Pseudo-telepathy: input cardinality and Bell-type inequalities. International Journal of Quantum Information 5(4), 525–534 (2007)
10. Green, A.S., Lumsdaine, P.L., Ross, N.J., Selinger, P., Valiron, B.: Quipper: a scalable quantum programming language. In: Boehm, H.J., Flanagan, C. (eds.) PLDI, pp. 333–342. ACM (2013)
11. Hasuo, I., Hoshino, N.: Semantics of higher-order quantum computation via geometry of interaction. In: LICS, pp. 237–246. IEEE Computer Society (2011)
12. Hoshino, N.: A modified GoI interpretation for a linear functional programming language and its adequacy. In: Hofmann, M. (ed.) FOSSACS 2011. LNCS, vol. 6604, pp. 320–334. Springer, Heidelberg (2011)
13. Laurent, O.: A token machine for full geometry of interaction. In: Abramsky, S. (ed.) TLCA 2001. LNCS, vol. 2044, pp. 283–297. Springer, Heidelberg (2001)
14. Mackie, I.: The geometry of interaction machine. In: POPL, pp. 198–208 (1995)
15. Mairson, H.G., Terui, K.: On the computational complexity of cut-elimination in linear logic. In: Blundo, C., Laneve, C. (eds.) ICTCS 2003. LNCS, vol. 2841, pp. 23–36. Springer, Heidelberg (2003)
16. Malherbe, O., Scott, P., Selinger, P.: Presheaf models of quantum computation: An outline. In: Coecke, B., Ong, L., Panangaden, P. (eds.) Computation, Logic, Games and Quantum Foundations. LNCS, vol. 7860, pp. 178–194. Springer, Heidelberg (2013)

17. Melliès, P.A.: Categorical semantics of linear logic. Panoramas et Synthèses, ch. 1, vol. 27, pp. 15–215. Société Mathématique de France (2009)
18. Nielsen, M.A., Chuang, I.L.: Quantum Computation and Quantum Information. Cambridge Univ. Press (2000)
19. Ömer, B.: Quantum programming in QCL. Master's thesis, Institute of Information Systems, Technical University of Vienna (2000)
20. Pinto, J.S.: Implantation Parallèle avec la Logique Linéaire (Applications des Réseaux d'Interaction et de la Géométrie de l'Interaction). Ph.D. thesis, École Polytechnique, Main text in English (2001)
21. Selinger, P., Valiron, B.: Quantum lambda calculus. In: Gay, S., Mackie, I. (eds.) Semantic Techniques in Quantum Computation, pp. 135–172. Cambridge Univ. Press (2009)
22. Terui, K.: Proof nets and boolean circuits. In: LICS [1], pp. 182–191
23. van Tonder, A.: A lambda calculus for quantum computation. SIAM J. Comput. 33(5), 1109–1135 (2004)
24. Yoshimizu, A., Hasuo, I., Faggian, C., Dal Lago, U.: Measurements in proof nets as higher-order quantum circuits. Extended version with proofs (2014), www-mmm.is.s.u-tokyo.ac.jp/~ayoshimizu

Automatic Termination Verification for Higher-Order Functional Programs*

Takuya Kuwahara[1], Tachio Terauchi[2], Hiroshi Unno[3], and Naoki Kobayashi[4]

[1] University of Tokyo
kuwahara@is.s.u-tokyo.ac.jp
[2] Nagoya University
terauchi@is.nagoya-u.ac.jp
[3] University of Tsukuba
uhiro@cs.tsukuba.ac.jp
[4] University of Tokyo
koba@is.s.u-tokyo.ac.jp

Abstract. We present an automated approach to verifying termination of higher-order functional programs. Our approach adopts the idea from the recent work on termination verification via transition invariants (a.k.a. binary reachability analysis), and is fully automated. Our approach is able to soundly handle the subtle aspects of higher-order programs, including partial applications, indirect calls, and ranking functions over function closure values. In contrast to the previous approaches to automated termination verification for functional programs, our approach is sound and complete, relative to the soundness and completeness of the underlying reachability analysis and ranking function inference. We have implemented a prototype of our approach for a subset of the OCaml language, and we have confirmed that it is able to automatically verify termination of some non-trivial higher-order programs.

1 Introduction

Recent years have witnessed a dramatic progress in automated verification of higher-order functional programs [27,31,24,11,16,33,37]. The line of work takes the ideas from the recent advances in the verification of non-functional programs, such as predicate abstraction, counterexample-guided abstraction refinement, and interpolation [1,9,21,10], to the verification of higher-order functional programs by way of refinement (dependent) types [36] and higher-order model checking [23,14].

However, except for the case when the base-type data is of a finite domain [15,20], the above line of work (to the extent of software model checking techniques for higher-order programs) has been limited to the verification of safety (i.e., reachability) properties. In particular, it is unable to verify liveness properties, such as termination.

For automated termination verification of higher-order programs, popular methods have been based on size-change termination [12,29,28] or TRS (term rewriting systems) techniques [6]. (Besides them, Xi [35] has proposed termination analysis based on dependent types, but his technique is not fully automated in the sense that users

---

* This work was supported by MEXT Kakenhi 23220001, 23700026, 25280023, and 25730035.

Z. Shao (Ed.): ESOP 2014, LNCS 8410, pp. 392–411, 2014.

```
let rec app f x () =
    if x>0 then app f (x-1) () else f x () in
let id () = () in
let rec g x = if x=0 then id else app g x in
let t = * in g t ()
```

Fig. 1. A non-terminating higher-order program

have to provide dependent types of recursive functions as witness of termination.) The current methods based on those approaches are not completely satisfactory, especially in terms of precision. Roughly, these techniques first construct a finite graph (called a static call graph [12,29,28] or a termination graph [6]) that over-approximates certain dependencies on termination, and then use techniques for first-order programs [19,7] to show that there is no cyclic dependency. In these two-phase approaches to termination, information is often lost in the first phase; see Section 5 for more details.

In the present paper, we follow an approach based on transition invariants [26,4,5], and extend it to deal with higher-order functional programs. The transition-invariant-based approach has emerged as a powerful technique for verifying termination of first-order imperative programs [26,4,5]. The technique iteratively reduces the termination verification problem to the problem of checking the *binary* reachability of program transition relations. It then delegates the binary reachability checking to a reachability checker by encoding the problem as a plain reachability problem via a program transformation. Advantages of this approach are that termination arguments can be flexibly adjusted for each program by choosing an appropriate binary reachability relation, and that precise flow information can be taken into account in the plain reachability verification phase. The latter advantage is particularly important since the termination property often depends on safety properties. For example, consider the program:

```
let f x = if p(x) then () else loop_forever()
```

Then, a call of f terminates if and only if p(x) is true, and the latter condition can be checked during the reachability verification. In the higher-order case, termination verification would be even more complicated since the condition can be passed as a parameter of f. This shows the advantage of reducing termination verification to reachability verification, where all the relevant information (such as value-dependent control flow and size change) is put together and precisely analyzed by taking advantage of the recent advance of reachability verification tools for higher-order programs.

The extension of the transition invariant-based technique for higher-order programs is non-trivial. To see why, let us consider the OCaml program P_0 shown in Figure 1. (Here, $*$ denotes a non-deterministic integer.) The program is non-terminating for any non-deterministic choice of t such that $t < 0$. For example, for $t = -1$, the program exhibits the following infinite reduction sequence.

$$g\ (-1)\ ()\ \to^*\ \mathrm{app}\ g\ (-1)\ ()\ \to^*\ g\ (-1)\ ()\ \to^*\ \mathrm{app}\ g\ (-1)\ ()\ \to^*\ \cdots$$

Note here that g is passed to and indirectly called by app, and there is no direct call to g in the definition of g. Moreover, g itself does not (totally) call app but returns a partially applied closure of the form app g n. Therefore, a termination verifier must soundly handle indirect calls and function closures to avoid incorrectly reporting that the program is terminating.

For a terminating example, let us consider a variation P_1 of the above program, obtained by replacing the branching condition x = 0 in g with x ≤ 0. To prove that P_1 is terminating for any non-deterministically chosen t (and any non-deterministic choice of the integers chosen inside g), we need to know that the sequence of the third arguments passed to the recursive calls to app is strictly decreasing and is bounded below by 0.

Our technique consists of: (i) a method to find an appropriate (disjunctively) well-founded relation, including those over function closure values, that over-approximates the binary reachability relation (the relation between two recursive function calls), (ii) a program transformation that reduces the binary reachability problem to the plain reachability problem, and (iii) a plain reachability analysis for higher-order programs. For (iii), we employ off-the-shelf reachability verification tools for higher-order programs [27,31,11,16,33,37]. For (i), we adopt the previous technique [33] for automatically inserting implicit integer parameters that represent information about function closures. We can then adopt the existing techniques to find ranking functions (on integer arguments) from counterexamples [25,3,5]. The most subtle part is (ii): how to reduce the binary reachability analysis to plain reachability analysis. Actually, Ledesma-Garza and Rybalchenko [18] has recently tackled this problem, but (as admitted in [18], Section 8), their solution does not work quite well in the presence of partial applications and indirect function calls. In fact, their method cannot properly deal with the programs P_0 and P_1 above (cf. Section 5 of this paper for more details). By contrast, the reduction from binary reachability to plain reachability presented in this paper is *sound* and *complete*.

Our contributions are: (i) The first sound approach to the termination verification of higher-order functional programs that is based on the transition invariant / binary reachability technique. The approach is also complete relative to the completeness of the backend reachability checker and the ranking function inference process. A notable aspect of our approach is an inference of ranking functions over closure values via the automatic inference of implicit parameter instantiations. (ii) A prototype implementation to show the effectiveness of the proposed approach.

The rest of the paper is organized as follows. We define the target functional language of termination verification in Section 2. Section 3 formalizes our termination verification method. Section 4 reports on a preliminary implementation and experiment results. We compare our method with related work in Section 5 and conclude the paper in Section 6. The extended report [17] contains extra materials and proofs of the theorems.

2 Preliminaries

In this section, we introduce a higher-order functional language L, which is the target of our termination verification. Figure 2 shows the syntax of L. Here, $\tilde{x}$ is an abbreviation for a (non-empty) variable sequence $x_1 \ x_2 \ \ldots \ x_k$. The meta-variables f, x, c and op range over the sets of function symbols, variables, constants, and binary operators respectively. We write $|\tilde{x}|$ for the length of $\tilde{x}$. The arity of function f_i, written $arity(f_i)$, is the number of formal parameters, i.e., $|\tilde{x}_i|$ in the function definition $f_i \ \tilde{x}_i = e_i$.

Programs $P ::= \{f_1 \, \tilde{x}_1 = e_1, \ldots, f_n \, \tilde{x}_n = e_n\}$

Expressions $e ::= v \mid x \mid \text{let } x = e_1 \text{ in } e_2 \mid e_1 \text{ op } e_2 \mid e_1 \, e_2 \mid \text{if } e_1 \text{ then } e_2 \text{ else } e_3 \mid *_{\text{int}}$

Values $v ::= c \mid f \mid f \, \tilde{v} \text{ (where } |\tilde{v}| < arity(f))$

Fig. 2. Syntax of L

Eval. contexts $E ::= [\,] \mid E \text{ op } e \mid v \text{ op } E \mid E \, e \mid v \, E \mid \text{let } x = E \text{ in } e$
$$\mid \text{ if } E \text{ then } e_1 \text{ else } e_2$$

$$E[c_1 \text{ op } c_2] \to_P E[[\![op]\!](c_1, c_2)]$$

$$\frac{n \in \mathbb{Z}}{E[*_{\text{int}}] \to_P E[n]}$$

$$E[\text{let } x = v \text{ in } e] \to_P E[[v/x]\,e]$$

$$E[\text{if true then } e_1 \text{ else } e_2] \to_P E[e_1]$$

$$\frac{f \, \tilde{x} = e \in P \qquad |\tilde{x}| = |\tilde{v}|}{E[f \, \tilde{v}] \to_P E[[\tilde{v}/\tilde{x}]\,e]}$$

$$E[\text{if false then } e_1 \text{ else } e_2] \to_P E[e_2]$$

Fig. 3. Operational semantics of L

We assume that the set of constants includes $()$, `true`, `false` and (unbounded) integers, and that the set of binary operators includes comparators: $>, <, \geq, \leq, =$ and boolean operators: $\wedge, \vee, \Rightarrow$. We also assume that a program has a special one-arity function named `main` that does not occur in the body of a function definition.

A program is a set of top-level function definitions; note that this does not lose generality because any functional program can be transformed to this form via λ-lifting. In the definition of the expression, $*_{\text{int}}$ evaluates to some integer in a non-deterministic manner. Note that the non-deterministic boolean, $*_{\text{bool}}$, can be defined as $*_{\text{int}} = 0$.

The set of evaluation contexts and the reduction relation are given in Figure 3. Here, $[\![op]\!]$ denotes the binary operation on constants denoted by op. Note that the evaluation is call-by-value and non-deterministic (because of $*_{\text{int}}$). We write $\to_P^*$ for the reflexive and transitive closure of $\to_P$, and $\to_P^+$ for the transitive closure of $\to_P$. When it is clear from the context, we omit the subscript P from the relations.

Example 1. The following program `fib` chooses an integer n non-deterministically and computes the n-th Fibonacci number.

$$\left\{ \begin{array}{l} \text{fib } n = \text{if } n < 2 \text{ then } 1 \text{ else fib}(n-1) + \text{fib}(n-2), \\ \text{main } () = \text{fib } *_{\text{int}} \end{array} \right\}$$

The following is a possible reduction sequence of the program:

$$\text{main } () \to_{\text{fib}} \text{fib } *_{\text{int}} \to_{\text{fib}} \text{fib}(2) \to_{\text{fib}}^* \text{fib}(1) + \text{fib}(0)$$
$$\to_{\text{fib}}^* 1 + \text{fib}(0) \to_{\text{fib}}^* 1 + 1 \to_{\text{fib}}^* 2$$

For readability, we often write a program in the OCaml-like syntax as shown below:

```
let rec fib n = if n < 2 then 1 else fib (n-1) + fib (n-2)
let main () = fib *int
```

Example 2. The following program `indirect` is a simplified variant of the program P_1 in Section 1, obtained by removing the then branch of `app` and moving the decrement operation (i.e., $x - 1$) to inside `g`.

$$\left\{ \begin{array}{l} \texttt{app f x u} = \texttt{f x u} \\ \quad\texttt{id u} = \texttt{u} \\ \quad\quad\texttt{g x} = \texttt{if } x \le 0 \texttt{ then id else app g } (x - 1) \\ \quad\texttt{main ()} = \texttt{g } *_{\texttt{int}} \texttt{ ()} \end{array} \right\}$$

The following is a possible reduction sequence of the program.

$$\begin{array}{l} \texttt{main ()} \rightarrow^* \texttt{g 2 ()} \rightarrow^* \texttt{app g 1 ()} \rightarrow^* \texttt{g 1 ()} \\ \rightarrow^* \texttt{app g 0 ()} \rightarrow^* \texttt{g 0 ()} \rightarrow^* \texttt{id ()} \rightarrow^* \texttt{()} \end{array}$$

Note that, although `g` is applied to two arguments in the reduction above, $arity(\texttt{g}) = 1$ in our definition (because `x` is the only formal parameter in the definition of `g`).

We define termination as follows.

Definition 1. *A program P is* terminating, *if there is no infinite reduction sequence* $\texttt{main ()} \rightarrow_P e_1 \rightarrow_P e_2 \rightarrow_P \cdots .$

Remark 1. The language L is untyped and therefore, a program evaluation may get stuck. We consider a reduction sequence that ends with a stuck expression as terminating. Our approach is sound and complete even for untyped languages. But, our implementation currently supports only the typed subset because it delegates the reachability checking to a higher-order program model checker for a typed language.

3   Termination Verification via Binary Reachability

This section describes our termination verification method. We give an informal overview of the whole process in Subsection 3.1, and discuss each step in a more detail in the later subsections.

3.1   Overview

We use `indirect` from Example 2 as a running example in this subsection. Our termination verification method is based on the observation that a functional program is terminating if and only if each of its *call tree*,[1] which expresses how the functions are called in an execution of the program, is finite. Figure 4 shows a call tree for `indirect`. Each node expresses a fully applied function call (a

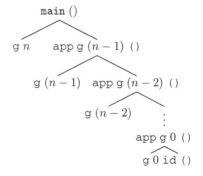

Fig. 4. A call tree of program `indirect`

---

[1] The call tree in this paper roughly corresponds to the *dynamic call graph* of [29].

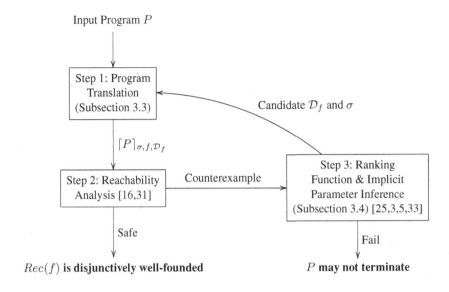

Fig. 5. Overview of the termination verification process

call of the form $f\,\widetilde{v}$ with $arity(f) = |\widetilde{v}|$), and an edge represents that the function call represented by the target node is made from the function call of the source node. For example, the edge from "app g $(n-1)$ ()" to "g $(n-1)$" means that g $(n-1)$ is called during evaluation of app g $(n-1)$ () (i.e., app g $(n-1)$ () $\rightarrow^+ E[\text{g}\,(n-1)]$ for some evaluation context E). For every (possibly infinite) reduction sequence, the corresponding call tree is finitely branching. Therefore, by König's lemma, to show that every call tree of the program is finite and therefore the program is terminating, it is sufficient to show that no call tree has an infinite path from the root. The latter is equivalent to showing that for every function f, there is no infinite path $f\,\widetilde{v}_1 \rhd f\,\widetilde{v}_2 \rhd f\,\widetilde{v}_3 \rhd \cdots$ where $f\,\widetilde{v} \rhd g\,\widetilde{w}$ means that $f\,\widetilde{v}$ is an ancestor of $g\,\widetilde{w}$ in the call tree. In the running example, the only non-trivial sequence is app g n_1 () $\rhd$ app g n_2 () $\rhd$ app g n_3 () $\rhd \cdots$ and this sequence must be finite since n_i is decreasing and bounded below by 0. Thus, we may conclude that `indirect` is terminating. We refer to Subsection 3.2 for the formal exposition of the above argument.

By the above argument, to show that the program terminates, it suffices to show that, for every function f, the relation $Rec(f) = \{(\widetilde{v}, \widetilde{v}') \mid f\,\widetilde{v} \rhd f\,\widetilde{v}'\}$ is well-founded, or disjunctively well-founded[2] [26] because $Rec_P(f)$ is transitive. Thus, as mentioned in Section 1, our termination verification method proceeds as follows.

(i) For each function f, guess a disjunctively well-founded relation $\mathcal{D}_f$ that over-approximates $Rec(f)$, and reduce the termination verification problem to the so called *binary reachability analysis* problem of showing $Rec(f) \subseteq \mathcal{D}_f$.

---

[2] A binary relation is *disjunctively well-founded* if it is a finite union of well-founded sets [26].

(ii) Use a program transformation to reduce the binary reachability problem to a plain reachability problem; and

(iii) Solve the plain reachability problem by using an off-the-shelf software model checker.

We express the disjunctively well-founded relation $\mathcal{D}_f$ by using a set of ranking functions, and gradually refine the set by using the technique of counterexample-guided abstraction refinement [25,3,5,33].

Figure 5 shows the overall flow of the process. We start with an empty set of ranking functions (i.e., with $\mathcal{D}_f = \emptyset$), and apply a program transformation to reduce the binary reachability analysis problem of deciding $Rec(f) \subseteq \mathcal{D}_f$ to the plain reachability analysis problem of deciding if an assertion failure is reachable in the translated program $\lceil P \rceil_{\sigma,f,\mathcal{D}_f}$ (Step 1 in Figure 5). Here, σ is a *candidate implicit parameter instantiation* and is used for ranking functions over higher-order values (i.e., function closures). For the purpose of the exposition, we focus on the case where the ranking functions are only over the first-order values in Subsections 3.2 and 3.3, and defer implicit parameters and ranking functions over higher-order values to Subsection 3.4. For simplicity, we write $\lceil P \rceil_{f,\mathcal{D}_f}$ for $\lceil P \rceil_{\sigma,f,\mathcal{D}_f}$ when implicit parameters are irrelevant to the discussion.

Informally, the idea of the program transformation is to pass around the argument $\widetilde{pv}$ of an ancestor call as an *extra argument*, and assert in the body of f that $\widetilde{pv}$ and the current argument $\widetilde{v}$ are related by $\mathcal{D}_f$. For the running example, the definition of app would be transformed as follows.

```
app s1 f s2 x s3 u = assert((s3,(f,x,u))∈ 𝒟_app); ...
```

Here, s1, s2, and s3 are the extra arguments that carry the arguments of ancestor calls to app. Because a function body does not evaluate until the function is fully applied, only s3 is relevant and is checked with the current arguments (f, x, u) for the candidate disjunctively well-founded relation $\mathcal{D}_{\texttt{app}}$. We use non-determinism to ensure that the extra parameter can be bound to the argument of an *arbitrary* ancestor call, so that the transformed program is assertion safe if and only if $Rec(f) \subseteq \mathcal{D}_f$. Because a function can be called indirectly in a higher-order program, we pass extra arguments at *all* call sites, including indirect calls, to account for all possible ancestor relations. Therefore, for the running example, we also transform the functions g and id to take extra parameters (but only track and check the arguments of app). This makes our approach sound and complete even in the presence of higher-order functions.[3] In this manner, the binary reachability problem is reduced to a plain reachability problem. We refer to Subsection 3.3 for a more formal exposition.

We proceed to the plain reachability analysis (Step 2 in Figure 5), to check if the inserted assertion may fail. If the assertion cannot fail, then we conclude that $Rec(f) \subseteq \mathcal{D}_f$ holds (and if that is the case for every function f in the program, we conclude that the program is terminating). Even if the program is terminating, however, an assertion failure may occur, because of a wrongly guessed $\mathcal{D}_f$. For our running example, in the initial

---

[3] This is a crucial difference with the previous approaches to automated termination verification for higher-order programs [30,28,29,6,12] that handle higher-order functions by approximating the call graph up front (e.g., via a control flow analysis), which can lose precision when the calls depend on non-trivial safety conditions.

iteration, we set $\mathcal{D}_{\mathtt{app}} = \emptyset$, and when the transformed program is given to a reachability verifier (e.g., MoCHi [16]), the verifier would return a concrete counterexample to the assertion safety. Suppose the following counterexample is returned.

$$\mathtt{main}\ () \to^* \mathtt{app}\ s_1\ \mathtt{g}\ s_2\ 0\ (\mathtt{g}, 1, ())\ () \to^* \mathtt{fail}$$

which corresponds to the following reduction sequence in the original program:

$$\mathtt{main}\ () \to^* \mathtt{g}\ 2\ () \to^* \mathtt{app}\ \mathtt{g}\ 1\ () \to^* \mathtt{app}\ \mathtt{g}\ 0\ ()$$

We analyze the counterexample, and infer a new ranking function to refine $\mathcal{D}_f$ (Step 3 in Figure 5). For the running example, we look for a ranking function r such that $r(\mathtt{g}, 1, ()) > r(\mathtt{g}, 0, ()) \geq 0$ and update $\mathcal{D}_{\mathtt{app}}$ to $\mathcal{D}_{\mathtt{app}} \cup \{((pf, px, pu), (f, x, u)) \mid r(pf, px, pu) > r(f, x, u) \geq 0\}$. To find a ranking function, we adopt the existing techniques for inferring ranking functions from counterexamples of first-order programs [25,5].[4] If no ranking function can be found, then we report that the program may not be terminating. This may happen either because the program is indeed non-terminating, or the method used for the ranking function synthesis is incomplete. We refer to Subsection 3.4 for a more formal exposition on this step.

Upon refining $\mathcal{D}_f$, we go back to Step 1 and repeat the process. If the program is terminating, and if the underlying reachability analysis tool and the ranking function synthesis *were* complete, the loop eventually terminates and we conclude that the program is terminating.

3.2 Termination and Binary Reachability

We discuss how termination verification is reduced to binary reachability analysis (to show $Rec(f) \subseteq \mathcal{D}_f$) more formally. First, we define the relations $\triangleright$ and $Rec(f)$.

Definition 2. *The* call relation $\triangleright_P$ *is the binary relation defined by:*

$$\triangleright_P := \{(f\ \widetilde{v}, g\ \widetilde{w}) \mid (\mathtt{main}\ () \to_P^* E_1\ [f\ \widetilde{v}]) \wedge (f\ \widetilde{v} \to_P^+ E_2\ [g\ \widetilde{w}]) \\ \wedge arity(f) = |\widetilde{v}| \wedge arity(g) = |\widetilde{w}|\}$$

We often use the infix notation $f\ \widetilde{v} \triangleright_P g\ \widetilde{w}$ for $(f\ \widetilde{v}, g\ \widetilde{w}) \in \triangleright_P$.

Definition 3. $Rec_P(f)$, *the* recursion relation *of f in P, is the binary relation defined by:*

$$Rec_P(f) := \{(\langle \widetilde{v_1} \rangle, \langle \widetilde{v_2} \rangle) \mid f\ \widetilde{v_1} \triangleright_P f\ \widetilde{v_2}\}$$

When it is clear from contexts, we omit the subscript P. Note that the relations $\triangleright_P$ and $Rec_P(f)$ are transitive.

Example 3. Recall program $\mathtt{fib}$ in Example 1. $Rec(\mathtt{fib})$ is:

$$(\{(n, n-1) \mid n > 1\} \cup \{(n, n-2) \mid n > 2\})^+ = \{(m, n) \mid m > n \geq 0\}$$

---

[4] To infer a ranking relation over function closure values, we use implicit parameters and infer sufficient instantiations for them to represent the closures. This is done by adopting the counterexample-guided technique from the previous work [33] (cf. Subsection 3.4).

As shown in the example below, $Rec(f)$ may be non-empty even if f is not recursively defined, and $Rec(f)$ may be empty even if f is recursively defined.

Example 4. Recall the program in Example 2. The recursion relations are:

$$Rec(\mathtt{app}) = \{(\langle \mathtt{g}, m, () \rangle, \langle \mathtt{g}, n, () \rangle) \mid m > n \geq 0\}$$
$$Rec(\mathtt{id}) = Rec(\mathtt{g}) = \emptyset$$

Note that g is defined recursively but does not cause a recursive call to g. Therefore, the relation $Rec(\mathtt{g})$ is empty. On the other hand, app is not recursively defined but $Rec(\mathtt{app}) \neq \emptyset$. This shows that we must check the disjunctive well-foundedness of $Rec(f)$ for each function f, regardless of whether f is recursively defined or not.

Next, we show the termination verification problem can be reduced soundly and completely to the problem of showing that $Rec(f)$ is disjunctively well-founded for every f.

We state the soundness and the completeness of the reduction.

Theorem 1 (Soundness). *A program P is terminating if $Rec_P(f)$ is disjunctively well-founded for every f defined in P.*

Theorem 2 (Completeness). *If a program P is terminating, then $Rec_P(f)$ is disjunctively well-founded for every f defined in P.*

3.3   From Binary Reachability to Plain Reachability

This subsection presents the reduction from the binary reachability problem of deciding $Rec_P(f) \subseteq \mathcal{D}_f$ to a plain reachability problem. As remarked in Subsection 3.1, we transform P to the program $\lceil P \rceil_{f,\mathcal{D}_f}$ that simulates the program P and asserts the property $(\widetilde{v'}, \widetilde{v}) \in \mathcal{D}_f$ whenever a recursive call relation $f \, \widetilde{v'} \rhd_P f \, \widetilde{v}$ is detected. Then, $Rec_P(f) \subseteq \mathcal{D}_f$ holds if and only if an assertion in $\lceil P \rceil_{f,\mathcal{D}_f}$ may fail.

The target language of the program transformation is an extension of L with tuples $\langle e_1, \ldots, e_k \rangle$, assertions $\mathtt{assert}(e_1); e_2$, and a special value $\bot$. The semantics of assertions is defined by:

$$E[\mathtt{assert}(\mathtt{true}); e] \rightarrow_P E[e] \qquad E[\mathtt{assert}(\mathtt{false}); e] \rightarrow_P \mathtt{fail}$$

where the evaluation contexts are extended accordingly: $E ::= \cdots \mid \mathtt{assert}(E); e$. The special value $\bot$ is used in place of the argument of an ancestor call, when there is no tracked ancestor call; see examples below.

Before we give the formal definition of the transformation, $\lceil \cdot \rceil_{f,\mathcal{D}_f}$, we informally describe the idea. The program $\lceil P \rceil_{f,\mathcal{D}_f}$ is obtained by adding extra function arguments that represent the arguments of past calls to f.

First we consider the simple case where the program only contains first-order functions. For example, let P be the Fibonacci program from Example 1. Let $\mathcal{D}_{\mathtt{fib}} = \{(\mathtt{pn}, \mathtt{n}) \mid \mathtt{pn} > \mathtt{n} \geq 0\}$. Then, $\lceil P \rceil_{\mathtt{fib}, \mathcal{D}_{\mathtt{fib}}}$ would be as follows.

```
1: let rec fib pn n =
2:   assert(pn>n && n≥0);
3:   let pn' = if *bool then pn else n in
4:   if n < 2 then 1 else fib pn' (n-1) + fib pn' (n-2)
5: let main () = fib ⊥ *int
```

We have added the formal argument pn that represents the argument of an ancestor call (i.e., a call that corresponds to an ancestor node in the call tree) for fib, and inserted the assertion that checks $(pn, n) \in \mathcal{D}_{fib}$ (lines 1-2). Accordingly, we have also inserted an extra parameter to each function call (calls in line 4). In line 3, we non-deterministically "update" the tracked argument to the current argument in order to compare the argument of the current call with a future call of fib. The extra parameter is initially set to $\bot$, to indicate that there is no ancestor call (line 5). We assume that $>$ is extended so that $\bot > n$ holds for every n. For the two recursive calls to fib in the definition of fib, pn or n is passed in a non-deterministic manner. Below is a possible reduction of the transformed program.

$$\begin{aligned}
&\mathtt{main}\ () \to^* \mathtt{fib}\ \bot\ 2 \to^* \mathtt{assert}(\bot > 2 \&\& 2 \geq 0); \cdots \\
&\to^* \mathtt{fib}\ 2\ 1 + \mathtt{fib}\ 2\ 0 \\
&\to^* (\mathtt{assert}(2 > 1 \&\& 1 \geq 0); \cdots) + \mathtt{fib}\ 2\ 0 \\
&\to^* 1 + \mathtt{fib}\ 2\ 0 \\
&\to^* 1 + (\mathtt{assert}(2 > 0 \&\& 0 \geq 0); \cdots) \\
&\to^* 1 + 1 \to^* 2
\end{aligned}$$

The subexpressions fib 2 1 and fib 2 0 capture the fact that fib 1 and fib 0 are called from fib 2 in the original program. It is easy to see that $Rec_P(\mathtt{fib}) \subseteq \mathcal{D}_{fib}$ if and only if $\lceil P \rceil_{fib, \mathcal{D}_{fib}}$ does not cause an assertion failure.

The transformation is more subtle for higher-order programs with partial applications and indirect calls. For example, let P be the program indirect from Example 2 and 4. Suppose that we wish to show $Rec_P(\mathtt{app}) \subseteq \mathcal{D}_{app}$ where $\mathcal{D}_{app} = \{((ph, pv, pu), (h, v, u)) \mid pv > v \geq 0\}$. Then, $\lceil P \rceil_{app, \mathcal{D}_{app}}$ would be as follows.

```
 1: let app _ h _ v (ph,pv,pu) u =
 2:    assert(pv>v && v≥0);
 3:    let (ph,pv,pu) = if *bool then (ph,pv,pu) else (h,v,u)
 4:    in
 5:        h (ph,pv,pu) v (ph,pv,pu) u
 6: let id (ph,pv,pu) u = u
 7: let rec g (ph,pv,pu) x =
 8:    if x≤0 then id
 9:    else app (ph,pv,pu) g (ph,pv,pu) (x-1)
10: let main () = g ⊥̃ *int ⊥̃ ()
```

Here, $\tilde{\bot}$ denotes $(\bot, \bot, \bot)$. As before, the extra parameter (ph, pv, pu) is inserted to represent the arguments of an ancestor call to app (line 1). Note that the extra parameter for this program takes a tuple of values, so that all three arguments of app can be tracked (i.e., h, v, and u). As before, the assertion is inserted at the beginning of the body of app to check $((\text{ph}, \text{pv}, \text{pu}), (\text{h}, \text{v}, \text{u})) \in \mathcal{D}_{\text{fib}}$ (line 2), and we update the tracked past arguments with the current arguments non-deterministically, in order to compare the arguments of the current call with a future call of the function (line 3).

To soundly and completely track the extra parameters through partial applications and indirect calls, we pass the extra parameter at *every* function application site (lines 5, 9, and 10). To be able to do this, note that we have also transformed the definitions of id and g to take the extra parameters and pass them at the applications that occur in their body (lines 6 and 7), and also transformed the definition of app to take an extra parameter argument just before h and v as well as just before u, even though app only checks the well-foundedness against the one passed just before u. (Note that _ in the definition of app is an unused argument.) This is needed, because, in general, we cannot statically decide which (indirect) function call is a fully applied function call, nor which is a call to the target function (i.e., app in the example). We note that it is possible to soundly eliminate some of the redundancy via a static analysis (see Example 5 below), but it is in general impossible to completely decide *a priori* which function is called in what context. In effect, the idea of our transformation is to delegate such tasks to the backend reachability checker.

Example 5. By using useless code elimination [34,13], we can simplify the above program to:

```
let app h v (ph,pv,pu) u =
  assert(pv>v && v≥0);
  let (ph,pv,pu) = if *bool then (ph,pv,pu) else (h,v,u) in
  h v (ph,pv,pu) u
let id (ph,pv,pu) u = u
let rec g x = if x≤0 then id else app g (x-1)
let main () = g *int ⊥ ()
```

Below is a possible reduction of $\lceil P \rceil_{\text{app},\mathcal{D}_{\text{app}}}$. (For simplicity, we use a reduction sequence from the optimized version in Example 5.)

$$\begin{aligned}
\text{main}() &\longrightarrow^* \text{g}\, 2\, \widetilde{\bot}\, () \longrightarrow^* \text{app}\, \text{g}\, 1\, \widetilde{\bot}\, () \\
&\longrightarrow^* \text{g}\, 1\, (\text{g}, 1, ())\, () \longrightarrow^* \text{app}\, \text{g}\, 0\, (\text{g}, 1, ())\, ()
\end{aligned}$$

Note that the reached state $\text{app}\, \text{g}\, 0\, (\text{g}, 1, ())\, ()$ captures the recursion relation $\text{app}\, \text{g}\, 1$ $()\, \triangleright_P \text{app}\, \text{g}\, 0\, ()$ of the original program P.

The Formal Definition of $\lceil \cdot \rceil_{f,\mathcal{D}}$

We now define the transformation formally. $\lceil P \rceil_{f,\mathcal{D}}$ is obtained by transforming each function definition:

$$\lceil P \rceil_{f,\mathcal{D}} = \{\lceil g\, \widetilde{x} = e \rceil_{f,\mathcal{D}} \mid g\, \widetilde{x} = e \in P\}$$

where the function definition transformation is defined as follows.

$$\lceil g\, x_1 \cdots x_k = e \rceil_{f,\mathcal{D}} =$$
$$\begin{cases} g\, s_1\, x_1 \cdots s_k\, x_k = \\ \quad \texttt{let}\ s = \mathbf{check\&upd}(\mathcal{D}, s_k, \langle x_1, \ldots, x_k \rangle)\ \texttt{in}\ \lceil e \rceil_s \\ \qquad\qquad\qquad\qquad\qquad\qquad\qquad\qquad\qquad \text{if } g = f \\ g\, s_1\, x_1 \cdots s_k\, x_k = \lceil e \rceil_{s_k} \qquad\qquad\quad\ \ \text{if } g \neq f \end{cases}$$

Note that an extra parameter s_i is added before every original parameter x_i of a function. Therefore, as opposed to the informal examples given above, the $\texttt{main}$ function in the target program now takes *two* arguments, the first of which is always instantiated to $\bot$. The code that checks the candidate well-foundedness and non-deterministically updates the arguments is inserted at the beginning of the body of the target function f. Here, $\mathbf{check\&upd}(\mathcal{D}, s_k, \langle x_1, \ldots, x_k \rangle)$ denotes the expression

$$\texttt{assert}(\mathcal{D}^\#(s_k, \langle x_1, \ldots, x_k \rangle));\, \texttt{if}\ *_{\texttt{bool}}\ \texttt{then}\ s_k\ \texttt{else}\ \langle x_1, \ldots, x_k \rangle.$$

where the relation $\mathcal{D}^\#$ is the extension of $\mathcal{D}$ defined by:

$$\mathcal{D}^\# = \{(\widetilde{\bot}, \langle v_1, \ldots, v_k \rangle) \mid v_1, \ldots, v_k \text{ are values}\} \cup$$
$$\{(\langle v_1', \ldots, v_k' \rangle, \langle v_1, \ldots, v_k \rangle) \mid (\langle \lfloor v_1' \rfloor, \ldots, \lfloor v_k' \rfloor \rangle, \langle \lfloor v_1 \rfloor, \ldots, \lfloor v_k \rfloor \rangle) \in \mathcal{D}\}$$

Here, $\lfloor v \rfloor$ is the value obtained by removing all the extra arguments from partial applications; see below for the definition. We assume that $\mathcal{D}^\#$ is represented by a formula of some logic. (In the implementation, we use the first-order logic with linear arithmetic.)

Note that the body e of each function definition is transformed by $\lceil e \rceil_s$ where s is the extra parameter passed just before the last argument (non-deterministically updated to the current arguments in the case of the target function). The expression transformation $\lceil e \rceil_s$ passes s at each application site in e, and is formally defined as follows.

$$\lceil c \rceil_s = c \qquad \lceil *_{\texttt{int}} \rceil_s = *_{\texttt{int}} \qquad \lceil f \rceil_s = f \qquad \lceil x \rceil_s = x$$
$$\lceil \texttt{let}\ x = e_1\ \texttt{in}\ e_2 \rceil_s = \texttt{let}\ x = \lceil e_1 \rceil_s\ \texttt{in}\ \lceil e_2 \rceil_s$$
$$\lceil e_1\ op\ e_2 \rceil_s = \lceil e_1 \rceil_s\ op\ \lceil e_2 \rceil_s$$
$$\lceil \texttt{if}\ e_1\ \texttt{then}\ e_2\ \texttt{else}\ e_3 \rceil_s = \texttt{if}\ \lceil e_1 \rceil_s \texttt{then}\ \lceil e_2 \rceil_s \texttt{else}\ \lceil e_3 \rceil_s$$
$$\lceil e_1\, e_2 \rceil_s = \lceil e_1 \rceil_s\ s\ \lceil e_2 \rceil_s$$

The operation $\lfloor e \rfloor$ for removing extra arguments (used in the definition of $\mathcal{D}^\#$) is defined as follows.

$$\lfloor c \rfloor = c \qquad \lfloor *_{\texttt{int}} \rfloor = *_{\texttt{int}} \qquad \lfloor f \rfloor = f \qquad \lfloor x \rfloor = x$$
$$\lfloor \texttt{let}\ x = e_1\ \texttt{in}\ e_2 \rfloor = \texttt{let}\ x = \lfloor e_1 \rfloor\ \texttt{in}\ \lfloor e_2 \rfloor$$
$$\lfloor e_1\ op\ e_2 \rfloor = \lfloor e_1 \rfloor\ op\ \lfloor e_2 \rfloor \qquad \lfloor e_1\ s\ e_2 \rfloor = \lfloor e_1 \rfloor\ \lfloor e_2 \rfloor$$
$$\lfloor \texttt{if}\ e_1\ \texttt{then}\ e_2\ \texttt{else}\ e_3 \rfloor = \texttt{if}\ \lfloor e_1 \rfloor \texttt{then}\ \lfloor e_2 \rfloor \texttt{else}\ \lfloor e_3 \rfloor$$

Note that $\lfloor \lceil e \rceil_s \rfloor = e$.

We prove the soundness and the completeness of the transformation. The following theorem states the soundness of the transformation. It says that the target program reaches an assertion failure when the recursion relation is not a subset of $\mathcal{D}$.

Theorem 3 (Soundness of $\lceil \cdot \rceil_{f,\mathcal{D}_f}$)
Suppose that $\mathtt{main}\,() \to_P^* E_1[f\,v_1\cdots v_k]$, $f\,v_1\cdots v_k \to_P^+ E_2[f\,w_1\cdots w_k]$, *and* $(\langle v_1,\ldots,v_k\rangle,\langle w_1,\ldots,w_k\rangle) \notin \mathcal{D}$. *Then,* $\mathtt{main}\,\bot\,() \to_{\lceil P\rceil_{f,\mathcal{D}}}^* \mathtt{fail}$.

The theorem below states the completeness. It says that the target program reaches an assertion failure only when the recursion relation is not a subset of $\mathcal{D}$.

Theorem 4 (Completeness of $\lceil \cdot \rceil_{f,\mathcal{D}_f}$)
If $\mathtt{main}\,\bot\,() \to_{\lceil P\rceil_{f,\mathcal{D}}}^* \mathtt{fail}$, *then* $\mathtt{main}\,() \to_P^* E_1[f\,\widetilde{v}]$ *and* $f\,\widetilde{v} \to_P^+ E_2[f\,\widetilde{w}]$, *and* $(\langle\widetilde{v}\rangle,\langle\widetilde{w}\rangle) \notin \mathcal{D}$ *for some* $E_1, E_2, \widetilde{v}, \widetilde{w}$.

3.4   Ranking Function Inference

This subsection details how we refine the candidate disjunctively well-founded relation $\mathcal{D}_f$. As remarked in Subsection 3.1, we actually infer both $\mathcal{D}_f$ and the *implicit parameter instantiation* σ. The implicit parameters are used to assert and check well-founded relation over function closure values.

We first describe the case where only $\mathcal{D}_f$ is inferred. (This happens, for example, when f is first-order and does not take function closures as arguments.) Recall that the inference is invoked when $Rec(f) \not\subseteq \mathcal{D}_f$ (cf. Step 3 of Figure 5), and in such a case, the reachability checker returns a counterexample of the form:

$$\mathtt{main}\,() \to^* E[f\,s_1\,v_1\,s_2\,v_2\cdots(v_1',\ldots,v_n')\,v_n]$$
$$\to \mathtt{assert}((v_1',\ldots,v_n'),(v_1,\ldots,v_n)) \in \mathcal{D}_f);\ldots \to \mathtt{fail}$$

As remarked in Subsection 3.3, this implies that $f\,v_1'\cdots v_n' \triangleright f\,v_1\cdots v_n$, and we have that $((v_1',\ldots,v_n'),(v_1,\ldots,v_n)) \in Rec(f)$ and $((v_1',\ldots,v_n'),(v_1,\ldots,v_n)) \notin \mathcal{D}_f$.

The goal of ranking function inference is to obtain a refined disjunctively well-founded relation $\mathcal{D}_f'$ such that

$$\mathcal{D}_f \cup \{((v_1',\ldots,v_n'),(v_1,\ldots,v_n))\} \subseteq \mathcal{D}_f'.$$

To this end, we infer a new ranking function $r(x_1,\ldots,x_n)$ such that $r(v_1',\ldots,v_n') > r(v_1,\ldots,v_n) \geq 0$ and let $\mathcal{D}_f' = \mathcal{D}_f \cup \{(\widetilde{x}',\widetilde{x}) \mid r(\widetilde{x}') > r(\widetilde{x}) \geq 0\}$. We adopt the constraint-based technique [25,5] to infer $r(\widetilde{x})$.

We overview the inference process. We prepare a ranking function *template* $c_0 + c_1x_1 + \cdots + c_nx_n$. Here, c_i's are fresh variables, serving as *unknowns*. Then, we solve for the assignments to c_i's that satisfy the constraint

$$\forall\widetilde{x}.[\![\pi]\!] \Rightarrow c_0 + c_1v_1' + \cdots + c_nv_n' > c_0 + c_1v_1 + \cdots + c_nv_n \geq 0$$

where $\widetilde{x}$ are the free variables in $[\![\pi]\!]$ and $v_1,\ldots,v_n,v_1',\ldots,v_n'$. Here, $[\![\pi]\!]$ is the strongest postcondition of the given counterexample π.[5] Finally, we set $r(x_1,\ldots,x_n) = \alpha_0 + \alpha_1x_1 + \cdots + \alpha_nx_n$ where each α_i is the assignment obtained for c_i.

Next, we extend the above process with *implicit parameters* to infer ranking functions over higher-order values. We illustrate the need for ranking functions over higher-order values with the following program $\mathtt{indirectHO}$.

---

[5] More precisely, we construct a corresponding straightline program from the counterexample, and take its strongest postcondition (cf. [16,33] and the extended report [17]).

```
let app h v = h () v
let id x = x
let rec g x u =
      if x <= 0 then id else app (g (x-1))
let main () = g *int () ()
```

The program is similar to indirect from Example 2 and 4, except that app no longer takes an integer argument and instead has the "decreasing" integer value captured inside the function closure passed as h. To show that this program is terminating, we need to show that the recursion relation for app is disjunctively well-founded. However, because app only takes function-type arguments (besides unit), ranking functions over first-order values are insufficient for this.

To this end, we adopt the idea from the previous work [33] and systematically add an integer-type *implicit parameter* just before each function-type parameter.[6] For indirectHO, we add an implicit parameter h_IMPARAM before h so that the program is now the following. (The added parts are underlined.)

```
let app h_IMPARAM h () = h () ()
let id x = x
let rec g x () =
      if x <= 0 then id else app σ(ℓ) (g (x-1))
let main () = g *int () ()
```

Here, σ is the *candidate implicit parameter instantiation* that maps each *instantiation site* ℓ to an arithmetic expression over the variables bound in the context of ℓ. Formally, an instantiation site is at an application of a function-type argument, and is syntactically determined (i.e., between $e_1\ e_2$ where e_2 is function-type). Clearly, the addition of implicit parameters and their instantiations do not affect the termination of the program, and so we may check the termination of the program with the implicit parameters added to check the termination of the original. The verification process starts by initializing the candidate instantiations to some arithmetic expression (e.g., 0), and refine them iteratively via a counterexample analysis (cf. Figure 5).

As remarked above, in the presence of implicit parameters, we infer both σ and $\mathcal{D}_f$ when given a counterexample. To this end, the above inference process is extended as follows. We prepare templates for the instantiation expressions in addition to the templates for the ranking functions. Then, when generating the constraints, we use the template instantiation expressions in the strongest postcondition of the counterexample, and solve for both the unknowns in the ranking function templates and the instantiation expression templates.

More formally, let $\Pi = \{\pi_1, \ldots, \pi_m\}$ be the set of counterexamples we have seen so far for f. We prepare a template instantiation map Δ that maps each ℓ to an expression of the form $c_0 + c_1 x_1 + \cdots + c_n x_n$ where c_i's are fresh unknowns and x_i's are the

---

[6] Implicit parameters are called "extra parameters" in [33]. We call them implicit parameters here to avoid confusion with the extra parameters in this paper which are used for a different purpose.

Table 1. Experiment results

program	ord	time	program	ord	time	program	ord	time
Ackermann	1	5.85	alias_partial	1	0.32	churchNum	4	3.13
Fibonacci	1	0.15	quicksort	2	timeout	CE-Jones_Bohr	4	0.71
McCarthy91	1	4.95	indirectIntro	2	4.76	up_down	2	0.65
loop2	1	0.61	indirect	2	1.36	map	2	1.59
append	1	0.14	indirectHO	2	7.75	toChurch	2	0.69
zip	1	0.15	CE-0CFA	2	0.14	x_plus_2^n	2	2.02
binomial	1	0.70	CE-1CFA	2	0.24	foldr	2	1.19

integer-type variables that are bound in the context of ℓ (which may include implicit parameters). Then, we form the following constraint

$$\bigwedge_{\pi \in \Pi} \forall \tilde{x}. [\![\pi \Delta]\!] \Rightarrow c_{\pi,0} + c_{\pi,1} v'_{\pi,1} + \cdots + c_{\pi,n} v'_{\pi,n} > c_{\pi,0} + c_{\pi,1} v_{\pi,1} + \cdots + c_{\pi,n} v_{\pi,n} \geq 0$$

where $c_{\pi,i}$'s are fresh unknowns, and $\tilde{x}$ are the free non-unknown variables in $[\![\pi \Delta]\!]$ and $v_1, \ldots, v_n, v'_1, \ldots, v'_n$. (Here, we assume that the counterexamples π explicitly use the instantiation sites ℓ as expressions.) We solve for the unknowns that satisfy the constraint to obtain implicit parameter instantiations and ranking functions that refute the counterexample. We obtain the new candidate disjunctive well-founded relation from the ranking functions: $\mathcal{D} = \bigcup_{\pi \in \Pi} \{(\tilde{x}', \tilde{x}) \mid r_\pi(\tilde{x}') > r_\pi(\tilde{x}) \geq 0\}$ where $r_\pi(\tilde{x}) = \alpha_{\pi,0} + \alpha_{\pi,1} x_1 + \cdots + \alpha_{\pi,n} x_n$ and each $\alpha_{\pi,i}$ is the obtained assignment for $c_{\pi,i}$. And, we substitute the assignments to the unknowns in Δ to obtain the new candidate implicit parameter instantiation. The extended report [17] contains details of the inference process applied to indirectHO.

4 Implementation and Experiments

We have implemented a prototype of the termination verifier for a subset of OCaml. We use MoCHi [16] as the backend reachability checker, and Z3 [22] as a constraint solver for ranking function inference. As an optimization, we have extended the ranking function inference described in Section 3.4 to also infer lexicographic linear ranking functions [5] whenever possible. The extended report [17] contains details of the lexicographic linear ranking function inference process.

We have tested our tool on various termination verification benchmark programs in literature, taken mostly from the previous work on termination verification of higher-order programs, as well as some synthetic but non-trivial examples. We ran the experiment on a machine with 3.20GHz CPU and 16GB of memory, with timeout of 600 seconds. The web interface of the verification tool and the programs used in the experiments are available online [17].

Table 1 summarizes the experiment results. The column "program" shows the names of programs, and the column "ord" shows the order of the program (where order-1 functions take only base type values, order-2 functions may take order-1 functions as arguments, etc., and the order of a program is the maximum order of the functions in the program). The column "time" shows the running time in seconds.

We briefly describe the benchmark programs. The seven programs in the left column and `alias_partial` are first-order (i.e., order-1) programs. The programs `append`, `zip`, and `binomial` are from [2]. `Ackermann` is the Ackermann's function, and is also used as examples in [2,35]. `McCarthy91` is the McCarthy's 91 function (used as a benchmark program in, e.g., [18][7]). `Fibonacci` is the Fibonacci number function from Example 1. The program `alias_partial` is from Section 8 of [18] and is given as an example on which their approach fails.

The program `quicksort` is from [35],[8] and is a second-order program where the list sorting function is parametrized by the "compare" function. We check the termination of a program that passes the sorting function a terminating compare function and an arbitrary list. (Our tool currently does not directly support lists, and so a list is represented by the integer denoting its length.) Our tool fails to verify the program within the time limit due to the underlying reachability checker MoCHi failing to verify the necessary assertion safety. This is not a fundamental limitation with our termination verification approach, and we expect further advances in reachability verification to allow our approach to verify instances like `quicksort`.

The rest of the programs are higher-order programs whose termination depends non-trivially on the functions passed as the arguments, and precise reasoning about the function arguments is required for proving termination. They are mostly from the examples and benchmarks in [12,28,29]. Many of these are difficult examples that the previous approaches cannot verify. (We have selected the ones given as examples where their approaches fail). We refer to the extended report [17] for further description of these programs. As seen in Table 1, the benchmark results are promising and show that our tool is able to automatically verify the difficult instances quickly, except `quicksort` whose reason for the failure is elaborated above.

5   Related Work

There have been three major approaches to automated termination verification for first-order programs: *transition invariants* [26,3,4], *size-change termination* [19], and *term rewriting* [7] (see also [32,8] for relationships between those approaches). The approaches have recently been extended to the termination verification of higher-order programs [18,30,28,29,6,12]. Below, we compare them with our approach.

5.1   Transition Invariants

Closest to our work is the work by Ledesma-Garza and Rybalchenko [18]. Similar to our work, they propose a program transformation to reduce the transition invariant verification problem (i.e., binary reachability analysis) to a plain reachability problem via a program transformation. Unfortunately, as also admitted in their paper (Section

---

[7] [18] is not fully automated and requires the user to provide the sufficient ranking functions as well as the predicates to be used for reachability checking.

[8] [35] is not automated.

8 of [18]), their approach has a limited applicability to the verification of higher-order programs because it does not correctly handle indirect calls and is actually unsound. For example, their approach would incorrectly report the program P_0 from Section 1 to be terminating. Moreover, their approach is not fully automated and requires a sufficient well-foundedness relation to be provided manually, and it also cannot handle well-foundedness relations over function closure values.

By contrast, we have proposed the first sound and (relatively) complete approach to termination verification of higher-order programs via binary reachability analysis. A key idea of our approach is the novel program transformation that precisely tracks the call-tree ancestor's arguments values through the higher-order control flow without a priori approximation. We have also presented a method to infer well-foundedness relations (including those over function closure values) from counterexamples returned by a higher-order program verifier, thus realizing a fully automated verification.

5.2 Size-Change Analysis

The size-change approach [19] to termination verification involves the following two steps: (1) an analysis of the program to construct a *size-change graph*, and (2) an analysis of the obtained graph to decide if the program is terminating. For functional programs, the size-change graph is a graph comprising functions in the program where the edges express the changes in the values that may be passed as arguments. Step (1) constructs the graph by statically approximating the possible calls that the program would make in its actual execution.

To apply size-change termination verification to higher-order programs, a control flow analysis (CFA) is employed to statically approximate the possible call relations as a call graph and construct a sound size-change graph from the call graph [30,28,29,12]. Therefore, the approach involves *a priori* approximation of the program, and can lead to loss in a precision when a precise graph cannot be constructed by the static analysis. For example, the approach may fail on cases where a non-terminating call depends on a safety property (recall the simple example from Section 1 where a non-terminating function is called if and only if the condition $p(x)$ is met). By contrast, our approach suffers no a priori loss in precision and is sound and complete.

Like our approach, the size-change approach to higher-order programs [30,28,29,12] can prove termination of programs that require well-foundedness relation over function closure values. For example, Jones and Bohr [12] and Sereni [28] order closure arguments by using the subtree relation on their tree representations. By contrast, we have presented a generic approach that uses implicit parameters and counterexample analysis to infer the appropriate instantiations for the implicit parameters. Our approach is more general in the sense that it is not fixed to one pattern of closure information to be used for the well-foundedness relation. For example, the subtree relation used in [12,28] can be expressed by inferring instantiations that encode the depth of the closures, and our prototype implementation automatically verifies examples in their paper that require such information (cf. Section 4 and the extended report [17]).

On the other hand, we employ counterexample analysis and constraint-based inference to automatically infer the instantiations, and so the approach of Jones, Bohr, and

Sereni that fixes the closure information to a pre-determined pattern may be more efficient on instances that are known to be verifiable with such information.

5.3 Term Rewriting

Similar to the size-change approach, the application of termination verification techniques for term rewriting systems to higher-order programs is done in a two-step process [6]. There, in the first step, a static analysis is employed to construct a term rewriting system that soundly approximates the given program such that the program is terminating if the constructed rewriting system is terminating. Then, the second step applies a termination verifier for term rewriting systems [7] to verify termination.

As with the size-change approach, this two-step approach can introduce a loss in precision because of the approximation in the first step. For example, Giesl et al. [6] show a simple program on which their approach fails because of this limitation (Example 4.12 in [6]).

6 Conclusion

We have presented a new automated approach to termination verification of higher-order functional programs. In stark contrast to the previous approaches, our approach is sound and complete relative to the soundness and completeness of the underlying reachability analysis and ranking function inference. Our approach is the first sound binary reachability analysis based approach to the termination verification of higher-order programs. The key features of our approach are the novel program transformation that correctly tracks the call-tree ancestor's arguments through the higher-order control flow, and the inference method for ranking functions over higher-order values via implicit parameter instantiation inference.

References

1. Ball, T., Rajamani, S.K.: The SLAM project: debugging system software via static analysis. In: POPL, pp. 1–3 (2002)
2. Chin, W.N., Khoo, S.C.: Calculating sized types. Higher-Order and Symbolic Computation 14(2-3), 261–300 (2001)
3. Cook, B., Podelski, A., Rybalchenko, A.: Abstraction refinement for termination. In: Hankin, C., Siveroni, I. (eds.) SAS 2005. LNCS, vol. 3672, pp. 87–101. Springer, Heidelberg (2005)
4. Cook, B., Podelski, A., Rybalchenko, A.: Termination proofs for systems code. In: PLDI, pp. 415–426. ACM (2006)
5. Cook, B., See, A., Zuleger, F.: Ramsey vs. lexicographic termination proving. In: Piterman, N., Smolka, S.A. (eds.) TACAS 2013. LNCS, vol. 7795, pp. 47–61. Springer, Heidelberg (2013)
6. Giesl, J., Raffelsieper, M., Schneider-Kamp, P., Swiderski, S., Thiemann, R.: Automated termination proofs for Haskell by term rewriting. ACM Transactions on Programming Languages and Systems 33(2), 7:1–7:39 (2011)
7. Giesl, J., Thiemann, R., Schneider-Kamp, P., Falke, S.: Automated termination proofs with AProVE. In: van Oostrom, V. (ed.) RTA 2004. LNCS, vol. 3091, pp. 210–220. Springer, Heidelberg (2004)

8. Heizmann, M., Jones, N.D., Podelski, A.: Size-change termination and transition invariants. In: Cousot, R., Martel, M. (eds.) SAS 2010. LNCS, vol. 6337, pp. 22–50. Springer, Heidelberg (2010)

9. Henzinger, T.A., Jhala, R., Majumdar, R., Sutre, G.: Lazy abstraction. In: POPL, pp. 58–70 (2002)

10. Jhala, R., Majumdar, R.: Software model checking. ACM Comput. Surv. 41(4) (2009)

11. Jhala, R., Majumdar, R., Rybalchenko, A.: HMC: Verifying functional programs using abstract interpreters. In: Gopalakrishnan, G., Qadeer, S. (eds.) CAV 2011. LNCS, vol. 6806, pp. 470–485. Springer, Heidelberg (2011)

12. Jones, N.D., Bohr, N.: Call-by-value termination in the untyped lambda-calculus. Logical Methods in Computer Science 4(1) (2008)

13. Kobayashi, N.: Type-based useless-variable elimination. Higher-Order and Symbolic Computation 14(2-3), 221–260 (2001)

14. Kobayashi, N.: Model checking higher-order programs. Journal of the ACM 60(3) (2013)

15. Kobayashi, N., Ong, C.H.L.: A type system equivalent to the modal mu-calculus model checking of higher-order recursion schemes. In: LICS, pp. 179–188. IEEE Computer Society (2009)

16. Kobayashi, N., Sato, R., Unno, H.: Predicate abstraction and CEGAR for higher-order model checking. In: PLDI, pp. 222–233. ACM (2011)

17. Kuwahara, T., Terauchi, T., Unno, H., Kobayashi, N.: Automatic termination verification for higher-order functional programs (2013),
http://www-kb.is.s.u-tokyo.ac.jp/~kuwahara/termination

18. Ledesma-Garza, R., Rybalchenko, A.: Binary reachability analysis of higher order functional programs. In: Miné, A., Schmidt, D. (eds.) SAS 2012. LNCS, vol. 7460, pp. 388–404. Springer, Heidelberg (2012)

19. Lee, C.S., Jones, N.D., Ben-Amram, A.M.: The size-change principle for program termination. In: POPL, pp. 81–92. ACM (2001)

20. Lester, M.M., Neatherway, R.P., Ong, C.H.L., Ramsay, S.J.: Model checking liveness properties of higher-order functional programs. In: Proceedings of ML Workshop 2011 (2011)

21. McMillan, K.L.: Lazy abstraction with interpolants. In: Ball, T., Jones, R.B. (eds.) CAV 2006. LNCS, vol. 4144, pp. 123–136. Springer, Heidelberg (2006)

22. de Moura, L.M., Bjørner, N.: Z3: An efficient SMT solver. In: Ramakrishnan, C.R., Rehof, J. (eds.) TACAS 2008. LNCS, vol. 4963, pp. 337–340. Springer, Heidelberg (2008)

23. Ong, C.H.L.: On model-checking trees generated by higher-order recursion schemes. In: LICS, pp. 81–90. IEEE Computer Society (2006)

24. Ong, C.H.L., Ramsay, S.: Verifying higher-order programs with pattern-matching algebraic data types. In: Proceedings of POPL 2011, pp. 587–598. ACM (2011)

25. Podelski, A., Rybalchenko, A.: A complete method for the synthesis of linear ranking functions. In: Steffen, B., Levi, G. (eds.) VMCAI 2004. LNCS, vol. 2937, pp. 239–251. Springer, Heidelberg (2004)

26. Podelski, A., Rybalchenko, A.: Transition invariants. In: LICS, pp. 32–41. IEEE Computer Society (2004)

27. Rondon, P.M., Kawaguchi, M., Jhala, R.: Liquid types. In: PLDI, pp. 159–169. ACM (2008)

28. Sereni, D.: Termination analysis of higher-order functional programs. Ph.D. thesis, Magdalen College (2006)

29. Sereni, D.: Termination analysis and call graph construction for higher-order functional programs. In: ICFP, pp. 71–84. ACM (2007)

30. Sereni, D., Jones, N.D.: Termination analysis of higher-order functional programs. In: Yi, K. (ed.) APLAS 2005. LNCS, vol. 3780, pp. 281–297. Springer, Heidelberg (2005)

31. Terauchi, T.: Dependent types from counterexamples. In: POPL, pp. 119–130. ACM (2010)

32. Thiemann, R., Giesl, J.: The size-change principle and dependency pairs for termination of term rewriting. Appl. Algebra Eng. Commun. Comput. 16(4), 229–270 (2005)
33. Unno, H., Terauchi, T., Kobayashi, N.: Automating relatively complete verification of higher-order functional programs. In: POPL, pp. 75–86. ACM (2013)
34. Wand, M., Siveroni, I.: Constraint systems for useless variable elimination. In: Proceedings of POPL 1999, pp. 291–302 (1999)
35. Xi, H.: Dependent types for program termination verification. In: LICS 2001, pp. 231–242. IEEE (2001)
36. Xi, H., Pfenning, F.: Dependent types in practical programming. In: POPL, pp. 214–227 (1999)
37. Zhu, H., Jagannathan, S.: Compositional and lightweight dependent type inference for ML. In: Giacobazzi, R., Berdine, J., Mastroeni, I. (eds.) VMCAI 2013. LNCS, vol. 7737, pp. 295–314. Springer, Heidelberg (2013)

An Abstract Domain to Infer
Ordinal-Valued Ranking Functions⋆

Caterina Urban and Antoine Miné

ÉNS & CNRS & INRIA, Paris, France
{urban,mine}@di.ens.fr

Abstract. The traditional method for proving program termination consists in inferring a ranking function. In many cases (i.e. programs with unbounded non-determinism), a single ranking function over natural numbers is not sufficient. Hence, we propose a new abstract domain to automatically infer ranking functions over ordinals.

We extend an existing domain for piecewise-defined natural-valued ranking functions to polynomials in ω, where the polynomial coefficients are natural-valued functions of the program variables. The abstract domain is parametric in the choice of the maximum degree of the polynomial, and the types of functions used as polynomial coefficients.

We have implemented a prototype static analyzer for a while-language by instantiating our domain using affine functions as polynomial coefficients. We successfully analyzed small but intricate examples that are out of the reach of existing methods.

To our knowledge this is the first abstract domain able to reason about ordinals. Handling ordinals leads to a powerful approach for proving termination of imperative programs, which in particular subsumes existing techniques based on lexicographic ranking functions.

1 Introduction

The traditional method for proving program termination [12] consists in inferring ranking functions, namely mappings from program states to elements of a well-ordered set (e.g. ordinals) whose value decreases during program execution.

Intuitively, we can define a partial ranking function from the states of a program to ordinal numbers in an incremental way: we start from the program final states, where the function has value 0 (and is undefined elsewhere); then, we add states to the domain of the function, retracing the program backwards and counting the maximum number of performed program steps as value of the function. In [10], this intuition is formalized into a most precise ranking function that can be expressed in fixpoint form by abstract interpretation [8] of the program maximal trace semantics.

⋆ The research leading to these results has received funding from the ARTEMIS Joint Undertaking under grant agreement no. 269335 (ARTEMIS project MBAT) (see Article II.9. of the JU Grant Agreement).

Z. Shao (Ed.): ESOP 2014, LNCS 8410, pp. 412–431, 2014.

However, the most precise ranking function is not computable. In [22], we present a decidable abstraction for imperative programs by means of piecewise-defined ranking functions over natural numbers. These functions are attached to the program control points and represent an upper bound on the number of program execution steps remaining before termination. Nonetheless, in many cases (i.e. programs with unbounded non-determinism), natural-valued ranking functions are not powerful enough. For this reason, we propose a new abstract domain to automatically infer ranking functions over ordinals.

We extend the abstract domain of piecewise-defined natural-valued ranking functions to *piecewise-defined ordinal-valued ranking functions* represented as polynomials in ω, where the polynomial coefficients are natural-valued functions of the program variables. The domain automatically infers such ordinal-valued functions through backward invariance analysis. To handle disjunctions arising from tests and loops, the analysis automatically partitions the space of values for the program variables into abstract program states, inducing a piecewise definition of the functions. Moreover, the domain naturally infers sufficient preconditions for program termination. The analysis is sound: all program executions respecting these sufficient preconditions are indeed terminating, while an execution that does not respect these conditions might not terminate.

The abstract domain is parametric in the choices of the state abstraction used for partitioning (in particular, we can abstract the program states using any convex abstract domain such as intervals [7], octagons [19], polyhedra [11], . . .), the maximum degree of the polynomials, and the type of functions used as polynomial coefficients of ω^k (e.g. affine, quadratic, cubic, exponential, . . .). We have implemented an instance of the abstract domain based on interval partitions and affine functions. We successfully analyzed small but intricate examples out of the reach of existing methods.

To our knowledge this is the first abstract domain able to reason about ordinals. We show that handling ordinals leads to a powerful approach for proving program termination of imperative programs which, in particular, subsumes existing techniques based on lexicographic functions.

Motivating Example. In order to motivate the need for ordinal numbers, let us consider the well-known program in Figure 1. At each loop iteration, either it decrements the value of x_2 or it decrements the value of x_1 and resets the value of x_2, until one of the variables becomes less than or equal to zero. The program presents unbounded non-determinism: there is a non-deterministic choice between the branches of the if statement at program point 2, and the value of the variable x_2 is chosen non-deterministically at program point 4 in the first branch of the if statement. The program terminates whatever the initial values for x_1 and x_2 are, and whatever the non-deterministic choices taken during execution.

In the graph of Figure 2, each node represents a state of the program (the nodes with a double outline are final states) and each edge represents a loop iteration. We define a ranking function for the program following the intuition described above: we start from the final states, where we assign value 0 to the function; then, we follow the edges backwards, and for each state that we

```
int : x₁, x₂
while ¹( x₁ ≥ 0 ∧ x₂ ≥ 0 ) do
    if ²( ? ) then
        ³x₁ := x₁ − 1
        ⁴x₂ := ?
    else
        ⁵x₂ := x₂ − 1
od⁶
```

Fig. 1. Motivating example. The symbol ? stands for a non-deterministic choice.

encounter we define the value of the ranking function as the maximum of all values of the function plus 1 for all successors of the state. Hence, we need a transfinite value whenever we encounter a state that leads through unbounded non-determinism to program executions of arbitrary length. In this example, in particular, we need ordinal numbers for all states where $x_1 > 1$ and $x_2 > 0$.

In Section 5 we will detail the analysis of the program by means of our abstract domain of ordinal-valued ranking functions.

It is also possible to prove the termination of the program using a lexicographic ranking function (x_1, x_2). Indeed, a lexicographic tuple $(f_n, \ldots, f_1, f_0)$ of natural numbers is an isomorphic representation of the ordinal $\omega^n \cdot f_n + \cdots + \omega \cdot f_1 + f_0$ [18]. However, reasoning directly with lexicographic ranking functions, poses the additional difficulty of finding an appropriate lexicographic order. Existing methods [1,3,5, etc.] use heuristics to explore the space of possible orders, which grows very large with the number of program variables. Instead, the interesting aspect of ordinal-valued ranking functions is that the coefficients $f_n, \ldots, f_1, f_0$ (and thus their order) are automatically inferred by the analysis. We refer to Section 7 for further discussion on the comparison between lexicographic and ordinal-valued ranking functions.

Our Contribution. In summary, in this paper we propose a parameterized abstract domain for proving termination of imperative programs by abstract interpretation. We introduce the abstract domain of *ordinal-valued* ranking functions, which we subsequently lift to *piecewise-defined* ranking functions. We also describe the implementation of an instance of the abstract domain based on affine functions, and we provide experimental evidence of its expressivity.

Outline of the Paper. Section 2 gives a brief overview of the theory of ordinals and ordinal arithmetic. In Section 3 we recall our concrete semantics, and in Section 4 we introduce the abstract domain of ordinal-valued ranking functions, which we extend to piecewise-defined ranking functions in Section 5. We describe the

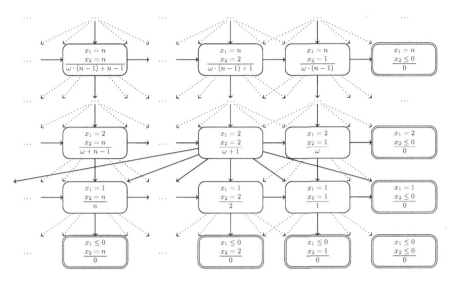

Fig. 2. Transitions between states at control point 1 for the program in Figure 1. There is an edge from any node where x_1 has value $k > 0$ (and $x_2 > 0$) to all nodes where x_1 has value $k - 1$ (and x_2 has any value). In every node we indicate the maximum number of loop iterations needed to reach a final state.

implementation of our prototype static analyzer and we experimentally evaluate our approach in Section 6. Section 7 discusses related work and Section 8 concludes.

2   Ordinals

A relation $<$ is *well-founded* if every $<$-decreasing sequence is finite. A *well-ordered set* is a pair $\langle X, \leq \rangle$ where $\leq$ is a *well-ordering*, i.e. a total order whose corresponding strict order $<$ is a well-founded relation over X. Two well-ordered sets $\langle X, \leq_X \rangle$ and $\langle Y, \leq_Y \rangle$ are *order-isomorphic* if there is a bijection $f : X \to Y$ such that, for all $x_1, x_2 \in X$, $x_1 \leq_X x_2$ if and only if $f(x_1) \leq_Y f(x_2)$. Two order-isomorphic well-ordered sets are said to have the same *order type*.

An *ordinal number* is defined as the order type of a well-ordered set. In the following, we will use lower case Greek letters to denote ordinals. In particular, a well-ordered set $\langle X, \leq \rangle$ with order type α is order-isomorphic to the set $\{x \in X \mid x < \alpha\}$ of all ordinals strictly less than the ordinal α itself. In fact, this property permits the representation of each ordinal as the set of all ordinals that precede it: the smallest ordinal is $\emptyset$, denoted as 0. The *successor* of an ordinal α is defined as $\alpha \cup \{\alpha\}$ and is denoted as $\alpha + 1$. Thus, the first successor ordinal is $\{0\}$, denoted as 1. The next is $\{0, 1\}$, denoted as 2. Continuing in this manner, we obtain all natural numbers (i.e. all *finite* ordinals). A *limit ordinal* is an ordinal number which is neither zero nor a successor ordinal. The set of all natural numbers, denoted as ω, is the first limit ordinal (and the first *transfinite* ordinal). In the following we will use $\langle \mathbb{O}, \leq \rangle$ to denote the well-ordered set of ordinals.

Ordinal Arithmetic. We recall the definition and some properties of addition, multiplication and exponentiation on ordinals [15].

Addition. Ordinal addition can be defined by transfinite induction:

$$\alpha + 0 = \alpha \qquad \text{(zero case)}$$
$$\alpha + (\beta + 1) = (\alpha + \beta) + 1 \qquad \text{(successor case)}$$
$$\alpha + \beta = \bigcup_{\gamma < \beta} (\alpha + \gamma) \qquad \text{(limit case)}$$

Note that addition is associative, i.e. $(\alpha + \beta) + \gamma = \alpha + (\beta + \gamma)$, but not commutative, e.g. $1 + \omega = \omega \neq \omega + 1$.

Multiplication. Ordinal multiplication can also be defined inductively:

$$\alpha \cdot 0 = 0 \qquad \text{(zero case)}$$
$$\alpha \cdot (\beta + 1) = (\alpha \cdot \beta) + \alpha \qquad \text{(successor case)}$$
$$\alpha \cdot \beta = \bigcup_{\gamma < \beta} (\alpha \cdot \gamma) \qquad \text{(limit case)}$$

Multiplication is associative, i.e. $(\alpha \times \beta) \times \gamma = \alpha \times (\beta \times \gamma)$, and left distributive, i.e. $\alpha \times (\beta + \gamma) = (\alpha \times \beta) + (\alpha \times \gamma)$. However, commutativity does not hold, e.g. $2 \times \omega = \omega \neq \omega \times 2$, and neither does right distributivity, e.g. $(\omega + 1) \times \omega = \omega \times \omega \neq \omega \times \omega + \omega$.

Exponentiation. We define ordinal exponentiation again by transfinite induction:

$$\alpha^0 = 1 \qquad \text{(zero case)}$$
$$\alpha^{\beta+1} = (\alpha^\beta) \cdot \alpha \qquad \text{(successor case)}$$
$$\alpha^\beta = \bigcup_{\gamma < \beta} (\alpha^\gamma) \qquad \text{(limit case)}$$

Cantor Normal Form. Using ordinal arithmetic, we can build all ordinal numbers up to ε_0 (i.e. the smallest ordinal such that $\varepsilon_0 = \omega^{\varepsilon_0}$):

$$0, 1, 2, \ldots, \omega, \omega + 1, \omega + 2, \ldots, \omega \cdot 2, \omega \cdot 2 + 1, \omega \cdot 2 + 2, \ldots, \omega^2, \ldots, \omega^3, \ldots, \omega^\omega, \ldots$$

In the following, we will use the representation of ordinals based on Cantor Normal Form [15], i.e. every ordinal $\alpha > 0$ can be uniquely written as

$$\omega^{\beta_1} \cdot n_1 + \cdots + \omega^{\beta_k} \cdot n_k$$

where k is a natural number, the coefficients $n_1, \ldots, n_k$ are positive integers and the exponents $\beta_1 > \beta_2 > \cdots > \beta_k \geq 0$ are ordinal numbers. Throughout the rest of the paper we will consider ordinal numbers only up to ω^ω.

3   Termination Semantics

We consider a programming language that allows non-deterministic assignments and non-deterministic tests. The *operational semantics* of a program is described by a transition system $\langle \Sigma, \tau \rangle$, where Σ is the set of program states and $\tau \subseteq \Sigma \times \Sigma$ is the program transition relation. Let $\beta_\tau \triangleq \{ s \in \Sigma \mid \forall s' \in \Sigma : \langle s, s' \rangle \notin \tau \}$ denote the set of final states. The *maximal trace semantics* [6] generated by a transition system is the set of all infinite traces over the states in Σ and all finite traces that end with a state in β_τ.

The traditional method for proving program termination [12] consists in inferring ranking functions, namely mappings from program states to elements of a well-ordered set (e.g. ordinals) whose value decreases during program execution.

Intuitively, we have seen that we can define a ranking function from the states of a program to ordinal numbers in an incremental way: starting from the program final states and retracing the program backwards while counting the maximum number of performed program steps as value of the function. In Section 1, we have justified the need for ordinal numbers in case of programs with unbounded non-determinism. In [10], Patrick Cousot and Radhia Cousot formalize this intuition and prove the existence of a *most precise ranking function* that can be expressed in fixpoint form by abstract interpretation of the program trace semantics. This partial function[1] $v \in \Sigma \rightharpoonup \mathbb{O}$ extracts the well-founded part of the transition relation τ: starting from the final states in β_τ and mapping each program state in Σ definitely leading to a final state (i.e. a program state such that all the traces to which it belongs end up at a final state in β_τ) to an ordinal in $\mathbb{O}$ representing an upper bound on the number of program execution steps remaining to termination. It is defined as the least fixpoint of the operator ϕ starting from the totally undefined function $\dot{\emptyset}$:

$$v \triangleq \mathsf{lfp}_{\dot{\emptyset}}^{\preccurlyeq} \phi$$

$$\phi(v) \triangleq \lambda s. \begin{cases} 0 & \text{if } s \in \beta_\tau \\ \sup\{ v(s') + 1 \mid \langle s, s' \rangle \in \tau \} & \text{if } s \in \widetilde{\mathsf{pre}}(\mathsf{dom}(v)) \\ \text{undefined} & \text{otherwise} \end{cases}$$

where $v_1 \preccurlyeq v_2 \triangleq \mathsf{dom}(v_1) \subseteq \mathsf{dom}(v_2) \wedge \forall x \in \mathsf{dom}(v_1) : v_1(x) \leq v_2(x)$ and $\widetilde{\mathsf{pre}}(X) \triangleq \{ s \in \Sigma \mid \forall s' \in \Sigma : \langle s, s' \rangle \in \tau \Rightarrow s' \in X \}$. Therefore v is a partial function the domain $\mathsf{dom}(v)$ of which is the set of states definitely leading to program termination: any trace starting in a state $s \in \mathsf{dom}(v)$ must terminate in at most $v(s)$ execution steps, while at least one trace starting in a state $s \notin \mathsf{dom}(v)$ does not terminate. Note that whenever $v(s) \geq \omega$, the programs still terminates, but the number of program execution steps before termination is unbounded.

The ranking function v constitutes a program semantics which is sound and complete to prove program termination (see [10]). However, it is usually not computable. In the following, we will present a decidable abstraction of v. The abstraction uses

---

[1] $A \rightharpoonup B$ is the set of partial maps from a set A to a set B.

the following approximation order (see [9] for further discussion on approximation and computational orders of an abstract domain):

$$v_1 \sqsubseteq v_2 \triangleq \mathsf{dom}(v_1) \supseteq \mathsf{dom}(v_2) \land \forall x \in \mathsf{dom}(v_2) : v_1(x) \leq v_2(x).$$

It computes an over-approximation of the value of the function v but it under-approximates its domain of definition $\mathsf{dom}(v)$. In this way, the abstraction provides sufficient preconditions for program termination: if the abstraction is defined on a program state, then all program execution traces branching from that state are definitely terminating.

4   Ordinal-Valued Ranking Functions

We derive an approximate program semantics by abstract interpretation [8]. First, we introduce the abstract domain of ordinal-valued ranking functions O, which abstracts ranking functions in $\Sigma \rightharpoonup \mathbb{O}$ by abstract ranking functions $o^\# \in \mathcal{O}^\#$ attached to program control points. Then, in the next section, we employ state partitioning to lift this abstraction to piecewise-defined ranking functions.

Let $\mathcal{X}$ be a finite set of program variables. We split the program state space Σ into program control points $\mathcal{L}$ and environments $\mathcal{S} \triangleq \mathcal{X} \rightarrow \mathbb{Z}$, which map each program variable to an integer value. No approximation is made on $\mathcal{L}$. On the other hand, each program control point $l \in \mathcal{L}$ is associated with an element $o^\# \in \mathcal{O}^\#$ of the abstract domain O. Specifically, $o^\#$ represents an abstraction of the function $o \in \mathcal{S} \rightharpoonup \mathbb{O}$ defined on the environments related to the program control point l:

$$\langle \mathcal{S} \rightharpoonup \mathbb{O}, \sqsubseteq \rangle \xleftarrow{\gamma_\mathsf{O}} \langle \mathcal{O}^\#, \sqsubseteq_\mathsf{O} \rangle.$$

Natural-Valued Functions. We assume we are given an abstraction $\langle \mathcal{S}^\#, \sqsubseteq_\mathsf{S} \rangle$ of environments: $\langle \mathcal{P}(\mathcal{S}), \subseteq \rangle \xleftarrow{\gamma_\mathsf{S}} \langle \mathcal{S}^\#, \sqsubseteq_\mathsf{S} \rangle$ (i.e. any abstract domain such as intervals [7], octagons [19], polyhedra [11], . . .), and an abstraction $\langle \mathcal{S}^\# \times \mathcal{F}^\#, \sqsubseteq_\mathsf{F} \rangle$ of $\langle \mathcal{S} \rightharpoonup \mathbb{O}, \sqsubseteq \rangle$ by means of *natural-valued* functions of the program variables:

$$\langle \mathcal{S} \rightharpoonup \mathbb{O}, \sqsubseteq \rangle \xleftarrow{\gamma_\mathsf{F}} \langle \mathcal{S}^\# \times \mathcal{F}^\#, \sqsubseteq_\mathsf{F} \rangle.$$

More specifically, the abstraction $\langle \mathcal{S}^\# \times \mathcal{F}^\#, \sqsubseteq_\mathsf{F} \rangle$ encodes a partial function $v \in \mathcal{S} \rightharpoonup \mathbb{O}$ by a pair of an abstract state $s^\# \in \mathcal{S}^\#$ and a natural-valued function (e.g. an affine function) of the program variables $f^\# \in \mathcal{F}^\#$ [22]. We can now use the abstractions $\mathcal{S}^\#$ and $\mathcal{F}^\#$ to build the abstract domain O.

Ordinal-Valued Functions. The elements of the abstract domain O belong to $\mathcal{O}^\# \triangleq \mathcal{S}^\# \times \mathcal{P}^\#$ where

$$\mathcal{P}^\# \triangleq \{\bot_\mathsf{P}\} \cup \left\{p^\# \mid p^\# = \sum_i \omega^i \cdot f_i^\#, f_i^\# \in \mathcal{F}^\#\right\} \cup \{\top_\mathsf{P}\}$$

is the set of ordinal-valued ranking functions of the program variables (in addition to the function $\perp_P$ representing potential non-termination, and the function $\top_P$ representing the lack of enough information to conclude). More specifically, an abstract function $o^\# \in \mathcal{O}^\#$ is a pair of an abstract state $s^\# \in \mathcal{S}^\#$ and a polynomial in ω (i.e. an ordinal number in Cantor Normal Form) $p^\#$:

$$p^\# \triangleq \omega^k \cdot f_k^\# + \cdots + \omega^2 \cdot f_2^\# + \omega \cdot f_1^\# + f_0^\# \qquad\qquad k > 0$$

where the coefficients $f_0^\#, f_1^\#, \ldots, f_k^\#$ belong to $\mathcal{F}^\#$. In the following, with abuse of notation, we use a map $s^\# \mapsto p^\#$ to denote the pair of $s^\# \in \mathcal{S}^\#$ and $p^\# \in \mathcal{P}^\#$.

The abstract domain O is parameterized by the choices of the state abstraction $\langle \mathcal{S}^\#, \sqsubseteq_S \rangle$, the maximum degree k of the polynomial, and the type (e.g. affine, quadratic, cubic, exponential, ...) of functions used as polynomial coefficients $f_0^\#, f_1^\#, f_2^\#, \ldots, f_n^\#$.

Concretization Function. The concretization function $\gamma_O \in \mathcal{O}^\# \to (\mathcal{S} \rightharpoonup \mathbb{O})$ depends on γ_S, which maps an abstract state $s^\# \in \mathcal{S}^\#$ to the corresponding set of program environments, and on γ_F, which maps a relation $v^\# \in \mathcal{S}^\# \times \mathcal{F}^\#$ to the corresponding partial function $v \in \mathcal{S} \rightharpoonup \mathbb{O}$:

$$\gamma_O(s^\# \mapsto \perp_P) = \dot{\emptyset}$$
$$\gamma_O(s^\# \mapsto p\#) = \lambda s \in \gamma_S(s^\#).\ p^\#(s)$$
$$\text{where } p^\#(s) = \sum_{i \leq k} \omega^i \cdot \gamma_F(s^\# \mapsto f_i^\#)(s)$$
$$\gamma_O(s^\# \mapsto \top_P) = \dot{\emptyset}$$

where $\dot{\emptyset}$ denotes the totally undefined function. Note that the concretization function γ_O forgets about all program states that are potentially non-terminating ($\perp_P$) and all program states for which there is not enough information ($\top_P$). This agrees with our goal to under-approximate the domain of definition of the most precise ranking function (cf. Section 3).

Order. To compare two abstract functions, we define the abstract approximation order $\sqsubseteq_O$ as the abstract counterpart of the approximation order $\sqsubseteq$:

$$(s_1^\# \mapsto p_1^\#) \sqsubseteq_O (s_2^\# \mapsto p_2^\#) \triangleq s_2^\# \sqsubseteq_S s_1^\# \wedge p_1^\# \sqsubseteq_P p_2^\#$$

where $p_1^\# \sqsubseteq_P p_2^\# \triangleq \forall s \in \gamma_S(s_2^\#) : p_1^\#(s) \leq p_2^\#(s)$.

In order for an abstract function $o_1^\#$ to be smaller than an abstract function $o_2^\#$, we require the domain of $o_2^\#$ to be included in the domain of $o_1^\#$ ($s_2^\# \sqsubseteq_S s_1^\#$) and, for all states in the domain of $o_2^\#$, we require $o_1^\#$ to have smaller (or equal) value than $o_2^\#$ ($p_1^\# \sqsubseteq_P p_2^\#$). The relative precision between abstract functions is preserved by the concretization function γ_O:

$$(s_1^\# \mapsto p_1^\#) \sqsubseteq_O (s_2^\# \mapsto p_2^\#) \Rightarrow \gamma_O(s_1^\# \mapsto p_1^\#) \sqsubseteq \gamma_O(s_2^\# \mapsto p_2^\#)$$

Join. The join operator $\sqcup_O$, given two abstract functions $o_1^\# \triangleq s_1^\# \mapsto p_1^\#$ and $o_2^\# \triangleq s_2^\# \mapsto p_2^\#$, determines the function $o^\# \triangleq s^\# \mapsto p^\#$, defined on their common domain $s^\# \triangleq s_1^\# \sqcap_S s_2^\#$ with value $p^\# \triangleq p_1^\# \sqcup_P p_2^\#$.

Specifically, the unification $p_1^\# \sqcup_P p_2^\#$ of two polynomials $p_1^\#$ and $p_2^\#$ is done in ascending powers of ω, joining the coefficients of similar terms (i.e. terms with the same power of ω). The join of two coefficients $f_1^\#$ and $f_2^\#$ is provided by $f^\# \triangleq f_1^\# \sqcup_F f_2^\#$ and is defined as a *natural-valued* function (of the same type of $f_1^\#$ and $f_2^\#$) greater than $f_1^\#$ and $f_2^\#$ (on the domain $s^\#$). Whenever such function does not exist, we force $f^\#$ to equal 0 and we carry 1 to the unification of terms with next higher degree (unless we have already reached the maximum degree for the polynomial, in which case we abandon to $\top_P$).

Example 1. Let $\mathcal{X} = \{x_1, x_2\}$ and let $\langle \mathcal{S}^\# \times \mathcal{F}^\#, \sqsubseteq_F \rangle$ be an abstraction of $\langle \mathcal{S} \rightharpoonup \mathbb{O}, \sqsubseteq \rangle$ that uses intervals [7] as state abstraction and affine functions as abstract functions $f^\# \in \mathcal{F}^\#$ [22]. We consider the join of the abstract functions:

$$o_1^\# \triangleq s_1^\# \mapsto p_1^\# \triangleq [-\infty, +\infty] \mapsto \omega \cdot x_1 + x_2$$
$$o_2^\# \triangleq s_2^\# \mapsto p_2^\# \triangleq [-\infty, +\infty] \mapsto \omega \cdot (x_1 - 1) - x_2$$

Their common domain is trivially $s^\# \triangleq [-\infty, +\infty]$. The unification of the two polynomials $p_1^\#$ and $p_2^\#$ starts from joining the functions $f_{0_1}^\# \triangleq x_2$ and $f_{0_2}^\# \triangleq -x_2$. However, there does not exist a *natural-valued* affine function $f_0^\#$ greater than $f_{0_1}^\#$ and $f_{0_2}^\#$ for all possible values of x_2 (since $s^\# \triangleq [-\infty, +\infty]$). We force $f_0^\#$ to equal 0 and we carry 1 to the unification of $f_{1_1}^\# \triangleq x_1$ and $f_{1_2}^\# \triangleq x_1 - 1$ which becomes $f_1^\# = x_1 + 1$ (i.e. x_1 after the unification, and $x_1 + 1$ after carrying). The result of the join is $o^\# \triangleq [-\infty, +\infty] \mapsto \omega \cdot (x_1 + 1)$. □

Intuitively, whenever natural-valued functions are not sufficient, we naturally resort to ordinal numbers. Let us consider the join $\omega^k \cdot f^\#$ of two terms $\omega^k \cdot f_1^\#$ and $\omega^k \cdot f_2^\#$. Forcing $f^\#$ to equal 0 and carrying 1 to the terms with next higher degree is exactly the same as considering $f^\#$ equal to ω (and applying the limit case of ordinal multiplication): $\omega^k \cdot f^\# = \omega^k \cdot \omega = \omega^{k+1} \cdot 1 + \omega^k \cdot 0 = \omega^{k+1}$.

Widening. The widening operator ∇_O summarizes two abstract functions $o_1^\# \triangleq s_1^\# \mapsto p_1^\#$ and $o_2^\# \triangleq s_2^\# \mapsto p_2^\#$ into a single one $o^\# \triangleq s^\# \mapsto p^\#$, where $s^\# \triangleq s_1^\# \sqcup_S s_2^\#$ and $p^\# \triangleq p_1^\# \sqcup_P p_2^\#$ (unless the two abstract functions are already defined on the same abstract state — i.e. $s_1^\# =_S s_2^\#$ — and $p_1^\# \sqsubseteq_P p_2^\#$, in which case $p^\# \triangleq \top_P$ to ensure convergence). Note that ∇_O differs from the join $\sqcup_O$ in that it widens the abstract state $s^\#$ to the union of $s_1^\#$ and $s_2^\#$. Indeed, the join is an upper-bound with respect to the approximation order $\sqsubseteq$, while the widening is an upper-bound with respect to the computational order $\preceq$ (cf. Section 3).

Assignments. In order to handle assignments, the abstract domain is equipped with an operation to substitute an arithmetic expression for a variable within a function $f^\# \in \mathcal{F}^\#$. Given an abstract function $o^\# \triangleq s^\# \mapsto p^\#$, an assignment is carried out independently on the abstract state $s^\#$ and on the polynomial $p^\#$. In particular, an assignment on $p^\#$ is performed in ascending powers of ω, possibly carrying 1 to the term with next higher degree, and is preceded by the addition of 1 to the polynomial constant (to take into account that one more program step is needed before termination). The need for carrying might occur in case of non-deterministic assignments: it is necessary to take into account all possible outcomes of the assignment, possibly using ω as approximation.

Example 2. Let $\mathcal{X} = \{x_1, x_2\}$. We consider the result of the non-deterministic assignment $x_1 := ?$ to the polynomial $p^\# \triangleq \omega \cdot x_1 + x_2$. First, we add 1 to the function $f_0^\# \triangleq x_2$ to *count* the assignment as an additional step needed before termination. Then, we perform the assignment on the terms of the polynomial: the function $f_0^\#$ remains unchanged (since the assignment involves only the variable x_1), whereas the coefficient $f_1^\# \triangleq x_1$ of ω is reset to 0 and carries 1 to the term with next higher degree ω^2. In fact, the assignment $x_1 := ?$ allows x_1 (and consequently $f_1^\#$) to take *any* value, but there does not exist a *natural-valued* function that properly abstracts all possible outcomes of the assignment. The resulting polynomial is $\bar{p}^\# \triangleq \omega^2 \cdot 1 + \omega \cdot 0 + x_2 + 1 = \omega^2 + x_2 + 1$. □

Tests. Test statements only affect the abstract states $s^\# \in \mathcal{S}^\#$ (and are managed by the state abstraction) and leave unchanged the polynomials $p^\# \in \mathcal{P}^\#$.

5   Piecewise-Defined Ranking Functions

In the following, we will briefly recall the abstract domain of piecewise-defined ranking functions [22]. Then, we describe our extension of this domain using the ordinal-valued ranking functions we presented in Section 4.

5.1   Piecewise-Defined Natural-Valued Ranking Functions

In [22], a decidable abstraction of the most precise ranking function $v \in \Sigma \rightharpoonup \mathbb{O}$ (cf. Section 3) is provided by the abstract domain $\mathsf{V}(\mathsf{F}(\mathsf{S}))$, where V is a functor abstract domain parameterized by S, an abstract domain for states, and F, an abstract domain based on natural-valued functions of the program variables.

The elements of the abstract domain belong to $\mathcal{V}^\# \triangleq \mathcal{P}(\mathcal{S}^\# \times \mathcal{F}^\#)$, where $\mathcal{S}^\#$ is the set of abstract program states (e.g. intervals [7]) and $\mathcal{F}^\#$ is the set of natural-valued functions of the program variables (e.g. affine functions). More specifically, an element $v^\# \in \mathcal{V}^\#$ has the form:

$$v^\# \triangleq \begin{cases} s_1^\# \mapsto f_1^\# \\ \quad \vdots \\ s_k^\# \mapsto f_k^\# \end{cases}$$

where the abstract states $s_1^{\#}, \ldots, s_k^{\#}$ induce a partition of the space of environments $\mathcal{S} \triangleq \mathcal{X} \to \mathbb{Z}$, and $f_1^{\#}, \ldots, f_k^{\#}$ are ranking functions.

The binary operators of the abstract domain rely on a partition unification algorithm that, given two piecewise-defined ranking functions $v_1^{\#}$ and $v_2^{\#}$, modifies the partitions on which they are defined into a common refined partition of the space of program environments. For example, in case of partitions determined by intervals with constant bounds, the unification simply introduces new bounds consequently splitting intervals in both partitions. Then, the binary operators are applied piecewise. The approximation order $\sqsubseteq_V$ and the computational order $\preccurlyeq_V$ return the conjunction of the piecewise comparisons. The piecewise join $\sqcup_V$ computes the piecewise-defined natural-valued ranking function greater than $v_1^{\#}$ and $v_2^{\#}$. The piecewise widening $\triangledown_V$ summarizes *adjacent* pieces of a function joining them into a single one. In this way, it prevents the number of pieces of an abstract function from growing indefinitely. It also prevents the indefinite growth of the *value* of an abstract function going to $\top$ on the partitions where the value of the ranking function has increased between iterations.

The unary operators for assignments and tests are also applied piecewise. In particular, assignments are carried out independently on each abstract state and each ranking function. Then, the resulting covering induced by the over-approximated abstract states is refined (joining overlapping pieces) to obtain once again a partition.

The operators of the abstract domain are combined together to compute an abstract ranking function for a program, through backward invariance analysis. The starting point is the constant function equal to 0 at the program final control point. The ranking function is then propagated backwards towards the program initial control point taking assignments and tests into account with join and widening around loops. As a consequence of the soundness of all abstract operators (see [22]), we can establish the soundness of the analysis for proving program termination: the program states, for which the analysis finds a ranking function, are states from which the program indeed terminates.

However, since the abstract domain V is limited to ranking functions over natural numbers, all program traces with unbounded non-determinism are disregarded by the abstraction. As a result, the abstract domain is not able to prove the termination of programs as the one in Figure 1. In the following, we describe how we extend this abstract domain to ranking functions over ordinal numbers.

5.2   Piecewise-Defined Ordinal-Valued Ranking Functions

We propose the abstract domain V(O(F(S))) obtained by extending V(F(S)) with the domain of ordinal-valued ranking functions O presented in Section 4.

An element $v^{\#} \in \mathcal{V}^{\#}$ of the abstract domain has now the form:

$$v^{\#} \triangleq \begin{cases} s_1^{\#} \mapsto p_1^{\#} \\ \quad\vdots \\ s_k^{\#} \mapsto p_k^{\#} \end{cases}$$

where the abstract states $s_1^{\#}, \ldots, s_k^{\#} \in \mathcal{S}^{\#}$ induce a partition of the space of environments $\mathcal{S}$ and $p_1^{\#}, \ldots, p_k^{\#}$ are ranking functions represented as polynomials $\omega^k \cdot f_k^{\#} + \cdots + \omega^2 \cdot f_2^{\#} + \omega \cdot f_1^{\#} + f_0^{\#}$ whose coefficients $f_0^{\#}, f_1^{\#}, f_2^{\#}, \ldots, f_n^{\#} \in \mathcal{F}^{\#}$ are natural-valued functions of the program variables.

The partition unification algorithm of $\mathsf{V}(\mathsf{O}(\mathsf{F}(\mathsf{S})))$ works exactly in the same way as that of $\mathsf{V}(\mathsf{F}(\mathsf{S}))$, while the piecewise operators of the domain now use the operators of O (which in turn exploit the operators of F for the polynomial coefficients) instead of using directly those of F. The soundness of all abstract operators of $\mathsf{V}(\mathsf{O}(\mathsf{F}(\mathsf{S})))$ follows by the soundness of all abstract operators of $\mathsf{V}(\mathsf{F}(\mathsf{S}))$, and by the soundness of all abstract operators of O with respect to ordinal arithmetic. Therefore, the abstract domain $\mathsf{V}(\mathsf{O}(\mathsf{F}(\mathsf{S})))$ is suitable to prove program termination and is more powerful than $\mathsf{V}(\mathsf{F}(\mathsf{S}))$ because it overcomes the limitations of natural-valued ranking functions. Indeed, $\mathsf{V}(\mathsf{O}(\mathsf{F}(\mathsf{S})))$ is able to prove the termination of the non-deterministic program in Figure 1.

Motivating Example (continued). Due to space constraints, we describe in some detail only a few interesting iterations of the (backward) analysis of the program in Figure 1. We invite the interested reader to refer to our prototype implementation [21] for a more complete and detailed program analysis.

The starting point is the constant function $f_6(x_1, x_2) = 0$ at the program final control point 6. We use a widening delay of 3 iterations. At the fourth iteration, the ranking function at the loop control point 1 is:

$$f_1^4(x_1, x_2) = \begin{cases} 1 & x_1 \leq 0 \vee x_2 \leq 0 \\ 3x_2 + 2 & x_1 = 1 \\ \bot & \text{otherwise} \end{cases}$$

In the second case, the function $3x_2 + 2$ comes out as a result of the widening between adjacent pieces with consecutive values for x_2 (i.e. between the pieces $(x_1 = 1 \wedge x2 = 1) \mapsto 5$ and $(x_1 = 1 \wedge x2 = 2) \mapsto 8$).

Ordinal numbers appear for the first time at program control point 4 due to the non-deterministic assignment to x_2:

$$f_4^4(x_1, x_2) = \begin{cases} 2 & x_1 \leq 0 \\ \omega & x_1 = 1 \\ \bot & \text{otherwise} \end{cases}$$

In the first case, the value of the function is simply increased (to count one more program step before termination) but (since x_2 can now have any value) its domain is modified forgetting all constraints on x_2 (i.e. $x_2 \leq 0$). In the second case, $3x_2 + 2$ is increased to $3x_2 + 3$ (to count one more program step) which then becomes ω (due to approximation of the non-deterministic assignment).

At the seventh iteration, at control point 1, we obtain the ranking function:

$$f_1^7(x_1, x_2) = \begin{cases} 1 & x_1 \leq 0 \vee x_2 \leq 0 \\ 3x_2 + 2 & x_1 = 1 \\ \omega + 3x_2 + 9 & x_1 = 2 \\ \bot & \text{otherwise} \end{cases}$$

as a result of the widening between the preceding iterate f_1^6:

$$f_1^6(x_1, x_2) = \begin{cases} 1 & x_1 \leq 0 \vee x_2 \leq 0 \\ 3x_2 + 2 & x_1 = 1 \\ \omega + 12 & x_1 = 2 \wedge x_2 = 1 \\ \omega + 15 & x_1 = 2 \wedge x_2 = 2 \\ \bot & \text{otherwise} \end{cases}$$

and the ranking function $f_1^{6'}$, obtained from f_1^6 after one loop iteration:

$$f_1^{6'}(x_1, x_2) = \begin{cases} 1 & x_1 \leq 0 \vee x_2 \leq 0 \\ 3x_2 + 2 & x_1 = 1 \\ \omega + 12 & x_1 = 2 \wedge x_2 = 1 \\ \omega + 15 & x_1 = 2 \wedge x_2 = 2 \\ \omega + 18 & x_1 = 2 \wedge 3 \leq x_2 \\ \bot & \text{otherwise} \end{cases}$$

In particular, widening occurs between the pieces where $x_1 = 2$. It is performed in ascending powers of ω: from the constants 12, 15 and 18 (all corresponding to consecutive values for x_2), it infers the affine function $3x_2 + 9$ (by classic join of affine functions); then, since for all pieces the coefficient of ω is equal to 1, the inferred coefficient of ω is again 1. Thus, the result of the widening for $x_1 = 2$ is $\omega + 3x_2 + 9$.

Finally, at the eleventh iteration, we reach a fixpoint f_1^{11}:

$$f_1^{11}(x_1, x_2) = \begin{cases} 1 & x_1 \leq 0 \vee x_2 \leq 0 \\ 3x_2 + 2 & x_1 = 1 \\ \omega + 3x_2 + 9 & x_1 = 2 \\ \omega \cdot (x_1 - 1) + 7x_1 + 3x_2 - 5 & \text{otherwise} \end{cases}$$

Note that the second and third expressions are particular cases (for $x_1 = 1$ and $x_1 = 2$ respectively) of the last expression and are explicitly listed only due to the amount of widening delay we used. The function $f(x_1, x_2) = \omega \cdot (x_1 - 1) + 7x_1 + 3x_2 - 5$ constitutes a ranking function[2] for the program loop, while the first case represents immediate program exit (without even entering the loop). □

---

[2] The reason why we obtain a different ranking function with respect to Figure 2 is because we count the number of program execution steps whereas, for convenience of presentation, in Figure 2 we count the number of loop iterations.

6   Implementation

We have incorporated the implementation of our abstract domain for ordinal-valued ranking functions O into our prototype static analyzer [21] based on piecewise-defined ranking functions.

The prototype accepts programs written in a small non-deterministic while-language. It is written in OCaml and, at the time of writing, the available abstraction for program states S is based on intervals [7] and the available abstraction for natural-valued functions F is based on affine functions represented as convex polyhedra [11]. The operators for the intervals and convex polyhedra abstract domains are provided by the Apron library [14]. The extension to ordinal-valued ranking functions is optional, but when activated it requires to choose a maximum degree for the abstract polynomials. It is also possible to tune the precision of the analysis by adjusting the widening delay.

The analysis proceeds by structural induction on the program syntax, iterating loops until an abstract fixpoint is reached. In case of nested loops, a fixpoint on the inner loop is computed for each iteration of the outer loop.

6.1   Examples

To illustrate the expressiveness of our domain, we consider two more examples, besides the one shown in Section 5.

Example 3. Let us consider the program in Figure 3 which is an involved variation of the one in Figure 1. The variables x_1 and x_2 can have any initial integer value, and the program behaves differently depending on whether x_1 is positive or negative. In case x_1 is positive, the program behaves exactly as in Figure 1. In case x_1 is negative, the program either increments the value of x_1 or it decrements the value of x_2 and resets x_1 to any value (possibly positive). The loop exits when x_1 is equal to zero or x_2 is less than zero.

Note that there does not exist a lexicographic ranking function for the loop. In fact, the variables x_1 and x_2 can be alternatively reset to any value at each loop iteration: the value of x_2 is reset at the program control point 5 (in the first branch of the first if statement, i.e. if $x_1 > 0$) while the value of x_1 is reset at the control point 10 (in the second branch of the first if statement, i.e. if $x_1 < 0$).

Nonetheless, the program always terminates, regardless of the initial values for x_1 and x_2, and regardless of the non-deterministic choices taken during execution. Let us consider the graph in Figure 5. Whenever x_2 is reset to any value, we move towards the final states decreasing the value of x_1, and whenever x_1 is reset to any value, we move towards the final states decreasing the value of x_2. Moreover, whenever x_1 is reset to a positive value, its value will only decrease until it reaches zero (or x_2 is reset to a value less than zero).

Our prototype is able to prove the program termination in about 10 seconds (with a widening delay of 3 iterations). We automatically infer the following piecewise-defined ranking function:

```
int : x₁, x₂
while ¹( x₁ ≠ 0 ∧ x₂ ≥ 0 ) do
    if ²( x₁ > 0 ) then
        if ³( ? ) then
            ⁴x₁ := x₁ - 1
            ⁵x₂ := ?
        else
            ⁶x₂ := x₂ - 1
    else
        if ⁷( ? ) then
            ⁸x₁ := x₁ + 1
        else
            ⁹x₂ := x₂ - 1
            ¹⁰x₁ := ?
od¹¹
```

Fig. 3. Program with no lexicographic ranking function

```
int : x₁, x₂
¹x₁ := N
while ²( x₁ ≥ 0 ) do
    ³x₂ := N
    while ⁴( x₂ ≥ 0 ) do
        ⁵x₂ := x₂ - 1
    od
    ⁶x₁ := x₁ - 1
od⁷
```

Fig. 4. Program with non-linear computational complexity

$$f(x_1, x_2) = \begin{cases} \omega^2 + \omega \cdot (x_2 - 1) - 4x_1 + 9x_2 - 2 & x_1 < 0 \wedge x_2 > 0 \\ 1 & x_1 = 0 \vee x_2 \leq 0 \\ \omega \cdot (x_1 - 1) + 9x_1 + 4x_2 - 7 & x_1 > 0 \wedge x_2 > 0 \end{cases}$$

In Figure 5, we justify the need for ω^2. Indeed, from any state where $x_1 < 0$ and $x_2 = k_2 > 0$, whenever x_1 is reset at program control point 10, it is possible to jump to any state where $x_2 = k_2 - 1$. In particular, for example from the state where $x_1 = -1$ and $x_2 = 2$, it is possible to jump through unbounded non-determinism to states with value of the most precise ranking function equal to an arbitrary ordinal number between ω and ω^2, which requires ω^2 as upper bound of the maximum number of loop iterations needed to reach a final state.

Finally, note the expressions identified as coefficients of ω: where $x_1 < 0$, the coefficient of ω is an expression in x_2 (since x_2 guides the progress towards the final states), and where $x_1 > 0$, the coefficient of ω is an expression in x_1 (because x_1 now rules the progress towards termination). The expressions are automatically inferred by the analysis without requiring assistance from the user.   □

Example 4. Let us consider the program in Figure 4. Since the program has quadratic time complexity, we cannot prove its termination limiting ourselves to piecewise-defined natural-valued *affine* ranking functions.

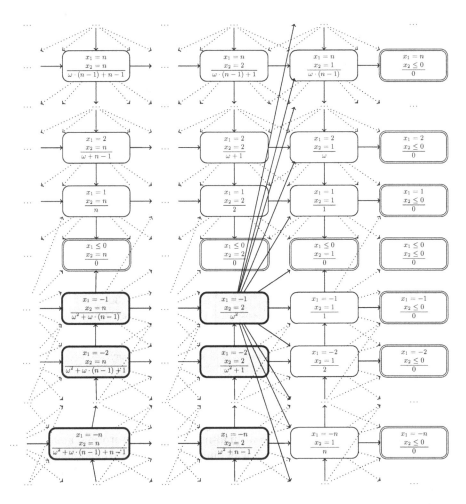

Fig. 5. Transitions between states at control point 1 for the program in Figure 3. There is an edge from any node where x_1 has value $k_1 > 0$ (and $x_2 > 0$) to all nodes where x_1 has value $k_1 - 1$ (and x_2 has any value); there is also an edge from any node where x_2 has value $k_2 > 0$ (and $x_1 < 0$) to all nodes where x_2 has value $k_2 - 1$ (and x_1 has any value). In every node we indicate the maximum number of loop iterations needed to reach a final state: the highlighted nodes require an ordinal greater than ω^2.

Program	Ranking Function
[1, Figure 1]	$f(x, y) = 57x + 3y + 28$ Time: < 3 s (Widening Delay: 2)
[4, Figure 1]	$f(x, y) = 7y + 3x - 5$ Time: < 1 s (Widening Delay: 2)
[5, Figure 7a]	$f(x, y, d) = \omega \cdot (y - 1) + 4x + 9y - 7$ Time: < 60 s (Widening Delay: 3)
[5, Figure 7b]	$f(x, y, z) = \omega^2 \cdot (y - 1) + \omega \cdot (y + z - 2) + 3x + 13y + 8z - 18$ Time: < 240 s (Widening Delay: 3)
[5, Figure 8a]	$f(x) = \begin{cases} -3x + 1 & x < 0 \\ 1 & x = 0 \\ 3x + 1 & x > 0 \end{cases}$ Time: < 1 s (Widening Delay: 2)
[23, MirrorIntervSim]	$f(x) = \begin{cases} 4 & x \leq -6 \\ \bot & -5 \leq x \leq -1 \\ 1 & x = 0 \\ 6 & x = 1 \\ 5x + 1 & 2 \leq x \leq 30 \\ \bot & 31 \leq x \leq 35 \\ 4 & x \geq 36 \end{cases}$ Time: < 1 s (Widening Delay: 2)

Fig. 6. Some of the benchmarks used in experiments

However, with the extension to ordinal-numbers, our prototype analyzes the program in about 2 seconds (with a widening delay of 2 iterations). The inferred ranking function is $f(x_1, x_2) = \omega + 2$, where ω constitutes an upper-bound on the number of program execution steps spent inside the while loop (i.e. it testifies that the number of execution step spent inside the while loop is *finite*), and the constant 2 takes into account the initialization step $x_1 := N$ and the test $x_1 < 0$ that enforces loop exit. This ordinal-valued ranking function represents a rough approximation of the program computational complexity, but allows nonetheless to prove its termination without requiring to handle ranking function more complex than affine functions.   □

6.2   Experiments

We have evaluated our prototype implementation against a set of benchmarks collected from publications in the area [1,4,5,23, etc.] or inspired from real code.

We analyzed 38 examples: 25 terminating loops and 13 conditionally terminating loops. Among them, nine are "simple loops" (i.e. loops with only variable updates in the loop body) and seven are nested loops. We successfully proved (conditional) termination for all simple loops but one, and for four out of the seven nested loops. Only two nested loops required the extension to ordinal numbers (to cope with a non-linear computational complexity). 13 of the 38 benchmarks are non-deterministic programs. We proved termination for ten of them, using ordinal numbers in five cases. In the other five cases, piecewise-defined natural-valued ranking functions were sufficient (even when the programs were presented in the literature as requiring a lexicographic ranking function). In summary, our prototype was able to automatically solve 30 of the 38 benchmarks we considered. Failure in the eight missing cases is due to the non-relational nature of partitioning with intervals and, in particular, is not related to the use of ordinal numbers. Almost all examples were analyzed in less than 60 seconds (only one example took aroud 240 seconds), with maximum polynomial degree of two and maximum widening delay of seven iterations. In Figure 6 are depicted some representatives of the benchmarks, together with our results.

7 Related Work

In the recent past, a large body of work has been devoted to proving program termination of imperative programs. To the best of our knowledge, in this setting, the inference of ordinal-valued ranking functions is unique to our work.

Aside from the use of ordinal numbers, the approach presented in this paper is mostly related to [1]: both techniques handle programs with arbitrary structure and infer ranking functions (that also provide information on the program computational complexity in terms of executions steps) attached to program control points. The technique proposed in [1] uses invariants (pre)computed for each program control point to infer lexicographic ranking functions (also attached to program points). On the other hand, with our approach, we infer ordinal-valued ranking functions *directly* as invariants attached to program control points. In [1], the problem of finding an appropriate lexicographic order is handled by a greedy algorithm, whereas dealing with ordinal numbers relieves us from the burden of finding lexicographic orders (cf. Section 1). In contrast, ordinal-valued ranking functions parameterized by functions with limited expressivity (e.g. affine functions) might produce a rough approximation of the program computational complexity (cf. Example 4). We plan to study these issues further and support non-linear functions as part of our future work.

In order to avoid lexicographic ranking functions, many other approaches rely on the transition invariants method introduced in [20]. The advantage of this method is that it only requires to find a *set* of ranking functions, without lexicographic ordering between them. However, the main drawback of the method is the cost of explicitly checking the validity of the termination argument. On the other hand, our approach also avoids explicit lexicographic orders, but in addition it does not suffer from this disadvantage because the validity of the termination argument is automatically enforced at each loop iteration.

In a different context, a large amount of research followed the introduction of size-change termination (SCT) [17]. The SCT approach consists in collecting a set of size-change graphs (representing function calls) and combining them into multipaths (representing program executions) in such a way that at least one variable is guaranteed to decrease. Compared to SCT, our approach avoids the exploration of the combinatorial space of multipaths with the explicit manipulation of ordinal numbers. In [16,2], algorithms are provided to derive explicit ranking functions from size-change graphs, but these ranking functions have a shape quite different from ours which makes it difficult for us to compare their expressiveness. For example, the derived ranking functions use lexicographic orders on variables while our polynomial coefficients are arbitrary linear combinations of variables. In general, an in-depth comparison between such fairly different methods is an open research topic (e.g. see [13] for the comparison of the transition invariants and the size-change termination methods).

Finally, we have seen that there exist programs (e.g., the program in Figure 3) for which there does not exist a lexicographic ranking function. In [5] the authors discuss the problem and propose some heuristics to circumvent it. Interestingly these heuristics rediscover exactly the need for piecewise-defined ranking functions, even if implicitly and in a roundabout way.

8   Conclusion

In this paper, we proposed a parameterized abstract domain for proving termination of imperative programs. The domain automatically infers sufficient conditions for program termination, and synthesizes piecewise-defined ordinal-valued ranking functions through backward invariance analysis.

We also described the implementation of an instance of the abstract domain based on affine functions, and we have provided experimental evidence of its expressivity. In particular, we have seen that inferring ranking functions over ordinals removes the burden of finding lexicographic orders (cf. Section 1 and Section 5), and overcomes the limitations of affine functions in case of programs with non-linear computational complexity (cf. Example 4). Finally, we have seen (cf. Example 3) that piecewise-defined ordinal-valued ranking functions are crucial where lexicographic ranking functions are not powerful enough.

It remains for future work to support *non-linear* functions (e.g. quadratic, cubic, exponential, ...) and *relational* abstract domains (e.g. octagons [19], polyhedra [11], ...) for better state partitioning.

Acknowledgments. We are very grateful to Damien Massé for the interesting discussions and his helpful suggestions. We also thank the anonymous reviewers for their careful reviews and their useful comments.

References

1. Alias, C., Darte, A., Feautrier, P., Gonnord, L.: Multi-Dimensional Rankings, Program Termination, and Complexity Bounds of Flowchart Programs. In: Cousot, R., Martel, M. (eds.) SAS 2010. LNCS, vol. 6337, pp. 117–133. Springer, Heidelberg (2010)

2. Ben-Amram, A.M., Lee, C.S.: Ranking Functions for Size-Change Termination II. Logical Methods in Computer Science 5(2) (2009)
3. Bradley, A.R., Manna, Z., Sipma, H.B.: Linear Ranking with Reachability. In: Etessami, K., Rajamani, S.K. (eds.) CAV 2005. LNCS, vol. 3576, pp. 491–504. Springer, Heidelberg (2005)
4. Cook, B., Podelski, A., Rybalchenko, A.: Proving Program Termination. Communications of the ACM 54(5), 88–98 (2011)
5. Cook, B., See, A., Zuleger, F.: Ramsey vs. Lexicographic Termination Proving. In: Piterman, N., Smolka, S.A. (eds.) TACAS 2013. LNCS, vol. 7795, pp. 47–61. Springer, Heidelberg (2013)
6. Cousot, P.: Constructive Design of a Hierarchy of Semantics of a Transition System by Abstract Interpretation. Electronic Notes in Theoretical Computer Science 6, 77–102 (1997)
7. Cousot, P., Cousot, R.: Static Determination of Dynamic Properties of Programs. In: Symposium on Programming, pp. 106–130 (1976)
8. Cousot, P., Cousot, R.: Abstract Interpretation: a Unified Lattice Model for Static Analysis of Programs by Construction or Approximation of Fixpoints. In: POPL, pp. 238–252 (1977)
9. Cousot, P., Cousot, R.: Higher Order Abstract Interpretation (and Application to Comportment Analysis Generalizing Strictness, Termination, Projection, and PER Analysis. In: ICCL, pp. 95–112 (1994)
10. Cousot, P., Cousot, R.: An Abstract Interpretation Framework for Termination. In: POPL, pp. 245–258 (2012)
11. Cousot, P., Halbwachs, N.: Automatic Discovery of Linear Restraints Among Variables of a Program. In: POPL, pp. 84–96 (1978)
12. Floyd, R.W.: Assigning Meanings to Programs. In: Proceedings of Symposium on Applied Mathematics, vol. 19, pp. 19–32 (1967)
13. Heizmann, M., Jones, N.D., Podelski, A.: Size-Change Termination and Transition Invariants. In: Cousot, R., Martel, M. (eds.) SAS 2010. LNCS, vol. 6337, pp. 22–50. Springer, Heidelberg (2010)
14. Jeannet, B., Miné, A.: APRON: A Library of Numerical Abstract Domains for Static Analysis. In: Bouajjani, A., Maler, O. (eds.) CAV 2009. LNCS, vol. 5643, pp. 661–667. Springer, Heidelberg (2009)
15. Kunen, K.: Set Theory: An Introduction to Independence Proofs. Studies in Logic and the Foundations of Mathematics (1980)
16. Lee, C.S.: Ranking Functions for Size-Change Termination. ACM Transactions on Programming Languages and Systems 31(3) (2009)
17. Lee, C.S., Jones, N.D., Ben-Amram, A.M.: The Size-Change Principle for Program Termination. In: POPL, pp. 81–92 (2001)
18. Manna, Z., Pnueli, A.: The Temporal Verification of Reactive Systems: Progress (1996)
19. Miné, A.: The Octagon Abstract Domain. Higher-Order and Symbolic Computation 19(1), 31–100 (2006)
20. Podelski, A., Rybalchenko, A.: Transition Invariants. In: LICS, pp. 32–41 (2004)
21. Urban, C.: FuncTion, http://www.di.ens.fr/~urban/FuncTion.html
22. Urban, C.: The Abstract Domain of Segmented Ranking Functions. In: Logozzo, F., Fähndrich, M. (eds.) SAS 2013. LNCS, vol. 7935, pp. 43–62. Springer, Heidelberg (2013)
23. Velroyen, H., Rümmer, P.: Non-Termination Checking for Imperative Programs. In: Beckert, B., Hähnle, R. (eds.) TAP 2008. LNCS, vol. 4966, pp. 154–170. Springer, Heidelberg (2008)

Model and Proof Generation
for Heap-Manipulating Programs*

Martin Brain, Cristina David, Daniel Kroening, and Peter Schrammel

University of Oxford
Department of Computer Science
`first.lastname@cs.ox.ac.uk`

Abstract. Existing heap analysis techniques lack the ability to supply counterexamples in case of property violations. This hinders diagnosis, prevents test-case generation and is a barrier to the use of these tools among non-experts. We present a verification technique for reasoning about aliasing and reachability in the heap which uses ACDCL (a combination of the well-known CDCL SAT algorithm and abstract interpretation) to perform interleaved proof generation and model construction. Abstraction provides us with a tractable way of reasoning about heaps; ACDCL adds the ability to search for a model in an efficient way. We present a prototype tool and demonstrate a number of examples for which we are able to obtain useful concrete counterexamples.

1   Introduction

Heap-manipulating programs are notoriously hard to verify. Although there are successful approaches to proving the safety of such programs, e.g. analyses based on three-valued logic [1] and separation logic [2, 3], these analyses are primarily concerned with proof generation and only very few provide a concrete countermodel when a property is violated [4, 5]. Such countermodels can be used as test cases that lead the program execution to the error, and hence, they are invaluable in debugging and understanding the nature of the defect.

As properties of dynamically allocated data structures involve quantifiers, inductive definitions and transitive closure, the concrete interpretation is impractical, and *abstraction* is used to give an approximate representation of sets of concrete values, providing an effective way of dealing with such specifications. In approaches based on abstract interpretation [6], the behaviour of a program is evaluated over the abstract domain using an abstract transformer, which is iterated until the set of abstract states saturates. The generated abstract fixed point is an over-approximation of the set of reachable states of the original program. Now, the difficulty is that, due to the precision loss involved in this analysis, an *abstract countermodel* might be spurious, i.e. it can reach the error state according to an abstract semantics, but not in the concrete semantics. Our goal

---

* Supported by the ARTEMIS VeTeSS project, UK EPSRC EP/J012564/1 and ERC project 280053.

Z. Shao (Ed.): ESOP 2014, LNCS 8410, pp. 432–452, 2014.

is hence to compute a *concrete countermodel*, i.e. a witness for the refutation of a property in the form of a concrete heap configuration that, starting from the initial program state, will reach an error state according to concrete semantics.

Generation of Concrete Countermodels. We identify and address two specific issues hindering the generation of concrete countermodels.

The first issue is the loss of precision caused by *join operators* when reasoning about multiple execution paths. Join operations are well-known for losing precision [7, 8]. One way to retain precision in such situations is to use disjunctive (powerset) abstractions that express all the possible behaviours individually, avoiding the need for an overapproximative join operator. However, disjunctive abstractions increase space and time requirements exponentially. Thus, in order to achieve scalability, shape analyses generally relinquish the precision offered by the powerset domain in favour of more practical solutions. Options include partially disjunctive heap abstractions [9], or special join operations for the separation logic domain which abstract information selectively [8]. However, due to the precision loss, generating counterexamples is difficult or even impossible.

We propose an analysis capable of regaining just the right amount of precision lost by the join *without* a powerset domain. This is achieved by exploiting recent results on embedding abstract domains inside the Conflict Driven Clause Learning (CDCL) algorithm used by SAT solvers, a framework known as *Abstract Conflict Driven Clause Learning* (ACDCL). As our main focus is on proving aliasing and reachability properties about the heap, we instantiate ACDCL with a heap domain. Our technique produces an abstract countermodel such that any concrete instantiation of it will always provide a valid concrete countermodel.

The second scenario where concrete countermodels are difficult to generate is in the presence of loops, when a *widening operator* may be required to accelerate convergence by extrapolation. For programs with loops, we propose using a combined approach based on loop unwinding and widening. Unwinding allows us to construct concrete refutation witnesses for property invalidations that appear within a certain number of loop unwindings. As this technique is inconclusive if no such invalidations appear for the specified number of unwindings, widening will be used to prove safety in such situations. Any abstract countermodel generated subsequent to widening may be spurious, i.e., may not correspond to any concrete execution in the original program. The experience from bounded model checking indicates that many bugs are found with a small number of loop unwindings.

Contributions. Our contributions are summarised as follows:

- An abstract domain specialised for heap-manipulating programs that is used to express aliasing and reachability facts about the heap.
- A verification technique for heap-manipulating programs that interleaves *model construction and proof generation* by exploiting recent results on embedding abstract domains inside the CDCL algorithm used by SAT solvers. As precision loss caused by joins is recovered through decisions and learning, our technique is capable of path-sensitive reasoning. Crucially, by

generalizing causes of conflict, stronger facts can be learned, avoiding case and path enumeration.

- In contrast to most other heap analysis techniques based on abstract interpretation, our analysis produces abstract countermodels that are under-approximations of concrete countermodels and can hence be used to diagnose the property violation. We provide an algorithm for obtaining concrete instantiations of our abstract countermodels.
- We present a prototype tool and demonstrate that we are able to obtain useful concrete counterexamples for typical list-manipulating programs and for benchmarks from SV-COMP'13 involving various kinds of lists and trees.

2   A Running Example

For illustration, let us consider the example in Fig. 1, with the corresponding CFG in Fig. 2. Function *running_example* takes as input two pointers x and y to singly-linked lists, and removes the head of the list x and frees it.

Property 1. We instrument the code with the assumption at Line 7, stating that y is non-dangling. At the end of the method we expect y not to be affected by the memory deallocation at Line 12, and to remain non-dangling. Accordingly, in the CFG representation, an error state is reached only if y is dangling at the end of the program. The fact that the error location can be reached is easily discovered by any heap verification technique (if x and y are aliases, the memory location pointed to by y does get deallocated, leaving y dangling at location N5). However, the join operation performed at location N5 will usually

```
1   typedef struct node {
2     int val;
3     struct node *n;
4   } List;
5
6   void running_example(List *x, List *y) {
7     assume(!Dangling(y));
8
9     if(x!=null) {
10      List *aux = x;
11      x = x->n;
12      free(aux);
13    }
14
15    assert(!Dangling(y)); // property 1
16  }
```

Fig. 1. Running example (with property 1)

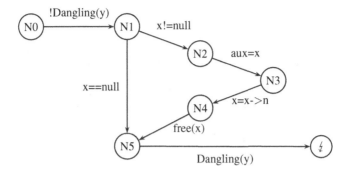

Fig. 2. CFG for the running example (with property 1)

```
void counterexample1() {

    List *x, *y;
    x = new(List);
    y = x;


    running_example(x,y);
}
```

```
void counterexample2() {

    List *x, *y;
    y = new(List);
    y->n = null;
    x = y;

    running_example(x,y);
}
```

Fig. 3. A concrete counterexample for property 1 of the running example

Fig. 4. A concrete counterexample for property 2 of the running example

lose the information about the two independent behaviours corresponding to whether or not x is *null*. This is due to the fact that the most precise property at the join point requires disjunction, and correspondingly a disjunctive domain.

We use a heap domain inside a Conflict-Driven Learning algorithm as used by SAT solvers to construct a countermodel consisting of reachability and aliasing facts without using a powerset domain. The generated abstract countermodel consists of the facts $x \neq null$ and $x = y$. A concrete instantiation of this counter-model as a test case that triggers the property violation is given in Fig. 3. We shall return with details on how the countermodel is generated for this example in Sec. 5, after describing the analysis.

Property 2. Now, let us consider a slightly more involved heap property. As-suming the existence of a path from y to *null* via field n at Line 7 in Fig. 1 (by replacing *assume*(!*Dangling*(y)) with *assume*(*Path*(y, *null*, n))), we want to check that this path is preserved at Line 15 (*assert*(!*Dangling*(y)) is re-placed by *assert*(*Path*(y, *null*, n))). The abstract countermodel constructed by our technique is such that, in order for the error location to be reached, x must

$$
\begin{aligned}
datat &:= struct\ C\ \{(typ\ v)^*\} \\
e &:= v \mid v{\rightarrow}f \mid \texttt{new}(C) \mid \texttt{null} \\
S &:= v{:=}e \mid v_1{\rightarrow}f{:=}v_2 \mid \texttt{free}(v) \mid S_1; S_2 \mid if\ (B)\ S_1\ else\ S_2 \mid \\
&\quad\ while\ (B)\ S \mid \texttt{assert}(\phi) \mid \texttt{assume}(\phi) \\
B &:= e_1{=}e_2 \mid e_1{\neq}e_2 \\
A &:= \neg A \mid Path(v_1, v_2, f) \mid OnPath(v_1, v_2, v_3, f) \mid Dangling(v) \\
\phi &:= A \mid B \mid \phi \wedge \phi \mid \phi \vee \phi
\end{aligned}
$$

Fig. 5. Programming Language

be on the path from y to *null*. A concrete countermodel obtained by instantiating the abstract countermodel is shown in Fig. 4.

3   Preliminaries

3.1   Programming Language

We use the sequential programming language in Fig. 5. It allows heap allocation and mutation, with v denoting a variable and f a pointer field. To simplify the presentation but without loss of expressiveness, we allow only one-level field access, denoted by $v{\rightarrow}f$. Chained dereferences of the form $v{\rightarrow}f_1{\rightarrow}f_2\ldots$ are handled by introducing auxiliary variables. The statement $assert(\phi)$ checks whether the given argument holds for the current program state, whereas $assume(\phi)$ constrains the program state. $Path(v_1, v_2, f)$ captures the fact that the heap location referenced by pointer variable v_2 is reachable from the memory location referenced by v_1 via the field f, whereas $OnPath(v_1, v_2, v_3, f)$ denotes the existence of a memory location referenced by v_3 on the path from v_1 to v_2 via the field f. The predicate $Dangling(v)$ indicates that a pointer v points to a non-allocated memory location, i.e. after a call to $free(v)$, pointer v still points to the deallocated memory location.

The predicates $Path$, $OnPath$, and $Dangling$ are used to instrument the code in order to prove the absence of memory safety errors such as null pointer dereferences, dangling pointer dereferences and double frees, for example.

3.2   Logical Encoding

We translate a program as defined in Sec. 3.1 to an equivalent logical formula. This is done in the spirit of [10] via transforming the program into static single assignment (SSA) form, where each variable is assigned to only once (auxiliary variables are introduced to record intermediate values). This encoding is purely syntactic and can be performed in linear time. It also makes explicit the state dependency of heap accesses and updates. Finally, the formula is translated into conjunctive normal form (CNF).

$v_1:=v_2\to f$	$\leadsto_M$	$v_1=sel(M,v_2,f)$
$v_1\to f:=v_2$	$\leadsto_M$	$M'=store(M,v_1,f,v_2)$
$\text{Path}(v_1,v_2,f)$	$\leadsto_M$	$Path(M,v_1,v_2,f)$
$\text{OnPath}(v_1,v_2,v_3,f)$	$\leadsto_M$	$OnPath(M,v_1,v_2,v_3,f)$
$\text{Dangling}(v)$	$\leadsto_M$	$Dangling(M,v)$
$v:=\text{new}(C)$	$\leadsto_M$	$M'=new(M,v,C)$
$\text{free}(v)$	$\leadsto_M$	$M'=free(M,v)$
$\text{assume}(\phi)$	$\leadsto_M$	ϕ
$\text{assert}(\phi)$	$\leadsto_M$	$\neg\phi$

Fig. 6. Logical encoding

Most constructs such as sequential statements and *if-else* are encoded as usual. *while* loops are unrolled up to a given bound. In Sec. 5 we give an example how iterations beyond this bound can be translated as a fixed point construct in order to prove unbounded safety. Unless otherwise stated, we assume in the sequel that loops have been unwound, and hence, programs are loop-free. For the heap-related statements the encoding rules are given in Fig. 6. We have to capture the effects that an update to a dynamically allocated data structure has on all the pointers referencing that memory location. To this end, we introduce an explicit notion of heap, updated via operators *store*, *new*, *free*. More precisely, if M denotes such a heap, then the encoding rules in Fig. 6 apply, where M' is the updated heap.

Note that for *assert(e)*, the negation of the asserted property is added to the formula. Thus, an unsatisfiable formula corresponds to the scenario when the assertion holds, whereas any model of the formula denotes a witness for the invalidation of the asserted property.

Example 1. Our example in Fig. 1 is translated to the following formula:

$$\begin{pmatrix} \neg Dangling(M_1,y_1)\ \wedge \\ Dangling(M_2,y_1) \end{pmatrix} \wedge \left(\begin{pmatrix} x_1\neq null \wedge aux_1=x_1\ \wedge \\ x_2=sel(M_1,x_1,n)\ \wedge \\ M_2=free(aux_1) \end{pmatrix} \vee \begin{pmatrix} x_1=null\ \wedge \\ M_1=M_2 \end{pmatrix} \right)$$

Transformed into CNF, we have:

$$\begin{array}{ccc} \neg Dangling(M_1,y_1) & \wedge & (aux_1=x_1 \vee x_1=null) \quad \wedge \\ (x_2=sel(M_1,x_1,n) \vee x_1=null) \wedge & (M_2=free(M_1,aux_1) \vee x_1=null) \wedge \\ (x_1\neq null \vee M_1=M_2) & \wedge & Dangling(M_2,y_1) \end{array}$$

3.3   Concrete Semantics

We define the concrete semantics of a program in terms of the logical formula obtained through the transformation described in the previous section.

Given the set *PVar* of pointer variables and *Fld* of pointer fields, a concrete program state ρ is defined as a triple (Obj,P,L), where *Obj* denotes the set of all

$$
\begin{aligned}
[\![v_1 = v_2]\!]\rho &\equiv L(v_1){=}L(v_2) \\
[\![M'{=}store(M, v_1, f, v_2)]\!]\rho &\equiv \rho \models_c M \Longrightarrow \\
&\quad (Env, Obj, P/P[(L(v_1), f){\mapsto}L(v_2)], L) \models_c M' \\
[\![M'{=}M]\!]\rho &\equiv \rho \models_c M \Longrightarrow \rho \models_c M' \\
[\![M'{=}free(M, v)]\!]\rho &\equiv \rho \models_c M \Longrightarrow (Env, Obj\backslash L(v), P, L) \models_c M' \\
[\![M'{=}new(M, v, C)]\!]\rho &\equiv \rho \models_c M \Longrightarrow \\
&\quad \exists o{\notin}Obj.\ (Env, Obj\cup\{o\}, P, L/L[v \mapsto o]) \models_c M' \\
[\![sel(M, v, f)]\!]\rho &\equiv P(L(v), f) \\
[\![Path(M, v_1, v_2, f)]\!]\rho &\equiv L(v_1){=}L(v_2)\ \vee
\begin{pmatrix}
\exists o{\in}Obj, v_3{\notin}PVar.P(L(v_1), f){=}o\ \wedge \\
[\![Path(v_3, v_2, f)]\!](Obj, P, L/L[v_3{\mapsto}o])\wedge \\
\neg[\![Path(M, v_2, v_1, f)]\!]\rho
\end{pmatrix} \\
[\![OnPath(M, v_1, v_2, v_3, f)]\!]\rho &\equiv
\begin{pmatrix}
[\![Path(M, v_1, v_3, f)]\!]\rho \wedge [\![Path(M, v_3, v_2, f)]\!]\rho\ \wedge \\
\neg Path(M, v_2, v_3, f)]\!]\rho
\end{pmatrix} \\
[\![Dangling(M, v)]\!]\rho &\equiv \nexists o{\in}Obj.\ L(v){=}o
\end{aligned}
$$

Fig. 7. Concrete semantics ded_c

the allocated heap nodes plus a distinguished *null* node, P is the set of points-to relations such that $P \subseteq Obj{\times}Fld{\times}Obj$, and L is the pointer variable labelling function, $L : PVar{\rightarrow}Obj$.

Before defining the concrete semantics in Fig. 7, we provide a consistency relation $\rho \models_c M$ between a concrete program state ρ and an explicit heap configuration M. The consistency relation states that the same reachability and aliasing facts must hold in both M and ρ.

$$
\rho \models_c M \iff \forall v, v_1, v_2 {\in} PVar, f {\in} Fld.[\![Path(M, v_1, v_2, f)]\!]\rho \wedge \\
[\![OnPath(M, v_1, v_2, v, f)]\!]\rho \wedge [\![Dangling(M, v)]\!]\rho
$$

Memory allocation $M'{=}new(M, v, C)$ assigns a new heap node to the pointer variable v, whereas the deallocation statement $M'{=}free(M, v)$ removes the deallocated heap node from Obj. As the mapping of v to the deallocated node is not removed from L, the variable points to an invalid memory location, i.e. v is dangling. Note that the definition of *Path* excludes circular paths. We add the predicate *OnPath* for notational convenience; it can be expressed with the help of *Path*.

We refer to concrete program states (Obj, P, L) as structures $Structs$, and the concrete domain of structures as $(\mathcal{P}(Structs), \subseteq, \cup, \cap)$. A structure ρ is called a model of φ if $[\![\varphi]\!]\rho = 1$, and a countermodel if $[\![\varphi]\!]\rho = 0$.

4   Our Approach

4.1   Abstract Conflict Clause Learning (ACDCL)

Conflict Driven Clause Learning (CDCL) [11] is used by all industrially-relevant propositional SAT solvers. It consists of two complementary phases, iterated until either a model is found or a proof is generated. The first phase, *model search*,

Algorithm 1. ACDCL Algorithm

```
 1  while true do
 2  |   S = ⊤ ;
 3  |   while true do                              /* PHASE 1: Model Search */
 4  |   |   repeat                                        /* deduction */
 5  |   |   |   S ← S ⊓ ded(S);
 6  |   |   until S=S ⊓ ded(S);
 7  |   |   if S=⊥ then break ;                              /* conflict */
 8  |   |   if complete(ded,S) then return (not ⊥,S);  /* return SAT model */
 9  |   |   S ← decision(S);                            /* make decision */
10  |   end
11  |   L ← analyse_conflict(S) ;          /* PHASE 2: Conflict Analysis */
12  |   if L=⊤ then return (⊥,L);                         /* return UNSAT */
13  |   ded ← ded ⊓ ded_L;               /* learn: refine transformer */
14  end
```

tries to construct a model by using a *partial assignment* of truth values for the propositional variables and extending it using deduction (unit clause propagation) and heuristic guesses. If this constructs a model, then it is returned and the algorithm terminates. If not, a conflicting partial assignment is produced and is passed, along with the reasons for each truth assignment, to the second phase. In contrast to the model-theoretic approach of the first phase, the second phase, *conflict analysis*, takes a proof-theoretic approach. The failed model search is used to guide resolution to produce a clause that allows deduction to avoid the conflict and others like it. If the learnt clause is empty, then the problem is unsatisfiable and the algorithm terminates. The key to the algorithm's effectiveness is the synergy between the two approaches; failed model generation targets the resolution so that high-value clauses are produced and these clauses in turn strengthen deduction and target the heuristics to improve model generation.

An alternative view of CDCL is that the partial assignments are an *over-approximation* of the space of full logical assignments [12]. Thus, the first phase is application of an over-approximate abstract transformer plus extrapolation and the second phase is using an underapproximation and interpolation to generalise the reason for the conflict and increase the precision of the abstract transformer. From this viewpoint it is possible to lift CDCL to give ACDCL [13], which applies the approach but works over a variety of abstract domains (see Alg. 1).

To use ACDCL we first need a concrete domain (a lattice) and a transformer. ACDCL determines whether the transformer projects all elements to ⊥. In the case of propositional SAT, the concrete domain is the lattice of sets of truth assignments and the transformer projects a set of assignments to the subset of them that are models of the formulae. If this is ⊥ for all points, then the formulae has no models (*UNSAT*), otherwise it has models (*SAT*). When applied to heaps, the concrete domain is $(\mathcal{P}(Structs), \subseteq, \cup, \cap)$ and the transformer projects sets of heaps to the subset of these that are models, thus proving the program safe (if the transformer projects all sets to ⊥) or finding counterexamples.

The second component needed for ACDCL is an abstract domain and an abstract transformer that over-approximates the concrete transformer. In the case of propositional SAT solvers, the abstract domain is partial assignments and the abstract transformer is unit propagation. In this work, *Heapdom* (see Sec. 4.2) is an abstract domain capable of capturing reachability and aliasing facts in the heap and *ded* (detailed in Sec. 4.3) is the abstract transformer.

The final components required are the completeness test and extrapolation used in the model search phase and the generalisation function used in the conflict analysis phase. Model search applies the abstract transformer until a fixed point is reached (Lines 4 to 6). It then tests for completeness (Line 8). In the case of propositional SAT solvers, this test is checking whether all variables have been assigned. In this work, it is the procedure *complete*, detailed in Sec. 4.4. If the abstract element is not complete (and not ⊥), then a heuristic guess is needed to add new information (Line 9). Modern propositional SAT solvers use a variant of the VSIDS heuristic, while the procedure *decision* given in Sec. 4.3 is used for heaps. If the model search phase reaches a ⊥, then the conflict analysis phase is run (Lines 11–13). This uses a generalisation function to underapproximate the reasons for the conflict. In the case of propositional SAT solvers, this is usually First-UIP based learning, while heaps use *analyse_conflict* given in Sec. 4.3.

4.2   Abstract Heap Domain

The structure of our abstract heap domain *Heapdom* is given in Fig. 8. An element S of *Heapdom* is a conjunction of predicates *pred* or their negation (literals *Heaplit*), represented as a set. *Heaplit*s are equalities/disequalities representing aliasing information, together with predicates describing reachability/validity facts about heap configurations ($Path^\sharp$, $OnPath^\sharp$ and $Dangling^\sharp$). *Heapdom* forms a lattice $\langle Heapdom, \supseteq, \cup, \cap, Heaplit, \emptyset \rangle$. Note that the meet operation ⊓ is the union of literals ∪, the join ⊔ is the intersection ∩, and inclusion ⊑ is ⊇. The top element ⊤ is the empty set and bottom ⊥ is the set of all literals *Heaplit*. For convenience, all inconsistent heap configurations will be projected to bottom, e.g., $pred \wedge \neg pred$ and $Path^\sharp(M, v_1, v_2, f) \wedge Dangling^\sharp(M, v_1)$ are ⊥.[1] Note that *Heapdom* is finite for programs with a finite number of pointer variables and loops being unwound a finite number of times.

From a *shape analysis* point of view, the reachability predicate $Path^\sharp(M, x, y, n)$ denotes a list segment from x to y, whereas $Path^\sharp(M, x, null, n)$ represents a full list. When interested in *heap reachability analysis*, our heap abstract domain is applicable to general heap-allocated data structures that go beyond linked lists.

Abstract Semantics. We define now the semantics of programs (as given in Sec. 3) in our abstract heap domain. In Fig. 9, the abstract semantics is given

---

[1] The intuition behind the latter case is that, in accordance with the semantics in Fig. 7, reachability facts can only involve pointers to allocated heap locations.

$$
\begin{aligned}
Heapdom &:= \mathcal{P}(Heaplit) \\
Heaplit &:= pred \mid \neg pred \\
pred &:= v{=}e \mid Path^{\sharp}(M, v_1, v_2, f) \mid OnPath^{\sharp}(M, v_1, v_2, v_3, f) \mid Dangling^{\sharp}(v) \\
e &:= null \mid v \mid sel^{\sharp}(M, v, f) \\
v &\in Var, f \in Fld
\end{aligned}
$$

Fig. 8. Abstract heap domain

in form of an abstract transformer $ded : Heapdom \rightarrow Heapdom$ that defines the effect $\llbracket p \rrbracket^{\sharp}$ of the predicates p in the logical encoding on abstract heap states S.

$Path$, $OnPath$, $Dangling$ and sel generate the corresponding abstract predicates $Path^{\sharp}$, $OnPath^{\sharp}$, $Dangling^{\sharp}$, and $sel^{\sharp}$. An equality between heaps $M = M'$ results in duplicating all facts for the new heap.

The transformers for *new*, *free*, and *store* are more complicated because they involve the creation of a new heap M' that is a modified version of the previous heap configuration M:

- *new* allocates a new memory location; disjoint from all the other allocated memory locations. Accordingly, the abstract transformer (see Fig. 11) adds a non-null, non-dangling pointer v (S_2), generates disequalities between the pointer to the newly allocated location and all the other non-dangling pointers (S_3), and copies all known facts to the new heap (S_1).
- *free* and *store* have to capture the effects of a *strong update* on the predicates describing heap facts.[2] Corresponding to the effects of a strong update, any pointer variable that is an alias of v_1 is pointing to the updated heap object in the new heap, while any pointer variable disjoint from v_1 points to the same heap object as it did before the update. Thus, the abstract transformers must capture the truth value of the predicates $Path$, $OnPath$ and $Dangling$ in the updated heap in a precise manner. For this purpose, there are transformers that define the effects of the memory update on the corresponding positive literal, i.e. whether or not the literal preserves its truth value in the new heap, as well as the effects on the negative literal. The abstract transformer for the *store* operator is the most complex and is shown in Fig. 11. The *free* operation is a simpler version of *store* (omitted here).

The copying of the facts from the previous heap configuration M that are unaffected by the heap update to the new heap M' is performed by the "heap copy" functions, also shown in Fig. 11. The *hcp* functions filter abstract elements present in both S and S_1 if the constraint c holds in S_1 while also substituting the heap configuration from M to M'. The $\hat{\in}$ operator in these definitions is given as $c_1 \wedge c_2 \mathbin{\hat{\in}} S \equiv c_1 \in S \wedge c_2 \in S$, and $c_1 \vee c_2 \mathbin{\hat{\in}} S \equiv c_1 \in S \vee c_2 \in S$.

---

[2] In shape analysis, a strong update to an abstract memory location overwrites its old content with a new value, whereas a weak update adds new values to the existing set of values associated with that memory location [1, 14].

$$
\begin{aligned}
&[\![v_1 = v_2]\!]^\sharp S &&\equiv \{v_1 = v_2\} \\
&[\![v = sel(M, v, f)]\!]^\sharp S &&\equiv \{v = sel^\sharp(M, v, f)\} \\
&[\![M' = store(M, v_1, f, v_2)]\!]^\sharp S &&\equiv ded_{M' = store(M, v_1, f, v_2)} &&\text{(see Fig. 11)} \\
&[\![M' = new(M, v, C)]\!]^\sharp S &&\equiv ded_{M' = new(M, v, C)} &&\text{(see Fig. 11)} \\
&[\![M' = free(M, v)]\!]^\sharp S &&\equiv ded_{M' = free(M, v)} &&\text{(see text)} \\
&[\![M' = M]\!]^\sharp S &&\equiv \{s[M/M'] \mid s \in S\} \\
&[\![Path(M, v_1, v_2, f)]\!]^\sharp S &&\equiv \{Path^\sharp(M, v_1, v_2, f)\} \\
&[\![OnPath(M, v_1, v_2, v_3, f)]\!]^\sharp S &&\equiv \{OnPath^\sharp(M, v_1, v_2, v_3, f)\} \\
&[\![Dangling(M, v)]\!]^\sharp S &&\equiv \{Dangling^\sharp(M, v)\}
\end{aligned}
$$

Fig. 9. Abstract semantics: abstract transformer ded

The concretisation function γ that relates abstract states S with concrete states ρ (cf. Fig. 7) is given in Fig. 10 with $\gamma(S) = \cap_{s \in S} \gamma_s$.

$$
\begin{aligned}
&\gamma_{v_1 = v_2} &&\equiv \{\rho \mid [\![v_1 = v_2]\!]\rho\} \\
&\gamma_{v = sel^\sharp(M, v, f)} &&\equiv \{\rho \mid [\![v = sel^\sharp(M, v, f)]\!]\rho\} \\
&\gamma_{Path^\sharp(M, v_1, v_2, f)} &&\equiv \{\rho \mid [\![Path(M, v_1, v_2, f)]\!]\rho\} \\
&\gamma_{OnPath^\sharp(M, v_1, v_2, v_3, f)} &&\equiv \{\rho \mid [\![OnPath(M, v_1, v_2, v_3, f)]\!]\rho\} \\
&\gamma_{Dangling^\sharp(M, v)} &&\equiv \{\rho \mid [\![Dangling(M, v)]\!]\rho\}
\end{aligned}
$$

Fig. 10. Concretisation function γ

We now state the theorems that establish the soundness of the abstraction:

Theorem 1. *The concrete domain* $\mathcal{P}(Structs)$ *and the abstract domain Heapdom form a Galois connection, i.e.* $(\mathcal{P}(Structs), \subseteq) \xleftarrow[\alpha]{\gamma} (Heapdom, \supseteq)$.

Theorem 2. *The abstract semantics is a sound over-approximation of the concrete semantics, i.e.* $(ded_c \circ \gamma)(S) \subseteq (\gamma \circ ded)(S)$.

The proofs establish the inclusion case by case over the structure of $\mathcal{P}(Structs)$ and *Heapdom*, respectively ded_c and ded.

4.3   ACDCL Instantiation

The ACDCL algorithm in Alg. 1 is instantiated using our abstract heap domain as follows:

Deduction. The abstract semantics in Sec. 4.2 defines an abstract transformer $ded : Heapdom \to Heapdom$, which can also be viewed as a set of deduction rules. During model search ACDCL applies the abstract transformer ded to deduce facts until saturation or detection of a conflict (the abstract value $\perp$).

$$[\textbf{DED--[NEW]}]$$

$$S_1 = hcp\left(\left\{\begin{array}{l} v_1=sel^\sharp(M,v_2,f),\ Path^\sharp(M,v_1,v_2,f), \\ OnPath^\sharp(M,v_1,v_2,v_3,f),\ Dangling^\sharp(M,v) \end{array}\right\},\textbf{true}\,,S,M,M'\right)$$
$$S_2 = \{v\neq null,\neg Dangling^\sharp(M',v)\}$$
$$S_3 = \{v\neq v' \mid v'\in PVar \wedge v\neq v' \wedge \neg Dangling^\sharp(M',v)\in S\}$$

$$\overline{ded_{M'=new(M,v,C)}(S) = (S_1 \cup S_2 \cup S_3)}$$

$$[\textbf{DED--[STORE]}]$$

$$S_1 = hcp\_pos(\{v_3=sel^\sharp(M,v_4,f)\},v_1\neq v_3,S,M,M')$$
$$S_2 = hcp\_pos(\{\neg(v_3=sel^\sharp(M,v_4,f))\},v_1\neq v_3 \vee v_2\neq v_4,S,M,M')$$
$$S_3 = hcp\_neg(\{\neg(v_3=sel^\sharp(M,v_4,f))\},v_1=v_3 \wedge v_2=v_4,S,M,M')$$
$$S_4 = hcp\_pos\left(\begin{array}{l}\{Path^\sharp(M,v_3,v_4,f)\}, \\ \neg Path^\sharp(M,v_3,v_1,f) \vee \neg OnPath^\sharp(M,v_3,v_4,v_1,f) \vee Path^\sharp(M,v_2,v_4,f), \\ S,M,M'\end{array}\right)$$
$$S_5 = hcp\_neg\left(\begin{array}{l}\{Path^\sharp(M,v_3,v_4,f)\}, \\ Path^\sharp(M,v_3,v_1,f) \wedge OnPath^\sharp(M,v_3,v_4,v_1,f) \wedge \neg Path^\sharp(M,v_2,v_4,f), \\ S,M,M'\end{array}\right)$$
$$S_6 = hcp\_pos(\{\neg Path^\sharp(M,v_3,v_4,f)\},\neg Path^\sharp(M,v_3,v_1,f) \vee \neg Path^\sharp(M,v_2,v_4,f),S,M,M')$$
$$S_7 = hcp\_neg(\{\neg Path^\sharp(M,v_3,v_4,f)\},Path^\sharp(M,v_3,v_1,f) \wedge Path^\sharp(M,v_2,v_4,f),S,M,M')$$
$$S_8 = hcp\_pos\left(\begin{array}{l}\{OnPath^\sharp(M,v_3,v_4,v_5,f)\}, \\ Path^\sharp(M,v_3,v_4,f) \wedge \left(\begin{array}{l}\neg Path^\sharp(M,v_3,v_1,f) \vee \\ \neg OnPath^\sharp(M,v_3,v_5,v_1,f) \wedge Path^\sharp(M,v_2,v_5,f)\end{array}\right), \\ S,M,M'\end{array}\right)$$
$$S_9 = hcp\_neg\left(\begin{array}{l}\{OnPath^\sharp(M,v_3,v_4,v_5,f)\}, \\ \neg Path^\sharp(M,v_3,v_4,f) \vee \left(\begin{array}{l}Path^\sharp(M,v_3,v_1,f) \wedge OnPath^\sharp(M,v_3,v_5,v_1,f) \\ \vee \neg Path^\sharp(M,v_2,v_5,f)\end{array}\right), \\ S,M,M'\end{array}\right)$$
$$S_{10} = hcp\_pos\left(\begin{array}{l}\{\neg OnPath^\sharp(M,v_3,v_4,v_5,f)\}, \\ \neg Path^\sharp(M,v_3,v_4,f) \vee \neg Path^\sharp(M,v_3,v_1,f) \vee \neg Path^\sharp(M,v_2,v_5,f), \\ S,M,M'\end{array}\right)$$
$$S_{11} = hcp\_neg\left(\begin{array}{l}\{\neg OnPath^\sharp(M,v_3,v_4,v_5,f)\}, \\ Path^\sharp(M,v_3,v_4,f) \wedge Path^\sharp(M,v_3,v_1,f) \wedge Path^\sharp(M,v_2,v_5,f), \\ S,M,M'\end{array}\right)$$
$$S_{12} = hcp\left(\left\{\begin{array}{l} v_1=sel^\sharp(M,v_2,f'),\ Path^\sharp(M,v_1,v_2,f'), \\ OnPath^\sharp(M,v_1,v_2,v_3,f'),\ Dangling^\sharp(M,v) \end{array}\right\},\textbf{true}\,,S,M,M'\right)$$
$$S_{13} = hcp\_pos(\{Dangling^\sharp(M,v_3)\},v_1\neq v_3,S,M,M')$$
$$S_{14} = \{v_2=sel^\sharp(M',v_1,f)\}$$

$$\overline{ded_{M'=store(M,v_1,f,v_2)}(S) = \begin{cases} \bot & \text{if } (Dangling^\sharp(M,v_1)\vee v_1=null)\,\hat{\in}\,S \\ \bigcup_{i=1..14} S_i & \text{otherwise} \end{cases}}$$

Functions for copying heap facts:		
$hcp(S,c,S_1,M,M')$	$=$	$\{s[M/M'] \mid s\in S\cap S_1 \wedge c\,\hat{\in}\,S_1\}$
$hcp\_pos(S,c,S_1,M,M')$	$=$	$\{s[M/M'] \mid s\in S\cap S_1 \wedge c\,\hat{\in}\,S_1\}$
$hcp\_neg(S,c,S_1,M,M')$	$=$	$\{\neg s[M/M'] \mid s\in S\cap S_1 \wedge c\,\hat{\in}\,S_1\}$

Fig. 11. Abstract transformers

In addition to the abstract transformer *ded*, we make use of a *transitive closure* transformer that infers all the possible new heap facts from existent ones, e.g. it infers $Path(M,v_1,v_3,f)$ from $Path(M,v_1,v_2,f)$ and $Path(M,v_2,v_3,f)$.

The transitive closure is also necessary to canonicalize abstract elements. This is in particular important for checking whether an abstract value is equivalent to $\bot$ (which has multiple representations).

We can show that the abstract transformer *ded* we presented in Sec. 4.2 is the best abstract transformer in our heap domain. However, this is not necessary for the completeness and termination of the ACDCL algorithm: less precise transformers can be used, as they will be subsequently refined through decisions and learning. This is frequently a worthwhile trade-off for performance.

Maintaining the Set of Relevant Decisions. During this propagation phase, we maintain a set H ("hints") of literals (*Heaplit*) for the benefit of the decision heuristic explained in the next section. The set H consists of those literals that appear in the transformer's hypothesis and are not present in the current abstract model S, and hence, they constitute the set of literals that guarantees that a decision actually triggers a deduction. Hints are collected during the application of the transformers based on the c, S_1 arguments to the heap copy functions (*hcp*, *hcp_pos*, *hcp_neg*):

$$extract\_hints(c, S_1) = \{h \mid h \in literals(c)\backslash S_1\}$$

where

$$literals(c) = \begin{cases} literals(c_1) \cup literals(c_2) & \text{if } c = (c_1 \wedge c_2) \\ literals(c_1) & \text{if } c = (c_1 \vee c_2) \\ \{s\} & \text{if } c = s \end{cases}$$

returns a set of literals in formula c that is sufficient to trigger a deduction: note that in the case of disjunction in the hypothesis c, only one disjunct is added in order to avoid unnecessary decisions. A consequence of this definition is that whenever the completeness test (Line 8 in Alg. 1) fails, there must be at least one hint in H.

Decisions. Once no new information can be deduced through propagation, the ACDCL algorithm makes a decision by guessing the truth value of a predicate and adding it to the partial abstract model S. As explained above, we collect the relevant potential decisions H during deduction in order to restrict the choices for decisions. We may use any decision heuristic *get_a_hint* to return (and remove) an element from H. A trivial option is to simply take the first element, but we could also use elaborate ranking heuristics in order to prioritise certain literals. The *decision* function (Line 9 in Alg. 1) adds the obtained literal to the abstract model:

$$decision_H \quad : Heapdom \rightarrow Heapdom$$
$$decision_H(S) = S \cup \{get\_a\_hint(H)\}$$

Conflict Analysis and Learning. In the conflict analysis phase, the learning function identifies the cause of the conflict:

$$analyse\_conflict \quad : Heapdom \rightarrow \mathcal{P}(Heapdom)$$
$$analyse\_conflict(S) = (generalise \circ complement)(decisions(S))$$

where *decisions* returns the set of decision literals in the current iteration of main (outer) iteration of the ACDCL algorithm. As a learning heuristic, the conjunction of all the decisions leading to conflict is initially complemented according to the *complement* function:

$$complement \quad : Heapdom \rightarrow \mathcal{P}(Heapdom)$$
$$complement(S) = \{\{\neg s\} \mid s \in S\}$$

Subsequently, the found cause of conflict is generalised using the *generalise* function:

$$generalise : \mathcal{P}(Heapdom) \rightarrow \mathcal{P}(Heapdom)$$

Generalisation is important to efficiently prune the search space so as to avoid case enumeration. Generalisation is based on heuristics (e.g. First-UIP in SAT solving). The *generalise* function we have implemented is for example able to perform the following generalisations:

- $x{=}y \implies \forall f \in Fld.Path^{\sharp}(x,y,f)$
- $\neg Path^{\sharp}(M,x,y,f) \implies x{\neq}y$.

The set $\mathcal{L}$ returned by *analyse_conflict* is then used to build the learned transformer $ded_{\mathcal{L}}$ that is used to refine the abstract transformer *ded* (Alg. 1, Line 13):

$$ded_{\mathcal{L}} \quad : Heapdom \rightarrow Heapdom$$
$$ded_{\mathcal{L}} = \bigsqcup_{\ell \in \mathcal{L}} ded_{\ell}$$

meaning $ded_{\mathcal{L}}(S) = \bigcap_{\ell \in \mathcal{L}}(S \cup \ell)$. In our implementation, transformer refinement is realised by conjoining the CNF formula corresponding to $\mathcal{L}$ with the formula.

4.4   Soundness and Completeness

Using various properties of the abstract domain, we show that the instantiation of the ACDCL framework given here is a decision procedure (i.e. it is sound, complete and terminating) for loop-free programs. Sketches of the heap-specific parts of the proof are given here, the correctness of the framework is shown in [13]. We recall the definition of γ-completeness:

Definition 1. *A transformer ded is γ-complete at $S \in Heapdom$ if* $\gamma(ded(S)) = ded_c(\gamma(S))$.

The way we construct the set of relevant possible decisions H enables a simple implementation of *complete*:

$$complete_H(ded, S) \equiv (H = \emptyset)$$

which has the following properties:

Lemma 1. *If $complete_H(ded, S)$ is true then ded is γ-complete at S. If $complete_H(ded, S)$ is false then the decision function refines the partial abstract model, $S \subset decision_H(S)$.*

Central to the correctness of the system is the invariant that *ded* is an over-approximation of ded_c and that each iteration of the outer loop strengthens it. This can be proven inductively; Theorem 2 gives the base case and the inductive step is a consequence of the next lemma:

Lemma 2. *Given ded, an over-approximation of ded_c, the second phase of the algorithm gives a strictly stronger over-approximation of ded_c.*

Given φ, a loop-free program with a finite number of variables, termination, soundness and completeness follow:

Theorem 3. *Alg. 1 terminates.*

Proof sketch. Heapdom is finite, and thus the application of *ded* will reach a fixed point. Likewise, owing to the second part of Lemma 1, the main loop of phase 1 will either exit as $complete_H(ded, S)$ is true or will eventually reach $\bot$. Finally, as *Heapdom* is finite, there are only a finite number of over-approximations of ded_c, so the invariant implies the main loop will terminate.

Theorem 4. *If Alg. 1 returns (not $\bot$, S) then $\forall \rho \in \gamma(S).\llbracket \varphi \rrbracket \rho = 1$*

Proof sketch. The preconditions of the statement that returns *not* $\bot$ include $complete_H(ded, S)$ and $S = ded(S)$. Using Lemma 1, $\gamma(S) = ded_c(\gamma(S))$, thus all elements of the concrete set are models. Note that $\gamma(S)$ can contain an infinite family of models; the next section shows how to produce counterexamples.

Theorem 5. *If Alg. 1 returns $\bot$ then $\forall \rho \in Structs.\llbracket \varphi \rrbracket \rho = 0$*

Proof sketch. The only statement that returns $\bot$ occurs when $\mathcal{L}=\top$, i.e. *ded* $\sqcap$ $ded_{\mathcal{L}}$ is the function that maps all abstract elements to $\bot$. Using the invariant this is an overapproximation, thus $ded_c(\top) = \bot$, thus there are no models of φ.

4.5   From Abstract to Concrete Countermodels

In Fig. 2 we provide a high-level overview of the algorithm for the generation of concrete countermodels from abstract ones. Our goal is to compute a concrete countermodel that contains only three types of elements: $v_1=v_2$, $v=null$ and $v_1=sel(M, v_2, f)$. Initially, the abstract model is split into positive reachability-based constraints (S_1), and the rest of the abstract model (S_2) (Lines 1 and 2, respectively). Subsequently, S_1 is used to infer candidate concrete models, which are exhaustively generated in C such that each path constraint in S_1 is concretised to a length of at most l (Line 5). The inner loop (Lines 6–13) iteratively attempts to find a valid concrete counterexample. In order to qualify, a candidate must be consistent with the rest of the abstract constraints in S_2. This consistency check translates into a satisfiability call to our instantiation of ACDCL (Line 10). If no candidate qualifies, the minimum length of the heap paths is incremented and the process is reiterated with new candidates.

Algorithm 2. Concretisation of Abstract Countermodels

---

1 $S_1 \leftarrow \{s|s \in S \text{ and } (s = Path(M, v_1, v_2, n) \text{ or } s = OnPath(M, v_1, v_2, v_3, n))\};$
2 $S_2 \leftarrow S \backslash S_1$;
3 $l = 0;$
4 **while** *true* **do**
5     $C \leftarrow \{c \mid c \text{ is a concrete model of } S_1 \text{ for paths of length } \le l\}$;
6   **while** $C \ne \emptyset$ **do**
7        $\pi \leftarrow choose \ a \ model \ from \ C;$
8        $C \leftarrow C \setminus \pi;$
9        $\forall s_i \in (\pi \cup S_2).\phi \leftarrow \bigwedge_i s_i$;
10   **if** ϕ *is SAT* **then**
11 | **return** $\pi;$
12   **end**
13   **end**
14    $l \leftarrow l + 1$
15 **end**

Theorem 6. *Given an abstract counterexample (an abstract element different from $\bot$ at which ded is γ-complete, then Alg. 2 always terminates with a finite concrete countermodel.*

Proof sketch. A partial ordering of the current variables can be computed such that $Path(M, v_1, v_2, n) \Rightarrow v_1 \preceq v_2$ and $OnPath(M, v_1, v_2, v_3, n) \Rightarrow v_1 \preceq v_3 \preceq v_2$. It is always possible to generate a countermodel from this ordering without introducing any auxiliary variables. As $S_1 \cup S_2 \ne \bot$, there must exist one such countermodel that satisfies both S_1 and S_2.

5 Experiments

We have implemented the ACDCL instantiation with the *Heapdom* domain described in Alg. 1 in a prototype solver and connected it to the Model Checker CBMC 4.6. The source code of the prototype tool and the benchmarks are available online.[3] The prototype was subsequently used to verify memory safety and reachability properties for some typical list-manipulating programs for singly-linked lists, e.g. filter, find, bubble sort, and benchmarks from the SV-COMP'13 *list-properties* and *memsafety-ext* sets.

In addition to checking memory safety, i.e. absence of null or dangling pointer dereferences, we have also added reachability assertions, e.g. the reachability predicate $Path(x, y, n)$ denotes a list segment from x to y, and $Path(x, null, n)$ represents a full list.

1. Countermodel Construction. In order to test the soundness of the tool and its capacity to construct witnesses for property refutation, we applied it

---

[3] http://www.cprover.org/svn/cbmc/branches/ESOP2014-heap

Table 1. Experimental results: lines of code (loc), clauses (cls) and analysis time (t, in seconds) for safe and unsafe versions of the benchmarks; timeout 15 minutes (t.o.). All experiments were performed with two loop unwindings.

Benchmark	loc	safe cls	safe t	unsafe cls	unsafe t	Benchmark	loc	safe cls	safe t	unsafe cls	unsafe t
bubble sort*	40	728	0.86	732	10.1	list	60	294	1.57	296	1.14
concat*	24	45	0.08	45	0.08	simple_built_from_end	34	124	0.17	120	0.16
copy*	40	159	0.20	158	1.50	simple	45	157	0.18	157	0.17
create*	27	100	0.15	100	0.15	splice	89	474	0.33	478	0.55
filter*	42	259	0.68	259	0.55	dll_extends_pointer	64	302	0.29	308	0.79
find*	23	47	0.09	35	0.08	skiplist_2lvl	91	520	t.o.	514	4.87
insert*	17	18	0.13	16	0.15	skiplist_3lvl	105	722	t.o.	726	15.5
reverse*	20	81	0.07	83	0.08	tree_cnstr	85	942	3.31	922	2.56
traverse*	15	16	0.08	18	0.07	tree_dsw	117	1037	2.43	984	3.24
alternating_list	65	278	0.21	282	0.28	tree_parent_ptr	95	844	0.43	811	45.9
list_flag	62	244	0.46	246	0.57	tree_stack	93	1413	0.50	1394	t.o.

to safe and unsafe, i.e. faulty, versions of our benchmarks (with loops unwound twice), followed by manually inspecting the countermodels generated for the unsafe versions. The results of these experiments are given in Table 1. Both the safe and unsafe versions of each program are instrumented with memory safety assertions. Those marked with a * have additional reachability assertions.

Example 2. We describe how countermodel construction proceeds for our running example in Fig. 1. Recall the corresponding logical encoding in Sec. 3.2.

Model Search (1). After the *first propagation*, the partial abstract model consists of the elements $\neg Dangling(M_1, y_1)$ and $Dangling(M_2, y_1)$, representing neither a conflict, nor a complete countermodel. Thus, a *decision* constrains x_1 to be not *null*, and the model search loop is reiterated. This time, the abstract transformers for $aux_1 = x_1$, $x_2 = sel(M_1, x_1, n)$ and $M_2 = free(M_1, aux_1)$ are applied. As the application of $M_2 = free(M_1, aux_1)$ is imprecise (no aliasing information for x_1 and y_1 is available), a second *decision* is made assuming that y_1 is not reachable from x_1, i.e. $\neg Path(M_1, x_1, y_1, n)$. Consequently, a new application of $M_2 = free(M_1, aux_1)$ will preserve the non-dangling knowledge about y_1 from M_1 to M_2, resulting in the *conflict* $\neg Dangling(M_2, y_1)$ and $Dangling(M_2, y_1)$.

Conflict Analysis (2). The cause of conflict is $x_1 \neq null \land \neg Path(M_1, x_1, y_1, n)$. Hence, one possible clause to be learned is $x_1 = null \lor Path(M_1, x_1, y_1, n)$. As we want to avoid case enumeration, we generalise the cause of conflict. For example, the fact that x_1 and y_1 are not aliases is more general than $\neg Path(M_1, x_1, y_1, n)$, i.e. $\neg Path(M_1, x_1, y_1, n) \Rightarrow x_1 \neq y_1$.[4] Thus, we learn $x_1 = null \lor x_1 = y_1$ and restart the model search phase.

Model Search (3). After a decision $x_1 \neq null$, the abstract element $x_1 = y_1$ is added to the abstract model and $M_2 = free(M_1, aux_1)$ is now complete. Thus,

---

[4] A heap path between two pointer variables may be empty (cf. Fig. 7).

the abstract transformer passes the completeness test, and the abstract counter-model $\{x_1 \neq null, x_1 = y_1\}$ is generated.

Concrete Countermodel Generation (4). Fig. 3 shows a test case triggering the property violation obtained from the abstract countermodel using Alg. 2.

2. Safety Proof Generation. When failing to construct a concrete refutation witness after a bounded number of unwindings, a safety proof is attempted by applying a fixed point computation. This computation makes use of a widening operator that loses information about individual points-to facts by generalising them to reachability facts, e.g. $y = sel(M, x, n)$ is generalised to $Path(M, x, y, n)$.

We do not detail the fixed point computation and the widening operator as they are both rather standard (in particular in the spirit of [15]). In order to investigate feasibility of our approach, we have experimented with the backend solver of our prototype by trying simple list-manipulating programs like filter, concat, copy, and reverse on singly-linked lists, where we computed invariants for each loop.

For instance, for the *concat* example in Fig. 12, we replace the while loop by the invariant $Path(x, curr, n) \wedge curr \rightarrow n = null$ resulting from the fixed point computation with widening. The transformer for the store $curr \rightarrow n = y$ joins this information yielding $Path(x, y, n)$, thus proving safety.

6   Related Work

ACDCL. We build on previous results on embedding abstract domains inside the Conflict Driven Clause Learning (CDCL) algorithm used by modern SAT solvers in a framework known as Abstract Conflict Driven Clause Learning (ACDCL) [13]. Other promising instances of this framework include a bit-precise decision procedure for the theory of binary floating-point arithmetic [16].

```
void concat(List *x, List *y) {
  List *curr;
  assume(!Path(x,y));
  if(x==null)  x = y;
  else {
    curr = x;
    while(curr->n != null) curr = curr->n;
    curr->n = y;
  }
  assert(Path(x,y));
}
```

Fig. 12. List concatenation

The ACDCL framework enables the design of *property-driven* analyses (analyses that propagate facts starting with states exhibiting a certain property of interest, e.g. backward under-approximation). The model search phase of the ACDCL framework exhibits the property-driven nature of backward analysis, while using transformers that are forward in nature. This differs from most abstract-interpretation-based analyses for heap-manipulating programs [8, 17, 1, 9], which perform exhaustive forward propagation.

Model vs. Proof Generation.   Among the successful approaches for proving safety of heap-manipulating programs, the most prominent ones are based on three-valued logic [1] and separation logic [2, 3]. Although the majority of these analyses are mainly concerned with proof generation and do not construct witnesses for the refutation of a property [8, 17, 9], there are recent advances in diagnosing failure with the purpose of refining shape abstractions [4, 5]. These works start with failed proofs, and subsequently try to find concrete counter-models from possible spurious abstract ones. Thus, the proof generation phase is *independent* from model construction. The same remark applies to an approach designed to find memory leaks in Android applications [18], which answers reachability queries by refining a points-to analysis through a backwards search for a witness. In contrast, the ACDCL framework, and hence our instantiation, exploits the *interleaving of model construction and proof generation* to mutually support model search and conflict analysis.

Decidable Logics.   Recently, several decidable logics for reasoning about linked lists have been proposed [19–23]. Piskac et al. provide a reduction of decidable separation logic fragments to a decidable first-order SMT theory framework [20]. A decision procedure for a new logic that is an alternation-free sub-fragment of first-order logic with transitive closure and no alternation between universal and existential quantifiers is described in [19]. While these works design decision procedures for handling quantified constraints, we use an abstract domain enabling us to employ the ACDCL framework. As a direct implication, we do not have a separation between propositional and theory-specific reasoning. Thus, theory-specific facts can be learned during conflict analysis, which may result in better pruning of the search space.

7   Conclusions

We have presented a verification technique for reasoning about aliasing and reachability in the heap which uses ACDCL to perform both proof generation and model construction. Proof generation benefits from model construction by learning how to refine the abstract transformer, and in turn, it assists in pruning the search space for a model. The ACDCL framework was instantiated with a newly designed abstract heap domain. From a shape analysis perspective, this domain allows expressing structural properties of list segments, whereas in a more general context of reachability analysis it can denote reachability facts regardless of the underlying data structure.

References

1. Sagiv, S., Reps, T.W., Wilhelm, R.: Parametric shape analysis via 3-valued logic. In: POPL, pp. 105–118 (1999)
2. Reynolds, J.C.: Separation logic: A logic for shared mutable data structures. In: LICS, pp. 55–74 (2002)
3. O'Hearn, P.W., Pym, D.J.: The logic of bunched implications. Bulletin of Symbolic Logic 5(2), 215–244 (1999)
4. Berdine, J., Cox, A., Ishtiaq, S., Wintersteiger, C.M.: Diagnosing abstraction failure for separation logic-based analyses. In: Madhusudan, P., Seshia, S.A. (eds.) CAV 2012. LNCS, vol. 7358, pp. 155–173. Springer, Heidelberg (2012)
5. Beyer, D., Henzinger, T.A., Théoduloz, G., Zufferey, D.: Shape refinement through explicit heap analysis. In: Rosenblum, D.S., Taentzer, G. (eds.) FASE 2010. LNCS, vol. 6013, pp. 263–277. Springer, Heidelberg (2010)
6. Cousot, P., Cousot, R.: Abstract interpretation: A unified lattice model for static analysis of programs by construction or approximation of fixpoints. In: POPL, pp. 238–252 (1977)
7. Laviron, V., Logozzo, F.: Refining abstract interpretation-based static analyses with hints. In: Hu, Z. (ed.) APLAS 2009. LNCS, vol. 5904, pp. 343–358. Springer, Heidelberg (2009)
8. Yang, H., Lee, O., Berdine, J., Calcagno, C., Cook, B., Distefano, D., O'Hearn, P.W.: Scalable shape analysis for systems code. In: Gupta, A., Malik, S. (eds.) CAV 2008. LNCS, vol. 5123, pp. 385–398. Springer, Heidelberg (2008)
9. Manevich, R., Sagiv, M., Ramalingam, G., Field, J.: Partially disjunctive heap abstraction. In: Giacobazzi, R. (ed.) SAS 2004. LNCS, vol. 3148, pp. 265–279. Springer, Heidelberg (2004)
10. Clarke, E.M., Kroening, D., Sharygina, N., Yorav, K.: Predicate abstraction of ANSI-C programs using SAT. FMSD 25(2-3), 105–127 (2004)
11. Silva, J.P.M., Lynce, I., Malik, S.: Conflict-driven clause learning SAT solvers. In: Handbook of Satisfiability, pp. 131–153. IOS Press (2009)
12. D'Silva, V., Haller, L., Kroening, D.: Satisfiability solvers are static analysers. In: Miné, A., Schmidt, D. (eds.) SAS 2012. LNCS, vol. 7460, pp. 317–333. Springer, Heidelberg (2012)
13. D'Silva, V., Haller, L., Kroening, D.: Abstract conflict driven learning. In: POPL, pp. 143–154 (2013)
14. Dillig, I., Dillig, T., Aiken, A.: Fluid updates: Beyond strong vs. weak updates. In: Gordon, A.D. (ed.) ESOP 2010. LNCS, vol. 6012, pp. 246–266. Springer, Heidelberg (2010)
15. Gulwani, S., Tiwari, A.: An abstract domain for analyzing heap-manipulating low-level software. In: Damm, W., Hermanns, H. (eds.) CAV 2007. LNCS, vol. 4590, pp. 379–392. Springer, Heidelberg (2007)
16. Haller, L., Griggio, A., Brain, M., Kroening, D.: Deciding floating-point logic with systematic abstraction. In: FMCAD, pp. 131–140 (2012)
17. Calcagno, C., Distefano, D., O'Hearn, P.W., Yang, H.: Compositional shape analysis by means of bi-abduction. J. ACM 58(6), 26 (2011)
18. Blackshear, S., Chang, B.Y.E., Sridharan, M.: Thresher: precise refutations for heap reachability. In: PLDI, pp. 275–286 (2013)
19. Itzhaky, S., Banerjee, A., Immerman, N., Nanevski, A., Sagiv, M.: Effectively-propositional reasoning about reachability in linked data structures. In: Sharygina, N., Veith, H. (eds.) CAV 2013. LNCS, vol. 8044, pp. 756–772. Springer, Heidelberg (2013)

20. Piskac, R., Wies, T., Zufferey, D.: Automating separation logic using SMT. In: Sharygina, N., Veith, H. (eds.) CAV 2013. LNCS, vol. 8044, pp. 773–789. Springer, Heidelberg (2013)
21. Yorsh, G., Rabinovich, A.M., Sagiv, M., Meyer, A., Bouajjani, A.: A logic of reachable patterns in linked data-structures. J. Log. Alg. Prog. 73(1-2) (2007)
22. Madhusudan, P., Parlato, G., Qiu, X.: Decidable logics combining heap structures and data. In: POPL, pp. 611–622 (2011)
23. Bouajjani, A., Drăgoi, C., Enea, C., Sighireanu, M.: Accurate invariant checking for programs manipulating lists and arrays with infinite data. In: Chakraborty, S., Mukund, M. (eds.) ATVA 2012. LNCS, vol. 7561, pp. 167–182. Springer, Heidelberg (2012)

REAP: Reporting Errors
Using Alternative Paths*

João Matos, João Garcia, and Paolo Romano

INESC-ID / Instituto Superior Técnico

Abstract. Software testing is often unable to detect all program flaws. These bugs are most commonly reported to programmers in error reports containing core dumps and/or execution traces that frequently reveal users' private information without providing all necessary information for effective debugging. Hence, these mechanisms are sparsely used due to users' data privacy concerns. This paper presents REAP, a new fault replication method, which allows for enhancing privacy protection while still providing software developers with the 'steps-to-reproduce' errors. REAP uses symbolic execution and randomized search heuristics to identify alternative execution paths leading to an observed error. We evaluated REAP using a testbed including real bugs of popular, large scale applications. The results show the high effectiveness of REAP in anonymizing user input: on average, REAP reveals only 16.78% of the bits in the original input, achieving an average residue (the number of common characters in the original and anonymized input) of 15.07%. Our evaluation also highlights that REAP significantly outperforms state of the art techniques in terms of achieved privacy and/or scalability.

Keywords: Software Bugs, Error Reporting, Fault-Replication, Privacy.

1 Introduction

It is common for software errors to manifest themselves after the software is released and persist long after that [1], despite more than half of the resources in a typical development cycle being invested in testing and bug fixing. Software bugs represent several billion dollars per year worth of maintenance costs in Europe and in the US alone [2]. Currently, the most popular tools to provide developers with information about application crashes (e.g. [3–5]) are error-reporting tools. These tools aim to allow software vendors to fix bugs in a timely manner. However, error reports usually include solely partial snapshots of the memory, stack traces of the failed process and a textual description of the faulty scenario, which is often insufficient to reproduce the error [6, 7]. Fault replication mechanisms address the shortcomings of classical error reports, by allowing engineers to reproduce, at the development site, a faulty execution taken place at the client side. These mechanisms monitor target applications on client devices in order to gather enough information for execution reproduction, while imposing the least overhead possible. Numerous fault-replication mechanisms have been

---

* This work was supported by national funds through FCT - Fundação para a Ciência e Tecnologia - under project PEst-OE/EEI/LA0021/2013, and by GreenTM project (EXPL/EEI-ESS/0361/2013).

Z. Shao (Ed.): ESOP 2014, LNCS 8410, pp. 453–472, 2014.

developed and are becoming more capable of efficient application monitoring and successful bug reproduction ([8–10] to name a few). Unfortunately, privacy and security concerns have prevented widespread adoption of many of these techniques and, because they rely on user participation, have ultimately limited their usefulness [11]. In fact, whether the user is working on a confidential document or has typed in personal information, sensitive private information is likely to be included either in the memory snapshot taken to generate an error report or in the non-deterministic sources logged by fault replication mechanisms [12].

A promising approach aimed at tackling these privacy concerns is based on the idea of obfuscating sensitive information inserted while ensuring the reproduction of the faulty execution ([11–13]). These mechanisms use symbolic execution (e.g. [14]) in order to derive a set of logical constraints of the user input, called *path condition* [15], that ensures the application will re-execute along the same execution path that previously led to failure. Alternative inputs, which reproduce the bug can then be drawn from the set of all inputs satisfying the identified path condition. This approach was shown to have the potential to achieve high obfuscation levels since large portion of the input data can often be replaced by alternative values derived from less constrained symbolic values. However, the degree of obfuscation achievable by these techniques is directly dependent on the restrictiveness of the path condition's constraints (i.e. on the cardinality of the set of inputs that match a given constraint), which can be critically affected by the application's structure and bug placement in the code.

In this paper we propose REAP (Reporting Errors using Alternative Paths), a novel approach based on the idea of increasing the degree of obfuscation by exploiting the presence of alternative execution paths leading to the same failure. REAP relies on symbolic execution techniques, and on lightweight search heuristics that perform bounded-depth detours from the original execution path in order to identify alternative, failure inducing paths (and their corresponding alternative user inputs). We provide a theoretical analysis of the search heuristics employed by REAP, establishing a conservative upper bound on the information leakage that it can achieve and the information that an attacker can derive on the original user input. We present the results of an extensive experimental analysis based on 6 publicly available applications, which includes popular, large scale software projects and privacy-sensitive applications from the financial and online dating domains. REAP's evaluation assesses the feasibility of the proposed solution in realistic settings, and quantifies the obfuscation quality enhancements achievable in comparison with state of the art solutions. The results show that, contrasted with state of the art solutions analyzing solely the conditions of the original execution path, REAP can achieve, with comparable execution times, up to an 83.22% average reduction in revealed input data. Furthermore, REAP can identify alternative inputs in a matter of minutes with large scale applications.

This paper is organized as follows. Section 2 overviews existing obfuscation mechanisms and discusses their main strengths and limitations. Section 3 presents the REAP system. We evaluate the proposed system in Sec. 4 before presenting some concluding remarks.

2   State of the Art and Motivations

2.1   Final Application State Error Reporting

Initial approaches to automatic error report, such as Windows Error Reporting [4] and Mozilla Crash Report [5] involved mainly information collected at the end of a failed program execution. When an application crashes, the error reporting system gathers information uncritically from the state of the process at the moment of the crash and submits it as an error report, if authorized by the user. Two major disadvantages of these methods stand out: i) there is no filtering of the submitted information regarding users' privacy preservation, which means that sensitive information may end up being incorporated in the dump of the application state performed upon the occurrence of the bug [12]; ii) the generated report does not provide any historical information on how the error was reached, which typically makes the reproduction of the bug a complex and time consuming task [6, 7].

One of the first systems to attempt to filter user private information from error reports was Scrash [16]. Applications have all their sensitive data marked as such during development, and allocated in a specially reserved area of memory. When an error report is submitted for a Scrash enabled application, all the sensitive variables are removed. This approach has three main problems. First, it requires access to an application's source code. Second, it assumes that the application programmers are trustworthy and will mark all sensitive data as such. And finally, error reports that have been amputated of relevant data may not allow for the full replay of the original error.

2.2   Input Anonymization in Fault Replication Systems

Fault replication systems that transmit the user input to the maintenance site arguably raise even larger privacy concerns. Two main approaches have been proposed to identify anonymized, failure-inducing inputs: input minimization [17] and path condition analysis [11, 12, 18].

Input minimization techniques [17] were originally designed to speed-up testing/debugging and attempt repeated random removals of input chunks, in order to identify input fragments that are irrelevant for the reproduction of the bug. By purging irrelevant inputs, these techniques can enhance privacy. However, as discussed in previous works [11, 12], due to their purely random nature, input minimization techniques typically fail in frequent scenarios in which valid inputs must respect precise structural conditions. (e.g. a credit card number must be composed of exactly 16 digits satisfying the Luhn checksumming algorithm; XML documents must comply with a defined structure).

Approaches based on path condition analysis [11, 12, 18] overcome these limitations, by reasoning on the logical constraints imposed by the conditional branches that were taken during a failure-inducing execution, i.e. its path condition. In other words, the logical restrictions imposed by a path condition delimit the domain from which input values can be chosen and still trigger the same error.

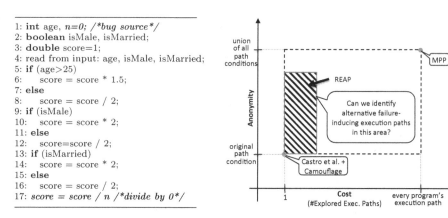

```
1: int age, n=0; /*bug source*/
2: boolean isMale, isMarried;
3: double score=1;
4: read from input: age, isMale, isMarried;
5: if (age>25)
6:    score = score * 1.5;
7: else
8:    score = score / 2;
9: if (isMale)
10:   score = score * 2;
11: else
12:   score=score / 2;
13: if (isMarried)
14:   score = score * 2;
15: else
16:   score = score / 2;
17: score = score / n /*divide by 0*/
```

Fig. 1. Example code excerpt   **Fig. 2.** Trade-off explored by REAP

Therefore, the degree of obfuscation attained by these approaches [11, 12, 18] is critically affected by the restrictiveness of the logical clauses in a path condition. The two main metrics to evaluate privacy in this context [11, 12] are the *number of leaked information bits* (henceforth called *leakage*) and the *residue*. The leakage of a particular path condition is calculated as $-\log_2(\alpha)$, where α is the fraction of the domain of the application input variables that satisfy the path condition. The residue is a more intuitive metric defined as the number of input characters that remain unchanged after the anonymization process.

The code excerpt in Figure 1 is used to motivate and illustrate the behavior of REAP. We note that the code excerpt exhibits a trivial bug (division by 0 caused by a wrong initialization of variable n in line 3, which manifests itself in line 17). The bug could be easily detected using classic debugging tools. However, despite its simplicity, the example clearly highlights the potentialities of REAP and the limitations of the two existing approaches. Now let us assume that the user input: $age = 26$, $isMale = true$, and $isMarried = false$. The path condition derived from the execution with this data yields the constraints:

$$age \in [25, MaxInt] \wedge isMale \wedge \overline{isMarried} \qquad (1)$$

In such a scenario, the age input by the user can be (partially) obfuscated by replacing it with any value larger than 25. The remaining input values, on the other hand, will have to be fully disclosed. It should be noted that in the program of Figure 1, it is actually possible to achieve total input anonymization, given that the bug manifests in all possible execution paths, and, hence, independently from the value of the user input. MPP [19] is, to the best of our knowledge, the only system that attempts to exploit the presence of multiple failure-inducing execution paths in order to maximize the obfuscation level of a bug report.

By considering the disjunction of the path conditions of *all* execution paths leading to a bug, MPP can achieve, at least for small-scale programs, the theoretical lower bound on information leakage, identifying *all* the possible inputs that replay the bug. Unfortunately, MPP suffers from severe scalability limitations for two main reasons. MPP relies on an off-line reachability analysis that performs a symbolic execution of the program, and produces as output, for all lines of code, a path condition and a triggering input for *all* the execution paths that traverse that line of code. As demonstrated by the experimental data presented in MPP's paper [19], and as confirmed by our experimental evaluation, the costs associated with MPP's off-line reachability analysis are prohibitive for applications other than small scale ones. Also, as not all the execution paths identified during the symbolic execution may actually trigger the bug, the client needs to re-execute all of them, in order to verify which subset of the paths actually reproduces the error. This can be quite inefficient especially if the bug is located in a line of code that happens to be reachable through a high number of paths.

In the considered code example, MPP would generate 8 path conditions, each one associated with different combinations of the three tests on the input variables. As all of these paths lead to the bug, the disjunction of their path conditions yields a total relaxation of the constraints on the input variables, and achieves perfect anonymization. Unfortunately, the price for attaining such a boost on input obfuscation grows exponentially with the number of tests on different input variables contained by the program.

As depicted in Fig. 2, REAP seeks an innovative balance between efficiency and anonymity in the design space of privacy preserving fault replication schemes. At the extreme of lowest anonymity are systems like in [11, 12, 18], which explore only the original execution path. On the other hand, by exploring all execution paths leading to the observed point of crash, MPP may provide the maximum possible anonymity, but suffer of severe scalability limitations. REAP strikes a balance between these two extremes, by taking advantage from alternative failure-inducing execution paths, while using scalable search heuristics that ensure its practicality even in large-scale, complex programs.

3   REAP

This section presents an overview of REAP's framework, used to generate search heuristics aimed at identifying alternative failure-inducing execution paths. It is also discussed the anonymization capabilities of REAP.

3.1   Overview of the System

The various stages of execution of REAP are illustrated by the diagram in Figure 3, and described in the following.

Original Input Anonymization Phase. Similarly to existing fault-replication systems [11, 12, 19], REAP relies on automatic code instrumentation to log user inputs in a transparent fashion. When an application failure f is detected, REAP re-executes symbolically the application feeding it with the original failure-inducing input I (just as in the systems in [11, 12]). The Original Input Anonymization

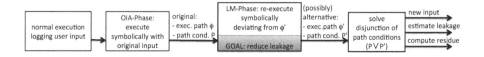

Fig. 3. Architectural Overview of REAP

(OIA) phase pursues a twofold goal: *i*) identifying the sequence of program state-ments composing the original failure-inducing execution path, denoted as ϕ; *ii*) computing the path conditions, P, associated with ϕ.

Leakage Minimization Phase. Next, REAP executes what we called *leak-age minimization* (LM) phase. In this phase REAP relies on randomized depth-bounded search heuristics that aim to identify an alternative failure-inducing execution path ϕ' by performing controlled detours from ϕ. To this end, we introduce a flexible search heuristics framework, which allows not only to con-trol the duration/extensiveness of the search phase, but also to customize the behavior of the search algorithm, i.e., the logic controlling the selection of the detouring points and the trajectories to explore once a detour is ongoing. In this work we show how REAP's search framework can be used to derive two alter-native heuristics for which we prove a fundamental property: if REAP identifies an alternative path ϕ', it guarantees that no attacker can deterministically de-duce ϕ, even if she is aware of the topology of the full execution graph and has unbounded processing capabilities. Beyond that, if such an attacker performed a probabilistic analysis of every possible failure-inducing path, it could only de-duce that the most likely original execution path coincides with that output by REAP (i.e., ϕ'), hence effectively concealing ϕ. Section 3.3 provides a theoretical analysis of REAP's anonymization capabilities.

Privacy Evaluation and Report Submission. Once ϕ' is obtained, REAP determines a feasible value for the input I' that triggers the execution path ϕ' by finding a solution to the corresponding path condition P'. Further, REAP computes the residue associated with I', and derives a conservative lower bound for the attained leakage level. Finally, the user is presented with the anonymized input, along with the corresponding leakage and residue values, and is asked to authorize the transmission of the bug report to the maintenance site.

3.2   Search Heuristics Framework

As we have already mentioned, REAP searches for alternative failure-inducing execution paths by performing detours of bounded length from the original faulty execution path ϕ. Before detailing the algorithms employed by REAP to this end, we introduce how an execution path is modeled in REAP.

REAP associates with the execution path ϕ of a program a directed acyclic graph where each node of the graph represents a sequence of statements comprised between two subsequent conditional tests on some input-dependent variable. The graph is built dynamically, during the symbolic execution of ϕ, adding a node to the graph (and connecting it to the previously generated node) every time that a branch of an input-dependent test is taken. Whenever a node is added to the graph, this is also labeled using the following triple: a location identifier composed by line of code and class signature; the current stack trace; the value of the current iteration of any cycle within which the node is being executed. This simple scheme allows us to avoid aliasing problems, ensuring that if a program statement is executed in two different execution contexts, two unique identifiers will be attributed to it. As in typical symbolic execution engines [20], an execution path is modeled assuming that each logical test generates only two edges[1], hence the execution graph is a binary tree.

We can now present the framework used to generate the search heuristics employed by REAP. The framework is embodied by the function ϕSEEKER, whose pseudocode is shown in Algorithm 1. This function encapsulates the logic of a generic search heuristic that, given the original execution path ϕ and a fault f^2, returns the path condition of a possible alternative failure-inducing execution path ϕ'. The behavior of ϕSEEKER is customizable via the following parameters:

- *numDetours:* the total number of detours the search heuristic should attempt.
- *maxDetourLength:* the maximum depth that the search heuristic can traverse after having performed a detour and before joining back the original path;
- *maxAttempts:* the maximum number of times that the LM-phase can be run;

and via the following two functions, whose implementation allows to flexibly derive a wide range of alternative search algorithms:

- DETOURSSELECTOR takes as input the original path ϕ, and the total number of detours that should be attempted, *numDetours*, and returns a set of *numDetours* nodes in ϕ from which ϕSEEKER should attempt a detour;
- PICKCHILD is used whenever a detour is being performed, to determine which of the two branches outgoing from a node (passed as input parameter) should be explored next. Both functions accept also as input parameter the identifier of the current search attempt, in order to allow the definition of adaptive policies whose behavior evolves across different attempts.

The heuristics' behavior is fully specified by defining how they implement the functions DETOURSSELECTOR and PICKCHILD, as well as they set the *numDetours* parameter. The parameters *maxDetourLength* and *maxAttempts* are used as tuning knobs to control, respectively, the radius of the search, and the maximum duration of the search. At each step of the search, the current node is executed symbolically and the corresponding logical constraint is added to the path condition P that identifies the domain of feasible input values that are able to replay the current execution path. The logical constraint for the first

---

[1] This simplifies reasoning on the execution graph, while still allowing capturing arbitrarily complex branching structures.

[2] We assume that faults are observable and uniquely identifiable as in [11, 12, 19].

Algorithm 1. Pseudocode defining the family of algorithms used to identify alternative paths

---

```
 1  function φSEEKER
    Input parameters:
      ExecPath φ;
      Fault f;
      int numDetours,maxDetourLength, maxAttempts;
      function Node PICKCHILD(Node n, int attempt);
      function Set<Node> DETOURSSELECTOR(ExecPath
    φ, int numDetours, int attempt);
    Output parameter:
      PathCondition;

 2  begin
 3    for int currAtt=0; currAtt < maxAtt; currAtt + + do
 4      Set<Node> detours=∅;
 5      PathCondition P=∅;
 6      detours = DETOURSSELECTOR(φ, numDetours, currAtt);
 7      if ( FORWARD(φ.getFirstNode(),P) ∧ P ≠ φ.getPathCondition() ) then
               // an alternative failure-inducing path was found
 8        if currAtt == 1 then
 9          return P;

10        else
11          return with probability 0.5 either P or φ.getPathCondition();

12    return φ.getPathCondition();

13  boolean FORWARD(Node n, PathCondition P)
14  begin
15    if n == null then
        return false;
16    execute n symbolically;
17    add to P the logical constraint of n;
18    if n reproduces f then
        return true;
19    Node next,checkp,current;
20    checkp = next = the successor of n that lays on the original path φ;
21    if n ∈ detours then
22      current = the successor of n that does not lay on the original path φ;
23      next = DETOUR(current,maxDetourLength, P);
24      if next == null then
          next = checkp; // detour failed, continue along the original path φ

25    return FORWARD(next, P);

26  Node DETOUR(Node n, int bound, PathCondition P)
27  begin
28    if bound == 0 then
        return null;
29    execute n symbolically;
30    Node next = PICKCHILD(n, currAtt);
31    if next ∈ φ then
          // the detour has re-joined the original path φ
32        add to P the logical constraints of this detour;
          return next;
33    return DETOUR(next,bound-1,P);
```

---

starting node of the program is void, but, for every other node n, it is equal to the logical condition imposed by the edge connecting n's predecessor to n.

Next, if the current node has been selected for a detour (line 21), a detour attempt is performed using the DETOUR function. This function implements a bounded-depth search in which, at each step, the next node to be explored is selected by means of the PICKCHILD method. If the detour joins back the original path (line 31), the path condition of the detour is added to that of the current execution path. Otherwise, if the detour reaches the upper bound on its length ($maxDetourLength$) without joining the original path, the detour attempt is aborted and the exploration proceeds along the original path (line 24).

The FORWARD function can terminate either because it reaches the same crash point as ϕ and does not reproduce f (line 15) - which can happen if one or more nodes of ϕ, required to reproduce f, were detoured - or because it replays f (line 18). Note that in the latter case, FORWARD may fail all the detour it attempts and return the original path. This case is detected in line 7, where it is accounted as a failed attempt. In case of successful identification of an alternative failure-inducing path, ϕSEEKER behaves differently depending on whether this is the first attempt or not. In the former case, the corresponding path condition P is returned. If REAP performs multiple attempts to find path ϕ' it may create a bias towards ϕ. For example, if only two failure inducing paths exist and $maxAttempts = \infty$, REAP eventually finds the alternative path with probability 1. Consequently the original path could be deduced deterministically by an attacker who knows REAP's behavior. To cope with this issue, if REAP requires more than one attempt to find an alternative path, it returns ϕ with probability 0.5 (line 11). As we will discuss in Section 3.3 this allows effectively concealing the original path ϕ in case an alternative path $\phi' \neq \phi$ is returned by ϕSEEKER. Finally, if no failure-inducing path is identified after $maxAttempts$ attempts, ϕSEEKER simply returns ϕ.

Below we describe two different search algorithms, which we called Bounded Random Walk (REAP-BRW) and Bounded Adaptive Greedy (REAP-BAG).

REAP-BRW: Bounded Random Walk. This algorithm has a similar behavior to a random walk, within the radius bounded by $maxDetourLength$ around ϕ. The value of $numDetours$ is picked at random between 0 and the length of ϕ. Further, DETOURSSELECTOR selects $numDetours$ nodes in ϕ as the source of a detour with uniform probability. Finally, the function PICKCHILD returns a child node at random, also with equal probability.

REAP-BAG: Bounded Adaptive Greedy. A logical test made on a set of input variables generates two edges that divide the input domain (of these variables), usually in a not equal way. This algorithm is biased to pick the edge outgoing from a node, whose path condition is satisfied by the largest number of input values (i.e., associated with the least restrictive path condition), a *broad edge*. We refer to the edge associated with the smaller part of the domain as *narrow edge*. This heuristic tends to choose *broad edges* over *narrow edges*, although with an adaptive probability, which decreases as the number of attempts performed so far increases. For this algorithm, the function SORTCHILD returns the child node that encompasses the largest fraction of the input domain. The SORTCHILD function implements the adaptive greedy policy, by selecting a broad edge from the currently visited node (automatically selected for the detour as $numDetours = |\phi|$) with probability $P(B)$:

$$P(B) = \frac{t+1}{2t} \qquad (2)$$

where t is the attempt being performed, and a narrow edge with the complementary probability $P(N) = 1 - P(B)$. This ensures that in the first iterations REAP-BAG will attempt with higher probability to follow the least restrictive execution paths, while converging the behavior towards the REAP-BRW heuristic as the number of attempts grows. We note that this heuristic is inspired to analogous policies used in the context of reinforcement learning problems to explore the trade-off between exploration and exploitation in face of uncertainty in [21]. In the cases where the input domain is divided equally, the edges are chosen with 0.5 probability, like in REAP-BRW. The DETOURSSELECTOR function selects the nodes in ϕ to be the source of a detour, with the probability given by equation 2.

3.3   Privacy

In this Section we analyze the privacy properties of $REAP\text{-}BRW$ and $REAP\text{-}BAG$.

Preliminary notations. We denote with $\mathcal{F}$ the set of all failure inducing paths and with $\mathcal{F}(\phi', MDL)$ the set of all failure-inducing paths from which the execution path ϕ' could be obtained via detours of maximum length equal to MDL. Further, we denote with i the original input that triggered the bug, and with $\mathcal{I}(\phi)$ the set of inputs triggering an execution path ϕ. Finally, we denote respectively $P(BRW \to \phi')$, $P(BAG \to \phi')$, the probability that REAP-BRW, REAP-BAG output an input associated with the failure-inducing path ϕ' starting from the failure-inducing path ϕ. When we refer to both REAP's variants we write, instead, $P(R \to \phi')$.

Proof overview. We demonstrate that the original path, denoted as ϕ, cannot be deduced from the path output by REAP, denoted as ϕ'. To do so, we first demonstrate that if REAP outputs a path ϕ', then ϕ' is the execution path in $\mathcal{F}(\phi', MDL)$ that is the most likely of being the original path. Next we discuss why, in case REAP outputs an alternative path $\phi' \neq \phi$, the information leakage of $\phi \cup \phi'$ and can be used as an upper bound of the information leakage reached by REAP. This result allows us to derive a methodology to quantify and report to end-users the information leakage allowed by REAP. Before presenting the proofs, we introduce some preliminary remarks.

Remark 1. In order for REAP to be application independent, its privacy guarantees (including the measurements of both leakage and residue) rely on the assumption of pure entropy, just like in all previous work [11, 12, 19]. Hence, we assume no *a priori* knowledge on the input structure nor on any information that can be deduced or contextualized in the program semantics.

Remark 2. Let ϕ^* be the original failure-inducing path in $\mathcal{F}(\phi', MDL)$ (note that this set also includes $\phi^* = \phi'$). We denote with $C(\phi^*, \phi')$ the set of edges in common between ϕ^* and ϕ', and with $D(\phi^*, \phi')$ the set of edges present in ϕ^* and not in ϕ'. The latter set contains the edges obtained when REAP performs a detour from ϕ^*, whereas the edges in $C(\phi^*, \phi')$ are obtained whenever a node of ϕ^* is not selected to perform a detour, or when a detour attempt starting from that node fails. Finally $|C(\phi^*, \phi')| + |D(\phi^*, \phi')| = |\phi'|$.

Remark 3. Both REAP-BRW and REAP-BAG, when executed with $MDL = d$ starting from an execution path ϕ, can only identify alternative paths ϕ' such that each sub-path (i.e., sequence of consecutive edges) $s_i \in D(\phi, \phi')$ has length at most d. This allows us to provide a more rigorous definition of the set of alternative failure-inducing paths identifiable starting from a path ϕ, which we denoted as $\mathcal{F}(\phi, d)$: $\phi^* \in \mathcal{F}(\phi, d) \Rightarrow \forall s_i \in D(\phi, \phi^*) \; |s_i| \leq d$.

Remark 4. Since we are assuming that the only source of non-determinism is the user input, then, given two execution paths ϕ and ϕ' where $\phi \neq \phi'$, it follows that, given two inputs[3] $i \in \mathcal{I}(\phi)$ and $i' \in \mathcal{I}(\phi')$, they must differ by at least one bit. Hence, $\mathcal{I}(\phi) \cap \mathcal{I}(\phi') = \emptyset$.

Theorem 1. *Assume REAP-BRW is provided with the execution path ϕ as input and that it returns a (possibly different execution path) ϕ'. Then among all paths $\phi^* \in \mathcal{F}(\phi', d)$, no path has higher probability of being the original path than ϕ'. Formally:* $\phi' \in \underset{\phi^* \in \mathcal{F}(\phi', d)}{argmax} \; P(BRW \to \phi' | i \in \mathcal{I}(\phi^*))$

Proof. For REAP-BRW to generate path ϕ' starting from path ϕ^*, with $\phi^* \neq \phi'$, in one of the *maxAttempts* attempts it performs the following must happen:

1. for all edges $c \in C(\phi^*, \phi')$, REAP-BRW must either i) not detour from the original path ϕ^*, or ii) detour from the original path and fail the detour attempt. As the start node, say n_c, of an edge $c \in C(\phi^*, \phi')$ is also in the original path ϕ^*, when REAP-BRW encounters n, it decides whether to detour with probability 0.5. Conversely, the probability of failing a detour attempt from node n depends on the actual topology of the execution graph of the program, but it is independent from the original path ϕ^*; we denote this probability as $P_{fd}(n_c)$ and assume it unknown in the following. Overall, the probability for REAP-BRW to generate all the edges $n_c \in C(\phi^*, \phi')$ starting from ϕ^* is:
$$\prod_{n_c \in C(\phi^*, \phi')} 0.5 + P_{fd}(n_c)$$

2. when it encounters the starting node, say n, of every edge $d_i \in D(\phi^*, \phi')$, REAP-BRW must select (between the two edges outgoing from n) the edge $d_i \in \phi'$. As REAP-BRW picks an edge during a detour with probability 0.5, the probability for REAP-BRW to generate the edges in $D(\phi^*, \phi')$ is $0.5^{|D(\phi^*, \phi')|}$.

---

[3] Recall that when we refer to an input $i \in \mathcal{I}(\phi)$, we mean the entire string of bytes provided as input to trigger the execution path ϕ.

Hence, the conditional probability that REAP-BRW identifies path ϕ' from any path $\phi^* \in \mathcal{F}(\phi', d)$ in a single attempt, given that the original user input was associated with ϕ^* is:

$$P(BRW \to \phi'|i \in \mathcal{I}(\phi^*)) = 0.5^{|D(\phi^*,\phi')|} \cdot \prod_{n_c \in C(\phi^*,\phi')} 0.5 + P_{fd}(n_c) \quad (3)$$

It is straightforward to observe that:

$$\phi' \in \underset{\phi^* \in \mathcal{F}(\phi',d)}{\operatorname{argmax}} \ P(BRW \to \phi'|i \in \mathcal{I}(\phi^*))$$

as i) the cardinality of $|C(\phi^*, \phi')|$ is maximum when $\phi^* = \phi'$, and ii) $P_{fd} \geq 0$. Hence, no path in $\mathcal{F}(\phi', d)$ is more likely to be the original path than ϕ', if REAP-BRW outputs ϕ' in a single attempt.

On the other hand, if REAP identifies an alternative path $\phi' \neq \phi$ using more than one attempt, it outputs, with probability 0.5, either ϕ or ϕ'. This guarantees that no path in $\mathcal{F}(\phi', d)$ has higher probability of being the original path than ϕ'. □

Theorem 2. *Assume REAP-BAG is provided with the execution path ϕ as input and that it returns a (possibly different execution path) ϕ'. Then among all paths $\phi^* \in \mathcal{F}(\phi', d)$, no path has higher probability of being the original path than ϕ'. Formally:* $\phi' \in \underset{\phi^* \in \mathcal{F}(\phi',d)}{\operatorname{argmax}} \ P(BAG \to \phi'|i \in \mathcal{I}(\phi^*))$

Proof. The proof structure is analogous to the one of Theorem 1, so only a sketch of proof is provided for space constraints. Consider the set of edges in $C(\phi^*, \phi')$, and denote with $B(C(\phi^*, \phi'))$, resp. $N(C(\phi^*, \phi'))$, the set of broad, resp. narrow, edges in $C(\phi^*, \phi')$. Also, denote with $E(C(\phi^*, \phi'))$ the set of edges that are neither broad, nor narrow - which we call *even* edges. Using the same arguments employed in the previous theorem, one can compute the probability that REAP-BAG generates all the edges $n_c \in C(\phi^*, \phi')$ starting from ϕ^*, denoted as $P_C(BAG \to \phi'|i \in \mathcal{I}(\phi^*))$, as:

$$\prod_{n_c \in E(C(\phi^*,\phi'))} 0.5 + P_{fd}(n_c) \prod_{n_c \in B(C(\phi^*,\phi'))} P(B) + P_{fd}(n_c) \prod_{n_c \in N(C(\phi^*,\phi'))} P(N) + P_{fd}(n_c)$$

and the probability $P_D(BAG \to \phi'|i \in \mathcal{I}(\phi^*))$ of yielding the edges in $D(\phi^*, \phi')$:

$$0.5^{|E(D(\phi^*,\phi'))|} \cdot P(B)^{|B(D(\phi^*,\phi'))|} \cdot P(N)^{|N(D(\phi^*,\phi'))|}$$

The probability $P(BAG \to \phi'|i \in \mathcal{I}(\phi^*))$, which is equal to:

$$P_C(BAG \to \phi'|i \in \mathcal{I}(\phi^*)) \cdot P_D(BAG \to \phi'|i \in \mathcal{I}(\phi^*)) \quad (4)$$

is maximum for $\phi^* = \phi'$, since $\forall \phi^* \in \mathcal{F}(\phi', d)$ with $\phi^* \neq \phi'$ it must be that $|C(\phi', \phi')| > |C(\phi^*, \phi')|$.

When considering scenarios in which an alternative path ϕ' is output after multiple attempts by REAP-BAG, the same considerations valid for REAP-BRW also apply to REAP-BAG. □

Theorem 3. *If REAP finds an alternative path ϕ' starting from a different path ϕ, the information leakage is at most equal to that computed by considering the logical disjunction of the path conditions associated with ϕ and ϕ'.*

Proof. Assume that an attacker was provided with the correct knowledge that, among all the paths in $\mathcal{F}(\phi', d)$, the actual original path may only be either ϕ or ϕ'. In this case, the uncertainty of the attacker is smaller than if she had to select among the entire set of paths in $\mathcal{F}(\phi', d)$ (as, in general, the paths in this set may have a non-null probability of being the original path). The uncertainty of this scenario is therefore a lower bound on the actual uncertainty of the attacker. Hence, the leakage results that we derive in the following represent a consistent upper bound on the actual leakage allowed by REAP.

Given that we are assuming that all inputs are equiprobable, and that we are only considering the paths ϕ and ϕ', it follows that the probability that the user original input lies on path ϕ, ϕ', denoted, resp., as $P(i \in \mathcal{I}(\phi))$, $P(i \in \mathcal{I}(\phi'))$, is:

$$P(i \in \mathcal{I}(\phi)) = \frac{|\mathcal{I}(\phi)|}{|\mathcal{I}(\phi \cup \phi')|}, \quad P(i \in \mathcal{I}(\phi')) = \frac{|\mathcal{I}(\phi')|}{|\mathcal{I}(\phi \cup \phi')|} \qquad (5)$$

where we denoted with $|\mathcal{I}(\phi)|$ the cardinality of the input domain associated with ϕ. The unconditional probability for both variants of REAP to output a failure inducing path ϕ' starting from a path $\phi^* \in \mathcal{F}(\phi', d)$ can hence be computed as:

$$P(R \to \phi' \wedge i \in \mathcal{I}(\phi^*)) = P(R \to \phi' | i \in \mathcal{I}(\phi^*)) \cdot P(i \in \mathcal{I}(\phi^*)) \qquad (6)$$

The attacker can compute the probability that ϕ is the original path given that REAP outputs ϕ', denoted as $P(i \in \mathcal{I}(\phi) | R \to \phi')$, as follows:

$$P\left(i \in \mathcal{I}(\phi) | R \to \phi'\right) = \qquad (7)$$

$$= \frac{P(R \to \phi' \wedge i \in \mathcal{I}(\phi))}{P(R \to \phi' \wedge i \in \mathcal{I}(\phi)) + P(R \to \phi' \wedge i \in \mathcal{I}(\phi'))} = \qquad (8)$$

$$= \frac{P(R \to \phi' | i \in \mathcal{I}(\phi)) \cdot P(i \in \mathcal{I}(\phi))}{P(R \to \phi' | i \in \mathcal{I}(\phi)) \cdot P(i \in \mathcal{I}(\phi)) + P(R \to \phi' | i \in \mathcal{I}(\phi')) \cdot P(i \in \mathcal{I}(\phi'))}$$

where, in order to derive Eq. 8 from Eq. 7, we have exploited Remark 4.

Since by Eq. 4 (for REAP-BAG) and Eq. 3 (for REAP-BRW) we have that $P(R \to \phi' | i \in \mathcal{I}(\phi)) \leq P(R \to \phi' | i \in \mathcal{I}(\phi'))$, we can obtain an upper bound for Eq. 7 by replacing in its denominator $P(R \to \phi' | i \in \mathcal{I}(\phi'))$ with $P(R \to \phi' | i \in \mathcal{I}(\phi))$, and simplifying the expression using Eq. 5:

$$P(i \in \mathcal{I}(\phi) | R \to \phi') \leq \frac{P(i \in \mathcal{I}(\phi))}{P(i \in \mathcal{I}(\phi)) + P(i \in \mathcal{I}(\phi'))} = \frac{|\mathcal{I}(\phi)|}{|\mathcal{I}(\phi)| + |\mathcal{I}(\phi')|} \qquad (9)$$

Finally, for the attacker to correctly guess the actual user input, in addition to identifying that the original path was not ϕ' but ϕ (whose probability is given by Eq. 7), she needs to pick the correct input among those in $\mathcal{I}(\phi)$. Since we are assuming that inputs are equiprobable, the latter probability, which we note $P(\text{right input in } \mathcal{I}(\phi) \text{ is guessed})$, is simply $|\mathcal{I}(\phi)|^{-1}$ hence:

$$P \text{ (original input is guessed} | R \to \phi') =$$
$$= P(i \in \mathcal{I}(\phi) | R \to \phi') \cdot P(\text{right input in } \mathcal{I}(\phi) \text{ is guessed}) \leq$$
$$\leq \frac{1}{|\mathcal{I}(\phi))| + |\mathcal{I}(\phi'))|} \tag{10}$$

Recalling that, by Remark 4, $\mathcal{I}(\phi) \cap \mathcal{I}(\phi') = \emptyset$, the claim follows.   □

3.4 Prototype Implementation

We implemented REAP for applications written in the Java language[4]. This tool has three main components: the execution monitor, the symbolic execution engine and the anonymizer. The execution monitor instruments the compiled Java application using the SOOT [22] bytecode instrumentation tool in order to log all user input in a transparent fashion. Note that, in order to ensure deterministic error replay, one should log all sources of non-determinism of the program, and not solely user input. On the other hand, dealing with other sources of non-determinism is out of the scope of the REAP system for the following two main reasons: i) different types of non-deterministic sources could be tackled using dedicated solutions aimed at supporting deterministic replay [23, 24]; ii) from the privacy perspective, which represents the focus of our work, user inputs are arguably the most critical sources of non-determinism. Our prototype of REAP supports multi-threaded programs (using the Java Pathfinder extension jpf-concurrent [25]) but, at this time, does not handle the reproduction of concurrency bugs. Coping with such kind of bugs would require instrumenting REAP to log, during the symbolic execution phase, any accesses to shared memory, analogously to other sources of non-determinism.

The symbolic execution engine is one of the most crucial components of REAP. REAP uses Java PathFinder [14, 20] (JPF) for this purpose. By default, all variables that are affected by the execution of read calls of the *java.io* library are assumed to be user input and are therefore marked as symbolic. Our anonymization tool is implemented in Java and uses JPF's constraint solving implementation to obtain new input from the path condition. The JPF solving implementation bridges JPF to the actual solver, which can be specified as a parameter. JPF's constraint solving implementation supports several constraint solvers, but in our work we used z3 [26].

4 Evaluation

In this section we evaluate REAP's anonymization quality and scalability. REAP was evaluated using six different applications, selected because they manage user sensitive private information, and/or due to their high popularity and to the availability of real bugs. We provide only a brief overview of these applications and of their bugs and references for detailed descriptions.

---

[4] The REAP prototype is open source:
http://sourceforge.net/projects/fastfixrsm/

In every plot in this section, the first data point (labeled '-' in the x-axis) represents the results of the OIA phase. Due to the non-deterministic properties of our algorithms, especially of the REAP-BRW, each point of the x-axis of each plot represents the average of 50 runs. The experimental platform used in this study is a machine running the MacOS X Lion operating system, with a 2.5 GHz Intel Core i5 processor and 4 GB of memory. In all experiments, we evaluate each of the algorithms presented in this paper with the test cases presented above for several values of $maxDetourLength$.

4.1 Subjects

• *Apache Tomcat* is a large and well-known Java web server (4213 classes, 188 kLOC) that powers numerous large-scale, mission-critical web applications across a diverse range of industries and organizations [27]. In our test case *Tomcat* crashes due to the bug reported in [28]. We aim to anonymize several properties such as security roles, application parameters, amongst many other fields.

• *Apache Xerces* [29] is a popular and large application for parsing and manipulating XML files (1436 classes, 90 kLOC). The bug reported in [30] causes a NullPointerException to be thrown when using external unparsed entities. In our test case *Xerces* parses a xml file that triggers this bug and REAP will attempt to anonymize its content.

• *MySQL/JDBC* [31] is the most popular open source Java database connector (752 classes, 85 kLOC). Our test case is based on the vulnerability reported in [32] and we intend to anonymize the content of the queries.

• *Apache Commons CLI* [33] is a well known application that provides an API for parsing command line options passed to programs (110 classes, 4145 LOC). The bug considered [34] throws an exception when the parser erroneously treats arguments as commands in case of syntax similarities. REAP is intended to anonymize the commands and arguments inserted by the user.

• *PaiNPai* [35] is an personal finances manager (108 classes, 5369 LOC). The bug in this subject is artificial. However, it is a great example of a program that deals with highly sensitive information, such as bank account numbers and other private information of the account holders. Given the confidential nature of such information we consider *PaiNPai* to be an important subject in our evaluation.

• *iDate* is a dating mobile application that finds people matching a specified profile. This application crashes when users use different versions of this application, as they differ in the representation of the input values. In similarity to the *PaiNPai* subject, *iDate* requires the input of very private information. The users devise a personal profile with information such as age, gender, height, weight and also their dating preferences, to be compared with the profiles of other users. We adapted *iDate* (3 classes, 1225 LOC) to run on a desktop computer.

4.2 Privacy

We measure privacy using two metrics: leakage, the amount of bits of the original input revealed by the new input, and residue, the amount of bytes of the

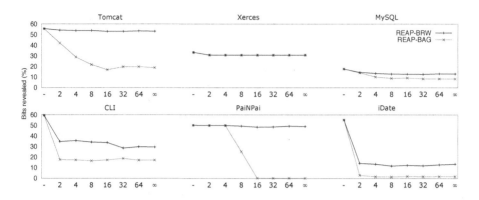

Fig. 4. Bar charts showing the leakage

original user input that remain unchanged in the new input. For each test case in every plot, the first point represents the privacy attainable by exploiting the path condition associated with the original execution path ϕ, generated by the OIA phase (which coincide with that achieved by the solutions in Castro et al. [12] and Clause and Orso [11]). Additionally these plots measure the impact on privacy due to choice of the value of $maxDetourLength$, which we treat as the independent parameter of our study.

Leakage. Figure 4 shows the amount of bits revealed in our experiments. The results suggest that even considering a conservative overestimation of the leakage allowed by REAP, evaluated by the path conditions in $\phi \cup \phi'$, REAP-BAG reveals considerably less information than state of the art solutions [11]. In this evaluation, REAP-BAG achieved anonymizations of 83, 22%, on average, and up to 99.84%, whereas REAP-BRW achieved an average of 68.18%. Comparing to the OIA phase, the LM phase of REAP-BAG was able to improve 28.34%, on average, and up to 53.88%, whereas REAP-BRW improved 13.30%. Specifically for each test case, the average improvement of REAP-BAG/REAP-BRW comparing to the OIA phase was respectively: 31.58%/2.07% for *Tomcat*, 2.55%/2.55% for *Xerces*, 8.22%/ 4.61% for *MySQL*, 42.09%/27.26% for *CLI*, 32.19/0.87% for *PaiNPai* and 53.43/42.45% for *iDate*. Figure 4 also suggests that increasing the value of $maxDetourLength$ may not provide a path that leaks less information, which was the case specially for *Xerces* and *iDate*. In some cases, REAP-BRW did not show significant improvements when compared to the OIA phase. This is due to its random nature that, in many cases, returns an alternative path that is mostly composed by *narrow* edges. These paths give very few additional solutions and therefore there is little gain in terms of leakage. In *Xerces*, REAP did not anonymize more than 70.15%, as many XML tags need to be fully disclosed if the failure is to be reproduced. Nevertheless these parts are merely XML structural terms and do not reveal sensitive information about the user.

Figure 4 suggests that many of our subjects perform several restrictive logical tests, which force the leakage of significant portion of the user input thereby

```
// each of the following tests fully leak the type of query
if ( StringUtils . startsWithIgnoreCaseAndWs ( noCommentSql , "INSERT" )
  || StringUtils . startsWithIgnoreCaseAndWs ( noCommentSql , "UPDATE" )
  || ( . . . )
```

Listing 1.1. MySQL/JDBC

```
//true iff the user
//is a minor
if ( IsNomineeMinor ) {
  ( . . . )
}
```

```
// if the value of the variable role is in
// securityRoles [] , it will be revelealed
for ( int i =0; i<securityRoles . length ; i++){
  if ( role . equals ( securityRoles [ i ]) )
    return ( true );
```

Listing 1.2. PaiNPai   **Listing 1.3.** Tomcat

Fig. 5. Code excerpts exemplifying restrictive logical tests

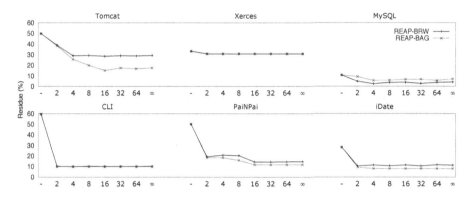

Fig. 6. Box plots showing the residue

reducing the effectiveness of an OIA-only approach. Figure 5 presents examples of code excerpts from some of our test cases. In these examples, a mechanism such as the OIA phase (or previous work [11, 12, 18]) would leak all the information introduced by the user. However, REAP may be able to circumvent those branches taken in ϕ, and find alternative solutions, as suggested in Fig. 4.

Residue. Figure 6 presents the residue measurements in our experiments. The results show that REAP is also able to considerably reduce the dissimilarity between the original input and the alternative input. In this evaluation REAP-BAG achieved, on average, residue reductions of 84.93% and REAP-BRW attained 83.07%. Compared with the OIA phase, the LM phase of REAP-BAG improved 23.42% and REAP-BRW improved 21.5%. This means that, before the report is sent, the user is be presented with a very dissimilar input from the one in the original execution.

The main lessons learned in this part of the evaluation are i) solutions that consider only the original execution path, such as the OIA phase and mechanisms presented in [11, 12, 18], often leak considerable amounts of information, ii) by detouring restrictive logical tests, REAP is able to further anonymize the

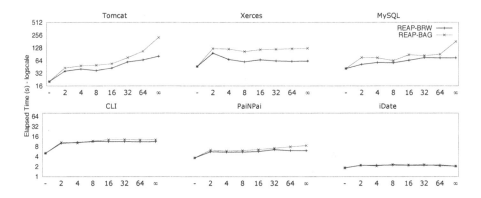

Fig. 7. Bar charts showing the execution time

input, *iii*) informed search heuristics, such as REAP-BAG, have the potential to significantly outperform pure random approaches, like REAP-BRW and *iv*) REAP is able to produce alternative inputs that are very dissimilar comparing to the original ones.

4.3   Scalability

Figure 7 gives a complete notion of the overhead of REAP when compared with the single phase process of obfuscating using only the original execution path. It is important to note that for each run (with the exception of OIA), the total execution time includes the execution time of the OIA phase and the execution time of the LM phase. The results show that REAP takes at most a few minutes to finish. This is, in practice, perfectly admissible, especially if one considers that REAP will run as a background task executing during idle periods.

Figure 7 suggests that REAP-BRW algorithm is faster than REAP-BAG. This is because, REAP-BRW is biased towards shorter paths. In fact, the number of constraints of the path conditions obtained by REAP-BRW was, on average, 77.23, which is much smaller than the average 223.22 of REAP-BAG and 134.31 of the OIA phase. Additionally REAP performed, on average, 1.09 attempts to reproduce the error. In other words, REAP seldom requires more than one attempt to reproduce the error. In terms of memory usage use REAP-BRW required, on average, 373MB and REAP-BAG 601MB.

We also ran MPP [19] with these subjects and, except for *iDate*, MPP either depleted all available memory or did not find any reproducible alternative path in the first 24 hours of execution. These results confirm what was already found in [19], i.e. it can be prohibitively expensive to compute all possible execution paths of medium/large sized programs, even if this is done offline. For iDate, which is by far the smallest subject in our testbed, the execution time of the MPP Client — even when provided with all pre-computed paths of MPP Server— was two orders of magnitude larger than REAP's (300 sec vs 2 sec).

The main lessons learned in this part of our evaluation are *i*) REAP is a feasible approach for large applications and may not require to be bounded to small values of *maxDetourLength*, *ii*) REAP-BAG is slower than REAP-BRW *iii*) REAP-BRW is likely to find shorter paths and *iv*) MPP is not a feasible approach for medium and large-sized applications.

5   Conclusions and Future Work

This paper presented REAP, a system that tackles the issue of user privacy in error reporting. REAP advances the state of the art by increasing privacy through the exploration of alternative execution paths using heuristics that perform bounded deviations in the surroundings of the original path in a scalable way. Our experimental study highlighted that the additional costs, in terms of computation time needed to identify alternative failure-inducing paths, were of at most a few minutes, even for complex applications. Our evaluation also demonstrated that REAP is able to reduce significantly the information leaked with respect to state of the art solutions [11, 12, 18] that do not identify alternative failure-inducing paths, achieving average leakage and residue reductions of 83.22% and 84.93% respectively. We conducted a rigorous analysis of the security properties and guarantees of REAP.

REAP was released as an open-source framework and designed to maximize flexibility and ease of extension. By open sourcing REAP, we hope to foster the interest of other researchers in investigating the design of alternative search algorithms aimed at further enhancing its performance and privacy.

Our future research direction aims at extending REAP in order to support the anonymization of concurrency bugs.

References

1. Zamfir, C., Candea, G.: Execution synthesis: A technique for automated software debugging. In: EUROSYS, pp. 321–334. ACM, New York (2010)
2. Research Triangle Institute: The Economic Impacts of Inadequate Infrastructure for Software Testing. Technical Report Planning Report 02-3, NIST (2002)
3. Apple Inc: Technical Note TN2123: CrashReporter (2010)
4. Microsoft Corporation: Windows Error Reporting (2012), http://msdn.microsoft.com/en-us/library/bb513641(VS.85).aspx
5. Mozilla Foundation: GNOME bug tracking (2013), http://bugzilla.gnome.org/
6. Bettenburg, N., Just, S., Schroter, A., Weiss, C., Premraj, R., Zimmermann, T.: What makes a good bug report? In: FSE, pp. 308–318. ACM, New York (2008)
7. Laukkanen, E., Mantyla, M.: Survey reproduction of defect reporting in industrial software development. In: ESEM, pp. 197–206 (2011)
8. Altekar, G., Stoica, I.: Odr: Output-deterministic replay for multicore debugging. In: SOSP, pp. 193–206. ACM, New York (2009)
9. Huang, J., Liu, P., Zhang, C.: Leap: Lightweight deterministic multi-processor replay of concurrent java programs. In: FSE, pp. 207–216. ACM, New York (2010)

10. Park, S., Zhou, Y., Xiong, W., Yin, Z., Kaushik, R., Lee, K.H., Lu, S.: Pres: Probabilistic replay with execution sketching on multiprocessors. In: SOSP, pp. 177–192. ACM, New York (2009)
11. Clause, J., Orso, A.: Camouflage: Automated anonymization of field data. In: ICSE, pp. 21–30. ACM, New York (2011)
12. Castro, M., Costa, M., Martin, J.P.: Better bug reporting with better privacy. In: ASPLOS, pp. 319–328. ACM, New York (2008)
13. Wang, R., Wang, X., Li, Z.: Panalyst: Privacy-aware remote error analysis on commodity software. In: Security, pp. 291–306. USENIX, Berkeley (2008)
14. Anand, S., Păsăreanu, C.S., Visser, W.: Jpf-se: A symbolic execution extension to java pathfinder. In: Grumberg, O., Huth, M. (eds.) TACAS 2007. LNCS, vol. 4424, pp. 134–138. Springer, Heidelberg (2007)
15. Snelting, G.: Combining slicing and constraint solving for validation of measurement software. In: Cousot, R., Schmidt, D.A. (eds.) SAS 1996. LNCS, vol. 1145, pp. 332–348. Springer, Heidelberg (1996)
16. Broadwell, P., Harren, M., Sastry, N.: Scrash: A system for generating secure crash information. In: Security. SSYM 2003, p. 19. USENIX, Berkeley (2003)
17. Zeller, A., Hildebrandt, R.: Simplifying and isolating failure-inducing input. IEEE TSE 28(2), 183–200 (2002)
18. Andrica, S., Candea, G.: Mitigating anonymity challenges in automated testing and debugging systems. In: ICAC, pp. 259–264. USENIX, Berkeley (2013)
19. Louro, P., Garcia, J., Romano, P.: Multipathprivacy: Enhanced privacy in fault replication. In: European Dependable Computing Conference, pp. 203–211 (2012)
20. National Aeronautics and Space Administration: Java Pathfinder (2013)
21. Sutton, R.S., Barto, A.G.: Reinforcement learning i: Introduction (1998)
22. Vallée-Rai, R., Hendren, L., Sundaresan, V., Lam, P., Gagnon, E., Co, P.: Soot - a Java Optimization Framework. In: CASCON, pp. 125–135 (1999)
23. Machado, N., Romano, P., Rodrigues, L.: Lightweight cooperative logging for fault replication in concurrent programs. In: DSN, pp. 1–12 (2012)
24. VMware: The Amazing VM Record/Replay Feature in VMware Workstation 6 (2011)
25. Ujma, M., Shafiei, N.: jpf-concurrent: An extension of java pathfinder for java.util.concurrent. CoRR abs/1205.0042 (2012)
26. de Moura, L., Bjørner, N.S.: Z3: An Efficient SMT Solver. In: Ramakrishnan, C.R., Rehof, J. (eds.) TACAS 2008. LNCS, vol. 4963, pp. 337–340. Springer, Heidelberg (2008)
27. Apache Foundation: Apache Tomcat (2013), http://tomcat.apache.org
28. Apache Foundation: Tomcat Bug Report 29688 (2004), https://issues.apache.org/bugzilla/show_bug.cgi?id=29688
29. Apache Foundation: Apache Xerces (2013), http://xerces.apache.org
30. Apache Foundation: Xerces Bug Report 4026 (2004), https://issues.apache.org/bugzilla/show_bug.cgi?id=4026
31. MySQL: Connector/J (2013), http://dev.mysql.com/downloads/connector/j/
32. MySQL: Bug Report 64731 (2012), http://bugs.mysql.com/bug.php?id=64731
33. Apache Foundation: CLI (2013), http://commons.apache.org/cli/
34. Apache Foundation: CLI bug report CLI-71 (2007), https://issues.apache.org/jira/browse/CLI-71
35. Ajey Joshi: PaiNPai (2013), http://painpai.sourceforge.net/

The Network as a Language Construct

Tony Garnock-Jones[1], Sam Tobin-Hochstadt[2], and Matthias Felleisen[1]

[1] Northeastern University, Boston, Massachusetts, USA
[2] Indiana University, Bloomington, Indiana, USA

Abstract. The actor model inspires several important programming languages. In this model, communicating concurrent actors collaborate to produce a result. A pure actor language tends to turn systems into an organization-free collection of processes, however, even though most applications call for layered and tiered architectures. To address this lack of an organizational principle, programmers invent design patterns.

This paper investigates integrating some of these basic patterns via a programming language construct. Specifically, it extends a calculus of communicating actors with a "network" construct so that actors can conduct scoped, tiered conversations. The paper then sketches how to articulate design ideas in the calculus, how to implement it, and how such an implementation shapes application programming.

1 Organizing Squabbling Actors

Hewitt's actor model [1] presents computation as a collaboration of concurrent and possibly parallel agents. Collaboration necessitates communication, and all communication among actors happens by message passing. The resulting separation of actors isolates resources and thus prevents conflicting use due to competing activities. Several programming languages and frameworks use the actor model as a design guideline, most prominently Erlang [2] and Scala [3].

Like the λ-calculus, the actor model is an elegant foundation for language design but fails to scale to real systems. Hence, a pure actor language turns programs and systems into organization-free "soups of processes." More precisely, the model provides no organizational principle that helps programmers arrange collections of actors into a layered or tiered architecture; also out of scope is the management and monitoring of actors via actors. Similarly, the model does not support common idioms of communication, such as multi-cast messaging, sessions, or connections. Finally, it ignores exceptions and errors, meaning it does not deal with partial failures.

Implementations of the actor model meet programmer demand for organizational principles with libraries whose APIs and protocols realize appropriate design patterns. Many such APIs hide a mini language that deserves the same kind of focused study that proper linguistic features earn. In this paper, we explain the *network* as such a hidden language feature. Our central innovation is the *Network Calculus*, which explains how to equip a given programming language with networks. Our prototype implementation of the calculus, *Marketplace*, illustrates the potential of the network as a language construct.

Z. Shao (Ed.): ESOP 2014, LNCS 8410, pp. 473–492, 2014.

2 Our Model of Actors

While Agha et al. [4] present an elegant operational semantics as a verification framework for imperative actors, our goal is to create a calculus of actors to articulate a language design idea. Specifically, we wish to show how to construct an actor language from an *arbitrary* base language via the addition of a fixed communication layer. To this end, we make the state of actors explicit, require their specification as a state-transition function, and demand that they interact exclusively via messages—not effects. This strict enforcement of the message-passing discipline does *not* prevent us from using an imperative base language, as long as its effects do not leak. In other words, the base could be a purely functional language such as Haskell, a higher-order imperative language such as Racket, or an object-oriented language such as JavaScript.[1]

The abstract syntax of our calculus is straightforward:

$$
\begin{array}{llll}
C = [\overline{\alpha}\,\overline{A}] & C_Q = [\cdot\,\overline{A_Q}] & \text{(Actor Configurations)} \\
A = x : \Sigma & A_Q = x : \Sigma_Q & \text{(Actors)} \\
\Sigma = \overline{a} \lhd B & \Sigma_Q = \cdot \lhd B & \text{(Actor States)} \\
B = f ; u & & \text{(Simple Behaviors)} \\
a = \alpha \mid A & & \text{(Actions)} \\
\alpha = \langle x, v \rangle & & \text{(Events)} \\
v = u \mid x \mid v, v & & \text{(Message Values)}
\end{array}
$$

We use $\overline{p}$ to denote a queue of ps. The xs in this grammar are drawn from an unspecified set of names or atoms; u ranges over base language values.

An actor configuration C consists of some actors $\overline{A}$ and a queue $\overline{\alpha}$ of pending events. An actor is a named (x) state that combines a behavior B with a queue $\overline{a}$ of pending actions. A behavior B pairs a function f with a state value u, both from the base language. We use A_Q to denote the set of *quiescent* actors, i.e., those with an empty queue of pending actions; a quiescent configuration C_Q has no pending events and all its actors are quiescent. Our actors may perform one of two actions: send a message or create another actor. The latter is specified as $x : \Sigma$, i.e., a complete actor, while $\langle x, v \rangle$ denotes a request to send message v to the actor named x. On receipt of a message, actor x computes the actions $\overline{a}$ it wishes to perform.

This response computation makes up the complete interface between the base language and the communication layer.[2] The interface consists of an $interp_0$ function, which interprets an actor-level event α and yields actor-level actions $\overline{a}$:

$$
interp_0 : f \times \alpha \times u \to \overline{a} \times u
$$

---

[1] In fact, each base actor could in principle use a different language, turning the network calculus into a semantics of middleware.

[2] The traditional actor model includes a **become** primitive, updating an actor's code and its state simultaneously. Such a primitive would require that the interpretation function delivers actions, a state, and a state-transformation function, i.e., $f \times \overline{a} \times u$.

The base language itself must also include facilities for analyzing and constructing representations of network-level events and actions, respectively.

We can now formulate the dispatch rule for communicating actors:

$$\frac{A_Q \xrightarrow{\alpha} A'}{[\alpha \overline{\alpha}_0 \; \overline{A_Q}] \longrightarrow [\overline{\alpha}_0 \; \overline{A'}]} \text{ (dispatch)}$$

To keep the interactions between the base and the network simple, the dispatch rule fires only when all the configuration's actors are quiescent. It relies on an event-indexed family of relations $\xrightarrow{\alpha}$ that dispatch events α to actors:

$$\frac{interp_0 \; f \; \alpha \; u = (\overline{a}, u')}{x : \cdot \lhd f; u \xrightarrow{\alpha} x : \overline{a} \lhd f; u'} \alpha = \langle x, v \rangle \qquad \frac{}{x : \Sigma \xrightarrow{\alpha} x : \Sigma} \alpha \neq \langle x, v \rangle$$

Since the dispatch rule adds actions to an actor's queue, we need two additional rules to interpret these actions:

$$[\overline{\alpha} \quad \overline{A_Q} \; (x : \langle y, v \rangle \overline{a} \lhd B) \; \overline{A}] \longrightarrow [\overline{\alpha} \langle y, v \rangle \quad \overline{A_Q} \; (x : \overline{a} \lhd B) \; \overline{A}] \qquad \text{(send)}$$
$$[\overline{\alpha} \quad \overline{A_Q} \; (x : A_{new} \overline{a} \lhd B) \; \overline{A}] \longrightarrow [\overline{\alpha} \quad \overline{A_Q} \; (x : \overline{a} \lhd B) \; \overline{A} \, A_{new}] \qquad \text{(spawn)}$$

Due to their syntactic constraints, dispatch and interpretation alternate, and messages sent by any given actor are received by peers in order.

While *spawn* is semantically straightforward, users of the model have a pragmatic hurdle to overcome if they wish to ensure *uniqueness* of actor names in a configuration. They may choose to use a "name-factory" service, to preallocate names, or any other of a wide range of appropriate strategies. Unique naming in a distributed setting is a well-known thorny issue, and it is one of our motivations in separating actor naming and addressing from actor identity below.

In our calculus, actors do not block; they remain responsive to inputs. Traditional behaviors such as "nested receive" and mailbox filtering are still expressible using well-known techniques [5].

Our actor calculus satisfies basic correctness theorems. First, the communication layer does not add any errors. Second, it is deterministic.

Theorem 1 (Soundness). *If $interp_0$ is total, an actor configuration C is either quiescent or there exists C' such that $C \longrightarrow C'$.*

Proof (Sketch). The lemma is a reasonably standard "progress lemma" and follows from a conventional proof approach [6]. □

Theorem 2 (Determinism). *For any actor configuration C, there is at most one C' such that $C \longrightarrow C'$ (modulo systematic actor renaming).*

Proof (Sketch). The lemma is a conventional diamond lemma and follows from an inspection of all possible critical pairs in the reduction relation. □

3   Making Networks a Proper Part of the Language

The actor model of computation comes with one special, built-in network that connects the actors to each other. Both our experience and the literature [7,8,9] lead us to argue, however, that programmers must be able to create and manage recursively-nestable networks. To make this point, we sketch and analyze the implementation of a chat room server, a typical example. We assume that users access this chat room over TCP via a `telnet`-like client and that the chat room broadcasts each "line" from one user to every other user. As users connect, these new connections are announced to the signed-up users, and the list of already-connected peers is sent to the new user. Disconnections are announced in a similar fashion.

A natural starting point is to create one actor per connecting user. Unfortunately the point-to-point messaging in an actor network conflicts with the desire to *broadcast* messages among users. One option is for each actor to maintain a list of peers, but synchronizing so much state becomes challenging as the number of participants grows. A more scalable, idiomatic option is to reify the medium of communication as a "broadcasting" actor, shown at right.

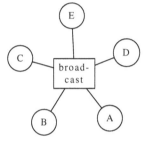

Our service now involves two different classes of actor: one for relaying to and from connected users and one for mediating the interactions of the former. The system cleanly divides responsibilities among the two. Each "relay" actor registers with the "chatroom" actor, relays messages from the chatroom to the associated TCP socket, and parses incoming utterances from the TCP socket, converting them into chatroom messages. The chatroom actor, for its part, must manage a directory of active relay actors, announce comings and goings, and broadcast chat messages received from the relays.

Both kinds of parties must detect failure in other actors. A failing relay actor should be treated as if the user had requested disconnection, causing both the closing of the associated TCP socket and an announcement of the departure of the user to the remaining users. Similarly, if the chatroom actor fails, each relay actor should take some emergency action such as announcing the problem and presumably closing its connection.

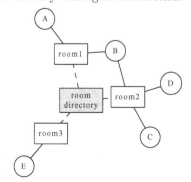

Now imagine that the service supports several named chat rooms and that connecting users may join any number of rooms. This refined design calls for a directory mapping room names to actor addresses. Again, it is natural to implement this service as an actor. This "room directory" actor maintains a directory of available chat rooms and responds to room lookup requests from relay actors. Each chatroom actor now registers itself with the room directory as it is created and relay actors query the room directory as users ask to join individual chatrooms. Finally, all three types of actor are now committed to monitoring the health of other actors to maintain their own state.

As simple as it is, the scenario exemplifies a number of classic patterns in actor architectures that internalize concepts from distributed object systems:

- dynamic *naming service*, illustrated by directory and chatroom actors;
- a *multicast medium*, implemented in the chatroom actor and also known as a data distribution service [10] or a publish/subscribe broker [11];
- dealing with *partial failure* [12]; each actor must detect and handle failures in the assembled system as part of its regular duties.

Furthermore, we can identify common patterns from layered architectures [13]:

- Members of each layer communicate using a layer-specific protocol. As messages cross layers, actors translate them from one protocol to another. In our example, relay actors translate from TCP to chat messages.
- Layers isolate components. Explicit relaying and message transformation protects services from external requests. For the chat service, the relay actors make up the periphery, protecting chat rooms and room directories.

The chat room scenario is simple but not special. Programmers re-implement naming services and multicast over and over. They ensure isolation and protection for layers of communication in actor systems. And they equip actors with code to detect and signal partial failures. This happens regardless of whether the system is sequential, concurrent or parallel, distributed or monolithic.

In response, we supply these services via a novel linguistic construct, dubbed "network" because it internalizes networking-style programming into actor systems. A network is a communications medium and a resource container [7,9] offering *naming*, *delivery*, *relaying*, and *multiplexing* services to its clients and enabling them to monitor the coming and going of their peers.

4   The Network Calculus

To address the design concerns raised above, we experimented with three generations of actor middleware and a number of full-scale applications. Here we distill our experience into a calculus of networks, which we consider a tool for language re-design. This section presents the calculus, again as a layer atop a sequential language, and sketches some variations. The next two illustrate how to "code" in the calculus and how to use it as a guide to language design.

The Calculus. We extend our actor calculus to the Network Calculus (NC) in three syntax design steps: (1) we turn the communications substrate into a linguistic construct; (2) we generalize from point-to-point messaging to broadcasts; and (3) we signal routing changes as events alongside regular messages.

The first step is to promote configurations to behavior status:

$$B = f; u \mid C \qquad B_Q = f; u \mid C_Q \qquad B_I = f; u \mid C_I \qquad \text{(Behaviors)}$$
$$C = [\overline{\alpha}\ \overline{\pi}\ \overline{A}] \qquad C_Q = [\cdot\ \overline{\pi}\ \overline{A_Q}] \qquad C_I = [\cdot\ \overline{\pi}\ \overline{A_I}] \qquad \text{(Configurations)}$$

This change allows programs to spawn entire networks recursively as actors. Multiple networks can thus exist side-by-side and nested within other configurations. Each actor, except for the root configuration, is contained in a configuration.

The second step introduces a form of publish-subscribe messaging that allows both point-to-point messaging and broadcasting. Actors thus no longer come with names but *subscriptions* $\overline{\pi}$ describing their interests, and a network maintains a set of subscriptions $\overline{\pi}$, describing the interests of its environment:

$$A = \overline{\pi} : \Sigma \qquad A_Q = \overline{\pi} : \Sigma_Q \qquad A_I = \overline{\pi} : \Sigma_I \qquad \text{(Actors)}$$
$$\Sigma = \overline{a} \lhd B \qquad \Sigma_Q = \cdot \lhd B \qquad \Sigma_I = \cdot \lhd B_I \qquad \text{(Actor States)}$$

In addition to quiescent configurations C_Q and actors A_Q, we now distinguish *inert* variations: $C_I \subset C_Q \subset C$ and $A_I \subset A_Q \subset A$. While a quiescent configuration has merely emptied its *local* queues, inert variants have empty queues at all levels. In other words, inert actors or networks are waiting for *external* events.

A subscription is an expression of interest in certain messages. Messages come in two, symmetric varieties: $\langle v \rangle$, an ordinary data-bearing message, and (v), a *feedback* message that travels along routes in the opposite direction to ordinary messages. Feedback messages are useful for flow-control and acknowledgement signalling. A message may also be prefixed by $i \geq 0$ downward arrows $\downarrow$, indicating that it should be relayed out to the ith-innermost containing network:

$$m = \langle v \rangle \mid (v) \mid \downarrow m \qquad \text{(Messages)}$$
$$v = u \mid x \mid v, v \qquad \text{(Message values)}$$

Messages carry binary trees[3] of values from the base language and atoms x from an unspecified set.

Equipped with messages, we can describe subscriptions:

$$\pi = \langle p \rangle_n \mid (p)_n \mid \downarrow \pi \qquad \text{(Subscriptions)}$$
$$p = u \mid x \mid p, p \mid \star \qquad \text{(Message patterns)}$$

Temporarily ignoring the subscripts, the syntax of a subscription specifies a tree over values and atoms and the wildcard $\star$. Semantically, a subscription π is an expression of interest in messages:

- $(p)_n$, a subscriber pattern specifies interest in receiving ordinary data messages and sending feedback messages,
- $\langle p \rangle_n$, a publisher pattern expresses an interest in receiving feedback messages and sending ordinary messages.

---

[3] Our choice of trees allows a convenient representation of arbitrary structured data along with a simple definition of pattern-matching. Many other suitable choices exist.

Just as for message transmission, prefixing a subscription with i downward arrows ($\downarrow i\,\pi$) indicates the subscription pertains to the ith-innermost containing network. A network aggregates subscriptions to form its routing table.

The third design step adds a novel form of event, a *routing event* $\overline{\pi}$.[4] Actions are extended in an analogous manner to match the new class of events:

$$\alpha = m \mid \overline{\pi} \qquad\qquad\text{(Events)}$$

$$a = \alpha \mid S \qquad\qquad\text{(Actions)}$$

$$S = \overline{\pi} : \overline{a} \triangleleft f; u \mid \cdot : \cdot \triangleleft [\cdot \cdot (\cdot : \overline{S} \triangleleft \cdot; \cdot)] \qquad\text{(Spawnable actors)}$$

Every time a network's routing table changes, it sends routing events $\overline{\pi}$ to its actors describing its current aggregate routing table. Each actor's view of the routing table is then filtered by its own subscriptions, and in particular by the *observer level* (subscript n) attached to each subscription: a subscription $(p_1)_n$ is only signalled to actors with matching subscriptions $\langle p_2 \rangle_m$ where both $m > n$ and $p_1 \parallel p_2$; see figure 1 for the definition of the matching functions ($\cdot \parallel \cdot$). Actors interested in participating in conversations without observing other participants subscribe at level $n = 0$; those interested in observing participants use $n = 1$; those interested in observing observers use $n = 2$; and so on.

To formulate the semantics of the NC, we need to introduce the notion of a *spawnable actor* because spawning an entire network requires restrictions to preserve routing table consistency. A spawned network holds a list of spawn actions, which start the configuration's processes. They run within a special, primordial process. A newly spawned actor whose subscription set is non-empty is effectively assigned responsibilities from the very first moments of its existence.

Actor configurations evolve via two reduction relations: $\Sigma \longrightarrow \Sigma'$ encodes internal reduction steps toward inertness, and $A \xrightarrow{\alpha} A'$ informs actors of the event α. Our formulation of the semantics relies on the definitions in figure 1.

When a configuration's actors are quiescent, it sends the next queued event:

$$\frac{A_Q \xrightarrow{\alpha} A'}{\overline{a} \triangleleft [\alpha \overline{\alpha}_0\, \overline{\pi}_1\, \overline{A_Q}] \longrightarrow \overline{a} \triangleleft [\overline{\alpha}_0\, \overline{\pi}_1\, \overline{A'}]} \text{ (dispatch)}$$

Dispatched events are matched against the active subscriptions of each actor. Events not matching are ignored,[5] while matching events are delivered:

$$\frac{}{\overline{\pi} : \Sigma \xrightarrow{\alpha} \overline{\pi} : \Sigma} \quad \alpha \parallel \overline{\pi} \text{ is undefined}$$

$$\frac{interp_0\, f\, (\alpha \parallel \overline{\pi})\, u = (\overline{a}, u')}{\overline{\pi} : \cdot \triangleleft f; u \xrightarrow{\alpha} \overline{\pi} : \overline{a} \triangleleft f; u'} \quad \alpha \parallel \overline{\pi} \text{ is defined}$$

$$\frac{inject(\alpha \parallel \overline{\pi})\, C = C'}{\overline{\pi} : \cdot \triangleleft C \xrightarrow{\alpha} \overline{\pi} : \cdot \triangleleft C'} \quad \alpha \parallel \overline{\pi} \text{ is defined}$$

---

[4] A routing event is, on the one hand, like "service presence" in XMPP [14] and, on the other hand, resembles route advertisements in distance-vector routing protocols [15].

[5] Inspired by the "discard" relation of Ene and Muntean's broadcast π-calculus [16].

$table : A \to \overline{\pi}$	Extracts the current subscription set from an actor
$lift : \overline{\pi} \to \overline{\pi}$	"Lifts" a subscription set by prepending $\downarrow$ to each subscription
$drop : \overline{\pi} \to \overline{\pi}$	Almost-inverse of $lift$: removes $\downarrow$ from subscriptions in a subscription set, omitting those lacking $\downarrow$.
$\alpha \parallel \overline{\pi} : \alpha \times \overline{\pi} \rightharpoonup \alpha$	Filter/restrict an event by a subscription set
	$(v) \parallel \overline{\pi} = (v)$, if $\exists \langle p \rangle_n \in \overline{\pi}$ such that $v \parallel_v p$
	$\langle v \rangle \parallel \overline{\pi} = \langle v \rangle$, if $\exists (p)_n \in \overline{\pi}$ such that $v \parallel_v p$
	$\downarrow m \parallel \overline{\pi} = \downarrow m$, if $m \parallel drop(\overline{\pi})$
	$\overline{\pi}_1 \parallel \overline{\pi}_2 = (\pi_{11} \parallel \pi_{21}) \cdots (\pi_{11} \parallel \pi_{2m})(\pi_{12} \parallel \pi_{21}) \cdots (\pi_{1n} \parallel \pi_{2m})$
	where $\pi_{11} \cdots \pi_{1n} = \overline{\pi}_1$ and $\pi_{21} \cdots \pi_{2m} = \overline{\pi}_2$
$\pi \parallel \pi : \pi \times \pi \rightharpoonup \pi$	Intersection of two subscriptions, respecting observer level
	$(p_1)_n \parallel \langle p_2 \rangle_m = (p_1 \parallel p_2)_n$, if $n < m$
	$\langle p_1 \rangle_n \parallel (p_2)_m = \langle p_1 \parallel p_2 \rangle_n$, if $n < m$
	$\downarrow \pi_1 \parallel \downarrow \pi_2 = \downarrow (\pi_1 \parallel \pi_2)$
$p \parallel p : p \times p \rightharpoonup p$	Intersection of patterns; standard unification-style algorithm
$v \parallel_v p : v \times p \rightharpoonup v$	Match v against p; standard unification-style algorithm

Fig. 1. Network Calculus metafunctions

The function *inject* transforms events from the outside world before adding them to a configuration's event queue. Incoming messages are marked as originating from one layer down and incoming routing table updates are similarly marked with *lift* before they are aggregated with the routes of the network itself:

$$inject : \alpha \times C \to C$$
$$inject\ m\ [\overline{\alpha}\ \overline{\pi}\ \overline{A}] = [\overline{\alpha} \downarrow m\ \ \overline{\pi}\ \ \overline{A}] \qquad \text{(relay-in)}$$
$$inject\ \overline{\pi}'\ [\overline{\alpha}\ \overline{\pi}\ \overline{A}] = [\overline{\alpha}\ \overline{\pi}_{total}\ \ \overline{\pi}_{new}\ \ \overline{A}] \qquad \text{(routes-in)}$$
$$\text{where } \overline{\pi}_{new} = lift(\overline{\pi}') \text{ and } \overline{\pi}_{total} = \overline{table(A)}\ \overline{\pi}_{new}$$

A dispatched event results in an enqueued action, which may trigger events within the local configuration, actions for the *containing* network, or both:

$$\overline{a}_0 \lhd [\overline{\alpha}\ \overline{\pi}_1\ \overline{A_Q}(\pi : \langle v \rangle \overline{a} \lhd B)\overline{A}] \longrightarrow \overline{a}_0 \lhd [\overline{\alpha}\langle v \rangle\ \overline{\pi}_1\ \overline{A_Q}(\pi : \overline{a} \lhd B)\overline{A}] \qquad \text{(send)}$$
$$\overline{a}_0 \lhd [\overline{\alpha}\ \overline{\pi}_1\ \overline{A_Q}(\pi : (v)\overline{a} \lhd B)\overline{A}] \longrightarrow \overline{a}_0 \lhd [\overline{\alpha}(v)\ \overline{\pi}_1\ \overline{A_Q}(\pi : \overline{a} \lhd B)\overline{A}] \qquad \text{(feedback)}$$
$$\overline{a}_0 \lhd [\overline{\alpha}\ \overline{\pi}_1\ \overline{A_Q}(\pi : \downarrow m\overline{a} \lhd B)\overline{A}] \longrightarrow \overline{a}_0 m \lhd [\overline{\alpha}\ \overline{\pi}_1\ \overline{A_Q}(\pi : \overline{a} \lhd B)\overline{A}] \qquad \text{(relay-out)}$$
$$\overline{a}_0 \lhd [\overline{\alpha}\ \overline{\pi}_1\ \overline{A_Q}(\pi : \overline{\pi}'\overline{a} \lhd B)\overline{A}] \longrightarrow \overline{a}_0 drop(\overline{\pi}'') \lhd [\overline{\alpha}(\overline{\pi}''\overline{\pi}_1)\ \overline{\pi}_1\ \overline{A_Q}(\pi' : \overline{a} \lhd B)\overline{A}]$$
$$\text{where } \overline{\pi}'' = \overline{table(A_Q)}\ \overline{\pi}'\ \overline{table(A)} \qquad \text{(routes-out)}$$

The rule for spawning new actors is complex. Its essence is as follows:

$$\overline{a}_0 \lhd [\overline{\alpha}\ \overline{\pi}_1\overline{A_Q}(\pi : A_{new}\overline{a} \lhd B)\overline{A}] \longrightarrow \overline{a}_0 \lhd [\overline{\alpha}\ \overline{\pi}_1\overline{A_Q}(\pi : \overline{a} \lhd B)\overline{A}A_{new}] \quad \text{(spawn, draft)}$$

The spawned actor A_{new} is lifted out of the spawning actor's action queue and placed at the end of the containing configuration's actor list. This first draft elides a critical detail, however. Since newly-spawned actors may arrive complete with non-empty subscription sets, the subscriptions must be incorporated into the configuration's routing tables and propagated to other interested parties:

$$\ldots \longrightarrow \overline{a}_0 \, drop(\overline{\pi}') \triangleleft [\overline{\alpha}(\overline{\pi}'\overline{\pi}_1) \ \overline{\pi}_1 \ \overline{A_Q}(\overline{\pi} : \overline{a} \triangleleft B)\overline{A} \ A_{new}]$$

$$\text{where } \overline{\pi}' = \overline{table(A_Q)} \ \overline{\pi} \ \overline{table(A)} \ table(A_{new}) \qquad \text{(spawn)}$$

The *entire* subscription table is sent to actors; if an actor needs the difference between the old and the new table, it must perform the computation on its own.

Finally, a network may step if a contained actor state can step:

$$\frac{\Sigma_Q \longrightarrow \Sigma'}{\overline{a}_0 \triangleleft [\cdot \, \overline{\pi}_1 \ \overline{A_I}(\overline{\pi} : \Sigma_Q)\overline{A_Q}] \longrightarrow \overline{a}_0 \triangleleft [\cdot \, \overline{\pi}_1 \ \overline{A_Q} \ \overline{A_I}(\overline{\pi} : \Sigma')]} \qquad \text{(schedule)}$$

This rule allows variations in scheduling. As written, the rule preserves deterministic stepping, picking the leftmost non-inert actor, and it rotates the queue of contained actors, giving each a chance to take a step.

NC satisfies the same basic correctness theorems as our actor calculus. First, the communication layer never fails. Second, the calculus remains deterministic.

Theorem 3 (Soundness). *If $interp_0$ is total, a behavior B is either inert or there exists some Σ' such that $\cdot \triangleleft B \longrightarrow \Sigma'$.*

Proof (Sketch). We employ the same Wright/Felleisen technique as for theorem 1, with a slight modification embodied in the progress lemma below.

Definition 1 (Height). *Let the height of an actor be defined as follows:*

$$height : A \to \mathbb{N}$$
$$height(\overline{\pi} : \overline{a} \triangleleft f; u) = 0$$
$$height(\overline{\pi} : \overline{a} \triangleleft [\overline{\alpha} \ \overline{\pi}_1 \ \overline{A}]) = 1 + max(\overline{height \ A})$$

Let the height of a configuration C be $height(\cdot : \cdot \triangleleft C)$.

Lemma 1 (Progress). *If $interp_0$ is total, for all $\overline{a} \triangleleft C$ and $H \in \mathbb{N}$ with $height(C) \leq H$, C is either inert or there exists some Σ' such that $\overline{a} \triangleleft C \longrightarrow \Sigma'$.*

Proof (Sketch). By nested induction on the height bound and structure of C. $\square$

Theorem 4 (Deterministic Evaluation). *For any actor state Σ there exists at most one Σ' such that $\Sigma \longrightarrow \Sigma'$ (modulo systematic renaming).*

Proof (Sketch). The proof shows that, due to the restrictions on the scheduling rule, the reduction system cannot create non-trivial diamonds. $\square$

We modeled NC with Redex [17] and Coq [18]; testing the theorems in the former and proving them in the latter.[6]

---

[6] Models and proofs available at http://www.ccs.neu.edu/home/tonyg/esop2014/.

An Interpretation. NC comes with several novelties, including concepts such as routing events, subscription, and connection. Together these concepts help address a number of programming problems:

Starting Up Services. Assembling service components into a complete application involves determining a suitable startup order. Otherwise a service may attempt to access another service before the latter is initialised. Routing events solve this problem in a natural fashion. Once a service is ready, it subscribes to incoming requests via $(service, \star)_0$ and therefore its clients can notice it via subscriptions to $\langle service, \star \rangle_1$.

Session Management. A connection is a relationship between two communicating stateful parties. If some peer A subscribes to $\langle A, c, \star \rangle_0$ (for connection identifier c) and $(B, c, \star)_1$ while B subscribes to $(A, c, \star)_1$ and $\langle B, c, \star \rangle_0$, they not only construct two unidirectional streams, but also each observes the presence of the other. During their conversation, if A receives a routing event in which $\langle B, c, \star \rangle_0$ is *absent*, it knows that B disconnected or faulted and that it may now release any state associated with the connection.

Demultiplexing. A network automatically demultiplexes incoming events via subscription-based message filtering. Imagine an NC program that implements an SSH server and uses an SSH-styled protocol. Each SSH packet carries a type identifier number. If each packet type handler subscribes with a pattern identifying a specific type number, e.g. $(ssh, 21, \star)_0$, and each actor responsible for dispatching incoming packets subscribes to $\langle ssh, \star, \star \rangle_1$, the dispatcher can use the resulting routing events to decide whether an "unhandled packet type" error response to an incoming packet is required.

Demand Tracking. By keeping track of active service instances and monitoring client connections via routing events, "management" actors can match supply to demand for a service, spawning new service instances as clients appear.

VPNs. With layering comes a need for coordinating actors, not just direct peers, but also those communicating across levels of containment. By tunneling encoded routing events as messages to remote parties, subscriptions can be propagated between subnets; the relaying actor becomes a proxy for remote peers. This approach is analogous to the topology notifications in distance-vector routing protocols; it yields a form of "virtual private network."

Design Variations. Like λ-calculus, NC is a flexible system that can easily serve as the basis for variations and extensions.

Non-determinism. While NC is intrinsically concurrent, connecting event-driven and message-exchanging actors, it remains deterministic. Its design carefully ensures that the addition of networks to a deterministic base language yields a deterministic result. Real-world communicating systems are often non-deterministic, however. There are two obvious ways to introduce forms of non-determinism that allow the calculus to exhibit parallelism and racing. First, we can loosen the quiescence and inertness restrictions on the reduction rules. Doing so introduces new interleavings that make the system truly parallel. Second, we can weaken the network's guarantee of delivering messages in order or at all.

For out-of-order delivery, the dispatch rule can be modified to select arbitrarily from the queue. For packet loss, the system needs a new rule for discarding messages from the queue. This form of non-determinism primitively reflects the uncertainty that comes with actors relaying messages across layers.

Routing. Since routing events do not distinguish entire networks from atomic actors, actors cannot tell the two apart. It is therefore possible to introduce new types of network with the same interface but different internal routing and delivery rules. For example, altering the dispatch rule for message events to select only the *first* actor matching the message, instead of all matching actors, gives "anycast" routing [19]. If, in addition, unroutable events are retained in the event queue until a matching subscription is created, the network behaves as a "message queue" in the terminology of messaging middleware [11].

Furthermore, protocol-specific routing optimizations can be applied to individual layers without breaking encapsulation. For example, IP datagrams are routed on target IP address alone; an IP-specific layer could restrict patterns to permit matching only on target IP address, enabling traditional routing table implementation techniques. In general, each network instance can enforce its own message formats and protocols, for which a session type system [20] is likely to provide the matching static checking.

Fairness. NC does not guarantee fairness. If an atomic actor constantly sends itself events, it can starve its siblings. To avoid such starvations, the network could buffer events for atomic actors or rotate the actor queue as part of every action-interpretation step.

Faults and Supervision. While the interpretation rule also assumes totality, a practical variant of NC can easily handle crashes. If $interp_0$ can return some *exception* token indicating failure, the rule

$$\frac{interp_0 \; f \; (\alpha \; || \; \overline{\pi}) \; u = exception}{\overline{\pi} : \cdot \lhd f; u \xrightarrow{\alpha} \overline{\pi} : (\cdot) \lhd \cdot; \cdot} \quad \alpha \; || \; \overline{\pi} \text{ is defined}$$

causes a crashing actor to retract its subscriptions. If a "supervisor" actor [2] exists, it may then deploy matching recovery strategies as failures are detected.

5   Programming with the Network Calculus

Network Calculus, like λ-calculus, is too spare for programming. To make such an exercise reasonably convenient, we assume a purely functional base language extended with a conventional pattern-matching facility. We choose to model atomic behaviors $f; u$ using functions in this base language, meaning that $interp_0 \; f \; \alpha \; u = f \; \alpha \; u$. This assumption also means that events α and actions a are data structures in the base language.

To illustrate NC, we implement the chat room of section 3. **Bold** identifiers denote NC terms, `monospace` literal atoms, and *italics* base language concepts.

The chat service is structured as a single network. Contained actors communicate with each other using a chat-network-specific protocol, namely the exchange of ⟨`chat`, *username*, *text*⟩ messages. Each such message conveys the information that *username* said *text*.

The chat users necessarily exist outside the service itself. Instead of regarding users and their `telnet` connections as meta-entities, we take advantage of the layered structure of NC. While our chat network communicates internally with a chat-specific protocol, we *simulate* the external world as if it were another network layer below the chat network. Actors receive and send messages on both the internal chat network and the simulated network that connects the entire service to the outside world. Ordinary messages are delivered to siblings within the chat network, while arrow-prefixed messages $\downarrow m$ are delivered to the outside world, where the users are. Figure 2 shows the layering.

Our `telnet`-like protocol rests on four message types: $\langle$`connect`, *username*$\rangle$, $\langle$`disconnect`, *username*$\rangle$, $\langle$`input`, *username*, *line*$\rangle$ and $\langle$`output`, *username*, *line*$\rangle$. The actors in our chat network are then responsible for (1) interpreting these messages and transforming them into messages for their direct peers on the inner, chat-specific network, and (2) vice versa.

The service's starting configuration **room** both creates the chat network and spawns within it the single stateless actor **acceptor**, which responds to `connect` messages received from the outer network:

$$\textbf{room} = \cdot : \cdot \vartriangleleft [\cdot \cdot (\cdot : \textbf{acceptor} \vartriangleleft \cdot ; \cdot)]$$
$$\textbf{acceptor} = \cdot : \downarrow(\textbf{connect}, \star)_0 \vartriangleleft acceptor; \cdot$$

The $\downarrow$ prefix on the acceptor's subscription indicates that it pertains to the network containing the whole service, shaded in figure 2, rather than the chat-specific inner network. The acceptor wishes to receive `connect` messages from the outside world, but takes action locally in response.

The base-language function *acceptor* implements **acceptor**'s behavior. When it receives a `connect` message, it spawns a relay actor responsible for managing communication with the newly-arrived user:

$$acceptor \ \downarrow\langle\textbf{connect}, user\rangle \ state = (\textbf{relay} \ user, state)$$
$$\textbf{relay} \ user = \cdot : (\downarrow(\textbf{input}, user, \star)_0$$
$$\downarrow\langle\textbf{output}, user, \star\rangle_0$$
$$\downarrow(\textbf{disconnect}, user)_0$$
$$\langle\textbf{chat}, user, \star\rangle_0$$
$$(\textbf{chat}, \star, \star)_1) \vartriangleleft relay; (user, \{\})$$

The **relay** actor advertises subscriptions for `telnet`-like input, output and disconnection events taking place in the outside world, and advertises its intent

Fig. 2. Chat service layering. Shaded regions are implicit, not part of the program.

to send chat messages into the inner network on behalf of the connected user. All these subscriptions are marked with a subscript 0, because **relay** is only interested in receiving these messages, and is *not* interested in receiving related routing event notifications. In contrast, its final subscription, $(\texttt{chat}, \star, \star)_1$, has a subscript of 1, indicating interest not only in receiving chat messages from the inner network, but also in hearing about related changes to the routing table.

As its peers come and go, their $\langle \texttt{chat}, user, \star \rangle_0$ subscriptions *match* the $(\texttt{chat}, \star, \star)_1$ subscription and are delivered to **relay** as routing events. The actor thus uses information about the routing table to inform the remote user of the arrival and departure of other users. In order to do so, it maintains in its actor state not only its own name but also the set of peers it has seen so far; initially, the empty set $\{\}$.

The base-language function *relay* handles both routing and message events:

$$relay \ \downarrow\langle \texttt{input}, user, line \rangle \ (user, peers) = (\langle \texttt{chat}, user, line \rangle, (user, peers))$$

$$relay \ \downarrow\langle \texttt{disconnect}, user \rangle \ (user, peers) = (\overline{\pi}', \texttt{nil}) \quad \text{where } \overline{\pi}' = \cdot$$

$$relay \ \langle \texttt{chat}, who, line \rangle \ (user, peers) =$$
$$(\downarrow\langle \texttt{output}, user, who \mathbin{+\!\!+} \text{`` says ''} \mathbin{+\!\!+} line \rangle, (user, peers))$$

$$relay \ \overline{\pi} \ (user, peers) = (arrvls \mathbin{+\!\!+} dprt, (user, peers'))$$
$$\text{where } \ peers' = \{u \mid \langle \texttt{chat}, u, \star \rangle_0 \in \overline{\pi}\}$$
$$arrvls = [\ \downarrow\langle \texttt{output}, user, u \mathbin{+\!\!+} \text{`` arrived''} \rangle \quad \mid \ u \in peers' - peers \ ]$$
$$dprt = [\ \downarrow\langle \texttt{output}, user, u \mathbin{+\!\!+} \text{`` departed''} \rangle \quad \mid \ u \in peers - peers' \ ] \quad (\dagger)$$

Text arriving from the user via the remote network is relayed to peers in the chat network. Next, a disconnection notice from the outside world translates into withdrawal of all the relay's subscriptions. Messages from peers are relayed to the user via **output** messages on the outer network. Finally, when a routing event arrives, *relay* computes routing table differences and announces corresponding arrivals and departures to its user.

The subscription withdrawals triggered by **disconnect** events cause routing events to be delivered to other relays. Because subscriptions are being withdrawn, the routing table has shrunk, and so $(peers - peers')$ on line $(\dagger)$ is nonempty, resulting in a "departed" notification being sent to the remaining users.

With the model in place, we can now simulate communication and computation using the *inject* metafunction from section 4. For example, to simulate the connection of user A, reduce the configuration state

$$\cdot \lhd (inject \ \langle \texttt{connect}, \texttt{A} \rangle \ \texttt{room})$$

to $\overline{a} \lhd C_I'$. The actions $\overline{a}$ include **output** messages for connected users, and C_I' is the final state of the server, waiting for the next event from the outside world.

In this way, *inject* and the resulting $\overline{a}$ provide an I/O interface between an NC program and its context. Our layered structure cleanly accounts for "real I/O" performed by a group of actors in a way that is impossible in a non-layered actor model, lacking any facility for distinguishing actions intended for sibling actors from actions intended for entities outside the actor configuration.

6   Implementing the Network Calculus

Marketplace is a Racket-based [21] implementation of NC. Event handlers are Racket functions, and data structures represent events and actions. Marketplace actor behaviors are also plain Racket functions, meaning $interp_0$ becomes `apply`. In turn, Marketplace's networks are ordinary actors. A second prototype, Marketplace/JS, uses Javascript as the base language and runs in the browser.

To connect to the outside world, Marketplace provides a *ground* network [22]. Its subscriptions are interpreted as subscriptions to Racket's I/O events. It observes the routing table and creates corresponding Racket event descriptors. For example, a Marketplace program may subscribe to a timer or a TCP socket.

Marketplace implements one of the variants of NC discussed in section 4. The Marketplace scheduler is fair. Exceptions thrown by Racket code are translated into failures of actors. Support libraries assist with the manipulation of subscriptions and the interpretation of routing events.

We have written a chat server in Marketplace, comparing it with Python, Haskell and Erlang implementations. Much socket- and state-management is automatic, a consequence of our routing events. Our Python and Haskell implementations initially came with subtle flaws in handling simultaneous disconnections; doing so corrupted shared state in the server. Marketplace avoids such problems *by construction*, with no shared state but the routing table, and no in-place mutation at all.

We have also implemented two major applications to explore Marketplace's potential: a DNS system and an SSH protocol implementation and server.[7]

Our Marketplace **DNS service** is a two-layered network system. While the bottom layer speaks UDP, the upper layer implements a DNS protocol. Relay actors encode and decode DNS packets as they traverse the UDP/DNS layer boundary. Within the DNS layer, actors cooperate to enact the DNS protocol for iteratively discovering the answers to incoming DNS questions. Questions are processed concurrently, with one actor allocated to each DNS inquiry. The system uses broadcasting to keep the internal DNS cache database up-to-date. The cache management actor subscribes to a wildcard so that it can eavesdrop on actors as they communicate DNS answers to each other; it populates the cache based on what it hears.

Our Marketplace **SSH server** consists of three network layers; see figure 3. Its organization directly matches the specification of the protocol [23]. Each new connection results in new Session and Application layer instances. Relay actors receive encrypted TCP data from the ground layer, decrypting and parsing it before sending the results into the session-specific layer. Packet-handler actors in that layer enact the SSH protocol, relaying application data packets to the innermost, application-specific layer. If any actor within the session layer exits unexpectedly, a "watchdog" supervisory actor notices via routing events and disconnects the session. Nesting of layers separates groups of related actors by

---

[7] All code is available via `http://www.ccs.neu.edu/home/tonyg/esop2014/`.

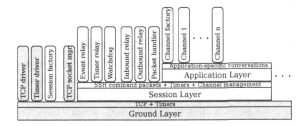

Fig. 3. Layered structure of the SSH implementation

clearly defining the available channels for communication between groups. Each network also provides a crisp boundary for the resources under its control.

Our prototype Marketplace implementations take a simple, unoptimized approach to routing. Nevertheless, the performance of our DNS resolver is adequate; it has been quietly serving web browsers in our lab for the past year.

7   Related Work

On the theoretical level, our work on NC extends previous work on event-driven systems [8], and invites comparison with process calculi and actor-based models of concurrency. On the practical level, our Marketplace language is comparable to actor-inspired languages and their libraries, especially Erlang, Scala, E and AmbientTalk.

In general, most related work concerns point-to-point communication between named entities within a single layer, dealing with broadcasting and layered architectures as derived concepts. In contrast, NC eschews names, treats broadcasting as fundamental, and adds novel routing events. The latter solve many problems: startup ordering, session lifetimes, failures, supervisors, etc. Lacking routing events completely, related systems address these problems on an ad-hoc basis, if at all, rather than as consequences of a unifying mechanism.

The Conversation Calculus. Spiritually closest to our work is the Conversation Calculus [24,25], based on π-calculus. Its *conversational contexts* scope multi-party interactions. Named contexts nest hierarchically, forming a tree. Processes running within a context may communicate with others in the same context and processes running in their context's immediate container. Contexts on distinct tree branches may share a name and thus connect transparently through hyperlinks. The Conversation Calculus also provides a Lisp-style `throw` facility that aborts to the closest `catch` clause. This mechanism enables supervisor-like recovery strategies for exceptions.

Although Conversational and NC serve different goals—the former is a calculus of services while the latter is a language design guideline—the two are strikingly similar. Like a network, a conversational context has both a spatial meaning as a location for computation and a behavioral meaning as a delimiter for a session or protocol instance. Both calculi permit communication *within* their respective kinds of boundary as well as *across* them.

The two calculi starkly differ in three aspects. First, NC cannot *transparently* link subnets into logical overlay networks because its actors are nameless. Instead, inter-subnet routing has to be implemented in an explicit manner, based on NC's routing events. Proxy actors tunnel events and actions across links between subnets; once such a link is established, actors may ignore the actual route. Any implementation of Conversation Calculus must realize just such explicit routing; NC can provide the same expressiveness as a library feature.

Second, Conversation Calculus lacks routing events and does not automatically signal peers when conversations come to an end—normally or through failure. Normal termination in Conversation Calculus is a matter of convention, while exceptions signal failure to containing contexts but *not* to remote participants in the conversational context. In contrast, Network Calculus's routing events signal failure to all interested parties transparently.

Finally, our implementation experiences with Marketplace suggest that mapping context names to "wire level" identifiers poses a steep obstacle for a similar effort for Conversation Calculus. After all, different parts of the system are going to be written in different base languages. With the explicit demultiplexing in Network Calculus, managing a heterogeneous system poses no problems.

Actors. One major family of Actor models is due to Agha and colleagues [4,26,27].

Varela and Agha's variation [27] groups actors into hierarchical *casts* via *director* actors, which control some aspects of communication between their casts and other actors. If multicast is desired, it must be explicitly implemented by a director. While casts and directors have some semblance to the layered Network Calculus, the two differ in many aspects. Our system's use of pub/sub automatically provides multicast without forcing all members of a layer to use the same conversational pattern. Directors are computationally active, but our networks are not. In their place, Network Calculus employs *relay actors* that connect adjacent layers. Finally, Varela and Agha's system lacks routing events and thus cannot deal with failures easily. They propose mobile *messenger* actors for localizing failure instead.

In Callsen and Agha's ActorSpace [26] actors join and leave *actorspaces*. Each actorspace provides a scoping mechanism for pattern-based multicast and anycast message delivery. Besides communication via actorspace, a separate mechanism exists to let actors address each other directly. In contrast, our system performs all communication with subscription-based routing and treats networks as specialized actors, enforcing abstraction boundaries and making it impossible to distinguish between a single actor or an entire network providing some service. Actors may join multiple actorspaces, whereas Network Calculus actors may only inhabit a single network, reflecting physical and logical layering of networks and giving an account of locality. In our system, actors join multiple networks by spawning proxy actors, which tunnel events and actions through intervening layered networks. Finally, ActorSpace does not specify a failure model, whereas Network Calculus signals failure with routing events.

All actor models lack an explicit interface to the outside world. I/O remains a brute-force side-effect instead of a messaging mechanism. Our functional approach to messaging and recursive layers empowers us to treat this question as an implementation decision.

Mobile Ambients. Cardelli and Gordon [28] describe the *Mobile Ambient Calculus.* An *ambient* is a nestable grouping of processes, an "administrative domain" within which computation and communication occur.

At first glance, the two pieces of work are duals. While Network Calculus focuses on routing data between domains, from which code mobility can be derived, Mobile Ambients derives message routing from a primitive notion of process mobility. By restricting ourselves to transporting *data* rather than *code* from place to place, we avoid a large class of mobility-related complication and closely reflect real networks, which transport only first-order data. Moving higher-order data (functions, objects) happens via encodings. Furthermore, mobility of code is inherently point-to-point, and the π-calculus-like names attached to ambients reflect this fact. Our pattern-based routing is a natural fit for a more general class of conversational patterns in which duplication of messages is desired.

Mobile Ambients can directly express *locks*, trading broadcast communication for the ability to express guaranteed-two-party atomic protocols. Network Calculus comes without such locks and guarantees, because communications are always broadcast even if they are intended to be two-party conversations. This seeming weakness is a reflection of our desire to align Network Calculus with the abilities of real networks, which likewise have no means of expressing atomic transfer of ownership. Hence, programs in Network Calculus must, like Actors, implement distributed locking algorithms explicitly.

Process Calculi. Fournet and Gonthier's *Distributed Join Calculus* [29] arranges processes in a tree of locations, with automatic mobility and communication between them; Network Calculus manages such nonlocal interaction explicitly. Similarly, neither first- nor higher-order π-calculi [30] represent layered or nested process groups; the spatial arrangement of their processes remains implicit.

Middleware. A comparison with publish/subscribe brokers [11] supplies an additional perspective. Essentially, a network corresponds to a broker: the routing table of a network is the subscription table of a broker; the network buffers are broker "queues;" characteristic protocols are used for communication between parties connected to a broker; etc. In short, Network Calculus can be viewed as the first formal semantics of brokers.

Erlang/OTP. The closest relative to Marketplace is Erlang/OTP [31,2]. Both support isolated "shared-nothing" message-passing processes; crash reporting in the form of explicit events to interested parties; and supervisory processes. Erlang's `gen_server` interface corresponds closely to our $interp_0$ signature.

Marketplace differs from Erlang in its use of: broadcasting in lieu of point-to-point communication; abstract topics to name services versus Erlang's use of process IDs; nesting to demultiplex conversations versus explicit demultiplexing; and routing events versus exit signals and process monitors.

Many of the OTP design patterns are linguistic constructs in Marketplace. For example, debugging and tracing of subsystems requires explicit handling of "debug facilities" and "system messages" by OTP processes, whereas in Marketplace the uniform type of an actor behavior allows tracing actors without changing any code. OTP's global service registries are Marketplace's built-in routing tables. Each Erlang application is responsible for solving its startup ordering problem, whereas Marketplace applications can use routing events to find the required topological dependency ordering implicitly.

Scala. Several Scala [3] libraries support Actor-style programming. Most of them implement Erlang-style actor supervision. Notable among the implementations is Akka, which arranges actors in a tree—spawned actors are considered children of the spawning actor—and uses the tree as the basis of supervision. Akka's tree arrangement does not constrain communication, and Akka does not support routing events. Akka's *multiple* distinct broadcast mechanisms, especially the EventBus, resemble our pub/sub mechanism. As in Erlang, no special support is provided for solving startup ordering problems.

E and AmbientTalk. The E programming language provides language-level support for *vats* [32], which like actors, take atomic *turns* at responding to events. Their state persists between turns for fault-tolerance and recovery. In addition to Miller and his colleagues [33,34], work on AmbientTalk [35] continues to explore vats. AmbientTalk adds distributed service discovery, error handling, anycast and multicast within a mobile, ad-hoc network context. In contrast to Marketplace, AmbientTalk lacks layering and does not exploit pub/sub communication for service discovery, failures, error handling, etc.

8 Conclusion

Existing programming languages fail to support layered communication architectures with linguistic constructs. Instead, programmers develop design patterns and support them with frameworks and libraries. The prevalence of these concepts suggests that language designers should consider the inclusion of appropriate programming constructs. In response, our paper presents a novel language idea—the network—in the form of the Network Calculus, building on existing actor-model designs. With the addition of a network construct, language designers can automatically provide services that programmers routinely redevelop. Programmers in turn can internalize idioms from the networking world to simplify their architectures.

The paper explains how to program in this calculus and how to use it as the basis for a language implementation. We have used Marketplace, our implementation of NC, to create and deploy two major systems. Our experience with this prototype suggests that the resulting applications are more modular than comparable systems while providing sufficient performance for daily use.

NC is a malleable design. In its basic form, it is a deterministic concurrency theory. As discussed, it can readily be extended to a parallel and non-deterministic variant and optimised in protocol-specific ways. We expect to explore both the theoretical framework and its implementation.

Acknowledgements. This work was supported in part by the DARPA CRASH program and NSF Infrastructure grant CNS-0855140. The authors would like to thank Olin Shivers and Mitch Wand for listening to many rough presentations on this material. In addition the participants of NU PLT's coffee round posed many helpful questions that helped hone this research.

References

1. Hewitt, C., Bishop, P., Steiger, R.: A universal modular ACTOR formalism for artificial intelligence. In: Proc. 3rd Int. Joint Conf. on Artificial Intelligence, pp. 235–245. Morgan Kaufmann Publishers Inc. (August 1973)
2. Ericsson(AB): Erlang/OTP Design Principles (2012), http://www.erlang.org/doc/design_principles/des_princ.html
3. Haller, P., Odersky, M.: Scala Actors: Unifying thread-based and event-based programming. Theoretical Computer Science 410(2-3), 202–220 (2009)
4. Agha, G.A., Mason, I.A., Smith, S.F., Talcott, C.L.: A Foundation for Actor Computation. J. Functional Programming 7(1) (1997)
5. Li, P., Zdancewic, S.: Combining Events and Threads for Scalable Network Services. In: Proc. Conf. on Programming Language Design and Implementation, pp. 189–199 (2007)
6. Wright, A.K., Felleisen, M.: A syntactic approach to type soundness. Information and Computation 115, 38–94 (1992)
7. Day, J.: Patterns in Network Architecture: A Return to Fundamentals. Prentice Hall (2008)
8. Felleisen, M., Findler, R.B., Flatt, M., Krishnamurthi, S.: A Functional I/O System. In: ICFP (2009)
9. Zave, P., Rexford, J.: The geomorphic view of networking: A network model and its uses. In: Proc. of the Middleware for Next Generation Internet Computing Workshop (2012)
10. Object Management Group: Data Distribution Service for Real-time Systems (January 2007)
11. Eugster, P.T., Felber, P.A., Guerraoui, R., Kermarrec, A.M.: The many faces of publish/subscribe. ACM Computing Surveys 35(2), 114–131 (2003)
12. Waldo, J., Wyant, G., Wollrath, A., Kendall, S.: A Note on Distributed Computing. Sun Microsystems Laboratories Technical Report SMLI TR-94-29 (November 1994)
13. Shaw, M., Garlan, D.: Software Architecture: Perspectives on an Emerging Discipline. Prentice Hall (1996)
14. Saint-Andre, P.: Extensible Messaging and Presence Protocol (XMPP): Core. RFC 6120 (March 2011)
15. Heart, F.E., Kahn, R.E., Ornstein, S.M., Crowther, W.R., Walden, D.C.: The interface message processor for the ARPA computer network. In: Proc. Spring Joint Computer Conference (AFIPS 19870), pp. 551–567 (May 1970)
16. Ene, C., Muntean, T.: A Broadcast-based Calculus for Communicating Systems. In: Proc. of the Workshop on Formal Methods for Parallel Programming (2001)

17. Felleisen, M., Findler, R.B., Flatt, M.: Semantics Engineering with PLT Redex. The MIT Press (2009)
18. The Coq development team: The Coq proof assistant reference manual. LogiCal Project, Version 8.0 (2004)
19. Partridge, C., Mendez, T., Milliken, W.: Host Anycasting Service. RFC 1546 (Informational) (November 1993)
20. Honda, K., Yoshida, N., Carbone, M.: Multiparty asynchronous session types. In: Proc. Symp. on Principles of Programming Languages, pp. 273–284 (January 2008)
21. Flatt, M.: PLT: Reference: Racket. Technical Report PLT-TR-2010-1, PLT Inc. (2010), http://racket-lang.org/tr1/
22. Lieberman, H.: Concurrent Object-Oriented Programming in Act 1. In: Yonezawa, A., Tokoro, M. (eds.) Object-Oriented Concurrent Programming. MIT Press (1987)
23. Ylonen, T., Lonvick, C.: The Secure Shell (SSH) Protocol Architecture. RFC 4251 (January 2006)
24. Caires, L., Vieira, H.T.: Analysis of Service Oriented Software Systems with the Conversation Calculus. In: Barbosa, L.S., Lumpe, M. (eds.) FACS 2010. LNCS, vol. 6921, pp. 6–33. Springer, Heidelberg (2012)
25. Vieira, H.T., Caires, L., Seco, J.C.: The conversation calculus: A model of service-oriented computation. In: Drossopoulou, S. (ed.) ESOP 2008. LNCS, vol. 4960, pp. 269–283. Springer, Heidelberg (2008)
26. Callsen, C.J., Agha, G.: Open Heterogeneous Computing in ActorSpace. J. Parallel and Distributed Computing 21(3), 289–300 (1994)
27. Varela, C.A., Agha, G.: A Hierarchical Model for Coordination of Concurrent Activities. In: Ciancarini, P., Wolf, A.L. (eds.) COORDINATION 1999. LNCS, vol. 1594, pp. 166–182. Springer, Heidelberg (1999)
28. Cardelli, L., Gordon, A.D.: Mobile ambients. Theoretical Computer Science 240(1), 177–213 (2000)
29. Fournet, C., Gonthier, G.: The Join Calculus: a Language for Distributed Mobile Programming. In: Applied Semantics: International Summer School (2000)
30. Sangiorgi, D., Walker, D.: The Pi-Calculus: A Theory of Mobile Processes. Cambridge University Press (October 2003)
31. Armstrong, J.: Making reliable distributed systems in the presence of software errors. PhD thesis, Royal Institute of Technology, Stockholm (2003)
32. Miller, M.S.: Robust composition: Towards a unified approach to access control and concurrency control. PhD thesis, Johns Hopkins University (2006)
33. Miller, M.S., Van Cutsem, T., Tulloh, B.: Distributed electronic rights in javaScript. In: Felleisen, M., Gardner, P. (eds.) ESOP 2013. LNCS, vol. 7792, pp. 1–20. Springer, Heidelberg (2013)
34. Yoo, S., Killian, C., Kelly, T., Cho, H.K., Plite, S.: Composable Reliability for Asynchronous Systems. In: Proc. USENIX Annual Technical Conference (June 2012)
35. Van Cutsem, T., Mostinckx, S., Gonzalez Boix, E., Dedecker, J., De Meuter, W.: AmbientTalk: Object-oriented Event-driven Programming in Mobile Ad hoc Networks. In: Intl. Conf. of the Chilean Society of Computer Science (SCCC), pp. 3–12. IEEE (November 2007)

Resolving Non-determinism in Choreographies *

Laura Bocchi[1], Hernán Melgratti[2], and Emilio Tuosto[3]

[1] Department of Computing, Imperial College London, UK
[2] Departamento de Computación, FCEyN, Universidad de Buenos Aires - Conicet, Argentina
[3] Department of Computer Science, University of Leicester

Abstract. Resolving non-deterministic choices of choreographies is a crucial task. We introduce a novel notion of realisability for choreographies –called *whole-spectrum implementation*– that rules out deterministic implementations of roles that, no matter which context they are placed in, will never follow one of the branches of a non-deterministic choice. We show that, under some conditions, it is decidable whether an implementation is whole-spectrum. As a case study, we analyse the POP protocol under the lens of whole-spectrum implementation.

1 Introduction

The Context. A *choreography* describes the expected interactions of a system in terms of the message exchanged between its components (aka *roles*):

> "Using the Web Services Choreography specification, a contract containing a global definition of the common ordering conditions and constraints under which messages are exchanged, is produced [...]. Each party can then use the global definition to build and test solutions that conform to it. The global specification is in turn realised by combination of the resulting local systems [...]"

The first part of the excerpt above taken from [15] envisages a choreography as a global contract regulating the exchange of messages; the last part identifies a distinctive element of choreographies: the global definition can be used to check the conformance of local components so to (correctly) realise the global contract. Choreographies allows for the combination of independently developed distributed components (e.g., services) while hiding implementation details. Moreover, the communication pattern specified in the choreography suffices to check each component.

For illustration, take a simple choreography, hereafter called *ATM*, involving the cash machine of a bank B and a customer C depicted as either of the following diagrams:

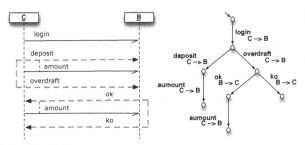

In the diagram on the left, the doubly stroked lines represent choices and the dashed lines connect interactions with the branches where they occur. On the right, *ATM* is expressed in terms of the conversation protocols of [12].

---

* This work has been partially sponsored by Projects: EU 7FP Grant 295261 (MEALS), AN-PCyT BID-PICT-2008-00319, Ocean Observatories Initiative and EPSRC EP/K034413/1.

Z. Shao (Ed.): ESOP 2014, LNCS 8410, pp. 493–512, 2014.

After successful authentication, B offers a deposit and an overdraft service to C. When opting for a deposit, C indicates the amount of money to be deposited. If C asks to overdraft then B can either grant or deny it; in the former case C will communicate the amount of money required.

On Realisations. A set of processes is a *realisation* of a choreography when the behaviour emerging from their concurrent execution matches the behaviour specified by the choreography. A choreography is *realisable* when it has a realisation.

A realisation of *ATM* can be given using two CCS-like processes [20] (augmented with internal $\_ \oplus \_$ and external $\_ + \_$ choice operators) for roles B and C:

$$T_B = \mathsf{login}.(\mathsf{deposit}.\mathsf{amount} + \mathsf{overdraft}.(\overline{\mathsf{ok}}.\mathsf{amount} \oplus \overline{\mathsf{ko}}))$$
$$T_C = \overline{\mathsf{login}}.(\overline{\mathsf{deposit}}.\overline{\mathsf{amount}} \oplus \overline{\mathsf{overdraft}}.(\mathsf{ok}.\overline{\mathsf{amount}} + \mathsf{ko}))$$

In words, T_B specifies that, after C logs in, B waits to interact either on deposit or on overdraft; in the latter case, B non-deterministically decides whether to grant or deny the overdraft; T_C is the dual of T_B. Note that *ATM* uses non-determinism to avoid specifying the criteria for B to grant or deny an overdraft. The use of non-determinism is also reflected in realisations, in fact T_B uses the internal choice operator $\_ \oplus \_$ to model the reaction when C requests an overdraft.

Choreographies can be interpreted either as *constraints* or as *obligations* of distributed interactions [19]. The former interpretation (aka *partial* [19] or *weak* [23]) admits a realisation if it exhibits a subset of the behaviour. For instance, take

$$T_B' = \mathsf{login}.(\mathsf{deposit}.\mathsf{amount} + \mathsf{overdraft}.\overline{\mathsf{ko}})$$

then T_B' and T_C form a partial realisation of *ATM* where requests of overdraft are consistently denied. On the contrary, when interpreting choreographies as obligations, a realisation is admissible if it is able to exhibit *all* interaction sequences (hence such realisations are also referred to as *complete* realisations [19]). For instance, T_B and T_C form a complete realisation of *ATM*.

The Problem. Choreographies typically yield non-deterministic specifications; here we explore the problem of resolving their non-determinism. In fact, despite being a valuable abstraction mechanism, non-determinism has to be implemented using deterministic constructs such as conditional branch statements.

Using again *ATM*, we illustrate that traditional notions of complete realisation are not fully satisfactory. The non-deterministic choice in T_B abstracts away from the actual conditions used in implementations to resolve the choice. This permits, e.g., different banks to adopt different policies depending, for instance, on the type of the clients' accounts. Consider the (deterministic) implementations B_1 and B_2 of T_B below (for brevity, each name refers to the interaction of *ATM* with the same initial):

$$B_i ::= l(c); (d(); a(x); Q + o(); P_i(c)) \quad \text{for } i = 1, 2 \quad (Q \text{ is immaterial})$$
$$P_1(c) ::= \text{if } check(c) : \overline{ok}.a(x) \text{ else } \overline{ko} \quad \text{and} \quad P_2(c) ::= \overline{ko}$$

The expression $check(c)$ in P_1 deterministically discriminates if the overdraft should be granted. Clearly both B_1 and B_2 can be used as implementations of T_B in *partial realisations* of the choreography.[1] (as e.g. in [11]).

---

[1] For instance, both B_1 and B_2 type-check against T_B considered as a session type due to the fact that subtyping for session types [13] is contra-variant with respect to internal choices (and covariant with respect to external choices).

Conversely, neither B_1 nor B_2 can be used in a *complete realisation*. This is straightforward for B_2 (unable to interact over ok after receiving an overdraft request), but not so evident for B_1. Depending on the credentials c sent by the customer to login, $check(c)$ will evaluate either to `true` or to `false`. Therefore, B_2 will be unable to exhibit both branches. This will be the case for any possible deterministic implementation of *ATM*: only one branch will be matched. Consequently, there is not a complete, deterministic realisation for *ATM*.

We prefer B_1 to B_2 arguing that they are not equally appealing when interpreting choreographies as obligations. In fact, B_2 consistently precludes one of the alternatives while B_1 guarantees only one or the other alternative (provided that *check* is not the constant map) depending on the deterministic implementation of the role T_C.

Contributions and Synopsis. We introduce *whole-spectrum implementation* (WSI), a new interpretation of choreographies as interaction obligations. A WSI of a role R guarantees that, whenever the choreography allows R to make an internal choice, there is a context (i.e., an implementation of the remaining roles) for which (the implementation of) R chooses such alternative. We illustrate the use of WSI to analyse the POP2 protocol (i.e., choreography § 2.2, implementation § 3.1, and verification § 5.1).

We develop our results in a behavioural typing framework since types directly relate specifications to implementations, but our results can be established in different contexts (c.f. [3, Appendix F]). Our technical contributions are a formalisation of WSI and a sound type system that guarantees that typable processes form WSIs. For instance, our type system validates B_1 against T_B while it discards B_2. Typing is decidable if so is the logic expressing internal conditions. We relate a denotational semantics of global types (featuring optional behaviours) to the operational semantics of local types (c.f. Thm. 3). Finally, the strong connection between local types and processes ensures that well-typed processes enjoy whole-spectrum implementability (c.f. Thm. 4).

2 Global and Local Types

Our types elaborate from [18] and use a more tractable form of iteration (discussed below). We fix a countably infinite set $\mathbb{C}$ of *(session channel) names* ranged over by $u, y, s, \ldots$ and a countably infinite set $\mathbb{P}$ of *(participants) roles* ranged over by $p, q, r, \ldots$ (with $\mathbb{C} \cap \mathbb{P} = \emptyset$). Basic data types, called *sorts*, (e.g., booleans `Bool`, integers `Int`, strings `Str`, record types, etc.) are assumed; U ranges over sorts.

Tuples are written in bold font and, abusing notation, we use them to represent their underlying set (e.g., if $\mathbf{y} = (y_1, y_2, y_3)$, we write $y_2 \in \mathbf{y}$ for $y_2 \in \{y_1, y_2, y_3\}$). Let $\#X$ denote the cardinality of a set X. Write $\{\_/\_\}$ for substitutions and in $\{\mathbf{y}/\mathbf{s}\}$ assume that $\mathbf{s}$ and $\mathbf{y}$ have the same length, that the components of $\mathbf{y}$ are pairwise disjoint, and that the i-th element of $\mathbf{y}$ is replaced by the i-th element of $\mathbf{s}$.

2.1 Types

A *global type term* (GTT, for short) G is derived by the following grammar:

$$G ::= p \rightarrow q : y \langle U \rangle \mid G + G \mid G \mid G \mid G; G \mid G^{*^f} \mid \text{end}$$

In words, a GTT can either be a single interaction, the non-deterministic ($\_+\_$), parallel ($\_\mid\_$), or sequential ($\_;\_$) composition of two GTTs, the iteration of a GTT ($\_^*$), or the empty term. Hereafter, we tacitly assume $p \neq q$ in any interaction $p \rightarrow q : y\langle U \rangle$. As in [7], we adopt a form of iteration to statically check for WSI (see § 4); in G^{*^f}, f injectively maps roles in G to pairs of channels and sorts; i.e., $f(p) = y\langle U \rangle$ is used to notify $p \in G$ when the iteration ends. We use $\text{cod}(f)$ to denote the set of channels appearing as first component in the image of f.

For a GTT G, $\text{ch}(G) \subseteq \mathbb{C}$ are the names, $\mathcal{P}(G)$ are the participants, and $\text{fst}(G)$ are the initially enabled input and output actions of each each participant in G; e.g., in

$$G_f = p \rightarrow q : y\langle U \rangle; \quad q \rightarrow s : z\langle U \rangle \tag{2.1}$$

$\text{ch}(G_f) = \{y, z\}$, $\mathcal{P}(G_f) = \{p, q, s\}$, and $\text{fst}(G_f) = \{(p, \bar{y}), (q, y), (s, z)\}$. Formal definitions of such maps are standard and relegated in [3, Appendix A].

A *global type* is defined by an equation $\mathcal{G}(\mathbf{y}) \stackrel{\triangle}{=} G$ where $\mathbf{y} \subseteq \mathbb{C}$ are pairwise distinct names and $\text{ch}(G) \subseteq \mathbf{y}$. The syntax of global types explicitly mentions names as they are needed when typing processes to check if they form a WSI (c.f. § 5). We write $\mathcal{G}(\mathbf{y})$ when the defining equation of a global type is understood or its corresponding GTT is immaterial; we write $\mathcal{G}$ or G instead of $\mathcal{G}(\mathbf{y})$ when parameters are understood.

GTTs are taken up to *structural congruence*, defined as the smallest congruence $\equiv$ such that $\_;\_$, $\_\mid\_$, and $\_+\_$ form a monoid with identity end and $\_\mid\_$ and $\_+\_$ are commutative. Two global types $\mathcal{G}_1(\mathbf{y}_1) \stackrel{\triangle}{=} G_1$ and $\mathcal{G}_2(\mathbf{y}_2) \stackrel{\triangle}{=} G_2$ are structurally equivalent when $G_1 \equiv G_2\{\mathbf{y}_2/\mathbf{y}_1\}$, in which case we write $\mathcal{G}_1 \equiv \mathcal{G}_2$.

We define the set of *ready participants* of G as follows.

$$\text{rdy}(p \rightarrow q : y\langle U \rangle) = \{p\} \quad \text{rdy}(G + G') = \text{rdy}(G \mid G') = \text{rdy}(G) \cup \text{rdy}(G') \quad \text{rdy}(\text{end}) = \emptyset$$
$$\text{rdy}(G; G') = \text{rdy}(G), \text{ if } \text{rdy}(G) \neq \emptyset \quad \text{rdy}(G; G') = \text{rdy}(G'), \text{ if } \text{rdy}(G) = \emptyset \quad G^{*^f} = \text{rdy}(G)$$

(note that for the GTT (2.1) $\text{rdy}(G_f) = \{p\}$). We extend $\mathcal{P}(\_)$ and $\text{rdy}(\_)$ to global types $\mathcal{G}(\mathbf{y}) \stackrel{\triangle}{=} G$ by defining $\mathcal{P}(\mathcal{G}) = \mathcal{P}(G)$ and $\text{rdy}(\mathcal{G}) = \text{rdy}(G)$.

As customary in session types, we restrict the attention to *well-formed* global types in order to rule out specifications that cannot be implemented distributively. A global type is *well-formed* when it enjoys the following properties: *linearity*, *single threadness*, *single selector* [14], *knowledge of choice* [14,7], and *single iteration controller*. All but the last condition are standard. The last condition is specific to our form of iteration; informally, it requires that in each interaction there is a unique participant that decides when to exit the loop (see [3, Appendix B] for its definition).

A *local type term* (LTT for short) T is derived by the following grammar:

$$T ::= \bigoplus_{i \in I} y_i!U_i; T_i \quad \Big| \quad \sum_{i \in I} y_i?U_i; T_i \quad \Big| \quad T_1; T_2 \quad \Big| \quad T^* \quad \Big| \quad \text{end}$$

An LTT is either an internal ($\bigoplus$) or external ($\sum$) guarded choice, the sequential composition of LTTs $\_;\_$, an iteration $\_^*$, or the empty term end. The set $\text{ch}(T)$ of channels of T is standard (see [3, Appendix A]).

A *local type* is defined by an equation $\mathcal{T}(\mathbf{y}) \stackrel{\triangle}{=} T$ where $\mathbf{y}$ are pairwise distinct names and $\text{ch}(T) \subseteq \mathbf{y}$. Hereafter, we write $\mathcal{T}(\mathbf{y})$ when the defining equation of a local type is understood or its corresponding LTT is immaterial; we may write $\mathcal{T}$ or T instead of $\mathcal{T}(\mathbf{y})$ when parameters are understood. We overload $\equiv$ to denote the structural congruence over local types defined as the least congruence such that internal and external choice are associative, commutative and have end as identity, while $\_;\_$ is associative. In the following, we consider types up-to structural congruence.

The projection operation extracts the local types from a global type. For a well-formed GTT G and $r \in \mathbb{P}$, $G{\upharpoonright}r$ is the *projection* of G on r and it is defined homomorphically on $\_ \oplus \_$, $\_ + \_$, and $\_;\_$ and as follows on the remaining constructs:

$$
G{\upharpoonright}r = \begin{cases}
y!U \quad (\text{ resp. } y?U) & \text{if } G = r \to p : y\langle U\rangle \ (\text{ resp. if } G = p \to r : y\langle U\rangle) \\
G_i{\upharpoonright}r & \text{if } G = G_1 \mid G_2 \text{ and } r \notin \mathcal{P}(G_j) \text{ with } j \neq i \in \{1,2\} \\
(G_1{\upharpoonright}r)^*; b_1!U_1;\ldots;b_n!U_n & \text{if } G = G_1^{*^f}, \text{cod}(f) = \{b_1\langle U_1\rangle,\ldots,b_n\langle U_n\rangle\}, \text{ and } r \in \text{rdy}(G_1) \\
(G_1{\upharpoonright}r)^*; b?U & \text{if } G = G_1^{*^f}, f(r) = b\langle U\rangle, \text{ and } r \notin \text{rdy}(G_1) \\
\text{end} & \text{if } G = p \to q : y\langle U\rangle \text{ and } r \neq p,q \text{ or if } G = \text{end} \\
\text{end} & \text{if } G = G_1^{*^f} \text{ and } r \notin \mathcal{P}(G_1) \text{ or } f(r) \text{ is undefined}
\end{cases}
$$

Our projection is total on well-formed global types. All but the clauses for the projections of iteration in the definition of $\_{\upharpoonright}\_$ are straightforward (c.f. [14]). Each iteration has a unique participant $r \in \text{rdy}(G_1)$ (by well-formedness) dictating when to stop the iteration, and a number of 'passive' participants. Projection sends messages from r to each passive participant to signal the termination of the iteration. The *projection* $\mathcal{G}(\mathbf{y}){\upharpoonright}r$ of a global type $\mathcal{G}(\mathbf{y}) \overset{\triangle}{=} G$ with respect to r is a local type $\mathcal{T}(\mathbf{y}) \overset{\triangle}{=} T$ where $T = G{\upharpoonright}r$.

Example 1. Let $G = G_f^{*^f}$, with G_f defined in (2.1), $f(q) = b_1\langle U_1\rangle$ and $f(s) = b_2\langle U_2\rangle$. Then, the projections of G are

$$G{\upharpoonright}p = (y!U)^*; b_1!U_1; b_2!U_2 \qquad G{\upharpoonright}q = (y?U; z!U)^*; b_1?U_1 \qquad G{\upharpoonright}s = (z?U)^*; b_2?U_2$$

2.2 Running Example

We illustrate our approach on a real yet tractable protocol, the Post Office Protocol - Version 2 (POP2) [5] between a client and a mail server. We describe POP2 with the following choreography where $G_{\text{EXIT}}=S \to C : \text{BYE}\langle\rangle$:

$$
\begin{aligned}
G_{\text{POP}} &= C \to S : \text{QUIT}\langle\rangle; G_{\text{EXIT}} + C \to S : \text{HELO}\langle\text{Str}\rangle; G_{\text{MBOX}} \\
G_{\text{MBOX}} &= S \to C : R\langle\text{Int}\rangle; G_{\text{NMBR}} + S \to C : E\langle\rangle; G_{\text{EXIT}} \\
G_{\text{NMBR}} &= (C \to S : \text{FOLD}\langle\text{Str}\rangle; S \to C : R\langle\text{Int}\rangle \\
&\qquad + C \to S : \text{READ}\langle\text{Int}\rangle; S \to C : R\langle\text{Int}\rangle; G_{\text{SIZE}})^{*S \mapsto \text{QUIT}\langle\rangle}; G_{\text{EXIT}} \\
G_{\text{SIZE}} &= (C \to S : \text{RETR}\langle\rangle; S \to C : \text{MSG}\langle\text{Data}\rangle.G_{\text{XFER}} \\
&\qquad + C \to S : \text{READ}\langle\text{Int}\rangle; S \to C : R\langle\text{Int}\rangle)^{*S \mapsto \text{FOLD}\langle\text{Str}\rangle}; S \to C : R\langle\text{Int}\rangle \\
G_{\text{XFER}} &= C \to S : \text{ACKS}\langle\rangle; S \to C : R\langle\text{Int}\rangle + C \to S : \text{ACKD}\langle\rangle; S \to C : R\langle\text{Int}\rangle \\
&\qquad + C \to S : \text{NACK}\langle\rangle; S \to C : R\langle\text{Int}\rangle
\end{aligned}
$$

The protocol G_{POP} starts with C sending S either an empty message along channel QUIT to quit the session, or a string on channel HELO representing C's password. In the first case, the protocol ends as per G_{EXIT} while in the latter case the G_{MBOX} is executed.

In G_{MBOX}, the server S either sends the number of messages in the default mailbox or it signals an error and ends the session as per G_{EXIT}. In the former case, G_{NMBR} establishes that C repeatedly asks either (a) to enter a folder (sending the folder's name on FOLD) and then receiving back the number of messages in that folder, or (b) to request a message by sending its index along READ and then receiving back the length of the message. In case (a), the loop is immediately repeated after S's reply, in case (b) the protocol continues as G_{SIZE} where another loop starts with C either (a) retrieving the message or (b) asking for another message (by interacting again on READ). For (a), C signals on RETR that it is ready to receive data that are sent by S on MSG (sort Data abstracts away the format of messages specified in [10]); after these interactions the choreography continues as G_{XFER} where the transmission is acknowledged by C with the interactions in G_{XFER}: ACKS keeps the message in the mailbox, ACKD deletes the message, NACK notifies that the message has not been received and must be kept in the mailbox; after any acknowledgement, S sends C the length of the next message. After some iterations in G_{SIZE}, C specifies a different folder and repeats G_{NMBR}.

The projection $T_S = G_{POP} \upharpoonright S$ of G_{POP} onto the server is below; $G_{POP} \upharpoonright C$ is dual.

$$T_S = \text{QUIT}?; T_{EXIT}$$
$$+ \text{HELO}?\text{Str}; T_{MBOX}$$
$$T_{MBOX} = \text{R}!\text{Int}; T_{NMBR} \oplus \text{E}!; T_{EXIT}$$
$$T_{EXIT} = \text{BYE}!$$

$$T_{NMBR} = (\text{FOLD}?\text{Str}; \text{R}!\text{Int} + \text{READ}?\text{Int}; \text{R}!\text{Int}; T_{SIZE})^*;$$
$$\text{QUIT}?; T_{EXIT}$$
$$T_{SIZE} = (\text{RETR}?; \text{MSG}!\text{Data}; T_{XFER} + \text{READ}?\text{Int}; \text{R}!\text{Int})^*;$$
$$\text{FOLD}?\text{Str}; \text{R}!\text{int}$$
$$T_{XFER} = \text{ACKS}?; \text{R}!\text{Int} + \text{ACKD}?; \text{R}!\text{Int} + \text{NACK}?; \text{R}!\text{Int}$$

The messages in T_S are as in G_{POP} and S iterates until either a signal on QUIT or on FOLD is sent by C.

In Ex. 2 we present, for illustrative purpose, a multiparty variant of G_{POP} where the authentication is outsourced.

Example 2. A multiparty variant of POP2 is given by G'_{POP} below where S uses a third-party authentication service A:

$$G'_{POP} = C \to S : \text{QUIT} \langle \rangle; G_{EXIT} + C \to S : \text{HELO} \langle \text{Str} \rangle; G'_{MBOX}$$
$$G'_{MBOX} = S \to A : \text{REQ} \langle \text{Str} \rangle; A \to S : \text{RES} \langle \text{Bool} \rangle;$$
$$S \to C : \text{R} \langle \text{Int} \rangle; G_{NMBR} + S \to C : \text{E} \langle \rangle; G_{EXIT}$$

where, on RES, A sends the result of the authentication of C (G_{NMBR} and G_{EXIT} remain unchanged). The projection of G'_{POP} on S is

$$T'_S = \text{QUIT}?; T_{EXIT} + \text{HELO}?\text{Str}; T_{AUTH} \qquad \blacklozenge$$
$$T_{AUTH} = \text{REC}!\text{Str}; \text{RES}?\text{Bool}; T'_{MBOX} \qquad T'_{MBOX} = \text{R}!\text{Int}; T_{NMBR} \oplus \text{E}!; T_{EXIT}$$

2.3 Behaviour of Types

The semantics of local types is given in terms of *specifications*, namely pairs of partial functions Γ and Δ such that Γ maps session names to global types and names to sorts, and Δ maps tuples of session names to local types. We use $\Gamma \bullet \Delta$ to denote a specification and adopt the usual syntactic notations for environments:

$$\Gamma ::= \emptyset \mid \Gamma, u : \mathcal{G} \mid \Gamma, x : \text{U} \qquad \Delta ::= \emptyset \mid \Delta, \mathbf{s} : \mathcal{T}$$

$$\frac{\Gamma(u)\equiv\mathcal{G}(\mathbf{y})}{\Gamma\bullet\Delta \xrightarrow{\overline{u}^n\mathbf{y}} \Gamma\bullet\Delta,\mathbf{y}:\mathcal{G}(\mathbf{y}){\upharpoonright}0} \text{[TReq]} \qquad \frac{\Gamma(u)\equiv\mathcal{G}(\mathbf{y})}{\Gamma\bullet\Delta \xrightarrow{u_i\mathbf{y}} \Gamma\bullet\Delta,\mathbf{y}:\mathcal{G}(\mathbf{y}){\upharpoonright}\mathtt{i}} \text{[TAcc]}$$

$$\frac{\mathbf{v}:\mathbf{U}_j \quad s_j\in\mathbf{s} \quad j\in I}{\Gamma\bullet\Delta,\mathbf{s}:\bigoplus_{i\in I}s_i!\mathbf{U}_i;\mathcal{T}_i \xrightarrow{\overline{s_j}\mathbf{v}} \Gamma\bullet\Delta,\mathbf{s}:\mathcal{T}_j} \text{[TSend]} \qquad \frac{\mathbf{v}:\mathbf{U}_j \quad s_j\in\mathbf{s} \quad j\in I}{\Gamma\bullet\Delta,\mathbf{s}:\sum_{i\in I}s_i?\mathbf{U}_i;\mathcal{T}_i \xrightarrow{s_j\mathbf{v}} \Gamma\bullet\Delta,\mathbf{s}:\mathcal{T}_j} \text{[TRec]}$$

$$\frac{\Gamma\bullet\Delta,\mathbf{s}:\mathcal{T} \xrightarrow{\alpha} \Gamma\bullet\Delta,\mathbf{s}:\mathcal{T}'}{\Gamma\bullet\Delta,\mathbf{s}:\mathcal{T};\mathcal{T}'' \xrightarrow{\alpha} \Gamma\bullet\Delta,\mathbf{s}:\mathcal{T}';\mathcal{T}''} \text{[TSeq]} \qquad \frac{\Gamma\bullet\Delta_1 \xrightarrow{\tau} \Gamma\bullet\Delta_1'}{\Gamma\bullet\Delta_1,\Delta_2 \xrightarrow{\tau} \Gamma\bullet\Delta_1',\Delta_2} \text{[TPar]}$$

$$\Gamma\bullet\Delta,\mathbf{s}:\mathcal{T}^* \xrightarrow{\tau} \Gamma\bullet\Delta,\mathbf{s}:\mathsf{end}[\text{TLoop1}] \qquad \Gamma\bullet\Delta,\mathbf{s}:\mathcal{T}^* \xrightarrow{\tau} \Gamma\bullet\Delta,\mathbf{s}:\mathcal{T};\mathcal{T}^*[\text{TLoop2}]$$

Fig. 1. Labelled transitions for specifications

as usual, when writing $\Delta,\mathbf{s}:\mathcal{T}$, $\mathbf{s}\notin\mathrm{dom}(\Delta)$ is implicitly assumed (likewise for $\Gamma,\_:\_$) and $\Delta_1,\Delta_2 \equiv \Delta_2,\Delta_1$.

The semantics of specifications is generated by the rules in Fig. 1 using the labels

$$\alpha ::= \overline{u}^n\mathbf{s} \mid u_i\mathbf{s} \mid \overline{s}v \mid sv \mid \tau \tag{2.3}$$

that respectively represent the request on u for the initialisation of a session among $n+1$ roles, the acceptance of joining a session of u as the i-th role, the sending of a value on s, the reception of a value on s, and the silent step.

Intuitively, the rules of Fig. 1 specify how a single participant behaves in a session $\mathbf{s}$ and are instrumental for type checking processes. Rules [TReq] and [TAcc] allow a specification to initiate a new session by projecting (on 0 and $\mathtt{i}$, resp.) the global type associated[2] to name u in Γ. By [TSend], if types are respected, a specification can send any value on one of the names in a branch of an internal choice. Dually, [TRec] accounts for the reception of a value. Note that values occur only on the label of the transitions and are not instantiated in the local types. Rule [TSeq] is trivial. Rule [TPar] allows part of a specification to make a transition. Finally, an iterative local type can either stop by rule [TLoop1] or arbitrarily repeat itself by rule [TLoop2].

3 Processes and Systems

As we will see (Def. 1 in § 4), global types are implemented by *systems*. Our systems exchange values specified by *expressions* having the following syntax:

$$e ::= x \mid \mathbf{v} \mid e_1 \text{ op } e_2 \qquad \ell ::= [e_1,\ldots,e_n] \mid e_1..e_2$$

An expression e is either a variable, or a value, or else the composition of expressions (we assume that expressions are implicitly sorted and do not include names). Lists $[e_1,\ldots,e_n]$ and numerical ranges $e_1..e_2$ are used for iteration; in the former case, all the items of a list have the same sort, in the latter case, both expressions are integers and

---

[2] The use of $\equiv$ in the premises caters for α-conversion of names $\mathbf{y}$. Also, $\mathbb{P}$ is the set of natural numbers (0 is the initiator of sessions) and for readability, in examples we use names to denote participants.

the value of e_1 is smaller than or equal to the value of e_2. The empty list is denoted as ε and the operations $\mathrm{hd}(\ell)$ and $\mathrm{tl}(\ell)$ respectively return the head and tail of ℓ (defined as usual). We write $\mathrm{var}(e)$ and $\mathrm{var}(\ell)$ for the set of variables of e and ℓ.

The syntax of processes and systems below relies on *queues* of basic values M and input-guarded non-deterministic sequential process N, respectively defined as

$$M ::= \mathbf{0} \mid \mathbf{v} \cdot M \qquad N ::= \sum_{i \in I} y_i(x_i); P_i$$

where $i \neq j \in I \implies y_i \neq y_j$; we define $\mathbf{0} \overset{\triangle}{=} \sum_{i \in \emptyset} y_i(x_i); P_i$.

The syntax of systems S and processes P is

$$P, Q ::= u_i(\mathbf{y}).P \mid \overline{u}^n(\mathbf{y}).P \mid N \mid \overline{s}e \mid \text{if } e : P \text{ else } Q$$
$$\mid P; P \mid \text{for } x \text{ in } \ell : P \mid \text{do } N \text{ until } b(x)$$
$$S ::= P \mid (\mathbf{vs})S \mid S \mid S \mid s : M$$

All constructions but loops are straightforward. In $\text{for } x \text{ in } \ell : P$, the body P is executed for each element in ℓ, while $\text{do } N \text{ until } b(x)$ repeats N until a message on b is received. Intuitively, the former construct is executed by the (unique) role that decides when to exit the iteration while the latter construct is used by the "passive" roles in the loop (see § 2.1 and § 5). Given a process P, $\mathrm{fv}(P)$ denotes the set of all variables appearing outside the scope of input prefixes in P. Also, we extend $\mathrm{var}(\_)$ to systems in the obvious way. In $(\mathbf{vs})S$, names $\mathbf{s}$ are bound (the set $\mathrm{fc}(S)$ of free session names of S is defined as expected); a system S is *closed* when $\mathrm{fc}(S) = \emptyset$ and it is *initial* when S does not contain runtime constructs, namely new session $(\mathbf{vs})S'$ and queues $s : M$. Formally, S is initial iff for each s and S', if $S \equiv (\mathbf{vs})S'$ then $\mathbf{s} \not\subseteq \mathrm{fc}(S')$.

The structural congruence $\equiv$ is the least congruence over systems closed with respect to α-conversion, such that $\_ \mid \_$ and $\_ + \_$ are associative, commutative and have $\mathbf{0}$ as identity, $\_; \_$ is associative and has $\mathbf{0}$ as identity, and the following axioms hold:

$$(\mathbf{vs})\mathbf{0} \equiv \mathbf{0} \qquad (\mathbf{vs})(\mathbf{vs'})S \equiv (\mathbf{vs'})(\mathbf{vs})S \qquad (\mathbf{vs})(S \mid S') \equiv S \mid (\mathbf{vs})S', \text{ when } \mathbf{s} \not\subseteq \mathrm{fc}(S)$$

The operational semantics of systems is in Fig. 2 where a store σ records the values assigned to variables, $e \downarrow \sigma$ is the evaluation of e (defined if $\mathrm{var}(e) \subseteq \mathrm{dom}(\sigma)$ and undefined otherwise), and $\sigma[x \mapsto \mathbf{v}]$ is the update of σ at x with $\mathbf{v}$. Labels are obtained by extending the grammar in (2.3) with the production $\alpha ::= e \vdash \alpha$ where e is a boolean expression used in conditional transitions $\langle S, \sigma \rangle \xrightarrow{e \vdash \alpha} \langle S', \sigma' \rangle$ representing the fact that $\langle S, \sigma \rangle$ has an α-transition to $\langle S', \sigma' \rangle$ provided that $e \downarrow \sigma$ actually holds. We may write α instead of $\mathtt{true} \vdash \alpha$ and $e \wedge e' \vdash \alpha$ instead of $e \vdash (e' \vdash \alpha)$.

We comment on the rules in Fig. 2 where $\mathrm{fc}(\alpha)$ is defined as $\mathrm{fc}(\overline{u}^n \mathbf{s}) = \mathrm{fc}(u_i \mathbf{s}) = \{u\}$, $\mathrm{fc}(\overline{s}\mathbf{v}) = \mathrm{fc}(s\mathbf{v}) = \{s\}$, and $\mathrm{fc}(\tau) = \emptyset$. Rules [SReq] and [SAcc] are for requesting and accepting new sessions; in their continuations, newly created session names $\mathbf{s}$ replace $\mathbf{y}$. Rule [SRec] is for receiving messages in an early style approach (variables are assigned when firing input prefixes); note that the store is updated by recording that x is assigned $\mathbf{v}$. Rule [SSend] is for sending values. Rules [SThen] and [SElse] handle 'if' statements as expected; their only peculiarity is that the guard is recorded on the label of the transition: this is instrumental for the correspondence between systems

$$\frac{s \notin \mathtt{fc}(P)}{\langle \bar{u}^n(\mathbf{y}).P, \sigma \rangle \xrightarrow{\bar{u}^n s} \langle P\{\mathbf{y}/s\}, \sigma \rangle} \; [\text{SReq}]$$

$$\frac{\ell \downarrow \sigma \neq \varepsilon \quad \langle P, \sigma[x \mapsto \mathtt{hd}(\ell \downarrow \sigma)] \rangle \xrightarrow{e \vdash \alpha} \langle P', \sigma' \rangle}{\langle \text{for } x \text{ in } \ell : P, \sigma \rangle \xrightarrow{e \vdash \alpha} \langle P'; \text{for } x \text{ in } \mathtt{tl}(\ell) : P, \sigma' \rangle} \; [\text{SFor}_2]$$

$$\frac{s \notin \mathtt{fc}(P)}{\langle u_i(\mathbf{y}).P, \sigma \rangle \xrightarrow{u_i s} \langle P\{\mathbf{y}/s\}, \sigma \rangle} \; [\text{SAcc}]$$

$$\frac{e \downarrow \sigma = \mathtt{true} \quad \langle P, \sigma \rangle \xrightarrow{e' \vdash \alpha} \langle P', \sigma' \rangle}{\langle \text{if } e : P \text{ else } Q, \sigma \rangle \xrightarrow{e \wedge e' \vdash \alpha} \langle P', \sigma' \rangle} \; [\text{SThen}]$$

$$\langle s(x); P+N, \sigma \rangle \xrightarrow{sv} \langle P, \sigma[x \mapsto v] \rangle \; [\text{SRec}]$$

$$\frac{e \downarrow \sigma = \mathtt{false} \quad \langle Q, \sigma \rangle \xrightarrow{e' \vdash \alpha} \langle Q', \sigma' \rangle}{\langle \text{if } e : P \text{ else } Q, \sigma \rangle \xrightarrow{\neg e \wedge e' \vdash \alpha} \langle Q', \sigma' \rangle} \; [\text{SElse}]$$

$$\frac{e \downarrow \sigma = v}{\langle \bar{s}e, \sigma \rangle \xrightarrow{\bar{s}v} \langle 0, \sigma \rangle} \; [\text{SSend}]$$

$$\langle \text{do } P \text{ until } b(x), \sigma \rangle \xrightarrow{bv} \langle 0, \sigma[x \mapsto v] \rangle \; [\text{SLoop}_1]$$

$$\frac{\langle P, \sigma \rangle \xrightarrow{e \vdash \alpha} \langle P', \sigma' \rangle}{\langle P; Q, \sigma \rangle \xrightarrow{e \vdash \alpha} \langle P'; Q, \sigma' \rangle} \; [\text{SSeq}]$$

$$\frac{\langle P, \sigma \rangle \xrightarrow{e \vdash \alpha} \langle P', \sigma' \rangle \quad b \notin \mathtt{fc}(\alpha)}{\langle \text{do } P \text{ until } b, \sigma \rangle \xrightarrow{e \vdash \alpha} \langle P'; \text{do } P \text{ until } b, \sigma' \rangle} \; [\text{SLoop}_2]$$

$$\frac{\ell \downarrow \sigma = \varepsilon}{\langle \text{for } x \text{ in } \ell : P, \sigma \rangle \xrightarrow{\tau} \langle 0, \sigma \rangle} \; [\text{SFor}_1]$$

$$\frac{P \equiv P' \quad \langle P', \sigma \rangle \xrightarrow{e \vdash \alpha} \langle Q', \sigma' \rangle \quad Q' \equiv Q}{\langle P, \sigma \rangle \xrightarrow{e \vdash \alpha} \langle Q, \sigma' \rangle} \; [\text{SStruct}]$$

$$\frac{s \notin \mathtt{fc}(P_i) \quad Q_i = P_i\{\mathbf{y}_i/s\} \text{ for } i = 0,\ldots,n}{\langle \bar{u}^n(\mathbf{y}_0).P_0 \mid u_1(\mathbf{y}_1).P_1 \mid \ldots \mid u_n(\mathbf{y}_n).P_n, \sigma \rangle \xrightarrow{\tau} \langle (vs)(Q_0 \mid \ldots \mid Q_n \mid s : \emptyset), \sigma \rangle} \; [\text{SInit}]$$

$$\frac{\langle P, \sigma \rangle \xrightarrow{e \vdash \bar{s}v} \langle P', \sigma' \rangle}{\langle P \mid s : M, \sigma \rangle \xrightarrow{e \vdash \tau} \langle P' \mid s : M \cdot v, \sigma' \rangle} \; [\text{SCom}_1]$$

$$\frac{\langle P, \sigma \rangle \xrightarrow{e \vdash sv} \langle P', \sigma' \rangle}{\langle P \mid s : v \cdot M, \sigma \rangle \xrightarrow{e \vdash \tau} \langle P' \mid s : M, \sigma' \rangle} \; [\text{SCom}_2]$$

$$\frac{\langle S, \sigma \rangle \xrightarrow{e \vdash \alpha} \langle S', \sigma' \rangle \quad s \notin \mathtt{fc}(\alpha)}{\langle (vs)S, \sigma \rangle \xrightarrow{e \vdash \alpha} \langle (vs)S', \sigma' \rangle} \; [\text{SNews}]$$

$$\frac{\langle S_1, \sigma \rangle \xrightarrow{e \vdash \alpha} \langle S_1', \sigma' \rangle \quad \mathtt{var}(S_1) \cap \mathtt{var}(S_2) = \emptyset}{\langle S_1 \mid S_2, \sigma \rangle \xrightarrow{e \vdash \alpha} \langle S_1' \mid S_2, \sigma' \rangle} \; [\text{SPar}]$$

Fig. 2. Labelled transitions for processes (top) and systems (bottom)

and their types (c.f. § 6). Rules [SFor$_1$], [SFor$_2$], [Sloop$_1$], [Sloop$_2$] unfold the corresponding iterative program in an expected way. Except for session initialisation, the remaining rules are standard. Rule [SInit] allows n roles to synchronise with $\bar{u}^n(\mathbf{y}_0).P_0$; in the continuation of each role i, the bound names $\mathbf{y}_i$ are replaced with a tuple of freshly chosen session names for which the corresponding queues are created. Such queues are used to exchange values as prescribed by rules [SCom$_1$] and [SCom$_2$]. Rule [SNews] is standard and allows an action α to pass a restriction that does not involve the names of α. Rule [SInit] requires the synchronisation of all roles. Since processes are single-threaded, this is only possible when each process plays exactly one role in that session. Note that the semantics relies on a global store σ. However, the condition $\mathtt{var}(S_1) \cap \mathtt{var}(S_2) = \emptyset$ in rule [SPar] ensures that each program has its own local (logical) store (i.e., there is no confusion between local variables of different programs).

Note that, in a sequential composition $P; Q$, the store σ allows us to extend the scope of names bound in P by input prefixes to Q.

3.1 Running Examples

In Ex. 3 we give the implementation of T_S (i.e., participant S of G_{POP}) from § 2.2. To ease the presentation, we use the following auxiliary functions.

- $\texttt{auth}:\texttt{Str}\to\texttt{Bool}$ that is used for authenticating clients;
- $\texttt{fn}:\texttt{Str}\to\texttt{Int}$ that given a folder name returns the number of messages in that folder (we assume $\texttt{inbox}$ to be the default folder);
- $\texttt{mn}:\texttt{Int}\to\texttt{Int}$ that given a message number returns its length (in bytes);
- $\texttt{data}:\texttt{void}\to\texttt{Data}$ that returns the current message;
- $\texttt{next}:\texttt{void}\to\texttt{Int}$ that returns the next message number;
- $\texttt{del}:\texttt{void}\to\texttt{Int}$ that returns the next message number and deletes the current message from the folder.

Let s_k denote the name in $\mathbf{s}$ corresponding to channel k in $\mathsf{G_{POP}}$ and likewise for $\mathsf{G'_{POP}}$.

Example 3. The process $P_{\texttt{INIT}}$ below implements POP2's server.

$$P_{\texttt{INIT}}=u_S(\mathbf{s}).P_S \qquad P_S=s_{\texttt{QUIT}}();P_{\texttt{EXIT}}+s_{\texttt{HELO}}(x);P_{\texttt{MBOX}} \qquad P_{\texttt{EXIT}}=\overline{s}_{\texttt{BYE}}$$

$$P_{\texttt{MBOX}} = \text{if } \texttt{auth}(x)\ :\ \overline{s_R}\texttt{fn}(\texttt{inbox});P_{\texttt{NMBR}} \text{ else } \overline{s_E};P_{\texttt{EXIT}}$$

$$P_{\texttt{NMBR}} = \text{do}(s_{\texttt{FOLD}}(x);\overline{s_R}\texttt{fn}(x) + s_{\texttt{READ}}(x');\overline{s_R}\texttt{mn}(x');P_{\texttt{SIZE}}) \text{ until } s_{\texttt{QUIT}}();P_{\texttt{EXIT}}$$

$$P_{\texttt{SIZE}} = \text{do}(s_{\texttt{RETR}}();\overline{s_{\texttt{MSG}}}\texttt{data}();P_{\texttt{XFER}} + s_{\texttt{READ}}(x');\overline{s_R}\texttt{mn}(x')) \text{ until } s_{\texttt{FOLD}}(x);\overline{s_R}\texttt{fn}(x)$$

$$P_{\texttt{XFER}} = s_{\texttt{ACKS}}();\overline{s_R}\texttt{mn}(\texttt{next}()) + s_{\texttt{ACKD}}();\overline{s_R}\texttt{mn}(\texttt{del}()) + s_{\texttt{NACK}}();\overline{s_R}\texttt{mn}(x')$$

Firstly, $P_{\texttt{INIT}}$ initiates a session of type $\mathsf{G_{POP}}$ as S then it behaves according to $\mathsf{T_S}$. The non-deterministic choice is resolved in the conditional statement of $P_{\texttt{MBOX}}$.   ◆

Ex. 4 gives an implementation of the server $\mathsf{T'_S}$ of the multiparty variant of POP2.

Example 4. Let $\mathsf{G'_{POP}}$ be as in Ex. 2 and $P'_{\texttt{INIT}}=u_S(\mathbf{s}).P'_S$ where

$$P'_S\ = s_{\texttt{QUIT}}();P_{\texttt{EXIT}}+s_{\texttt{HELO}}(x);P_{\texttt{AUTH}}$$

$$P_{\texttt{AUTH}} = \overline{s_{\texttt{REQ}}}x;s_{\texttt{RES}}(y);P'_{\texttt{MBOX}}$$

$$P'_{\texttt{MBOX}} = \text{if } \texttt{auth}(x)\wedge y\ :\ \overline{s_R}\texttt{fn}(\texttt{inbox});P_{\texttt{NMBR}} \text{ else } \overline{s_E};P_{\texttt{EXIT}}$$

Here, $P'_{\texttt{INIT}}$ resolves the non-deterministic choice in $P'_{\texttt{MBOX}}$ by taking into account both the value returned by $\texttt{auth}(\_)$ and the feedback of A stored in variable y.   ◆

4   Whole-Spectrum Implementation

Definition 1 below introduces the notion of candidate implementation of a global type, that is a system consisting of one process for each role in the global type.

Definition 1 (Implementation). *Given* $\mathcal{G}(\mathbf{y})\overset{\triangle}{=}\mathsf{G}$ *s.t.* $\mathcal{P}(\mathcal{G})=\{\mathsf{p}_1,\dots,\mathsf{p}_n\}$ *and a mapping* ι *assigning a process to each* $\mathsf{p}\in\mathcal{P}(\mathcal{G})$, *a* ι-*implementation of* $\mathcal{G}$ *is a system* $I_{\mathcal{G}}^{\iota}$ *such that either (i)* $I_{\mathcal{G}}^{\iota}\equiv\iota(\mathsf{p}_1)\mid\dots\mid\iota(\mathsf{p}_n)$ *and* $\mathbf{y}\cap\texttt{fc}(\iota(\mathsf{p}_1))=\dots=\mathbf{y}\cap\texttt{fc}(\iota(\mathsf{p}_n))=\emptyset$ *or (ii)* $I_{\mathcal{G}}^{\iota}\equiv(\nu\mathbf{y})(\iota(\mathsf{p}_1)\mid\dots\mid\iota(\mathsf{p}_n)\mid\mathbf{y}:\mathbf{M})$.

In case (*i*) the session that implements $\mathcal{G}$ is not initiated. For simplicity, we assume that roles do not use the channels defined by the global type before initiating the corresponding session (i.e., $\mathbf{y}\cap\texttt{fc}(\iota(\mathsf{p}_i))=\emptyset$). This is not a limitation since channel names can always be renamed to avoid clashes. Case (*ii*) captures already initiated sessions; wlog, we assume that the system and the global type use the same session channels $\mathbf{y}$.

We characterise WSI as a relation between the execution traces of a global type $\mathcal{G}$ and its implementations $I_{\mathcal{G}}^{\iota}$. An execution trace of $I_{\mathcal{G}}^{\iota}$ is a sequence of input and output actions decorated with the role that performs them (in symbols $\langle\mathsf{p},s!U\rangle$ and $\langle\mathsf{p},s?U\rangle$).

Let $\langle \iota(p), \sigma \rangle \xrightarrow{e' \vdash \alpha} \langle \iota'(p), \sigma' \rangle$ stand for $\langle \iota(p), \sigma \rangle \xrightarrow{e' \vdash \alpha} \langle P, \sigma' \rangle$ and $\iota' = \iota[p \mapsto P]$

$$\frac{\langle I_G^\iota, \sigma \rangle \xrightarrow{e \vdash \tau} \langle I_G^{\iota'}, \sigma' \rangle \quad \langle \iota(p), \sigma \rangle \xrightarrow{e' \vdash \alpha} \langle \iota'(p), \sigma' \rangle \quad \text{fc}(\alpha) \cap \mathbf{y} \neq \emptyset \quad r \in \mathcal{R}_u(\langle I_G^{\iota'}, \sigma' \rangle) \quad \text{obj}(\alpha) : \mathtt{U}}{\langle p, \alpha\{\text{obj}(\alpha)/\mathtt{U}\}\rangle r \in \mathcal{R}_u(\langle I_G^\iota, \sigma \rangle)} \text{[RRInt]} \qquad \frac{\langle I_G^\iota, \sigma \rangle \nrightarrow}{\varepsilon \in \mathcal{R}_u(\langle I_G^\iota, \sigma \rangle)} \text{[RREnd]}$$

$$\frac{\langle I_G^\iota, \sigma \rangle \xrightarrow{e \vdash \alpha} \langle I_G^{\iota'}, \sigma' \rangle \quad u \notin \text{fc}(\alpha) \quad \langle \iota(p), \sigma \rangle \xrightarrow{e' \vdash \beta} \langle \iota'(p), \sigma' \rangle \quad \text{fc}(\beta) \cap \mathbf{y} = \emptyset \quad r \in \mathcal{R}_u(\langle I_G^{\iota'}, \sigma' \rangle)}{r \in \mathcal{R}_u(\langle I_G^\iota, \sigma \rangle)} \text{[RRExt]}$$

Fig. 3. Runs of implementations

Definition 2 (Runs of implementations). *Let I_G^ι be an implementation of $G(\mathbf{y}) \overset{\triangle}{=} \mathtt{G}$. The set $\mathcal{R}_u(\langle I_G^\iota, \sigma \rangle)$ of runs of I_G^ι initiated on u with store σ is the least set closed with respect to the rules in Fig. 3. We write $\mathcal{R}_u(I_G^\iota)$ for $\mathcal{R}_u(\langle I_G^\iota, \emptyset \rangle)$. The runs of a set of implementations $\mathbb{I}$ is $\mathcal{R}_u(\mathbb{I}) = \cup_{I \in \mathbb{I}} \mathcal{R}_u(I)$.*

Rules in Fig. 3 rely on the semantics of Fig. 2. In rule [RRInt] (where $\text{obj}(\alpha) = \mathtt{v}$ for $\alpha = \bar{s}\mathtt{v}$ or $\alpha = s\mathtt{v}$), a system reduces when some process $\iota(p)$ in the implementation interacts over a session channel (i.e., α is either $\bar{y}\mathtt{v}$ or $y\mathtt{v}$ with $y \in \mathbf{y}$). Since the action α performed by $\iota(p)$ involves a session channel of the global type, an event α associated to the role p is added to the trace. Note that the actual value of the message α is substituted by its type, i.e., $\alpha\{\text{obj}(\alpha)/\mathtt{U}\}$ in place of α. Rule [RREnd] is straightforward. Rule [RRExt] accounts for a computation step that does not involve session channels, i.e., an internal transition τ in a role, a communication over a channel not in $\mathbf{y}$, or a session initiation. This rule allows a process to freely initiate sessions over channels different from u (i.e., sessions that do not corresponds to the global type $\mathtt{G}$). On the contrary, when a role attempts to initiate a session over u, rule [RRExt] requires all roles in the implementation to initiate the session (this behaviour is imposed by the premise $u \notin \text{fc}(\alpha)$). We assume that any role in the implementation will execute exactly one action over the channel u which also matches the role assigned by ι. Nested sessions are handled by assuming that all sessions are created over different channels that have the same type. This is just a technical simplification analogous to the possibility of having annotations to indicate the particular instance of the session under analysis.

For global types, we deviate from standard definition of traces [9,7] and use, for technical convenience, *annotated traces* that distinguish mandatory from optional actions. We write $[r]$ to denote the optional sequence r. Moreover, we consider an asynchronous communication model as in [16] and a trace implicitly denotes the equivalence class of all traces obtained by permuting causally independent actions.

Definition 3 (Runs of a global type). *Given a global type term $\mathtt{G}$, the set $\mathcal{R}(\mathtt{G})$ denotes the runs allowed by $\mathtt{G}$ and is defined as the least set closed under the rules in Fig. 4.*

The first four rules are straightforward. Rule [RGPar] considers just the sequential composition of the traces corresponding to the two parallel branches (recall that a trace denotes an equivalence class of executions). The traces of an iterative type $\mathtt{G}^{*^f}$ are given

$$\frac{}{\varepsilon \in \mathcal{R}(\mathtt{end})}[\texttt{RGEnd}] \qquad\qquad \frac{}{\langle \mathtt{p}, s!\mathtt{U}\rangle\langle \mathtt{q}, s?\mathtt{U}\rangle \in \mathcal{R}(\mathtt{p} \to \mathtt{q}: s\langle\mathtt{U}\rangle)}[\texttt{RGComm}]$$

$$\frac{r \in \mathcal{R}(\mathtt{G}_1) \cup \mathcal{R}(\mathtt{G}_1)}{r \in \mathcal{R}(\mathtt{G}_1 + \mathtt{G}_2)}[\texttt{RGCh}] \qquad\qquad \frac{r_1 \in \mathcal{R}(\mathtt{G}_1) \quad r_2 \in \mathcal{R}(\mathtt{G}_2)}{r_1 r_2 \in \mathcal{R}(\mathtt{G}_1;\mathtt{G}_2)}[\texttt{RGSeq}]$$

$$\frac{r_1 \in \mathcal{R}(\mathtt{G}_1) \quad r_2 \in \mathcal{R}(\mathtt{G}_2)}{r_1 r_2 \in \mathcal{R}(\mathtt{G}_1 \mid \mathtt{G}_2)}[\texttt{RGPar}] \quad \frac{r_1 \in \mathcal{R}(\mathtt{G})}{r_1 \in \widetilde{\mathcal{R}}(\mathtt{G}^{*f})}[\texttt{RG*1}] \quad \frac{r_1 \in \widetilde{\mathcal{R}}(\mathtt{G}^{*f}) \quad r_2 \in \mathcal{R}(\mathtt{G})}{[r_1]r_2 \in \widetilde{\mathcal{R}}(\mathtt{G}^{*f})}[\texttt{RG*2}]$$

$$\frac{r \in \widetilde{\mathcal{R}}(\mathtt{G}^{*f}) \quad \mathtt{rdy}(\mathtt{G}) = \{\mathtt{p}\} \quad \mathcal{P}(\mathtt{G}) = \{\mathtt{p},\mathtt{p}_1,\dots,\mathtt{p}_n\} \quad \forall 1 \leq i \leq n: f(p_i) = s_i \langle \mathtt{U}_i \rangle}{r\langle \mathtt{p}, s_1!\mathtt{U}_1\rangle \dots \langle \mathtt{p}, s_n!\mathtt{U}_n\rangle \langle \mathtt{p}_1, s_1?\mathtt{U}_1\rangle \dots \langle \mathtt{p}_n, s_n?\mathtt{U}_n\rangle \quad \in \quad \mathcal{R}(\mathtt{G}^{*f})}[\texttt{RGIter}]$$

Fig. 4. Runs of a global type

by the rule [RGIter]; the set $\widetilde{\mathcal{R}}(\mathtt{G}^{*f})$ in the premise contains the traces of the unfolding of $\mathtt{G}^{*f}$ defined by the rules [RG*1] and [RG*2]. Optional events are introduced when unfolding an iterative type (rule [RG*2]). The main motivation is that an iterative type $\mathtt{G}^{*f}$ denotes an unbounded number of repetitions G (i.e., an infinite number of traces). Note that $\widetilde{\mathcal{R}}(\mathtt{G}^{*f}) = \{r_1, [r_1]r_2, [[r_1]r_2]r_3, \dots\}$ with $r_i \in \mathcal{R}(\mathtt{G})$. When implementing an iterative type, we will allow the implementation to perform just a finite number of iterations (but we require at least once iteration). Annotation of optional events are instrumental to the comparison of traces associated with iterative types (which is defined below). Rule [RGIter] adds the events associated to the termination of an iteration: (i) the ready role p sends the termination signal to any other role by using the dedicated channels specified by f (i.e., $\langle \mathtt{p}, s_1!\mathtt{U}_1\rangle \dots \langle \mathtt{p}, s_n!\mathtt{U}_n\rangle$), and (ii) the waiting roles receive the termination message (i.e., $\langle \mathtt{p}_1, s_1?\mathtt{U}_1\rangle \dots \langle \mathtt{p}_n, s_n?\mathtt{U}_n\rangle$). As for parallel composition, we just consider one of the possible interleavings for the receive events (that can actually happen in any order).

We use the operator $\lessdot$ to compare annotated traces, which is defined as the least preorder satisfying the following rules

$$[r] \lessdot \varepsilon \qquad \varepsilon \lessdot r \qquad r \lessdot r' \implies [r] \lessdot [r'] \qquad r_1 \lessdot r_1' \wedge r_2 \lessdot r_2' \implies r_1 r_2 \lessdot r_1' r_2'$$

Basically, $r \lessdot r'$ means that r' matches all mandatory actions of r and all optional actions in r' are also optional in r. Let R_1 and R_2 be two sets of annotated traces, we write $R_1 \Subset R_2$ if $r \in R_1$ implies $\exists r' \in R_2$ such that $r \lessdot r'$.

Definition 4 (Whole-spectrum implementation). *A set $\mathbb{I}$ of implementations covers a global type* G *with respect to u iff* $\mathcal{R}(\mathtt{G}) \Subset \mathcal{R}_u(\mathbb{I})$. *A process P is a* whole-spectrum *implementation of* $\mathtt{p}_i \in \mathcal{P}(\mathtt{G}) = \{\mathtt{p}_0, \dots, \mathtt{p}_n\}$ *when there exists a set* $\mathbb{I}$ *of implementations that covers* G *with respect to u s.t.* $I_\mathtt{G}^\mathfrak{l} \in \mathbb{I}$ *implies* $\iota(\mathtt{p}_i) = P$.

A whole-spectrum implementation (WSI) of a role $\mathtt{p}_i$ is a process P such that any expected behaviour of the global type can be obtained by putting P into a proper context. For iteration types, the comparison of annotated traces implies that the implementation has to be able to perform the iteration body at least once but possibly many times.

Remark 1. A set of implementations covering a global type $\mathcal{G}$ can exhibit more behaviour than the runs of $\mathcal{G}$. Nonetheless, we use WSI with the usual soundness requirement (given in § 6) to characterise valid implementations.

5 Typing Rules

We now give a typing system to guarantee that well-typed systems are a WSI of their global type. Systems are typed by judgements of the form $C \,\lrcorner\, \Gamma \;\vdash\; S \rhd \Delta \;\divideontimes\; \Gamma'$ stipulating that, under condition C and environment Γ, system S is typed as Δ and yields Γ' (where environments Γ, Γ' and Δ are as in § 2.3). Condition C is called *context assumption*; it is a logical formula derivable by the grammar

$$C ::= e \mid \neg C \mid C \wedge C \qquad \text{where } e \text{ is of type } \mathtt{bool}$$

that identifies the assumptions on variables taken by processes in S. The map Γ' extends Γ with the sorts for the names bound in S. This is needed to correctly type $P;Q$ where in fact a free name of Q could be bound in P.

Due to space limits, Fig. 5 gives only the typing rules to validate processes (the rules for systems are adapted from [14] and detailed in [3, Appendix C]). Condition $C \not\vdash \bot$ is implicitly assumed among the hypothesis of each rule of Fig. 5. Rule [VReq] types session requests of the form $\bar{u}^n(\mathbf{y}).P$; its premise checks that P can be typed by extending Δ with the mapping from session names $\mathbf{y}$ to the projection of the global type $\Gamma(u)$ on the 0-th role. Dually, rule [VAcc] types the acceptance of a session request as i-th role. Rule [VRec] types an external choice $P = \sum_{i \in I} y_i(x_i); P_i$ checking that each branch P_i can be typed against the respective continuation of the type, $\Delta, \mathbf{y} : \mathcal{T}_i$ (once Γ is updated with the type assignment on the bound name x_i); rule [VRec] cannot be applied (making the validation fail) when the names in $\mathtt{fv}(P) \cup \mathtt{fc}(P)$ are not mapped to the same sorts in all environments Γ_i. Rule [VSend] is trivial.

Rules [VThen] and [VElse] handle the cases in which the guard of the conditional statement is either a tautology or a contradiction. Rule [VCond] ensures that both branches can be selected by fixing a proper assumption (i.e., both $C \wedge e$ and $C \wedge \neg e$ are consistent). Note that C is augmented with the condition e (resp. $\neg e$) for typing the 'then'-branch (resp. 'else'-branch). The resulting type is $\Delta_1 \bowtie \Delta_2$ defined in Fig. 6. The merge $\Delta_1 \bowtie \Delta_2$ is defined only when Δ_1 and Δ_2 are *compatible*, namely iff

$$\forall \mathbf{s}_1 \in \mathrm{dom}(\Delta_1), \mathbf{s}_2 \in \mathrm{dom}(\Delta_2) : \mathbf{s}_1 \cap \mathbf{s}_2 \neq \emptyset \implies \mathbf{s}_1 = \mathbf{s}_2$$

For $\mathbf{s} \notin \mathrm{dom}(\Delta_1) \cap \mathrm{dom}(\Delta_2)$, the merging behaves as the union of environments Δ_1 and Δ_2, otherwise it returns the merging of the local types $\mathcal{T}_1 = \Delta_1(\mathbf{s})$ and $\mathcal{T}_2 = \Delta_2(\mathbf{s})$; in turn, $\mathcal{T}_1 \bowtie \mathcal{T}_2$ yields an internal choice of $\mathcal{T}_1$ and $\mathcal{T}_2$, but for a common sequence of outputs. Rule [VFor1] assigns the type $\mathcal{T}^*$ to a for loop when its body P has type $\mathcal{T}$ under C extended with $x \in \ell$, and the environment Γ extended with $x : \mathtt{U}$. Rule [VFor2] is for empty lists. By rule [VLoop], the type of a loop is $\mathcal{T}^*; b?\mathtt{U}$ when its body P has type $\mathcal{T}$ and b is the channel used to receive the termination signal. Notice that the environments of the rules [VFor1] and [VLoop] include only one session (respectively $\mathbf{y} : \mathcal{T}^*$ and $\mathbf{y} : \mathcal{T}^*; b?\mathtt{U}$), hence the body can only perform actions within a single session.

$$\frac{\Gamma(u)\equiv\mathcal{G}(\mathbf{y}) \qquad C\lrcorner\Gamma \;\vdash\; P \triangleright \Delta,\mathbf{y}:\mathcal{G}(\mathbf{y})\lceil 0 \;*\; \Gamma'}{C\lrcorner\Gamma \;\vdash\; \bar{u}^n(\mathbf{y}).P \triangleright \Delta \;*\; \Gamma'}\;[\text{VReq}]$$

$$\frac{\Gamma(u)\equiv\mathcal{G}(\mathbf{y}) \qquad C\lrcorner\Gamma \;\vdash\; P \triangleright \Delta,\mathbf{y}:\mathcal{G}(\mathbf{y})\lceil i \;*\; \Gamma'}{C\lrcorner\Gamma \;\vdash\; u_i(\mathbf{y}).P \triangleright \Delta \;*\; \Gamma'}\;[\text{VAcc}]$$

$$\frac{\begin{array}{c}P = \sum_{i\in I} y_i(x_i);P_i \qquad \forall i:y_i\in\mathbf{y}\text{ and } C\lrcorner\Gamma,x_i:\mathsf{U}_i \;\vdash\; P_i \triangleright \Delta,\mathbf{y}:\mathcal{T}_i \;*\; \Gamma_i \\ \Gamma'=\bigcap_{i\in I}\Gamma_i \qquad \mathbf{fv}(P)\cup\mathbf{fc}(P)\subseteq\mathrm{dom}(\Gamma')\end{array}}{C\lrcorner\Gamma \;\vdash\; P \triangleright \Delta,\;\mathbf{y}:\sum_{i\in I}y_i?\mathsf{U}_i;\mathcal{T}_i \;*\; \Gamma'}\;[\text{VRec}]$$

$$\frac{\Gamma(e)=\mathsf{U} \qquad y\in\mathbf{y}}{C\lrcorner\Gamma \;\vdash\; \bar{y}e \triangleright \mathbf{y}:y!\mathsf{U} \;*\; \Gamma}\;[\text{VSend}] \qquad\qquad \frac{\Delta(\mathbf{s})=\mathsf{end} \quad \forall\mathbf{s}\in\mathrm{dom}(\Delta)}{C\lrcorner\Gamma \;\vdash\; \mathbf{0} \triangleright \Delta \;*\; \Gamma}\;[\text{VEnd}]$$

$$\frac{C\lrcorner\Gamma \;\vdash\; P_1 \triangleright \Delta_1 \;*\; \Gamma_1 \qquad C\lrcorner\Gamma_1 \;\vdash\; P_2 \triangleright \Delta_1 \;*\; \Gamma_2}{C\lrcorner\Gamma \;\vdash\; P_1;P_2 \triangleright \Delta_1;\Delta_2 \;*\; \Gamma_2}\;[\text{VSeq}]$$

$$\frac{\Gamma(e)=\mathsf{bool} \qquad C\wedge e \not\vdash \bot \qquad C\wedge\neg e \vdash \bot \qquad C\wedge e\lrcorner\Gamma \;\vdash\; P \triangleright \Delta \;*\; \Gamma'}{C\lrcorner\Gamma \;\vdash\; \mathsf{if}\;e: P\;\mathsf{else}\;Q \triangleright \Delta \;*\; \Gamma'}\;[\text{VThen}]$$

$$\frac{\Gamma(e)=\mathsf{bool} \qquad C\wedge e \vdash \bot \qquad C\wedge\neg e \not\vdash \bot \qquad C\wedge\neg e\lrcorner\Gamma \;\vdash\; Q \triangleright \Delta \;*\; \Gamma'}{C\lrcorner\Gamma \;\vdash\; \mathsf{if}\;e: P\;\mathsf{else}\;Q \triangleright \Delta \;*\; \Gamma'}\;[\text{VElse}]$$

$$\frac{\begin{array}{c}\Gamma(e)=\mathsf{bool} \qquad C\wedge e \not\vdash \bot \qquad C\wedge\neg e \not\vdash \bot \\ C\wedge e\lrcorner\Gamma \;\vdash\; P \triangleright \Delta_1 \;*\; \Gamma_1 \qquad C\wedge\neg e\lrcorner\Gamma \;\vdash\; Q \triangleright \Delta_2 \;*\; \Gamma_2\end{array}}{C\lrcorner\Gamma \;\vdash\; \mathsf{if}\;e: P\;\mathsf{else}\;Q \triangleright \Delta_1 \bowtie \Delta_2 \;*\; \Gamma_1\cap\Gamma_2}\;[\text{VCond}]$$

$$\frac{\Gamma(\ell)=[\mathsf{U}] \qquad C\vdash\ell\neq\varepsilon \qquad C\wedge x\in\ell\lrcorner\Gamma,x:\mathsf{U} \;\vdash\; P \triangleright \mathbf{y}:\mathcal{T} \;*\; \Gamma'}{C\lrcorner\Gamma \;\vdash\; \mathsf{for}\;x\;\mathsf{in}\;\ell: P \triangleright \mathbf{y}:\mathcal{T}^* \;*\; \Gamma'}\;[\text{VFor1}]$$

$$\frac{C\vdash\ell=\varepsilon}{C\lrcorner\Gamma \;\vdash\; \mathsf{for}\;x\;\mathsf{in}\;\ell: P \triangleright \mathbf{y}:\mathsf{end} \;*\; \Gamma'}\;[\text{VFor2}]$$

$$\frac{C\lrcorner\Gamma \;\vdash\; N \triangleright \mathbf{y}:\mathcal{T} \;*\; \Gamma'}{C\lrcorner\Gamma \;\vdash\; \mathsf{do}\;N\;\mathsf{until}\;b(x) \triangleright \mathbf{y}:\mathcal{T}^*;b?\mathsf{U} \;*\; \Gamma',x:\mathsf{U}}\;[\text{VLoop}]$$

Fig. 5. Typing rules for processes

Iterations involving messages over multiple sessions could not be checked compositionally since the conformance of a process to a local type would not be sufficient to ensure the correct coordination of a 'for'-iteration with the corresponding 'loop'-iterations. Rule [VEnd] types idle processes with a Δ that maps each session $\mathbf{s}$ to the end type. Rule [VSeq] checks sequential composition. Here $\Delta_1;\Delta_2$ is the pointwise sequential composition of Δ_1 and Δ_2, i.e., $(\Delta_1;\Delta_2)(\mathbf{s}) = \mathcal{T}_1;\mathcal{T}_2$ where $\mathcal{T}_i = \Delta_i(\mathbf{s})$ if $\mathbf{s}\in\mathrm{dom}(\Delta_i)$ and $\mathcal{T}_i = \mathsf{end}$ otherwise, for $i=1,2$. Note that P_2 is typed under the environment Γ_1, which contains the names bound by the input prefixes of P_1.

The following result ensures that type checking is decidable (it follows from the obvious recursive algorithm and decidability of the underlying logic).

$$(\Delta_1 \bowtie \Delta_2)(s) = \begin{cases} \Delta_1(s) & \text{if } s \in \text{dom}(\Delta_1) \setminus \text{dom}(\Delta_2) \\ \Delta_2(s) & \text{if } s \in \text{dom}(\Delta_2) \setminus \text{dom}(\Delta_1) \\ \Delta_1(s) \bowtie \Delta_2(s) & \text{if } s \in \text{dom}(\Delta_1) \cap \text{dom}(\Delta_2) \end{cases}$$

$$T_1 \bowtie T_2 = \begin{cases} T_1 \oplus T_2 & \text{if } T_1 = y_1!U_1; T_1', \ T_2 = y_2!U_2; T_2', \ y_1 \neq y_2 \\ y!U; (T_1' \bowtie T_2') & \text{if } T_1 = y!U; T_1', \ T_2 = y!U; T_2' \\ \bot & \text{otherwise} \end{cases}$$

Fig. 6. Composition of types

Theorem 1. *Given* C, Γ, Γ', S *and* Δ, *then the provability of* $C \_ \Gamma \vdash S \triangleright \Delta \divideontimes \Gamma'$ *is decidable.*

Our proof system discerns between B_1 and B_2 in the introduction (i.e., only B_1 is validated) due to the rules for conditional statements and to the lack of a rule for type refinement. In fact, after a few verification steps on B_1 (resp. B_2) we would reach the following scenario: $P_1(c) = \text{if } c : \overline{s_{OK}}; s_{AMOUNT}(x) \text{ else } \overline{s_{KO}}$ (resp. $P_2(c) = \overline{s_{KO}}$) and $\Delta = s : \text{OK!}; \text{AMOUNT?} \oplus \text{KO!}$. The verification of $P_1(c)$ terminates successfully after an application of [VCond]. In the case of $P_2(c)$ the only rule for a sending process, [VSend], cannot be applied against a type with a choice.

5.1 Running Examples

We now apply our typing to different implementations of POP2.

Example 5. The first few verification steps of P_{INIT} from Ex. 3 are shown below. By rule [VAcc], the newly created session is added to the session environment, then the verification of the external choice is split by [VRec] into the verification of each branch. As we omit the whole derivation, just assume that P_{INIT} yields $\Gamma' = \Gamma, x : \text{Str}$.

$$\cfrac{\cfrac{\Gamma(u) \equiv G_{POP}(s) \quad \text{true} \_ \Gamma \vdash s_{QUIT}(); P_{EXIT} + s_{HELO}(x); P_{MBOX} \triangleright s : T_S \divideontimes \Gamma'}{\cfrac{\text{true} \_ \Gamma \vdash P_{EXIT} \triangleright s : T_{EXIT} \divideontimes \Gamma' \quad \text{true} \_ \Gamma, x : \text{Str} \vdash P_{MBOX} \triangleright s : T_{MBOX} \divideontimes \Gamma'}{} \text{[VRec]}}{\text{true} \_ \Gamma \vdash u_s(s).P_S \triangleright \emptyset \divideontimes \Gamma'} \text{[VAcc]}}$$

Consider the second branch P_{MBOX}; assuming that $\text{true} \wedge \text{auth}(x)$ is neither a tautology nor a falsum, we apply [VCond] (if it was, the verification would terminate unsuccessfully as the only possible branch would not validate against the choice in T_{MBOX}).

$$\cfrac{\text{auth}(x) \_ \Gamma, x : \text{Str} \vdash \overline{s_R}\text{mn}(\text{inbox}); P_{NMBR} \triangleright s : \text{R!Int}; T_{NMBR} \divideontimes \Gamma' \quad \neg\text{auth}(x) \_ \Gamma, x : \text{Str} \vdash \overline{s_E}; P_{EXIT} \triangleright s : \text{E!}; T_{EXIT} \divideontimes \Gamma'}{\text{true} \_ \Gamma, x : \text{Str} \vdash P_{MBOX} \triangleright s : T_{MBOX} \divideontimes \Gamma'} \text{[VCond]}$$

The rest is trivial observing $s : T_{MBOX} = s : \text{R!Int}; T_{NMBR} \bowtie s : \text{E!}; T_{EXIT}$.   ◆

Ex. 6 types the multiparty variant given in Ex. 4.

Example 6. Assume $\Gamma(u) \equiv G'_{POP}$. The first steps are as in Ex. 5 by rules [VAcc] and [VRec]. We focus on the second branch that in this case is P_{AUTH} and apply [VSeq].

$$\cfrac{\text{true} \_ \Gamma, x : \text{Str} \vdash \overline{s_{REQ}}x \triangleright s : \text{REQ!Str} \divideontimes \Gamma' \quad \text{true} \_ \Gamma, x : \text{Str} \vdash s_{RES}(y); P'_{MBOX} \triangleright s : \text{RES?Bool}; T_{AUTH} \divideontimes \Gamma'}{\text{true} \_ \Gamma, x : \text{Str} \vdash \overline{s_{REQ}}x; s_{RES}(y); P'_{MBOX} \triangleright s : T_{AUTH} \divideontimes \Gamma'} \text{[VSeq]}$$

We show the verification of the first branch

$$\frac{\dfrac{\overline{}}{\text{true} \_\Gamma,x:\text{Str} \ \vdash\ \mathbf{0} \rhd \mathbf{s}:\text{end} \ * \ \Gamma'} \ [\text{VEnd}]}{\text{true} \_\Gamma,x:\text{Str} \ \vdash\ \overline{s_{\text{REQ}}}x \rhd \mathbf{s}:\text{REQ!Str} \ * \ \Gamma'} \ [\text{VSend}]$$

and the successive steps for the second branch:

$$\frac{\text{true} \_\Gamma,x:\text{Str},y:\text{Bool} \ \vdash\ P'_{\text{MBOX}} \rhd \mathbf{s}:\text{T}'_{\text{MBOX}} \ * \ \Gamma'}{\text{true} \_\Gamma,x:\text{Str} \ \vdash\ s_{\text{RES}}(y);P'_{\text{MBOX}} \rhd \mathbf{s}:\text{RES?Bool};\text{T}'_{\text{MBOX}} \ * \ \Gamma'} \ [\text{VRec}]$$

The verification of P'_{MBOX} proceeds with an application of [VCond], [VIf] or [VElse] depending on $\text{auth}() \wedge y$. If $\text{auth}()$ is not a contradiction then [VCond] can be applied as the condition depends from the context (that is the administrator). This leads to a successful validation. In this case, unlike in Ex. 5, the implementation is whole-spectrum even if $\text{auth}()$ is a tautology. If $\text{auth}()$ is a falsum then [VElse] is applied and the process will not validate against the type which has a choice. ◆

Ex. 7 deals with a process implementing two interleaved sessions. Ex. 7 shows that the verification scales to more complex processes that compose different protocols.

Example 7. We give a process that, upon request, engages as a server in a session G_{POP} (§ 2.2), and as a client in a session G_{ADMIN} to outsource the authentication. Instead of embedding in the same session this extra interactions with the administrator, as we did in Ex. 2, we represent the multiparty interaction as two interleaved sessions.

$$\text{G}_{\text{ADMIN}} = \text{C} \to \text{A}:\text{REQ} \langle \text{Str} \rangle; \text{A} \to \text{C}:\text{RES} \langle \text{Bool} \rangle \qquad \text{T}_{\text{C}} = \text{REQ!Str};\text{RES?Bool}$$

In G_{ADMIN}, the client C sends the administrator A a password and A replies along RES. T_{C} is the projection on G_{ADMIN} on C. We assume $\Gamma(u) \equiv \text{G}_{\text{POP}}$ and $\Gamma(v) \equiv \text{G}_{\text{ADMIN}}$. Process P_{INIT} starts, upon request, a session of type G_{POP} and then requests to start a session of type G_{ADMIN}. We omit the definition of processes P_{NMBR} and P_{EXIT} which are as in Ex. 3.

$$P''_{\text{INIT}} = u_{\text{S}}(\mathbf{s}).\bar{v}^{\text{C}}(\mathbf{t}).P''_{\text{S}} \qquad\qquad P''_{\text{S}} = s_{\text{QUIT}}();P_{\text{EXIT}} + s_{\text{HELO}}(x);P_{\text{AUTH}}$$
$$P_{\text{AUTH}} = \overline{t_{\text{REQ}}}x;t_{\text{RES}}(y);P''_{\text{MBOX}} \qquad P''_{\text{MBOX}} = \text{if } y:\ \overline{s_{\text{R}}}\text{fn}(\text{inbox});P_{\text{NMBR}} \text{ else } \overline{s_{\text{E}}};P_{\text{EXIT}}$$

The authentication is delegated to the administrator in session $\mathbf{t}$ via the message along t_{REQ}. Session $\mathbf{s}$ continues using the information in y, which stores the last message received in session $\mathbf{t}$. The first verification steps are by rules [VAcc], [VReq] and [VRec].

$$\frac{\begin{array}{c}\text{true} \_\Gamma \ \vdash\ P_{\text{EXIT}} \rhd \mathbf{s}:\text{T}_{\text{EXIT}},\mathbf{t}:\text{T}_{\text{S}} \ * \ \Gamma' \\ \text{true} \_\Gamma,x:\text{Str} \ \vdash\ P_{\text{AUTH}} \rhd \mathbf{s}:\text{T}_{\text{MBOX}},\mathbf{t}:\text{T}_{\text{S}} \ * \ \Gamma' \\ \hline \Gamma(u) \equiv \text{G}_{\text{POP}}(\mathbf{s}) \quad \Gamma(v) \equiv \text{G}_{\text{POP}}(\mathbf{t}) \quad \text{true} \_\Gamma \ \vdash\ P''_{\text{S}} \rhd \mathbf{s}:\text{T}_{\text{S}},\mathbf{t}:\text{T}_{\text{S}} \ * \ \Gamma' \end{array}}{\text{true} \_\Gamma \ \vdash\ u_{\text{S}}(\mathbf{s}).\bar{v}^{\text{S}}(\mathbf{t}).P''_{\text{S}} \rhd \emptyset \ * \ \Gamma'} \begin{array}{l}[\text{VRec}] \\ \\ [\text{VAcc}],[\text{VReq}]\end{array}$$

The verification of the second branch P_{AUTH} proceeds with one application of [VSeq] where $(\mathbf{s}:\text{T}_{\text{MBOX}},\mathbf{t}:\text{T}_{\text{S}}) \equiv (\mathbf{s}:\text{end},\mathbf{t}:\text{REQ!Str});(\mathbf{s}:\text{T}_{\text{MBOX}},\mathbf{t}:\text{RES?Bool})$.

Let $\mathrm{push}([\_], s!\mathrm{v}) = s!\mathrm{v}[\_]$ and $\mathrm{push}(s_1!\mathrm{v}_1; \ldots; s_n!\mathrm{v}_n[\_], s!\mathrm{v}) = s_1!\mathrm{v}_1; \ldots; s_n!\mathrm{v}_n; s!\mathrm{v}[\_]$

$$\Gamma \bullet \Delta, \mathbf{s} : s!\mathrm{v}; \mathbb{M} @\, \mathrm{p} \xrightarrow{\overline{s\mathrm{v}}} \Gamma \bullet \Delta, \mathbf{s} : \mathbb{M} @\, \mathrm{p} \quad [\text{TQueue}]$$

$$\frac{\Gamma \bullet \mathbf{s} : \mathcal{T} \xrightarrow{\overline{s\mathrm{v}}} \Gamma \bullet \mathbf{s} : \mathcal{T}' \quad \mathbb{M}'[\_] = \mathrm{push}(\mathbb{M}[\_], s!\mathrm{v})}{\Gamma \bullet \Delta, \mathbf{s} : \mathbb{M}[\mathcal{T}] @\, \mathrm{p} \xrightarrow{\tau} \Gamma \bullet \Delta, \mathbf{s} : \mathbb{M}'[\mathcal{T}'] @\, \mathrm{p}} \quad [\text{TCom1}]$$

$$\frac{\Gamma \bullet \mathbf{s} : \mathcal{T} \xrightarrow{s\mathrm{v}} \Gamma \bullet \mathbf{s} : \mathcal{T}'}{\Gamma \bullet \mathbf{s} : s!\mathrm{v}; \mathbb{M}_1 @\, \mathrm{p}, \ \mathbb{M}_2[\mathcal{T}] @\, \mathrm{q} \xrightarrow{\tau} \Gamma \bullet \mathbf{s} : \mathbb{M}_1 @\, \mathrm{p}, \ \mathbb{M}_2[\mathcal{T}'] @\, \mathrm{q}} \quad [\text{TCom2}]$$

$$\frac{u \in \mathrm{dom}(\Gamma) \quad \Gamma(u) \equiv \mathcal{G}(\mathbf{s}) \stackrel{\triangle}{=} \mathrm{G} \quad \mathcal{P}(\mathrm{G}) = \{\mathrm{p}_1, \ldots, \mathrm{p}_n\}}{\Gamma \bullet \Delta \xrightarrow{\tau} \Gamma \bullet \Delta, \mathbf{s} : (\mathrm{G} \!\upharpoonright\! \mathrm{p}_1) @\, \mathrm{p}_1, \ldots, \mathbf{s} : (\mathrm{G} \!\upharpoonright\! \mathrm{p}_n) @\, \mathrm{p}_n} \quad [\text{TInit}]$$

Fig. 7. Additional labelled transitions (to those of Fig. 1) for runtime specifications

$$\frac{\begin{array}{l} \mathrm{true} \_\Gamma, x : \mathrm{Str} \ \vdash \ \overline{t_{\mathrm{REQ}} x} \ \triangleright \ \Delta \ \divideontimes \ \mathbf{s} : \mathrm{end}, \mathbf{t} : \mathrm{REQ!Str} \\ \mathrm{true} \_\Gamma, x : \mathrm{Str} \ \vdash \ t_{\mathrm{RES}}(y); P''_{\mathrm{MBOX}} \ \triangleright \ \mathbf{s} : \mathrm{T}_{\mathrm{MBOX}}, \mathbf{t} : \mathrm{RES?Bool} \ \divideontimes \ \Gamma' \end{array}}{\mathrm{true} \_\Gamma, x : \mathrm{Str} \ \vdash \ \overline{t_{\mathrm{REQ}} x}; t_{\mathrm{RES}}(y); P''_{\mathrm{MBOX}} \ \triangleright \ \mathbf{s} : \mathrm{T}_{\mathrm{MBOX}}, \mathbf{t} : \mathrm{T}_{\mathbf{S}} \ \divideontimes \ \Gamma'} \quad [\text{VSeq}]$$

Focusing on the second branch we apply [VRec]

$$\frac{\mathrm{true} \_\Gamma, x : \mathrm{Str}, y : \mathrm{Bool} \ \vdash \ P''_{\mathrm{MBOX}} \ \triangleright \ \mathbf{s} : \mathrm{T}_{\mathrm{MBOX}}, \mathbf{t} : \mathrm{end} \ \divideontimes \ \Gamma'}{\mathrm{true} \_\Gamma, x : \mathrm{Str} \ \vdash \ t_{\mathrm{RES}}(y); P''_{\mathrm{MBOX}} \ \triangleright \ \mathbf{s} : \mathrm{T}_{\mathrm{MBOX}}, \mathbf{t} : \mathrm{RES?Bool} \ \divideontimes \ \Gamma'} \quad [\text{VRec}]$$

Rule [VCond] can be applied since condition y of the conditional statement in P''_{MBOX} is neither a tautology nor a contradiction. The rest is as in Ex. 5.   ◆

6   Properties of the Type System

Runtime Types. The properties of our type system are stated in terms of the behaviour of local types. As in [14], *runtime types* extend local types with *message contexts* $\mathbb{M}$ of the form $s_1!\mathrm{v}_1; \cdots; s_n!\mathrm{v}_n[\_]$ with $n \geq 0$, namely $\mathbb{M}$ is a sequence of outputs followed by a hole $[\_]$. To model asynchrony, we stipulate the equality

$$s_1!\mathrm{v}_1; s_2!\mathrm{v}_2; \mathbb{M} \approx s_2!\mathrm{v}_2; s_1!\mathrm{v}_1; \mathbb{M} \qquad \text{if } s_1 \neq s_2$$

A *runtime type* is either a message context $\mathbb{M}$ or a "type in context", that is a term $\mathbb{M}[\mathcal{T}]$. We extend environments so to map session names $\mathbf{s}$ to runtime types of roles in $\mathbf{s}$; we write $\Delta, \mathbf{s} : \mathbb{M}[\mathcal{T}] @\, \mathrm{p}$ to specify that (1) the runtime type of $\mathrm{p} \in \mathbb{P}$ in $\mathbf{s}$ is $\mathbb{M}[\mathcal{T}]$ and (2) that for any $\mathbf{s} : \mathbb{M}'[\mathcal{T}'] @\, \mathrm{q}$ in Δ we have $\mathrm{q} \neq \mathrm{p}$.

The semantics of runtime types is obtained by adding the rules in Fig. 7 to those in Fig. 1. Rule [TQueue] removes a message from of a queue. Rules [TCom1] and [TCom2] establish how runtime specifications send and receives messages (the transition in their premises are derived from the rules in Fig. 1). Rule [TInit] initiates a new session by mapping the new session $\mathbf{s}$ to the projections of the global type assigned by Γ.

Soundness. The typing rules in § 5 ensure the semantic conformance of processes with the behaviour prescribed by their types. Here, we define conformance in terms of *conditional simulation* that relates states and specifications. Our definition is standard, except for input actions, for which specifications have to simulate only inputs of messages with the expected type (i.e., systems are not responsible when receiving ill-typed messages).

Define $\xRightarrow{\alpha} \ = \xrightarrow{\tau} {}^* \xrightarrow{\alpha}$. Let $\Gamma \bullet \Delta \xRightarrow{s}$ shorten $\exists \Delta' \exists \mathrm{v} : \Gamma \bullet \Delta \xRightarrow{s\mathrm{v}} \Gamma \bullet \Delta'$.

Definition 5 (Conditional simulation). *A relation* $\mathbb{R}$ *between states and specifications is a* conditional simulation *iff for any* $(\langle S, \sigma \rangle, \Gamma \bullet \Delta) \in \mathbb{R}$, *if* $\langle S, \sigma \rangle \xrightarrow{e \vdash \alpha} \langle S', \sigma' \rangle$ *then*

1. *if* $\alpha = sv$ *then* $\Gamma \bullet \Delta \xrightarrow{s}$ *and if* $\Gamma \bullet \Delta \xRightarrow{sv}$ *then there is* $\Gamma \bullet \Delta'$ *such that* $\Gamma \bullet \Delta \xRightarrow{sv}$ $\Gamma \bullet \Delta'$ *and* $(\langle S', \sigma' \rangle, \Gamma \bullet \Delta') \in \mathbb{R}$
2. *otherwise,* $\Gamma \bullet \Delta \xRightarrow{\alpha} \Gamma \bullet \Delta'$ *and* $(\langle S', \sigma' \rangle, \Gamma \bullet \Delta') \in \mathbb{R}$.

We write $\langle S, \sigma \rangle \precsim \Gamma \bullet \Delta$ *if there is a conditional simulation* $\mathbb{R}$ *s.t.* $(\langle S, \sigma \rangle, \Gamma \bullet \Delta) \in \mathbb{R}$.

By (1), only inputs of S with the expected type have to be matched by $\Gamma \bullet \Delta$ (recall rule [TRec] in Fig. 1), while it is no longer expected to conform to the specification after an ill-typed input (i.e., not allowed by $\Gamma \bullet \Delta$).

Def. 6 establishes consistency for stores in terms of preservation of variables' sorts.

Definition 6 (Consistent store). *Given an environment* Γ, *a context assumption* C, *and a state* $\langle S, \sigma \rangle$ *with* $\text{var}(S) \subseteq \text{dom}(\sigma)$, *store* σ *is* consistent *for* S *with respect to* Γ *and* C *iff* $\forall x \in \text{dom}(\sigma)$, $\sigma(x) : \Gamma(x)$, *and* $C \downarrow \sigma = \text{true}$.

Theorem 2 (Subject reduction). *Assume that*

$$C \lrcorner \Gamma \vdash S \triangleright \Delta * \Gamma' \quad and \quad \langle S, \sigma \rangle \xrightarrow{e \vdash \alpha} \langle S', \sigma' \rangle$$

with σ *consistent for* S *with respect to* Γ *and* C. *Then*

1. *if* $\alpha = sv$ *then* $\Gamma \bullet \Delta \xRightarrow{s}$ *and if* $\Gamma \bullet \Delta \xRightarrow{sv}$ *then there is* $\Gamma \bullet \Delta'$ *such that* $\Gamma \bullet \Delta \xRightarrow{sv}$ $\Gamma \bullet \Delta'$ *with* $\mathtt{v} : \mathtt{U}$ *and* $C \wedge e \lrcorner \Gamma, x : \mathtt{U} \vdash S' \triangleright \Delta' * \Gamma''$ *for some* x *and some* $\Gamma'' \supseteq \Gamma'$
2. *otherwise* $\Gamma \bullet \Delta \xRightarrow{\alpha} \Gamma \bullet \Delta'$ *and* $C \wedge e \lrcorner \Gamma \vdash S' \triangleright \Delta' * \Gamma''$ *for some* $\Gamma'' \supseteq \Gamma'$.

Corollary 1 (Soundness). *If* $C \lrcorner \Gamma \vdash S \triangleright \Delta * \Gamma'$ *then* $\langle S, \sigma \rangle \precsim \Gamma \bullet \Delta$ *for all* σ consistent store for S with respect to Γ and C.

WSI by typing

We show that well-typed processes are WSIs (Def. 4). First, we relate the runs of a global type with those of its corresponding runtime types. Then, we state the correspondence between the runs of runtime types and well-typed implementations.

Definition 7 (Runs of runtime types). *The set* $\mathcal{R}_\mathbf{s}(\Delta)$ *denotes the runs of events over the channels in* $\mathbf{s}$ *generated by* Δ, *and is inductively defined by the rules in Fig. 8.*

Rule [RTCom] builds the runs for two communicating types. Rules [RTIt1] and [RTIt2] unfold the runs of an iterative type. Note that the mandatory actions of runs associated to recursive types are those requiring at least one execution of the iteration body, while additional executions are optional. The remaining rules are self-explanatory. (The correspondence between the operational and denotational semantics is in [3, Appendix E].)

Thm. 3 ensures that well-formed global types are covered by their projections, while Thm. 4 states that the set of well-typed implementation covers its specification.

Theorem 3. *For any global type* $\mathcal{G}(\mathbf{s})$, $\mathcal{R}(\mathcal{G}(\mathbf{s})) \Subset \mathcal{R}_\mathbf{s}(\{\mathbf{s} : (\mathcal{G}(\mathbf{s}) \restriction \mathtt{p}) @ \mathtt{p}\}_{\mathtt{p} \in \mathcal{P}(\mathcal{G}(\mathbf{s}))})$.

Theorem 4. *Let* $\mathcal{G}(\mathbf{s}) \stackrel{\triangle}{=} \mathtt{G}$ *be a global type. Fix* $\mathtt{p} \in \mathcal{P}(\mathtt{G})$ *and* P *a well-typed implementation of* $\mathtt{p}$. *Define*

$$\mathbb{I}_{\mathtt{p},P} = \{I_G^1 | \iota(\mathtt{p}) = P, \forall \mathtt{q} \in \mathcal{P}(\mathtt{G}) : \text{true} \lrcorner \Gamma, u : \mathcal{G}(\mathbf{s}) \vdash \iota(\mathtt{q}) \triangleright \Delta, \mathbf{s} : \mathcal{G}(\mathbf{s}) \restriction \mathtt{q} * \Gamma'\}$$

then, $\mathcal{R}_\mathbf{s}(\{\mathbf{s} : (\mathcal{G}(\mathbf{s}) \restriction \mathtt{p}) @ \mathtt{p}\}_{\mathtt{p} \in \mathcal{P}(\mathcal{G})}) \quad \Subset \quad \mathcal{R}_u(\mathbb{I}_{\mathtt{p},P})$.

$$\dfrac{r \in \mathcal{R}_{\mathfrak{s}}(\Delta, \mathbf{s} : \mathbb{M}[T_k] @ \mathsf{p}, \ \mathbb{M}'[T_k'] @ \mathsf{q}) \qquad k \in J}{\langle \mathsf{p}, s_k!\mathsf{U}_k \rangle \langle \mathsf{q}, s_k?\mathsf{U}_k \rangle r \in \mathcal{R}_{\mathfrak{s}}(\Delta, \mathbf{s} : \mathbb{M}[s_k!\mathsf{U}_k ; T_k] @ \mathsf{p}, \ \mathbb{M}'[\sum_{j \in J} s_j?\mathsf{U}_j ; T_j'] @ \mathsf{q})} \ [\mathrm{RTCom}]$$

$$\dfrac{r \in \mathcal{R}_{\mathfrak{s}}(\Delta, \mathbf{s} : T_i ; T_j @ \mathsf{p})}{r \in \mathcal{R}_{\mathfrak{s}}(\Delta, \mathbf{s} : T_i^* ; T_j @ \mathsf{p})} \ [\mathrm{RTIt1}] \qquad \dfrac{rr' \in \mathcal{R}_{\mathfrak{s}}(\Delta, \mathbf{s} : T_i ; T_i^* ; T_j @ \mathsf{p}) \quad r' \in \mathcal{R}_{\mathfrak{s}}(\Delta \mathbf{s} : T_i ; T_j @ \mathsf{p})}{[r] r' \in \mathcal{R}_{\mathfrak{s}}(\Delta, \mathbf{s} : T_i^* ; T_j @ \mathsf{p})} \ [\mathrm{RTIt2}]$$

$$\dfrac{r \in \mathcal{R}_{\mathfrak{s}}(\Delta) \qquad \mathbf{s} \neq \mathbf{r}}{r \in \mathcal{R}_{\mathfrak{s}}(\Delta, \mathbf{r} : T)} \ [\mathrm{RTPar}] \qquad \dfrac{r \in \mathcal{R}_{\mathfrak{s}}(\Delta)}{r \in \mathcal{R}_{\mathfrak{s}}(\Delta, \mathbf{s} : \mathsf{end} @ \mathsf{p})} \ [\mathrm{RTEnd1}] \qquad \varepsilon \in \mathcal{R}_{\mathfrak{s}}(\emptyset) \ [\mathrm{RTEnd2}]$$

$$\dfrac{r \in \mathcal{R}_{\mathfrak{s}}(\Delta, \mathbf{s} : s_j!\mathsf{U}_j ; T_j @ \mathsf{p}) \qquad j \in I}{r \in \mathcal{R}_{\mathfrak{s}}(\Delta, \mathbf{s} : \bigoplus_{i \in I} s_i!\mathsf{U}_i ; T_i @ \mathsf{p})} \ [\mathrm{RTCh}]$$

Fig. 8. Runs of runtime local types

7   Conclusion and Related Work

WSI forbids implementations of a role that persistently avoid the execution of some alternative branches in a choreography. Although WSI is defined as a relation between the traces of a global type and those of its candidate implementations, it can be checked by using multiparty session types. Technically, we show that (i) the sets of the projections of a global type G preserves all the traces in G (Thm. 3); and (ii) any trace of a local type can be mimicked by a well-typed implementation, if interacting in a proper context (Thm. 4). The soundness of our type system (Corollary 1) ensures that well-typed implementations behave as prescribed by the choreography.

We are currently working on the extension of WSI to other models of choreography as e.g. those based on automata [12], which poses the classical question about the decidability of the notion of realisability (see [1]). To the best of our knowledge, the only proposal dealing with complete (i.e., exhaustive) realisations in a behavioural context is [7] but this approach focuses on non-deterministic implementation languages. Our type system is more restrictive than [14,2,4,8,6]. We do not consider subtyping because the liberal elimination of internal choices prevents WSI. The investigation of suitable forms of subtyping for WSIs is scope for future work.

WSI coincides with projection realisability [17,22,7] when implementation languages feature non-deterministic internal choices. On the contrary, WSI provides a finer criterion to distinguish deterministic implementations, as illustrated by the motivating example in the introduction. To some extent our proposal is related to the fair subtyping approach in [21], where refinement is studied under the fairness assumption: Fair subtyping differs from usual subtyping when considering infinite computations but WSI differs from partial implementation also when considering finite computations.

The static verification of WSI requires a form of recursion more restrictive than the one in [14,2], where the number of iterations is limited. This restriction is on the lines of [7] that also considers finite traces. The extension of our theory with a more general form of iteration is scope for future work.

Acknowledgements. We thank the reviewers for their insightful and helpful comments.

References

1. Basu, S., Bultan, T., Ouederni, M.: Deciding choreography realizability. In: POPL (2012)
2. Bettini, L., Coppo, M., D'Antoni, L., De Luca, M., Dezani-Ciancaglini, M., Yoshida, N.: Global progress in dynamically interleaved multiparty sessions. In: van Breugel, F., Chechik, M. (eds.) CONCUR 2008. LNCS, vol. 5201, pp. 418–433. Springer, Heidelberg (2008)
3. Bocchi, L., Melgratti, H., Tuosto, E.: Extended version of this paper (2014) http://publicaciones.dc.uba.ar/Publications/2014/BMT14c/
4. Bravetti, M., Zavattaro, G.: A theory of contracts for strong service compliance. MSCS 19(3) (2009)
5. Butler, M., Postel, J., Chase, D., Goldberger, J., Reynoldsa, J.: Post office protocol - version 2. RFC 918 (February 1985), http://tools.ietf.org/html/rfc937
6. Caires, L., Vieira, H.T.: Conversation types. In: Castagna, G. (ed.) ESOP 2009. LNCS, vol. 5502, pp. 285–300. Springer, Heidelberg (2009)
7. Castagna, G., Dezani-Ciancaglini, M., Padovani, L.: On global types and multi-party session. LMCS 8(1) (2012)
8. Castagna, G., Padovani, L.: Contracts for mobile processes. In: Bravetti, M., Zavattaro, G. (eds.) CONCUR 2009. LNCS, vol. 5710, pp. 11–228. Springer, Heidelberg (2009)
9. Chen, T.-C., Honda, K.: Specifying stateful asynchronous properties for distributed programs. In: Koutny, M., Ulidowski, I. (eds.) CONCUR 2012. LNCS, vol. 7454, pp. 209–224. Springer, Heidelberg (2012)
10. Crocker, D.: Standard for the format of arpa internet text messages. RFC 822 (February 1982), www.ietf.org/rfc/rfc0822.txt
11. Dezani-Ciancaglini, M., de'Liguoro, U.: Sessions and session types: An overview. In: Laneve, C., Su, J. (eds.) WS-FM 2009. LNCS, vol. 6194, pp. 1–28. Springer, Heidelberg (2010)
12. Fu, X., Bultan, T., Su, J.: Realizability of conversation protocols with message contents. Int. J. Web Service Res. 2(4), 68–93 (2005)
13. Gay, S., Hole, M.: Subtyping for Session Types in the Pi-Calculus. Acta Inf. 42(2/3), 191–225 (2005)
14. Honda, K., Yoshida, N., Carbone, M.: Multiparty asynchronous session types. In: POPL (2008)
15. Kavantzas, N., Burdett, D., Ritzinger, G., Fletcher, T., Lafon, Y. (2004), http://www.w3.org/TR/2004/WD-ws-cdl-10-20041217
16. Lamport, L.: Time, clocks, and the ordering of events in a distributed system. CACM 21(7), 558–564 (1978)
17. Lanese, I., Guidi, C., Montesi, F., Zavattaro, G.: Bridging the gap between interaction-and process-oriented choreographies. In: SEFM (2008)
18. Lange, J., Tuosto, E.: Synthesising choreographies from local session types. In: Koutny, M., Ulidowski, I. (eds.) CONCUR 2012. LNCS, vol. 7454, pp. 225–239. Springer, Heidelberg (2012)
19. Lohmann, N., Wolf, K.: Decidability results for choreography realization. In: Kappel, G., Maamar, Z., Motahari-Nezhad, H.R. (eds.) Service Oriented Computing. LNCS, vol. 7084, pp. 92–107. Springer, Heidelberg (2011)
20. Milner, R.: Communication and Concurrency. Prentice Hall (1989)
21. Padovani, L.: Fair subtyping for multi-party session types. In: De Meuter, W., Roman, G.-C. (eds.) COORDINATION 2011. LNCS, vol. 6721, pp. 127–141. Springer, Heidelberg (2011)
22. Salaün, G., Bultan, T.: Realizability of choreographies using process algebra encodings. In: Integrated Formal Methods (2009)
23. Su, J., Bultan, T., Fu, X., Zhao, X.: Towards a theory of web service choreographies. In: Dumas, M., Heckel, R. (eds.) WS-FM 2007. LNCS, vol. 4937, pp. 1–16. Springer, Heidelberg (2008)

A Correspondence between Two Approaches to Interprocedural Analysis in the Presence of Join

Ravi Mangal[1], Mayur Naik[1], and Hongseok Yang[2]

[1] Georgia Institute of Technology
[2] University of Oxford

Abstract. Many interprocedural static analyses perform a lossy join for reasons of termination or efficiency. We study the relationship between two predominant approaches to interprocedural analysis, the summary-based (or functional) approach and the call-strings (or k-CFA) approach, in the presence of a lossy join. Despite the use of radically different ways to distinguish procedure contexts by these two approaches, we prove that post-processing their results using a form of garbage collection renders them equivalent. Our result extends the classic result by Sharir and Pnueli that showed the equivalence between these two approaches in the setting of distributive analysis, wherein the join is lossless.

We also empirically compare these two approaches by applying them to a pointer analysis that performs a lossy join. Our experiments on ten Java programs of size 400K–900K bytecodes show that the summary-based approach outperforms an optimized implementation of the k-CFA approach: the k-CFA implementation does not scale beyond k=2, while the summary-based approach proves up to 46% more pointer analysis client queries than 2-CFA. The summary-based approach thus enables, via our equivalence result, to measure the precision of k-CFA with unbounded k, for the class of interprocedural analyses that perform a lossy join.

1 Introduction

Two dominant approaches to interprocedural static analysis are the summary-based approach and the call-strings approach. Both approaches aim to analyze each procedure precisely by distinguishing calling contexts of a certain kind. But they differ radically in the kind of contexts used: the summary-based (or functional) approach uses input abstract states whereas the call-strings (or k-CFA) approach uses sequences of calls that represent call stacks.

Sharir and Pnueli [SP81] showed that, in the case of a finite, distributive analysis, the summary-based approach is equivalent to the unbounded call-strings approach (hereafter called ∞-CFA). In this case, both these approaches maintain at most one abstract state at each program point under a given context of its containing procedure, applying a join operation to combine different abstract states at each program point into a single state. The distributivity condition ensures that this join is *lossless*. As a result, both approaches compute the precise meet-over-all-valid-paths (MVP) solution, and are thus equivalent.

Z. Shao (Ed.): ESOP 2014, LNCS 8410, pp. 513–533, 2014.

Many useful static analyses using the summary-based approach, however, lack distributivity. They too use a join, in order to maintain at most one abstract state at each program point under a given context, and thereby scale to large programs (e.g., [FYD+08]). But in this non-distributive case, the join is *lossy*, leading such analyses to compute a solution less precise than the MVP solution.

We study the relationship between the summary-based and call-strings approaches, in the presence of a lossy join. Our main result is that these two approaches are equivalent in precision despite their use of radically different ways to distinguish procedure contexts. This result yields both theoretical and practical insights. The theoretical insight includes two new proof techniques. The first is a form of garbage collection on the results computed by the non-distributive summary-based approach. This garbage collection removes entries of procedure summaries that are used during analysis but not in the final analysis results. It provides a natural way for connecting the results of the summary-based approach with those of ∞-CFA. The other is a new technique for proving that a fixpoint of a non-monotone function is approximated by a pre-fixpoint of the function. Standard proof techniques do not apply because of non-monotonicity, but such an approximation result is needed in our case because non-distributive summary-based analyses use non-monotone transfer functions.

On the practical side, our equivalence result provides, for the class of non-distributive interprocedural analyses, a feasible approach to determine how precise k-CFA can get using arbitrary k. This feasible approach is the summary-based one, which scales much better than k-CFA. State-of-the-art algorithms for k-CFA do not scale to beyond small values of k, as the number of call-string contexts in which they analyze procedures grows exponentially with k. As a concrete example, we compare the performance of the summary-based approach to an optimized BDD-based implementation of k-CFA for a non-distributive pointer analysis for object-oriented programs. On ten Java programs each of size 400K-900K bytecodes from the DaCapo benchmark suite, we find that the k-CFA implementation does not scale beyond $k=2$, and even for $k=2$, it computes 4X–7X more contexts per benchmark than the summary-based approach. Furthermore, for three clients of the pointer analysis—downcast safety, call graph reachability, and monomorphic call inference—the summary-based approach proves up to 46% more client queries per benchmark than 2-CFA, providing an upper bound on the number of queries that is provable by k-CFA using arbitrary k.

2   Example

We illustrate various interprocedural approaches by means of a pointer analysis on the Java program in Figure 1. All the approaches infer points-to information— aliasing relationships among program variables and heap objects—but differ in their treatment of methods. We illustrate five key aspects of these approaches: (i) 0-CFA produces imprecise results; (ii) using k-CFA with $k > 0$ helps to address this imprecision but hurts scalability; (iii) summary-based analysis (hereafter called SBA) causes no loss in precision compared to k-CFA; (iv) the lossy join

```
                                   class C {
                                     static Container foo() {
                                 h1:   Container s1 = new Container();
                                 h2:   A a = new A();
class A {}                       i1:   s1.add(a);
                                       return s1;
                                     }
class B {}                           static Container bar() {
                                 h3:   Container s2 = new Container();
class Container {                h4:   B b = new B();
   Object holder;                i2:   s2.add(b);
   Container() { holder = null; }      return s2;
   void add(Object x) {               }
     if (x.equals(holder)) return;    static void taz(Container s){...}
     holder = x;                      static void main() {
   }                                    Container s=(*) ? foo() : bar();
   bool isEmpty() {             j1:    // join point
     return (holder==null);     i3:    s.isEmpty();
   }                            i4:    s.isEmpty();
}                               i5:    taz(s);
                                     }
                                   }
```

Fig. 1. Example Java program

operation in SBA allows analyzing methods in fewer contexts and thereby improves scalability; and (v) SBA can merge multiple k-CFA contexts of a method into a single SBA context which also improves scalability.

We start with 0-CFA which treats method calls in a context insensitive manner. This means that the analysis does not differentiate different call sites to a method, and merges all the abstract states from these call sites into a single input. For instance, consider the program in Figure 1, where the main() method calls either foo() or bar(), creates a container object s containing an A or B object, and operates on this container s by calling isEmpty() and taz(). When the pointer analysis based on 0-CFA is applied to main, it imprecisely concludes that the returned container from foo() may contain an A or B object, instead of the true case of containing only an A object. Another imprecise conclusion is what we call *call graph reachability*. The analysis infers that at one point of execution, the call stack may contain both foo() and B::equals(), the second on top of the first, i.e., B::equals() is reachable from foo(). Note that this reachability never materializes during the execution of the program. The main source of both kinds of imprecision is that 0-CFA does not differentiate between the calls to add() from **i1** in foo() and **i2** in bar(). It merges the abstract states from both call sites and analyzes add() under the assumption $[x \rightarrow \{h_2, h_4\}]$, which means that x points to a heap object allocated at h_2 or h_4, so the object

x has type A or B. Note that once this assumption is made, the analysis cannot avoid the two kinds of imprecision discussed above.

One way to resolve 0-CFA's imprecision is to use an analysis based on k-CFA with $k > 0$, which analyzes method calls separately if the call stacks at these call sites store sufficiently different sequences of call sites. For instance, the pointer analysis based on 1-CFA analyzes a method multiple times, once for each of its call sites. Hence, when it is applied to our example, it differentiates two call sites to add() (i.e., i1 and i2), and analyzes add() twice, once for the call site i1 with the assumption $[x \rightarrow \{h_2\}]$ on the parameter x, and again for the call site i2 with the assumption $[x \rightarrow \{h_4\}]$. This differentiation enables the analysis to infer that the returned container from foo() contains objects of the type A only, and also that B::equals() is not reachable from foo(). In other words, both kinds of imprecision of 0-CFA are eliminated with 1-CFA.

An alternative solution to the imprecision issue is to use SBA. Unlike k-CFA, SBA does not distinguish contexts based on sequences of call sites stored in the call stack. Instead, it decides that two calling contexts differ when the abstract states at call sites are different. SBA re-analyzes a method in a calling context only if it has not seen the abstract state τ of this context before. In Figure 1, the abstract states at call sites i1 and i2 are, respectively, $[s_1 \rightarrow \{h_1\}, a \rightarrow \{h_2\}]$ and $[s_2 \rightarrow \{h_3\}, b \rightarrow \{h_4\}]$, which become the following input abstract states to add() after the actual parameters are replaced with the formal parameters; $[this \rightarrow \{h_1\}, x \rightarrow \{h_2\}]$ and $[this \rightarrow \{h_3\}, x \rightarrow \{h_4\}]$. Since these inputs are different, SBA analyzes method add() separately for the calls from i1 and i2, and reaches the same conclusion about the return value of foo() and call graph reachability as that of 1-CFA described previously. This agreement in analysis results is not an accident. We prove in Section 3 that SBA's results always coincide with those of ∞-CFA, a version of k-CFA that does not put a bound on the length of call-strings.

An important feature of SBA is that at every control-flow join point in a program, incoming abstract states to this point are combined to a single abstract state via a lossy join operator (if they all originate from the same input abstract state to the current method). This greatly helps the scalability of SBA, because it leads to fewer distinct abstract states at call sites and reduces the number of times that each method should be analyzed. For instance, when SBA analyzes the program in Figure 1, it encounters two incoming abstract states at the join point j1, $\tau_1 = [s \rightarrow \{h_1\}]$ from the true branch and $\tau_2 = [s \rightarrow \{h_3\}]$ from the false branch. The analysis combines τ_1 and τ_2 using a lossy join operator, and results in $\tau' = [s \rightarrow \{h_1, h_3\}]$. As a result, at the subsequent call site i5, the analysis has only one input abstract state τ', instead of two (i.e., τ_1 and τ_2), and it analyzes the method taz() only once.

Using a lossy join operator differentiates SBA from the well-known distributive summary-based analysis [RHS95, SP81], which uses a lossless join. If such an analysis were applied to our program, it would collect τ_1, τ_2 as the set $\{\tau_1, \tau_2\}$ at the join point j1, and analyze the call to taz() twice. As a result, the co-incidence between the results of SBA and ∞-CFA does not follow from what

$$
\begin{array}{rl}
\text{(method)} & m \ \in \ \mathbf{M} = \{\ m_{main}, ... \ \}\\
\text{(atomic command)} & a \ \in \ \mathbf{A}\\
\text{(method call)} & i \ \in \ \mathbf{I}\\
\text{(statement)} & s \ \in \ \mathbf{S} \triangleq (\mathbf{A} \cup \mathbf{I})\\
\text{(CFG node)} & n \ \in \ \mathbf{N}\\
\text{(CFG edge)} & e \ \in \ \mathbf{E} \subseteq \mathbf{N} \times \mathbf{S} \times \mathbf{N}\\
& e \ \triangleq \ \langle n_1, s, n_2 \rangle\\
& p \ \in \ \mathbf{P} \triangleq (\mathbf{N} \cup \mathbf{E})
\end{array}
$$

$$
\begin{array}{rl}
origin(\langle n_1, s, n_2 \rangle) \triangleq & n_1\\
stmt(\langle n_1, s, n_2 \rangle) \triangleq & s\\
target(\langle n_1, s, n_2 \rangle) \triangleq & n_2\\
callEdge(\langle n_1, a, n_2 \rangle) \triangleq & false\\
callEdge(\langle n_1, i, n_2 \rangle) \triangleq & true\\
\text{(method of node/edge)} \ method \in & \mathbf{P} {\to} \mathbf{M}\\
\text{(entry node of method)} \ entry \in & \mathbf{M} {\to} \mathbf{N}\\
\text{(exit node of method)} \ exit \in & \mathbf{M} {\to} \mathbf{N}
\end{array}
$$

Fig. 2. Notation for interprocedural control flow graphs

was established previously by Sharir and Pnueli. In fact, proving it requires new proof techniques, as we explain in Section 3.

According to our experiments reported in Section 5, SBA scales better than k-CFA for high k values. This is because SBA usually distinguishes calling contexts of a method less than k-CFA, and re-analyzes the method less often than k-CFA. Concretely, a method may be invoked multiple times with call stacks storing different sequences of call sites but with the same abstract state. In this case, k-CFA re-analyzes the method for each call sequence in the stack, but SBA analyzes the method only once and reuses the computed summary for all the invocations of this method. In effect, SBA merges multiple k-CFA contexts into a single SBA context in this case. This phenomenon can be seen in Figure 1 at the two calls to isEmpty() in i3 and i4. Since these call sites are different, isEmpty() would be analyzed twice by k-CFA with $k \geq 1$. However, the abstract state at both of the call sites is the same $[s \to \{h_1, h_3\}]$. Hence, SBA analyzes the method only once and reuses the computed summary for the second call.

3 Formal Description and Correspondence Theorem

This section formalizes an unbounded k-CFA and a summary-based interprocedural analysis. The former is an idealization of usual k-CFA that does not put a bound on the length of tracked call strings (i.e., sequences of call sites in the call stack), and records analysis results separately for each call string. To emphasize the absence of bound, we call this analysis ∞-CFA. The summary-based analysis is a non-distributive variant of the standard summary-based approach for distributive (and disjunctive) analyses [RHS95]. It treats join points approximately using a lossy join operator, unlike the standard approach, and trades precision for performance. The main result of the section is that the summary-based analysis has the same precision as ∞-CFA, despite the lossy join.

3.1 Interprocedural Control Flow Graph

In our formalism, we assume that programs are specified in terms of interprocedural control flow graphs $\mathcal{G} = (\mathbf{M}, \mathbf{A}, \mathbf{I}, \mathbf{N}, \mathbf{E}, method, entry, exit)$ in Figure 2. Set $\mathbf{M}$ consists of method names in a program, and $\mathbf{A}$ and $\mathbf{I}$ specify available

$$\begin{array}{ll}
\text{(abstract state)} & \tau \in \mathbf{\Gamma} = \{\, \tau_{init}, \dots \,\} \\
\text{(lattice operations)} & \bigsqcup, \sqcap \in \mathcal{P}(\mathbf{\Gamma}) \to \mathbf{\Gamma} \quad \perp, \top \in \mathbf{\Gamma} \quad \sqsubseteq \subseteq \mathbf{\Gamma} \times \mathbf{\Gamma} \\
\text{(transfer functions)} & [\![a]\!] \in \mathbf{\Gamma} \to \mathbf{\Gamma} \\
\text{(targets of call)} & calls(s, \tau) \in \mathcal{P}(\mathbf{M}) \\
\text{(call string)} & \pi \in \mathbf{\Pi} \triangleq \bigcup_{n \geq 0} (\mathbf{M} \cup \mathbf{E})^n \\
\text{(∞-CFA annotation)} & \kappa \in \mathbf{A}_{\mathsf{cfa}} = (\mathbf{P} \times \mathbf{\Pi}) \to \mathbf{\Gamma} \\
\text{(SBA annotation)} & \sigma \in \mathbf{A}_{\mathsf{sba}} = (\mathbf{P} \times \mathbf{\Gamma}) \to \mathbf{\Gamma}
\end{array}$$

Fig. 3. Analysis domains and transfer functions

$$F_{\mathsf{cfa}}(\kappa)(n, \pi) = \begin{cases} \bigsqcup \{\, \kappa(e, \pi) \mid n = target(e) \,\} & \text{if } \nexists m : n = entry(m) \\ \bigsqcup \{\, \tau \mid \exists e, \pi_1 : callEdge(e) \wedge \pi = m \oplus e \oplus \pi_1 & \text{if } n = entry(m) \\ \quad \wedge \tau = \kappa(origin(e), \pi_1) \wedge m \in calls(stmt(e), \tau) \,\} \end{cases}$$

$$F_{\mathsf{cfa}}(\kappa)(e, \pi) = \begin{cases} [\![stmt(e)]\!](\kappa(origin(e), \pi)) & \text{if } \neg callEdge(e) \\ \bigsqcup \{\, \tau \mid \exists \tau_1, m : \tau_1 = \kappa(origin(e), \pi) & \text{if } callEdge(e) \\ \quad \wedge m \in calls(stmt(e), \tau_1) \wedge \tau = \kappa(exit(m), m \oplus e \oplus \pi) \,\} \end{cases}$$

Fig. 4. Transfer function F_{cfa} on ∞-CFA annotations

atomic commands and method call instructions. Sets $\mathbf{N}$ and $\mathbf{E}$ determine nodes and intraprocedural edges of a control flow graph. Each node in this graph belongs to a method given by the function *method*. The functions *entry* and *exit* decide the entry and exit nodes of each method. The figure also shows defined entities—*origin*, *stmt*, *target*, and *callEdge*, which can be used to obtain components of an edge and to decide the type of the edge. We assume all the five sets in a control flow graph are finite.

Our control flow graphs are required to satisfy well-formedness conditions. First, $m_{main} \in \mathbf{M}$. Second, for all $m \in \mathbf{M}$ and $e \in \mathbf{E}$,

$$entry(m) \neq exit(m) \wedge (method \circ entry)(m) = (method \circ exit)(m) = m \, \wedge$$
$$(method \circ target)(e) = (method \circ origin)(e) = method(e).$$

The first conjunct means that the entry node and the exit node of a method are different, the second says that *entry* and *exit* pick nodes belonging to their argument method, and the last conjunct states that an edge and its source and target nodes are in the same method.

3.2 Formal Description of Analyses

Both ∞-CFA and the summary-based analysis assume $(\mathbf{\Gamma}, \tau_{init}, [\![\_]\!], calls)$ in Figure 3, which are needed for performing an intraprocedural analysis as well as processing dynamically dispatched method calls. Component $\mathbf{\Gamma}$ is a finite complete lattice, and consists of abstract states used by the analysis. The next $\tau_{init} \in \mathbf{\Gamma}$ is an initial abstract state to the root method m_{main}, and $[\![a]\!]$ represents abstract transfer functions for atomic commands a. The final component *calls* takes a

$$F_{\mathsf{sba}}(\sigma)(n,\tau) = \begin{cases} \bigsqcup \{\,\sigma(e,\tau) \mid n = \mathit{target}(e)\,\} & \text{if } \nexists m : n = \mathit{entry}(m) \\ \bigsqcup \{\,\tau \mid \exists e, \tau_1 : \mathit{callEdge}(e) \wedge \tau = \sigma(\mathit{origin}(e), \tau_1) & \text{if } n = \mathit{entry}(m) \\ \qquad \wedge\, m \in \mathit{calls}(\mathit{stmt}(e), \tau)\,\} \end{cases}$$

$$F_{\mathsf{sba}}(\sigma)(e,\tau) = \begin{cases} [\![\mathit{stmt}(e)]\!](\sigma(\mathit{origin}(e),\tau)) & \text{if } \neg\mathit{callEdge}(e) \\ \bigsqcup \{\,\tau' \mid \exists \tau_1, m : \tau_1 = \sigma(\mathit{origin}(e),\tau) & \text{if } \mathit{callEdge}(e) \\ \qquad \wedge\, m \in \mathit{calls}(\mathit{stmt}(e),\tau_1) \wedge \tau' = \sigma(\mathit{exit}(m),\tau_1)\,\} \end{cases}$$

Fig. 5. Transfer function F_{sba} on SBA annotations

pair (s, τ), and conservatively estimates target methods of a call s in (concrete) states described by τ, if s is a method call. Otherwise, it returns the empty set.

We require that the components of the analysis satisfy the following properties: (i) $\tau_{init} \neq \bot$; (ii) $\mathit{calls}(s, \_)$ and $[\![a]\!]$ are monotone with respect to the order in Γ or the subset order[1]; (iii) $\mathit{calls}(s, \bot) = \emptyset$ and $[\![a]\!](\bot) = \bot$; (iv) for all s and τ, $m_{main} \notin \mathit{calls}(s, \tau)$, and if s is not a method call, $\mathit{calls}(s, \tau) = \emptyset$.

∞-**CFA Analysis.** The ∞-CFA analysis is an interprocedural analysis that uses call strings of arbitrary length as calling contexts and analyzes a method separately for each call string. If a reader is familiar with k-CFA, we suggest to view ∞-CFA as the limit of k-CFA with k tending towards ∞. Indeed, ∞-CFA computes a result that is as precise as any k-CFA analysis.

The ∞-CFA works by repeatedly updating a map $\kappa \in \mathbf{A}_{\mathsf{cfa}} = (\mathbf{P} \times \mathbf{\Pi}) \to \Gamma$, called ∞-**CFA annotation**. The first argument p to κ is a program node or an edge, and the second π a call string defined in Figure 3, which is a finite sequence of method names and edges. A typical call string is $m_2 \oplus e_2 \oplus m_1 \oplus e_1 \oplus m_{main}$. It represents a chain of calls $m_{main} \to m_1 \to m_2$, where m_1 is called by the edge e_1 and m_2 by e_2. The function κ maps such p and π to an abstract state τ, the current estimation of concrete states reaching p with π on the call stack.

We order ∞-CFA annotations pointwise: $\kappa \sqsubseteq \kappa' \iff \forall p, \pi : \kappa(p, \pi) \sqsubseteq \kappa'(p, \pi)$. This order makes the set of ∞-CFA annotations a complete lattice. The ∞-CFA analysis computes a fixpoint on ∞-CFA annotations:

$$\kappa_{\mathsf{cfa}} = \mathsf{leastFix}\ \lambda\kappa.\ (\kappa_I \sqcup F_{\mathsf{cfa}}(\kappa)). \tag{1}$$

Here κ_I is the initial ∞-CFA annotation, and models our assumption that a given program starts at m_{main} in a state satisfying τ_{init}:

$$\kappa_I(p, \pi) = \text{if } ((p, \pi) = (\mathit{entry}(m_{main}), m_{main})) \text{ then } \tau_{init} \text{ else } \bot.$$

Function F_{cfa} is the so called transfer function, and overapproximates one-step execution of atomic commands and method calls in a given program. Figure 4 gives the definition of F_{cfa}. Although this definition looks complicated, it comes from a simple principle: F_{cfa} updates its input κ simply by propagating abstract states in κ to appropriate next nodes or edges, while occasionally pushing or popping call sites and invoked methods in the tracked call string.

---

[1] This means $\forall \tau, \tau' \in \Gamma : \tau \sqsubseteq \tau' \implies (\mathit{calls}(s, \tau) \subseteq \mathit{calls}(s, \tau') \wedge [\![a]\!](\tau) \sqsubseteq [\![a]\!](\tau'))$.

We make two final remarks on ∞-CFA. First, F_{cfa} is monotone with respect to our order on ∞-CFA annotations. This ensures that the least fixpoint in (1) exists. Although the monotonicity is an expected property, we emphasize it here because the transfer function of our next interprocedural analysis SBA is not monotone with respect to a natural order on analysis results. Second, the domain of ∞-CFA annotations is infinite, so a finite number of iterations might be insufficient for reaching the least fixpoint in (1). We are not concerned with this potential non-computability, because we use ∞-CFA only as a device for comparing the precision of SBA in the next subsection with that of k-CFA.

Summary-Based Analysis. The summary-based analysis SBA is another approach to analyze methods context-sensitively. Just like ∞-CFA, it keeps separate analysis results for different calling contexts, but differs from ∞-CFA in that it uses input abstract states to methods as contexts, instead of call strings. The main data structures of SBA are **SBA annotations** σ:

$$\sigma \in \mathbf{A}_{\mathsf{sba}} = (\mathbf{P} \times \mathbf{\Gamma}) \to \mathbf{\Gamma}.$$

An SBA annotation σ specifies an abstract state $\sigma(p, \tau)$ at each program point p for each calling context τ. Recall that a calling context here is just an initial abstract state to the current method. SBA annotations are ordered pointwise: $\sigma \sqsubseteq \sigma' \iff \forall p, \tau : \sigma(p, \tau) \sqsubseteq \sigma'(p, \tau)$. With this order, the set of SBA annotations forms a complete lattice. Further, it is finite as $\mathbf{P}$ and $\mathbf{\Gamma}$ are finite.

The summary-based analysis is an iterative algorithm for computing a fixpoint of some function on SBA annotations. It starts with setting the current SBA annotation to σ_I below:

$$\sigma_I(p, \tau) = \text{if } ((p, \tau) = (entry(m_{main}), \tau_{init})) \text{ then } \tau_{init} \text{ else } \bot,$$

which says that only the entry node of m_{main} has the abstract state τ_{init} under the context τ_{init}. Then, it repeatedly updates the current SBA annotation using the transfer function F_{sba} in Figure 5. The function propagates abstract states at all program nodes and edges along interprocedural control-flow edges. In doing so, it approximates one-step execution of every atomic command and method call in a given program. The summary-based analysis does the following fixpoint computation and calculates σ_{sba}:

$$\sigma_{\mathsf{sba}} = \mathsf{fix}^{\sigma_I} \, (\lambda\sigma. \, \sigma \sqcup F_{\mathsf{sba}}(\sigma)). \tag{2}$$

Let $G = (\lambda\sigma. \, \sigma \sqcup F_{\mathsf{sba}}(\sigma))$. Here $(\mathsf{fix}^{\sigma_I} G)$ generates the sequence $G^0(\sigma_I)$, $G^1(\sigma_I)$, $G^2(\sigma_I)$, ..., until it reaches a fixpoint $G^n(\sigma_I)$ such that $G^n(\sigma_I) = G^{n+1}(\sigma_I)$. This fixpoint $G^n(\sigma_I)$ becomes the result σ_{sba} of $\mathsf{fix}^{\sigma_I} G$.

Note that fix always reaches a fixpoint in (2). The generated sequence is always increasing because $\sigma \sqsubseteq G(\sigma)$ for every σ. Since the domain of SBA annotations is finite, this increasing sequence should reach a fixpoint. One might wonder why SBA does not use the standard least fixpoint. The reason is that our transfer function F_{sba} is not monotone, so the standard theory for least fixpoints does not apply. This is in contrast to ∞-CFA that has the monotone transfer function.

Non-monotone transfer functions commonly feature in program analyses for numerical properties that use widening operators [Min06, CC92], and the results of these analyses are computed similarly to what we described above (modulo the additional use of a widening operator).

3.3   Correspondence Theorem

The main result of this section is the Correspondence Theorem, which says that ∞-CFA and SBA have the same precision.

Recall that the results of SBA and ∞-CFA are functions of different types: the domain of σ_{sba} is $\mathbf{P} \times \mathbf{\Gamma}$, whereas that of κ_{cfa} is $\mathbf{P} \times \mathbf{\Pi}$. Hence, to connect the results of both analyses, we need a way to relate functions of the first kind with those of the second. For this purpose, we use a particular kind of functions:

Definition 1. *A* **translation function** η *is a map of type* $\mathbf{M} \times \mathbf{\Pi} \to \mathbf{\Gamma}$.

Intuitively, $\eta(m, \pi) = \tau$ expresses that although a call string π and an abstract state τ are different types of calling contexts, we will treat them the same when they are used as contexts for method m.

One important property of a translation function η is that it induces maps between SBA and ∞-CFA annotations:

$$L(\eta, -) : \mathbf{A}_{\mathsf{sba}} \to \mathbf{A}_{\mathsf{cfa}} \quad L(\eta, \sigma) = \lambda(p, \pi). \, \sigma(p, \eta(method(p), \pi)),$$
$$R(\eta, -) : \mathbf{A}_{\mathsf{cfa}} \to \mathbf{A}_{\mathsf{sba}} \quad R(\eta, \kappa) = \lambda(p, \tau). \bigsqcap \{\kappa(p, \pi) \mid \tau \sqsubseteq \eta(method(p), \pi)\}.$$

Both L and R use η to convert calling contexts of one type to those of the other. The conversion in $L(\eta, \sigma)$ is as we expect; it calls η to change an input call string π to an input abstract state $\eta(method(p), \pi)$, which is then fed to the given SBA annotation σ. On the other hand, the conversion in $R(\eta, \kappa)$ is unusual, but follows the same principle of using η for translating contexts. Conceptually, it changes an input abstract state τ to a set of call strings π that would be translated to an overapproximation of τ by η (i.e., $\tau \sqsubseteq \eta(method(p), \pi)$), looks up the values of κ at these call strings, and combine the looked-up values by the meet operation. The following lemma relates $L(\eta, -)$ and $R(\eta, -)$:

Lemma 1. *For all* σ *and* κ, *if* $\sigma \sqsubseteq R(\eta, \kappa)$, *then* $L(\eta, \sigma) \sqsubseteq \kappa$.

The definition of a translation function does not impose any condition, and permits multiple possibilities. Hence, a natural question is: what is a good translation function η that would help us to relate the results of the SBA analysis with those of the ∞-CFA analysis? The following lemma suggests one such candidate η_{sba}, which is constructed from the results σ_{sba} of the SBA analysis:

Lemma 2. *There exists a unique translation function* $\eta : \mathbf{M} \times \mathbf{\Pi} \to \mathbf{\Gamma}$ *such that for all* $m \in \mathbf{M}$, $e \in \mathbf{E}$ *and* $\pi \in \mathbf{\Pi}$,

$$\eta(m_{main}, m_{main}) = \tau_{init},$$
$$\eta(m, m \oplus e \oplus \pi) = if \ (m \in calls(stmt(e), \sigma_{\mathsf{sba}}(origin(e), \eta(method(e), \pi)))$$
$$\wedge \ callEdge(e)) \ then \ \sigma_{\mathsf{sba}}(origin(e), \eta(method(e), \pi)) \ else \perp,$$
$$\eta(m, \pi) = \perp \quad (for \ all \ the \ other \ cases).$$

We denote this translation with η_{sba}.

Intuitively, for each call string π, the translation η_{sba} in the lemma follows the chain of calls in π while tracking corresponding abstract input states stored in σ. When this chasing is over, it finds an input abstract state τ corresponding to the given π. For instance, given a method m_2 and a call string $m_2 \oplus e_2 \oplus m_1 \oplus e_1 \oplus m_{main}$, if all the side conditions in the lemma are met, η_{sba} returns abstract state $\sigma_{\mathsf{sba}}(origin(e_2), \sigma_{\mathsf{sba}}(origin(e_1), \tau_{init}))$. This corresponds to the input abstract state to method m_2 that arises after method calls first at e_1 and then e_2.

Another good intuition is to view η_{sba} as a *garbage collector*. Specifically, for each method m, the set

$$\Gamma_m = \{\eta_{\mathsf{sba}}(m, \pi) \mid \pi \in \mathbf{\Pi}\}. \tag{3}$$

identifies input abstract states for m that contribute to the analysis result σ_{sba} along some call chain from m_{main} to m; every other input abstract state τ for m is garbage even if it was used during the fixpoint computation of σ_{sba} and so $\sigma_{\mathsf{sba}}(entry(m), \tau) \neq \bot$.

Our Correspondence Theorem says that the SBA analysis and the ∞-CFA analysis compute the same result modulo the translation via $L(\eta_{\mathsf{sba}}, -)$.

Theorem 2 (Correspondence). $L(\eta_{\mathsf{sba}}, \sigma_{\mathsf{sba}}) = \kappa_{\mathsf{cfa}}$.

One important consequence of this theorem is that both analyses have the same estimation about reachable concrete states at each program point, if we garbage-collect the SBA's result using η_{sba}:

Corollary 1. *For all $p \in \mathbf{P}$ and $m \in \mathbf{M}$, if $method(p) = m$, then*

$$\{\kappa_{\mathsf{cfa}}(p, \pi) \mid \pi \in \mathbf{\Pi}\} = \{\sigma_{\mathsf{sba}}(p, \tau') \mid \tau' \in \Gamma_m\}, \text{ where } \Gamma_m \text{ is defined by (3)}.$$

Overview of Proof of the Correspondence Theorem. Proving the Correspondence Theorem is surprisingly tricky. A simple proof strategy is to show that the relationship in the theorem is maintained by each step of the fixpoint computations of ∞-CFA and SBA, but this strategy does not work. Since ∞-CFA and SBA treat the effects of method calls (i.e., call edges) very differently, the relationship in the theorem is not maintained during fixpoint computations. Further difficulties arise because the SBA analysis uses a non-monotone transfer function F_{sba} and does not necessarily compute the least fixpoint of $\lambda\sigma.\ \sigma_I \sqcup F_{\mathsf{sba}}(\sigma)$—these render standard techniques for reasoning about fixpoints no longer applicable.

In this subsection, we outline our proof of the Correspondence Theorem, and point out proof techniques that we developed to overcome difficulties mentioned above. The full proof is included in the Appendix.

Let $G_{\mathsf{cfa}} = \lambda\kappa.\ \kappa_I \sqcup F_\kappa(\kappa)$ and $G_{\mathsf{sba}} = \lambda\sigma.\ \sigma_I \sqcup F_{\mathsf{sba}}(\sigma)$. Recall that the ∞-CFA analysis computes the least fixpoint of G_{cfa} while the SBA analysis computes some pre-fixpoint of G_{sba} (i.e., $G_{\mathsf{sba}}(\sigma_{\mathsf{sba}}) \sqsubseteq \sigma_{\mathsf{sba}}$) via an iterative process. Our proof consists of the following four main steps.

1. First, we prove that $G_{\mathsf{cfa}}(L(\eta_{\mathsf{sba}}, \sigma_{\mathsf{sba}})) \sqsubseteq L(\eta_{\mathsf{sba}}, \sigma_{\mathsf{sba}})$. That is, $L(\eta_{\mathsf{sba}}, \sigma_{\mathsf{sba}})$ is a pre-fixpoint of G_{cfa}. This implies

$$\kappa_{\mathsf{cfa}} \sqsubseteq L(\eta_{\mathsf{sba}}, \sigma_{\mathsf{sba}}), \tag{4}$$

a half of the conclusion in the Correspondence Theorem. To see this implication, note that the function G_{cfa} is monotone and works on a complete lattice, and the analysis computes the least fixpoint κ_{cfa} of G_{cfa}. According to the standard result, the least fixpoint is also the least pre-fixpoint, so κ_{cfa} is less than or equal to another pre-fixpoint $L(\eta_{\mathsf{sba}}, \sigma_{\mathsf{sba}})$.

2. We next construct another translation, denoted η_{cfa}, this time from the result of the ∞-CFA analysis: $\eta_{\mathsf{cfa}} = \lambda(m, \pi). \kappa_{\mathsf{cfa}}(entry(m), \pi)$. Then, we show

$$\sigma_{\mathsf{sba}} \sqsubseteq R(\eta_{\mathsf{cfa}}, \kappa_{\mathsf{cfa}}). \tag{5}$$

The proof of this inequality uses our new technique for verifying that an SBA annotation overapproximates σ_{sba}, a pre-fixpoint of a non-monotone function G_{sba}. We will explain this technique at the end of this subsection.

3. Third, we apply Lemma 1 to the inequality in (5), combine the result of this application with (4), and derive

$$L(\eta_{\mathsf{cfa}}, \sigma_{\mathsf{sba}}) \sqsubseteq \kappa_{\mathsf{cfa}} \sqsubseteq L(\eta_{\mathsf{sba}}, \sigma_{\mathsf{sba}}). \tag{6}$$

4. Finally, using the relationship between σ_{sba} and κ_{cfa} in (6), we show that $\eta_{\mathsf{cfa}} = \eta_{\mathsf{sba}}$. Note that conjoined with the same relationship again, this equality entails $L(\eta_{\mathsf{sba}}, \sigma_{\mathsf{sba}}) = \kappa_{\mathsf{cfa}}$, the claim of the Correspondence theorem.

Before finishing, let us explain a proof technique used in the second step. An SBA annotation σ is **monotone** if $\forall p, \tau, \tau' : \tau \sqsubseteq \tau' \implies \sigma(p, \tau) \sqsubseteq \sigma(p, \tau')$. Our proof technique is summarised in the following lemma:

Lemma 3. *For all SBA annotations σ, if σ is monotone, $G_{\mathsf{sba}}(\sigma) \sqsubseteq \sigma$ and*

$$\forall m : \tau \sqsubseteq \sigma(entry(m), \tau), \tag{7}$$

then $\sigma_{\mathsf{sba}} \sqsubseteq \sigma$.

We remind the reader that if G_{sba} is a monotone function and σ_{sba} is its least fixpoint, we do not need the monotonicity of σ and the condition in (7) in the lemma. In this case, $\sigma_{\mathsf{sba}} \sqsubseteq \sigma$ even without these conditions. This lemma extends this result to the non-monotone case, and identifies additional conditions.

The conclusion of the second step in our overview above is obtained using Lemma 3. In that step, we prove that (1) $R(\eta_{\mathsf{cfa}}, \kappa_{\mathsf{cfa}})$ is *monotone*; (2) it is a pre-fixpoint of G_{sba}; (3) it satisfies the condition in (7). Hence, Lemma 3 applies, and gives $\sigma_{\mathsf{sba}} \sqsubseteq R(\eta_{\mathsf{cfa}}, \kappa_{\mathsf{cfa}})$.

A final comment is that when the abstract domain of a static analysis is infinite, if it is a complete lattice, we can still define SBA similar to our current definition. The only change is that the result of SBA, σ_{sba}, is now defined in terms of the limit of a potentially infinite chain (generated by the application of G_{sba} and the least-upper-bound operator for elements at limit ordinals), instead of a finite chain. This new SBA is not necessarily computable, but we can still ask whether its result coincides with that of ∞-CFA. We believe that the answer is yes: most parts of our proof seem to remain valid for this new SBA, while the remaining parts (notably the proof of Lemma 3) can be modified relatively easily to accommodate this new SBA. This new Coincidence theorem, however, is limited; it does not say anything about analyses with widening.

4   Application to Pointer Analysis

We now show how to apply the summary-based approach to a pointer analysis for object-oriented programs, which also computes the program's call graph.

The input to the analysis is a program in the form of an interprocedural control flow graph (defined in Section 3.1). Figure 6 shows the kinds of statements it considers: atomic commands that create, read, and write pointer locations, via local variables v, global variables (i.e., static fields) g, and object fields (i.e., instance fields) f. We label each allocation site with a unique label h. We elide statements that operate on non-pointer data as they have no effect on our analysis. For brevity we presume that method calls are non-static and have a lone argument, which serves as the receiver, and a lone return result. We use functions arg and ret to obtain the formal argument and return variable, respectively, of each method. Finally, our analysis exploits type information and uses function

(allocation site)	$h \in \mathbf{H}$	(subtypes)	$sub \in \mathbf{T} \to \mathcal{P}(\mathbf{T})$
(local variable)	$v \in \mathbf{V}$	(class hierarchy analysis)	$cha \in (\mathbf{M} \times \mathbf{T}) \to \mathbf{M}$
(global variable)	$g \in \mathbf{G}$	(method argument)	$arg \in \mathbf{M} \to \mathbf{V}$
(object field)	$f \in \mathbf{F}$	(method result)	$ret \in \mathbf{M} \to \mathbf{V}$
(class type)	$t \in \mathbf{T}$	(abstract contexts)	$\Gamma = \mathbf{V} \to \mathcal{P}(\mathbf{H})$
(atomic command)	$a ::= v = null \mid$	(points-to of locals)	$\mathsf{ptsV} \in \mathbf{V} \to \mathcal{P}(\mathbf{H})$

$v = new\ h \mid v = (t)\ v' \mid g = v \mid$ 　(points-to of globals)　$\mathsf{ptsG} \in \mathbf{G} \to \mathcal{P}(\mathbf{H})$
$v = g \mid v.f = v' \mid v' = v.f$ 　(points-to of fields)　$\mathsf{ptsF} \in (\mathbf{H} \times \mathbf{F}) \to \mathcal{P}(\mathbf{H})$
　(method call)　$i ::= v' = v.m()$ 　(call graph)　$\mathsf{cg} \subseteq (\Gamma \times \mathbf{E} \times \Gamma \times \mathbf{M})$
(allocation type) $type \in \mathbf{H} \to \mathbf{T}$

Fig. 6. Data for our pointer analysis

$$[\![v = null]\!](\mathsf{ptsV}) = \mathsf{ptsV}[v \mapsto \emptyset] \tag{8}$$

$$[\![v = new\ h]\!](\mathsf{ptsV}) = \mathsf{ptsV}[v \mapsto \{\,h\,\}] \tag{9}$$

$$[\![g = v]\!](\mathsf{ptsV}) = \mathsf{ptsV} \tag{10}$$

$$[\![v.f = v']\!](\mathsf{ptsV}) = \mathsf{ptsV} \tag{11}$$

$$[\![v' = (t)\ v]\!](\mathsf{ptsV}) = \mathsf{ptsV}[v' \mapsto \{\,h \in \mathsf{ptsV}(v) \mid type(h) \in sub(t)\,\}] \tag{12}$$

$$[\![v = g]\!](\mathsf{ptsV}) = \mathsf{ptsV}[v \mapsto \mathsf{ptsG}(g)] \tag{13}$$

$$[\![v' = v.f]\!](\mathsf{ptsV}) = \mathsf{ptsV}[v' \mapsto \bigcup\{\mathsf{ptsF}(h,f) \mid h \in \mathsf{ptsV}(v)\}] \tag{14}$$

$$calls(v' = v.m(), \mathsf{ptsV}) = \{\,cha(m, type(h)) \mid h \in \mathsf{ptsV}(v)\,\} \tag{15}$$

$$[\![g = v]\!](\mathsf{ptsG}) = \lambda g'.\ \text{if}\ (g' = g)\ \text{then}\ (\mathsf{ptsG}(g) \cup \mathsf{ptsV}(v))\ \text{else}\ \mathsf{ptsG}(g) \tag{16}$$

$$[\![v.f = v']\!](\mathsf{ptsF}) = \lambda(h, f').\ \text{if}\ (h \in \mathsf{ptsV}(v) \wedge f' = f) \tag{17}$$
$$\text{then}\ (\mathsf{ptsF}(h, f') \cup \mathsf{ptsV}(v'))\ \text{else}\ \mathsf{ptsF}(h, f')$$

Fig. 7. Transfer functions for our pointer analysis

type to obtain the type of objects allocated at each site, function *sub* to find all the subtypes of a type, and function $cha(m, t)$ to obtain the target method of calling method m on a receiver object of run-time type t.

We specify the analysis in terms of the data $(\mathbf{\Gamma}, \tau_{init}, [\![\_]\!], calls)$ in Section 3. Abstract states $\tau \in \mathbf{\Gamma}$ in our analysis are abstract environments ptsV that track points-to sets of locals. Our analysis uses allocation sites for abstract memory locations. Thus, points-to sets are sets of allocation sites. The lattice operations are standard, for instance, the join operation takes the pointwise union of points-to sets: $\bigsqcup \{\mathsf{ptsV}_1, ..., \mathsf{ptsV}_n\} = \lambda v. \bigcup_{i=1}^n \mathsf{ptsV}_i(v)$. The second component τ_{init} is the abstract environment $\lambda v.\emptyset$ which initializes all locals to empty points-to sets. The remaining two components $[\![\_]\!]$ and *calls* are shown in Figure 7. We elaborate upon them next. Equations (8)–(14) show the effect of each statement on points-to sets of locals. We explain the most interesting ones. Equation (12) states that cast statement $v' = (t)\ v$ sets the points-to set of local v' after the statement to those allocation sites in the points-to set of v before the statement that are subtypes of t. Equations (13) and (14) are transfer functions for statements that read globals and fields. Since ptsV tracks points-to information only for locals, we use separate data ptsG and ptsF to track points-to information for globals and fields, respectively. These data are updated by transfer functions for statements that write globals and fields, shown in Equations (16) and (17). Since the transfer functions both read and write data ptsG and ptsF, the algorithm for our combined points-to and call graph analysis has an outer loop that calls the SBA algorithm from Section 3 until ptsG and ptsF reach a fixpoint, starting with empty data for them in the initial iteration, $\lambda g.\emptyset$ and $\lambda(h, f).\emptyset$. This outer loop implements a form of the reduced product [CC79] of our flow-sensitive points-to analysis for locals and the flow-insensitive analysis for globals and fields.[2] It is easy to see that the resulting algorithm terminates as $\mathbf{\Gamma}$ is finite.

Finally, in addition to points-to information, our analysis produces a context sensitive call graph, denoted by a set cg containing each tuple (τ_1, e, τ_2, m) such that the call at control-flow edge e in context τ_1 of its containing method may call the target method m in context τ_2. It is straightforward to compute this information by instrumenting the SBA algorithm to add tuple (τ_1, e, τ_2, m) to cg whenever it visits a call site e in context τ_1 and computes a target method m and a target context τ_2.

5   Empirical Evaluation

We evaluated various interprocedural approaches on our pointer analysis using ten Java programs from the DaCapo benchmark suite (`http://dacapobench.org`), shown in Table 1. All experiments were done using Oracle HotSpot JVM 1.6.0 on a Linux machine with 32GB RAM and AMD Opteron 3.0GHz processor. We also measured the precision of these approaches on three different clients of the pointer analysis. We implemented all our approaches and clients using the Chord

---

[2] We used flow-insensitive analysis for globals and fields to ensure soundness under concurrency—many programs in our experiments are concurrent.

Table 1. Program statistics by flow and context insensitive call graph analysis ($0CFA_I$)

	brief description	classes		methods		bytecode (KB)		KLOC	
		app	total	app	total	app	total	app	total
antlr	parser/translator generator	109	1,091	873	7,220	81	467	26	224
avrora	microcontroller simulator/analyzer	78	1,062	523	6,905	35	423	16	214
bloat	bytecode optimization/analysis tool	277	1,269	2,651	9,133	195	586	59	258
chart	graph plotting tool and pdf renderer	181	1,756	1,461	11,450	101	778	53	366
hsqldb	SQL relational database engine	189	1,341	2,441	10,223	190	670	96	322
luindex	text indexing tool	193	1,175	1,316	7,741	99	487	38	237
lusearch	text search tool	173	1,157	1,119	7,601	77	477	33	231
pmd	Java source code analyzer	348	1,357	2,590	9,105	186	578	46	247
sunflow	photo-realistic rendering system	165	1,894	1,328	13,356	117	934	25	419
xalan	XSLT processor to transform XML	42	1,036	372	6,772	28	417	9	208

program analysis platform for Java bytecode (http://jchord.googlecode.com). We next describe the various approaches and clients.

Interprocedural Approaches. The approaches we evaluated are shown in Table 2. They differ in three aspects: (i) the kind of implementation (tabulation algorithm from [RHS95] called RHS for short vs. BDD); (ii) the degree of call-strings context sensitivity (i.e., the value of k); and (iii) flow sensitive vs. flow insensitive tracking of points-to information for locals. The approach in Section 4 is the most precise one, SBA_S. It is a non-distributive summary-based approach that yields unbounded k-CFA context sensitivity, tracks points-to information of locals flow sensitively, and does heap updates context sensitively. It is implemented using RHS. Doing context sensitive heap updates entails SBA_S calling the tabulation algorithm repeatedly in an outer loop that iterates until points-to information for globals and fields reaches a fixpoint (each iteration of this outer loop itself executes an inner loop—an invocation of the tabulation algorithm—that iterates until points-to information for locals reaches a fixpoint). We confirmed that the non-distributive aspect (i.e., the lossy join) is critical to the performance of our RHS implementation: *it ran out of memory on all our benchmarks without lossy join*. In fact, the lossy join even obviated the need for other optimizations in our RHS implementation, barring only the use of bitsets to represent points-to sets.

It is easy to derive the remaining approaches in Table 2 from SBA_S. $0CFA_S$ is the context insensitive version of SBA_S. It also uses the RHS implementation and leverages the flow sensitive tracking of points-to information of locals in the tabulation algorithm. We could not scale the RHS implementation to simulate k-CFA for $k > 0$. Hence, our evaluation includes a non-RHS implementation: an optimized BDD-based one that tracks points-to information of locals flow insensitively but allows us to do bounded context sensitive k-CFA for $k > 0$. Even this optimized implementation, however, ran out of memory on all our benchmarks beyond $k = 2$. Nevertheless, using it up to $k = 2$ enables us to gauge the precision and performance of a state-of-the-art bounded k-CFA approach.

Table 2. Interprocedural approaches evaluated in our experiments

	kind of implementation	context sensitivity degree (k)	flow sensitivity for locals?
SBA_S	RHS	∞	yes
$0CFA_S$	RHS	0	yes
$kCFA_I$	BDD	0,1,2	no

To summarize, the relative precision of the approaches we evaluate is: $SBA_S \preceq$ $0CFA_S \preceq 0CFA_I$ and $SBA_S \preceq 2CFA_I \preceq 1CFA_I \preceq 0CFA_I$. In particular, the only incomparable pairs are $(0CFA_S, 1CFA_I)$ and $(0CFA_S, 2CFA_I)$.

Pointer Analysis Clients. We built three clients that use the result of our pointer analysis: downcast safety, call graph reachability, and monomorphic call site inference. The result used by these clients is the context sensitive call graph, $cg \subseteq (\mathbf{C} \times \mathbf{E} \times \mathbf{C} \times \mathbf{M})$, and context sensitive points-to sets of locals at each program point, $pts \in (\mathbf{N} \times \mathbf{C}) \to \mathbf{\Gamma}$, where contexts $c \in \mathbf{C}$ are abstract environments (in domain $\mathbf{\Gamma}$) for the SBA_* approaches and bounded call strings (in domain $\mathbf{\Pi}$) for the CFA_* approaches. The above result signatures are the most general, for instance, a context insensitive approach like $0CFA_I$ may use a degenerate $\mathbf{C}$ containing a single context, and a flow insensitive approach like $kCFA_I$ may ignore program point n in $pts(n, c)$, giving the same points-to information at all program points for a local variable of a method under context c. We next formally describe our three clients using the above results.

Downcast Safety. This client statically checks the safety of downcasts. A safe downcast is one that cannot fail because the object to which it is applied is guaranteed to be a subtype of the target type. Thus, safe downcasts obviate the need for run-time cast checking. We define this client in terms of the downcast predicate: $downcast(e) \iff \exists c : \{ type(h) \mid h \in pts(n, c)(v) \} \not\subseteq sub(t)$, where the command at control-flow edge e with $origin(e) = n$ is a cast statement $v' = (t) \, v$. The predicate checks if the type of some allocation site in the points-to set of v is not a subtype of the target type t. Each query to this client is a cast statement at e in the program. It is proven by an analysis if $downcast(e)$ evaluates to false using points-to information pts computed by the analysis.

Call Graph Reachability. This client determines pairwise reachability between every pair of methods. The motivation is that the different approaches in Table 2 may not differ much in broad statistics about the size of the call graph they produce, such as the number of reachable methods, but they can differ dramatically in the number of paths in the graph. This metric in turn may significantly impact the precision of call graph clients.

We define this client in terms of the reach predicate:

$reach(m, m') \iff \exists c, e, c' : method(e) = m \land (c, e, c', m') \in R,$
(where $R = \mathsf{leastFix} \, \lambda X. (cg \cup \{(c, e, c'', m) \mid \exists c', m', e' : method(e') = m' \land$
$(c, e, c', m') \in X \land (c', e', c'', m) \in cg\}))$.

The above predicate is true if there exists a path in the context sensitive call graph from m to m'. The existence of such a path means that it may be possible

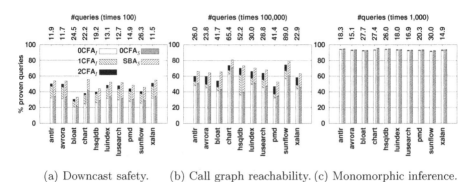

(a) Downcast safety.   (b) Call graph reachability. (c) Monomorphic inference.

Fig. 8. Precision of various interprocedural approaches on clients of pointer analysis

Table 3. Statistics of call graphs computed by various interprocedural approaches

		antlr	avrora	bloat	chart	hsqldb	luindex	lusearch	pmd	sunflow	xalan
	$0CFA_I$	26,871	25,427	42,766	41,655	38,703	28,064	27,978	32,447	49,502	25,037
number of edges	$1CFA_I$	95.8	96.3	96.4	96.0	92.5	96.3	96.7	96.8	94.2	96.3
in call graph	$2CFA_I$	93.6	93.9	94.7	94.6	90.8	94.0	94.3	94.7	91.7	93.8
as % of $0CFA_I$	$0CFA_S$	98.0	98.6	98.6	81.3	97.2	98.7	98.7	98.2	95.6	98.6
	SBA_S	91.4	91.5	92.4	75.8	87.4	91.9	91.6	91.9	86.8	91.5
	$0CFA_I$	7,220	6,905	9,133	11,450	10,223	7,741	7,601	9,105	13,356	6,772
number of	$1CFA_I$	98.7	99.0	99.1	99.0	99.1	99.0	99.1	99.2	99.2	99.0
reachable methods	$2CFA_I$	98.0	98.3	98.6	98.6	98.5	98.4	98.4	98.7	98.6	98.3
as % of $0CFA_I$	$0CFA_S$	98.9	99.2	99.2	81.8	98.1	99.3	99.3	99.1	95.9	99.2
	SBA_S	96.8	97.1	97.3	80.3	96.6	97.3	97.3	97.4	94.4	97.1
total # contexts	$1CFA_I$	5.3	5.1	6.9	5.2	5.1	5.1	5.1	5.0	4.9	5.1
total # methods	$2CFA_I$	41.9	41.8	54.6	35.7	34.3	38.8	39.9	35.9	31.5	42.4
	SBA_S	6.7	6.4	9.9	7.2	6.6	6.4	6.2	6.8	7.4	6.4

to invoke m' while m is on the call stack, either directly or transitively from a call site in the body m. Each query to this client is a pair of methods (m, m') in the program. This query is proven by an analysis if $\mathsf{reach}(m, m')$ evaluates to false using the call graph cg computed by that analysis—no path exists from m to m' in the graph.

Monomorphic Call Inference. Monomorphic call sites are dynamically dispatched call sites with at most one target method. They can be transformed into statically dispatched ones that are cheaper to run. We define a client to statically infer such sites, in terms of the $\mathsf{polycall}$ predicate: $\mathsf{polycall}(e) \iff |\{ m \mid \exists c, c' : (c, e, c', m) \in \mathsf{cg}\}| > 1$, where the command at control-flow edge e is a dynamically dispatching call. Each query to this client is a dynamically dispatched call site e in the program. The query is proven by an analysis if $\mathsf{polycall}(e)$ evaluates to false using call graph cg computed by that analysis.

We next summarize our evaluation results, including precision, interesting statistics, and scalability of the various approaches on our pointer analysis and its three clients described above.

Table 4. Running time of pointer analysis using various approaches

	antlr	avrora	bloat	chart	hsqldb	luindex	lusearch	pmd	sunflow	xalan
0CFA$_I$	1m45s	1m42s	3m10s	4m40s	3m29s	2m34s	2m22s	3m52s	5m00s	2m32s
1CFA$_I$	40m	38m	82m	121m	74m	41m	43m	61m	148m	36m
2CFA$_I$	72m	68m	239m	256m	158m	83m	80m	112m	279m	82m
0CFA$_S$	23m	26m	38m	30m	34m	35m	24m	34m	58m	23m
SBA$_S$	21m	17m	60m	51m	37m	27m	16m	29m	72m	16m

Precision on Clients. Figure 8 shows the precision of the approaches on the three clients. We measure the precision of an approach on a client in terms of how many queries posed by the client can be proven by the approach on each benchmark. The total number of queries is shown at the top. For instance, for antlr, there are 11.9×10^2 queries by the downcast safety client.

The stacked bars in the plots show the fraction of queries proven by the various approaches. We use separate bars for the flow-insensitive and flow-sensitive approaches, and vary only the degree of context sensitivity within each bar. At the base of each kind of bar is the fraction of queries proven by the context insensitive approaches (0CFA$_I$ and 0CFA$_S$). The bars stacked above them denote fractions of queries proven exclusively by the indicated context sensitive approaches. For instance, for the downcast safety client on antlr, the left bar shows that 0CFA$_I$ proves 32% queries, 1CFA$_I$ proves an additional 15% queries (for a total of 47% proven queries), and 2CFA$_I$ proves another 3% queries (for a total of 50% proven queries). The right bar shows that 0CFA$_S$ proves 34% queries, and SBA$_S$ proves an additional 20% queries (for a total of 54% proven queries). We next briefly summarize the results.

The SBA$_S$ approach is theoretically the most precise of all five approaches. Compared to the next most precise approach 2CFA$_I$, it proves 12% more downcast safety queries on average per benchmark, and 9% more call graph reachability queries, but only 0.6% more monomorphic call site inference queries. The largest gain of SBA$_S$ over 2CFA$_I$ is 21.3%, and occurs on bloat for the call graph reachability client. The relatively lower benefit of increased context sensitivity for the monomorphic call site inference client is because the context insensitive approaches are themselves able to prove over 90% of the queries by this client on each benchmark. We also observe that 0CFA$_S$ proves only slightly more queries than 0CFA$_I$ for each client on each benchmark, suggesting that flow sensitivity is ineffective without an accompanying increase in context sensitivity. In particular, with the exception of chart, 0CFA$_S$ proves less queries than 1CFA$_I$.

Call Graph Statistics. We found it instructive to study various statistics of the call graphs computed by the different approaches. The first two sets of rows in Table 3 show the number of reachable methods and the number of edges in the call graphs computed by the different approaches. Both decrease with an increase in the precision of the approach, as expected. But the reduction is much smaller compared to that in the number of unproven queries for the call graph reachability client, shown in Figure 8(b). An unproven $reach(m, m')$ query indicates the presence of one or more paths in the call graph from m to m' and the higher the number of such unproven queries, the higher the number of paths in the call graph. The average reduction in the number of such unproven queries from $0CFA_I$ to SBA_S is 41%, but the corresponding average reduction in the number of call graph edges is only 10.8%, and that in the number of reachable methods is even smaller, at 4.8%. From these numbers, we conclude that the various approaches do not differ much in coarse-grained statistics of the call graphs they produce (e.g., the number of reachable methods) but they can differ dramatically in finer-grained statistics (e.g., the number of paths), which in turn can greatly impact the precision of certain clients.

Scalability. Lastly, we compare the scalability of the different approaches. Table 4 shows their running time on our pointer analysis, exclusive of the clients' running time which is negligible. The running time increases from $0CFA_I$ to $2CFA_I$ with large differences between the different flow insensitive approaches. The similar running times of $0CFA_S$ and SBA_S is because of the use of the tabulation algorithm with almost identical implementation for both. Finally, SBA_S runs much faster than $2CFA_I$ on all benchmarks.

The improved performance of SBA_S over $2CFA_I$ can be explained by the ratio of the number of contexts to that of reachable methods computed by each approach. This ratio is shown in the bottom set of rows in Table 3 for $1CFA_I$, $2CFA_I$, and SBA_S. (It is not shown for context insensitive approaches $0CFA_I$ and $0CFA_S$ as it is the constant 1 for them.) These numbers elicit two key observations. First, the rate at which the ratio increases as we go from $0CFA_I$ to $2CFA_I$ suggests that call-strings approaches with $k \geq 3$ run out of memory by computing too many contexts. Second, $2CFA_I$ computes almost 4X-7X more contexts per method than SBA_S on each benchmark, implying that the summary-based approach used in SBA_S is able to merge many call-string contexts.

The primary purpose of the empirical evaluation in this work was to determine how precise k-CFA can get using arbitrary k. The proof of equivalence between ∞-CFA and SBA enabled us to use SBA_S for this evaluation. However, other works [MRR05, LH08] have shown that, in practice, using *object-sensitivity* [MRR02, SBL11] to distinguish calling contexts for object-oriented programs is more precise and scalable than k-CFA. Though call string and object-sensitive contexts are incomparable in theory, an interesting empirical evaluation in future work would be to compare the precision of ∞-CFA with analyses using object-sensitive contexts.

6   Related Work

This section relates our work to existing equivalence results, work on summary-based approaches, and work on cloning-based approaches of which call-strings approaches are an instance.

Equivalence Results. Sharir and Pnueli [SP81] prove that the summary-based and call-strings approaches are equivalent in the finite, distributive setting. They provide constructive algorithms for both approaches in this setting: an iterative fixpoint algorithm for the summary-based approach and an algorithm to obtain a finite bound on the lengths of call strings to be computed for the call-strings approach. They prove each of these algorithms equivalent to the meet-over-all-valid-paths (MVP) solution (see Corollary 3.5 and Theorem 5.4 in [SP81]). Their equivalence proof thus relies on the distributivity assumption. Our work can be viewed as an extension of their result to the more general non-distributive setting. Also, they do not provide any empirical results, whereas we measure the precision and scalability of both approaches on a widely-used pointer analysis, using real-world programs and clients.

For points-to analyses, Grove and Chambers [GC01] conjectured that Agesen's Cartesian Product Algorithm (CPA) [Age95] is strictly more precise than ∞-CFA, and that SBA(which they refer as SCS for Simple Class Set)has the same precision as ∞-CFA. The first conjecture was shown to be true by Besson [Bes09] while we proved that the second conjecture also holds in this work.

Might et al. [MSH10] show the equivalence between k-CFA in the object-oriented and functional paradigms. The treatment of objects vs. closures in the two paradigms causes the same k-CFA algorithm to be polynomial in program size in the object-oriented paradigm but EXPTIME-complete in the functional paradigm. Our work is orthogonal to theirs. Specifically, our formal setting is agnostic to language features, assuming only a finite abstract domain Γ and monotone transfer functions $[\![\_]\!]$, and indeed instantiating these differently for different language features can cause the k-CFA algorithm to have different complexity.

Summary-Based Interprocedural Analysis. Sharir and Pnueli [SP81] first proposed using functional summaries to solve interprocedural dataflow problems precisely. Later, Reps et al. [RHS95] proposed an efficient quadratic representation of functional summaries for finite, distributive dataflow problems, and the tabulation algorithm based on CFL-reachability to solve them in cubic time. More recent works have applied the tabulation algorithm in non-distributive settings, ranging from doing a fully lossy join to a partial join to a lossless join. All these settings besides lossy join are challenging to scale, and either use symbolic representations (e.g., BDDs in [BR01]) to compactly represent multiple abstract states, or share common parts of multiple abstract states without losing precision (e.g., [YLB+08, MSRF04]) or at the expense of precision (e.g., [BPR01]). Summary-based approaches like CFA2 [VS10] have also been proposed for functional languages to perform fully context-sensitive control-flow analysis. Our work is motivated by the desire to understand the formal relationship between the widely-used summary-based approach in non-distributive settings and the call-strings approach, which is also prevalent as we survey next.

Cloning-Based Interprocedural Analysis. There is a large body of work on bounded call-string-like approaches that we collectively call *cloning-based* approaches. Besides k-CFA [Shi88], another popular approach is *k-object sensitive analysis* for object-oriented programs [MRR02, SBL11]. Many recent works express cloning-based pointer analyses in Datalog and solve them using specialized Datalog solvers [Wha07, BS09]. These solvers exploit redundancy arising from large numbers of similar contexts computed by these approaches for high k values. They either use BDDs [BLQ+03, WL04, ZC04] or explicit representations from the databases literature [BS09] for this purpose. Most cloning-based approaches approximate recursion in an ad hoc manner. An exception is the work of Khedker et al. [KMR12, KK08] which maintains a single representative call string for each equivalence class. Unlike the above approaches, it does not approximate recursion in an ad hoc manner, and yet it is efficient in practice by avoiding the computation of redundant call-string contexts. Our pointer analysis achieves a similar effect but by using the tabulation algorithm.

7   Conclusion

We showed the equivalence between the summary-based and unbounded call-strings approaches to interprocedural analysis, in the presence of a lossy join. Our result extends the formal relationship between these approaches to a setting more general than the distributive case in which this result was previously proven. We presented new implications of our result to the theory and practice of interprocedural analysis. On the theoretical side, we introduced new proof techniques that enable to reason about relationships that do not hold between two fixpoint computations at each step, but do so when a form of garbage collection is applied to the final results of those computations. On the practical side, we empirically compared the summary-based and bounded call-strings approaches on a widely-used pointer analysis with a lossy join. We found the summary-based approach on this analysis is more scalable while providing the same precision as the unbounded call-strings approach.

Acknowledgement. We thank the anonymous reviewers for insightful comments. This work was supported by DARPA under agreement #FA8750-12-2-0020, NSF award #1253867, gifts from Google and Microsoft, and EPSRC. The U.S. Government is authorized to reproduce and distribute reprints for Governmental purposes notwithstanding any copyright notation thereon.

References

[Age95]   Agesen, O.: The cartesian product algorithm. In: Olthoff, W. (ed.) ECOOP 1995. LNCS, vol. 952, pp. 2–26. Springer, Heidelberg (1995)

[Bes09]   Besson, F.: CPA beats ∞-CFA. In: FTfJP (2009)

[BLQ+03]   Berndl, M., Lhoták, O., Qian, F., Hendren, L., Umanee, N.: Points-to analysis using BDDs. In: PLDI (2003)

[BPR01]   Ball, T., Podelski, A., Rajamani, S.K.: Boolean and cartesian abstraction for model checking C programs. In: Margaria, T., Yi, W. (eds.) TACAS 2001. LNCS, vol. 2031, pp. 268–283. Springer, Heidelberg (2001)

[BR01]   Ball, T., Rajamani, S.: Bebop: a path-sensitive interprocedural dataflow engine. In: PASTE (2001)

[BS09]   Bravenboer, M., Smaragdakis, Y.: Strictly declarative specification of sophisticated points-to analyses. In: OOPSLA (2009)

[CC79]   Cousot, P., Cousot, R.: Systematic design of program analysis frameworks. In: POPL (1979)

[CC92]   Cousot, P., Cousot, R.: Abstract interpretation frameworks. Journal of Logic and Computation 2(4) (1992)

[FYD+08]   Fink, S., Yahav, E., Dor, N., Ramalingam, G., Geay, E.: Effective typestate verification in the presence of aliasing. ACM TOSEM 17(2) (2008)

[GC01]   Grove, D., Chambers, C.: A framework for call graph construction algorithms. ACM TOPLAS 23(6) (2001)

[KK08]   Khedker, U.P., Karkare, B.: Efficiency, precision, simplicity, and generality in interprocedural dataflow analysis: Resurrecting the classical call strings method. In: Hendren, L. (ed.) CC 2008. LNCS, vol. 4959, pp. 213–228. Springer, Heidelberg (2008)

[KMR12]   Khedker, U.P., Mycroft, A., Rawat, P.S.: Liveness-based pointer analysis. In: Miné, A., Schmidt, D. (eds.) SAS 2012. LNCS, vol. 7460, pp. 265–282. Springer, Heidelberg (2012)

[LH08]   Lhoták, O., Hendren, L.: Evaluating the benefits of context-sensitive points-to analysis using a BDD-based implementation. ACM TOSEM 18(1) (2008)

[Min06]   Miné, A.: The octagon abstract domain. Higher-Order and Symbolic Computation 19(1) (2006)

[MRR02]   Milanova, A., Rountev, A., Ryder, B.: Parameterized object sensitivity for points-to and side-effect analyses for Java. In: ISSTA (2002)

[MRR05]   Milanova, A., Rountev, A., Ryder, B.G.: Parameterized object sensitivity for points-to analysis for Java. ACM TOSEM 14(1) (2005)

[MSH10]   Might, M., Smaragdakis, Y., Horn, D.: Resolving and exploiting the k-CFA paradox: illuminating functional vs. oo program analysis. In: PLDI (2010)

[MSRF04]   Manevich, R., Sagiv, M., Ramalingam, G., Field, J.: Partially disjunctive heap abstraction. In: Giacobazzi, R. (ed.) SAS 2004. LNCS, vol. 3148, pp. 265–279. Springer, Heidelberg (2004)

[RHS95]   Reps, T., Horwitz, S., Sagiv, M.: Precise interprocedural dataflow analysis via graph reachability. In: POPL (1995)

[SBL11]   Smaragdakis, Y., Bravenboer, M., Lhoták, O.: Pick your contexts well: understanding object-sensitivity. In: POPL (2011)

[Shi88]   Shivers, O.: Control-flow analysis in scheme. In: PLDI (1988)

[SP81]   Sharir, M., Pnueli, A.: Two approaches to interprocedural data flow analysis. In: Program Flow Analysis: Theory and Applications, ch. 7. Prentice-Hall (1981)

[VS10]   Vardoulakis, D., Shivers, O.: CFA2: A Context-Free Approach to Control-Flow Analysis. In: Gordon, A.D. (ed.) ESOP 2010. LNCS, vol. 6012, pp. 570–589. Springer, Heidelberg (2010)

[Wha07]   Whaley, J.: Context-Sensitive Pointer Analysis using Binary Decision Diagrams. PhD thesis, Stanford University (March 2007)

[WL04]   Whaley, J., Lam, M.: Cloning-based context-sensitive pointer alias analysis using binary decision diagrams. In: PLDI (2004)

[YLB+08]   Yang, H., Lee, O., Berdine, J., Calcagno, C., Cook, B., Distefano, D., O'Hearn, P.W.: Scalable shape analysis for systems code. In: Gupta, A., Malik, S. (eds.) CAV 2008. LNCS, vol. 5123, pp. 385–398. Springer, Heidelberg (2008)

[ZC04]   Zhu, J., Calman, S.: Symbolic pointer analysis revisited. In: PLDI (2004)

Targeted Update – Aggressive Memory Abstraction Beyond Common Sense and Its Application on Static Numeric Analysis

Zhoulai Fu[*]

IMDEA Software

Abstract. Summarizing techniques are widely used in the reasoning of unbounded data structures. These techniques prohibit strong update unless certain restricted safety conditions are satisfied. We find that by setting and enforcing the analysis boundaries to a limited scope of program identifiers, called *targets* in this paper, more cases of strong update can be shown sound, not with regard to the entire heap, but with regard to the targets. We have implemented the analysis for inferring numeric properties in Java programs. The experimental results show a tangible precision enhancement compared with classical approaches while preserving a high scalability.

Keywords: abstract interpretation, points-to analysis, abstract numeric domain, abstract semantics, strong update.

1   Introduction

Static analysis of heap-manipulating programs has received much attention due to its fundamental role supporting a growing list of other analyses (Blanchet et al., 2003b; Chen et al., 2003; Fink et al., 2008). *Summarizing* techniques, where the heap is partitioned into finite groups,can manipulate unbounded data structures through *summarized dimensions* (Gopan et al., 2004). These techniques have many possible uses in heap analyses, such as points-to analysis (Emami et al., 1994) and TVLA (Lev-Ami and Sagiv, 2000), and also have been investigated as a basis underpinning the extension of classic numeric abstract domains to pointer-aware programs (Fu, 2013). Most of these analyses follow the *strong/weak update paradigm* (Chase et al., 1990) to model the effects of assignments on summarized dimensions. A strong update overwrites the data that may be accessed with a new value, whereas a weak update adds a new value to the summarized dimensions and preserves their old values. Strong update is desired whenever safe as it provides better precision.

Applying strong update to a summarized dimension requires that it represent a single run-time memory. This requirement poses a difficulty for applying

---

[*] In addition to research facilities granted by IMDEA Software, this work has also received financial support from AX – L'Association des Anciens Élèves et Diplômés de l'École polytechnique at 5, rue Descartes 75005 Paris.

Z. Shao (Ed.): ESOP 2014, LNCS 8410, pp. 534–553, 2014.

strong update as it is usually hard to know the element number represented by a summarized dimension. Efforts have been made to use sophisticated heap disambiguation techniques (Sagiv et al., 1999). While such approaches indeed help to find out more strong update circumstances, many of the proposed algorithms, such as *focus* and *blur* operations in shape analysis, are often hard to implement or come with a considerable complexity overhead.

The paper presents a new memory abstraction that makes strong update possible for summarized dimensions even if they do not necessarily represent a singleton. The approach is called *targeted update*. It extends the traditional notion of soundness in heap analysis by focusing the abstract semantics on a selected set of program identifiers, called *targets*.

Our major finding can be summarized as follows: By focusing on the targets, we are able to perform an aggressive analysis even if the traditional safety condition for strong update fails.

A motivating example. Consider the assignment y.f = 7. Assume that the memory state before the assignment is informally represented in Fig. 1. The two access paths $x.f$ and $y.f$ are of integer type. The two gray clouds denoted by δ_1 and δ_2 represent two disjoint summarized dimensions. They initially store numeric values in the range of $[0,5]$ and $[0,9]$ respectively. An edge from an access path to a cloud indicates a may-access relation.

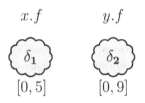

Fig. 1. Memory state before statement y.f = 7

The memory state does not tell which summarized dimension (δ_1 or δ_2) should be updated. In addition, more than one concrete memory cell may be associated with δ_1 or δ_2. Thus, traditional analysis of $y.f = 7$ performs weak update on δ_1 and δ_2. The abstract state after the assignment becomes $\delta_1 \in [0,7] \wedge \delta_2 \in [0,9]$, following which we infer $x.f \in [0,7] \wedge y.f \in [0,9]$. We call this approach *common sense strong/weak update paradigm*.

Now we present the targeted update approach. In this approach, a set of access paths needs to be selected before the analysis. The selected set is called target set. Here, if we set $\{y.f\}$ as target set, we are able to apply strong update on both δ_1 and δ_2. This is because making wrong assertions on the concrete memories of δ_1 or δ_2 that are not pointed to by $y.f$ does not contravene *the soundness with regard to the targets*: The two clouds are at most pointed to by $x.f$ and $y.f$, yet $x.f$ is not a target. The described approach is called *targeted update*. Applying targeted update with target set $\{y.f\}$ allows for precise analysis of $y.f$, but the value of the non-target $x.f$ is not tracked. The obtained $\delta_1 = 7 \wedge \delta_2 = 7$ only infers $y.f = 7$. There is no information concerning $x.f$.

It can be seen that depending on specific analysis requirement, the target set $\{y.f\}$ may not be appropriate. Imagine that we want to verify this post-condition of the statement y.f = 7

$$x.f \in [0,7] \wedge y.f \in [0,7] \tag{1}$$

This property cannot be verified by the strong/weak update paradigm, neither by the targeted update using $\{y.f\}$ as the target set. To use targeted update with the target set $T = \{x.f, y.f\}$ solves the problem. The summarized dimension δ_1 is now pointed to by both targets, and δ_2 by one target. Targeted update weakly updates δ_1 because updating δ_1 has an effect on both $x.f$ and $y.f$ that are targets. It strongly updates δ_2 because it is a region that can only be "observed" from $y.f$: For the concrete memories represented by δ_2 that are not pointed to by $y.f$, nothing is wrong to associate whatever values with δ_2; for the concrete memories represented by δ_2 that are truly pointed to by $y.f$, the values associated with δ_2 due to targeted update are correct. Finally, targeted update obtains $\delta_1 \in [0, 7] \wedge \delta_2 = 7$, from which we infer (1).

In summary, targeted update has only responsibilities for its targets, namely, the objects pointed to by these targets, and it has no obligation to be sound with regard to the entire heap as in the common sense approach. As illustrated by the example, targeted update has two major characteristics: 1) More strong update cases on summarized dimensions can be discovered by targeted update. 2) Picking up right target set is a trade-off problem since targeted update can be very precise for targets, but it does not track non-targets.

This paper makes the following key contributions:

- We introduce the concept of *targets* and formalize the soundness notion with regard to targets (Sect. 3). The crucial insight lies in the fundamental difference of this notion of soundness with that in the common sense strong/weak paradigm.
- We derive an aggressive abstract semantics (Sect. 4 and 5) from the notion of targets. This is made possible due to a simple condition we have discovered that allows *targeted update* to be safely applied. We have formalized and proved the soundness of targeted update.
- Important design choices are discussed in Sect. 6. The implemented analyzer was tested on the SPECjvm98 benchmark suite, composed of 10 real-world Java programs.

2   Preliminaries

This section gives a brief review of some basic concepts from static program analysis that are used in this paper. A companion report of this paper is provided [1] with more details, including the notions of abstract interpretation, the semantics of points-to graph, the resolution of an access path, etc.

General Notations. For a given set U, the notation $U_\perp$ represents the disjoint union $U \cup \{\perp\}$. Given a mapping $m \in A \to B_\perp$, we express the fact that m is undefined in a point x by $m(x) = \perp$. We write $post[m] \in \wp(A) \to \wp(B)$ for the mapping $\lambda A_1.\{b \mid \exists a \in A_1 : m(a) = b\}$.

---

[1] http://hal.inria.fr/hal-00921702/en

Syntactical Notations. The primary data types include scalar numbers in $\mathbb{I}$, where $\mathbb{I}$ can be integers, rationals or reals, and pointers (or references) in *Ref*. The primary syntactical entities include the universe of *local variables* and *fields*. They are denoted by *Var* and *Fld* respectively. An *access path* (Landi and Ryder, 1992) is either a variable or a variable followed by a sequence of fields. The universe of access paths is denoted by *Path*. We subscript Var_τ, Fld_τ, $Path_\tau$ and their elements with $\tau \in \{n, p\}$ to indicate their types as scalar number or reference. We use $\mathtt{Imp}_n$ to refer to the basic statements involving only numeric variables and use the meta-variables s_n to range over these statements. Similarly, we let $\mathtt{Imp}_p$ be the statements that use only pointer variables and let s_p range over these statements. Below we show the main syntactical categories and the meta-variables used in the paper.

$$
\begin{array}{ll}
k \in \mathbb{I} & \text{scalar numbers} \\
r \in Ref & \text{concrete references} \\
x_\tau, y_\tau \in Var_\tau & \text{numeric/pointer variables} \\
f_\tau, g_\tau \in Fld_\tau & \text{numeric/pointer fields} \\
\boldsymbol{u}_\tau, \boldsymbol{v}_\tau \in Path_\tau & \text{numeric/pointer access paths} \\
s_n \in \mathtt{Imp}_n & x_n = k \mid x_n = y_n \mid x_n = y_n \diamond z_n \mid x_n \bowtie y_n \\
s_p \in \mathtt{Imp}_p & x_p = \mathbf{new} \mid x_p = \mathbf{null} \mid x_p = y_p.f_p \mid x_p = y_p \mid x_p.f_p = y_p
\end{array}
$$

where $\diamond \in \{+, -, *, /\}$, and $\bowtie$ is an arithmetic comparison operator.

Analysis of $\mathtt{Imp}_n$. We express a *numeric property* by a conjunction of arithmetic formulae such as $\{x+y \leq 1, x \leq 0\}$. The universe of the numeric properties is denoted by $Num^\sharp$. As usual, an *environment* maps variables to their values. We consider *numeric environments* $Num \triangleq Var_n \to \mathbb{I}_\perp$. The relationship between an environment and a property can be formalized by the relation of *valuation*. We say that $\mathsf{n} \in Num$ is a valuation of $\mathsf{n}^\sharp \in Num^\sharp$, denoted by

$$\mathsf{n} \models \mathsf{n}^\sharp \tag{2}$$

if $\mathsf{n}^\sharp$ becomes a tautology after each of its free variables is replaced by its corresponded value in n. For example, if $\mathsf{n} = \{x \to 7, y \to 7\}$, and $\mathsf{n}^\sharp = \{x + y < 15\}$ then we have $\mathsf{n} \models \mathsf{n}^\sharp$. For each statement s_n of $\mathtt{Imp}_n$, the concrete semantics is given by a standard rule of state transition $\xrightarrow{Num} (s_n) \in Num \to Num$. We write $\sqcup$ and $\triangledown$ for the join and widening operator.

In this paper, we assume that a sound abstract semantics of s_n of signature $\lVert \cdot \rVert_n^\sharp \in \mathtt{Imp}_n \to (Num^\sharp \to Num^\sharp)$ is available to us. The abstract semantics is assumed to be sound with regard to the concrete $\xrightarrow{Num}$: For any n, $\mathsf{n}^\sharp$ and $s_n \in \mathtt{Imp}_n$, $\mathsf{n} \models \mathsf{n}^\sharp \Rightarrow \xrightarrow{Num} (s_n)(\mathsf{n}) \models \lVert s_n \rVert_n^\sharp (\mathsf{n}^\sharp)$.

Analysis of $\mathtt{Imp}_p$. A concrete state in $\mathtt{Imp}_p$ is thought of as a graph-like structure representing the *environment* and *heap*. The universe of the concrete states is denoted by *Pter*. We write p to range over them.

$$\mathsf{p} \in Pter \triangleq (Var_p \to Ref_\perp) \times ((Ref \times Fld_p) \to Ref_\perp) \qquad (3)$$

Points-to analysis is a dataflow analysis for detecting pointer relations. The essential process is to partition Ref into a finite set H and then to summarize the run-time pointer relations via elements of H and program variables. The elements of H are called *allocation sites* or *abstract references*. The process can be interfaced with a function $\triangleright$ called *naming scheme*.

$$\triangleright \in Ref \to H \qquad (4)$$

In this paper, we consider a standard naming scheme that names heap objects after the control points where the objects are allocated. We assume that the naming scheme is flow-independent. That is to say, the analysis of two control branches uses the same naming scheme. Note that this is the case for points-to analysis but not for shape-analysis.

Definition 1 (Interface of traditional points-to analyzer)

$$(\mathtt{Imp}_p, Pter, \xrightarrow{Pter}, Pter^\sharp, \gamma_p, [\![\cdot]\!]_p^\sharp)$$

The universe of the concrete states is denoted by $Pter$, and the concrete transition rule is denoted by $\xrightarrow{Pter} \in \mathtt{Imp}_p \to (Pter \to Pter)$. The universe of the abstract states is denoted by $Pter^\sharp$. We write $\mathsf{p}^\sharp$ to range over them.

$$\mathsf{p}^\sharp \in Pter^\sharp \triangleq (Var_p \to \wp(H)) \times ((H \times Fld_p) \to \wp(H)) \qquad (5)$$

Each abstract state is called a points-to graph. *The* concretization function $\gamma_p : Pter^\sharp \to \wp(Pter)$ *specifies the semantics of points-to graph. The abstract semantics $[\![\cdot]\!]_p^\sharp$ is assumed to be sound with regard to the concrete $\xrightarrow{Pter}$: For any* $\mathsf{p}, \mathsf{p}^\sharp$ *and* $s_p \in \mathtt{Imp}_p$, $\mathsf{p} \models \mathsf{p}^\sharp \Rightarrow \xrightarrow{Pter} (s_p)(\mathsf{p}) \in \gamma_p \circ [\![s_p]\!]_p^\sharp (\mathsf{p}^\sharp)$.

3 Summarizing Technique with Targets

In this section, we introduce the concept of targets and how summarizing technique with targets differs from classic summarizing technique.

The Analyzed Language. This paper focuses on how to deal with language $\mathtt{Imp}_{np}$. The statements in $\mathtt{Imp}_{np}$ include these in $\mathtt{Imp}_n$ and $\mathtt{Imp}_p$, and statements in the forms of $y_p.f_n = x_n$ and $x_n = y_p.f_n$. We write s_{np} to range over $\mathtt{Imp}_{np}$.

$$s_{np} ::= s_n \mid s_p \mid y_p.f_n = x_n \mid x_n = y_p.f_n \qquad (6)$$

We call $y_p.f_n = x_n$ or $y_p.f_n = k$ a *write access* and $x_n = y_p.f_n$ a *read access*.

A Non-standard Concrete Semantics. A concrete state in $\mathtt{Imp}_{np}$ is an environment mapping variables to values and a mapping from fields of references to values. By grouping the numeric and pointer parts, we formalize the universe of the concrete states as

$$State = \overbrace{(Var_n \rightarrow \mathbb{I}_\perp) \times ((Ref \times Fld_n) \rightarrow \mathbb{I}_\perp)}^{Num[\,Var_n \cup (Ref \times Fld_n)\,]} \qquad (7)$$

$$\underbrace{\times\, (Var_p \rightarrow Ref_\perp) \times ((Ref \times Fld_p) \rightarrow Ref_\perp)}_{Pter} \qquad (8)$$

Thus, a state is a pair (n, p) where n can be regarded as a concrete state of $\mathtt{Imp}_n$ over $Var_n \cup (Ref \times Fld_n)$, and p as a concrete state of $\mathtt{Imp}_p$. In the companion report, we express the concrete semantics of $\mathtt{Imp}_{np}$, denoted by $\longrightarrow^\natural$, via $\overset{Num}{\longrightarrow}$ and $\overset{Pter}{\longrightarrow}$.

Example 1 Consider the following program:

```
1              List tmp = null, hd;
2              int idx;
3              for (idx = 0; idx < 3; idx++){
4                  hd = new List();   // allocation site h
5                  hd.val = idx;
6                  hd.next = tmp;
7                  tmp = hd;
8              }
```

The integers $0, 1$ and 2 are stored iteratively on the heap. The head of the list is pointed to by the variable hd. The concrete state at the end of the program can be specified as (n, p). We write r_0, r_1 and r_2 for the concrete memories allocated at allocation site h.

$$\mathsf{n} = \{(r_0, val) \rightarrow 0, (r_1, val) \rightarrow 1, (r_2, val) \rightarrow 2, idx \rightarrow 3\}$$
$$\mathsf{p} = \{hd \rightarrow r_2, tmp \rightarrow r_2, (r_2, next) \rightarrow r_1, (r_1, next) \rightarrow r_0\} \qquad (9)$$

Common Sense Summarizing Technique. A naming scheme $\rhd \in Ref \rightarrow H$ is assumed for the analysis of $\mathtt{Imp}_{np}$. In this context, the idea of summarizing technique is to use the names computed by the naming scheme to create summarized dimensions that represent the numeric values stored on the heap.

Below we show an abstraction of the concrete state (9).

$$(\mathsf{n}^\sharp, \mathsf{p}^\sharp) = \left(\delta_{h,val} \in [0, 2], idx = 3, \qquad hd \longrightarrow h \overset{\curvearrowright}{\bigcirc} next \right) \qquad (10)$$

In this abstraction, the naming scheme maps the concrete r_0, r_1 and r_2 to an abstract reference $h \in H$. We can perform pointer analysis based on the naming scheme and, on the other hand, summarize numeric information on the *val* field of r_0, r_1 and r_2 by a summarized dimension related to h and *val*, denoted by $\delta_{h,val}$. The summarized dimension in this context is an element $H \times Fld_n$.

In the following, we denote $H \times Fld_n$ by Δ, and use δ to range over the pairs in Δ. We also write δ_{h,f_n} to indicate the summarized dimension corresponding to the allocation site h and the field f_n.

Definition 2 *An abstract state is defined to be a pair* $(\mathsf{n}^\sharp, \mathsf{p}^\sharp)$ *of*

$$NumP^\sharp \triangleq Num^\sharp[Var_n \cup \Delta] \times Pter^\sharp \tag{11}$$

where $Num^\sharp[Var_n \cup \Delta]$ *is similar to* $Num^\sharp$, *but defined over* $Var_n \cup \Delta$, *and* $Pter^\sharp$ *is the universe of points-to graphs (Sect. 2).*

The summarizing process can be formalized through the extended naming scheme on $Ref \times Fld_n \to H \times Fld_n$, defined as $\lambda(r, f_n).(\triangleright(r), f_n)$. By abuse of notation, we still write $\triangleright$ for the extended naming scheme. For example, the naming scheme used in (10) satisfies $\triangleright(r_i, f) = \delta_{h,f}$ for $i = 0, 1$ and 2. In (10), $\delta_{h,val} \to [0, 2]$ asserts that its concrete state (n, p) must satisfy

$$\forall(r, val) \in \triangleright^{-1}(\delta_{h,val}) : \mathsf{n}(r, val) \in [0, 2] \tag{12}$$

This is common sense — a summarized dimension represents a set of concrete locations, and the fact over the summarized dimension translates to *all* the heap locations represented by the summarized dimension. Although it seems natural to require (12), we find that this kind of "contract" between the abstract and concrete states can be in some circumstances, too strong to be useful.

Assume that we have an extra statement `hd.val = 0` after l. 8. Imagine that we only want to ensure that *hd.val* becomes 0 after the statement. We cannot update $\delta_{h,val}$ to 0 because that would mean all $(r, val) \in \triangleright^{-1}(\delta_{h,val})$ store the value 0, which is clearly unsound. To make a more precise analysis in this situation, we need to relax the condition (12) so that a fact over a summarized dimension does not always translate to *all* their represented concrete heap locations.

This is where *targeted update* comes in. It allows a subset $S \subseteq \triangleright^{-1}(\delta_{h,val})$ in (12) to be specified so that the abstract semantics only needs to guarantee $\mathsf{n}(r, val) \in [0, 2]$ for (r, val) belonging to the specified subset S.

Targets. In the context of Imp_{np}, a *target set*, or *targets*, is a set of access paths holding numeric values on the heap. These access paths should not be local variables, and may not occur in the analyzed program syntax.

We use two operations on targets: Let t be an access path of a target set, $\mathsf{p} \in Pter$, $d \in Ref \times Fld_n$. Then $d = \mathsf{p}(t)$ reads as t *resolves to* or *points to* d under p. If p has an arc from variable x to r, then $\mathsf{p}(x.f_n) = (r, f_n)$; $\delta \in \mathsf{p}^\sharp(t)$ reads as t *resolves to* or *points to* δ under $\mathsf{p}^\sharp$. For example, in Fig. 1, we have $\mathsf{p}^\sharp(x.f) = \{\delta_1\}$ and $\mathsf{p}^\sharp(y.f) = \{\delta_1, \delta_2\}$. See the companion report for their formal definitions.

Below we write $\mathsf{p} \in \gamma_p(\mathsf{p}^\sharp)$ to denote that p is abstracted by $\mathsf{p}^\sharp$; we write $\mathsf{n} \models [ins]\mathsf{n}^\sharp$ to denote that n is a valuation (the symbol $\models$ is introduced in Sect. 2) of $\mathsf{n}^\sharp$ with its variables substituted following *ins*. For example, let *ins* = $\{\delta_1 \to d_1, \delta_2 \to d_2\}$ and $\mathsf{n}^\sharp = \{\delta_1 + \delta_2 > 0, \delta > 10\}$. Then we have $[ins]\mathsf{n}^\sharp = \{d_1 + d_2 > 0, d_2 > 10\}$.

If a target set is selected and the soundness is enforced with regard to the targets, the abstract state $(\mathsf{n}^\sharp, \mathsf{p}^\sharp)$ represents all concrete states (n, p) as long as p is abstracted by $\mathsf{p}^\sharp$ and n can be abstracted by whatever $\mathsf{n}^{\sharp\prime}$ that is $\mathsf{n}^\sharp$ with its summarizing dimensions $\delta_1, \ldots, \delta_m$ instantiated with some $d_1, \ldots, d_m$ satisfying: For $1 \leq i \leq m$, $\rhd(d_i) = \delta_i$ and d_i can be reached by targets, *i.e.*, $\exists t \in T : d_i = \mathsf{p}(t)$.

Definition 3 *Let T be the target set. The concretization of a state $(\mathsf{n}^\sharp, \mathsf{p}^\sharp) \in NumP^\sharp$ is defined as*

$$\gamma_{\langle T \rangle}(\mathsf{n}^\sharp, \mathsf{p}^\sharp) \triangleq \{(\mathsf{n}, \mathsf{p}) \mid \mathsf{p} \in \gamma_p(\mathsf{p}^\sharp), \forall ins \in Ins_\mathsf{p}\langle T \rangle : \mathsf{n} \models [ins](\mathsf{n}^\sharp)\} \quad (13)$$

with $Ins_\mathsf{p}\langle T \rangle \triangleq \{ins \in \Delta \to D \mid \forall(\delta, d) \in ins : \rhd(d) = \delta \,\wedge\, d \in post[\mathsf{p}](T)\}$. Read it as, an element (n, p) is in the concretization $\gamma_{\langle T \rangle}(\mathsf{n}^\sharp, \mathsf{p}^\sharp)$, if p is in the concretization of $\mathsf{p}^\sharp$, and n is in the concretization of $[ins]\mathsf{n}^\sharp$ where ins is called an instantiation *mapping summarized dimensions to concrete $d \in D$ that are pointed to by the targets T.*

Below, we present the abstract semantics of statements in $\mathtt{Imp}_{np}$, called *targeted update*.

4   Targeted Update — The Case of Write Access $y_p.f_n = x_n$

Algorithm. Targeted update uses two operators: The *local strong update* operator $[\![\delta = x_n]\!]^S$ assigns x_n to δ, regarding x_n and δ as scalar variables. For example, if it is interval domain on which targeted update is built, we have

$$[\![\delta = x_n]\!]^S (\{\delta \in [1, 2], x_n \in [3, 4]\}) = \{\delta \in [3, 4], x_n \in [3, 4]\} \quad (14)$$

Another operator $[\![\delta = x_n]\!]^W$ is called *local weak update* operator. It assigns x_n to δ and then joins the result with its original state, for example,

$$[\![\delta = x_n]\!]^W (\{\delta \in [1, 2], x_n \in [3, 4]\}) = \{\delta \in [1, 4], x_n \in [3, 4]\} \quad (15)$$

It is clear that both operators can be computed from traditional numeric domains.

The input of targeted update is an abstract state $(\mathsf{n}^\sharp, \mathsf{p}^\sharp) \in NumP^\sharp$ and a pre-selected target set T. We do not care about how this set is selected for now. Targeted update first computes the summarized dimensions to which $y_p.f_n$ resolves, namely $\mathsf{p}^\sharp(y_p.f_n)$. Each summarized dimension δ is then treated one by one.[2] If the following condition holds:

$$\delta \text{ is pointed to by no target in } T \backslash \{y_p.f_n\} \quad (TU)$$

---

[2] Dealing with δ in different orders could have an influence on precision, but this point is not studied in the paper.

then local strong update will be performed on δ; otherwise, local weak update has to be performed on δ. The above condition is referred to as (TU) condition subsequently. This algorithm for the abstract semantics is presented in Algo. 1.

Algorithm 1. TARGETED UPDATE FOR $y_p.f_n = x_n$

    Input: Abstract state $(n^\sharp, p^\sharp)$, targets T
    Output: The abstract state after targeted update $[\![y_p.f_n = x_n]\!]^\sharp_{\langle T \rangle}(n^\sharp, p^\sharp)$

1 $n^\sharp{}' \leftarrow n^\sharp$
2 **for** $\delta \in p^\sharp(y_p.f_n)$ **do**
3   **if** *there exists no* $t \in T \backslash \{y_p.f_n\}$ *satisfying* $\delta \in p^\sharp(t)$ **then**
4 | $n^\sharp{}' \leftarrow [\![\delta = x_n]\!]^S(n^\sharp{}')$
5   **else**
6 | $n^\sharp{}' \leftarrow [\![\delta = x_n]\!]^W(n^\sharp{}')$
7   **end if**
8 **end for**
9 **return** $n^\sharp{}', p^\sharp$

Remark 1 Automatically finding targets adapted to specific problem requirements is a problem in itself. In our implementation, we use the *numeric access paths* (excluding scalar variables) that appear syntactically in the program as targets.

Comparison with Strong/Weak Update. Below, we present a case study. It shows how targeted update works and in which way it differs from the common sense strong/weak update paradigm.

Example 2 Assume that a program has three numeric access paths: t, $y_p.f_n$ and s, and there are three summarized dimensions: δ_1, δ_2 and δ_3. Assume that the access paths resolve to summarized dimensions as depicted:

$$\tag{16}$$

namely, $p^\sharp(t) = \{\delta_3\}$, $p^\sharp(y_p.f_n) = \{\delta_1, \delta_2, \delta_3\}$, $p^\sharp(s) = \{\delta_2, \delta_3\}$. We shall compare targeted update and strong/weak update paradigm of $y_p.f_n = x_n$.

The concrete semantics of $y_p.f_n = x_n$ is known: It modifies one element of $d \in \triangleright^{-1}(\delta_1) \cup \triangleright^{-1}(\delta_2) \cup \triangleright^{-1}(\delta_3)$. It is clear that the information from (16) does not help to identify the one among δ_1, δ_2, and δ_3 that will be modified by the statement. In addition, this specific δ may have more than one concrete represented element. Thus, the traditional approach performs weak update which amounts to a conservative join of $[\![\delta_1 = x_n]\!]^W(n^\sharp)$, $[\![\delta_2 = x_n]\!]^W(n^\sharp)$ and $[\![\delta_3 = x_n]\!]^W(n^\sharp)$. Formally, the weak update is defined as

$$\llbracket y_p.f_n = x_n \rrbracket^\sharp (\mathsf{n}^\sharp, \mathsf{p}^\sharp) \triangleq \left(\sqcup_{\delta \in \mathsf{p}^\sharp(y_p.f_n)} \llbracket \delta = x_n \rrbracket^W (\mathsf{n}^\sharp) \right), \mathsf{p}^\sharp \qquad (17)$$

Now, let us consider targeted update. Assume that all three access paths are targets, $T = \{t, y_p.f_n, s\}$. Because only δ_1 satisfies (TU) condition, targeted update abstracts $y_p.f_n = x_n$ as a composition of local weak update of δ_2 and δ_3, and local strong update of δ_1, namely, $\llbracket \delta_3 = x_n \rrbracket^W \circ \llbracket \delta_2 = x_n \rrbracket^W \circ \llbracket \delta_1 = x_n \rrbracket^S$. Formally, we define targeted update as follows.

Definition 4 *Let T be a set of targets, $(\mathsf{n}^\sharp, \mathsf{p}^\sharp) \in NumP^\sharp$. Define the targeted update for $y_p.f_n = x_n$:*

$$\llbracket y_p.f_n = x_n \rrbracket^\sharp_{\langle T \rangle} (\mathsf{n}^\sharp, \mathsf{p}^\sharp) \triangleq \llbracket \delta_1 = x_n \rrbracket^{\eta(\delta_1)} \circ \cdots \circ \llbracket \delta_M = x_n \rrbracket^{\eta(\delta_M)} \mathsf{n}^\sharp, \mathsf{p}^\sharp \qquad (18)$$

with $\{\delta_1, \ldots, \delta_M\} = \mathsf{p}^\sharp(y_p.f_n)$,

$$\eta \triangleq \lambda \delta : \mathsf{p}^\sharp(y_p.f_n). \begin{cases} S & \text{if } \{t \in T \mid t \neq y_p.f_n \wedge \delta \in \mathsf{p}^\sharp(t)\} = \emptyset \\ W & \text{otherwise} \end{cases} \qquad (19)$$

Correctness. The correctness of the abstract semantics can be formalized as follows.

Theorem 1 *Let T be a target set. For any abstract state $(\mathsf{n}^\sharp, \mathsf{p}^\sharp)$ of $NumP^\sharp$ and any $(\mathsf{n}, \mathsf{p}) \in \gamma_{\langle T \rangle}(\mathsf{n}^\sharp, \mathsf{p}^\sharp)$. We have*

$$\longrightarrow^\sharp (y_p.f_n = x_n)(\mathsf{n}, \mathsf{p}) \in \gamma_{\langle T \rangle} \circ \llbracket y_p.f_n = x_n \rrbracket^\sharp_{\langle T \rangle} (\mathsf{n}^\sharp, \mathsf{p}^\sharp) \qquad (20)$$

We need a lemma for the proof. If the (TU) condition holds, the summarized dimension δ specified in the condition is pointed to by at most one target. Observationally, δ is a singleton representing only one object, although δ may represent more than one object that is not necessarily pointed to by targets.

   This intuition is formalized as the lemma below. We write $tu(T, \mathsf{p}^\sharp, y_p.f_n, \delta)$ as a shortcut for (TU), namely $\nexists t \in T \setminus \{y_p.f_n\} : \delta \in \mathsf{p}^\sharp(y_p.f_n)$. The proof of the lemma needs a property as stated of points-to graph: For any concrete p and abstract $\mathsf{p}^\sharp$ such that $\mathsf{p} \in \gamma_p(\mathsf{p}^\sharp)$, if access path $\boldsymbol{u}$ resolves to $d \in Ref \times Fld_n$, i.e. $\mathsf{p}(\boldsymbol{u}) = d$, then we have $\rhd(d) \in \mathsf{p}^\sharp(\boldsymbol{u})$. This property ensures, for example, if $\mathsf{p}(x) = r$ in the concrete, then $\mathsf{p}^\sharp(x)$ has to contain $\rhd(r)$.

Lemma 1 *Assume that $tu(T, \mathsf{p}^\sharp, y_p.f_n, \delta)$ holds. Then, for any $\mathsf{p} \in \gamma_p(\mathsf{p}^\sharp)$ and $ins \in Ins_\mathsf{p}\langle T \rangle$, we have $ins(\delta) = \mathsf{p}(y_p.f_n)$.*

Proof (Proof of Lem. 1) Because $ins \in Ins_\mathsf{p}\langle T \rangle$, we have $ins(\delta)$ must be pointed to by targets in T.

$$ins(\delta) \in \{p(t) \mid t \in T, t \neq y_p.f_n\} \cup \{p(y_p.f_n)\} \tag{21}$$

Condition (TU) combined with the semantics of points-to graph tells that the first part of (21) has to be empty. Otherwise, we have some $t \in T\backslash\{y_p.f_n\}$ pointing to δ, which contradicts $tu(T, p^\sharp, y_p.f_n, \delta)$. By consequence, we have $ins(\delta) = p(y_p.f_n)$. □

This lemma plays a crucial role in proving the correctness of the abstract semantics. We give a proof sketch in the companion report.

5 Targeted Update — The Case of Read Access $x_n = y_p.f_n$, s_n and s_p

We have developed an abstract semantics for the write access statement using the soundness notion with regard to targets. This section presents our abstract semantics for other types of statements in Imp_{np}.

Case for $x_n = y_p.f_n$. Assume that $y_p.f_n$ only resolves to δ. It is tempting, but wrong, to abstract statement as in traditional numeric analysis, *i.e.*, $[\![x_n = \delta]\!]_n^\sharp$. Consider `a = x.f; b = y.f; if (a < b){...}`. Assume that $p^\sharp(x.f) = p^\sharp(y.f) = \{\delta\}$. If the abstract semantics relates a (resp. b) with δ after $a = x.f$ (resp. $b = y.f$), the analysis will wrongly argue that the following `if` branch can never be reached. The above reasoning is wrong because we should not, in general, correlate a summarized dimension with a scalar variable.

Gopan *et al.* have pointed out that to assign a summarized dimension δ to a non-summarized dimension x_n takes three steps: First, *extend* δ to a fresh dimension δ' (using the operator $\mathrm{expand}_{\delta,\delta'}^\sharp$ that copies dimensions). Then, *relate* x_n with δ' using traditional abstract semantics for assignment $[\![x_n = \delta']\!]_n^\sharp$. Finally, the newly introduced dimension δ' has to be *dropped* (using the operator $\mathrm{drop}_{\delta'}^\sharp$ that removes dimensions). See (Gopan et al., 2004) for the details of $\mathrm{drop}_{\delta'}^\sharp$ and $\mathrm{expand}_{\delta,\delta'}^\sharp$.

In summary, Gopan's operator *copies* the values of the summarized dimension to the scalar variable but keeps them uncorrelated. The following operator is used to assign a summarized dimension δ to a scalar variable x_n.

$$G(x_n, \delta) \triangleq \lambda n^\sharp. \mathrm{drop}_{\delta'}^\sharp \circ [\![x_n = \delta']\!]_n^\sharp \circ \mathrm{expand}_{\delta,\delta'}^\sharp \, n^\sharp \tag{22}$$

For example, the property $G(x_n = \delta)\{\delta > 1\} = \{x_n > 1, \delta > 1\}$ after applying $x = \delta$. We see that scalar variable x_n and summarized dimension δ cannot be related, even if the underlined numeric domain is relational.

Remark 2 The lack of correlation between δ and x_n reveals another source of imprecision of the classic soundness notion, besides its weak update semantics.

Sharper analysis can be obtained thanks to the notion of targets. In Lem. 1, we have shown an important consequence of (TU), that is, the underlined summarized dimension δ represents a single concrete object among the objects pointed to by the targets. This lemma allows us to deal with δ satisfying (TU) as a scalar variable.

Consider the read access $x_n = y_p.f_n$. Let $(\mathsf{n}^\sharp, \mathsf{p}^\sharp)$ be the input abstract state, T be the targets. If $y_p.f_n \notin T$, we have to unconstrain x_n. If $y_p.f_n \in T$ and $\mathsf{p}^\sharp(y_p.f_n) = \{\delta_1, \dots, \delta_M\}$, targeted update joins the effects of assigning δ_i to x_n for $1 \le i \le M$. For each δ_i, if (TU) satisfies, the effect of assigning δ_i to x_n is the same as $[\![x_n = \delta_i]\!]_n^\sharp (\mathsf{n}^\sharp)$, as if δ_i is a scalar variable; if (TU) fails, the best we can do is to copy the possible values of δ_i into x_n, which amounts to using Gopan's operator (22). This is summarized in Algo. 2. That is,

$$[\![x_n = y_p.f_n]\!]_{\langle T \rangle}^\sharp (\mathsf{n}^\sharp, \mathsf{p}^\sharp) \triangleq \begin{cases} [\![x_n =?]\!]_n^\sharp \mathsf{n}^\sharp, \mathsf{p}^\sharp & y_p.f_n \notin T \\ \bigsqcup_{\delta \in \mathsf{p}^\sharp(y_p.f_n)} [\![x_n = \delta]\!]^{\eta(\delta)} \mathsf{n}^\sharp, \mathsf{p}^\sharp & y_p.f_n \in T \end{cases} \quad (23)$$

where the operator $[\![x_n =?]\!]_n^\sharp$ unconstrains x_n, η is the shortcut defined in (19), and

$$[\![x_n = \delta]\!]^S \triangleq [\![x_n = \delta]\!]_n^\sharp, \qquad [\![x_n = \delta]\!]^W \triangleq G(x_n, \delta) \quad (24)$$

Algorithm 2. TARGETED UPDATE FOR $x_n = y_p.f_n$

Input: Abstract state $(\mathsf{n}^\sharp, \mathsf{p}^\sharp)$, targets T
Output: The abstract state after targeted update $[\![x_n = y_p.f_n]\!]_{\langle T \rangle}^\sharp (\mathsf{n}^\sharp, \mathsf{p}^\sharp)$

1 **if** $y_p.f_n \notin T$ **then**
2   **return** $[\![x_n =?]\!]_n^\sharp (\mathsf{n}^\sharp), \mathsf{p}^\sharp$
3 $\mathsf{n}^\sharp\prime \leftarrow \bot$
4 **for** $\delta \in \mathsf{p}^\sharp(y_p.f_n)$ **do**
5   **if** *there exists no* $t \in T \backslash \{y_p.f_n\}$ *satisfying* $\delta \in \mathsf{p}^\sharp(t)$ **then**
6        $\mathsf{n}^\sharp\prime \leftarrow \mathsf{n}^\sharp\prime \sqcup [\![x_n = \delta]\!]_n^\sharp (\mathsf{n}^\sharp\prime)$
7   **else**
8        $\mathsf{n}^\sharp\prime \leftarrow \mathsf{n}^\sharp\prime \sqcup G(x_n, \delta)$
9   **end if**
10 **end for**
11 **return** $\mathsf{n}^\sharp\prime, \mathsf{p}^\sharp$

Case for s_n. If s_n is an assignment in $\mathtt{Imp}_n$, it can be treated in the same way as in traditional numeric analysis using its abstract transfer function $[\![\cdot]\!]_n^\sharp$ (Sect. 2). In this paper, the transfer function for updating $(\mathsf{n}^\sharp, \mathsf{p}^\sharp)$ with s_n is defined as:

$$[\![s_n]\!]_{\langle T \rangle}^\sharp (\mathsf{n}^\sharp, \mathsf{p}^\sharp) \triangleq ([\![s_n]\!]_n^\sharp \mathsf{n}^\sharp, \mathsf{p}^\sharp) \quad (25)$$

Case for s_p. Targeted update tracks the heap objects pointed to by the targets. An important thing to note is that s_p may cause changes to what objects the access paths are pointing—necessitating changes to the numeric portion of the abstract state. Subsequently, we write s_p in the form of '$l=r$'.

Given a target set T and an abstract state $(\mathsf{n}^\sharp, \mathsf{p}^\sharp) \in NumP^\sharp$. Taking an arbitrary $(\mathsf{n}, \mathsf{p}) \in \gamma_{\langle T \rangle}(\mathsf{n}^\sharp, \mathsf{p}^\sharp)$, we want to find $\mathsf{n}^{\sharp\prime}$ so that $(\mathsf{n}, \xrightarrow{Pter} (s_p)\mathsf{p})$ is in the concretization of $(\mathsf{n}^{\sharp\prime}, \|s_p\|_p^\sharp (\mathsf{p}^\sharp))$. The hypothesis $(\mathsf{n}, \mathsf{p}) \in \gamma_{\langle T \rangle}(\mathsf{n}^\sharp, \mathsf{p}^\sharp)$ states that $\mathsf{n} \models [ins]\mathsf{n}^\sharp$ for any $ins \in Ins_\mathsf{p}\langle T \rangle$; for the sake of soundness, the updated $\mathsf{n}^{\sharp\prime}$ has to satisfy $\mathsf{n} \models [ins]\mathsf{n}^{\sharp\prime}$ for any $ins \in Ins_{\xrightarrow{Pter}(s_p)\mathsf{p}}\langle T \rangle$. Following Def. 3, it suffices to unconstrain all summarized dimensions of $\mathsf{n}^{\sharp\prime}$ in the form of $\rhd(d)$ with $d \in post[\xrightarrow{Pter} (s_p)\mathsf{p}](T) \setminus post[\mathsf{p}](T)$. Let $M \triangleq post[\xrightarrow{Pter} (s_p)\mathsf{p}](T) \cap post[\mathsf{p}](T)$. We can show that $M \supseteq \{\mathsf{p}(t) \mid t \in T, t$ does not have l as prefix$\}$. This is because for any $\mathsf{p}(t)$ such that $t \in T$ and t does not have l as prefix, $\mathsf{p}(t) \in post[\mathsf{p}](T)$ immediately implies $\mathsf{p}(t) \in post[\xrightarrow{Pter} (s_p)](T)$.

In conclusion, a conservative way to model s_p is to unconstrain targets that do not necessarily point to where they previously pointed. Thus, we unconstrain all $\mathsf{p}^\sharp(t)$ such that $t \in T$ and t has l as prefix. For example, in x = new; we unconstrain δ if it is pointed to by the target $x.val$. The transfer function for s_p is modeled as:

$$\|s_p\|_{\langle T \rangle}^\sharp (\mathsf{n}^\sharp, \mathsf{p}^\sharp) \triangleq \bigsqcup_{\delta \in uncons_{\langle T \rangle}(s_p, \mathsf{p}^\sharp)} \|\delta =?\|_n^\sharp \mathsf{n}^\sharp, \quad \|s_p\|_p^\sharp \mathsf{p}^\sharp \qquad (26)$$

Here, $uncons_{\langle T \rangle}(s_p, \mathsf{p}^\sharp) \triangleq \{\delta \mid s_p = \text{'}l=r\text{'}, \exists t \in T : t$ has l as prefix $\wedge \delta \in \mathsf{p}^\sharp(t)\}$.

6   A Discussion of Some Important Design Choices

Targets. Our implementation uses the numeric access paths excluding variables that appear syntactically in the program as targets. Without prior knowledge of specific program properties to be verified, this design choice seems to give a trade-off between expressiveness and precision. Although this target set may appear large, our experiments (Sect. 8) show that targeted update using this target set still provides a significant precision enhancement while covering common cases where program properties to be expressed only use program syntax.

Join and Widening. The design of the join operator is usually a difficult step for developing abstract domains. We have assumed (Sect. 2) that the naming scheme should be flow independent. Thanks to the naming scheme hypothesis, our join operator seems to be delightfully uncomplicated: We just compute the join (or widening) component-wise. Then, if a concrete state (n, p) is in $\gamma_{\langle T \rangle}(\mathsf{n}_1^\sharp, \mathsf{p}_1^\sharp)$ or in $\gamma_{\langle T \rangle}(\mathsf{n}_2^\sharp, \mathsf{p}_2^\sharp)$, it is also in the concretization of $(\mathsf{n}_1^\sharp \sqcup \mathsf{n}_2^\sharp, \mathsf{p}_1^\sharp \cup \mathsf{p}_2^\sharp)$. The case for widening is similar.

$$(n_1^\sharp, p_1^\sharp) \sqcup^\sharp (n_2^\sharp, p_2^\sharp) = (n_1^\sharp \sqcup n_2^\sharp, p_1^\sharp \cup p_2^\sharp) \tag{27}$$

$$(n_1^\sharp, p_1^\sharp) \triangledown^\sharp (n_2^\sharp, p_2^\sharp) = (n_1^\sharp \triangledown n_2^\sharp, p_1^\sharp \cup p_2^\sharp) \tag{28}$$

Constraint System with a Flow-Insensitive Points-to Analysis. As in the implementation of (Fu, 2014), we use a flow-insensitive points-to analysis to simplify the states propagation. The analysis is done in a pre-analysis phase and does not participate with the propagation of numeric lattices. The obtained flow-insensitive points-to graph is then used at each control point as a superset of the flow-sensitive points-to graph.

Using flow-insensitive variant does not cause any soundness issue. This is because the soundness of our analysis is based on the soundness of its component numeric domains and pointer analysis. Using the single flow-insensitive points-to graph for all program control points can be modeled as an analysis that is initialized with an over-approximation of the least fixpoint of a flow-sensitive analysis that propagates in the style of `skip`.

Let $F^\sharp(s) \triangleq \lambda n^\sharp.fst \circ [\![s]\!]^\sharp_{\langle T \rangle} (n^\sharp, p_{fi}^\sharp)$, where $p_{fi}^\sharp$ is the flow-insensitive points-to graph, and fst is the operator that extracts the first element from a pair of components. We use the following the constraint system that operates on numeric lattice $n^\sharp$ only (rather than on $(n^\sharp, p^\sharp)$ pair):

$$\overline{n^\sharp}[l] \sqsupseteq F^\sharp(s)(\overline{n^\sharp}[l']) \tag{29}$$

where we write $\overline{n^\sharp}[l]$ (resp. $\overline{n^\sharp}[l']$) for the numeric component of $NumP^\sharp$ at control point l (resp. l'), l' is the control point of statement s, and (l', l) is an arc in the program control flow.

Intra-procedural Numeric Analysis. While the points-to graph is computed by an interprocedural pointer analysis, the static numeric anlaysis is intentionally left intra-procedural.

Existing numeric domains, in particular the relational ones, are generally sensitive to the size of the program and number of variables. The objective of scalability is hard to achieve if the problem solving has to iterate through all the program call-graph. To take variables in all the procedures as a whole necessarily incurs a high complexity for the numeric part in our analysis. To give an idea of this complexity, our experiments on the abstract domains in PPL show that octagonal analysis can hardly run on several hundreds of variables, and polyhedral analysis can quickly time out with more than 30 variables; on the other hand, a real-world Java program, with all its procedures put in together, could easily reach tens of thousands of variables to be analyzed.

A known workaround exists. The pre-analysis of *variable packing* technique allows ASTREE (Blanchet et al., 2003a) to successfully scale up to large sized C programs. We regard intra-procedural numeric analysis as a lightweight alternative to variable packing: Variables are related only if they are in the same procedure. In this way, we do not need to invent strategies to pack variables.

7 An Example

We discuss a Java program with interesting operations on a single linked list. Fig. 2 presents the program. Here, our goal is to show how targeted update works in practice and to prove two properties that are challenging for a human. The analysis results from our implemented analyzer are shown in the companion report.

```
1   List  hd,  node;    int  idx;
2   hd = new  List ();  //allocation  site  h₁
3   hd.val  =  0;
4   hd.next  =  null;
5   for  (idx  =  -17;  idx  <  42;  idx++){
6         node  =  new  List ();  //allocation  site  h₂
7         node.val  =  idx;
8         node.next  =  hd.next;
9         hd.next  =  node;
10        hd.val  =  hd.val  +  1;
11  }
12  return;
```

Fig. 2. A Java program

Example 3 Observe that there are two allocation sites h_1 and h_2 in the program, with the head of the list stored in h_1 and the body of the list stored in h_2. The head node has a special meaning. It is used to indicate of length of the list. From l. 1 to l. 4, the program creates an empty list with a single head node. From l. 5 to l. 11, a list of integers is iteratively stored on the list. Within the loop, the head node is updated (l. 10) to track list length whenever a new list cell is created.

Targeted update, instantiated with polyhedral analysis, is able to infer the following properties:

- *Prop1:* At the loop entry (l. 5), $hd.val \in [0, 60] \land hd.val - idx = 17$.
- *Prop2:* From l. 5 to l. 10, $hd.val - node.val = 17$.
- *Prop3:* At the exit of the loop (l. 12), $hd.val = 60$.

Targeted update works as follows: First, it pre-analyzes the program with flow-insensitive points-to analysis.

$$(30)$$

All numeric access paths appeared in program syntax that are not variables are taken as targets: $T = \{hd.val, node.val\}$. By computing $\{\delta \mid \exists t \in T, \delta \in p_{f_i}^{\sharp}(t)\}$, targeted update obtains two summarized dimensions $\delta_{h_1,val}$ and $\delta_{h_2,val}$. The initial abstract state is set to $\{\delta_{h_1,val} \rightarrow \top, \delta_{h_2,val} \rightarrow \top, idx \rightarrow \top\}$. Then, we apply transfer functions of targeted update and solve the constraint system (29). For example, the statements at l. 3 and l. 7 are treated as write access $y_p.f_n = x_n$. The statement at l .10 is transformed by SOOT into three short ones: `tmp1 = hd.val`, `tmp2 = tmp1 + 1` and `hd.val = tmp2`. They are treated as read access, s_n and write access statements, respectively. Finally, targeted update obtains (1) at l. 5: $\delta_{h_1.val} \in [0, 60] \wedge \delta_{h_1,val} - idx = 17$, (2) at l. 5 to l. 10: $\delta_{h_1.val} - \delta_{h_2.val} = 17$ and (3) At l. 12: $\delta_{h_1.val} = 60$. From these, we deduce *Prop1*, *Prop2* and *Prop3* respectively (based on the concretization function defined in Def. 3).

These properties are interesting and useful. *Prop1* tells a non-trivial loop invariant involving access paths and scalar variables. *Prop2* is particularly difficult to infer: $hd.val$ and $node.val$ have an invariant difference 17 because this is the case at the loop entry; in addition, $node.val$ increments by one (because it is correlated with the idx at l. 7) at each iteration, and $hd.val$ increments by one as well (l. 10). *Prop3* gives a precise value stored in the head node, indicating that the list length is tracked as 60, precisely.

Remark 3 Targeted update is able to infer these relations because the summarized dimensions $\delta_{h_1,val}$ and $\delta_{h_2,val}$ lose their original sense: They can be correlated with scalar variables and strongly updated because (TU) condition is satisfied there. In addition, since targeted update is built on traditional numeric domains, we can take the best from these, such as the very precise polyhedral abstraction and the widening/narrowing techniques (Cousot and Cousot, 1992) used in this example.

8   Experiments

The implemented targeted update is built on the static numeric analyzer NumP developed in (Fu, 2014). Our implementation of targeted update is called T-NumP. The analyzed language of T-NumP is Jimple (Vallée-Rai et al., 1999). The compiler framework SOOT is used as the analysis front-end. It offers a range of pointer analyses as well, including the points-to analysis and the side-effect analysis (to approximate the effects of invocation). The default flow-insensitive points-to analysis used in SOOT is denoted by Pter subsequently. For the purpose of comparison, we have implemented a traditional static numeric analyzer for Java by wrapping abstract domains in PPL. The implemented analyzer is called Num.

Assessment. To demonstrate the effectiveness of our technique, we evaluate it on the SPECjvm98 benchmark suite. The experiments were performed on a 3.06 GHz Intel Core 2 Duo with 4 GB of DDR3 RAM laptop with JDK 1.6.

We tested all the 10 benchmarks in SPECjvm98. The corresponding results are given in Tab. 1 and 2. The characteristics of the benchmarks are presented by the number of the analyzed Jimple statements (col. 2, STATEMENT), the number of write access statements in the form of $y_p.f_n = x_n$ or $y_p.f_n = k$ (col. 3, WA), and the number of read access statements in the form of $x_n = y_p.f_n$ (col. 4, RA). Experimental results are shown in Tab. 1 where we use the interval domain Int64_Box of PPL.

Table 1. Evaluation of targeted update on the benchmark suite SPECjvm98: Interval + Spark

Benchmark Characteristics				Precision			Time			Metrics			
BENCHMARK	STATEMENT	WA	RA	TU	PRCS	SCALAR	T_NUM	T_PTER	T_TNUMP	Q_TU	Q_PRCS	Q_SCALAR	Q_T
_200_check	2307	25	48	19	18	6	00m12s	02m36s	03m13s	76%	72%	13%	115%
_201_compress	2724	96	142	89	55	9	00m07s	02m39s	03m34s	93%	57%	6%	129%
_202_jess	12834	232	646	212	102	2	00m16s	02m43s	05m02s	91%	44%	0%	169%
_205_raytrace	5465	53	64	52	24	0	00m05s	02m35s	03m35s	98%	45%	0%	134%
_209_db	2770	32	65	31	19	0	00m04s	02m41s	03m47s	97%	59%	0%	138%
_213_javac	25973	342	1362	312	143	25	00m12s	04m15s	10m12s	91%	42%	2%	229%
_222_mpegaudio	14604	138	247	124	62	6	00m18s	02m50s	04m15s	90%	45%	2%	136%
_227_mtrt	5466	53	64	52	24	0	00m06s	02m40s	03m42s	98%	45%	0%	134%
_228_jack	12221	462	414	436	102	7	00m31s	02m45s	06m03s	94%	22%	2%	185%
_999_checkit	3038	38	53	29	19	0	00m05s	02m38s	03m44s	76%	50%	0%	137%
Mean										90%	48%	3%	151%

Three parameters TU, PRCS, and SCALAR (col. 5-7) are measured to estimate the precision gain. The parameter TU counts the number of write access statements before which condition (TU) is satisfied. We record PRCS for the number of the write access statements after which the obtained invariants are strictly more precise than Num. Improvement on scalar variables is assessed by the number of read-access statements after which the obtained numeric invariant by T-NumP is strictly more precise than Num in terms of scalar variables (summarized dimensions are unconstrained for this comparison). The execution time is measured for Num, Pter, and T-NumP (col. 8-10). The parameters T_Num and T_Pter are the times spent by Num and Pter when they analyze individually. The parameter T_TNUMP records the time of our analysis.

The last four columns compute the metrics for assessment. The metrics Q_TU $\triangleq$ TU/WA and Q_PRCS $\triangleq$ PRCS/WA (col. 11-12) are the ratios of TU and PRCS to the number of write access statements. The metrics Q_SCALAR $\triangleq$ SCALAR/RA (col. 13) is defined with regard to read-access statements. The metric Q_T $\triangleq$ T_TNUMP/(T_Num+T_Pter) (col. 14) records the ratio of the time spent by our analysis to the total time of its component analyses.

The size of the analyzed Jimple statements ranges from 2307 (_200_check) to 25973 (_213_javac).[3] We observe that T_Pter is always much larger than T_Num. This is because the points-to analysis is interprocedural while the numeric analysis is run procedures by procedures. Our analysis relies on the pointer analysis and is thus bottlenecked by it in terms of efficiency. Still, the time spent

---

[3] The Jimple statements are generally less than in the source program, because SOOT typically analyzes a subset of its call-graph nodes.

for the benchmark takes several minutes, with an average Q_T = 151%. The average precision metrics is calculated on the last row of Tab. 1. Q_TU = 90%, Q_PRCS = 48% show a clear precision enhancement of our approach over traditional approaches.

Please mind the gap between TU and PRCS in Tab. 1 (and between Q_TU nd Q_PRCS as well). Besides the non-monotonicity of widening operators (Cortesi and Zanioli, 2011), we observe that the practical reason causing this disparity is that targeted update, in the context of non-relational analysis (as the interval analysis above), is helpless in dealing with write-access statements in the form of $y_p.f_n = x_n$ as long as no information on x_n has been gathered.

This point can be remedied by relational analysis. Tab. 2 shows our experimental results with octagonal analysis and the same points-to analysis as above. Since the condition (TU) can not be influenced by numeric analysis, we obtain the same Q_TU as in Tab. 1. The parameters Q_PRCS and Q_SCALAR can be greatly improved due to the relational analysis, with similar time overhead Q_TU as in Tab. 1.

Table 2. Evaluation of targeted update on the benchmark suite SPECjvm98: Octagonal + Spark

Benchmark Characteristics				Precision			Time			Metrics			
BENCHMARK	STATEMENT	WA	RA	TU	PRCS	SCALAR	T_NUM	T_PTER	T_TNUMP	Q_TU	Q_PRCS	Q_SCALAR	Q_T
_200_check	2307	25	48	19	19	6	00m13s	02m44s	03m48s	76%	76%	13%	129%
_201_compress	2724	96	142	89	93	70	00m09s	03m18s	05m16s	93%	97%	49%	153%
_202_jess	12834	232	646	212	215	52	00m36s	02m46s	06m38s	91%	93%	8%	197%
_205_raytrace	5465	53	64	52	52	8	00m10s	02m38s	03m52s	98%	98%	13%	138%
_209_db	2770	32	65	31	31	13	00m08s	02m42s	03m51s	97%	97%	20%	136%
_213_javac	25973	342	1362	312	244	156	02m35s	05m31s	14m28s	91%	71%	11%	179%
_222_mpegaudio	14604	138	247	124	117	36	00m39s	02m45s	06m44s	90%	85%	15%	198%
_227_mtrt	5466	53	64	52	52	8	00m21s	02m37s	03m58s	98%	98%	13%	134%
_228_jack	12221	462	414	436	410	168	00m34s	02m43s	08m06s	94%	89%	41%	247%
_999_checkit	3038	38	53	29	28	6	00m09s	02m52s	04m46s	76%	74%	11%	158%
Mean										90%	88%	19%	167%

The experimental results show that targeted update discovers significantly more program properties in summarized dimensions and scalar variables as well, at a cost comparable to that of running the numeric and pointer analysis separately.

9   Related Work

This research continues the work in (Fu, 2014) that addresses the general issue of lifting numeric domains to heap-manipulating programs.

Memory abstraction using strong and weak updates (Chase et al., 1990; Wilson and Lam, 1995) is common sense. Efforts have been made to enable safe application of strong update. Sagiv *et al.* used the *focus* operation (that isolates individual elements of the summarized dimensions) of shape analysis (Sagiv et al., 1999) to apply strong update. Fink *et al.* (Fink et al., 2008) used a uniqueness analysis based on must-alias and liveness information to facilitate the verification of whether a summarized node represents more than one concrete reference.

The recency abstraction (Balakrishnan and Reps, 2006) is a simple and elegant technique that enables strong update by distinguishing the objects recently allocated from those created earlier. This approach allows strong update to be applied whenever a write access immediately follows an allocation, which is usually the case for initialization. Although the objective of recency abstraction is similar to targeted update, it uses a different abstraction that is not comparable to ours.

The issue of strong/weak update has been mostly studied for array structures. Cousot *et al.* (Cousot et al., 2010) proposed an efficient solution based on the ordering of array indexes. It may be not easy to generalize their method to the analysis of the pointer access. Fluid update (Dillig et al., 2010) is much closer to our approach. It is an abstract semantics that provides a sharp analysis for the array structure. The authors used bracket constraints to refine points-to information on arrays, which was shown to be effective to disambiguate array indexes. This approach was also extended in (Dillig et al., 2011) to deal with containers and other non-array structures.

10   Conclusion

Targeted update introduces a novel dimension in program analysis for tuning precision and efficiency. We have derived the abstract semantics from the concept of targets. This approach is validated on the benchmark suite SPECjvm98. The experimental results show a tangible precision enhancement compared with classical approaches while preserving a high scalability.

Acknowledgments. The author wishes to thank Laurent Mauborgne for his thoughtful feedback.

References

Balakrishnan, G., Reps, T.W.: Recency-abstraction for heap-allocated storage. In: Yi, K. (ed.) SAS 2006. LNCS, vol. 4134, pp. 221–239. Springer, Heidelberg (2006)

Blanchet, B., Cousot, P., Cousot, R.: A static analyzer for large safety-critical software. In: PLDI, pp. 196–207 (2003a)

Blanchet, B., Cousot, P., Cousot, R., et al.: A static analyzer for large safety-critical software. In: PLDI, pp. 196–207 (2003b)

Chase, D.R., Wegman, M.N., Zadeck, F.K.: Analysis of pointers and structures (with retrospective). In: Best of PLDI, pp. 343–359 (1990)

Chen, P.S., Hung, M.Y., Hwang, Y.S.: et al. Compiler support for speculative multithreading architecture with probabilistic points-to analysis. In: PPoPP, pp. 25–36 (2003)

Cortesi, A., Zanioli, M.: Widening and narrowing operators for abstract interpretation. Computer Languages, Systems & Structures 37(1), 24–42 (2011)

Cousot, P., Cousot, R.: Comparing the Galois connection and widening/narrowing approaches to Abstract interpretation. In: Bruynooghe, M., Wirsing, M. (eds.) PLILP 1992. LNCS, vol. 631, pp. 269–295. Springer, Heidelberg (1992)

Cousot, P., Cousot, R., Mauborgne, L.: A scalable segmented decision tree abstract domain. In: Manna, Z., Peled, D.A. (eds.) Pnueli Fetschrift. LNCS, vol. 6200, pp. 72–95. Springer, Heidelberg (2010)

Dillig, I., Dillig, T., Aiken, A.: Fluid updates: Beyond strong vs. weak updates. In: Gordon, A.D. (ed.) ESOP 2010. LNCS, vol. 6012, pp. 246–266. Springer, Heidelberg (2010)

Dillig, I., Dillig, T., Aiken, A.: Precise reasoning for programs using containers. In: POPL, pp. 187–200 (2011)

Emami, M., Ghiya, R., Hendren, L.J.: Context-sensitive interprocedural points-to analysis in the presence of function pointers. In: PLDI, pp. 242–256 (1994)

Fink, S.J., Yahav, E., Dor, N., et al.: Effective typestate verification in the presence of aliasing. ACM Trans. Softw. Eng. Methodol. 17(2) (2008)

Fu, Z.: Static Analysis of Numerical Properties in the Presence of Pointers. PhD thesis, Université de Rennes 1 – INRIA, Rennes, France (2013)

Fu, Z.: Modularly combining numeric abstract domains with points-to analysis, and a scalable static numeric analyzer for java. In: McMillan, K.L., Rival, X. (eds.) VMCAI 2014. LNCS, vol. 8318, pp. 282–301. Springer, Heidelberg (2014)

Gopan, D., DiMaio, F., Dor, N., Reps, T., Sagiv, M.: Numeric domains with summarized dimensions. In: Jensen, K., Podelski, A. (eds.) TACAS 2004. LNCS, vol. 2988, pp. 512–529. Springer, Heidelberg (2004)

Landi, W., Ryder, B.G.: A safe approximate algorithm for interprocedural pointer aliasing. In: PLDI, pp. 235–248 (1992)

Lev-Ami, T., Sagiv, M.: TVLA: A system for implementing static analyses. In: SAS 2000. LNCS, vol. 1824, pp. 280–302. Springer, Heidelberg (2000)

Sagiv, M., Reps, T., Wilhelm, R.: Parametric shape analysis via 3-valued logic. In: POPL, pp. 105–118 (1999)

Vallée-Rai, R., Co, P., Gagnon, E., Hendren, L.J., Lam, P., Sundaresan, V.: Soot - a Java bytecode optimization framework. In: CASCON, p. 13 (1999)

Wilson, R.P., Lam, M.S.: Efficient Context-Sensitive Pointer Analysis for C Programs. In: PLDI, pp. 1–12 (1995)

Affine Parallelization of Loops with Run-Time Dependent Bounds from Binaries

Aparna Kotha, Kapil Anand, Timothy Creech, Khaled ElWazeer,
Matthew Smithson, and Rajeev Barua

University of Maryland,
College Park, MD 20742
{akotha,kapil,tcreech,wazeer,msmithso,barua}@umd.edu

Abstract. An automatic parallelizer is a tool that converts serial code to parallel code. This is an important tool because most hardware today is parallel and manually rewriting the vast repository of serial code is tedious and error prone. We build an automatic parallelizer for binary code, *i.e.* a tool which converts a serial binary to a parallel binary. It is important because: (i) most serial legacy code has no source code available; (ii) it is compatible with all compilers and languages.

In the past binary automatic parallelization techniques have been developed and researchers have presented results on small kernels from polybench. These techniques are a good start; however they are far from parallelizing larger codes from the SPEC2006 and OMP2001 benchmark suites which are representative of real world codes. The main limitation of past techniques is the assumption that loop bounds are statically known to calculate loop dependencies. However, in larger codes loop bounds are only known at run-time; hence loop dependencies calculated statically are overly conservative making binary parallelization ineffective.

In this paper we present a novel algorithm that enhancing past techniques significantly by guessing the most likely loop bounds using only the memory expressions present in that loop. It then inserts run-time checks to see if these guesses were indeed correct and if correct executes the parallel version of the loop, else the serial version executes. These techniques are applied to the large affine benchmarks in SPEC2006 and OMP2001 and unlike previous methods the speedups from binary are as good as from source. We also present results on the number of loops parallelized directly from a binary with and without this algorithm. Among the 8 affine benchmarks among these suites, the best existing binary parallelization method achieves an average speedup of 1.74X, whereas our method achieves a speedup of 3.38X. This is close to the speedup from source code of 3.15X.

Keywords: Automatic Parallelization, Binary Rewriting, Affine loop parallelization, Run-time dependent loop bounds.

1 Introduction

With the advent of multi-core machines it is most efficient to run parallel code on them. However, most code ever written is serial. Several methods have been

Z. Shao (Ed.): ESOP 2014, LNCS 8410, pp. 554–574, 2014.

proposed to parallelize serial code which include: (i) explicitly rewriting serial code using Message Passing Interface (MPI), pthreads, Threading Building Blocks (TBB) etc; (ii) using program directives such as Open Multi-Processing (OMP) to specify parallelism in serial code and (iii) using an automatic parallelizer to convert serial code to parallel without any human intervention. Automatic parallelizer is more attractive than the first two methods since: (i) it is not prone to human error; (ii) programmers do not need to be trained to think and program in parallel. Hence, we choose automatic parallelization to bridge the gap between serial code and parallel hardware.

In this paper we develop mechanisms to implement an automatic parallelizer within a binary rewriter. i.e. we develop *a tool that takes as input serial binary code and produces as output a parallel binary.* The advantages of parallelizing binary code include: (i) it works on old legacy code for which no source code is available; (ii) it works for all binaries of an instruction set irrespective of the language/compiler they come from; (iii) it works on hand-coded assembly language programs as well; (iv) it can be used by the end user who does not have access to the source code.

In the past a few attempts have been made to parallelize affine codes directly from binaries Kotha et al. (2010); Pradelle et al. (2012). Though these papers present good foundational ideas and results on polybench kernels, they are only a start to parallelizing large real world affine codes. The major limitation of these methods is that their algorithms are not powerful enough to handle loops with run-time dependent loop bounds and such loops are present in abundance in real life code. In this paper we present a novel algorithm to work on such loops whose bounds are run-time dependent or statically unknown. The idea is that we guess the most likely loop bounds using the memory expressions present in the loop and add run-time checks to see if these were indeed correct before executing the parallel version of the loop. These run-time checks may slow down the program in the worst case but open up for more possible parallelism. Our results show that affine benchmarks from the SPEC2006 and OMP2006 benchmark suites (much larger benchmarks representative of real world codes) can be parallelized with our techniques.

Further, this paper is arranged as follows. Section 2 presents the closest related work contrasting our techniques to them. Section 3 presents the limitations of the present binary affine parallelization techniques using an example and motivates the algorithm followed by a brief algorithm and more examples in section 4. The core algorithm is presented in section 5 followed by the description of our infrastructure in section 6 and the results in section 7.

2 Related Work

In this section, we present potentially competing related work contrasting it to this paper in the following categories: (i) static automatic parallelization of binaries; (ii) dynamic automatic parallelization of binaries; (iii) automatic vectorization of binaries and (iv) array delinearization techniques.

Static Automatic Parallelization of Binaries: Kotha et al. (2010) and Pradelle et al. (2012) are the only two static methods we are aware of that have done automatic parallelization in a binary rewriter. Both these methods present results on small kernels that are a part of the polybench benchmark suite. Pradelle et al. (2012) automatically parallelizes binaries by feeding the binary intermediate form to the polyhedral compiler. Its results are only on the polybench benchmark suite. Kotha et al. (2010) statically parallelizes binaries by using dependence information determined from binaries. However, its methods are limited to affine loops where loop bounds are known and hence, it also can only parallelize small kernels from the polybench benchmark suite. Both these methods present a brief section on run-time dependent loop bounds and suggest adding run-time checks to check if different accesses were indeed to different arrays. Their methods are highly lacking since they have no mechanisms to reason about dependencies between accesses to the same array and in the absence of such a mechanism it will be conservative and not parallelize real world code. We build on this work and have devised a novel algorithm to guess the possible loop bounds of affine loops. We are able to parallelize affine benchmarks from the SPEC2006 and OMP2001 benchmark suites.

Dynamic Automatic Parallelization of Binaries: Dynamic automatic parallelization techniques present in literature are   Yardimci and Franz (2006), Wang et al. (2009) and J. Yang and Whitehouse (2011). Yardimci and Franz (2006) focuses on a dynamic method to detect non-affine parallelism. Wang et al. (2009) presents a dynamic method to parallelize binaries using speculative slicing and J. Yang and Whitehouse (2011) presents a method to use run-time information to parallelize binary code. All the three methods are dynamic. Hence, they suffer from run-time overheads from analysis. Most importantly, they do not optimize for affine loops whereas our method does.

Vectorization of Binaries: Nakamura et al. (2011) and Dasgupta and Dasgupta (2003) present techniques to analyze binaries and vectorize them. Their analysis is limited to vectorization of binaries and do not attempt to parallelize using threads like we do.

Array Delinearization Techniques: Array Delinearization methods Maslov (1992) Franke and O'boyle (2003) take source code with linearized multi-dimensional accesses, and convert them to multi-dimensional accesses when possible. Ideally, if we delinearize array accesses in a binary we can parallelize them as effectively as from source. However, source-level methods to delinearize array accesses cannot be adapted to binaries easily. Delinearization methods such as Maslov (1992), Franke and O'boyle (2003) require high level intermediate C like representation which is not available from binary code. They use symbolic information which contains information about the number, location, and dimension sizes of arrays, to delinearize arrays. Finding this information in the general case from stripped binaries (*i.e.* those without symbolic information) is impossible since it is discarded by the linker. Hence, delinearization methods cannot be adapted for binary code.

The method in this paper circumvents the problem of missing array information in binaries by not attempting to recover guaranteed information about array locations and dimension sizes. Instead it guesses the possible bounds for loops. When the guesses are correct, the code can be parallelized. Run-time checks ensure that when the guessed bounds are wrong, the serial code is executed. No previous method guesses loop bounds from binaries, or uses run-time checks like our method. *The result is that our method is the first to parallelize binary code with unknown loop bounds.*

3 Motivation

To parallelize affine loops, traditional techniques calculate distance vectors for each loop and use them to reason about parallelizing the loop. In this section we first describe the best-known methods for obtaining distance vectors from source code for affine loops with run-time determined loop bounds. We then present the limitations of the existing binary method for the same and briefly describe our method.

```
int A[20,50]
for i = 0 → ub_i step 1
  for j = 0 → ub_j step 1
    A[i,j] = A[i,j] + 10
```

The code shows a normalized loop, *i.e.* a loop with a lower bound of zero and a step of one. Loops can be normalized using existing methods such as the normalization pass in LLVM.

Fig. 1. Code Example

Distance vectors from source for code in figure 1 are calculated as follows. Existing methods make the assumption that row and column accesses are within the bounds of the array's dimensions. They solve for two iterations that refer to the same memory location in the infinite space for each dimension separately. If no solution exists, like in this example, they conclude that no two iterations ever access the same memory. This implies that iterations of the j loop can execute in parallel (i.e., the component of the distance vector for j dimension is zero.) Similarly, they proves that the loop i is parallel.

To obtain distance vectors from binary for this code we cannot use the above source method since it relies on known affine expressions for array indexes in terms of induction variables, which are not apparent from the binary. Instead we start with the existing method for binaries in Kotha et al. (2010). It shows that we can recover linearized expressions for memory accesses from a binary, and solving these linearized expressions gives us distance vectors. In the presence of loop bounds the solutions from binaries are very powerful, and can handle most linear algebraic kernels as presented in Kotha et al. (2010). However, when loop bounds are run-time dependent, we need to solve these linearized expressions in the infinite space (since we need to assume that the loop bounds can take any value at run-time). This greatly reduces the precision of the analysis.

Let us apply the existing binary method to code in figure 1. From its binary, we recover a memory expression of the form $Base_A + 200i + 4j$ which corresponds to the A[i,j] access (assuming the element size is 4). The "200" in $200i$ is because the size of a row is 50 elements, each of 4 bytes. We need to reason about this access in the infinite space for i and j since the loop bounds are unknown. In the infinite space, iterations $(2, 0)$, $(1, 50)$ and $(0, 100)$ refer to the same memory location. All the iterations except $(2, 0)$ are not possible since the legal range of j is $[0,49]$ and beyond 49 the code accesses columns out of bounds wrapping into rows. Source code methods assume that such iterations are not possible; hence proving the loop is parallel. However, the binary method in Kotha et al. (2010) cannot make any such assumptions about iterations remaining within array bounds, since array bounds and dimensions are not known. As a result, without loop bounds, the binary method in Kotha et al. (2010) fails to prove that this loop is parallel because false loop-carried dependence appears.

In this paper we present a method to statically guess the most likely upper bounds of loops when loop bounds are statically unknown. We then use run-time checks to see if the loop bounds were indeed within the guessed range and execute the parallel version when the run-time checks succeed, else we execute the serial version. For example, for code in figure 1, using the theory presented in Kotha et al. (2010) we discover the memory expression for the A[i][j] access to be $Base_A + 200i + 4j$. We then look at the coefficients multiplying the induction variables in this memory expression and guess that the likely limit of the induction variable with the smallest coefficient (i.e. j, as the immediately higher coefficient divided by the coefficient of this induction variable; i.e. in this example we guess the limit on j as (Coefficient of i/Coefficient of j) (i.e. $\frac{200}{4} = 50$). By guessing that j is less than 50 no two iterations will access the same memory location because now j has been prevented to wrap into i. At run-time, we check if j is indeed less than 50. In this case, this check will always succeed and we will always execute the parallel version of the loop.

4   Examples

In this section we first briefly describe the steps of the algorithm described in section 5 and then apply it to four code examples to show how their loops can be parallelized from a binary even though the loop bounds are run-time dependent.

First, we state the algorithm that we use to guess the loop bounds for a loop directly from a binary and then present details in section 5.

Step 1: Divide memory accesses (both reads and writes) in a loop into *Dependence Groups (DGs)*. Intuitively, a DG is a subset of memory addresses in the loop that are sufficiently close to one another.

Step 2: Arrange all DGs in ascending order of their base addresses, from DG_1 to DG_T.

Step 3: For all the DGs that have writes in them make best guesses for the possible range for induction variables. These guesses are called intra-group constraints, since they are obtained by working on one DG at a time.

Step 4: Initiate worklist with DGs that have constraints remaining after step 3.

Step 5: Work on each DG_i in the worklist and solve for the values of induction variables such that the accesses in DG_i do not overlap with those in $DG_{(i+1)}$.

This generates further guesses on the induction variables. Merge these new constraints with existing constraints for the same induction variable by choosing the minimum. These guesses are called inter-group constraints because they are obtained by constraining DG_i to not overlap $DG_{(i+1)}$.

```
int A[20,50]
int B[20,50]
for i = 0 → ubᵢ step 1
  for j = 0 → ubⱼ step 1
    B[i,j] = A[i,j] + 10
```
(a) Example 1

```
int A[20,50]
for i = 0 → ubᵢ step 1
  for j = 0 → ubⱼ step 1
    A[2i,j] = 10*i+j
```
(b) Example 2

```
int A[100]
for i = 0 → ubᵢ step 1
  A[i] = i;
  A[i+50] = i + 50;
```
(a) Example 3

Example 1: The memory address expressions that we recover from the binary of example 1 are of the form $Base_A + 200i + 4j$ and $Base_B + 200i + 4j$ (Assuming that the size of an integer is 4.). $Base_A$ and $Base_B$ will at least differ by 4000, since the size of each array is 4000 bytes. Without loss of generality let's assume we recover the following from the binary $100 + 200i + 4j$ and $4100 + 200i + 4j$.

When the code above is compiled to a striped binary, all symbolic information is lost. Hence we no longer know the location or dimension sizes (20, 50) of array A. Hence we can no longer infer (as we implicitly do from source) that $ub_i < 20$ and $ub_j < 50$. Instead we must assume that the loop bounds can take any value.

We now show briefly how our algorithm is applied to these accesses to guess the bounds on i and j. In Step 1, we check to see if the accesses belong to different DGs. The heuristic we use is that the difference of the bases is greater than a factor (5 for our experiments) of the highest coefficient; $i.e.$ $Base_B - Base_A > 5 \times 200$ $i.e.$ (4100-100) $> 5 \times 200$. Since this is true both the accesses will belong to different DGs. In Step 2, we arrange the DGs in ascending order of their bases. $100 + 200i + 4j$ belongs to DG_1 because its base is lower than the second access which belongs to DG_2. In Step 3, we solve for intra-group constraints in DG_2 since it contains a write. We guess the bound on j by dividing the co-efficient multiplying i (the just higher co-efficient in the linearized equation) by the co-efficient of j $i.e.$ ($\frac{200}{4} = 50$). Hence, we guess that j must belong to $[0, 49]$. In step 4, we create a worklist with all DGs that have constraints remaining. In this example both the DGs have constraints remaining on i; hence both of them will belong to the worklist. In step 5, we guess the bound on i by solving that DG_1 $i.e.$ $100 + 200i + 4j$ does not overlap with DG_2 $i.e.$ $4100 + 200i + 4j$ given the highest possible value for j is 49; $i.e.$ $100 + 200i + 4*49 < 4100$. Hence, i must be less than 19.02 or in the range $[0, 19]$. Since DG_2 is the highest DG we do not solve for it overlapping with any other DG.

After we have applied our algorithm to this loop, our guess for i is $[0, 19]$ and j is $[0, 49]$. We now solve for dependencies within this range for the loop and discover that the loop can be parallelized. We also add lightweight run-time checks before the parallel version of the loop (which will always succeed for this loop).

Example 2: The memory address expression that we recover from the binary in example 2 is $Base_A + 400i + 4j$. Since there is only one access, step 1 and 2 will result in placing it in DG_1. In step 3, we guess that the bound of j is ($\frac{400}{4} = 100$) or the range of j is guessed to be $[0, 99]$. There would be no step 4 and 5 for this loop since there is only one DG.

Next we calculate dependencies assuming the range of j is $[0, 99]$ and i can take any value and discover that the loop can be parallelized. In reality however the range of j will not exceed $[0, 49]$. But our larger discovered bounds work well since even if they did exceed 49 and be below 99 this loop can still be parallelized *i.e.* if the programmer decided to access two rows using a column increment (which most programmers would not do) it is still a parallel loop. From the binary this means that we see array A of size $[20,50]$ as an array of size $[10,100]$. However, this is fine since we reason about the dependencies in the correct way and parallelize the loop only when our run-time checks succeed.

Example 3: The equations we will recover from the binary of example 3 are $Base_A + 4i$ and $Base_A + 200 + 4i$. After step 1, we will place them in different DGs since the difference between the bases (200) is greater than 5 times the highest co-efficient 4. After arranging the DGs in ascending order in step 2, $Base_A + 4i$ will belong to DG_1 and $Base_A + 200 + 4i$ will belong to DG_2. No intra-group guesses are calculated in step 3 since the recovered equations are single dimensional. After step 4, the worklist is populated with both the DGs since both contain i for which there is no guess as yet. In step 5, we solve for inter-group guesses such that DG_1 does not overlap with DG_2, *i.e.* $4i < 200$ or $i < 50$. Hence, the range we guess for i is $[0, 49]$ which is also the actual limit on i from source. The run-time check will always succeed in binary code and we will execute the parallel version of this loop. This is correct because, regardless of the value of ub_i, the two array references access non-intersecting portions of the array. Our method correctly treats these non-intersecting portions as different arrays.

5   Algorithm to Guess Loop Bounds

In this section we describe in detail the algorithm briefly presented in section 4. First we describe which loops from binary code we work on and then in subsequent subsections we describe the steps of the algorithm in detail.

First, we would like to present to you the kind of loops on which our algorithm is applied on and the kind of loops on which our algorithm is effective. We apply our method to every loop that has only affine accesses in them *i.e.* accesses of the form A[i+3][5j], A[i+j][k+i], A[j][j] etc are all processed by our method. We also apply our method only on loops whose bounds are loop invariant. Our method is able to effectively parallelize loop nests with array accesses of the form A[i][2j], A[3j][i+100], and A[j][i] *i.e.* normalized accesses with induction variables in any order; however affine accesses having multiple induction variables in a single array index expression (such as A[i+j]) or having repeated induction variables (such as A[j][j]) are not currently effectively parallelized by our method. Our guesses may be incorrect for these loops. Hence, the run-time checks might fail for these loops and the serial version of the code may be executed. However, these kinds of accesses are rare in real code and hence our method is nearly as powerful from binary as from source.

Every affine memory address that we recover from the binary is a linearized multidimensional equation of the form Kotha et al. (2010):

$$\texttt{MemAddr(Base, d)} = \texttt{Base} + \sum_{j=1}^{n} d_j \times i_j \qquad (1)$$

(where $\texttt{Base}$ and d's are constants or loop invariant quantities, i's are induction variables, and $d_1 >= d_2 >= \; >= d_n$). We arrange the memory expression with d's in this order since in the algorithm we use the immediately higher coefficient while guessing the value of a particular induction variable, $i.e.$ we use $d_{(m+1)}$ when guessing the values of induction variable i_m. We will refer to memory addresses from binary using $\texttt{MemAddr(Base, d)}$ throughout the paper. Different memory addresses from binary will have different $\texttt{Base}$ and $\texttt{ds}$. Since we work on loops with only affine accesses in them, if we discover that a loop contains an access that is not affine $i.e.$ we cannot discover a linearized expression for it then we do not work that loop.

In the following subsections we first describe our algorithm and then present an intuition for it.

5.1   Step 1: Divide the Accesses into DGs

A DG is a subset of memory references in the loop that are sufficiently close to one another and these set of references most likely do not overlap with other DGs. Intuitively, while dividing memory references into DGs we try to guess all the references which access the same array, or a region of an array not overlapping with other regions. This is not immediately apparent since binaries lack symbolic information containing the locations and sizes of arrays.

We create DGs using the following method. We look at the address of each memory reference and place it in an already present DG if it is sufficiently close to the addresses already in that DG; else we create a new DG with this memory address. We define that two accesses are sufficiently close to one another if the difference between the bases is within a factor (5) of the highest coefficient in the memory expression. The formal algorithm is presented in algorithm 1. We use a factor 5 which we find effective in most cases; however any other method can be used as well to determine which accesses are close to each other.

We now describe some of the terms used in the algorithm. $\texttt{DGlist}$ is the list of DGs that is initialized to NULL and then populated as we consider every memory access in the loop. d_1 is the highest coefficient in the memory expression; hence, if the difference between the base and any of the bases already in a DG is within a factor of it, we guess that it most likely belongs to the same memory array and place this reference in that DG. $\texttt{CD}_{\text{Thres}}$ is a number that guesses the maximum difference between references in the same DG. Currently we set $\texttt{CD}_{\text{Thres}}$ to 5. With $\texttt{CD}_{\text{Thres}} = 5$, two accesses to A[i] and A[i+4] will belong to the same DG, whereas two accesses to A[i] and A[i+10] will belong to different DGs.

We manually looked at many affine benchmarks and determined that having accesses A[i] and A[i+e] where e > 5 in the same loop is relatively rare in affine codes; as most constants in affine codes are less than 5. Most of the codes only look at neighbouring values ($i.e.$ use constants ± 2) to update an array. Hence, even if we had accesses to A[i+2] and A[i-2], the difference 4 is still lower than the factor 5 we choose. If the rare case occurs, and there are accesses to A[i] and A[i+e] (e > 5), we would treat them as accesses to two different arrays. Accesses to different arrays A and B will belong to different DGs unless the highest dimension of A has size less than 5 (which again is very rare) and B immediately follows A in the binary's data layout. Most often in affine codes, the array sizes are relatively huge running into thousands. If this rare case appears we will treat both A and B as the same array. In both the above cases, the run-time checks will fail and the serial version of the loop will be executed. Hence, the loop may run slower than from source, but correctness is always maintained.

Algorithm 1. Step 1: Algorithm to divide accesses into DGs

Input: $MemAddr(Base, d)$ for all accesses in loop
Output: $DGlist$ has the accesses divided into DGs
Require: Initialize $DGlist$ to NULL
  for all $MemAddr(Base, d)$ in loop **do**
    Initialize $TmpDGlist$ to NULL
    for all DG_i in $DGlist$ **do**
      if $|Base - \text{Any base in } DG_i| < d_1 \times CD_{Thres}$ **then**
        Put $MemAddr(Base, d)$ in DG_i
        Put DG_i in $TmpDGlist$
      end if
    end for
    if sizeof $TmpDGList > 1$ **then**
      Merge all the DGs in $TmpDGList$
    end if
    if sizeof $TmpDGList == 0$ **then**
      A new DG with $MemAddr$ in it is added to $DGlist$
    end if
  end for

5.2   Step 2: Arrange DGs in Ascending Order

In this step we reorganize the DGs in DGlist in ascending order of the bases present in them. After arranging those in ascending order the following will be true:

All bases in DG_1 < All bases in DG_2 < $\cdots$ < All bases in DG_T (This will be < since if they are equal they would belong to the same DG). We call this ordering of DGs, the *FullList*.

5.3   Step 3: Induce Intra-group Dependencies

In this step we make our best guesses for all array bounds, and hence induction variables, except the array bound of the highest dimension in an array reference. We make the guesses based on the assumption that array references accesses arrays within the bounds of each dimension.

We apply step 3 to every DG that has a write in it. The reason we apply it to DGs with writes in them is that even if a read accesses across bounds it does not create a

---

Algorithm 2. Step 3.1: Guesses for induction variables using one access

---

Input: All DGs that have a write in them
Output: Initial guesses for the induction variables
Require: Initialize each of $g_1, g_2, \cdots, g_n$ to TOP
  for all DG_i in FullList that has a write in it **do**
    for all $MemAddr(Base, d)$ in DG_i **do**
      for $k = 2 \to n$ **do**
        $g_{1k} = \lfloor \frac{d_{(k-1)}}{d_k} \rfloor$
        $g_k = min(g_k, g_{1k})$
      end for
    end for
  end for

---

loop dependency that prevents parallelization; hence guessing bounds considering DGs with only reads is not necessary. For example, if there is an affine loop that only reads from an array, there is no need to guess bounds for such a loop as it is parallel in the infinite space as long as there is no scalar dependency in it.

Step 3 is divided into two sub steps 3.1 and 3.2. Step 3.1 is applied to every access in a DG and step 3.2 is applied to a pair of accesses in a DG. We first present the algorithms for both the sub steps before presenting intuitions for them.

Step 3.1: The formal algorithm for step 3.1 is presented in algorithm 2. We are working on loop nests with induction variables say $i_1, i_2, \cdots, i_n$ and guesses for each $g_1, g_2, \cdots, g_n$. First, we initialize the guesses for each of these induction variables to TOP representing infinity which is what we know about each of the induction variables before the start of this step. Then we look at every memory access which is of the form MemAddr(Base, d) (from eq(1)) and make guesses for each induction variable as follows.

$$\text{The guess on } i_k, \text{ } g_{1k} = \lfloor \tfrac{d_{(k-1)}}{d_k} \rfloor \text{ } \forall k \in [2, n] \tag{2}$$

We then update the guess already in g_k for i_k using

$$g_k = min(g_k, g_{1k}) \tag{3}$$

Note: $min(TOP, g_{1k}) = g_{1k}$ since TOP represents infinity.

We apply this to every memory access in every DG that has a write and guess for every induction variable other than the highest dimension i_1. Note that we cannot make a guess for i_1 since there is no d_0 in the equation. Hence, we do not have a guess for i_1 in this step. The guess for i_1 is made in step 5 and will be described later.

Step 3.2: After we have applied step 3.1 to all DGs that have a write in them, we work on the same DGs considering pairs of accesses in them and apply step 3.2 on them. This algorithm is presented in algorithm 3.

We now describe the algorithm briefly. We first initialize $x_1, x_2, \cdots, x_n$ to zeroes. These represent the adjustment we need to make to each of the induction variable bound guesses at the end of this step. Then we consider pairs of accesses in this DG, if the bases are different then we store the absolute difference in Base$_{diff}$. We then run a loop that checks to see which factor of this difference came from which

---

Algorithm 3. Step 3.2: Guesses for induction variables using pair of accesses

---

Input: All DG_is that have a write in them and $g_1, g_2, \cdots, g_n$ from step 3.1
Output: Refined guesses for induction variables
Require: Initialize $x_1, x_2, \cdots, x_n$ to zeroes
 for $MemAddr_1(Base_1, d), MemAddr_2(Base_2, e)$ in DG_i **do**
  $Base_{diff} = \mid Base_1 \text{ - } Base_2 \mid$
  for $k = 1 \rightarrow n$ **do**
   if $\frac{Base_{diff}}{gcd(d_k, e_k)} \geq 1$ **then**
    $x_{11} = \lfloor \frac{Base_{diff}}{gcd(d_k, e_k)} \rfloor$
    $x_k = max(x_k, x_{11})$
    $Base_{diff} = Base_{diff} - \lfloor \frac{Base_{diff}}{gcd(d_k, e_k)} \rfloor \times gcd(d_k, e_k)$
   end if
  end for
 end for
 for $k = 1 \rightarrow n$ **do**
  $g_k = g_k - x_k$
 end for

---

co-efficient and keep track of that in d_ks. Later these are subtracted from the guesses for induction variables g_k from step 3.1.

It is important to make this adjustment to the guesses on loop bounds from step 3.1 since by doing so we are making sure that each of the accesses do not run into the higher dimension of the other. After this adjustment we will not have spurious dependencies from binary that prevent prallelization. We will present further intuition to this step below.

Intuition for Step 3.1: Let us assume that the binary code we are accessing came from source code where the loop nest had induction variables (say $i_1, i_2, \cdots, i_n$) and an array accesses $A[C_1 \times i_1 + B_1][C_2 \times i_2 + B_2] \cdots [C_n \times i_n + B_n]$ in the loop and the size of array A is $[n1][n2] \cdots [nn]$. Assume that none of the induction variables is repeated; however any ordering of the induction variables is allowed. This access when recovered from the binary will be of the form.

$$(\text{Base}_A + \sum_{j=1}^{n} B_j \times \prod_{m=j+1}^{n} n_m) + \sum_{j=1}^{n} C_j \times \prod_{m=j+1}^{n} n_m \times i_j \qquad (4)$$

(This assumes an element size of 1; else each one of the terms will be multiplied by the element size.) The algorithm is correct even if the compiler uses the column-major layout; we assume the row-major layout only for explaining the intuition. Our results also include FORTRAN benchmarks for which the gfortran compiler uses the column-major layout. Base_A and all the terms containing B's (shown in parenthesis above) are rolled into the constant term when recovered from the binary. We know that the memory address that we recover from binary is of the form $\text{MemAddr}(\text{Base}, d)$ (from eq.(1)).

Equating (4) and (1) we get:

$$\text{Base} = \text{Base}_A + \sum_{j=1}^{n} B_j \times \prod_{m=j+1}^{n} n_m \qquad (5)$$

$$\text{and, } d_j = C_j \times \prod_{m=j+1}^{n} n_m \qquad (6)$$

First, let us calculate the actual upper bounds of the induction variables from source. From source we know that the array indices do not access arrays out of their bounds. Hence, each dimension index must be less than the actual size of that dimension.

$$i.e. \; C_k \times i_k + B_k < n_k \tag{7}$$

$$\text{Rearranging the terms, } i_k < \frac{(n_k - B_k)}{C_k} \tag{8}$$

Hence, the upper bound of i_k from source is $\frac{(n_k - B_k)}{C_k}$.

Second, let us see what our guess for induction variable i_k is by applying step 3.1 to this access. Our guess for induction variable i_k is obtained by substituting eq(6) in eq(2)

$$i.e. \; g_{1k} = \lfloor \frac{C_{(k-1)} \times n_k}{C_k} \rfloor \; \forall k \in [2, n] \tag{9}$$

Next taking the minimum of g_{1k} and TOP (the initialized value) we get,

$$g_k = \min(\text{TOP}, g_{1k}) = g_{1k} = \lfloor \frac{C_{(k-1)} \times n_k}{C_k} \rfloor \; \forall k \in [2, n] \tag{10}$$

We now show that the guesses for induction bounds are greater than or equal to the actual loop bounds. This is important because if the guesses were lower than the actual loop bounds our run-time checks would fail. We have already seen that the guess on the induction variable $i_k = \frac{C_{(k-1)} \times n_k}{C_k}$, this is greater than the actual limit of i_k, which is $\frac{(n_k - B_k)}{C_k}$ from eq.(8). We observe that if $C_{(k-1)}$ is 1 and B_k is 0, then the value we would have guessed is the same as the actual upper bound. Further, if C_k is 1 as well, the guess for i_k is n_k, which is the size of that array dimension. Every guess we make for the induction variables is actually higher than or equal to its actual bound as shown above. By taking the minimum at every step we have a guess that is at least its actual bound.

Intuition for step 3.2: Let us assume that there is a second accesses to A, $A[C_1 \times i_1 + B_1 + E_1] \cdots [C_n \times i_n + B_n + E_n]$ in this loop where Es are small numbers < 5. The memory address for this access from binary will be of the form:

$$\text{Base}_A + \sum_{j=1}^{n} (B_j + E_j) \times \prod_{x=j+1}^{n} n_x + \sum_{j=1}^{n} C_j \times \prod_{x=j+1}^{n} n_x \times i_j \tag{11}$$

Recollect that this access when recovered from the binary will be of the form MemAddr(Base_2, e), from equation (1):

$$\text{MemAddr}(\text{Base}_2, e) = \text{Base}_2 + \sum_{j=1}^{n} e_j \times i_j \tag{12}$$

Equating eq.(11) and eq.(12), we get:

$$\text{Base}_2 = \text{Base}_A + \sum_{j=1}^{n} (B_j + E_j) \times \prod_{x=j+1}^{n} n_x \tag{13}$$

$$\text{and, } e_j = C_j \times \prod_{x=j+1}^{n} n_x \tag{14}$$

First, let us prove that both the references belong to the same DG using step 1 since we would apply step 3.2 to them only if both of them belong to the same DG. From step 1 we know that if the difference between the bases is $< d_1 \times \text{CD}_{\text{Thres}}$, then they will belong to the same DG.

$$i.e. \text{ if } |\text{Base}_2 - \text{Base}| < d_1 \times \text{CD}_{\text{Thres}} \tag{15}$$

then, both the accesses will belong to this DG.

The difference between the bases from eq.(13) and eq.(5) is

$$\text{Base}_2 - \text{Base} = \sum_{j=1}^{n} E_j \times \prod_{x=j+1}^{n} n_j \tag{16}$$

We know from eq.(14) and eq.(6) that:

$$d_1 = e_1 = C_1 \times \prod_{m=2}^{n} n_m \qquad (17)$$

Now, substituting eq.(16) and eq.(17) in eq.(15) we get:

$$\text{If } \sum_{j=1}^{n} E_j \times \prod_{x=j+1}^{n} n_j < C_1 \times \prod_{m=2}^{n} n_m \times CD_{\text{Thres}} \qquad (18)$$

, then both the accesses will belong to this DG

$$\Rightarrow \frac{E_1}{C_1} + \frac{E_2}{C_1 \times n_2} + \cdots + \frac{E_n}{C_1 \times \prod_{m=2}^{n} n_m} < CD_{\text{Thres}} \qquad (19)$$

(which will be true in most cases since C_1 and ES are small positive numbers < 5 and $n_2 \cdots n_n$ are relatively large, and CD_{Thres} is 5 in our experiments.)

Hence, both these accesses represented by `MemAddr(Base, d)` and `MemAddr(Base2, e)` from the binary will belong to the same DG.

First, let us see what the bounds for the induction variable from source would be in the presence of the second access as well. We know that accesses from source do not access out of bounds in correct programs. We have seen that the bounds for each induction variable (i_k) only considering the first access is $\frac{(n_k - B_k)}{C_k}$ as shown in eq.(8). Now considering that the second access does not access out of bounds we get:

$$C_k \times i_k + B_k + E_k < n_k \qquad (20)$$

$$\text{Rearranging the terms, } i_k < \frac{(n_k - (B_k + E_k))}{C_k} \qquad (21)$$

The difference between the bounds calculated from eq.(8) and eq.(21) is $\frac{E_k}{C_k}$

Now let us apply algorithm 3 to both these accesses.

We know that $\text{Base}_{\text{diff}} = \sum_{j=1}^{n} E_j \times \prod_{x=j+1}^{n} n_j$. By dividing it with $\gcd(d_k, e_k) = d_k$ (since $d_k = e_k$ in our case) repeatedly in loop and keeping the remainder of it for the next iteration we recover x_ks of the form $\lfloor \frac{E_k}{C_k} \rfloor$ as long as C_ks are factors of E_ks. By subtracting x_ks from the already present guesses of the induction variables we get $g_k = \frac{C_{(k-1)} \times n_k}{C_k} - \frac{E_k}{C_k}$. Many of the ES will be zeroes, hence we will not make adjustment to many bounds, however we will make adjustment to the bounds that have small constant ES in their terms. Further, it is good to note that the term we subtract using algorithm 3 is equivalent to the difference of the bounds as shown above.

It is important to note at this point that by subtracting from the already guessed bounds, we are making sure that the second access which accesses a few extra elements in some dimensions does not run into the higher dimension of the first access. This is very important because if we do not make this adjustment we will have extra dependencies from binary which will prevent parallelization and by subtracting the extra from bounds we will not see those spurious dependencies. Also it is important to note that the new guess we have for the bounds is also higher than or equal to the actual bounds of the loop.

5.4   Step 4: Create the Worklist

In this step we create a worklist with DGs that have accesses with remaining constraints so that we can apply step 5 on them to guess the upper bounds for the remaining induction variables. After step 3 we have upper bound constraints for all the induction variables in the memory addresses other than the ones that correspond to the highest dimension in the write accesses. We need a method to guess the upper bound on these induction variables as well. This method is step 5. Hence, we now create a worklist with all DGs in which there is an induction variable for which we do not have an upper bound guess as yet. These would be the highest dimension induction variables since we do not have guesses for those after step 3. This worklist will enable us to work on only those DGs that have remaining constraints.

5.5   Step 5: Work on Inter-group Constraints

In this step we look at all DGs in the worklist created in step 4 (recall that these DGs have induction variables for which we have no guesses as yet) and solve for this DG not overlapping with the immediately following DG in the FullList. While creating DGs we assumed that each DG corresponds to a non-overlapping array region. Hence, it is required that different DGs do not overlap with each other; else this would generate false dependencies from binaries. Solving this generates further guesses on the remaining induction variables. These guesses are called inter-group constraints.

The formal method for solving that DG_i from worklist does not overlap with $DG_{(i+1)}$ (the immediately following DG in the FullList of DGs) is presented in algorithm 4, we describe it briefly here. For every DG_i that has constraints remaining we substitute the guesses for all induction variables other than the highest one in all its memory expressions and require that this be less than the lowest base in $DG_{(i+1)}$. Solving the above constraint we can obtain an higher bound for the highest induction variable. We then choose the minimum of the present guess and the already present minimum guess for that induction variable. This way we ensure that all our guesses are respected.

Algorithm 4. Step 5: Algorithm for Inter-group constraints

Input: Worklist from step 4 and guesses $g_1, g_2, \cdots, g_n$ from step 3.2
Output: Final guesses for bounds $g_1, g_2, \cdots, g_n$
for all DG_i in worklist after step 4 **do**
    for all $MemAddr(Base, d)$ in DG_i **do**
        $Base_{low}$ = Lowest Base from $DG_{(i+1)}$ in FullList
        $g_{11} = \lfloor \dfrac{Base_{low} - Base - (\sum\limits_{j=2}^{n} d_2 * g_2)}{d_1} \rfloor$
        $g_1 = min(g_1, g_{11})$
    end for
end for

Intuition for step 5: Now that we have presented an algorithm for calculating the bounds on the highest induction variable, let us apply this to an access from source code, to show that our method guesses the value for the highest induction variable that is $\geq$ to the actual bound on that induction variable.

In step 3 we assumed we were working with loop nests comprising of the following induction variables $(\text{say}, i_1, i_2, \cdots i_n)$ and array accesses $A[C_1 \times i_1 + B_1] \cdots [C_n \times i_n + B_n]$ in the loop, and the size of array A is $[n_1][n_2] \cdots [n_n]$. Let this access belong to DG_i.

First, let us recollect the guesses for all induction variables except the highest induction variable from step 3. One of the guesses we would have made for induction variable i_k (where $k \in [2,n]$) is $\frac{C_{(k-1)} \times n_k}{C_k}$ (eq.(9)). Hence, the final guess after step 4 will be equal to or lower than this guess.

Next, let us assume that there is an access to array B in the same loop belonging to $DG_{(i+1)}$, $i.e.$ the immediately following DG in the FullList. If this second array B is laid immediately after A in the binary, then $Base_B$ will be at least:

$$Base_B = Base_A + \prod_{j=1}^{n} n_j \text{ (this term is the size of A)} \qquad (22)$$

Let us assume that all accesses corresponding to B belong to $DG_{(i+1)}$. The lowest address of $DG_{(i+1)}$ will be $Base_B$.

Next, we apply the method in algorithm 4 for solving DG_i not overlapping with $DG_{(i+1)}$ from source to derive the guess for i_1 and then verify that this guess is correct. For doing so we must substitute our guesses for all the induction variables except the highest dimension induction variable in the expression of memory address A and this must be less than $Base_B$. The expression for memory address A obtained by substituting the intra-group guesses eq.(9) in eq.(4) is:

$$Base_A + \sum_{j=1}^{n} B_j \times \prod_{x=j+1}^{n} n_x + C_1 \times \prod_{x=2}^{n} n_x \times i_1 + \sum_{j=2}^{n} C_j \times \prod_{x=j+1}^{n} n_x \times \left(\frac{C_{j-1} \times n_j}{C_j} - 1\right) \qquad (23)$$

The only unknown in eq.(23) is i_1. This must be less than $Base_B$ (from eq.(22)). Hence,

$$Base_A + \sum_{j=1}^{n} B_j \times \prod_{x=j+1}^{n} n_x + C_1 \times \prod_{x=2}^{n} n_x \times i_1 + \sum_{j=1}^{n} C_j \times \prod_{x=j+1}^{n} n_x - \sum_{j=2}^{n} C_j \times \prod_{x=j+1}^{n} n_x$$

$$\leq Base_A + \prod_{j=1}^{n} n_j \qquad (24)$$

Rearranging the terms we get,

$$i_1 \leq \frac{\prod_{j=1}^{n} n_j - \left(C_1 \times \prod_{x=2}^{n} n_x + \sum_{j=1}^{n} B_j \times \prod_{x=j+1}^{n} n_x\right)}{C_1 \times \prod_{x=2}^{n} n_x} \qquad (25)$$

Further,

$$i_1 \leq \frac{n_1}{C_1} - 1 - \frac{B_1}{C_1} - \frac{\left(\sum_{j=2}^{n} B_j \times \prod_{x=j+1}^{n} n_x\right)}{C_1 \times \prod_{x=2}^{n} n_x} \qquad (26)$$

$$i.e. \ i_1 \leq \frac{n_1}{C_1} - 1 - \frac{B_1}{C_1} - (\Delta) \qquad (27)$$

The remaining values are small since the constant C's and B's are small and the sizes of arrays in affine code are generally large.

Hence, the guess for i_1 will be:

$$g_1 = \left\lfloor \frac{(n_1 - B_1)}{C_1} - 1 \right\rfloor \qquad (28)$$

As seen before from source we require that the array expression must not exceed the size of the array dimension. Hence the highest dimension array expression $(C_1 \times i_1 + B_1)$ must not exceed the highest dimension (n_1).

$$i.e. \ C_1 \times i_1 + B_1 < n_1 \qquad (29)$$

Rearranging the terms $i_1 < \frac{(n_1 - B_1)}{C_1}$

Hence, the maximum value i_1 can take is $\frac{(n_1 - B_1)}{C_1} - 1$ and this is what we get by solving the equations from binary.

We have now seen that the algorithm 4 to calculate the bounds on the highest dimension induction variable yields a limit on it that is the true limit on it even from source code.

At the end of step 5, we now have made best guesses for all induction variables in the loop that appear in a memory address. If there is an induction variable that does not appear in any memory access, then we just assume that it can take any value since we have no way of determining its bounds. This does not hurt our method and is reasonable since even from source if an induction variable does not appear in any of the memory addresses present in the loop it could take any value at run-time and this would be legal.

For array accesses that came from dynamically allocated memory we apply the same algorithm described above. It is important to note that all ds in the MemAddr(Base, d) expression would be loop invariant symbols rather than constants. In many cases the memory expression we recover from binary code for these accesses will be of the form

$$\texttt{Base} + x_1 \times x_2 \cdots x_n \times i_1 + x_2 \times x_3 \cdots x_n \times i_2 + \cdots + x_n \times i_n \tag{30}$$

where all the xs and Base are loop invariant quantities. By applying the algorithm to such an access we guess that the bound on i_k is $x_{(n-1)}$. We then check that the actual bounds are less than this loop invariant quantity (this check would succeed) before executing the parallel version of the loop.

Now that we have constraints on all the induction variables, we calculate the distance vectors and take parallelizing decisions for this loop assuming these as loop bounds. We then clone this loop and run the parallel version of the loop when the run-time checks for all induction variables succeed; else we run the serial version of the loop. Since we check at run-time that the loop bounds that we have guessed are actually correct we will always be conservatively correct. Please note that using the distance vector method to parallelize is our implementation method, one may use any parallelizing decision algorithm including polyhedral methods.

6   Implementation-SecondWrite

In this section we describe the binary rewriting infrastructure, SecondWrite Kotha et al. (2010); O'Sullivan et al. (2011); Anand and et. al. (2013) used for this research and how the automatic parallelizer interacts with rest of the system.

Architecture of Binary Rewriter called SecondWrite is presented in figure 2. SecondWrite's custom binary reader and de-compiler modules translate the input x86 binary into the intermediate representation (IR) of the LLVM compiler. LLVM is a well-known open-source compiler Lattner and Adve (2004) developed at the University of Illinois, and is now maintained by Apple Inc. LLVM IR is language and machine independent. Thereafter the LLVM IR produced is optimized using LLVM's pre-existing optimizations, as well as our enhancements, including automatic parallelization. Our new algorithm is implemented within this static

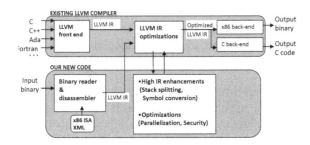

Fig. 2. SecondWrite

affine automatic parallelizer. Finally, the LLVM IR is code generated to output x86 code using LLVM's existing x86 code generator.

Currently SecondWrite rewrites x86 binaries from both Linux and Windows. It successfully rewrites binaries coming from source totaling over 2 million lines of code, including all of the SPEC2006 benchmarks. Real world programs such as the apache web server (230K+ LOC), Lynx browser (135K+ LOC) and MySQL (1.7M LOC) are also successfully rewritten. Rewritten benchmark binaries on average run 10% faster than highly optimized input binaries, and 45% faster than unoptimized input binaries because of the existing optimizations in LLVM not including parallelization.

SecondWrite is able to rewrite binaries without relocation information Smithson et al. (2010). SecondWrite implements various mechanisms O'Sullivan et al. (2011); Anand and et. al. (2013) to obtain an intermediate representation which contains features like procedure arguments, return values, types, high-level control flow, symbols and aggregate data structures. Second-Write also employs extra mechanisms to safely handle indirect calls and indirect branches Smithson et al. (2010). It employs alias analysis frameworks present in LLVM to discover all the possible target procedures at indirect callsites, given by the points-to set of the operand in indirect call instruction. An edge is added from the indirect call-site to all its possible target procedures. Indirect branches are mostly present due to jump tables in the binary. Procedure boundary determination techniques are devised to limit the possible branch targets within the current procedure and extra control flow edges are added corresponding to the possible targets determined by alias analysis. If one of the target is outside procedure boundary, it is handled as an indirect call.

The algorithm presented in section 5 can be implemented in any static or dynamic binary rewriter as long as symbol recognition and induction variable analysis is implemented in the system.

7   Results

We use "-O3" optimized binaries from gcc-4.3 and gfortran-4.3 as input to SecondWrite, which includes the new algorithm proposed in this paper within a static affine parallelizer. The static affine automatic parallelizer, that is in SecondWrite works on LLVM IR. We build a source automatic parallelizer by feeding it LLVM IR generated from *clang* LLVM (2007) (a C language front-end for llvm) for the 'C' benchmarks and LLVM IR generated using the *dragonegg* LLVM (2009) plugin (a plugin that integrates the LLVM optimizers and code generator with GCC) for the FORTRAN benchmarks. The LLVM IR fed to the stand-alone automatic parallelizer contains array location and dimension information, hence the source parallelizer uses it to take parallelization decisions. We run all the binaries on the AMD Opteron(TM) processor 6212 and present results.

In this section we present our results on parallelizing binaries from SPEC2006 and OMP2001 using our new algorithm. First, we introduce our benchmarks. Second, we present the speedups we have from source and binary. For the binary numbers, we present results for speedups both with and without the new algorithm. Third, we present the actual number of affine loops that are parallelized from the binary with and without the algorithm. We measure speedups by measuring the clock time to run the programs on 1 thread and 8 threads.

Table 1. Description of Benchmarks

Benchmark	Language	# LOC	Suite		Benchmark	Language	# LOC	Suite
swim	Fortran	275	OMP2001		quake	C	1151	OMP2001
bwaves	Fortran	680	SPEC2006		libquantum	C	2605	SPEC2006
mgrid	Fortran	789	OMP2001		milc	C	9575	SPEC2006
lbm	C	908	SPEC2006		cactus	Fortran + C	59827	SPEC2006

First, table 1 lists the 8 affine benchmarks that we present our results on. Our source and binary parallelizers correctly parallelize every benchmark from both the benchmark suites; however do not give any speedup on the remaining benchmarks since those benchmarks do not contain affine rich regions. We have picked only the affine rich benchmarks from the SPEC2006 and OMP2001 benchmark suites. We manually profiled every benchmark belonging to both the benchmark suites and after examining the hot regions classified benchmarks as affine or not affine. We present our results on all the affine benchmarks discovered from both the benchmark suites. The benchmarks *swim, mgrid* and *quake* belong to the OMP2001 benchmark suite and *bwaves, lbm, libquantum, milc* and *cactus* belong to the SPEC2006 benchmark suite. These benchmarks range from 275 to 59,827 lines of code as shown in table 1.

Second, figure 3 presents the speedup for 8 threads from source and binary for each of the benchmarks w.r.t the gcc "-O3" compiled single thread version of the benchmark. There are three bars for each benchmark; (i) the first bar is the speedup of the benchmark from source code for 8 threads; (ii) the second bar is the speedup of the binary for 8 threads without the new algorithm using only the theory presented in Kotha et al. (2010) and (iii) the third bar is the speedup of the binary for 8 threads using the new algorithm presented in this paper. We observe that *swim, bwaves, mgrid, quake, milc* and *cactus* gain significant speedups when the new algorithm presented in this paper is present in the static affine binary parallelizer.

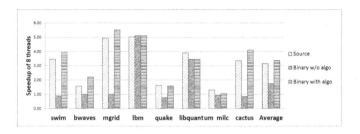

Fig. 3. Speedup of 8 threads for the affine benchmarks from SPEC2006 and OMP2001

The significant affine loops in these benchmarks have run-time determined loop bounds and hence using our new algorithm we are able to parallelize these loops that were not parallelized using the theory developed before. The benchmarks *lbm* and *libquantum* do not have any difference in the speedups with and without the algorithm. The reason being; (i) in *lbm*, the loops bounds are statically known and hence the theory in Kotha et al. (2010) is sufficient to parallelize the affine loops in it and (ii) in *libquantum* the loops are single dimensional with a write to one single dimensional memory accesses. These loops can be parallelized without the new algorithm and hence we see a speedup in *libquantum* even without the new algorithm. Overall the average speedup for 8 threads for the 8 benchmarks from binaries increases from 1.75X to 3.38X with the addition of the new algorithm. Our binaries run slightly faster than source since SecondWrite is able to rewrite "-O3" binaries to run 10% faster than the input binaries.

Table 2. Number of loops parallelized with and without the new algorithm

Benchmark	# loops w/o algo	# loops with algo	Benchmark	# loops w/o algo	# loops with algo
swim	6	18	quake	7	9
bwaves	0	1	libquantum	18	18
mgrid	0	6	milc	37	43
lbm	4	4	cactus	112	126

Third, table 2 presents the number of loops that are parallelized from the binary with and without the new algorithm. We observe that in the benchmarks *lbm* and *libquantum* the number of loops parallelized with and without the algorithm do not change. The reasons for this have been explained earlier. In *swim*, *quake*, *milc* and *cactus*, a number of loops are parallelized even when the new algorithm is not present in the static affine binary parallelizer; however, these loops are small and do not contribute to the run-time of the benchmark. Hence, these loops do not result in a speedup from 8 threads for these benchmarks. We make this comparison to show that it is not the number of loops that are parallelized that matter, but it is important to parallelize the run-time intensive loops that can be parallelized by our new algorithm.

8   Discussion and Future Directions

In this section we describe few salient aspects of our algorithm choice and alternate ideas that can be tested in the future.

8.1   Choice of a Heuristic Based Method

In the algorithm presented in this paper, one observes that we are solving a system of equations using a set of constraints to obtain loop bounds. We also observe that the number of constraints we have are not sufficient to solve for definite solutions for loop bounds. In this scenario, there are two possible methods to obtain a solution: (i) using a linear systems of equation solver that gives all possible solutions; and (ii) using a heuristic based solution relying on assumptions about loop structure and memory accesses, which gives one solution.

We choose a heuristic based approach over an equation solver for the following reasons: (i) it gives only one definite solution that can be used to insert run-time checks in the code and execute the parallel version only if the check succeeds; and (ii) it arrives at a solution in linear time complexity. One way of looking at our heuristic based algorithm is that it picks the one solution from all the possible solutions (that can be obtained using a solver) making assumptions on the loop structure most amenable to parallelization. Hence, even though there are many other solutions, this is the one that is mostly likely correct and going to yield from parallelization. Further, using our method we obtain the solution in linear time as against in exponential time complexity using a solver.

8.2   Future Directions

The present algorithm is two-dimensional; *i.e.* if the guess is wrong then at run-time it uses the fall-back solution and executes the serial version of the loop. In the future the following ideas can be used to enhance it.

1. If a run-time checks fails, then the loop bounds for that loop can be written to a log file and in future they can be used to parallelize the loop. That way in future with some run-time feedback, the algorithm to parallelize affine loops can be enhanced further.

2. In the present algorithm, we make a lot of assumptions to arrive at one set of loop bounds. In future, we will look into refining our assumptions to arrive at a few possible loop bounds and then use run-time feedback to use a different one in the next execution if this set fails in this run. This will provide fall-back solutions beyond serial execution.

3. In the present algorithm, we do not include any mechanism for user feedback. In future, we envision a system where the user can explicitly turn off parallelization of certain loops it they know that it would not be as profitable.

References

Anand, K., et al.: A compiler level intermediate representation based binary analysis and rewriting system. In: Proceedings of the 8th ACM European Conference on Computer Systems (2013)

Dasgupta, A., Dasgupta, A.: Vizer: A framework to analyze and vectorize intel x86 binaries (2003)

Franke, B., O'boyle, M.: Array recovery and high-level transformations for dsp applications. ACM Trans. Embed. Comput. Syst. (2003)

Yang, J., Soffa, M.L., Skadron, K., Whitehouse, K.: Feasibility of dynamic binary parallelization (2011)

Kotha, A., Anand, K., Smithson, M., Yellareddy, G., Barua, R.: Automatic parallelization in a binary rewriter. In: Proceedings of the 2010 43rd Annual IEEE/ACM International Symposium on Microarchitecture (2010)

Lattner, C., Adve, V.: LLVM: A compilation framework for lifelong program analysis & transformation. In: Proceedings of the International Symposium on CGO (2004)

LLVM, clang: a C language family frontend for LLVM (2007), http://clang.llvm.org/

LLVM, DragonEgg - Using LLVM as a GCC backend (2009), http://dragonegg.llvm.org/

Maslov, V.: Delinearization: an efficient way to break multiloop dependence equations. In: Proc. the SIGPLAN 1992 Conference on Programming Language Design and Implementation, pp. 152–161 (1992)

Nakamura, T., Miki, S., Oikawa, S.: Automatic vectorization by runtime binary translation. In: Proceedings of the 2011 Second International Conference on Networking and Computing (2011)

O'Sullivan, P., Anand, K., Kotha, A., Smithson, M., Barua, R., Keromytis, A.D.: Retrofitting security in cots software with binary rewriting. In: Proceedings of the 26th International Information Security Conference (2011)

Pradelle, B., Ketterlin, A., Clauss, P.: Polyhedral parallelization of binary code. ACM Trans. Archit. Code Optim. (2012)

Smithson, M., Anand, K., Kotha, A., Elwazeer, K., Giles, N., Barua, R.: Binary rewriting without relocation information. Technical report, University of Maryland, College Park (2010)

Wang, C., Wu, Y., Borin, E., Hu, S., Liu, W., Sager, D., Ngai, T.-F., Fang, J.: Dynamic parallelization of single-threaded binary programs using speculative slicing. In: Proceedings of the 23rd International Conference on Supercomputing, ICS 2009 (2009)

Yardimci, E., Franz, M.: Dynamic parallelization and mapping of binary executables on hierarchical platforms. In: Proceedings of the 3rd Conference on Computing Frontiers (2006)

Author Index